Strategies & Tactics® for the MBE

Multistate Bar Exam

Kimm Walton, J.D.
and
Steve Emanuel, J.D.

ASPEN
PUBLISHERS

1185 Avenue of the Americas, New York NY 10036
www.aspenpublishers.com

Permissions
Aspen Publishers
1185 Avenue of the Americas
New York, NY 10036

Printed in the United States of America

ISBN 0-7355-4418-2

This book is intended as a general review of a legal subject. It is not intended as a source for advice for the solution of legal matters or problems. For advice on legal matters, the reader should consult an attorney.

About Aspen Publishers

Aspen Publishers, headquartered in New York City, is a leading information provider for attorneys, business professionals, and law students. Written by preeminent authorities, our products consist of analytical and practical information covering both U.S. and international topics. We publish in the full range of formats, including updated manuals, books, periodicals, CDs, and online products.

Our proprietary content is complemented by 2,500 legal databases, containing over 11 million documents, available through our Loislaw division. Aspen Publishers also offers a wide range of topical legal and business databases linked to Loislaw's primary material. Our mission is to provide accurate, timely, and authoritative content in easily accessible formats, supported by unmatched customer care.

To order any Aspen Publishers title, go to *www.aspenpublishers.com* or call 1-800-638-8437.

To reinstate your manual update service, call 1-800-638-8437.

For more information on Loislaw products, go to *www.loislaw.com* or call 1-800-364-2512.

For Customer Care issues, e-mail *CustomerCare@aspenpublishers.com*; call 1-800-234-1660; or fax 1-800-901-9075.

Aspen Publishers
A Wolters Kluwer Company

TABLE OF CONTENTS

ABOUT THE MBE

If you're like most students, there's quite a bit about the Multistate Bar Exam that you don't know. Here are the answers to some of the questions we hear most frequently.

Is the MBE required in every state?

Almost. As of July, 2003, only two states — Louisiana and Washington — *don't* administer the MBE.

Also, the District of Columbia, the Virgin Islands, Guam, the Northern Mariana Islands and Palau require the MBE.

When is the MBE given?

In most states, the MBE is given twice each year — on the last Wednesday in February and on the last Wednesday in July — but a few states offer the MBE only once a year. Most states also administer their own, state-specific exams on the day(s) immediately before or after the MBE; these state-specific exams usually consist of essays covering a variety of subjects. In addition, other multistate exams, such as the Multistate Essay Examination (MEE) and the new Multistate Performance Test (MPT), take place on the day(s) immediately before or after the MBE.

What's the format of the MBE?

The Multistate Bar Examination is a six-hour examination consisting of 200 questions. The exam is divided into two parts: Part I is administered in the morning and Part II is administered in the afternoon. Each part takes three hours and contains 100 questions.

What subjects are covered on the Multistate Bar Exam?

Currently, there are six subjects on the MBE: Constitutional Law, Contracts, Criminal Law, Evidence, Real Property, and Torts.

Many students believe that Civil Procedure is tested on the MBE. It's not. The MBE currently covers only the six subjects listed above.

How many questions are there on each subject?

As of July, 2003, the MBE is made up of 34 questions each on Contracts and Torts, and 33 questions each on Constitutional Law, Criminal Law, Evidence, and Real Property (for a total of 200 questions). In other words *all six subjects on the MBE are given substantially equal weight*.[1]

This means that, if your jurisdiction considers a raw score of 120 to be a "passing score," you could get every single question in any one subject wrong and still pass the MBE, so long as you scored well enough on all the

---

1. Prior to 1997, Contracts and Torts each had 40 questions, with the others having 30. Since some of the past released questions in this book date from before 1997, this book has more Contracts and Torts questions than questions from the other subjects. Don't feel you have to do every Contracts or Torts question in the book — spend about the same amount of time on each of the six subjects.

other subjects. In fact, in some jurisdictions you could, theoretically, miss *every* question in *two* subjects and still pass the MBE, but you'd have to miss virtually no questions on the other subject areas.

What's the format of MBE questions?

The MBE is an "objective" exam; that is, it's *multiple-choice from a given set of facts*. Each question has four possible answer options, with one correct answer and three incorrect choices.

What order are the questions in?

Questions on the MBE are presented in a completely *random* manner. Both the level of difficulty and the subject matter may vary from one question to the next. This means that your first MBE question may be very difficult, but the following question may be relatively easy. Since MBE test questions are set up in a random order of difficulty, the MBE is different from many other standardized tests you've taken (such as the SAT), where the questions become progressively more difficult within each section of the test.

MBE questions are also random in subject matter, so a Property question may be followed by a Torts question, which may be followed by a Contracts question. Note also that you won't be told the subject matter of any question; you have to figure out what area is being tested by carefully reading the question itself.

Are all the questions on the MBE given the same weight?

Yes; difficult questions are worth no more than easy ones.

How is the MBE graded?

Each question is worth one point, making a total possible "raw" score of 200. Because the difficulty of the MBE may vary from one exam to another (for example, the July 2003 MBE may be somewhat more difficult than the February 2002 MBE), "raw" scores are not comparable from year to year. To handle this problem, the Bar Examiners use a statistical procedure, called "equating," to produce what are called "scaled" scores-- raw scores that have been adjusted so that the performance of Bar Examinees can be compared from exam to exam (within the limitations of measurement and equating error). For instance, if the July, 2003 MBE turns out to be more difficult than previous MBEs, the scores of students who took the July exam would be adjusted ("scaled") upward to account for this difference in difficulty. If, on the other hand, the July, 2003 exam was easier than previous MBEs, then the scores of those who took it would be adjusted ("scaled") downward to account for that difference. This scoring procedure helps to ensure that no applicant is unfairly penalized or rewarded for taking a particular version of the exam.

Keep in mind that no credit is given for any answer except the best one. Also, if you fill in more than one answer to a question, you'll get no credit for the question (even if one of your answers is the correct one).

Will I lose points for wrong answers?

No. The MBE isn't like the SAT or "Jeopardy" — you aren't penalized for wrong answers. (And you don't have to state your answer in the form of a question.) In other words, even if you don't have any idea what the right answer is to a particular question, *it's best to guess!* You've got nothing to lose, and, if you follow the advice in this book, you've got everything to gain.

Are the official answers to the MBE ever wrong?

The answer to this has to be a "qualified yes."

Even though the MBE is exceptionally carefully prepared, sometimes questions don't operate as the Bar Examiners expected them to. In order to compensate for this, the Bar Examiners use a process called "early item analysis." The process works this way: immediately after each MBE is administered, the answer sheets of approximately 1,500 applicants in several different jurisdictions are quickly scored and analyzed. If a large number of the applicants who score the highest on the entire exam marked the wrong option to any particular question, then the official, "correct" answer is considered suspect. All suspect questions are sent back to the drafting committee that prepared them, and the committees then reexamine the questions. If they find that any question is confusing, they change the answer key in the following manner. In the rare cases where a committee finds that an entire question is faulty, everyone gets credit for his answer regardless of his choice. More often, however, two rejected choices are clearly wrong, and it has simply proven too difficult to select accurately between the two remaining answer choices. In such cases, credit is given only to applicants who marked either of the two remaining answers. Once the "early item analysis" process is completed, all answer sheets are scored using the corrected key.

Do not let the fact that the Bar Examiners use this "early item analysis" process to correct for faulty questions influence you too much. If you enter the MBE anticipating that one or more questions are going to be reviewed and discarded, you may prematurely decide that some questions are unanswerable. If you do this and just mark an answer choice randomly, figuring that you'll get credit even if you're wrong, you'll be making a **big mistake**. The question may simply be a difficult one that requires a bit more analysis. Also, the drafters simply don't make many mistakes — certainly no more than a handful on each exam — so deciding that a particular question is flawed is not good strategy.

What score do I need to pass?

The score needed to pass the MBE varies according to **where you're taking the exam**, because the Bar Examiners of each jurisdiction use the MBE in different ways. In some states, if you score high enough on the MBE, the Bar Examiners won't even look at your essays, since they assume that, if you did very well on the MBE, you're likely to score well on the essays, too, so there's really no need to grade your essays.

Most states, however, establish a specific score needed to "pass" their individual bar exams by combining MBE and essay scores. States use one of three formulas to combine the two scores: the standard deviation method, the comparative range method, and the equi-percentile method. All three methods are quite complex, and explaining them would be beyond the scope of this book. What you need to know is that, even if the MBE isn't the sole determining factor in your passing the bar exam, it contributes significantly to the result.

As a general rule, if you can get 130 "raw" questions correct, you should be on track to pass even in a tough jurisdiction. For instance, in July, 2001 (the latest year for which the NCBE has published statistics as of this writing), California had the lowest passing rate, 57%.[1] On that July 2001 MBE, the mean raw score nationally was 128.72. And the standard deviation on that exam was 19.46. If we do some statistical manipulation, and if we make the reasonable assumption that the applicants in California were exactly as good on the MBE as the applicant pool nationally was, to be just barely on track to pass in California (i.e., to be better than exactly 43% of the other applicants), you would have needed to get a raw score of 125 on that exam (which would have equated to a scaled score of about 140).

Or, consider a more typical jurisdiction, with a pass rate of 67% for July takers. (Michigan in July 2001 passed 66%, for instance.) Again assuming that this state's takers are exactly as strong as the national average, you would have to get just 120 raw questions correct to be on track to just barely pass (i.e., to be beating 33% of the other applicants).

So this is not an exam where you're expected to score a "90%" or anything close to it. If you can answer two-thirds of the questions correctly, and you perform at that same relative level of competence on your state's essay and/or performance test, you're nearly certain to pass.

Who writes MBE questions?

As you may imagine, drafting MBE questions is an involved process that involves many people. Each of the six major subjects is handled by a committee of five people — three law professors and two bar examiners. At semiannual meetings, each committee, along with special question writers, drafts 30 or 40 MBE questions. Each committee then meets for two days with experts on testing, after which the questions are redrafted. After the semiannual meeting, each committee member reviews the questions and then, a few weeks later, reviews the final form of the questions. The questions are also subject to a final review by a practicing attorney and, usually, by a law professor who is not a member of the drafting committee.

Since the MBE is so important (it is, after all, part of almost every jurisdiction's bar examination), the bar examiners of each participating jurisdiction are given an opportunity to review the test in its final stages. At that time, the entire test can be accepted or rejected; in addition, the local bar examiners may suggest changing only parts of the exam. Each drafting committee considers these suggestions and makes any changes the committee decides are needed.

---

1. In virtually all states and in every year, the mean score on the February exam is significantly lower than on the July exam. That's because February has many more repeaters. The mean scaled score in February tends to be about 6 lower than in July. Pass rates are also lower in February. To pick one example, only 37% passed the Feb. 2001 California exam, compared with 57% passing the July 2001 California exam.

HOW TO USE THIS BOOK

If you use this book correctly, it can have a dramatic impact on your MBE performance. In this introductory section, we'll discuss how you can get the most out of this book.

First, it's important to know what this book can do for you, and what it can't. Correctly preparing for the MBE involves developing two skills: a **complete grasp of the substantive law**, and the **ability to analyze MBE questions**. This book deals with the second skill: analysis. Substantive review, on the other hand, is the task of learning all the law you need to know in order to pass the MBE. You may think, "But I'm going to do every single question in this book! Shouldn't I know the law by then?" Unfortunately, the answer is no. Many students every year try to learn the law simply by doing thousands of simulated MBE questions. This is not good enough. Studying by answering MBE questions, even actual ones from past exams, such as the ones in this book, can't substitute for a good review of substantive law; it can only **supplement** it. While answering MBE questions will help reinforce many of the principles you need to know, it will provide only a random review and the **techniques** for exam-taking; it's not guaranteed to teach you all the law you need to know. Studying just by answering questions would be like attempting to write a short story by writing random sentences that sound good, all the while hoping that, when you're done, you'll have put together enough sentences to make a whole story. This is a less-than-effective way to review **every** aspect of the law.

The most effective way to review all the substantive law you need for the MBE is to review substantive material, to the level of detail you need, in an organized fashion. The *Law In A Flash* Multistate Bar Review Set is an easy and effective way to review all the substantive detail you need to know for the MBE. If you bought this book as part of the Multistate Review Set, then you have everything you need to prepare for the MBE; if not, you can purchase the set from your local bookstore or from us directly at (800) EMANUEL. Regardless of your source of study, you shouldn't rely exclusively on this book, or on practice MBE questions of any kind, for your substantive review.

HOW THIS BOOK IS ORGANIZED

Here are the major features in this book:

- First, we give you **details about the MBE** and advice on **how you should attack it**.

- Next, we give you **"Strategies and Tactics"** for each of the six subjects on the MBE.

- These are followed immediately by **questions** on that particular MBE subject, so that you can practice the strategies. These are **actual past MBE questions**, which we are reprinting under special license from the MBE examiners. (Many are from the recently-released July 1998 exam.)

- We then give you an **Answer Key** (at the beginning of the answers for that subject) so you can quickly score yourself.

- Then, perhaps most important, we give you full **explanatory answers** for each question in that subject, with detailed explanations both of why the "correct" answer is the best one and why the other answer choices are not as good.

- Next, we give you a full-length, **practice MBE (again entirely from past actual MBE questions)**, with Answer Key and full explanatory answers.

• Lastly, we give you ***answer sheets***, so you can practice doing questions under simulated exam conditions.

ATTACKING THE MBE

The first thing to read is our description of the MBE and our advice on attacking it. Those sections will give you pointers on studying and analyzing questions — on learning, in fact, to think like the Bar Examiners.

STRATEGIES AND TACTICS FOR EVERY MAJOR SUBJECT: TIMING YOURSELF

After reading "How to Attack the MBE," you should choose the subject you want to review first and read the "Strategies and Tactics" section for that subject; then, complete the practice questions in that subject. While the MBE is a timed test, try to avoid timing yourself when you first begin to practice. When you actually sit for the MBE, you'll have about 1.8 minutes to answer each question (assuming you don't fall behind). Right now, though, you aren't sitting for the MBE; you're learning how to take it. The important things to learn are, first, the black-letter law, followed by the nuances of the language the Bar Examiners use, the nature of the details they test, and, in effect, how to think the way they do. Learning these things necessarily requires more than a minute or so per question. Take your time on each question, and you'll benefit in the long run. As you become more proficient at answering MBE questions and learn more black-letter law through your substantive review, your speed will naturally increase.

USING ANSWER SHEETS

When you answer the questions on each subject or take the practice exam, use the scoring sheets provided in the back of the book. If you need more sheets, make copies of the ones provided. These scoring sheets are replicas of those you will use on the actual MBE. As you answer each question, make a note on a separate sheet of paper, mark those answers which were only your best guesses and not based on a sure knowledge of the law; in this way, you can check those answers more carefully against the full answers given in this book.

SCORING YOUR PERFORMANCE

At the beginning of each Answer section, we give you an Answer Key to let you quickly score yourself.

When you compute your raw score for a given subject, (the number correct), keep in mind that the subjects vary somewhat in the mean scores produced by applicants. Here's a table of raw scores for the July 2001 test, to give you some idea of relative difficulties:

Table 1: Subject Difficulty on The July 2001 MBE

Raw scores	Con Law	Contracts	Crim. Law	Evidence	Real Prop.	Torts
Mean # correctly answered	22.9	21.8	21.6	21.4	19.2	21.9
# of Q's	33	34	33	33	33	34
Correct answers as % of Total	69.4%	64.1%	65.5%	64.8%	58.2%	64.4%
Rank order of difficulty	6 (easiest)	2	5	4	1 (hardest)	3

So Real Property was far and away the hardest (applicants got, on average, only 58.2 % of the questions correct), Con Law was by far and away the easiest (applicants got an average of 69.4% correct), and the other four subjects were tightly clustered between 64.1% and 65.5%. One of the lessons is that you shouldn't waste too much time on the (many) very long and very difficult Real Property questions, because you won't get enough extra ones right to make a difference anyway. Conversely, you've got to "make hay while the sun shines" on the relatively easy (and short) Con Law questions. These results are fairly typical of July exams across many years.

When you score yourself using the Answer Key, compute the % correct that you got, and compare: (1) how your own performance varies from subject to subject, to let you know where you need to spend the most time; and (2) how your performance in a subject compares with the national averages, again to get a clue to where you're most relatively deficient.

READ THE EXPLANATORY ANSWERS!

For every question you try, please you *read the explanatory answer*; if you do, you'll find that the answers in this book go far beyond telling you the basic principle involved in each question. We also analyze the specific error contained in every wrong answer; we even discuss what principles you may have been thinking about if you picked that answer. If your time is limited, you don't have to read every part of our explanatory answer to every question; you can choose to read only the discussion of the answer you chose, as well as the discussion of the correct choice (if you didn't pick the correct answer). If, however, you were unsure of one of the other answer choices (for example, if you originally marked choice A as the correct answer but then changed your mind), you may want to read the discussion of that answer as well. Remember, your goal in using this book is to become intimately familiar with MBE questions and how to answer them; reaching that goal requires that you feel comfortable with as many answer choices in this book as possible. In fact, you may even become frustrated sometimes, because you feel you're reading the same principles (for instance, the elements of strict product liability) over and over again, but that's intentional. We repeat those principles, in full, every time they're applicable, so that, by the time you take the MBE, those principles will be *second nature* to you. In our opinion, it's better that you overlearn basic principles than that your knowledge be so tentative that you forget the principles when you take the MBE.

THE PRACTICE MBE

Some good advice — complete the simulated full-length MBE in our Practice MBE. By doing so, you may be able to save hundreds of dollars on Multistate seminars, which essentially give you a practice MBE and then tell you what your weak points are.

If you want to duplicate the "look and feel" of the real test, make sure the circumstances under which you take our Practice MBE are as similar as possible to those of the real MBE. First, time yourself! Second, sit in one room (perhaps a library) and work straight through, duplicating the two three-hour sessions of the actual MBE. Break only to use the bathroom, if necessary, but don't give yourself extra time for that (you won't get any on the MBE). Follow all the advice in our "Attacking the MBE" section when you take the practice MBE. Simulating the actual MBE in this way can significantly cut your anxiety when it's time for you to face the real thing: taking the practice MBE under exam conditions gives you experience at actually sitting for the whole exam; you'll find that it's quite different from doing 25 or even 50 questions at a time. The experience of sitting for a practice MBE, both in simulating the environment and in practicing how your mind will organize, process, and function during the test (i.e., attacking the MBE), really is worth the 6 hours of time spent taking the Practice MBE.

WHAT TO DO WHEN YOUR STUDY TIME IS LIMITED

Ideally, you would have a month in which to use this book, so that you could cover an average of 20 pages a day. You may find, though, that you don't have the time to go through this entire process. If that's the case, you'll still find this book an invaluable study tool. You should prioritize your studies this way:

    ❶ Read "How to Attack the MBE."

    ❷ Read the Strategies and Tactics section for each subject, paying special attention to the coverage of each topic on the MBE.

    ❸ Do the practice questions for each subject, starting with Torts and Contracts.

    ❹ Do the Practice MBE.

In terms of your substantive review, if you don't have time to study every topic in every subject, pay special attention to the topics which are heavily tested by the MBE. You'll find that information in the outlines at the beginning of the "Strategies and Tactics" sections for every subject. For instance, there are 34 questions each on Torts and Contracts, and 33 each on the other four major subjects (Evidence, Criminal Law, Property, and

Constitutional Law). In Torts, half of the questions test only Negligence; thus, almost 8.5% of the entire MBE is on Negligence, so you'd be wise to learn it very well! Contrast that with Future Interests: generally, the MBE will have no more than nine questions on all of Future Interests (and that's at the very outside); so, considering the low number of questions, coupled with the fact that Future Interests is extremely difficult for many people, you may want to allot very little study time to it if your time is limited.

In addition, keep in mind that some MBE subjects are easier than others, so, barring individual variables (e.g., you happen to be an expert on a difficult subject), you may want to concentrate your limited study time on questions in subject areas that are likely to be easiest for you to answer. (See "Scoring Your Performance" above for more details.)

While the MBE requires a substantial amount of preparation, remember that time spent preparing should be rewarded; your success will be proportionate to the amount of time you spend in reviewing the law and in understanding the techniques used by MBE examiners.

HOW TO ATTACK
THE MBE

*"How often have I said to you, that when you
have eliminated the impossible, whatever
remains, however impossible, must be the truth."*

— *Sherlock Holmes*

UNDERSTANDING THE NATURE OF THE BEAST

Let's say that you had both a photographic memory and unlimited time in which to study for the Multistate Bar Exam. In addition, you had time to read every textbook and every treatise concerning every subject on the MBE. Would you still need to know how to analyze MBE questions? The simple answer is — *no,* provided of course, that you could read and understand exam fact patterns. Your substantive knowledge would always lead you to the correct answer.

For most of us, that's just not reality — we don't have photographic memories, and we don't have unlimited time to study. That's why using this book is so important. In this section, you'll learn **how to analyze MBE questions**. This section gives you basic tips on how to study, advice on how to time yourself on the MBE, other general advice on taking the exam, how to analyze the facts in MBE questions, how to use process of elimination to arrive at the correct answer, and how to guess at the best response when your reasoning fails you (as it does the best of us).

Learning how to attack the MBE requires, first, that you understand why it's such a difficult test. Not all objective tests are difficult, but this one is. Take a look at the following hypothetical question:

> Laurel and Hardy, who've never seen each other before, are guests at a party. Laurel is standing in a corner minding his own business, holding a cream pie. Hardy walks over and snatches the cream pie out of Laurel's hands, for no apparent reason, and frightens him. If Laurel sues Hardy, the claim most likely to succeed will be
>
> A. Battery
> B. Murder
> C. Conspiracy
> D. Breach of contract

It doesn't take a rocket scientist to figure out that A is the correct answer, does it? No. That's because none of the other answers are even close to being correct — so A *must* be the best answer.

Let's change the question a bit, though. Same facts — different answers.

> A. Assault, because although Hardy intended to frighten Laurel, he didn't touch him
> B. Battery, because it isn't necessary that the person himself be touched for the claim to succeed
> C. Intentional infliction of emotional distress, because Hardy intended to frighten Laurel
> D. There is no likely claim, because Hardy's conduct wasn't tortious

We've taken a simple objective question and made it into one that's far more difficult. Why is it more difficult? Because even though the answer's the same — battery, you need a **much more detailed knowledge** of Tort law to answer the second version. In the second question, we've "masked" the correct answer with very similar answers, so it's harder to figure out what the correct answer is. That's why we call incorrect answers "distractors": they're designed to **distract** you by tempting you to pick a similar, but wrong, answer.

If you were the National Conference of Bar Examiners, and you wanted a test that would distinguish the examinees with the best grasp of the substantive law from those who didn't know the law as well, which question would you ask? The second one. And that's exactly what they do.

HOW TO STUDY FOR THE MULTISTATE BAR EXAM

In the "About the MBE" section of this book, we told you that each of the six subjects on the MBE is treated with virtually equal weight. There are 33 questions on each subject, except for Contracts and Torts, which have 34 each. The Bar Examiners have decided that each subject should be treated equally on the bar exam, and you should divide your study time accordingly. As we've said before, however, this doesn't mean that all topics within a given subject are treated equally—e.g., negligence.

When planning your study for the MBE, take into consideration two aspects for your substantive review — the **scope** of what you need to study, and the **depth** to which you have to study.

The scope of what you need to study about each subject is covered in the "Strategies and Tactics" sections in this book, which you'll find at the beginning of every subject area. As you'll see, the subject coverage is **broad**; the MBE is likely to contain a couple of questions on each of a variety of topics, not many on any one topic in particular. That's straightforward. The depth to which you must study each subject, on the other hand, is worth addressing.

First, and most importantly, keep in mind that the exam is given **nation-wide**. This means that, in general, you must learn the majority principles and ignore the vagaries of local law. You must know what the **majority approach** is on any given topic, since that's typically what you'll be asked. It doesn't do you any good on the MBE to know that there are two or more views on a topic; you have to know which is the current prevailing view.

The sample questions in this book will, first, give you a feel for the details you need to master in order to pass the MBE — make no mistake about it, **the MBE tests details, not broad concepts of law**. The explanatory answers will then give you further understanding of the majority views on a wide variety of principles. Thus, when you study, make sure you're noting the not-so-obvious details and that you understand the aims and the rationales of rules. For instance, you probably already know that, in Contracts, third party intended beneficiaries have rights under a contract, while incidental beneficiaries do not. On the MBE, though, if you're given a question on third party beneficiaries, you're unlikely to be tested on something so basic. Instead, you may need to know, for instance, when an intended beneficiary's rights "vest". The Bar Examiners know that, if you have only a superficial knowledge of the subject, you'll see that a question deals with third party beneficiaries, decide that the beneficiary mentioned is an "intended" beneficiary, and therefore give him enforceable rights on that basis. This will probably not be correct. The Bar Examiners want to reward students with more thorough knowledge of beneficiaries, students who know that, before a beneficiary's rights vest, he doesn't have enforceable rights under a contract.

Here's another example. If you remember the "Mercy Rule" from Evidence, you probably remember that it allows the defendant in a criminal case to introduce evidence of his good character. If you see a MBE question concerning the Mercy Rule, and that's all you remember about the Rule, you'll probably get the answer wrong. Why? Because there are **two other important points** to remember about the Mercy Rule. First, the character evidence must be **pertinent** (probative) in order to be admissible. Thus, in an MBE question, you may see evidence that a defendant charged with fraud was a "peaceful" man. You should realize, though, that his peacefulness is unrelated to the crime with which he's charged, so the Mercy Rule wouldn't make the evidence admissible. Second, under the Mercy Rule, the character evidence can only be offered in the form of **reputation or opinion**; it can't be evidence of specific instances of conduct. So, even if a criminal defendant charged with fraud introduced evidence of his honesty, if the evidence was in the form of a specific instance ("He was honest in his dealings with me when he sold me his car"), it wouldn't be admissible. Once again, the Bar Examiners hope to catch those students with incomplete knowledge about the Rule. Even if you know the basics of the Rule, you could miss two questions, because you don't know the Rule in enough depth to apply it to pertinence and specific facts!

As these examples indicate, your substantive review for the Multistate must teach you to think about details; you simply cannot go into the MBE armed with only general superficial principles of law.

REMEMBER WHO WILL BE "TRIPPED UP" ON MBE QUESTIONS

Knowing what kind of person will be fooled by MBE questions can help you avoid becoming such a person. There are three general types of victims; they are those who

1. panic;

2. operate by instinct, and

3. are **unprepared.**

If you analyze MBE questions, keeping in mind that these are the three kinds of people who will pick an incorrect answer, you can avoid the answers **they'd** pick and improve your chances of choosing the correct answers. Let's look at what each of these people might do on the MBE.

1. Panickers.

Unfortunately, there are many completely justifiable reasons to approach the MBE in a sweat. For instance, you may have a job riding on your passing the Bar Exam. You may feel you didn't prepare enough. You may face a couple of very tough questions early on that torpedo your confidence. Remember, though, that, no matter what causes it, panic can have disastrous effects on your performance.

What does panicking do? For one thing, severe anxiety actually inhibits your memory from functioning well. As you've probably experienced, the more anxious you are about remembering something, the less likely you are to remember it. The only real cure for this is **adequate preparation**. If you've prepared sufficiently, both substantively and by practicing MBE questions (and keeping in mind you need nowhere near a perfect score to pass the MBE), you should be able to keep your nerves from undermining your performance. Remember, you're not shooting for an A+ here; law school is **over**. Many people carry over their law school mentality of "I have to get the best score in the class" to the bar exam. That's a mistake! On the bar exam, there's no difference between a student who passes by 5 points and a student who passes by 55 points; **both pass**, and that's all that matters.

What we're primarily concerned about **here,** though, is not your attitude coming into the exam, but its impact on your ability to analyze questions. If you panic, you will not read questions carefully enough to pick the right response. Keep this in mind as you study the questions in this book. It's clear from past MBEs that the Bar Examiners know what people will overlook when they panic — some answers are clearly incorrect simply because they misapply some very basic fact in the question! Understanding what a panicker will do can help you avoid the same mistake.

2. People who operate by instinct.

You've probably heard the old saying a million times — "Your first instinct is generally correct." On the MBE, **ignore this advice at all costs.** The Bar Examiners aren't looking for lawyers who fly by the seat of their pants; they want lawyers who can apply legal principles to factual situations in a rational, disciplined manner. You should, therefore, follow an instinct only if you can tie that instinct to a principle of law.

How can your instincts hurt you on the MBE? One, they may make you overlook stated facts. Suppose, for example, that, in a Criminal Law question, you're asked if the defendant will be found guilty under the facts. One of the elements of the crime described is intent, and the only evidence on this issue is the defendant's own testimony, in which he states that he didn't intend to commit the crime. The facts tell you to **assume the jury believes the defendant.** Now, your instincts may tell you that the defendant is lying through his teeth and that no one over the age of five would believe him, so you leap for the answer that says the defendant will be found guilty. Watch out! If the facts tell you that the jury believes him, your instincts shouldn't matter. If you follow your instincts, you'll pick an incorrect response. **The facts** tell you that the jury will find that the defendant lacked intent and so isn't guilty.

Here's another mistake you'll make if you follow your instincts. You probably remember from Evidence class that no piece of evidence is ever **really** inadmissible; virtually everything is admissible, somehow. If you let your instinct guide you on the MBE, therefore, you'd **never** pick the "inadmissible as hearsay not within any exception" response. And you'd be wrong fairly regularly. (For more on how to deal with this specific problem, see the "Strategies and Tactics" for Evidence.)

If you let your instincts guide you, you may also let your emotions control your reasoning. Look at this example from a past MBE:

Dutton, disappointed by his 8-year-old son's failure to do well in school, began systematically depriving the child of food during summer vacation. Although his son became seriously ill from malnutrition, Dutton failed to call a doctor. He believed that, as a parent, he had the sole right to determine whether the child was fed or received medical treatment. Eventually the child died. An autopsy disclosed that the child had suffered agonizingly as a result of the starvation, that a physician's aid would have alleviated the suffering, and that, although the child would have died in a few months from malnutrition, the actual cause of death was an untreatable form of cancer.

The father was prosecuted for murder, defined in the jurisdiction as "unlawful killing of a human being with malice aforethought." The father should be

- A. acquitted, because of the defendant's good-faith belief concerning parental rights in supervising children

- B. acquitted, because summoning the physician or feeding the child would not have prevented the child's death from cancer

- C. convicted, because the father's treatment of his son showed reckless indifference to the value of life

- D. convicted, because the child would have died from malnutrition had he not been afflicted with cancer

What's your gut reaction? Dutton is a slimeball, right? Sure he is — but the fact is that he **didn't** cause his child's death; the child died of cancer, so Dutton can't be liable for the child's death. If you let your instincts overwhelm you, you'll pick C — after all, Dutton **was** recklessly indifferent to his child's welfare and deserves to be punished. If you do this, you'll get this question wrong. Remember: in real life, being an emotional, caring person is an asset, but on the MBE, it's not — you have to be robot-like in applying the law to the facts you're given. The correct answer is B.

3. Those who are unprepared.

Obviously, the person the Bar Examiners most certainly intend to snare is the one who is unprepared for the MBE. Simply put, **if you don't know the law, you shouldn't be a lawyer**. A person unprepared for the MBE will make mistakes, such as remembering only snippets of rules or forgetting how theories apply to facts. Of course, it's not possible to be completely prepared for every single legal issue on the MBE, so, to some extent, you're bound to be underprepared. If, though, you've recently completed law school when you take the MBE, you'll probably be able to answer as many as half of the MBE questions correctly simply on the basis of your classroom knowledge. If you review and understand the substantive law and learn from this book how to analyze questions, you should be able to answer enough of the remaining questions to pass.

HOW TO ANALYZE MBE QUESTIONS

The advice in this section addresses the MBE in general. The "Strategies and Tactics" section for each subject will give you specific tips on handling each particular subject, so you should always read the "Strategies and Tactics" before you attempt to answer any questions on a subject.

As you read further, you may find the process of analysis outlined here a bit overwhelming at first; you may even be tempted to skip over it. **Don't!** If you follow the procedure given below faithfully when you begin to practice answering questions, it will become second nature, and you'll be able to apply it almost automatically. As a result, you'll be able to analyze MBE questions quickly and accurately, and you'll enter the MBE with a significant advantage.

A. Analyzing the facts of the question.

a. The composition of MBE questions.

Almost every MBE question will give you a factual setting and then a specific inquiry. In some cases, one common set facts will be given and will form the basis for a whole series of questions. Here's an example of a typical set of facts:

Al and Bill are identical twins. Al, angry at David, said, "You'd better stay out of my way. The next time I find you around here, I'll beat you up." Two days later, while in the neighborhood, David saw Bill coming toward him. As Bill came up to David, Bill raised his hand. Thinking Bill was Al, and fearing bodily harm, David struck Bill.

If Bill asserts a claim against David, and David relies on the privilege of self-defense, David will

- A. not prevail, because Bill was not an aggressor

- B. not prevail unless Bill intended his gesture as a threat

- C. prevail, if David honestly believed that Bill would attack him

- D. prevail only if a reasonable person under the circumstances would have believed that Bill would attack him

The first paragraph is the factual setting. The final sentence, beginning with "If Bill..." is the specific inquiry or "the call of the question".

b. Read carefully.

In general, because of the time constraints of the MBE, you'll only have time to read a factual setting in detail once, so make that reading count! You have to read carefully in order to answer correctly, because many wrong answers ("distractors") are aimed at people who skip over important facts. As you read a question, you may want to highlight important points (you're allowed to mark in the question book), but watch your time.

The following example from a past MBE illustrates the importance of careful reading.

> Lester, the owner in fee simple of a small farm consisting of thirty acres of land improved with a house and several outbuildings, leased the same to Tanner for a ten-year period. After two years had expired, the government condemned twenty acres of the property and allocated the compensation award to Lester and Tanner according to their respective interest so taken. It so happened, however, that the twenty acres taken embraced all of the farm's tillable land, leaving only the house, outbuildings, and a small woodlot. There is no applicable statute in the jurisdiction where the property is located, nor any provision in the lease relating to condemnation. Tanner quit possession, and Lester brought suit against him to recover rent. Lester will
>
> A. lose, because there has been a frustration of purpose which excuses Tanner from further performance of his contract to pay rent
>
> B. lose, because there has been a breach of the implied covenant of quiet enjoyment by Lester's inability to provide Tanner with possession of the whole of the property for the entire term
>
> C. win, because of the implied warranty on the part of the tenant to return the demised premises in the same condition at the end of the term as they were at the beginning
>
> D. win, because the relationship of landlord and tenant was unaffected by the condemnation, thus leaving Tanner still obligated to pay rent

If you read that question quickly, you might have overlooked the fact that ***Tanner was already compensated for his loss by the condemnation award*** and choose A or B. If, instead, you read the question carefully, you could eliminate choices A and B, since under both of those choices Tanner prevails, and his prior recovery alone should suggest to you that he shouldn't. You could, therefore, narrow your choice down to C or D. (In fact, the correct response is D.) See how important it is to read the facts carefully?

c. Don't assume facts.

A corollary to the "read carefully" rule is that you should be careful not to read facts that aren't there into the questions on the MBE. The MBE is a meticulously crafted test; the facts you need in order to answer the question will be given to you, so you must rely only on those facts and on reasonable inferences from them. (This has important ramifications in choosing a correct response, which we'll discuss in detail a little later on.)

d. Choose the simple interpretation.

Don't make problems more complex than they really are. If there are multiple ways to interpret a question, one which makes the problem straightforward, and others which make it very difficult, choose the straightforward interpretation.

e. "Trigger" factors to watch for in reading MBE questions.

While you should read every question carefully, there are a few "trigger" items which are extremely likely to determine the correct answer.

1. Statutes.

Some MBE questions contain statutes. A statute may be given for two reasons:

a. There are conflicting common law rules, but no one majority rule.

For instance, burglary is subject to several different rules: some states limit burglary to a residence and to nighttime; others require neither or only one of these. The same conflict is evident in defining degrees of murder. If a question involves that kind of precise issue, you'll almost certainly be given a statute to guide you as to which rule applies.

b. The Examiners want to see if you can ignore your instincts.

Sometimes you'll be given a statute that doesn't comport with what you think ought to happen. For example, a criminal statute may require knowledge, but your gut reaction is that the conduct described need only constitute *negligence* to result in liability. Follow the statute, not your instinct.

As both (a) and (b) indicate, the most important things to do when you're faced with a statute are to read it carefully and to apply it *mechanically*. If a question contains a statute, the statute almost certainly determines the central issue, and answering correctly almost certainly depends upon interpreting the statute as it was written.

Here's an example from a past MBE:

> A state statute requires any person licensed to sell prescription drugs to file with the State Board of Health a report listing the types and amounts of such drugs sold, if his sales of such drugs exceed $50,000 during a calendar year. The statute makes it a misdemeanor to "knowingly fail to file" such a report.
>
> Nelson, who is licensed to sell prescription drugs, sold $63,000 worth of prescription drugs during 1976 but did not file the report. Charged with committing the misdemeanor, Nelson testifies that he did a very poor job of keeping records and did not realize that his sales of prescription drugs had exceeded $50,000. If the jury believes Nelson, he should be found
>
> A. guilty, because this is a public welfare offense
>
> B. guilty, because he cannot be excused on the basis of his own failure to keep proper records
>
> C. not guilty, because the statute punishes omissions and he was not given fair warning of his duty to act
>
> D. not guilty, because he was not aware of the value of the drugs he had sold

Here, you're probably tempted to choose choice B, because you figure that if Nelson is such a bonehead that he doesn't keep complete records, he should be liable — it's really not fair for him to rely on his sloppiness to avoid liability. Focus on the statute, though. The statute requires "knowing" behavior, so if Nelson's behavior wasn't "knowing," he can't be guilty. Since he didn't realize he'd sold more than $50,000 worth of prescription drugs, he didn't act knowingly when he failed to file the report, so he can't be guilty under the statute. Mechanically applying the statute to these facts will lead you straight to the correct response: D.

2. Pay special attention to seemingly meaningless details about people.

While the Bar Examiners do sometimes give you a *deliberate* red herring, you should always assume that every fact in every question is important. For instance, normally, you won't be told any personal characteristics about people in the questions; you'll typically see only statements such as: "Able contracted with Baker" or "Jones shot Smith," and you can generally assume that all the people mentioned are sane, responsible adults. If, therefore, a question does tell you more about a person, such as that "Able, a ten-year-old, contracted with Baker," the extra information given is likely to be important, so you should note it and use it. In Contract law, what does including Able's age suggest? An incapacity to contract. The same kind of thing is true in the following examples. Say you're told that "Lee, a chronically unemployed person, is testifying." Since the question has given you an additional fact about Lee, look at that fact. What does "chronically unemployed" tell you? It tells you, for one thing, that Lee probably can't be an expert witness so probably can't offer certain kinds of opinion testimony. Say you're told that "Fred, a pharmacist, offers to sell his snow blower to Arnie." Ask yourself, what does Fred's being a pharmacist suggest? For one thing, that he's not a merchant dealing in snow blowers, so his offer *can't* be irrevocable without consideration. See how it works? Here's another example, this time from a past MBE:

> Addle, who has been in the painting and contracting business for ten years and has a fine reputation, contracts to paint Boone's barn. Boone's barn is a standard red barn with loft. The contract has no provision regarding assignment. If Addle assigns the contract to Coot, who has comparable experience and reputation, which of the following statements is correct?
>
> A. Addle is in breach of contract
>
> B. Boone may refuse to accept performance by Coot

C. Boone is required to accept performance by Coot

D. There is a novation

Focus specifically on the description after Coot's name in the question — "who has comparable experience and reputation." What does this suggest to you? If you remember the rules on assignment, you know that, to be valid, an assignment cannot increase the risk that the promisee (here, Boone) will not receive the promised performance. What does Coot's comparable experience and reputation suggest? That this risk won't be increased, and that the assignment is likely to be valid! Of course, assignments have other elements as well, but if you focused on the additional information given and **applied** it, you'd clearly eliminate choices A and B, and that would give you a 50-50 chance of choosing the correct answer. (In fact, the correct response is C. Choice D is wrong because a novation requires the consent of the promisee to performance by the assignee.)

f. Handling the specific inquiry in each question.

1. Reword the inquiry.

Most questions on the MBE are framed in the positive; that is, you're told to look, for example, for the "most likely outcome" or the "claim that is most likely to succeed" or the "best defense." You may find such questions difficult unless you reword them. This is how to do it:

Question: "What is the most likely outcome?"
Reword to: "What will the result be — and why?"

Question: "Which claim is most likely to succeed?
Reword to: "Which is the *only* claim that can succeed on these facts — and why?"

Question: "What is Defendant's best defense?"
Reword to: "Why *won't* the defendant be guilty on these facts?"

Question: "If party X loses, the most likely basis for the judgment is that..."
Reword to: "Party X loses because..."

What does this rewording do? It makes you look for one correct answer. In the overwhelming majority of MBE questions, there is only one possible correct answer, because the other alternatives are somehow defective — i.e., they misstate the facts, the law, or both. If you reword the specific inquiry and thus focus your mind on finding one correct answer, you're less likely to be seduced by distractors.

In a **few** MBE questions, the specific inquiry or "call" will be worded **in the negative**; that is, you are asked to determine, for example, "which claim won't succeed," "which is the least sufficient basis for admitting the evidence," "of which crime is Defendant least likely to be guilty," etc. The primary difference between handling negative as opposed to positive inquiries is in **how you apply a process of elimination** to arrive at the correct response (this will be discussed in detail below). The process for **rewording,** however, is the same. Here's an example from a past MBE:

In a narcotics conspiracy prosecution against Daly, the prosecutor offers in evidence a tape recording of a telephone call allegedly made by Daly. A lay witness is called to testify that the voice on the recording is Daly's. Her testimony to which of the following would be the LEAST sufficient basis for admitting the recording?

A. She had heard the same voice on a similar tape recording identified to her by Daly's brother.

B. She had heard Daly speak many times, but never over the telephone

C. She had, specifically for the purpose of preparing to testify, talked with Daly over the telephone at a time after the recording was made

D. She had been present with Daly when he engaged in the conversation in question but had heard only Daly's side of the conversation

You should reword the question to read: "When **won't** the recording be admissible?" This forces you to look for the only insufficient basis for authentication and not to engage in drawing fine lines as to which type of authentication will be best. You'll find that rewording such questions makes it considerably easier to answer them. (In fact, the correct response is A, since it's the only one where the witness has no personal knowledge of Daly's voice.)

2. Summon the applicable test immediately.

If you're asked if a certain result should occur, *immediately* summon to your mind the appropriate test under the rules you've learned . For example, if you're asked whether Defendant will be guilty of murder, focus on what murder requires — an unlawful killing, neither justifiable nor excusable, with malice aforethought. If you're asked if a state statute is constitutional, think immediately of the three-prong standard for constitutionality of state statutes — within state's power, not violating any person's constitutional rights, not an undue burden on interstate commerce. Sometimes you won't know the nature of a claim or of an argument until you read each answer choice; strategies for dealing with that situation are discussed elsewhere. If, however, you're asked about a certain result in the question itself, immediately calling to mind the applicable rule or test will help prevent you from being seduced into choosing a distractor.

B. Analyzing responses — the process of elimination.

The MBE is like other standardized tests in one very important respect — the best, and sometimes only, way to arrive at the correct answer is to use a process of elimination. Basically, you should arrive at the correct answer by eliminating, one by one, any answer which clearly *cannot* be correct.

Think about it: in theory, for each MBE question, you should be able to eliminate three answers as definitely wrong, and, by doing that, get a perfect score — without knowing that any answer was definitely correct! Of course, this would never happen in reality, but it does indicate the value of knowing how to eliminate incorrect responses.

On the MBE, knowing how to recognize a bad response is *your most valuable analytical skill,* and we'll teach you how to do it in this section. First, we'll discuss the basic procedure for eliminating incorrect responses (issue spotting and modifiers), and then we'll discuss how answer choices can be wrong.

a. The basic concept.

First, let's take a look at a question and go over the basics of the process of elimination as applied to the MBE. Here's a question from a past MBE.

> Statutes in the jurisdiction define criminal assault as "an attempt to commit a criminal battery" and criminal battery as "causing an offensive touching."
>
> As Edward was walking down the street, a gust of wind blew his hat off. Edward reached out, trying to grab his hat, and narrowly missed striking Margaret in the face with his hand. Margaret, fearful of being struck by Edward, pushed Edward away.
>
> If charged with criminal assault, Edward should be found
>
>   A. guilty, because he caused Margaret to be in apprehension of an offensive touching
>
>   B. guilty, because he should have realized he might strike someone by reaching out
>
>   C. not guilty, because he did not intend to hit Margaret
>
>   D. not guilty, because he did not hit Margaret

In applying the process of elimination, you should analyze each answer choice separately, determining if it's a possible correct answer or if it can be eliminated. Remember, in order for an answer to be correct, *every aspect* of it must be correct: it must correctly characterize the facts, it must state the correct law, its result must be consistent with its reasoning (if it's a "two part" answer), and it must address and resolve a central issue. If a response is *potentially* correct, mark a "Y" for "yes" next to the answer in the question booklet; if not, eliminate it with an "N" for "no."

Let's look at each of the responses for the question above.

> As we discussed above, when you're told the nature of a claim in a specific question, you should *immediately* think of the test for that claim. The task is made easy for you here, because the definition of criminal assault — "an attempt to commit a criminal battery" — is provided by the statute in the problem. Keeping this in mind, analyze each response. Choice A correctly characterizes the facts, but it understates the *mens rea* required for the crime: it suggests that merely causing apprehension is sufficient for guilt. Your knowledge of substantive law should, however, tell you that "attempt" requires *intent,* but choice A suggests that causing an apprehension of imminent contact is a criminal act, without regard to the accused's *mens rea*; thus, choice A is definitely incorrect, and you should mark an "N" next to it.

Choice B is, similarly, plausible on the facts, but it also misstates the law. The "should have realized" language in choice B suggests that ***negligence*** is the standard required by the statute. In fact, this understates the mental element required. By requiring attempt, the statute clearly requires intent, not mere negligence. Thus, choice B cannot be correct, and you should mark an "N" next to it, as well.

Choice C suggests that Edward should not be guilty because he didn't intend to hit Margaret. Choice C thus identifies the correct mental element, and it reflects some of the question's facts — that Edward didn't intend to hit Margaret but rather intended only to retrieve his hat. Furthermore, Edward's lack of intent is a central issue, because the lack of this element of the crime would result in his acquittal. Finally, choice C's result agrees with its reasoning. Choice C is, therefore, a very strong likelihood, and you should mark a "Y" next to it.

Finally, choice D states that Edward can't be guilty, because he didn't actually hit Margaret. As discussed above, focus in on the language of the statute. The statute cited doesn't actually require a touching; a mere *attempt* to touch is enough to satisfy the statute. Choice D misstates the law, so it cannot be a correct response. Mark it with an "N."

Process of elimination on this question, then, leaves you with three "N's" and only one "Y." The "Y" response must be the correct one and, in fact, it is.

You may feel that this is a laborious way to go about answering MBE questions, especially since you'll be working under time constraints when you actually take the MBE Actually, it's the best way to master the MBE process. In fact, on many questions, you'll go through this process very quickly, because you'll immediately spot the best response and quickly eliminate the other three. When that happens, ***great!*** Just mark the correct response on your answer sheet and keep moving. When you begin practicing for the exam, though, use as much time as you need to master the process. You'll speed up as you practice.

A few paragraphs back, we told you that, sometimes, process of elimination is the only way to arrive at a correct response to an MBE question. Just look at the following question, from a past MBE:

> Tess occupied an apartment in a building owned by Len. She paid rent of $125 in advance each month. During the second month of occupancy, Tess organized the tenants in the building as a tenants' association and the association made demands of Len concerning certain repairs and improvements the tenants wanted. When Tess tendered rent for the third month, Len notified her that rent for the fourth and subsequent months would be $200 per month. Tess protested and pointed out that all other tenants paid rent of $125 per month. Thereupon, Len gave the required statutory notice that the tenancy was being terminated at the end of the third month. By an appropriate proceeding, Tess contests Len's right to terminate. If Tess succeeds, it will be because
>
> A. a periodic tenancy was created by implication
> B. the doctrine prohibiting retaliatory eviction is part of the law of the jurisdiction
> C. the $200 rent demanded violates the agreement implied by the rate charged to other tenants
> D. the law implies a term of one year in the absence of any express agreement

You can, if you like, go through a detailed "Y" and "N" elimination with each response here. (In fact, this question appears in the Practice MBE in this book, as question 136, and each response is analyzed in detail in the answer to that question.) We include this question here, though, to point out that there are times when a correct answer can only be deduced by a process of elimination. Here, with a basic knowledge of Property law, you'd be able to eliminate choices A, C, and D conclusively. That would leave B, a response you'd be unlikely to choose as the correct answer under any other circumstances. For one thing, the MBE is a national exam, and choice B addresses local law; furthermore, the doctrine of retaliatory eviction is a very minor point of Property law, one you probably never covered in law school. If you've used the process of elimination, however, you know that the other three answers are unquestionably wrong under the rules which you have learned, so choice B ***must*** be the right response. And it is.

b. How to eliminate incorrect responses.

Now that you've got the basic concept down, let's address some specifics on how to eliminate incorrect responses.

l. Issue spotting on the MBE.

Your ability to identify and resolve the central issue in each question is crucial to your ability to answer MBE questions correctly. To do this, you must not only spot issues in the facts themselves, but also be sensitive to nuances in the answer choices. The "Strategies and Tactics" sections address this in detail for each subject, so we'll examine only some basic principles here.

If you're used to taking essay exams in school, you already know the importance of issue spotting. Since the MBE is an *objective* test, you may be tempted to believe you won't need to spot issues. That's only *partially* correct. The MBE requires only *modified* issue spotting, because you're working with a limited set of possibilities: one of the choices *must* identify and resolve a central issue. You don't have to **supply** the right answer—you only have to **recognize** it.

Don't get too excited, though; you aren't completely off the hook, because you *also* have to be able to (1) identify *what issue each response is addressing*, and (2) identify *the central issue in the problem*. If the central issue isn't obvious to you, based on your reading of the facts, you can sometimes use the answer choices to help identify what the central issue must be, if you work correctly and in a disciplined fashion.

Let's address the "central issue in the problem" aspect of issue spotting first. This requires you to ask yourself, "what, *in theory*, is going on in this problem?" Say, for instance, that the question asks if plaintiff's claim for negligence will succeed. You must know that, to prove negligence, the plaintiff will have to prove duty, breach, causation, and damages; you must also know that the plaintiff will only succeed if the defendant doesn't have a valid defense. An issue raising one of these elements must be present in the facts of the question; the correct response will be the one that addresses and resolves that issue.

Suppose, instead, that you're trying to solve a problem for which you must pick which plaintiff's claim is "most likely to succeed." To do this, you must find the answer choice which most closely addresses, and overcomes, the greatest obstacle to the plaintiff's success. You'll have to: (1) think of what, theoretically, the plaintiff must prove; (2) identify which element of his position is weakest (or which defense is strongest); and, (3) choose an answer which states a valid argument for overcoming that obstacle.

To practice further, suppose you're faced with an Evidence question that asks you to identify the "most likely" basis on which a piece of evidence will be admissible. Ask yourself: What's the most likely reason the evidence *wouldn't* be admissible? Is it hearsay? Opinion? Character evidence? The correct response will have to address that central reason; by reading each of the choices, you'll find out, one way or another, what that issue is. Every answer choice, either explicitly or implicitly, addresses some issue. For example, in Torts questions, if an answer uses phrases such as "should have known," "reasonable care," and the like, the language used tells you that it must be addressing the issue of negligence.

Let's look at a fairly simple question from a past MBE.

> Pitt sued Dow for damages for injuries that Pitt incurred when a badly rotted limb fell from a curbside tree in front of Dow's home and hit Pitt. Dow claimed that the tree was on city property and thus was the responsibility of the city. At trial, Pitt offered testimony that, a week after the accident, Dow had cut the tree down with a chainsaw. The offered evidence is
>
> A. inadmissible, because there is a policy to encourage safety precautions
>
> B. inadmissible, because it is irrelevant to the condition of the tree at the time of the accident
>
> C. admissible to show the tree was on Dow's property
>
> D. admissible to show the tree was in a rotted condition

What's going on here? Pitt is offering evidence of something Dow did *after* an incident to fix a dangerous condition. What, in legal terms, is Pitt doing? He's offering evidence of a *subsequent remedial measure,* and the fact that Dow denied ownership of the property suggests that Pitt is offering the evidence to prove that the tree is on Dow's property. Remember that, while subsequent remedial measures are inadmissible to prove negligence or wrongdoing (due to the public policy concern of encouraging safety precautions), such evidence *is* admissible to prove ownership and control. Now look at the answer choices. Choice A states the general rationale of the subsequent remedial measure rule. Even if you didn't realize that the central issue in this problem was the admissibility of evidence of subsequent remedial measures, the language in A would suggest that you go back to the facts and see if you can't spot that issue. What does choice B do? It suggests that the evidence is inadmissible because it doesn't make any issue in the case any more or less likely — the choice raises the issue of relevancy. Choice C *implicitly* recognizes that the problem is one of admitting evidence of subsequent remedial measures *by invoking an exception to the general rule: proving ownership*. Choice D implicitly states that the evidence should be admissible because it's relevant to the facts at issue — that is, Dow's chopping the tree down a week after the accident indicates that it was, in fact, in a rotted condition.

Once you've broken down the answer choices into their theoretical bases, it becomes much simpler to spot both the central issue and the choice which correctly resolves it: C. The example also reinforces how important it is for you to be able to determine what *exact issue* a response is addressing, because that isn't always straightforward.

Generally, the central issue of each question is reasonably obvious in the fact pattern. Sometimes, though, the only way to spot the central issue is to determine the focus of the answer choices. Here's an example from a past MBE.

> Miller is tried for armed robbery of the First Bank of City. The prosecution, in its case in chief, offers evidence that, when Miller was arrested one day after the crime, he had a quantity of heroin and a hypodermic needle in his possession. This evidence should be
>
> A. admitted to prove Miller's motive to commit the crime
>
> B. admitted to prove Miller's propensity to commit crimes
>
> C. excluded, because its probative value is substantially outweighed by the danger of unfair prejudice
>
> D. excluded, because such evidence may be offered only to rebut evidence of good character offered by defendant

Let's focus on choice C. It suggests that the evidence is inadmissible because it's not legally relevant — that is, its probative value is substantially outweighed by the danger of unfair prejudice. To see if that's the correct response, you'd have to go back to the facts and, in essence, "spot" the issue. Is there a legal relevance problem in these facts? There *is*, because the evidence is sufficiently "shocking" that a jury could give it undue weight and probably use it for purposes other than those which are proper under these facts (considering the choices here, the evidence offered could only be used to prove motive, i.e., that he needed money to purchase drugs). You can see that the MBE format can actually benefit you; with an objective test, issue spotting is simplified, because the central issue *must* be resolved by at least one of the answer choices. Note, though, that issue spotting is still a vital skill, a skill you must have in order to answer most MBE questions correctly.

2. Language specifics.

On the MBE, in order to distinguish correct from incorrect answers choices, you must meticulously read the alternatives.

a. Glance at the modifier quickly, then study the reasoning and, finally, the result.

Many MBE answers will have three distinct parts: the result, the reasoning to support that result, and a *modifier* linking the two. For instance, an answer might read, "Admissible, because the statement is an admission of a party-opponent," or, "liable, only if she was negligent," or, "guilty, because they planned and conspired to steal the stamps." The portion *before* the comma is the "result"; the *first word after* the comma (because, if, unless, since) is the "modifier"; the portion *after* the modifier is the "reasoning."

When you first look at the alternative answers after reading a question, glance quickly at the modifier. Usually, the modifier is "because." If it's *something else*, such as "if," "unless," "but," "only if," or the like, make special note of this. We'll discuss why in a moment.

After you've glanced at the modifier, you should analyze the reasoning to see if it's correct (this may seem counterintuitive, since you're likely to want to look at the result next). The reasoning can be incorrect due to misstating the facts, misstating the law, or both (more on this below). If the reasoning is incorrect, the answer cannot be correct; you can eliminate it and move on.

If the reasoning is correct, you have to take another look at the modifier. Here's how you should deal with the three most common modifiers: "because," "if," and "unless."

1. **Where "because" is the modifier.**

   As we said earlier, *"because"* is by far the most common modifier on the MBE. If "because" is used as the modifier, the answer can be correct only if:

   ➡ The reasoning addresses and resolves a central issue (or at least a more central issue than any other response);

   ➡ The facts in the question *completely satisfy* the reasoning (that is, if the reasoning says, "because he was drunk," the facts must state or imply *unequivocally* that he was drunk); and

   ➡ The result is consistent with the reasoning (for instance, if the reasoning states, "because the statement was an admission by a party-opponent," the result *must* be "admissible" in order for the answer to be correct).

   Keep in mind that there are synonyms for "because" which are used on the MBE; these include *"since"* and *"as"* (for example, "admissible *as* a prior identification" really means "admissible *because it (*the statement) is a prior identification").

   Now, let's take a look at those modifiers we told you to watch for: "if" and "unless."

2. **Where "if" is the modifier.**

   Where "if" is the modifier, in order to be correct, the reasoning need only be *plausible* under the facts (that is, there can't be anything in the facts to suggest the reasoning *couldn't* be true), the reasoning must address a central issue, and the result and the reasoning must agree.

   As you can see, the big difference between "because" and "if" is that the "because" reasoning must flow unequivocally from the facts; the "if" reasoning must be *only plausible.* Take a look at the following example.

   > Husband and Wife, walking on a country road, were frightened by a bull running loose on the road. They climbed over a fence to get onto the adjacent property, owned by Grower. After climbing over the fence, Husband and Wife damaged some of Grower's plants which were near the fence. The fence was posted with a large sign, "No Trespassing."
   >
   > Grower saw Husband and Wife and came toward them with his large watchdog on a long leash. The dog rushed at Wife. Grower had intended only to frighten Husband and Wife, but the leash broke, and before Grower could restrain the dog, the dog bit Wife. If Husband asserts a claim based on assault against Grower, will Husband prevail?
   >
   > A. Yes, because the landowner did not have a privilege to use excessive force
   >
   > B. Yes, if Husband reasonably believed that the dog might bite him
   >
   > C. No, if the dog did not come in contact with him
   >
   > D. No, if Grower was trying to protect his property

   Let's look at choice B. Remember, before you even got to choice B, you should have thought of the elements for tortious assault — an act creating in plaintiff a reasonable apprehension of immediate harmful or offensive contact with plaintiff's person, intent to create this apprehension, and causation. You also should have noted that choices B, C, and D all use the modifier "if" (which is quite unusual, since "because" is the normal modifier). So much for preliminaries. Let's go through the "if" reasoning to see if choice B could be correct. First, is the reasoning plausible on the facts? Well, there's nothing to indicate that it *couldn't* be true, and since you could *infer from the facts* (remember, inferences are permissible) that Husband was physically close to *Wife* when the dog attacked her, it's plausible that *Husband* feared he'd be bitten, too. Second, does the choice resolve a central issue? Yes — it satisfies the apprehension element of assault, and that's the central issue on these facts, since it was Wife who was bitten, and so there would be some question as to whether Husband was put in apprehension of immediate contact. Finally, the reasoning and the result match: if Husband was put in fear, assuming the other elements of assault (which are not very much in question on these facts) were met, Husband would prevail. Of course, you'd have to eliminate the other possibilities to determine *conclusively* that B is correct, but it's clear from this analysis that B is the correct response.

Let's take a quick look at choice C to see how a response with an "if" modifier can be incorrect. First, is the reasoning plausible on the facts? Yes — it's possible that the dog didn't come into contact with Husband, because the facts don't state otherwise. Second, does this choice address and resolve a central issue? *No* — this is where choice C falls apart. Assault doesn't require contact; battery does. Thus, the fact that the dog didn't come into contact with Husband would not determine if he'd prevail. Choice C can't, therefore, be the best response.

Keep in mind that "if" also has **synonyms** or **equivalents** ("as long as," for example); if you see such a synonym, your analysis should be the same.

3. **When "unless" is the modifier.**

    Now let's look at "unless" as a modifier. When this modifier is used, the reasoning must be the only circumance under which the result *cannot* occur. If you can think of even *one other way* the result might come about, the response cannot be correct. Let's look at an example from a past MBE.

    > Carver is a chemical engineer. She has no interest in or connection with Chemco. Carver noticed that Chemco's most recent, publicly issued financial statement listed, as part of Chemco's assets, a large inventory of a certain special chemical compound. This asset was listed at a cost of $100,000, but Carver knew that the ingredients of the compound were in short supply and that the current market value of the inventory was in excess of $1,000,000. There was no current public quotation of the price of Chemco stock. The book value of Chemco stock, according to the statement, was $5 a share; its actual value was $30 a share.
    >
    > Knowing these facts, Carver offered to purchase from Page, at $6 a share, the 1,000 shares of Chemco stock owned by Page. Page and Carver had not previously met. Page sold the stock to Carver for $6 a share.
    >
    > If Page asserts a claim based on misrepresentation against Carver, will Page prevail?
    >
    > A. Yes, because Carver knew that the value of the stock was greater than the price she offered
    >
    > B. Yes, if Carver did not inform Page of the true value of the inventory
    >
    > C. No, unless Carver told Page that the stock was not worth more than $6 a share
    >
    > D. No, if Chemco's financial statement was available to Page

    Let's focus on choice C, which uses "unless" as a modifier. Using our method, when you look at choice C, you should say to yourself: "Is there any way Page could prevail if Carver didn't tell her the stock was worth more than $6 a share?" Remember, as soon as you read the specific inquiry in this question, you should have summoned to your mind the elements of misrepresentation: Defendant's misrepresentation of a material past or present fact, Defendant's knowledge of falsity/reckless disregard for falsity, Defendant's intent to induce Plaintiff's reliance, Plaintiff's actual and justifiable reliance, and damages. You should also remember other substantive law: that misrepresentation can take the form of nondisclosure only when there exists a duty to disclose, due to special circumstances (such as a fiduciary relationship between the two parties). Beyond that, you should recognize that the facts give you additional personal information — that Carver and Page had **never met** — which should strongly suggest to you that Carver didn't owe Page a duty of disclosure as to the real value of the stock; without such a duty, Carver's nondisclosure couldn't be actionable as misrepresentation. Thus, what choice C states is true: without Carver's representation to Page that the stock was worth **more** than Carver paid for it, there is **no way** for Page to prevail! C is the correct response.

    Before we leave this question, let's look at choice B, which uses "if" as a modifier. Go through your analysis process. First, is the reasoning plausible on the facts? Yes. There's nothing to suggest that Carver **did** inform Page of the inventory's true value. Second, does this resolve a central issue? No. It doesn't resolve Carver's liability, which must be based on the element of duty. The central issue here concerns Carver's duty to disclose the value of the stock, so the result choice B reaches, that Page will prevail, cannot be reached on its reasoning; it would **have** to provide a basis for liability. Since it doesn't, it can't be the best response.

Finally, look at choice A, which uses the "because" modifier. Remember, with "because," the reasoning must be unequivocally shown in the facts. Here, it is — you're expressly told that Carver knew that the value of the Chemco stock was far greater than Page offered. But that fact doesn't resolve a central issue! Misrepresentation in the form of nondisclosure, as we discussed two paragraphs back, requires a duty to disclose. No such duty exists here. Thus, Carver's knowledge of the true value of the stock **doesn't** make her liable, contrary to what choice A states. (Incidentally, if the representation here were "positive" — e.g., Carver told Page, "This stock isn't worth more than $6" — then Carver's knowledge of its value **would** be one element supporting a misrepresentation claim.)

Remember that we told you to look at the reasoning before the result? After doing all this work with modifiers, you should see why. Modifiers like "if" and "unless" can **change the result** — they're "catch words". If you only looked at the answer choices to find a specific result, you couldn't isolate and reject an incorrect answer.

c. How answer choices can be wrong.

Having discussed the threshold issues of issue spotting and modifiers, let's examine how answer choices can be wrong.

In the last section, we told you that your most important analysis skill on the MBE is the ability to identify when an answer choice is definitely wrong. In this section, we'll address the different ways in which choices can be wrong and the order in which you should analyze each choice.

There are three general ways in which an answer choice can be wrong: (1) it can mischaracterize the facts; (2) it can misstate the law; and/or (3) it can ignore a central issue in the question. This is the order in which you should address each of these possibilities. Remember, if a choice fails in **any respect,** you can stop your analysis, eliminate it, and move on; in order to be correct, an answer choice must be correct **in every respect**.

Let's look at each of these elements in detail.

1. The reasoning mischaracterizes the facts.

If the reasoning doesn't reflect either the facts as they appear in the question or reasonable inferences drawn from those facts, the answer choice **cannot** be correct. This can happen in several ways.

a. A blatant contradiction of the facts as stated.

Look at this example from a past MBE:

> Jim watched a liquor store furtively for some time, planning to hold it up. He bought a realistic-looking toy gun for the job. One night, just before the store's closing time, he drove to the store, opened the front door, and entered. He reached in his pocket for the toy gun, but he became frightened and began to move back toward the front door. However, the shopkeeper had seen the butt of the gun. Fearing a hold up, the shopkeeper produced a gun from under the counter, pointed it at Jim, and yelled, "Stop!" Jim ran to the door and the toy gun fell from his pocket. The shopkeeper fired. The shot missed Jim but struck and killed a passerby outside the store.
>
> A statute in the jurisdiction defines burglary as "breaking and entering any building or structure with the intent to commit a felony or to steal therein." On a charge of burglary, Jim's best defense would be that
>
> A. the intent required was not present
> B. the liquor store was open to the public
> C. he had a change of heart and withdrew before committing any crime inside the store
> D. he was unsuccessful, and so at most could only be guilty of attempted burglary

Look at choice A, which states that Jim lacked the requisite intent. This is clearly wrong on the facts: Jim planned a hold up and entered the store intending to hold it up. Thus, his best defense **couldn't** be that he lacked the requisite intent, because **the facts indicate otherwise**. You don't have to spend any more time here; since choice A misstates the facts, it can't be correct — you can drop that choice without going further: you don't have to analyze the law or determine if the choice addresses a central issue more precisely than the other choices.

Look at another example dealing with misstating facts:

House owns his home in City. On the lawn in front of his home and within five feet of the public sidewalk there was a large tree. The roots of the tree caused the sidewalk to buckle severely and become dangerous. An ordinance of City requires adjacent landowners to keep sidewalks in a safe condition. House engaged Contractor to repair the sidewalk, leaving it to Contractor to decide how the repair should be made.

Contractor dug up the sidewalk, cut back the roots of the tree, and laid a new sidewalk. Two days after House had paid Contractor the agreed price of the repair, the tree fell over onto the street and damaged a parked car belonging to Driver.

Driver has asserted claims against House and Contractor, and both defendants admit that cutting the roots caused the tree to fall.

In the claim of Driver against Contractor, the best defense of Contractor is that

    A. the tree was on the property of House

    B. he repaired the sidewalk at the direction of House

    C. he could not reasonably foresee that the tree would fall

    D. he was relieved of liability when House paid for the repair

Look at choice B. You're told in the facts that House left "it to Contractor to decide how the repair should be made." Choice B directly contradicts this by stating that Contractor repaired the sidewalk at House's direction. You know, therefore, that choice B cannot be correct.

You may already have guessed the reason you should eliminate factually incorrect choices; these choices often contain reasoning which is *legally correct* and would resolve a central issue in the question if it reflected the facts. As a result, you could easily be seduced (distracted) into choosing these choices if you didn't immediately check the facts and eliminate them from contention!

The examples we've looked at so far are examples of answer choices that directly contradict the facts. Be aware, however, that answer choices can be factually incorrect in *other* ways. Let's look at the other major ways an answer choice can misstate the facts.

b. The answer choice goes beyond the facts.

Look at this question from a past MBE:

Jack and Paul planned to hold up a bank. They drove to the bank in Jack's car. Jack entered while Paul remained as lookout in the car. After a few moments, Paul panicked and drove off. Jack looked over the various tellers, approached one and whispered nervously, "Just hand over the cash. Don't look around, don't make a false move — or it's your life." The teller looked at the fidgeting Jack, laughed, flipped him a dollar bill and said, "Go on, beat it." Flustered, Jack grabbed the dollar and left.

Soon after leaving the scene, Paul was stopped by the police for speeding. Noting his nervous condition, the police asked Paul if they might search the car. Paul agreed. The search turned up heroin concealed in the lid of the trunk.

The prosecution's best argument to sustain the validity of the search of Jack's car would be that

    A. the search was reasonable under the circumstances, including Paul's nervous condition

    B. the search was incident to a valid arrest

    C. Paul had, under the circumstances, sufficient standing and authority to consent to the search

    D. exigent circumstances, including the inherent mobility of the car, justified the search

Look specifically at choice B, which presupposes there's been a valid arrest. The facts don't mention or imply an arrest; thus, choice B goes beyond the facts, and, as a result, it can't possibly be correct. This example illustrates how these answer choices can be dangerous distractors: if the facts were as B stated them to be, B could be a correct response, since it states a correct rule of law. Its misstatement of the facts, nonetheless, makes it unquestionably incorrect.

c. The answer choice assumes a fact in dispute.

Sometimes, a choice will characterize a fact as settled when, in actuality, the facts don't show such a clear-cut resolution. Here's an example from a past MBE.

> Albert, the owner of a house and lot, leased the same to Barnes for a term of five years. In addition to the house, there was also an unattached, two-car brick garage located on the lot. Barnes earned his living as an employee in a local grocery store, but his hobby consisted of wood carving and the making of small furniture. Barnes installed a work bench, electric lights, and a radiator in the garage. He also laid pipes connecting the radiator with the heating plant inside the house. Thereafter Albert mortgaged the premises to Good Bank to secure a loan. Barnes was not given notice of the mortgage, but the mortgage was recorded. Still later, Albert defaulted on the mortgage payments, and Good Bank began foreclosure proceedings, as it was entitled to do under the terms of the mortgage. By this time Barnes's lease was almost ended. Barnes began the removal of the equipment he had installed in the garage. Good Bank brought an action to enjoin the removal of the equipment mentioned above. Both Barnes and Albert were named as defendants.
>
> If the court refuses the injunction, it will be because
>
> A. Barnes was without notice of the mortgage
>
> B. the circumstances reveal that the equipment was installed for Barnes's exclusive benefit
>
> C. in the absence of a contrary agreement, a residential tenant is entitled to remove any personal property he voluntarily brings upon the premises
>
> D. the Statute of Frauds precludes the Bank from claiming any interest in the equipment

Look at choice C. Its reasoning characterizes the work bench, lights, and radiator *conclusively* as personal property. In fact, the central legal issue here is the characterization of those items — namely, whether they are personal property (and thus not subject to the mortgage) or "fixtures" (and thus subject to the mortgage). This is an issue because the items are of a type which *could* be subject to permanent annexation to the realty, depending on the intent of the annexor (here, Barnes) and other circumstances. They probably *aren't* fixtures here, though, because Barnes didn't intend to annex them permanently to the realty. Whatever the result, the point here is that choice C *assumes an essential fact which is the very issue to be resolved:* whether or not the the items are personalty.

2. The reasoning is legally wrong.

Once you've determined that the reasoning in an answer choice represents the facts, you should determine whether it's legally correct. This is where careful substantive preparation will pay off!

Just as an answer choice can be *factually* incorrect in several ways, it can contain a number of different kinds of *legal* errors, too: it may overstate the requirements of a crime, tort, or admissibility of evidence; it may state an antiquated or otherwise inapplicable rule; it may state a rule that has no application to the facts; it may make an overinclusive statement of the law, which will be wrong even if it happens to be correct on the facts; or it may overstate or understate the correct legal standard. We'll look at each of these possibilities separately, but first, let's stress once again how important it is to determine what words a response is using in stating a legal *theory*. Remember, we addressed this in the "issue spotting" section. It's real importance, however, is in determining the legal validity of each response. Simply put, you can't determine if a response is legally correct if you don't understand what legal principle it's addressing.

With that in mind, let's look, in detail, at the major ways in which an answer choice can be legally incorrect.

a. Reasoning that overstates the requirements of a crime, tort, or admissibility of evidence.

This is a common kind of legal inaccuracy. For instance, you may face a question in which someone is claiming negligence, but the answer choice states that the defendant can't be guilty because he didn't act intentionally. Or a choice may tell you that a piece of hearsay evidence is inadmissible as an "excited utterance," because the declarant is available to testify — but unavailability is not a requirement of the "excited utterance" hearsay exception. Or you may be told that a criminal defendant cannot be guilty of murder because he didn't intentionally kill his victim — but "depraved heart" murder does not require intent. As these examples indicate, the most frequent kind of legal misstatement is one that does define accurately the requirements of **some legal principle**, but the elements of which are not relevant to the question you're addressing. If you don't have your principles memorized correctly, you can be fooled by these misstatements, because they **sound** as though they should be correct.

b. **Reasoning that uses antiquated rules or rules from inapplicable bodies of law.**

If a rule is not the modern one, or it doesn't reflect the body of law on which the MBE relies, it can't be the basis of a correct response. For example, a husband is no longer vicariously liable for his wife's torts simply because they're married, and the attractive nuisance doctrine no longer requires that a child be lured onto property by the attractive nuisance. If an answer choice states an outmoded rule like these, it **cannot** be correct.

Similarly, you need to keep in mind the bodies of law on which the MBE relies. For instance, in Evidence law, the MBE applies the Federal Rules of Evidence, **not the common law**. Invariably, when the correct answer to a question involves a matter in which the FRE and the common law differ, one of the distractors will state the common law rule. A frequently used distractor is _res gestae; res gestae_ is a common law concept not recognized by the FRE. Thus, **an answer choice relying on res gestae as the source of admissibility for hearsay can't be correct.** Similarly, where transactions in goods are involved, the MBE relies on the UCC, Article 2. If you apply a contradictory common law rule to questions in which a transaction in goods is involved, you'll get the wrong answer — you can be sure that there are distractors tailor-made for just such a mistake!

c. **Reasoning applying rules that do not apply to the facts.**

A response can correctly characterize the facts but then state a rule of law which is inapplicable to those facts. Here's an example from a prior MBE.

> Miller is tried for armed robbery of the First Bank of City. At the request of police, the teller who was robbed prepared a sketch bearing a strong likeness to Miller, but the teller died in an automobile accident before Miller was arrested. At trial the prosecution offers the sketch. The sketch is
>
> A. admissible as an identification of a person after perceiving him
> B. admissible as past recollection recorded
> C. inadmissible as hearsay not within any exception
> D. inadmissible as an opinion of the teller

Look at choice A. Teller's action concerning Miller is an "identification" in the actual, physical sense, since she did "identify" him. While a prior identification can be admissible as an exception to the hearsay rule (and thus choice A may suggest the application of a correct rule) it doesn't apply to these facts — these identifications are admissible only if the one who made the identification is a testifying witness. Here, you're told that Teller died, and that does a fairly complete job of eliminating the possibility that she's a testifying witness. Thus, even though prior identification is a valid principle of Evidence law, it simply doesn't apply to these facts. A can't be correct. (In fact, C is the best response.)

d. **Answer choices that make overinclusive statements of the law; these choices are wrong even if they happen to apply to these facts.**

An answer choice which misstates the law **cannot** be correct, even if there is a piece of truth in the statement, as it applies to the facts. Suppose, for example, that a factual setting involves testimony that is inadmissible hearsay. One of the choices states that the testimony is "inadmissible, because hearsay is inadmissible." Now, under these specific facts, it's true that the testimony is inadmissible hearsay, but that's **not because hearsay in general is inadmissible** — as you know, there are lots of exceptions and exclusions to the hearsay rule. Thus, the choice cannot be correct, because it makes an overinclusive statement of the law of hearsay evidence.

e. **Answer choices which overstate or understate the applicable legal standard.**

Remember the "Three Bears," in which Goldilocks sought the porridge that was neither too hot nor too cold? Well, on some MBE questions, you'll undertake an analogous task: picking the appropriate legal standard from among others which are too strict or too lenient. Here's an example from a past MBE (only the pertinent part of the question is reproduced):

> During 1976 a series of arsons, one of which damaged the Humongous Store, occurred in the City of Swelter. In early 1977 Swelter's City Council adopted this resolution:
>
> The City will pay $10,000 for the arrest and conviction of anyone guilty of any of the 1976 arsons committed here.
>
> The foregoing was telecast by the city's sole television station once daily for one week. Thereafter, in August, 1977, the City Council by resolution repealed its reward offer and caused this resolution to be broadcast once daily for a week over two local radio stations, the local television station having meanwhile ceased operations.
>
> If the city's reward offer was revocable, revocation could be effectively accomplished only
>
> A. by publication in the legal notices of a local newspaper
> B. in the same manner as made, i.e., by local telecast at least once daily for one week
> C. in the same manner as made or by a comparable medium and frequency of publicity
> D. by notice mailed to all residents of the city and all other reasonably identifiable, potential offerees

Your job here is to choose the minimum that City must do to revoke its offer. The rule on revoking "general offers" is that the offer must be revoked by **equivalent notice** to the original offerees — typically via an ad in the same medium as the offer. Here, you have to face the additional obstacle that the original medium, the local TV station, is no longer available (note that this makes B an incorrect response — and one you'd have chosen if you misread the facts). Of the remaining three answer choices, D overstates the standard, and A, in a sense, understates it, because a newspaper ad wouldn't reach the same audience. That leaves choice C as "Baby Bear's porridge" — that is, the choice which states the correct legal standard.

f. **CAVEAT: Answer choices stating only a snippet of a legal rule, which address a central issue.**

Make a special note of one exception to our rule that reasoning which makes an under- or overinclusive statement of the law cannot be correct. Be particularly careful about the following type of "underinclusive" legal statement. MBE answer choices don't usually state **every** element of the crime in the reasoning when the "call" asks if a particular crime has been committed. Instead, the reasoning will most likely state only one essential piece of the principle; the answer can be correct only if that piece satisfies the central issue in the facts (remember our discussion about determining "central issues"). Look at this example from a past MBE:

> Johnson wanted to purchase a used motor vehicle. The used car lot of Car Company, in a remote section away from town, was enclosed by a ten-foot chain link fence. While Johnson and Sales Representative, an employee of Car Company, were in the used car lot looking at cars, a security guard locked the gate at 1:30 p.m., because it was Saturday and the lot was supposed to be closed after 1:00 p.m. Saturday until Monday morning. At 1:45 p.m., Johnson and Sales Representative discovered they were locked in.
>
> There was no traffic in the vicinity and no way in which help could be summoned. After two hours, Johnson began to panic at the prospect of remaining undiscovered and without food and water until Monday morning. Sales Representative decided to wait in a car until help should come. Johnson tried to climb over the fence and, in doing so, fell and was injured. Johnson asserts a claim based on false imprisonment against Car Company for damages for his injuries. Will Johnson prevail?

A. Yes, because he was confined against his will

B. Yes, because he was harmed as a result of his confinement

C. No, unless the security guard was negligent in locking the gate

D. No, unless the security guard knew that someone was in the lot at the time the guard locked the gate

Look at choice D. False imprisonment requires: (1) a Defendant's act or omission which confines or restraints plaintiff to a bounded area (such that plaintiff believes there's no reasonable means of escape); (2) Defendant must have intended to confine or restrain the plaintiff; and (3) causation. Choice D doesn't mention anything about Johnson's belief that there was no reasonable means of escape. The only element on which it focuses is the security guard's knowledge that someone was in the lot when he locked the gate. In spite of that, D is the correct response. Why? Because there's only one real issue here — the guard's intent. All the other elements are quite plainly satisfied by the facts or inferences drawn from them. Thus, choice D is correct; it focuses on the central issue here, ***even though it's an incomplete statement of a prima facie case of false imprisonment.***

3. **An answer choice can be wrong even if it's factually and legally correct, if it's not as precise or effective as another answer choice.**

Until now, we've addressed choices that cannot be correct because they include mistakes, either legal or factual. Here is something more subtle — an answer choice that, although correct, is less correct than one of the other choices and thus isn't the best response.

An answer choice can be incorrect simply because it doesn't meet the "call" as effectively as another choice. For instance, if, under a given set of facts, there are two potential defenses available to a defendant; if one of those defenses meets an obstacle posed by the facts more effectively than the other, that will be the correct response. (Remember, we discussed this under "issue spotting.") Here are two rules to apply in determining which is the most "effective" of several potentially correct choices:

a. **An answer choice that is easier to prove is more likely to be correct than an answer choice which is difficult to prove.**

If you're asked for plaintiff's best claim, and there are two potential claims, the better claim will generally be the one most easily proven on the facts. If you're asked the defendant's best defense, the same measure will apply: the easier, the better. Here's an example from a past MBE:

Jack and Paul planned to hold up a bank. They drove to the bank in Jack's car. Jack entered while Paul remained as lookout in the car. After a few moments, Paul panicked and drove off.

Jack looked over the various tellers, approached one and whispered nervously, "Just hand over the cash. Don't look around, don't make a false move — or it's your life." The teller looked at the fidgeting Jack, laughed, flipped him a dollar bill and said, "Go on, beat it." Flustered, Jack grabbed the dollar and left.

Soon after leaving the scene, Paul was stopped by the police for speeding. Noting his nervous condition, the police asked Paul if they might search the car. Paul agreed. The search turned up heroin concealed in the lid of the trunk. The prosecution's best argument to sustain the validity of the search of Jack's car would be that

A. the search was reasonable under the circumstances, including Paul's nervous condition

B. the search was incident to a valid arrest

C. Paul had, under the circumstances, sufficient standing and authority to consent to the search

D. exigent circumstances, including the inherent mobility of a car, justified the search

You'll remember that we analyzed this question earlier in the "misstating the facts" section. Here we're faced with a more difficult task: choosing from among the three potential answers, A, C, and D (remember that we eliminated B). While it's certainly true that exigent circumstances ***can*** provide the basis for a valid search, this would require that the prosecution introduce all sorts of evidence bearing on the reasonableness of the officers' belief that a search was merited. Choice A would also raise issues of reasonableness. If, on the other hand, the prosecutor relies on Paul's consent, assuming Paul was in a position to offer his consent, the prosecutor's task will be straightforward: prove that Paul consented, that he had the authority to consent, and that's it — the search is valid. Thus, of the three potential answers here, a "consent" search is the easiest to prove, making it the prosecutor's best argument, so choice C is correct.

b. A more precise answer is better than a less precise answer.

What do we mean by "precision?" Think of the question as a bull's-eye with many concentric circles. Precision means that one answer *covers more of the bull's-eye than any other,* i.e., *it either addresses the factual situation in more respects* than another, or it *addresses more issues* in the fact pattern than another. For instance, if you're asked whether a piece of evidence will be admissible, and you have two potential answers — "admissible even though its hearsay" or "admissible under the 'present sense impression' exception to the hearsay rule" — the latter would be more precise and is more likely to be correct. Here's an example from a past MBE.

> All lawyers practicing in the state of Erewhon must be members of the State Bar Association, by order of the state supreme court. Several state officials serve on the Bar Association's Board of Bar Governors. The Board of Bar Governors authorizes the payment of dues for two staff members of the Cosmopolitan Club, a private dining club licensed to sell alcoholic beverages. The Cosmopolitan Club is frequented by affluent businessmen and professionals and by legislators. It is generally known that the purpose of the membership of the Bar Association staff is to enable them to go where members of the "elite" meet and to lobby for legislation in which the Bar Association is interested. The State Bar Association has numerous committees and subcommittees concerned with family law, real estate law, unauthorized practice, etc., and its recommendations often influence state policy. Some committee meetings are held at the Cosmopolitan Club. The club is known to have rules which restrict membership by race, religion, and sex.

> Plaintiffs, husband and wife, who are members of the Erewhon Bar Association, petition the Board of Bar Governors to adopt a resolution prohibiting the payment of club dues to and the holding of meetings of the Bar Association or its committees at places which discriminate on the basis of race, religion, or sex. After substantial public discussion, the Board of Bar Governors, by a close vote, fails to pass such a resolution. These events receive extensive coverage in the local newspapers. Plaintiffs bring an action in federal court seeking an injunction against such payments and the holding of meetings in such places as the Cosmopolitan Club.

> The strongest argument for plaintiffs is

> A. private rights to discriminate and associate freely must defer to a public interest against discrimination on the basis at race, religion, or sex

> B. the failure of the State Bar Association to pass a resolution forbidding discrimination on the basis of race, religion, or sex constitutes a denial of equal protection

> C. the State Bar Association is an agency of the state and its payment of dues to such private clubs promotes discrimination on the basis of race, religion, and sex

> D. the State Bar Association's payment of dues to such private clubs promotes discrimination on the basis of race, religion, and sex

Here, look at choices C and D. They are very similar, except that choice C has an element which D is missing: it characterizes the State Bar Association as an *agency of the state.* This cements the possibility that there's *state action* involved here, and that's an important issue, since it enables plaintiffs to claim discrimination under the Fourteenth Amendment (the Fourteenth Amendment doesn't bar purely private acts of discrimination). If there were no choice C, choice D would be a reasonably good answer. Taking into account choice C's greater precision (it covers more of the bull's-eye), though, D is not the best response — C is.

c. How to guess intelligently when your reasoning fails you.

No matter how well prepared you are for the MBE, there will be questions you simply can't figure out. ***Don't be lured into unthinking, unsophisticated guessing on those questions!*** Instead, keep in mind the tips outlined below. Remember, if there's one thing the Bar Examiners know how to do, it's write good "wrong" answers, and the reason those "wrong" answers are good is because they sound as though they should be correct!

1. Ignore some things you may already know about objective tests.

If you took objective tests in law school, this will be both a benefit ***and*** a detriment on the MBE. Obviously, you'll benefit from knowing how to take objective law exams, but this is a double-edged sword; many of the techniques of "gamesmanship" that may have helped you in law school ***won't*** help you on the MBE. There's a good reason for this — your law school professors were experts on law, not test-making, and they most likely made mistakes that the Bar Examiners simply don't make. For instance, inexperienced test-makers leave the correct answer until C or D. The Bar Examiners don't do this. Inexperienced test-makers offer answers that are ***inadvertently*** overinclusive or underinclusive. Again, this is a mistake the Bar Examiners won't make. Inexperienced test-makers offer clues to later questions in "series" questions. The Bar Examiners make sure that no early questions or answers give clues to later answers. We could go on, but you get the point: don't waste your time searching for lapses in test construction or reasoning.

2. Don't guess until you've eliminated all the definitely wrong responses.

Even if a question has you stumped, you'll almost certainly be able to eliminate at least one or two responses as definitely wrong. Don't try to guess until you've eliminated those responses. After all, if you can narrow your choice down to two potential answers, you've got a 50-50 chance of picking the best response, as opposed to the 1 in 4 chance you have if you choose at random.

3. Factors that should influence your guess.

Keep in mind that you should apply the following advice only ***when your reasoning fails you.*** You can undoubtedly think of exceptions to each one of these suggestions. Their only purpose is to state what's most likely to apply in the absence of other facts.

a. Look at the facts, and ask yourself, "So what?"

If you can't pick up what the central issue is from the four responses, go back and look at the fact pattern and see if there's an issue you may have missed before and that seems to predominate. If there is, then it's likely that the correct answer will address that issue.

b. Beware of "seducers."

We'll only touch on this issue here, since it's addressed in significant detail in each of the "Strategies and Tactics" sections at the beginning of each subject. In short, "seducers" exist in every subject. They're those terms which ***seem*** as though they ought to apply to a wide variety of facts, but that actually have no application to the particular fact situation. For instance, take the "prior identifications" hearsay exception in Evidence law. In lay terms, a prior identification would de defined as an identification made by one party of another at any time prior to a specified event. Wouldn't it be easy if that were all the hearsay exception required? In fact, the hearsay exception for prior identifications is just a siren's song on the MBE, because it's ***very*** technical and won't make otherwise excludable evidence admissible in the vast majority of cases. Another example? The Privileges and Immunities Clause of the Fourteenth Amendment in Constitutional Law questions. As a practical matter, there aren't any laws that are made unconstitutional for violating this clause, but it sounds as though it ought to make a whole variety of laws unconstitutional. That's why it's an MBE favorite. Make sure you pay close attention to these and similar seducers in every subject.

c. Beware of certainties.

As you know by now, there are few definites in law. So be careful when an answer choice uses the words "always," "never," "cannot," "must," and the like. If a choice states something as a certainty, and you can think of even one situation where it ***doesn't*** apply, it can't be the best response!

d. Beware of responses that rely on "people" relationships.

As a general rule, the fact that people are related doesn't change the rules of Contract law, or Criminal law, or Tort law (with the most obvious exception being the fiduciary duty that parents owe to their children). Generally, if an answer choice implies that one's duties toward someone else are somehow different because of a familial relationship, barring other facts the answer is less likely to be correct than the others.

e. Beware of answers that focus only on results.

No one is liable solely because of the results of his or another's acts or omissions. For instance, in Criminal law, one can only be liable for a criminal act or omission; it those don't exist, the results of one's behavior won't make one guilty. In Negligence, if there's no duty and so no breach of a duty, there can't be liability, regardless of the results of one's actions. Here's an example from a past MBE.

> Si was in the act of siphoning gasoline from Neighbor's car in Neighbor's garage and without his consent when the gasoline exploded and a fire followed. Rescuer, seeing the fire, grabbed a fire extinguisher from his car and put out the fire, saving Si's life and Neighbor's car and garage. In doing so, Rescuer was badly burned.
>
> If Rescuer asserts a claim against Si for personal injuries, Rescuer will
>
> A. prevail, because he saved Si's life
>
> B. prevail, because Si was at fault in causing the fire
>
> C. not prevail, because Rescuer knowingly assumed the risk
>
> D. not prevail, because Rescuer's action was not a foreseeable consequence of Si's conduct

Look at Choice A. This states only **the results** of all the acts described. It doesn't deal with the other essential elements of negligence liability. The **results** of Rescuer's acts could be relevant only if there was a statement of **causation**. Thus, as a general rule, if there's no issue of causation, a response finding liability only on the basis of results, is unlikely to be correct. (In fact, the correct answer here is B.)

f. Be wary of answer choices from unrelated subjects.

As we've noted elsewhere, what makes the MBE an excellent objective test is the fact that distractors are likely to resemble correct responses in some important respect. Thus, it stands to reason that a response that addresses a totally unrelated subject is **less likely** to be correct. Here's an example from a past MBE.

> Adams, Bennett, and Curtis are charged in a common law jurisdiction with conspiracy to commit larceny. The state introduced evidence that they agreed to go to Nelson's house to take stock certificates from a safe in Nelson's bedroom, that they went to the house, and that they were arrested as they entered Nelson's bedroom.
>
> Adams testified that he thought the stock certificates belonged to Curtis, that Nelson was improperly keeping them from Curtis, and that he went along to aid in retrieving Curtis' property. Bennett testified that he suspected Adams and Curtis of being thieves and joined up with them in order to catch them. He also testified that he made an anonymous telephone call to the police alerting them to the crime and that the call caused the police to be waiting for them when they walked into Nelson's bedroom.
>
> Curtis did not testify. If the jury believes both Adams and Bennett, it should find Curtis
>
> A. guilty, because there was an agreement and the entry into the bedroom is sufficient for the overt act
>
> B. guilty, because he intended to steal
>
> C. not guilty, because a conviction would penalize him for exercising his right not to be a witness
>
> D. not guilty, because Adams and Bennett did not intend to steal

Look at choice C — it sticks out like a sore thumb. In every other respect, this question is a Criminal Law question, but up pops choice C, stating a (bogus) principle of Constitutional Criminal Procedure. The mere fact that choice C is from another subject makes it less likely to be the correct answer. (In fact, the correct response is D.)

g. If two answers are opposites, one is probably true.

This is a traditional rule of objective tests that holds true on the MBE. If there are two answers which are direct opposites, the test maker is probably testing your knowledge of the correct rule, so one of those two answers will likely be correct.

h. Look for a common issue, if you're asked to argue both ways.

Sometimes, especially in a series of Constitutional Law questions based on one factual setting, you'll be asked, first, for the plaintiff's best argument, and, next, for the defendant's best argument. When this happens, and you're stumped on at least one of the questions, look for a common issue between the two. The biggest obstacle for one side will likely be the strongest argument for the other.

i. Remember minority rules.

Sometimes, if you're stuck when trying to find a party's best argument, it may help to think of minority rules. After all, if no other response makes sense to you, it could be that the case is taking place in a jurisdiction that recognizes a minority rule, and this makes an otherwise unattractive option the party's best argument. *This doesn't mean that you should gear your studying to memorizing minority positions, because that is not a sensible use of your study time.* If, however, you're reduced to guessing and you just happen to remember a minority rule, it might be worth applying it.

j. Choose the longest response.

If you've narrowed the responses down but simply cannot choose among the remaining answers, choose the longer one; since it probably contains more reasoning, it's more likely to be precise, and thus more likely to be the correct response (barring any clear facts indicating otherwise).

k. Most importantly, don't get bogged down on questions you don't know!

As you practice, learn to apply these guessing techniques quickly. When you're reduced to guessing, the most important thing is put down at least a *tentative* answer and move on to questions you're more likely to know. Remember, you're likely to answer about half the MBE questions fairly easily. If you waste time on questions you really don't know and can't reasonably guess, you run the risk of not having time to work on those you're capable of answering.

- What you might do is keep a list on a piece of scratch paper of the questions you want to come back to, if you have the time at the end of the session. Of course, as you answer each question, you should mark the responses you definitively eliminated as incorrect responses, so that, if you do have time to re-analyze the question, you won't waste time going over incorrect responses twice.

HOW TO TAKE THE MBE

So much for specifics on how to study and how to analyze questions. Let's focus on more general advice for taking the MBE.

1. How to prep physically for the test.

You've heard a million times that it's important to be sufficiently well-rested before you face an important exam, and that you shouldn't spend the evening before an exam popping stay-awake pills and cramming. That's true. Watch out, though. You may be tempted to do the opposite, to get twelve hours of sleep. If you're not used to that, it will have just as soporific an effect on you as getting too little sleep! Instead, for a week or so before the exam, try getting up at the hour you'll have to get up on the day of the exam (including travel time, etc., in your wake-up time estimate). That way, you can be sure you'll be alert when you have to be.

As to advice about what to eat, what to wear, what to take to the exam — we're confident that you, as a law school graduate, know perfectly well without being told that you shouldn't wear clothing that cuts off circulation to your extremities or causes difficulty breathing, and that you shouldn't breakfast on Twinkies and Hershey bars when you have to spend the day thinking (not to mention sitting still).

2. When you take the exam itself.

a. Timing.

It's imperative that you stick to a schedule when you take the MBE. With a hundred questions to answer in each of the two, three-hour sessions, you should finish 17 questions every half hour. Whatever you do, don't get behind! Otherwise, you may chew up time on questions you don't know and run out of time for questions you do know (remember, the questions occur randomly, so there are just as likely to be easy questions at the end of the test as at the beginning!).

b. Remember that you can write in the question booklet.

You don't have to leave your question booklet in pristine condition. Take whatever notes help you, highlight whatever you feel needs highlighting, and mark correct and incorrect responses in the margins (given the time constraints). Of course, remember that this *isn't* true of the answer sheet — mark only one answer choice for each question on the sheet and make sure that you don't leave any stray marks.

c. Advice on "skipping around."

On some standardized tests, you have enough time to make a general pass through every question and then go back and answer them. You can't do this on the MBE — there just isn't time. The *worst* thing you can do is read every fact pattern, answer the questions you know, and go back to the ones you don't. You'll undoubtedly find that you won't have time to go back.

However, if you find while practicing that answering a series of long questions fatigues you, you may need to give your mind a rest and answer a few short questions. This is fine, so long as you *check carefully to make sure you're marking the matching boxes on the answer sheet*. Note that this advice is not inconsistent with the advice in the last paragraph, because here we're saying that, if you *must* skip around, just glance at the sheer length of questions without reading them at all.

d. Answer questions in an episodic fashion.

Don't let your reaction to any one question influence how you face ensuing questions. For instance, there will frequently be questions you'll find very easy. If this happens, thank your lucky stars, fill in the answer sheet, and go on. By the same token, if you're stunned by a tough question, make your best guess and then *start completely fresh* on the next question — don't go on thinking about a question you had some doubt about (although, as we've discussed, you can answer tentatively and make a list of questions to return to, if you have the time).

e. Maintain your concentration all the way through.

You'll probably find that it's difficult to concentrate in the last hour or so of each session. If you have to, get up and get a drink of water, bite the inside of your cheek, dig your fingernails into your palms — do anything you have to do to stay focused on your work. The questions are randomly organized, so, if you don't concentrate towards the end, you're likely to miss some questions you'd otherwise find simple.

A FINAL WORD OF ADVICE

When it comes time to take the MBE, and you've prepared as much as you can . . . *relax!* Tens of thousands of people every year pass their state's bar exam, and they aren't any smarter than you are. By working with this book, you've indicated your determination to succeed. We wish you the best of luck, both on the bar exam and in your legal career.

STRATEGIES AND TACTICS

CONSTITUTIONAL LAW

If you think for a minute about Constitutional Law, it's a strange subject to appear on the MBE — it's more theoretical than the other subjects covered on the exam.

In a way, the unique nature of Constitutional Law can **help** you on the MBE. With a multiple-choice test like the MBE, it's impossible to have the type of open-ended discussions that your Constitutional Law class in law school probably involved, discussions such as how this justice or that justice might decide a case. Instead, you have to treat Constitutional Law as you do every other subject on the MBE — apply rules. Given the nature of Constitutional Law, though, you should be familiar with case law in order to see how various rules have been applied in different contexts. Why? You really can't be asked "pure" hypotheticals, because you're expected to know the law, not to read the minds of the Supreme Court justices. In many cases you simply can't know how a test applies to a given set of facts unless the Supreme Court has **already considered** that set of facts.

You'll notice that the discussion on Study Strategies is considerably longer for this subject than it is for any other. Our goal here is to get you to think about Constitutional concepts in such a way that you can apply them to multiple-choice questions. Keep in mind, however, that the sole purpose of this is to alert you to tricky topics you might otherwise overlook. This section is **not** intended to be an exhaustive, substantive review of Constitutional Law; you should rely on other materials for that. (The *Law In A Flash* set on *Constitutional Law*, for example, is an excellent tool for learning how Constitutional principles apply to hundreds of different fact patterns.)

OUTLINE OF COVERAGE

You will face 33 questions on Constitutional Law on the MBE. (Note that the terms "Constitution," "constitutional," and "unconstitutional" refer to the federal Constitution, unless otherwise indicated.)

The following outline for the Constitutional Law portion of the MBE has been adopted by the Bar Examiners for all MBEs given on or after July, 2003. It was designed to clarify what's covered on the Con Law portion of the exam. This is the most up-to-date outline of coverage released by the Bar Examiners, and your substantive study for Constitutional Law should be centered around it.

Here's what you need to know:

I. The nature of judicial review
   A. Organization and relationship of state and federal courts in a federal system
   B. Jurisdiction
      1. Constitutional basis
      2. Congressional power to define and limit
   C. Judicial review in operation
      1. The "case or controversy" requirement including standing, ripeness, and mootness
      2. Political questions and justiciability
      3. The "adequate and independent state ground"
II. The separation of powers
   A. The powers of Congress
      1. Commerce, taxing and spending
      2. Power over federal property
      3. War and defense powers
      4. Power to enforce the 13th, 14th, and 15th Amendments
   B. The powers of the President
      1. As chief executive
      2. As commander-in-chief
      3. Treaty and foreign affairs powers

    4. Appointment and removal of officials
  C. Federal interbranch relationships
    1. Congressional limits on the executive
    2. The President's power to veto or to withhold action
    3. Delegation doctrine
    4. Executive, legislative, and judicial immunities
III. The relation of nation and states in a federal system
  A. Intergovernmental immunities
    1. Federal immunity from state law
    2. State immunity from federal law
  B. The authority reserved to the states
    1. Negative implications of the commerce clause
    2. Tenth Amendment
    3. Other
  C. National power to override or extend state authority
    1. Preemption
    2. Authorization of otherwise invalid state action
  D. Relations among states
    1. Interstate compacts
    2. Full faith and credit
IV. Individual rights
  A. "State action" and the role of the courts
  B. Due process
    1. Substantive due process
      a. Fundamental rights
      b. Other rights
    2. Takings
    3. Procedural due process
  C. Equal protection
    1. Fundamental rights
    2. Other rights
    3. Suspect classifications
    4. Other classifications
  D. Privileges and immunities clauses
  E. Obligation of contracts, bills of attainder, *ex post facto* laws
  F. First Amendment freedoms
    1. Freedom of religion and separation of church and state
      a. Free exercise
      b. Establishment
    2. Freedom of expression and association
      a. Regulation of content of expression
      b. Regulation of time, manner, and place of expression
      c. Regulation of unprotected expression
        i. Obscenity
        ii. Other
      d. Regulation of commercial speech
      e. Regulation of, or impositions upon, public employment, licenses, or benefits based upon exercise of expressive or associational rights
      f. Regulation of association
      g. Regulation of defamation and invasions of privacy

WHAT TO EXPECT

About half of the 33 Constitutional Law questions on the exam will come from category IV — Individual Rights; the other half will come from categories I, II, and III. There will be questions from each of the roman numeral topics on the exam, but not necessarily from each of the sub-topics.

There are two common types of Constitutional Law MBE questions:

  1. You're asked about the ***validity of a statute***; or
  2. You're asked to identify the ***best or worst argument*** for upholding or overturning a statute.

STUDY STRATEGIES

1. Determine what the various constitutional clauses do.

First, you have to make two determinations:

1. *To whom does the clause apply?* Federal government, states, or both?
2. *What does the clause do?* Is it a source of power — or does it prohibit something?

Here's a rundown on some major clauses you should remember. Other major clauses, such as equal protection and due process, will be addressed separately.

A. Commerce Clause, Article I, § 8, Clause 3.
Applies to: Federal Government
Source or prohibition: Source

The Commerce Clause power is exceptionally broad. Congress can regulate *three categories* of activities involving interstate commerce: *channels* of interstate commerce, *instrumentalities* of interstate commerce, and activities *"substantially affecting"* commerce. What does this mean on the MBE? Basically, in determining whether Congress can regulate an activity, you need only determine that (1) the activity is *commercial*, and (2) the activity "substantially affects" interstate commerce. If both are true, then the statute is valid under the Commerce Clause. Note that most Commerce Clause questions on the MBE involve the *sale* or *distribution* of an item, usually in a *commercial* setting. (If, on the other hand, the activity involves a non-commercial activity, the test is stricter: you must find a "pretty obvious connection" between the activity and interstate commerce for the statute to be valid under the Commerce Clause.)

You may remember discussing the somewhat surprising *U.S. v. Lopez* decision in your Constitutional Law class. In *Lopez*, the Supreme Court actually *struck down* a federal "no guns in schools" statute on the grounds that it went *beyond* Congress's Commerce Clause power! Amazing, huh? Don't worry; since most MBE Commerce Clause questions focus on the *sale or distribution* of an item at the end of the stream of interstate commerce (not its *use* once it's *left* the stream of interstate commerce, which the *Lopez* statute did), you shouldn't have to worry about *Lopez* at all.

Here's an example of how broad the commerce power is. Say Old Mac — a farmer — grows corn on his farm to feed only himself and his pigs. You're likely to think, "Well, there's no impact on interstate commerce whatsoever, so Congress can't regulate Old Mac's corn production, right?" *Wrong.* The commerce power would allow Congress to regulate Old Mac's production: the activity (farming) is commercial, and the cumulative (or aggregate) effect of many farmers' production could substantially affect the supply and demand of commodities interstate. (You may remember these facts from *Wickard v. Filburn* (1942)). After you've gone to some pains to show how broad the commerce power is in real life, don't forget that the Supreme Court *has* recently shown that there are limits to how broad the Commerce Clause power is. Take a step back, though, and remember that we're talking about the MBE, which is purely theoretical. If the activity being regulated involves the use of an item after it's finished traveling through interstate commerce, or if the activity being regulated is non-commercial, the statute may have gone too far. Keep this in mind when you're asked the source of power for a federal enactment.

CAVEAT: State power under the Commerce Clause.

Just as the Commerce Clause is a *source* of power for the federal government, it's also a *limitation* on the power of the states. No need to worry, though; the only time you analyze state statutes' impact on interstate commerce under the Commerce Clause is when there's *no relevant federal legislation*. Then you have to determine if a state regulation unduly burdens interstate commerce (see the discussion on validity of state statutes under #3 below). If relevant federal legislation exists, then your analysis falls under the *Supremacy Clause*. There are two questions you have to ask:

1. Did Congress expressly authorize or prohibit state regulation? If so, that controls. If *not* —
2. With no express authorization or prohibition by Congress, you have to determine if the federal law *preempts* the state law. If the state law *directly contradicts* the federal law, it will be preempted. If there's no direct conflict, you have to determine if Congress intended the federal law to occupy the *entire* field. Look at four factors to determine if that is the case: (1) whether the subject matter is traditionally classified as local or federal; (2) how pervasive the federal regulation is; (3) how similar the state and federal laws are (the more they coincide, the more likely it is that federal law was intended to supersede state law); and (4) whether there's a need for uniform federal regulation. You can remember this with a mnemonic — **PUSH** (**P**ervasiveness, **U**niformity, **S**imilarity,

History).

Note that preemption is an issue *any* time a state law conflicts with a federal law (or is in the same field). However, it's most likely to be applied in the area of interstate commerce.

B. Welfare Clause, Article I, § 8.
Applies to: Federal government.
Source or prohibition: Source.

The Welfare Clause gives Congress the power to *tax and spend* for the general welfare. Any federal legislation reasonably related to this power will be valid (assuming it doesn't violate some other Constitutional provision, such as Equal Protection). Pretty straightforward. So why is it here at all? Because it's easy to forget the limitations on the Welfare power. Tax and spend. That's it. Congress does *not* have the power to enact any legislation that promotes the general welfare of the nation under the Welfare Clause, even though that's what you'd expect from its name. Just remember — tax and spend is the scope of the power.

Incidentally, keep in mind that *states* do have the power to legislate for the general welfare, but only under their *police* power, not under the Welfare Clause. (Don't forget that there is no *federal* police power — see #2B, below.)

C. Contracts Clause, Article I, § 10.
Applies to: States *only*.
Source or prohibition: Prohibition.

The Contracts Clause, or "Obligations of Contracts" Clause, prohibits states from passing any law which impairs the obligations of contracts. It's usually correctly applied when the state seems to be trying to *escape its own obligations.*

The most important thing to remember here is that, as a prerequisite for protection under this clause, the contract must have existed when the statute was passed. States *can* regulate contract formation *prospectively.* Thus, when the "Contracts Clause" is an answer choice, the first thing you should do is check to see if the contract in question predates the offending statute. If not, then the Contracts Clause is irrelevant.

That's the most important thing to remember, but there are a couple of other points to keep in mind. First, not *all* contract impairments are invalid under the Contracts Clause. If they *were*, people could insulate themselves from state regulation simply by entering into contracts. Instead, state modifications of contracts *will* be permissible if the modifications (1) serve an *important and legitimate public interest* and (2) are *necessary* to achieve that public interest; and if, (3) the contract impairment is *reasonable* under the circumstances.

Also, keep in mind that the state has more leeway when the state *itself* was a party to the contract. Beyond the rules on modification applicable to *all* contracts (see last paragraph) the state needn't adhere to a contract where it surrenders, from the start, an "essential attribute" of its sovereignty (such as the police power or eminent domain).

Here's an example of the Contracts Clause "in action":

A statute of the state of Tuscarora made it a misdemeanor to construct any building of more than five stories without an automatic fire sprinkler system.

A local construction company built a ten-story federal office building in Tuscarora. It constructed the building according to the precise specifications of a federal contract authorized by federal statutes. Because the building was built without the automatic fire sprinkler system required by state law, Tuscarora prosecutes the private contractor.

Which of the following is the company's strongest defense to that prosecution?

A. The state sprinkler requirement denies the company property or liberty without due process

B. The state sprinkler requirement denies the company equal protection of the laws

C. As applied, the state sprinkler requirement violates the supremacy clause

D. As applied, the state sprinkler requirement violates the obligations of contracts clause

Remember, when you're considering the obligations of contracts issue, the first thing you have to do is see if the contract predates the statute. Here, it apparently doesn't. That means that the contracts clause does not invalidate the statute, and D can't be the best response. (In fact, choice C is the best response.)

D. Privileges and Immunities Clauses — *both of them.*
Privileges & Immunities of the Fourteenth Amendment.
Applies to: States.
Source or Limitation: Limitation.

"Interstate" Privileges & Immunities Clause, Article IV, § 2.
Applies to: States.
Source or Limitation: Limitation.

It's important to keep these two clauses separate in your mind, because one of them has practical effect — it actually prohibits things — and the other *doesn't*. When the MBE refers to either, it'll be distinguishable by the language used; the MBE will tell you their source: "Privileges and Immunities Clause of the Fourteenth Amendment" or "Privileges & Immunities Clause of Article IV."

1. Privileges & Immunities Clause of the Fourteenth Amendment.

This voids state enactments which clearly infringe on the privileges of *national citizenship*. The protection is limited to the fundamental rights shared by all citizens, namely the right to travel freely from state to state, to petition Congress for redress of grievances, to vote for national officers, to assemble peaceably, and to discuss matters of national legislation.

To say that this clause is construed narrowly is understating the matter (it's like saying law students do little studying). In fact, reliance on this clause usually yields a *wrong* answer on the MBE. Here's why: These same rights are protected against state encroachment by the Due Process and Equal Protection Clauses of the Fourteenth Amendment, so, wherever Privileges and Immunities seems to apply, Due Process or Equal Protection would be a stronger argument against the constitutionality of the state action in question. Consequently, though there may be no such thing as a guarantee on the MBE, when you see "Privileges and Immunities Clause of the Fourteenth Amendment" as a possible answer for invalidating a state statute, you can be pretty sure it's just a distractor.

2. "Interstate" Privileges & Immunities Clause (Article IV).

Unlike its Fourteenth Amendment counterpart, *this* clause has some teeth. Here's what it does: it prevents states from discriminating against out-of-state citizens and residents in matters concerning "essential activities" (e.g., pursuing one's livelihood, owning property) and "basic rights" (e.g., medical care, court access), unless the discrimination is closely related to a substantial state purpose (e.g., protecting natural resources by the state) and there are no less restrictive means available to achieve the purpose. It's important to remember that this provision doesn't protect corporations or aliens — just out-of-state, human, U.S. citizens.

E. Eleventh Amendment.
Applies to: Individuals.
Source or Limitation: Limitation.

The important thing to remember about the Eleventh Amendment is how *narrow* it is. This is all it does: it forbids most actions in federal court for damages against states, when the claim is based on past conduct and where the damages will be payable from state funds. Given its narrow scope, you should remember what the Eleventh Amendment *doesn't* cover. It *doesn't*, for instance, prevent suits by the federal government against states; or suits by anyone against state subdivisions (e.g., cities or counties); or suits looking for *prospective* relief (an injunction as opposed to money damages for past acts); or suits where a state official has violated the claimant's constitutional rights (even if the official's act was permissible under *state* law).

F. Thirteenth Amendment.
Applies to: Anyone — government or private individual.
Source or Limitation: Limitation.

The Thirteenth Amendment outlaws any "badges or incidents" of slavery. It gives Congress the power to prohibit virtually *any* discrimination against blacks, or whites (and it may cover other kinds of discrimination). The thing to remember about the Thirteenth Amendment is that it's the *only* constitutional provision **explicitly limiting private acts by individuals**. No state action is required. Contrast this with the Fourteenth Amendment, which also prohibits discrimination under its Equal Protection Clause but only limits **state** action — not private action.

2. Determining the validity of statutes.

Many Constitutional Law questions on the MBE ask you to determine if a given statute is valid. Here's a logical way for you to attack these questions:

A. Determine first if the statute is a federal statute or a state statute.

This isn't difficult to determine — the question will tell you.

B. Analyze the validity of federal statutes or actions.

Congress can act only pursuant to its enumerated powers under the Constitution. Thus, any valid federal statute must be **rationally related to an enumerated power**, or it must be **necessary and proper to effectuate an enumerated power**.

As a result, you'll probably find it useful to keep in mind the major powers of Congress. Here they are:

Civil Rights
Elections (Congressional)
Admiralty
Taxation
Eminent Domain
Spending/Taxing for General Welfare
Defense
Interstate Commerce
Citizenship
External (Foreign) Affairs

Here's a mnemonic for this: CREATES DICE

Keep in mind that this is not an **exhaustive** list. For instance, Congress has virtually exclusive power over federally-owned lands under the Property Clause; it controls Bankruptcy. Furthermore, Congress has **"state-like" powers over the District of Columbia** (where, for instance, it could regulate marriages, education, and other state-oriented areas). This list does, however, represent the major Congressional powers, and so, in the vast majority of cases, any valid federal law will have to be rationally related to one of these powers (or necessary and proper to effectuate one of them).

If Congress tries to legislate **beyond** its powers, it violates the Tenth Amendment. The Tenth Amendment reserves to the states (and the people) those powers not expressly delegated to Congress by the Constitution, nor prohibited to the States.

Note that the list above is interesting for what's missing: a police power. **There is no federal police power!** Only the states have police powers. Congress **can** use its commerce power to do "police-like" things, e.g., prohibiting interstate transportation of stolen property, misbranded goods, lottery tickets, etc., but this doesn't change the fact that Congress doesn't have police powers. Don't forget this!

C. Determining the validity of state statutes.

In order to be valid, a state enactment must meet a three-part test:

1. The law must be enacted within the state's powers (e.g., police powers);
2. It must not violate any person's Constitutional rights; and
3. It must not unduly burden interstate commerce.

If a state statute passes this test, it's valid. Let's look at each element a little more closely.

1. State powers.

The police powers are the most common source of state authority. State legislation is enacted under the police powers if it involves the **public health, safety, welfare or morals**. As you can see, this is a pretty broad spectrum of authority: it covers everything from family issues to education to a whole variety of economic and social legislation. Of course, states have other powers, such as controlling in-state property, but police powers are the **most** significant.

2. Constitutional rights: due process and equal protection.

The two most frequent ways in which a state statute can violate the Constitution involve due process and equal protection. These will be discussed in detail below in their own section.

3. Interstate commerce.

As discussed earlier, Congress has a complete lock on interstate commerce. This doesn't mean, however, that a state can't place **any** burden on interstate commerce — it just can't **unduly** burden interstate commerce. Determining if an undue burden exists requires the application of a balancing test: is the burden on interstate commerce outweighed by **legitimate interests** of the state in protecting its citizens, taking into account less burdensome alternatives? Also, the regulation must be **nondiscriminatory**, unless the state has no reasonable, non-discriminatory alternatives in its effort to protect health and safety.

This is one of those loosy-goosy constitutional tests that is virtually impossible to apply. We'll look at some examples instead. For instance, a state statute forbidding tandem trucks on its highways, in the light of proof that such trucks are more dangerous than tractor-trailers, has been found to be an **impermissible** burden on interstate commerce. *Raymond Motor Transport v. U.S.* (1978). Change the facts a bit; say the statute only barred tandem trucks on **local** roads (**not** highways). This would impose a lesser burden on interstate commerce and thus **could** be valid. Here's another one. Say a state charges trucks involved in interstate commerce $25/year for the privileges of using state highways. The revenues are used to defray the costs of maintaining the roads. This is a **permissible** burden on interstate commerce, because the state interest is substantial and the burden is slight. Say instead that the fee was the same, but it was applied only against out-of-state truckers and was intended to protect in-state truckers by making it more expensive for out-of-state truckers to operate in the state. This would be **impermissible**. Even though amount of the burden is the same, the regulation is **discriminatory**, and, since there are other, non-discriminatory ways to raise revenue, the statute would be an invalid burden on interstate commerce.

3. Due Process and Equal Protection.

These two Constitutional clauses show up with such frequency, both as correct responses and as distractors, that we'll go into each one in depth.

A. Distinguishing due process problems from equal protection problems.

On the MBE, you'll face questions that ask you for the clearest Constitutional violation posed by a set of facts. Even though due process and equal protection can overlap, there's a simple test you can use to determine which of the two applies: ***see if a classification is built into the statute*** (such as residents vs. non-residents, men vs. women, legitimate children vs. illegitimate children). Here's an example:

> The State of Missoula has enacted a new election code designed to increase voter responsibility in the exercise of the franchise and to enlarge citizen participation in the electoral process. None of its provisions conflicts with federal statutes.
>
> Which of the following is the strongest reason for finding unconstitutional a requirement in the Missoula election code that each voter must be literate in English?
>
> A. The requirement violates Article I Section 2 of the Constitution, which provides that representatives to Congress be chosen "by the People of the several States"
>
> B. The requirement violates Article I, Section 4 of the Constitution, which gives Congress the power to "make or alter" state regulations providing for the "Times" and "Manner" of holding elections for senators and representatives
>
> C. The requirement violates the due process clause of the Fourteenth Amendment
>
> D. The requirement violates the equal protection of the laws clause of the Fourteenth Amendment

Remember: look for a ***classification***. Is there one here? Sure — English-speakers vs. non-English-speakers. A classification is the hallmark of an equal protection problem. (Incidentally, the correct answer is, in fact, D.)

1. If there's a classification: How to analyze equal protection problems.

Once you've determined there's a classification, you have to determine what that classification is based on. Why? Because the nature of the classification determines the level of scrutiny the statute will be subjected to in order to determine its validity — and the level of scrutiny, to a large extent, will determine if the statute will be upheld.

However, there is a threshold issue to address first. If the statute is a federal statute, there's no equal protection problem, *because the equal protection clause does not apply to the federal government*.

Another threshold to remember — the equal protection clause applies only to *government action* (also called "*state action*", even when applied to federal action), not to actions taken by purely private parties and in which government played no substantial role. On the MBE, you'll have to be able to decide quickly which activities constitute state action and which don't. If a state or federal government is enacting a law (which is usually the case in MBE questions), then, obviously, you have state action. If a private individual or group of individuals is involved, you need to look for two things. First, ask yourself if there's a significant "nexus" of government involvement (i.e., whether the government encourages or benefits from the private conduct). Second, ask yourself if the private conduct has a "public function" that's normally exclusively reserved to the state. If you answer either "yes," then there's state action.

Where discrimination is the issue, you also need to remember that, in order for a statute to be held invalid, it must be found to be discriminatory in one of the following ways: it must be discriminatory on its face, or be facially neutral but unequally administered, or have an impermissible motive — the intent to discriminate. The statute won't be found invalid if the discrimination results merely *from its impact.* Given these requirements, if you're faced with a newly enacted statute but you're not told anything about its background, it can be held invalid *only* because it's invalid on its face (since it hasn't been applied, evenly or unevenly, and since you know of no improper motive).

LEVELS OF SCRUTINY:

a. Strict scrutiny.

This applies *only* to these types of classifications.

1. The classification is "suspect" — that is, it's based on race or alienage; *OR*
2. The classification relates to *who may exercise a fundamental right*.

The fundamental rights, for purposes of equal protection, are:

➡ Freedom of association
➡ Interstate travel (look for *residency* requirements as conditions to receipt of welfare benefits, medical care, or voting rights — *vital* governmental services only — *not* tuition reduction or the right to a divorce)
➡ Privacy (marriage, procreation, abortion)
➡ Voting (requirements other than age, residency, and citizenship)

Note that the freedom of expression *is* also a fundamental right, but, because it's riddled with so many rules, it will discussed separately below. Religion is also addressed separately.

Where a classification involves these fundamental rights, it's generally subject to strict scrutiny — the "compelling interest" test: it must be *necessary* to promote a *compelling* governmental interest. This is pretty much the kiss of death for a statute, since laws almost never survive this test.

You should keep one element in mind when considering a problem where alienage (i.e., non-citizenship) is the basis of the classification. A state needs only a rational basis for discriminating against non-citizens in the context of essential state functions. Thus, a state can require that state police, public school teachers, probation officers, and others be U.S. citizens.

b. Intermediate scrutiny.

This applies to the following "quasi-suspect" classifications:

Gender
Legitimacy

Under intermediate scrutiny, a law must be *substantially* related to an *important state interest* in order to be valid.

The only real way to know what a "substantial relation" is or to know which state interests are "important" is to examine the kinds of statutes that have passed muster in the past. For instance, say a state statute prohibits illegitimate children from inheriting from their father in intestacy, unless paternity was established during the father's lifetime. The state's interest in promoting orderly property distribution has been held to justify such a statute. *Lalli v. Lalli* (1978). Take another example. A state statute requires that a paternity suit, for the purpose of obtaining support from the father, must be brought before the child is two years old. This is unconstitutional as a burden on equal protection. While the state's interest is important — preventing stale or fraudulent claims — the "substantial relation" is missing; two years doesn't allow a reasonable opportunity to bring a claim, and the threat of stale or fraudulent claims isn't sufficiently great to justify a two-year deadline.

c. Rational relation.

This level of scrutiny will be applied to *everything* else. When faced with an equal protection question, then, you should methodically run through the suspect and quasi-suspect categories, and, if the classification you're examining doesn't fit one of those classification, then it's subject to the rational relation test: if there is a set of facts imaginable that would make the law a reasonable way to achieve a legitimate governmental purpose, the law is valid. Given that test, if you correctly identify that a statute should be reviewed under this test, the statute should almost certainly be upheld.

Needless to say, there's a whole world of classifications which are analyzed under rational relation. All purely economic and social legislation is usually subject to the rational relation test. So are some classifications you might be tempted to classify as suspect or quasi-suspect; classifications based on poverty/wealth, age, and mental retardation, for instance, are subject only to the rational relation test.

2. Where there's no classification — due process problems.

Both federal and state governments are subject to due process constraints. There are two types of due process problems: procedural and substantive.

a. Procedural due process.

This addresses the fairness of the procedure used to deprive someone of a significant interest, typically in property, but also in life (e.g., capital punishment) or liberty (e.g., incarceration). In general, when you're dealing with procedural due process, you'll ask if *notice and a hearing* are necessary when a right is removed.

When dealing with procedural due process, keep in mind, first, that "property," in this context, doesn't necessarily mean actual, tangible land or chattels — "property" can also mean an interest already acquired in specific benefits. For instance, a doctor has a property right in his license to practice medicine; a welfare recipient has a property right in continued benefits. The most common "property" question on the MBE involves *government jobs.* People typically *don't* have a property right in continued public employment — unless something in the facts of a question suggests otherwise (such as mention of tenure or of a contract provision requiring that an employee can only be fired for "cause"). Note that a person's mere *expectations* of maintaining benefits or a job aren't enough to make their expectations into a property right — there must be a law — whether federal, state, or local — under which the person has a *legitimate claim* to the benefits.

b. Substantive due process.

Substantive due process is a much more likely source of difficulty on the MBE than procedural due process. Substantive due process becomes an issue when state action substantially interferes with a *"fundamental"* right. If the right interfered with is "fundamental," a statute must meet the same "strict scrutiny" test as in equal protection law or it won't be upheld. If the right is *not* fundamental, the statute is subject to the same "rational relation" test as in equal protection law. Remember, though, that only *personal* rights are considered "fundamental" under substantive due process: First Amendment rights (in general; note that, as to the right to vote, restrictions as to age, residency, and citizenship are valid), the right of privacy (contraception, procreation, marriage, abortion), and the right to interstate (and probably international) travel.

One end-run the Bar Examiners like to do around your knowledge of substantive due process is to ask you who has the *burden of persuasion* in a due process problem. Here's the rule: if the impaired right is fundamental, then the burden of persuasion is on the *government* to defend its action; if the right is non-fundamental, then the burden of persuasion is on the *person attacking* the government's action. We'll discuss this in #6, below.

3. Putting it all together.

Here are a few examples to show you how due process and equal protection relate to each other.

➡ Say there's a state statute that forbids unmarried people from buying contraceptives. Equal protection or due process problem? It's equal protection. There's a classification — married vs. unmarried people. What does the classification do? It limits who may use contraceptives, which falls under the right of privacy — a fundamental right. Since the classification defines who may exercise a fundamental right, it's subject to strict scrutiny, and on that basis, it will likely fail. Note, incidentally, that the problem is also, theoretically, a due process problem, because it infringes on the fundamental right to privacy. The important thing for you to remember, in terms of the MBE, is that the existence of a classification makes it more obviously an equal protection problem.

➡ Change the above facts so it's a federal statute instead of a state statute. Still an equal protection problem? It **can't** be — the Equal Protection Clause applies only to the states. In any case, the statute isn't likely to be valid, because the Due Process Clause of the Fifth Amendment covers instances of unreasonable discrimination by the national government. In addition, it's not clear on what basis Congress could enact such legislation. Compare the statute to the list of congressional powers, *supra,* and see for yourself.

➡ Back to the state statute. Say, instead of only forbidding unmarried people from using contraceptives, the statute stopped **everyone** from using them. Equal protection or due process? It can't be equal protection, because there's no classification involved; however, such a statute **does** infringe a personal right, so there's a due process problem. Since contraceptives involve the right of privacy, the right is "fundamental," and, as in the equal protection analysis, the statute will be subject to strict scrutiny — and will probably fail.

4. Freedom of expression.

You may think, "Wait a minute. Freedom of expression is a fundamental right. Why not just lump it together with the other fundamental rights?" That really can't be done, because what we're focusing on here is applying general constitutional principles on the MBE, and there are so many special rules which apply to freedom of expression that considering it as just another fundamental right would confuse you more than help you. If the only thing you remember is that any statute impinging on freedom of expression must pass the "strict scrutiny" test, you'll be in trouble.

Keep in mind, first of all, that "freedom of expression" actually covers several distinct yet related rights: the freedoms of **speech**, **press**, **assembly**, and **association**.

Also keep in mind that any statute regulating freedom of speech (or association) must contain **narrow and definite standards** in order to be upheld. This involves the twin doctrines of **overbreadth** and **vagueness**. If a statute prohibits not only unprotected speech, but some **protected** speech as well, it's unconstitutionally **overbroad**. If the conduct prohibited by a statute is so unclearly defined that a reasonable person would have to **guess at its meaning**, it's unconstitutionally **vague**. Note that statutes which are unconstitutionally overbroad are usually unconstitutionally vague, too.

Here's an example of overbreadth:

A newly-enacted state criminal statute provides, in its entirety, "No person shall utter to another person in a public place any annoying, disturbing, or unwelcome language." Smith followed an elderly woman for three blocks down a public street, yelling offensive four-letter words in her ear. The woman repeatedly asked Smith to leave her alone, but he refused.

In the subsequent prosecution of Smith, the first under this statute, Smith

A. can be convicted

B. cannot be convicted, because speech of the sort described here may not be punished by the state because of the First and Fourteenth Amendments

C. cannot be convicted, because, though his speech here may be punished by the state, the state may not do so under this statute

D. cannot be convicted, because the average user of a public street would think his speech/action here was amusing and ridiculous rather than "annoying," etc.

Under the Constitution, language can be annoying without being subject to prohibition. Thus, even if Smith's language could constitutionally be prohibited on some grounds (as, for instance, with obscenity), it can't be prohibited under the statute here. C is, thus, the best response. (Incidentally, note the fact that this prosecution is the *first under this statute*. A statute that is otherwise unconstitutionally vague and overbroad could be saved by a judicial interpretation which limited it enough to make it valid. The question here avoids this problem by stating that there's never been a judicial interpretation of the statute.)

So much for what any statute limiting speech must do to be valid. Let's look at a few special situations.

A. Defamation, obscenity, and "fighting words."

As shown by case law, these types of language are not considered to be "speech" protected by the First Amendment. Defamation is covered in detail in the Torts section of this book. Fighting words are those personally abusive epithets likely to incite immediate physical retaliation in the ordinary citizen. Obscenity — well, use your imagination or rent a George Carlin video (after all, he's quite famous for his seven dirty words). In any case, since none of these constitute "speech," they don't get First Amendment protection; as long as a statute contains narrow and definite standards, such speech can be prohibited without meeting the "compelling interest" test.

B. Advocacy of unlawful conduct — the "clear and present danger" test.

Government action *can* prohibit advocacy of illegal conduct if it meets the "clear and present danger" test from *Brandenberg v. Ohio*: If (1) the advocacy is *intended* to produce or incite *imminent* illegal action, and (2) the advocacy is *likely* to produce or incite such action, then it can be prohibited.

C. Prior restraints.

A prior restraint is a governmental action that prohibits speech before it takes place. As you can imagine, these actions are *presumptively invalid*, due, generally, to their vagueness or to their placing too much discretion in the hands of the public officials (those responsible, say, for granting licenses to hold demonstrations). Prior restraints can be valid, though, where the mere existence of the communication is proven to create some *special harm to society* (e.g., prohibiting publication of planned army movements in wartime would be valid). Otherwise, in the licensing situation, you should apply the time, place and manner standards in **E.**, below.

D. Commercial speech.

Commercial speech is speech whose primary goal is a *commercial transaction*. You know, Joe Isuzu-type speech. The thing to remember about commercial speech is that, although it's somewhat protected, it can be subject to *greater regulation* than non-commercial speech (e.g., it's permissible to prohibit misleading ads).

E. Public speech — time, place, and manner regulations.

If you determine that the speech in a given fact pattern is constitutionally protected, don't stop there; constitutionally protected speech *is* subject to reasonable time, place and manner regulations. In order to be valid, such a regulation:

1. Must be *neutral* as to the *content* of the speech, both on it's face and as applied (this is referred to as the requirement that the speech be "content-neutral");
2. Must further a *significant governmental interest* not capable of accomplishment by less restrictive means (e.g., maintaining traffic flow); and
3. Must allow for adequate alternative channels for communicating the information.

Here's an example:

> John Doe, the owner of a milk container manufacturing firm, sought to focus public attention on the milk packaging law of the State of Clinton in order to have it repealed. On a weekday at 12:00 noon, he delivered an excited, animated, and loud harangue on the steps of the State Capitol in front of the main entryway. An audience of 200 onlookers, who gathered on the steps, heckled him and laughed as he delivered his tirade. Doe repeatedly stated, gesturing expressively and making faces, that "the g-d damned milk packaging law is stupid," and that "I will strangle every one of those g-d damned legislators I can get hold of because this law they created proves they are all too dumb to live." After about fifteen minutes, Doe stopped speaking, and the amused crowd dispersed. A relevant statute of the State of Clinton prohibits "all speech making, picketing, and public gatherings of every sort on the Capitol steps in front of the main entryway between 7:45 a.m.-8:15 a.m., 11:45 a.m.-12:15 p.m., 12:45 p.m.-1:15 p.m., and 4:45 p.m.-5:15 p.m., on Capitol working days."
>
> This statute is probably

A. constitutional both on its face and as applied to Doe

B. constitutional on its face but unconstitutional as applied to Doe

C. unconstitutional on its face, because it applies to all working days

D. unconstitutional on its face, because it concerns the State Capitol

Here, public speech is involved, since the Capitol steps would be considered a public forum. Public speech can be subject to time, place, and manner restrictions. Here, the statute implies a governmental concern with traffic flow, since the statute only forbids speech during "peak periods" or "rush" times at the building. As such, it's a valid restriction on speech, and it will be constitutional both on its face and as applied to Doe (so A is the best response).

MBE questions will sometimes involve an attempt by a group or an individual to obtain a **permit or license**, as required by an ordinance or regulation, before that group or individual can speak or demonstrate. Be sure to apply the three-part test in this situation. Note that the ordinance or regulation must set out the grounds for **denying** a permit in **narrow and specific** language which curtails the discretion of local officials. (If it doesn't, the ordinance or regulation is probably overbroad.)

5. Freedom of religion.

Freedom of religion, like freedom of expression, is a fundamental right. It's considered separately here, because, as with freedom of expression, courts apply special rules to it.

Under the First Amendment, the government can neither **outlaw or seriously burden** a person's pursuit of religion (the "Free Exercise Clause"), nor **endorse or support** a particular religion ("the Establishment Clause"). The upshot is that the government has to be **religion neutral**. Your analysis of religion questions will differ slightly, depending on whether a statute **hurts** religion or **helps** it. In general, any government action must conform with the following test, from *Lemon v. Kurtzman* (1971):

1. the government action must have a **secular (i.e., non-religious) purpose**;
2. the **primary or principal effect** of the action must **not** be the **advancement of religion;** and
3. the government action must **not foster excessive governmental entanglement** with religion.

In general, when a law **burdens** the free exercise of religion, you have to perform a **balancing** test to determine if the statute is valid. Weigh the magnitude of the burden against the strength of the state interest, taking into account whether there are less burdensome means of accomplishing the state's goal.

Here are a couple points to remember about freedom of religion.

A. The government can only regulate the *practice* of religion.

You can't be told what to believe — for instance, the government can't prohibit you from believing in a specific religion. The government may, however, burden the **practice** of your beliefs, if the burden meets the balancing test described above.

B. The kinds of beliefs that are covered.

"Could it be magic?" says the Barry Manilow song. Sure, but don't expect First Amendment protection for it. The First Amendment's religion clauses only protect those beliefs paralleling traditional religious views. Thus, a mere political or philosophical view won't be protected, whereas something as bizarre as devil worship will be.

Why is this important? Because it limits what a court can look into when deciding a religion case. If your belief parallels a traditional religion, it doesn't matter if your deities are Coca-Cola bottles — your belief will be protected to the same extent as, say, Catholicism. The court simply cannot investigate the reasonableness of your religious views. Note, though, that, in applying the balancing test — strength of state interest vs. magnitude of burden on free exercise — the court **can** determine how important a particular practice is to the exercise of a religion.

C. Aid to private, religious schools.

There's a potential Establishment Clause problem any time the government helps out **private, religious schools**, even if that help is on the same as given to public schools. (Remember that the *Lemon v. Kurtzman* test applies to these situations.) There are two specific guidelines that will help you: first, the aid **must** be for secular (non-religious) instruction; second, aid to post-secondary schools (e.g., colleges) is more likely to be upheld than aid to elementary or secondary schools, because there's less perceived risk of religious indoctrination of college-aged people.

Beyond that, there are very few guidelines as to exactly which aid programs will be permissible and which won't. In fact, MBE questions on this topic tend to stay very close to actual cases, since that's the only sure way to know if a particular kind of aid to religious-oriented schools is valid. When in doubt, guess that the particular kind of aid is valid, since in recent years the Court has become much more inclined to find aid OK (e.g., vouchers for private-school tuition, even though 96% of participants use them for religious schools — *Zelman v. Simmons-Harris* (2002)).

Something you should watch for particularly is the "no fostering of excessive government entanglement" element of the *Lemon v. Kurtzman* test. For instance, where any kind of government aid to a parochial school would require that the government keep close surveillance on how the funds are dispensed (e.g., grants for salaries of teachers of secular subjects only), the entanglement required to monitor such a program — even though it would otherwise be constitutional — would make the grant impermissible.

6. Burden of persuasion.

To wrap up the area of fundamental rights, remember our discussion of who has to prove what in these cases. To recap, the rule is this: If the validity of a statute will be determined by the "rational relation" test, the plaintiff — that is, the one whose rights have ostensibly been violated — bears the burden of persuasion. *If*, however, the validity of the statute is determined by the "strict scrutiny" test, once the right has been shown to be impacted, *the government bears the burden of proving that the statute is valid*. This is important to remember, because it's counter-intuitive; in a normal civil case, the plaintiff typically bears the burden of persuasion. Of course, the fact that this isn't true for cases addressing fundamental rights is what makes it such an attractive issue for the MBE.

7. Standing.

Standing is a sneaky little issue that can come up and torpedo you. Keep in mind that standing is a prerequisite for *every* case; if the plaintiff doesn't have it, it doesn't matter how worthwhile his claim is; the case must be dismissed. There is a section on standing in the "Tactics" section, below, but here's the test for standing itself: standing exists only if the action challenged has caused, or is imminently likely to cause, an injury to the party seeking review. That's all there is to it.

You are likely to encounter this problem on the MBE in the area of *taxpayer standing*. As a general rule, taxpayers don't have standing. There is a very narrow exception to this rule, which typically only applies to cases involving religion based on the Establishment Clause. Technically, a federal taxpayer can gain standing to challenge spending matters if he can show two things: that the federal tax was invalidly applied to him, making the injury personal, *or* that the expenditures in question **both** exceeded a specific constitutional limitation on the taxing and spending powers, **and** that they were part of a federal spending program. This, as a rule, restricts taxpayer standing to *religion* cases. (Note that this is the rule for federal taxpayers. For state and municipal taxpayers, the outcome is similar: they can normally challenge state or municipal expenditures, limited typically to religion cases, e.g., local busing of parochial school students.)

You should also know when a plaintiff has standing to assert *someone else's* constitutional rights in federal court. In general, this is possible only where the plaintiff is injured because someone else's constitutional rights have been violated, or where those who are injured simply cannot assert their own rights. For instance, a beer distributor could challenge a state law which prohibits the sale of beer to men under 21 while allowing women as young as 18 to purchase it, since the equal protection violation to the 18-21 year old men adversely impacts the distributor's business. Similarly, say a state law unconstitutionally compels disclosure of NAACP membership lists. The NAACP would have standing to file suit on behalf of its members, claiming breach of the members' freedom of association rights, because, if the members themselves filed suit, they'd have to reveal their identities — which is what they wanted to avoid in the first place.

8. Jurisdiction.

Jurisdiction brings back happy memories of Civil Procedure for you, doesn't it? There are several facets of jurisdiction (principally federal court jurisdiction) that you should keep in mind on the Constitutional Law questions of the MBE.

First, keep in mind that Congress has the power to create courts inferior to the Supreme Court, and, as a result, Congress can control the jurisdiction of those lower federal courts, as long as it stays within the boundaries of Article III (e.g., Congress couldn't give federal courts the power to render *advisory opinions*). Congress can also control the appellate jurisdiction of the Supreme Court. For instance, Congress could stop the Supreme Court from hearing abortion cases. The only thing it really couldn't do, in this arena, is monkey with the Supreme Court's *original jurisdiction* (e.g., where an Ambassador, a state, or the United States itself is a party).

Second, remember that diversity jurisdiction isn't the only basis of federal court jurisdiction. Diversity cases — i.e., cases between citizens of different states in which at least $50,000 (exclusive of interest or costs) is at stake — are probably the most common federal court cases, but there are several other kinds. You undoubtedly remember federal question jurisdiction from Civil Procedure. Under federal question jurisdiction, if a case arises under a federal statute, a treaty, or the Constitution, a federal court has jurisdiction over the case. There are other kinds of federal jurisdiction, too — e.g., cases between a state and a citizen of another state — but diversity and federal question jurisdiction are the two biggies.

Third, you may want to remember the **means** by which a case can reach the Supreme Court. This depends on two factors: whether the source of the case is a federal court or the highest court of a state, and whether Supreme Court review is sought by *appeal* (review as of right) or by *writ of certiorari* (discretionary review). Keep in mind that the scope of discretionary review is far wider than review as of right, which means that every case subject to review as of right is within discretionary review, but not vice versa.

1. Appeal from a state's highest court
   Cases where a state court held a federal statute/treaty invalid or held a state statute valid in the face of a claim of invalidity under the Constitution or a federal law.

2. Writ of certiorari from a state's highest court
   Cases where a state court addressed a constitutional or federal statutory claim (where there was a challenge to the constitutionality of a federal law, a challenge to a state statute on the grounds of being unconstitutional or contrary to federal law, or any claim asserted under the Constitution or a federal law).

3. Appeal from a lower federal court
   Cases where a lower federal court held a federal statute invalid in a civil action in which the U.S. is a party, or found a state statute **invalid** under federal law or the Constitution.

4. Writ of certiorari — Lower federal court
   Any case, civil or criminal, regardless of whether a constitutional issue is involved.

You may not want to try and remember all of this, but it would probably pay to remember that, in order to get to the Supreme Court at all, a state court case must address a federal question. Furthermore, if a state case rests on adequate and independent **state** grounds, even if it also address a federal question, the Supreme Court won't review the case (because it doesn't matter how the federal question is resolved — the federal question is moot). In questions where a federal claim is presented in state court, you may be tempted to assume that the case is reviewable by the Supreme Court, but **watch out!** There may be "adequate and independent state grounds" for the state court decision; if so, the Supreme Court won't review the case.

Fourth, federal courts will not address **"political questions."** Political questions are those issues the Constitution commits to other governmental branches, as well as issues the judicial process is inherently incapable of resolving and enforcing. Foreign relations is the most obvious example. Foreign affairs are the domain of Congress and the President; thus, a lawsuit by any person or organization which challenged the handling of foreign affairs would not be heard by a federal court.

Fifth, federal courts will not issue **"advisory opinions."** An advisory opinion is one that answers a legal question when **none** of the parties before the court either has suffered or will face specific injury related to that question; remember, a federal court has jurisdiction **only** over "cases and controversies."

Sixth, keep in mind other factors that contribute to whether a federal court will hear a claim: specifically, the issue can be neither **moot** nor **unripe**. A case is moot if it's been resolved or rendered academic before it reaches the court. There are, however, lots of exceptions to this rule — for instance, say a pregnant woman challenges a state's restrictions on abortion. By the time her case winds its way up to federal court, she probably won't be pregnant any more. The issue is, therefore, moot, but this type of case fits into one of the exceptions to the "moot" rule: if an event is recurring but **will always evade review**, the court will address the issue anyway (otherwise, the issue may never be resolved). Class actions, too, can proceed so long as any of the claims remains valid, even if the claim of the representative of the class becomes moot (e.g., because it's settled). You get the idea.

"Ripeness" is really an aspect of standing. A case is "unripe" if it doesn't present an **immediate** threat of harm. Here's an example:

> The state of Champlain enacts the Young Adult Marriage Counseling Act, which provides that, before any persons less than 30 years of age may be issued a marriage license, they must receive at least five hours of marriage counseling from a state-licensed social worker. This counseling is designed to insure that applicants for marriage licenses know their legal rights and duties in relation to marriage and parenthood, that they understand the "true nature" of the marriage relationship, and that they

understand the procedures for obtaining divorce.

Pine, aged 25, contemplated marrying Ross, aged 25. Both are residents of the state of Champlain. Pine has not yet proposed to Ross because he is offended by the counseling requirement.

Pine sues in court, seeking a declaratory judgment that the Young Adult Marriage Counseling Act is unconstitutional. Which of the following is the clearest ground for dismissal for this action by the court?

   A. Pine and Ross are residents of the same state
   B. No substantial federal question is presented
   C. The suit presents a nonjusticiable political question
   D. The suit is unripe

Here, you can see that Pine hasn't even proposed to Ross, and so there is no immediate threat of harm. That makes the issue "unripe," so D's the best response. (Note that this question also addresses two issues of jurisdiction we've already discussed. Choice A impliedly addresses federal court diversity jurisdiction and suggests that, if the parties are residents of the same state, there can't be federal court jurisdiction at all. This ignores the existence of federal question jurisdiction, which would exist here, because Pine is questioning the validity of a state statute **under the federal Constitution**. That also knocks out choice B, since it ignores the existence of a federal question.)

9. Separation of powers.

You may find this a bit bewildering on the MBE, because it's unlikely your Constitutional Law professor spent much time on this issue in law school. While a complete review of the powers of each governmental branch is best left to your substantive review, don't forget the basics: Congress makes the laws, the President executes the laws, and the judiciary interprets the laws. For instance, Congress can't determine the constitutionality of its enactments, and it can't institute or enforce its own laws; the President, who has executive powers, only has legislating abilities to the extent that Congress delegates such powers to him.

On the MBE, you're most likely to see separation-of-powers questions involving a President's attempt to **impound funds** appropriated by Congress. If you face such a question, just remember that, as long as Congress specifies that the funds are to be spent, the Executive branch **must** spend the funds; if it doesn't, there's a separation-of-powers violation.

10. Bills of attainder.

A "bill of attainder" is a law, either federal or state, that punishes, without a trial, past or future conduct of specifically named individuals or ascertainable groups. Bills of attainder are **impermissible**. Bills of attainder are an occasional answer choice on the MBE. Just remember the hallmark of a bill of attainder: punishment on the basis of political beliefs or activities. For instance, a statute that bans members of the Communist Party from taking leadership positions in labor unions would be an invalid bill of attainder. *United States v. Brown* (1965).

EXAM TACTICS

1. When asked the validity of a law, check first to see if it's a federal or a state law.

As noted in the "Study Strategies" section, it's important to distinguish federal laws from state laws. If you do this, you'll frequently be able to eliminate at least one distractor. Here's an example:

The strongest constitutional basis for the enactment of a federal statute requiring colleges and universities receiving federal funds to offer student aid solely on the basis of need is the

   A. police power
   B. war and defense power
   C. power to tax and spend for the general welfare
   D. power to enforce the privileges and immunities clause of the Fourteenth Amendment

Here, take note of the fact that this is a **federal** statute. You know that the federal government has no police powers, so choice A can't be the best response. (In fact, the correct answer is C. Incidentally, this indicates how Congress can use its strongest powers — namely, spending and interstate commerce — to legislate in areas not delegated to it by the Constitution. In this case, that's education — a traditional state function.)

2. When asked about a plaintiff's standing, ignore substance.

If you're asked about a plaintiff's standing, remember what standing requires: the plaintiff must either have suffered or be imminently likely to suffer an injury due to the challenged action. What you must do is focus on that requirement and *ignore issues of substance* in the plaintiff's claim. Here's an example:

> As part of a comprehensive federal aid-to-education program, Congress included the following provisions as conditions for state receipt of federal funds: (1) Whenever textbooks are provided to students without charge, they must include no religious instruction and must be made available on the same terms to students in all public and private schools accredited by the state educational authority. (2) Salary supplements can be paid to teachers in public and private schools, up to ten percent of existing salary schedules, where present compensation is less than the average salary for persons of comparable training and experience, provided that no such supplement is paid to any teacher who instructs in religious subjects. (3) Construction grants can be made toward the cost of physical plant at private colleges and universities, provided that no part of the grant is used for buildings in which instruction in religious subject matters is offered.
>
> Federal taxpayer Allen challenges the provision that allows the distribution of free textbooks to students in a private school where religious instruction is included in the curriculum. On the question of the adequacy of Allen's standing to raise the constitutional question, the most likely result is that standing will be
>
> A. sustained, because any congressional spending authorization can be challenged by any taxpayer
>
> B. sustained, because the challenge to the exercise of congressional spending power is based on a claimed violation of specific constitutional limitations on the exercise of such power
>
> C. denied, because there is insufficient nexus between the taxpayer and the challenged expenditures
>
> D. denied, because, in the case of private schools, no state action is involved

Here, choice D depends on a substantive issue in the case, that is, whether there is state action involved. The question only asked about standing, though. To determine standing, a court looks solely at whether the plaintiff is legally qualified to press a claim, not whether his claim has merit. Thus, D can't be the best response. (In fact, B is the best response.)

3. Avoid answers which state that a statute is constitutional because the plaintiff's interest is a "privilege, not a right."

Sometimes an answer choice will suggest that a statute is valid, in the face of a due process challenge, because plaintiff's interest is a "privilege" and not a "right." This is a distinction without a difference. If a governmental action impinges on a plaintiff's personal, fundamental interest, it doesn't matter if the interest is characterized as a privilege instead of a right. As a result, the "privilege and not a right" answer choice is almost certainly a distractor.

4. When you're asked to argue both ways, look for a common issue.

Constitutional law MBE questions are unusual in that you'll frequently find two questions on the same fact pattern, one asking the strongest argument for holding the statute constitutional, and the other asking the strongest argument for striking down the statute. If you're stumped, it may help to look for a common issue in the answer choices of the two questions. After all, the strongest argument for one side is likely to be the greatest weakness for the other.

5. What to do with economic legislation.

When you're faced with a purely economic or social statute, remember that there's *no due process or equal protection problem*, because the statute will be subject only to the "rational relation" test. It's easy to read too much into such a question; don't be tempted to do so. For instance, say a state, as an environmental protection measure, bans plastic, nonreturnable milk cartons but allows milk to be sold in cardboard milk cartons. There's no due process or equal protection issue here. *Minnesota v. Cloverleaf Creamery Co.* (1981).

QUESTIONS
CONSTITUTIONAL LAW

QUESTIONS

CONSTITUTIONAL LAW

Question 1

A statute of the state of Texona prohibits any retailer of books, magazines, pictures, or posters from "publicly displaying or selling to any person any material that may be harmful to minors because of the violent or sexually explicit nature of its pictorial content." Violation of this statute is a misdemeanor.

Corner Store displays publicly and sells magazines containing violent and sexually explicit pictures. The owner of this store is prosecuted under the above statute for these actions.

In defending against this prosecution in a Texona trial court, the argument that would be the best defense for Corner Store is that the statute violates the

(A) First Amendment as it is incorporated into the Fourteenth Amendment, because the statute is excessively vague and overbroad.

(B) First Amendment as it is incorporated into the Fourteenth Amendment, because a state may not prohibit the sale of violent or sexually explicit material in the absence of proof that the material is utterly without any redeeming value in the marketplace of ideas.

(C) equal protection of the laws clause, because the statute irrationally treats violent and sexually explicit material that is pictorial differently from such material that is composed wholly of printed words.

(D) equal protection of the laws clause, because the statute irrationally distinguishes between violent and sexually explicit pictorial material that may harm minors and such material that may harm only adults.

Question 2

Congressional legislation authorizing marriages and divorces as a matter of federal law on prescribed terms and conditions could most easily be upheld if it

(A) applied only to marriages and divorces in which at least one of the parties is a member of the armed forces.

(B) applied only to marriages performed by federal judges and to divorces granted by federal courts.

(C) implemented an executive agreement seeking to define basic human rights.

(D) applied only to marriages and divorces in the District of Columbia.

Question 3

Assume for the purposes of this question that you are counsel to the state legislative committee that is responsible for the real estate laws in your state.

The committee wants you to draft legislation to make all restrictions on land use imposed by deeds (now or hereafter recorded) unenforceable in the future so that public land-use planning through zoning will have exclusive control in matters of land use. Which of the following is LEAST likely to be a consideration in the drafting of such legislation?

(A) Compensation for property rights taken by public authority.

(B) Impairment of contract.

(C) Sovereign immunity.

(D) Police power.

Question 4

Congress recently enacted a statute imposing severe criminal penalties on anyone engaged in trading in the stock market who, in the course of that trading, takes "unfair advantage" of other investors who are also trading in the stock market. The statute does not define the term "unfair advantage." There have been no prosecutions under this new statute. The members of an association of law school professors that is dedicated to increasing the clarity of the language used in criminal statutes believe that this statute is unconstitutionally vague. Neither the association nor any of its members is currently engaged in, or intends in the future to engage in, trading in the stock market. The association and its members bring suit against the Attorney General of the United States in a federal district court, seeking an injunction against the enforcement of this statute on the ground that it is unconstitutional.

May the federal court determine the merits of this suit?

(A) Yes, because the suit involves a dispute over the constitutionality of a federal statute.

(B) Yes, because the plaintiffs seek real relief of a conclusive nature — an injunction against enforcement of this statute.

(C) No, because the plaintiffs do not have an interest in the invalidation of this statute that is adequate to ensure that the suit presents an Article III controversy.

(D) No, because a suit for an injunction against enforcement of a criminal statute may not be brought in federal court at any time prior to a bona fide effort to enforce that statute.

Question 5

Company wanted to expand the size of the building it owned that housed Company's supermarket by adding space for a coffeehouse. Company's building was located in the center of five acres of land owned by Company and devoted wholly to parking for its supermarket customers.

City officials refused to grant a required building permit for the coffeehouse addition unless Company established in its store a child care center that would take up space at least equal to the size of the proposed coffeehouse addition, which was to be 20% of the existing building. This action of City officials was authorized by provisions of the applicable zoning ordinance.

In a suit filed in state court against appropriate officials of City, Company challenged this child care center requirement solely on constitutional grounds. The lower court upheld the requirement even though City officials presented no evidence and made no findings to justify it other than a general assertion that there was a shortage of child care facilities in City. Company appealed.

The court hearing the appeal should hold that the requirement imposed by City on the issuance of this building permit is

(A) constitutional, because the burden was on Company to demonstrate that there was no rational relationship between this requirement and a legitimate governmental interest, and Company could not do so because the requirement is reasonably related to improving the lives of families and children residing in City.

(B) constitutional, because the burden was on Company to demonstrate that this requirement was not necessary to vindicate a compelling governmental interest, and Company could not do so on these facts.

(C) unconstitutional, because the burden was on City to demonstrate that this requirement was necessary to vindicate a compelling governmental interest, and City failed to meet its burden under that standard.

(D) unconstitutional, because the burden was on City to demonstrate a rough proportionality between this requirement and the impact of Company's proposed action on the community, and City failed to do so.

Question 6

The mineral alpha is added to bodies of fresh water to prevent the spread of certain freshwater parasites. The presence of those parasites threatens the health of the organisms living in rivers and streams throughout the country and imperils the freshwater commercial fishing industry. Alpha is currently mined only in the state of Blue.

In order to raise needed revenue, Congress recently enacted a statute providing for the imposition of a $100 tax on each ton of alpha mined in the United States. Because it will raise the cost of alpha, this tax is likely to reduce the amount of alpha added to freshwater rivers and streams

and, therefore, is likely to have an adverse effect on the interstate freshwater commercial fishing industry. The alpha producers in Blue have filed a lawsuit in federal court challenging this tax solely on constitutional grounds.

Is this tax constitutional?

(A) No, because only producers in Blue will pay the tax and, therefore, it is not uniform among the states and denies alpha producers the equal protection of the laws.

(B) No, because it is likely to have an adverse effect on the freshwater commercial fishing industry and Congress has a responsibility under the commerce clause to protect, foster, and advance such interstate industries.

(C) Yes, because the tax is a necessary and proper means of exercising federal authority over the navigable waters of the United States.

(D) Yes, because the power of Congress to impose taxes is plenary, this tax does not contain any provisions extraneous to tax needs or purposes, and it is not barred by any prohibitory language in the Constitution.

Questions 7-8 are based on the following fact situation.

A recently enacted state law forbids aliens from owning more than 100 acres of land within the state and directs the state attorney general to bring an action of ejectment whenever an alien owns such land.

Zane, a resident alien, located and purchased 200 acres of land in the state after passage of that law. He brings an action in federal court to enjoin the state attorney general from enforcing the statute against him. The defendant moves to dismiss the complaint.

Question 7

The strongest argument for Zane is that

(A) states are forbidden by the commerce clause from interfering with the rights of aliens to own land.

(B) the state statute violates the equal protection clause of the Fourteenth Amendment.

(C) the state statute adversely affects Zane's right to travel.

(D) the state statute violates the obligation of contracts clause.

Question 8

The federal court should

(A) dismiss the action, because under the Constitution aliens may not sue in federal court.

(B) dismiss the action, because a state has unlimited power to determine the qualifications for landholding within its boundaries.

(C) hear the action, because the United Nations Charter forbids such discrimination.

(D) hear the action, because a federal question is presented.

Question 9

An ordinance of Central City requires every operator of a taxicab in the city to have a license and permits revocation of that license only for "good cause." The Central City taxicab operator's licensing ordinance conditions the issuance of such a license on an agreement by the licensee that the licensee "not display in or on his or her vehicle any bumper sticker or other placard or sign favoring a particular candidate for any elected municipal office." The ordinance also states that it imposes this condition in order to prevent the possible imputation to the city council of the views of its taxicab licensees and that any licensee who violates this condition shall have his or her license revoked.

Driver, the holder of a Central City taxicab operator's license, decorates his cab with bumper stickers and other signs favoring specified candidates in a forthcoming election for municipal offices. A proceeding is initiated against him to revoke his taxicab operator's license on the sole basis of that admitted conduct.

In this proceeding, does Driver have a meritorious defense based on the United States Constitution?

(A) No, because he accepted the license with knowledge of the condition and, therefore, has no standing to contest it.

(B) No, because a taxicab operator's license is a privilege and not a right and, therefore, is not protected by the due process clause of the Fourteenth Amendment.

(C) Yes, because such a proceeding threatens Driver with a taking of property, his license, without just compensation.

(D) Yes, because the condition imposed on taxicab operators' licenses restricts political speech based wholly on its content, without any adequate governmental justification.

Question 10

Leonard was the high priest of a small cult of Satan worshippers living in New Arcadia. As a part of the practice of their religious beliefs, a cat was required to be sacrificed to the glory of Satan after a live dissection of the animal in which it endured frightful pain. In the course of such religious sacrifice, Leonard was arrested on the complaint of the local Humane Society and charged under a statute punishing cruelty to animals. On appeal, a conviction of Leonard probably will be

(A) sustained on the grounds that belief in or worship of Satan does not enjoy constitutional protection.

(B) sustained on the grounds that sincere religious belief is not an adequate defense on these facts.

(C) overturned on the grounds that the constitutionally guaranteed freedom of religion and its expression was violated.

(D) overturned on the grounds that the beliefs of the cult members in the need for the sacrifice might be rea-

sonable, and their act was religious.

Question 11

An appropriations act passed by Congress over the President's veto directs that one billion dollars "shall be spent" by the federal government for the development of a new military weapons system, which is available only from the Arms Corporation. On the order of the President, the Secretary of Defense refuses to authorize a contract for the purchase of the weapons system. The Arms Corporation sues the Secretary of Defense alleging an unlawful withholding of these federal funds.

The strongest constitutional argument for the Arms Corporation is that

(A) passage of an appropriation over a veto makes the spending mandatory.

(B) Congress' power to appropriate funds includes the power to require that the funds will be spent as directed.

(C) the President's independent constitutional powers do not specifically refer to spending.

(D) the President's power to withhold such funds is limited to cases where foreign affairs are directly involved.

Question 12

Doctor, a resident of the city of Greenville in the state of Green, is a physician licensed to practice in both Green and the neighboring state of Red. Doctor finds that the most convenient place to treat her patients who need hospital care is in the publicly owned and operated Redville Municipal Hospital of the city of Redville in the state of Red, which is located just across the state line from Greenville. For many years Doctor had successfully treated her patients in that hospital. Early this year she was notified that she could no longer treat patients in the Redville hospital because she was not a resident of Red, and a newly adopted rule of Redville Municipal Hospital, which was adopted in conformance with all required procedures, stated that every physician who practices in that hospital must be a resident of Red.

Which of the following constitutional provisions would be most helpful to Doctor in an action to challenge her exclusion from the Redville hospital solely on the basis of this hospital rule?

(A) The bill of attainder clause.

(B) The privileges and immunities clause of Article IV.

(C) The due process clause of the Fourteenth Amendment.

(D) The ex post facto clause.

Question 13

State Y has a state employee grievance system that requires any state employee who wishes to file a grievance against the state to submit that grievance for final resolution to a panel of three arbitrators chosen by the parties from a statewide board of 13 arbitrators. In any given case, the grievant and the state alternate in exercising the right of each party to eliminate five members of the board, leaving a panel of three members to decide their case. At the present time, the full board is composed of seven male arbitrators and six female arbitrators.

Ellen, a female state employee, filed a sexual harassment grievance against her male supervisor and the state. Anne, the state's attorney, exercised all of her five strikes to eliminate five of the female arbitrators. At the time she did so, Anne stated that she struck the five female arbitrators solely because she believed women, as a group, would necessarily be biased in favor of another woman who was claiming sexual harassment. Counsel for Ellen eliminated four males and one female arbitrator, all solely on grounds of specific bias or conflicts of interest. As a result, the panel was all male.

When the panel ruled against Ellen on the merits of her case, she filed an action in an appropriate state court, challenging the panel selection process as a gender-based denial of equal protection of the laws.

In this case, the court should hold that the panel selection process is

(A) unconstitutional, because the gender classification used by the state's attorney in this case does not satisfy the requirements of intermediate scrutiny.

(B) unconstitutional, because the gender classification used by the state's attorney in this case denies the grievant the right to a jury made up of her peers.

(C) constitutional, because the gender classification used by the state's attorney in this case satisfies the requirements of the strict scrutiny test.

(D) constitutional, because the gender classification used by the state's attorney in this case satisfies the requirements of the rational basis test.

Question 14

In recent years, several large corporations incorporated and headquartered in State A have suddenly been acquired by out-of-state corporations that have moved all of their operations out of State A. Other corporations incorporated and headquartered in State A have successfully resisted such attempts at acquisition by out-of-state corporations, but they have suffered severe economic injury during those acquisition attempts.

In an effort to preserve jobs in State A and to protect its domestic corporations against their sudden acquisition by out-of-state purchasers, the legislature of State A enacts a statute governing acquisitions of shares in all corporations incorporated in State A. This statute requires that any acquisition of more than 25% of the voting shares of a corporation incorporated in State A that occurs over a period of less than one year must be approved by the holders of record of a majority of the shares of the corporation as of the day before the commencement of the acquisition of those shares. The statute expressly applies to acquisitions of State A corporations by both in-state and out-of-state entities.

Assume that no federal statute applies.
Is this statute of State A constitutional?

(A) No, because one of the purposes of the statute is to prevent out-of-state entities from acquiring corporations incorporated and headquartered in State A.

(B) No, because the effect of the statute will necessarily be to hinder the acquisition of State A corporations by other corporations, many of whose shareholders are not residents of State A and, therefore, it will adversely affect the interstate sale of securities.

(C) Yes, because the statute imposes the same burden on both in-state and out-of-state entities wishing to acquire a State A corporation, it regulates only the acquisition of State A corporations, and it does not create an impermissible risk of inconsistent regulation on this subject by different states.

(D) Yes, because corporations exist only by virtue of state law and, therefore, the negative implications of the commerce clause do not apply to state regulations governing their creation and acquisition.

Question 15

Central City in the state of Green is a center for businesses that assemble personal computers. Components for these computers are manufactured elsewhere in Green and in other states, then shipped to Central City, where the computers are assembled. An ordinance of Central City imposes a special license tax on all of the many companies engaged in the business of assembling computers in that city. The tax payable by each such company is a percentage of the company's gross receipts.

The Green statute that authorizes municipalities to impose this license tax has a "Green content" provision. To comply with this provision of state law, the Central City license tax ordinance provides that the tax paid by any assembler of computers subject to this tax ordinance will be reduced by a percentage equal to the proportion of computer components manufactured in Green.

Assembler is a company that assembles computers in Central City and sells them from its offices in Central City to buyers throughout the United States. All of the components of its computers come from outside the state of Green. Therefore, Assembler must pay the Central City license tax in full without receiving any refund. Other Central City computer assemblers use components manufactured in Green in varying proportions and, therefore, are entitled to partial reductions of their Central City license tax payments.

Following prescribed procedure, Assembler brings an action in a proper court asking to have Central City's special license tax declared unconstitutional on the ground that it is inconsistent with the negative implications of the commerce clause.

In this case, the court should rule

(A) against Assembler, because the tax falls only on companies resident in Central City and, therefore, does not discriminate against or otherwise adversely affect interstate commerce.

(B) against Assembler, because the commerce clause does not interfere with the right of a state to foster and support businesses located within its borders by encouraging its residents to purchase the products of those businesses.

(C) for Assembler, because any tax on a company engaged in interstate commerce, measured in whole or in part by its gross receipts, is a per se violation of the negative implications of the commerce clause.

(D) for Assembler, because the tax improperly discriminates against interstate commerce by treating in-state products more favorably than out-of-state products.

Question 16

Agitator, a baseball fan, has a fierce temper and an extremely loud voice. Attending a baseball game in which a number of calls went against the home team, Agitator repeatedly stood up, brandished his fist, and angrily shouted, "Kill the umpires." The fourth time he engaged in this conduct, many other spectators followed Agitator in rising from their seats, brandishing fists, and shouting, "Kill the umpires."

The home team lost the game. Although no violence ensued, spectators crowded menacingly around the umpires after the game. As a result, the umpires were able to leave the field and stadium only with the help of a massive police escort.

For his conduct, Agitator was charged with inciting to riot and was convicted in a jury trial in state court. He appealed. The state supreme court reversed his conviction. In its opinion, the court discussed in detail decisions of the United States Supreme Court dealing with the First Amendment free speech clause as incorporated into the Fourteenth Amendment. At the end of that discussion, however, the court stated that it "need not resolve how, on the basis of these cases," the United States Supreme Court would decide Agitator's case. "Instead," the court stated, "this court has always given the free-speech guarantee of the state's constitution the broadest possible interpretation. As a result, we hold that in this case, where no riot or other violence actually occurred, the state constitution does not permit this conviction for incitement to riot to stand."

The United States Supreme Court grants a writ of certiorari to review this decision of the state supreme court.

In this case, the United States Supreme Court should

(A) affirm the state supreme court's decision, because Agitator's ballpark shout is commonplace hyperbole that cannot, consistently with the First and Fourteenth Amendments, be punished.

(B) remand the case to the state supreme court with directions that it resolve the First and Fourteenth Amendment free-speech issue that it discussed in such detail.

(C) dismiss the writ as improvidently granted, because the state supreme court's decision rests on an independent and adequate state law ground.

(D) reverse the decision of the state supreme court, because incitement to violent action is not speech protected by the First and Fourteenth Amendments.

Questions 17-18 are based on the following fact situation.

As part of a comprehensive federal aid-to-education program, Congress included the following provisions as conditions for state receipt of federal funds: (1) Whenever textbooks are provided to students without charge, they must include no religious instruction and must be made available on the same terms to students in all public and private schools accredited by the state educational authority. (2) Salary supplements can be paid to teachers in public and private schools, up to ten percent of existing salary schedules, where present compensation is less than the average salary for persons of comparable training and experience, provided that no such supplement is paid to any teacher who instructs in religious subjects. (3) Construction grants can be made toward the cost of physical plant at private colleges and universities, provided that no part of the grant is used for buildings in which instruction in religious subject matters is offered.

Question 17

Federal taxpayer Allen challenges the provision that allows the distribution of free textbooks to students in a private school where religious instruction is included in the curriculum. On the question of the adequacy of Allen's standing to raise the constitutional question, the most likely result is that standing will be

(A) sustained, because any congressional spending authorization can be challenged by any taxpayer.

(B) sustained, because the challenge to the exercise of congressional spending power is based on a claimed violation of specific constitutional limitations on the exercise of such power.

(C) denied, because there is insufficient nexus between the taxpayer and the challenged expenditures.

(D) denied, because in the case of private schools, no state action is involved.

Question 18

Federal taxpayer Bates also challenges the construction grants to church operated private colleges and universities. The most likely result is that the construction grants will be

(A) sustained, because aid to one aspect of an institution of higher education not shown to be pervasively sectarian does not necessarily free it to spend its other resources for religious purposes.

(B) sustained, because bricks and mortar do not aid religion in a way forbidden by the establishment clause of the First Amendment.

(C) held unconstitutional, because any financial aid to a

church-operated school strengthens the religious purposes of the institution.

(D) held unconstitutional, because the grants involve or cause an excessive entanglement with religion.

Question 19

The governor of the state of Green proposes to place a Christmas nativity scene, the components of which would be permanently donated to the state by private citizens, in the Green Capitol Building rotunda where the Green Legislature meets annually. The governor further proposes to display this state-owned nativity scene annually from December 1 to December 31, next to permanent displays that depict the various products manufactured in Green. The governor's proposal is supported by all members of both houses of the legislature.

If challenged in a lawsuit on establishment clause grounds, the proposed nativity scene display would be held

(A) unconstitutional, because the components of the nativity scene would be owned by the state rather than by private persons.

(B) unconstitutional, because the nativity scene would not be displayed in a context that appeared to depict and commemorate the Christmas season as a primarily secular holiday.

(C) constitutional, because the components of the nativity scene would be donated to the state by private citizens rather than purchased with state funds.

(D) constitutional, because the nativity scene would be displayed alongside an exhibit of various products manufactured in Green.

Question 20

A city owns and operates a large public auditorium. It leases the auditorium to any group that wishes to use it for a meeting, lecture, concert, or contest. Each user must post a damage deposit and pay rent, which is calculated only for the actual time the building is used by the lessee. Reservations are made on a first-come, first-served basis.

A private organization that permits only males to serve in its highest offices rented the auditorium for its national convention. The organization planned to install its new officers at that convention. It broadly publicized the event, inviting members of the general public to attend the installation ceremony at the city auditorium. No statute or administrative rule prohibits the organization from restricting its highest offices to men.

An appropriate plaintiff sues the private organization seeking to enjoin it from using the city auditorium for the installation of its new officers. The sole claim of the plaintiff is that the use of this auditorium by the organization for the installation ceremony is unconstitutional because the organization disqualifies women from serving in its highest offices.

Will the plaintiff prevail?

(A) Yes, because the Fourteenth Amendment prohibits such an organization from discriminating against women in any of its activities to which it has invited members of the general public.

(B) Yes, because the organization's use of the city auditorium for this purpose subjects its conduct to the provisions of the Fourteenth Amendment.

(C) No, because the freedom of association protected by the Fourteenth Amendment prohibits the city from interfering in any way with the organization's use of city facilities.

(D) No, because this organization is not a state actor and, therefore, its activities are not subject to the provisions of the Fourteenth Amendment.

Question 21

Kelly County, in the state of Green, is located adjacent to the border of the state of Red. The communities located in Kelly County are principally suburbs of Scarletville, a large city located in Red, and therefore there is a large volume of traffic between that city and Kelly County. While most of that traffic is by private passenger automobiles, some of it is by taxicabs and other kinds of commercial vehicles.

An ordinance of Kelly County, the stated purpose of which is to reduce traffic congestion, provides that only taxicabs registered in Kelly County may pick up or discharge passengers in the county. The ordinance also provides that only residents of Kelly County may register taxicabs in that county.

Which of the following is the proper result in a suit brought by Scarletville taxicab owners challenging the constitutionality of this Kelly County ordinance?

(A) Judgment for Scarletville taxicab owners, because the fact that private passenger automobiles contribute more to the traffic congestion problem in Kelly County than do taxicabs indicates that the ordinance is not a reasonable means by which to solve that problem.

(B) Judgment for Scarletville taxicab owners, because the ordinance unduly burdens interstate commerce by insulating Kelly County taxicab owners from out-of-state competition without adequate justification.

(C) Judgment for Kelly County, because the ordinance forbids taxicabs registered in other counties of Green as well as in states other than Green to operate in Kelly County and, therefore, it does not discriminate against interstate commerce.

(D) Judgment for Kelly County, because Scarletville taxicab owners do not constitute a suspect class and the ordinance is reasonably related to the legitimate governmental purpose of reducing traffic congestion.

Question 22

The King City zoning ordinance contains provisions restricting places of "adult entertainment" to two specified city blocks within the commercial center of the city. These provisions of the ordinance define "adult entertainment" as "live or filmed nudity or sexual activity, real or simulated, of an indecent nature."

Sam proposes to operate an adult entertainment establishment outside the two-block area zoned for such establishments but within the commercial center of King City. When his application for permission to do so is rejected solely because it is inconsistent with provisions of the zoning ordinance, he sues the appropriate officials of King City, seeking to enjoin them from enforcing the adult entertainment provisions of the ordinance against him. He asserts that these provisions of the ordinance violate the First Amendment as made applicable to King City by the Fourteenth Amendment.

In this case, the court hearing Sam's request for an injunction would probably hold that the adult entertainment provisions of the King City zoning ordinance are

(A) constitutional, because they do not prohibit adult entertainment everywhere in King City, and the city has a substantial interest in keeping the major part of its commercial center free of uses it considers harmful to that area.

(B) constitutional, because adult entertainment of the kind described in these provisions of the King City ordinance is not protected by the free speech guarantee of the First and Fourteenth Amendments.

(C) unconstitutional, because they prohibit in the commercial area of the city adult entertainment that is not "obscene" within the meaning of the First and Fourteenth Amendments.

(D) unconstitutional, because zoning ordinances that restrict freedom of speech may be justified only by a substantial interest in preserving the quality of a community's residential neighborhoods.

Question 23

City enacted an ordinance banning from its public sidewalks all machines dispensing publications consisting wholly of commercial advertisements. The ordinance was enacted because of a concern about the adverse aesthetic effects of litter from publications distributed on the public sidewalks and streets. However, City continued to allow machines dispensing other types of publications on the public sidewalks. As a result of the City ordinance, 30 of the 300 sidewalk machines that were dispensing publications in City were removed.

Is this City ordinance constitutional?

(A) Yes, because regulations of commercial speech are subject only to the requirement that they be rationally related to a legitimate state goal, and that requirement is satisfied here.

(B) Yes, because City has a compelling interest in protecting the aesthetics of its sidewalks and streets, and such a ban is necessary to vindicate this interest.

(C) No, because it does not constitute the least restrictive means with which to protect the aesthetics of City's sidewalks and streets.

(D) No, because there is not a reasonable fit between the legitimate interest of City in preserving the aesthetics of its sidewalks and streets and the means it chose to advance that interest.

Question 24

John is a licensed barber in State A. The State A barber licensing statute provides that the Barber Licensing Board may revoke a barber license if it finds that a licensee has used his or her business premises for an illegal purpose.

John was arrested by federal narcotics enforcement agents on a charge of selling cocaine in his barbershop in violation of federal laws. However, the local United States Attorney declined to prosecute and the charges were dropped.

Nevertheless, the Barber Licensing Board commenced a proceeding against John to revoke his license on the ground that John used his business premises for illegal sales of cocaine. At a subsequent hearing before the board, the only evidence against John was affidavits by unnamed informants, who were not present or available for cross-examination. Their affidavits stated that they purchased cocaine from John in his barbershop. Based solely on this evidence, the board found that John used his business premises for an illegal purpose and ordered his license revoked.

In a suit by John to have this revocation set aside, his best constitutional argument is that

(A) John's inability to cross-examine his accusers denied him a fair hearing and caused him to be deprived of his barber license without due process of law.

(B) the administrative license revocation proceeding was invalid, because it denied full faith and credit to the dismissal of the criminal charges by the United States Attorney.

(C) Article III requires a penalty of the kind imposed on John to be imposed by a court rather than an administrative agency.

(D) the existence of federal laws penalizing the illegal sale of cocaine preempts state action relating to drug trafficking of the kind involved in John's case.

Question 25

Alex contracted for expensive cable television service for a period of six months solely to view the televised trial of Clark, who was on trial for murder in a court of the state of Green.

In the midst of the trial, the judge prohibited any further televising of Clark's trial because he concluded that the presence of television cameras was disruptive.

Alex brought an action in a federal district court against the judge in Clark's case asking only for an injunction that would require the judge to resume the televising of Clark's trial. Alex alleged that the judge's order to stop the televising of Clark's trial deprived him of property—his investment in cable television service—without due process of law.

Before Alex's case came to trial, Clark's criminal trial concluded in a conviction and sentencing. There do not appear to be any obvious errors in the proceeding that led to the result in Clark's case. After Clark's conviction and sentencing, the defendant in Alex's case moved to dismiss that suit.

The most proper disposition of this motion by the federal court would be to

(A) defer action on the motion until after any appellate proceedings in Clark's case have concluded, because Clark might appeal, his conviction might be set aside, he might be tried again, and television cameras might be barred from the new trial.

(B) defer action on the motion until after the Green Supreme Court expresses a view on its proper disposition, because the state law of mootness governs suits in federal court when the federal case is inexorably intertwined with a state proceeding.

(C) grant the motion, because the subject matter of the controversy between Alex and the defendant has ceased to exist and there is no strong likelihood that it will be revived.

(D) deny the motion, because Alex has raised an important constitutional question—whether his investment in cable service solely to view Clark's trial is property protected by the due process clause of the Fourteenth Amendment.

Question 26

Nora, executive director of an equal housing opportunity organization, was the leader of a sit-in at the offices of a real estate management company. The protest was designed to call attention to the company's racially discriminatory rental practices. When police demanded that Nora desist from trespassing on the company's property, she refused and was arrested. In Nora's trial for trespass, the prosecution peremptorily excused all nonwhites from the jury, arguing to the court that even though Nora was white, minority groups would automatically support Nora because of her fight against racism in housing accommodations.

If Nora is convicted of trespass by an all-white jury and appeals, claiming a violation of her constitutional rights, the court should

(A) affirm the conviction, because Nora was not a member of the class discriminated against.

(B) affirm the conviction, because peremptory challenge of the nonwhites did not deny Nora the right to an impartial jury.

(C) reverse the conviction, because racially based peremptory challenges violate equal protection of the law.

(D) reverse the conviction, because Nora was denied the right to have her case heard by a fair cross section of the community.

Question 27

The state of Green imposes a tax on the "income" of each of its residents. As defined in the taxing statute, "income" includes the fair rental value of the use of any automobile provided by the taxpayer's employer for the taxpayer's personal use. The federal government supplies automobiles to some of its employees who are resident in Green so that they may perform their jobs properly. A federal government employee supplied with an automobile for this purpose may also use it for the employee's own personal business.

Assume there is no federal legislation on this subject.

May the state of Green collect this tax on the fair rental value of the personal use of the automobiles furnished by the federal government to these employees?

(A) No, because such a tax would be a tax on the United States.

(B) No, because such a tax would be a tax upon activities performed on behalf of the United States, since the automobiles are primarily used by these federal employees in the discharge of their official duties.

(C) Yes, because the tax is imposed on the employees rather than on the United States, and the tax does not discriminate against persons who are employed by the United States.

(D) Yes, because an exemption from such state taxes for federal employees would be a denial to others of the equal protection of the laws.

Question 28

A city ordinance requires a taxicab operator's license to operate a taxicab in King City. The ordinance states that the sole criteria for the issuance of such a license are driving ability and knowledge of the geography of King City. An applicant is tested by the city for these qualifications with a detailed questionnaire, written and oral examinations, and a practical behind-the-wheel demonstration.

The ordinance does not limit the number of licenses that may be issued. It does, however, allow any citizen to file an objection to the issuance of a particular license, but only on the ground that an applicant does not possess the required qualifications. City licensing officials are also authorized by the ordinance to determine, in their discretion, whether to hold an evidentiary hearing on an objection before issuing a license.

Sandy applies for a taxicab operator's license and is found to be fully qualified after completing the usual licensing process. Her name is then posted as a prospective licensee, subject only to the objection process. John, a licensed taxicab driver, files an objection to the issuance of such a license to Sandy solely on the ground that the grant of a license to Sandy would impair the value of John's existing license. John demands a hearing before a license is issued to Sandy so that he may have an opportunity to prove his claim. City licensing officials refuse to hold such a hearing, and they issue a license to Sandy. John petitions for review of this action by city officials in an appropriate court, alleging that the Constitution requires city licensing officials to grant his request for a hearing before issuing a license to Sandy.

In this case, the court should rule for

(A) John, because the due process clause of the Fourteenth Amendment requires all persons whose property may be adversely affected by governmental action to be given an opportunity for a hearing before such action occurs.

(B) John, because the determination of whether to hold a hearing may not constitutionally be left to the discretion of the same officials whose action is being challenged.

(C) city officials, because John had the benefit of the licensing ordinance and, therefore, may not now question actions taken under it.

(D) city officials, because the licensing ordinance does not give John any property interest in being free of competition from additional licensees.

Question 29

Current national statistics show a dramatic increase in the number of elementary and secondary school students bringing controlled substances (drugs) to school for personal use or distribution to others. In response, Congress enacted a statute requiring each state legislature to enact a state law that makes it a state crime for any person to possess, use, or distribute, within 1,000 feet of any elementary or secondary school, any controlled substance that has previously been transported in interstate commerce and that is not possessed, used, or distributed pursuant to a proper physician's prescription.

This federal statute is

(A) unconstitutional, because Congress has no authority to require a state legislature to enact any specified legislation.

(B) unconstitutional, because the possession, use, or distribution, in close proximity to a school, of a controlled substance that has previously been transported in interstate commerce does not have a sufficiently close nexus to such commerce to justify its regulation by Congress.

(C) constitutional, because it contains a jurisdictional provision that will ensure, on a case-by-case basis, that any particular controlled substance subject to the terms of this statute will, in fact, affect interstate commerce.

(D) constitutional, because Congress possesses broad authority under both the general welfare clause and the commerce clause to regulate any activities affecting education that also have, in inseverable aggregates, a substantial effect on interstate commerce.

Question 30

A federal statute provides that the United States Supreme Court has authority to review any case filed in a United States Court of Appeals, even though that case has not yet been decided by the court of appeals.

The Environmental Protection Agency (EPA), an agency in the executive branch of the federal government, issued an important environmental rule. Although the rule had not yet been enforced against them, companies that would be adversely affected by the rule filed a petition for review of the rule in a court of appeals, seeking a declaration that the rule was invalid solely because it was beyond the statutory authority of the EPA. The companies made no constitutional claim. A statute specifically provides for direct review of EPA rules by a court of appeals without any initial action in a district court.

The companies have filed a petition for a writ of certiorari in the Supreme Court requesting immediate review of this case by the Supreme Court before the court of appeals has actually decided the case. The EPA acknowledges that the case is important enough to warrant Supreme Court review and that it should be decided promptly, but it asks the Supreme Court to dismiss the petition on jurisdictional grounds.

The best constitutional argument in support of the EPA's request is that

(A) the case is not within the original jurisdiction of the Supreme Court as defined by Article III, and it is not a proper subject of that court's appellate jurisdiction because it has not yet been decided by any lower court.

(B) the case is appellate in nature, but it is beyond the appellate jurisdiction of the Supreme Court, because Article III states that its jurisdiction extends only to cases arising under the Constitution.

(C) Article III precludes federal courts from reviewing the validity of any federal agency rule in any proceeding other than an action to enforce the rule.

(D) Article III provides that all federal cases, except those within the original jurisdiction of the Supreme Court, must be initiated by an action in a federal district court.

Question 31

Congress enacts a criminal statute prohibiting "any person from interfering in any way with any right conferred on another person by the equal protection clause of the Fourteenth Amendment."

Application of this statute to Jones, a private citizen, would be most clearly constitutional if Jones with threats of violence coerces

(A) a public school teacher to exclude Black pupils from her class, solely because of their race.

(B) Black pupils, solely because of their race, to refrain from attending a privately owned and operated school licensed by the state.

(C) the bus driver operating a free school bus service under the sponsorship of a local church to refuse to allow Black pupils on the bus, solely because of their race.

(D) the federal office in charge of distributing certain federal benefits directly to students from distributing them to Black pupils, solely because of their race.

Question 32

The vaccination of children against childhood contagious diseases (such as measles, diphtheria and whooping cough) has traditionally been a function of private doctors and local and state health departments. Because vaccination rates have declined in recent years, especially in urban areas, the President proposes to appoint a Presidential Advisory Commission on Vaccination which would be charged with conducting a national publicity campaign to encourage vaccination as a public health measure. No federal statute authorizes or prohibits this action by the President. The activities of the Presidential Advisory Commission on Vaccination would be financed entirely from funds appropriated by Congress to the Office of the President for "such other purposes as the President may think appropriate."

May the President constitutionally create such a commission for this purpose?

(A) Yes, because the President has plenary authority to provide for the health, safety, and welfare of the people of the United States.

(B) Yes, because this action is within the scope of executive authority vested in the President by the Constitution, and no federal statute prohibits it.

(C) No, because the protection of children against common diseases by vaccination is a traditional state function and, therefore, is reserved to the states by the Tenth Amendment.

(D) No, because Congress has not specifically authorized the creation and support of such a new federal agency.

Question 33

The state of Brunswick enacted a statute providing for the closure of the official state records of arrest and prosecution of all persons acquitted of a crime by a court or against whom criminal charges were filed and subsequently dropped or dismissed. The purpose of this statute is to protect these persons from further publicity or embarrassment relating to those state proceedings. However, this statute does not prohibit the publication of such information that is in the possession of private persons.

A prominent businessman in Neosho City in Brunswick was arrested and charged with rape. Prior to trial, the prosecutor announced that new information indicated that the charges should be dropped. He then dropped the charges without further explanation, and the records relating thereto were closed to the public pursuant to the Brunswick statute.

The Neosho City *Times* conducted an investigation to determine why the businessman was not prosecuted, but was refused access to the closed official state records. In an effort to determine whether the law enforcement agencies involved were properly doing their duty, the *Times* filed suit against appropriate state officials to force opening of the records and to invalidate the statute on constitutional grounds.

Which of the following would be most helpful to the state in defending the constitutionality of this statute?

(A) The fact that the statute treats in an identical manner the arrest and prosecution records of all persons who have been acquitted of a crime by a court or against whom criminal charges were filed and subsequently dropped or dismissed.

(B) The argument that the rights of the press are no greater than those of citizens generally.

(C) The fact that the statute only prohibits public access to these official state records and does not prohibit the publication of information they contain that is in the possession of private persons.

(D) The argument that the state may seal official records owned by the state on any basis its legislature chooses.

Question 34

Congress wishes to enact legislation prohibiting discrimination in the sale or rental of housing on the basis of the affectional preference or sexual orientation of the potential purchaser or renter. Congress wishes this statute to apply to all public and private vendors and lessors of residential property in this country, with a few narrowly drawn exceptions.

The most credible argument for congressional authority to enact such a statute would be based upon the

(A) general welfare clause of Article I, Section 8, because the conduct the statute prohibits could reasonably be deemed to be harmful to the national interest.

(B) commerce clause of Article I, Section 8, because, in inseverable aggregates, the sale or rental of almost all housing in this country could reasonably be deemed to have a substantial effect on interstate commerce.

(C) enforcement clause of the Thirteenth Amendment, because that amendment clearly prohibits discrimination against the class of persons protected by this statute.

(D) enforcement clause of the Fourteenth Amendment, because that amendment prohibits all public and private actors from engaging in irrational discrimination.

Question 35

Congress enacts a statute punishing "each and every conspiracy entered into by any two or more persons for the purpose of denying Black persons housing, employment, or education, solely because of their race." Under which of the following constitutional provisions is the authority of Congress to pass such a statute most clearly and easily justifiable?

(A) The obligation of contracts clause.
(B) The general welfare clause of Article I, §8.
(C) The Thirteenth Amendment.
(D) The Fourteenth Amendment.

Question 36

A federal statute with inseverable provisions established a new five-member National Prosperity Board with broad regulatory powers over the operation of the securities, banking, and commodities industries, including the power to issue rules with the force of law. The statute provides for three of the board members to be appointed by the President with the advice and consent of the Senate. They serve seven-year terms and are removable only for good cause. The other two members of the board were designated in the statute to be the respective general counsel of the Senate and House of Representatives Committees on Government Operations. The statute stipulated that they were to serve on the board for as long as they continued in those positions.

Following all required administrative procedures, the board issued an elaborate set of rules regulating the operations of all banks, securities dealers, and commodities brokers. The Green Light Securities Company, which was subject to the board's rules, sought a declaratory judgment that the rules were invalid because the statute establishing the board was unconstitutional.

In this case, the court should rule that the statute establishing the National Prosperity Board is

(A) unconstitutional, because all members of federal boards having broad powers that are quasi-legislative in nature, such as rulemaking, must be appointed by Congress.
(B) unconstitutional, because all members of federal boards exercising executive powers must be appointed by the President or in a manner otherwise consistent with the appointments clause of Article II.
(C) constitutional, because the necessary and proper clause authorizes Congress to determine the means by which members are appointed to boards created by Congress under its power to regulate commerce among the states.
(D) constitutional, because there is a substantial nexus between the power of Congress to legislate for the general welfare and the means specified by Congress in this statute for the appointment of board members.

Question 37

Water District is an independent municipal water-supply district incorporated under the applicable laws of the state of Green. The district was created solely to supply water to an entirely new community in a recently developed area of Green. That new community is racially, ethnically, and socioeconomically diverse, and the community has never engaged in any discrimination against members of minority groups.

The five-member, elected governing board of the newly created Water District contains two persons who are members of racial minority groups. At its first meeting, the governing board of Water District adopted a rule unqualifiedly setting aside 25% of all positions on the staff of the District and 25% of all contracts to be awarded by the District to members of racial minority groups. The purpose of the rule was "to help redress the historical discrimination against these groups in this country and to help them achieve economic parity with other groups in our society." Assume that no federal statute applies.

A suit by appropriate parties challenges the constitutionality of these set-asides.

In this suit, the most appropriate ruling on the basis of applicable United States Supreme Court precedent would be that the set-asides are

(A) unconstitutional, because they would deny other potential employees or potential contractors the equal protection of the laws.
(B) unconstitutional, because they would impermissibly impair the right to contract of other potential employees or potential contractors.
(C) constitutional, because they would assure members of racial minority groups the equal protection of the laws.
(D) constitutional, because the function and activities of Water District are of a proprietary nature rather than a governmental nature and, therefore, are not subject to the usual requirements of the Fourteenth Amendment.

Question 38

Congress passes an act requiring that all owners of bicycles in the United States register them with a federal bicycle registry. The purpose of the law is to provide reliable evidence of ownership to reduce bicycle theft. No fee is charged for the registration. Although most stolen bicycles are kept or resold by the thieves in the same cities in which the bicycles were stolen, an increasing number of bicycles are being taken to cities in other states for resale.

Is this act of Congress constitutional?

(A) Yes, because Congress has the power to regulate property for the general welfare.
(B) Yes, because Congress could determine that in inseverable aggregates bicycle thefts affect interstate commerce.
(C) No, because most stolen bicycles remain within the state in which they were stolen.
(D) No, because the registration of vehicles is a matter reserved to the states by the Tenth Amendment.

Question 39

The legislature of State X enacts a statute that it believes reconciles the state's interest in the preservation of human life with a woman's right to reproductive choice. That statute permits a woman to have an abortion on demand during the first trimester of pregnancy but prohibits a woman from having an abortion after that time unless her physician determines that the abortion is necessary to protect the woman's life or health.

If challenged on constitutional grounds in an appropriate court, this statute will probably be held

(A) constitutional, because the state has made a rational policy choice that creates an equitable balance between the compelling state interest in protecting fetal life and the fundamental right of a woman to reproductive choice.

(B) constitutional, because recent rulings by the United States Supreme Court indicate that after the first trimester a fetus may be characterized as a person whose right to life is protected by the due process clause of the Fourteenth Amendment.

(C) unconstitutional, because the state has, without adequate justification, placed an undue burden on the fundamental right of a woman to reproductive choice prior to fetal viability.

(D) unconstitutional, because a statute unqualifiedly permitting abortion at one stage of pregnancy, and denying it at another with only minor exceptions, establishes an arbitrary classification in violation of the equal protection clause of the Fourteenth Amendment.

Question 40

Congress enacts a law providing that all disagreements between the United States and a state over federal grant-in-aid funds shall be settled by the filing of a suit in the federal district court in the affected state. "The judgment of that federal court shall be transmitted to the head of the federal agency dispensing such funds, who, if satisfied that the judgment is fair and lawful, shall execute the judgment according to its terms." This law is

(A) constitutional, because disagreements over federal grant-in-aid funds necessarily involve federal questions within the judicial power of the United States.

(B) constitutional, because the spending of federal monies necessarily includes the authority to provide for the effective settlement of disputes involving them.

(C) unconstitutional, because it vests authority in the federal court to determine a matter prohibited to it by the Eleventh Amendment.

(D) unconstitutional, because it vests authority in a federal court to render an advisory opinion.

Question 41

The President of the United States recognizes the country of Ruritania and undertakes a diplomatic relations with its government through the Secretary of State. Ruritania is governed by a repressive totalitarian government.

In an appropriate federal court, Dunn brings a suit against the President and Secretary of State to set aside this action on the ground that it is inconsistent with the principles of our constitutional form of government. Dunn has a lucrative contract with the United States Department of Commerce to provide commercial information about Ruritania. The contract expressly terminates, however, "when the President recognizes the country of Ruritania and undertakes diplomatic relations with its government."

Which of the following is the most proper disposition of the Dunn suit by federal court?

(A) Suit dismissed, because Dunn does not have standing to bring this action.

(B) Suit dismissed, because there is no adversity between Dunn and the defendants.

(C) Suit dismissed, because it presents a non-justiciable political question.

(D) Suit decided on the merits.

Question 42

A generally applicable state statute requires an autopsy by the county coroner in all cases of death that are not obviously of natural causes. The purpose of this law is to ensure the discovery and prosecution of all illegal activity resulting in death. In the 50 years since its enactment, the statute has been consistently enforced.

Mr. and Mrs. Long are sincere practicing members of a religion that maintains it is essential for a deceased person's body to be buried promptly and without any invasive procedures, including an autopsy. When the Longs' son died of mysterious causes and an autopsy was scheduled, the Longs filed an action in state court challenging the constitutionality of the state statute, and seeking an injunction prohibiting the county coroner from performing an autopsy on their son's body. In this action, the Longs claimed only that the application of this statute in the circumstances of their son's death would violate their right to the free exercise of religion as guaranteed by the First and Fourteenth Amendments. Assume that no federal statutes are applicable.

As applied to the Longs' case, the court should rule that the state's autopsy statute is

(A) constitutional, because a dead individual is not a person protected by the due process clause of the Fourteenth Amendment.

(B) constitutional, because it is a generally applicable statute and is rationally related to a legitimate state purpose.

(C) unconstitutional, because it is not necessary to vindicate a compelling state interest.

(D) unconstitutional, because it is not substantially related to an important state interest.

Question 43

A statute of State X permits a person's name to appear on the general election ballot as a candidate for statewide public office if the person pays a $100 filing fee and provides proof from the State Elections Board that he or she was nominated in the immediately preceding primary election by one of the state's two major political parties. It also permits the name of an independent candidate or a candidate of a smaller party to appear on the general election ballot if that person pays a filing fee of $1,000, and submits petitions signed by at least 3% of the voters who actually cast ballots for the office of governor in the last State X election. State X maintains that these filing requirements are necessary to limit the size of the election ballot, to eliminate frivolous candidacies, and to help finance the high cost of elections.

Historically, very few of State X's voters who are members of racial minority groups have been members of either of the two major political parties. Recently, a new political party has been formed by some of these voters.

Which of the following constitutional provisions would be most helpful to the new political party as a basis for attacking the constitutionality of this statute of State X?

(A) The First Amendment.
(B) The Thirteenth Amendment.
(C) The Fourteenth Amendment.
(D) The Fifteenth Amendment.

Question 44

A federal statute appropriated $7 million for a nationwide essay contest on "How the United States Can Best Stop Drug Abuse." The statute indicates that its purpose is to generate new, practical ideas for eliminating drug abuse in the United States.

Contest rules set forth in the statute provide that winning essays are to be selected on the basis of the "originality, aptness, and feasibility of their ideas." The statute expressly authorizes a first prize of $1 million, 50 second prizes of $100,000 each, and 100 third prizes of $10,000 each. It also states that judges for the contest are to be appointed by the President of the United States with the advice and consent of the Senate, and that all residents of the United States who are not employees of the federal government are eligible to enter and win the contest. A provision of the statute authorizes any taxpayer of the United States to challenge its constitutionality.

In a suit by a federal taxpayer to challenge the constitutionality of the statute, the court should

(A) refuse to decide its merits, because the suit involves policy questions that are inherently political and, therefore, nonjusticiable.
(B) hold the statute unconstitutional, because it does not provide sufficient guidelines for awarding the prize money appropriated by Congress and, therefore, unconstitutionally delegates legislative power to the contest judges.
(C) hold the statute unconstitutional, because its relationship to legitimate purposes of the spending power of Congress is too tenuous and conjectural to satisfy the necessary and proper clause of Article I.

(D) hold the statute constitutional, because it is reasonably related to the general welfare, it states concrete objectives, and it provides adequate criteria for conducting the essay contest and awarding the prize money.

Question 45

Senator makes a speech on the floor of the United States Senate in which she asserts that William, a federal civil servant with minor responsibilities, was twice convicted of fraud by the courts of State X. In making this assertion, Senator relied wholly on research done by Frank, her chief legislative assistant. In fact, it was a different man named William and not William the civil servant, who was convicted of these crimes in the state court proceedings. This mistake was the result of carelessness on Frank's part.

No legislation affecting the appointment or discipline of civil servants or the program of the federal agency for which William works was under consideration at the time Senator made her speech about William on the floor of the Senate.

William sues Senator and Frank for defamation. Both defendants move to dismiss the complaint.

As a matter of constitutional law, the court hearing this motion should

(A) grant it as to Frank, because he is protected by the freedom of speech guarantee against defamation actions by government officials based on his mere carelessness; but deny it as to Senator, because, as an officer of the United States, she is a constituent part of the government and, therefore, has no freedom of speech rights in that capacity.
(B) grant it as to both defendants, because Senator is immune to suit for any speech she makes in the Senate under the speech or debate clause of Article I, Section 6, and Frank may assert Senator's immunity for his assistance to her in preparing the speech.
(C) deny it as to both defendants, because any immunity of Senator under the speech or debate clause does not attach to a speech that is not germane to pending legislative business, and Frank is entitled to no greater immunity than the legislator he was assisting.
(D) deny it as to Frank, because he is not a legislator protected by the speech or debate clause; but grant it as to Senator, because she is immune from suit for her speech by virtue of that clause.

Questions 46-47 are based on the following fact situation.

Three states, East Winnetka, Midland, and West Hampton, are located next to one another in that order. The states of East Winnetka and West Hampton permit the hunting and trapping of snipe, but the state of Midland strictly forbids it in order to protect snipe, a rare species of animal, from extinction. The state of Midland has a state statute that provides, "Possession of snipe traps is prohibited. Any game warden finding a snipe trap within the state shall seize and destroy it." Snipe traps cost about $15 each.

Prentis is a resident of West Hampton and an ardent snipe trapper. She drove her car to East Winnetka to purchase a new improved snipe trap from a manufacturer there. In the course of her trip back across Midland with the trap in her car, Prentis stopped in a Midland state park to camp for a few nights. While she was in the park, a Midland game warden saw the trap, which was visible on the front seat of her car. The warden seized the trap and destroyed it in accordance with the Midland statute after Prentis admitted that the seized item was a prohibited snipe trap. No federal statutes or other federal administrative regulations apply.

Question 46

For this question only, assume that Prentis demonstrates that common carriers are permitted to transport snipe traps as cargo across Midland for delivery to another state and that in practice, the Midland statute is enforced only against private individuals transporting those traps in private vehicles. If Prentis challenges the application of the Midland statute to her on the basis only of a denial of equal protection, this application of the statute will probably be found

(A) constitutional, because the traps constitute contraband in which Prentis could have no protected property interest.

(B) constitutional, because there is a rational basis for differentiating between the possession of snipe traps as interstate cargo by common carriers and the possession of snipe traps by private individuals.

(C) unconstitutional, because the state cannot demonstrate a compelling public purpose for making this differentiation between common carriers and such private individuals.

(D) unconstitutional, because interstate travel is a fundamental right that may not be burdened by state law.

Question 47

For this question only, assume that a valid federal administrative rule, adopted under a federal consumer product safety act, regulates the design of snipe traps. The rule was issued to prevent traps from causing injury to human beings, e.g. by pinching fingers while persons were setting the traps. No other federal law applies. Which of the following best states the effect of the federal rule on the Midland state statute?

(A) The federal rule preempts the Midland state statute, because the federal rule regulates the same subject-matter, snipe traps.

(B) The federal rule preempts the Midland state statute, because the federal rule does not contain affirmative authorization for continued state regulation.

(C) The federal rule does not preempt the Midland state statute, because the Midland state statute regulates wild animals, a field of exclusive state power.

(D) The federal rule does not preempt the Midland state

statute, because the purposes of the federal rule and the Midland state statute are different.

ANSWERS
CONSTITUTIONAL LAW

Answer Key

Use this Answer Key to quickly identify the correct answer to each question.

(1) A	(11) B	(21) B	(31) A	(41) C
(2) D	(12) B	(22) A	(32) B	(42) B
(3) C	(13) A	(23) D	(33) C	(43) C
(4) C	(14) C	(24) A	(34) B	(44) D
(5) D	(15) D	(25) C	(35) C	(45) B
(6) D	(16) C	(26) C	(36) B	(46) B
(7) B	(17) B	(27) C	(37) A	(47) D
(8) D	(18) A	(28) D	(38) B	
(9) D	(19) B	(29) A	(39) C	
(10) B	(20) D	(30) A	(40) D	

ANSWERS

CONSTITUTIONAL LAW

Answer 1

(A) is the best response,

because the statute bars some protected conduct, and leaves the public uncertain about what conduct is and isn't forbidden.

A statute is *overbroad* if, in addition to proscribing activities which may constitutionally be forbidden, it also sweeps within its coverage a substantial amount of speech or conduct which is protected by the guarantees of free speech. The doctrine of *vagueness* is similar but not identical to that of overbreadth. A statute will be void for vagueness if the conduct forbidden by it is so unclearly defined that persons of common intelligence would have to guess at its meaning and would differ as to its application.

The statute here is both overbroad and vague. It is overbroad because it covers (or appears to cover) a substantial amount of conduct protected by the First Amendment. One big problem is that the way the statute is written, if the material might be harmful to minors, it may not be sold to (or displayed to) *adults*, either. And adults have a First Amendment right to read even sexually explicit materials, if they aren't "obscene." So the statute probably denies to adults massive amounts of non-obscene — and thus protected — sexually explicit materials (e.g., *Playboy*), since these "may" be harmful to minors. That makes the statute overbroad.

And the statute is vague, as well, because it doesn't give even an approximate definition of either the term "sexually explicit nature" or the term "harmful." So a reader of the statute would be left to guess just how great the degree of sexual explicitness (are topless women covered, no pun intended?), or how great the likelihood of harm (chance that one in 1,000 minor readers would have a nightmare?) needs to be.

(B) is not the best response,

because this is a corrupted version of a now-outmoded test for obscenity, and is therefore not the relevant test.

At one time, to sustain an obscenity prosecution, prosecutors had to prove that the material was utterly without "the slightest redeeming social importance," a standard somewhat similar to the one in this choice. But that's no longer the test for obscenity: now, a "patently offensive" portrayal of "sexual conduct" that is "specifically defined" by state law may be prohibited, provided only that the work, taken as a whole, lacks "serious literary, artistic, political, or scientific value." (*Miller v. Cal.* (1973)). So the presence of the smallest

"redeeming value in the marketplace of ideas" (as this choice states) wouldn't protect against a finding of obscenity.

But even if this choice had the right test for obscenity, it would miss the fact that, as the Court held in *Ginsberg v. N.Y.* (1968), states *may* prohibit the sale *to minors* of sexually explicit material that doesn't meet the definition of obscenity. The big problem with the statute is that (as described in Choice (A)) it bars adults from seeing or buying non-obscene materials on grounds that these might harm minors, and Choice (B) doesn't capture this difficulty at all.

(C) is not the best response,

because the distinction between written and pictorial material would not be found to be wholly irrational.

Where a statute treats two different classes of things or people in two different ways, unless a suspect category or fundamental right is involved, only a completely irrational classification will be found to violate equal protection. So here, if a plaintiff could convince the court that it is irrational to treat people who want to buy sexually-explicit pictorial materials differently from those who want to buy sexually-explicit materials consisting solely of words, the plaintiff might prevail with an equal protection argument.

The problem is that it is very unlikely that a court would agree that it's completely irrational to distinguish between pictures and words. It might be rational, for example, for a state to conclude that the harmful impact of sexually explicit pictures on men with a latent tendency to impose sexually-sadistic violence on women is greater than the impact on the same men of works consisting solely of words. In summary, the equal protection argument is far less likely to succeed than the overbreadth and vagueness arguments used in Choice (A).

(D) is not the best response,

because there is a rational distinction that may be made between minors and adults.

Where a statute treats two different classes of things or people in two different ways, unless a suspect category or fundamental right is involved, only a completely irrational classification will be found to violate equal protection. So here, if a plaintiff could convince the court that it is wholly irrational to treat violent or sexually-explicit pictorial materials differently depending on whether they harm minors or just adults, the claim might work.

But a plaintiff would be exceptionally unlikely to succeed in making such a showing. The Court has previously held (in *Ginsberg v. N.Y.* (1968), a First Amendment case), that the states may prohibit the sale to minors of sexually explicit material that doesn't meet the definition of obscenity, on the grounds that minors are more impressionable. So a court now would be unlikely to conclude that it's wholly irrational for materials that might harm minors in this way to be distinguished from those that would "only" harm adults. (Besides, any materials that would harm adults would be likely to harm minors as well, making the statute's distinction even less irrational.)

Answer 2

(D) is the best response,

because it recognizes an area over which Congress would clearly have authority to legislate marriages and divorces.

The central obstacle under this problem is that the states have the general power to legislate regarding marriage and divorce, because family-oriented legislation is not within Congress's enumerated powers. Congress only has power to the extent of its enumerated powers under the Constitution. In order to be valid, a federal statute must be rationally related to an enumerated power, or be a necessary and proper means of effectuating such power. These are the major powers of Congress: Civil Rights, Elections (Congressional), Admiralty, Taxation, Eminent Domain, Spending for General Welfare, Defense, Interstate Commerce, Citizenship, and External (Foreign) Affairs.

What option D does is to avoid the whole issue of Congressional power vis-a-vis state power. Under Article I, §8 of the Constitution, Congress is expressly given the power to govern the District of Columbia. This, in effect, gives it "state-like" control over the District of Columbia, and this neatly avoids the obstacle in this problem – namely, that marriage and divorce is neither one of Congress's enumerated powers, nor is its legislation necessary and proper to effectuating an enumerated power. Since legislation concerning marriage and divorce would clearly be part of "governing" the District of Columbia, such Congressional legislation would be valid. This is admittedly a bit of a tricky question, since you don't often come across questions concerning Congress's power over the District of Columbia. However, under these facts, this power provides the best means of regulating marriages and divorces, and since D recognizes this, it's the best response.

(A) is not the best response,

because although Congress has power over the military, legislating marriages of members of the armed forces would not be sufficiently close to the military power to merit Congressional control.

Congress only has power to the extent of its enumerated powers under the Constitution. In order to be

valid, a federal statute must be rationally related to an enumerated power, or be a necessary and proper means of effectuating such a power. These are the major powers of Congress: Civil Rights, Elections (Congressional), Admiralty, Taxation, Eminent Domain, Spending for General Welfare, Defense, Interstate Commerce, Citizenship, and External (Foreign) Affairs. The central focus of the legislation here – marriage and divorce – is a family law matter traditionally reserved to the states. The military power, found in Article I, §8 of the Constitution, grants Congress the power, in general, to declare war, raise armies, maintain a navy, create rules regulating the armed forces, and otherwise organize, discipline, arm, and call forth the militia. Regulating the marriages of military personnel could only be tenuously related to this power. Thus, the military power would not be a good basis on which Congress could regulate marriage and divorce. Since A doesn't recognize this, it's not the best response.

(B) is not the best response,

because Congress's power over the jurisdiction of federal courts would not be a strong basis on which to uphold legislation concerning marriages and divorces.

Congress only has power to the extent of its enumerated powers under the Constitution. In order to be valid, a federal statute must be rationally related to an enumerated power, or be a necessary and proper means of effectuating such a power. These are the major powers of Congress: Civil Rights, Elections (Congressional), Admiralty, Taxation, Eminent Domain, Spending for General Welfare, Defense, Interstate Commerce, Citizenship, and External (Foreign) Affairs. The central focus of the legislation here – marriage and divorce – is a family law matter traditionally reserved to the states. It's true that Congress has great control over the jurisdiction of the lower federal courts, since it was given the power to create such lower courts in Article III, §2 of the Constitution. This theoretically would give Congress the power to regulate marriages performed by federal judges and divorces granted by federal courts. However, due to Congress's lack of enumerated power over marriage and divorce, this argument would not be tremendously strong, especially in light of the fact that there's another option – D – which provides a clear area of Congressional power. As a result, B is not the best response.

(C) is not the best response,

because it does not overcome the central obstacle here – that is, that marriage and divorce is an area traditionally controlled by the states, not the federal government.

Congress only has power to the extent of its enumerated powers under the Constitution. In order to be valid, a federal statute must be rationally related to an enumerated power, or be a necessary and proper means of effectuating such a power. These are the major powers of Congress: Civil Rights, Elections

(Congressional), Admiralty, Taxation, Eminent Domain, Spending for General Welfare, Defense, Interstate Commerce, Citizenship, and External (Foreign) Affairs.

While Congress has considerable power over human rights under amendments like the Fourteenth Amendment, this wouldn't as a general matter give it the power to legislate concerning marriage and divorce. The fact that there's an executive agreement involved doesn't create for Congress power it doesn't otherwise have. Since option C doesn't recognize this, it's not the best response.

Answer 3

(C) is the best response,

because it offers the consideration least likely to impact how the legislation is drafted.

The states enjoy freedom from *federal* court suits brought by their own citizens under the Eleventh Amendment (although it does not bar suits against subdivisions of the state, like cities, and local agencies, like school boards). The specific type of lawsuit that's barred is a claim seeking damages, based on past conduct, where the damages will be payable from state funds. Whether or not the legislation here is valid, as drafted, would not be impacted by sovereign immunity. Instead, the validity of the legislation will depend on whether it meets these requirements: One, whether it's enacted within the state's powers (e.g., police powers); two, whether it violates any person's constitutional rights; and three, when it improperly burdens interstate commerce. If it meets these three requirements, it will be valid. If it doesn't, the validity of the statute can be challenged by anyone injured by the statute or imminently likely to be injured by the statute, regardless of sovereign immunity. As a result, sovereign immunity will not impact the way the legislation is drafted. Since the question is looking for the option that is least likely to be a consideration in drafting the legislation, C is the best response.

(A) is not the best response,

because eminent domain will have a clear impact on the drafting of such land use legislation.

The power of eminent domain is indirectly recognized in the Fifth Amendment. Eminent domain is the power of government (federal, state or local) to seize private property, for public use, upon payment of just compensation.

In this question, you have to determine if eminent domain will impact state legislation invalidating all future land use restrictions in deeds. As with any state enactment, in order for such legislation to be valid, it must meet three requirements: It must be enacted within the state's powers (e.g., police powers); it must not violate any person's constitutional rights; and it must not improperly burden interstate commerce. Eminent domain addresses the second issue – violating

constitutional rights. If the legislation was drafted so that it denied any landholder of significant enjoyment of his land, he'd be entitled to just compensation under the Fifth Amendment. Alternatively, the legislation would have to make clear that the taking would be for *public* use, since eminent domain has that limitation (even though the state can take the land and turn it over to a private entity, e.g., a utility). Either of these would have an impact on whether the legislation is valid, so eminent domain will clearly have an impact on how the legislation is drafted. Since the question is looking for the option which is least likely to be a consideration in drafting the legislation, A can't be the best response.

(B) is not the best response,

because the Contracts Clause could be violated by the proposed legislation, if the legislation is not drafted properly.

As a general rule, the Contracts Clause prohibits states (not the federal government) from passing any law which impairs the obligations of contracts. The contract must exist at the time the regulation was passed in order to be impaired by it, since states *can* regulate contract formation *prospectively.*

Under these facts, deed restrictions are sought to be invalidated. Deed restrictions are generally the result of private contracts between people – for instance, a property owner paying another for an easement. If the legislation made deed restrictions unenforceable in the future, this would impair contracts already in place, and would, as a result, likely violate the Contracts Clause. Since this consideration will impact how the legislation is drafted, and this question is looking for the option which is least likely to be a consideration in drafting the legislation, B can't be the best response.

(D) is not the best response,

because the state's police power will likely be the source of the state's power to draft the legislation, so it will clearly impact the legislation.

In order to be valid, a state enactment must satisfy three requirements: It must be enacted within the state's powers (e.g., police powers); it must not violate any person's constitutional rights; and it must not improperly burden interstate commerce. The police power gives the state the power to achieve a legitimate state interest when the public health, safety, welfare, or morals is concerned. The state's determination of how land should be used could be based on the public welfare. Thus, the police power is likely to impact how the legislation is formulated, since it's likely to give the state the power to enact the legislation in the first place. Since the question is looking for the option which is least likely to be a consideration in drafting the legislation, D isn't the best response.

Answer 4

(C) is the best response,

because none of the members of the association has been injured or will be injured, making the organization lack standing.

Standing is an interest in the outcome of a controversy. An organization has standing to challenge government actions that cause an injury in fact to its members if the organization can demonstrate the following: (1) that there is an injury in fact to some members of the organization that would give these individual members a right to sue on their own behalf; (2) that the injury to the members is related to the organization's purpose; and (3) that neither the nature of the claim nor the relief requested requires participation of the individual members in the lawsuit. *Hunt v. Wash. Apple* (1977).

Here, the organization cannot satisfy (at least) requirement (1). The facts carefully specify that no member currently trades or expects to do so in the future. Consequently, no member could either be prohibited by the statute from conduct they would otherwise engage in, or even benefit from the statute's protections. Therefore, no member has standing to bring an individual action, and thus the organization does not have standing either.

(A) is not the best response,

because the mere fact that a suit involves a "dispute over the constitutionality of a federal statute" does not dispense with the need for standing.

It's true that, as this choice suggests, a federal suit (at least one not based on diversity) must involve a federal question, that is, a question arising under the constitution or under a federal statute. So the fact that the constitutionality of a federal statute is at issue certainly satisfies the "must pose a federal question" requirement. But there is an additional requirement that the plaintiffs have standing, and for the reasons discussed in Choice (C) above, that requirement is not satisfied.

(B) is not the best response,

because the fact that the suit seeks "relief of a conclusive nature" is irrelevant.

Where plaintiffs lack standing, the fact that they are seeking "relief of a conclusive nature" does not nullify the non-justiciability of their claim. This organization lacks standing for the reasons discussed in Choice (C). If Choice (B) were correct, it would follow that any person or organization, no matter how little their practical stake in the outcome, could sue for an injunction against any statute's enforcement. This would make a mockery of the constitutional requirement that each federal suit involve a "case or controversy."

(D) is not the best response,

because a suit for an injunction preventing enforcement of the statute *could* be brought.

It's true that if the court were convinced that enforcement of the statute was extremely unlikely to occur in the reasonable future, the court might exercise its discretion to conclude that the suit shouldn't be heard because it wasn't ripe. But this choice says far more than that — it asserts that the mere fact that there has not yet been a "bona fide effort" to enforce the statute means an injunction suit can't be brought. And that's clearly not true. See, e.g., *Epperson v. Arkansas* (1968) (Court hears case involving ban on teaching evolution, which ban hadn't ever been enforced during its entire 40 years on the books.)

Answer 5

(D) is the best response,

because without this showing of "rough proportionality," the ordinance violates the Takings clause.

In *Dolan v. City of Tigard* (1994), the Court held that when a city conditions a building permit on some "give back" by the owner, there must be a "rough proportionality" between the burdens on the public that the building permit would bring about, and the benefits to the public from the give-back. There's nothing in the facts to suggest that the city ever made the required showing here. (Indeed, the facts tell us that City officials presented no evidence of any sort, so they certainly didn't produce evidence either about the size of the public burden from allowing the coffeehouse or the size of the corresponding benefit from the new child care facility they were requiring here.)

(A) is not the best response,

because mere-rationality is not the standard where, as here, a city requires the dedication of private property for public uses.

As is described in the discussion of Choice (D) above, when a city conditions a building permit on some "give back" by the owner, there must be a "rough proportionality" between the burdens on the public that the building permit would bring about, and the benefits to the public from the give-back. In other words, the existence of a "rational relationship" between the city requirement and a legitimate governmental interest will no longer suffice (if it ever would have) to withstanding a Takings clause attack like the one here.

(B) is not the best response,

because strict scrutiny is not the standard, and if it were, the burden of proof would be on City, not Company.

As is described in the discussion of Choice (D) above, when a city conditions a building permit on some "give back" by the owner, there must be a "rough proportionality" between the burdens on the public that the building permit would bring about, and the benefits to the public from the give-back. This is probably a less difficult-to-satisfy burden than strict scrutiny. But if strict scrutiny *were* the standard, the burden would be on

City to show that the standard had been satisfied, not on Company to show that it hadn't. (And in any event, Company *would* almost certainly be able to show that the requirement was not "necessary to vindicate a compelling governmental interest," in view of the complete lack of evidence from the City about how great the need for extra child care was.)

(C) is not the best response,

because strict scrutiny is not the standard.

As is described in the discussion of Choice (D) above, when a city conditions a building permit on some "give back" by the owner, there must be a "rough proportionality" between the burdens on the public that the building permit would bring about, and the benefits to the public from the give-back.

This is probably a less difficult-to-satisfy burden than strict scrutiny. So if strict scrutiny were the proper standard, this choice would be correct in saying both that (1) the burden was on City to show that the standard was satisfied; and (2) City failed to meet that standard. But the choice is wrong because the correct standard is "rough proportionality" (which is still a standard City hasn't met).

Answer 6

(D) is the best response,

because the purpose of the tax is to raise revenue.

Article 1, §8, cl. 1 of the Constitution gives Congress the power to "lay and collect Taxes ... and Excises, to pay the Debts and provide for the Common Defence and general Welfare of the United States." So Congress can tax for the purpose of "provid[ing] for the ... general Welfare." That's what it's doing here. Because the power is plenary (i.e., complete) a tax measure will be upheld so long as it bears some reasonable relationship to revenue production, and does not violate any specific constitutional provision.

Here, the purpose of the tax is to raise revenue, so the requirement of "reasonable relationship to revenue production" (expressed in the choice as not having any "provisions extraneous to tax needs or purposes") is satisfied. There is no provision in the Constitution that this tax would violate. Therefore, it's valid.

(A) is not the best response,

because the tax is uniform in its application.

It's true that Article 1, §8, cl. 1, which grants the power to tax, also requires that "all Duties, Imposts and Excises shall be uniform throughout the United States." However, this requirement merely means that any excise tax (and this is one, since it's imposed on the sale or production of a particular product) may not discriminate *among states* — it does not matter that only some individuals (and only residents of one state) pay the tax because they're the ones who produce or sell the product.

The tax on alpha here meets the requirement of uniformity, because it applies the same way on each ton of alpha mined in the country — so while alpha is currently mined only in the state of Blue, if it is ever mined in another state the tax will also apply there.

(B) is not the best response,

because it misstates the operation of the "commerce clause."

If the phrase "commerce clause" is intended to mean "commerce power," the fact that Congress has the *power* to regulate interstate commerce doesn't impose on Congress any affirmative *obligation* to do any regulating of any sort, so Congress is free to take an action that would inhibit (rather than fostering) a particular "interstate industry." If the phrase "commerce clause" is intended to mean the "dormant commerce clause," this is a limitation on what the states may do, not an affirmative requirement on Congress. So there is no plausible meaning for the phrase "commerce clause" that would impose on Congress an obligation to "protect ... such interstate industries."

(C) is not the best response,

because the issue is the power to tax, not navigable waterways.

Congress has no special authority over the "navigable waters" of the U.S. (The federal judicial power extends to "all Cases of admiralty and maritime Jurisdiction," but this doesn't add anything to Congress' powers.) While it's true that Congress' commerce power would probably give it authority to regulate navigable waters because they affect commerce, this power is far more tangential to the problem here than is Congress' power to tax for the general welfare. So Choice (C) reaches the correct conclusion, but for the wrong reason.

Answer 7

(B) is the best response,

because it correctly identifies that the most likely basis on which the statute is illegal is its violation of the Equal Protection Clause.

In order to be valid, a state law – like the one here – must meet three requirements:

1. It must be enacted within the state's powers (e.g., police powers);
2. It must not violate any person's constitutional rights; and
3. It must not improperly burden interstate commerce.

The problem here is with the second requirement. Under these facts, you have an enactment which creates a classification that determines people's rights. That is, the statute mandates that only U.S. citizens can own more than 100 acres of land in-state. In order to determine whether the statute is valid under equal protection, you have to determine the basis of the classification, and then apply the appropriate test to it (strict scrutiny, intermediate scrutiny, or mere rationality). When the classification relates to who may exercise a fundamental right (freedom of association and speech, interstate travel, privacy, voting), or when it is based on a suspect classification (race or alienage), the classification will be subject to strict scrutiny.

What the statute here does is to make a classification based on alienage: It treats citizens and non-citizens differently. Alienage is considered a "suspect classification," meaning that in order for the statute to be valid, it must meet the "strict scrutiny" test. Strict scrutiny requires that the classification must be necessary to promote a compelling governmental interest. As you know, this is the kiss of death for a statute; the strict scrutiny test is virtually impossible to pass. Thus, Zane's best argument is that the statute violates equal protection. Since option B recognizes this, it's the best response.

(A) is not the best response,

because the commerce clause does not prevent states from interfering with aliens' rights to own land.

In order to be valid, a state statute – like the one here – must meet three requirements:

1. It must be enacted within the state's powers (e.g., police powers);
2. It must not violate any person's constitutional rights; and
3. It must not improperly burden interstate commerce.

The problem with this statute is the second element – the statute is an equal protection violation. Contrary to what A states, there's no problem with the Commerce Clause, and, in any case, the Commerce Clause doesn't do what option A says it does.

The Commerce Clause, Article I, §8, Clause 3 of the Constitution, gives Congress the right to regulate interstate commerce. This is interpreted extremely broadly; however, states can regulate commerce to the extent that Congress intended that the states be able to regulate the activity in question, and where the nature of the activity in question suggests that its regulation is local, not federal. This isn't an issue here, because the commerce clause doesn't forbid states from interfering with the rights of aliens to own land; it prevents states from unduly burdening interstate commerce. Since A misapplies the Commerce Clause, and doesn't recognize that equal protection is Zane's strongest argument, it's not the best response.

(C) is not the best response,

because it misstates the facts: The statute does not adversely affect Zane's right to travel, and in any case, Zane, as an alien, doesn't have a right to travel under the privileges and immunities clause of the Fourteenth Amendment.

In order to be valid, a state statute – like the one here – must meet three requirements:

1. It must be enacted within the state's powers (e.g., police powers);

2. It must not violate any person's constitutional rights; and
3. it must not improperly burden interstate commerce.

By invoking Zane's right to travel, option C suggests that the second element is a problem. While this itself is true, it's not because Zane's right to travel has been violated. First of all, the right to travel is one of the privileges and immunities protected by the Privileges and Immunities Clause of the Fourteenth Amendment. That Clause, which is interpreted extremely narrowly, voids those state enactments which clearly infringe privileges enjoyed by U.S. citizens. The right to travel freely from state to state is one of these. However, it is only enjoyed by U.S. citizens, not aliens, and Zane is an alien.

Even if you analyzed the statute in terms of Zane's right to interstate travel, a fundamental right under which Zane is entitled to due process protection, you'd still be skirting the principal obstacle with this option, which is that this statute doesn't adversely affect Zane's right to travel. It only stops him from buying more than 100 acres of land in-state. If anything, in a perverse way, it *encourages* him to travel, because it stops him from owning significant amounts of property in-state. Instead, the far more likely constitutional obstacle with this statute is that it creates an impermissible classification – based on alienage – and as a result is an equal protection violation. Since C misapplies the right to travel to these facts, and ignores the equal protection issue, it's not the best response.

(D) is not the best response,

because there's no evidence of a Contracts Clause violation under these facts.

The Contracts Clause prohibits the state from passing any law which impairs the obligations of contracts. As a prerequisite, then, the contract in question must exist at the time the regulation was passed in order to be impaired by it, since states *do* have the power to regulate contract formation prospectively. Here, you're told that Zane purchased his 200 acres of land after the statute was passed. Thus, the contract under which he bought the land didn't exist when the statute was passed, and it couldn't have been impaired by the statute. Had Zane entered into a land sale contract before the statute was passed, and the contract couldn't be enforced because of the statute, *then* there would be a Contracts Clause problem. However, under the facts as they exist, there's no problem with the Contracts Clause, and since option D doesn't recognize this, it's not the best response.

Answer 8

(D) is the best response,

because it correctly identifies the basis of the federal court's jurisdiction.

What this question impliedly addresses is whether

the federal court can hear the case. The jurisdiction of the federal courts is addressed in Article III, §2 of the Constitution. Among other cases, federal courts may hear cases between citizens of different states ("diversity" jurisdiction), cases arising under the Constitution or a federal law or treaty ("federal question" jurisdiction), and those where the U.S. is a party.

Option D suggests that there's federal question jurisdiction under these facts. If you look at Zane's claim, you can deduce that it'll address an equal protection violation, since the statute under which he's been injured creates a suspect classification: It forbids aliens from owning over 100 acres of land, and alienage is a suspect classification. Equal protection is protected by the federal Constitution, so Zane's claim would "arise" under the Constitution, giving the federal court federal question jurisdiction over the case. Since option D recognizes this, it's the best response.

(A) is not the best response,

because it misstates federal court jurisdiction.

Article III, §2 of the Constitution gives the Supreme Court original jurisdiction over cases where a state is a party, as here. Congress has the power to create lower federal courts, and give them jurisdiction concurrent with the Supreme Court. In fact, Congress specifically authorized federal courts to hear cases brought by aliens against states. As a result, A is incorrect in stating that aliens may not sue in federal court, making it not the best response.

(B) is not the best response,

because while the state typically has power over in-state land, this power is not unlimited.

In order to be valid, a state law – like the one here – must meet three requirements:

1. It must be enacted within the state's powers (e.g., police powers);
2. It must not violate any person's constitutional rights; and
3. It must not improperly burden interstate commerce.

While regulating in-state land is one of the state's powers, this regulation must still meet the other two requirements. Here, the statute is an impermissible regulation principally because it violates the Equal Protection Clause, by setting up a classification based on alienage. Since option B incorrectly states that the state's right to regulate in-state land is unlimited, it's not the best response.

(C) is not the best response,

because violation of the U.N. Charter, by itself, would not give the federal court power to hear the lawsuit.

The jurisdiction of the federal courts is determined in Article III, §2 of the Constitution, and as provided by Congress (which can regulate the appellate jurisdiction of federal courts). One source of federal court jurisdic-

tion is "federal question" jurisdiction, which gives federal courts the power to hear cases arising under the Constitution or a federal law or treaty. If you chose this response, you may have thought of the U.N. Charter as a treaty; in fact, it's not, and there's nothing under these facts to suggest that it's been adopted as a treaty. On the other hand, you may have been taking a wild stab in the dark in choosing this response, which is unavoidable once in a while. In any case, there is a federal question presented by these facts, which is what gives the court jurisdiction to hear the case. Zane would most likely be arguing that the state statute violated the federal Constitution, by violating the Equal Protection Clause. Since option C doesn't recognize this, it's not the best response.

Answer 9

(D) is the best response,

because the operator's ordinance is a content-based restriction on core political speech, and cannot survive strict scrutiny.

It is presumptively unconstitutional for the government to place burdens on speech because of its content. To justify such content-based regulation of speech, the government must show that the regulation is necessary to achieve a compelling state interest and is narrowly defined to achieve that end. (That is, the regulation must survive strict scrutiny.)

By conditioning a taxicab operating license on an agreement not to display any bumper sticker or placard favoring a particular candidate for any elected public office, Central City is effectively banning a certain type of political speech solely because of its content. The fact that Central has done this not by an outright ban on all bumper stickers, but by conditioning a government benefit (cab license) on agreement not to display the messages, makes no difference — Central is intentionally rendering a particular type of expression significantly harder to make, and this triggers the strict scrutiny given to content-based speech regulations. This ordinance can't survive that scrutiny, because there is no indication that there is any meaningful risk that members of the public might incorrectly think that the slogans are attributable to council members; thus no compelling state interest is being pursued.

(A) is not the best response,

because the ordinance is unconstitutional and Driver has not waived his rights to challenge the ordinance.

It is presumptively unconstitutional for the government to place burdens on speech because of its content. To justify such content-based regulation of speech, the government must show that the regulation is necessary to achieve a compelling state interest and is narrowly defined to achieve that end. The fact that Central City has not made display of all political messages a crime, and has instead used its power to deny a hack license as a "club" to induce some people (cab drivers) to "voluntarily" surrender their right to transmit those messages, is no defense. And the fact that Driver knew of the condition when he applied for his license would not cause him to lose standing to contest this clear unconstitutionality.

(B) is not the best response,

because calling a government-bestowed benefit a "privilege" does not entitle the government to condition that benefit on the beneficiary's renunciation of the right to constitutionally-protected speech.

As a general matter (subject to some exceptions not relevant here), government may not condition the receipt of a government-conferred benefit upon the beneficiary's willingness to forego the exercise of some constitutional right. So, for instance, government can't say, "We hereby fire any public employee who is a member of the Communist Party," if government wouldn't have the power under the First Amendment to ban Communist Party membership. *Elfbrandt v. Russell* (1966).

Here, since the display of political messages on bumper stickers is protected by the First Amendment (a ban on such messages would be an intentional and content-based interference with political speech, and would be strictly scrutinized and summarily struck down), the City cannot condition a government-bestowed "privilege" (a cab license) on the driver's willingness to forego the right to make such a display.

(C) is not the best response,

because the ordinance is merely a regulation, not a "taking."

The 5th Amendment provides that private property shall not be taken for public use without paying just compensation to the owner. If Central City confiscated cab licenses so that, say, it could operate all cabs itself for profit — and then refused to pay the former license-holders anything — the licensees might have a "taking" argument. But here, what is occurring is merely regulation, and regulation of a sort that falls far short of denying the licensee all economically viable use of his property (the standard for when a "taking" is deemed to have occurred). Therefore, the takings clause has not been violated.

Answer 10

(B) is the best response,

because it impliedly recognizes that the statute is a reasonable restriction on the free exercise of religion.

The "free exercise" part of the First Amendment's religion clause guarantees the right to free exercise of religion. However, as with the First Amendment rights of speech, assembly, and association, this right is not absolute. Instead, reasonable regulation is permissible. The reasonableness of regulations burdening the free exercise of religion is determined with a balancing test, considering:

1. The magnitude of the burden;
2. The strength of the state interest; and
3. Whether there are less burdensome alternative means to accomplish the same goal.

A threshold issue, which B addresses, is whether or not a belief in Satan would be considered a "religious belief" in the context of the First Amendment. In order to be considered a religious belief, the belief need only parallel an orthodox religious belief; it cannot be a purely political or philosophical view. Worshipping Satan could well be considered a religious belief, and here, this is not a particular problem because you're told in the question that feline sacrifice is part of the practice of the group's "religious beliefs," so you can assume that those beliefs would qualify for First Amendment protection.

As to the balancing test, the burden on Leonard's religious beliefs would be considered slight. The state's police power would have been the basis of enacting the "cruelty to animals" legislation, and by the same token it would be the interest to be balanced here. With a slight burden and a strong state interest, the statute would be considered a valid burden on the right to free exercise of religion. Since B recognizes this, it's the best response.

(A) is not the best response,

because a belief in Satan *could* enjoy constitutional protection, and A makes the blanket statement that it cannot.

The "free exercise" part of the First Amendment's religion clause guarantees the right to free exercise of religion. In order to gain protection a religious belief must be held in good faith, and it must parallel an orthodox religious belief; it cannot be merely a political or philosophical view. United States v. Seeger (1965). Thus, a belief in Satan could constitute a religious belief. If Leonard, in fact, had a religious belief in Satan, and the statute here violated his right to the free exercise of religion, his conviction would be overturned. Since A doesn't recognize this, it's not the best response.

(C) is not the best response,

because applying this statute to Leonard would not violate Leonard's right to freedom of religion.

The "free exercise" part of the First Amendment's religion clause guarantees the right to free exercise of religion. However, as with the First Amendment rights of speech, assembly, and association, this right is not absolute. Instead, reasonable regulation is permissible. The reasonableness of regulations burdening the free exercise of religion is determined with a balancing test, considering:

1. The magnitude of the burden;
2. The strength of the state interest; and
3. Whether there are less burdensome alternative means to accomplish the same goal.

Here, the burden on Leonard's religious beliefs would be considered slight. The state's police power would have been the basis of enacting the "cruelty to animals" legislation, and by the same token it would be the interest to be balanced here. With a slight burden and a strong state interest, the statute would be considered a valid burden on the right to free exercise of religion.

Incidentally, note that while the conduct of religion can be regulated, the beliefs themselves cannot. The right to *hold* religious beliefs is considered absolute.

Since option C does not take into account the balancing test to determine the validity of regulations impacting the free exercise of religion, it's not the best response.

(D) is not the best response,

because it does not apply the correct test to these facts.

The statute here impacts Leonard's exercise of his religious beliefs. Thus, the "free exercise" part of the First Amendment's religion clause, guaranteeing the right to free exercise of religion, is called into question. This right, as with the First Amendment rights of speech, assembly, and association, is not absolute. Instead, reasonable regulation is permissible. The reasonability of regulations burdening the free exercise of religion is determined with a balancing test, considering:

1. The magnitude of the burden;
2. The strength of the state interest; and
3. Whether there are less burdensome alternative means to accomplish the same goal.

D ignores this test, and instead has the court considering whether the need for sacrifice, in worshipping Satan, is reasonable. This implies that a religious practice is only protected if it is reasonable in light of the particular religious belief. That's not the case. Instead, if a religious belief parallels an orthodox religious belief, and exceeds a purely political or philosophical view, it will be protected. A court will not delve into whether a particular belief is reasonable.

Furthermore, the mere fact that an act is religious does not determine whether it will be protected. As the balancing test above suggests, the religious nature of the act will be balanced against the state's interest in determining if the restriction on the exercise of religious beliefs is valid. Here, the state's interest would be pursuant to its police power to protect the general welfare of its citizens. Since option D ignores this balancing test entirely, it's not the best response.

Answer 11

(B) is the best response,

because it's the only one that addresses the central issue under these facts, impoundment, and offers a solid argument for Arms Corporation.

"Impoundment" is the President's refusal to spend funds appropriated by Congress. The rule is that the President does not have the power to refuse to spend appropriated funds under an express mandate from Congress that such funds be spent. Kendall v. United State (1838). (Note, incidentally, that the extent to which "impoundment" is a settled issue only goes as far as funds that Congress has expressly mandated be spent. Beyond that, the President *may* have the power to impound funds.) Here, Congress mandated that the billion dollars "shall be spent" for the weapons system. Thus, the President *must* authorize the contract for purchase of the system. Option B recognizes that this is Arms Corporation's strongest constitutional argument in challenging the withholding of the funds.

Note, incidentally, that Arms Corporation has the standing to challenge the impoundment, because it has been harmed by the withholding of funds, since it's the only supplier of the weapons system. Also, since Congress has the power to spend for the general welfare, and to arm the armed forces, the bill authorizing the weapons system would be a valid exercise of Congressional power.

In any case, since option B recognizes that impoundment is the central issue here, and offers an argument in Arms Corporation's favor, it's the best response.

(A) is not the best response,

because passing an appropriation over a veto does not, in fact, make spending mandatory.

A veto occurs when the President refuses to sign a bill passed by Congress. Congress can override a Presidential veto with a two-thirds vote of both houses. Regardless of whether the President signs a bill into law, or the bill becomes law in spite of a Presidential veto, this doesn't address an argument for the President's withholding funds authorized by Congress. Instead, the issue addressed here is executive impoundment, since a president is said to "impound" when he withholds (or delays) spending funds appropriated by Congress. Since option A ignores the central issue, it's not the best response.

(C) is not the best response,

because the argument it makes would not authorize the President to withhold spending funds appropriated by Congress.

It's true that Congress holds the enumerated power to tax and spend for the general welfare. The President, on the other hand, has the power to enforce laws, which includes carrying out spending programs authorized by Congress, once those programs become law (either because the President signed the bill authorizing the program, or Congress passed the bill over the President's veto). However, this doesn't address specifically whether the President can withhold spending funds appropriated by Congress. Instead, this is an issue of "impoundment." "Impoundment" is the President's refusal to spend funds appropriated by Congress. The rule is that the President does not have the power to refuse to spend appropriated funds under an express mandate from Congress that such funds be spent. Kendall v. United State (1838). (Note, incidentally, that the extent to which "impoundment" is a settled issue only goes as far as funds that Congress has expressly mandated be spent. Beyond that, the President *may* have the power to impound funds.) Here, Congress mandated that the billion dollars "shall be spent" for the weapons system. Thus, the President *must* authorize the contract for purchase of the system.

Since C does not address the issue of impoundment, it's not the best response.

(D) is not the best response,

because the subject matter of the legislation does not specifically address the President's ability to withhold spending funds appropriated by Congress.

It's true that the President holds broad powers in respect to foreign affairs, and it's possible that, since the spending here involves a weapons system, the President's power would control. If it *did,* this certainly wouldn't be a good argument for Arms Corporation, which would be trying to argue that the President has no power to withhold spending funds Congress appropriated, and in this question you're looking for Arms Corporation's best argument.

In fact, this ignores the central issue under these facts: impoundment. "Impoundment" is the President's refusal to spend funds appropriated by Congress. The rule is that the President does not have the power to refuse to spend appropriated funds under an express mandate from Congress that such funds be spent. Kendall v. United State (1838). (Note, incidentally, that the extent to which "impoundment" is a settled issue only goes as far as funds that Congress has expressly mandated be spent. Since D does not address the issue of impoundment, it's not the best response.

Answer 12

(B) is the best response,

because the Art. IV P&I clause imposes near-strict scrutiny on any state's infringement of out-of-staters' right to practice their business or profession.

When a state (or subdivision of a state, like a city and its municipally-owned operations) regulates a right that is "fundamental to national unity," and does so in a way that disadvantages out-of-staters, that regulation will essentially be subject to strict scrutiny under the Art. IV Privileges and Immunities clause. (Among other things, the state must show that the discrimination against non-residents bears a "substantial relationship" to the problem the state is attempting to solve.) Practice of one's business or profession is a right "fundamental to national unity" for P&I purposes.

The case here is on all fours with *New Hampshire v. Piper* (1985), where the Court held that New Hampshire's attempt to restrict the right to practice law to

state residents violated the Art. IV P&I clause. So since there's no showing that out-of-state doctors are the peculiar source of any special problem that the hospital is trying to solve, the restriction violates the P&I Clause.

(By the way, there's no exception under the P&I Clause for activities in which the city or state is a "market participant," as there is under the Commerce Clause. *United Bldg and Constr. Trades Counc. v. Camden* (1984). So the fact that the city owns the hospital that's making the rule doesn't help it, as it would against a Commerce Clause attack.)

(A) is not the best response,

because the legislature of state Red did not make Doctor liable for a crime.

A bill of attainder is a legislative act that inflicts punishment for a crime without a judicial trial upon individuals who are designated by name or in terms of past conduct.

The constitutional prohibition against a bill of attainder would not be helpful to Doctor because the hospital here merely changed the residency requirement for practicing medicine at the hospital. No public entity named Doctor as a criminal, or changed medical licensing requirements in such a way that only Doctor was affected, which is what a bill of attainder would have done.

(C) is not the best response,

because Doctor would have to show that the licensing requirement was not rationally related to a legitimate government interest, a showing Doctor probably couldn't make.

The Due Process clause of the 14th Amendment provides that no state shall make or enforce any law which shall deprive any person of life, liberty, or property, without due process of law. When a fundamental right is not involved, substantive due process requires only that a law be "rationally related" to the achievement of a "legitimate government interest."

A Due Process argument would not be the most helpful to Doctor because she would have to prove that state Red's new residency requirement was not rationally related to some legitimate government purpose. This standard is very lenient and easy-to-satisfy. Here, for instance, the hospital could plausibly claim that it wants to have on staff only doctors who live very nearby, and that it's entitled to use state of residence as a proxy for nearbyness. Although the fit between means and end isn't very tight under this rationale, it's almost certainly tight enough to meet the extremely lenient rational-relation standard.

(D) is not the best response,

because state Red was not legislating against past acts.

The Ex Post Facto clauses, Article I, §9 and §10, prohibit both the federal government and the state, respectively, from passing legislation that retroactively alters the criminal law as to offenses or punishments, in a substantially prejudicial manner. A retroactive change in civil regulations, such as licensing requirements, cannot violate the prohibition, since the prohibition applies only to "penal," i.e., punitive, measures.

Here, the facts make it clear that the hospital was not making a rule penalizing past acts, but was instead making residency a requirement to practice medicine in state Red going forward. So the Ex Post Facto clause would not apply.

Answer 13

(A) is the best response,

because peremptory challenges based on gender violate equal protection.

Gender-based classifications are subject to intermediate scrutiny, which requires that the government show that the classification be substantially related to an important government objective. The use of peremptory challenges to exclude all women from a jury cannot survive mid-level review because it fails to further the state's legitimate interest in achieving a fair trial, while reinforcing stereotypical assumptions about women. *J.E.B. v. Alabama* (1994).

This rationale should apply to invalidate the state's action here, even though a non-jury adjudication method has been used. Anne used all of her peremptory challenges to eliminate women from the arbitrator's panel because she believed that they would necessarily be biased in favor of another woman claiming sexual harassment. Her reasoning reinforced the stereotypical assumption about women. By removing only women from the panel she did not substantially further State Y's legitimate interest in ensuring the employee grievance system provides a fair trial for employers and employees; therefore her actions were unconstitutional.

(B) is not the best response,

because a participant in an arbitration does not have a constitutional right to have the arbitration panel made up of the participant's peers. That is a right that is limited to formal jury trials.

(C) is not the best response,

because gender-based classifications are examined under intermediate scrutiny, not strict scrutiny, and the state's action could not survive strict scrutiny

Gender-based classifications are subject to intermediate scrutiny, which requires that the government show that the classification is substantially related to an important government objective. As described in the analysis of Choice (A), the state's strike-all-female-arbitrators action here does not satisfy this intermediate-level standard.

Choice (C) is wrong for two reasons. First, it applies the wrong standard, strict scrutiny instead of the proper intermediate-level scrutiny. Second, the state's action cannot even survive the intermediate-level scrutiny (see the analysis of Choice (C) for why), so it certainly couldn't survive strict scrutiny, as choice (C) says it could.

(D) is not the best response,

because gender-based classifications are examined under intermediate scrutiny, not rational-basis review.

Gender-based classifications are subject to intermediate scrutiny, which requires that the government show that the classification be substantially related to an important government objective. Thus rational-basis review (under which the action will be upheld if the means chosen are "rationally related" to the achievement of a "legitimate" state interest) is not the right standard. (It probably is true that if rational-basis review were the correct standard, the state would survive that review here, though this is not absolutely certain.)

Answer 14

(C) is the best response,

because State A's statute does not violate the dormant commerce clause, in that it neither unduly burdens, nor intentionally discriminates against, out-of-state economic interests.

Congress has the power to regulate interstate commerce. However, that power is non-exclusive — if Congress has not enacted laws regarding the subject, a state or local government may regulate aspects of interstate commerce. But the "dormant commerce clause" (i.e., the principle that state regulation may not unduly interfere with Congress' power to regulate commerce) says that the regulation will be valid only if it satisfies two tests: (1) it does not intentionally discriminate against out-of-state competition to benefit local economic interests; and (2) it is not unduly burdensome, which is to say that the incidental burden on interstate commerce does not outweigh the legitimate local benefits produced by the regulation.

The statute of State A is constitutional because it passes both tests. As to the first test: although the statute seeks to benefit local economic interests, it does not discriminate against out-of-state competition in the method it employs to protect domestic corporations. That is so because the statute, by requiring that any acquisition of more than 25% of the voting shares of a corporation incorporated in State A be approved by the holders of record of a majority of the corporation, imposes exactly the same burden on both in-state and out-of-state entities wishing to acquire a State A corporation.

The second requirement is that the regulation not be "unduly burdensome" to interstate commerce. The State A statute regulates only the acquisition of State A corporations, and there is no obvious large burden on out-of-staters that want to acquire in-state corporations. Since only corporations incorporated in State A are covered by the statute, one important form of undue burden — the inconsistent state-by-state regulation of a corporation incorporated in another state — does not occur. Thus the second prong of the test is satisfied.

The act here is similar to one upheld by the Court against Commerce Clause attack in *CTS Corp. v. Dynamics Corp. of Amer.* (1987) (anti-takeover attack upheld because, "to the limited extent that the Act affects interstate commerce, this is justified by the State's interests in defining the attributes of shares in its corporations and in protecting shareholders.")

(A) is not the best response,

because the fact that one purpose of the statute may be to prevent out-of-state acquisitions is not fatal, where the provision applies equally to in-state and out-of-state acquirers.

Dormant Commerce Clause attacks generally won't succeed unless the plaintiff shows either a discriminatory intent (less-favored treatment of out-of-staters than in-staters) or an "undue burden" on commerce. (See the discussion of Choice (C) above.) The mere fact that one of the purposes is to prevent out-of-staters from doing something unsatisfactory won't be enough, if in-staters are also prevented (since then there is no discrimination.)

(B) is not the best response,

because the presence of an "adverse effect" on an interstate market does not suffice for a violation of the dormant commerce clause.

As is discussed more fully in the treatment of Choice (C) above, a plaintiff in a dormant commerce clause case must generally show either discrimination against interstate commerce, or a "substantial burden" on it. Choice (B), by making the test be whether there is any sort of "adverse effect" at all, is not the right test.

(D) is not the best response,

because it's an incorrect statement about what the dormant commerce clause prohibits.

It's true that corporations exist only by virtue of state law. It's also true that a state probably has greater freedom in how it regulates its own domestic (i.e., state-chartered) corporations than in some other areas of regulation. But an anti-takeover statute, even if applied only to state-chartered targets, would still violate the dormant commerce clause if it *discriminated against* — i.e., treated less favorably — out-of-state acquirers than in-state acquirers (for instance, by requiring a higher percentage of target stockholders to approve an out-of-state takeover than a domestic takeover). So when Choice (D) says that the "negative implications of the commerce clause" (an accurate way to refer to the dormant commerce clause) "do not apply to state regulations governing [domestic corporations'] creation and

acquisition," the choice is not stating the law correctly.

Answer 15

(D) is the best response,

because the tax discriminates against out-of-state manufacturers.

Congress' power over interstate commerce is non-exclusive: If Congress has not enacted laws regarding the subject, a state or local government may regulate aspects of interstate commerce if (and only if) the regulation: (1) does not discriminate against out-of-state competition to benefit local economic interests; and (2) does not unduly burden interstate commerce. This limit on the powers of state or local governments to regulate or affect interstate commerce is sometimes called the "dormant commerce clause."

By reducing the amount of taxes paid by assemblers of computers in an amount equal to the portion of computer components manufactured in Green, Central City is discriminating against out-of-state competition to benefit local economic interests. This discrimination causes the tax measure to violate test (1) above. Consequently, the ordinance violates the dormant commerce clause principle.

(A) is not the best response,

because the ordinance has the effect of making parts manufactured outside of Green more expensive.

It is true that the tax falls only on companies resident in Central City. But the *effect* of the tax is to make components manufactured in Green less expensive than those manufactured outside of Green. Consequently, companies like Assembler are induced to favor in-state component-makers over out-of-state ones. This intentional discrimination against out-of-staters violates the no-discrimination-against-out-of-staters component of dormant commerce clause principles (described more fully in the discussion of choice (D) above).

(B) is not the best response,

because the dormant commerce clause places limits on a state's right to foster resident corporations.

Although a state may sometimes foster local businesses by encouraging its residents to "buy local," some methods of encouragement violate the dormant commerce clause. Where a state uses its tax system to confer a direct financial benefit to those who buy locally-manufactured goods, at the expense of out-of-state makers of goods, the state crosses the line into forbidden "economic protectionism," and violates the dormant commerce clause. That's what the tax here does.

(C) is not the best response,

because taxes based on gross receipts are not a per se violation of dormant commerce clause principles.

Some tax schemes violate the dormant commerce clause because they either discriminate against, or unduly burden, interstate commerce. But the mere fact that a tax is "measured in whole or in part by [the tax-payer's] gross receipts" does not automatically mean that either forbidden discrimination or an undue burden on commerce is present.

It's true that if a state enacted a tax on a multi-state taxpayer's gross receipts, and made no distinction between receipts from in-state activities and those from out-of-state activities, that tax might well be found to be an undue burden on commerce, and thus a violation of the dormant commerce clause. But Choice (C) goes way beyond this principle, and doesn't tie in to the problem with the tax here (which is that it intentionally discriminates against out-of-state component makers.)

Answer 16

(C) is the best response,
because the decision for Agitator was reached entirely on state grounds.

The Supreme Court may hear a case from a state only if the state court judgment turned on federal grounds. The Court must refuse jurisdiction if it finds adequate and independent nonfederal grounds to sup-port the state decision. To be "adequate," the non-fed-eral grounds must be fully dispositive of the case. To be "independent," the state court's interpretation of the state provision must be based on the court's own rea-soning about state law, not based in whole or part on the state court's conclusion about what federal law pro-vides.

Here, the state grounds mentioned by the state supreme court were "adequate" to support the deci-sion, because that court's decision was based entirely on its own practice of giving the broadest possible interpretation to the state constitution's free-speech guarantee. The state grounds were "independent" because although the state court discussed in detail the Supreme Court's 1st and 14th Amendment deci-sions, the state court specifically stated that its deter-mination was independent of how the Supreme Court would decide the federal constitutionality of the statute.

Because there were both adequate and independent state grounds, the Court can and should dismiss the writ of certiorari as improvidently granted.

(A) is not the best response,
because it is an incorrect statement of the law.

First, the Court may not hear the case at all, for the reason given in Choice (C). But even if the Court did hear the case, Choice (A) would not explain what the Court should do.

One of the categories of speech unprotected by the 1st Amendment is "fighting words," that is words that are likely to induce the person to whom they are addressed commit an immediate act of violence. (To constitute "fighting words" it is not enough that the speaker's words make the listeners angry — an incite-ment to immediate violence is required.) Agitator's ball-park shout could constitutionally be punished under this "fighting words" doctrine, because it tended to incite the other spectators to violence.

(B) is not the best response,
because the state court's decision was reached on independent state grounds.

The Court may not hear the case due to the presence of a independent and adequate state ground, as described in the discussion of Choice (C). Therefore, the Court does not have jurisdiction to issue a "remand" (which is itself an exercise of federal jurisdic-tion, and thus inappropriate here).

(D) is not the best response,
because the Court does not have jurisdiction.

The Court may not hear the case due to the presence of a independent and adequate state ground, as described in the discussion of Choice (C). Therefore, the Court does not have jurisdiction to reverse the state-court decision. (If the Court *did* have jurisdiction, because the state court had rested its decision partly or fully on federal-constitutional grounds, then this choice (D) would be a correct statement of what the Supreme Court should do, since incitement to violent action is not protected speech, under the "fighting words" doc-trine.)

Answer 17

(B) is the best response,
because it identifies the central reason Allen will have standing to challenge the provision concerning distribu-tion of free textbooks to parochial schools.

The issue of standing determines whether, as a threshold matter, a plaintiff may press his claim. Stand-ing requires that the government action challenged must have caused, or is imminently likely to cause, an injury to the party seeking review. Where the issue is a spending program and the plaintiff's only connection with that spending is his status as taxpayer, the injury issue is generally quite remote. In fact, a person's sta-tus as a federal taxpayer only gives him standing in limited matters. Principally, a taxpayer can gain stand-ing in spending matters if he can show that:

1. The federal tax was invalidly applied against him (making the "injury" personal) OR
2. The expenditure in question exceeded a specific constitutional limitation on the taxing and spend-ing powers, AND
3. They were part of a federal spending program. *Flast v. Cohen* (1968).

This is, in fact, a very narrow exception; taxpayers generally have standing only in religion cases, based on the Establishment Clause. Thus, under these facts, Allen will have standing because Congress is not allowed to spend money in derogation of the Establish-ment Clause of the First Amendment.

Incidentally, state or municipal taxpayers can normally challenge state or municipal *measurable* expenditures (e.g., local busing of parochial school students).

In any case, since B is the only option that addresses precisely why Allen will have standing under these facts, it's the best response.

(A) is not the best response,

because it overstates the scope of taxpayer standing.

A person's status as a federal taxpayer only gives him standing in limited matters. Contrary to what A states, it's not *any* congressional spending that can be challenged. Principally, a taxpayer can gain standing in spending matters if he can show that:

1. The federal tax was invalidly applied against him (making the "injury" personal) OR
2. The expenditure in question exceeded a specific constitutional limitation on the taxing and spending powers, AND
3. They were part of a federal spending program. *Flast v. Cohen* (1968).

This is, in fact, a very narrow exception; taxpayers generally have standing only in religion cases, based on the Establishment Clause. Thus, under these facts, Allen will have standing because Congress is not allowed to spend money in derogation of the Establishment Clause of the First Amendment. While A recognizes that Allen will have standing, it overstates the scope of federal taxpayer standing, so it can't be the best response.

(C) is not the best response,

because it misstates the standard for determining federal taxpayer standing, and it fails to recognize that Allen will have standing under these facts.

A person's status as a federal taxpayer only gives him standing in limited matters. This is not determined on the basis of a nexus between the taxpayer and the challenged spending. Principally, a taxpayer can gain standing in spending matters if he can show that:

1. The federal tax was invalidly applied against him (making the "injury" personal) OR
2. The expenditure in question exceeded a specific constitutional limitation on the taxing and spending powers, AND
3. They were part of a federal spending program. *Flast v. Cohen* (1968).

This is, in fact, a very narrow exception; taxpayers generally have standing only in religion cases, based on the Establishment Clause. Thus, under these facts, Allen will have standing because Congress is not allowed to spend money in derogation of the Establishment Clause of the First Amendment.

If you chose this response, you may have been thinking of the older rule, or you may have been thinking of the rule under which a state may tax non-resident individuals or companies doing business in state. The traditional rule is that a taxpayer had no standing to challenge federal expenditures. However, this rule has

been supplanted by the rule from Flast v. Cohen. As to state taxation of non-resident individuals and companies, the cornerstone of such taxation is that a substantial nexus must exist between the activity taxed and the state (and if such nexus doesn't exist the state lacks jurisdiction over the activity, and taxing it would be a due process violation). This clearly doesn't fit the facts here. Since C doesn't cite the correct rule, it's not the best response.

(D) is not the best response,

because it addresses the wrong issue, and beyond that, it incorrectly analyzes that issue.

Here, the question is specifically addressing Allen's *standing* to challenge the federal expenditures on private, religious schools. Whether or not the provision will be upheld depends to a large extent on whether state action exists, because the Constitution does not outlaw purely private acts of discrimination. However, this issue is *substantive*. Standing is a threshold issue which determines whether the plaintiff in a case is in a position to press his claim. Thus, the existence of state action is not determinative of standing, contrary to what D states.

Assuming arguendo that this question did address the substantive issue of state action, D would still miss the mark. It's true that the Constitution does not outlaw purely private acts of discrimination; some "state action" must be involved. However, under these facts there is obvious state action in the form of spending governmental funds; furthermore, the statute here is *federal,* not a state statute, so "state action" is not an issue. Nonetheless, the central issue is Allen's standing, and since D doesn't address this, it's not the best response.

Answer 18

(A) is the best response,

because it recognizes the central reason the provision for construction of buildings to be used for secular purposes, at religious colleges and universities, is constitutional.

Under the First Amendment, the government must be "religion-neutral"; that is, it can't respect an establishment of religion, and it can't prohibit the free exercise of religion. Here, you have Congress subsidizing construction of buildings at private, and potentially religious, colleges and universities. Thus, there's a potential Establishment Clause problem. In such situations, the test used to determine if the enactment is constitutional is from *Lemon v. Kurtzman* (1971):

1. The statute must have a secular purpose;
2. It must have as its principal or primary effect neither the advancement nor inhibition of religion;
3. It must not foster excessive government entanglement with religion.

Option A implicitly recognizes that this test is met.

The central issue here is the third element, "excessive entanglement", because it is purely judgmental – the only real way to know if a particular provision constitutes excessive entanglement is to see if the Supreme Court has already addressed the issue. And, by gum, with this one, it has. The issue of government grants for construction of buildings to be used exclusively for secular education, at religious colleges and universities, was addressed in *Tilton v. Richardson* (1971). The grants were upheld, on the basis that, as long as the schools involved were not "permeated with religion," the grants didn't involve excessive entanglement with religion. A correctly addresses this.

There is a caveat to this, in the sense that almost no direct aid to primary and secondary religious schools would be permissible, since such aid is considered "excessive entanglement" (in that religious indoctrination of younger students is more of a problem than with older, university-age students). In any case, since option A recognizes that the specific provision involved here is constitutional, it's the best response.

(B) is not the best response,

because it does not identify the central reason the building grant will be constitutional.

Under the First Amendment, the government must be "religion-neutral"; that is, it can't respect an establishment of religion, and it can't prohibit the free exercise of religion. Here, you have Congress subsidizing construction of buildings at private, and potentially religious, colleges and universities. Thus, there's a potential Establishment Clause problem. In such situations, the test used to determine if the enactment is constitutional is from *Lemon v. Kurtzman* (1971):

1. The statute must have a secular purpose;
2. It must have as its principal or primary effect neither the advancement nor inhibition of religion;
3. It must not foster excessive government entanglement with religion.

Here, option B states that it's the bricks and mortar themselves that do not foster religion. However, say the facts were different, and the bricks and mortar were to be used to build a chapel. This would clearly violate the Establishment Clause, although the reasoning in B would still make the grant valid.

Instead, the reason the grants here will be valid is that they are to be used for secular education only, and thus don't respect an establishment of religion or involve excessive government entanglement with religion. While the "excessive entanglement" issue involves line-drawing, the Supreme Court addressed this specific issue in *Tilton v. Richardson* (1971), and decided such grants were valid. Since B does not recognize the specific reason the grants will be valid, it's not the best response.

(C) is not the best response,

because it fails to recognize that aid for *secular* pur-

poses can be constitutional even if the recipient is a private, religious school.

Under the First Amendment, the government must be "religion-neutral"; that is, it can't respect an establishment of religion, and it can't prohibit the free exercise of religion. Here, you have Congress subsidizing construction of buildings at private, and potentially religious, colleges and universities. Thus, there's a potential Establishment Clause problem. In such situations, the test used to determine if the enactment is constitutional is from *Lemon v. Kurtzman* (1971):

1. The statute must have a secular purpose;
2. It must have as its principal or primary effect neither the advancement nor inhibition of religion;
3. It must not foster excessive government entanglement with religion.

The key point here is that financial aid to church-operated schools can be valid if it meets this test, because it's possible to aid the secular goals of schools without violating the *Lemon v. Kurtzman* test. While this would, tangentially perhaps, strengthen the religious purposes of the school, this would be sufficiently outweighed by the government's interest in the general welfare of students to allow limited financial aid to religious schools.

There is a caveat to this, in the sense that almost no direct aid to primary and secondary religious schools would be permissible, since such aid is considered "excessive entanglement" (in that religious indoctrination of younger students is more of a problem than with older, university-age students). In any case, since C would prohibit any financial help to religious schools, when in fact there are limited circumstances (including those here) where such aid would be permissible, C cannot be the best response.

(D) is not the best response,

because the aid here would not be considered "excessive entanglement," and the grants would, in fact, be considered constitutional.

Under the First Amendment, the government must be "religion-neutral"; that is, it can't respect an establishment of religion, and it can't prohibit the free exercise of religion. Here, you have Congress subsidizing construction of buildings at private, and potentially religious, colleges and universities. Thus, there's a potential Establishment Clause problem. In such situations, the test used to determine if the enactment is constitutional is from *Lemon v. Kurtzman* (1971):

1. The statute must have a secular purpose;
2. It must have as its principal or primary effect neither the advancement nor inhibition of religion;
3. It must not foster excessive government entanglement with religion.

It's the third element that option D calls into question. In fact, if you chose this option, this is a perfectly understandable mistake to make, because the "excessive entanglement" issue is purely judgmental – the only real way to know if a particular provision constitutes excessive entanglement is to see if the Supreme Court has already addressed the issue. And, by gum, with this one, it has. The issue of government grants for construction of buildings to be used exclusively for secular education, at religious colleges and universities, was addressed in *Tilton v. Richardson* (1971). The grants were upheld, on the basis that, as long as the schools involved were not "permeated with religion," the grants didn't involve excessive entanglement with religion. Since D states otherwise, it's not the best response.

Answer 19

(B) is the best response,

because based on the facts, a reasonable observer would likely believe the government of state Green was endorsing the nativity scene as a religious symbol.

The constitutionality of the display of a religious symbol such as a nativity scene will be a question of fact. The most important single factor seems to be the context in which the religious symbol is displayed: If the religious symbol is presented by itself in what is clearly a space reserved by the government for its own property and its own messages, the Court is likely to conclude that a reasonable observer would believe that the government was endorsing the religious message. Conversely, the presence of other non-religious symbols nearby, or the existence of a sign indicating that the display was furnished by private parties, may well be enough to lead a reasonable observer to the conclusion that the government was *not* endorsing religion. See *Allegheny County v. ACLU* (1989) (nativity scene displayed in a courthouse violated the Establishment Clause, in part because the absence of any nearby non-religious symbols as part of the display would lead a reasonably observer to conclude that the city was endorsing a religious observance, not merely celebrating the secular holiday season.)

On this standard, the proposed display of the nativity scene would be unconstitutional. The nativity scene would not be surrounded by non-religious symbols having to do with the holiday season, a fact which would rebut the implication that the nativity scene was just part of a secular celebration of the holiday season. The whole presentation (and the fact that the governor and legislature supported it) would create in a reasonable observer the impression that the government was endorsing a religious message.

(A) is not the best response,

because the ownership of the display would not be dispositive on the issue of whether government seemed to be endorsing religion.

If the scene here seemed to be a celebration of Christmas as a primarily secular holiday, the fact that the government owned the display would not be fatal. But (for the reasons discussed in Choice (B) above),

the context of the display here would suggest to a reasonable observer that the state was endorsing religion. Consequently, the display violates the Establishment Clause. Thus Choice (A) reaches the correct result, but for the wrong reason.

(C) is not the best response,

because donation would be only one element considered in the total context of the display.

If the display made it clear to the public that private citizens had donated the components, this would indeed be one factor (but just one) tending to demonstrate that the display was not a forbidden government endorsement of religion. But there's no indication that the fact of private donations would be disclosed to the public. Furthermore, this fact, even if disclosed, probably wouldn't be enough to overcome the otherwise-powerful impression that the government is endorsing a religious message.

(D) is not the best response,

because displaying the scene next to the products would not rebut the impression that the state was endorsing the nativity scene's religious message.

When a religious symbol such as a nativity scene is displayed in a public place, the issue is whether a reasonable observer would believe that the government is endorsing a religious method. Context is all-important. If the nativity scene were displayed next to other objects that pertain to December as a primarily secular holiday (e.g., a Santa Claus figure), the impression of an endorsement of religion would be rebutted. But putting the scene next to the year-round display of in-state-manufactured products would not rebut the impression of an endorsement of religion, because an observer would realize that the two displays were separate, and that the nativity scene was its own stand-alone display on an explicitly religious topic.

Answer 20

(D) is the best response,

because there is no evidence of the city's involvement with the private organization beyond the renting of the auditorium.

The Fourteenth Amendment provides that no State shall make or enforce any law which shall deny to any person within its jurisdiction the equal protection of the laws. This Amendment, and thus the Equal Protection Clause contained in it, applies *only to government action*, not to action by private citizens. This is known as the requirement of *"state action,"* and whenever you have an equal protection or due process question, you should check to see that it's satisfied.

There are several ways in which the state can become so involved with private citizens' discriminatory actions that the discrimination will be attributable to the state for state-action purposes. For instance, perhaps the state has become so involved with the private action that the two become symbiotic, which is to say there is a mutually beneficial relation between the state and the private discriminator (e.g., state gets revenue from leasing space in a public parking garage to a discriminatory restaurant; *Burton v. Wilmington Parking Auth.* (1961)). Or, perhaps the state has somehow encouraged the private discrimination.

But here, the state involvement with the private action here is so limited, and so independent of the discrimination, that no state action will be found. The state will rent to anyone, and charges the same hourly rate to everyone, so the fact that the state is renting to the all-male organization here does not constitute any kind of endorsement or encouragement by the state of (or unusual benefit to the state from) the discrimination. Consequently, there is no state action, and the organization's conduct won't be subject to the Fourteenth Amendment.

(A) is not the best response,
because inviting members of the general public does not make private organization a state actor.

It's probable that if this organization were a public organization (e.g., organized by and run by a city), the all-male-officers rule would violate the Fourteenth Amendment. But as described in Choice (D) above, there is no state action here. Therefore, Choice (A) cannot be correct in suggesting that the Fourteenth Amendment applies. And that's true even though this private organization has invited members of the public to some of its activities.

(B) is not the best response,
because renting the auditorium does not make the private organization a state actor.

As is described in Choice (D) above, the mere occasional first-come-first-served rental of a city auditorium to a discriminatory private group is not enough to transform the private group's conduct into the requisite state action. If the city encouraged, or substantially benefitted from, the discrimination in some way, that might be enough to constitute state action. But the rental here — which is on the same basis as it would be for any other group, discriminatory or not — does not come close to being state action.

(C) is not the best response,
because the absence of state action prevents the court from even getting to the Fourteenth Amendment issue.

First of all, this choice is wrong because although there is a constitutionally-protected interest in freedom of association, it's conferred by the First Amendment (as a variant of the freedom of expression), not by the Fourteenth Amendment. Second, whatever freedom-of- association claim the organization might have would not be strong enough to prohibit interference "in any way" with the organization's use of city facilities. (The organization's freedom-of-association rights might be strong enough to interfere with *some* efforts

by the city to reduce discrimination. See, e.g., *Boy Scouts of America v. Dale* (2002), holding that because opposition to homosexuality is part of the Scouts' 'expressive message,' the Scouts freedom of association was violated by a state anti-discrimination law that barred the group from excluding gay members.)

But the biggest reason why this choice is wrong is that due to the lack of "state action" here (see Choice (D) above), the court would never even get to the point of analyzing whether the freedom of association blocked the application of the Fourteenth Amendment.

Answer 21

(B) is the best response,
because lessening congestion by allowing only Kelly County cabs to do business is an undue burden on interstate commerce.

Under the dormant commerce clause, a state regulation that substantially affects interstate commerce must meet each of the following requirements to be upheld: (1) the regulation must pursue a legitimate end; (2) the regulation must be rationally related to that legitimate end; and (3) the regulatory burden imposed by the state on interstate commerce, and any discrimination against interstate commerce, must be outweighed by the state's interest in enforcing the regulation. Protection of a state's economic interests is generally not considered to be a legitimate state objective, where the pursuit of that objective materially affects interstate commerce.

The stated purpose of the regulation, reducing traffic congestion in Kelly County, is a general-welfare-and-safety concern that would be provisionally considered by the Court to be a legitimate state end, pending the rest of the analysis. The ordinance is also rationally related to that legitimate state end. The ordinance fails, however, in that its effect imposes an *undue burden* on interstate travel. The practical effect of this ordinance is to preclude taxicab drivers from state Red from doing business in Kelly County in state Green — they cannot pick up passengers in Kelly, nor can they drop off passengers in Kelly, even passengers who originated in state Red. So the ordinance functionally eliminates from the competition for business anyone not from Kelly County. Reduction of some degree of traffic congestion would not be enough of a benefit to justify this sort of protectionism against out-of-staters. (And the fact that the governmental body is a county rather than state, or the fact that in-staters from outside the county are also discriminated against, makes no difference.)

(A) is not the best response,
because there is no requirement that the means used be the best way of achieving the ends.

Under the dormant commerce clause, a state regulation which affects interstate commerce must meet each of the following requirements to be upheld: (1) the regulation must pursue a legitimate end; (2) the regulation must be rationally related to that legitimate end; and (3) the regulatory burden imposed by the state on interstate commerce, and any discrimination against interstate commerce, must be outweighed by the state's interest in enforcing the regulation.

The fact that the means used is not the "best" means of solving the problem — i.e., is not the means having the tightest possible fit with the governmental objection — is irrelevant under this test. (Factor (2) above requires just a "rational relation" between means and end, a very easy-to-satisfy test.) So the fact that the County has tried to solve its congestion problem "one step at a time" (by eliminating some sources of congestion but not the biggest source) is also irrelevant — as long as the County has eased the problem somewhat, that's all that's required as to the means-end fit.

(C) is not the best response,

because unlawful discrimination against interstate commerce is not rebutted by showing that in-staters from a different part of the state are also being discriminated against.

Under the dormant commerce clause, as long as the business efforts of out-of-staters are being discriminated against or unduly burdened, the fact that in-staters from other part of the state (in this case, those living in Green state but not in Kelly county) are also being discriminated against is irrelevant.

(D) is not the best response,

because the answer applies a Due Process analysis to a dormant commerce clause issue.

Suspect classes are part of a Due Process analysis. The issue here is whether the restriction violates the dormant commerce clause. The appropriate analysis under the dormant commerce clause is the balance between the burden on interstate commerce imposed by the state, and the state's interest in enforcing the regulation. Suspect classes have nothing to do with that analysis.

Answer 22

(A) is the best response,

because the ordinance here is a content-neutral one that allows reasonable alternatives for the type of expression at issue.

The Court has held that a city may confine sexually-explicit land uses (like "adult theaters") to a single part of town, as part of a content-neutral attempt to regulate the bad "secondary effects" (e.g., increased crime, declining property values) of such uses. *Renton v. Playtime Theatres* (1986). The ordinance here is exactly on point with Renton. (By the way, a 2000 case, *Erie v. Pap's A.M.*, seems to go even further, apparently holding that a city may combat the secondary effects of adult activity like nude dancing by completely banning the activity, not just limiting it to a

defined zone.)

The key to the analysis is that the city is (supposedly) not engaging in "content based" discrimination, because it's attacking not the "message" of the adult activity, but merely its "secondary effects" (bad effects not associated with the precise message, like extra crime). Therefore, this is to be analyzed as a time-place-and-manner restriction (valid if it is substantially related to an important government objective, and it leaves open reasonable alternatives for the same type of expression) rather than as a content-based restriction (subject to strict scrutiny and almost certainly struck down).

(B) is not the best response,

because adult entertainment *is* protected by the 1st and 14th Amendments.

Certain types of expression, while not directly suppressible on the grounds of their content, have been treated by the Court as being inherently less valuable, so that they may be regulated more extensively than speech close to the "core" of the First Amendment values, such as political speech. This less-favored category of speech includes speech that is "indecent," such as the adult entertainment here.

So the zoning ordinance here is constitutional, but not for the reason stated. While not afforded the protection of speech at the core of the First Amendment, such as political speech, public adult sexual expression is protected to some extent.

(C) is not the best response,

because non-obscene adult entertainment may nonetheless be regulated despite its First Amendment protection.

It's true that, as Choice (C) suggests, some adult entertainment as defined in the zoning ordinance is non-obscene, and may therefore not be banned on obscenity grounds. But as described in Choice (A) above, because of the "secondary effects" associated with adult entertainment (e.g., extra crime and declining property values), the city may make a time-place-and-manner regulation of such adult entertainment, by limiting it to a particular area of the city.

(D) is not the best response,

because there are allowable reasons for regulating speech beyond protecting "a community's residential neighborhoods."

As Choice (A) above describes, a city may confine sexually-explicit land uses like "adult theaters" to a single part of town, as part of a content-neutral attempt to regulate the bad "secondary effects" of such uses. The secondary effects that may be combatted are not limited to (though they may include) declining quality of the community's residential neighborhoods. (For instance, a city might ban adult entertainment from the core business district because such entertainment increases street crime, reduces commercial property values, etc.) So Choice (D) is wrong because it dramatically understates the bad secondary effects that a city is permitted to combat by zoning of otherwise-protected expression.

Answer 23

(D) is the best response,

because the ordinance removes only one box in ten from the streets.

Commercial speech, if it is not misleading or concerning unlawful activity, is covered by the First Amendment and may be regulated only if the state shows that the regulation (1) directly advances, (2) a substantial governmental interest, (3) in a way that is reasonably tailored to achieve that objective.

While the ordinance here directly advances the city's governmental interest in preventing the adverse effects of publication-caused litter on public sidewalks and streets, the ordinance fails the last part of the Court's test. The facts state that the city's ordinance removed just 30 of the existing 300 sidewalk machines that were dispensing publications. And there's no indication that publications containing solely advertising will result in more litter per-publication than those that have some non-advertising content. An ordinance which removes only one box in ten, and with no indication why that one poses more of a litter problem, is not reasonably tailored to achieving the city's legitimate interest of combatting litter.

(A) is not the best response,

because this choice states the wrong test.

As is described in Choice (D) above, the Court applies what is essentially mid-level review to regulations of commercial speech. Since Choice (A) says that the review is the easy-to-satisfy rational-relation standard, it's wrong.

(B) is not the best response,

because the answer is based on a test that is inapplicable to the facts.

This choice propounds the strict-scrutiny standard used for content-based restrictions. What's at issue here, however, is a time-place-and-manner regulation aimed at the secondary effects (litter) of a certain method of disseminating written material. The appropriate standard is the intermediate-level review described in Choice (D). Furthermore, if strict-scrutiny *were* the correct standard, the ordinance here would clearly not satisfy the standard, since it's attacking only one-tenth of the problem (by removing only one-tenth of the boxes), meaning that the means chosen are not a very good method of achieving the objective.

(C) is not the best response,

because the applicable test is reasonable-fit, not least-restrictive means.

Commercial speech, if it is not misleading or concerning unlawful activity, is covered by the 1st Amendment and may be regulated only if the state shows that the regulation (1) directly advances, (2) a substantial governmental interest, (3) in a way that is reasonably tailored to achieve that objective.

The Court has indicated that showing (3) does not require that there not be any less-restrictive alternative, merely that there be a fairly close relationship between means and end. In fact, the scheme here doesn't even meet this reasonably-tailored test, but Choice (C) is wrong because it states an incorrectly-strict test for the means-end fit.

Answer 24

(A) is the best response,

because his barber license was "property," which the state could not take away from him without due process.

Where a state-issued license is required to pursue a business or profession, a person who has already obtained the license has a "property" interest in that license for Fourteenth Amendment due process purposes. Consequently, that property may not be taken away without due process of law.

Precisely what procedural safeguards John is entitled to is not certain, but the more serious the threatened loss of property or liberty, the wider the array of procedural safeguards required. Here, the threatened loss (right to practice one's profession) is serious, so extensive safeguards ought to be given. Since the proceeding is analogous to a criminal trial — the Board is determining whether John used his premises to commit a crime — he's got a strong claim of entitlement to the sorts of procedures used in criminal trials, including the right to cross-examine his accusers. There's no guarantee that John would win with this due process argument, but it's clearly the most likely to succeed of the four choices.

(B) is not the best response,

because the United States Attorney dropped the case before a judgment was entered.

Article IV, §1 states that Full Faith and Credit shall be given by each state to public acts and judicial proceedings of every other state. By extension of this principle, the states must give full faith and credit to federal proceedings as well.

However, the decision by the local United States Attorney not to prosecute John was not a judicial decision deserving full faith and credit, because it was not the final outcome of a judicial proceeding. (The case was dropped, not decided, and so there would be nothing to give full faith and credit to.) Consequently, Choice (B) is not correct.

(C) is not the best response,

because Article III has nothing to do with state proceedings, and any way this is not the sort of "penalty" that must be conferred by a court rather than an agency.

Article III prescribes the judicial power of the United States, i.e., the limits of the power of the *federal* judiciary. It says nothing about how the states must exercise their judicial power. Since this is a state proceeding, Article III is irrelevant.

Furthermore, even if this were a federal license-revocation proceeding, nothing in Article III specifies that the license could only be revoked by an Article III court rather than administrative agency. If this were a truly "penal" proceeding (e.g., a proceeding to institute a criminal conviction or a fine intended to punish), it would have to be in an Article III court (i.e., before a judge with a lifetime term). But this is a non-penal administrative proceeding, so it need not be before an Article III court.

(D) is not the best response,

because federal drug laws are not so extensive as to force aside state laws.

Under the Supremacy Clause of Article IV, §2, even absent explicit language, Congress' intent to supersede state law altogether may be found from a scheme of federal regulation so pervasive as to make reasonable the inference that Congress left no room to supplement it.

However, there's nothing in the facts here to suggest that when Congress made it a federal crime to sell cocaine, it intended to preempt the states from also criminalizing cocaine sales. (Indeed, as to virtually all federal drug crimes, the states have concurrent jurisdiction to criminalize the same conduct.) So the states would even be free to prosecute John for the state crime of cocaine selling. Beyond that, the state proceeding here is a non-penal civil proceeding, so it certainly wouldn't be preempted by the existence of a federal statute criminalizing the same conduct.

Answer 25

(C) is the best response,

because the case is now moot.

A case is moot if it raised a justiciable controversy at the time the complaint was filed but events occurring after the filing have deprived the litigant of an ongoing stake in the controversy and it is not likely the case will be revived.

Alex was seeking only an injunction (not, for instance, damages). And the facts tell us that this is the only criminal trial he was counting on seeing via cable tv. So unless this criminal trial has a significant likelihood of continuing, there is no ongoing damage to Alex, and thus no need for an injunction. The facts tell us that there were no obvious errors in the trial, so it's unlikely that the case will be reversed and remanded for a new trial. Consequently, there is virtually no possibility of new proceedings that could be televised, and

thus no live controversy about whether the injunction sought by Alex should be granted.

(A) is not the best response,

because the likelihood of a live controversy is remote, thus dictating dismissal rather than deferral.

It is appropriate for a court to defer decision in a case where later events will or may likely occur that would make the case more suitable for decision than it is now. So if there were a good likelihood that a new trial would occur, deferral might be the right course. But here, we're told that there are no obvious errors, so it's unlikely that there will be an appellate reversal and a new criminal trial. Since likelihood of a new trial that would raise the "do we televise?" issue is remote, the court should dismiss rather than merely defer.

(B) is not the best response,

because the Green Supreme Court will not have occasion to say anything about the case's merits.

Alex's case presents a pure question of federal (constitutional) law. While principles of concurrent jurisdiction would probably have permitted him to bring the case in state court, he didn't choose to do that. Therefore, the Green Supreme Court won't ever have occasion to express an opinion. In any event, this choice's statement that "state law of mootness governs suits in federal court..." is basically gibberish — it's up to the federal courts to say, as a federal constitutional matter, when a controversy is moot.

(D) is not the best response,

because however important the constitutional question raised by Alex, it's moot due to the fact that there's no longer a criminal trial about which to grant the requested injunctive relief.

A case will be dismissed as moot if the relief sought no longer makes sense. That's true even if, in the abstract, the case presents "an important constitutional question." So Choice (D), by ignoring the mootness problem and relying solely on the importance of the issue, is wrong.

Answer 26

(C) is the best response,

because the prosecution's dismissal of jurors solely on racial grounds violates the defendant's equal protection rights.

A state may not permit litigants (including litigants who are state actors, such as prosecutors) to exclude jurors based solely on racial grounds. This constitutes a violation of the other litigant's equal protection rights. *Batson v. Ky.* (1986). And that's especially true where the exclusion is based upon the reasoning that "the jurors would decide the case solely on racial considerations," as the prosecution is claiming here.

(A) is not the best response,

because Nora's race wouldn't matter.

Prosecutors may not use peremptory challenges to dismiss potential jurors based solely on the race of the juror. (See Choice (C) above.) That's true regardless of whether the litigant who is raising the equal protection argument (here, Nora) is or isn't a member of the race being discriminated against.

(B) is not the best response,

because the use of peremptory challenges to dismiss potential jurors based solely on the juror's race is automatically deemed to be a denial of an impartial jury.

The use of peremptory challenges based solely on the race of the potential jurors violates equal protection. *Batson v. Ky.* (1986). The litigant who is objecting to the practice doesn't have to make a specific showing that this exclusion denied her an impartial jury — the mere fact of intentional exclusion suffices to create an equal protection violation.

(D) is not the best response,

because "fair cross section of the community" is not the appropriate legal standard.

When a litigant excludes potential jurors based solely on racial grounds, the other litigant's equal protection rights have been violated. (See Choice (C) above.) A litigant has the right to an "impartial" jury, and a jury of her peers. But there is no right to a jury consisting of "a fair cross section of the community."

Answer 27

(C) is the best response,

because employees of the federal government are not immune from state taxes.

The federal government is immune from taxation by any state. Federal immunity from state taxation exists only in these situations where the "legal incidence" of the tax is on the United States. Employees of the federal government are not immune from state taxation. Since the legal incidence of the tax here is on the employee, not the government, there is no immunity from the tax. (If the tax were on the deemed value of the business use of the auto, so that the U.S. was in effect being taxed, the result might be different. But the facts make it clear that it's only the employee's personal use that's being taxed, so the case is an easy one.)

(A) is not the best response,

because a tax on federal employees is not a tax on the United States government.

The federal government is immune from taxation by any state. Federal immunity from state taxation exists only in these situations where the "legal incidence" of the tax is on the United States. The tax here is not on the government or a government entity, but upon employees of the federal government, and they are not immune from state taxation.

(B) is not the best response,

because only the value of the personal use is taxed, not the value of the use generally.

The federal government is immune from taxation by any state. Federal immunity from state taxation exists only in these situations where the "legal incidence" of the tax is on the United States. Employees of the federal government are not immune from state taxation.

Green probably could not tax government employees for the use of automobiles in discharge of government duties, because in that case the legal incidence of the tax would be on the United States. But the tax here applies only to the fair value of the personal use, not the use for the U.S.'s benefit. (The fact that the *car* is primarily used for federal government purposes is irrelevant, since it's only the value of the personal use that's being taxed.)

(D) is not the best response,

because it reaches the right result but for the wrong reason.

If the state were to give federal employees a total tax exemption on the value of the personal use of the car, this would probably *not* be an equal protection violation. That's because the standard would be whether there was a rational relation between the means chosen by the state (exemption) and some legitimate state objective. A court would probably hold that it's rational for a state to conclude that state-federal relations would benefit from this sort of exemption.

Answer 28

(D) is the best response,

because there is no right to a hearing unless one has been deprived of liberty or property, and John hasn't been so deprived.

A person who is affected by governmental action doesn't thereby automatically get the right to a hearing. Instead, only those whose "property" or "liberty" are being affected have the right to due process (and even then, these due process rights won't necessarily entail the right to a formal hearing).

Here, nothing the city has ever done has created in John a property interest in being free of additional taxi competition. Indeed, the facts demonstrate the contrary — there is no limit to the number of licenses that may be issued, and the only required qualifications are driving ability and geographic knowledge. So John has not been deprived of a property (or liberty) interest, and the court will never even reach the issue of what procedures (such as a hearing) were due to him — none were.

(A) is not the best response,

because this is not a correct statement of who gets the protection of due process.

For the reason stated in Choice (D) above, this Choice is exactly wrong about when the due process clause applies — only those deprived of "property" or "liberty" by the government, not all those "adversely affected by government action," have a due process interest.

(B) is not the best response,

because John never had a right to a hearing at all.

For the reasons stated in Choice (D), John had no due process rights that were implicated here, and therefore had no right to a hearing. Thus the court would never reach the issue of who may decide whether he gets a hearing

(C) is not the best response,

because the fact that John once got the benefit of the ordinance has nothing to do with whether his due process rights have been violated here.

The licensing ordinance might have been written in such a way that John would get a property interest in not having new competition. (For instance, this would probably be so if the ordinance set the number of licenses at a fixed total, and charged a substantial fee for each one.) In that event, John would be permitted to assert his due process claim even though he originally benefitted from the same ordinance. The reason John loses is because he had no property interest in being free from additional competition (see the discussion of Choice (D) above), not because he previously benefitted from the ordinance.

Answer 29

(A) is the best response,

because any attempt by Congress to force a state to enact particular legislation would violate the Tenth Amendment.

Although the Tenth Amendment today doesn't pose much of a limit for Congress, it does prevent Congress (or any other part of the federal government) from compelling a state to enact or enforce a particular law. *N.Y. v. U.S.* (1992). That's what Congress has purported to do here, by requiring each state to make certain conduct a crime. (Congress could use the power of the purse to coerce states into acting, by denying federal funds to states that don't pass the statute. But that's not what Congress is doing here.)

(B) is not the best response,

because banning controlled substances that had moved in interstate commerce *does* have a sufficient nexus with commerce to allow congressional regulation.

The examiners are trying to trick you by making you thinking that *U.S. v. Lopez* (1995) (Congress can't ban guns near schools, because there's not enough connection to interstate commerce) applies. But the federal statute in *Lopez* banned *all* guns — even those that had never travelled in interstate commerce. Had it banned just guns that had moved in interstate commerce, the result in *Lopez* would almost certainly have been different. So here, a direct ban by Congress on the sale or use near schools of drugs that had moved

in commerce would be enough to bring the statute within the commerce power.

The problem is that Congress hasn't done the banning directly — instead, it's tried to force the states to do it. And that violates the Tenth Amendment, as described in Choice (A).

(C) is not the best response,

because the jurisdictional statement doesn't take care of the fact that Congress is unconstitutionally ordering states to enact statutes.

If Congress were passing a statute that made the drug-related conduct here a federal crime, the jurisdictional statute would indeed be enough create a sufficient nexus to interstate commerce. (See the discussion of *Lopez* in Choice (B) above.)

But that's not what Congress is doing. Instead, it's ordering states to enact statutes containing the jurisdictional provision. And with or without jurisdictional provisions, ordering a state to enact a statute violates the Tenth Amendment, as discussed in Choice (A).

(D) is not the best response,

because it ignores the Tenth Amendment problem, and also incorrectly asserts that there is a "general welfare clause."

First, as discussed in Choice (A), Congress violates the Tenth Amendment when it orders a state to enact a particular statute. Second, Choice (D) suggests that there is an independent Congressional power to act for "the general welfare." This is not so — there's a power to "*tax and spend* ... for the general welfare," but that's not what's at issue here (because Congress is doing pure regulating, not taxing or spending). So this choice is wrong in both result and reasoning, and the reasoning is wrong in two different respects.

Answer 30

(A) is the best response,

because no lower court has yet reached a decision in the case.

The best argument in support of the EPA's request that the Supreme Court dismiss the petition on jurisdictional grounds is that the case is within neither the Court's original or appellate jurisdiction.

Original jurisdiction: Under Article III, §2, the Supreme Court has original jurisdiction in (and only in) all cases affecting Ambassadors, other public Ministers and Counsels, and those in which a State shall be a party. The case here does not involve any of those categories, so original jurisdiction does not exist.

Appellate jurisdiction: Article III, §2 also provides that in those cases arising under the Constitution, by an Act of Congress, or by treaty, the Supreme Court shall have appellate jurisdiction. It's true that, as the facts tell us, a federal statute gives the Supreme Court the authority to review any case filed in a United States Court of Appeals, even though that case has not yet been decided by the court of appeals. But that statute presumes a decision by a lower court, which hasn't yet happened in this case. Indeed, for the Supreme Court to hear this case, in the absence of any lower-court decision, would not be an exercise of "appellate" jurisdiction at all — there is no decision being appealed from.

(B) is not the best response,

because the answer is an inaccurate statement of what Article III provides.

Article III, §2 provides that in addition to cases arising under the Constitution, the Supreme Court shall have appellate jurisdiction in cases arising relating to an Act of Congress or a treaty. So insofar as this choice says that the Supreme Court's appellate jurisdiction extends "only" to cases "arising under the Constitution" (and implies that there is no jurisdiction over cases arising under federal statutes), it's flatly wrong.

(C) is not the best response,

because the answer is an inaccurate statement of the law.

Article III, §2 limits federal court jurisdiction to "cases" and "controversies" and so the federal courts may not issue "advisory opinions" (i.e., opinions giving advice about particular legislative or executive action, when no party is before the court who has suffered or imminently faces specific injury). Federal courts can, however, issue *declaratory judgments*, where the court is not requested to award damages or an injunction, but rather is requested to state what the legal effect would be of proposed conduct by one of the parties. Because an action for declaratory judgment would be within federal courts' Article III power, yet such an action would not be an "action to enforce the rule," Choice (C) is wrong.

(D) is not the best response,

because the answer is an inaccurate statement of the law.

Choice (D) states that all federal cases not falling with the Supreme Court's original jurisdiction must be "initiated by an action in federal district court." This is simply an untrue statement. For example, the Court may hear a case originally filed with and heard by a U.S. Court of Appeals, if Congress authorizes this arrangement. So Choice (D) is simply an incorrect statement of the law.

Answer 31

(A) is the best response,

because it identifies most closely the situation in which "state action" is involved.

The question here asks you for the facts under which the statute is most likely to be constitutional. To determine this, you have to identify first why the statute might not be constitutional. The problem is the "state

action" requirement of the Fourteenth Amendment. That is, the Fourteenth Amendment only addresses *governmental* action. Specifically, the Equal Protection Clause forbids governmental discrimination, not private discrimination. Thus, the correct response would have to involve "state action" in promoting discrimination.

That's what option A does. A public school is an agency of the state, and as such any action taken by it would be considered "state action." Here, as an agent of the school, a teacher's discriminating on the basis of race would be considered an Equal Protection violation. Jones's actions, in threatening the teacher with violence if she didn't comply, would satisfy the "interference" part of the statute. As a result, the statute could be applied to Jones, making A the best response.

(B) is not the best response,

because the acts Jones encouraged would not involve "state action."

The question here asks you for the facts under which the statute is most likely to be constitutional. To determine this, you have to identify first why the statute might not be constitutional. The problem is the "state action" requirement of the Fourteenth Amendment. That is, the Fourteenth Amendment only addresses *governmental* action. Specifically, the Equal Protection Clause forbids governmental discrimination, not private discrimination. Thus, the correct response would have to involve "state action" in promoting discrimination.

Here, the actions of the black students, in refraining from attending a private school, would not be considered "state action." Thus, Jones's actions, in threatening them with violence if they attended class, would not be promoting an Equal Protection violation, and the statute would not apply. Since B doesn't recognize this, it's not the best response.

(C) is not the best response,

because the acts Jones encouraged would not involve "state action."

The question here asks you for the facts under which the statute is most likely to be constitutional. To determine this, you have to identify first why the statute might not be constitutional. The problem is the "state action" requirement of the Fourteenth Amendment. That is, the Fourteenth Amendment only addresses *governmental* action. Specifically, the Equal Protection Clause forbids governmental discrimination, not private discrimination. Thus, the correct response would have to involve "state action" in promoting discrimination.

Here, the bus driver works for a local church. The actions of the church would not constitute "state action." Thus, Jones's coercing the bus driver into refusing to allow black children onto his bus would not be "interfering" with a right conferred by the Equal Protection Clause. Since C doesn't recognize this, it's not the best response.

(D) is not the best response,

because the acts Jones encouraged would not involve "state action."

The question here asks you for the facts under which the statute is most likely to be constitutional. To determine this, you have to identify first why the statute might not be constitutional. The problem is the "state action" requirement of the Fourteenth Amendment. That is, the Fourteenth Amendment only addresses *governmental* action. Specifically, the Equal Protection Clause forbids governmental discrimination, not private discrimination. Thus, the correct response would have to involve "state action" in promoting discrimination.

Here, the official Jones coerced was a *federal* official, not a *state* official, and the Equal Protection Clause only applies to states, not the federal government. Thus, any action taken by the federal official could not be considered an Equal Protection violation. Had the facts been different, and the official was a state official instead of a federal official, the "state action" requirement would be met, and Jones could be convicted under the statute. However, since the "state action" requirement is missing, D is not the best response.

Answer 32

(B) is the best response,

because the Commission is a temporary agency set up for a specific purpose.

An advisory commission, such as the one here, comes within the President's executive powers. Congress has the right to earmark specified federal monies to be spent as the President shall determine. Therefore, nothing about this arrangement violates any Constitutional provision.

(A) is not the best response,

because it is not a correct statement of law.

The President does not have "plenary power to provide for the health, safety, and welfare of the people..." For instance, the President does not have power to spend federal money for what he determines to be the health needs of "the people." This answer ignores both the source of the president's authority (the executive power, that is, the power to see that the laws are carried out) and the need for all funding to be appropriated by Congress.

(C) is not the best response,

because it incorrectly states the effect of the Tenth Amendment.

The Tenth Amendment states that the powers not delegated to the federal government by the Constitution, and not prohibited to the states, are reserved to the states. The Tenth Amendment has relatively little force today as a limit on federal power. (About the only force it has as a limit on federal powers is to prevent Congress from directly forcing the states to enact or enforce federal policies).

The Amendment does not mean that the federal government may not exercise power over a "traditional state function." So the fact that vaccination has traditionally been a function handled by the states does not mean that the Tenth Amendment bars the federal government from taking action with respect to vaccinations.

(D) is not the best response,

because Congress does not need to authorize the creation of a temporary commission.

An Advisory Commission on Vaccination is not a new federal agency. It is an advisory group, set up for a specific purpose and having a temporary existence. The President does not need Congressional approval to create such an organization. Nor has Congress prohibited its creation, because as the facts state no federal statute authorizes or prohibits this action.

Answer 33

(C) is the best response,

because there is no constitutional principle requiring the government to divulge information it possesses.

The suit here is claiming that some constitutional principle (presumably the First Amendment) is violated by the statute. This amounts to a claim that government is sometimes required by the First Amendment to divulge information that it possesses. However, the Supreme Court has never squarely found that the First Amendment ever requires the release of government information.

The First Amendment does, however, prevent government from imposing a "prior restraint," that is, from prohibiting private individuals (including the media) from publishing information that they possess, except in the most extraordinary instances (e.g., troop movements in time of war). So if the statute did prohibit newspapers from publishing information it already possessed about the businessman (or about the prosecution's decision not to prosecute him), it would almost certainly violate this prohibition on prior restraints.

Since Choice (C) is the only choice that distinguishes between compelling the disclosure by the government of information it holds, and publication of privately-held information that originally comes from government records, it is the correct choice.

(A) is not the best response,

because the answer doesn't address the issue the court would address.

This choice sounds as though it would be relevant in defending against an equal protection claim, but it is irrelevant to defending against a First Amendment claim. For instance, if the statute prohibited newspapers from publishing the name of any person prosecuted and not convicted, the fact that it treated those who are acquitted the same as those against whom filed charges are dropped would be completely irrelevant — the statute would still be a prior restraint that violated the First Amendment.

(B) is not the best response,

because even if the press doesn't have greater rights than citizens generally, this would not be a defense against the claim here.

First, it's not clear whether the press has greater rights than those of citizens generally — the Court has never definitively decided this.

Second, even if the press didn't have greater rights, that wouldn't necessarily help the state defend the statute. For instance, a court might hold that anyone — newspaper or private citizen — had the right to compel disclosure of this information. So the argument is irrelevant to the attack that's been made here.

(D) is not the best response,

because the answer incorrectly states the applicable law.

When the choice says that the state may "seal official records," it's implying that the state could make it a crime to print the contents of those records regardless of the legislature's reasons. This is clearly not the case — if the state prohibited newspapers, say, from printing the contents of state records of which the newspaper gained possession, this would be an invalid prior restraint unless it were strictly necessary to achieve a compelling governmental purpose. So on this reading of the word "seal," this choice simply states an incorrect legal principle.

If the choice, when it refers to the state's right to "seal" records, merely means that the state may "refuse to disclose the contents of" the records, the question is closer. But some Court cases (e.g., *Richmond Newspapers v. Virginia* (1989)) seem to suggest that the press may have some limited right of access to certain types of government-controlled information (e.g., contents of certain trials), if the state interest in non-disclosure is weak. So this choice, by indicating that no legislative objective is too weak to prevail, is probably wrong.

Answer 34

(B) is the best response,

because the "substantial effect on commerce" rationale has been accepted by the Supreme Court.

In *Wickard v. Filburn* (1942), the Court held that Congress could regulate even the consumption of wheat on the farm where it was produced, because such intrastate uses had a substantial effect on interstate commerce. The same principle would apply here — a local sale or rental of property would indirectly affect interstate commerce.

(A) is not the best response

because Congress has no power to regulate for the general welfare.

Congress does not have the power to enact regulatory legislation for the general welfare. Art. I § 8 gives Congress the power to *"tax and spend"* for the general welfare, but that's not what's happening here — what's happening here is pure regulation. (By the way, this "general welfare" wrong answer is perhaps the single most frequently-sprung trap in the history of MBE Con Law questions. Rare is the MBE that doesn't use it at least once.)

(C) is not the best response,

because the Thirteenth Amendment cannot be used to protect against sexual-orientation discrimination.

The Thirteenth Amendment expressly protects against slavery. Its enforcement clause has been interpreted to allow Congress to legislate against the "badges of slavery," and to prohibit even private actors from practicing racial discrimination. The Court has never held that the Amendment may be used outside of the racial area. It's possible (though not certain) that Congress could rely on the Amendment to prohibit private discrimination on the basis of ethnicity and national origin in addition to race, since these are similar to racial discrimination. But it's very unlikely that the Amendment can be used to bar private discrimination on grounds so distinct from slavery as sexual orientation.

{D) is not the best response,

because it is a misstatement of law, in that the Fourteenth Amendment does not prohibit private actors from engaging in discrimination (whether irrational or not).

The Equal Protection clause of the Fourteenth Amendment bars discrimination when there is state action. When a purely private actor practices discrimination, Congress' Fourteenth Amendment § 5 remedial powers do not permit it to prohibit that discrimination. So although Congress could probably rely on its § 5 powers to prohibit public entities (states and cities, for instance) from discriminating on grounds of sexual orientation, it cannot do so with respect to purely private discrimination. See *U.S. v. Morrison* (2000) (Congress can't use its 14th Amendment § 5 powers to let victims of gender-motivated violent crimes sue in federal court.)

Answer 35

(C) is the best response,

because the Thirteenth Amendment addresses *private acts.*

Here, Congress is trying to eliminate private discrimination through this statute. That's the central obstacle to the validity of the statute, because the most likely source of constitutionality for statutes eliminating discrimination is the Fourteenth Amendment, which, problematically, only eliminates *state action* in promoting or authorizing discrimination. The Thirteenth Amendment is, in fact, the only constitutional provision explicitly limiting private acts by individuals. Under it, if Congress could rationally determine that the conduct it is prohibiting imposes a "badge or incident" of slavery on a victim, the statute will be valid. *Jones v. Alfred H. Mayer Co.* (1968). This provision is exceptionally broad, giving Congress the power to prohibit virtually all racial discrimination against blacks, and whites, for that matter.

Here, the statute will serve to eliminate racial discrimination against blacks, and Congress could rationally determine that when people conspire to deny blacks housing, employment, or education due to their race, this constitutes a "badge or incident" of slavery. As a result, the statute will be valid, and the Thirteenth Amendment will be the source of the validity. Since C recognizes this, it's the best response.

(A) is not the best response,

because the Contracts Clause is a limitation on the states, not a source of power for the federal government.

The Contracts Clause, Article I, §10 of the Constitution, prohibits states from passing any law which impairs the obligations of existing contracts. A law "impairs" contracts by substantially invalidating, releasing, or extinguishing obligations under a contract, or, alternatively, derogating rights under a contract that are substantial.

Here, there is a federal law involved, not a state law. Furthermore, the question is asking you for a basis on which the statute is *justifiable,* not one on which it is unconstitutional. As a result, the Contracts Clause cannot be the right answer, making A not the best response.

(B) is not the best response,

because the Welfare Clause could not be a source of constitutionality for this statute.

The Welfare Clause, Article I, §8 of the Constitution, empowers Congress to collect taxes and spend money and to provide for the general welfare, and to make all laws which are necessary and proper to implement those powers. The statute here is designed to eliminate discrimination through regulating behavior. It doesn't address taxing or spending, so the Welfare Clause cannot be a source of power for it. Since B doesn't recognize this, it's not the best response.

(D) is not the best response,

because the Fourteenth Amendment doesn't address *private* discrimination.

Under the Fourteenth Amendment, the states are forbidden from, among other things, discriminating on the basis of race. If a state does so, an Equal Protection violation exists. However, one of the requirements of the Fourteenth Amendment is *state action.* Here, on the other hand, Congress is trying to eliminate *private*

discrimination, which is not covered by the Fourteenth Amendment. Furthermore, the Fourteenth Amendment Equal Protection Clause only addresses *state* action, not *federal* action. As a result, the Fourteenth Amendment is not a good source of constitutionality for the statute, making D not the best response.

Answer 36

(B) is the best response,

because Congress cannot constitutionally designate two members of this board.

The President, not Congress, is given the power to appoint federal officers. Article 2, §2, the "Appointments Clause," provides that the President shall "nominate, and by and with the Advice and Consent of the Senate, shall appoint Ambassadors ... Judges of the Supreme Court, and all other Officers of the United States..." A key aspect of the Appointments Clause is that *Congress itself may not make any appointments of federal officials who exercise executive power.*

Although the statute here endowed the board with broad regulatory powers over the operations of the securities, banking and commodities industries, it also gave the board the power to issue rules with the force of law. This is an executive power — that is, the power to see that the laws are carried out. Under similar facts, the Court has held that where the tasks performed by the board are executive in nature, Article 2, §2 means that these tasks can only be exercised by Officers of the United States who are appointed by the President. *Buckley v. Valeo* (1976). So here, the fact that two of the board's five members were designated by Congress violates the Appointments Clause.

(A) is not the best response,

because it is the President, not Congress, that has the power of appointment.

Congress may make its own appointments of persons to exercise powers that are essentially of an investigative and informative nature. But where the appointee's powers are essentially rule-making rather than investigative, this is an executive function, not a legislative function. Consequently, as described in Choice (B) above, it is the President, not Congress, that has the right of appointment. So this choice is correct that the statute is unconstitutional on account of separation-of-powers problems, but incorrect about what those problems are.

(C) is not the best response,

because although the Necessary and Proper Clause gives the Congress the power to create the board, it does not give Congress the power to appoint the board's members.

It's true that where Congress is exercising one of its enumerated powers, it may enact any law which is "necessary and proper for carrying into execution" that power. So Congress can regulate the securities and banking industries pursuant to its commerce power, and it can enact laws to carry out that regulation. But as explained in the discussion of Choice (B), the Appointments Clause means that the power to appoint members of the board (who are "federal officers") falls to the President under the Appointments Clause. Nothing in the Necessary and Proper Clause overcomes this Appointments-Clause problem.

(D) is not the best response,

because (1) it ignores the Appointments-Clause problem described in the discussion of Choice (B); and (2) it falsely indicates that Congress has a free-standing power to pass laws that are for the "general welfare."

As to (1), the Appointments Clause, as interpreted by the Court, means that "Officers of the United States" must be appointed by the President, not Congress. The board members here are federal officers, so the fact that two of them are appointed by Congress violates this Clause.

As to (2), the General Welfare clause, Article 1, §8, states that Congress shall have the power to lay and collect taxes, to pay debts and to provide for the common defense and the general welfare. This clause gives Congress the substantive power to tax and appropriate money. But it does not confer on Congress a free-standing power to regulate to achieve the general welfare. So Congress' General Welfare power is irrelevant to the constitutionality of the regulatory statute here.

Answer 37

(A) is the best response,

because the rule would not survive strict scrutiny.

Equal protection requires race-based affirmative action plans to be subject to the same strict scrutiny as are governmental actions that intentionally discriminate against racial minorities. Any governmental action that is explicitly race-based must be "necessary" to achieve a "compelling" governmental interest. Minority set-aside programs enacted by a city or state will be subjected to strict scrutiny and will usually be found unconstitutional on equal protection grounds. *Richmond v. J.A. Croson Co.* (1989).

The set-aside plan here is unconstitutional. Although the Water District claims to be pursuing the objective of overcoming past discrimination, *Richmond v. Croson* establishes that a desire to overcome broad historical "societal" discrimination is *not* a compelling governmental interest. Therefore, the fact that racial minorities have been discriminated against "in this country" does not suffice (and the facts make it very clear that the community to be served by the Water District has never discriminated).

(B) is not the best response,

because the impairment-of-contracts clause has nothing to do with the set-aside here.

The obligation-of-contracts clause protects solely against governmental actions that have the effect of interfering with contractual obligations that were undertaken *before the governmental action.* Nothing in the clause prevents government from making it harder for people to make a certain kind of contract after the enactment. Since the set-aside here would apply only to hiring and contracting occurring after the set-aside was enacted, the contracts clause would have no application to these facts.

(C) is not the best response,

because racial set-asides have to pass a strict scrutiny test.

Equal protection requires race-based affirmative action plans to be subject to the same strict scrutiny as are governmental actions that intentionally discriminate against racial minorities. (See the discussion in Choice (A)). In other words, the Supreme Court takes the view that when minority groups are given express racially-oriented preferences, they are not receiving "equal protection" — they are instead receiving a preference, one which may well constitute a denial of equal protection to the members of the non-favored (majority) racial group. Here, because the government entity giving the preference has not been shown to have discriminated in the past, the preference would fail the required strict scrutiny. So Choice (C) is wrong both as to the theory it espouses and as to the result it predicts.

(D) is not the best response,

because state actions, whether involving governmental or proprietary functions, are reviewed under strict scrutiny.

The examiners are hoping you'll think about the equal protection voting cases (e.g., *Ball v. James* (1981)) holding that where a governmental unit has a limited purpose which disproportionately affect only one group (e.g., landowners), the right to vote for positions governing that unit may be limited to the affected group. So here, the right to elect members of the Water District's governing board may indeed be limited to landowners.

But once the District is formed, it can't give out "goodies" (staff positions and private-sector contracts) on a racially-discriminatory basis unless the scheme survives strict scrutiny. For the reasons described in Choice (C), the scheme here would fail that strict scrutiny. The fact that this was a special-purpose body whose governors could be elected solely by landowners doesn't change this result in the slightest.

Answer 38

(B) is the best response,

because it recognizes the central reason the statute will be valid: It's within Congress's commerce power.

In order for a Congressional statute to be valid, it must be enacted within Congress's enumerated powers, or it must be necessary and proper to effectuate an enumerated power. Here, the most likely source of power for the statute is the Commerce Clause, Article I, §8, clause 3. The Commerce Clause gives Congress exceptionally broad power to regulate interstate commerce; under the "affectation doctrine," in fact, Congress can regulate any activity that has any appreciable direct or indirect effect on interstate commerce. Here, Congress could rationally believe that the cumulative effect of many stolen bicycles travelling interstate could impact interstate commerce. As such, its federal bicycle registry would be valid. Wickard v. Filburn (1942). In fact, what this question indicates is that Congress's commerce power is potentially all-pervasive. Since option B recognizes this, it's the best response.

(A) is not the best response,

because Congress's general welfare power could not be a source of authority to pass the bicycle registration law.

In order for a Congressional statute to be valid, it must be enacted within Congress's enumerated powers, or it must be necessary and proper to effectuate an enumerated power. Option A suggests that the source of power for the bicycle statute should be the Welfare Clause, Article I, §8 of the Constitution. However, the Welfare Clause only empowers Congress to *collect taxes and spend money* for the general welfare. Here, the statute is regulatory, and doesn't involve money at all. Thus, it can't be based on the Welfare Power. Since A doesn't recognize this, it's not the best response.

(C) is not the best response,

because it doesn't properly state the scope of Congress's power over interstate commerce.

By suggesting that most bicycles stay in-state, option C is implying that Congress's power over interstate commerce could not be a source of power for the statute, since the "interstate" element is missing. However, this misstates the Commerce Power. Under the "affectation doctrine," Congress can regulate any activity that has any appreciable direct or indirect effect on interstate commerce. Even where an individual activity – here, a stolen bicycle – may not seem to have any effect whatsoever on interstate commerce, Congress may still regulate it if the cumulative effect of many stolen bicycles travelling interstate could impact interstate commerce. Thus, it doesn't matter that most stolen bicycles remain in-state, and option C attaches significance to this element that doesn't, in fact, exist. As a result, C is not the best response.

(D) is not the best response,

because it ignores the impact of Congress's commerce power.

In order for a Congressional statute to be valid, it must be enacted within Congress's enumerated pow-

ers, or it must be necessary and proper to effectuate an enumerated power. Here, the most likely source of power for the statute is the Commerce Clause, Article I, §8, clause 3. The Commerce Clause gives Congress exceptionally broad power to regulate interstate commerce; under the "affectation doctrine," in fact, Congress can regulate any activity that has any appreciable direct or indirect effect on interstate commerce. Here, Congress could rationally believe that the cumulative effect of many stolen bicycles travelling interstate could impact interstate commerce. As such, its federal bicycle registry would be valid.

This doesn't mean that the states *couldn't* register bicycles for themselves, as well. However, to the extent that stolen bicycles impact interstate commerce, registering vehicles is not a matter reserved to the states by the Tenth Amendment, since the Tenth Amendment only reserves to the states (or the people) those powers not delegated to the federal government by the Constitution, nor prohibited by it to the states. The Commerce Power is one of Congress's enumerated powers, so it's not reserved to the states under the Tenth Amendment (although states may be able to regulate commerce, depending on the nature of the activity in question, and whether Congress intended that the states be able to regulate the activity). Since option D doesn't recognize this, it's not the best response.

Answer 39

(C) is the best response,

because the state may not, up to the point where the fetus is viable, unduly burden a woman's fundamental right to choose whether to continue the pregnancy.

The Court has held that the right of privacy includes the right of a woman to have an abortion under certain circumstances without undue interference from the state. Up until the time the fetus is viable, a state may adopt regulations protecting the mother's health and the life of the fetus only if the regulation does not impose an undue burden or substantial obstacle to the woman's right to have an abortion. Then, once the fetus becomes viable, the state's interest in the fetus' life can override the woman's right to choose and abortion. *Planned Parenthood v. Casey* (1992).

The fetus is not yet viable in many pregnancies that have gone beyond the first trimester. (Typically, viability occurs late in the second or early in the third trimester.) Since the statute here forbids the mother from ending such a post-first-trimester-but-not-yet-viable pregnancy unless her life or health is in danger, a court would almost certainly hold that the statute "unduly burdens" the mother's fundamental rights.

(A) is not the best response,

because, prior to viability, the state does not have a compelling state interest in preserving fetal life.

Under *Planned Parenthood v. Casey* (1992), a

woman's right to reproductive choice — and to not be "unduly burdened" in the exercise of that reproductive choice — extends beyond the first trimester, all the way to viability. Before viability, the state's interest in fetal life is not compelling. Therefore, Choice (A)'s statement that before viability the state can seek an "equitable balance" between its compelling interest protecting fetal life and the woman's fundamental right to reproductive choice is inconsistent with *Casey*, and thus wrong.

(B) is not the best response,

because the fetus doesn't become a "person" after the first trimester, merely a potential life which the state has an interest in protecting.

Even after the point of viability, the Supreme Court has never said that the fetus is a "person" whose right to life is protected by the due process clause. Furthermore, even if the Court had said this, Choice (B) would still be wrong, because that choice falsely states that the fetus is a person where the first trimester is over but viability not yet reached. (As applied to such cases the statute is in fact *un*constitutional, because the woman's right to abort a non-viable fetus can't be "unduly burdened," and an outright prohibition of pre-viability abortions not needed to protect that woman's life or health would certainly be an undue burden.)

(D) is not the best response,

because the answer is based on equal protection analysis, rather than the proper substantive-due-process analysis.

The Court has never used equal protection analysis in abortion cases. If it did, the statute here would probably be constitutional, because it would not be irrational for a state to decide that abortions after the end of the first trimester harm the state's interest in protecting fetal life more than those that occur during the first trimester. The essence of the Court's analysis of abortion rights has always been substantive due process, not equal protection. And, under that substantive due process analysis, it's the existence of a fundamental right to reproductive choice prior to viability that is the focus of the analysis.

Answer 40

(D) is the best response,

because it correctly identifies that Congress cannot enlarge federal court jurisdiction to include advisory opinions.

Article III, §2 of the Constitution gives Congress the power to create federal courts beneath the Supreme Court, and also the power to determine the jurisdiction of those courts. However, there is a limitation on this power — Congress cannot expand federal court jurisdiction beyond the boundaries prescribed by Article III. The "case and controversy" requirement is one such boundary. Federal courts can only render opinions

where there is an actual controversy – they cannot offer advisory opinions. That is, the matter in controversy must be definite and concrete, touching the legal relations of parties having adverse legal interests, and – here's the problem here – there must be a real and substantial controversy *capable of specific relief through a decree of a conclusive character*. Aetna Life Insurance Co. v. Haworth (1937).

Here, an advisory opinion is exactly what the statute calls for. The federal courts are not being used to resolve disputes – rather, they are rendering opinions which will be taken under advisement by the administrator of the federal agency which is dispersing the funds in question. Such advisory opinions are prohibited, and since option D recognizes this, it's the best response.

(A) is not the best response,

because it fails to recognize that the statute expands federal court jurisdiction beyond the bounds of Article III, and thus is invalid.

Article III, §2 of the Constitution gives Congress the power to create federal courts beneath the Supreme Court, and also the power to determine the jurisdiction of those courts. As option A implicitly recognizes, one of the bases of federal court jurisdiction is "federal question" jurisdiction – that is, cases which arise under the Constitution, or a federal law or treaty. Where federal grant-in-aid funds are in question, "federal question" jurisdiction would, in fact, exist. However, this *alone* doesn't determine if the federal court can hear the case. For instance, the plaintiff must have standing to present the claim in question, and there must be a "case or controversy." This is where option A falls down, because the statute here improperly authorizes federal courts to render advisory opinions. Under this statute, the federal courts are not being used to resolve disputes – rather, they are rendering opinions which will be taken under advisement by the administrator of the federal agency which is dispersing the funds in question. Since option A doesn't recognize that this makes the statute invalid, it's not the best response.

(B) is not the best response,

because it misstates the law.

Congress has the power to legislate, and this power includes the power to decide how federal funds will be spent. The President has the power to execute such appropriations. However, the power to resolve disputes about how funds are distributed would not, contrary to what option B suggests, give Congress the power to use federal courts as tribunals. While Congress can set up tribunals to resolve disputes, it cannot use Article III courts for this purpose. To do so would require federal courts to render advisory opinions, which is something prohibited by Article III. Since option B doesn't recognize this, it's not the best response.

(C) is not the best response,

because the Eleventh Amendment would not bar suits under this statute.

The Eleventh Amendment, as a general matter, bars a citizen from suing a state in federal court without that state's consent. In general, the only suits that are prohibited are those which would require a federal court to award money damages for past conduct, where the damages will be payable from the state treasury.

Here, the lawsuits covered by the statute are between states and the federal government. The Eleventh Amendment does *not* bar federal court suits by the federal government against the states. Thus, the statute here cannot be unconstitutional due to operation of the Eleventh Amendment. Instead, what makes this statute unconstitutional is that it authorizes federal courts to render advisory opinions, which they are prohibited from doing under Article III of the Constitution. Since option C doesn't recognize the correct basis for the statute's unconstitutionality, it's not the best response.

Answer 41

(C) is the best response,

because it recognizes the central reason for dismissing the suit: It involves a nonjusticiable issue.

There are several limitations on the jurisdiction of federal courts. For instance, the plaintiff must have standing to press his claim, there must be some basis for federal court jurisdiction (e.g., diversity, federal question), there must be a "case or controversy," and – the issue that's involved here – a "political question" cannot be presented.

A "political question" is one which the Constitution commits to another governmental branch, which the judicial process is inherently incapable of resolving and enforcing. These are the criteria for determining political questions:

1. A "textually demonstrable" constitutional commitment of the issue to the political branches;
2. Lack of manageable standards for judicial resolution;
3. A need for finality in the action of the political branches; and
4. Difficulty or impossibility of devising effective judicial remedies.

Foreign relations is a classic source of "political questions." Congress and the President control foreign affairs exclusively, and the nature of foreign affairs is such that the judiciary cannot intrude. Here, Dunn is seeking to forbid the President from recognizing Ruritania, due to its totalitarian government. This is a purely political question, and as such the court should dismiss the suit. Since C recognizes this, it's the best response.

(A) is not the best response,

because Dunn *does* have standing to bring the action.

In order to press a claim, a plaintiff requires standing. Standing requires that the action challenged must have caused, or is imminently likely to cause, an injury to the party seeking review. Here, if the President recognizes Ruritania (which he is empowered to do), Dunn's contract with the Department of Commerce will terminate.Thus, Dunn is imminently likely to suffer an injury due to the action he's challenging, and he will have standing on that basis. Since A doesn't recognize this, it's not the best response.

(B) is not the best response,

because there *is* adversity between the parties.

Here, Dunn is bringing suit in federal court. The federal court requirements for jurisdiction, found in Article III of the Constitution, include the requirement that the federal courts can only hear "cases and controversies." One element of a "case and controversy" is that the parties must have adverse legal interests. Thus, B is correct in implying that adversity is a requirement of a federal court suit – but it's not correct in stating that there's no adversity here. The President wants to recognize Ruritania, and Dunn doesn't want him to recognize Ruritania. Thus, it can't be the lack of adversity that makes the suit improper. Rather, it's the fact that the conduct of foreign relations is the basis of the suit, and this is a nonjusticiable "political question" that will require that the suit be dismissed. Since B doesn't recognize that adversity exists here, and it ignores the real reason for dismissing the suit, it's not the best response.

(D) is not the best response,

because the federal court will not hear the case on its merits.

There are several limitations on the jurisdiction of federal courts. For instance, the plaintiff must have standing to press his claim, there must be some basis for federal court jurisdiction (e.g., diversity, federal question), there must be a "case or controversy," and – the issue that's involved here – a "political question" cannot be presented.

A "political question" is one which the Constitution commits to another governmental branch, which the judicial process is inherently incapable of resolving and enforcing. These are the criteria for determining political questions:

1. A "textually demonstrable" constitutional commitment of the issue to the political branches;
2. Lack of manageable standards for judicial resolution;
3. A need for finality in the action of the political branches; and
4. Difficulty or impossibility of devising effective judicial remedies.

Foreign relations is a classic source of "political questions." Congress and the President control foreign affairs exclusively, and the nature of foreign affairs is such that the judiciary cannot intrude. Here, Dunn is asking the court to forbid the President from recognizing Ruritania. This is a purely political question, and as such the court should dismiss the suit. Since D doesn't recognize this, it's not the best response.

Answer 42

(B) is the best response,

because free exercise rights must yield to a rational and generally-applicable law even if that law proscribes conduct required by religion.

This case is governed by *Employment Div. v. Smith* (1990), in which the Court held that "the right of free exercise does not relieve an individual of the obligation to comply with a *valid and neutral law of general applicability* on the ground that the law proscribes ... conduct that his religion prescribes." Here, the law states that "there must be an autopsy" (in certain cases), and the Longs claim that their religion prohibits autopsies. So *Smith* applies: we have a "valid and neutral law of general applicability" (i.e., a law that's not motivated by anti-religious bias, that applies to all cases of non-natural death, and that's rationally related to the legitimate state purpose of detecting illegal activity). That law is proscribing certain conduct (refusing an autopsy), and it's applicable to conduct that the plaintiff's religion prescribes, or requires (refusing an autopsy). So *Smith* requires that the law be enforced notwithstanding the Longs' objection, even though the effect would be to impair their free exercise of their religion.

(A) is not the best response,

because while the statute is constitutional, it is not constitutional for the reason stated in this choice.

It's in a sense true that a "dead individual is not a person protected by the due process clause..." But the Longs' claim is not based on their son's due process rights, but on their own free-exercise rights (as made applicable to the states through the Fourteenth Amendment's due process clause). So the fact that the son has no relevant rights is irrelevant. Instead, the statute is constitutional for the reason discussed in Choice (B).

(C) is not the best response,

because strict scrutiny is not the appropriate standard for the statute here.

Employment Div. v. Smith (1990) says that where a valid generally-applicable statute requires certain conduct, the statute must be obeyed even by a person whose religion proscribes that conduct. So the Court does not strictly scrutinize the statute, as this choice implies that it should. Instead, the Court gives just the lowest-level mere-rationality review, which the statute here easily passes.

(D) is not the best response,

because mid-level review is not the appropriate standard for the statute here.

Employment Div. v. Smith (1990) says that where a valid generally-applicable statute requires certain conduct, the statute must be obeyed even by a person whose religion proscribes that conduct. So the Court does not give mid-level review to the statute, as this choice implies that it should. Instead, the Court gives just the lowest-level mere-rationality review, which the statute here easily passes.

Answer 43

(C) is the best response,

because access to the ballot is protected by the Equal Protection clause of the Fourteenth Amendment.

Access to the ballot is protected by the Equal Protection clause of the Fourteenth Amendment. The Court gives relatively deferential review to state burdens on a political party's ability to get on the ballot. However, the Court has sometimes struck down state rules limiting minor parties' ballot access, on the grounds that the rules are so stringent that they give new or minor parties no realistic change of getting on the ballot, and thus violate those parties' (and their members') equal protection rights. See, e.g., *Williams v. Rhodes* (1968). While the equal protection argument might not win, it is the only argument of the four presented that has even a reasonable chance of success.

(A) is not the best response,

because while speech is protected by the First Amendment, access to the ballot is protected by the Fourteenth Amendment.

A political party's argument that it is being denied ballot access might theoretically be based on freedom-of-association concepts. But the Court has tended to decide such ballot-access cases on equal protection grounds, not First Amendment grounds. On the facts here, the state is not saying that people may not get together to join the new political party that is the plaintiff here — the state is merely making it tough for that party to get on the ballot. Since the essence of the party's claim is that the state is preferring the two established parties over newcomer parties, that's really an "unequal treatment" claim, i.e., an equal protection claim.

(B) is not the best response,

because while the members of the new political party are racial minorities, this issue is access to the ballot, not the badges and incidents of slavery.

The Thirteenth Amendment, §1, provides that "neither slavery nor involuntary servitude, except as a punishment for a crime... shall exist in the United States." §2 allows Congress to pass "all laws necessary and proper for abolishing all badges and incidents of slavery." While the members of the new party that is the plaintiff here are racial minorities, the connection between a state's making it hard for a minority-based party to get on the ballot and the institution of slavery would almost certainly be held to be too attenuated to constitute a Thirteenth Amendment violation.

(D) is not the best response,

because the statute's requirements are not a denial of the right to vote.

The Fifteenth Amendment is a limitation on both the states and the federal government. It prohibits either from denying any citizen the right to vote for reasons of race or color. But the state statute here isn't inhibiting anyone's right to vote, it's directed at who may be on the ballot. And traditionally, the Court has viewed ballot-access restrictions as implicating the equal protection clause, not the Fifteenth Amendment right to vote.

Answer 44

(D) is the best response,

because Congress provided clear standards for the contest.

The General Welfare clause, Article 1, §8, states that Congress shall have power to "lay and collect Taxes ... to pay the Debts and provide for the ... general Welfare of the United States." This clause gives Congress the substantive power to tax and spend, limited only by the requirement that the taxing and spending be for the general welfare. Congress may delegate its legislative power as long as the person or body receiving the delegated power is directed to conform to an intelligible principle set forth by Congress.

The statute here is valid under these rules: (1) eradication of drug abuse would contribute to the "general welfare," and the contest is a rational way of using federal funds to generate ideas for doing this (it is exceptionally rare for the Court to conclude that a particular taxing or spending scheme doesn't bear the requisite connection to "the general welfare"); and (2) the contest rules, and the structure for running the contest, are sufficiently specific that the requirement of an "intelligible principle" guiding the delegation would be found to be satisfied.

(A) is not the best response,

because the contest's constitutionality is a simple matter to decide.

The requirement of a justiciable Article III controversy is deemed to carry with it a limitation against the deciding of purely "political questions." The court will leave the resolution of such political questions to the other departments of government. The primary earmarks of a nonjusticiable political question are: (1) the presence of a "textually demonstrable" constitutional commitment of the issue to the political branches (Congress and the executive branch) for resolution; (2) a need for the political branches' decision on the issue to be final, and not subject to judicial second-guessing; (3) a lack of adequate standards for judicial resolution of the issue; and (4) the presence of issues that are too controversial or could involve enforcement problems.

None of these factors are present here. There is no reason why the court cannot quickly determine that the spending here is rationally related to pursuit of the general welfare, and that the guidance given to the contest administrators is reasonably specific.

(B) is not the best response,

because the statute sets out very clear standards.

Congress may delegate its legislative power (here, the spending power) as long as the person or body receiving the delegated power is directed to conform to an intelligible principle set forth by Congress. Here, the guidelines for awarding the prize money appropriated by Congress are very clearly set out in the statute, so there is no problem of inappropriately-vague delegation.

(C) is not the best response,

because the statute is a legitimate use of Congress' power to appropriate funds to end drug abuse.

The General Welfare clause, Article 1, §8, states that Congress shall have power to "lay and collect Taxes ... to pay the Debts and provide for the ... general Welfare of the United States." This clause gives Congress the substantive power to tax and spend, limited only by the requirement that the taxing and spending be reasonably related to the pursuit of the general welfare.

The requirement that the taxing and spending have a rational relation to the attainment of the general welfare has very little "bite" — the Court rarely (if ever) concludes that a particular taxing or spending scheme doesn't bear the requisite connection to "the general welfare." Here, given the size of the drug abuse problem, and the relatively small sum proposed, it's wildly unlikely that the Court would conclude that the relationship between the contest and the elimination of drug abuse is "too tenuous and conjectural" to pass muster.

Answer 45

(B) is the best response,

because the statements were made during the legislative process.

Article 1, §6 states that for any speech or debate in either the House of Representatives or the Senate, members of Congress shall not be questioned in any other place. This is the "Speech and Debate" Clause.

The clause clearly applies to Senator's statement: the statement was made on the floor of the Senate, so it falls within even the most narrowly-defined construction of the Speech and Debate Clause. (The fact that the speech didn't relate to current legislation is irrelevant — as long as the words were spoken on the floor during the session, that's enough.)

With respect to Frank, the clause itself, by its literal terms, seems not to apply. But the Court has held that the clause applies "not only to a Member but also to his aides insofar as the conduct of the latter would be a protected legislative act if performed by the Member himself." *Gravel v. U.S.* (1972). Thus since Senator is covered, so is Frank.

Neither (A), (C) and (D) is the best answer, since each asserts that at least one of the defendants is not covered by the Speech and Debate Clause. Both defendants are in fact covered, as explained in the discussion of Choice (B) above.

Answer 46

(B) is the best response,

because it correctly recognizes that the statute here will be valid under the "rational relation" test.

Here, the statute is a state statute. In order to be valid, a state statute must be enacted within the state's powers (e.g., police powers), it must not improperly burden a person's constitutional rights, and it must not unduly burden interstate commerce.

Here, Paula's claim suggests that the statute is an equal protection violation. Equal protection is triggered by the existence of a classification which determines people's rights. If the classification is "suspect," or determines who may exercise a fundamental right, it's subject to strict scrutiny. Suspect classifications are race and alienage; the fundamental rights are the First Amendment rights, interstate travel, voting, and privacy. Where the statute instead is only economic or social legislation, the "rational relation" test will be used. Here, the statute as applied distinguishes between who may transport snipe traps through Midland: common carriers are not prohibited from carrying snipe traps, and private individuals are. This does not involve a suspect classification or a fundamental right, so it will be subject to the rational relation test. Here, there is a rational basis on which to make the distinction, since it's likely that common carriers would not have Midland as their destination, where a private person quite possibly could. Furthermore, prohibiting common carriers from transporting snipe traps through Midland would be an impermissible burden on interstate commerce, so the state *could not* constitutionally prohibit common carriers from transporting snipe traps. Since option B recognizes that the distinction is constitutional, due to the rational basis for distinguishing common carriers from private individuals, it's the best response.

(A) is not the best response,

because it doesn't address the constitutionality of the statute as applied to Paula.

Here, the statute is a state statute. In order to be valid, a state statute must be enacted within the state's powers (e.g., police powers), it must not improperly burden a person's constitutional rights, and it must not unduly burden interstate commerce.

Here, Paula's claim suggests that the statute is an equal protection violation. Equal protection is triggered by the existence of a classification which determines people's rights. If the classification is "suspect," or

determines who may exercise a fundamental right, it's subject to strict scrutiny. Suspect classifications are race and alienage; the fundamental rights are the First Amendment rights, interstate travel, voting, and privacy. Where the statute instead is only economic or social legislation, the "rational relation" test will be used. Here, the statute as applied distinguishes between who may transport snipe traps through Midland: common carriers are not prohibited from carrying snipe traps, and private individuals are. This does not involve a suspect classification or a fundamental right, so it will be subject to the rational relation test. Here, there is a rational basis on which to make the distinction, since it's likely that common carriers would not have Midland as their destination, where a private person quite possibly could. More importantly, prohibiting common carriers from transporting snipe traps through Midland would be an impermissible burden on interstate commerce, so the state *could not* constitutionally prohibit common carriers from transporting snipe traps. As a result, it's not the lack of permissible reasons why Prentis might have the snipe trap that makes the statute constitutional, but rather the rational reason for distinguishing between common carriers and individuals transporting snipe traps. Since option A doesn't recognize this, it's not the best response.

(C) is not the best response,

because it overstates the level of scrutiny to which the statute will be subject.

Here, the statute is a state statute. In order to be valid, a state statute must be enacted within the state's powers (e.g., police powers), it must not improperly burden a person's constitutional rights, and it must not unduly burden interstate commerce.

Here, Paula's claim suggests that the statute is an equal protection violation. Equal protection is triggered by the existence of a classification which determines people's rights. If the classification is "suspect," or determines who may exercise a fundamental right, it's subject to strict scrutiny. Suspect classifications are race and alienage; the fundamental rights are the First Amendment rights, interstate travel, voting, and privacy. Where the statute instead is only economic or social legislation, the "rational relation" test will be used. Here, the statute as applied distinguishes between who may transport snipe traps through Midland: common carriers are not prohibited from carrying snipe traps, and private individuals are. This does not involve a suspect classification or a fundamental right, so it will be subject to the rational relation test.

If you chose this response, you may have thought that the statute impermissibly burdens private individuals' fundamental right to interstate travel. However, the statute doesn't burden interstate travel, just the transportation of snipe traps. Prentis was free to travel interstate, it's just that she couldn't possess a snipe trap in Midland. As a result, the right to interstate travel would not be called into question. Since the rational basis test would be the appropriate test here, and option C doesn't recognize this, it's not the best response.

(D) is not the best response,

because the statute here doesn't burden the right to interstate travel.

Here, the statute is a state statute. In order to be valid, a state statute must be enacted within the state's powers (e.g., police powers), it must not improperly burden a person's constitutional rights, and it must not unduly burden interstate commerce.

Here, Paula's claim suggests that the statute is an equal protection violation. Equal protection is triggered by the existence of a classification which determines people's rights. If the classification is "suspect," or determines who may exercise a fundamental right, it's subject to strict scrutiny. Suspect classifications are race and alienage; the fundamental rights are the First Amendment rights, interstate travel, voting, and privacy. Where the statute instead is only economic or social legislation, the "rational relation" test will be used. Here, the statute as applied distinguishes between who may transport snipe traps through Midland: common carriers are not prohibited from carrying snipe traps, and private individuals are. This does not involve a suspect classification or a fundamental right, so it will be subject to the rational relation test.

If you chose this response, you may have thought that since the statute burdened Prentis's right to travel through Midland with snipe traps, it unconstitutionally burdened her fundamental right to interstate travel. However, the statute doesn't really burden her right to interstate travel at all. When you're talking about impermissible burdens on interstate travel, you're generally talking about waiting periods before new residents may receive crucial governmental benefits or services. Here, Prentis is free to move in and out of Midland – she just can't have a snipe trap while she's there. Since option D incorrectly states that Prentis's right to interstate travel is burdened by this statute, it's not the best response.

Answer 47

(D) is the best response,

because it recognizes why preemption will not make the state statute invalid.

The doctrine of preemption comes into play when there's a power is held by both the federal government and the states – i.e., the power is "concurrent" – and there's a state law and a federal law on the same subject. In determining whether the federal law "preempts" the state law, the court will determine whether the general intent of the federal statute either authorizes or forbids the state law.

Where preemption is an issue, you must first determine if there's a direct conflict between the state and federal law. If there *is,* then the federal law will take precedence under the Supremacy Clause, Article VI, §2. If there's no direct conflict, you have to determine if Congress intended to "preempt" the entire field in question. To determine this, you examine four factors:

1. The traditional classification of the subject matter, whether historically local or federal;
2. Pervasiveness of the federal regulation;
3. Similarity between state and federal law (the more they coincide, the more likely federal law intended to supersede state law); and
4. The need for uniform national regulation.

As option D correctly recognizes, there's no need to go into the second part of the analysis, because there's no direct conflict between the two statutes. The federal statute addresses the design of snipe traps. This would be a valid federal law, probably under Congress's commerce power. The state law, prohibiting possession of snipe traps, is intended to protect snipe, an endangered species. This would be a valid exercise of Midland's police powers. The federal law is designed to make snipe traps safe (say *that* three times fast); the state law is designed to protect snipe. Since the two laws have very different purposes, there's no conflict, and thus the laws can coexist without the federal law preempting the state law.

Incidentally, note that preemption only comes into play when there's a federal law on the same subject. There's a different rule when a state's discriminates against interstate commerce on a subject on which Congress *hasn't enacted any relevant legislation.* When that's the case, courts judge state regulation of interstate commerce under the Commerce Clause, and will allow state regulation of interstate commerce *only* when Congress expressly authorizes such regulation (although Congress can't authorize states to violate the Equal Protection Clause).

In any case, the preemption doctrine would come into play under these facts due to the existence of both a federal and state law on the same subject; and since option D correctly recognizes that the laws can coexist, it's the best response.

(A) is not the best response,

because it misstates the facts – the two laws do not address the same *specific* subject matter.

The doctrine of preemption comes into play when there's a power is held by both the federal government and the states – i.e., the power is "concurrent" – and there's both a federal law and a state law on the same subject. In determining whether the federal law "preempts" the state law, the court will determine whether the general intent of the federal statute either authorizes or forbids the state law.

Where preemption is an issue, you must first determine if there's a direct conflict between the state and federal law. If there *is,* then the federal law will take precedence under the Supremacy Clause, Article VI, §2. If there's no direct conflict, you have to determine if

Congress intended to "preempt" the entire field in question. To determine this, you examine four factors:

1. The traditional classification of the subject matter, whether historically local or federal;
2. Pervasiveness of the federal regulation;
3. Similarity between state and federal law (the more they coincide, the more likely federal law intended to supersede state law); and
4. The need for uniform national regulation.

Option A incorrectly states that there's a similarity in subject matter. The federal statute addresses the design of snipe traps. This would be a valid federal law, probably under Congress's commerce power. The state law, prohibiting possession of snipe traps, is intended to protect snipe, an endangered species. This would be a valid exercise of Midland's police powers. The federal law is designed to make snipe traps safe (say *that* three times fast); the state law is designed to protect snipe. Since the two laws have very different purposes, there's no conflict, contrary to what option A states. As a result, the laws can coexist, and A is not the best response.

(B) is not the best response,

because it ignores the fact that Congress has passed legislation concerning snipe traps.

The issue here is preemption. The doctrine of preemption comes into play when there's a power is held by both the federal government and the states – i.e., the power is "concurrent" – and there's both a federal law and a state law on the same subject. In determining whether the federal law "preempts" the state law, the court will determine whether the general intent of the federal statute either authorizes or forbids the state law. However, you must first determine if there's any direct conflict between the two laws – if there isn't, the state law can be valid without the federal law authorizing continued state regulation.

If you chose this response, you were thinking of a state's discrimination against interstate commerce when Congress *hasn't enacted any relevant legislation.* When that's the case, courts judge state regulation of interstate commerce under the Commerce Clause, and will allow state regulation of interstate commerce *only* when Congress expressly authorizes such regulation (although Congress can't authorize states to violate the Equal Protection Clause). Thus, if you chose this response, you were thinking of situations where there's no relevant federal legislation. Here, there's a federal statute concerning snipe traps – it addresses the safety of those traps. Since Congress has addressed the area, the doctrine of preemption is triggered. Applying that doctrine to these facts, you find that the state statute will stand, because there's no direct conflict between the two statutes. The federal statute addresses the safety of snipe traps, and the state statute protects snipe themselves. Since option B implicitly states that there's no Congressional legislation in the area, when in fact there is under these facts, B is not the best response.

(C) is not the best response,

because although it arrives at the correct conclusion, it mischaracterizes the power exercised here as an exclusive state power.

Although states have, in general, power over in-state property, the existence of Congressional power permits Congress to regulate certain aspects of in-state property, as well. For instance, although a state has power over in-state property, it could not pass legislation forbidding aliens from owning property, because this would violate the Equal Protection Clause. When both the state and federal government have powers that potentially conflict (as is the case here) preemption becomes an issue. In fact, option C is internally inconsistent, because in an area where a state has exclusive power, there can't be preemption – preemption is only an issue when valid federal and state laws conflict.

Here, the federal statute addresses the design of snipe traps. This would be a valid federal law, probably under Congress's commerce power. The state law, prohibiting possession of snipe traps, is intended to protect snipe, an endangered species. This would be a valid exercise of Midland's police powers. Thus, the issue becomes one of whether or not the federal law preempts the state law. The initial question you must ask is whether there's a direct conflict between the two laws. In fact, there isn't one, because the federal law addresses the safety of snipe traps, whereas the state law focuses on protecting snipe, and isn't at all concerned with the safety of snipe traps. Thus, option C correctly concludes that the federal law will not preempt the state law. However, since it mischaracterizes the regulation here as an exclusive power of the state, it's not the best response.

STRATEGIES AND TACTICS

CONTRACTS

Contracts and Sales questions are alike in every way on the MBE except one — the **source of law** involved. Contracts questions rely on the common law, while Sales questions rely on the UCC. Because of their similarities, we'll address them together here. For simplicity, we'll use "Contracts" to refer to both Contracts and Sales.

OUTLINE OF COVERAGE

You should be familiar with the provisions of Articles I and II of the Uniform Commercial Code and assume that they have been adopted for the purpose of answering Contracts questions on the MBE. As we'll discuss below, approximately 25% of the Contracts questions on the MBE will involve the Uniform Commercial Code.

The following outline of coverage for the Contracts portion of the MBE was adopted by the Bar Examiners for all MBEs given on or after July, 2003. It was designed to clarify what's covered on the Contracts portion of the exam. This is the most up-to-date outline of coverage released by the Bar Examiners, and your substantive study for Contracts should be centered around it.

Here's what you need to know:

I. Formation of Contracts
    A. Mutual assent
        1. Offer and acceptance
        2. Mistake, misunderstanding, misrepresentation, nondisclosure, confidential relationship, fraud, undue influence, and duress
        3. Problems of communication and "battle of the forms"
        4. Indefiniteness or absence of terms
    B. Capacity to contract
    C. Illegality, unconscionably, and public policy
    D. Implied-in-fact contract and quasi-contract
    E. "Pre-contract" obligations based on detrimental reliance
    F. Express and implied warranties in sale-of-goods contracts
II. Consideration
    A. Bargain and exchange
    B. "Adequacy" of consideration: mutuality of obligation, implied promises, and disproportionate exchanges
    C. Modern substitutes for bargain: "moral obligation," detrimental reliance, and statutory substitutes
    D. Modification of contracts: preexisting duties
    E. Compromise and settlement of claims
III. Third-party beneficiary contracts
    A. Intended beneficiaries
    B. Incidental beneficiaries
    C. Impairment or extinguishment of third-party rights by contract modification or mutual rescission
    D. Enforcement by the promisee
IV. Assignment of rights and delegation of duties
V. Statute of frauds
VI. Parol evidence and interpretation
VII. Conditions
    A. Express
    B. Constructive
        1. Conditions of exchange: excuse or suspension by material breach
        2. Immaterial breach and substantial performance

      3. Independent covenants
      4. Constructive conditions of non-prevention, non-hindrance, and affirmative cooperation
   C. Obligations of good faith and fair dealing in performance and enforcement of contracts
   D. Suspension or excuse of conditions by waiver, election, or estoppel
   E. Prospective inability to perform: effect on other party
VIII.Remedies
   A. Total and partial breach of contract
   B. Anticipatory repudiation
   C. Election of substantive rights and remedies
   D. Specific performance; injunction against breach; declaratory judgment
   E. Rescission and reformation
   F. Measure of damages in major types of contract and breach
   G. Consequential damages: causation, certainty, and foreseeability
   H. Liquidated damages and penalties
   I. Restitutionary and reliance recoveries
   J. Remedial rights of defaulting parties
   K. Avoidable consequences and mitigation of damages
IX. Impossibility of performance and frustration of purpose
X. Discharge of contractual duties

WHAT TO EXPECT

There will be 34 questions on Contracts on the MBE. 60% of the questions will cover categories I, VII, and VIII, above (Formation of Contracts, Parol Evidence, and Remedies); the remaining 40% will cover categories II, III, IV, V, VI, IX, and X. There will be questions from each of the roman numeral topics on the exam, but not necessarily from each of the sub-topics.

Important note: Remember that *approximately 25%* of the Contracts questions on each MBE will be based on the Uniform Commercial Code, Articles 1 and 2 (in other words, they'll be Sales questions).

Types of questions

Many Contracts and Sales questions are "series" questions — that is, you'll be given 2-5 questions based on a single set of facts. In addition, you should also be aware that you may be asked many types of contract questions. These include:

    1. Plaintiff's or defendant's best argument or theory for recovery
    2. How contractual terms should be construed (e.g., as conditions)
    3. How to characterize facts (e.g., if certain acts constitute an offer, acceptance, contract)
    4. Whether plaintiff will succeed
    5. Legal effect of additional facts
    6. If court decides for a specified party, the reason why
    7. How a goal could be accomplished (e.g., offer accepted or revoked)
    8. Which of two or three alternatives are correct, or would influence outcome of case.

STUDY STRATEGIES

1. Common law vs. UCC.

Remember the ***distinctions between the common law and the UCC***. For example, look at the subject of contract ***modifications***: At common law, modifications require consideration. Under the UCC, modifications require only good faith. ***Irrevocable offers*** are also different under common law and the UCC. At common law, an offer can be made irrevocable only with consideration — in general, the offeree must pay for the irrevocability and thus create an option contract. Under the UCC, merchants (not non-merchants) can make irrevocable, or "firm," offers without consideration, so long as the offers are in writing and signed.

Another difference to watch for is ***delays***. At common law, a reasonable delay is only a minor breach of contract unless the contract provides that time is of the essence — or unless the breaching party knew, when the contract was created, of some extraordinary fact which made the deadline essential. If time is of the essence, any delay is a major breach (the difference being that, with a minor breach, the other party must perform and sue for damages; with a major breach, the other party needn't perform and can still sue for damages). Under the UCC's "perfect tender" rule, every deadline must be met precisely, and any delay is a major breach. Note, however, that the exceptions to the UCC rule make it considerably less harsh in practice (e.g., with notice to the buyer, a seller can cure defective performance if there's time left for performance; also, even if the time for performance has passed, seller can still cure if the buyer rejected nonconforming tender that the seller had reasonable grounds to believe the buyer would accept. § 2-508(2)).

These kinds of distinctions are easy to overlook and are, thus, attractive targets for MBE questions.

2. Unilateral vs. bilateral contracts.

In real life, an offeror rarely desires *only* a unilateral contract; almost every contract offer could be interpreted as seeking a bilateral contract, as well. Remember, however, that you're preparing not only for real life but also for the MBE; you will need to know and apply the distinctions between offers for bilateral and for unilateral contracts:

➡ An offer for a bilateral contract seeks a promise in return, not performance.

➡ An offer for a unilateral contract seeks performance in return, not a promise.

As an example, let's talk about a typical reward offer. The offeror isn't interested in obtaining a promise from someone that he'll perform some act (such as, "I promise I'll try to find your dog if you pay me the reward"); the offeror is interested only in the performance (the actual return of the dog, instead of a promise to look). Thus, a reward offeror must be seeking a unilateral contract. (Incidentally, the modern view is that the offeree need only complete performance with knowledge of a reward offer [or a public offer of any kind], in order to earn the reward. Contrast this with the traditional rule — that the public offer must have provoked the offeree's performance.)

Look at another example. Say that an offeror states, "I'll pay you $50 if you paint my house." Because either a promise to paint or the actual painting of the house would suffice, this offer could be interpreted as seeking either a bilateral or a unilateral contract.

Here's a less obvious example, from the MBE:

> Duffer and Slicker, who lived in different suburbs twenty miles apart, were golfing acquaintances at the Interurban Country Club. Both were traveling salesmen — Duffer for a pharmaceutical house and Slicker for a widget manufacturer. Duffer wrote Slicker by United States mail on Friday, October 8:

> > I need a motorcycle for transportation to the country club, and will buy your Suzuki for $1,200 upon your bringing it to my home address above [stated in the letterhead] on or before noon, November 12 next. This offer is not subject to countermand.
> >
> > Sincerely,
> >
> > [signed] Duffer

> Slicker replied by mail the following day:

> > I accept your offer, and promise to deliver the bike as you specified.
> >
> > Sincerely,
> >
> > [signed] Slicker

> This letter although properly addressed, was misdirected by the postal service and not received by Duffer until November 10. Duffer had bought another Suzuki bike from Koolcat for $1,050 a few hours before.

> Koolcat saw Slicker at the Interurban Country Club on November 11 and said: "I sold my Suzuki to Duffer yesterday for $1,050. Would you consider selling me yours for $950?" Slicker replied: "I'll let you know in a few days."

> On November 12, Slicker took his Suzuki to Duffer's residence; he arrived at 11:15 a.m. Duffer was asleep and did not answer Slicker's doorbell rings until 12:15 p.m. Duffer then rejected Slicker's bike on the ground that he had already bought Koolcat's.

> In a lawsuit by Slicker against Duffer for breach of contract, what would the court probably decide regarding Slicker's letter of October 9?

> A. The letter bound both parties to a unilateral contract as soon as Slicker mailed it

> B. Mailing of the letter by Slicker did not, of itself, prevent a subsequent, effective revocation by Duffer of his offer

C. The letter bound both parties to a bilateral contract, but only when received by Duffer on November 10

D. Regardless of whether Duffer's offer had proposed a unilateral or a bilateral contract, the letter was an effective acceptance upon receipt, if not upon dispatch

Look at Duffer's original letter. He didn't say, "I'll buy your Suzuki for $1,200 if you promise to bring it to my home address...." He was looking only for performance in return: Slicker's bringing the Suzuki to Duffer's house before noon on November 12. Since Duffer was seeking *return performance*, he made an offer for a unilateral contract; thus, Slicker's *promise* to perform couldn't constitute acceptance — Slicker could accept the offer only by performing. As a result, Slicker's promise was meaningless, so the unaccepted offer remained revocable. (Choice B recognizes this, making it the best response.)

3. Issues of consideration.

A. Consideration itself.

Let's get back to basics for a minute. Any enforceable agreement requires consideration or a substitute for consideration (such as promissory estoppel). You also undoubtedly remember the definition of consideration: a bargained-for exchange, plus either detriment to the promisee or benefit to the promisor (and typically both).

The key here is the *bargain*. Both parties must view the return promise (or performance) as the "price" of the contract. If they don't, there's no consideration.

The most important function of the "bargain" element is that *it makes promises to make a gift unenforceable.* The best way to distinguish a gift from a bargain is to look at whether or not the promisor is *getting something in return* for his/her promise or action. If not, then it's a gift, and the promise is unenforceable (unless promissory estoppel applies [see **D.**, below]).

B. Consideration in the form of surrendering a legal claim.

OK, here's the situation. Larry and Curly are painters. In a fit, Larry hits Curly on the head with a paintbrush. Curly threatens to sue Larry for assault and battery. Larry tells him, "If you promise not to sue me, I'll give you $500." Curly agrees. Consideration for the agreement? Curly's surrendering his claim! It was bargained for, and it constitutes a detriment to him (as promisee) and a benefit to Larry (as promisor). That's pretty straightforward.

What's trickier is the situation where the claim is *invalid*. Although it seems strange, surrendering an invalid claim can *still* be consideration, if two requirements are met:

1. A reasonable person could believe the claim is well-founded; and
2. It can be pursued in good faith.

Note that the mind-set of the one who's surrendering the claim is all-important *and that the other party's belief is irrelevant*. Say Curly's claim against Larry is no good, but Curly reasonably believes it's valid even though Larry believes it isn't. Larry's belief is unimportant, since the two requirements for consideration — reasonableness and good faith — are met. If the situation were *reversed* — that is, it's reasonable to believe the claim is well-founded, Larry believes it's good, but Curly knows it isn't — there's *no consideration*, since Curly, knowing the claim is invalid, couldn't pursue it in good faith. Here's another example, this time from the MBE:

Neff and Owens owned adjoining residences in Smithville. In 1971, they hired a contractor to lay sidewalks in front of both of their homes. Each man was to pay the contractor for that part of the work attributable to his property. After he had paid the bill which the contractor had submitted to him, Neff became convinced that the contractor had erred and had charged him for labor and materials which were used for part of the sidewalk in front of Owens' property. Neff thereupon asked Owens to reimburse him for the amount which he assumed he had erroneously paid the contractor. After a lengthy discussion, and although he was still convinced that he owed Neff nothing, Owens finally said: 'I want to avoid trouble, and so if you agree not to sue for reimbursement, I'll employ a caretaker for a three-year term to keep our sidewalks free of ice and snow." Neff orally assented.

Although he could have hired the man for three years, Owens hired Parsons in October, 1971, to keep the snow and ice off the sidewalks for the winter, November 1971-March 1972. During the early fall of 1972, Owens decided to go to Florida for the winter. He told his nephew, Morse, that he could live in Owens' house for the winter provided Morse would hire someone to keep the snow and ice off the walks in front of both Neff's and Owens' properties, and suggested that

Morse could hire Parsons for that task at relatively little cost. Morse moved into Owens' home in October, 1972, but moved out November, 1972, prior to any icing or snowfall. He did not employ anyone to remove snow and ice in front of either property. Owens did not know that Morse had moved out of his home until he returned to Smithville in the spring. During the winter Neff had kept his own walks clean. No one cleaned the snow and ice from the walks in front of Owens' property.

Assume that the contractor had made no error and that Neff had paid only for labor and materials for the walk in front of his own property. Was Owens' promise to hire a caretaker supported by consideration?

- A. Yes
- B. No, because Owens did not believe that Neff had a valid claim
- C. No, because Neff's claim was groundless
- D. No, because Owens' promise to employ the caretaker was aleatory

If you apply the rule on invalid claims, you can see that it's Neff's belief in the validity of the claim that counts, as long as it's reasonable to believe the claim is valid. Both of these requirements for consideration are satisfied here, regardless of what Owens believes. Thus, the correct response is A.

C. Consideration in a unilateral contract.

Remember that, in a unilateral contract, the offeror seeks return performance, not a return promise. Under such circumstances, it can be confusing figuring out what the consideration for the agreement is. In fact, it's the offeree's performance. That's all there is to it.

D. Promissory estoppel.

An agreement can be enforceable without consideration as long as there's a substitute for consideration — typically, promissory estoppel. Promissory estoppel can act as a substitute for consideration in order to avoid injustice. It's triggered by a gratuitous promise which is likely to, and does, induce the promisee's reliance. It's not true consideration, because there's no bargain, but it does result in the promise's being **enforceable**. The most important thing to remember is that the **lack of an otherwise enforceable contract** is a prerequisite for promissory estoppel; if there's an enforceable contractual promise, there **can't** be promissory estoppel!

E. Quasi-contract.

Quasi-contract, like promissory estoppel, requires that there be **no enforceable contract.** If there **is** one, quasi-contract can't apply.

Courts typically apply quasi-contract rules if a plaintiff has conferred a benefit on the defendant under circumstances where the defendant would be **unjustly enriched** if he were allowed to retain the benefit without paying for it. Thus, once you've established that there's no enforceable contract, you have to determine if there's unjust enrichment. If you find enrichment, but it's not unjust, you can't have a quasi-contractual recovery. Keep in mind, also, that there can't be unjust enrichment if the performing party suffered no detriment.

4. Conditions.

The bar exam frequently tests conditions, because it's easy to confuse the different types. Remember the basic definition of a condition: an event, other than the mere passage of time, that triggers, limits, or extinguishes an absolute duty to perform of one party to a contract.

There are two different ways to categorize conditions. The first is to categorize them according to how the condition came about; there are three types: **express**, **implied**, and **constructive** conditions. The most important thing to remember here is the level of compliance required by each type. If a condition is express — that is, the parties explicitly included it in the contract — it must be **strictly complied with**. Substantial performance won't suffice, so, if there's substantial, but not complete, performance, the non-breaching party doesn't have to perform at all. On the other hand, with implied and constructive conditions, substantial performance is sufficient (note that, if performance isn't complete, the other party will be able to recover damages but still has to perform).

The second way to categorize conditions is by the time of performance. This is the part of the law of conditions which you're likely to find confusing. There are three categories here: **conditions precedent, concurrent**, and **subsequent.** We'll look at each one separately.

a. Conditions precedent.

A condition precedent is an event or act which must occur first in order to trigger a party's absolute duty of performance. These are easy to spot. Just ask this question: is there an enforceable duty before the required event happens? If you answer no, that's a condition precedent. For example, let's say I tell you, "If the Yankees make it to the World Series, I'll buy your tickets for $500." You agree. Ask yourself, do I owe you any duty if the Yankees don't make it to the World Series? No. Thus, the Yankees making it to the World Series is a *condition precedent* to my duty to perform (and to your duty to tender tickets, as well). The Yankees making it to the World Series triggers my duty to pay, as well as your duty to tender tickets.

b. Concurrent conditions.

Concurrent conditions exist where each party's duty to perform is conditioned on the other party's performance. Say, for instance, Laurel offers to sell Hardy his piano for $200. Hardy agrees. Hardy's tendering the piano is a condition to Laurel's duty to pay; Laurel's tendering the $200 is a condition to Hardy's duty to hand over the piano. The thing to remember about concurrent conditions is that they have to be capable of simultaneous performance. With the Laurel and Hardy agreement, this requirement is satisfied, since a transfer is physically possible, and they didn't provide for any special order of performance.

Let's change the facts. Say Dorothy agrees to whitewash Auntie Em's fence for $100. Whitewashing the fence and tendering the cash can't be concurrent conditions, because they can't be accomplished at the same time. (In fact, since Dorothy's performance will take a period of time to complete and Em's won't, Dorothy's performance would impliedly have to precede Em's duty to perform — that is, Dorothy's performance would be an implied condition precedent to Em's duty to perform. If Dorothy doesn't perform, Em has no duty to pay.)

Let's change the facts again. Say David agrees to sell his golden gun to Glenn for $1,000. David is to deliver the gun on February 1, and Glenn is to pay on February 15. No concurrent conditions here, since the parties can't perform simultaneously. Say, instead, that the two make no provision about when Glenn is to pay; they provide only that David is to deliver the gun February 1. A court would imply concurrent conditions, since time is set for one performance — David's — and the parties *can* perform simultaneously. Finally, assume no time is set for either party to perform (this is analogous to the original Laurel and Hardy example, where performance could be simultaneous). There would be implied concurrent conditions.

c. Conditions subsequent.

We saved the toughest one for last. A condition subsequent *discharges a previously absolute duty to perform.* A common circumstance for this type of condition is an insurance contract, where the insurance company's duty to pay is discharged if the insured doesn't sue within, say, six months of an accident. Conditions subsequent are very rare, so you need to *be careful* not to say that some occurrence is a condition subsequent just because it happens *after* something else. Take the Dorothy and Auntie Em hypo again, in which Dorothy agreed to whitewash Auntie Em's fence for $100. Dorothy's duty to whitewash is a condition precedent to Auntie Em's duty to pay — but Auntie Em's duty to pay is *not* a condition subsequent to Dorothy's duty to whitewash! The thing to look for is whether the condition subsequent *discharges* a duty that was already absolute. If the duty wasn't already absolute, it can't be subject to discharge by a condition subsequent. Here's an example:

> Paul and Daniel entered into a contract in writing on November 1, the essential part of which read as follows: "Paul to supply Daniel with 200 personalized Christmas cards on or before December 15, 1970, bearing a photograph of Daniel and his family, and Daniel to pay $100 thirty days thereafter. Photograph to be taken by Paul at Daniel's house. Cards guaranteed to be fully satisfactory and on time." Because Daniel suddenly became ill, Paul was unable to take the necessary photograph of Daniel and his family until the first week of December. The final week's delay was caused by Paul's not being notified promptly by Daniel of his recovery. Before taking the photograph of Daniel and his family, Paul advised Daniel that he was likely to be delayed a day or two beyond December 15 in making delivery because of the time required to process the photograph and cards. Daniel told Paul to take the photograph anyway. The cards were finally delivered by Paul to Daniel on December 17, Paul having diligently worked on them in the interim. Although the cards pleased the rest of the family, Daniel refused to accept them because, as he said squinting at one of the cards at arm's length without bothering to put on his reading glasses, "The photograph makes me look too old. Besides, the cards weren't delivered on time."

> Which of the following statements is most accurate?

A. Payment by Daniel of the $100 was a condition precedent to Paul's duty of performance

B. The performances of Paul and Daniel under the contract were concurrently conditional

C. Payment by Daniel of the $100 was a condition subsequent to Paul's duty of performance

D. Performance by Paul under the contract was a condition precedent to Daniel's duty of payment of the $100

Under the contract, Daniel had no duty to perform until Paul performed by supplying satisfactory Christmas cards. The performances couldn't occur simultaneously, and Daniel's payment of $100 doesn't discharge a previously absolute duty to perform. Thus, Paul's duty must be a condition precedent to Daniel's duty. Choice D is the correct response.

5. Interpretation.

Some MBE questions require you to interpret contract provisions. The general rule is that contract terms are to be interpreted **objectively**, by determining what interpretation a reasonable person, knowing all the parties know, would place on the terms. You want to avoid any extraordinary or unusually strict interpretation of contract language. Here's an example:

In the application for a life insurance policy, Mary answered in the negative the question, "Have you ever had any heart disease?" Both the application and the insurance policy which was issued provided: "Applicant warrants the truthfulness of the statements made in the application and they are made conditions to the contract of insurance." Unknown to Mary, she had had a heart disease at a very early age. The policy provided that the proceeds were not to be paid over to the named beneficiary, Mary's daughter, Joan, "until she reaches the age of 21." No contingent beneficiary was named in the policy. Mary was killed in an automobile accident two months after the policy was issued. Joan died one month later at the age of 19 from injuries incurred in the same accident. If the question is raised in an action against the insurance company, how is the court likely to construe the clause dealing with the truthfulness of statements in the application?

A. The clause is a condition, and because the condition was not met, the company will not be liable

B. The clause is a condition, but it will be interpreted to mean, "truthfulness to the best of my knowledge"

C. The clause is not a condition, and therefore the company may be liable even though Mary's statement was not true

D. The clause is not a condition but is a promise, and therefore the company will have a cause of action against Mary's estate for any losses it suffered because of Mary's misstatement

Here, it wouldn't be reasonable for the insurance company to expect people to disclose diseases they didn't know about, so a court would adopt a **reasonable** interpretation of the clause and require truthfulness only to the best of an applicant's knowledge. That makes B the best response.

In interpreting contracts, keep in mind that you shouldn't imply promises when the parties have expressly dealt with a set of circumstances in the contract. If the parties addressed a situation, or determined who should bear the risk of a certain kind of loss, a court will not look outside the "four corners" of the contract.

6. The Statute of Frauds.

If a contract falls within the Statute of Frauds (SOF), it must be **in writing** to be enforceable. Thus, the first thing you have to know is which kinds of contracts are covered by the SOF; then, when you encounter a problem on the MBE in which the enforceability of an oral contract is in question, check it against your list of SOF rules **methodically**. Overcome the temptation to put contracts **under** the Statute of Frauds even though they don't belong there. If a contract doesn't fall within the SOF, it's enforceable even though it's oral. That's all there is to it.

The Statute of Frauds coverage varies from state to state, but here are seven, basic types of contracts which generally fall under the SOF (of course, an MBE question could offer a Statute of its own which may vary from the usual):

1. Contracts of **suretyship** (i.e., a contract to answer for another's debt or default — a guarantee of performance);

2. Contracts for the **sale of an interest in land** (which includes leases of one year or longer);

3. Contracts for the **sale of goods worth more than $500** (UCC § 2-201) (except specially manufactured goods, or where there is partial performance);

4. Contracts which **cannot possibly be performed within a year**;

5. Contracts for the sale of securities (UCC § 8-319);
6. Regardless of cost, contracts for the sale of personal property other than goods with a value of more than $5,000, e.g., royalty rights (UCC § 1-206);
7. Contracts in consideration of marriage.

Here's a mnemonic to help you remember this list: **MP SIGNS** (**M**arriage; **P**ersonal property more than $5,000; **S**uretyship; **I**nterest in land; **G**oods more than $500; **N**ot performable within a year; **S**ecurities). Of theses seven types, only numbers 1 through 4 appear with regularity on the MBE.

You also need to know when the need for a writing will be excused. At common law, there are five circumstances under which a contract within the SOF will be enforceable even without a writing:

1. Full performance by both sides;
2. Seller conveys property to buyer;
3. Buyer pays all or part of the purchase price AND performs some act explainable only by the contract's existence (e.g., constructing buildings on land);
4. Promissory estoppel;
5. Waiver (e.g., by not affirmatively pleading the Statute of Frauds as a defense).

Under the UCC, courts will excuse the necessity for a writing under several circumstances. Where a transaction in goods is involved, part performance removes the writing requirement (but only to the extent of performance), as does an admission in court by the party denying the contract's existence. In addition, specially manufactured goods don't require a writing once the seller has begun manufacture or made commitments to procure the goods, § 2-201(3)(a), and a letter of confirmation can also satisfy the Statute of Frauds if the transaction is between merchants.

You should also remember the "main purpose" exception to the SOF as regards contracts of suretyship (where one person promises to pay for the debts of another); if the surety's **main purpose** is to further his/her **own interest**, then the promise does **not** fall within the Statute of Frauds.

Here's an example of a Statute of Frauds question from the MBE:

In September, 1970, Joe Smith, twenty-three years old and unmarried, was beginning his third year of law school. At that time he entered into a written lease with Landlord for the lease of an apartment for the nine-month school year ending on May 31, 1971, at $150 a month payable in advance on the first day of each month. Joe paid the rent through December 1, but did not pay the amount due on January 1, nor has he paid any since.

On January 15, 1971, Landlord threatened to evict Joe if he did not pay the rent. That night Joe called his father, Henry, and told him that he did not have the money with which to pay the rent nor did he have the money with which to pay his tuition for the second semester. Henry told Joe that if he agreed not to marry until he finished law school, Henry would pay his tuition, the $150 rent that was due on January 1, the rent for the rest of the school year, and $100 a month spending money until he graduated. Joe, who was engaged to be married, at that time agreed that he would not marry until after he graduated.

On January 16, Henry wrote to Landlord the following letter which Landlord received on January 17: "Because of the love and affection which I bear my son, Joe, if you do not evict him, I will pay the rent he now owes you and will pay you his $150 rent on the first day of each month through May, 1971. If I do not hear from you by January 25, I will assume that this arrangement is all right with you. (Signed) Henry Smith."

Landlord did not reply to Henry's letter and he did not evict Joe. Henry died suddenly on January 26. Joe continued to live in the apartment through May 31, 1971, but paid no more rent. He did not marry and graduated from law school. Henry had paid Joe's tuition for the spring semester but had paid no money to either Landlord or Joe.

Joe's claim against Henry's estate having been denied by the executor, Joe brought suit against the estate in June, 1971, asking for a judgment of $400 ($100 spending money for each of the months, February through May). In this action, Joe probably will be

A. successful

B. unsuccessful, because his contract with Henry was illegal

C. unsuccessful, because Henry's death terminated the offer

D. unsuccessful, because his contract with Henry was not in writing and signed by Henry

The specific agreement on which Joe is suing — the $100 per month spending money — doesn't fit into any of the Statute of Frauds categories—not even the made "in consideration of marriage" category, because this promise was to delay marriage (a contract in consideration of marriage would arise, say, if Joe had promised to pay his fiancee's tuition if she agreed to marry him). Since Joe's agreement isn't covered by the Statute of Frauds, it's enforceable without a writing, so choice D can't be right. That's all there is to it. (Choice A is the best response).

Remember, even if a contract fails for non-compliance with the Statute of Frauds, a party may be entitled to quasi-contractual recovery for the reasonable value of his part performance, and to restitution of any other benefits he may have conferred.

7. Third party beneficiaries.

If the promisee of a contractual promise intends that her performance should benefit someone outside the contract, that other person is called the intended third party beneficiary, and, as you know, only intended, not incidental, beneficiaries have enforceable rights. Remember, though, that a beneficiary's rights aren't enforceable until those rights vest. Why is that a big deal? Because, before that, the parties to the contract can modify or even rescind it **without regard to the beneficiary.** Once the rights vest, however, any modification **requires the beneficiary's consent.**

Traditionally, determining when the beneficiary's rights vest depends on whether a beneficiary is a creditor beneficiary or a donee beneficiary; most modern courts, however, agree with the Restatement 2d of Contracts, § 311, which ignores the donee-creditor distinction and views the beneficiary's rights as vesting when one of three events occurs:

1. the beneficiary manifests assent to the promise;
2. the beneficiary sues to enforce the promise; or
3. the beneficiary justifiably relies on the promise to his detriment.

Remember, the **third party beneficiary's rights can't vest until he knows about the contract**. Thus, before a third party beneficiary finds out about a contract, it can be modified or rescinded, with no regard for the beneficiary's rights.

8. Assignment and delegation.

You need to remember two things about assignment and delegation: first, what can/can't be assigned or delegated; second, the effect of contract prohibitions on assignment and delegation.

a. Assignment — what *can* be assigned.

Under both the common law and the UCC, the only rights that **can't** be assigned are those which would materially change the other party's duty, risk, or chance of receiving return performance. That includes things like personal services, rights under future contracts, requirements and output contracts, and assignments contrary to public policy (such as government pensions and alimony payments). All other rights can be assigned.

b. Delegation — what can be delegated.

Determining which duties can be delegated is a bit more complicated. The easiest way to do this is with a two-tier analysis:

1. Ask if the duty is "impersonal." If not — it can't be delegated.
   (An "impersonal" duty is one in which the one receiving performance has no particular interest in limiting performance only to the one from whom he expected performance. Personal duties include services of people like lawyers, doctors, architects, and portrait painters.)
2. If you determine that the duty *is* impersonal, ask if the delegation materially alters performance. If not — it's delegable.

Keep in mind that an "assignment of the contract" **impliedly** includes a delegation of duties as well, unless circumstances suggest otherwise (e.g., the contract is only assigned as security for a loan, which would indicate that the duties weren't delegated as part of the assignment of the contract).

c. Contract prohibitions on assignments and delegations.

The rules in (a) and (b) on assignments and delegations apply when the contract contains nothing **preventing** transfer. A contract prohibition throws a wrench into the works, but exactly what the prohibition does is totally dependent on how the prohibition is worded. Look at these examples:

1. "Assignment of rights under this contracted is prohibited," or similar language.

   The assignment is valid. The other party can sue only for damages for breach of covenant. Note that, under the UCC, § 9-318(4), assignment of the right to receive payment generally *cannot* be prohibited (and any prohibition is invalid).

2. "Assignment of rights under this contract is void," or similar language.

   The assignment is voidable at the other party's option. Note that, under the UCC, § 9-318(4), assignment of the right to receive payment generally cannot be prohibited (and any prohibition is invalid).

3. The contract prohibits assignment "of the contract."

   This bars only delegation of duties, not assignment of rights. While such provisions are upheld, they are narrowly construed. UCC § 2-210(3) and common law.

9. Integration and the parol evidence rule.

These two concepts are flip sides of the same coin; in order to determine if the parol evidence rule bars evidence of contract terms, you have to determine if the contract is "completely integrated."

Under the parol evidence rule, a writing that is "completely integrated" cannot be contradicted or supplemented by prior written or oral agreements, or by contemporaneous oral agreements. A "completely integrated" agreement is one the parties intended to be a *final and complete statement* of their agreement.

You need to know two things here: first, what the exceptions to parol evidence are, and second, what happens if an agreement *isn't* completely integrated.

First — the exceptions. The parol evidence rule doesn't bar evidence of defects in contract formation, such as lack of consideration, fraud, and duress.

Second — the ramifications of an incomplete, or partial, integration. A partially integrated agreement is one that doesn't reflect the *complete* agreement of the parties. Even if a court determines that a contract is only partially integrated, though, it's not open season on evidence of other terms. The written agreement will be considered final as to the terms it states, but the agreement may be *supplemented* by consistent, additional terms. Say, for example, that Bluto agrees to loan Wimpy $500, at 15% interest, to buy hamburgers, with a due date of Tuesday on the loan. They reduce the agreement to a writing which mentions their names, the amount, and the term of the loan, but not the interest rate. They couldn't have intended the writing to reflect their complete agreement, because they agreed on interest, and it's not in the writing. Thus, the agreement can be only partially integrated (assuming they intended it to be final as to the terms it *does* state). If they end up in court, either one can offer evidence, in the form of oral testimony or other notes, as to their agreement on the interest rate, since that's a consistent additional term. They could not, however, dispute the amount of the loan, since that was fully integrated in the writing and thus can't be contradicted.

In real life, there are several different, rather complex rules for determining if an agreement is "completely integrated." On the MBE, your job is made easier by the limited number of answer choices: if an answer choice addresses a material term that wasn't in the written agreement, chances are that the agreement was only partially integrated.

Here is an example from the MBE:

> The Kernel Corporation, through its president, Demeter Gritz, requested from Vault Finance, Inc., a short-term loan of $100,000. On April 1, Gritz and Vault's loan officer agreed orally that Vault would make the loan on the following terms: (1) the loan would be repaid in full on or before the following July 1 and would carry interest at an annual rate of 15 percent (a lawful rate under the applicable usury law); and (2) Gritz would personally guarantee repayment. The loan was approved and made on April 5. The only document evidencing the loan was a memorandum, written and supplied by Vault and signed by Gritz for Kernel, that read in its entirety:

> April 5

> in consideration of a loan advanced on this date, Kernel Corporation hereby promises to pay Vault Finance, Inc., $100,000 on September 1.

> Kernel Corporation

> by /s/ Demeter Gritz
> Demeter Gritz, President

Kernel Corporation did not repay the loan on or before July 1, although it had sufficient funds to do so. On July 10, Vault sued Kernel as principal debtor and Gritz individually as guarantor for $100,000, plus 15 percent interest from April 5.

At the trial, can Vault prove Kernel's oral commitment to repay the loan on or before July 1?

    A. Yes, because the oral agreement was supported by an independent consideration

    B. Yes, because the evidence of the parties' negotiations is relevant to their contractual intent concerning maturity of the debt

    C. No, because such evidence is barred by the preexisting duty rule

    D. No, because such evidence contradicts the writing and is barred by the parol evidence rule

Here, the element Vault wants to prove **directly contradicts** a term in the written agreement — the due date of the loan; thus, it doesn't matter if the agreement is fully or partially integrated — no evidence will be admitted on the matter. D is, therefore, the best answer.

EXAM TACTICS

1. Once you've determined that a question is Contracts-oriented, check immediately to see if a transaction in goods is involved.

If the facts involve a transaction in goods, UCC Article II applies. You need to make this distinction early, because, when a question addresses an issue on which the common law and the UCC differ, one of the incorrect answers will inevitably try to mislead you by addressing the rule from the law that **doesn't** apply. Remember, approximately 1 in every 4 Contracts questions will involve a transaction in goods! Here's an example from the MBE:

> On May 1 Ohner telegraphed Byer, "Will sell you any or all of the lots in Grove subdivision at $5,000 each. Details follow in letter." The letter contained all the necessary details concerning terms of payment, insurance, mortgages, etc., and provided, "This offer remains open until June 1." On May 2, after he had received the telegram but before he had received the letter, Byer telegraphed Ohner, "Accept your offer with respect to lot 101." Both parties knew that there were fifty lots in the Grove subdivision and that they were numbered 101 through 150.
>
> Assume that Ohner and Byer were bound by a contract for the sale of lot 101 for $5,000, and that on May 3 Ohner telephoned Byer that because he had just discovered that a shopping center was going to be erected adjacent to the Grove subdivision, he would "have to have $6,000 for each of the lots including lot 101," that Byer thereupon agreed to pay him $6,000 for lot 101, and that on May 6 Byer telegraphed, "Accept your offer with respect to the rest of the lots." Assuming that two contracts were formed and that there is no controlling statute, Byer will most likely be required to pay
>
>   A. only $5,000 for each of the fifty lots
>
>   B. only $5,000 for lot 101, but $6,000 for the remaining forty-nine lots
>
>   C. $6,000 for each of the fifty lots
>
>   D. $6,000 for lot 101, but only $5,000 for the remaining forty-nine lots

If you failed to determine that the common law applies here, since this is a sale of an interest in land, you might mistakenly apply the UCC and choose choice C, which reflects the UCC rule on modifications — that no consideration is required for modifications as long as they are made in good faith. § 2-209. Remember, the UCC, Article II, can't apply here because there's **no transaction in goods**. The correct answer is B, which reflects the common law "pre-existing" duty rule as to modifications — that modifications require consideration. In fact, you should spot yet another common law/UCC difference here: at common law, an irrevocable offer requires consideration in order to make it a valid "option;" under the UCC, § 2-205, merchants can make irrevocable, or "firm," offers, without consideration, as long as the offer is embodied in a signed writing. Under these facts, then, Ohner's letter didn't create an irrevocable offer (if you mistakenly applied the UCC as to this element, you'd have picked choice A).

2. Handling questions with a combination of alternatives.

In some Contracts and Sales questions, you'll be given a choice of two or three alternatives, and then you'll have to decide which combination of these answers is correct. You should apply a standard process of elimination to the alternatives, eliminating those you **know** are wrong. Here's an example of this kind of question:

Reggie offered Harriet $200 for a 30-day option to buy Harriet's land, Grandvale, for $10,000. As Harriet knew, Reggie, if granted the option, intended to resell Grandvale at a profit. Harriet declined, believing that she could find a desirable purchaser herself. Reggie thereupon said to Harriet, "Make me a written 30-day offer, revocable at your pleasure, to sell me Grandvale at a sale price of $10,000, and tomorrow I will pay you $200 for so doing." Harriet agreed and gave Reggie the following document:

For 30 days I offer my land known as Grandvale to Reggie for $10,000, this offer to be revocable at my pleasure at any time before acceptance.

[Signed] Harriet

Later that day Harriet's neighbor, Norma, said to Harriet, "I know someone who would probably buy Grandvale for $15,000." Harriet asked, "Who?" and Norma replied, "My cousin Portia." Harriet thanked Norma. Several hours later, Norma telephoned Harriet and said, "Of course, if you sell to Portia I will expect the usual 5 percent brokerage fee for finding a buyer." Harriet made no reply. The next day Harriet telephoned Reggie, declared that her written offer to him was revoked, and demanded payment of $200. Reggie refused to pay. Harriet subsequently sold Grandvale to Portia for $15,000 but refused to pay Norma anything.

In a lawsuit by Harriet against Reggie to recover $200, which of the following arguments would plausibly support Reggie's position?

I.   Any promise implied by Harriet in making her offer was illusory because of the revocability provision.

II. Since Harriet's offer, if any, was in writing and involved realty, it could not be revoked by telephone.

III. Enforced payment of $200 by Reggie to Harriet would defeat Reggie's reasonable expectation if Harriet's offer was legally open for only one day.

    A. I and II only

    B. I and III only

    C. II and III only

    D. I, II, and III

Here, let's say you could only eliminate one alternative as definitely wrong — alternative II. You should, therefore, eliminate every answer choice that includes alternative II, so you could wipe out A, C, and D. By identifying just one incorrect alternative, you have found the correct answer: here, only choice B is left as the correct response (in fact, it is the best response).

3. **Read the facts *very carefully*.**

While this is true of every MBE question, it's especially true for Contracts and Sales questions, which are frequently in the form of "series" questions — that is, you'll face several issues based on the same interlocking set of facts. If you find it helpful, you can diagram each fact to determine what each does to your application of the law. This is particularly helpful if one of the questions asks the status of the parties at some point before the facts have all developed — for example, the events in the facts go from March 1 to April 1, and a question asks you the status of the parties after a letter is sent on March 15. Under these circumstances, it's crucial to isolate that date and ***ignore whatever happens thereafter.***

4. **Find that a contract exists, wherever possible.**

Traditionally, a contract requires an offer, acceptance, and consideration (or some consideration substitute). If a contract exists, then concepts like promissory estoppel and quasi-contract don't apply, and you have to analyze the problem under the contract: what are the parties' duties, what relieves those duties, what triggers them, etc.

5. **Pay attention when you're told a seemingly meaningless detail about someone.**

In most MBE questions, you're not told anything about the parties except their names. If a question does tell you something more, watch out — those facts are often relevant to the status of the person described. Here's an example from the MBE:

In a telephone call on March 1, Adams, an unemployed, retired person, said to Dawes, "I will sell my automobile for $3,000 cash. I will hold this offer open through March 14." On March 12, Adams called Dawes and told her that he had sold the automobile to Clark. Adams in fact had not sold the automobile to anyone. On March 14, Dawes learned that Adams still owned the automobile, and on that date called Adams and said, "I'm coming over to your place with $3,000." Adams replied, "Don't bother, I won't deliver the automobile to you under any circumstances." Dawes protested, but made no further attempt to pay for or take delivery of the automobile.

In an action by Dawes against Adams for breach of contract, Dawes probably will

    A. succeed, because Adams had assured her that the offer would remain open through March 14

    B. succeed, because Adams had not in fact sold the automobile to Clark

    C. not succeed, because Dawes had not tendered the $3,000 to Adams on or before March 14

    D. not succeed, because on March 12 Adams had told Dawes that he had sold the automobile to Clark

Here, the first thing you're told is Adams is an "unemployed, retired person." This is certainly out of the ordinary as descriptions on the MBE go — and, in fact, it's very significant. As you know, where the sale of goods are concerned, only a merchant in those goods can make an offer irrevocable in the absence of consideration. When the question tells you that Adams is an "unemployed, retired person," it's really telling you that he's **not a merchant**. Thus, for the offer to be irrevocable, it would have to be supported by consideration (making it an enforceable "option" contract). Since the offer here wasn't supported by consideration, it was revocable, and when Adams' acted inconsistently with the offer — by telling Dawes that he had sold the automobile to Clark — he terminated Dawes's ability to accept the offer. Thus, D is the best response. If you ignored the added information about Adams, you might have believed that Adams was a merchant and that the offer was **irrevocable**, so you'd have chosen choice A.

6. What to do when you're told a party wins a case, and that outcome doesn't seem correct to you.

In some Contracts and Sales questions, you'll be told a party prevailed and be asked why. If the victory doesn't make sense to you, ask yourself why — the best response will undoubtedly address your doubts. Here's an example:

> Blackacre is a three-acre tract of land with a small residence. Olga, the owner of Blackacre, rented it to Terrence at a monthly rental of $200. After Terrence had been in possession of Blackacre for several years, Terrence and Olga orally agreed that Terrence would purchase Blackacre from Olga for the sum of $24,000, payable at the rate of $200 a month for ten years and also would pay the real estate taxes and the expenses of insuring and maintaining Blackacre. Olga agreed to give Terrence a deed to Blackacre after five years had passed and $12,000 had been paid on account and to accept from Terrence a note secured by a mortgage for the balance. Terrence continued in possession of Blackacre and performed his obligations as orally agreed. Terrence, without consulting Olga, made improvements for which he paid $1,000. When Terrence had paid $12,000, he tendered a proper note and mortgage to Olga and demanded the delivery of the deed as agreed. Olga did not deny the oral agreement but told Terrence that she had changed her mind, and she refused to complete the transaction. Terrence then brought an action for specific performance. Olga pleaded the Statute of Frauds as her defense. Olga wins, because
>
>   A. nothing Terrence could have done would have overcome the original absence of a written agreement
>
>   B. the actions and payments of Terrence are as consistent with his being a tenant as with an oral contract
>
>   C. Terrence did not secure Olga's approval for the improvements that he made
>
>   D. Olga has not received any unconscionable benefit, and, therefore, Terrence is not entitled to equitable relief

Here, the fact that Olga won probably threw you for a loop. If it did, it's probably because you relied on the Statute of Frauds rule that partial performance — the buyer, apart from paying part of the purchase price, does something unequivocally referable to the existence of an oral agreement — removes a land sale contract from the Statute of Frauds. Terrence's $1,000 in improvements did just that. Your first reaction gives you a clue to the right response —since Olga won, it must be that something in the possible choices overcame the fact that Terrence spent $1,000 on improvements to the land. There's only one answer choice that addresses this problem: choice B, which is the correct response.

7. Distinguish *third party beneficiaries* and *assignees*.

This is an easy one. Frequently, in questions dealing with third party beneficiaries, one of the responses will mention a rule relating to assignees (and vice versa). Remember — a beneficiary is created in the contract; an assignee gains his rights only sometime later, when a party transfers his contract rights to the assignee. Thus, a person who doesn't have rights created and arising in the contract *can't* be a beneficiary. Here's an example. Cleopatra contracts to sell her asp to Mark Antony for $100 and provides, in their contract, that Antony should pay the contract price to Julius Caesar. Since Caesar's rights are created in the contract, he's a third party beneficiary. Say, instead, that the contract doesn't mention paying Caesar. After the contract is created, Cleopatra transfers her right to payment to Caesar. Did he have rights when the contract was created? No. His rights were created later. Thus, he must be an assignee.

QUESTIONS
CONTRACTS

QUESTIONS
CONTRACTS

NOTE: For ease of study, we've put all questions involving **Sales** (i.e., UCC Article 2) at the end of the section, beginning with Question 46.

Questions 1-2 are based on the following fact situation.

Gourmet, a famous chef, entered into a written agreement with his friend Deligor, a well-known interior decorator respected for his unique designs, in which Deligor agreed, for a fixed fee, to design the interior of Gourmet's new restaurant, and, upon Gourmet's approval of the design plan, to decorate and furnish the restaurant accordingly. The agreement was silent as to assignment or delegation by either party. Before beginning the work, Deligor sold his decorating business to Newman under an agreement in which Deligor assigned to Newman, and Newman agreed to complete, the Gourmet-Deligor contract. Newman, also an experienced decorator of excellent repute, advised Gourmet of the assignment, and supplied him with information confirming both Newman's financial responsibility and past commercial success.

Question 1

Is Gourmet obligated to permit Newman to perform the Gourmet-Deligor agreement?

(A) Yes, because the agreement contained no prohibition against assignment or delegation.

(B) Yes, because Gourmet received adequate assurances of Newman's ability to complete the job.

(C) No, because Deligor's duties were of a personal nature, involving his reputation, taste, and skill.

(D) No, because Deligor's purported delegation to Newman of his obligations to Gourmet effected a novation.

Question 2

If Gourmet allows Newman to perform and approves his design plan, but Newman fails without legal excuse to complete the decorating as agreed, against whom does Gourmet have an enforceable claim for breach of contract?

(A) Deligor only, because Deligor's agreement with Newman did not discharge his duty to Gourmet, and Newman made no express promise to Gourmet.

(B) Newman only, because Deligor's duty to Gourmet was discharged when Deligor obtained a skilled decorator (Newman) to perform the Gourmet-Deligor contract.

(C) Newman only, because Gourmet was an intended beneficiary of the Deligor-Newman agreement, and Deligor's duty to Gourmet was discharged when Gourmet permitted Newman to do the work and approved Newman's design.

(D) Either Deligor, because his agreement with Newman did not discharge his duty to Gourmet; or Newman, because Gourmet was an intended beneficiary of the Deligor-Newman agreement.

Questions 3-4 are based on the following fact situation.

Neff and Owens owned adjoining residences in Smithville. In 1991, they hired a contractor to lay sidewalks in front of both of their homes. Each man was to pay the contractor for that part of the work attributable to his property. After he had paid the bill which the contractor had submitted to him, Neff became convinced that the contractor had erred and had charged him for labor and materials that were used for part of the sidewalk in front of Owens' property. Neff thereupon asked Owens to reimburse him for the amount which he assumed he had erroneously paid the contractor. After a lengthy discussion, and although he was still convinced that he owed Neff nothing, Owens finally said: "I want to avoid trouble, and so if you agree not to sue for reimbursement, I'll employ a caretaker for a three-year term to keep our sidewalks free of ice and snow." Neff orally assented.

Although he could have hired the man for three years, Owens hired Parsons in October 1991, to keep the snow and ice off the sidewalks for the winter, November 1991-March 1992. During the early fall of 1992, Owens decided to go to Florida for the winter. He told his nephew, Morse, that he could live in Owens' house for the winter provided that Morse would hire someone to keep snow and ice off the walks in front of both Neff's and Owens' properties, and suggested that Morse could hire Parsons for that task at relatively little cost. Morse moved into Owens' home in October 1992, but moved out in November 1992, prior to any icing or snowfall. He did not employ anyone to remove snow and ice in front of either property. Owens did not know that Morse had moved out of his home until he returned to Smithville in the spring. During the winter Neff had kept his own walks clean. No one cleaned the ice and snow from the walks in front of the Owens' property.

Question 3

Assume that the contractor had made no error and that Neff had paid only for the labor and materials for the walk in front of his own property. Was Owens' promise to hire a caretaker supported by consideration?

(A) Yes.

(B) No, because Owens did not believe that Neff had a valid claim.

(C) No, because Neff's claim was groundless.

(D) No, because Owens' promise to employ the caretaker was aleatory.

Question 4

Assuming there is an enforceable contract between Owens and Morse, does Neff have an action against Morse?

(A) Yes, because Neff is a creditor third-party beneficiary of the contract.

(B) Yes, because Neff is a donee third-party beneficiary of the contract.

(C) No, because Neff is only an incidental beneficiary of the contract.

(D) No, because there was no privity between Neff and Morse.

Questions 5-6 are based on the following fact situation.

On May 1, Ohner telegraphed Byer, "Will sell you any or all of the lots in Grover subdivision at $5,000 each. Details follow in letter." The letter contained all the necessary details concerning terms of payment, insurance, mortgages, etc., and provided, "This offer remains open until June 1." On May 2, after he had received the telegram but before he had received the letter, Byer telegraphed Ohner, "Accept your offer with respect to lot 101." Both parties knew that there were fifty lots in the Grove subdivision and that they were numbered 101 through 150.

Question 5

For this question only, assume that Ohner and Byer were bound by a contract for the sale of lot 101 for $5,000, that on May 3, Ohner telephoned Byer that because he had just discovered that a shopping center was going to be erected adjacent to the Grove subdivision, he would "have to have $6,000 for each of the lots including lot 101", that Byer thereupon agreed to pay him $6,000 for lot 101 and that on May 6, Byer telegraphed, "Accept your offer with respect to the rest of the lots." Assuming that the two contracts were formed and that there is no controlling statute, Byer will most likely be required to pay

(A) only $5,000 for each of the fifty lots.

(B) only $5,000 for lot 101, but $6,000 for the remaining forty-nine lots.

(C) $6,000 for each of the fifty lots.

(D) $6,000 for lot 101, but only $5,000 for the remaining forty-nine lots.

Question 6

For this question only, assume that on May 5, Ohner telephoned Byer that he had sold lots 102 through 150 to someone else on May 4 and that Byer thereafter tele-

graphed Ohner, "Will take the rest of the lots." Assume further that there is no controlling statute. In an action by Byer against Ohner for breach of contract, Byer probably will

(A) succeed, because Ohner had promised him that the offer would remain open until June 1.

(B) succeed, because Ohner's attempted revocation was by telephone.

(C) not succeed, because Byer's power of acceptance was terminated by Ohner's sale of the lots to another party.

(D) not succeed, because Byer's power of acceptance was terminated by an effective revocation.

Question 7

Vetter and Prue each signed a memorandum which stated that Vetter agreed to sell and Prue agreed to purchase a tract of land and that the contract should be closed and conveyance made and accepted "by tender of general warranty deed conveying a good and marketable title" on a date specified. The memorandum signed by the parties contains all of the elements deemed essential and necessary to satisfy the Statute of Frauds applicable to the transaction except that there was omission of a recitation of the purchase price agreed upon. Vetter has refused to perform the contract, and in action by Prue for specific performance, Vetter relies upon the Statute of Frauds as a defense. If Prue offers evidence, in addition to the written memorandum, that the parties discussed and agreed upon a purchase price of $35,000 just prior to signing, Prue should

(A) succeed, because Vetter is estopped to deny that such agreed price is a fair and equitable one, which will be implied by law as a term of the written memorandum

(B) succeed, because the law implies that the parties contracted for the reasonable market value of the land, although the price paid may not necessarily be that orally agreed upon

(C) fail, because the price agreed upon is an essential element of the contract and must be in writing

(D) fail, because the evidence does not show that the price agreed upon is in fact the reasonable market value of the land.

Questions 8-9 are based on the following fact situation.

In a single writing, Painter contracted with Farmer to paint three identical barns on her rural estate for $2,000 each. The contract provided for Farmer's payment of $6,000 upon Painter's completion of the work on all three barns. Painter did not ask for any payment when the first barn was completely painted, but she demanded $4,000 after painting the second barn.

Question 8

Is Farmer obligated to make the $4,000 payment?

(A) No, because Farmer has no duty under the contract to pay anything to Painter until all three barns have been painted.

(B) No, because Painter waived her right, if any, to payment on a per-barn basis by failing to demand $2,000 upon completion of the first barn.

(C) Yes, because the contract is divisible.

(D) Yes, because Painter has substantially performed the entire contract.

Question 9

For this question only, assume that Farmer rightfully refused Painter's demand for payment.

If Painter immediately terminates the contract without painting the third barn, what is Painter entitled to recover from Farmer?

(A) Nothing, because payment was expressly conditioned on completion of all three barns.

(B) Painter's expenditures plus anticipated "profit" in painting the first two barns, up to a maximum recovery of $4,000.

(C) The reasonable value of Painter's services in painting the two barns, less Farmer's damages, if any, for Painter's failure to paint the third barn.

(D) The amount that the combined value of the two painted barns has been increased by Painter's work.

Questions 10-11 are based on the following fact situation.

On March 1, Green and Brown orally agreed that Brown would erect a boathouse on Green's lot and dig a channel from the boathouse, across Clark's lot, to a lake. Clark had already orally agreed with Green to permit the digging of the channel across Clark's lot. Brown agreed to begin work on the boathouse on March 15, and to complete all the work before June 1. The total price of $10,000 was to be paid by Green in three installments: $2,500 on March 15; $2,500 when the boathouse was completed; $5,000 when Brown finished the digging of the channel.

Question 10

Assume that Green tendered the $2,500 on March 15, and Brown refused to accept it or to perform. In an action by Green against Brown for breach of contract, which of the following can Brown successfully use as a defense?

   I.   The Clark-Green agreement permitting the digging of the channel across Clark's lot was not in writing.

   II. The Green-Brown agreement was not in writing.

(A) I only.

(B) II only.

(C) Both I and II.

(D) Neither I nor II.

Question 11

Assume that Green paid the $2,500 on March 15 and that Brown completed the boathouse according to specifications, but that Green then refused to pay the second installment and repudiated the contract. Assume further that the absence of a writing is not raised as a defense. Which of the following is(are) correct?

   I.   Brown has a cause of action against Green and his damages will be $2,500.

   II. Brown can refuse to dig the channel and not be liable for breach of contract.

(A) I only.

(B) II only.

(C) Both I and II.

(D) Neither I nor II.

Question 12

Assume that Green paid the $2,500 on March 15, that Brown completed the boathouse, that Green paid the second installment of $2,500, and that Brown completed the digging of the channel but not until July 1. Assume further that the absence of a writing is not raised as a defense. Which of the following is(are) correct?

   I.   Green has a cause of action against Brown for breach of contract.

   II. Green is excused from paying the $5,000.

(A) I only.

(B) II only.

(C) Both I and II.

(D) Neither I nor II.

Questions 13-14 are based on the following fact situation.

Tortfeasor tortiously injured Victim in an auto accident. While Victim was consequently hospitalized in Hospital, Tortfeasor's liability insurer, Insurer, settled with Victim for $5,000. Victim gave Insurer a signed release and received a signed memorandum wherein Insurer promised to pay Victim $5,000 by check within thirty days. When Victim left Hospital two days later, Hospital demanded payment of his $4,000 stated bill. Victim thereupon gave Hospital his own negotiable promissory note for $4,000 payable to Hospital's order in thirty days, and also, as security, assigned to Hospital the Insurer settlement memorandum. Hospital promptly assigned for value the settlement memorandum and negotiated the note to Holder, who took the note as a holder in due course. Subsequently, Victim misrepresented to Insurer that he had lost the settlement memorandum and needed another. Insurer issued another memorandum identical to the first, and Victim assigned it to the ABC Furniture to secure a $5,000 credit sale contract. ABC immediately notified Insurer of this assignment. Later it was discovered that Hospital had mistakenly overbilled Victim by an amount of $1,000 and that Tortfeasor was an irresponsible minor.

Question 13

If Victim starts an action against Insurer forty days after the insurance settlement agreement, can Victim recover?

(A) Yes, because his attempted assignment of his claims against Insurer were ineffective, inasmuch as Insurer's promise to pay "by check" created a right in Victim that was too personal to assign.

(B) No, because he no longer has possession of Insurer's written memorandum.

(C) No, because Tortfeasor's minority and irresponsibility vitiated the settlement agreement between Victim and Insurer.

(D) No, because he has made at least one effective assignment of his claim against Insurer, and Insurer has notice thereof.

Question 14

In view of Tortfeasor's age and irresponsibility when Insurer issued his liability policy, can Holder and ABC Furniture recover on their assignments?

(A) Neither can recover because Victim, the assignor, is a third-party beneficiary of the liability policy whose rights thereon can be no better than Tortfeasor's.

(B) Neither can recover unless Insurer knowingly waived the defense of Tortfeasor's minority and irresponsibility.

(C) Neither can recover because the liability policy and settlement thereunder are unenforceable on account of Tortfeasor's minority.

(D) Either Holder or ABC Furniture, depending on priority, can recover as an assignee (or subassignee) on Victim's claim because the latter arose from Insurer's settlement agreement, the latter agreement not being vitiated by Tortfeasor's minority and irresponsibility when he obtained the policy.

Question 15

Kontractor agreed to build a power plant for a public utility. Subbo agreed with Kontractor to lay the foundation for $200,000. Subbo supplied goods and services worth $150,000, for which Kontractor made progress payments aggregating $100,000 as required by the subcontract. Subbo then breached by refusing unjustifiably to perform further. Kontractor reasonably spent $120,000 to have the work completed by another subcontractor.

Subbo sues Kontractor for the reasonable value of benefits conferred, and Kontractor counterclaims for breach of contract.

Which of the following should be the court's decision?

(A) Subbo recovers $50,000, the benefit conferred on Kontractor for which Subbo has not been paid.

(B) Subbo recovers $30,000, the benefit Subbo conferred on Kontractor minus the $20,000 in damages incurred by Kontractor.

(C) Kontractor recovers $20,000, the excess over the contract price that was paid by Kontractor for the performance it had bargained to receive from Subbo.

(D) Neither party recovers anything, because Subbo committed a material, unexcused breach and Kontractor received a $50,000 benefit from Subbo for which Subbo has not been paid.

Question 16

In September, 1990, Joe Smith, twenty-three years old and unmarried, was beginning his third year of law school. At that time he entered into a written lease with Landlord for the lease of an apartment for the nine-month school year ending on May 31, 1991, at $150 a month payable in advance on the first day of each month. Joe paid the rent through December 1, but did not pay the amount due on January 1, nor has he paid any since.

On January 15, 1991, Landlord threatened to evict Joe if he did not pay the rent. That night Joe called his father, Henry, and told him that he did not have the money with which to pay the rent nor did he have the money with which to pay his tuition for the second semester. Henry told Joe that if he agreed not to marry until he finished law school, Henry would pay his tuition, the $150 rent that was due January 1, the rent for the rest of the school year, and $100 a month spending money until he graduated. Joe, who was engaged to be married at that time, agreed that he would not marry until after he graduated.

On January 16, Henry wrote to Landlord the following letter which Landlord received on January 17: "Because of the love and affection which I bear my son, Joe, if you do not evict him, I will pay the rent he now owes you and will pay you his $150 rent on the first day of each month through May, 1991. If I do not hear from you by January 25, I will assume that this arrangement is all right with you. (Signed) Henry Smith."

Landlord did not reply to Henry's letter and he did not evict Joe. Henry died suddenly on January 26. Joe continued to live in the apartment through May 31, 1991, but paid no more rent. He did not marry and graduated from law school. Henry had paid Joe's tuition for the spring semester, but had paid no money to either Landlord or Joe.

Joe's claim against Henry's estate having been denied by the executor, Joe brought suit against the estate in June, 1991, asking for a judgment of $400 ($100 spending money for each of the months, February through May). In this action, Joe probably will be

(A) successful.

(B) unsuccessful, because his contract with Henry was illegal.

(C) unsuccessful, because Henry's death terminated the offer.

(D) unsuccessful, because his contract with Henry was not in writing and signed by Henry.

Questions 17-18 are based on the following fact situation.

Alpha and Beta made a written contract pursuant to which Alpha promised to convey a specified apartment house to Beta in return for Beta's promise (1) to convey a 100-acre farm to Alpha and (2) to pay Alpha $1,000 in cash six months after the exchange of the apartment house and the farm. The contract contained the following provision: "It is understood and agreed that Beta's obligation to pay $1,000 six months after the exchange of the the apartment house and the farm shall be voided if Alpha has not, within three months after the aforesaid exchange, removed the existing shed in the parking area in the rear of the said apartment house."

Question 17

Which of the following statements concerning the order of performances is LEAST accurate?

(A) Alpha's tendering of good title to the apartment house is a condition precedent to Beta's duty to convey good title to the farm.

(B) Beta's tendering of good title to the farm is a condition precedent to Alpha's duty to convey good title to the apartment house.

(C) Beta's tendering of good title to the farm is a condition subsequent to Alpha's duty to convey good title to the apartment house.

(D) Alpha's tendering of good title to the apartment house and Beta's tendering of good title to the farm are concurrent conditions.

Question 18

Alpha's removal of the shed from the parking area of the apartment house is

(A) a condition subsequent in form but precedent in substance to Beta's duty to pay the $1,000.

(B) a condition precedent in form but subsequent in substance to Beta's duty to pay the $1,000.

(C) a condition subsequent to Beta's duty to pay the $1,000.

(D) not a condition, either precedent or subsequent, to Beta's duty to pay the $1,000.

Question 19

Gourmet purchased the front portion of the land needed for a restaurant he desired to build and operate, but the back portion was the subject of a will dispute between Hope and Faith (two sisters). Hope's attorney advised her that her claim was doubtful. Gourmet, knowing only that the unresolved dispute existed, agreed in a signed writing to pay Hope $6,000, payable $1,000 annually, in exchange for a quitclaim deed (a deed containing no warranties) from Hope, who promptly executed such a deed to Gourmet and received Gourmet's first annual payment. Shortly thereafter, the probate court handed down a decision in Faith's favor, ruling that Hope had no interest in the land. This decision has become final. Gourmet subsequently defaulted when his second annual installment came due.

In an action against Gourmet for breach of contract, Hope will probably

(A) lose, because she was aware at the time of the agreement with Gourmet that her claim to the property quitclaimed was doubtful.

(B) lose, because Hope suffered no legal detriment in executing the quitclaim deed.

(C) win, because Gourmet bargained for and received in exchange a quitclaim deed from Hope.

(D) win, because Gourmet, by paying the first $1,000 installment, is estopped to deny that his agreement with Hope is an enforceable contract.

Question 20

Loyal, aged 60, who had no plans for early retirement, had worked for Mutate, Inc., for 20 years as a managerial employee-at-will when he had a conversation with the company's president, George Mutant, about Loyal's post-retirement goal of extensive travel around the United States. A month later, Mutant handed Loyal a written, signed resolution of the company's Board of Directors stating that when and if Loyal should decide to retire, at his option, the company, in recognition of his past service, would pay him a $2,000-per-month lifetime pension. (The company had no regularized retirement plan for at-will employees.) Shortly thereafter, Loyal retired and immediately bought a $30,000 recreational vehicle for his planned travels. After receiving the promised $2,000 monthly pension from Mutate, Inc., for six months, Loyal, now unemployable elsewhere, received a letter from Mutate, Inc., advising him that the pension would cease immediately because of recessionary budget constraints affecting in varying degrees all managerial salaries and retirement pensions.

In a suit against Mutate, Inc., for breach of contract, Loyal will probably

(A) win, because he retired from the company as bargained-for consideration for the Board's promise to him of a lifetime pension.

(B) win, because he timed his decision to retire and to buy the recreational vehicle in reasonable reliance on the Board's promise to him of a lifetime pension.

(C) lose, because the Board's promise to him of a lifetime pension was an unenforceable gift promise.

(D) lose, because he had been an employee-at-will throughout his active service with the company.

Questions 21-24 are based on the following fact situation.

On November 1, the following notice was posted in a privately operated law school:

> The faculty, seeking to encourage legal research, offers to any student at this school who wins the current National

Obscenity Law Competition the additional prize of $500. All competing papers must be submitted to the Dean's office before May 1.

(The National Competition is conducted by an outside agency, unconnected with any law school.) Student read this notice on November 2, and thereupon intensified his effort to make his paper on obscenity law, which he started in October, a winner. Student also left on a counter in the Dean's office a signed note saying, "I accept the faculty's $500 Obscenity Competition offer." This note was inadvertently placed in Student's file and never reached the Dean or any faculty member personally. On the following April 1, the above notice was removed and the following substituted therefore:

The faculty regrets that our offer regarding the National Obscenity Law Competition must be withdrawn.

Student's paper was submitted through the Dean's office on April 15. On May 1, it was announced that Student had won the National Obscenity Law Competition and the prize of $1,000. The law faculty refused to pay anything.

Question 21

Assuming that the faculty's notice of November 1 was posted on a bulletin board or other conspicuous place commonly viewed by all persons in the law school, such notice constituted a

(A) preliminary invitation to deal, analogous to newspaper advertisements for the sale of goods by merchants.
(B) contractual offer, creating a power of acceptance.
(C) preliminary invitation, because no offeree was named therein.
(D) promise to make a conditional, future gift of money.

Question 22

As to Student, was the offer effectively revoked?

(A) Yes, by the faculty's second notice.
(B) No, because it became irrevocable after a reasonable time had elapsed.
(C) No, because of Student's reliance, prior to April 1, on the offer.
(D) No, unless Student became aware of the April 1 posting and removal before submitting the paper.

Question 23

The offer proposed a

(A) unilateral contract only.
(B) bilateral contract only.
(C) unilateral contract or bilateral contract at the offeree's option.
(D) unilateral contract which ripened into a bilateral contract, binding on both parties, as soon as Student

intensified his effort in response to the offer.

Question 24

The promise of the faculty on November 1 was

(A) enforceable on principles of promissory estoppel.
(B) enforceable by Student's personal representative even if Student has been killed in an accident on April 16.
(C) not enforceable on policy grounds because it produced a noncommercial agreement between a student and his teachers, analogous to intramural family agreements and informal social commitments.
(D) not enforceable because Student, after entering the National Competition in October, was already under a duty to perform to the best of his ability.

Questions 25-27 are based on the following fact situation.

Paul and Daniel entered a contract in writing on November 1, the essential part of which read as follows: "Paul to supply Daniel with 200 personalized Christmas cards on or before December 15, 1990, bearing a photograph of Daniel and his family, and Daniel to pay $100 thirty days thereafter. Photograph to be taken by Paul at Daniel's house. Cards guaranteed to be fully satisfactory and on time." Because Daniel suddenly became ill, Paul was unable to take the necessary photograph of Daniel and his family until the first week of December. The final week's delay was caused by Paul's not being notified promptly by Daniel of his recovery. Before taking the photograph of Daniel and his family, Paul advised Daniel that he was likely to be delayed a day or two beyond December 15 in making delivery because of the time required to process the photograph and cards. Daniel told Paul to take the photograph anyway. The cards were finally delivered by Paul to Daniel on December 17, Paul having diligently worked on them in the interim. Although the cards pleased the rest of the family, Daniel refused to accept them because, as he said squinting at one of the cards at arm's length without bothering to put on his reading glasses, "The photograph makes me look too old. Besides, the cards weren't delivered on time."

Question 25

In an action by Paul against Daniel, which of the following would be Daniel's best defense?

(A) The cards, objectively viewed, were not satisfactory.
(B) The cards, subjectively viewed, were not satisfactory.
(C) The cards were not delivered on time.
(D) Daniel's illness excused him from further obligation under the contract.

Question 26

Which of the following statements is most accurate?

(A) Payment by Daniel of the $100 was a condition precedent to Paul's duty of performance.

(B) The performances of Paul and Daniel under the contract were concurrently conditional.

(C) Payment by Daniel of the $100 was a condition subsequent to Paul's duty of performance.

(D) Performance by Paul under the contract was a condition precedent to Daniel's duty of payment of the $100.

Question 27

Which of the following statements regarding the legal effect of Daniel's illness is LEAST accurate?

(A) Daniel's illness and the related developments excused Paul from his obligations to deliver the cards on or before December 15.

(B) Prompt notice by Daniel to Paul of Daniel's recovery from illness was an implied condition of Paul's duty under the circumstances.

(C) Paul was under a duty of immediate performance of his promise to deliver the cards, as of December 15, by reason of the express language of the contract and despite the illness of Daniel and the related developments.

(D) Daniel's conduct after his illness constituted a waiver of the necessity of Paul's performing on or before December 15.

Question 28

A written construction contract, under which Contractor agreed to build a new house for Owner at a fixed price of $200,000, contained the following provision:

Prior to construction or during the course thereof, this contract may be modified by mutual agreement of the parties as to "extras" or other departures from the plans and specifications provided by Owner and attached hereto. Such modifications, however, may be authorized only in writing, signed by both parties.

During construction, Contractor incorporated into the structure overhanging gargoyles and other "extras" orally requested by Owner for orally agreed prices in addition to the contract price. Owner subsequently refused to pay anything for such extras, aggregating $30,000 at the agreed prices, solely on the ground that no written, signed authorization for them was ever effected.

If Contractor sues Owner on account of the "extras," which, if any, of the following will effectively support Owner's defense?

    I. The parol evidence rule.

    II. The preexisting duty rule.

    III. Failure of an express condition.

    IV. The statute of frauds.

(A) I and III only.

(B) I and IV only.

(C) II and IV only.

(D) Neither I, II, III, nor IV.

Question 29-31 are based on the following fact situation.

Brill saved the life of Ace's wife, Mary, who thereafter changed her will to leave Brill $1,000. However, upon Mary's death she had no property except an undivided interest in real estate held in tenancy by the entirety of Ace. The property had been purchased by Ace from an inheritance.

After Mary died, Ace signed and delivered to Brill the following instrument: "In consideration of Brill's saving my wife's life and his agreement to bring no claims against my estate based on her will, I hereby promise to pay Brill $1,000."

Upon Ace's death, Brill filed a claim for $1,000. Ace's executor contested the claim on the ground that the instrument was not supported by sufficient consideration.

Question 29

In most states, would Brill's saving of Mary's life be regarded as sufficient consideration for Ace's promise?

(A) Yes, because Ace was thereby morally obligated to Brill.

(B) Yes, because Ace was thereby materially benefitted.

(C) No, because Ace had not asked Brill to save her.

(D) No, because the value of Brill's act was too uncertain.

Question 30

With respect to the recital that Brill had agreed not to file a claim against Ace's estate, what additional fact would most strengthen Brill's claim?

(A) Brill's agreement was made in a writing he signed.

(B) Brill reasonably believed he had a valid claim when the instrument was signed.

(C) Mary had contributed to accumulation of the real property.

(D) Brill paid Ace $1 when he received the instrument

Question 31

On which of the following theories would it be most likely that Brill could recover?

(A) Ace and Brill have made a compromise.

(B) Ace must give restitution for benefits it would be unjust to retain.

(C) Ace is bound by promissory estoppel.

(D) Ace executed a binding unilateral contract.

Question 32

In exchange for a valid and sufficient consideration, Goodbar orally promised Walker, who had no car and wanted a minivan, "to pay to anyone from whom you buy a minivan within the next six months the full purchase-price thereof." Two months later, Walker bought a used minivan on credit from Minivanity Fair, Inc., for $8,000. At the time, Minivanity Fair was unaware of Goodbar's earlier promise to Walker, but learned of it shortly after the sale.

Can Minivanity Fair enforce Goodbar's promise to Walker?

(A) Yes, under the doctrine of promissory estoppel.

(B) Yes, because Minivanity Fair is an intended beneficiary of the Goodbar-Walker contract.

(C) No, because Goodbar's promise to Walker is unenforceable under the suretyship clause of the statute of frauds.

(D) No, because Minivanity Fair was neither identified when Goodbar's promise was made nor aware of it when the minivan-sale was made.

Questions 33-34 are based on the following fact situation.

When Esther, Gray's 21-year-old daughter, finished college, Gray handed her a signed memorandum stating that if she would go to law school for three academic years, he would pay her room, board, and tuition and would "give her a $1,000 bonus" for each "A" she got in law school. Esther's uncle, Miller, who was present upon this occasion, read the memorandum and thereupon said to Esther, "and if he doesn't pay your expenses, I will." Gray paid her tuition, room, and board for her first year but died just before the end of that year. Subsequently, Esther learned that she had received two "A's" in the second semester. The executor of Gray's estate has refused to pay her anything for the two "A's" and has told her that the estate will no longer pay her tuition, room, and board in law school.

Question 33

In an action by Esther against Miller on account of the executor's repudiation of Gray's promise to pay future tuition, room and board, which of the following would be Miller's strongest defense?

(A) The parties did not manifestly intend a contract.

(B) Gray's death terminated the agreement.

(C) The agreement was oral.

(D) The agreement was divisible.

Question 34

In an action against Gray's estate for $2,000 on account of the two "A's", if the only defense raised is lack of consideration, Esther probably will

(A) succeed under the doctrine of promissory estoppel.

(B) succeed on a theory of bargained-for exchange for her father's promise.

(C) not succeed, because the $1,000 for each "A" was promised only as a bonus.

(D) not succeed, because Esther was already legally obligated to use her best efforts in law school.

Question 35

Osif owned Broadacres in fee simple. For a consideration of $5,000, Osif gave Bard a written option to purchase Broadacres for $300,000. The option was assignable. For a consideration of $10,000, Bard subsequently gave an option to Cutter to purchase Broadacres for $325,000. Cutter exercised his option.

Bard thereupon exercised his option. Bard paid the agreed price of $300,000 and took title to Broadacres by deed from Osif. Thereafter, Cutter refused to consummate his purchase.

Bard brought an appropriate action against Cutter for specific performance, or, if that should be denied, then for damages. Cutter counterclaimed for return of the $10,000. In this action, the court will

(A) grant money damages only to Bard.

(B) grant specific performance to Bard.

(C) grant Bard only the right to retain the $10,000.

(D) require Bard to refund the $10,000 to Cutter.

Questions 36-38 are based on the following fact situation.

A written contract was entered into between Bouquet, a financier-investor and Vintage Corporation, a winery and grape-grower. The contract provided that Bouquet would invest $1,000,000 in Vintage for its capital expansion and, in return, that Vintage, from grapes grown in its famous vineyards, would produce and market at least 500,000 bottles of wine each year for five years under the label "Premium Vintage Bouquet."

The contract included provisions that the parties would share equally the profits and losses from the venture and that, if feasible, the wine would be distributed by Vintage only through Claret, a wholesale distributor of fine wines. Neither Bouquet nor Vintage had previously dealt with Claret. Claret learned of the contract two days later from reading a trade newspaper. In reliance thereon, he immediately hired an additional sales executive and contracted for enlargement of his wine storage and display facility.

Question 36

If Vintage refuses to distribute the wine through Claret and Claret then sues Vintage for breach of contract, is it likely that Claret will prevail?

(A) Yes, because Vintage's performance was to run to Claret rather than to Bouquet.

(B) Yes, because Bouquet and Vintage could reasonably foresee that Claret would change his position in reliance on the contract.

(C) No, because Bouquet and Vintage did not expressly agree that Claret would have enforceable rights under their contract.

(D) No, because Bouquet and Vintage, having no apparent motive to benefit Claret, appeared in making the contract to have been protecting or serving only their own interests.

Question 37

For this question only, assume the following facts. Amicusbank lent Bouquet $200,000 and Bouquet executed a written instrument providing that Amicusbank "is entitled to collect the debt from my share of profits, if any, under the Vintage-Bouquet contract." Amicusbank gave prompt notice of this transaction to Vintage.

If Vintage thereafter refuses to account for any profits to Amicusbank and Amicusbank sues Vintage for Bouquet's share of profits then realized, Vintage's strongest argument in defense is that

(A) the Bouquet-Vintage contract did not expressly authorize an assignment of rights.

(B) Bouquet and Vintage are partners, not simply debtor and creditor.

(C) Amicusbank is not an assignee of Bouquet's rights under the Bouquet-Vintage contract.

(D) Amicusbank is not an intended third-party beneficiary of the Bouquet-Vintage contract.

Question 38

For this question only, assume the following facts. Soon after making its contract with Bouquet, Vintage, without Bouquet's knowledge or assent, sold its vineyards but not its winery to Agribiz, a large agricultural corporation. Under the terms of this sale, Agribiz agreed to sell to Vintage all grapes grown on the land for five years. Agribiz's employees have no experience in wine-grape production, and Agribiz has no reputation in the wine industry as a grape producer or otherwise. The Bouquet-Vintage contract was silent on the matter of Vintage's selling any or all of its business assets.

If Bouquet seeks an appropriate judicial remedy against Vintage for entering into the Vintage-Agribiz transaction, is Bouquet likely to prevail?

(A) Yes, because the Vintage-Agribiz transaction created a significant risk of diminishing the profits in which Bouquet would share under his contract with Vintage.

(B) Yes, because the Bouquet-Vintage contract did not contain a provision authorizing a delegation of Vintage's duties.

(C) No, because Vintage remains in a position to perform under the Bouquet-Vintage contract.

(D) No, because Vintage, as a corporation, must necessarily perform its contracts by delegating duties to individuals.

Questions 39-40 are based on the following fact situation.

Mater, a wealthy widow, wishing to make a substantial and potentially enduring gift to her beloved adult stepson Prodigal, established with the Vault Savings and Loan Association a passbook savings account by an initial deposit of $10,000.

Question 39

For this question only, assume the following facts. The passbook was issued solely in Prodigal's name; but Mater retained possession of it, and Prodigal was not then informed of the savings account. Subsequently, Mater became disgusted with Prodigal's behavior and decided to give the same savings account solely to her beloved adult daughter Distaff. As permitted by the rules of Vault Savings and Loan, Mater effected this change by agreement with Vault. This time she left possession of the passbook with Vault. Shortly thereafter, Prodigal learned of the original savings account in his name and the subsequent switch to Distaff's name.

If Prodigal now sues Vault Savings and Loan for $10,000 plus accrued interest, will the action succeed?

(A) Yes, because Prodigal was a third-party intended beneficiary of the original Mater-Vault deposit agreement.

(B) Yes, because Prodigal was a constructive assignee of Mater's claim, as depositor, to the savings account.

(C) No, because Prodigal never obtained possession of the passbook.

(D) No, because Prodigal's rights, if any, to the funds on deposit were effectively abrogated by the second Mater-Vault deposit agreement.

Question 40

For this question only, assume the following facts. The passbook was issued by Vault to Mater solely in her own name. That same day, disinterested witnesses being present, she handed the passbook to Prodigal and said, "As a token of my affection and love for you, I give you this $10,000 savings account." Shortly thereafter, she changed her mind and wrote to Prodigal, "I hereby revoke my gift to you of the $10,000 savings account with Vault Savings and Loan Association. Please return my passbook immediately. Signed: Mater." Prodigal received the letter, but ignored it and Mater died unexpectedly a few days later.

In litigation between Prodigal's and Mater's estate, which of the following is a correct statement of the parties' rights with respect to the money on deposit with Vault?

(A) The estate prevails, because Mater's gift to Prodigal was revocable and was terminated by her death.

(B) The estate prevails, because Mater's gift to Prodigal was revocable and was terminated by her express revocation.

(C) Prodigal prevails, because he took Mater's claim to the savings account by a gratuitous but effective and irrevocable assignment from Mater.

(D) Prodigal prevails, because his failure to reject the gift, even if the assignment was revocable, created an estoppel against Mater and her estate.

Questions 41-42 are based on the following fact situation.

Fifty-year old Ginrus wrote to Collatera, his unemployed adult niece and said: "If you come and live with me and take care of me and my property, Twin Oaks, for the rest of my life, I will leave Twin Oaks to you in my will." Collatera immediately moved in with Ginrus and took care of him and Twin Oaks until he was killed instantly in an automobile accident two weeks later. By his will, Ginrus left his entire estate, including Twin Oaks, to his unmarried sister, Sibling. Twin Oaks was reasonably worth $75,000.

Question 41

Which of the following best states the rights of Collatera and Ginrus' estate (or Sibling)?

(A) Collatera is entitled to receive the reasonable value of her two weeks services only, because two weeks service would be inadequate consideration for the conveyance of Twin Oaks.

(B) Collatera is entitled to receive the reasonable value of her two weeks services only, because Ginrus's letter was an invalid promise to make a will.

(C) Collatera is entitled to receive a conveyance of Twin Oaks, because the letter and her services created a valid contract between her an Ginrus.

(D) The estate (or Sibling) has the right to rescind the contract, if any, because Ginrus' death within two weeks after the agreement was a circumstance apparently unforeseen by the parties at the time they entered into the agreement.

Question 42

For this question only, assume that two days before Ginrus was killed, Collatera made an offer in writing to Drei to sell Twin Oaks to Drei for $75,000 when she should receive the property. If Drei has not accepted by the date of Ginrus' death, may Collatera effectively revoke her offer?

(A) Yes, because she could not make a valid offer to sell property she did not own.

(B) Yes, because there was no option contract with Drei.

(C) No, because a reasonable length of time had not elapsed since she made the offer.

(D) No, because the offer became irrevocable upon Ginrus' death.

Question 43

In March, when Ohm was 17, Stereo delivered to Ohm a television set. At that time Ohm agreed in writing to pay $400 for the set on July 1 when he would reach his eighteenth birthday. Eighteen is the applicable statutory age of majority, and on that date Ohm was to receive the proceeds of a trust. On July 1, when the reasonable value of the television set was $250, Ohm sent Stereo a signed letter stating, "I'll only pay you $300; that is all the set is worth."

In an action against Ohm for money damages on July 2, what is the maximum amount that Stereo will be entitled to recover?

(A) nothing.

(B) $250, the reasonable value of the set.

(C) $300, the amount Ohm promised to pay in his letter of July 1.

(D) $400, the original sale price.

Questions 44-45 are based on the following fact situation.

On April 1, Owner and Buyer signed a writing in which Owner, "in consideration of $100 to be paid to Owner by Buyer," offered Buyer the right to purchase Greenacre for $100,000 within 30 days. The writing further provided, "This offer will become effective as an option only if and when the $100 consideration is in fact paid." On April 20, Owner, having received no payment or other communication from Buyer, sold and conveyed Greenacre to Citizen for $120,000. On April 21, Owner received a letter from Buyer enclosing a cashier's check for $100 payable to Owner and stating, "I am hereby exercising my option to purchase Greenacre and am prepared to close whenever you're ready."

Question 44

Which of the following, if proved, best supports Buyer's suit against Owner for breach of contract?

(A) Buyer was unaware of the sale to Citizen when Owner received the letter and check from Buyer on April 21.

(B) On April 15, Buyer decided to purchase Greenacre, and applied for and obtained a commitment from Bank for a $75,000 loan to help finance the purchase.

(C) When the April 1 writing was signed, Owner said to Buyer, "Don't worry about the $100; the recital of `$100 to be paid' makes this deal binding."

(D) Owner and Buyer are both professional dealers in real estate.

Question 45

For this question only, assume that, for whatever reason, Buyer prevails in the suit against Owner.

Which of the following is Buyer entitled to recover?

(A) Nominal damages only, because the remedy of specific performance was not available to Buyer.

(B) The fair market value, if any, of an assignable option to purchase Greenacre for $100,000.

(C) $20,000, plus the amount, if any, by which the fair market value of Greenacre on the date of Owner's breach exceeded $120,000.

(D) The amount, if any, by which the fair market value of Greenacre on the date of Owner's breach exceeded $100,000.

[START OF SALES QUESTIONS]

Questions 46-47 are based on the following fact situation.

Computers, Inc., contracted in writing with Bank to sell and deliver to Bank a mainframe computer using a new type of magnetic memory, then under development but not perfected by Computers, at a price substantially lower than that of a similar computer using current technology. The contract's delivery term was "F.O.B. Bank, on or before July 31."

Question 46

For this question only, assume that Computers tendered the computer to Bank on August 15, and that Bank rejected it because of the delay.

If Computers sues Bank for breach of contract, which of the following facts, if proved, will best support a recovery by Computers?

(A) The delay did not materially harm Bank.

(B) Computers believed, on the assumption that Bank was getting a "super deal" for its money, that Bank would not reject because of the late tender of delivery.

(C) Computers' delay in tender was caused by a truckers' strike.

(D) A usage in the relevant trade allows computer sellers a 30-day leeway in a specified time of delivery, unless the usage is expressly negated by the contract.

Question 47

For this question only, assume the following facts. After making the contract with Bank, Computers discovered that the new technology it intended to use was unreliable and that no computer manufacturer could yet build a reliable computer using that technology. Computers thereupon notified Bank that it was impossible for Computers or anyone else to build the contracted-for computer "in the present state of the art."

If Bank sues Computers for failure to perform its computer contract, the court will probably decide the case in favor of

(A) Computers, because its performance of the contract was objectively impossible.

(B) Computers, because a contract to build a machine using technology under development imposes only a duty on the builder to use its best efforts to achieve the result contracted for.

(C) Bank, because the law of impossibility does not apply to merchants under the applicable law.

(D) Bank, because Computers assumed the risk, in the given circumstances, that the projected new technology would not work reliably.

Questions 48-49 are based on the following fact situation.

On December 15, Lawyer received from Stationer, Inc., a retailer of office supplies, an offer consisting of its catalog and a signed letter stating, "We will supply you with as many of the items in the enclosed catalog as you order during the next calendar year. We assure you that this offer and the prices in the catalog will remain firm throughout the coming year."

Question 48

For this question only, assume that no other correspondence passed between Stationer and Lawyer until the following April 15 (four months later), when Stationer received from Lawyer a faxed order for "100 reams of your paper, catalog item #101."

Did Lawyer's April 15 fax constitute an effective acceptance of Stationer's offer at the prices specified in the catalog?

(A) Yes, because Stationer had not revoked its offer before April 15.

(B) Yes, because a one-year option contract had been created by Stationer's offer.

(C) No, because under applicable law the irrevocability of Stationer's offer was limited to a period of three months.

(D) No, because Lawyer did not accept Stationer's offer within a reasonable time.

Question 49

For this question only, assume that on January 15, having at that time received no reply from Lawyer, Stationer notified Lawyer that effective February 1, it was increasing the prices of certain specified items in its catalog.

Is the price increase effective with respect to catalog orders Stationer receives from Lawyer during the month of February?

(A) No, because Stationer's original offer, including the price term, became irrevocable under the doctrine of promissory estoppel.

(B) No, because Stationer is a merchant with respect to office supplies; and its original offer, including the price term, was irrevocable throughout the month of February.

(C) Yes, because Stationer received no consideration to support its assurance that it would not increase prices.

(D) Yes, because the period for which Stationer gave assurance that it would not raise prices was longer than three months.

Question 50

On July 15, in a writing signed by both parties, Fixtures, Inc., agreed to deliver to Druggist on August 15 five storage cabinets from inventory for a total price of $5,000 to be paid on delivery. On August 1, the two parties orally agreed to postpone the delivery date to August 20. On August 20, Fixtures tendered the cabinets to Druggist, who refused to accept or pay for them on the ground that they were not tendered on August 15, even though they otherwise met the contract specifications.

Assuming that all appropriate defenses are seasonably raised, will Fixtures succeed in an action against Druggist for breach of contract?

(A) Yes, because neither the July 15 agreement nor the August 1 agreement was required to be in writing.

(B) Yes, because the August 1 agreement operated as a waiver of the August 15 delivery term.

(C) No, because there was no consideration to support the August 1 agreement.

(D) No, because the parol evidence rule will prevent proof of the August 1 agreement.

Questions 51-52 are based on the following fact situation.

In a written contract, Singer agreed to deliver to Byer 500 described chairs at $20 each F.O.B. Singer's place of business. The contract provided that "neither party will assign this contract without the written consent of the other." Singer placed the chairs on board a carrier on January 30. On February 1, Singer said in a signed writing, "I hearby assign to Wheeler all my rights under the Singer-Byer contract." Singer did not request and did not get Byer's consent to this transaction. On February 2, the chairs while in transit were destroyed in a derailment of the carrier's railroad car.

Question 51

In an action by Wheeler against Byer, Wheeler probably will recover

(A) $10,000, the contract price.

(B) the difference between the contract price and the market value of the chairs.

(C) nothing, because the chairs had not been delivered.

(D) nothing, because the Singer-Byer contract forbade an assignment.

Question 52

In an action by Byer against Singer for breach of contract, Byer will probably

(A) succeed, because the carrier will be deemed to be Singer's agent.

(B) succeed, because the risk of loss was on Singer.

(C) not succeed, because of impossibility of performance.

(D) not succeed, because the risk of loss was on Byer.

Question 53

Zeller contracted in writing to deliver to Baker 100 bushels of wheat on August 1 at $3.50 a bushel. Because his suppliers had not delivered enough wheat to him by that time, Zeller on August 1 only had 95 bushels of wheat with which to fulfill his contract with Baker.

If Zeller tenders 95 bushels of wheat to Baker on August 1, and Baker refused to accept or pay for any of the wheat, which of the following best states the legal relationship between Zeller and Baker?

(A) Zeller has a cause of action against Baker, because Zeller has substantially performed his contract.

(B) Zeller is excused from performing his contract because of impossibility of performance.

(C) Baker has a cause of action against Zeller for Zeller's failure to deliver 100 bushels of wheat.

(D) Baker is obligated to give Zeller a reasonable time to attempt to obtain the other five bushels of wheat.

Questions 54-55 are based on the following fact situation.

On June 1, Seller and Buyer contracted in writing for the sale and purchase of Seller's cattle ranch (a large single tract), and to close the transaction on December 1.

Question 54

For this question only, assume the following facts. On October 1, Buyer told Seller, "I'm increasingly unhappy about our June 1 contract because of the current cattle market, and do not intend to buy your ranch unless I'm legally obligated to do so."

If Seller sues Buyer on October 15 for breach of contract, Seller will probably

(A) win, because Buyer committed a total breach by anticipatory repudiation on October 1.

(B) win, because Buyer's October 1 statement created reasonable grounds for Seller's insecurity with respect to Buyer's performance.

(C) lose, because the parties contracted for the sale and conveyance of a single tract, and Seller cannot bring suit for breach of such a contract prior to the agreed closing date.

(D) lose, because Buyer's October 1 statement to Seller was neither a repudiation nor a present breach of the June 1 contract.

Question 55

For this question only, assume the following facts. Buyer unequivocally repudiated the contract on August 1. On August 15, Seller urged Buyer to change her mind and proceed with the scheduled closing on December 1. On October 1, having heard nothing further from Buyer, Seller sold and conveyed his ranch to Rancher without notice to Buyer. On December 1, Buyer attempted to close under the June 1 contract by tendering the full purchase price to Seller. Seller rejected the tender.

If Buyer sues Seller for breach of contract, Buyer will probably

(A) win, because Seller failed seasonably to notify Buyer of any pending sale to Rancher.

(B) win, because Seller waived Buyer's August 1 repudiation by urging her to retract it on August 15.

(C) lose, because Buyer did not retract her repudiation before Seller materially changed his position in reliance thereon by selling the ranch to Rancher.

(D) lose, because acceptance of the purchase price by Seller was a concurrent condition to Seller's obligation to convey the ranch to Buyer on December 1.

Question 56

By the terms of a written contract signed by both parties on January 15, M.B. Ram, Inc., agreed to sell a specific ICB personal computer to Marilyn Materboard for $3,000, and Materboard agreed to pick up and pay for the computer at Ram's store on February 1. Materboard unjustifiably repudiated on February 1. Without notifying Materboard, Ram subsequently sold at private sale the same specific computer to Byte, who paid the same price ($3,000) in cash. The ICB is a popular product. Ram can buy from the manufacturer more units than it can sell at retail.

If Ram sues Materboard for breach of contract, Ram will probably recover

(A) nothing, because it received a price on resale equal to the contract price that Materboard had agreed to pay.

(B) nothing, because Ram failed to give Materboard proper notice of Ram's intention to resell.

(C) Ram's anticipated profit on the sale to Materboard plus incidental damages, if any, because Ram lost that sale.

(D) $3,000 (the contract price), because Materboard intentionally breached the contract by repudiation.

Questions 57-58 are based on the following fact situation.

Landholder was land-rich by inheritance but money-poor, having suffered severe losses on bad investments, but still owned several thousand acres of unencumbered timberland. He had a large family, and his normal, fixed personal expenses were high. Pressed for cash, he advertised a proposed sale of standing timber on a choice 2,000-acre tract. The only response was an offer by Logger, the owner of a large, integrated construction enterprise, after inspection of the advertised tract.

Question 57

For this question only, assume the following facts. Logger offered to buy, sever, and remove the standing timber from the advertised tract at a cash price 70% lower than the regionally prevailing price for comparable timber rights. Landholder, by then in desperate financial straits and knowing little about timber values, signed and delivered to Logger a letter accepting the offer.

If, before Logger commences performance, Landholder's investment fortunes suddenly improve and he wishes to get out of the timber deal with Logger, which of the following legal concepts affords his best prospect of effective cancellation?

(A) Bad faith.

(B) Equitable estoppel.

(C) Unconscionability.

(D) Duress.

Question 58

For this question only, assume the following facts. Logger offered a fair price for the timber rights in question, and Landholder accepted the offer. The 2,000-acre tract was an abundant wild-game habitat and had been used for many years, with Landholder's permission, by area hunters. Logger's performance of the timber contract would destroy this habitat. Without legal excuse and over Landholder's strong objection, Logger repudiated the contract before commencing performance. Landholder could not afford to hire a lawyer and take legal action, and made no attempt to assign any cause of action he might have had against Logger.

If Logger is sued for breach of the contract by Landholder's next-door neighbor, whose view of a nearby lake is obscured by the standing timber, the neighbor will probably

(A) lose, as only an incidental beneficiary, if any, of the Logger-Landholder contract.

(B) lose, as a maintainer of nuisance litigation.

(C) prevail, as a third-party intended beneficiary of the Logger-Landholder contract.

(D) prevail, as a surrogate for Landholder in view of his inability to enforce the contract.

Questions 59-60 are based on the following fact situation.

Fixtures, Inc., in a signed writing, contracted with Apartments for the sale to Apartments of 50 identical sets of specified bathroom fixtures, 25 sets to be delivered on March 1, and the remaining 25 sets on April 1. The agreement did not specify the place of delivery, or the time or place of payment.

Question 59

Which of the following statements is correct?

(A) Fixtures must tender 25 sets to Apartments at Apartments' place of business on March 1, but does not have to turn them over to Apartments until Apartments pays the contract price for the 25 sets.

(B) Fixtures has no duty to deliver the 25 sets on March 1 at Fixtures' place of business unless Apartments tenders the contract price for the 25 sets on that date.

(C) Fixtures must deliver 25 sets on March 1, and Apartments must pay the contract price for the 25 sets within a reasonable time after their delivery.

(D) Fixtures must deliver 25 sets on March 1, but Apartments' payment is due only upon the delivery of all 50 sets.

Question 60

For this question only, make the following assumptions. On March 1, Fixtures tendered 24 sets to Apartments and explained, "One of the 25 sets was damaged in transit from the manufacturer to us, but we will deliver a replacement within 5 days."

Which of the following statements is correct?

(A) Apartments is entitled to accept any number of the 24 sets, reject the rest, and cancel the contract both as to any rejected sets and the lot due on April 1.

(B) Apartments is entitled to accept any number of the 24 sets and to reject the rest, but is not entitled to cancel the contract as to any rejected sets or the lot due on April 1.

(C) Apartments must accept the 24 sets but is entitled to cancel the rest of the contract.

(D) Apartments must accept the 24 sets and is not entitled to cancel the rest of the contract.

Question 61

Breeder bought a two-month-old registered boar at auction from Pigstyle for $800. No express warranty was made. Fifteen months later, tests by experts proved conclusively that the boar had been born incurably sterile. If this had been known at the time of the sale, the boar would have been worth no more than $100.

In an action by Breeder against Pigstyle to avoid the contract and recover the price paid, the parties stipulate that, as both were and had been aware, the minimum age at which the fertility of a boar can be determined is about 12 months.

Which of the following will the court probably decide?

(A) Breeder wins, because the parties were mutually mistaken as to the boar's fertility when they made the agreement.

(B) Breeder wins, because Pigstyle impliedly warranted that the boar was fit for breeding.

(C) Pigstyle wins, because Breeder assumed the risk of the boar's sterility.

(D) Pigstyle wins, because any mistake involved was unilateral, not mutual.

Question 62

Retailer, a dry goods retailer, telephoned Manufacturer, a towel manufacturer, and offered to buy for $5 each a minimum of 500 and a maximum of 1,000 large bath towels, to be delivered in 30 days. Manufacturer orally accepted this offer and promptly sent the following letter to Retailer, which Retailer received two days later: "This confirms our agreement today by telephone to sell you 500 large bath towels for 30-day delivery. /s/ Manufacturer." Twenty-eight days later, Manufacturer tendered to Retailer 1,000 (not 500) conforming bath towels, all of which Retailer rejected because it had found a better price term from another supplier. Because of a glut in the towel market, Manufacturer cannot resell the towels except at a loss.

In a suit by Manufacturer against Retailer, which of the following will be the probable decision?

(A) Manufacturer can enforce a contract for 1,000 towels, because Retailer ordered and Manufacturer tendered that quantity.

(B) Manufacturer can enforce a contract for 500 towels, because Manufacturer's letter of confirmation stated that quantity term.

(C) There is no enforceable agreement, because Retailer never signed a writing.

(D) There is no enforceable agreement, because Manufacturer's letter of confirmation did not state a price term.

Question 63

Buyer mailed a signed order to Seller that read: "Please ship us 10,000 widgets at your current price." Seller received the order on January 7 and that same day mailed to Buyer a properly stamped, addressed, and signed letter stating that the order was accepted at Seller's current price of $10 per widget. On January 8, before receipt of Seller's letter, Buyer telephoned Seller and said, "I hereby revoke my order." Seller protested to no avail. Buyer received Seller's letter on January 9. Because of Buyer's January 8 telephone message, Seller never shipped the goods.

Under the relevant and prevailing rules, is there a contract between Buyer and Seller as of January 10?

(A) No, because the order was an offer that could be accepted only by shipping the goods; and the offer was effectively revoked before shipment.

(B) No, because Buyer never effectively agreed to the $10 price term.

(C) Yes, because the order was, for a reasonable time, an irrevocable offer.

(D) Yes, because the order was an offer that Seller effectively accepted before Buyer attempted to revoke it.

Question 64

Bye Bye telegraphed Vendor on June 1, "At what price will you sell 100 of your QT-Model garbage-disposal units for delivery around June 10?" Thereafter, the following communications were exchanged:

1. Telegram from Vendor received by Bye Bye on June 2: "You're in luck. We have only 100 QT's, all on clearance at 50% off usual wholesale of $120 per unit, for delivery at our shipping platform on June 12."

2. Letter from Bye Bye received in U.S. mail by Vendor on June 5: "I accept. Would prefer to pay in full 30 days after invoice."

3. Telegram from Vendor received by Bye Bye on June 6: "You must pick up at our platform and pay C.O.D."

4. Letter from Bye Bye received in U.S. mail by Vendor on June 9: "I don't deal with people who can't accommodate our simple requests."

5. Telegram from Bye Bye received by Vendor on June 10, after Vendor had sold and delivered all 100 of the QT's to another buyer earlier that day: "Okay. I'm over a barrel and will pick up the goods on your terms June 12."

Bye Bye now sues Vendor for breach of contract.

Which of the following arguments will best serve Vendor's defense?

(A) Vendor's telegram received on June 2 was merely a price quotation, not an offer.

(B) Bye Bye's letter received on June 5 was not an acceptance because it varied the terms of Vendor's initial telegram.

(C) Bye Bye's use of the mails in response to Vendor's initial telegram was an ineffective method of acceptance.

(D) Bye Bye's letter received on June 9 was an unequivocal refusal to perform that excused Vendor even if the parties had previously formed a contract.

Answer Key

Use this Answer Key to quickly identify the correct answer to each question.

(1) C	(11) B	(21) B	(31) A	(41) C	(51) A	(61) C
(2) D	(12) A	(22) C	(32) B	(42) B	(52) D	(62) B
(3) A	(13) D	(23) A	(33) C	(43) C	(53) C	(63) D
(4) A	(14) D	(24) B	(34) B	(44) A	(54) D	(64) D
(5) B	(15) C	(25) B	(35) B	(45) D	(55) C	
(6) D	(16) A	(26) D	(36) D	(46) D	(56) C	
(7) C	(17) C	(27) C	(37) C	(47) D	(57) C	
(8) A	(18) A	(28) D	(38) A	(48) A	(58) A	
(9) C	(19) C	(29) C	(39) D	(49) B	(59) B	
(10) D	(20) B	(30) B	(40) C	(50) B	(60) D	

ANSWERS

CONTRACTS

Answer 1

(C) is the best response,

because contracts involving artistic services are not delegable.

Delegation is a transfer of one's duties under a contract. Assignment is a transfer of one's rights under a contract. If a party to a contract wishes to have another person perform his duties under the contract, he delegates them. There are certain kinds of duties that are non-delegable. In general a duty or performance is delegable unless the obligee has a substantial interest in having the delegator perform. UCC § 2-210(1). Contracts which call for the promisor's use of his own particular skills are normally not delegable. Thus, contracts involving artistic performances or professional services are generally not delegable.

Here, Gourmet hired Deligor because of his own particular, artistic skills. Therefore, the rule that duties involving artistic performance are not delegable applies. Thus, when Deligor sold his decorating business to Newman, Gourmet was not obligated to permit Newman to perform the Gourmet-Deligor contract, even though Newman was also an experienced decorator of excellent repute.

(A) is not the best response,

because there would be no need for a non-delegation clause.

Delegation is a transfer of one's duties under a contract. There are certain kinds of duties that are non-delegable, including tasks that call for the promisor's use of his own particular skills. Thus, contracts involving artistic performances or professional services are not delegable.

The agreement between Gourmet and Deligor would not have to contain a prohibition on delegation, because contracts involving the use of particular skills or artistic performances, such as the design of the interior of Gourmet's new restaurant, are not delegable.

(B) is not the best response,

because the choice would be Gourmet's.

Delegation is a transfer of one's duties under a contract. There are certain kinds of duties that are non-delegable. In general a duty or performance is delegable unless the obligee has a substantial interest in having the delegator perform. Contracts which call for the promisor's use of his own particular skills, such as contracts involving artistic performances or professional services, are normally not delegable.

Under this rule, Gourmet is not obligated to permit Newman to perform the Gourmet-Deligor agreement. And that's true no matter how great Newman's ability to do the job was.

(D) is not the best response,

because only Gourmet, not Deligor, could effect a novation.

Delegation is a transfer of one's duties under a contract. If a party to a contract wishes to have another person perform his duties under the contract, he delegates them. If the obligee under the original contract, the person to whom the duty was owed, agrees to relieve the obligor of all liability after the delegation, a novation is said to have occurred. The effect of a novation is to substitute for the original obligor a stranger to the original contract.

Here, Deligor's purported delegation to Newman of his obligations did not effect a novation. For a novation to occur, Gourmet, the person to whom Deligor's duty of design was owed, would have had to agree to relieve the obligor, Deligor, of all liability. It would not be in either Deligor's or Newman's power to effect a novation by themselves.

Answer 2

(D) is the best response,

because delegators remain liable and Gourmet was an intended beneficiary.

Understanding this answer turns on understanding two principles: a delegator's liability, and intended beneficiaries. When the performance of a duty is delegated, the delegator remains liable. An intended beneficiary is one to whom it would be appropriate to give the right to sue to effectuate the intentions of the parties. The test for determining whether someone is an intended beneficiary is to pose the following question: "To whom is performance to be given according to the language of the contract?"

Here, Gourmet has a breach of contract claim against Deligor, because Deligor's delegation to Newman did not end Deligor's liability under the Gourmet-Deligor contract.

Gourmet also has a breach of contract claim against Newman, because Gourmet was the intended beneficiary of the Deligor-Newman agreement. That is, Gourmet was the person to whom performance (the design, decoration and furnishing of the restaurant) was to be given according to the language of the agreement between Deligor and Newman; that makes

Gourmet the intended beneficiary of Newman's promise to perform, and thus gives Gourmet the right to sue on the promise.

(A) is not the best response,
because express promises do not have to be made to intended beneficiaries.

Gourmet has an enforceable breach of contract claim against both Deligor and Newman. Gourmet has a breach of contract claim against Newman whether or not Newman made any express promises to Gourmet, because Gourmet was the intended beneficiary of the Deligor-Newman agreement. That is, Gourmet was the person to whom performance (the design, decoration and furnishing of the restaurant) was to be given according to the language of the agreement between Deligor and Newman, and the person to whom the promised performance is to be given will normally be an intended beneficiary.

(B) is not the best response,
because Deligor cannot discharge his duty merely by assigning

When the performance of a duty is delegated, the delegator remains liable. So here, Gourmet has a breach of contract claim against Deligor because Deligor's delegation to Newman — no matter how skilled Newman was — did not end Deligor's liability under the Gourmet-Deligor contract.

(C) is not the best response,
because allowing the delegatee to work does not free the delegator from liability.

When the performance of a duty is delegated, the delegator remains liable. So here, Gourmet has a breach of contract claim against Deligor, because neither Deligor's delegation to Newman, nor Gourmet's permitting Newman to do the work, ended Deligor's liability under the Gourmet-Deligor contract.

Answer 3

(A) is the best response,
because it's the only response that recognizes that the agreement is supported by consideration.

A valid agreement has three basic elements: Offer, acceptance, and consideration (or some substitute for consideration, like promissory estoppel). Consideration is a bargained-for exchange and either detriment to the promisee or benefit to the promisor, and typically both. The central issue here is whether Neff's promise not to sue for reimbursement would be sufficient to constitute consideration. In fact, it would, because consideration in the form of detriment to the promisee *can* take the form of promisee's refraining from doing something he's legally entitled to do – like pressing a valid legal claim. As long as this is bargained-for, it'll satisfy the consideration requirement. Here, it is bargained-for, because Owens exchanged his promise to pay for the

caretaker for Neff's promise not to sue.

Thus, as long as Neff has a good faith belief in the validity of the claim, it's consideration enough for the agreement. Since A recognizes this, it's the best response.

(B) is not the best response,
because it's not *Owens's* perception of validity that's relevant, but Neff's.

A valid agreement has three basic elements: Offer, acceptance, and consideration (or some substitute for consideration, like promissory estoppel). Consideration is a bargained-for exchange and either detriment to the promisee or benefit to the promisor, and typically both. The central issue here is whether Neff's promise not to sue for reimbursement would be sufficient to constitute consideration. In fact, it would, because consideration in the form of detriment to the promisee *can* take the form of promisee's refraining from doing something he's legally entitled to do – like pressing a legal claim. As long as this is bargained-for, it'll satisfy the consideration requirement. Here, it is bargained-for, because Owens exchanged his promise to pay for the caretaker for Neff's promise not to sue. Thus, Owens's belief as to the validity of the claim doesn't matter; even if the claim is *invalid,* as long as Neff has a good faith belief in the validity of his own claim, and a reasonable person could believe the claim is well-founded, that will suffice. Since B doesn't recognize this, it's not the best response.

(C) is not the best response,
because it wouldn't be determinative of whether consideration exists. Even if the claim is groundless, it's consideration if Neff had a good-faith belief in its validity.

A valid agreement has three basic elements: Offer, acceptance, and consideration (or some substitute for consideration, like promissory estoppel). Consideration is a bargained-for exchange and either detriment to the promisee or benefit to the promisor, and typically both. The central issue here is whether Neff's promise not to sue for reimbursement would be sufficient to constitute consideration. In fact, it would, because consideration in the form of detriment to the promisee *can* take the form of promisee's refraining from doing something he's legally entitled to do – like pressing a valid legal claim. As long as this is bargained-for, it'll satisfy the consideration requirement. Here, it is bargained-for, because Owens exchanged his promise to pay for the caretaker for Neff's promise not to sue. Thus, even though the claim may be groundless, the agreement is still supported by consideration. Note that even if the claim is *invalid,* as long as Neff has a good faith belief in the validity of his own claim, and a reasonable person could believe the claim is well-founded, that will suffice. Since C places unwarranted importance on the groundlessness of the claim, it's not the best response.

(D) is not the best response,

because the contract here is *not* aleatory, and even if it was, aleatory contracts are enforceable.

An aleatory contract is one where the duty to perform is conditional upon an occurrence which is uncertain. Accident insurance is one example. Such contracts *are* enforceable, since the conditional obligation to pay is considered adequate consideration to enforce the other party's duties.

Here, the contract wasn't aleatory, because Owens's duty to hire a caretaker was firm – he didn't, say, only have to hire a caretaker if it snowed, he had to hire a caretaker no matter what.

Now, confess – if you chose this response, you probably did so because you used a process of elimination and were left with this response, and since it had a word whose definition you couldn't remember, you took a chance. As a rule, that's a dangerous policy. In fact, the right answer here is that the contract *was* supported by consideration, in the form of Neff's agreeing not to press a legal claim in which he had a good-faith belief of validity. Since D doesn't recognize this, it's not the best response.

Answer 4

(A) is the best response,

because it correctly characterizes Neff, and this determines why he'll prevail against Morse.

When two parties form a contract, there are two general types of beneficiaries which may be created: *Intended* beneficiaries and *incidental* beneficiaries. Only intended beneficiaries have enforceable rights under the contract. Of intended beneficiaries, there are two types: *Creditor* and *donee* beneficiaries. The way you tell the difference between the two is to determine if the beneficiary is a creditor beneficiary; if he's not, he *must* be a donee beneficiary. A creditor beneficiary is one to whom the promisee owes a pre-existing duty, which the promisor's performance will fulfill. Here, the promise to maintain the sidewalk is Morse's, in return for Owens's promise to let Morse live in Owens's house rent-free. Thus, as to the promise for which Neff is the beneficiary – keeping the sidewalk clear – Morse is the promisor and Owens is the promisee. The promise to keep the sidewalk clear discharges Owens's previous duty to Neff to maintain the sidewalk. Thus, Neff is a creditor beneficiary to the Owens-Morse contract, *not* a donee beneficiary. If there hadn't been a prior agreement between Owens and Neff, and Owens was keeping Neff's sidewalk clear out of the kindness of his heart, Neff would be a *donee* beneficiary, due to the lack of a pre-existing duty to Neff.

Since option A correctly states why Neff will be able to maintain an action against Morse, it's the best response.

(B) is not the best response,

because it mischaracterizes Neff: He's a *creditor* bene-

ficiary, not a *donee* beneficiary.

When two parties form a contract, there are two general types of beneficiaries which may be created: *Intended* beneficiaries and *incidental* beneficiaries. Only intended beneficiaries have enforceable rights under the contract. Of intended beneficiaries, there are two types: *Creditor* and *donee* beneficiaries. The way you tell the difference between the two is to determine if the beneficiary is a creditor beneficiary; if he's not, he *must* be a donee beneficiary. A creditor beneficiary is one to whom the promisee owes a pre-existing duty, which the promisor's performance will fulfill. Here, the promise to maintain the sidewalk is Morse's, in return for Owens's promise to let Morse live in Owens's house rent-free. Thus, as to the promise for which Neff is the beneficiary – keeping the sidewalk clear – Morse is the promisor and Owens is the promisee. The promise to keep the sidewalk clear discharges Owens's previous duty to Neff to maintain the sidewalk. Thus, Neff is a creditor beneficiary to the Owens-Morse contract, *not* a donee beneficiary. If there hadn't been a prior agreement between Owens and Neff, and Owens was keeping Neff's sidewalk clear out of the kindness of his heart, Neff would be a *donee* beneficiary, due to the lack of a pre-existing duty to Neff.

If you chose this response, keep in mind that the only relevance of the creditor-donee distinction is when the beneficiary's rights "vest," making those rights enforceable. Traditionally, a creditor beneficiary's rights vest when he has detrimentally relied on the contract, under the majority view. A donee beneficiary's rights vest upon justified detrimental reliance OR when he manifests assent to the agreement, which can be implied to occur as soon as he finds out about it. However, most modern courts follow the Restatement 2d of Contracts, §311, which ignores the donee-creditor distinction, and rather views the rights of both as vesting when one of these three events occurs:

1. The beneficiary manifests assent to the promise;
2. The beneficiary sues to enforce the promise; or
3. The beneficiary justifiably relies on the promise to his detriment.

In fact, this isn't an issue in this question, because the fact that Neff is an intended beneficiary gives him the ability to sue Morse, regardless of whether he's a creditor or donee beneficiary. Nonetheless, since B mischaracterizes Neff, it can't be the best response.

(C) is not the best response,

because it mischaracterizes Neff – he's an *intended* beneficiary, not an *incidental* beneficiary.

When two parties form a contract, there are two general types of beneficiaries which may be created: *Intended* beneficiaries and *incidental* beneficiaries. Only intended beneficiaries have enforceable rights under the contract.

The way you tell the difference is to look at the intent of the *promisee* (the one to whom the duty in question is owed). If it's his primary intent that the third party receive benefit from promisor's performance, the third party is an intended beneficiary – otherwise, the third party is an incidental beneficiary with no enforceable rights. Criteria to examine in making this determination include:

1. A statement of intent in the contract;
2. Close relationship between promisee and beneficiary;
3. Identifiability of the beneficiary (before contract is discharged, not at formation);
4. Promisor's performance directly to third party.

Under these facts, the duty in question is keeping Neff's sidewalk clear. Under the Morse-Owens contract, this is Morse's promise, in return for Owens's promise of free rent. Thus, Morse is the promisor as to the sidewalk clearing, and Owens is the promisee. Thus, if it's Owens's intent that Morse keep the sidewalk clear for Neff's benefit, Neff is an intended beneficiary. Given that Owens previously owed Neff the duty of keeping the sidewalk clear, Neff would be an intended beneficiary. In fact, Neff is, more specifically, a *creditor* beneficiary under the contract, because Morse's performance would discharge a duty Owens owed Neff (the other type of intended beneficiary is a donee beneficiary). Since he's an intended beneficiary, once his rights "vest" under the contract, he has enforceable rights under the contract and can sue Morse. Since C mischaracterizes Neff, it's not the best response.

(D) is not the best response,

because although it's theoretically correct, it's not determinative of Neff's recovery.

While it's true that there is no privity of contract between Neff and Morse, this does not torpedo Neff's claim, because it ignores the possibility of Neff's recovery as an intended beneficiary under the Owens-Morse contract. A third party beneficiary, by dint of *being* a third party beneficiary, is not in privity with a party – however, if a third party is an intended beneficiary of a contract, he'll have enforceable rights in the absence of privity.

Under these facts, Neff's recovery is predicated on his being an intended beneficiary under the Morse-Owens contract. He's an intended beneficiary because as to the duty in question – keeping the sidewalk clear – Owens was the promisee, and it was his intent that Neff benefit from Morse's performance. Note that if Neff *were* in privity with Morse, he could recover without turning to a third party beneficiary theory. However, the fact that he lacks privity doesn't stop him from recovering. Since D doesn't recognize this, it's not the best response.

Answer 5

(B) is the best response,

because it correctly applies the common law rules on irrevocability and modifications to these facts.

First, you have to determine whether the common law or the UCC will control. Since it's the sale of *land* that's involved, not a transaction in *goods,* the common law will control.

Second, you have to analyze what each communication *does.* The first is Ohner's May 1 telegram to Byer. It is sufficiently definite to constitute an offer to sell any or all lots in the subdivision for $5,000 each. Byer's May 2 telegram to Ohner constituted an *acceptance* as to lot 101 at $5,000, and inherently rejected the offer as to the other 49 lots. As a result, Ohner's offer as to all the other lots terminated, because his original offer to keep the offer open until June 1 was not supported by consideration, so it *was* revocable. Even if Byer's acceptance as to lot 101 *didn't* terminate the offer, Ohner's subsequently raising the price to $6,000 *did* revoke the original offer and created a new one, at $6,000.

Thus, the price on the latter 49 lots was $6,000. The *original* lot, #101, had a price of $5,000, because Byer originally accepted at that price. Thus, once Byer accepted at $5,000, there was a contract formed as to lot 101. The subsequent change to $6,000 would thus be a modification, and since there was no consideration, the modification as to lot 101 was unenforceable under the pre-existing duty rule. As a result, the contract price is $5,000 for lot 101 and $6,000 for the rest.

This question indicates why it's so important to segregate UCC and non-UCC cases *before* you analyze them. Here, the rule on modifications under the UCC is very different from the common law. Under §2-209, modifications are valid without consideration as long as they are in good faith. At common law, consideration is required under the "pre-existing duty" rule. As to irrevocability, at common law, consideration is required to form an option contract; under §2-205, merchants can make irrevocable, or "firm" offers, without consideration. Both of these would lead you astray on these facts. However, since B correctly applies the common law rules, it's the best response.

(A) is not the best response,

because it ignores the fact that only lot 101 is subject to the $5,000 offer – the remaining lots will cost $6,000.

First, you have to determine whether the common law or the UCC will control. Since it's the sale of *land* that's involved, not a transaction in *goods,* the common law will control.

Second, you have to analyze what each communication *does.* The first is Ohner's May 1 telegram to Byer. It is sufficiently definite to constitute an offer to sell any or all lots in the subdivision for $5,000 each. Byer's May 2 telegram to Ohner constituted an *acceptance* as to lot 101 at $5,000, and inherently rejected the offer as to the other 49 lots. As a result, Ohner's offer as to all the other lots terminated, because his original offer to keep the offer open until June 1 was not supported by consideration, so it *was* revocable. Even if Byer's acceptance as to lot 101 *didn't* terminate the offer, Ohner's subsequently raising the price to $6,000 *did* revoke the original offer and created a new one, at $6,000.

Thus, the price on the latter 49 lots was $6,000. The *original* lot, #101, had a price of $5,000, because Byer originally accepted at that price. Thus, once Byer accepted at $5,000, there was a contract formed as to lot 101. The subsequent change to $6,000 would thus be a modification, and since there was no consideration, the modification as to lot 101 was unenforceable under the pre-existing duty rule. As a result, the contract price is $5,000 for lot 101 and $6,000 for the rest.

If you chose this response, you were thinking of the UCC rule as to irrevocable offers. Under UCC §2-205, a merchant in the goods may make an offer irrevocable for up to three months, as long as the offer is in a signed writing. Here, there's no transaction in goods, so the common law applies. At common law, as "option contracts," consideration is required to make an offer irrevocable.

In any case, if the UCC applied, then every lot would be $6,000, due to operation of the UCC rule on modifications. Under §2-209, modifications do not require consideration as long as they are made in good faith. Here, Ohner didn't know about the shopping center when he made the offer, and there are no other facts suggesting bad faith, so his modification as to lot 101 would probably be enforceable.

In any case, the UCC does not apply, and application of common law rules results in a contract price of $5,000 for lot 101 and $6,000 for the rest. Since option A doesn't recognize this, it's not the best response.

(C) is not the best response,

because it ignores the fact that lot 101 will only cost $5,000, although it's correct in stating that the other 49 will be $6,000 each.

First, you have to determine whether the common law or the UCC will control. Since it's the sale of *land* that's involved, not a transaction in *goods,* the common law will control.

Second, you have to analyze what each communication *does.* The first is Ohner's May 1 telegram to Byer. It is sufficiently definite to constitute an offer to sell any or all lots in the subdivision for $5,000 each. Byer's May 2 telegram to Ohner constituted an *acceptance* as to lot 101 at $5,000, and inherently rejected the offer as to the other 49 lots. As a result, Ohner's offer as to all the other lots terminated, because his original offer to keep the offer open until June 1 was not supported by consideration, so it *was* revocable. Even if Byer's acceptance as to lot 101 *didn't* terminate the offer,

Ohner's subsequently raising the price to $6,000 *did* revoke the original offer and created a new one, at $6,000.

Thus, the price on the latter 49 lots was $6,000. The *original* lot, #101, had a price of $5,000, because Byer originally accepted at that price. Thus, once Byer accepted at $5,000, there was a contract formed as to lot 101. The subsequent change to $6,000 would thus be a modification, and since there was no consideration, the modification as to lot 101 was unenforceable under the pre-existing duty rule. As a result, the contract price is $5,000 for lot 101 and $6,000 for the rest.

If you chose this response, you correctly applied the UCC to this problem – the only hitch being that, since there's a sale of land, and not a transaction in goods involved, the UCC doesn't apply. What's central to the UCC under these facts is the UCC rule on modifications, under §2-209. Modifications in sale of goods contracts do not require consideration as long as they are made in good faith. Here, Ohner didn't know about the impending shopping center when he made the offer, and there are no other facts suggesting bad faith, so his modification as to all the lots would probably be enforceable.

In any case, since the UCC doesn't apply here, and option C doesn't recognize this, it's not the best response.

(D) is not the best response,

because it doesn't correctly state the price as to *either* lot 101 *or* the remaining 49 lots – in fact, it has the prices reversed.

First, you have to determine whether the common law or the UCC will control. Since it's the sale of *land* that's involved, not a transaction in *goods,* the common law will control.

Second, you have to analyze what each communication *does.* The first is Ohner's May 1 telegram to Byer. It is sufficiently definite to constitute an offer to sell any or all lots in the subdivision for $5,000 each. Byer's May 2 telegram to Ohner constituted an *acceptance* as to lot 101 at $5,000, and inherently rejected the offer as to the other 49 lots. As a result, Ohner's offer as to all the other lots terminated, because his original offer to keep the offer open until June 1 was not supported by consideration, so it *was* revocable. Even if Byer's acceptance as to lot 101 *didn't* terminate the offer, Ohner's subsequently raising the price to $6,000 *did* revoke the original offer and created a new one, at $6,000.

Thus, the price on the latter 49 lots was $6,000. The *original* lot, #101, had a price of $5,000, because Byer originally accepted at that price. Thus, once Byer accepted at $5,000, there was a contract formed as to lot 101. The subsequent change to $6,000 would thus be a modification, and since there was no consideration, the modification as to lot 101 was unenforceable under the pre-existing duty rule. As a result, the contract price is $5,000 for lot 101 and $6,000 for the rest.

If you chose this response, you mistakenly believed the modification as to lot 101 was valid, but that the original offer as to the other lots was irrevocable. Since neither one of these is true, due to operation of the common law rules on modification (not valid without consideration) and irrevocable offers (no irrevocability without consideration), D isn't the best response.

Answer 6

(D) is the best response,

because it correctly identifies the central reason Ohner will prevail: The offer had been revoked, so Byer no longer had the power to accept it.

A revocation is offeror's retraction of the offer. Once there's an effective revocation, the offeree *cannot* accept the offer.

A revocation can be direct – by expressly terminating the offer – or indirect, by offeror's performing an act inconsistent with the offer, which terminates the offer as soon as the offeree knows about it. Here, Ohner sold the subject of the offer – the lots – to someone else. Thus he impliedly revoked the offer to Byer, and once Byer knew about the sale, he couldn't accept. Note that it's not selling the land to someone else that is, *by itself,* a revocation – but Byer's *knowledge* of that sale. Since D impliedly recognizes that this forms an effective revocation, and that Ohner will prevail as a result, it's the best response.

(A) is not the best response,

because the offer was not, in fact, irrevocable. As a result, Ohner's telling Byer that the lots had been sold to someone else amounted to a revocation of the offer.

First, you have to determine if the UCC applies here. Since the contract involves the sale of land, not a transaction in goods, the common law controls, *not* the UCC.

Now, look at the offer itself. On May 1, Ohner, in writing, assured Byer that he'd leave the offer open until June 1. The rule at common law is that the only way to make an offer irrevocable (i.e., to create an "option"), is with consideration. Under these facts, Byer didn't pay for the option (or supply any other consideration), so the offer was revocable. A revocation can take the form of offeree's knowledge of an act by offeror which is inconsistent with the offer. Here, selling the subject of the offer – the lots – to someone else would certainly qualify, once Byer knew of the sale.

If you chose this response, you were thinking of the UCC. This is an easy trap to fall into in this question, because every requirement of an irrevocable offer under the UCC is satisfied – except that the UCC itself doesn't apply! Under §2-205, irrevocable offers, or "firm offers" as they are called, are binding only where the offeror is a merchant and the offer of irrevocability is made in a "signed writing" (also, the time period involved cannot exceed three months). Thus, here, the

offer of irrevocability would qualify if a transaction in goods were involved. Since option A fails to recognize that the sale here involves *land,* it's not the best response.

(B) is not the best response,

because Ohner's revocation by phone would be effective.

A revocation is offeror's retraction of the offer. There is no requirement that it be in writing. Here, Ohner's telling Byer over the phone that he had sold the lots to someone else would be an effective revocation, thus terminating Byer's power to accept the offer.

If you chose this response, you were probably thinking about the traditional (not modern) rule on acceptances (not revocations). In the old days, an acceptance was only effective if it was communicated by a medium expressly or impliedly authorized by the offeror – meaning that unless the offeror specified otherwise, the manner he used (e.g., a letter) was the appropriate means of responding. However, under modern rules, an offeree may accept via any means reasonable in the circumstances Restatement 2d of Contracts §30 (the UCC also holds this view, §2-206). In any case, this doesn't refer to revocations, only acceptances.

You may also have been tripped up by the Statute of Frauds, since the sale of land is involved. However, only a contract for the sale of land need be in writing to be enforceable, *not* a revocation of an offer. You may have even been thinking of rescissions (cancellations) of contracts covered by the Statute of Frauds, which must be in writing. However, that's only for contracts already formed, *not* for offers.

The upshot is that Ohner's telephoned revocation was valid, and since option B doesn't recognize this, it's not the best response.

(C) is not the best response,

because it ignores a key element of indirect revocation.

C is correct in implying that an offeror's revocation need not be directly or expressly made in order to be valid, and that it's Ohner's selling the land to someone else that's the lynchpin of his revocation. In fact, an offer may be terminated by any act by the offeror which is inconsistent with the offer – but *not until the offeree knows about it.* If, for instance, Ohner had sold to someone else but Byer didn't know about it, from Ohner or anyone else, then Byer would still be able to accept! Since C ignores a crucial element of the revocation, it's not the best response.

Answer 7

(C) is the best response,

because it correctly identifies that the missing price term will render the agreement unenforceable.

Contracts for the sale of an interest in land fall within the Statute of Frauds, and thus require a writing in order to be enforceable (unless they are partially performed). In order to suffice, the writing must specify with reasonable certainty

1. the contract's subject matter;
2. parties' identities;
3. promises, by whom and to whom made, and essential terms and conditions;
4. signature of the party to be charged (the one who denies the contract's existence).

In many states, the contract requires a recital of consideration as well.

Under these facts, the price would be considered an essential term, so the written agreement would be unenforceable without it. Since C recognizes this, it's the best response.

(A) is not the best response,

because the price term, since it's "essential," would not be implied by the court.

Contracts for the sale of an interest in land fall within the Statute of Frauds, and thus require a writing in order to be enforceable (unless they're partially performed). In order to suffice, the writing must specify with reasonable certainty

1. the contract's subject matter;
2. parties' identities;
3. promises, by whom and to whom made, and essential terms and conditions;
4. signature of the party to be charged (the one who denies the contract's existence).

In many states, the contract requires a recital of the consideration, as well.

Under these facts, the price would be considered an essential term, so the written agreement would be unenforceable without it.

If you chose this response, you were probably thinking of the modern trend concerning *reliance*. In a growing number of states, and under the Restatement, the court will estop a party from asserting the Statute of Frauds as a defense due to the other party's reliance. Restatement of Contracts 2d §139. According to the Restatement, enforcing a promise that is within the Statute of Frauds, due to reliance, depends on several factors:

1. The availability of other remedies (in particular, restitution);
2. the extent to which the promisee's detrimental reliance was foreseeable and reasonable, and how substantial the reliance was; and
3. the extent to which the reliance itself, and other evidence, agrees with the oral agreement.

Under these facts, there's no evidence of any reliance at all; and if there were, and the majority of states followed the rule on reliance, the court would have to determine what the agreed price was, not whether it was fair and equitable.

Since A fails to realize that the contract is not enforceable without the price term, it's not the best

response.

(B) is not the best response,

because it reflects the UCC rule, not the common law.

Here, a contract for the sale of an interest in land is involved. Article 2 of the UCC only covers transactions in goods. Thus, the common law controls.

Contracts for the sale of an interest in land fall within the Statute of Frauds, and thus require a writing in order to be enforceable (unless they are partially performed). In order to suffice, the writing must specify with reasonable certainty

1. the contract's subject matter;
2. parties' identities;
3. promises, by whom and to whom made, and essential terms and conditions;
4. signature of the party to be charged (the one who denies the contract's existence).

In many states, the contract requires a recital of consideration as well.

Under these facts, the price would be considered an essential term, so the written agreement would be unenforceable without it.

If you chose this response, you were thinking of the UCC Statute of Frauds, which is considerably more liberal than the common law. Under UCC §2-201, the writing must

1. be evidence of a contract (i.e., it must provide a basis for believing that the offered oral evidence rests on a real transaction;
2. be signed; and
3. show quantity.

Thus, price, time, and place of payment or delivery, warranties and quality of goods may all be missing, leaving the contract enforceable nonetheless – although the more missing terms there are, the less likely it is the parties intended to be bound.

Here, under the UCC the contract would be enforceable, although the court would include the price as the parties intended it (*not* reasonable market value). However, B fails to realize that the UCC does not apply to these facts, and since the controlling rule at common law is different, B is not the best response.

(D) is not the best response,

because although its result is correct, its reasoning is irrelevant.

As a general rule, parties are free to set the terms of their agreement as they see fit. Barring fraud, their agreed price may represent a bargain to one party, while leaving the agreement enforceable.

Option D, in fact, reaches the correct conclusion, but the reason for the conclusion is that, since price is an essential term and the contract is covered by the Statute of Frauds, the contract will be *unenforceable* without a writing.

Contracts for the sale of an interest in land fall within

the Statute of Frauds, and thus require a writing in order to be enforceable (unless they are partially performed). In order to suffice, the writing must specify with reasonable certainty

1. the contract's subject matter;
2. parties' identities;
3. promises, by whom and to whom made, and essential terms and conditions;
4. signature of the party to be charged (the one who denies the contract's existence).

In many states, the contract requires a recital of consideration as well.

Under these facts, the price would be considered an essential term, so the written agreement would be unenforceable without it. Since D ignores this, it's not the best response.

Answer 8

(A) is the best response,

because the contract did not alter the default rule that where one performance takes time and the other doesn't, the former must be completed before the latter.

Rest. 2d § 234(2), on order of performances, says that "where the performance of only one party under ... an exchange [of promises] *requires a period of time*, his performance is *due at an earlier time* than that of the other party, unless the language or circumstances indicate the contrary." Since Painter's performance (painting) took a "period of time," and Farmer's performance (payment) didn't, this rule applies, and meant that Painter had to fully perform before Farmer's performance was due, unless "the language or circumstances indicate the contrary." Nothing in the contract language or the circumstances indicated the contrary (indeed, the document says explicitly that payment is due upon "completion of the work on all three barns," making the case especially easy.)

(B) is not the best response,

because (1) nothing in these circumstances indicates that Painter ever had a right to payment on a per-barn basis; and (2) even if Painter had such a right, his failure to demand payment after the first barn would not be a waiver of his right to demand payment after the second barn.

Under the analysis in Choice (A), Painter never had a right to payment on a per-barn basis. (She might have negotiated such a right, of course, but she didn't.) So there couldn't have been any waiver.

Furthermore, even if Painter did have such a right, it's unlikely that her failure to exercise it after the first barn would cost her the right to demand payment after the second. That's so because even if Painter was held to have "waived" the right to demand payment on a barn-by-barn basis when she didn't demand payment after the first one and went on working, that waiver was

revocable at any time before Farmer materially relied on it. Therefore, when Painter demanded full payment for two barns after the second one was done, she would have been making an enforceable revocation of any waiver that might have occurred (since there's no indication that Farmer could have materially relied on the waiver).

(C) is not the best response,

because the contract is not divisible, since the parties did not agree that painting of a single barn and payment of $2,000 were agreed equivalents.

If indeed this contract was "divisible," this choice would be correct. As the Restatement puts the idea (while not using the word "divisible"), "If the performances to be exchanged under an exchange of promises can be apportioned into corresponding pairs of part performances so that the parts of each pair are *properly regarded as agreed equivalents*, a party's performance of his part of such a pair has the same effect on the other's duties to render performance of the agreed equivalent as it would have if only that pair of performances had been promised." Rest. § 240.

The problem for Painter is that here, the painting of each barn and payment for that barn are not "properly regarded as agreed equivalents," because the contract established that payment was due after painting of all three barns. In other words, the contract was not in fact set up by the parties as a divisible one.

(D) is not the correct response,

because performance of 2/3's of the work would not constitute substantial performance.

If Painter had truly "substantially performed," he would indeed be entitled to the contract price, less damages for his less-than-perfect performance. But 2/3's performance is very unlikely to be found to constitute substantial performance. Furthermore, the question asks you whether he's entitled to be paid $4,000, not whether he's entitled to payment of any amount. So even if the court found he'd substantially performed, Painter would be entitled only to the contract price less damages for the non-performance, and that wouldn't necessarily come out at the full $6,000 amount less exactly $2,000 for the unpainted last barn. (Farmer might now have to spend more than $2,000 to get the last barn painted by itself, for instance, leading to damages equalling this greater amount.)

Answer 9

(C) is the best response,

because it correctly states the damages available under a quasi-contract theory.

Where a defaulting plaintiff has rendered some performance of value to the defendant, but has not substantially performed, the plaintiff may not recover "on the contract." But he may recover on a *quasi-contract* or *quantum meruit* ("as much as he deserved") theory

— the court uses its equity-like powers to prevent unjust enrichment of the defendant.

If Farmer didn't have to pay anything, he'd have been unjustly enriched (at least with respect to the two painted barns, putting aside his damage from not getting the agreed-upon painting of the third bard) by the "value" to him of the painting of two barns. So the court would start by awarding Painter this value. But then, Farmer would be entitled to be made whole for the damages to him from not getting all three barns painted for the agreed-upon $6,000. So the court would compute how much it would now cost Farmer to get that single barn painted. If that cost would be $2,000 or less, Farmer's damages would be zero. But if it would cost more, then the difference would be deducted from Painter's quasi-contract "value of the services of painting two barns" recovery.

(A) is not the best response,

because even though the painting of all three barns was an express condition of payment under the contract, the court can and would still award a quasi-contract recovery.

A party who makes some performance but materially breaches may nonetheless recover the reasonable value of his services on a quasi-contract or quantum meruit theory, as detailed in Choice (C). That's true even though the return performance was expressly conditioned on the defaulting party's making of full performance.

(B) is not the best response,

because Painter, as a material breacher, is not entitled to any recovery that takes into account the profits Painter would have made had she performed.

For the reasons described in Choice (C), Painter is only entitled to a quasi-contract recovery, not to recover "on the contract." So any formula keyed to Painter's anticipated "profit" is irrelevant — it's the value to the defendant, not the profit that would have been made by the breaching plaintiff, that is the starting point. (Profits that would have been made by the plaintiff are relevant only where it's the defendant, not the plaintiff, who breached.)

(D) is not the correct response,

because this formula doesn't take into account Farmer's right to deduct damages for Painter's failure to paint the third barn.

If the contract had involved only two barns, and Painter's breach was a failure to substantially complete that painting (let's say Painter used the wrong type of paint, or painted only one and a half barns), this formula would probably be the correct measure of Painter's quasi-contract recovery. But while Farmer must pay Painter the reasonable value of Painter's work in painting the two barns, Farmer is entitled to deduct his damages for breach of contract (i.e., for the fact that he didn't collect on his bargain to have all

three barns painted for a single $6,000 price). Since this choice doesn't deduct anything for Farmer's damages, it's wrong.

Answer 10

(D) is the best response.

As to alternative I: This is not a good defense for Brown because although the Clark-Green agreement would have to be in writing to be enforceable, Brown could not rely on this to excuse his own performance. That's because third parties to a contract *cannot* assert the Statute of Frauds as a defense.

A contract need only be in writing to be enforceable if it falls within the Statute of Frauds. Although the Statute of Frauds varies from state to state, a writing is generally required for contracts incapable of performance in less than one year, in consideration of marriage, to answer for another's debt or default, as required by the UCC (which doesn't control here, since there's no transaction in goods), or – the one most likely to apply to these facts – for the sale of an interest in land.

Here, the channel *is* an interest in land in the form of an *easement* – a non-possessory interest in land, such that one has the right to use another's land. However, the reason this doesn't do Brown any good is that he can't rely on it to excuse his performance; only Clark could use it to make the agreement unenforceable. Here, Brown agreed to build a boathouse as well as dig the channel; he has neither rights nor duties, and thus no excuses, under the Clark-Green agreement.

Had Brown started to dig the channel and Clark had enjoined him from proceeding, *then* Brown would have an excuse. However, under these facts, Brown has not undertaken to perform at all, not even to build the boathouse. Note that if Brown *had* commenced construction, the writing requirement, in a claim between Green and Clark, would probably be excused on grounds of promissory estoppel. However, since the Statute of Frauds is not available to Brown, as a third party to the contract, alternative I can't be correct.

As to alternative II: This is not a good defense for Brown, because the contract falls *outside* the Statute of Frauds, and as a result is enforceable without a writing.

A contract need only be in writing to be enforceable if it falls within the Statute of Frauds. Although the Statute of Frauds varies from state to state, a writing is generally required for contracts incapable of performance in less than one year, in consideration of marriage, to answer for another's debt or default, as required by the UCC (which doesn't control here, since there's no transaction in goods), or – the one most likely to apply to these facts – for the sale of an interest in land.

Here, Green only contracted for Brown's services as a contractor, and since this is not within the Statute of Frauds, no writing will be required to make the contract enforceable. Since II doesn't recognize this, it can't be correct.

Answer 11

(B) is the best response.

As to alternative I: The problem here is that it may or may not reflect Brown's damages – you can't tell from these facts. However, if alternative I is taken to mean that Brown is only entitled to the contract price of the boathouse ($5,000 all together), it's incorrect.

In construction contracts, the builder's damages depend on whether the buyer's material breach occurs before, during, or after builder's performance. Here, Green breached the contract during construction. As a result, this formula will determine Brown's damages:

> Contract price (here, $10,000)
> less
> Cost to complete (here, unknown)
> and less
> Amount already paid (here, $2,500)

In addition, savings due to mitigation (if available) must be deducted. Since $2,500 may or may not represent this amount, alternative I isn't correct.

As to alternative II: This is true, because by repudiating the contract Green has committed a major breach, relieving Brown of his duty to perform under the contract.

At common law (not under the UCC), when a party breaches a contract, the other party's duty to perform under the contract depends on whether the breach was material (major) or minor. A material breach relieves the aggrieved party of his contractual duty to perform; a minor breach means the aggrieved party must perform and then sue for damages.

The Restatement of Contracts §275 offers six factors to determine if a breach is material, weighing them according to what's critical in each case:

1. To what extent has the injured party received benefits?
2. Can the injured party be adequately compensated in damages?
3. Is the breaching party "close" to full performance?
4. Will the breaching party face great hardship if termination is permitted?
5. How willful is the breach?
6. How great is the certainty of completion?

Here, the fact that Green's breach was willful, by itself, would indicate that the breach is material. As a result, Brown can refuse to perform under the contract any further (and, naturally, recover damages). Since alternative II recognizes this, it's correct.

Answer 12

(A) is the best response.

As to alternative I: This is correct because, although Brown's breach would only be considered minor, Green would nonetheless have a claim for breach of contract (although he *will* have to perform under the contract).

If a party *materially* breaches a contract, the other party is excused from performing under the contract. If the breach is only *minor,* the other party must perform and sue for damages.

In non-UCC cases, a reasonable delay is generally considered only a minor breach. Here, since there's no transaction in goods involved, the common law will control. Thus, absent extraordinary circumstances known to Brown when the contract was created that would make the June 1 deadline essential, or an express "time is of the essence" term in the contract, the delay would be a minor breach, thus requiring that Green perform but also giving Green a claim for breach of contract.

The only way Green would not have a claim for breach would be if Brown's delay were not considered a breach *at all.* Since it would be considered a minor breach, and alternative I recognizes this, alternative I is correct.

As to alternative II: This is *not* correct, because Green would not be excused from performing under the contract.

If a party *materially* breaches a contract, the other party is excused from performance under the contract; where the breach is only minor, the other party must perform and sue for breach. Thus, the only way Green's performance would be excused is if the delay were considered a material breach.

In non-UCC cases, a reasonable delay is generally considered only a minor breach. Here, since there's no transaction in goods involved, the common law will control. Thus, absent extraordinary circumstances known to Brown when the contract was created that would make the June 1 deadline essential, or an express "time is of the essence" term in the contract, the delay would be a minor breach. This would require that Green perform, but it would also give Green a claim for breach of contract.

Keep in mind that under the UCC "perfect tender" rule, the stance on delays is quite different – any delay excuses performance. However, this is sharply curtailed by the seller's right to cure defective performance, so in practice it isn't quite buyer's heaven.

Since alternative II mistakenly states that a minor breach relieves the other party's duty of performance, it can't be correct.

Answer 13

(D) is the best response,

because it identifies the reason that Victim will be unable to recover: He has no rights under the contract to enforce.

Most contract rights are assignable. The common law rule, embodied in UCC §2-210(2), allows assignment unless the assignment would:

1. Materially change the other party's duty;

2. Materially increase the risk the contract imposes; or

3. Materially impair the other party's chance of receiving return performance.

Exceptions to assignability include personal services, rights under future contracts, requirements and output contracts, and assignments contrary to public policy (e.g., government pensions and alimony payments).

Thus, an assignment by Victim would be effective. Which of ABC and Hospital is the assignee depends on which claim has priority – however, as to Victim's recovery this is irrelevant, since by transferring away his rights he retains *no* rights under the contract. Until the obligor (here, Insurer) has notice of the assignment, he can pay the assignor without risking double liability; once he has notice, he must pay the assignee. Here, ABC notified Insurer of its assignment, so Insurer *couldn't* pay Victim. As a result, Victim cannot prevail in a claim against Insurer. Since D recognizes this, it's the best response.

(A) is not the best response,
because the right to receive payment *would* be assignable.

The common law rule on assignability of rights, as embodied in UCC §2-210(2), allows assignment unless the assignment would:

1. Materially change the other party's duty;

2. Materially increase the risk the contract imposes; or

3. Materially impair the other party's chance of receiving return performance.

Exceptions to assignability include personal services, rights under future contracts, requirements and output contracts, and assignments contrary to public policy (e.g., government pensions and alimony payments).

Here, the right Victim assigned was the right to receive payment. Insurer's duty to pay someone other than Victim doesn't materially alter its rights or performance under the contract. Thus, the right would not be too personal to assign, contrary to what A states.

Since the assignment was effective, Victim, as the assignor, is left with no rights under the contract, and as a result he cannot succeed in a claim against Insurer. Since option A doesn't recognize this, it's not the best response.

(B) is not the best response,
because Victim's possession of the memorandum is not relevant to his claim.

Here, Victim's recovery depends on whether he has the right to receive payment. If he *does,* and since the contract doesn't fall within the Statute of Frauds, Victim could enforce the contract without a writing *at all,* let alone a writing in his possession.

Even with a written memorandum evidencing Insurer's contractual obligation, Victim need not possess the memorandum in order to recover. The only

time possession of a writing is necessary to recovery is in cases where documents like negotiable instruments are involved – that is, where the writing contains the right, and the right doesn't exist without the writing.

That's not the case here. Instead, what defeats Victim's claim is that he assigned his right to receive payment, and thus has no rights under the contract anymore. Since B doesn't recognize this, it's not the best response.

(C) is not the best response,
because the validity of the agreement isn't dependent on Tortfeasor's responsibility.

There's only two ways Tortfeasor's responsibility could determine the validity of the agreement: If it was a condition, or it was consideration. As to the condition argument, there's nothing in these facts to suggest that Insurer conditioned its liability on Tortfeasor's responsibility. As to consideration, Insurer could argue that without Tortfeasor's responsibility, its promise to pay Victim was gratuitous. However, as with all settlements, a good-faith belief in the validity of the claim, even if the claim turns out to be valueless, is sufficient for consideration. Thus, Tortfeasor's responsibility is not relevant to Victim's recovery.

Instead, the reason Victim can't recover is that he assigned away his rights under the contract, and thus has no rights left to enforce. Since C doesn't recognize this, even though it arrives at the correct result, it's not the best response.

Answer 14

(D) is the best response,
because it identifies the central reason why Insurer will be liable to Holder or ABC, whichever assignee has priority.

The rights of either Holder or ABC stem from the Victim-Insurer settlement agreement. In order to be valid, a contract requires consideration, which is bargained-for exchange and either benefit to the promisor or detriment to the promisee (and typically both). Under these facts, Victim had a good faith belief in the validity of his claim against Insurer. Thus, the settlement agreement between them, whereby Victim surrendered his claim, was supported by consideration.

Then, because the right to receive payment is assignable, Victim assigned his right to either Holder or ABC (depending on which had priority). As assignee, Holder or ABC assumed Victim's rights under the contract, and could enforce Insurer's promise to pay. In fact, Hospital's original assignment was irrevocable, since it gave up valuable consideration – its right to collect from Victim – for it. Thus, when Victim assigned to ABC, Victim would be liable for breach of the implied warranty that he wouldn't interfere with his assignee's rights.

Thus, while Tortfeasor's minority may release *him* from liability, leaving Insurer holding the ball, that's just too bad. Insurer must live up to his promise under the Insurer-Victim contract, and since that was not predicated on Insurer's ability to enforce a contract with Tortfeasor, and D recognizes this, it's the best response.

(A) is not the best response,

because Victim's rights under the contract with Insurer have nothing to do with Tortfeasor.

The rights of either Holder or ABC stem from the Victim-Insurer settlement agreement. In order to be valid, a contract requires consideration, which is bargained-for exchange and benefit to the promisor or detriment to the promisee, and typically both. Under these facts, Victim had a good faith belief in the validity of his claim against Insurer. Thus, the settlement agreement between them, whereby Victim surrendered his claim, was supported by consideration. Thus, when Victim assigned his rights away, they were his *own* rights under his contract with Insured, with no regard to Tortfeasor at all. Victim was entitled to assign whatever right to payment he had under the contract, and that's what he did. His rights did not spring from any beneficiary status under the Insurer-Tortfeasor agreement, and since A states otherwise, it can't be the best response.

(B) is not the best response,

because Insurer will be liable under his contract with Victim, regardless of Tortfeasor's ultimate irresponsibility.

The rights of either Holder or ABC stem from the Victim-Insurer settlement agreement. In order to be valid, a contract requires consideration, which is bargained-for exchange and benefit to the promisor or detriment to the promisee, and typically both. Under these facts, Victim had a good faith belief in the validity of his claim against Insurer. Thus, the settlement agreement between them, whereby Victim surrendered his claim, was supported by consideration.

Then, because the right to receive payment is assignable, Victim assigned his right to either Holder or ABC (depending on which had priority). As assignee, Holder or ABC assumed Victim's rights under the contract, and could enforce Insurer's promise to pay. Thus, Tortfeasor's irresponsibility is irrelevant, and Insurer's waiver of that irresponsibility as a defense would not be a prerequisite to recovery. Since B states otherwise, it's not the best response.

(C) is not the best response,

because Tortfeasor's minority is not relevant to either Holder's or ABC's rights as assignees of Victim's rights.

The rights of either Holder or ABC stem from the Victim-Insurer settlement agreement. In order to be valid, a contract requires consideration, which is bargained-for exchange and benefit to the promisor or detriment to the promisee, and typically both. Under these facts, Victim had a good faith belief in the validity of his claim against Insurer. Thus, the settlement agreement

between them, whereby Victim surrendered his claim, was supported by consideration.

Then, because the right to receive payment is assignable, Victim assigned his right to either Holder or ABC (depending on which had priority). As assignee, Holder or ABC assumed Victim's rights under the contract, and could enforce Insurer's promise to pay.

Thus, while Tortfeasor's minority may release *him* from liability, leaving Insurer holding the ball, that's just too bad. Insurer must live up to his promise under the Insurer-Victim contract, and since that was not predicated on Insurer's ability to enforce a contract with Tortfeasor, C isn't the best response.

Answer 15

(C) is the best response,

because this will put Kontractor in the position it would have been in had Subbo performed.

The standard measure of contract damages is the expectation measure, which attempts to put the plaintiff in the position he would have been in had the contract been performed. Here, performance meant that Kontractor would have a foundation, at a total cost to it of $200,000. Kontractor paid Subbo $100,000, then paid another $120,000 to the replacement subcontractor, for a total of $220,000. So Kontractor is $20,000 worse off than had Subbo performed. Kontractor will recover this $20,000 in order to be in the position that performance would have left it.

(A) is not the best response,

because Subbo's restitutionary recovery must be computed after subtracting breach damages owed by Subbo.

A materially-breaching plaintiff may recover in quasi-contract for the value to the defendant of the rendered performance. But this recovery must be computed on a "net" basis, by subtracting from the unpaid-for value rendered to the defendant any damages caused by the breach. So in this case, if Kontractor had been able to finish the work for, say, $10,000 (so that it would have spent a total of $130,000), Subbo would have been entitled to recover in quasi-contract the $50,000 difference between the $150,000 value that it rendered to Kontractor and the $100,000 Kontractor had made in progress payments (since Subbo's breach would not have caused any damages to Kontractor).

But on the actual facts here, even if Subbo recovered nothing in quasi-contract, Kontractor would still have been damaged by $20,000 (as analyzed in Choice (C)). So Subbo obviously can't recover anything in quasi-contract, since each dollar given to it would just make Kontractor's net damages worse. Instead, Subbo owes Kontractor the $20,000 needed to make Kontractor whole.

Furthermore, in many jurisdictions a plaintiff who "wilfully" breaches isn't even eligible for a quasi-contract recovery, so in such a jurisdiction we wouldn't even get to the point of calculating whether Subbo was entitled to anything.

(B) is not the best response,
because this would not leave Kontractor whole.

Kontractor has $20,000 in damages (see Choice (C)) only on the assumption that Kontractor doesn't have to pay Subbo anything in the litigation on a quasi-contract theory. If Subbo recovered $50,000, Kontractor's net damages would mount to $70,000 from the original $20,000. The overriding principle is that Kontractor, as a non-breaching counterclaimer, gets expectation damages to put it in the net position it would have been in had the contract been performed. Obeying this principle means that Subbo not only gets $0 in quasi-contract, but has to write out a check to Kontractor for $20,000.

(D) is not the best response,
because this would not leave Kontractor whole.

The overriding principle is that Kontractor, as a non-breaching counterclaimer, gets expectation damages to put it in the net position it would have been in had the contract been performed. If Subbo didn't have to pay anything (and didn't receive anything), Kontractor would be $20,000 worse off than if the contract had been performed. (Kontractor has paid a total of $220,000 to the two subs, versus $200,000 that it would have paid had Subbo performed.)

Answer 16

(A) is the best response,
because it's the only option that recognizes that Joe's claim will succeed.

There are a few major obstacles Joe's claim would have to overcome, under these facts. First, you may have noticed the unconventional consideration in the contract – Henry gets nothing but peace of mind out of the deal. Second, the contract involves delaying marriage, and that brings up public policy concerns. Finally, there's a Statute of Frauds gloss, since the payment of another's debts is involved (to the extent of the rent provision, *not* the spending money provision).

As to the consideration issue, consideration requires a bargained-for exchange, as well as either detriment to the promisee or benefit to the promisor (or typically both). While Joe (as promisee) clearly suffered a detriment by delaying his wedding, it's not as clear what the benefit to Henry (as promisor) was. As a matter of fact, peace of mind or personal satisfaction is sufficient to qualify as a benefit. Thus, Henry's ensuring that his son complete school before being distracted by a wedding would be sufficient to support a contract. Furthermore, since Joe delayed the marriage at Henry's request, it was "bargained for." As a result, there's no problem with consideration.

As to the public policy concerns, it's only contracts in *derogation* of marriage that are considered illegal (and

thus enforceable). If Henry had offered to pay Joe to *divorce,* instead of to delay his marriage, such an agreement would be unenforceable. As it is, there's no public policy problem with the contract.

Finally, there's no Statute of Frauds problem, because the spending money agreement doesn't fall within the Statute of Frauds, and thus is enforceable without a writing. It's the promise to pay Joe's rent that's within the Statute of Frauds, as a promise to pay the debt of another. But that's not the issue here, so the contract is enforceable without a writing.

Since A correctly characterizes the contract as enforceable, it's the best response.

(B) is not the best response,
because the contract was not illegal.

A contract is illegal if it is contrary to public policy when made (it need not involve criminal or tortious conduct). Such contracts include contracts which are usurious, or obstruct justice, defraud a third party, involve the commission of crimes or torts, or – the one you probably thought of if you chose this response – contracts in derogation of marriage. However, contracts in derogation of marriage involve a divorce (e.g., "Divorce that bum and I'll give you $100,000"). Here, Henry only wanted Joe to postpone his wedding until graduation. Thus, the contract was not illegal, and in fact was enforceable. Since there was a bargained-for exchange, and detriment to the promisee (Joe – in terms of delaying his marriage) and benefit to the promisor (Henry – in terms of personal satisfaction), the contract was supported by consideration. Furthermore, it didn't fall within the Statute of Frauds (as to the spending money provision), so it would be enforceable without a writing. Since B incorrectly states that the contract was illegal and thus unenforceable, it's not the best response.

(C) is not the best response,
because although it correctly states a *theoretical* rule – death of the offeror terminates an offer – it does not apply here, because there was already an enforceable contract when Henry died, and so the enforceability of the offer is irrelevant.

A contract requires an offer, acceptance, and consideration (or some substitute for consideration). Here, Henry offered to pay Joe's rent and give him spending money if he delayed his marriage. Joe did so, and this was his detriment (and Henry's benefit, in terms of personal satisfaction), so the contract was supported by consideration and thus enforceable. Henry's death *after* the contract was created would not discharge his (or his estate's) duty of performance, because his estate can carry out the payment – his personal contribution is not necessary to the contract (if it *were,* as say he was to paint Joe's portrait, it *would* be discharged by his death). Since option C mischaracterizes the contract as being only at the offer stage, and not an intact contract, it's not the best response.

(D) is not the best response,

because the contract is enforceable without a writing.

Option D suggests that the contract is not enforceable because it falls within the Statute of Frauds, and thus, in general, requires a writing. This is a bit sneaky because the part of the contract to which Joe's claim refers – the agreement to provide $100 spending money every month – does *not* fall within the Statute of Frauds, and thus is enforceable without a writing! It's the part of the contract addressing Henry's agreement to pay Joe's rent which must be in writing to be enforceable, since it's an agreement to pay the debt of another, and as such falls within the Statute of Frauds. Since the agreement that forms the basis of Joe's claim, the "spending money" agreement, does not fall within the Statute of Frauds, and D fails to recognize this, it's not the best response.

Answer 17

(C) is the best response,

because it's the only response that offers an inaccurate description of the facts.

Option C discusses conditions subsequent. Conditions can be classified in accordance with their time of performance: Precedent, concurrent, and subsequent. (The other way to classify conditions addresses how they were created: Express, implied, or constructive.) A condition in general is the occurrence or non-occurrence of an event (not merely the passage of time) that triggers, limits, or extinguishes an absolute duty to perform in one party to the contract. A condition subsequent is an event which, pursuant to the agreement of the parties, discharges a duty to perform that had become absolute. True conditions subsequent are very rare, one of the few situations in which you find them is insurance claims (where, for instance, the insured's failure to sue in a certain period of time discharges the insurer's duty to pay, which was otherwise absolute).

Here, each party's performance is a condition to the other party's performance. Since they are to exchange performance simultaneously, each party's duty is a concurrent condition. You could even, perhaps, characterize each party's performance as a condition precedent to the other party's performance, since tendering good title "triggers" the other party's duty to do likewise. However, there's no way to characterize the duty to tender good title as a condition *subsequent,* by either party, since tendering good title constitutes a condition to the other party's performance and performance itself, but *not* a discharge of a previously absolute duty to perform. Since C mischaracterizes the facts, making it the least accurate statement of these four options, it's the best response.

(A) is not the best response,

because Alpha's tendering the title to the apartment

house *could* be characterized as a condition precedent to Beta's duty to hand over title to the farm (and vice versa, by the way).

This is a tricky question because it asks you the *worst* way to characterize the facts, not the *best way.* Thus, three of the answers are good, and only one is bad. Since option A is a fairly good representation of the facts, it can't be the best response.

Option A discusses a condition precedent. Conditions can be classified in accordance with their time of performance: Precedent, concurrent, and subsequent. (The *other* way to classify conditions is how they came about: Express, implied, and constructive.) A condition in general is the occurrence or non-occurrence of an event (not merely the passage of time) that triggers, limits, or extinguishes an absolute duty to perform in one party to the contract. A condition *precedent* is an event or an act which must occur in order to trigger a party's absolute duty of performance.

Here, there's no language about either party's duty being expressly conditioned on the other party's duty. Since they can both perform at the same time, each party's performance would be constructively conditioned on the other party's performance. That is, Alpha's tendering the title to the apartment house is a condition to Beta's duty to tender the title to the farm, and vice versa. While this may be more properly characterized as a concurrent condition, since the parties will exchange performance simultaneously, it *could* be considered a condition precedent, since Alpha must tender the title in order to trigger Beta's duty. Since this is a fair characterization of the facts, and the question asks you for the least accurate depiction of the facts, A isn't the best response.

(B) is not the best response,

because Beta's tendering the title to the farm *could* be characterized as a condition precedent to Alpha's duty to tender the title to the apartment house (and vice versa).

Option B discusses a condition precedent. Conditions can be classified in accordance with their time of performance: Precedent, concurrent, and subsequent. (The *other* way to classify conditions is how they came about: Express, implied, and constructive.) A condition in general is the occurrence or non-occurrence of an event (not merely the passage of time) that triggers, limits, or extinguishes an absolute duty to perform in one party to the contract. A condition *precedent* is an event or an act which must occur in order to trigger a party's absolute duty of performance.

Here, there's no language about either party's duty being expressly conditioned on the other party's duty. Since they can both perform at the same time, each party's performance would be constructively conditioned on the other party's performance. That is, Alpha's tendering the title to the apartment house is a condition to Beta's duty to tender the title to the farm, and vice versa. While this may be more properly characterized as a concurrent condition, since the parties will exchange performance simultaneously, it *could* be considered a condition precedent, since Alpha must tender the title in order to trigger Beta's duty. Since this is a fair characterization of the facts, and the question asks you for the least accurate depiction of the facts, B isn't the best response.

(D) is not the best response,

because it represents the *most* accurate way to classify Alpha's and Beta's duties, and the question wants the *least* accurate description. If you chose this response, you probably misread this, and looked for the most accurate response instead of the least accurate one.

Option D discusses concurrent conditions. Conditions can be classified in accordance with their time of performance: Precedent, concurrent, and subsequent. (The other way to classify conditions addresses how they came about: Express, implied, constructive.) A condition in general is the occurrence or non-occurrence of an event (not merely the passage of time) that triggers, limits, or extinguishes an absolute duty to perform in one party to the contract. A "concurrent condition" provides that the parties must exchange performance simultaneously; each party's duty to perform is dependent on the other's. Courts will find concurrent conditions where there are no conditions precedent, express or implied, and both parties *can* perform simultaneously.

Here, Alpha's tendering the title to the apartment house is a condition to Beta's tendering the title to the farm, and Beta's tendering the title to the farm is a condition to Alpha's tendering title to the apartment house. Thus, both parties' performances are concurrent conditions. Since D recognizes this, and the question is looking for the *least* accurate statement, D can't be the best response.

Answer 18

(A) is the best response,

because it most accurately describes how removing the shed should be characterized.

A condition precedent is an event or an act which must occur in order to trigger a party's absolute duty of performance. In other words, the party has no duty to perform *unless* the condition occurs. A condition *subsequent,* on the other hand, is one that discharges a duty that had *already* become absolute. You most often see conditions subsequent in the insurance context, where, say, an insurer's duty to pay is *discharged* if the insured doesn't sue within a stated period of time.

The tricky thing here is that the hallmark of a condition subsequent is language like "the contract will be void if…" While that's the language used here, making the condition a condition subsequent *in form,* if you look closely at what's happening you can see that

removing the shed is *actually* a condition *precedent* to Beta's duty to pay the additional $1,000. That's because Alpha's removing the shed *must* occur before Beta has *any* duty to pay. If Alpha doesn't remove the shed within three months, Beta's duty to pay never comes into being. Thus, removing the shed is a condition precedent. For a condition subsequent, the duty must have been absolute, and the occurrence of an event must extinguish it. That's not the case here, even though the language is suggestive of a condition subsequent. Since option A recognizes this precisely, it's the best response.

(B) is not the best response,

because it mischaracterizes the removal of the shed – it's subsequent in form and precedent in substance, not the other way around.

A condition is the occurrence or non-occurrence of an event (not merely the passage of time) that triggers, limits, or extinguishes an absolute duty to perform in one party to a contract. Conditions can be classified in accordance with their time of performance: Precedent, concurrent, or subsequent.

A condition precedent is an event or an act which must occur in order to trigger a party's absolute duty of performance. In other words, the party has no duty to perform *unless* the condition occurs. A condition *subsequent,* on the other hand, is one that discharges a duty that had *already* become absolute. You most often see conditions subsequent in the insurance context, where, say, an insurer's duty to pay is *discharged* if the insured doesn't sue within a stated period of time.

The tricky thing here is that the hallmark of a condition subsequent is language like "the contract will be void if…" While that's the language used here, making the condition a condition subsequent *in form,* if you look closely at what's happening you can see that removing the shed is *actually* a condition *precedent* to Beta's duty to pay the additional $1,000. That's because Alpha's removing the shed *must* occur before Beta has *any* duty to pay. If Alpha doesn't remove the shed within three months, Beta's duty to pay never comes into being. Thus, removing the shed is a condition precedent. For a condition subsequent, the duty must have been absolute, and the occurrence of an event must extinguish it. That's not the case here, even though the language is suggestive of a condition subsequent. Since option B reverses the form and substance descriptions, it's not the best response.

(C) is not the best response,

because removing the shed is a condition *precedent* to Beta's duty to pay $1,000, not subsequent – even though it looks like a condition subsequent.

A condition is the occurrence or non-occurrence of an event (not merely the passage of time) that triggers, limits, or extinguishes an absolute duty to perform in one party to a contract. Conditions can be classified in accordance with their time of performance: Precedent, concurrent, or subsequent.

A condition precedent is an event or an act which must occur in order to trigger a party's absolute duty of performance. In other words, the party has no duty to perform *unless* the condition occurs. A condition *subsequent,* on the other hand, is one that discharges a duty that had *already* become absolute. You most often see conditions subsequent in the insurance context, where, say, an insurer's duty to pay is *discharged* if the insured doesn't sue within a stated period of time.

The tricky thing here is that the hallmark of a condition subsequent is language like "the contract will be void if..." While that's the language used here, making the condition a condition subsequent *in form,* if you look closely at what's happening you can see that removing the shed is *actually* a condition *precedent* to Beta's duty to pay the additional $1,000. That's because Alpha's removing the shed *must* occur before Beta has *any* duty to pay. If Alpha doesn't remove the shed within three months, Beta's duty to pay never comes into being. Thus, removing the shed is a condition precedent. For a condition subsequent, the duty must have been absolute, and the occurrence of an event must extinguish it. That's not the case here, even though the language is suggestive of a condition subsequent.

Since option C mischaracterizes the status of removing the shed, it's not the best response.

(D) is not the best response,

because it mischaracterizes removing the shed – it *is,* in fact, a condition.

A condition is the occurrence or non-occurrence of an event (not merely the passage of time) that triggers, limits, or extinguishes an absolute duty to perform in one party to a contract. Conditions can be classified in accordance with their time of performance: Precedent, concurrent, or subsequent.

A condition precedent is an event or an act which must occur in order to trigger a party's absolute duty of performance. In other words, the party has no duty to perform *unless* the condition occurs. A condition *subsequent,* on the other hand, is one that discharges a duty that had *already* become absolute. You most often see conditions subsequent in the insurance context, where, say, an insurer's duty to pay is *discharged* if the insured doesn't sue within a stated period of time.

The tricky thing here is that the hallmark of a condition subsequent is language like "the contract will be void if..." While that's the language used here, making the condition a condition subsequent *in form,* if you look closely at what's happening you can see that removing the shed is *actually* a condition *precedent* to Beta's duty to pay the additional $1,000. That's because Alpha's removing the shed *must* occur before Beta has *any* duty to pay. If Alpha doesn't remove the shed within three months, Beta's duty to pay never

comes into being. Thus, removing the shed is a condition precedent. For a condition subsequent, the duty must have been absolute, and the occurrence of an event must extinguish it. That's not the case here, even though the language is suggestive of a condition subsequent.

If removing the shed *weren't* a condition, this would mean that Beta's duty to pay the $1,000 after six months was absolute. In fact, it's not – if the shed isn't removed, Beta doesn't have to pay. Since D mischaracterizes removing the shed, it's not the best response.

Answer 19

(C) is the best response,

because Gourmet's promise of payment to Hope was supported by consideration.

When Hope issued the quitclaim deed, she was effectively settling — by assigning to Gourmet — her claim against the property. So the question is whether one who promises to make payment in exchange for the surrender of an invalid claim has received consideration. (If Gourmet didn't receive consideration in return for his promise, that promise wouldn't be enforceable.)

The answer is that the surrender of the claim that turns out to be invalid nonetheless constitutes consideration if *either*: (1) the claim is *in fact doubtful* because of uncertainty as to the facts or the law; or (2) the surrendering party *believes* that the claim may be valid. Rest. 2d, § 74(1). Here, (1) was the case (since Hope's attorney told her her claim was doubtful, not that it was definitely invalid). Since Hope's surrender of the claim in a bargained-for exchange in return for Gourmet's promise of payment constituted consideration, Gourmet's promise is enforceable.

(A) is not the best response,

because surrender of a claim that the claimant believes to be doubtful (but not definitely invalid) constitutes consideration.

If Hope had *known* that her claim was totally invalid at the time she surrendered it (by issuing the quitclaim deed), her surrender would not be consideration for Gourmet's promise, and his promise would therefore be unenforceable. But the mere fact that Hope knew that her claim was doubtful — as opposed to invalid — is not enough to prevent her surrender from being consideration. See the more full discussion of when surrender of an invalid claim will be consideration, in Choice (C) above.

(B) is not the best response,

because surrender of a possibly valid claim *does* constitute legal detriment.

If Hope had surrendered a claim that she knew was definitely invalid, that surrender (by issuance of the quitclaim deed) would indeed not be a "legal detriment" — she would not have worsened her legal position. But because what Hope surrendered was a "doubtful" claim rather than a claim she knew to be invalid, her surrender is deemed to constitute consideration. See the further analysis in Choice (C) above.

(D) is not the best response,

because there would be no estoppel here.

This choice seems to be suggesting that there is no consideration to support Gourmet's promise, but that the doctrine of promisory estoppel would apply to make the promise binding without consideration. However, this analysis is wrong for two reasons: (1) as described in Choice (C), Hope's surrender of her doubtful claim *was* consideration for Gourmet's return promise; and (2) if the surrender of the claim wasn't consideration, promissory estoppel wouldn't apply because there's no indication that Hope relied to her detriment on the promise (and reasonable reliance is a pre-condition to the application of promissory estoppel).

Answer 20

(B) is the best response,

because Loyal's reasonable reliance caused Mutate's promise, though not supported by consideration, to be binding under the doctrine of promissory estoppel.

Mutate's promise was not supported by consideration, since Loyal didn't confer any benefit to Mutate, or undergo any legal detriment, in exchange for the promise. (See Choice (A) for more details about why this is so.) However, the doctrine of promissory estoppel applies to make Mutate's promise enforceable even without consideration.

Rest. 2d § 90(a) (the most famous section in the entire Restatement) says that "A promise which the promisor should *reasonably expect to induce action or forbearance* on the part of the promisee or a third person and which *does induce* such action or forbearance is *binding if injustice can be avoided* only by enforcement of the promise." This section applies here. It was reasonably foreseeable to Mutant that when it made the "you'll get a pension if you retire" offer to Loyal, he would or might rely on it by retiring, rather than staying on or taking another job. The promise then did in fact induce the foreseeable reliance: Loyal relied by not only retiring but by buying the RV and not taking another position somewhere else. Furthermore, that reliance has made Loyal unemployable elsewhere, so that without enforcement of the promise Loyal won't have any means of support. Consequently, all the requirements of promissory estoppel are satisfied, making the promise enforceable despite the lack of consideration.

Notice, by the way, that neither the correct choice nor any other choices here mentions the doctrine of promissory estoppel. That's typical of MBE fact patterns where the correct answer is p.e.: the examiners try to allude to the doctrine without mentioning it explicitly, because they believe that mentioning it will tip you off

and make the question too easy.

(A) is not the best response,

because the Board did not bargain to have Loyal retire.

A promise or act (here, Loyal's retirement) can be consideration for a counter-promise only if the promise or act was "bargained for or given in exchange" for the counter-promise. So here, Loyal's retirement would be consideration for the promise of a pension only if the Board bargained for that retirement, or received it in exchange for the promise. But here, there is no indication that Board was bargaining for his retirement, or that it promised the pension in exchange for that retirement. (Apparently Mutant didn't care too much whether Loyal stayed on the job or retired, as evidenced by the fact that the resolution said that the pension would be payable whenever Loyal, at his own option, made the decision to retire.) Consequently, Loyal's retirement was not consideration for Mutant's pension promise, making Choice (A) wrong. (In reality, the promise is enforceable even without consideration, as described in Choice (B).)

(C) is not the best response,

because although the promise of a pension was an otherwise-unenforceable promise to make a gift, it became enforceable under the doctrine of promissory estoppel once Loyal relied on it to his detriment.

A promise to make a gift can become enforceable when the promisee foreseeably relies on it to his detriment, and injustice can be avoided only by enforcing the promise. (See Choice (B) above.) Since Choice (C) asserts that the promise is unenforceable, it's wrong.

(D) is not the best response,

because the promise became enforceable via the doctrine of promissory estoppel, notwithstanding Loyal's at-will status.

It's true that Mutate could simply have fired Loyal at any time without any pension payments or other payments. But once Mutate made its promise to pay a pension and Loyal reasonably relied on it, the fact that Loyal was an at-will employee ceased to matter — the doctrine of promissory estoppel made the promise binding.

Answer 21

(B) is the best response,

because it correctly states that the notice fulfills the requirements of a public offer.

A public offer requires sufficient definiteness to qualify as an offer at all. The key factors to consider are whether it contains the language of an offer, and a quantity term (if it *doesn't*, it will be considered merely an invitation for offers). Here, the offer was specific as to quantity – only one student could win – and it contains the language of a promise – "The faculty...offers." As such, the notice creates an offer for a unilateral contract, which any student could accept by winning the competition, having completed performance with knowledge of the offer.

Since B correctly identifies the notice as containing a contractual offer, it's the best response.

(A) is not the best response,

because the notice is sufficiently definite to constitute an offer.

The key here is distinguishing a public offer from an invitation for offers, which most ads are. The distinction is important because a public offer creates a power of acceptance in offerees, such that if offeree accepts, a binding contract will be formed. An invitation for offers, on the other hand, doesn't give anyone the power to create a binding contract.

The thing that normally makes an ad an invitation instead of an offer is that it is indefinite, specifically in terms of the lack of language of a promise, and quantity. That's not the case here. The notice is specific as to quantity (only one student could win), price ($500), and is worded as a promise ("The faculty...offers"). As such, it creates an immediate power of acceptance in any student, such that if a student wins the competition having completed performance with knowledge of the offer, the faculty will be bound. (Note that the offer is for a *unilateral* contract, since it can only be accepted by performance, not a return promise.) Since option A mischaracterizes the notice as only an invitation to deal, it's not the best response.

(C) is not the best response,

because failure to identify the offeree, in the context of a public offer, would not destroy the offer.

A public offer requires sufficient definiteness to qualify as an offer at all. The key factors to consider are whether it contains the language of an offer, and a quantity term (if it *doesn't,* it will be considered merely an invitation for offers). Here, the offer is specific as to quantity – only one student could win – and it contains the language of a promise – "The faculty...offers." As such, the notice creates an offer for a unilateral contract, which any student could accept by winning the competition, having completed performance with knowledge of the offer.

Thus, while a typical offer must identify the offeree, a public offer (like the offer of a reward) cannot, by dint of its nature, identify the offeree. However if it's sufficiently definite as to the language of a promise, and quantity, it's an offer nonetheless. Since C doesn't recognize this, it's not the best response.

(D) is not the best response,

because the promise made by the faculty in the notice was a *bargain* promise, not a *conditional* promise.

This is an important distinction, because a conditional promise is not enforceable, whereas a bargain promise, when it's in the form of an offer (as here), cre-

ates the power of acceptance in an offeree.

The difference between the two turns on whether the parties consider performing the condition as the "price" of the promise; if they do, it's an enforceable, bargain promise. If not, it's a conditional promise. Say these facts were different, and Student had received a note from the law school dean after winning the contest, saying, "Congratulations on winning the *^!#{+ obscenity contest. I have a check from the school for $500 for you, and I'll give it to you if you come to my office at 2 p.m." This is a conditional promise, because the dean intended to make a gift, and Student's going to the office couldn't be construed as the *price* of the promise for $500. Under the facts as they are in the question, however, things are entirely different. It's clear that both the faculty and Student considered the condition stated – winning the contest – as the price for the offer of $500. Thus, the promise was a bargain promise for a unilateral contract, which Student accepted by winning the contest (having completed performance with knowledge of the offer). Since D mischaracterizes the promise, it's not the best response.

Answer 22

(C) is the best response,

because Student's reliance on the offer prior to the April 1 revocation would make the offer irrevocable as to him. In fact, his reliance consists of his part performance with knowledge of the offer and intent to accept it.

Here, the November 1 notice created a public offer for a unilateral contract. That is, a student could accept only by winning the contest. The modern view as to public offers is that acceptance is satisfied by offeree's completing performance with knowledge of the offer.

As to *irrevocability,* a unilateral offer becomes irrevocable once the offeree has partially performed. When that occurs, the offer must remain open for a reasonable period of time to give the offeree a chance to complete performance. Here, Student intensified his efforts on the contest when he saw the notice, indicating his intent to accept (since, in a unilateral offer, the offeree must intend to accept). Thus, since he partially performed before he saw the revocation, the offer was irrevocable as to him.

Incidentally, note that the intent to accept is only necessary in a *unilateral* contract. That's because bilateral contracts are governed by the objective theory of contracts, such that if a reasonable offeror could believe that the offeree had accepted, even if in fact the offeree didn't mean to accept or even know about the offer, there's a contract. This can't happen in a unilateral contract, where intent to accept must exist.

Since option C identifies why the offer was irrevocable as to Student, it's the best response.

(A) is not the best response,

because, as to Student, the offer was *irrevocable*

because he'd already begun performance, and had knowledge of the offer.

Here, the original notice created an offer for a unilateral contract, because it requested performance in return, not a return promise (which would be a *bilateral* contract). As a result, a student could only accept by winning the contest. Where unilateral contracts are concerned, the offer becomes irrevocable when the offeree partially performs, with intent to accept the offer, such that he must be given an opportunity to complete performance (which, under these facts, would constitute submitting a paper). The wrinkle here is that Student had already begun to write the paper *before* he learned of the offer. However, the modern view is that it's sufficient that the offeree *complete* performance with knowledge of the offer. (The older view was that he had to know of the offer when he *started* to perform.) Thus, once Student learned of the offer, and intended to accept it (indicated by his intensified efforts on the contest), it became irrevocable as to him. He saw the notice on November 2, and the offer wasn't revoked until April 1. Student had begun to perform in October. Thus, the second notice didn't revoke the offer as to Student. (Note that the revocation was proper as to students who hadn't partially performed. As a public offer, a revocation must be by the same or similar media and frequency. Here, another notice posted on the same board would suffice.)

Incidentally, note that Student's note of acceptance is irrelevant, since the offer was for a *unilateral* contract, not a *bilateral* contract, and could thus be accepted only by performance – viz., winning the contest. While most offers could be construed as bilateral, the offer here is in the nature of a reward, which is one of the few types of offers which clearly seek *only* performance in return. Here, the faculty has no interest in a promise to perform. If it *had* sought a promise in return, Student's acceptance would have been binding when "sent" (here, put on the desk) regardless of whether it ever actually reached the Dean or a faculty member. In any case, since the offer here was for a unilateral contract, and it was irrevocable as to Student before the revocation was posted, A isn't the best response.

(B) is not the best response,
    because it misstates the law.

    At common law, an offer only becomes irrevocable if either the offeree *pays* for the irrevocability (creating an "option"), or by accepting the offer (by a return promise under a bilateral contract, or part performance under a unilateral contract), or through promissory estoppel (triggered by a gratuitous promise that is likely to, and does, induce promisee's reliance). Here, the offer in the notice was for a unilateral contract: Thus, it sought performance, in the form of winning the contest, *not* a return promise. The rule is that once the offeree has partially performed, the offer is irrevocable as to that offeree. When the offer is a *public* offer, as here, it's

sufficient that offeree complete performance with knowledge of the offer, having intended to accept the offer. Thus, the offer as to *Student* was irrevocable, but only because he knew about it before he completed performance. It's not because the offer becomes irrevocable after a reasonable time goes by, as B states – because that is, in fact, the opposite of the actual rule. The rule is that, if nothing else terminates the offer, the lapse of a reasonable time does so. Since B misstates this rule, even though the offer as to Student was irrevocable, B is not the best response.

(D) is not the best response,
    because Student's awareness of the revocation notice would not revoke the offer as to him.

    Here, the November 1 notice created a public offer for a unilateral contract. That is, Student could accept only by winning the contest. The modern view as to public offers is that acceptance is satisfied by offeree's completing performance with knowledge of the offer.

    As to *irrevocability*, a unilateral offer becomes irrevocable once the offeree has partially performed. When that occurs, the offer must remain open for a reasonable period of time to give the offeree the chance to complete performance. Here, Student intensified his efforts on the contest when he saw the notice, indicating his intent to accept (since a unilateral contract requires intent to accept); thus, since he partially performed before he saw the revocation, the offer was irrevocable as to him. That makes the faculty's April 1 notice irrelevant as to Student; it would only revoke the offer as to students who hadn't partially performed with knowledge of the original offer. Since D is not correct as it applies to Student, it's not the best response.

Answer 23

(A) is the best response,
    since it correctly identifies that only winning the contest would constitute acceptance; a promise to win wouldn't suffice.

    An offer is a promise to do something in exchange for something else. If the offer seeks a return promise, it proposes a *bilateral* contract; if it proposes a *unilateral* contract, it seeks performance, not a return promise.

    Here, you can tell that the offer is seeking only a unilateral contract, because what the faculty wants is someone to *win* the contest, not someone *promising* to win the contest. Thus, Student's winning the contest constitutes acceptance; his promise to win is meaningless.

    There are, in fact, very few situations where an offer *clearly* seeks performance instead of a return promise. One clear case is the offer of a reward; another is where offeror specifically limits the acceptance to performance. Here, the public offer would be analogous to a reward offer, and thus it could only be accepted by performance. Thus, the offer only seeks a unilateral contract, and offeree cannot create a bilateral contract with a return promise. (Note that this is the common law rule. Under the UCC, §2-206, the rule on ambiguity is the same: An offer to buy goods which is ambiguous as to means of acceptance can be accepted either by a prompt promise to ship *or* prompt shipment).

Since option A correctly identifies that the offer here proposes only a unilateral contract, it's the best response.

(B) is not the best response,

because the offer proposes only a *unilateral* contract, not a bilateral contract.

An offer is a promise to do something in exchange for something else. If the offer proposes a *bilateral* contract, it seeks a return promise; if it proposes a *unilateral* contract, it seeks performance, not a promise. You can tell that the offer here seeks performance, since what the faculty is looking for is someone winning the contest, not someone promising to win the contest (thus, Student's *promise* to perform would not constitute acceptance).

Note that there are very few situations where an offer clearly seeks performance instead of a return promise. One clear case is the offer of a reward; another is where offeror specifically limits the acceptance to performance. Here, the public offer would be analogous to a reward offer. Most other offers *could* be seeking a bilateral contract; and where the offer is ambiguous as to whether it's seeking a unilateral or a bilateral contract, the offeree has his choice of performing or promising to perform. (Note that this is the common law rule. Under the UCC, §2-206, the rule on ambiguity is the same: An offer to buy goods which is ambiguous as to means of acceptance can be accepted either by a prompt promise to ship *or* prompt shipment).

Here, since the offer unambiguously seeks return performance, it's only proposing a unilateral contract. Since B doesn't recognize this, it's not the best response.

(C) is not the best response,

because there's only one choice of acceptance open to offerees: Return performance, creating a *unilateral* contract.

An offer is a promise to do something in exchange for something else. If the offer seeks a return promise, it proposes a *bilateral* contract; if it proposes a *unilateral* contract, it seeks performance, not a return promise.

Here, you can tell that the offer is seeking only a unilateral contract, because what the faculty wants is someone to *win* the contest, not someone *promising* to win the contest. Thus, Student's winning the contest constitutes acceptance; his promise to win is meaningless.

What option C states is the rule where the offer is ambiguous as to whether it's seeking a unilateral or bilateral contract. When that's the case, the offeree has his choice of performing or promising to perform.

There are, in fact, very few situations where an offer *clearly* seeks performance instead of a return promise. One clear case is the offer of a reward; another is where offeror specifically limits the acceptance to performance. Here, the public offer would be analogous to a reward offer, and thus it could only be accepted by performance. Thus, the offer only seeks a unilateral contract, and offeree cannot create a bilateral contract with a return promise. (Note that this is the common law rule. Under the UCC, §2-206, the rule on ambiguity is the same: an offer to buy goods which is ambiguous as to means of acceptance can be accepted either by a prompt promise to ship *or* prompt shipment).

Since C gives offeree the option of creating a bilateral contract where that option doesn't exist under these facts, C isn't the best response.

(D) is not the best response,

because Student's intensifying his efforts doesn't make a unilateral contract into a bilateral contract; it only makes the faculty offer as to Student irrevocable.

An offer is a promise to do something in exchange for something else. If the offer seeks a return promise, it proposes a *bilateral* contract; if it proposes a *unilateral* contract, it seeks performance, not a return promise.

Here, you can tell that the offer is seeking only a unilateral contract, because what the faculty wants is someone to *win* the contest, not someone *promising* to win the contest. Thus, Student's winning the contest constitutes acceptance; his promise to win is meaningless.

Where there is a public offer for a unilateral contract, an offeree accepts by completing performance with knowledge of the offer and intent to accept it. Once he partially performs, the offer as to that offeree is irrevocable, until he has a reasonable opportunity to complete performance. Here, Student knows of the offer, and intensifying his effort to win indicates his intent to accept. Thus, his intensifying his effort makes the offer irrevocable as it applies to him – it doesn't make what's otherwise a unilateral contract into a bilateral contract. Student's winning ripens an offer into a unilateral contract, not a unilateral contract into a bilateral contract.

Note that option D highlights the distinction between unilateral and bilateral contracts. In a unilateral contract, there is no obligation on offeree to perform, but if he doesn't, offeror isn't obligated to perform either. Under these facts, since the offer seeks a unilateral contract and Student accepts by performing, D misstates the facts and is thus not the best response.

Answer 24

(B) is the best response,

because it implicitly recognizes that the promise was enforceable, that Student performed under the contract, and that as a result his estate can collect the $500.

Here, the original notice created a public offer proposing a unilateral contract. As a result, a student could accept only by performing – that is, winning the obscenity contest. By winning the contest, having completed performance knowing of the offer and intending to accept it, Student accepted the faculty's offer, making the faculty's promise to pay binding. (In fact, once Student completed his performance, it wouldn't change the result if he died *before* the winner was decided.) The revocation wasn't relevant because Student had already begun to perform, making the offer irrevocable until Student was given a reasonable time in which to complete performance. Once his essay won the contest, the faculty's duty to pay became absolute, and enforceable by Student's estate.

It's when the contract has not yet been formed, and there's only been an offer, that the death of the offeror, or a *specific* offeree (not when there's a public offer, as here), that the offer is terminated. Alternatively, when there's already a binding contract, if the personal services of one party are necessary to the contract, his death will excuse performance (e.g., an architect's services). However, neither of these are the case here. Since B correctly identifies that the promise is enforceable even if Student doesn't survive to enforce it, B is the best response.

(A) is not the best response,

because the promise of the faculty is enforceable on grounds of an enforceable contract, and thus there is no need to turn to promissory estoppel.

Promissory estoppel is a substitute for consideration, used to avoid injustice. It is triggered by a gratuitous promise that is likely to, and does, induce promisee's detrimental reliance. Thus, you need only look at promissory estoppel when consideration is lacking.

Here, the November 1 notice created an offer seeking a unilateral contract. That is, it could be accepted only by a student's performance – winning the obscenity contest. Student's completing performance, knowing of the offer and intending to accept it, would constitute acceptance and performance. The consideration in a unilateral contract is provided by the promisee's continued performance. Thus, once Student saw the offer and intended to accept it (as indicated by his intensified effort on the contest), the consideration was supplied by his continued effort. Since consideration isn't lacking, there's no need to turn to promissory estoppel to enforce the faculty's promise. Thereafter, Student's winning the contract triggered the faculty's duty to pay. Since A doesn't recognize that there's no need to rely on promissory estoppel, it's not the best response.

(C) is not the best response,

because it mischaracterizes the facts.

C is theoretically correct in the sense that informal social commitments and intramural family agreements do not create legally enforceable commitments. However, that's because in those situations there is a rea-

sonable factual presumption that the parties didn't *intend* legal ramifications. A contrary intent can overcome this presumption, so it's not the policy aspect that determines the enforceability of such agreements, but presumptions as to the intent of the parties. Here, there's no real analogy to these kinds of situations, since the conduct of the parties indicate they both intended to be bound. By posting a public offer, containing the language of a promise ("The faculty…offers"), and a quantity term, the faculty made an offer for a unilateral contract. Student accepted this contract by winning the contest, having completed performance knowing of the offer and intending to accept it. The relationship of the parties doesn't suggest a mere informal agreement without legal consequences. The faculty intended to encourage students to enter and win the contest, and with Student's acceptance, they got what they bargained for. Since C mischaracterizes the facts, it can't be the best response.

(D) is not the best response,

because the faculty's promise as to Student is enforceable due to his winning the contest, knowing of the offer and intending to accept it.

What option D suggests is that the faculty offer was unenforceable as to Student due to lack of consideration under the pre-existing duty rule. Under the pre-existing duty rule, a promise to perform something one is already obliged to do is unenforceable due to a lack of consideration. That's because consideration requires bargained-for exchange and either detriment to the promisee or benefit to the promisor (and typically both); where the promise is to perform an act one is already obliged to perform, there's no detriment and thus no consideration.

What makes this inapplicable here is that there *was* no pre-existing duty. Student had already begun his work on his contest paper, but he was under no duty to continue working, or make any kind of serious effort.

What may have tripped you up, if you chose this response, is the fact that Student didn't commence his performance in response to the faculty's offer; he was already working on his paper before he learned of the offer. The older view is that the offeree, in a unilateral offer situation, must know of the offer when he starts performance to provide valid consideration. However, the modern view is that it's sufficient that offeree *complete* performance with knowledge of the offer. Here, Student accepted the offer by winning the contest, having completed performance with knowledge of the offer and the intent to accept it (as evidenced by Student's intensified efforts after he saw the notice). Since option D mistakenly states the offer was unenforceable due to a pre-existing duty, it's not the best response.

Answer 25

(B) is the best response,

because Daniels' dissatisfaction, if in good faith, would

relieve him of performing under the contract, and would thus be a good defense.

First, look at the contract and determine what the satisfaction clause *does*. Whether satisfaction is objective or subjective depends on the subject matter of the contract. In a construction or manufacturing contract, a satisfaction clause will require the satisfaction of a reasonable person. If personal taste or judgment is involved, only subjective satisfaction is required (e.g., medical services, paintings, and the like). Here, since a photograph is involved, Daniel's *personal*, subjective satisfaction is all that's required; as long as he operates in good faith, he can reject performance and avoid liability under the contract, even if the photograph is *objectively* satisfactory. As option B points out, this would, as a result, be a good defense for Daniel.

Note that Daniel couldn't argue, under these facts, that the pictures are *objectively* unsatisfactory, because everyone else likes them, and thus they are presumably objectively satisfactory. Also, if David doesn't act in good faith, the condition (satisfaction) would be excused, and Daniel's duty to perform would be absolute. However, under these facts there's no indication of bad faith, so Daniel's dissatisfaction will be a good defense. Since B recognizes this, it's the best response.

(A) is not the best response,

because it mischaracterizes the facts.

Here, the contract was conditioned on Daniel's "full satisfaction." Whether satisfaction is objective or subjective depends on the subject matter of the contract. In a construction or manufacturing contract, a satisfaction clause will require the satisfaction of a reasonable person. If personal taste or judgment is involved, only subjective satisfaction is required (e.g., medical services, paintings, and the like). Here, since a photograph is involved, Daniel's *personal*, subjective satisfaction is all that's required; as long as he operates in good faith, he can reject performance and avoid liability under the contract, even if the photograph is *objectively* satisfactory.

The problem with option A is that you're asked for Daniel's best defense, and arguing that the cards are objectively unsatisfactory wouldn't help him, since the facts tell you that the rest of the family is pleased; it's only Daniel who's displeased. If you infer that the family is "reasonable" in its assessment of the cards, then the cards *are* objectively satisfactory.

Thus, what Daniel must try *instead* is to condition the contract on his own, *personal* satisfaction. "Fully satisfactory," in light of the subject matter of the contract, would be interpreted to mean *Daniel's* full satisfaction, since he is purchasing Paul's services, and photographs would be difficult to assess objectively. If Daniel argued that his personal satisfaction is required, all he'd have to do is act in good faith in rejecting the cards (since his good faith would provide the consider-

ation for the contract).

In any case, arguing that the cards are objectively unsatisfactory wouldn't help Daniel, because it doesn't comport with the facts. Since A doesn't recognize this, it's not the best response.

(C) is not the best response,

because Daniel waived the condition that the cards be delivered on time, so arguing that he should be excused from performance due to the delay would not help Daniel.

Under the contract, time was made "of the essence" by expressly providing that the cards must be delivered "on time." Even if the contract hadn't specifically provided for delivery on time, the fact that the cards were Christmas cards, and Christmas time was fast approaching, suggests that time was of the essence.

As a result, under normal circumstances, *any* delay would be considered a major breach, relieving Daniel of the duty to perform under the contract. However, conditions can be excused by waiver, and that's what happened here. When Paul told Daniel that Daniel's inability to have his picture taken earlier would mean a delay in the completion date, by telling Paul to go ahead and take the picture, Daniel was *waiving* delivery on December 15th, and thereby excusing the delivery-on-time express condition. Thereafter, Daniel could not rely on breach of the condition as a defense.

Even if Daniel had *not* expressly waived the condition, his subsequent failure to notify Paul of his recovery would excuse the delivery-on-time condition, since, had Daniel notified Paul immediately of his recovery, Paul could have performed on time. Thus, Daniel's own failure to notify Paul created the delay, and thus the time condition will be excused by *prevention* – that is, Daniel's own wrongful conduct prevented the condition from occurring, and so he can't rely on failure of the condition to avoid liability under the contract.

Since C focuses on the delivery provision, on which Daniel cannot rely, it's not the best response.

(D) is not the best response,

because Daniel's illness wouldn't excuse him from performing under the contract.

If Daniel's illness *had* prevented him from performing under the contract, then he would have a valid impossibility defense, and would avoid liability under the contract. But that's not what the facts here tell you. Paul's final delivery of the pictures was only two days late. Thus, it's not Daniels' illness that caused the delay, but his failure to notify Paul of his recovery until one week after he recovered.

Under these facts, the "on time" provision in the contract made time of the essence, such that delivering the pictures on time was an express condition to Daniel's duty to pay. Thus, *any* delay at all would be a major breach, relieving Daniel of the duty to perform under the contract. However, a condition can be excused in a number of ways, one of which is *prevention* – that is, a party cannot take advantage of his own wrongful act to avoid contractual liability. Here, Daniel's failure to call Paul, for a week after he recovered, prevented Paul from fulfilling the "on time" condition.

Thus, it's not Daniel's illness that excuses his performance under the contract, since it didn't relieve him of the duty to perform. Instead, since the contract was also conditioned on personal satisfaction, Daniel *could* argue that he, in good faith, wasn't satisfied with the pictures, and he could avoid liability that way. Since D doesn't recognize this, it's not the best response.

Answer 26

(D) is the best response,

because it correctly characterizes the facts.

A condition is the occurrence or non-occurrence of an event (not merely the passage of time) that triggers, limits, or extinguishes an absolute duty to perform in one party to the contract. Conditions can be classified in accordance with their time of performance: Precedent, concurrent, and subsequent. (The other way to classify conditions is how they came about: Express, implied, and constructive.)

A condition precedent is an event or act which must occur in order to trigger a party's absolute duty of performance. Until the condition occurs, there's no enforceable duty owed.

Here, until (and unless) Paul performs under the contract, Daniel owes him no duty to pay. Thus, Paul's performance must be a condition precedent to Daniel's performance. Since D recognizes this, it's the best response.

(A) is not the best response,

because it's got the parties the wrong way around: It's Paul's performance that's a condition precedent to Daniel's duty to perform.

A condition is the occurrence or non-occurrence of an event (not merely the passage of time) that triggers, limits, or extinguishes an absolute duty to perform in one party to the contract. Conditions can be classified in accordance with their time of performance: Precedent, concurrent, and subsequent. (The other way to classify conditions is how they came about: Express, implied, and constructive.) A condition precedent is an act or event which must occur in order to trigger a party's absolute duty of performance. Until the condition occurs, there's no enforceable duty owed.

Here, until (and unless) Paul performs under the contract, Daniel owes him no duty. Thus, Paul's performance must be a condition precedent to Daniel's performance. If you "plug" the parties into this formula as option A suggests, you'd have Paul not obligated to provide the pictures until Daniel pays him the $100. That doesn't reflect what the contract says, so it can't be correct, making A not the best response.

(B) is not the best response,

because under the terms of the contract, the duties are not performable simultaneously, so they *can't* be concurrent conditions.

A condition is the occurrence or non-occurrence of an event (not merely the passage of time) that triggers, limits, or extinguishes an absolute duty to perform in one party to the contract. Conditions can be classified in accordance with their time of performance: Precedent, concurrent, and subsequent. (The other way to classify conditions is how they came about: Express, implied, and constructive.)

Where conditions are concurrent, the parties exchange performance simultaneously, such that each party's duty to perform is dependent on the other party's. For instance, say Paul agrees to sell Daniel a camera for $1,000. Barring any contract provision otherwise, a court would imply delivery of the camera and payment of the $1,000 as being concurrent conditions.

The most significant element of concurrent conditions is that the performances must be capable of simultaneous performance. In general, where one party promises to perform *before* the other party promises to perform under the contract, the *earlier* performance is considered a condition precedent of the *later* performance. Here, Paul's performance – taking satisfactory pictures – *must* occur before Daniel is required to pay for them, since Daniel is not required to pay until 30 days later. Even if there hadn't been a 30 day payment provision, they *still* couldn't be concurrent conditions, because Paul's performance takes time, and Daniel's takes only a moment, and the rule in such cases is that the lengthy performance is a condition precedent to the momentary one. Thus, Paul's performance is a condition precedent to Daniel's performance – they can't be concurrent. Since B doesn't recognize this, it can't be the best response.

(C) is not the best response,

because Daniel's payment of $100 *isn't* a condition subsequent to Paul's duty to perform, since Daniel's payment doesn't extinguish Paul's previously absolute duty to perform (and that's what a condition subsequent does).

A condition is the occurrence or non-occurrence of an event (not merely the passage of time) that triggers, limits, or extinguishes an absolute duty to perform in one party to the contract. Conditions can be classified in accordance with their time of performance: Precedent, concurrent, and subsequent. (The other way to classify conditions is how they came about: Express, implied, and constructive.)

A condition subsequent is an event which discharges a duty to perform that had become absolute. You most often see conditions subsequent in the insurance context, where, say, an insurer's duty to pay is *discharged* if the insured doesn't sue within a stated period of time. A condition subsequent is typically (but not always) indicated by language like "The contract will be void if..."

Here, Daniel's payment doesn't discharge Paul's previous duty to provide photographs. In fact, Daniel doesn't have a duty to pay until thirty days after Paul provides the photos. If you chose this response, it's probably because you saw that Daniel's performance wasn't due until 30 days after Paul's, and thus applied "subsequent" in its literal sense, meaning later in time. However, that's not what it means in the context of conditions. What this illustrates is that one party's performance can be a condition precedent to the other party's performance – here, Paul's performance is a condition precedent to Daniel's duty to perform, since it triggers Daniel's duty to perform — without the reverse being true. That is, Paul's performance being a condition precedent to Daniel's performance doesn't make Daniel's performance a condition subsequent to Paul's performance.

Since option C mischaracterizes the facts, it's not the best response.

Answer 27

(C) is the best response,

because Paul won't be bound by the December 15 deadline, contrary to what C states – and the question is looking for the least accurate option.

Here, the contract expressly provided for a December 15 deadline, and made time "of the essence" by guaranteeing delivery on time. What this would normally do is make *any* delay a *material* breach of contract, meaning Daniel wouldn't be required to pay and could sue for damages (under normal circumstances, where time is not of the essence, a minor delay is normally only a minor breach). However, here you have a unique situation, because Paul's timely performance *depends* on Daniel's cooperation – sitting for the photographs.

You have to analyze two discrete time frames: Daniel's illness for a week, and then the week when he failed to notify Paul of his recovery. As to the week of the illness, Paul's duty of timely performance would be excused due to failure of an implied condition. As to the week *after* the illness, Paul's duty of timely performance would be excused due to failure of the implied condition of good faith – since Daniel's non-notification would be considered uncooperative and thus in bad faith. Keeping in mind that Paul's performance was only two days late, failure of either of these two conditions would excuse his timely performance.

Beyond that, Daniel *waived* his right to insist on timely performance by both failing to notify Paul of his recovery *and* his express relinquishment of that right, by telling Paul to go ahead and take the photo *knowing* that delivery would be one or two days late.

Both of these – failure of an implied condition, and waiver – would override the express condition of timely

performance in the contract. Since C doesn't recognize this, it's not accurate. Since the question asks you for the least accurate option, C is the best response.

(A) is not the best response,

because Daniel's illness and related developments *would* excuse Paul's performance by the December 15 deadline, and the question here asks you for the *least* accurate response.

Under these facts, in order to fulfill his duty under the contract, Paul requires Daniel's participation – sitting for the photograph. Thus, since the contract doesn't expressly provide for Daniel's participation, it's an *implied* condition to Paul's duty to perform. Thus, when Daniel became ill, Paul's duty to perform was excused at least as to that week, due to failure of an implied condition. As to Daniel's failure to notify Paul of his recovery for a week after he recovered, this would constitute failure of the implied condition of good faith, and would excuse Paul's performance further. Thus, while Paul's performance is not made impossible due to Daniel's illness and failure to notify Paul of his recovery, it *would* excuse Paul's duty to perform by the deadline of December 15. As a result, A correctly characterizes these facts, and since the question asks you for the least accurate response, A isn't the best response.

(B) is not the best response,

because Daniel's notifying Paul of his recovery *would* be an implied condition of Paul's duty to perform, and the question asks you for the *least* accurate response.

Under these facts, in order to fulfill his duty under the contract, Paul requires Daniel's participation – sitting for the photograph. Thus, since the contract doesn't expressly provide for Daniel's participation, it's an *implied* condition to Paul's duty to perform.

As to Daniel's sitting for the photograph, you have two discrete problems: One, his week's illness, over which he had no control; and his week's failure to notify Paul of his recovery, which he *could* have prevented. Option B tells you that Daniel's failure to notify Paul of his recovery was a failure of an implied condition, and that's correct, because *every* contract has an implied condition of good faith. By failing to notify Paul and giving him an opportunity to perform, Daniel acted in bad faith. This would excuse Paul's providing the photos on time (since Daniel delayed a week, and Paul, working diligently, was only two days late). Since B correctly characterizes the facts, and the question requests the least accurate response, B can't be the best response.

(D) is not the best response,

because Daniel *did* waive the deadline requirement, and the question asks you for the *least* accurate response.

Here, the contract expressly provided for a December 15 deadline, and made time "of the essence" by guaranteeing delivery on time. What this would normally do is make *any* delay a *material* breach of contract, meaning Daniel wouldn't be required to pay and could sue for damages (under normal circumstances, where time is not of the essence, a minor delay is normally only a minor breach). However, here you have a unique situation, because Paul's timely performance *depended* on Daniel's cooperation – sitting for the photographs. Ignoring any issue of failure of conditions for the moment, Daniel *did* waive the on-time requirement. A waiver is a knowing, voluntary relinquishment of a right. Assuming Daniel had the right to insist on timely delivery, his statement to Paul – to go ahead and take the photograph in spite of a one or two day delay in delivery – would constitute a waiver of the right to insist on the December 15 deadline.

Note that, irrespective of the waiver, Daniel's inability to sit for a photograph due to his illness, followed by his failure to notify Paul of his recovery, would constitute failure of an implied condition of cooperation. What makes his conduct after his illness a waiver is that it was *voluntary,* whereas his illness itself presumably wasn't voluntary and thus couldn't be a waiver, only failure of a condition to Paul's timely performance. Since D correctly characterizes the facts, and the question is looking for the least accurate option, D can't be the best response.

Answer 28

(D) is the best response,
because none of the options will support Owner's defense.

(I) The parol evidence rule:
The parol evidence rule provides that a writing intended by the parties to be a full and final expression of their agreement may not be supplemented or contradicted by any oral or written agreements made *prior* to the writing, or by an oral agreement that is *contemporaneous* with the writing. The rule does not apply to proof that the parties orally modified the writing after it was made. Since Owner is attempting to bar evidence of the oral agreements made *after*, not before, the contract between Owner and Contractor was signed, the parol evidence rule won't help Owner. Therefore Choice I is wrong.

(II) The preexisting duty rule:
The preexisting duty rule is a concept concerning consideration. It states that if a party does or promises to do something that he is already obligated to do, or forbears or promises to forbear from doing something which he is not legally entitled to do, he has not incurred the kind of detriment necessary for his performance or forbearance to constitute consideration. The rule does not, however, apply to prevent a promise to do something extra (beyond what the party is already obligated to do) from constituting consideration for a return promise.

Here, suppose Owner had promised to pay more

than the contracted-for price merely because Contractor threatened to walk off the job if he didn't get more money. Owner's promise would be rendered unenforceable by the pre-existing duty rule (since Contractor would have merely promised not to walk off, i.e., promised to do the work he was already legally obligated to do). But here, Contractor promised to do extra work beyond that which he was already obligated to do; that "extra" promise was consideration for Owner's promise to pay more. So the preexisting duty rule has no application.

(III) Failure of an express condition:
It's possible that the "no oral modifications" clause would be interpreted to make Owner's duty to pay for modifications expressly conditional on the modifications' being authorized in a writing signed by both parties. (It's not certain that an express condition would be found, but it might well be.)

However, even if such a condition were found here, Owner's right to benefit from it would be nullified by the doctrine of *waiver*. A person who knowingly receives benefits under a contract and retains them while remaining silent will normally be found to have waived the benefit of a condition to his duty to pay for those benefits. Since Owner remained silent about the need for a writing when Contractor incorporated the extras into the structure, and since strict enforcement of the N.O.M. clause would cause Contractor to suffer a "forfeiture" (complete lack of payment in return for a valuable benefit), the court will find that Owner waived the benefits of the clause. Therefore, Choice III is wrong.

(IV) Statute of Frauds:
The Statute of Frauds requires that certain types of contracts must be in writing to be enforceable. One of the kinds of contracts that needs to be in writing is a promise to transfer an interest in land. But it is irrelevant that the performance of the contract will create a structure on land — if the subject matter of the contract itself is not the transfer of or creation of an *interest* in land, the contract does not fall within the statute. Therefore, this contract to build a building does not fall within the statute, since the contract does not call for the creation of an interest in land. Consequently, Choice IV is wrong.

Answer 29

(C) is the best response,
because it correctly identifies that Ace didn't bargain for Brill's saving Mary's life, so that act can't constitute consideration.

In order to be an enforceable agreement, a contract requires consideration or some substitute for consideration (e.g., promissory estoppel). Consideration is a bargained-for exchange, as well as either detriment to the promisee or benefit to the promisor (and, in practice, both). Here, as to the promise to pay $1,000, Ace is the promisor and Brill is the promisee. Thus, Brill's saving Mary's life would be a detriment to him, and a benefit to Ace, and it would constitute consideration *if it had been bargained for.* However, under these facts, Brill had *already* saved Mary's life when Ace made his promise. Thus, there's no bargain, and regardless of the benefit to Ace, there's no consideration.

What makes this question tricky is that Ace's promise *is* supported by consideration – but Brill's saving Mary's life doesn't provide it! What provides consideration for Ace's promise is not Brill's saving Mary's life, but his surrendering his claim against the estate – a claim which he presumably reasonably believed, in good faith, to be valid. Surrendering a legal claim is considered a detriment sufficient to constitute consideration. Since C recognizes that it's not Brill's saving Mary's life that constitutes consideration, it's the best response.

(A) is not the best response,

because a moral obligation does not, in and of itself, typically engender legal liability.

In order to be an enforceable agreement, a contract requires consideration or some substitute for consideration (e.g., promissory estoppel). Consideration is a bargained-for exchange, as well as either detriment to the promisee or benefit to the promisor (and, in practice, both). Certainly saving his wife's life would make Ace morally obligated to Brill, and Brill will probably always be on Ace's Christmas card list. However, as to saving Mary's life *only* (not surrendering his claim against the estate) there's no detriment to Brill (as the promisee of Ace's promise to pay $1,000), because he'd already saved Mary's life; he didn't save Mary in response to Ace's promise. Thus, Brill's act of saving Mary's life, while creating a moral obligation, doesn't constitute consideration sufficient for a legal obligation.

This isn't to say a moral obligation can *never* constitute consideration – under very limited circumstances, it can. For instance, say Ace owed Brill $1,000, but the debt was unenforceable due to operation of law (e.g., discharged through bankruptcy or barred by the Statute of Limitations), and Ace subsequently promised to pay the debt anyway. Under these circumstances, the moral obligation *would* be enforceable (although most jurisdictions would require that the subsequent promise be in writing).

Back to these facts. What makes this question tricky is that Ace's promise *is* supported by consideration – but Brill's saving Mary's life doesn't provide it! What provides consideration for Ace's promise is not Brill's saving Mary's life, but Brill's surrendering his claim against the estate – a claim which he presumably reasonably believed, in good faith, to be valid. Surrendering a legal claim is considered a detriment sufficient to constitute consideration. Since A ignores this, it's not the best response.

(B) is not the best response,

because mere benefit to Ace would not be sufficient for consideration. Consideration requires a bargained-for exchange.

In order to be an enforceable agreement, a contract requires consideration or some substitute for consideration (e.g., promissory estoppel). Consideration is a bargained-for exchange, as well as either detriment to the promisee or benefit to the promisor (and, in practice, both). Here, as to the promise to pay $1,000, Ace is the promisor and Brill is the promisee. Thus, Brill's saving Mary's life would be a detriment to him, and a benefit to Ace, and it would constitute consideration *if it had been bargained for.* However, under these facts, Brill had *already* saved Mary's life when Ace made his promise. Thus, there's no bargain, and regardless of the benefit to Ace, there's no consideration.

If you chose this response, you were thinking of quasi-contract, where a party is bound even without a promise. Quasi-contract is typically implied where plaintiff confers a benefit on the defendant, under circumstances where the defendant would be unjustly enriched if he were allowed to retain the benefit without paying for it. At that point, a duty to pay is implied even though no contractual duty exists. The reason this doesn't apply here is that there's no unjust enrichment, and material benefit *alone* isn't sufficient for quasi-contract. In any case, since B ignores the fact that the benefit wasn't bargained for and thus can't constitute consideration, it's not the best response.

(D) is not the best response,

because Brill's act would have sufficient value to constitute consideration, *if* it were bargained for.

In order to be an enforceable agreement, a contract requires consideration or some substitute for consideration (e.g., promissory estoppel). Consideration is a bargained-for exchange, as well as either detriment to the promisee or benefit to the promisor (and, in practice, both). Here, as to the promise to pay $1,000, Ace is the promisor and Brill is the promisee. Thus, Brill's saving Mary's life would be a detriment to him, and a benefit to Ace, and it would constitute consideration *if it had been bargained for.* However, under these facts, Brill had *already* saved Mary's life when Ace made his promise. Thus, there's no bargain, and regardless of the benefit to Ace, there's no consideration.

The concept of value only arises in the consideration context in the form of legal value, which is detriment to the promisee or benefit to the promisor (and is thus an element of consideration). Courts in general don't look at the *adequacy* of consideration, although when consideration is grossly inadequate, it may indicate fraud, duress, or a similar problem which the court *would* address. However, under these facts, you're told only that Brill saved Mary's life. This could be anything from snatching her from the slavering jaws of a saber-toothed tiger to lifting a car off of her, but whatever it was, you could safely assume that it was "adequate" for consideration. Its actual monetary value would only be at issue if Brill were recovering under quasi-contract, where the value of his services would have to be determined, and even then you wouldn't get into metaphysical questions of the value of life itself. Since D states otherwise, it's not the best response.

Answer 30

(B) is the best response,

because it offers an element Brill must prove in order to prevail.

In order for an agreement to be enforceable, it must be supported by consideration (or some substitute for consideration, like promissory estoppel). Consideration requires a bargained-for exchange as well as either detriment to the promisee or detriment to the promisor (and, in practice, both are required).

Here, Brill's agreement not to file a claim against Mary's estate *could* constitute valid consideration, because it constitutes a legal detriment.

Even if the claim isn't ultimately valid, it can still qualify. Surrendering invalid claims can be valid consideration as long as a reasonable person could believe the claim is well-founded, and it could be pursued in good faith. Thus, Brill's reasonable belief in the validity of his claim would be crucial to his prevailing against Ace, since it provides the consideration for the agreement with Ace. Since this will make Brill's claim valid, and B recognizes this, it's the best response.

(A) is not the best response,

because the agreement is not covered by the Statute of Frauds, and thus the non-existence of a writing would have no impact on Brill's claim.

If an agreement falls within the Statute of Frauds, it requires a writing in order to be enforceable (although under some circumstances the writing requirement will be excused). Such contracts include those for the sale of an interest in land, those incapable of performance in less than one year, for the sale of goods with a price of $500 or more (UCC §2-201), and to answer for another's debt or default. The agreement here – not to claim against the estate in return for $1,000 – doesn't fall under the statute, and thus would be enforceable without a writing. As a result, the existence of the writing wouldn't strengthen Brill's claim.

Assuming arguendo a writing *were* required, the writing that exists in the facts would suffice. The letter from Ace clearly delineates the terms of the agreement. The Statute of Frauds also requires that the writing be signed by the "party to be charged" – that is, the one who's denying the agreement. Here, the party in concern is Ace, not Brill, and Ace signed the agreement, and as the party to be charged, his signature alone is sufficient (note that if Ace were suing Brill and Brill denied the agreement, only Brill's signature would be necessary).

In any case, this all ignores the central issue. The facts tell you that Ace contested the suit on grounds of lack of consideration. Option A addresses the Statute of Frauds, which deals with the enforceability of oral contracts, not consideration. As a result, A is not the best response.

(C) is not the best response,

because Mary's having contributed to the purchase of the property would not help Brill's case.

What option C suggests is that Brill's gift under Mary's will should be enforceable to the extent of her contribution to the real estate. In fact, this isn't helpful due to the nature of the tenancy by which the property was held: A tenancy by the entirety. A tenancy by the entirety is a marital estate, with the right of survivorship. That means that Ace, as Mary's husband, gets the property at Mary's death *regardless* of any provisions to the contrary in her will. Thus, her contribution to the purchase price would not impact Brill's claim. Since C states otherwise, it's not the best response.

(D) is not the best response,

because it would not make a contract otherwise unsupported by consideration, enforceable.

In order to be enforceable, a contract requires an offer, acceptance, and consideration (or some substitute for consideration, e.g., promissory estoppel). Consideration requires a bargained-for exchange as well as either detriment to the promisee or benefit to the promisor (and, in practice both are required). What D implies, then, is that Brill's claim was otherwise unsupported by consideration, and that his paying $1 in return for the promise to pay $1,000 is a detriment to Brill, as promisee, and thus constitutes consideration.

The problem with this is that if the underlying premise were true – Ace's promise was not supported by consideration – the $1 payment wouldn't help because it would be considered "nominal" consideration, which is *insufficient* to support a contract. Consideration must represent the "price" the parties put on the contract. Where the consideration is grossly inadequate – here, $1 in return for $1,000 – it's clear that the parties were only trying to give an unenforceable gift the window-dressing of a bargain, so as to make it enforceable. In such situations the "consideration" won't support a contract. Thus, proving such a payment by Brill wouldn't strengthen his case. Since D states otherwise, it's not the best response.

Answer 31

(A) is the best response,

because it provides Brill's best argument for recovery: An enforceable contract.

A valid contract requires an offer, acceptance, and consideration (or a substitute for consideration, like promissory estoppel). Consideration is the sticky point here. Consideration requires a bargained-for exchange, and detriment to the promisee or benefit to the promisor (in practice, both are required). Here, as to the promise to pay, Ace is the promisor and Brill is the promisee. By agreeing to give up his claim, Brill has suffered a detriment, and Ace has benefitted. Thus, there's consideration. Even if the claim would be invalid ultimately, it would still be valid consideration, as long as a reasonable person could believe the claim is well-founded, and it's pursued in good faith. There's nothing in these facts to suggest otherwise. Thus, the compromise is enforceable, as a bilateral contract – a promise for a promise.

Incidentally, note that Brill's saving Mary's life *wouldn't* be consideration, because it wasn't bargained-for; he saved Mary *before* his agreement with Ace (or Mary, for that matter). If Ace's promise were solely in return for Brill's saving Mary's life, then, it wouldn't be enforceable. It's the compromise that makes it enforceable. Since A recognizes this, it's the best response.

(B) is not the best response,
because Ace has not received any unjust benefits, and even if he had, restitution would not apply to these facts.

Restitution is a remedy under which the parties are returned to their position before the contract was formed. (Compare this with the damages remedy, wherein the non-breaching party is put in the situation he would have been in had the contract been fulfilled). Restitution is measured by the value rendered to defendant. It is appropriate in three general situations: The contract formulation involves mutual mistake; contract formulation involves unilateral mistake due to fraud, duress, or undue influence; or the breacher has committed a material breach.

The problem here is that restitution is an equitable remedy, and thus is only applicable to avoid injustice. Here, there's no injustice to remedy; Ace hasn't benefitted unjustly from Brill's performance. In any case, Brill has a valid claim at law, for breach of contract, since his agreement with Ace was enforceable (the consideration being supplied by Brill's detriment in not pursuing his claim). Since B doesn't recognize this, it's not the best response.

(C) is not the best response,
because it misstates the facts: Ace would not be bound by promissory estoppel, because he'd be bound by a valid contract.

Promissory estoppel is a *substitute* for consideration, used to avoid injustice. It is triggered by a gratuitous promise that is likely to, and does, induce promisee's detrimental reliance.

The reason promissory estoppel doesn't apply here is that there's an enforceable contract, and you only turn to promissory estoppel in the *absence* of an enforceable promise. A contract requires an offer,

acceptance, and consideration, or a substitute for consideration (of which promissory estoppel is the most obvious one). The sticky issue here is consideration. Consideration requires bargained-for exchange, and either benefit to the promisor or detriment to the promisee (and, in practice, both). Here, the consideration is provided by Brill's surrendering his claim against the estate, which constitutes valid consideration. Even if the claim is ultimately *invalid,* it's sufficient for consideration as long as a reasonable person could believe it's well-founded, and it could be pursued in good faith. Thus, it's apparent that the claim here was supported by consideration and thus the contract between Ace and Brill is supportable. As a result, there's no need to turn to promissory estoppel. Since C doesn't recognize this, it's not the best response.

(D) is not the best response,
because it mischaracterizes the facts: The contract was bilateral, not unilateral.

A valid contract requires an offer, acceptance, and consideration (or some substitute for consideration, like promissory estoppel). An offer for a *bilateral* contract seeks a promise in return; one for a *unilateral* contract seeks performance. Here, Ace's letter says he was offering $1,000 in return for Brill's *agreement* (read: promise) not to sue. Thus, since Ace was seeking a promise, he wanted a bilateral, not a unilateral contract. (A unilateral offer from Ace to Brill would have been: "I'll pay you $1,000 to rescue my wife." This seeks return performance, not a promise.)

As to the contract's being binding, option D is correct. The consideration for the agreement was provided by Brill's surrendering his legal claim. However, since D mischaracterizes the contract as unilateral instead of bilateral, it's not the best response.

Answer 32

(B) is the best response,
because Minivanity meets all the requirements necessary to be an intended beneficiary.

For a third party to be an intended beneficiary, it must first of all be the case that giving him the right to sue would be appropriate to effectuate the intentions of the parties. If he meets this test, he must further fit into one of the two following categories: (1) either the performance of the promise will satisfy an obligation of the promisee to pay money to the beneficiary; or (2) the circumstances indicate that the promisee intends to give the beneficiary the benefit of the promised performance.

Minivanity meets these requirements, and is thus an intended beneficiary of Goodbar's promise. First, giving Minivanity the right to sue would effectuate the intentions of the parties — Goodbar intended to help Walker get a minivan by his promise to pay, and letting the seller sue on the promise is consistent with that intention. Next, Walker (the promisee), has promised to pay money to Minivanity (the beneficiary), so enforcing the promise satisfies alternate test (1) above. Having met the requirements of an intended beneficiary, Minivanity can enforce Goodbar's promise to Walker.

(A) is not the best response,

because Minivanity was not a party to Goodbar's promise to Walker.

The essence of the promissory estoppel idea is that the maker of a promise may be bound by that promise, even though it is not supported by consideration, if the promisee relies upon that promise to his detriment, and the promisor should have foreseen the reliance. The doctrine gives only the promisee the right to sue.

For Minivanity to enforce the Goodbar promise to Walker under a promissory estoppel theory, some promise would have to have been made *to Minivanity*, since only the promisee may sue. Goodbar's promise was made only to Walker, not to Walker and Minivanity. (In fact, Minivanity did not even learn of the promise made by Goodbar until he sold the minivan to Walker.) So while Minivan can enforce Goodbar's promise, he cannot do so for the reasons stated.

(C) is not the best response,

because Goodbar made no promise to Minivanity.

The statute of frauds requires that certain types of contracts be in writing. One type of agreement that has to be in writing in order to be enforceable is a suretyship agreement, which is the promise to pay the debt of another.

Goodbar's promise does not fall within the suretyship clause of the statue of frauds, because Goodbar did not make a promise to Minivanity. For Goodbar to be a surety of Walker, Goodbar would have had to make a promise *to Minivanity* (the creditor), which Goodbar didn't do. So the fact that Goodbar promised Walker (the debtor) that Goodbar would make good on the debt is irrelevant for purposes of the suretyship provision.

(D) is not the best response,

because intended beneficiaries do not have to be identified or aware that a promise was made.

For a third party to be an intended beneficiary, it must first of all be the case that giving him the right to sue would be appropriate to effectuate the intentions of the parties. If he meets this test, he must further fit into one of the two following categories: (1) either the performance of the promise will satisfy an obligation of the promisee to pay money to the beneficiary; or (2) the circumstances indicate that the promisee intends to give the beneficiary the benefit of the promised performance.

There is no requirement that the intended beneficiary be identified when the promise is made, or that he be aware that it was made at any particular moment. Therefore, the fact that Minivanity was neither identi-fied, nor aware of the promise when it was made, is irrelevant — Minivanity meets all the requirements of an intended beneficiary and so would be able to sue to enforce Goodbar's promise to Walker.

Answer 33

(C) is the best response,

because it recognizes a defense on which Miller can prevail.

Here, Gray agreed to pay Esther's expenses (plus bonuses) if she attended law school for three years. Miller agreed to pay if Gray didn't pay. Here, after one year of law school, Gray died and his estate refused to pay Esther. Thus, if Miller's promise was enforceable, he'd have to pay since the condition precedent to his promise – Gray's not paying – occurred. However, "enforceable" is the operative word here. As a promise to assume another's debt or default, and covering a promise which is incapable of performance in less than one year, Miller's promise falls within the Statute of Frauds, and thus must be in writing to be enforceable (barring an excuse). Since it's not in writing, it's not enforceable, and *that's* Miller's best defense.

Incidentally, note that Esther's going to law school provides the consideration for both Gray's and Miller's promises. Gray's offer proposed a unilateral contract – payment in return for performance (attending law school). Esther commenced law school in response to *both* Gray's and Miller's promises. Thus, had Miller's promise been in writing, it would have been enforceable.

Since C recognizes a valid defense, it's the best response.

(A) is not the best response,

because it misstates the facts.

As a general rule, in order for there to be a legally enforceable agreement, there must be a reasonable, factual presumption that the parties actually intended a legal obligation. While the relationship between the parties (here, Uncle and Niece) would be relevant, the nature of the agreement suggests that the parties intended the agreement to be enforceable. The agreement was embodied in a memorandum, which Miller read. His promise to pay Esther's expenses if Gray didn't does *not* suggest that the promise was merely "social" and not intended to be enforceable. Instead, when you talk about lack of intent to contract, you're talking about things like promises to go out to dinner with someone, or a casual arrangement to split housekeeping duties, not an agreement like the one here. On the contrary, what makes the contract unenforceable – and is thus Miller's best defense – is that the agreement was oral.

Under these facts, Gray proposed a unilateral contract, which Esther accepted by performing – attending law school. Thus, once Esther began school, Gray was obligated to pay her expenses and a $1,000 bonus for each "A" she earned. Miller's promise was a promise to answer for Gray's debt to Esther. Furthermore, it is incapable of performance in less than a year. As such, it falls within the Statute of Frauds, and will generally require a writing. Note that there's nothing to excuse a writing (e.g., promissory estoppel, or full performance by both sides). Thus, the promise will be unenforceable because it was oral. Since A doesn't recognize this, and it mischaracterizes the facts, it's not the best response.

(B) is not the best response,

because Gray's death would not terminate the agreement: His estate could carry out his obligation. Furthermore, this doesn't address *Miller's* obligations, and it ignores the fact that Miller can't be bound because his promise was not in writing.

Under these facts, Gray's originally handing the memo to Esther was an offer proposing a unilateral contract, since he was seeking performance – attending law school for three years – not a promise, in return. Esther accepted the promise, thus creating a binding contract, by attending law school. Thereafter, all Gray had to do was pay her expense and $1,000 for each "A" she received. His death would not terminate the contract because his personal contribution wasn't necessary for the contract. It wasn't as though he'd contracted to paint Esther's portrait; he was just paying her bills, and "A" bonuses. Paying money is something his estate could carry out equally well.

If you chose this response, you may have been thinking of *offers,* which are terminated by the death of the offeror or the offeree. Here, a contract exists, sine Esther as offeree had began performance under a unilateral contract. Thus, Gray's death wouldn't be a good defense for Miller.

In any case, this doesn't address *Miller* at all. Neither Miller nor Esther died, so death isn't an issue as to Miller's obligation to Esther. Instead, what makes the contract unenforceable – and is thus Miller's best defense – is that the agreement was oral. Under these facts, Gray proposed a unilateral contract, which Esther accepted by performing – attending law school. Thus, once Esther began school, Gray was obligated to pay her expenses and a $1,000 bonus for each "A" she earned. Miller's promise was a promise to answer for Gray's debt to Esther. Furthermore, it is incapable of performance in less than a year. As such, it falls within the Statute of Frauds, and requires a writing. Note that there's nothing to excuse a writing (e.g., promissory estoppel, or full performance by both sides). Thus, the promise will not be enforceable because it was oral. Since B doesn't recognize this, it's not the best response.

(D) is not the best response,

because it probably mischaracterizes the facts, and even if it *did* reflect the facts, it wouldn't be a good defense for Miller.

Here, Gray agreed to pay Esther's expenses (plus bonuses) if she attended law school for three years. Miller agreed to pay if Gray didn't pay. Here, after one year of law school, Gray died and his estate refused to pay Esther. Thus, if Miller's promise was enforceable, he'd have to pay since the condition precedent to his promise – Gray's not paying – occurred. However, "enforceable" is the operative word here. As a promise to assume another's debt or default, and covering a promise which is incapable of performance in less than one year, Miller's promise falls within the Statute of Frauds, and thus must be in writing to be enforceable (barring an excuse). Since it's not in writing, it's not enforceable, and *that's* Miller's best defense.

Thus, an argument focusing on the contract's divisibility wouldn't be helpful to Miller. In fact, it's probably not an accurate depiction of the facts. A contract is divisible if each party's performance is divided into at least two parts, the performance of each part by one party corresponding to the other party's performance of that part. Installment contracts and employment contracts (e.g., working for $1,000/week) are examples of divisible contracts. Divisibility is only relevant where there's a material breach of contract. Under a divisible contract, even where there's a material breach of the whole contract, a party can recover for a divisible portion if it's been substantially performed. Thus, say Einstein contracts to work for Nuclear Toyco for one year at $10,000/month. After one month, Einstein wrongfully quits. He's entitled to $10,000 because he substantially performed one portion of the contract – one month.

As this example indicates, the concept of divisibility isn't applicable to the problem here. While you could theoretically divide the contract into three portions – for the three years of law school – the contract wouldn't be considered divisible because Gray wouldn't have been seeking Esther's performance in portions. Instead, he wanted her to complete law school, and that happens to require three years. Since D states otherwise, and ignores a sound defense for Miller, it's not the best response.

Answer 34

(B) is the best response,

because it correctly identifies that the "A" provision is an enforceable promise.

In order to be enforceable, an agreement must be supported by consideration, or a substitute for consideration (e.g., promissory estoppel). Consideration requires a bargained-for exchange, and either detriment to the promisee, or benefit to the promisor (and typically both). Here, Gray made an offer to Esther proposing a unilateral contract – that is, he requested her *performance* in return, in the form of attending law school for three years. Esther, as promisee, suffered a detriment by doing something she wasn't legally obligated to do – attending law school. Gray enjoyed a benefit, in the form of personal satisfaction due to his daughter's attending law school, and presumably being able to brag about this to all of his buddies. Finally, by performing at Gray's request, Esther satisfied the bargain element of consideration.

Note that Gray's promise had two elements – paying expenses and paying $1,000 for every "A". Gray's calling the "A" provision a bonus doesn't make it a gratuitous promise. The fact is, it was part and parcel of the offer Esther accepted by attending law school and earning "A"'s. Presumably, Esther worked harder at law school than she might have otherwise, knowing each "A" would mean $1,000 to her, in response to Gray's promise. Her extra effort alone would be sufficient to provide consideration for the "A" provision. Since B recognizes this, it's the best response.

(A) is not the best response,

because there's consideration to support a contract, and as a result there's no need to turn to promissory estoppel.

To be enforceable, an agreement must be supported by consideration (or a substitute for consideration). Promissory estoppel is a substitute for consideration, used to avoid injustice. It is triggered by a gratuitous promise that is likely to, and does, induce promisee's detrimental reliance. What distinguishes promissory estoppel from consideration is the bargained-for exchange. Here, Gray bargained for – and got – Esther's attending law school. Stated differently, Esther's detriment, going to law school, was at Gray's request. Thus, there was detriment to Esther, in attending law school, and benefit to Gray, in the form of personal satisfaction, thus satisfying the detriment and/or benefit element of consideration. Say the facts had been different, and Gray had promised to give Esther $10,000 as a gift, knowing she wanted to go to law school. Relying on the promise, Esther enrolled in law school. Here, there's no bargain, but Gray's promise to give Esther $10,000 would be enforceable on promissory estoppel grounds, since Gray's promise was likely to, and did, result in Esther's reliance.

However, the facts as presented in the question indicate a bargain. Sine the presence of consideration *precludes* application of promissory estoppel, A isn't the best response.

(C) is not the best response,

because the bonus for the "A's" was part of what Esther bargained for, and thus the promise to pay for the "A's" would be supported by consideration.

In order to be enforceable, an agreement must be supported by consideration (or some substitute for consideration). Consideration requires bargained-for exchange and either detriment to the promisee or benefit to the promisor (and typically, both).

Here, Gray made an offer to Esther proposing a unilateral contract – he wanted Esther to perform in return for his promise, viz., attend law school for three years.

The promise Gray made had two elements: paying Esther's expenses, and paying her $1,000 for every "A". Gray's calling the "A" provision a bonus doesn't make it a gratuitous promise. The fact is, it was part and parcel of the offer Esther accepted by attending law school, and earning "A"'s.

What C suggests is that the "A" bonus was a gratuitous promise. Say the facts were different, and Gray didn't make *any* promise to Esther until after the first year of law school, during which she earned two A's. At a party shortly after the first year, Gray told Esther, "In consideration of your earning two "A"'s, I promise to give you $2,000." This *would* be gratuitous because there was no bargain, and it didn't induce any requested detriment in Esther, as promisee.

In the facts in the question, Esther's attending law school and earning the "A"'s was in response to Gray's *entire* promise, including the "A" bonus. Since C doesn't recognize this, it's not the best response.

(D) is not the best response,

because Esther was under no duty to use her best efforts in law school.

What option D suggests is that Esther was under a pre-existing duty to perform, and thus she didn't suffer any detriment in response to Gray's promise, making the promise "illusory" (unsupported by consideration). In fact, no such duty existed; Esther hadn't even *applied* to law school when Gray made his offer.

In order to be enforceable, an agreement must be supported by consideration, or a substitute for consideration (e.g., promissory estoppel). Consideration requires a bargained-for exchange, and either detriment to the promisee, or benefit to the promisor (and typically, both). Here, Gray made an offer to Esther proposing a unilateral contract – that is, he requested her *performance* in return, in the form of attending law school for three years. Esther, as promisee, suffered a detriment by doing something she wasn't legally obligated to do – attending law school. Gray enjoyed a benefit, in the form of personal satisfaction due to his daughter's attending law school, and presumably being able to brag about this to all of his buddies. Finally, by performing at Gray's request, Esther satisfied the bargain element of consideration.

Say the facts were different, and once Esther was in law school, Gray told her, "I'll only continue to pay your expenses if you maintain a 4.0 average." Here, Gray was already contractually bound by his first promise, and since there's no additional consideration for this latter request, it's unenforceable due to a pre-existing duty. (Under the UCC, the rule is different: modifications are enforceable, without consideration, as long as they're made in good faith.)

Incidentally, the "best efforts" language of option D is the language sometimes used to make an otherwise illusory promise enforceable. Say Esther quit law school and decided to become a stand-up comic. Gray agreed to use his best efforts to promote her, in return for 10% of her earnings. Without the "best efforts" provision, Gray would have a completely unrestricted right to renege on his promise, and thus there'd be no consideration. The "best efforts" provision restricts his freedom of action, and thus supplies consideration.

In any case, under the facts in the question, Esther performed in response to Gray's request, which forms the basis of an enforceable contract. Since D ignores this, it's not the best response.

Answer 35

(B) is the best response,
because it correctly identifies that Bard is entitled to the remedy he wanted: Specific performance.

Understanding why specific performance is the appropriate remedy requires that you analyze the facts with two rules in mind: First, specific performance is an equitable remedy requiring, as a prerequisite, that there be no adequate remedy "at law" (that is – money damages). This occurs, typically, where the subject is unique – e.g., a piece of land or an antique – and/or the money value is not ascertainable. Second, in land sale contracts, when the seller refuses to convey the property, the buyer can seek specific performance. That's pretty straightforward. But the rule that's *less* obvious is that if the *buyer* refuses to carry out the sale, the *seller* can compel performance – even though the buyer will only be paying money, as he would in a damages claim! This is generally explained by the "affirmative mutuality of remedy" – since the buyer can insist on specific performance, so can the seller.

With that in mind, look closely at what happens in these facts. Bard has an option to buy Broadacre for $300,000. He then makes an irrevocable offer to Cutter to purchase Broadacre for $325,000. Cutter exercises his option, meaning Bard is bound to exercise his own option. Bard exercises his option, pays the $300,000, and takes the deed to Broadacre. Only at *that* point does Cutter renege on the deal. Thus, what you have is Bard holding the title to Broadacre, and Cutter refusing to carry out an enforceable duty – taking title to Broadacre. Thus, what's involved is a land sale contract – a classic specific performance situation! Note that the reason damages are inadequate in a case like this – where the buyer refuses to carry out a land sale contract, is that it doesn't give the seller the full benefit of his bargain. The measure of *damages* in such cases is the difference between the market value of the property and the contract price, as well as consequential damages (e.g., expenses of finding another buyer, additional insurance, mortgage payments). The problem is that this wouldn't reflect what the seller *thought* he was getting when he entered the contract, and the goal of the damages remedy is to put the non-breaching party in the position he would have been in had the contract been performed.

Since option B doesn't recognize that specific perfor-

mance is appropriate here, it's not the best response.

(C) is not the best response,
because it understates Bard's recovery – he's entitled to specific performance of the contract.

If you chose this response, you probably overlooked the fact that Bard exercised is *own* option. If he is unable to recover under the contract with Cutter, he'll be out-of-pocket for the amount he spent to buy Broadacre. The only circumstance under which Bard would be limited to the $10,000 is if Cutter had not exercised his option. An option is a contract under which an offer is made irrevocable for a given period of time. Had Cutter not exercised the option, Bard would keep the $10,000, since Cutter got what he bargained for – an irrevocable offer for a certain time period.

What C ignores is that Bard will be entitled to specific performance. In order to see why, you have to keep two rules in mind as you analyze the facts: First, specific performance is an equitable remedy requiring, as a prerequisite, that there be no adequate remedy "at law" (that is – money damages). This occurs, typically, where the subject is unique – e.g., a piece of land or an antique – and/or the money value is not ascertainable. Second, in land sale contracts, when the seller refuses to convey the property, the buyer can seek specific performance. That's pretty straightforward. But the rule that's *less* obvious is that if the *buyer* refuses to carry out the sale, the *seller* can compel performance – even though the buyer will only be paying money, as he would in a damages claim! This is generally explained by the "affirmative mutuality of remedy"": since the buyer can insist on specific performance, so can the Seller.

With that in mind, look closely at what happens in these facts. Bard has an option to buy Broadacre for $300,000. He then makes an irrevocable offer to Cutter to purchase Broadacre for $325,000. Cutter exercises his option, meaning Bard is bound to exercise his own option. Bard exercises his option, pays the $300,000, and takes the deed to Broadacre. Only at *that* point does Cutter renege on the deal. Thus, what you have is Bard holding the title to Broadacre, and Cutter refusing to carry out an enforceable duty – taking title to Broadacre. Thus, what's involved is a land sale contract – a classic specific performance situation! Since C doesn't recognize this, it's not the best response.

(D) is not the best response,
because it ignores entirely the fact that Cutter breached the contract with Bard, and thus Bard will be entitled to *some* kind of remedy. In fact, Bard will be entitled to the remedy he requested – specific performance.

In order to see why specific performance is the appropriate remedy, you have to keep two rules in mind as you analyze the facts: First, specific performance is an equitable remedy requiring, as a prerequisite, that there be no adequate remedy "at law" (that is – money damages). This occurs, typically, where the subject is unique – e.g., a piece of land or an antique – and/or the money value is not ascertainable. Second, in land sale contracts, when the seller refuses to convey the property, the buyer can seek specific performance. That's pretty straightforward. But the rule that's *less* obvious is that if the *buyer* refuses to carry out the sale, the *seller* can compel performance – even though the buyer will only be paying money, as he would in a damages claim! This is generally explained by the "affirmative mutuality of remedy" – since the buyer can insist on specific performance, so can the Seller.

With that in mind, look closely at what happens in these facts. Bard has an option to buy Broadacre for $300,000. He then makes an irrevocable offer to Cutter to purchase Broadacre for $325,000. Cutter exercises his option, meaning Bard is bound to exercise his own option. Bard exercises his option, pays the $300,000, and takes the deed to Broadacre. Only at *that* point does Cutter renege on the deal. Thus, what you have is Bard holding the title to Broadacre, and Cutter refusing to carry out an enforceable duty – taking title to Broadacre. Thus, what's involved is a land sale contract – a classic specific performance situation! Since D ignores the fact that Bard is entitled to recovery, it's not the best response.

Answer 36

(D) is the best response,

because it recognizes the central reason Claret can't recover under the contract: He is an incidental beneficiary, and thus he has no rights under the contract.

When two parties enter into a contract, there are two types of beneficiaries which may be created: Intended beneficiaries, and incidental beneficiaries. Only intended beneficiaries have enforceable rights under the contract. You determine whether a beneficiary is intended by looking at the intent of the promisee (the one to whom the duty in question is owed). If it is his primary intent that the third party receive benefit from promisor's performance, the third party is an intended beneficiary; if not, he has no enforceable rights under the contract.

The central element which is missing *here* is that there was no intent to benefit Claret: The facts instead suggest that the parties intended to distribute through Claret in order to ensure that the wine is distributed correctly, and thus the use of Claret was intended to benefit the parties *themselves,* not Claret. This prevents Claret from being an intended beneficiary. Since option D correctly recognizes that this leaves Claret with no rights to enforce under the contract, it's the best response.

(A) is not the best response,

because it attaches too much importance to the fact that Vintage's performance will run to Claret. In fact,

Claret is only an incidental beneficiary under the Vintage-Banquet contract, and thus has no enforceable rights under it.

When two parties enter into a contract, there are two types of beneficiaries which may be created: Intended beneficiaries, and incidental beneficiaries. Only intended beneficiaries have enforceable rights under the contract. You determine whether a beneficiary is intended by looking at the intent of the promisee (the one to whom the duty in question is owed). If it is his primary intent that the third party receive benefit from promisor's performance, the third party is an intended beneficiary. Criteria to examine include:

1. A statement of intent in the contract;
2. Close relationship between promisee and beneficiary; and
3. Promisor's performance directly to third party.

What option A does is to focus on the third element – performance directly to Claret – and implicitly conclude that Claret is an intended beneficiary under the contract, with enforceable rights under it. The problem is that A places too much emphasis on the third element alone, and ignores the central issue in identifying an intended beneficiary: The promisee's intent that the third party benefit from performance. Here, the facts suggest that the parties intended to distribute through Claret in order to ensure that the wine is distributed correctly, and thus the use of Claret was intended to benefit the parties *themselves,* not Claret. Since they didn't intend to benefit Claret, Claret is only an *incidental* beneficiary to the contract, and thus has no enforceable rights under the contract.

Say the facts were slightly different, and the parties *had* intended to benefit Claret. Then the only question would be if Claret's rights had "vested," such that it could enforce it rights. Traditionally, to determine vesting, you had to determine whether Claret was a creditor or donee beneficiary. Since the performance to Claret doesn't discharge a pre-existing duty – neither party had previously dealt with Claret – he's a donee, not a creditor, beneficiary. Traditionally, a donee beneficiary's rights would vest only when he manifested assent to the agreement (implied through knowledge of it), or he justifiably relied on it to his detriment. Most modern courts follow the Restatement 2d of Contracts, §311, which ignores the donee-creditor distinction, and rather views the rights of both as vesting when one of these three events occurs:

1. The beneficiary manifests assent to the promise;
2. The beneficiary sues to enforce the promise; or
3. The beneficiary justifiably relies on the promise to his detriment.

Here, if Claret was an intended beneficiary, he justifiably relied on the contract by hiring new help and expanding his facilities; thus, his rights had vested, and he could enforce the distribution provision.

However, under these facts, Claret has no enforceable rights. Since A places too much emphasis on only one element used to determine an intended beneficiary, it's not the best response.

(B) is not the best response,
because reasonable foreseeability of reliance is not an adequate basis on which Claret could recover.

In order for a third party to have enforceable rights under a contract, one must either be a beneficiary of that contract, or have rights assigned to him under the contract. (The difference between the two is that a beneficiary is created when the contract is created; an assignee only gets his right thereafter.) Here, whatever rights Claret got, he got when the contract was created. Thus, in order to recover, he'd have to have been an intended beneficiary under the Vintage-Bouquet contract.

When two parties enter into a contract, there are two types of beneficiaries which may be created: Intended beneficiaries, and incidental beneficiaries. Only intended beneficiaries have enforceable rights under the contract. You determine whether a beneficiary is intended by looking at the intent of the promisee (the one to whom the duty in question is owed). If it is his primary intent that the third party receive benefit from promisor's performance, the third party is an intended beneficiary; if not, he has no enforceable rights under the contract.

Thus, the mere foreseeability of Claret's reliance wouldn't be enough to give him enforceable rights under the contract. If you chose this response, you were probably thinking of promissory estoppel: However, that only kicks in when there's no enforceable contractual promise. Promissory estoppel is a substitute for consideration to avoid injustice. It is triggered by a gratuitous promise that is likely to, and does, induce promisee's detrimental reliance. Here, no one made a promise to Claret, so he can't be a promisee, and thus his reliance creates no liability for Vintage. (Also, in the *assignment* context, an otherwise revocable assignment becomes *irrevocable* if the assignee has relied on the assignment to his detriment, and such reliance should have been foreseeable to the assignor. Here, Claret *can't* be an assignee because an assignment requires a transfer of rights under an already-existing contract. Here, if Claret has *any* rights, they're in the original contract itself, so Claret could *only* be a third party beneficiary.)

Reliance *can* be relevant in the third party beneficiary context, in determining when the intended beneficiary's rights "vest" (before vesting, the parties can modify or rescind the contract without the beneficiary's consent). Traditionally, a creditor beneficiary's rights vested when he detrimentally relied on the contract; a donee beneficiary's rights vested on detrimental reliance or when he manifested assent to the agreement, which could be implied to occur as soon as he had knowledge of it. However, most modern courts agree with the Restatement 2d of Contracts §311, which ignores the donee-creditor distinction, and rather views the rights of both as vesting when one of these three events occurs:

1. The beneficiary manifests assent to the promise;
2. The beneficiary sues to enforce the promise; or
3. The beneficiary justifiably relies on the promise to his detriment.

(Here, if Claret *had* been an intended beneficiary, he'd be a *donee* beneficiary because the performance wouldn't discharge a prior duty owed to him.)

In any case, since option B focuses on an element which is not relevant under these facts, it's not the best response.

(C) is not the best response,
because it overstates what's necessary to create an intended beneficiary. Claret *could,* in theory, have enforceable rights under the contract without there being an express provision in the contract.

When two parties enter into a contract, there are two types of beneficiaries which may be created: Intended beneficiaries, and incidental beneficiaries. Only intended beneficiaries have enforceable rights under the contract. You determine whether a beneficiary is intended by looking at the intent of the promisee (the one to whom the duty in question is owed). If it is his primary intent that the third party receive benefit from promisor's performance, the third party is an intended beneficiary; if not, he has no enforceable rights under the contract.

Thus, it would be possible for Claret to have enforceable rights under the contract without the parties expressly providing for it, as long as Claret was intended to benefit from performance. Criteria that would indicate this *include* a statement of intent under the contract, but this isn't necessary. However, the central element which is missing *here* is that there was no intent to benefit Claret: The facts instead suggest that the parties intended to distribute through Claret in order to ensure that the wine is distributed correctly, and thus the use of Claret was intended to benefit the parties *themselves,* not Claret. This prevents Claret from being an intended beneficiary, and thus he cannot claim under the contract. Since C overlooks this, even though it arrives at the correct result, it's not the best response.

Answer 37

(C) is the best response,
because it states an argument which will release Vintage from liability to Amicusbank.

There are two ways a third party could gain rights under a contract: at the inception of the contract, as an intended beneficiary; or thereafter, if one of the parties assigns its rights under the contract to the third party. Here, since the facts involve a post-formation transfer of rights, if Amicusbank has rights at all under the contract, it will be as an assignee. A valid assignment requires the assignor's clear intent to transfer his rights completely, and immediately, to a third party. (It also requires identification of the rights to be assigned; intent must be addressed to the assignee or assignee's representative; and the assignee must accept the rights, although this is generally presumed if the assignment is beneficial.)

What's missing under these facts, as C impliedly recognizes, is the *intent* requirement. Banquet didn't intend to relinquish his rights under the contract with Vintage; he only offered the rights as security for a $200,000 loan. Since the intent element is missing, there's no assignment, and Vintage could safely perform its duty under the contract to Bouquet, under the original contract. Since this would relieve Vintage of liability to Amicusbank, it's Vintage's best defense, making C the best response.

(A) is not the best response,

because an effective assignment does not require express authorization in the contract.

In fact, the rule is almost exactly the reverse of this. Most rights are assignable, under both the UCC and the common law. An assignment is only prohibited if the assignment would materially change the other party's duty, materially increase the risk the contract imposes, or materially impair the other party's chance of receiving return performance. (Exceptions to assignability include personal services, rights under future contracts, requirement and output contracts, and assignments contrary to public policy, e.g., government pensions and alimony payments.)

Thus, without a provision otherwise, the right here – to receive payments under the contract – would be assignable. Had the question been different and the contract had prohibited assignment of rights, the prohibition would be void under UCC §9-318 (since prohibitions of the right to receive payment are invalid). At common law, such prohibitions are not favored. However, what's important here is that a valid assignment doesn't require express authorization, contrary to what A states. As a result, A would not be a good argument for Vintage, who's trying to argue *against* assignment. Since A states otherwise, it's not the best response.

(B) is not the best response,

because although it correctly characterizes Bouquet and Vintage as partners, it doesn't address whether or not Amicusbank is an assignee under the contract.

Under these facts, Bouquet and Vintage are partners to an enforceable contract. There are two ways a third party could gain rights under a contract: at the inception of the contract, as an intended beneficiary; or thereafter, if one of the parties assigns its rights under the contract to the third party. Here, since the facts involve a post-formation transfer of rights, if Amicusbank has rights at all under the contract, it will be as an assignee. A valid assignment requires the assignor's

clear intent to transfer his rights completely, and immediately, to a third party. (It also requires identification of the rights to be assigned; intent must be addressed to the assignee or assignee's representative; and the assignee must accept the rights, although this is generally presumed if the assignment is beneficial.) Thus, it doesn't matter if the parties to the contract are considered partners, debtor and creditor, or a vaudeville act, for that matter, as long as the elements of an assignment are fulfilled. As a result it wouldn't do Vintage any good to claim that he and Bouquet are partners, not debtor and creditor, since this doesn't undermine the potential existence of a valid assignment. If there's a valid assignment, Vintage has been notified of it, and he refuses to perform to the assignee, he'll be liable. Since option B doesn't address a good defense for Vintage, it's not the best response.

(D) is not the best response,

because if Amicusbank is a valid assignee of the contract, it can recover without being an intended third party beneficiary of the contract.

There are two ways a third party could gain rights under the contract: as an intended beneficiary *or* as an assignee. The difference is that the rights of third party beneficiaries are created *in* the contract; an assignment involves the subsequent transfer of rights under the contract. If a third party is *either* an intended beneficiary or an assignee, he has rights under the contract; he needn't be both.

Thus, if the transfer from Bouquet to Amicusbank was a valid assignment, Vintage will be liable to Amicusbank, since he'd been notified of the assignment (and thus could no longer perform to the assignor, Bouquet). Since option D states an argument which does not relieve Vintage's potential liability to Amicusbank, it's not the best response.

Answer 38

(A) is the best response,

because it correctly identifies why Bouquet will prevail: The wine-grape growing duty was not delegable to Agribiz.

This is the rule on delegating contractual duties. Any "impersonal" duties may be delegated, as long as the delegation does not materially alter performance. "Impersonal" duties are those in which the obligee has no particular interest in receiving performance from a particular obligor, such that delegation would not materially alter performance. Personal duties can include services of lawyers, doctors, portrait painters, architects, and the like. Note that even if the delegation is valid, the delegator (here, Vintage) remains liable unless he's expressly released (making the delegation a novation).

The key here is that, by delegating its duties to Agribiz, which has no experience in the wine grape business, Vintage has materially diminished the chances that Bouquet will receive similar profits to those it would have received from Vintage. The delegation, while not a breach of contract itself, becomes anticipatory repudiation if the original promisee (Vintage) lets the obligee (Bouquet) know that he won't perform personally. Since option A recognizes this, it's the best response.

(B) is not the best response,

because it misstates the law: A delegation *can* be valid without a contract provision expressly authorizing delegation.

This is the rule on delegating contractual duties. Any "impersonal" duties may be delegated, as long as the delegation does not materially alter performance. "Impersonal" duties are those in which the obligee has no particular interest in receiving performance from a particular obligor, such that delegation would not materially alter performance. Personal duties can include services of lawyers, doctors, portrait painters, architects, and the like. Note that even if the delegation is valid, the delegator (here, Vintage) remains liable unless he's expressly released (making the delegation a novation).

The key here is that, by delegating its duties to Agribiz, which has no experience in the wine grape business, Vintage has materially diminished the chances that Bouquet will receive similar profits to those it would have received from Vintage. Thus, even though the contract doesn't expressly prohibit delegation, *this* delegation would be invalid (regardless of whether grape growing is considered "personal" or "impersonal").

Incidentally, if the contract *had* a provision prohibiting delegation, the court would uphold the provision. (This is different from prohibitions of *assignment*, which are disfavored.) Since B ignores the fact that the delegation here was invalid even though the contract didn't prohibit it, it's not the best response.

(C) is not the best response,

because Bouquet will prevail even though Vintage can still perform under the contract. Bouquet will prevail because the delegation was *invalid*, regardless of Vintage's ability to perform.

This is the rule on delegating contractual duties. Any "impersonal" duties may be delegated, as long as the delegation does not materially alter performance. "Impersonal" duties are those in which the obligee has no particular interest in receiving performance from a particular obligor, such that delegation would not materially alter performance. Personal duties can include services of lawyers, doctors, portrait painters, architects, and the like. Note that even if the delegation is valid, the delegator (here, Vintage) remains liable unless he's expressly released (making the delegation a novation).

The key here is that, by delegating its duties to Agribiz, which has no experience in the wine grape business, Vintage has materially diminished the chances that Bouquet will receive similar profits to those it would have received from Vintage.

Thus, Vintage's *ability* to perform is irrelevant. In fact, when Vintage notifies Bouquet that he won't perform personally, he'll be liable for anticipatory repudiation. The significance of Vintage's remaining able to perform is its ability to *revoke* the repudiation, which is possible, as to *Bouquet,* as long as Bouquet hasn't relied on the repudiation in the interim (e.g., by filing suit). Since Bouquet filed suit here, Vintage could no longer revoke its repudiation (and, in any case, Vintage could be liable to Agribiz if it revoked the repudiation). In any case, since Vintage will be liable to Bouquet due to material alteration of performance under the contract, and C states otherwise, C isn't the best response.

(D) is not the best response,

because it misstates the law.

Here, Bouquet contracted with Vintage Corporation. As part of the bargain, Bouquet expected to receive the services of Vintage's employees, who have experience in growing wine grapes. Thus, while individuals *must* perform the work of a corporation, under the contract Bouquet was entitled to the services of individuals under Vintage's auspices, not Agribiz's. By delegating its duties under the contract to Agribiz, Vintage materially altered the performance Bouquet would likely receive under the contract, since Agribiz has no experience in growing wine grapes. Thus, the duty was not delegable, and the delegation, while not a breach of contract itself, becomes anticipatory repudiation if the original promisee (Vintage) lets the obligee (Bouquet) know he won't perform personally. Since option D doesn't recognize this, it's not the best response.

Answer 39

(D) is the best response,

because it implicitly recognizes that Prodigal's rights as an intended third party beneficiary under the original Mater-Vault agreement hadn't "vested," so he couldn't block the modification.

When two parties form an agreement, two types of third party beneficiaries may be created: Intended and incidental beneficiaries. Only intended beneficiaries have enforceable rights. An intended beneficiary is one whom the promise*e* (here, Mater) intends to benefit from the promisor's (here, Vault's) performance; all others are incidental beneficiaries. Here, since Mater intended Prodigal to benefit from the savings account at Vault, Prodigal was an intended beneficiary.

Having established that, you have to determine when Prodigal's rights would "vest," such that the agreement couldn't be modified or rescinded without his consent. This traditionally depended on whether Prodigal was a donee or creditor beneficiary. Since Mater didn't owe Prodigal a prior duty that setting up the savings account would discharge, he's a donee beneficiary. Traditionally, a donee beneficiary's rights only vested on justified detrimental reliance OR when he manifested assent to the agreement, which could be implied to occur as soon as he had knowledge of it. However, most modern courts agree with the Restatement 2d of Contracts, §311, which ignores the donee-creditor distinction, and rather views the rights of both as vesting when one of these three events occurs:

1. The beneficiary manifests assent to the promise;
2. The beneficiary sues to enforce the promise; or
3. The beneficiary justifiably relies on the promise to his detriment.

Here, Prodigal didn't even know about the contract when it was modified, so he can't contest the modification.

Note that even if Mater had transferred the account to him *after* she created it – thus making him an assignee – she could *still* have rescinded it, because the assignment was revocable. The things most likely to make it irrevocable – foreseeable reliance by Prodigal, or transferring to him the bank book, or his paying for the assignment, or his receiving performance from Vault as obligor – hadn't occurred. Thus, even if you mischaracterized Prodigal as an assignee, you'd *still* choose option D, the correct response.

(A) is not the best response,

because even if Prodigal is an intended beneficiary to the original Mater-Vault deposit agreement, Prodigal's rights under the contract did not "vest" before the account was transferred to Distaff. Thus, Prodigal couldn't stop the transfer.

Under these facts, the original agreement, under which Prodigal would gain any rights, was between Mater and Vault. There are two ways a third party can gain rights under a contract: As an intended beneficiary, or as an assignee. The difference is that the rights of third party beneficiaries are created in the contract, an assignment involves a subsequent transfer of rights under a contract.

Since the original passbook account was entered in Prodigal's name, he could be considered an intended beneficiary. That's because, as to Vault's duty, Mater is the promisee, and her intent is that Prodigal benefit from Vault's performance under the contract. As an intended beneficiary, Prodigal has enforceable rights under the contract, such that one his rights vest, the contract couldn't be modified or rescinded without his consent. "Vesting" is the key here. Traditionally, the time of vesting depends on whether the beneficiary is a *creditor* or a *donee* beneficiary. One is a creditor beneficiary only if the promisor's duty (here, Vault's) will discharge a duty promisee (Mater) previously owed the beneficiary. Here, Mater owes Prodigal nothing, so if he's an intended beneficiary at all, he must be a donee beneficiary.

Traditionally, the rule on vesting for a donee benefi-

ciary is that his rights only vest on justified detrimental reliance OR when he manifests assent to the agreement, which can be implied to occur as soon as he has knowledge of it. However, most modern courts agree with the Restatement of Contracts 2d, §311, which ignores the donee-creditor distinction, and rather views the rights of both as vesting when one of these three events occurs:

1. The beneficiary manifests assent to the promise;
2. The beneficiary sues to enforce the promise; or
3. The beneficiary justifiably relies on the promise to his detriment.

Here, Mater modified the contract – to make Distaff the beneficiary – before Prodigal even *knew* about the account. Thus, he couldn't prevent the transfer, and is left with no rights under the contract. Since option A ignores the vesting issue, it's not the best response.

(B) is not the best response,

because Prodigal could not be considered an assignee of any kind of the savings account, and even if he could, his right was validly revoked by the transfer to Distaff.

A constructive assignment occurs when a fraudulent or preferential transfer is converted, pursuant to statute, into an assignment that benefits creditors. Here, since Prodigal was not a creditor of Mater's, there could be no constructive assignment to him.

What option B seeks to do with the "constructive" language is to avoid a missing element of a regular assignment under these facts. In order to transfer rights under an existing contract, the assignor (here, Mater) must clearly intend to transfer his rights to a third party, the rights must be identified, and the intent must be addressed to the assignee or his representative, who must accept the assignment (although acceptance of a beneficial assignment is normally presumed). Here, Prodigal didn't *know* about the transfer, so there's no assignment. Apart from that, the transfer here would not be an assignment, because an assignment involves the transfer of rights under an already-existing contract. Here, Prodigal's rights were created in the original agreement between Mater and Vault. Thus, if he has any rights at all, they're due to his status as an intended third party beneficiary, *not* as an assignee.

In fact, Prodigal will not prevail in his claim, because his rights under the agreement had not vested before Mater modified it. As a donee beneficiary (since Mater owed him no pre-existing duty which the deposit would discharge), he would at least have had to *know* about the contract in order for his rights to vest, and here, he didn't, when the modification took place. Since option B mischaracterizes Prodigal, and arrives at the wrong result, it's not the best response.

(C) is not the best response,

because it presupposes Prodigal was an assignee,

where in fact he was only a third party beneficiary to the Mater-Vault agreement.

What option C impliedly addresses is the revocability of an assignment. In general, assignments are revocable, unless:

1. The assignee gave valuable consideration for the assignment;
2. The assignee has relied on the assignment to his detriment, and such reliance should have been foreseeable to the assignor;
3. The assignee has received payment or performance from the obligor;
4. A symbol of the assignment (e.g., a bank book) has been transferred.

Thus, if the transaction here *had* involved an assignment to Prodigal, Mater's failure to give him the passbook would make the assignment revocable. However, what makes option C incorrect is that Prodigal wasn't an assignee under the Mater-Vault contract.

In order to transfer rights under an existing contract, the assignor (here, Mater) must clearly intend to transfer his rights to a third party, the rights must be identified, and the intent must be addressed to the assignee or his representative, who must accept the assignment (although acceptance of a beneficial assignment is normally presumed). Here, Prodigal didn't *know* about the transfer, so there's no assignment. Apart from that, the transfer here would not be an assignment, because an assignment involves the transfer of rights under an already-existing contract. Here, Prodigal's rights were created in the original agreement between Mater and Vault. Thus, if he has any rights at all, they're due to his status as an intended third party beneficiary, *not* as an assignee.

In fact, Prodigal will not prevail in his claim, because his rights under the agreement had not vested before Mater modified it. As a donee beneficiary (since Mater owed him no pre-existing duty which the deposit would discharge), he would at least have had to *know* about the contract in order for his rights to vest, and here, he didn't, when the modification took place.

Thus, even though C arrives at the correct result, it mischaracterizes Prodigal, so it can't be the best response.

Answer 40

(C) is the best response,

because it correctly identifies that the assignment was *irrevocable,* and thus neither Mater's revocation nor her death can result in revocation.

Under these facts, Mater's original agreement, concerning her deposit, was with Vault. When Mater presented the passbook to Prodigal, she assigned her right to him. The central issue here is whether or not the assignment was revoked. In general, assignments are revocable, with four major exceptions:

1. The assignee gave valuable consideration for the

assignment;
2. The assignee has relied on the assignment to his detriment, and such reliance should have been foreseeable to the assignor;
3. The assignee has received payment or performance from the obligor;
4. A symbol of the assignment (e.g., a bank book) has been transferred (also, in some states, a written assignment is irrevocable).

Here, it's the fourth exception (transfer of a symbol of the assignment) that makes the assignment irrevocable. As a result, no subsequent acts by Mater will revoke the gift.

Since C correctly identifies this, it's the best response.

(A) is not the best response,

because the gift was irrevocable. Thus, Mater's death would have no impact on it.

Under these facts, Mater's original agreement, concerning her deposit, was with Vault. When Mater presented the passbook to Prodigal, she assigned her right to him. The central issue here is whether or not the assignment was revoked. In general, assignments are revocable, with four major exceptions:

1. The assignee gave valuable consideration for the assignment;
2. The assignee has relied on the assignment to his detriment, and such reliance should have been foreseeable to the assignor;
3. The assignee has received payment or performance from the obligor;
4. A symbol of the assignment (e.g., a bank book) has been transferred (also, in some states, a written assignment is irrevocable).

Here, it's the fourth exception (transfer of a symbol of the assignment) that makes the assignment irrevocable. As a result, no subsequent acts by Mater will revoke the gift.

Had the gift been revocable it could be revoked by the death of the assignor (Mater), by a subsequent assignment to someone else, or by notifying the assignee (Prodigal) or the obligor (Vault) of the revocation. Thus, while option A is theoretically correct in stating that Mater's death would revoke a revocable assignment, it ignores her prior revocation – sending Prodigal a letter to that effect – which would have revoked the assignment under these facts. However, the lynchpin here is that the gift was irrevocable. Since A doesn't recognize this, it's not the best response.

(B) is not the best response,

because the gift was irrevocable, an thus Mater's revocation would have no effect on it.

Under these facts, Mater's original agreement, concerning her deposit, was with Vault. When Mater presented the passbook to Prodigal, she assigned her right to him. The central issue here is whether or not the assignment was revoked. In general, assignments are revocable, with four major exceptions:

1. The assignee gave valuable consideration for the assignment;
2. The assignee has relied on the assignment to his detriment, and such reliance should have been foreseeable to the assignor;
3. The assignee has received payment or performance from the obligor;
4. A symbol of the assignment (e.g., a bank book) has been transferred (also, in some states, a written assignment is irrevocable).

Here, it's the fourth exception (transfer of a symbol of the assignment) that makes the assignment irrevocable. As a result, no subsequent acts by Mater will revoke the gift.

Had the facts been different – say, Mater hadn't handed over the passbook – and the gift *was* revocable, option B would be correct. A revocable gift can be revoked by the death of the assignor (Mater), by a subsequent assignment to someone else, or by notifying the assignee (Prodigal) or the obligor (Vault) of the revocation. Here, Mater's letter would have served as a revocation, had the gift been revocable. However, since it wasn't revocable, the letter had no effect, and Prodigal will prevail. Since B ignores this, it's not the best response.

(D) is not the best response,

because although it arrives at the correct result, it ignores the central reason why Prodigal will prevail: The gift was irrevocable.

What option D suggests is that Mater is estopped to deny the validity of the gift, even if the gift was revocable. However, this can't be true, because it's internally inconsistent. If the gift was revocable, Mater can revoke it, even though she of course *intended* a gift when she made it. The basis of estoppel is that someone relies on a promise to his detriment, the reliance was foreseeable, and thus the promisor can't deny the promise. While this would be a form of estoppel, it would make an otherwise revocable assignment *irrevocable.* Thus, you can't have a revocable assignment to which estoppel applies.

In fact, the reason Prodigal will prevail is that the assignment was irrevocable. Under these facts, Mater's original agreement, concerning her deposit, was with Vault. When Mater presented the passbook to Prodigal, she assigned her right to him. The central issue here is whether or not the assignment was revoked. In general, assignments are revocable, with four major exceptions:

1. The assignee gave valuable consideration for the assignment;
2. The assignee has relied on the assignment to his detriment, and such reliance should have been foreseeable to the assignor;
3. The assignee has received payment or perfor-

mance from the obligor;
4. A symbol of the assignment (e.g., a bank book) has been transferred (also, in some states, a written assignment is irrevocable).

Here, it's the fourth exception (transfer of a symbol of the assignment) that makes the assignment irrevocable. As a result, no subsequent acts by Mater will revoke the gift. Since D ignores this, it's not the best response.

Answer 41

(C) is the best response,

because it correctly identifies that Collatera will be entitled to Twin Oaks due to a valid, enforceable contract with Ginrus.

Under these facts Ginrus made Collatera an offer, in his letter – that is, a promise to do something in return for something else. He promised to will Twin Oaks to Collatera in return for her caring for him and the property for the rest of his life. Since he sought performance in return, not a promise, he proposed a unilateral, not a bilateral, contract. By moving in with him and commencing taking care of him and the property, Collatera accepted his offer. By remaining at Twin Oaks until his death, Collatera fully performed under the contract, thus entitling her to Ginrus's return performance: Transferring Twin Oaks to her. Since C identifies this, it's the best response.

(A) is not the best response,

because the consideration would be adequate to support the contract.

In order to be enforceable, an agreement must be supported by consideration, or some substitute for consideration (e.g., promissory estoppel). Consideration requires a bargained-for exchange and either detriment to the promisee or benefit to the promisor, and typically both. Here, as to the promise to transfer Twin Oaks, Ginrus is the promisor and Collatera is the promisee. By coming to take care of Ginrus, Collatera created a binding, unilateral contract. However, the issue here isn't whether there was consideration at all – Collatera clearly suffered *some* detriment and Ginrus enjoyed a benefit – but whether the consideration was adequate to support a transfer of Twin Oaks.

Consideration is only inadequate if it doesn't represent the "price" of the bargain; that is, there's a donative promise in the guise of a legal enforceable one. That's not the case here. Ginrus intended to will Twin Oaks to Collatera only if she moved in, cared for him, and maintained the property for the rest of his life. Both of them clearly saw her performance as the "price" of the bargain. The fact that he lived only two weeks doesn't make otherwise satisfactory consideration, unsatisfactory. Since A doesn't recognize this, it's not the best response.

(B) is not the best response,

because Ginrus's promise was not an invalid promise to make a will, but an enforceable, contractual promise.

Here, Ginrus made Collatera an offer – that is, a promise to do something in return for something else. He promised to will Twin Oaks to Collatera in return for her caring for him and the property for the rest of his life. Since he sought performance in return, not a promise, he proposed a unilateral contract. Collatera accepted by moving in with him and taking care of him and Twin Oaks. By remaining at Twin Oaks until his death, Collatera was entitled to return performance: conveyance of Twin Oaks. Thus, what makes the promise binding is that it was performance owed to Collatera under a contract – it wasn't just a promise to make a will. Since B doesn't recognize this, it's not the best response.

(D) is not the best response,

because Ginrus's untimely demise would not make an otherwise enforceable contract, unenforceable.

One of the underlying purposes of a contract is the allocation of risk. Here, by entering into a contract to take care of Ginrus for the rest of his life, Collatera took on the risk that Ginrus might live for many decades to come. By the same token, Ginrus ran the risk that he might die imminently, making the deal for Twin Oaks a much less attractive one for his estate. While the parties may not have foreseen Ginrus's death two weeks hence when they made the contract, death is not an event that could be considered unforeseeable, so as to excuse performance under the contract.

The language in option D concerning "unforeseen" circumstances is the language of impossibility and frustration, two means of discharging contractual duties. Under the doctrine of impossibility, where circumstances unanticipated by the parties make contract performance vitally different from what the parties contemplated, their duties under the contract are discharged, unless the adversely affected party assumed the risk the contingency might happen. Frustration of purpose relieves a duty to perform if the purpose of the contract is destroyed by a supervening act or event, which was unforeseeable when the parties entered into the contract. Here again, if the risk is considered foreseeable, a court would assign the risk to one party or the other. Neither of these would apply here, because Collatera was able to perform under the contract, it's only that her length of service was briefer than either party anticipated. However, she contracted to take care of Ginrus for the rest of his life, and she did so, so she's entitled to Twin Oaks.

Even if Ginrus's death *was* unforeseeable, assuming the contract itself was valid, rescission by the estate would not be an available remedy. Rescission by one party requires, in general, mistake (under limited circumstances), fraud, or duress. None of these exist here. The closest ground would be mutual mistake, whereby the parties made some mistake as to a basic assumption of fact. However, the length of Ginrus's life would be a matter of prediction, not fact, when the contract was entered into. Thus, unilateral rescission would not be a remedy.

In fact, Collatera is entitled to Twin Oaks because she performed under the contract. Since D doesn't recognize this, it's not the best response.

Answer 42

(B) is the best response,

because it correctly identifies that Collatera's offer was revocable.

Under these facts, Collatera made an offer to Drei. If Drei accepted the offer, Collatera's promise would be subject to a condition precedent: Ginrus's death. Thus, if Drei accepted Collatera's offer, Ginrus's death would trigger Collatera's duty to perform: that is, sell Twin Oaks for $75,000. Until Drei accepted the offer, Collatera was free to revoke it. That's because, at common law, an offer can only be made irrevocable if the irrevocability is supported by consideration, thereby creating an "option" contract. Here, Drei didn't pay to make the offer irrevocable, and thus Collatera could revoke it. Note that the only significance Ginrus's death has is that it would trigger Collatera's performance under a contract; here, there is no contract, so Ginrus's death has no impact on the offer. Since B correctly identifies this, it's the best response.

(A) is not the best response,

because it mischaracterizes the facts. Collatera wasn't selling something she didn't own; she was making a conditional promise, the condition to trigger her performance being Ginrus's death. Even if she was offering to sell something she didn't own, this wouldn't provide a justification for her revoking her offer. (Had she offered to sell something she didn't own, Drei could presumably void the contract due to fraud.)

Under these facts, Collatera made an offer to sell Twin Oaks for $75,000 when she receives it. That is, if Drei accepts her offer, her performance would be subject to a condition precedent: Ginrus's death. His death triggers her duty to perform; until then, neither party need perform. Thus, the offer is a valid, conditional promise.

Option A arrives at the correct result, but ignores the correct reasoning. Collatera may revoke her offer because it was revocable, and Drei hadn't yet accepted the offer. At common law, an offer can only be made irrevocable if it is supported by consideration – that is, the offeree pays for the irrevocability, making it an "option" contract. Here, there was no option. Thus, before Drei accepted, Collatera was entitled to revoke. Since A doesn't recognize this, it's not the best response.

(C) is not the best response,

because it understates the means by which an offer can be revoked.

There are six, basic ways by which an offer may terminate, other than by acceptance: Revocation, death or insanity of either party, intervening illegality, rejection or counter-offer, lapse of reasonable time, or destruction of the subject matter.

Thus, while option C is correct in stating that lapse of a reasonable time is *one* means of terminating the offer, it's not the *only* way. As long as the offer is revocable, the offeror can revoke the offer any time before the offeree accepts it. Here, Drei hadn't paid to make the offer irrevocable, and he hadn't accepted the offer, so Collatera was free to revoke it. Since C ignores this, it's not the best response.

(D) is not the best response,

because Ginrus's death would not make an otherwise revocable offer, irrevocable.

Under these facts, Colatera made an offer to Drei. If Drei accepted the offer, Collatera's promise would be subject to a condition precedent: Ginrus's death. Thus, if Drei accepted Collatera's offer, Ginrus's death would trigger Collatera's duty to perform: That is, sell Twin Oaks for $75,000.

However, Ginrus's death isn't relevant here, because Drei hadn't accepted the offer. Instead, under these facts, Collatera's offer was revocable, because Drei didn't pay to make it irrevocable (by creating an "option"), and he hadn't accepted the offer. Since Ginrus's death does not impact the offer, D is not correct in stating that the offer became irrevocable on Ginrus's death. As a result, it's not the best response.

Answer 43

(C) is the best response,

because it correctly identifies that Stereo can only recover to the extent Ohm ratified the contract when he reached age 18 – $300.

Under these facts, Ohm entered into a contract for a non-necessary item – a TV set – when he was a minor. As a result, his initial promise was voidable at his option due to his incapacity to contract. Thus, had Ohm not ratified the contract when he reached the age of majority, he could have avoided the contract all together (although Stereo could seek return of the set via restitution, if it was still in Ohm's possession when he disaffirmed the contract). By ratifying the contract when he reached 18, Ohm made the original promise to pay enforceable, *but only to the extent he ratified it –* $300.

Incidentally, note that Ohm wrote the letter to Stereo on his 18th birthday. This is relevant, in that, had he kept the TV for some time thereafter, this could be considered ratification by conduct manifesting such an intent, and he could have been liable for the entire

$400. Similarly, had he failed to disaffirm within a reasonable time after reaching 18, this could be considered a ratification of his original promise. Thus, by sending the letter, Ohm avoided the promise to pay $400. Since C recognizes this, it's the best response.

(A) is not the best response,

because Stereo will be able to recover damages to the extent Ohm ratified the contract when he reached 18: $300.

Under these facts, Ohm entered into a contract for a non-necessary item – a TV set – when he was a minor. As a result, his initial promise was voidable at his option due to his incapacity to contract. Thus, had Ohm not ratified the contract when he reached the age of majority, he could have avoided the contract all together (although Stereo could seek return of the set via restitution, if it was still in Ohm's possession when he disaffirmed the contract).

However, what this ignores is that Ohm ratified the contract when he reached 18. Thus, the promise to pay would be enforceable without consideration or promissory estoppel, but only to the extent Ohm ratified the contract – that is, $300. Since A ignores the fact that Ohm ratified the contract when he reached 18, it's not the best response.

(B) is not the best response,

because it understates Stereo's damages: He will be able to recover to the extent Ohm ratified the contract at age 18, that is, $300.

Under these facts, Ohm entered into a contract for a non-necessary item – a TV set – when he was a minor. As a result, his initial promise was voidable at his option due to his incapacity to contract. Thus, had Ohm not ratified the contract when he reached the age of majority, he could have avoided the contract all together (although Stereo could seek return of the set via restitution, if it was still in Ohm's possession when he disaffirmed the contract). However, by ratifying the contract when he reached 18, Ohm made the original promise to pay enforceable to the extent he reaffirmed it – $300.

If you chose this response, you were thinking of the rule relating to "necessaries." When a minor contracts to purchase necessaries, he may be bound to pay for the reasonable value of those items. Necessaries are those things including clothing, shelter, food, or other items necessary to sustain the minor, considering his age and station in life. If you chose this response, it's fair to say that a lot of people would agree that a TV would be *more* necessary than food, shelter, or clothing – especially if it has a remote control. Alas, the law wouldn't consider a TV a "necessary," so the reasonable value rule wouldn't apply. Since option B doesn't recognize this, it's not the best response.

(D) is not the best response,

because it overstates Stereo's damages. Ohm is only

liable to the extent he ratified the contract – $300.

Under these facts, Ohm entered into a contract for a non-necessary item – a TV set – when he was a minor. As a result, his initial promise was voidable at his option due to his incapacity to contract. Thus, had Ohm not ratified the contract when he reached the age of majority, he could have avoided the contract all together (although Stereo could seek return of the set via restitution, if it was still in Ohm's possession when he disaffirmed the contract). If you chose this response, you probably thought that ratification means the whole obligation is revivified – however, that's not the rule. Say the facts were different, and Ohm didn't disaffirm the contract within a reasonable time after reaching 18. *This* would be considered a ratification of the original promise, and he'd be obligated to pay the $400. In other words, a ratification needn't be express; conduct manifesting intent, or failure to disaffirm within a reasonable time after reaching majority, can do the trick as well. Since D overstates the actual damages here, it's not the best response.

Answer 44

(A) is the best response,

because Buyer still had the power of acceptance on April 21.

The statement in the document that the officer "will become effective as an option only if and when the $100 consideration is in fact paid" will be enforced. However, even before payment of the $100, Owner had made both an offer to sell the property, and an offer to grant an option. Each of those offers remained open unless something happened to either terminate it or cause it to be accepted.

Owner's sale of the property to Citizen on April 20 did not terminate either offer, because this inconsistent sale could terminate the offers only if it was a revocation, and a revocation does not become effective until received by the offeree. So the revocation could not have become effective until Buyer *learned* of the inconsistent sale, which (according to Choice (A)) had not yet happened by the time Buyer accepted the option offer by delivering his check to Owner. Once that happened, the offer to sell the property became temporarily irrevocable under the option.

(B) is not the best response,

because actions taken in preparation to perform cannot keep open a revoked offer.

An offeree can make an offer temporarily irrevocable if the offeree makes preparations that are not explicitly required by the contract but which are necessary before performance can begin. The Restatement (in § 87(2)) provides that an offer which the offeror should reasonably expect to induce action or forbearance of substantial character on the part of the offeree before acceptance, and which does induce such action or forbearance, is binding as an option contract to the extent

necessary to avoid injustice. But there are two problems for Buyer with this approach: (1) it's highly unlikely that the effort in applying for a loan constitutes action of a "substantial character"; and (2) it's also highly unlikely that enforcing the contract at all would be "necessary to avoid injustice," in view of the trivial reliance interest that Buyer has here.

(C) is not the best response,

because Buyer's evidence would not change the requirement of the contract.

In general, a party's oral statement, made prior to or simultaneously with the signing of the document, that a clause of the document doesn't mean what it seems to mean won't be effective to vary the contract. (This stems from the parol evidence rule.) Since the document clearly says that the option won't be binding without actual payment of the $100, Owner's statement to the contrary won't change this. (If Buyer can show that Owner intentionally mislead him, Buyer might have a claim for fraud. But if Owner was simply mistaken about the law on recitals of consideration, his oral statement will have no legal effect.)

The examiners are trying to confuse you, thinking that you may remember the general rule that where a contract recites the existence of consideration, the court won't ordinarily insist on proof that the recited consideration wasn't paid. But here, the document deals expressly with the issue, by not simply reciting that consideration "has been paid," but by explicitly saying that "consideration hasn't been paid and the option contract won't be binding until consideration *is* paid." So here, the general rule that the court will not go behind recitations of consideration won't apply.

(D) is not the best response,

because option contracts for the sale of real estate need consideration to be binding.

The examiners are trying to trick you, by inducing you to think that this contract is covered by the special UCC rule on firm offers. It's true that UCC § 2-205 says that "An offer by a merchant to buy or sell goods in a signed writing which by its terms gives assurance that it will be held open is not revocable, for lack of consideration, during the time stated..." But UCC applies only to contracts for the sale of goods, not real estate. There's no comparable firm-offer provision in the general common-law principles that deal with real estate. Therefore, the fact that both parties are "professional dealers in real estate" makes no difference.

Answer 45

(D) is the best response,

because Buyer would be awarded expectation damages.

Expectation damages are the usual measure of damages. In awarding expectation damages, the court attempts to put the plaintiff in the position he would have been in had the contract been performed by the defendant. Normally, this means that the plaintiff is awarded the profits he would have made had the contract been performed. That's the case here.

Choice (D) best states this principle: in giving Buyer "the amount, if any, by which the fair market value of Greenacre on the date of [the] breach exceeded [the contract price]," the court will be giving Buyer the "benefit of his bargain," i.e., the profit he would have been able to make immediately by reselling the property.

(A) is not the best response,

because Buyer was harmed and the amount of damage is provable.

Nominal damages are awarded when a right of action for breach exists but no harm has been done or is provable. Nominal damages are a small sum that is fixed without regard to the amount of harm. Here, for the reasons stated in the analysis of Choice (D), Buyer would be entitled to the amount by which the fair market value of the property exceeded the contract price (i.e., his expectation damages). The fact that an equitable remedy (injunction) isn't available doesn't prevent Buyer from collecting expectation damages.

(B) is not the best response,

because the value of an assignable option is not a measure of expectation damages.

When Buyer sent the $100, he was exercising the option, and thus binding himself to purchase the property. Prior to that moment, it's possible that the measure of damages would be the value of the option (less the $100 price to "buy" that option). But once Buyer exercised by sending the $100, the option was no longer significant — there was a contract fully binding on both sides, and the usual measure of damages for a buyer whose seller breaches the contract of sale (benefit of the bargain) applied.

(C) is not the best response,

because the fair market value of the property on the date of sale to Citizen might have been more or less than $120,000.

If the sale price to Citizen was the definitive proof of the market value of the property, this choice might be an accurate formulation. But that sale price is not legally dispositive, merely *evidence* of the fair market value. For instance, the sale to Citizen might have been at a price that the court finds to be greater than the actual market value on that day. In that event, guaranteeing Buyer a minimum recovery of $20,000 would be legally incorrect. (True, it seems unlikely that anyone would pay greater than the then "fair market value" on the day of sale. But the point is that the legal standard is "fair market value less plaintiff's contract price," not "the price paid by the third party less the plaintiff's contract price or the fair market value less the plaintiff's contract price, whichever is greater.")

Answer 46

(D) is the best response,

because this trade usage makes Computers' performance timely.

For one-shot (non-installment) sales contracts like the one here, § 2-601 states what is, in effect, a perfect tender rule: "[I]f the goods or the tender of delivery fail *in any respect* to conform to the contract, the buyer may (a) reject the whole[.]" So Computers will lose unless it finds a defense that is not inconsistent with the perfect-tender rule of § 2-601.

§ 1-205(3) says that "[A]ny usage of trade in the vocation or trade in which [the parties] are engaged or of which they are or should be aware *give[s] particular meaning to and supplement or qualify terms* of an agreement." So if Computers can indeed show that under trade usage in the purchase of computers, an apparently fixed delivery date really means "plus or minus 30 days on either side of the specified date," the contract will be interpreted in light of this usage. In other words, § 2-601 will still entitle Bank to reject if delivery were untimely, but the delivery won't in fact be deemed untimely because of the trade usage.

(A) is not the best response,

because the UCC requires tenders to be perfect, so that a defense based on lack of material harm won't work.

As described further in Choice (D) above, § 2-601 allows the buyer to reject (at least in one-shot, i.e., non-installment contracts like the one here) if the goods or tender of delivery "fail *in any respect* to conform to the contract." The phrase "in any respect" is intended to foreclose exactly the sort of "there was no material harm from the deviation" argument that Choice (A) hypothesizes.

(B) is not the best responses,

because the goodness of the deal Bank was getting would not entitled Computers to relief from the perfect-tender rule.

As described further in Choice (D) above, § 2-601 allows the buyer to reject (at least in one-shot, i.e., non-installment contracts like the one here) if the goods or tender of delivery "fail *in any respect* to conform to the contract." Under this version of the perfect-tender rule, there is certainly no room for an argument that "because the deal was an unusually good one for the buyer, the buyer loses its right to reject for late delivery or other non-conformity."

(C) is not the best response,

because a trucker's strike would not excuse a delay in tender of the mainframe.

The fact that the contract stated "F.O.B. Bank" hurts Computers' ability to rely on the truckers' strike. § 2-319(1)(b) says that "when the [shipment] term is F.O.B. the place of destination, the seller must at his own expense *and risk* transport the goods to that place and there tender delivery of them..." So a court would probably hold that use of the F.O.B. destination clause shifted to Computers the risk of a problem with Computers' choice of delivery methods.

The defense of commercial impracticability might seem relevant here. UCC § 2-615(1) provides that the seller's non-delivery, or a delay in delivery, will not constitute a breach "if performance as agreed has been made impracticable by the occurrence of a contingency the non-occurrence of which was a basic assumption on which the contract was made..." Computers might (though not necessarily, in view of the risk-shifting that might be found to be implicit in the term "F.O.B. Bank") be able to use this provision to escape *monetary liability* (damages) for breach. But the section wouldn't allow it to insist that Bank must take delivery late; the most that would happen is that both parties would be *discharged*, with neither paying anything to the other.

Answer 47

(D) is the best response,
because Computers assumed the risk of making the necessary technological breakthrough.

Computers' defense would have to be based on the UCC's version of the doctrine of commercial impracticability. § 2-615(a) says that "Delay in delivery or non-delivery in whole or in part by a seller ... is not a breach of his duty under a contract for sale if performance as agreed has been made impracticable by the occurrence of a contingency *the non-occurrence of which was a basic assumption on which the contract.*" So if Computers can convince the court that the non-occurrence of the unreliability of the new technology was a "basic assumption" behind the contract, Computers would get off the hook.

The problem for Computers is that in determining whether the non-occurrence of condition X was a "basic assumption," the court will look to whether the parties implicitly or explicitly *allocated to one party* the *risk of the non-occurrence* of condition X. If the party seeking to use commercial impracticability was allocated this risk during the negotiations, that party can't use the defense. Where one party (the seller) is going to manufacturer a device reliant on new and untested technology, a court would almost certainly hold that that party, not the buyer, implicitly bore the risk that the anticipated technological breakthrough would fail to materialize.

(A) is not the best response,
because Computers assumed the risk of objective impossibility.

As described in the analysis of Choice (D) above, even if performance by Computers was objectively impossible, this won't get Computers off the hook, because it would be found to have assumed the risk that the anticipated breakthrough would not material-

ize.

(B) is not the best response,
because Computers assumed the risk of objective impossibility.

Choice (B) is simply not a correct statement of the law. When a seller contracts to build and deliver a machine incorporating new and heretofore untested technology, the seller has a binding obligation to deliver it, unless the court finds that the parties intended to excuse performance in the event the technology does not come through. There's nothing in these facts to indicate that the parties intended such an excuse here. On the contrary, a court would almost certainly find (as detailed in the treatment of Choice (D) above) that Computers assumed the risk that it would be unable to make the needed breakthrough.

(C) is not the best response,
because the defense of impossibility applies to merchants under the UCC, in the form of the commercial impracticability defense.

It's true that the UCC doesn't use the word "impossibility." But § 2-615 gives a defense called "excuse by failure of presupposed conditions," a defense which is usually referred to as "commercial impracticability." If the contract hadn't implicitly placed on Computers the risk that the anticipated breakthrough would fail to materialize, Computers would indeed have been able to rely on § 2-615 as a defense. So this choice specifies the right outcome, but for the wrong reason.

Answer 48

(A) is the best response,
because, although the offer was no longer irrevocable on April 15, it had not been revoked, and was therefore capable of being accepted.

§ 2-205 of the UCC allows merchants to make "firm offers," i.e., offers that are irrevocable for a limited period even without consideration. (See the next question for more about this.) § 2-205 says that the period of irrevocability "in no event may ... exceed three months." So by April 15, the offer was no longer irrevocable, and Stationer was therefore free to revoke it.

But Stationer did not in fact revoke. (The revocation could only have occurred if Lawyer had learned that Stationer was no longer sticking to the offer.) Nor did the offer lapse on account of the passage of time, because the circumstances indicate that a "reasonable time for acceptance" was any time during the following year. There is no other event that caused the offer to terminate. Consequently, Lawyer's fax was a valid acceptance.

(B) is not the best response,
because at the time of acceptance this was not an option contract any more.

For the reasons stated in the analysis of Choice (A)

above, the period of irrevocability — i.e., the period during which there was an option contract — was only three months, not one year. So Lawyer's acceptance was effective not because there was an option contract at the time he accepted, but because the non-option-contract offer was unrevoked as of the moment of his acceptance (as described in Choice (A)).

(C) is not the best response,

because although Stationer's offer was irrevocable for only three months, it was still in force (though revocable) when Lawyer accepted.

It's true that, as this choice states, an offer by a merchant under § 2-205 may remain "firm," i.e., irrevocable, only for three months at maximum. But after that time expires, a firm offer doesn't automatically terminate — it merely becomes revocable. Stationer didn't exercise its right to terminate the offer, so it was still in force when Lawyer accepted it on April 15.

(D) is not the best response,

because in this case a reasonable time for acceptance was the entire year.

It's true that, as this choice suggests, an offer that has no express acceptance deadline will lapse after a "reasonable time." But here, the letter's reference to "the next calendar year" indicates that a reasonable time for acceptance was the entire next year. After three months, Stationer had the right to termination by revocation, but it didn't do so. Since there was no termination by lapse of a reasonable time for acceptance, the April 15 occurred while the offer was still open, and was therefore effective.

Answer 49

(B) is the best response,

because the December 15 offer made the price list irrevocable for a period of three months.

The "Firm Offer" section of the UCC, § 2-205, provides that an offer made by a merchant (i.e., a person dealing professionally in the kinds of goods in question) to buy or sell goods is irrevocable if the offer meets two conditions: (1) it is in a signed writing, and (2) it gives explicit assurance that the offer will be held open. Whether or not a time period is stated, under the firm offer section an offer cannot be made irrevocable for a period longer than three months.

This was a firm offer that met the requirements of § 2-205, since it was (1) by a merchant; (2) in a letter signed by the offeror; and (3) it promised that the offeror would sell all items at the catalog price for a year (a promise to hold the offer open). It's true that this promise of irrevocability didn't legally extend beyond three months (despite what it said), but the three months was enough to cover February.

(A) is not the best response,

because Lawyer did not detrimentally rely on Statio-

ner's offer.

The doctrine of promissory estoppel or detrimental reliance by the offeree may render an offer temporarily irrevocable. But this occurs only if the promisee substantially relies on the offer, and then, the offer will be enforced only to the extent needed to avoid injustice. (Rest. § 87(2).

Here, Lawyer has not relied at all, so far as the facts suggest, and he certainly hasn't relied substantially. So promissory estoppel won't apply.

(C) is not the best response,

because the UCC does not require consideration for an offer to be irrevocable.

The whole point of § 2-205 firm-offer provision is that qualifying offers by merchants will be irrevocable even though not supported by consideration. Since the offer here met the irrevocability requirements of § 2-205 (see the analysis of Choice (B) above), it was irrevocable for three months even though Lawyer gave no consideration for that irrevocability.

(D) is not the best response,

because even though the letter's attempt to confer more than three months of irrevocability failed, this attempt didn't prevent the initial three months of irrevocability, which were enough.

It's true that, as this choice suggests, the maximum period of irrevocability for firm orders under UCC § 2-205 is three months. But where an offer promises more than three months' irrevocability, the offer (assuming it meets the firm-offer requirements, such as having the irrevocability clause signed, and being by a merchant), will nonetheless be irrevocable for three months. Therefore, Choice (D) gives the wrong result, based upon incorrect implicit reasoning.

Answer 50

(B) is the best response,

because the UCC allows the attempt at modification to serve as a waiver.

Waiver is a party's manifestation of willingness to forego the benefit of a condition which occurs after the contract is formed but before the condition fails to occur. So here, Druggist's oral agreement on Aug. 1 that the cabinets didn't have to be delivered until Aug. 20 meets the requirement of a waiver.

The real issue in this question is the effect of the statute of frauds. Under § 2-201(1), a sales contract for $500 or more must be supported by a signed writing. The question is whether, in a contract that falls within § 2-201(1)'s statute of frauds requirement (because it's for more than $500) and that initially satisfies that requirement, any modification must be in writing. § 2-209(3), on modifications, says that "the requirements of the statute of frauds section ... must be satisfied if the contract as modified is within its provisions." Courts are in confusion about whether and when this sentence requires the modification itself to be in writing. But on these facts it doesn't matter, because according to § 2-209(4), "Although an attempt at modification or rescission does not satisfy the requirements of [the statute of frauds], it can *operate as a waiver.*" So Druggist's oral promise to take a later delivery, although oral, will still be able to act as a waiver. Although Druggist might have had the power to retract the waiver (see § 2-209(5), allowing retraction unless retraction would be "unjust in view of a material change of position in reliance on the waiver"), there's no indication in these facts that Druggist ever retracted. So he's bound by the waiver, and Fixtures will win.

(A) is not the best response,

because the July 15 contract would have to be in writing per the Statute of Frauds, but the oral change would nonetheless be binding as a waiver.

Under § 2-201(1), a sales contract for $500 or more must be supported by a signed writing. So this contract had to be in writing, as it was. Consequently, Choice (A) is flatly wrong.

Fixtures will win, but not for the reason given. Instead, it will win because the Aug. 1 agreement (whether or not it had to be in writing to be a full, non-retractable change to the agreement) served as a waiver, and as described in the analysis of Choice (B) above waivers will be enforced even though they are oral.

(C) is not the best response,

because the UCC does not require consideration for agreements modifying a pre-existing contract. See § 2-209(1): "An agreement modifying a contract within this Article needs no consideration to be binding."

(D) is not the best response,

because the parol evidence rule does not apply.

The parol evidence rule as integrated into the UCC holds that where a writing is a final expression of the parties' agreement (i.e., an integration), it may not be contradicted by evidence of any *prior* agreement, whether written or oral, nor of any oral agreement that is *contemporaneous* with the writing.

The Aug. 1 agreement occurred after, not before or simultaneous with, the execution of the signed writing. Therefore, the parol evidence rule has no application on the issue of whether the Aug. 1 agreement is enforceable though oral.

Answer 51

(A) is the best response,

because it correctly identifies that Wheeler will be able to recover the entire contract amount.

Arriving at this result requires resolving two major issues: (1) Whether the assignment to Wheeler was valid, and (2) Whether the risk of loss had passed to Byer.

First, the assignment was valid, even though the contract expressly prohibited assignment without the other party's permission. The reason this assignment was valid anyway is because, under UCC §2-210(3), barring circumstances to the contrary, prohibiting assignment "of the contract" refers only to *delegating duties*, not assigning contractual rights, as Singer did here. Here, Singer had already performed, so his right to payment was the only thing he had left.

Second, the risk of loss had passed to Byer, because of the "F.O.B. Singer's place of business" term. Under that term, the risk of loss passed to Byer as soon as Singer placed the chairs on board the carrier. Since the chairs were destroyed *after* Singer did so, while the chairs were in transit, *Byer* will bear the loss (note that Singer and Byer could have distributed the loss as they saw fit – if they provided "F.O.B. Byer's place of business," Singer would have borne the loss). Since option A correctly identifies the result under these facts, it's the best response.

(B) is not the best response,

because it does not use the correct formula in determining Wheeler's damages.

The central issue in determining Wheeler's recovery is resolving (1) the validity of the assignment clause, and (2) whether the risk of loss had passed to Byer when the railroad car derailed. If Singer could validly assign his interest to Wheeler, then Wheeler can recover whatever Singer could recover. First, the assignment was valid, even though the contract expressly prohibited assignment without the other party's permission. The reason this assignment was valid anyway is because, under UCC §2-210(3), barring circumstances to the contrary, prohibiting assignment "of the contract" refers only to *delegating duties*, not assigning contractual rights, as Singer did here. Here, Singer had already performed, so his right to payment was the only thing he had left. Second, since the contract called for F.O.B. Singer's place of business, the risk of loss passed from Singer to Byer as soon as Singer placed the chairs aboard the carrier, so that Byer will bear the entire loss. The upshot is that Wheeler will be able to recover the entire $10,000 from Byer.

If you chose this response, you were thinking of the buyer's remedy one he's accepted goods, and sues for breach, because option B represents the formula for calculating these damages. This clearly doesn't reflect what's going on here; apart from anything else, Wheeler is the *seller,* not the buyer. Since B applies the wrong formula to these facts, it can't be the right response.

(C) is not the best response,

because it fails to recognize that Byer will be liable *even though* the chairs hadn't been delivered.

Determining who's responsible for the loss – Singer

or Byer – depends on determining whether the risk of loss had passed from Singer to Byer. The relevant term is the F.O.B. term – here, it's for Singer's place of business. Thus, once Singer places the goods on board the carrier, the risk of loss passes to Byer.

If the term had been F.O.B. *Byer's* place of business, option C would be right, because Byer wouldn't bear the risk of loss until the chairs reached him. What option C *does* implicitly realize is that Singer was free to assign his right to Wheeler; however, since option C doesn't correctly analyze the risk of loss issue, it's not the best response.

(D) is not the best response,

because it doesn't recognize that Singer can assign his rights under the contract *despite* the contract prohibition.

Here, Singer and Byer agreed not to "assign the contract" without the written consent of the other party. There are two UCC provisions relevant to analyzing this provision under the facts in this question. First, under UCC §2-210(3), barring circumstances to the contrary, prohibiting assignment "of the contract" refers only to *delegating duties*, not assigning contractual rights, as Singer did here. Second, under UCC §9-318, the right to receive payment *cannot be prohibited* from assignment in a contract. Here, the only element of the contract left as to Singer is the right to receive payment.

If you chose this response, you were probably thinking of the common law view, under which prohibitions against assignment of contracts are valid (albeit narrowly construed by courts). However, since a transaction in goods is involved here, the UCC controls. Since the assignment will be valid in spite of the contractual provision providing otherwise, D is not the best response.

Answer 52

(D) is the best response,

because it correctly identifies the reason Byer won't prevail: the risk of loss had passed to Byer.

The F.O.B. term here discloses that the risk of loss passes to Byer at "Singer's place of business." Thus, once Singer placed the chairs on board the train, the risk of loss passed to Byer. UCC §2-613. As a result, when the chairs were destroyed, Byer bore the loss. Thus, Byer could not prevail against Singer in a breach of contract suit. Since D correctly identifies this, it's the best response.

(A) is not the best response,

because the carrier would not be considered Singer's agent.

The principal-agent relationship would require a degree of control that would not exist in a typical customer-railroad agreement. Without more, the simple fact that Singer chose to send the chairs via railroad

makes the railroad no more Singer's agent than does your mailing a letter make the U.S. Postal Service *your* agent.

What A fails to realize is that Byer will lose since the risk of loss had passed to him, under the "F.O.B. Singer's place of business" term – once Singer placed the chairs on board the train, the risk of loss passed to Byer. UCC §2-613. As a result, A is not the best response.

(B) is not the best response,

because the risk of loss was on *Byer*, not Singer.

The term that tells you this is the "F.O.B." term, which means that the risk of loss passes from Singer to Byer at Singer's place of business. UCC §2-613. The seller and buyer are free to divide the risk of loss as they see fit. Since the contract here provided for the risk of loss to pass at Singer's place of business, and the damage occurred when the goods were en route, Byer will bear the loss. Had the F.O.B. term referred to *Byer's* place of business, the risk of loss wouldn't pass to Byer until the chairs reached him. However, here, the risk of loss passes to Byer once the chairs are on board the carrier. Since B doesn't recognize this, it's not the best response.

(C) is not the best response,

because the doctrine of impossibility would not apply to these facts.

The UCC approach to impossibility is embodied in §2-613. It provides that if the goods are identified when the contract is made are destroyed, through no fault of either party, *before* the risk of loss passes to the buyer, the seller can *avoid* the contract.

Here, the risk of loss had already passed to Byer, due to operation of the F.O.B. term. By stating "F.O.B. Singer's place of business," the risk of loss passed to Byer when Singer placed the chairs on board the carrier. UCC §2-613. Since C doesn't recognize this, it's not the best response.

Answer 53

(C) is the best response,

because it correctly states that Baker has a valid claim against Zeller for breach of contract.

Under UCC §2-601, the buyer, in a single delivery (not installment) contract, has the right to reject the goods if they "fail in any respect to conform to the contract." However, the seller will have the right to cure defects, under §2-508, under two circumstances, as long as seller notifies buyer of his intent to cure:

1. The time for performance has not run out, and seller can cure within that time, or
2. Seller has reason to believe buyer would accept non-conforming goods – in which case seller can go reasonably *beyond* the time allowed for performance in curing the defects.

Here, neither of these exceptions will apply. The contract called for Zeller to deliver August 1, which he did; thus, there's no time left for performance. Second, there's nothing in these facts to give Zeller a reasonable belief that Baker would accept non-conforming goods. As a result, the general rule will apply, and Baker will have a claim for breach (since Baker rightfully rejected the goods). Since C recognizes this, it's the best response.

(A) is not the best response,

because it does not reflect the UCC view on performance.

Under the UCC, the general rule is that the buyer in a single delivery contract has the right to reject the goods if they "fail in any respect to conform to the contract." §2-601. In fact this is *not* the panacea it sounds, since the seller has a right to cure defects, pursuant to §2-508, if he notifies buyer of the intent to cure, and:

1. The time for performance has not run out, and seller can cure within that time, or
2. Seller has reason to believe buyer would accept non-conforming goods – in which case seller can go reasonably *beyond* the time allowed for performance in curing the defects.

Neither of these exceptions would benefit Zeller under these facts, because the time for performance expired the same day Zeller delivered the defective shipment, and there's nothing under these facts to give Zeller a reasonable belief Baker would accept non-conforming goods. Thus, Baker would have a valid claim against Zeller for failure to deliver the 100 bushels of wheat.

If you chose this response, you were thinking of the common law rule, under which a minor contractual breach (which is what this would be considered) does not relieve the aggrieved party of his duty to perform; instead, he must perform and sue for damages. However, since a transaction in goods is involved here, the UCC controls, and since option A doesn't reflect the UCC stance, it's not the best response.

(B) is not the best response,

because Zeller would not be excused from performing on grounds of impossibility.

Under UCC §2-613, a seller can only avoid a contract due to impossibility if the goods are identified when the contract is made, and the goods are destroyed, through no fault of either party, before the risk of loss passes to the buyer. Here, the goods weren't identified when the contract was made; the contract was for any 100 bushels of wheat.

Instead, Zeller will be liable to Baker for failure to deliver the wheat, since the time for performance ended the day Zeller delivered the 95 bushels to Baker, and Zeller had no reason to believe Baker would give him extra time in which to cure the defect. Since B doesn't recognize this, it's not the best response.

(D) is not the best response,

because Baker had no duty to give Zeller the opportunity to cure the defect.

The general rule is that, in single delivery contracts (*not* installment contracts), the buyer has the right to reject the goods if they "fail in any respect to conform to the contract." UCC §2-601. This isn't quite as strict as it sounds, because the seller has a right to cure defects under one of two exceptions from §2-608, as long as seller notifies buyer of his intent to cure:

1. The time for performance has not run out, and seller can cure within that time, or
2. Seller has reason to believe buyer would accept non-conforming goods – in which case seller can go reasonably *beyond* the time allowed for performance in curing the defects.

Here, neither one of these would apply so as to give Zeller a chance to cure. First, the contract called for delivery August 1, and Zeller delivered the defective shipment August 1, so the time for performance had run out. Second, under these facts, Zeller had no grounds to believe Baker would accept a defective shipment. Thus, Baker had no obligation to accept the shipment.

If you chose this response, you *may* have been thinking of buyer's obligation under an *installment* contract, not a single delivery contract like the one involved here. Where installment contracts are concerned, the buyer can *only* reject non-conforming installments if the non-conformity substantially impairs the value of that installment *and* the defect can't be cured. If the seller gives adequate assurances of cure, the buyer *must* accept the installment. Thus, under an installment contract, Zeller could have additional time to get his hands on more wheat, and Baker probably would have to accept the 95 bushels. However, since the rule for single-delivery contracts is different, and a single delivery contract is involved here, D isn't the best response.

Answer 54

(D) is the best response,

because Buyer stated she would buy the ranch if legally obligated to do so.

An anticipatory repudiation is a clear statement by a party, made before performance under a contract is due, that the party does not intend to perform. For a statement by the promisor to constitute a repudiation, it must appear to the promisee that the promisor is quite unlikely to perform. It is not enough that the promisor states vague doubts about his willingness or ability to perform.

Buyer's statement here does not meet these requirements. Buyer has not made it clear that she probably won't perform — indeed, just the contrary, since she's indicated that she *will* perform if legally required to do so.

An anticipatory repudiation is treated as if it were a

present breach. But since the statement here is not an anticipatory repudiation, and since there is no other present breach (the time for performance won't arrive until December), there has been no breach, and Seller will lose if the case is decided before December.

(A) is not the best response,

because Buyer stated she would buy if legally obligated to do so.

As described in the discussion of Choice (D) above, Buyer's statement did not meet the requirements for an anticipatory repudiation, because Buyer indicated that she would perform if required to do so.

(B) is not the best response,

because Seller has not yet requested assurances.

A party to a contract has the right to demand reasonable assurances when the other party to a contract gives an ambiguous indication of not performing. If the latter fails to provide these assurances, this failure will itself be considered a repudiation, and a breach.

Buyer's October 1 statement indeed created reasonable grounds for Seller's insecurity with respect to Buyer's performance. However, before Seller could sue for breach of contract, he was obligated to request assurances from Buyer. If Buyer then did not give Seller the requested assurances, Seller could treat this failure as a repudiation. However, under these facts, Seller has not yet requested assurances, and so Seller cannot successfully claim that a breach has occurred.

(C) is not the best response,

because Seller can bring suit prior to closing if Buyer anticipatorily repudiates.

One of the major purposes of the anticipatory repudiation doctrine is that it allows the repudiatee to bring an immediate suit for breach, before the time for performance has arrived. So if Buyer had anticipatorily repudiated, Seller could bring an immediate suit, and Choice (C) would be an incorrect statement.

Beyond this problem, of course, there is the additional difficulty (for Seller) that Buyer's words "I won't perform unless legally obligated" are not an anticipatory repudiation, for the reasons described in Choice (D).

Answer 55

(C) is the best response,

because Buyer did not retract her repudiation.

The Second Restatement states that a repudiation may be retracted until the aggrieved party has either (i) sued for breach, (ii) changed his position materially in reliance on the repudiation, or (iii) stated that he regards the repudiation as final. Rest. 2d § 256(1).

Under these facts, Buyer had from August 1, when she unequivocally repudiated the contract, to October 1 to retract her unequivocal repudiation. Buyer didn't do so. Buyer's right to retract her repudiation and per-

form under the contract ended when Seller materially changed his position in reliance on the repudiation, by selling to Rancher.

The fact that Seller initially urged Buyer to change her mind does not alter the analysis. Under the modern view, the repudiatee's exhortation to the repudiator to perform does not "reinstate the contract," and does not impair the repudiatee's right to cancel the contract or change position in reliance on the repudiation.

(A) is not the best response,

because Seller had no obligation to notify Buyer that Seller was viewing the contract as being in material breach.

A repudiation may be retracted until the aggrieved party has either (i) sued for breach, (ii) changed his position materially in reliance on the repudiation, or (iii) stated that he regards the repudiation as final. Rest. 2d § 256(1). When Seller sold the property to someone else, this was a material change of position in reliance on the repudiation, and immediately terminated Buyer's right to retract the repudiation. While Seller had the *right* to notify Buyer that Seller was viewing the contract as terminated and preparing to sell to someone else (and such a notice would have ended Buyer's right to retract the repudiation, under the third branch of the Restatement test cited above), Seller did not have the *obligation* to give this notice.

(B) is not the best response,

because Seller did not waive the repudiation by urging performance. Under the modern view, the repudiatee's exhortation to the repudiator to perform does not "reinstate the contract," and does not impair the repudiatee's right to cancel the contract or change position in reliance on the repudiation. (Under the older view, the repudiatee's urging to perform might have had this effect.)

(D) is not the best response,

because Buyer repudiated her rights under the contract, and the contract was cancelled once Seller sold to someone else.

Even had no repudiation occurred, this choice would not be a correct statement of the law. For instance, suppose that Buyer never repudiated, tendered the contract price on December 1, and Seller refused either to accept the money or convey the ranch — in that scenario Buyer would win, whereas the language of Choice (D) says that Buyer would lose. Beyond that, of course, the fact that Buyer had repudiated long before Dec. 1 entitled Seller to cancel the contract and convey to someone else, making Buyer's later tender of the contract price irrelevant.

Answer 56

(C) is the best response,

because Ram is a "lost volume" seller.

A "lost volume" seller is one who can obtain as many items from a supplier as she can sell. When the customer of such a seller breaches his contract, and the seller resells the item to another customer at the same price, the seller will end up making one fewer sale because of the breach. This is because the new customer would have bought an item anyway, regardless of whether the first customer had breached. Damages available to a lost volume seller under the UCC are the profits, including reasonable overhead, which the seller would have made from full performance by the buyer, together with any incidental damages. UCC § 2-708(2).

Ram is a "lost volume" seller, because as the facts state, Ram can buy more ICB personal computers than it can sell. Ram contracted with Marilyn Materboard for the sale of an ICB personal computer for $3,000. Materboard repudiated and Ram sold at private sale the same specific computer to Byte, who paid the same price. Ram did not lose any money on the sale of the specific computer, but as a lost-volume seller, Ram made one fewer sale. Ram's damages would include the profit from the lost sale to Materboard plus any incidental damages.

(A) is not the best response,

because damages to a "lost volume" seller include lost profits and incidental damages.

A "lost volume" seller is one who can obtain as many items from a supplier as she can sell. When the customer of such a seller breaches his contract, and the seller resells the item to another customer at the same price, the seller will end up making one fewer sale because of the breach. This is because the new customer would have bought an item anyway, regardless of whether the first customer had breached. Damages available to a lost volume seller under the UCC are the profits, including reasonable overhead, which the seller would have made from full performance by the buyer, together with any incidental damages.

Ram is a "lost volume" seller, because as the facts state, Ram can buy more ICB personal computers than it can sell. So the fact that Ram sold the unit in question to a different buyer for the same price is irrelevant — Ram has still lost one net sale. Under the UCC, damages available to a "lost volume" seller include the profits from Ram's lost sale to Materboard plus any incidental damages.

(B) is not the best response,

because notice of intent to resell is not required where the recovery is on a "lost volume" basis.

When the seller elects the remedy of "cover" — i.e., the right to resell and collect the difference between the resale price and the (higher) contract price — and the resale is at a private sale, the seller is required to give the buyer "reasonable notification of his intention to resell." § 2-706(3). Since we're told here that Ram's sale to Byte is "at private sale," Ram would be required

to give notice of intent to resell to Materboard if Ram wanted to recover the resale/contract-price differential under § 2-706(3).

However, Ram is *not* recovering on this resale/contract-price basis. That's because that basis would give him $0. Instead, he's recovering his lost profits as a lost-volume seller under § 2-708(2). (See Choice (C) for an analysis.) There's no pre-sale notice requirement for recoveries on this lost-volume basis.

(D) is not the best response,

because the damages available to a lost volume seller are not the contract price.

As the discussion of Choice (C) describes, Ram is a "lost volume" seller, who has lost one net sale and is entitled under UCC § 2-708(2) to the profits which he would have made from full performance by the buyer, together with any incidental damages. Nothing in the UCC provides for a different measure of damages — such as the full contract price — merely because the buyer has "unjustifiably repudiated." (Giving Ram the entire contract price would obviously over-compensate him, since he has avoided having to pay the wholesale purchase price to the manufacturer.)

Answer 57

(C) is the best response,

because unconscionability would allow Landholder to argue the contract was one-sided.

The concept of unconscionability is a defense to the enforcement of a contract that allows a court to refuse to enforce a provision or an entire contract to avoid unconscionable terms. UCC § 2-302(1). The principle behind the provision is the prevention of oppression and unfairness. The basic test is whether, in light of the general commercial background and needs of the particular parties, the clauses involved are so one-sided as to be unconscionable under the circumstances existing at the time the contract was formed. The unconscionability concept is often applied to one-sided bargains where one of the parties to the contract has substantially superior bargaining power and can dictate the terms of the contract to the other party with inferior bargaining power.

The concept of unconscionability affords Landholder his best prospect for effective cancellation. The test for unconscionability is whether in light of the general commercial background and the commercial needs of the particular parties, the contract is so one-sided as to be unconscionable. Landholder, the facts state, was pressed for cash because he had high, fixed personal expenses. When in desperate financial straits and knowing little about timber values, he entered into a contract with Logger at a price 70% lower than the prevailing price for comparable timber rights. These facts would provide a sound basis from which Landholder could argue that the contract he entered into with Logger was so one-sided as to be unconscionable and should therefore be canceled.

(A) is not the best response,

because Logger has not behaved in bad faith.

A buyer who proposes a very below-market price has not thereby behaved in bad faith. In any event, "bad faith" in some abstract sense is not grounds for cancelling a transaction to which the other party has agreed, in the absence of misrepresentation or unconscionability.

(B) is not the best response,

because Landholder did not make a misrepresentation.

Equitable estoppel, also known as estoppel in pais, is a doctrine applied by courts of equity when a person (1) misrepresents a fact, (2) on which the other party justifiably relies, (3) injuriously. Whereas promissory estoppel applies to situations where a contract has not been formed, equitable estoppel is applied to cancel formed contracts. Equitable estoppel will prevent a person from insisting on his strict legal rights when it would be inequitable for him to do so, in light of the prior dealings between the parties.

Equitable estoppel would not be Landholder's best prospect for effective cancellation because Landholder would have to show that Logger misrepresented the value of the timber rights. Under these facts, it is not likely that Landholder could make that showing. Landholder advertised a proposed sale of the timber rights and Logger was the only bidder. Even though Logger's bid was 70% lower than the regionally prevailing price, Logger's bid was not a misrepresentation, and Landholder was free to accept the bid or not.

(D) is not the best response,

because Logger did not use coercion to enter the contract.

The concept of duress is a defense to contract based on a lack of capacity. Contracts induced by duress and coercion are voidable by a court and may be rescinded as long as they are not affirmed. Duress will usually not be found, however, where one party merely takes economic advantage of the other's pressing need to enter the contract.

For the concept of duress to provide a good prospect of effective cancellation of the contract, Landholder would have to argue that Logger coerced Landholder into entering the contract. There are no facts here to show coercion. All Logger did was take advantage of Landholder's scant knowledge about timber values and his pressing need for immediate money.

Answer 58

(A) is the best response,

because Landholder's neighbor was not an intended beneficiary of the contract, and therefore may not enforce it.

An incidental beneficiary is a person who may derive benefit from performance of a contract, though that person is neither the promisee nor the one to whom performance is to be rendered. Since there will often be many people indirectly or even directly benefited by any given contractual performance, the term incidental beneficiary is used to describe those persons who would benefit by the performance but who were not intended by the parties to be benefited and who thus cannot enforce the contract.

Landholder's neighbor's rights under the Landholder-Logger contract are those of an incidental beneficiary, at best. Landholder's neighbor's rights are not directly related to the contract, as say a mill to which Logger would take the cut timber, but even more derivative or remote. Landholder's neighbor's interest in the contract has nothing to do with the timber, beyond having it removed so he can see the lake. Since Landholder's neighbor is only an incidental beneficiary of the contract, he cannot sue for enforcement of it.

(B) is not the best response,

because a nuisance-litigation suit could only be brought later (by Logger, after he won the suit brought by the neighbor).

The fact that a suit is "nuisance litigation" will not be a ground on which the defendant to the suit can win. Instead, if the defendant wins, the fact that the suit was so meritless as to have been a nuisance might be grounds for the original defendant to win a tort-like recovery from the original plaintiff in a second suit, brought by the original defendant for wrongful use of civil proceedings.

Thus here, Logger will have to win (and will win) the suit brought by the neighbor on the underlying merits of third-party beneficiary law (as described in Choice (A) above.) Once Logger does so, then, and only then, might he be able to recover affirmatively from the neighbor in a new suit for "nuisance litigation," i.e., the wrongful use of civil proceedings.

(C) is not the best response,

because Landholder's neighbor was not an intended beneficiary.

For a third party to be an intended beneficiary, it must first of all be the case that giving that party the right to sue would be appropriate to effectuate the intentions of the parties. The circumstances must also indicate that the promisee intends to give the beneficiary the benefit of the intended promise.

Landholder's neighbor is not an intended beneficiary of the Landholder-Logger contract, because neither party intended to give Landholder's neighbor the right to enforce the contract. Landholder, who was in desperate financial straits, entered the contract with Logger to raise funds to meet his expenses. Logger's intention was to make money on the timber severed from Landholder's property. Neither party contemplated Landholder's neighbor's benefit, nor intended to make him a beneficiary of their contract.

(D) is not the best response,

because no rights were transferred to Landholder's neighbor to allow him to sue as a surrogate.

Landholder's neighbor cannot claim to be a surrogate standing in to enforce Landholder's rights under the contract, unless he can show some relation to the contract. The facts state that Landholder has made no attempt to assign to his neighbor any cause of action he might have against Logger. Nor do the facts state any other legal relationship between Landholder and his neighbor. Without such an assignment or relationship, Landholder's neighbor cannot assert Landholder's rights as a surrogate.

Answer 59

(B) is the best response,

because the answer correctly states the UCC's noncarrier rules for delivery and payment.

Under the UCC, noncarrier cases are those instances where the parties did not intend that the goods be moved by carrier. That is the case here, since there's no indication that either party thought a carrier would be used. In noncarrier cases, unless the contract provides otherwise, "payment is due at the time and place at which the buyer is to receive the goods." UCC § 2-310(a). In other words, this was to be a cash sale, with payment due when the goods were delivered. Furthermore, under § 2-308(a), the place for delivery was "the seller's place of business..." So if Apartments didn't tender cash on March 1 at the seller's place of business, Fixture had no duty to deliver the goods. (Nor was Apartments entitled to wait until all 50 had been delivered — see the discussion of Choice (D).)

(A) is not the best response,

because delivery would not be to Apartments' place of business.

Under § 2-308(a), unless the contract provided otherwise (which it didn't) the place for delivery was "the seller's place of business..." Since Choice (A) says that the fixtures must be delivered at Apartments' place of business, it's wrong.

(C) is not the best response,

because payment is due concurrently with Fixture's delivery.

Under UCC § 2-310(a), unless otherwise agreed, "payment is *due at the time* and place at which the *buyer is to receive the goods* even though the place of shipment is the place of delivery." Since the parties made no plans for shipment by common carrier, the place for delivery was seller's premises (see discussion of Choice (A).) Therefore, payment was due concurrently with delivery, i.e., buyer was not entitled to even brief credit. (Nor was Apartments entitled to wait

until all 50 had been delivered — see the discussion of Choice (D).)

(D) is not the best response,

because payment is due only on the 25 sets delivered.

Under UCC § 2-307, unless otherwise agreed, "where the circumstances give either party the right to make or demand delivery in lots the price if it can be apportioned may be demanded for each lot." Since the agreement contemplates that delivery would occur separately for each of the two lots, and since the price can easily be apportioned (because the sets are usable independently of each other), the quoted provision applies. Therefore, Fixtures was entitled to demand that payment for the first 25 sets be made at the time these sets were delivered.

Answer 60

(D) is the best response,

because Fixtures can cure and must be given the right to do so.

Installment contracts under the UCC are contracts with several deliveries. In an installment contract, a non-conforming installment can be rejected only if the nonconformity substantially impairs the value of that installment and cannot be cured. UCC § 2-612(2). The seller can cure by giving reasonable notice and making a new tender of conforming goods, which the buyer must then accept. A deficiency in quantity may be cured by an additional delivery.

The contract between Fixtures and Apartments is an installment contract, because it calls for deliveries of 25 sets on March 1 and 25 sets on April 1. Apartments cannot reject the 24 sets because the nonconformity does not substantially impair the value of the installment, and Fixtures has given adequate assurance that the nonconformity can and will be cured. That is, Apartments can take and install the 24 bathroom fixtures now and then, shortly thereafter, install the replacement unit when it arrives. There is nothing in the facts to indicate that this brief delay in the last unit would "substantially impair the value" of the first 25-lot installment. Indeed, the fact that there is another 25-lot installment due one month latter indicates just the contrary, since it makes clear that the project won't be completed until after the second lot has been delivered and installed.

Because the installment's value is not substantially impaired and seller has given adequate assurances of cure, Apartments must both: (1) accept the first, 24-unit lot (subject to cure as to the 25th unit); and (2) leave the second part of the contract in force.

(A) is not the best response,

because Apartments has to accept the shipment and has no right to cancel the contract, for the reasons described in Choice (D).

(B) is not the best response,

because Apartments has to accept all 24 sets, and keep the contract in force.

It is true that as a general principle, where the goods "fail in any respect to conform to the contract," the buyer may (among other choices) "accept any commercial unit or units and reject the rest." UCC § 2-601. So if the whole contract consisted of just the 25 March 1 units, Apartments would be entitled to take whichever it wanted and reject the rest. But § 2-601 is made subject to the provision on breach in installment contracts, covered in § 2-612. And as described in the answer to Choice (D), because of the easy availability of cure and the lack of substantial impairment of the installment, Apartments is required both to allow Fixtures time to cure the first installment, and to leave the second installment in place.

(C) is not the best response,

because Apartments cannot cancel the rest of the contract.

According to § 2-612(3), "Whenever non-conformity or default with respect to one or more installments substantially impairs the value of the whole contract there is a breach of the whole." So if Fixtures' non-conformity as to the first installment substantially impaired the value of the whole 50-unit set, Apartments would be entitled to cancel the rest of the contract (though it wouldn't have to accept the 24 units in that event). But because Fixtures can timely cure the non-conformity, there is no substantial impairment of the value of the whole contract here. § 2-612(2). Consequently, the problem is governed not by the above-quoted language of § 2-612(3), but by the language of § 2-612(2), discussed in the treatment of Choice (D) above.

Answer 61

(C) is the best response,

because Pigstyle made no warranty about sterility.

A warranty, as the term is used in the UCC, is a kind of guarantee or promise by a seller of goods that they have certain characteristics. Where a seller at the time of contracting has reason to know any particular purpose for which the goods are required and that the buyer is relying on seller's judgment to furnish suitable goods, the seller is deemed to make an implied warranty that the goods will be fit for such purpose. If Pigstyle were found to have made an implied warranty that the boar was fit for breeding, Pigstyle would probably lose.

However, a court would decide that no warranty was made here. The facts state that no express warranty was made. Nor would there be an implied warranty of fitness for particular purpose, because there is no indication that Breeder "relied on the seller's skill or judgment to select or furnish suitable goods," a requirement under UCC § 2-315 for creation of an implied warranty of fitness for a particular purpose.

If no express or implied warranties were made by Pigstyle, then Breeder assumed the risk of the boar's sterility, and there would be no basis for recovery.

(A) is not the best response,

because the parties stipulated that the fertility of the boar was not known by either party at the time of the sale.

Mutual mistake allows a party to avoid a contract based on a mistake made by both parties. The Second Restatement imposes three requirements which must be satisfied before the adversely affected party may avoid the contract on account of mutual mistake: (1) the mistake must concern a basic assumption on which the contract was made; (2) the mistake must have a material effect on the agreed exchange of performances, and (3) the adversely affected party must not bear the risk of the mistake. Rest. 2d § 152. The basic idea of the last requirement is that the party who knows that his knowledge is incomplete but who elects to proceed anyway must bear the risk that what he doesn't know can hurt him.

Here, none of these requirements is satisfied: (1) there was no "basic assumption" of fertility, since both parties knew that fertility couldn't yet be known; (2) even if there was a "mistake" about fertility, the mistake couldn't have had a "material effect" on the exchange, since both parties must have adjusted the price to compensate for the fact that fertility couldn't yet be known; and most of all, (3) by proceeding in the face of known uncertainty about fertility, Breeder bore the risk of being wrong in his hopes.

(B) is not the best response,

because no implied warranty was made.

As the discussion of choice (C) covers in more detail, an implied warranty of fitness for a particular purpose is deemed made only where the buyer relies on the seller's "skill or judgment to select or furnish suitable goods." UCC § 2-315. Since both parties knew that fertility could not yet be known, and since there is no indication that Pigstyle said anything to indicate to Breeder that Pigstyle believed the boar would likely be good for breeding, there is no evidence of Breeder's reliance on Pigstyle's selection skills. Therefore, no implied warranty of fitness for breeding was made.

(D) is not the best response,

because no "mistake" was made (whether unilateral or mutual), and because even the existence of a unilateral mistake here would not support recovery.

The same three requirements are imposed for unilateral mistake as for mutual mistake, but in addition, either of two things must be shown: (1) that the mistake is such that enforcement of the contract would be unconscionable, or (2) that the other party had reason to know of the mistake or his fault caused the mistake.

Breeder could not prove a mutual mistake was made,

because, as described in the discussion of choice (A), Breeder knew that he didn't know anything about the boar's fertility, and thus did not make a "mistake." Nor could Breeder show either of the two additional elements needed to prove unilateral mistake: (1) The deal was not unconscionable, since unconscionability is very rare in commercial settings, and since the price here was implicitly set by market conditions, and factored in the risk of infertility. (2) Nor did Pigstyle have reason to know of the mistake: it was impossible for either party to have known the fertility of a two-month-old boar.

Answer 62

(B) is the best response,

because the confirmation sent by Manufacturer became binding on Retailer when he failed to object.

In sales-of-goods cases, a writing signed by the party against whom enforcement is sought is required for contracts aggregating $500 or more. § 2-201(1), first sentence. However, there is a very important exception: a merchant who *receives a signed confirmation from the other party* will be bound by it just as if he had signed it, unless the recipient of the confirmation objects within 10 days. UCC § 2-201(2).

Both Retailer, a dry goods retailer, and Manufacturer, a towel manufacturer, are merchants. Manufacturer confirmed in writing the agreement it reached with Retailer on the phone. Under § 2-201(2), if Retailer did not want to enter into a contract under those terms, Retailer was obligated to object in writing within 10 days. Since Retailer did not object, the contract is enforceable under the terms listed in the confirmation.

The fact that Retailer originally offered to buy somewhere between 500 and 1000 towels is irrelevant. Under the last sentence of § 2-201(1), where a memorandum (writing) of the agreement exists, "the contract is not enforceable ... beyond the quantity of goods shown in such writing." Since under § 2-201(2) the confirmation serves as the type of memorandum required in § 2-201(1), the 500-unit quantity listed in the confirmation is the maximum quantity for which the contract is enforceable.

(A) is not the best response,

because the written confirmation stated a term of 500 towels.

As described more fully in the last sentence of the discussion of Choice (B) above, the contract was not enforceable beyond the quantity stated in the confirmation. UCC §§ 2-201(1) and (2).

(C) is not the best response,

because as a confirmation between merchants, the agreement does not need to be signed.

Under UCC § 2-201(2), a merchant who receives a signed confirmation from the other party will be bound by it just as if he had signed it, unless the recipient of

the confirmation objects in writing within 10 days. Since both Manufacturer and Retailer were merchants, when Retailer failed to object in writing within 10 days of getting Manufacturer's signed letter (a confirmation), Retailer is bound even though he never signed a writing.

(D) is not the best response,

because the absence of a price term from the memorandum will not make a contract unenforceable.

In sale-of-goods cases, a memorandum is required if the total sale amount is $500 or more. But the memorandum need not recite all terms — according to the last sentence of § 2-201(1), "A writing is not insufficient because it omits or incorrectly states a term agreed upon ..." So the fact that the price was omitted is irrelevant. (Manufacturer will be permitted to prove that the parties orally agreed on the $5 price.)

Answer 63

(D) is the best response,

because Seller's acceptance was effective on dispatch.

First, Buyer's signed order was an offer. How could this offer be accepted? Well, under UCC § 2-206(1), "Unless otherwise unambiguously indicated by the language or circumstances ... (b) an order or other offer to buy goods for prompt or current shipment shall be construed as inviting acceptance either by a prompt promise to ship or by the prompt or current shipment of conforming or non-conforming goods[.]" So this order authorized Seller to accept by either promising to ship or shipping.

Next, we have to figure out whether and/or when Seller accepted that offer. Acceptance by mail was reasonable under the circumstances (see § 2-206(1)(a): acceptance normally may be made "in any manner and by any medium reasonable in the circumstances.") The "mailbox rule" (a common-law rule that applies in the UCC context because nothing in Article displaces it, and under § 1-103 common-law rules apply in the UCC unless expressly displaced by the Code) states that acceptance is effective immediately upon proper dispatch. The Second Restatement states the rule this way: "An acceptance made in a manner and by a medium invited by an offer is operative and completes the manifestation of mutual assent *as soon as put out of the offeree's possession*, without regard to whether it ever reaches the offeror." Rest.2d § 63(a). So under this common-law rule, Seller accepted by mailing, since at that moment the acceptance document (his letter) was "put out of the offeree's possession."

Since there was a contract at the moment Seller mailed the acceptance on Jan. 7, Buyer's purported Jan. 8 revocation was ineffective.

(A) is not the best response,

because the offer could be accepted by a promise to ship, not just by shipment.

Under § 2-206(1) (quoted more fully in Choice (D) above), Buyer's order authorized acceptance "either by a prompt promise to ship or by the prompt or current shipment of conforming or non-conforming goods[.]" So although Seller could have accepted by shipment, he was alternatively entitled to accepted by promise to ship, which he did. Therefore, Choice (A) is wrong. (Since acceptance occurred at the moment of promise by Seller — i.e., the mailing of the acceptance letter — the bargain was concluded before Buyer could revoke the next day.)

(B) is not the best response,

because Seller's order, although it supplied a price not previously mentioned by Buyer, was effective as an acceptance.

Buyer's offer indicated his willingness to buy at Seller's "current price." Therefore, although Seller's reply document was the first to mention the $10 price (and although Buyer never expressly committed to the $10 price), since the $10 was indeed Seller's current price, Seller's reply matched the offer well enough to qualify as an acceptance.

(C) is not the best response,

because nothing made Buyer's offer irrevocable for any length of time.

Offers ordinarily are not irrevocable. It's true that § 2-205 authorizes "firm offers" (i.e., irrevocable ones) even without consideration for the irrevocability. But under § 2-205, an offer is not "firm" unless it "by its terms gives assurance that it will be held open[.]" Nothing in Buyer's order "by its terms" gave that assurance. Therefore, Buyer had the usual common-law right to revoke before acceptance. (His problem was that his revocation didn't happen until after the acceptance, for the reason described in Choice (D)).

Answer 64

(D) is the best response,

because it correctly makes the case that Bye Bye's June 9 letter was either a rejection or a breach.

Vendor's June 2 telegram was probably specific enough to be an offer, since it including price, quantity and delivery terms. The fact that it did not include a time-for-payment term would not prevent the telegram from functioning as an offer, because time-for-payment terms are not so important that their absence indicates that no offer is present, and because the UCC stands by with an appropriate gap-filler (§ 2-310(a): "Unless otherwise agreed (a) payment is due at the time and place at which the buyer is to receive the goods even though the place of shipment is the place of delivery.")

Bye Bye's June 5 letter was probably an acceptance, even though Bye Bye said that he'd "prefer to pay in full 30 days after invoice." This is probably an acceptance because § 2-207(1) says that "A definite and seasonable expression of acceptance ... operates as an

acceptance even though it states terms additional to or different from those offered or agreed upon, unless acceptance is expressly made conditional on assent to the additional or different terms." Here, Bye Bye is not saying in effect, "I'm only accepting if you agree that I can pay in 30 days" — he's saying something more like "I'm accepting. I hope that the contract we're making will include 30 days to pay." So his response is not "expressly made conditional on assent to the different [30 days to pay] terms," and is thus a "definite and seasonable expression of acceptance [that] operates as an acceptance even though it states terms additional to or different from those offered or agreed upon."

If the June 5 letter was an acceptance, the 30-days-credit request was, under § 2-207(2), an "additional term[] [that is] to be construed as [a] proposal[] for addition to the contract." § 2-207(2)(b) then says that "Between merchants [which is what both Bye Bye and Vendor are] such [additional] terms become part of the contract unless: ... (b) [the additional term] materially alter[s] [the contract]." A court would almost certainly conclude that when the offer demands C.O.D. payment, a proposal for credit constitutes a "material alteration." In that event, the contract that, by hypothesis, was formed on June 5 did not include the 30-days-credit term, since a proposal in the acceptance for a "different" term doesn't enter the contract if it "materially alters" the contract. So the contract that was formed required C.O.D. payment.

If Bye Bye's June 5 letter indeed formed a contract, then his June 9 "I don't deal with people who can't accommodate our simple requests" letter was a repudiation (and thus a breach). That's because the June 9 letter unequivocally stated that Bye Bye wouldn't be performing ("deal[ing] with" Vendor) on account of Vendor's refusal to give him credit, and no credit was required under the contract. A refusal to perform unless the other party gives up a right under the contract is a repudiation and a breach. So by the "unequivocal refusal to perform" defense asserted in Choice (D), Vendor wins even if the "parties had previously formed a contract."

Now, what happens if Bye Bye's June 5 letter *didn't* form a contract? In that event, this letter was probably a counter-offer. If it was a counter-offer, then either: (a) Vendor's June 6 "You must pay C.O.D." telegram was a rejection, causing the counter-offer to terminate; or (b) the counter-offer survived Vendor's June 6 telegram, in which case Bye Bye's June 9 "I don't deal" letter was a revocation of the counter-offer. In either scenario, there was no offer open to accept by the time Bye Bye changed his mind and purported to accept on June 10.

So in summary, (1) if there was a contract formed prior to June 9, Bye Bye's June 9 "I don't deal" letter was a repudiatory breach, so he loses because he materially breached; and (2) if there wasn't a contract formed prior to June 9, no offer was open by Bye Bye's

June 10 purported acceptance, so he loses because there was never a contract.

(A) is not the best response,

because a court could find that the June 2 letter was an offer.

It is true that this argument *might* work — the court might conclude that the June 2 letter was indeed only a price quote and not an offer. If the court reached this conclusion, Vendor would probably win, because nothing else that happened later would be likely to be found to constitute an offer-and-acceptance.

However, the court probably will not agree with Vendor's contention that the June 2 letter was not an offer, for several reasons. First, Bye Bye's June 1 telegram was pretty clearly an attempt to solicit an offer (not just to solicit a quote), since it specified precise quantity and delivery-time terms — a court would probably presume that the response to this solicitation-of-offer was in fact an offer. Second, the quote mentioned the exact quantity the seller had for sale, and when the quantity in stock is mentioned a court is likely to find an offer rather than merely a quote. If the court did fine that the June 2 letter was an offer, then it would probably find that Bye Bye accepted on June 5, and that Vendor breached by selling the units to someone else.

So this "quote not an offer" approach is merely one that possibly succeeds, whereas choice (D) almost definitely succeeds.

(B) is not the best response,

because it misstates how the UCC operates.

UCC § 2-207(1) provides that any timely and definite "expression of acceptance" operates as an acceptance, "even though it states terms additional to or different from those offered ... unless acceptance is expressly made conditional on assent to the additional or different terms." Here, Bye Bye's June 5 letter was clearly timely and definite, and didn't say that the acceptance was "expressly ... conditional on [Vendor's] assent to" any additional or different terms. So the fact that the June 5 letter included an "additional" term (request for 30 days credit) did not prevent the letter from being an acceptance. (Whether the credit request became part of the contract is a different story — that would depend on whether this was a "material alteration," which it probably was. In that event, the credit term would not have become part of the contract.)

Notice that this answer is wrong because it (incorrectly) assumes that the common-law "mirror image" rule (in which a not-perfectly-matching response cannot be an offer) applies in a UCC context — as the above analysis show, the UCC rejects this common-law approach.

(C) is not the best response,

because a use of the mails would have been a valid method of acceptance.

It's true that an offer (which we can assume, for purposes of this discussion, was what Vendor's June 2 telegram was) can state the method by which acceptance is to be made. But Vendor did not do this. The mere fact that Vendor used a telegram doesn't mean that Vendor was in effect saying, "you must accept, if at all, by a telegram." So Bye Bye was free to accept by any method that was reasonable under the circumstances. (See § 2-206(1): "Unless otherwise unambiguously indicated by the language or circumstances (a) an offer to make a contract shall be construed as inviting acceptance in any manner and by any medium reasonable in the circumstances[.]") And given that there was no indication that the market price was changing rapidly or the items perishable, acceptance by letter was reasonable here.

STRATEGIES AND TACTICS

CRIMINAL LAW

OUTLINE OF COVERAGE

The following outline for the Criminal Law portion of the MBE was adopted by the Bar Examiners for all MBEs given on or after July, 2003. It was designed to clarify what's covered on the Crim Law portion of the exam. This is the most up-to-date outline of coverage released by the Bar Examiners, and your study for Criminal Law should be centered around it.

Here's what you need to know:

I. Homicide
   A. Intended killings
      1. Premeditation — deliberation
      2. Provocation
   B. Unintended killings
      1. Intent to injure
      2. Reckless and negligent killings
      3. Felony — murder
      4. Misdemeanor — manslaughter

II. Other crimes
   A. Theft
      1. Larceny
      2. Embezzlement
      3. False pretenses
   B. Receiving stolen goods
   C. Robbery
   D. Burglary
   E. Assault and battery
   F. Rape; statutory rape
   G. Kidnapping
   H. Arson

III. Inchoate crimes; parties
   A. Inchoate offenses
      1. Attempts
      2. Conspiracy
      3. Solicitation
   B. Parties to crime

IV. General principles
   A. State of mind
      1. Required mental state
      2. Strict liability
      3. Mistake of fact or law
   B. Responsibility
      1. Mental disorder
      2. Intoxication
   C. Causation
   D. Justification and excuse

V. Constitutional protection of accused persons (i.e., Criminal Procedure)
   A. Arrest, search and seizure
   B. Confessions and privilege against self-incrimination
   C. Lineups and other forms of identification

    D. Right to counsel
    E. Fair trial and guilty pleas
    F. Double jeopardy

Of the 33 "Criminal Law" questions on the MBE, 60% (about 19-20 questions) will cover categories I through IV (i.e., "substantive" Criminal Law); 40% (about 13-14 questions) will cover category V (i.e., Criminal Procedure). There will be questions from each of the roman numeral topics on the exam, but not necessarily from each of the sub-topics.

WHAT TO EXPECT

Criminal law questions on the MBE are not as difficult as those on other subjects, such as Property. Here are a few of the major types of questions:

1. You're asked whether, under the facts given, the defendant should be guilty;
2. You're asked the prosecutor's (or defendant's) best argument;
3. You're asked which of four precedents is the best one for the facts given;
4. You're asked the most serious crime for which the defendant could be convicted;
5. You're asked which of four fact patterns most closely fits a certain type of crime (e.g., felony murder).

STUDY STRATEGIES

1. Learn the differences between degrees and types of homicides.

You must keep the different types of homicides clear in your mind. Keep in mind that the common law did **not** recognize degrees of murder; therefore, if an MBE question wants to discuss degrees of murder, it will supply an appropriate statute.

In studying homicide, begin with murder. At common law, murder is an unlawful killing (neither justifiable nor excusable) with malice aforethought. Remember, "malice" **doesn't mean intent**. The Bar Examiners use this as a common MBE trap. While the malice element **can** be satisfied by an intent either to kill or to cause serious injury, or by felony murder, it can **also** be satisfied by a "depraved heart" — that is, the actor disregards an unreasonably high risk of harm to human life. In some states, testing "unreasonable risk" is purely objective (i.e., extreme negligence); in others, the defendant must consciously disregard the risk (i.e., recklessness). Either way, it's possible to be convicted of murder **without** intending to kill!

if a defendant satisfies the test for intentional murder, always look to see if there's sufficient provocation by the victim to knock the conviction down to voluntary manslaughter. Keep in mind that provocation is both subjective and objective: the provocation must be enough to anger this defendant, **and** it should be of a type that would provoke a reasonable person to kill; furthermore, this defendant must not have cooled off when the killing takes place, **and** a reasonable person would not have cooled off in these circumstance (a "heat of passion" killing).

If a defendant is charged with a killing that doesn't satisfy the requirements for murder, check for involuntary manslaughter; there are two types: **criminal negligence** and **misdemeanor manslaughter.** Criminal negligence means that the defendant ignores a risk of harm to human life which is **less** than the risk represented by depraved heart murder. Misdemeanor manslaughter is the misdemeanor equivalent of felony murder. What's important to remember here? Two things. First, don't get hung up on the difference between "extreme negligence" for depraved heart murder and "gross negligence" for criminal negligence involuntary manslaughter. On the MBE, such differences will be fairly obvious, since they're difficult to quantify. A simple way to remember the difference between depraved heart murder and criminal negligence manslaughter is to remember this example: Two men set out in separate cars. One drives through town and shoots a gun into the window of a house where a crowded party is being held. He doesn't intend to kill anyone, but he does. The other man drives out to the country and fires a gun into the window of an abandoned hunting cabin. He doesn't intend to kill anyone, but he hits and kills a bag person who's taken refuge in the cabin. The man who drove through the city committed depraved heart murder, due to the **extreme** negligence of his act (firing into a house crowded with people). The one who drove through the country is liable for criminal negligence involuntary manslaughter (his act was criminal negligence).

Here's a sample question from the MBE concerning homicide:

in which of the following situations is Defendant most likely to be guilty of common-law murder?

    A. Angered because his neighbor is having a noisy party, Defendant fires a rifle into the neighbor's house. The bullet strikes and kills a guest at the party

B. During an argument, Harry slaps Defendant. Angered, Defendant responds by shooting and killing Harry

C. Defendant drives his car through a red light and strikes and kills a pedestrian who is crossing the street

D. Using his fist, Defendant punches Walter in the face. As a result of the blow, Walter falls and hits his head on a concrete curb, suffers a concussion, and dies

This question covers the spectrum of homicides. As outlined above, you should start with the definition of murder: an unlawful killing with malice aforethought. Keep in mind that malice doesn't mean intent, but can be satisfied by extreme negligence or depraved heart. Applying this definition, you should find that choices C and D are eliminated. Driving through a red light, in the absence of other facts, would certainly be considered negligent, but not *extremely* negligent (which is what depraved heart murder requires), so it's highly unlikely to be considered murder. Choice D, similarly, involves a non-intentional killing; punching someone in the face would show intent to injure, but not to injure seriously enough for intentional murder. Furthermore, D would not involve negligence extreme enough to satisfy depraved heart murder. Your choice is now between A and B. As outlined above, the second thing you should do on a homicide question is to analyze whether there is provocation sufficient to make the killing voluntary manslaughter. Remember, the provocation must be serious enough to provoke a reasonable person to kill, not just serious enough to provoke this defendant. Applying this to A and B, you'll see provocation in both; however, in A, the provocation — a noisy party — would not be enough to cause a *reasonable* person to kill. The provocation in B — being slapped during an argument — could well be enough (although it's not a certainty). Thus, you wind up with one answer choice that clearly fits murder, one that doesn't fit very well, and two that definitely don't work, so the one that fits, choice A, must be the best response.

2. Know the basic definitions of crimes against people and property.

It may seem too good to be true, but many Criminal Law MBE questions require nothing more than a mechanical application in which you compare the elements of different crimes to the facts you're given. The most important crimes to know are larceny, robbery, and burglary. (The following are common law definitions — if an MBE question wants you to deal with differences found in modern rules, it will state them). Larceny is a trespassory taking and carrying away of the personal property of another with the intent to steal it. Robbery is very similar; it's simply a larceny from a person which is accomplished by force or fear. Burglary is the breaking and entering of the dwelling house of another, at night, with the intent to commit a felony therein. While you'll also need to know the elements of false pretenses, embezzlement, larceny by trick, and other larceny-related crimes against the person, larceny, robbery and burglary are the main crimes to remember.

3. Appreciate "hidden" Issues — causation and intent.

MBE questions rarely focus on *obvious* issues. That's why it's important to know elements of crimes *flawlessly*. Even if you do, though, it's easy to miss issues like causation, as the following question illustrates:

Dutton, disappointed by his 8-year-old son's failure to do well in school, began systematically depriving the child of food during summer vacation. Although his son became seriously ill from malnutrition, Dutton failed to call a doctor. He believed that as a parent he had the sole right to determine whether the child was fed or received medical treatment. Eventually, the child died. An autopsy disclosed that the child had suffered agonizingly as a result of the starvation, that a physician's aid would have alleviated the suffering, and that although the child would have died in a few months from malnutrition, the actual cause of death was an untreatable form of cancer.

The father was prosecuted for murder, defined in the jurisdiction as "unlawful killing of a human being with malice aforethought." The father should be

A. acquitted, because of the defendant's good-faith belief concerning parental rights in supervising children

B. acquitted, because summoning the physician or feeding the child would not have prevented the child's death from cancer

C. convicted, because the father's treatment of his son showed reckless indifference to the value of life

D. convicted, because the child would have died from malnutrition had he not been afflicted with cancer

Your gut reaction to facts like these is probably that the father is guilty because of his heinous behavior. If you read the facts closely, however, you should notice that the father *didn't cause his son's death:* the child died of untreatable cancer. Since the father didn't cause the death, he may be liable for other statutory crimes, but he can't be liable for any kind of homicide. As a result, B is the best response.

Another issue which can trip you up is *intent*. You need to remember how intent applies to the different crimes. For instance, note how intent affects conspiracy, accomplice liability, larceny, and robbery. In conspiracy, the conspirators must not only intend to agree, but must also intend the criminal goal of the conspiracy. For a defendant to be liable as an accomplice, he must intend that his principal carry out the criminal act. (Thus, if one offers help without that intent, he *cannot* be liable as an accomplice.) In larceny, the trespassory taking must be done with the *intent to steal*. If the actor intends only to *borrow* another's property, there's *no intent to steal* and thus no larceny; however, if he plans to steal when he takes the goods but changes his mind later and returns them, he's still liable — he took the goods with the requisite intent. Burglary is similar in that it requires breaking and entering another's dwelling house, at night, *with the intent to commit a felony therein*. If defendant intends to go in and play Scrabble, there's no burglary. If he mistakes the house for his own, goes in, and removes jewelry, believing it's his own, there's no intent to commit a felony, and thus no burglary. Keep in mind that, where intent is concerned, *even an unreasonable belief* can be a defense, *if it negates intent*. In real life, a defendant's unreasonable belief may make it far less likely a jury will believe him, but this doesn't change the legal rule that even an unreasonable belief can negate intent.

Intent is also important to remember when dealing with crimes that punish a defendant for doing one act while intending to perform another. The defendant is liable *even if* the second crime is not performed! This applies, of course, to the inchoate crimes of conspiracy and attempt, but also to crimes like larceny and burglary. For instance, burglary requires breaking and entering another's dwelling house, at night, with the intent to commit a felony therein. Thus, once the criminal actor has broken and entered with the appropriate intent, the crime is complete. Even if he has a change of heart once he's inside, he's still liable! Larceny requires the intent to steal. Once a person takes another's property with the intent to steal, a change of heart won't exonerate him, because the crime was *complete* when the taking occurred!

4. For Criminal Procedure, study cases.

In many instances, Criminal Procedure MBE questions resemble actual Supreme Court cases very closely; thus, you should become as familiar as you can with the fact patterns of *actual cases*.

5. Distinguish types of warrantless searches.

Remember to keep the different types of warrantless searches distinct in your mind. They are: (1) search incident to arrest; (2) inventory searches; (3) exigent circumstances; (4) plain view doctrine; (5) automobile searches; (6) consent searches; (7) stop and frisk; and (8) regulatory inspections (actually, you do need a warrant for this last one, but the requirements to obtain a warrant aren't as stringent). Questions involving warrantless searches show up *a lot* on the MBE, so study the scope of each type very carefully. Frequently, Criminal Procedure MBE questions will involve one kind of search, but some of the answer choices will try to confuse you by relying on a *different* type of search.

Also, remember that the Fourth Amendment applies only to searches and seizures done by the *police* or by people working under the direction of the police.

6. Keep in mind when *Miranda* kicks in.

Custodial interrogations/confessions is one of the Bar Examiners' favorite Crim Pro topics, so be sure to have a really good understanding of this part of Criminal Procedure.

Also, remember that *Miranda* warnings are required only when the police intend to conduct a *custodial* interrogation. "Custodial" means the suspect is *not free to leave*. Thus, if the police arrest someone and have no intent to question him — no *Miranda*. If the suspect volunteers a confession — no *Miranda*. Note also that a custodial interrogation *can* take place away from the police station, and it *can* be conducted of someone who *isn't* under arrest or even a suspect, but it *must* be administered by the police (or an agent of the police) — not by just a civilian).

EXAM TACTICS

l. Apply statutes.

Some criminal law questions on the MBE will contain statutes. If you come upon one of these, apply the statute to the facts *verbatim.* In many cases, simply doing this will lead you to the correct response. Here's an example:

> While testifying as a witness in a civil trial, Walters was asked on cross-examination if he had been convicted in the circuit court of Jasper County of stealing $200 from his employer on August 16, 1977. Walters said, "No, I have never been convicted of any crime." In fact, Walters had pleaded guilty to such a charge and had been placed on probation.
>
> Walters was then charged with perjury on the ground that his statement denying the conviction was false. A statute in the jurisdiction defines perjury as knowingly making a false statement while under oath.
>
> At trial, the state proved Walters' statement and the prior conviction. Walters testified that the attorney who represented him in the theft case had told him that, because he had been placed on probation, he had not been convicted of a crime. Walters had served his probationary period satisfactorily and been discharged from probation. The alleged advice of the attorney was incorrect.
>
> If the jury believes Walters, it should find him
>
> A. guilty, because his mistake was one of law
>
> B. guilty, because reliance on the advice of an attorney is not a defense
>
> C. not guilty, if the jury also finds that his reliance on the attorney's advice was reasonable
>
> D. not guilty, because he lacked the necessary mental state

Here, the statute states that perjury requires *knowingly* making a false statement while under oath. Regardless of whether Walters should or shouldn't have relied on his attorney's opinion, he *didn't know-ingly make a false statement*. Since that's what the statute requires, Walters simply *cannot* be guilty; he lacks the necessary mental state. Choice D correctly identifies this. To answer this question, then, all you have to do is mechanically apply the statute.

Note also that, in questions based on statutes, the correct response *must* agree with the statute. If an answer refers to a common law rule that conflicts with the statute, it *cannot* be the best response, even if the common law rule strikes you as being more "correct." Here's an example:

> Defendant became intoxicated at a bar. He got into his car and drove away. Within a few blocks, craving another drink, he stopped his car in the middle of the street, picked up a brick, and broke the display window of a liquor store. As he was reaching for a bottle, the night watchman arrived. Startled, Defendant turned and struck the watchman on the head with the bottle, killing him. Only vaguely aware of what was happening, Defendant returned to his car, consumed more liquor, and then drove off at a high speed. He ran a red light and struck and killed a pedestrian who was crossing the street.
>
> Relevant statutes define burglary to include "breaking and entering a building not used as a dwelling with the intent to commit a crime therein." Manslaughter is defined as the "killing of a human being in a criminally reckless manner." Criminal recklessness is "consciously disregarding a substantial and unjustifiable risk resulting from the actor's conduct." Murder is defined as "the premeditated and intentional killing of another or the killing of another in the commission of committing rape, robbery, burglary, or arson." Another statute provides that intoxication is not a defense to crime unless it negates an element of the offense.
>
> Defendant was charged with the murder of the watchman and manslaughter in the death of the pedestrian. Assume he is tried separately on each charge.
>
> As to the death of the pedestrian, Defendant pleads intoxication as a defense. The state's best argument to counter the intoxication issue in the manslaughter death of the pedestrian is that
>
> A. intoxication is no defense to the crime charged, because manslaughter is historically a general intent crime
>
> B. intoxication is a defense only to a specific intent crime, and no specific intent is involved in the definition of the crime of manslaughter
>
> C. conscious risk-taking refers to Defendant's entire course of conduct, including drinking with the knowledge that he might become intoxicated and seriously injure or kill someone while driving
>
> D. whether Defendant was intoxicated or not is not the crucial issue here; the real issue is whether the manner in which Defendant was operating his car can be characterized under the facts as criminally reckless

As you can see, choices A, B, and D ignore the terms of intoxication statute given in the facts, and, as a result, cannot be correct. That leaves only one alternative — C — which is in fact the correct response.

2. Remember causation.

Causation is a tricky issue, because it will never "pop out" of the page at you. In some MBE questions, the causation issue is carefully masked but nonetheless central to finding the correct answer. Remember — causation is **always** required for criminal liability. If the defendant's conduct did not cause the victim's injury, there's no criminal liability.

3. Remember that forgiveness or condonation by the victim, or return of stolen property, doesn't negate criminal liability.

For example, the crime of larceny is complete once one has taken someone else's property with the intent to steal it, whether or not the the actor later decides to return the property. Likewise, the crime of burglary is complete once one has broken and entered another's dwelling house at night with the intent to commit a felony therein, even if the person later reconsiders. The fact that the victim subsequently forgives the criminal actor **does not** mean that the actor cannot be convicted, because crimes are considered wrongs against the **state**, not against the individual (this is the primary distinction between crimes and torts).

Unfortunately, questions involving issues like this are sneaky. Your gut reaction will probably be that the defendant **shouldn't be found guilty**, because he's either renounced his criminal purpose or settled with the victim. Beware! You have to analyze these problems coldly and apply the elements of crimes **mechanically**. Here's an example:

> Johnson took a diamond ring to a pawnshop and borrowed $20 on it. It was agreed that the loan was to be repaid within 60 days and if it was not, the pawnshop owner, Defendant, could sell the ring. A week before expiration of the 60 days, Defendant had an opportunity to sell the ring to a customer for $125. He did so, thinking it unlikely that Johnson would repay the loan and if he did, Defendant would be able to handle him somehow, even by paying him for the ring if necessary. Two days later, Johnson came in with the money to reclaim his ring. Defendant told him that he had sold the ring because he thought Johnson would not reclaim it, and offered to give Johnson $125. Johnson demanded his ring. Defendant said, "Look buddy, that's what I got for it and it's more than it's worth." Johnson reluctantly took the money. Larceny, embezzlement, and false pretenses are separate crimes in the jurisdiction. Defendant could most appropriately be found guilty of
>
> A. Larceny
> B. Embezzlement
> C. False pretenses
> D. None of the above

Here, your gut reaction is likely lead to choice D because you think that Defendant should not be found guilty, because, after all, he gave Johnson the money he got for the ring and so didn't profit from his conduct. According to the law, though, once Defendant misappropriated property in his possession, he became liable for embezzlement, **regardless** of the fact that he turned over the proceeds to Johnson. This   makes B the best response. (Choices A and C identify the wrong crimes.) You can see from this example how important it is to analyze MBE problems coldly and mechanically.

4 How to handle questions that ask for defendant's "best defense."

Seeing the words "best defense" may strike fear in your heart, because you think you'll have to do some fine line-drawing as to the quality of various defenses. Have no fear. Just approach these questions this way: one of the answer choices will acquit the defendant, and three of them **won't**. To make that distinction, analyze the choices as follows:

a. Does this answer choice apply to the facts?

If the answer choice does not correctly characterize the facts — e.g., the choice states the defendant acted without intent when the facts show he did — it cannot be the best response, even if it's theoretically correct.

b. Is this answer choice a correct statement of the law?

This is where you have to dig into your memory bank. The answer choice must correctly reflect the law in order to be the best response.

c. Is the argument sufficient to acquit defendant?

Apart from being faithful to the facts and citing the correct law, the answer choice must identify the **central issue** in the facts. It must also negate an element of the crime or provide a valid defense to it. Watch for intent, defenses and causation, which frequently are hidden issues. Here's an example:

Harry met Bill, who was known to him to be a burglar, in a bar. Harry told Bill that he needed money. He promised to pay Bill $500 if Bill would go to Harry's house the following night and take some silverware. Harry explained to Bill that, although the silverware was legally his, his wife would object to his selling it.

Harry pointed out his home, one of a group of similar tract houses. He drew a floor plan of the house that showed the location of the silverware. Harry said that his wife usually took several sleeping pills before retiring, and that he would make sure that she took them the next night. He promised to leave a window unlocked.

Everything went according to the plan except that Bill, deceived by the similarity of the tract houses, went to the wrong house. He found a window unlocked, climbed in and found silver where Harry had indicated. He took the silver to the cocktail lounge where the payoff was to take place. At that point police arrested the two men.

If Harry were charged with burglary, his best argument for acquittal would be that

    A. there was no breaking

    B. he consented to the entry

    C. no overt act was committed by him

    D. there was no intent to commit a felony

The key fact to note here is that the mental element of burglary is missing. Burglary is breaking and entering the dwelling house of another, at night, with the intent to commit a felony therein. Thus, either Harry or Bill had to *intend* to commit a felony. Neither did, since they both believed Bill entered to retrieve silverware which *belonged* to Harry; if Bill had gone to the right house, his acts would not have been felonious. D is, therefore, the best response. The remaining three choices illustrate the other two steps in your "best defense" analysis. A and B both represent misstatements of the facts, since there was a breaking (opening a window), and there was no consent to entry (since Harry was not authorized to consent to the entry of another person's house). Choice C, although it does correctly state the facts, ignores the legal principle that an accessory can be liable without an overt act of his own. That leaves D, which comports with both the facts and the law and acquits Harry.

By the same token, questions that ask for the **_prosecutor's_** best argument involve the same kind of analysis, but from the other side. That is, one of the answer choices will result in the defendant's conviction, and the other three won't. You'd simply ask whether the answer choice applies to the facts, if it's legally correct, and if it addresses a central issue that will result in defendant's conviction.

5. In Procedure questions involving a search, determine the purpose of the search first.

Categorizing the type of search first is crucial, since what's valid in one set of circumstances — e.g., a valid custodial arrest — will differ from what's OK in another — e.g., a stop and frisk. Here's an example:

Police Officer stopped Dexter for speeding late one night. Noting that Dexter was nervous, he ordered him from the car and placed him under arrest for speeding. By state law, Police Officer was empowered to arrest Dexter and take him to the nearest police station for booking. He searched Dexter's person and discovered a package of heroin in his jacket pocket.

Dexter is charged with possession of heroin. At trial, Dexter's motion to prevent introduction of the heroin into evidence, on the ground that the search violated his federal constitutional rights, will most probably be

    A. denied, because the search was incident to a valid custodial arrest

    B. denied, because Police Officer acted under both a reasonable suspicion and legitimate concern for his own personal safety

    C. granted, because there was no reasonable or proper basis upon which to justify conducting the search

    D. granted if Police Officer was not in fear and had no suspicion that Dexter was transporting narcotics

It may seem basic, but the important thing here is to identify that this is a search incident to a valid custodial arrest. If you do that, you should be able to eliminate both answers B and D immediately, because they deal with the standard for a "stop and frisk." Since a search incident to a valid custodial arrest is justified, C is wrong. That leaves you with A — the correct response.

6. In Procedure questions, watch for the "hidden" issue of standing.

Keep in mind that a person can object to a search **only** if he has a legitimate expectation of privacy as to the place searched. This is likely to be an issue if something incriminating one person is seized from someone else's home, car, office, etc. Here's an example:

Downs was indicted in state court for bribing a public official. During the course of the investigation, police had demanded and received from Downs's bank the records of Downs's checking account for the preceding two years. The records contained incriminating evidence.

On the basis of a claim of violation of his constitutional rights, Downs moves to prevent the introduction of the records in evidence. His motion should be

    A. granted, because a search warrant should have been secured for seizure of the records

    B. granted, because the records covered such an extensive period of time that their seizure unreasonably invaded Downs's right of privacy

    C. denied, because the potential destructibility of the records, coupled with the public interest in proper enforcement of the criminal laws, created an exigent situation justifying the seizure

    D. denied, because the records were business records of the bank in which Downs had no legitimate expectation of privacy

Standing to object to a search is a threshold issue — if a person has no legitimate expectation of privacy as to the premises searched, he has no right to challenge the search. Here, once the checking account records are in the bank's hands, Downs doesn't have a legitimate expectation of privacy concerning them (since, apart from anyone else, everyone working at the bank has access to them). Thus, choice D is the best response.

7. Appreciate the difference between choices with the modifier "because" and those with the modifier "if."

This difference can decide a question. Remember our discussion of modifiers in the "How to Attack the MBE" section of this book. If an answer choice says, for instance, "guilty, because..." and states facts, those facts must both reflect the facts in the question itself **and** address a central issue correctly. If, instead, a choice says, "guilty, if..." the facts following the word *if* will be **additional** to the facts in the question, so all you need to do is determine whether the choice as stated correctly addresses an issue central to Defendant's guilt.

8. How to handle questions which deal with testimony and include the statement "If the jury believes him . . . ."

If a question states that the jury believes a piece of testimony, treat that testimony as **fact**. Why is this something to watch out for? Two reasons. First, it will inevitably appear when the defendant is testifying on his own behalf and your gut reaction is that he's lying through his teeth. If the jury believes him, though, you have to ignore your own feelings and treat the testimony as fact. Second, the testimony will **probably** address the issue of state of mind, so watch for **intent** problems when you see such testimony. Here's an example of these principles:

Dunbar and Balcom went into a drugstore, where Dunbar reached into the cash register and took out $200. Stone, the owner of the store, came out of a back room, saw what had happened, and told Dunbar to put the money back. Balcom then took a revolver from under his coat and shot and killed Stone.

Dunbar claims that Stone owed her $200 and that she went to the drugstore to try to collect the debt. She said that she asked Balcom to come along just in case Stone made trouble but that she did not plan on using any force and did not know that Balcom was armed.

If Dunbar is prosecuted for murder on the basis of felony murder and the jury believes her claim, she should be found

    A. guilty, because her companion, Balcom, committed a homicide in the course of a felony

    B. guilty, because her taking Balcom with her to the store created the risk of death that occurred during the commission of a felony

    C. not guilty, because she did not know that Balcom was armed and thus did not have the required mental state for felony murder

    D. not guilty, because she believed she was entitled to the money and thus did not intend to steal

Your first reaction to Dunbar's testimony was probably, "Oh, sure, and I'm the tooth fairy." If you read the facts carefully, though, you should have noticed that the **jury believed her claim**. That means you have to accept, as a fact, that Dunbar went to the store intending to retrieve her own money. What is that important? It eliminates a necessary element, her intent to steal, and thus removes the possibility of a felony; without a felony or an attempted felony, there can't be felony murder. Since D recognizes this, it's not only the best answer but also shows how important testimony can be in MBE questions.

9. **How to handle questions asking which answer choice represents the most likely case in which defendant will be convicted.**

This type of question requires you to mechanically apply the law. If you do, you'll find that, in three of the answers, at least one element of the crime in question is missing, or that there's a valid defense, or that causation is lacking. Only one answer will satisfy all the requirements of the crime. Here's an example:

In which of the following situations is Defendant most likely to be guilty of larceny?

    A. defendant took Sue's television set, with the intention of returning it the next day. However, he dropped it and damaged it beyond repair.

    B. defendant went into Tom's house and took $100 in the belief that Tom had damaged Defendant's car to that amount.

    C. mistakenly believing that larceny does not include the taking of a dog, Defendant took his neighbor's dog and sold it.

    D. unreasonably mistaking George's car for his own, Defendant got into George's car in the parking lot and drove it home.

Remember, in analyzing this problem, you'll find three answer choices that result in Defendant being acquitted and one that results in his being convicted. If you mechanically apply the elements of larceny to each choice, you'll find only one that fits the crime. Larceny requires a trespassory taking and carrying away of another's personal property, with the intent to steal it. In choice A, Defendant has no intent to steal, since he intends to return the TV set the next day. That choice is out. In choice B, Defendant has no intent to steal, because he intends the $100 to pay for damage to his own car. That choice is out. In choice D, Defendant's mistake — however unreasonable — would provide a defense, since it negates his intent to steal. That choice is out. You're left with choice C. Defendant's mistake is a mistake of law, which, as a general principle, is not a valid defense. Otherwise, choice C satisfies the elements of larceny, so it's the best response.

10. **How to apply questions which apply precedents.**

You may see questions on the MBE which ask you to determine the best precedent for a set of facts. Each answer choice will then list the facts of a potential precedent.

Naturally, you need to identify which answer choice most closely resembles the given facts in key respects. The problem with this type of question is that it's typically very long, complex, and difficult. As a result, you may want to consider skipping over this type of question on the MBE, coming back to it only if you have the time. If you do, remember to **mark** your answer form **carefully** so that you don't answer succeeding questions out of order.

QUESTIONS
CRIMINAL LAW

QUESTIONS

CRIMINAL LAW

NOTE: For ease of study, we've put all questions involving **Criminal Procedure** at the end of the section, beginning with Question 47.

Question 1

Jim watched a liquor store furtively for some time, planning to hold it up. He bought a realistic-looking toy gun for the job. One night, just before the store's closing time, he drove to the store, opened the front door and entered. He reached in his pocket for the toy gun, but he became frightened and began to move back toward the front door. However, the shopkeeper had seen the butt of the gun. Fearing a hold up, the shopkeeper produced a gun from under the counter, pointed it at Jim, and yelled, "Stop!" Jim ran to the door and the toy gun fell from his pocket. The shopkeeper fired. The shot missed Jim, but struck and killed a passerby outside the store.

A statute in the jurisdiction defines burglary as "breaking and entering any building or structure with the intent to commit a felony or to steal therein." On a charge of burglary, Jim's best defense would be that

(A) the intent required was not present

(B) the liquor store was open to the public

(C) he had a change of heart and withdrew before committing any crime inside the store

(D) he was unsuccessful, and so at most could only be guilty of attempted burglary

Questions 2-3 are based on the following fact situation.

Jackson and Brannick planned to break into a federal government office to steal food stamps. Jackson telephoned Crowley one night and asked whether Crowley wanted to buy some "hot" food stamps. Crowley, who understood that "hot" meant stolen, said, "Sure, bring them right over." Jackson and Brannick then successfully executed their scheme. That same night they delivered the food stamps to Crowley, who bought them for $500. Crowley did not ask when or by whom the stamps were stolen. All three were arrested. Jackson and Brannick entered guilty pleas in federal court to a charge of larceny in connection with the theft. Crowley was brought to trial in the state court on a charge of conspiracy to steal food stamps.

Question 2

On the evidence stated, Crowley should be found

(A) guilty, because when a new confederate enters a conspiracy already in progress, he becomes a party to it

(B) guilty, because he knowingly and willingly aided and abetted the conspiracy and is chargeable as a principal

(C) not guilty, because although Crowley knew the stamps were stolen, he neither helped to plan nor participated or assisted in the theft

(D) not guilty, because Jackson and Brannick had not been convicted of or charged with conspiracy, and Crowley cannot be guilty of conspiracy by himself

Question 3

If Jackson and Brannick are charged with conspiracy to steal the stamps in the state court, they should, on the evidence stated, be found

(A) not guilty, because the charge of conspiracy is a lesser included offense in the charge of larceny

(B) not guilty, because to charge them with conspiracy after their conviction of larceny would constitute double jeopardy

(C) not guilty, because the state prosecution is barred by the prosecution in federal court

(D) guilty, because they planned and conspired to steal the stamps

Question 4

Jack and Paul planned to hold up a bank. They drove to the bank in Jack's car. Jack entered while Paul remained as lookout in the car. After a few moments, Paul panicked and drove off.

Jack looked over the various tellers, approached one and whispered nervously, "Just hand over the cash. Don't look around, don't make a false move – or it's your life." The teller looked at the fidgeting Jack, laughed, flipped him a dollar bill and said, "Go on, beat it." Flustered, Jack grabbed the dollar and left.

Soon after leaving the scene, Paul was stopped by the police for speeding. Noting his nervous condition, the police asked Paul if they might search the car. Paul agreed. The search turned up heroin concealed in the lid of the trunk.

Paul's best defense to a charge of robbery would be that

(A) Jack alone entered the bank

(B) Paul withdrew before commission of the crime when he fled the scene

(C) Paul had no knowledge of what Jack whispered to the teller

(D) the teller was not placed in fear by Jack

Question 5

Adam and Bailey, brothers, operated an illicit still. They customarily sold to anyone unless they suspected the person of being a revenue agent or an informant. One day when Adam was at the still alone, he was approached by Mitchell, who asked to buy a gallon of liquor. Mitchell was in fact a revenue officer. After Adam had sold him the liquor, Mitchell revealed his identity. Adam grabbed one of the rifles that the brothers kept handy in case of trouble with the law, and shot and wounded Mitchell. Other officers, hiding nearby, overpowered and arrested Adam.

Shortly thereafter, Bailey came on the scene. The officers in hiding had been waiting for him. One of them approached him and asked to buy liquor. Bailey was suspicious and refused to sell. The officers nevertheless arrested him.

Adam and Bailey were charged with conspiracy to violate revenue laws, illegal selling of liquor, and battery of the officer.

On the charge of battery, which statement concerning Adam and Bailey is true?

(A) Neither is guilty.

(B) Both are guilty.

(C) Adam is guilty but Bailey is not, because the conspiracy had terminated with the arrest of Adam.

(D) Adam is guilty but Bailey is not, because Adam's act was outside the scope of the conspiracy.

Question 6

Defendant was driving his automobile at a legal speed in a residential zone. A child darted out in front of him and was run over and killed before Defendant could prevent it. Defendant's driver's license had expired three months previously; Defendant had neglected to check when it was due to expire. Driving without a valid license is a misdemeanor in the jurisdiction. On a charge of manslaughter, Defendant should be found

(A) guilty under the misdemeanor-manslaughter rule

(B) guilty because the licensing requirements are to protect life, and failure to obey is negligence

(C) not guilty because the offense was not the proximate cause of the death

(D) not guilty because there was no criminal intent

Question 7

During an altercation between Oscar and Martin at a company picnic, Oscar suffered a knife wound in his abdomen and Martin was charged with assault and attempted murder. At his trial, Martin seeks to offer evidence that he had been drinking at the picnic and was highly intoxicated at the time of the altercation.

In a jurisdiction that follows the common-law rules concerning admissibility of evidence of intoxication, the evidence of Martin's intoxication should be

(A) admitted without limitation.

(B) admitted subject to an instruction that it pertains only to the attempted murder charge.

(C) admitted subject to an instruction that it pertains only to the assault charge.

(D) excluded altogether.

Question 8

Defendant was tried for robbery. Victim and Worth were the only witnesses called to testify. Victim testified that Defendant threatened her with a knife, grabbed her purse, and ran off with it. Worth testified that he saw Defendant grab Victim's purse and run away with it but that he neither saw a knife nor heard any threats. On this evidence, the jury could properly return a verdict of guilty of

(A) robbery only

(B) larceny only

(C) either robbery or larceny

(D) both robbery and larceny

Question 9

After being fired from his job, Mel drank almost a quart of vodka and decided to ride the bus home. While on the bus, he saw a briefcase he mistakenly thought was his own, and began struggling with the passenger carrying the briefcase. Mel knocked the passenger to the floor, took the briefcase, and fled. Mel was arrested and charged with robbery.

Mel should be

(A) acquitted, because he used no threats and was intoxicated.

(B) acquitted, because his mistake negated the required specific intent.

(C) convicted, because his intoxication was voluntary.

(D) convicted, because mistake is no defense to robbery.

Question 10

While browsing in a clothing store, Alice decided to take a purse without paying for it. She placed the purse under her coat and took a couple of steps toward the exit. She then realized that a sensor tag on the purse would set off an alarm. She placed the purse near the counter from which she had removed it.

Alice has committed

(A) no crime, because the purse was never removed from the store.

(B) no crime, because she withdrew from her criminal enterprise.

(C) only attempted larceny, because she intended to take the purse out of the store.

(D) larceny, because she took the purse from its original location and concealed it with the intent to steal.

Question 11

Sam decided to kill his boss, Anna, after she told him that he would be fired if his work did not improve. Sam knew Anna was scheduled to go on a business trip on Monday morning. On Sunday morning, Sam went to the company parking garage and put a bomb in the company car that Anna usually drove. The bomb was wired to go off when the car engine started. Sam then left town. At 5 a.m. Monday, Sam, after driving all night, was overcome with remorse and had a change of heart. He called the security officer on duty at the company and told him about the bomb. The security officer said he would take care of the matter. An hour later, the officer put a note on Anna's desk telling her of the message. He then looked at the car but could not see any signs of a bomb. He printed a sign saying "DO NOT USE THIS CAR," put it on the windshield, and went to call the police. Before the police arrived, Lois, a company vice president, got into the car and started the engine. The bomb went off, killing her.

The jurisdiction defines murder in the first degree as any homicide committed with premeditation and deliberation or any murder in the commission of a common-law felony. Second-degree murder is defined as all other murder at common law. Manslaughter is defined by the common law.

Sam is guilty of

(A) murder in the first degree, because, with premeditation and deliberation, he killed whoever would start the car.

(B) murder in the second degree, because he had no intention of killing Lois.

(C) manslaughter, because at the time of the explosion, he had no intent to kill, and the death of Lois was in part the fault of the security officer.

(D) only attempted murder of Anna, because the death of Lois was the result of the security officer's negligence.

Question 12

In which of the following situations would Defendant's mistake most likely constitute a defense to the crime charged?

(A) A local ordinance forbids the sale of alcoholic beverages to persons under 18 years of age. Relying on false identification, Defendant sells champagne to a 16-year-old high school student. Defendant is charged with illegal sale of alcoholic beverages.

(B) Mistaking Defendant for a narcotics suspect, an undercover police officer attempts to arrest him. Defendant, unaware that the person who has grabbed him is an officer, hits him and knocks him unconscious. Defendant is charged with assault.

(C) Defendant, aged 23, has sexual intercourse with a 15-year-old prostitute who tells Defendant that she is 18. Defendant is charged with the felony of statutory rape under a statute that makes sexual relations with a child under 16 a felony.

(D) Relying on erroneous advice from his attorney that, if his wife has abandoned him for more than a year, he is free to marry, Defendant remarries and is subsequently charged with bigamy.

Question 13

On a charge of murdering Vic, Sam is

(A) not guilty, because his words did not create a "clear and present danger" not already existing

(B) not guilty, because mere presence and oral encouragement, whether or not he has the requisite intent, will not make him guilty as an accomplice

(C) guilty, because, with the intent to have Bill kill Vic, he shouted encouragement to Bill

(D) guilty, because he aided and abetted the murder through his mere presence plus his intent to see Vic killed

Question 14

On a charge of murdering Vic, Tom is

(A) not guilty, because mere presence, coupled with silent approval and intent, is not sufficient

(B) not guilty, because he did not tell Bill ahead of time that he hoped Bill would murder Vic

(C) guilty, because he had a duty to stop the killing and made no attempt to do so

(D) guilty, because he was present and approved of what occurred

Question 15

At a party, Diane and Victor agreed to play a game they called "spin the barrel." Victor took an unloaded revolver, placed one bullet in the barrel, and spun the barrel. Victor then pointed the gun at Diane's head and pulled the trigger once. The gun did not fire. Diane then took the gun, pointed it at Victor, spun the barrel, and pulled the trigger once. The gun fired, and Victor fell over dead.

A statute in the jurisdiction defines murder in the first degree as an intentional and premeditated killing or one occurring during the commission of a common-law felony, and murder in the second degree as all other murder at common law. Manslaughter is defined as a killing in the heat of passion upon an adequate legal provocation or a killing caused by gross negligence.

The most serious crime for which Diane can properly be convicted is

(A) murder in the first degree, because the killing was intentional and premeditated and, in any event, occurred during commission of the felony of assault with a deadly weapon.

(B) murder in the second degree, because Diane's act posed a great threat of serious bodily harm.

(C) manslaughter, because Diane's act was grossly negligent and reckless.

(D) no crime, because Victor and Diane voluntarily agreed to play a game and each assumed the risk of death.

Question 16

Matt and his friend Fred were watching a football game at Matt's home when they began to argue. Fred became abusive, and Matt asked him to leave. Fred refused, walked into the kitchen, picked up a knife, and said he would cut Matt's heart out. Matt pulled a gun from under the sofa, walked to his front door, opened it, and again told Fred to leave. Fred again refused. Instead, he walked slowly toward Matt, brandishing the knife in a threatening manner. Matt, rather than running out the door himself, shot in Fred's direction, intending only to scare him. However, the bullet struck Fred, killing him instantly.

Charged with murder, Matt should be

(A) convicted, because the use of deadly force was unreasonable under the circumstances.

(B) convicted, because he had a clear opportunity and duty to retreat.

(C) acquitted, because he did not intend to kill Fred.

(D) acquitted, because he was acting in self-defense and had no duty to retreat.

Questions 17-18 are based on the following fact situation.

Johnson took a diamond ring to a pawnshop and borrowed $20 on it. It was agreed that the loan was to be repaid within 60 days and if it was not, the pawnshop owner, Defendant, could sell the ring. A week before expiration of the 60 days, Defendant had an opportunity to sell the ring to a customer for $125. He did so, thinking it unlikely that Johnson would repay the loan and if he did, Defendant would be able to handle him somehow, even by paying him for the ring if necessary. Two days later, Johnson came in with the money to reclaim his ring. Defendant told him that it had been stolen when his shop was burglarized one night and that therefore he was not responsible for its loss.

Larceny, embezzlement, and false pretenses are separate crimes in the jurisdiction.

Question 17

It is most likely that Defendant has committed which of the following crimes?

(A) Larceny

(B) Embezzlement

(C) Larceny by trick

(D) Obtaining by false pretenses

Question 18

Suppose that, instead of denying liability, Defendant told Johnson the truth – that he sold the ring because he thought Johnson would not reclaim it – and offered to give Johnson $125. Johnson demanded his ring. Defendant

said, "Look, buddy, that's what I got for it and it's more than it's worth." Johnson reluctantly took the money. Defendant could most appropriately be found guilty of

(A) Larceny

(B) Embezzlement

(C) False pretenses

(D) None of the above

Questions 19-20 are based on the following statute.

VEHICULAR MANSLAUGHTER. Whoever in the course of driving a motor vehicle as defined in the Vehicle Code is criminally negligent in driving such vehicle or omits to do anything that is his duty to do and shows a wanton and reckless disregard for the safety of other persons and as a result of such act or omission causes the death of a human being is guilty of vehicular manslaughter.

Vehicular manslaughter is punishable by a sentence of not more than 10 years in the state prison or not more than one year in the county jail.

Question 19

Defendant, driving along at a reasonable rate of speed, was distracted by a child carrying a silver balloon. He went through a boulevard stop light and killed a pedestrian. He is charged with vehicular manslaughter. Of the following proposed definitions of criminal negligence, which is most favorable to the Defendant?

(A) Criminal negligence is something more than the slight negligence necessary to support a civil action for damages. It means disregard for the consequences of the act and indifference to rights of others.

(B) Any person who drives a motor vehicle should realize the danger to others. If he fails to respond to surrounding circumstances, he is criminally negligent. Criminal negligence involves reckless disregard for the lives or safety of others.

(C) To find the defendant guilty of criminal negligence, the jury must find as a fact that he intentionally did something he should not have done or intentionally failed to do something which he should have done under circumstances that demonstrate a conscious disregard of a known danger that his conduct would produce the result which it did produce.

(D) Criminal negligence is something more than the slight negligence usually required for tort liability. It is something less than the wanton misconduct required for civil liability under the guest statute. It is, of course, conduct that demonstrates something less than the abandoned and malignant heart required for murder.

Question 20

In a particular jurisdiction there are no statutory standards for the amount of alcohol required to be in the blood to create the presumption that a person is under the influence of alcohol. Defendant, an alcoholic, while driving his motor vehicle, collided with another vehicle. A passenger was killed. Defendant is charged with vehicular manslaughter. Experts will testify that a person with blood alcohol of 0.00 to 0.05 per cent is not under the influence. From 0.05 to 0.10 per cent he may be under the influence. Most of those with 0.10 to 0.15 per cent are under the influence. All of those with over 0.15 per cent are under the influence. Defendant consented to and was given a blood alcohol test 60 minutes after the accident. The test showed 0.11 per cent alcohol. Of the following, what is Defendant's most appropriate argument to the jury?

(A) Assuming the jury finds that the Defendant was driving under the influence of alcohol, they cannot convict him if he lacked the capacity to have the mental state of criminal negligence.

(B) The results of the blood tests were improperly admitted in evidence because there are no statutory standards for the interpretation of such tests.

(C) The blood test should merely be one more factor in the jury's determination along with such things as the police officers' opinion as to sobriety.

(D) Any statute which makes it a crime to kill someone while under the influence of alcohol is unconstitutional; alcoholism is a disease and cannot be punished any more than narcotic addiction.

Question 21

Linda was fifteen years old, but she appeared and acted older. When asked, she always said she was twenty-two, and she carried false identification saying she was that old. She frequented taverns and drank heavily. One evening in a bar she became acquainted with Duke. He believed her when she told him her claimed age. They had several drinks and became inebriated. Later, they drove in Duke's car to a secluded spot. After they had necked for a while, Duke propositioned Linda and she consented. Before Duke achieved penetration, Linda changed her mind, saying, "Stop! Don't touch me! I don't want to do it." When Duke did not desist, Linda started to cry and said, "I am only fifteen." Duke immediately jumped from the car and ran away. Duke was indicted for attempted rape, assault with intent to rape, contributing to the delinquency of a minor, and attempted statutory rape. The age of consent in the jurisdiction is sixteen. The attempted rape charge can only be sustained if

(A) the jury acquits Duke on all other charges

(B) the State can show that Duke thought Linda was over the age of consent

(C) the jury finds that Linda was resisting force used by Duke to accomplish an act of intercourse

(D) evidence of Duke's flight is not admitted by the trial judge

Question 22

Joe and Marty were coworkers. Joe admired Marty's wristwatch and frequently said how much he wished he

had one like it. Marty decided to give Joe the watch for his birthday the following week.

On the weekend before Joe's birthday, Joe and Marty attended a company picnic. Marty took his watch off and left it on a blanket when he went off to join in a touch football game. Joe strolled by, saw the watch on the blanket, and decided to steal it. He bent over and picked up the watch. Before he could pocket it, however, Marty returned. When he saw Joe holding the watch, he said, "Joe, I know how much you like that watch. I was planning to give it to you for your birthday. Go ahead and take it now." Joe kept the watch.

Joe has committed

(A) larceny.

(B) attempted larceny.

(C) embezzlement.

(D) no crime.

Question 23

Grace, while baby-sitting one night, noticed that Sam, who lived next door, had left his house but that the door did not close completely behind him. Grace said to Roy, the 11-year-old boy she was baby-sitting with, "Let's play a game. You go next door and see if you can find my portable television set, which I lent to Sam, and bring it over here." Grace knew that Sam had a portable television set and Grace planned to keep the set for herself. Roy thought the set belonged to Grace, went next door, found the television set, and carried it out the front door. At that moment, Sam returned home and discovered Roy in his front yard with the television set. Roy explained the "game" he and Grace were playing. Sam took back his television set and called the police.

Grace is

(A) not guilty of larceny or attempted larceny, because Roy did not commit any crime.

(B) not guilty of larceny but guilty of attempted larceny, because she never acquired possession of the television set.

(C) guilty of larceny as an accessory to Roy.

(D) guilty of larceny by the use of an innocent agent.

Question 24

Brown suffered from the delusion that he was a special agent of God. He frequently experienced hallucinations in the form of hearing divine commands. Brown believed God told him several times that the local Roman Catholic bishop was corrupting the diocese into heresy, and that the bishop should be "done away with." Brown, a devout Catholic, conceived of himself as a religious martyr. He knew that shooting bishops for heresy is against the criminal law. He nevertheless carefully planned how he might kill the bishop. One evening Brown shot the bishop, who was taken to the hospital where he died two weeks later.

Brown told the police he assumed the institutions of society would support the ecclesiastical hierarchy, and he expected to be persecuted for his God-inspired actions. Psychiatrist Stevens examined Brown and found that Brown suffered from schizophrenic psychosis, that in the absence of this psychosis he would not have shot the bishop, and that because of the psychosis Brown found it extremely difficult to determine whether he should obey the specific command that he do away with the bishop or the general commandment "Thou shalt not kill." Brown was charged with murder.

If Brown interposes an insanity defense and the jurisdiction in which he is tried has adopted only the M'Naghten test of insanity, then the strongest argument for the defense under that test is that

(A) Brown did not know the nature of the act he was performing

(B) Brown did not know that his act was morally wrong

(C) Brown did not know the quality of the act he was performing

(D) Brown's acts were the product of a mental disease

Question 25

Eighteen-year-old Kenneth and his 14-year-old girlfriend, Emma, made plans to meet in Kenneth's apartment to have sexual intercourse, and they did so. Emma later told her mother about the incident. Kenneth was charged with statutory rape and conspiracy to commit statutory rape.

In the jurisdiction, the age of consent is 15, and the law of conspiracy is the same as at common law.

Kenneth was convicted of both charges and given consecutive sentences. On appeal, he contends that his conspiracy conviction should be reversed.

That conviction should be

(A) affirmed, because he agreed with Emma to commit the crime.

(B) reversed, because Emma could not be a conspirator to this crime.

(C) reversed, because the crime is one that can only be committed by agreement and thus Wharton's Rule bars conspiracy liability.

(D) reversed, because one cannot conspire with a person too young to consent.

Question 26

In which of the following situations is Defendant most likely to be guilty of the crime charged?

(A) Without the permission of Owner, Defendant takes Owner's Car with the intention of driving it three miles to a grocery store and back. Defendant is charged with larceny.

(B) Defendant gets permission to borrow Owner's car for the evening by falsely promising to return it, although he does not intend to do so. Two days later, he changes his mind and returns the car. Defendant is charged with larceny by trick.

(C) Defendant gets permission to borrow Owner's car for the evening by misrepresenting his identity and falsely claiming he has a valid driver's license. He returns the car the next day. Defendant is charged with obtaining property by false pretenses.

(D) With permission, Defendant, promising to return it by 9:00 p.m., borrows Owner's car. Later in the evening, Defendant decides to keep the car until the next morning and does so. Defendant is charged with embezzlement.

Question 27

While testifying as a witness in a civil trial, Walters was asked on cross-examination if he had been convicted in the circuit court of Jasper County of stealing $200 from his employer on August 16, 1977. Walters said, "No, I have never been convicted of any crime." In fact, Walters had pleaded guilty to such a charge and had been placed on probation.

Walters was then charged with perjury on the ground that his statement denying the conviction was false. A statute in the jurisdiction defines perjury as knowingly making a false statement while under oath.

At trial, the state proved Walters' statement and the prior conviction. Walters testified that the attorney who represented him in the theft case had told him that, because he had been placed on probation, he had not been convicted of a crime. Walters had served his probationary period satisfactorily and been discharged from probation. The alleged advice of the attorney was incorrect.

If the jury believes Walters, it should find him

(A) guilty, because his mistake was one of law

(B) guilty, because reliance on the advice of an attorney is not a defense

(C) not guilty if the jury also finds that his reliance on the attorney's advice was reasonable

(D) not guilty, because he lacked the necessary mental state

Question 28

In which of the following situations is defendant most likely to be guilty of common-law murder?

(A) During an argument in a bar, Norris punches Defendant. Defendant, mistakenly believing that Norris is about to stab him, shoots and kills Norris.

(B) While committing a robbery of a liquor store, Defendant accidentally drops his revolver, which goes off. The bullet strikes and kills Johnson, a customer in the store.

(C) While hunting deer, Defendant notices something moving in the bushes. Believing it to be a deer, Defendant fires into the bushes. The bullet strikes and kills Griggs, another hunter.

(D) In celebration of the Fourth of July, Defendant discharges a pistol within the city limits in violation of a city ordinance. The bullet ricochets off the street and strikes and kills Abbott.

Question 29

At 11:00 p.m., John and Marsha were accosted in the entrance to their apartment building by Dirk, who was armed as well as masked. Dirk ordered the couple to take him into their apartment. After they entered the apartment, Dirk forced Marsha to bind and gag her husband John and then to open a safe which contained a diamond necklace. Dirk then tied her up and fled with the necklace. He was apprehended by apartment building security guards. Before the guards could return to the apartment, but after Dirk was arrested, John, straining to free himself, suffered a massive heart attack and died.

Dirk is guilty of

(A) burglary, robbery, and murder.
(B) robbery and murder only.
(C) burglary and robbery only.
(D) robbery only.

Question 30

Martha's high school teacher told her that she was going to receive a failing grade in history, which would prevent her from graduating. Furious, she reported to the principal that the teacher had fondled her, and the teacher was fired. A year later, still unable to get work because of the scandal, the teacher committed suicide. Martha, remorseful, confessed that her accusation had been false.

If Martha is charged with manslaughter, her best defense would be that she

(A) committed no act that proximately caused the teacher's death.
(B) did not intend to cause the teacher's death.
(C) did not act with malice.
(D) acted under extreme emotional distress.

Question 31

Beth wanted to make some money, so she decided to sell cocaine. She asked Albert, who was reputed to have access to illegal drugs, to supply her with cocaine so she could resell it. Albert agreed and sold Beth a bag of white powder. Beth then repackaged the white powder into smaller containers and sold one to Carol, an undercover police officer, who promptly arrested Beth. Beth immediately confessed and said that Albert was her supplier. Upon examination, the white powder was found not to be cocaine or any type of illegal substance.

If Albert knew the white powder was not cocaine but Beth believed it was, which of the following is correct?

(A) Both Albert and Beth are guilty of attempting to sell cocaine.
(B) Neither Albert nor Beth is guilty of attempting to sell cocaine.
(C) Albert is guilty of attempting to sell cocaine, but Beth is not.

(D) Albert is not guilty of attempting to sell cocaine, but Beth is.

Question 32

In a jurisdiction that has abolished the felony-murder rule, but otherwise follows the common law of murder, Sally and Ralph, both armed with automatic weapons, went into a bank to rob it. Ralph ordered all the persons in the bank to lie on the floor. When some were slow to obey, Sally, not intending to hit anyone, fired about 15 rounds into the air. One of these ricocheted off a stone column and struck and killed a customer in the bank.

Sally and Ralph were charged with murder of the customer.

Which of the following is correct?

(A) Sally can be convicted of murder, because she did the act of killing, but Ralph cannot be convicted of either murder or manslaughter.
(B) Neither can be guilty of murder, but both can be convicted of manslaughter based upon an unintentional homicide.
(C) Sally can be convicted only of manslaughter, but Ralph cannot be convicted of murder or manslaughter.
(D) Both can be convicted of murder.

Question 33

Homer lived on the second floor of a small convenience store/gas station that he owned. One night he refused to sell Augie a six-pack of beer after hours, saying he could not violate the state laws. Augie became enraged and deliberately drove his car into one of the gasoline pumps, severing it from its base. There was an ensuing explosion causing a ball of fire to go from the underground gasoline tank into the building. As a result, the building burned to the ground and Homer was killed.

In a common-law jurisdiction, if Augie is charged with murder and arson, he should be

(A) convicted of both offenses.
(B) convicted of involuntary manslaughter and acquitted of arson.
(C) convicted of arson and involuntary manslaughter.
(D) acquitted of both offenses.

Question 34

Defendant is charged with murder. The evidence shows that she pointed a gun at Victim and pulled the trigger. The gun discharged, killing Victim. The gun belonged to Victim.

Defendant testifies that Victim told her, and she believed, that the "gun" was a stage prop that could fire only blanks, and that she fired the gun as part of rehearsing a play with Victim at his house.

If the jury believes Defendant's testimony and finds that her mistaken belief that the gun was a prop was reasonable, they should find her

(A) guilty of murder.

(B) guilty of manslaughter.

(C) guilty of either murder or manslaughter.

(D) not guilty of murder or manslaughter.

Question 35

Dobbs, while intoxicated, drove his car through a playground crowded with children just to watch the children run to get out of his way. His car struck one of the children, killing her instantly.

Which of the following is the best theory for finding Dobbs guilty of murder?

(A) Transferred intent

(B) Felony murder, with assault with a deadly weapon as the underlying felony

(C) Intentional killing, since he knew that the children were there and he deliberately drove his car at them

(D) Commission of an act highly dangerous to life, without an intent to kill but with disregard of the consequences

Question 36

Which of the following is most likely to be found to be a strict liability offense?

(A) A city ordinance providing for a fine of not more than $200 for shoplifting

(B) A federal statute making it a felony to possess heroin

(C) A state statute making it a felony to fail to register a firearm

(D) A state statute making the sale of adulterated milk a misdemeanor

Question 37

Donaldson broke into Professor Ruiz' office in order to look at examination questions. The questions were locked in a drawer, and Donaldson could not find them. Donaldson believed that looking at examination questions was a crime, but in this belief he was mistaken.

Charged with burglary, Donaldson should be

(A) acquitted, because he did not complete the crime and he has not been charged with attempt

(B) acquitted, because what he intended to do when he broke in was not a crime

(C) convicted, because he had the necessary mental state and committed the act of breaking and entering

(D) convicted, because factual impossibility is not a defense

Question 38

Dent, while eating in a restaurant, noticed that a departing customer at the next table had left a five-dollar bill as a tip for the waitress. Dent reached over, picked up the five-dol-

lar bill, and put it in his pocket. As he stood up to leave, another customer who had seen him take the money ran over to him and hit him in the face with her umbrella. Enraged, Dent choked the customer to death.

Dent is charged with murder. He requests the court to charge the jury that they can find him guilty of voluntary manslaughter rather than murder. Dent's request should be

(A) granted, because the jury could find that Dent acted recklessly and not with the intent to cause death or serious bodily harm

(B) granted, because the jury could find that being hit in the face with an umbrella constitutes adequate provocation

(C) denied, because the evidence shows that Dent intended to kill or to cause serious bodily harm

(D) denied, because the evidence shows that Dent provoked the assault on himself by his criminal misconduct

Question 39

Rachel, an antique dealer and a skilled calligrapher, crafted a letter on very old paper. She included details that would lead knowledgeable readers to believe the letter had been written by Thomas Jefferson to a friend. Rachel, who had a facsimile of Jefferson's autograph, made the signature and other writing on the letter resemble Jefferson's. She knew that the letter would attract the attention of local collectors. When it did and she was contacted about selling it, she said that it had come into her hands from a foreign collector who wished anonymity, and that she could make no promises about its authenticity. As she had hoped, a collector paid her $5,000 for the letter. Later the collector discovered the letter was not authentic, and handwriting analysis established that Rachel had written the letter.

In a jurisdiction that follows the common-law definition of forgery, Rachel has

(A) committed both forgery and false pretenses.

(B) committed forgery, because she created a false document with the intent to defraud, but has not committed false pretenses, since she made no representation as to the authenticity of the document.

(C) not committed forgery, because the document had no apparent legal significance, but has committed false pretenses, since she misrepresented the source of the document.

(D) not committed forgery, because the document had no apparent legal significance, and has not committed false pretenses, since she made no representation as to authenticity of the document.

Question 40

Dann was an alcoholic who frequently experienced auditory hallucinations that commanded him to engage in bizarre and sometimes violent behavior. He generally obeyed their commands. The hallucinations appeared more frequently when he was intoxicated, but he sometimes experienced them when he had not been drinking. After Dann had been drinking continuously for a three day period, an elderly woman began to reproach him about his drunken condition, slapping him on the face and shoulders as she did so. Dann believed that he was being unmercifully attacked and heard the hallucinatory voice telling him to strangle his assailant. He did so, and she died.

If Dann is charged with second degree murder, Dann's best chance of acquittal would be to rely on a defense of

(A) intoxication

(B) lack of malice aforethought

(C) self-defense

(D) insanity

Question 41

James and Mary Green were walking to their car one evening after having seen a movie. As they were passing a dark alleyway, Daves leaped out brandishing a gun. He pushed Mary against the wall of a nearby building, held the gun to her head, and demanded money from James. James handed over his cash. Daves grabbed the cash and ran away.

Which of the following, listed in descending order of seriousness, is the most serious crime for which Daves may be convicted?

(A) Robbery from James Green

(B) Larceny from James Green

(C) Assault on James and Mary Green

(D) Assault on Mary Green

Question 42

Smart approached Johnson and inquired about hiring someone to kill his girlfriend's parents. Unknown to Smart, Johnson was an undercover police officer who pretended to agree to handle the job and secretly taped subsequent conversations with Smart concerning plans and payment. A few days before the payment was due, Smart changed his mind and called the plan off. Nevertheless, Smart was charged with solicitation to commit murder.

Smart should be

(A) acquitted, because he withdrew before payment and commission of the act.

(B) acquitted, because no substantial acts were performed.

(C) convicted, because the offense was completed before his attempt to withdraw.

(D) convicted, because Johnson agreed to commit the offense.

Question 43

Hannah, who was homeless, broke into the basement of a hotel and fell asleep. She was awakened by a security guard, who demanded that she leave. As Hannah was leaving, she cursed the security guard. Angered, the guard began to beat Hannah on her head with his flashlight. After the second blow, Hannah grabbed a fire extinguisher and sprayed the guard in his face, causing him to lose his sight in one eye.

The jurisdiction defines aggravated assault as assault with intent to cause serious bodily injury.

The most serious crime for which Hannah could properly be convicted is

(A) aggravated assault.

(B) burglary.

(C) assault.

(D) trespass.

Question 44

Damson was short of money. He decided to go into Waters' house to take Waters' silverware and then to sell it. That night, while Waters' was away, Damson entered by picking the lock on the front door. He picked up a chest of silverware from the dining room and went out the front door of the house to his car. As he was putting the chest of silverware into the trunk, he had second thoughts and decided that he did not wish to become a thief. He reentered the house and replaced the chest of silverware where he had found it. As he came out of the house the second time, he was arrested by the police, who had been called by a neighbor.

Damson is

(A) guilty of burglary and larceny

(B) guilty of burglary and attempted larceny

(C) guilty of burglary but not guilty of any larceny offense

(D) not guilty of burglary or any larceny offense

Question 45

Which of the following is LEAST likely to be the underlying felony in a prosecution for felony murder?

(A) Arson

(B) Manslaughter

(C) Attempted rape

(D) Burglary

Question 46

Sam and two of his friends were members of a teenage street gang. While they were returning from a dance late one evening, their car collided with a car driven by an elderly woman. After an argument, Sam attacked the elderly woman with his fists and beat her to death. Sam's two friends watched, and when they saw the woman fall to the ground they urged Sam to flee. Sam was eventually apprehended and tried for manslaughter, but the jury could not decide on a verdict.

If Sam's companions are subsequently tried as accomplices to manslaughter, they should be

(A) acquitted, because Sam was not convicted of the offense.

(B) acquitted, because they did not assist or encourage Sam to commit the crime.

(C) convicted, because they urged him to flee.

(D) convicted, because they made no effort to intervene.

[START OF CRIMINAL PROCEDURE QUESTIONS]

Question 47

Jack and Paul planned to hold up a bank. They drove to the bank in Jack's car. Jack entered while Paul remained as lookout in the car. After a few moments, Paul panicked and drove off.

Jack looked over the various tellers, approached one and whispered nervously, "Just hand over the cash. Don't look around, don't make a false move – or it's your life." The teller looked at the fidgeting Jack, laughed, flipped him a dollar bill and said, "Go on, beat it." Flustered, Jack grabbed the dollar and left.

Soon after leaving the scene, Paul was stopped by the police for speeding. Noting his nervous condition, the police asked Paul if they might search the car. Paul agreed. The search turned up heroin concealed in the lid of the trunk.

The prosecution's best argument to sustain the validity of the search of Jack's car would be that

(A) the search was reasonable under the circumstances, including Paul's nervous condition

(B) the search was incident to a valid arrest

(C) Paul had, under the circumstances, sufficient standing and authority to consent to the search

(D) exigent circumstances, including the inherent mobility of a car, justified the search

Question 48

Detective received information from Informant, who had given reliable information many times in the past, that Harry was a narcotics dealer. Specifically, Informant said that, two months before, he had visited Harry's apartment with Bill and that on that occasion he saw Harry sell Bill some heroin. Detective knew that Informant, Harry, and Bill were friends. Thereafter, Detective put all this information into an affidavit form, appeared before a magistrate, and secured a search warrant for Harry's apartment. The search turned up a supply of heroin. Harry's motion to suppress introduction of the heroin into evidence will most probably be

(A) granted, because a search warrant cannot validly be issued solely on the basis of an informant's information.

(B) granted, because the information supplied to Detective concerned an occurrence too remote in time to justify a finding of probable cause at the time of the search.

(C) granted, because a search for "mere evidence" alone is improper and illegal.

(D) denied, because Informant had proven himself reliable in the past and the information he gave turned out to be correct.

Question 49

Defendant sold heroin to Morgan. Morgan was later stopped by police for speeding. The police searched Morgan's car and found the heroin concealed under the rear seat. Defendant is charged with illegally selling heroin.

Defendant's motion to prevent introduction of the heroin into evidence will most probably be

(A) granted, because the heroin was not in plain view

(B) granted, because the scope of the search was excessive

(C) denied, because Defendant has no standing to object to the search

(D) denied, because the search was proper as incident to a valid full custodial arrest

Question 50

Scott held up a drugstore at 10:30 at night, and drove away. His car broke down in an isolated area just outside the small city in which the crime occurred. Scott walked to the nearest house and asked Henry, the homeowner, if he could stay until the next morning, explaining that he had been searching for his sister's home and had run out of gas. Henry agreed to let him sleep on a couch in the basement. During the course of the night, Henry began to doubt the story Scott had told him. Early the next morning, Henry called the police and said he was suspicious and frightened of a stranger whom he had allowed to stay the night. The police went immediately to the house to assist Henry and walked through the open front door. They found Scott and Henry drinking coffee in the kitchen. When they saw Scott, they realized he matched the description of the drugstore robber. They arrested Scott and in his jacket they found drugs taken during the robbery.

Scott moves to suppress the evidence of the drugs.

If the court finds that the police did not have probable cause to believe Scott was the robber until they saw him inside Henry's house and realized he matched the description, the court should

(A) grant the motion, because, as a guest, Scott has sufficient standing to contest the entry of the house without a warrant.

(B) grant the motion, because, as a guest, Scott has sufficient standing to contest the lack of probable cause at the time of the entry.

(C) deny the motion, because Scott had no ownership or other possessory interest in the premises.

(D) deny the motion, because the police had the permission of the owner to enter the house.

Questions 51-53 are based on the following fact situation.

The police had, over time, accumulated reliable information that Jason operated a large cocaine-distribution network, that he and his accomplices often resorted to violence, and that they kept a small arsenal of weapons in his home.

One day, the police received reliable information that a large brown suitcase with leather straps containing a supply of cocaine had been delivered to Jason's home and that it would be moved to a distribution point the next morning. The police obtained a valid search warrant to search for and seize the brown suitcase and the cocaine and went to Jason's house.

The police knocked on Jason's door and called out, "Police. Open up. We have a search warrant." After a few seconds with no response, the police forced the door open and entered. Hearing noises in the basement, the police ran down there and found Jason with a large brown suitcase with leather straps. They seized the suitcase and put handcuffs on Jason. A search of his person revealed a switchblade knife and a .45-caliber pistol. Jason cursed the police and said, "You never would have caught me with the stuff if it hadn't been for that lousy snitch Harvey!"

The police then fanned out through the house, looking in every room and closet. They found no one else, but one officer found an Uzi automatic weapon in a box on a closet shelf in Jason's bedroom.

In addition to charges relating to the cocaine in the suitcase, Jason is charged with unlawful possession of weapons.

Jason moves pretrial to suppress the use as evidence of the weapons seized by the police and of the statement he made.

Question 51

As to the switchblade knife and the .45-caliber pistol, Jason's motion to suppress should be

(A) granted, because the search and seizure were the result of illegal police conduct in executing the search warrant.

(B) granted, because the police did not inform Jason that he was under arrest and did not read him his Miranda rights.

(C) denied, because the search and seizure were incident to a lawful arrest.

(D) denied, because the police had reasonable grounds to believe that there were weapons in the house.

Question 52

As to Jason's statement, his motion to suppress should be

(A) granted, because the entry by forcing open the door was not reasonable.

(B) granted, because the police failed to read Jason his Miranda rights.

(C) denied, because the statement was volunteered.

(D) denied, because the statement was the product of a lawful public safety search.

Question 53

As to the Uzi automatic weapon, Jason's motion to suppress should be

(A) granted, because the search exceeded the scope needed to find out if other persons were present.

(B) granted, because once the object of the warrant—the brown suitcase—had been found and seized, no further search of the house is permitted.

(C) denied, because the police were lawfully in the bedroom and the weapon was immediately identifiable as being subject to seizure.

(D) denied, because the police were lawfully in the house and had probable cause to believe that weapons were in the house.

Questions 54-55 are based on the following fact situation.

In 1991 two police officers in a squad car received a radio message from headquarters to be on the lookout for a large green sedan occupied by two men who had just committed a bank robbery. An hour later they saw the car heading out of town. They had the car pull to the side of the road and walked over to the car. One of the officers told the occupants that they were under arrest for bank robbery. Thereupon Dean, the driver, suddenly put the car in gear and drove off. One officer clung to the car. The other officer pursued in the squad car. Unable to overtake the car and afraid he would lose sight of it in heavy traffic, the officer fired, first a warning shot and then at the car. He struck Evans, the passenger sitting next to Dean.

Dean was caught five minutes later. Evans died from loss of blood. Dean was taken to the police station.

The bank robbers had handed the teller a handwritten note, demanding the money. Dean was required over his protest, to write out the words of the note and have his fingerprints taken. He was then, for the first time, allowed to telephone a lawyer, who thereafter represented him. Dean was charged with the murder of Evans.

Question 54

The prosecution, after introducing the robbers' note to the teller, also offers in evidence Dean's writing of the words on the note at the request of the police. On appropriate action, the court should rule this

(A) admissible

(B) inadmissible, because he was not advised that his handwriting sample could be admitted into evidence against him

(C) inadmissible, because he was not advised of his right to refuse to give a handwriting sample

(D) inadmissible, because he had not been informed he had a right to have counsel present

Question 55

Suppose the jury finds Dean guilty of the murder of Evans. Before passing sentence, the judge hears argument by both parties. The prosecutor introduces the criminal record of Dean, showing two prior convictions for felony. Defense counsel admits the correctness of the record. The court imposes the maximum sentence of life imprisonment. On appeal, the appellate court should hold that this sentence

(A) violated Dean's right to due process, in that it deprived him of a fair and unbiased tribunal

(B) was in error because the introduction of new evidence after the trail deprived Dean of a fair trial

(C) was not in error

(D) deprived Dean of the right to confront the witness against him

Question 56

A grand jury was investigating a bank robbery. The only information known to the prosecutor was a rumor that Taylor might have been involved. The grand jury subpoenaed Taylor. He refused to answer questions about the robbery and was granted use immunity. He then testified that he and Simmons had robbed the bank. The grand jury indicted both Taylor and Simmons for the bank robbery. The prosecutor had no evidence as to the identity of the robbers except the testimony of Simmons and Taylor.

At Taylor's trial, his objections to Simmons' being permitted to testify should be

(A) sustained, because the prosecutor may not bargain away the rights of one codefendant in a deal with another

(B) sustained, because Simmons' testimony was acquired as a result of Taylor's grand jury testimony

(C) overruled, because the police suspected Taylor even before he testified in the grand jury hearing

(D) overruled, because a witness cannot be precluded from testifying if his testimony is given voluntarily

Question 57

Davison was driving through an apartment building area plagued with an unusually high incidence of burglaries and assaults. Acting pursuant to a police department plan to combat crime by the random stopping of automobiles in the area between midnight and 6:00 a.m., a police officer stopped Davison and asked him for identification. As Davison handed the officer his license, the officer directed a flashlight into the automobile and saw what appeared to be the barrel of a shotgun protruding from under the front seat on the passenger side of the car. The officer ordered Davison from the car, searched him, and discovered marijuana cigarettes and a shotgun.

At Davison's trial for unlawful possession of narcotics, his motion to suppress the use of the marijuana as evidence should be

(A) sustained, because the marijuana was discovered as a result of the unlawful stopping of Davison's automobile

(B) sustained, because the use of the flashlight constituted a search of the interior of Davison's automobile without probable cause

(C) denied, because the officer's conduct was consistent with the established police plan

(D) denied, because the discovery of the gun in plain view created the reasonable suspicion necessary to justify the   arrest and search of Davison

Question 58

On May 1, 1987, a car driven by Debra struck Peggy, a pedestrian. On July 1, 1987, with regard to this incident, Debra pleaded guilty to reckless driving (a misdemeanor) and was sentenced to 30 days in jail and a fine of $1,000. She served the sentence and paid the fine. On April 1, 1988, Peggy died as a result of the injuries she suffered in the accident. On March 1, 1991, a grand jury indicted Debra on a charge of manslaughter of Peggy. On May 15, 1991, trial had not begun and Debra filed a motion to dismiss the indictment on the ground of double jeopardy in that her conviction of reckless driving arose out of the same incident, and on the ground that the three-year statute of limitations for manslaughter had run.

Debra's motion should be

(A) granted only on double jeopardy grounds.

(B) granted only on statute of limitations grounds.

(C) granted on either double jeopardy grounds or statute of limitations grounds.

(D) denied on both grounds.

Question 59

Alford was a suspect in a homicide committed during a robbery of a liquor store. Barber was a friend of Alford. Police telephoned Barber and asked if he would help locate Alford. Barber agreed and met the police officers at headquarters later that night.

After a discussion during which police asked questions about Alford and the homicide, Barber said that he wanted to get something "off his chest" and advised the officers that he was in on the robbery but that Alford had shot the owner of the store without his permission or prior knowledge. The officers then for the first time gave Barber his Miranda warnings.

Barber was indicted for felony murder. He moved to prevent the introduction of his statement into evidence. His motion should be

(A) granted, because Barber was effectively in custody and entitled to receive Miranda warnings at the beginning of the discussion

(B) granted, because Barber's rights to counsel and to due process were violated by the interrogation at police headquarters

(C) denied, because his statement was freely and voluntarily given and he was not entitled to Miranda warnings

(D) denied, because by visiting headquarters voluntarily, Barber waived his right to have Miranda warnings at the beginning of the discussion

Question 60

State X enacted a statute "to regulate administratively the conduct of motor vehicle junkyard businesses in order to deter motor vehicle theft and trafficking in stolen motor vehicles or parts thereof." The statute requires a junkyard owner or operator "to permit representatives of the Department of Motor Vehicles or of any law enforcement agency upon request during normal business hours to take physical inventory of motor vehicles and parts thereof on the premises." The statute also states that a failure to comply with any of its requirements constitutes a felony.

Police officers assigned to Magnolia City's Automobile Crimes Unit periodically visited all motor vehicle junkyards in town to make the inspections permitted by the statute. Janet owned such a business in Magnolia City. One summer day, the officers asked to inspect the vehicles on her lot. Janet said, "Do I have a choice?" The officers told her she did not. The officers conducted their inspection and discovered three stolen automobiles.

Janet is charged with receiving stolen property. Janet moves pretrial to suppress the evidence relating to the three automobiles on the ground that the inspection was unconstitutional.

Her motion should be

(A) sustained, because the statute grants unbridled discretion to law enforcement officers to make warrantless searches.

(B) sustained, because the stated regulatory purpose of the statute is a pretext to circumvent the warrant requirement in conducting criminal investigations.

(C) denied, because the statute deals reasonably with a highly regulated industry.

(D) denied, because administrative searches of commercial establishments do not require warrants.

Question 61

Suspecting that Scott had slain his wife, police detectives persuaded one of Scott's employees to remove a drinking glass from Scott's office so that it could be used for fingerprint comparisons with a knife found near the body. The fingerprints matched. The prosecutor announced that he would present comparisons and evidence to the grand jury. Scott's lawyer immediately filed a motion to suppress the evidence of the fingerprint comparisons to bar its consideration by the grand jury, contending that the evidence was illegally acquired.

The motion should be

(A) granted, because, if there was no probable cause, the grand jury should not consider the evidence

(B) granted, because the employee was acting as a police agent and his seizure of the glass without a

warrant was unconstitutional

(C) denied, because motions based on the exclusionary rule are premature in grand jury proceedings

(D) denied, because the glass was removed from Scott's possession by a private citizen and not a police officer

Question 62

Miller was indicted in a state court in January 1985 for a robbery and murder that occurred in December 1982. He retained counsel, who filed a motion to dismiss on the ground that Miller had been prejudiced by a 25-month delay in obtaining the indictment. Thereafter, Miller, with his counsel, appeared in court for arraignment and stated that he wished to plead guilty. The presiding judge asked Miller whether he understood the nature of the charges, possible defenses, and maximum allowable sentences. Miller replied that he did, and the judge reviewed all of those matters with him. He then asked Miller whether he understood that he did not have to plead guilty. When Miller responded that he knew that, the judge accepted the plea and sentenced Miller to 25 years.

Six months later, Miller filed a motion to set aside his guilty plea on each of the following grounds.

Which of these grounds provides a constitutional basis for relief?

(A) The judge did not rule on his motion to dismiss before accepting the guilty plea

(B) The judge did not determine that Miller had robbed and killed the victim

(C) The judge did not determine whether Miller understood that he had a right to jury trial

(D) The judge did not determine whether the prosecutor's file contained any undisclosed exculpatory material

Questions 63-64 are based on the following fact situation.

Jones, a marijuana farmer, had been missing for several months. The sheriff's department received an anonymous tip that Miller, a rival marijuana farmer, had buried Jones in a hillside about 200 yards from Miller's farmhouse. Sheriff's deputies went to Miller's farm. They cut the barbed wire that surrounded the hillside and entered, looking for the grave. They also searched the adjacent fields on Miller's farm that were within the area enclosed by the barbed wire and discovered clothing that belonged to Jones hanging on a scarecrow. Miller observed their discovery and began shooting. The deputies returned the fire. Miller dashed to his pickup truck to escape. Unable to start the truck, he fled across a field toward the barn. A deputy tackled him just as he entered the barn.

As Miller attempted to get up, the deputy pinned his arms behind his back. Another deputy threatened, "Tell us what you did with Jones or we will shut you down and see your family on relief." Miller responded that he had killed Jones in a fight but did not report the incident because he did not want authorities to enter his land and discover his marijuana crop. Instead, he buried him behind the barn.

Miller was thereafter charged with murder.

Question 63

If Miller moves to suppress his admission about killing his neighbor, the court should

(A) grant the motion, because Miller did not voluntarily waive his right to silence.

(B) grant the motion, because the statement was the product of the warrantless entry and search of Miller's farm.

(C) deny the motion, because the deputy was in hot pursuit when he questioned Miller.

(D) deny the motion, because Miller was questioned during a police emergency search.

Question 64

If Miller moves to exclude the introduction of Jones's clothing into evidence, the court should

(A) grant the motion, because the deputies had not obtained a warrant.

(B) grant the motion, because the deputies' conduct in its entirety violated Miller's right to due process of law.

(C) deny the motion, because Miller had no expectation of privacy in the fields around his farmhouse.

(D) deny the motion, because the clothing was not Miller's property.

Answer Key

Use this Answer Key to quickly identify the correct answer to each question.

(1) B	(11) A	(21) C	(31) D	(41) A	(51) C	(61) C
(2) C	(12) B	(22) A	(32) D	(42) C	(52) C	(62) C
(3) D	(13) C	(23) D	(33) A	(43) D	(53) A	(63) A
(4) D	(14) A	(24) B	(34) D	(44) A	(54) A	(64) C
(5) D	(15) B	(25) B	(35) D	(45) B	(55) C	
(6) C	(16) D	(26) B	(36) D	(46) B	(56) B	
(7) A	(17) B	(27) D	(37) B	(47) C	(57) A	
(8) C	(18) B	(28) B	(38) B	(48) B	(58) D	
(9) B	(19) C	(29) A	(39) C	(49) C	(59) C	
(10) D	(20) C	(30) A	(40) D	(50) D	(60) C	

ANSWERS

CRIMINAL LAW

Answer 1

(B) is the best response,

because it is plausible under these facts, and negates one of the elements of burglary. Under the statute, burglary requires breaking and entering any building or structure with the intent to commit a felony or to steal therein. However, a structure that is open to the public *cannot* be "broken and entered," at least as to areas where, and times when, the public is welcome. Since the liquor store was open to the public, and Jim entered it during its business hours, he could not satisfy the "breaking and entering" element of burglary. Since B cites a fact that will exonerate Jim, and it fits these facts, it's the best response.

(A) is not the best response,

because it misstates the facts. The facts state that Jim intended to hold up the liquor store. The statute requires that the actor intend to commit a felony or to steal something from within a building or structure. Thus, Jim had the requisite intent, and, since A states otherwise, it's not the best response.

(C) is not the best response,

because the fact it cites occurred too late to exonerate Jim. The act of burglary is complete when the breaking and entry takes place – the wrongdoer need not actually commit the felony therein, under the statute given. Even if abandonment *were* a possible defense once Jim entered the building, it would not exonerate him here, because the facts suggest that he does not satisfy the elements of the abandonment defense. In order to successfully claim abandonment, the abandonment must be completely voluntary, and not made due to problems in completing the crime or the risk of getting caught; and it must represent a full renunciation of the criminal purpose. Here, the facts tell you only that Jim became "frightened." This does not suggest necessarily that his abandonment was completely voluntary. (A voluntary abandonment could be, for instance, Jim's suddenly feeling sorry for the shopkeeper, and deciding against stealing from him.) Since C identifies a fact that will not exonerate Jim, it's not his best argument, and as a result C is not the best response.

(D) is not the best response,

because Jim's lack of success would not exonerate him. The statute only requires that one break and enter a building or structure with the intent to commit a felony or to steal therein. Once inside, the crime is complete, *regardless* of whether one successfully carries out his intent. Since D cites a fact that will not exonerate Jim it's not his best argument, making D not the best response.

Answer 2

(C) is the best response,

because it arrives at the correct response, and correctly analyzes the central reason why Crowley will be acquitted. A conspiracy requires an agreement between at least two people, the intent to enter into such an agreement, and the intent to achieve the agreement's unlawful objective. Here, Crowley didn't have the intent to enter into an agreement to steal food stamps, or the intent to steal food stamps; he only had the intent to buy stolen food stamps. As a result, he was not part of a conspiracy to actually steal the food stamps. Had he actually helped to plan or participated in or assisted the theft, these acts would be evidence of his agreement to take part in the conspiracy; but he didn't. Since C correctly identifies that Crowley won't be guilty, and the central reason why he'll be exonerated, it's the best response.

(A) is not the best response,

because although it states a correct rule of law, it does not apply to these facts, and arrives at an incorrect result. Option A states as a given that Crowley has entered the conspiracy. This overlooks the central issue under these facts: Whether or not Crowley actually entered the conspiracy. A conspiracy requires an agreement, an intent to enter into such an agreement, and the intent to achieve the agreement's objectives. Here, Crowley did not conspire to actually steal the food stamps, because he didn't intend to steal the food stamps and didn't agree to enter into a plan to effect the stealing of the food stamps. As a result, he can't be liable for conspiracy to steal the food stamps, and thus A cannot be the best response.

(B) is not the best response,

because it mischaracterizes the facts, and arrives at an incorrect result. Crowley did not knowingly and willingly aid and abet the *theft;* he had no agreement regarding the theft, no intent to enter into such an agreement, and no intent to steal the food stamps. He merely agreed to buy stolen goods. As a result, his involvement is too late for him to be considered a conspirator with respect to stealing the food stamps, since he only agreed to buy them once they actually were stolen. Since B misstates the facts, and cites an argument which would not, in fact, result in Crowley's being convicted, it cannot be the best response.

(D) is not the best response,

because it misstates the law. A conspiracy requires that there be an agreement between at least two people, but it doesn't require that they all be charged with conspiracy. Beyond the agreement requirement, conspiracy requires that the defendant have intended to enter such an agreement, and have the intent to achieve the agreement's unlawful objective (at common law, a conspiracy could alternatively involve a lawful ultimate act, to be done unlawfully). If you chose this response, you may have mistaken these facts for a situation where there are two parties to a conspiracy who are both charged with conspiracy, and one is acquitted. The rule under those circumstances is that the other could not be convicted, because it takes at least two guilty parties to have a conspiracy (likewise, with a conspiracy of three persons, and all three are charged with conspiracy, if two are acquitted, the third would have to be also). However, the facts here state that *only Crowley has been charged.* Thus, this rule would not apply. Since D misstates the law, it's not the best response.

Answer 3

(D) is the best response,

because it correctly identifies the result, and identifies the central reason why Jackson and Brannick will be convicted. A conspiracy conviction requires an agreement between at least two people, an intent to enter into such an agreement, and the intent to achieve the agreement's unlawful objective (or alternatively, at common law, a lawful ultimate act to be done unlawfully). The facts here clearly state that Jackson and Brannick *planned* to steal the food stamps. Since there are no facts here that suggest the earlier larceny prosecution forbids the latter prosecution, and the facts support a finding of guilty for conspiracy, D is the best response.

(A) is not the best response,

because it misstates the law: in fact, conspiracy is a distinct offense which is *not* merged into the crime which is the object of the conspiracy. A conspiracy requires an agreement between at least two people, an intent to enter into such an agreement, and the intent to achieve the agreement's unlawful objective (or, at common law, a lawful ultimate act to be done unlawfully). The conspiracy is complete once the agreement is entered into, at common law (the modern rule is to require an act in furtherance of the conspiracy); it does not encompass the ultimate act. If you chose this response, it could be because you confused conspiracy with attempt. Attempt is merged into the completed crime, so that the accused can only be convicted of attempt OR the completed offense, but not both. How-

ever, as stated, conspiracy is a separate and distinct offense, which doesn't merge into the completed crime. Since A misstates the law, it's not the best response.

(B) is not the best response,

because it misstates the law, and arrives at an incorrect result: in fact, conspiracy is a separate and distinct offense from the crime which is the object of the conspiracy. Thus, being tried for it after pleading guilty to larceny would not be considered double jeopardy. Double jeopardy only attaches when two prosecutions meet two requirements: they must be based on the same conduct, AND they must both require proof of *the same facts* (double jeopardy also applies when you make it through the single jeopardy round on TV, with a score of greater than zero). Larceny and conspiracy require proof of quite different facts. Conspiracy focuses on the agreement aspect, and is complete once the agreement is made; conspiracy requires the actual larcenous taking of the stamps. Since B mistakenly states the double jeopardy would attach under these facts, it's not the best response.

(C) is not the best response,

because it misstates the law. The facts in this problem suggest that the latter prosecution would not be barred. A state prosecution after a federal prosecution would be forbidden under two circumstances: Either due to double jeopardy, or a kind of collateral estoppel: the earlier, federal prosecution was resolved in defendant's favor due to a factual finding that would bar a later conviction in state court (e.g., an alibi was upheld). Neither of these exist under these facts. Larceny and conspiracy are two separate and distinct crimes, and the proof that would be necessary for them would be largely different. Double jeopardy would not attach to the federal larceny conviction, and there is nothing under these facts to suggest that resolution of a factual issue precludes conviction in the later state prosecution. As a result, C cannot be the best response.

Answer 4

(D) is the best response,

because it addresses the fact that is most likely to exonerate Paul from culpability for robbery: No robbery took place. A robbery is a larceny from either a person or a person's presence, by either force or fear. Under the facts here, Jack did not use force, and the teller was clearly not put in fear. As a result, although there may be another crime, there's no robbery. If there's no robbery, nobody, including Paul, could be liable for robbery. This is a clever question in that it leads you down the garden path, focusing on Paul's actions, not Jack's. Thus, whenever accomplice liability is involved, check first to see if the actual crime took place. If it didn't, the accomplice can't possibly be liable. (Note that if the robbery had taken place, Paul would be liable as an accomplice, since he procured, counseled or commanded the commission of a felony.) Since D states the fact that will exonerate Paul, it's the best response.

(A) is not the best response,

because the fact it states would not exonerate Paul, and thus it would not make a good defense. Paul *could,* in theory, be convicted as an accomplice to robbery *even though* Jack was the only one who entered the bank. Robbery is a crime requiring larceny from a person or a person's presence, by either force or fear. An accomplice is one who procures, counsels or commands the commission of a felony. (Modern courts do not recognize a difference between accessories before the fact and principals in the second degree, but instead call them both accomplices. At common law, the difference between the two is that a principal is actually or constructively present at the commission of the criminal act, and the accessory is not. Here, it's likely Paul would be considered a principal in the second degree, since he was at the bank, albeit not inside it.) Thus, it isn't necessary that the accomplice actually participate in the criminal act itself. Since option A would condition Paul's culpability on whether or not he entered the bank, it can't be the best response.

(B) is not the best response,

because the fact it states would not exonerate Paul, and thus it would not make a good defense. B implies that Paul would have a valid defense due to withdrawal. In fact, Paul withdrew too late for withdrawal to serve as a defense, and, in any case, on these facts it is not clear that Paul's withdrawal reflects a renunciation of the criminal purpose, which a valid withdrawal requires – these facts only indicate that Paul "panicked." This suggests that he became nervous about the odds of success, which is not a valid withdrawal. As to timing, an accessory cannot withdraw once the chain of events has become "unstoppable." Here, Paul planned the crime with Jack, and drove Jack to the bank. If the crime had taken place, Paul would be liable, since he did *everything* before its commission that he intended to do. Since B addresses an argument that will not exonerate Paul, it's not his best defense, and thus not the best response.

(C) is not the best response,

because the fact it states would not exonerate Paul, and thus would not make a good defense. As an accomplice to a robbery, one must intend that the robbery be committed, and aid in its commission, but he needn't know the details of how the robbery is actually carried out. Here, Paul planned the robbery with Jack, and actually drove him to the bank. He intended that the robbery take place, and only chickened out while he was at the scene. Since Paul had the requisite intent, and helped in executing the ostensible robbery, it doesn't matter that he didn't know exactly what Jack said to the teller. As a result, C is not the best response.

Answer 5

(D) is the best response,

because it correctly identifies that Adam will be liable and Bailey will not, and identifies the central reason why. The key here is identifying the *scope of the conspiracy.*

Under the facts given, Adam is clearly liable for battery, since a battery is the unlawful application of force to the person of another, resulting in bodily injury or offensive touching. There was no excuse or justification for his doing so. However, if the conspiracy to make and sell liquor had a scope large enough to include the shooting, Bailey would be liable as well. The sticky point here is that the scope of a conspiracy only includes crimes committed in furtherance of the conspiracy's objectives, which are foreseeable. Here, the goal of the conspiracy was to make and sell liquor, not to shoot revenue agents. There are no facts, except for the rifles kept nearby, to suggest that shooting revenue agents would be part of the deal, and that wouldn't be enough to convict Bailey. (Bailey is similarly innocent as an accessory, since he didn't procure, counsel or command Adam to shoot Mitchell; in fact, Bailey didn't intend for Adam to shoot Mitchell at all.) Since D correctly identifies that Adam will be guilty and Bailey won't, and overcomes the argument most likely to result in Bailey's conviction (the conspiracy theory), it's the best response.

(A) is not the best response,

because it wrongly exonerates Adam (although it correctly finds Bailey not guilty). A battery is the unlawful application of force to the person of another, resulting in bodily injury or offensive touching. Adam's shooting and wounding Mitchell clearly qualifies as a battery, since there was no excuse or justification for his action. While option A correctly identifies that Bailey will not be liable, it wrongly exonerates Adam, so it is not the best response.

(B) is not the best response,

because it wrongly convicts Bailey (although it correctly finds Adam guilty). In order to be liable for Adam's shooting Bailey, Bailey would have to have agreed to the shooting or intended that it happen. He'd have to be liable on either an accessory or conspiracy basis. He wouldn't be liable as an accessory, because he didn't procure, counsel or command the commission of the act. He couldn't be liable on a conspiracy basis, because although operating the still involved a conspiracy, the shooting would be outside the scope of the conspiracy. An act is only within the scope of the conspiracy when it is committed in furtherance of the conspiracy's objectives, and the crime is foreseeable. While Adam and Bailey had a conspiracy concerning the still, shooting Mitchell would not be considered sufficiently in furtherance of the conspiracy's objectives or foreseeable enough to bind Bailey. As a result, B is not the best response.

(C) is not the best response,

because although it arrives at the correct response, the reasoning is faulty. Even if the conspiracy *did* end when Adam was arrested, the shooting occurred *before* Adam was arrested, so the termination of the conspiracy when Adam was arrested would not exonerate Bailey. Thus, if there was an agreement as to shooting revenue agents like Mitchell, or if Bailey had procured, counseled or commanded Adam to shoot Mitchell, Bailey would have been liable on either a conspiracy theory or an accessory theory. Since C focuses on an element which will not exonerate Bailey, even though it correctly identifies that Adam alone will be liable, it's not the best response.

Answer 6

(C) is the best response,

because it correctly identifies that Defendant will not be guilty, and it cites the central reason why.

The key here is that there's no relation between the licensing violation and the death. Apart from that, these facts indicate that *Defendant did nothing wrong* – these facts indicate that it was the child's fault that he got run over, since the facts state that *the child was killed before Defendant could prevent it.* Since Defendant was not even negligent, he couldn't be liable.

Misdemeanor manslaughter is a killing that occurs as a result of or during a *malum in se* misdemeanor, or a felony that is not sufficient for felony murder. Here, Defendant's misdemeanor – failing to renew his driver's license – neither resulted in the child's death, nor is the type of inherently bad misdemeanor appropriate for misdemeanor manslaughter. The other type of manslaughter, criminal negligence manslaughter, would require that Defendant engaged in a criminally negligent course of behavior, which resulted in the child's death. Here again, the causal connection is lacking. The simple fact is that Defendant's failure to renew his license had *no bearing* on the death of the child; in fact, under these facts, it's fairly clear that the child's own negligence resulted in his death. Defendant did not in fact behave negligently under these facts. Since C correctly identifies there's no causal connection between Defendant's negligence in failing to renew his license and the child's death, it's the best response.

(A) is not the best response,

because there's no causation between Defendant's misdemeanor and the death, and, beyond that, the misdemeanor involved is not the type that can be the subject of misdemeanor-manslaughter. Misdemeanor manslaughter is a killing that occurs as a result of or during a *malum in se* misdemeanor, or a felony that is not sufficient for felony murder. Here, Defendant's misdemeanor – failing to renew his driver's license – neither resulted in the child's death, nor is the type of

inherently bad misdemeanor appropriate for misdemeanor manslaughter. As a result, A is not the best response.

(B) is not the best response,

because it ignores causation, and as a result arrives at the wrong result. It may be true that the purpose of the licensing requirement is to protect life, and that driving without a license is negligent – but this does not change the fact that there would have to be a causal connection between Defendant's negligence and the child's death in order to find him guilty of manslaughter. Under these facts, it's fairly clear that the child's death was the fault of the child, not the Defendant (as indicated by the language: *...killed before Defendant could prevent it).* Thus, it's irrelevant that Defendant may have been negligent in failing to get his license reviewed. Look at it this way: Even if Defendant's license was valid, it would not have had a bearing on his liability for manslaughter in running over the child. Since B ignores causation, it's not the best response.

(D) is not the best response,

because it misstates the law: Defendant *could* be guilty without criminal intent. Under these facts, it so happens he's not guilty, but it's not because he lacked criminal intent: it's because the element of causation is missing. Defendant could be liable for manslaughter without intent, since, under criminal negligence type manslaughter, he's liable for manslaughter if a killing occurs through his gross or criminal negligence, either by act or omission. Thus, his act must create an unreasonable risk of harm. This does not require intent, and since option D states as a general principle that a manslaughter conviction is not possible without intent, it's not the best response.

Answer 7

(A) is the best response,

because evidence of intoxication might negate the requisite intent for both crimes.

Voluntary intoxication evidence may be offered, when the defendant is charged with a crime that requires purpose or intent, to establish that the intoxication may have prevented the defendant from formulating the requisite intent.

Each of the crimes charged here requires a particular intent. Assault requires an intent to cause bodily harm. Attempt murder requires an intent to kill. If Martin was intoxicated, this fact might (would not necessarily, but might) indicate that Martin could not or did not form the required intent. Therefore, the evidence is relevant to both crimes, and must be admitted.

(B) is not the best response,

because evidence of intoxication should be admitted as to assault, since it might negate the specific intent required for assault (intent to cause bodily harm).

(C) is not the best response,

because evidence of intoxication should be admitted as to attempted murder, since it might negate the specific intent required for attempted murder (intent to kill).

(D) is not the best response,

because evidence of intoxication might negate the requisite intent for both crimes. See the discussion of Choice (A) for more analysis.

Answer 8

(C) is the best response,

because it correctly identifies that the jury could find Defendant guilty of either robbery or larceny, but not both.

There are two keys here: One is realizing that larceny is a lesser-included offense to robbery; and, second, that the jury could properly decide either way on the use of force and fear (the knife and the threats).

The jury, as finder of fact, could believe or disbelieve any testimony. The key fact here involves the use of the knife and the threats: If the jury believes the victim, it would find Defendant guilty of robbery; if it doesn't, which would be reasonable since Worth, a witness, wasn't aware of the knife or threats, then it would find Defendant guilty of larceny. Robbery requires a larceny from a person or a person's presence, by either force or fear. The use of the knife and/or the threats in the act described in these facts would thus satisfy robbery. Larceny is the trespassory taking and carrying away of another's personal property with intent to steal. The act described in these facts is sufficient for larceny, if the knife and threats were not used. Note, however, that the jury couldn't properly find Defendant guilty of both robbery and larceny, since larceny is a lesser-included offense of robbery (requiring proof of some, but not all, of the elements of robbery, and no other elements). Since C correctly identifies that the jury could find Defendant guilty of either robbery or larceny but not both, it's the best response.

(A) is not the best response,

because it is too narrow: The jury could also properly return a verdict of guilty of larceny. The key here is whether the jury believes Defendant used the knife and/or made the threats, because this will determine whether or not it finds him guilty of robbery or larceny. Larceny requires a trespassory taking and carrying away of another's personal property with intent to steal. Robbery additionally requires that the larceny be from a person or in the presence of a person, by either force or fear. The jury, as the finder of fact, would be entitled – under these facts – to believe the victim, and find that force and fear were used, making Defendant liable for robbery, or not to believe the victim (due to Worth's testimony) and find only a larceny took place. Since A incorrectly limits the jury to robbery only, it's not the best response.

(B) is not the best response,

because it is too narrow: The jury could also properly return a verdict of guilty of robbery. The key here is whether the jury believes Defendant used the knife and/or made the threats, because this will determine whether or not it finds him guilty of robbery or larceny. Larceny requires a trespassory taking and carrying away of another's personal property with intent to steal. Robbery additionally requires that the larceny be from a person or in the presence of a person, by either force or fear. The jury, as the finder of fact, would be entitled – under these facts – to believe the victim, and find that force and fear were used, making Defendant liable for robbery, or not to believe the victim (due to Worth's testimony) and find only a larceny took place. Since B limits the jury to finding larceny only, it's not the best response.

(D) is not the best response,

because the jury *could not* properly find Defendant guilty of both robbery and larceny, since larceny is a lesser-included offense of robbery. A lesser included offense is one which requires proof of some but not all of the elements of another offense, and no other elements. Larceny requires a trespassory taking and carrying away of another's personal property with intent to steal. Robbery requires larceny from a person or the presence of a person, by either force or fear. As a result, Defendant *could not* properly be convicted of both charges. Furthermore, the jury could properly find that Defendant did not use a knife or threats. Since robbery requires the use of either force or fear, if the jury didn't believe the victim's testimony about those two factors, it couldn't find Defendant guilty of robbery. Since D incorrectly states that the jury could properly find Defendant guilty of both robbery and larceny, it's not the best response.

Answer 9

(B) is the best response,

because Mel's mistaken belief that the briefcase was his own prevented him from having the required mental state for robbery.

Robbery is the: (1) taking, (2) of personal property of another, (3) from the other's person or presence, (4) by force or intimidation, (5) with the intent to permanently deprive him of it.

The intent required for robbery is the intent to use force to take "the property of another." Therefore, if D mistakenly (even unreasonably) believes that the property in question is his own, the required "intent to take the property of another" is lacking. The fact that that mistake was brought about by voluntary intoxication — and the fact that the mistake may have been "unreasonable" — makes no difference.

(A) is not the best response,

because (1) the absence of threats would not prevent

this from being robbery; and (2) the intoxication would not necessarily prevent this from being robbery.

Robbery is the taking of personal property of another from the latter's person or presence, "by force or intimidation." A taking can involve force without involving threats. Here, Mel struggled with the owner, and knocked him to the floor, so the requisite force was present even though Mel made no threats.

Also, the fact that Mel was drunk would not necessarily prevent him from being guilty — it was only Mel's mistaken belief that the briefcase was his that caused him to avoid guilt. (It's true that the intoxication may have been what caused Mel to have the mistaken belief — but no matter why the mistaken belief occurred, Mel would have avoided guilt.) To the extent that this choice relies on an absence of threats, and the existence of the intoxication, to explain the result, it's twice-wrong even though it states the correct outcome.

(C) is not the best response,
because voluntary intoxication can still prevent the required specific intent from existing.

Robbery requires an intent to take "the property of another." If D fails to have the requisite intent, whatever the reason, the crime has not been committed. Here, Mel thought the briefcase was his, so he lacked the requisite intent to take "property of another." The fact that the intoxication was "voluntary" would not make a difference, if for any reason (including intoxication) he lacked the requisite intent.

(D) is not the best response,
because mistake *can* be a defense to specific intent crimes.

If a mistake of fact prevents the defendant from having the requisite intent for a "specific intent" crime, that mistake is indeed a defense. Here, robbery requires an intent to take "the property of another." If a mistake causes D to believe (whether reasonably or not) that the property is his own rather than another's, that mistake causes D not to meet the intent element for the crime.

Answer 10

(D) is the best response,
because Alice's actions satisfied all the elements of larceny.

Larceny is the: (1) taking and (2) carrying away, of the (3) tangible property, (4) of another, (5) by trespass or without consent, (6) with the intent to permanently deprive the person of his interest in property.

Alice committed larceny: (1) She picked up the purse, a taking. (2) She moved it from its original position when she placed it under her coat and took a few steps toward the exit, a carrying away. (3) & (4) The purse is a tangible item owned by another, the clothing store. (5) Alice took it without the clothing store's consent. (6) When she picked up the purse (exerted con-

trol over it) the facts state that she did so with the intent to take it without paying for it. Alice's actions therefore satisfy all the requirements of larceny.

The fact that Alice did not exit from the store with the property is irrelevant — the crime was complete once she exerted dominion and carried the item a small distance, while intending to keep it. Nor does the fact that Alice took only couple of steps with the purse prevent the "carrying away" element from being satisfied — even the smallest movement of the item will suffice.

(A) is not the best response,
because Alice completed the crime once she exerted dominion over the purse and carried it a small distance, while intending to keep it. See the analysis of Choice (D) above.

(B) is not the best response,
because Alice completed the crime when her actions matched her intent.

The crime was complete once Alice exerted dominion over the purse and carried it a small distance, while intending to keep it. Nothing she did thereafter — including "withdrawing" from the "criminal enterprise" — could undo the completed crime.

(C) is not the best response,
because the crime of larceny was complete once Alice moved the item with intent to take it.

By the analysis in Choice (D) above, the crime was complete once Alice exerted dominion over the purse and carried it a small distance, while intending to keep it. Since Choice (C) says that only attempted, not completed, larceny has occurred, it's wrong.

Answer 11

(A) is the best response,
because Sam acted with the intent to kill whoever started the car, and then killed that person.

This is basically a problem involving "concurrence" — the examiners are thinking (maybe hoping) you'll reason, "The requisite intent no longer existed at the time of the explosion, therefore the requirement of concurrence between act and mental state has not been satisfied."

It's true that "concurrence" is required. But in the case of a crime defined in terms of a particular result (like murder), the requisite concurrence is between *mental state and act, not* between *mental state and result*. In other words, at the moment D takes the act that brings about the result, D must be actuated by the appropriate intent; it doesn't matter whether D still has that intent when the result finally occurs.

Here, the "act" was the setting of the bomb. When Sam planted the bomb, he was actuated by an intent to kill Anna. The fact that before the bomb went off (producing death as a result) he had changed his mind is irrelevant.

There's a further element to worry about: the fact that an unintended victim (Lois), not the intended victim (Anna) was killed. But this makes no difference either, under the familiar doctrine of transferred intent, by which, if the type of harm intended is the type that results, the fact that a different victim ended up suffering that harm is irrelevant.

Lastly, the fact that the security guard had the opportunity to avoid the harm but failed to do so is irrelevant — Sam intended to bring about a death by bomb, and his act was the but-for cause of that death by bomb, so the fact that some other actor failed in a chance to avoid the harm makes no difference. And that's true even if the failure by the other person amounted to negligence.

(B) is not the best response,

because Sam killed with premeditation and deliberation, making him guilty of first degree murder.

Under the analysis in Choice (A), two things prevent this choice (B) from being correct: (1) Sam's intent is measured as of the moment he planted the bomb (and the fact that by the time of death he no longer intended to kill anyone is irrelevant); and (2) Sam's intent to kill Anna is deemed "transferred" to Lois.

(C) is not the best response,

because, under the analysis in Choice (A), two things prevent this choice (C) from being correct: (1) Sam's intent is measured as of the moment he planted the bomb (and the fact that by the time of death he no longer intended to kill anyone is irrelevant); and (2) the fact that the security officer had a good opportunity to avoid the harm does not prevent Sam's act from being the legal cause of the harm.

(D) is not the best response,

because Sam is guilty of murder, not just attempted murder.

Under the analysis in Choice (A), the fact that the security officer had a good opportunity to avoid the harm does not prevent Sam's act from being the legal cause of the harm. And that's true even if the security guard's failure amounted to negligence. Sam's act of planting the bomb was clearly a "but-for" cause of the death, and was so closely connected with the death that it was certainly a "legal" or "proximate" cause of that death. (The fact that the guard's negligence may have *also* been a proximate cause [and a but-for cause] won't save Sam from guilt for the death.) Since Sam caused the death by an act that was intended to cause the death, he's guilty of murder, not just attempted murder.

Answer 12

(B) is the best response,

because the right to use self-defense is not lost where the defendant makes a reasonable mistake about the need to use self-defense.

The defense of self-defense states that an individual who is not the aggressor may use such force as reasonably appears necessary to protect himself from the imminent use of unlawful force upon himself. The defendant does not lose the defense merely because he is reasonably mistaken about some aspect of the situation, such as the legality of the force being used against him. So here, the fact that Defendant mistakenly (but not unreasonably, so far as we're aware from the facts) believes that the person who has grabbed him is not privileged to do, does not cause Defendant to lose the right to use a reasonable level of force to resist the attack.

(A) is not the best response,

because public welfare offenses are strict liability crimes.

"Public welfare" offenses are strict liability offenses, because they generally involve a relatively low penalty and are not regarded by the community as involving significant moral impropriety. Ordinances forbidding the sale of alcohol to minors generally fall into this public-welfare-offense category. Consequently, such ordinances typically do not recognize the defense of mistake (even reasonable mistake).

(C) is not the best response,

because statutory rape is a strict liability crime.

Most statutory rape statutes impose strict liability. In particular, they reject the defense of "I didn't know she was underage," precisely because that defense is so often asserted and so hard for the prosecution to rebut.

(D) is not the best response,

because reliance on mistaken advice about how a crime is defined is not a defense to most crimes, and certainly not to the crime of bigamy.

There are crimes that are defined to require a "knowing" violation. (Income-tax evasion falls into this category, for instance.) For such a crime, the fact that D reasonably relied on counsel's advice that the proposed conduct was legal would be a defense.

But most crimes are *not* defined to make knowledge of illegality an element of the crime. Bigamy is like most crimes in this respect — a mistaken (even reasonably mistaken) belief that the law treats abandonment as being the automatic equivalent of a divorce does not furnish a defense. The colloquial expression "ignorance of the law is no excuse" is in fact a generally correct statement, and it's correct on the facts here.

Answer 13

(C) is the best response,

because it arrives at the correct result, and cites the principal reason for that result. One is liable for a crime, as an accomplice, if he procures, counsels, or commands the commission of a felony. Naturally, this would require that he intend that the felony be committed. Here, Sam's liability would rest on his statement "Kill him." Intent could be established by presumption, since a person of sufficient intelligence to understand the nature of his actions is presumed to intend the natural and probable consequences of his actions. Here, Sam encouraged Bill to kill Vic, so it could be said that Sam intended that Bill kill Vic. Furthermore, his statement would be considered counselling or commanding the commission of a felony – murder. As a result, Sam will be liable as an accomplice for murder. Since C states the correct result, backs this up with reasoning, and focuses on the central issues in the case, it's the best response.

(A) is not the best response,

because it arrives at the wrong result, and it applies the wrong rule to these facts. The "clear and present danger" test is the test used to determine the validity of a law designed to forbid advocacy of unlawful conduct. It provides that advocacy can only be forbidden if its aim is to produce or incite imminent illegal action, and it is likely to produce or incite such action. Whether Sam's speech is protected by the First Amendment is not the issue here; instead, the issue is whether Sam can be held liable for murder for encouraging Bill to kill Vic. Since A does not apply the correct rule, and, beyond that, arrives at the wrong result, it's not the best response.

(B) is not the best response,

because it's too broad. Given the requisite intent, "mere presence and oral encouragement" are sufficient to make Sam guilty as an accomplice. An accomplice is one who procures, counsels, or commands the commission of a felony (it encompasses two common law parties to a felony: accessory before the fact and principal in the second degree). Option B implies that "mere presence and oral encouragement" are insufficient to make one liable as an accomplice; however, under the definition of accomplice, encouragement would constitute "counseling" or "commanding," and so could create liability as an accomplice. This is an attractive choice, because your gut reaction could be that the mere encouragement of a bystander would be insufficient to create liability for murder. However, mechanical application of the rule indicates that this is possible. Since B states otherwise, it's not the best response.

(D) is not the best response,

because although it arrives at the correct result, the reasoning it gives would not be sufficient to hold Sam liable for murder. It's not Sam's presence and his intent which make him liable, as D suggests – rather, it's his act of encouraging the killing that makes him liable. Mere presence wouldn't make him liable, since, in general, one is not obligated to act affirmatively for the benefit of others; furthermore, his intent is not sufficient

to create liability, since intent is merely a state of mind and, with nothing more, it's not criminal (until it produces action to bring about the desired results). It's Sam's active encouragement – "kill him" – which makes him liable. Since D states incorrect reasoning despite a correct result, it's not the best response.

Answer 14

(A) is the best response,

because it arrives at the correct result, and identifies the principal reason why Tom will be acquitted. Under these facts, Tom has done nothing to subject himself to liability. The most promising element for liability is the fact that he hoped Bill would kill Vic. However, even if he intended that Bill kill Vic, all that's involved is a state of mind which, with nothing more, is not criminal. His failure to aid Vic would not subject him to liability because the law imposes no general duty to act affirmatively for the benefit of others, in the absence of some special pre-existing relationship between the defendant and the victim (e.g., defendant's negligence created the peril, or a special relationship mandates affirmative acts [parent and child, for instance]). Liability for murder would have required that Tom do *something* – either helping to plan Vic's murder, or aiding it in some other way – to make him liable under a conspiracy or accomplice theory. Under these facts, no such action exists. Since A correctly identifies that Tom will not be guilty, and the basis on which he'll be exonerated, it's the best response.

(B) is not the best response,

because although it arrives at the correct result, the reasoning it offers would not exonerate Tom. Option B suggests that Tom could only be liable if he told Bill ahead of time that he hoped Bill would murder Vic. This is both too narrow and too broad a statement of the applicable law. First, merely stating "I hope you kill Vic" might not be enough to make Tom liable, if he didn't plan the killing with Bill (conspiracy) or aid in any way (accomplice liability). Second, prior encouragement isn't the only way Tom could be liable; had he encouraged Bill at the scene of the crime – as Sam did – he'd be liable for murder as an accomplice. Since B does not give the correct reasoning, it cannot be the best response.

(C) is not the best response,

because it arrives at an incorrect result, and misstates the law. As a general rule, an individual has no duty to act affirmatively for the benefit of others. Although certain relationships between the defendant and the one in peril change this (e.g., defendant's negligence created the peril, or a special relationship mandates affirmative acts [parent-child, for instance]), no such facts exist in this question. Since no duty to aid exists, and Tom did nothing to plan or aid in committing the killing, he cannot be liable for murder. Since C imposes a duty that does not exist, and arrives at the wrong result, it's not the best response.

(D) is not the best response,

because it arrives at an incorrect result, and misstates the law. In order to be found guilty of murder, Tom would have to undertake some type of activity – be it planning or aiding in the killing. Mere presence and tacit approval are insufficient for liability as a conspirator or as an accomplice. Presence is not sufficient for liability, since, as a general rule, the law imposes no duty to act affirmatively for the benefit of others, in the absence of some special pre-existing relationship between the defendant and the victim (e.g., defendant's negligence created the peril, or a special relationship mandates affirmative acts [parent and child, for instance]). Even coupling this with tacit approval is insufficient, since approval is a mere state of mind which, with nothing more, is not criminal. Since D states insufficient grounds for a guilty verdict, and arrives at an incorrect result, it's not the best response.

Answer 15

(B) is the best response,

because Diane's actions fit the requirements for the "reckless indifference to the value of human life" variety of murder, which is second-degree murder in this jurisdiction.

The act here cannot be first-degree murder. It is not "intentional and premeditated killing" murder, because there's no evidence that Diane desired to kill Victor. And it can't be "killing during the commission of a common-law felony" murder because assault or battery are generally deemed to be lesser-included offenses that can't be bootstrapped into felony-murder. (Indeed, it's not even clear that assault or battery existed here, since there's not much evidence that Diane had any of the possible mental states for assault or battery — she apparently didn't desire to hurt Victor or even cause him fear of bodily harm).

On the other hand, the facts do fit the definition of murder of the "extreme indifference to the value of human life" (or "depraved heart") variety. Diane has intentionally or recklessly disregarded what she knows is an extremely high risk of death or serious bodily harm to Victor. Since extreme-indifference murder is a form of common-law murder, and since it doesn't fall within one of the two types of first-degree murder in this jurisdiction (intent-to-kill and in-the-course-of-a-common-law-felony), it's second-degree.

(A) is not the best response,

because Diane's actions do not fit the given definition for first degree murder. See the analysis of Choice (B) for why this is so.

(C) is not the best response,

because Diane's actions matched the requirements for

second-degree murder, a more serious crime than manslaughter. The analysis in Choice (B) shows why Diane qualifies for extreme-indifference second-degree murder.

(D) is not the best response,

because assumption of risk is a defense in torts but normally not in criminal law.

Consent of the victim is no defense in criminal law, unless the consent negates an element of the offense. The victim's consent does not negate an element of the crime of murder, because murder is defined as a killing under any of several mental states, and none of versions of murder is defined to include lack of the victim's consent as an element of the crime. (For instance, if H kills his painfully-dying wife W at her urging, her consent is not a defense to a "mercy killing" murder prosecution of H.)

Answer 16

(D) is the best response,

because Matt reasonably believed he faced death and was under no duty to retreat in his home.

A person may use deadly force in self-defense if he: (1) is confronted with unlawful force; (2) reasonably believes he is threatened with imminent death or great bodily harm; and (3) uses no greater force that he reasonably believes is required to avoid the danger.

Here, Matt was certainly faced with "unlawful force" (the threatened knife attack), and reasonably believed that this attack threatened him with death or great bodily harm. Nor was the level of force used greater than Matt reasonably believed was necessary, given that Matt was not trying to actually hit Fred. (If he had shot to kill, rather than just to frighten or wound, this might have been greater force than was reasonably believed necessary, which would have been a violation of requirement (3) above.)

Notice that it's important that Matt did not instigate the confrontation — if Matt had been the initial aggressor, in an unlawful and physical way, he would have forfeited his right to use self-defense on that occasion.

The most interesting question in this fact-pattern is whether, since Matt could have run out the door, he was required to *retreat* in this way rather than use deadly force. Some courts impose a general duty to retreat if the actor can safely do so, but even these courts do not require a person to retreat in or from his *home*. Therefore, in all courts Matt (since he was in his home) was permitted to use a reasonable though deadly level of force rather than retreating. Thus Matt met all requirements for self-defense, which is a complete defense to a criminal charge.

(A) is not the best response,

because the use of deadly force here was not unreasonable.

Even when D is threatened with unlawful force that

threatens imminent death or great bodily harm, D may only use the lowest level of force that's reasonable in the circumstances. But here, nothing in the fact pattern indicates that Matt used greater (or more deadly) force than seemed to him reasonably required. First, Matt tried to impose a solution (that Fred would leave) that would not have involved actual use of deadly force. Then, Matt tried to use the deadly object in a non-deadly way (aiming to frighten, not wound or kill). Given that the knife threat from Jeff posed the imminent risk of death to Matt, and given the absence of other solutions (apart from retreating, which Matt was not required to do in his home), Matt's intent here was to use no more force than reasonably appeared necessary. The fact that Matt unintentionally hit and killed Fred does not retroactively transform Matt's conduct into the unreasonable use of force — D's act is to be evaluated by the reasonableness of his conduct and beliefs, not by reference to an unexpectedly harmful outcome.

(B) is not the best response,

because Matt had no duty to retreat in his home.

As described in the analysis of Choice (D) above, even courts imposing a general duty to retreat before the use of deadly force do not impose that duty when the defendant is in his own home. Therefore, Matt had no duty to retreat even though he may have had the clear opportunity to do so.

(C) is not the best response,

because in the absence of a defense of self-defense Matt's conduct might well be extreme-indifference murder despite his lack of intent to kill.

As the analysis in Choice (D) above shows, the defense of self-defense will result in Matt's acquittal. Therefore, any choice that doesn't refer to this defense cannot be the best response.

In any event, if self-defense were not available, Choice (C) would still not be the best response. That's because, on these facts, the fact that Matt didn't have an intent to kill Fred would not necessarily entitle him to an acquittal.

There are multiple states of mind that may suffice for murder, and intent-to-kill is only one. Another is "extreme indifference to the value of human life" (sometimes called a "depraved heart.") Where D fires a loaded gun in the direction of V, intending only to frighten him, D might well be found to have exhibited extreme indifference to the value of human life, in which case he would be guilty of murder if the shot proved fatal, despite the lack of an intent to kill. So Choice (C), in stating that the absence of an intent to kill means that Matt must be acquitted, is incorrect.

Answer 17

(B) is the best response,

because it correctly characterizes the facts. Embezzle-

ment involves the wrongdoer's acquiring title to property in his lawful possession, by converting or appropriating it. That's what Defendant did here — he had lawful possession of the diamond ring, but within the first sixty days, he was not authorized to sell it. Selling it within that period of time amounted to embezzlement. Note that the distinction between all of these "property" crimes – larceny, larceny by trick, embezzlement, and false pretenses – frequently involves a difference of only one element. For instance, the difference between embezzlement and larceny is that embezzlement requires conversion, not movement; larceny involves wrongful *possession*. Embezzlement differs from larceny by trick in that larceny by trick involves obtaining possession, but not title; embezzlement occurs when the wrongdoer already has lawful possession, but he obtains title to the property by converting or appropriating it. Since option B makes the fine line distinction between these crimes correctly, it's the best response.

(A) is not the best response,

because an element of larceny is missing in these facts: Wrongful possession. Larceny requires a trespassory taking and carrying away of personal property of another, with intent to steal it. This is not satisfied by the facts here, because there was no "carrying away" of another's personal property; Defendant had rightful *possession* of the property. Embezzlement requires conversion as opposed to movement; it occurs when someone misappropriates property of which he has lawful possession. Since not every element of larceny is present in these facts, it's not the best response.

(C) is not the best response,

because an element of larceny by trick is not satisfied under these facts. Larceny by trick is essentially larceny, but instead of a physical taking of property, the taking occurs through fraud. (As an example, say Red Riding Hood gives Big Bad Wolf $50 upon his promise to buy groceries for her grandmother. If Wolf absconds with the cash, he'll be liable for larceny by trick.) Under these facts, Defendant is liable for embezzlement, not larceny by trick. The difference between the two is that, in larceny by trick, the wrongdoer obtains possession, but not title; in embezzlement, the wrongdoer already has lawful possession, but he obtains title to the property by converting or appropriating it. That's what happened here. There's nothing fraudulent about the way Defendant obtained possession of the ring – Johnson pawned it. What creates liability instead is that Defendant wrongfully converted the ring by selling it when he wasn't authorized to do so. Since the facts represent embezzlement instead of larceny by trick. C is not the best response.

(D) is not the best response,

because there was no misrepresentation involved in Defendant's taking possession of the diamond ring.

False pretenses involves obtaining legal title to property by false and fraudulent misrepresentations of fact. (As an example, say Louis obtains title to Alex's taxi by falsely convincing him that the transfer of title will result in a tax benefit to him. Louis is liable for false pretenses.) Here, Defendant didn't employ misrepresentation to obtain title; he simply converted goods in his possession. Converting or appropriating goods in one's lawful possession – which is what Defendant did – is *embezzlement.* Since the facts do not satisfy the elements of false pretenses, D is not the best response.

Answer 18

(B) is the best response,
because it correctly identifies that Defendant will be liable for embezzlement. Embezzlement occurs when someone misappropriates property of which he has lawful possession. That's the case here. Defendant had rightful possession of the diamond ring. However, he misappropriated it by selling it. The wrinkle in these facts is that he turned over the proceeds of the sale to Johnson. However, that's no defense to embezzlement. The intent to restore equivalent property is not a defense to embezzlement, since embezzlement requires only a fraudulent conversion of property by one with lawful possession of the property. As long as these elements are satisfied, there will be liability for embezzlement. Under these facts, they are – so B is the best response.

(A) is not the best response,
because the wrongful possession element of larceny is missing. Larceny requires a trespassory taking and carrying away of personal property of another with intent to steal it. Here, it's not possession that Defendant wrongfully took, but *title,* by selling the ring. Note, however, that giving Johnson the proceeds of the sale *does not exonerate Defendant of embezzlement.* An important thing to remember in Criminal Law is that the condonation of the victim *does not* change the criminal nature of Defendant's act! For instance, say Defendant *had* wrongfully taken the ring from Johnson, and was guilty of larceny. Giving Johnson the money wouldn't change this fact, because it wouldn't negate any of the elements of larceny. If, however, Defendant took the ring only intending to *borrow* it, then he *wouldn't* be guilty of larceny, *because the "intent to steal" element would be missing.* However, under these facts, it's clear that Defendant is liable for embezzlement, not larceny, so A cannot be the best response.

(C) is not the best response,
because an element of larceny by trick is not satisfied under these facts. Larceny by trick is essentially larceny, but instead of a physical taking of property, the taking occurs through fraud. (As an example, say Red Riding Hood gives Big Bad Wolf $50 upon his promise to buy groceries for her grandmother. If Wolf absconds

with the cash, he'll be liable for larceny by trick.) Under these facts, Defendant is liable for embezzlement, not larceny by trick. The difference between the two is that, in larceny by trick, the wrongdoer obtains possession, but not title; in embezzlement, the wrongdoer already has lawful possession, but he obtains title to the property by converting or appropriating it. That's what happened here. There's nothing fraudulent about the way Defendant obtained possession – Johnson pawned it. What creates liability instead is that Defendant wrongfully converted the ring by selling it when he wasn't authorized to do so. Say that the facts were different, and the Defendant *had* obtained the ring by false pretenses. Would his paying Johnson the $125 exonerate him? No – as with embezzlement, the intent to restore (or replace) the goods is *not* a good defense, since there's no requirement that the property be *stolen.* In any case, the intent would be applied to the time when the taking took place – not what happened subsequently. Since these facts represent embezzlement, C cannot be the best response.

(D) is not the best response,
because it fails to realize that Defendant will be guilty of embezzlement. If you chose this response, it's probably because you thought that Defendant turning over the proceeds of the sale would exonerate him. It doesn't, because the intent to restore equivalent property is not a defense to embezzlement. Embezzlement requires only a fraudulent conversion of property by one with lawful possession of the property. Since these elements are satisfied here, Defendant will be guilty of embezzlement. Since D fails to recognize this, it's not the best response.

Answer 19

(C) is the best response,
because it introduces the strongest subjective element into the definition of criminal negligence.

The key here is that the question is asking *the most favorable definition for the Defendant,* not the most reasonable definition. The way to determine this is to identify the response which creates the most difficult standard to meet, since that's the definition under which Defendant will most likely be exonerated. To do *that,* you should identify the standard which has the *strongest subjective element* – and that's option C.

By stating that criminal negligence requires the defendant to intentionally do something he shouldn't have done or intentionally fail to do something he should have done, indicating a conscious disregard of a known danger, option C makes it unlikely that Defendant will be convicted – since while his behavior was probably negligent from an objective viewpoint, he probably did not consciously disregard a known danger. While it may seem strange to have a strong subjective element in negligence, since negligence in tort is judged purely objectively, a few states use a subjective standard in determining criminal negligence, so it's not unheard of. Since C identifies the negligence standard that will be most difficult to meet, of these four options, it's the best definition for Defendant, and thus the best response.

(A) is not the best response,
because it does not offer a definition that's particularly helpful to the Defendant. By merely stating that criminal negligence is something more than slight negligence, Defendant is left open to liability, because he clearly disregarded the consequences of his act – not watching where he was going – and displayed indifference to the rights of others. Since Defendant would likely be guilty under the definition given in option A, it's not the definition most favorable to him, and as a result A is not the best response.

(B) is not the best response,
because it is not favorable to Defendant. The failure to respond to surrounding circumstances would cook Defendant's goose, because that's what he did – he failed to respond to the stop light. Furthermore, the concept of reckless disregard has both an objective and a subjective element: objectively, the individual must have undertaken an unjustifiable risk, and subjectively, he must have consciously disregarded the risk. Ideally, a definition favorable to Defendant would have as strong a subjective element as possible, because he clearly did not intend to run over the pedestrian. Since there is an option which has a stronger subjective element to its definition than option B, B is not the best response.

(D) is not the best response,
because it offers a definition under which Defendant would likely be found guilty. A definition favorable to Defendant would provide as strict a definition as possible of criminal negligence. By characterizing criminal negligence as something more than slight negligence in tort, but less than wanton misconduct, option D virtually invites a guilty verdict – since Defendant's conduct in ignoring a stop light and killing a pedestrian on a crosswalk could easily be characterized as gross negligence. The best thing for Defendant is to offer a definition which includes as strong a subjective element as possible, since Defendant clearly did not intend to kill the pedestrian. Since D does not offer a strong definition with Defendant's interests in mind, it's not the best response.

Answer 20

(C) is the best response,
because both credible and it serves Defendant's cause. What Defendant wants to do is minimize the importance the jury attaches to the expert testimony, since the expert testimony would tend to establish that Defendant was driving drunk, which the jury could interpret as a wanton and reckless disregard for the safety of others, or alternatively criminal negligence, and convict Defendant on that basis. Option C indicates the best way to achieve this goal, of these four options – to suggest that the blood test only be a factor in the jury determining whether Defendant was actually under the influence. Since Defendant is an alcoholic, the 0.11 reading on him may not, in fact, have as much of an influence on his coordination and perception as a person not addicted to alcohol. Option C offers an argument that is rationally based on the facts in the problem, while at the same time it helps Defendant's case. The other options are not as satisfactory because they either fail to help Defendant significantly, or they are not legally sound. As a result, C is the best response.

(A) is not the best response,
because it ignores the central issue in the question: How to minimize the effect of the expert testimony on the jury, while still offering a credible argument. Furthermore, if Defendant admits to driving under the influence of alcohol, that act *itself* could be considered criminal negligence, and probably recklessness, thus encouraging the jury to find Defendant guilty. Criminal negligence in most jurisdictions is an objective standard under which defendant will be liable for taking an action which creates an unreasonable risk of harm, in a grossly negligent fashion. Even though option A suggests that Defendant cannot be found guilty unless he was criminally negligent, admitting to being under the influence would encourage the jury to find criminal negligence on that fact alone. Since A does not provide an appropriate argument to the jury on Defendant's behalf, it's not the best response.

(B) is not the best response,
because it's a misstatement of the law. Expert testimony is appropriate whenever specialized knowledge will assist the trier of fact to understand the evidence or to determine a fact in issue. FRE 702. In fact, this is almost the opposite of what option B suggests, because if there were a statutory standard for interpreting blood tests, expert testimony would be *less* necessary than it is. What Defendant should, in fact, do, is minimize the importance the jury will attach to the expert testimony. Since B does not address this, it's not the best response.

(D) is not the best response,
because it offers an argument that does not apply to these facts, even though it is theoretically correct. Crimes that punish status (instead of acts or omissions) are considered unconstitutional as a violation of due process, and the prohibition of cruel and unusual punishment under the Eighth Amendment. The fallacy to this argument on these facts is that a state *can* outlaw an *act* as a result of the addiction, e.g., driving drunk, or possessing narcotics. What Defendant is

being tried for under these facts isn't *being* drunk, but *driving* drunk. Since option D does not address this, it's not the best response.

Answer 21

(C) is the best response,

because it negates an element of attempted rape. Note the way this question is worded: The attempted rape charge can *only be sustained if...* That means that, if the facts the correct option gives are *removed,* then Duke *could not* be convicted. Thus, the way to analyze questions like this is actually to analyze the facts in light of removing what the option states, and seeing if the defendant could still be convicted. If (s)he *could,* then the option is not the best response.

Attempted rape requires proof that Defendant attempted unlawful intercourse, with one other than his wife, without the victim's consent. Here, if Linda did not resist, coupled with the facts given in the problem, consent would be a valid defense. The thing that makes this problem tricky is that Linda is fifteen; however, this question focuses on the *attempted rape* charge, not the attempted *statutory* rape charge. For statutory rape, *consent is no defense.* The question here involves a charge for which consent *could be* a valid defense. Since the facts C gives would exonerate Duke, it's the best response.

(A) is not the best response,

because Duke could be convicted of both attempted rape and at least one of the other charges. If A were a lesser included offense of the other charges, or vice versa, that would preclude conviction of both or all of the charges involved. A lesser included offense is one which requires proof of some, but not all, of the elements of another offense, based on the same conduct. At least one of the other offenses – contributing to the delinquency of a minor – could involve different elements than attempted rape, even if it involved the same conduct. Since A states otherwise, it's not the best response.

(B) is not the best response,

because it does not state the only way Duke could be convicted of attempted rape. In order to be convicted of attempted rape, all the state must show is that Duke attempted to have unlawful intercourse, with one other than his wife, without the victim's consent. It's possible to be convicted of attempted rape of someone under the age of consent (however, when the female is under the age of consent, the defendant can also be charged with statutory rape. When one is charged with statutory rape, his knowledge of the female's being under age is irrelevant). Since B does not state a condition necessary to convicting Duke of attempted rape, it's not the best response.

(D) is not the best response,

because Duke could be convicted of attempted rape even if evidence of his flight is admitted. Attempted rape requires proof of attempted unlawful intercourse, with one other than the defendant's wife, without the victim's consent. An attempt to commit a crime requires that one have the intent to commit a crime, along with an overt act done in furtherance of the intent, beyond mere preparation. An abandonment is only a valid defense to attempt when it is completely voluntary, and not made due to problems in completing the crime or the risk of getting caught, and it represents a full renunciation of the criminal purpose. Under these facts, it's clear that Duke would be liable for attempt, and that his flight would not exonerate him – since he'd already done everything necessary for attempted rape, and his flight took place too late. Since D states an element which would not stop Duke from being convicted of attempted rape, it's not the best response.

Answer 22

(A) is the best response,

because the crime of larceny was complete when Joe picked up the watch with an intent to steal it.

Larceny is the: (1) taking, and (2) carrying away, (3) of the tangible property, (4) of another, (5) by trespass or without consent, (6) with the intent to permanently deprive the person of his interest in property.

Under these facts Joe met all the requirements of the crime of larceny as soon as he picked up the watch. The only one of the above requirements that could possibly be in doubt as of that moment was whether Joe satisfied the "carrying away" requirement. However, courts hold that even a small movement of the entire object will suffice. So the fact that Joe "picked up" the watch was enough.

Once he picked the watch up with intent to permanently deprive Marty of it, the crime was complete. Nothing that Marty did after that — including giving title to Joe — could undo the fact of the completed crime.

(B) is not the best response,

because Joe completed the crime of larceny when he picked up the watch.

Criminal attempt is an act that although done with the intent of committing a crime falls short of completing the crime. Since according to the analysis in Choice (A) above the crime was complete as soon as Joe picked up the watch, there has been actual larceny, not just attempted larceny.

(C) is not the best response,

because Joe was never in lawful possession of the watch.

Embezzlement is the: (1) fraudulent, (2) conversion, (3) of property, (4) of another, (5) by a person in lawful possession of that property. So at the moment of the fraudulent conversion, defendant must have been already in lawful possession of the property.

That wasn't the case here — at the moment Joe picked up the watch (the moment when he arguably "converted" it), he was not already in lawful possession. That's because as of that moment, Marty hadn't yet relinquished possession to Joe — he had merely left the watch on the blanket, intending to reserve possession to himself.

(D) is not the best response,

because Joe committed larceny, as described in the analysis of Choice (A) above.

Answer 23

(D) is the best response,

because Grace knowingly directed Roy to steal the television set.

Larceny is the: (1) taking, and (2) carrying away, of the (3) tangible property, (4) of another, (5) by trespass or without consent, (6) with the intent to permanently deprive the person of his interest in property.

Anyone who intentionally acts through an innocent agent is classified as a principal.

Grace is guilty of larceny, even though she herself did not take television set. She knowingly created a mistake of fact in the mind of Roy, and intentionally induced him to commit acts satisfying the first five elements of the crime of larceny. Since Roy was an innocent agent who acted at the behest of Grace, Roy's acts will be ascribed to Grace as if she had done them herself. Grace herself satisfies the sixth requirement (intent to permanently deprive the owner). Therefore, Grace is guilty of larceny.

(A) is not the best response,

because as an innocent agent of Grace's, Roy's actions are imputed to Grace.

It's true that Roy did not commit any crime. But as an innocent agent, his acts are ascribed to the principal. Therefore, his own innocence is irrelevant to whether Grace is guilty. See the analysis in Choice (D) above.

(B) is not the best response,

because her innocent agent acquired possession.

When a person intentionally causes an innocent agent to perform an act, the agent's act is attributed to the principal. So once Roy took and carried away possession of the set, this act is ascribed to Grace as if she had done it herself. Therefore, it's not accurate to say, as this choice does, that Grace "never acquired possession."

(C) is not the best response,

because Roy was not guilty of larceny, and Grace is a principal, not an accessory.

A principal is one who with the requisite mental state, actually engages in the act or omission that causes the criminal result. An accessory is one who aids or coun-

sels a principal in the completion of a crime. If Roy had been a principal, then Grace would probably have been an accessory.

In this case, however, Grace is not guilty as an accessory, because she was the principal. Roy acted without criminal intent after being misled by Grace. Therefore (as explained more fully in the analysis of Choice (D) above), Roy was an innocent agent and Grace a principal in this crime.

Answer 24

(B) is the best response,

because it's *possible* that it will exonerate Brown (depending on how the jurisdiction interprets M'Naghten), and it's provable on these facts.

Here, it's key to appreciate what the "best" defense will be: It must be the one that correctly states the M'Naghten Rule AND is the most easily provable on the facts given. Thus, your first step is to recall the M'Naghten Rule, and analyze each option under it.

Under M'Naghten, a person is legally insane if, at the time of committing the crime, he was acting under a defect of reason, caused by a disease of the mind, such that he *either* 1/ was unable to understand the nature and quality of his actions, OR 2/ if he *did* know the nature and quality, he was unable to know that what he was doing was wrong. The "wrong" referred to here is interpreted by most courts to refer to *legally* wrong, not *morally* wrong. However, some courts *do* hold that the inability to know one's act was *morally* wrong is enough to declare one insane. Under the facts in this question, you aren't told which of these two interpretations the jurisdiction follows – "legal" wrong or "moral" wrong. Since there's a chance it could follow the "moral" wrong option, Brown *could* be exonerated due to insanity; it's clear that he cannot appreciate the moral wrongness of his action even though he fully realizes it's legally wrong. Since there's a possibility option B could exonerate Brown, and the other three options do not offer strong defenses, B is the best response.

(A) is not the best response,

because although, if it were true, it would exonerate Brown under the M'Naghten Rule, it does not apply to these facts. Under M'Naghten, a person is legally insane if, at the time of committing the crime, he was acting under a defect of reason, caused by a disease of the mind, such that he *either* 1/ was unable to understand the nature and quality of his actions, OR 2/ if he *did* know the nature and quality, he was not able to know that what he was doing was wrong. Option A, in using the term "nature," is referring to the "nature and quality" part of M'Naghten; thus, option A is *theoretically* correct in stating that the inability to know the nature of the act performed would exonerate Brown. However, this refers to the inability to understand the physical consequences of his act – for instance, a man hitting his wife in the head with a baseball bat, believing her head is a baseball. This is clearly not applicable to these facts, because Brown knows that shooting the bishop is likely to kill him. Thus, Brown *does* appreciate the nature and quality of his act, and the statement in option A cannot exonerate him. As a result, A is not the best response.

(C) is not the best response,
because although, if it were true, it would exonerate Brown under the M'Naghten Rule, it does *not* apply to these facts. Option C is essentially a restatement of option A, and is incorrect on the same grounds. Under M'Naghten, a person is legally insane if, at the time of committing the crime, he was acting under a defect of reason, caused by a disease of the mind, such that he *either* 1/ was unable to understand the nature and quality of his actions, OR 2/ if he *did* know the nature and quality, he was not able to know that what he was doing was wrong. Option C, in using the term "quality," is referring to the "nature and quality" part of M'Naghten; thus, Option C is *theoretically* correct in stating that the inability to understand the physical consequences of his act – for instance, a man squeezing the neck of a woman believing she's a lemon. This is clearly not applicable to these facts, because Brown knows that shooting the bishop is likely to kill him, appreciating the physical consequences of his act. Thus, Brown *does* appreciate the nature and quality of his act, and the statement in option C cannot exonerate him. As a result, C is not the best response.

(D) is not the best response,
because it is not a correct statement of the M'Naghten Rule – thus, even if Brown's acts *were* the product of a mental disease, as option D states, Brown would not be exonerated under M'Naghten. The rule D states is the Durham Rule, which is followed by a small minority of jurisdictions. M'Naghten, which is followed by the jurisdiction in the question here, states that a person is legally insane if, at the time of committing the crime, he was acting under a defect of reason, caused by a disease of the mind, such that he *either* 1/ was unable to understand the nature and quality of his actions, OR 2/ if he *did* know the nature and quality, he was unable to know that what he was doing was wrong. Thus, even if Brown's acts were the product of a mental disease, he wouldn't be exonerated unless he *also* satisfied the "nature and quality" or "knowledge of wrong" element of M'Naghten. Even though option D is amenable to the facts here, since it will not exonerate Brown, it's not his strongest argument. Thus, D is not the best response.

Answer 25

(B) is the best response,
because as a member of a protected class, Emma could not conspire to commit statutory rape.

Members of a protected class cannot be members of a conspiracy to commit the crime that is designed to protect that class of people. At common law (as the facts specify to be the relevant law of conspiracy) if only two people are involved, the person who is not in the protected class cannot be guilty of criminal conspiracy on the basis of an agreement with a member in the protected class.

Emma, as a 14-year-old, was part of the class the statute was designed to protect, and so could not be a member to a conspiracy to commit the crime. Because, under these facts, there are only two parties involved and one could not be a party to a conspiracy, Kenneth could not be guilty of conspiracy either, under the common-law approach.

(A) is not the best response,
because as a member of a protected class, Emma could not conspire to commit statutory rape.

As described in the analysis of (B) above, where two people are charged with common-law conspiracy and one is not guilty because she is a member of the protected class, the other cannot be guilty either.

(C) is not the best response,
because Wharton's Rule does not apply to offenses that can possibly be committed by a single person.

Wharton's Rule says that where an offense is defined so as to necessarily require the guilty participation of more than one person, and no more than the logically-minimum number of participants are involved, a charge of conspiracy to commit that offense cannot be brought, because every substantive violation would logically include a conspiracy. (Example: Adultery).

However, statutory rape is *not* an offense so defined that more than one person's knowing and guilty participation is required. It's true that two people must be "involved," but by definition one of those two is a minor who cannot give consent. In other words, the over-age person can be (and usually is) the only person guilty of the substantive crime of statutory rape. Therefore, the crime is not the type of "two or more participants logically required" crime to which Wharton's Rule applies.

(D) is not the best response,
because the answer incorrectly states the law.

Conspiracy is an agreement between two or more persons to accomplish some criminal or unlawful purpose.

Kenneth's conviction should be reversed, but not for the reason given, which is a misstatement of the law. One *can* conspire with someone too young to consent, provided the person below the age of consent meets the mental requirements for the substantive crime that is the object of the conspiracy. For instance, Kenneth could conspire with Emma to commit robbery or some other crime. What Kenneth could not do is conspire with Emma to commit statutory rape, because Emma is a member of the class the law is intended to protect (as described in the analysis of Choice (B)).

Answer 26

(B) is the best response,

because Defendant satisfies all the elements of larceny by trick.

The question asks the option where Defendant is *most likely* to be convicted. This means in one option Defendant *will* be guilty, and in the other three he *won't*. So you had to determine the elements in each option, and apply them mechanically, to arrive at the best response.

Larceny by trick is different from larceny in the way that the property is acquired; larceny by trick involves a fraudulent taking, which negates the owner's apparent consent. Every other element is the same: The carrying away of another's personal property, with intent to steal it. Under the facts here, these elements are satisfied: Defendant obtains possession by misrepresenting his intent to return the car. The wrinkle here is that, after taking the car, Defendant decides to return it after all. However, Defendant's subsequent actions are not relevant to his guilt – once he has fulfilled all the requirements of larceny by trick, his subsequent repentance cannot exonerate him. Thus, Defendant is likely to be guilty, making B the best response.

(A) is not the best response,

because one of the elements of larceny – the intent to steal – is not satisfied, so Defendant cannot be convicted. Larceny requires the trespassory taking and carrying away of personal property of another with intent to steal it. Here, Defendant does not intend to steal the car – instead, he intends to borrow it and return it after driving it only six miles in total. Although every other element of larceny is satisfied, with the intent to steal element missing, Defendant will be acquitted. Since the question asks which option states facts under which Defendant will most likely be convicted, A cannot be the best response.

(C) is not the best response,

because Defendant is not likely to be convicted of false pretenses. False pretenses requires a misrepresentation of a material fact, which prompts the victim to pass title to his property to the defendant, who knows the misrepresentation is false and intends to defraud the victim. There is one element missing here: The victim here did not pass *title* to the car, only possession for the evening. Say that the facts were different, and Defendant got Owner to give him the car by falsely convicting Owner that transferring title will result in a tax benefit to Owner. That *would* be false pretenses, because there *title* was involved, not just *possession*. Under the facts in option C, Defendant's lie prompts Owner to surrender possession of the car for an evening, not title. While Defendant's lie about having a

driver's license prompted Owner to give up his car for an evening, it didn't make him surrender title. As a result, Defendant can't be convicted of false pretenses, making C not the best response.

(D) is not the best response,

because the act of interference with the rights of the owner was not serious enough to be considered a conversion. Embezzlement occurs when someone misappropriates property of which he has lawful possession. It requires conversion of the property. Conversion is a *serious* act of interference with the rights of the owner. Say the facts in the problem were different, so that Defendant used Owner's car as collateral for a bank loan, and returned it. This would be an interference significant enough to be grounds for embezzlement. However, under the facts here, Defendant only kept the car a few hours longer than Owner intended him to have it. This is not serious enough to constitute conversion, and thus Defendant cannot be guilty of embezzlement. Since the question here asks for the option under which Defendant is most likely to be convicted, D cannot be the best response.

Answer 27

(D) is the best response,

because it cites the central reason Walters will be acquitted, and arrives at the correct result: Not guilty. This requires a mechanical application of the statute in the question. The statute requires that one *knowingly* make a false statement while under oath. Mistake is a valid defense where it negates an element of the crime. That's the case here. The lawyer's erroneous advice *itself* is not a defense, but rather it contributed to Walters' *lack of knowledge* that he was lying on the witness stand, which *is* a defense. Since D correctly identifies that Walters will not be guilty because he lacked the requisite mental state, it's the best response.

(A) is not the best response,

because "mistake of law" is not applicable to these facts, and, in any case, Walters is not guilty. Defendant makes a mistake of law when he either believes his acts are not proscribed, or he is simply unaware of the law proscribing his behavior. A mistake of law does *not* exonerate defendant. Mistake of law arises only when the defendant's behavior fits the crime. Here, Walters will be exonerated because his act simply does not meet the statutory definition of perjury – he didn't *knowingly* make a false statement under oath, because he didn't know he'd been convicted of a crime. Since A mistakenly applies "mistake of law" to these facts, and erroneously finds Walters guilty, it's not the best response.

(B) is not the best response,

because although it states a correct rule of law, it does not apply to these facts, and it arrives at the wrong conclusion. It is true that reliance on erroneous advice from a lawyer is no defense. However, that's not applicable to these facts, because what exonerates Walters is the fact that he does not satisfy all the elements of the crime of perjury: he didn't *knowingly* make a false statement under oath. The issue of whether he has a valid defense due to mistake would only come into play if he *satisfied* all the elements of perjury, and needed a way out. The key is that the erroneous legal advice here is what *created* Walters' mistaken belief – but it's not the legal advice that's central to Walters' innocence but rather the fact that he lacks the mental element the crime requires. Since B states a rule that does not apply to these facts, and arrives at the wrong conclusion, it's not the best response.

(C) is not the best defense,

because reasonable reliance on the erroneous advice will not exonerate Walters. The actual rule is that reliance on erroneous advice of a lawyer is no defense, no matter how reasonable the reliance is. The key to Walters' innocence is that he lacked the requisite mental state – knowledge. Thus, the jury will find him not guilty if he lacked the requisite mental state, *regardless* of how that mental state came about. For instance, his reliance could have been *unreasonable,* and the fact would still remain that he did not knowingly make a false statement under oath. Since C focuses on an element that will not exonerate Walters and mistakenly says that it *will*, it's not the best response.

Answer 28

(B) is the best response,

because it represents the facts here under which Defendant is most likely to be guilty of murder.

The key here is realizing that common-law murder does not require *intent.* Murder is an unlawful killing with malice aforethought. Malice is satisfied by either intent to kill or do serious bodily injury, depraved heart, or felony murder. The most applicable category here is felony murder. Felony murder is a killing committed during the course of a "dangerous" felony (or an attempt), even though there is *no intent* to kill or cause serious bodily harm. That's exactly the case here. Armed robbery is a classic dangerous felony. The facts explicitly state that Defendant killed Johnson "while committing a robbery." Even though the killing was accidental, felony murder does not require intent, so this fact will not exonerate Defendant. Since Defendant satisfies the elements of felony murder, B is the best response.

(A) is not the best response,

because Defendant would most likely be liable for manslaughter, not murder. While Defendant is unlikely to be exonerated from *any* liability, he'd likely be liable only for manslaughter, not murder, under the imperfect self-defense doctrine. Under that doctrine, Defendant

will be liable for manslaughter instead of murder, when he intentionally kills another, if either: 1/ He was the aggressor in a fight (and therefore not entitled to a self-defense claim), or 2/ Defendant honestly but unreasonably believed deadly force was necessary. While the facts in Option A don't tell who started the fight or if the belief was reasonable, the facts do indicate that at most Defendant will likely be liable only for manslaughter. Since the question is looking for the option most likely representing common-law murder, Option A is not the best response.

(C) is not the best response,

because Defendant would be unlikely to be liable for common-law murder. Common-law murder is an unlawful killing with malice aforethought. While "malice" can be satisfied by depraved heart murder, "depraved heart" occurs when the defendant engages in extremely negligent conduct, which a reasonable man would realize creates a very high degree of risk to human life, and which results in death. While Defendant's action in option C was negligent, it is unlikely to be considered serious enough to satisfy depraved heart murder. After all, he was in the woods, hunting deer. Were there other facts – for instance, the woods were crawling with hunters – the result might be different. As the facts are, Defendant's negligence simply would not rise to the level of depraved heart murder, but would likely be criminal negligence manslaughter. Also, Defendant did not intend to kill Griggs and was not committing a felony, so his conduct does not satisfy other types of malice, and he cannot be guilty of common law murder. As a result, C is not the best response.

(D) is not the best response,

because Defendant's act is not serious enough to characterize as common law murder. Murder is an unlawful killing with malice aforethought. Malice can be intent to kill or do serious bodily injury, depraved heart, or felony murder. There are two facts of particular note here: First, the city ordinance; and second, the culpability of Defendant regardless of the ordinance. The ordinance gives rise to the issue of felony murder. However, violation of a city ordinance is typically a misdemeanor, not a felony, so felony murder could not apply. Analyzing Defendant's act without the ordinance requires focusing on depraved heart murder, since there's clearly no intent here. "Depraved heart" exists when the Defendant engages in extremely negligent conduct, which a reasonable man would realize creates a very high degree of risk to human life, and which results in death. Here, Defendant was aiming at the street, the bullet bounced up and killed Abbott. While this was undoubtedly negligent, without more facts it would be difficult to say that it was *extremely* negligent. For instance, if Abbott were part of a crowd, it *would* be; if he were alone, and the angle of the ricochet were unusual, it would be closer to a "freak" accident. As it stands, there are insufficient facts to conclude that Defendant would likely be guilty of murder. Rather, he'd most likely satisfy criminal-negligence manslaughter or misdemeanor manslaughter. Since he won't likely be guilty of murder, D isn't the best response.

Answer 29

(A) is the best response,

because Dirk can be found guilty of all three crimes.

Let's take the crimes one at a time.

First, let's look at burglary. Burglary is: (1) the breaking, (2) and entering, (3) of the dwelling, (4) of another, (5) at night time, (6) with the intent to commit a felony within.

Dirk's actions satisfy all the requirements for burglary. Requirements (1) and (6) are the only ones that are even worth discussing here. As to (1) (breaking), courts recognize "constructive breaking" — if D uses fraud or threat of force to induce the occupants to let him in, that counts as breaking. That's what happened here.

As to (6) (intent to commit a felony within), where D commits a felony once inside the premises, courts will in the absence of other evidence presume that D had the intent to commit that felony at the time of entry. So here, Dirk would readily be found to have intended, at the time he entered, to commit the felony of robbery once he was inside. Thus the requisite intent-to-commit-a-felony-within is satisfied.

Next, let's examine robbery. Robbery is: (1) a taking, (2) of the personal property of another, (3) from the other's person or presence, (4) by force or intimidation, (5) with the intent to permanently deprive. Here, the only interesting question is whether taking the property from the safe (rather than directly from the person) of the victim meets requirement (3). But the taking will suffice if it's from the "person or presence" of the owner, and the safe would be found to have been within John and Marsha's presence at the time Dirk took the necklace.

Finally, let's look at murder. There are of course multiple types — ways of committing — murder. Here, the relevant type of murder is felony murder. Felony murder is a killing, even an accidental one, committed during the commission of a dangerous felony.

Dirk's actions satisfy the requirements of felony murder. Dirk was committing robbery, and robbery is one of the "dangerous" felonies recognized at common law as a predicate-crime for felony-murder. The interesting question is whether the fact that Dirk was arrested before John had his heart attack prevents John's death from being "during the commission of" the robbery. Notice that John's death was very closely causally related to the robbery — John had his heart attack because he was trying to free himself from his bonds and gag, and he was bound and gagged because, and solely because, Dirk wanted to commit, and escape

from, the robbery. Where there is a close causal relationship between the underlying felony (or the attempt to escape from it) and the death, the requirement of a death "during the commission of" the felony is generally deemed satisfied, even if the death doesn't come until after the felony-and-escape period is in some sense over.

(B), (C) and (D) are not the best response,

because each fails to cover at least one of the three crimes that in fact was committed, as described in Choice (A).

Answer 30

(A) is the best response,

because the facts of the case make proximate cause the best defense.

Manslaughter is death caused by criminal negligence. Proximate cause is that which in a natural and continuous sequence, unbroken by any intervening cause, produces injury and without which the injury would not have occurred.

Martha can plausibly try to show at trial that the teacher was depressed about other things as well, not just the lack of work, so that the firing was not sufficiently closely causally related to the death to meet the requirement of proximate cause. And, Martha can argue that a death by suicide is not a "natural and probable consequence" of being fired or falsely accused, which is the standard for proximate cause in many jurisdictions.

Finally, the relatively long time period — about a year — between false accusation and death tends to weaken the causal connection. Indeed, notice that the facts say that the suicide occurred "a year later." If there was slightly *more* than a year between false accusation and death, then the common-law "year and a day" rule — by which a death happening more than a year and a day after the actus reus would be conclusively deemed not to be the proximate result of the act — might apply. (Some jurisdictions apply this rule to manslaughter cases, not just murders.)

There is no guarantee that this proximate-cause defense will work — indeed, perhaps it's not even "more likely than not" to work. But of the four choices, it's the only one that has a plausible chance. (For why each of the others won't work, read the discussions of those choices below.)

(B) is not the best response,

because Martha's actual intent would not be an issue in an involuntary manslaughter case.

The prosecution here would have to be for involuntary manslaughter, not voluntary manslaughter. Involuntary manslaughter is generally defined as death caused by gross criminal negligence (or, sometimes, "recklessness").

The fact that Martha did not intend to cause the

teacher's death could not possibly be a defense here, because Martha's subjective intent would not be the issue where the question is whether she acted with gross negligence or recklessness about the risk of death. Instead, the issue is whether a reasonable person in Martha's position would have known that a false accusation like the one she made posed a great risk of the teacher's eventual suicide. (Indeed, intent-to-cause-death is almost *never* present in successful prosecutions for involuntary manslaughter, because if it were present, the case would be a murder prosecution instead.)

(C) is not the best response,

because malice is relevant to the wrong state of mind.

As described in Choice (B) above, the relevant mental state in this involuntary manslaughter prosecution is gross negligence or recklessness. The fact that Martha lacked "malice" is not relevant at all. (It's relevant to some types of murder, as in the phrase "with malice aforethought," used to describe the mental state for garden-variety intent-to-kill murder.)

(D) is not the best response,

because her emotional distress would be relevant to sentencing, but not to whether she is guilty of the substantive crime.

"Extreme emotional distress" is not generally a substantive defense to crime. Instead, it can be a mitigating factor at sentencing. Even if extreme distress *were* in theory a defense, it would not apply here, where making a false sexual-misconduct accusation would hardly be an excusable response to being upset about a failing grade.

Answer 31

(D) is the best response,

because Albert did not have the intent to sell cocaine, while Beth did.

The prosecution of Beth poses the classic question of whether "factual impossibility" can be a defense. Factual impossibility is not a defense. That is, impossibility is no defense to an attempt prosecution in those cases where, had the facts been as D believed them to be, D would have had the mental state required for the substantive crime. Here, had the facts been as Beth believed (that the vials contained cocaine), Beth would have had the mental state required for sale of cocaine. Therefore, she had the mental state for attempt. And, since she carried out the physical act of selling the substance, she meets the actus reus requirement for attempted drug sale as well.

On the other hand, Albert does not have the mental state required for attempted sale of cocaine. The mens rea for an attempt to commit substantive crime X is the desire to commit acts which, if they were committed, would constitute the commission of crime X. Therefore, the mens rea for an attempt to sell drugs is the intent to

sell drugs. Since Albert didn't intent to sell drugs, he can't be liable for attempted sale of drugs.

(A), (B) and (C) are not the best response,

because each is inconsistent with the analysis in (D) above.

Answer 32

(D) is the best response,

because Sally acted with a reckless indifference and because Ralph was her accomplice.

Let's first discuss Sally's guilt. The mental state for murder, in a jurisdiction that has abolished the felony-murder rule, is any of the following: (1) intent to kill; (2) intent to inflict great bodily harm; or a (3) reckless indifference to an unjustifiably high risk to human life.

Here, a court would probably (though not certainly) hold that a person who (1) brings automatic weapons with her to a bank robbery; and then (2) fires those weapons into the ceiling, with lots of people around, meets the standard for "reckless indifference to an unjustifiably high risk to life." Bear in mind that (1) Sally's conduct is of as little redeeming social utility as it can be (so that a lower degree of risk to others should suffice for "reckless indifference" than if Sally were pursuing some socially-worthwhile goal, e.g., speeding to the hospital with her deathly ill child); and (2) any reasonable person ought to know of the large danger of ricocheting bullets, especially where the bullets are fired in a bank containing stone columns and lots of people. Since Sally has proximately caused a death, while satisfying one of the mental-state requirements for common-law murder, she's guilty of murder.

Now, on to Ralph. A person who intentionally aids, abets or encourages another to commit substantive crime X is himself guilty of substantive crime X as an accomplice. The accomplice needs, however, to have the (or a) mental state required for crime X. So here, the question is whether Ralph can be guilty of murder as an accomplice to Betty's commission of murder.

If a court is willing to find that Betty had the "reckless indifference" mental state that will suffice for murder, the court will probably also find that Ralph had that mental state. (This is not certain — Ralph might have strongly believed that neither he nor Sally would fire the weapons, in which case it wouldn't be logically inconsistent for the court to conclude that Sally, by not only carrying but firing her automatic weapon, met the reckless-indifference standard, but that Ralph didn't. *Probably*, however, the court would conclude that one who carries automatic weapons into a bank robbery, and who accompanies a co-felon who he knows is also carrying such weapons, has behaved with the requisite reckless indifference to the great danger of death from the joint conduct. In that event Ralph would be found to meet the reckless-indifference standard.)

There is the further question of whether Ralph meets the actus reus requirement for reckless-indifference murder. Ralph has clearly given knowing assistance to Betty's commission of this recklessly-dangerous armed bank robbery. Therefore, his assistance to her, in what we've concluded is murder by her, will also be deemed to be the actus reus for accomplice liability in that murder by her. Since he's satisfied both the mental-state requirement for reckless-indifference murder and the actus-reus requirement for reckless-indifference murder (knowing assistance to a person who herself commits reckless-indifference murder), Ralph is guilty of being an accomplice to the substantive crime of reckless-indifference murder. That makes him, too, guilty of the substantive crime of reckless-indifference murder. Whew!

(A), (B) and (C) are not the best response,

because each of them fails to recognize at least one defendant's guilt of murder.

Answer 33

(A) is the best response,

because Augie is guilty of common-law arson, and is guilty of felony-murder because of the arson.

Arson, as defined by the common law, is the: (1) malicious, (2) burning, (3) of the dwelling, (4) of another. Malice for arson does not require a specific intent, only that the defendant have acted with *either*: (1) the intent or knowledge that the structure would burn, or (2) the reckless disregard of an obvious risk that the structure would burn.

Under this definition, Augie is guilty. Since as noted common-law arson does not require that D had a particular desire to burn down the building, only that he acted with a reckless disregard for an obvious risk of burning, Augie's intentional driving into the pump qualifies — a court or jury would be justified in concluding that intentionally driving a car into a gas pump manifests a reckless disregard of the high risk of fire and/or explosion. Once the intent element of malice is satisfied the other elements of arson are clearly satisfied — there was a burning; the building that burned contained not only the convenience store but Homer's dwelling on the second floor; and the building was not Augie's but another's, Homer's.

Now, on to murder. Felony-murder occurs where D commits a killing — even an accidental one — which occurs during the course of, and as a result of, D's commission of any of a series of defined dangerous felonies.

Arson is one of the "dangerous felonies" for common-law felony murder. Since as described above Augie is guilty of arson, and since the death of Homer occurred during, and as the direct result of, the arson, Augie is also guilty of felony murder.

(B), (C) and (D) are not the best response,

because each choice fails to make Augie guilty of both murder and arson.

Answer 34

(D) is the best response,

because on these facts Defendant does not have the mental state for either murder or manslaughter.

Murder is the unlawful killing of another human being with malice aforethought. Malice aforethought is deemed to exist if the defendant has any of the following states of mind: (1) intent to kill; (2) intent to inflict great bodily harm; (3) a reckless indifference to an unjustifiably high risk to human life; or (4) the intent to commit a felony.

Here, since by hypothesis the jury believes that Defendant thought the gun was empty, none of the required states of mind can exist: (1) D clearly didn't intend to kill; (2) D clearly didn't intend to inflict great bodily harm; (3) D wasn't recklessly indifferent to an unjustifiably high risk to human life (since we're told the jury thinks D's mistaken belief that the gun contained blanks was "reasonable"); and (4) D didn't intend to commit any felony.

Involuntary manslaughter is death caused by gross negligence or recklessness. Since we're told to assume that the jury believes both that D thought the gun had blanks and that this belief was reasonable, D has not manifested either gross negligence nor recklessness. Therefore, she can't be guilty of involuntary manslaughter.

Nor can D be guilty of voluntary manslaughter — that crime requires an intent to kill or seriously injure, under partly extenuating circumstances (e.g., extreme provocation). Since there was no intent to kill or seriously injure, voluntary manslaughter can't exist.

(A), (B) and (C) are not the best responses,

because each of them makes Defendant guilty of either murder or manslaughter.

Answer 35

(D) is the best response,

because it most closely mirrors the facts, and offers a basis on which Dobbs could be found guilty of murder.

The key here is that Dobbs had no *intent* to kill or cause a serious injury. Note that the question asks for the *best* theory for convicting Dobbs. That means the best option will be the one that is most closely related to the facts, and legally correct. Note also that this means *one* of these options will result in Dobbs's conviction, and the other three *won't*.

Murder is an unlawful killing with malice aforethought. Malice aforethought requires either intent to kill or do serious bodily injury, felony murder, or depraved heart murder. Depraved heart murder occurs where Defendant engages in extremely negligent conduct, which a reasonable man would realize creates a very high degree of risk to human life, and which results in death. Option D, with its language "without an intent to kill but with disregard of the consequences" coupled with an act highly dangerous to life, essentially reflects this rule. The key is that D recognizes murder does *not* require *intent*. That's important here because Dobbs clearly didn't intend to kill the children, and probably didn't even know death was likely to result, so he *couldn't* be liable for any intent-related crime. Since D recognizes this, and provides a theoretical basis on which Dobbs could be convicted of murder, it's the best response.

(A) is not the best response,

because it misapplies the doctrine of transferred intent. Under transferred intent, a person intending to commit one crime accidentally commits another. His intent will be "transferred" from the person he intended to harm to the person he *actually* harmed. Say the facts here were different, and Dobbs, aiming to run over Little Penny, accidentally ran over Little Bobo instead. Under "transferred intent," his intent would be transferred from Penny to Bobo, and he'd be liable for intentional murder on that basis. What's missing under these facts is Dobbs's intent to kill in the first place – he doesn't intend to kill or even injure *anyone*. If anything, he intends for the children to run out of the way and *not* be injured. Since he has no criminal intent, it can't be transferred. Since A misapplies the doctrine of transferred intent, it can't be the best response.

(B) is not the best response,

because the felony is not sufficiently "independent" from homicide to be covered by the felony murder rule. The felony murder rule is as follows: Where a killing is committed during the course of a "dangerous" felony (or an attempt), the homicide is considered first degree murder, even though there is no intent to kill or cause great bodily harm. Such "dangerous" felonies typically include rape, kidnapping, mayhem, arson, robbery and burglary. The kind of conduct involved in an assault with a deadly weapon is the kind of personal violence that kills. In fact, assault with a deadly weapon would itself require the intent to do serious bodily harm, or to kill, so the "independence" required by the felony murder rule would be lacking. As a result, Dobbs could not be found guilty of felony murder, making B not the best response.

(C) is not the best response,

because the reasoning it states is insufficient to convict Dobbs of intentional killing. While intentional killing is sufficient for murder, intent must be one of two types: Either the actor must consciously desire a result, regardless of the likelihood his conduct will cause it; or, alternatively, he must know the result is practically certain to result from his conduct, regardless of whether he wants it to happen. Thus, under the facts in this question, Dobbs would have to want to kill the children, or know he was practically certain to kill one if he drove toward them. Thus, C is incorrect in stating that knowing they were there and deliberately driving at them

would be sufficient to convict Dobbs – in addition, he'd have to know that driving at them would result in one being killed. In fact, Dobbs believes they will run to get out of the way – he doesn't know he's practically certain to kill one. Since C does not correctly state the reasoning under which Dobbs could be found guilty of intentional killing, and in fact Dobbs wouldn't be liable for intentional killing, C is not the best response.

Answer 36

(D) is the best response,

because it most closely fits the classic attributes of a strict liability offense.

Note that the question here asks which crime is *most likely* to be found a strict liability offense. Thus, you must consider the elements of a strict liability crime, and see which option is the best fit. This requires comparing options, since all of them will have some elements of a strict liability offense.

The purpose of strict liability crimes is to help the prosecution where the mental element will be difficult to prove, or the harm caused is such that it's worth convicting people who lack "guilty minds." Strict liability crimes generally have the following attributes: (1) They are regulatory in nature; (2) They do not involve serious penalties; (3) They involve serious harm to the public; and (4) it's easy to determine true facts (e.g., for crime of selling narcotics, element of defendant's knowledge as to whether what he's selling *is* a narcotic – e.g., mistaking cocaine for powdered sugar – is easy to check, so it's appropriate for strict liability). In fact, statutes regulating food, drugs and misbranded articles, as well as hunting license requirements and the like, are all common forms of valid strict liability statutes. (Compare this with statutes imposing strict liability for failure to register as a felon, which would be a due process violation – since there would be no circumstances to "move one to inquire" as to the necessity to register.) Furthermore, making such a crime a strict liability crime would not be consistent with the purposes of strict liability: That is, to help the prosecution where the mental element will be difficult to prove, or the harm caused is such that it's worth convicting people who lack "guilty minds." D involves the sale of adulterated milk. The seriousness of the harm to the public, the fact that it's a misdemeanor instead of a felony, and the difficulty of proof of a "guilty mind" all make it a candidate for strict liability. Since D recognizes this, and none of the other options are as satisfactory, D is the best response.

(A) is not the best response,

because it's highly unlikely shoplifting would be regarded a strict liability crime, even if the statute did not specify which *mens rea* it would require. Strict liability crimes generally have the following attributes: (1) They are regulatory in nature; (2) They do not involve serious penalties; (3) They involve serious harm to the public; and (4) it's easy to determine true facts (e.g., for crime of selling narcotics, element of defendant's knowledge as to whether what he's selling *is* a narcotic – e.g., mistaking cocaine for powdered sugar – is easy to check, so it's appropriate for strict liability). Here, what would make this statute a less-than-perfect candidate for strict liability is that shoplifting is a type of larceny, and thus a court would likely imply a *mens rea* requirement – that is, the intent to steal. Furthermore, shoplifting is not regulatory in nature (e.g., firearms registration, hunting license requirements, and the like), and so is not a likely strict liability offense. Most importantly, another option – D – gives a crime which is a classic strict liability offense. As a result, A is not the best response.

(B) is not the best response,

because it's unlikely possessing heroin, as a felony, would be a strict liability crime, even if the statute did not mention a *mens rea*. Strict liability crimes generally have the following attributes: (1) They are regulatory in nature; (2) They do not involve serious penalties; (3) They involve serious harm to the public; and (4) it's easy to determine true facts (e.g., for crime of selling narcotics, element of defendant's knowledge as to whether what he's selling *is* a narcotic – e.g., mistaking cocaine for powdered sugar – is easy to check, so it's appropriate for strict liability). Here, the crime is a *felony*, so it's unlikely it would be a strict liability crime. Furthermore, making such a crime a strict liability crime would not be consistent with the purposes of strict liability: That is, to help the prosecution where the mental element will be difficult to prove, or the harm caused is such that it's worth convicting people who lack "guilty minds." A "possession" statute would be aimed at people who knowingly possess heroin. Thus, the statute in option B would be an unlikely candidate for strict liability, making B not the best response.

(C) is not the best response,

but it's close. Strict liability crimes generally have the following attributes: (1) They are regulatory in nature; (2) They do not involve serious penalties; (3) They involve serious harm to the public; and (4) it's easy to determine true facts (e.g., for crime of selling narcotics, element of defendant's knowledge as to whether what he's selling *is* a narcotic – e.g., mistaking cocaine for powdered sugar – is easy to check, so it's appropriate for strict liability). The thing that makes this option difficult is that firearms registration statutes are classic strict liability offenses. *However,* the wrinkle here is that it's a *felony* – thus, with a stiff penalty, a *mens rea* is likely to be required. Since this makes it a less-than-perfect choice for a strict liability offense, and, more importantly, there's another option that's more appropriate, C is not the best response.

Answer 37

(B) is the best response,

because it correctly identifies the key factor which will exonerate Donaldson: His mistake negates the necessary *mens rea* for burglary.

The key here is to remember the elements of burglary, the defenses that apply, and apply them strictly.Common law burglary requires the breaking and entering of the dwelling house of another, at night, with the intent to commit a felony therein. Most states broaden this to include entry at all times in all kinds of structures (thus eliminating the breaking, dwelling house, and nighttime requirements). Here, what Donaldson's mistake – believing looking at the exam questions is criminal when, in fact, it isn't – does is to negate his *mens rea*. There's no burglary when a defendant breaks and enters to commit a non-felony. The defense that covers these facts is legal impossibility – that is, what he intended to do was not criminal. Since this negates the required intent for burglary, he'll be acquitted.

What this problem points out is how important it is to remember that burglary and larceny are a kind of "inchoate" crime. That is, they are correct once defendant does something – in burglary, breaking and entering, in larceny, taking and carrying away personal property – with the *intent* to do something else – in burglary, committing a felony, and in larceny, stealing. However, the crimes are *complete* once the first act is done, *if there's the appropriate mental state* – intent. Since B correctly identifies that legal impossibility means there's no intent under these facts, it's the best response.

(A) is not the best response,

because it does not correctly apply the burglary definition to these facts. At common law, burglary requires breaking and entering the dwelling house of another, at night, with intent to commit a felony therein. Under most modern statutes, entry at all times in all kinds of structures are covered (thus eliminating the breaking, dwelling house, and nighttime requirements). Thus, the crime is *complete* once the breaking and entering with the appropriate intent has taken place. It's not necessary that the person actually *commit* the felony therein – he need only *intend* to do so. Thus, option A's language about Donaldson not completing the crime *cannot* be correct, since if he avoids liability for burglary, it cannot be on that basis. For the same reason, the statement about attempted burglary does not apply to these facts. Attempted burglary would apply under these facts, for instance, to Donaldson being caught *just before* he broke into Professor Ruiz's office (since attempt requires, at common law, proximity to the actual crime). In fact, what will exonerate Donaldson is his mistaken belief that what he intended to do – look at exam questions – was a crime. This is legal impossibility – that is, what Donaldson intended to do was not a crime – and it is a valid defense. Since A misstates the reason why Donaldson will be acquitted, it's not the best response.

(C) is not the best response,

because it does not apply to these facts, and arrives at the wrong result. If Donaldson *had* the correct mental state, his breaking and entering would make him liable for burglary. At common law, burglary requires breaking and entering the dwelling house of another, at night, with the intent to commit a felony therein (most modern statutes broaden this to include entry at all times in all kinds of structures, thus eliminating the breaking, dwelling house, and nighttime requirements). Thus, the "mental state" to which C refers is *intent*. Although it *seems* as though Donaldson had the right mental state, his mistaken belief that what he was doing was criminal, when in fact it *wasn't*, will exonerate him – since his mistake negates his intent to commit a felony. There's no burglary when Defendant breaks and enters to commit a non-felony. Since option C does not recognize the "mistake" defense, it's not the best response.

(D) is not the best response,

because it misstates the facts – what's involved here is *legal* impossibility, not *factual* impossibility. Factual impossibility occurs when completion of the crime is impossible due to physical facts not known to the defendant, e.g., a pickpocket picking an empty pocket. As D states, factual impossibility is no defense. However, what's involved here is *legal* impossibility, which arises when what defendant intends to do is not criminal. It is a valid defense, and applies to these facts. It will exonerate Donaldson because it negates the intent requirement of burglary. Common law burglary requires the breaking and entering of the dwelling house of another at night with the intent to commit a felony therein. Most states broaden burglary to cover entry at all times in all kinds of structures. Either way, without the intent to commit a felony once inside, defendant cannot be convicted. Here, the legal impossibility defense removes the intent. Since D does not apply the correct rule to these facts, and arrives at an incorrect result, it's not the best response.

Answer 38

(B) is the best response,

for three principal reasons: One, it arrives at the correct result; two, it ascribes to the jury its correct role as finder of facts; and three, it offers reasoning that would, indeed, result in a manslaughter conviction instead of murder.

This is a somewhat tricky question because it's a hybrid – you need to know the procedural rule that the jury decides issues of fact, and the judge decides issues of law.

As a general rule, if the evidence would be sufficient for conviction of a lesser offense (here, manslaughter), the issue should be submitted to the jury. By stating that whether the issue of manslaughter should go to the jury based on what the jury could find, instead of what the judge believes the evidence shows, B correctly states this rule. Furthermore, the reasoning in B correctly identifies a basis on which the jury could find Dent guilty only of manslaughter. Voluntary manslaughter is a murder committed under adequate provocation. Murder is an unlawful killing committed with malice aforethought. Thus, if the jury finds that an act by the other customer sufficiently provoked Dent, it will find him guilty of voluntary manslaughter instead of murder. Being hit in the face with an umbrella is just the sort of thing that *could* be considered provocation sufficient to reduce Dent's liability to manslaughter. A wrinkle in this problem is that Dent, in a way, provoked the provocation by stealing the tip. That's not relevant for Dent's liability in *this* question (whereas it would be relevant to the customer's liability in attacking Dent, since she would have a crime prevention argument). Since B correctly identifies the result, the jury's role, and the basis on which Dent may be liable for only manslaughter instead of murder, it's the best response.

(A) is not the best response,

because it does not apply the correct rule to voluntary manslaughter. In order to be found liable for only manslaughter instead of murder, the jury would have to find that Dent acted under provocation; that is, he committed an unlawful killing with malice aforethought, but was provoked. If you chose option A, you probably did so because you confused the rule for voluntary manslaughter with that of depraved heart murder, which is what A states. Thus, if the jury found that Dent acted recklessly and not with the intent to kill or seriously injure, it would *still* find him guilty of depraved heart murder. A does however correctly identify two things: One, that the request should be granted; and two, that granting the request should be on the basis of how the jury could find, *not* on the basis of what the evidence shows. Despite this, since A applies the wrong test to these facts, it's not the best response.

(C) is not the best response,

because it arrives at an incorrect result, and does not allow the jury to find voluntary manslaughter, which is possible from these facts. First, option C states that the request should be denied because of what the evidence shows. In fact, in its role as the finder of *facts*, the jury should have the option to find a result which is possible on these facts – voluntary manslaughter. The reason the jury *could* find this is because they *could* find adequate provocation to reduce murder to manslaughter. Thus, option C's statement that Dent intended to kill or cause serious harm doesn't go far enough, because even if he *did* act with intent, if he did so under adequate provocation he'll only be liable for voluntary manslaughter. Since C denies the jury the opportunity to make a finding which is possible under these facts, it's not the best response.

(D) is not the best response,

for three principal reasons: One, it arrives at the wrong result; two, it denies the jury its role as finder of fact; and three, it does not cite an appropriate reason as to why the request should be denied. In its role as finder of fact, if the evidence would be sufficient for conviction of a lesser offense (here, manslaughter), the issue should be submitted to the jury. Thus, the test is not what the evidence shows, but how the jury could find. D is also incorrect in the reasoning it provides, because Dent's provoking the assault on himself would *not* prevent him from being found guilty of manslaughter, but would, instead, go against a defense of self-defense under the "imperfect self-defense doctrine," a modern rule adopted by some states. Under it, when the defendant intentionally kills another, he'll be liable for manslaughter if either he was the aggressor in a fight (and therefore not entitled to a self-defense claim), *or* he honestly but unreasonably believed deadly force was necessary. The reason that the judge would deny Dent's request would be if the jury could *not* find him liable for manslaughter instead of murder. By offering reasoning that would make Dent guilty of manslaughter, D does just the opposite: Since it arrives at an incorrect result, pre-empts the jury, and employs incorrect reasoning, D is not the best response.

Answer 39

(C) is the best response,

because the answer correctly identifies the essential element of each crime under these facts.

Forgery is the: (1) fraudulent (2) making of a (3) false writing (4) having apparent legal significance.

Rachel did not commit forgery because element (4) is not satisfied — the document had no apparent legal significance. If the document had been a check, or a will, creating it with intent to defraud would have been a forgery. But since the document here merely purported to be a routine letter without legal significance, its creation cannot be forgery.

False pretenses is the: (1) obtaining of title, (2) to the property of another, (3) by an intentional false statement of existing fact, (4) with the intent to defraud the other.

Rachel meets these requirements, and is thus guilty of false pretenses. (1) She obtained title to the $5,000 fee. (2) The fee was the property of another (the collector). (3) By saying she had gotten the document from a foreign anonymous collector, she made an intentional false statement of existing fact. And (4) she intended to defraud the collector who bought from her, by inducing him to pay for something she knew was not what she caused him to believe it was. The fact that Rachel didn't make a direct claim of authenticity doesn't prevent the elements of false pretenses from being satis-

fied.

(A) is not the best response,

because while Rachel has committed false pretenses, she would not be guilty of forgery, pursuant to the reasoning above.

(B) is not the best response,

because both answers are incorrect — Rachel would not be guilty of forgery but did commit false pretenses, pursuant to the reasoning above.

(D) is not the best response,

because the second clause is wrong in that Rachel *has* committed false pretenses: She represented that she had gotten the document from a foreign collector, which was a misrepresentation of fact. (All the other elements of false pretenses are also satisfied — see the discussion of Choice (C) above.) The fact that Rachel didn't also make a misrepresentation as to authenticity is irrelevant.

Answer 40

(D) is the best response,

because it most closely applies to these facts, and it provides a valid defense to murder. Note that the question asks Dann's "best chance" of being acquitted. That means three of these options will result in a conviction, and one won't.

The most common test for insanity is the M'Naghten Rule, which requires that defendant have a diseased mind which caused a defect of reason, such that when Defendant acted he *either* didn't know his act was wrong *or* he didn't understand the nature and quality of his actions (e.g., mistaking someone's head for a baseball and hitting it with a bat). Here, it's not necessary to do a strict analysis under M'Naghten to appreciate the fact that Dann's off his rocker, and didn't know what he was doing was wrong. Since the facts indicate Dann has a promising insanity defense, and insanity is a good defense to murder, D is the best response.

(A) is not the best response,

because an intoxication defense would not exonerate Dann under a murder charge. Murder requires an unlawful killing with malice aforethought. Malice can take the form of intent to kill or inflict great bodily injury, felony murder, or "depraved heart" – acting in spite of an unjustifiably high risk to human life. Voluntary intoxication, which is involved here, is only a defense to prove a lack of capacity for specific intent crimes – it cannot be used if the *mens rea* requirement is only recklessness or negligence. Since depraved heart does not require intent, voluntary intoxication cannot be a valid defense to garden-variety murder. If you chose this response, it could be because you were thinking of *involuntary* intoxication, which could, theoretically, be a defense to a murder charge. Involuntary intoxication only applies when the defendant is misled about the nature of what he's taking, or where the defendant is physically forced to take the intoxicant – like Cary Grant in the movie *North by Northwest.* Involuntary intoxication is a valid defense if it prevents the defendant from understanding the criminal nature of his conduct. Thus, it resembles an insanity defense. Under the facts here, this *might* be a defense, although there would be a problem with causation (since Dann hallucinates *without* alcohol, as well). In any case, since the intoxication here is voluntary, and thus not be a valid defense, A is not the best response.

(B) is not the best response,
because it misstates the facts here. It's true that murder requires an unlawful killing with malice aforethought. Malice aforethought can take the form of intent to kill or do great bodily harm, felony murder, or acting in spite of an unjustifiably high risk to human life ("depraved heart"). Under these facts, the last type of malice aforethought would likely be satisfied, since it does not have, in most states, a subjective element – it's only viewed objectively. By strangling the old woman, Dan clearly acted in spite of an unjustifiably high risk to human life. As a result, a "lack of malice aforethought" defense would be unlikely to succeed, making B not the best response.

(C) is not the best response,
because self-defense would not be a valid defense to murder on these facts. Self-defense has both an objective and a subjective element: The defendant must *in fact* believe the danger exists (the subjective part), and the defendant must be *reasonable* in this belief (the objective part). Here, Dann misapprehended the danger – the old woman was only slapping him, and thus deadly force was not required. Since Dann's perception of danger was not reasonable, self-defense will not be available as a defense, and C will not be the best response.

Answer 41

(A) is the best response,
because it identifies the most serious crime, of these four, for which Daves can be convicted. Robbery is a larceny from the person accomplished with violence or intimidation. (Larceny is a trespassory taking and carrying away of personal property of another, with intent to steal it). The wrinkle here is that the victim, James, is not in fear for himself, and the violence is not directed at him. However, the rule is that the threat can be made to relatives or a companion. Since the facts here satisfy robbery, the question tells you that robbery is the most serious crime of the four options, and the question asks for the most serious crime for which Daves can be convicted, A is the best response.

(B) is not the best response,
because although Daves could be convicted of larceny, he could be convicted of a more serious crime – robbery. Larceny requires a trespassory taking and carrying away of personal property, of another, with intent to steal it. These elements are satisfied by the facts here. Specifically, it would be called "larceny from the person." However, these facts *also* indicate two *additional* elements, which raise the "larceny from the person" to robbery: the use of force or fear. What may have tricked you into choosing this response is that the force was directed at *Mary,* not the victim – James. However, the rule is that the threat can be made to relatives or a companion. Since these facts are covered by this, Daves will be guilty of robbery from James Green. Since he'll be liable for a more serious crime than larceny, and the question asks for the most serious crime for which he can be convicted, B is not the best response.

(C) is not the best response,
because Daves will be liable for robbery, a more serious crime than assault. Criminal assault can take one of two forms: either an attempt to commit a battery, or the intentional and physical creation of fear of imminent bodily harm in the mind of the victim. Under these facts, Daves would be liable for assault on Mary and James Green for the period of time when he leaped out of the dark alleyway brandishing a gun. However, he will *also* be liable for *at least* battery on Mary, and robbery from James. If you chose this response, you overlooked the robbery. Daves will be liable for robbery from James Green, because his act satisfies all the elements: A larceny from a person or a person's presence, by either force or fear. Here, the threat against Mary is sufficient for the force or fear element of robbery, since the force or fear *can* be directed at the victim's relative or companion. Since Daves satisfies the robbery elements, the question tells you that robbery is a more serious crime than assault, and the question asks for the most serious crime for which Daves can be convicted, C is not the best response.

(D) is not the best response,
because Daves will be liable for a more serious crime than assault. Criminal assault can take one of two forms: either an attempt to commit a battery, or the intentional and physical creation of fear of imminent bodily harm in the mind of the victim. Under these facts, Daves would be liable for assault on Mary for the period of time when he leaped out of the dark alleyway brandishing a gun. However, Daves will also be liable for more serious crimes, as well: Assault on *both* Mary and James Green, larceny from James Green, and robbery from James Green. Daves's act satisfies all the elements of robbery: a larceny from a person or a person's presence, by force or fear. Here, the threat against Mary is sufficient for the force or fear element, since the force or fear can be directed at the victim's

relative or companion. Since Daves satisfies the robbery elements, the question tells you robbery is a more serious crime than assault, and the question asks for the most serious crime for which Daves can be convicted, D is not the best response.

Answer 42

(C) is the best response,
because the crime of solicitation is completed with the concurrence of act and intent.

Solicitation consists of inciting, inducing, or urging another to commit a felony with the specific intent that the person solicited commit the crime. The offense is complete at the time the solicitation is made, whether the solicitee agrees or not. Therefore, Smart's effort to withdraw a few days before payment was due would not be a defense to the crime of solicitation — the crime was already completed. (Nor does it make any difference that the solicitee was only pretending to agree to commit the underlying crime.)

(A) is not the best response,
because the crime was completed as soon as Smart made his proposal to Johnson. Nothing that happened after that — including Smart's withdrawal — could undo the crime.

(B) is not the best response,
because the crime was completed once Smart made his proposal to Johnson. The fact that no "substantial act" was performed by either Smart or Johnson was irrelevant.

(D) is not the best response,
because Smart would be convicted even if Johnson had not agreed. Solicitation consists of inciting, inducing, or urging another to commit a felony with the specific intent that the person solicited commit the crime. The offense is complete at the time the inciting, inducing or urging of the other occurs. Even if the solicitee does not agree to do the requested act, the solicitor is guilty. So Choice (D), insofar as it recites Johnson's agreement as being the reason for Smart's guilt, is the wrong explanation for the correct result.

Answer 43

(D) is the best response,
because Hannah did not have the mental state for burglary or any form of assault.

Let's look first at assault. An assault is either (1) an attempt to commit a battery or (2) an intentional placing of another in apprehension of receiving an immediate battery. (Also, any completed battery contains an assault.) Since Hannah intentionally sprayed the guard with a harmful or offensive substance, she meets the prima facie requirement for type (1) assault (since she was trying to commit a battery, i.e., trying to cause a

harmful or offensive contact.) The question is whether she has a valid defense.

Here, Hannah has a valid claim of self-defense — she was acting to prevent the attack against her. It's true that the defense of self-defense doesn't apply where the defendant was the aggressor, but neither the fact that Hannah was a trespasser, nor the fact that she cursed at the guard, made her into an aggressor for purposes of losing the right to defend herself.

Since Hannah acted under the right of self-defense, this will be a complete defense to aggravated assault as well as to simple assault.

Nor is this burglary. Burglary is the breaking and entering of the dwelling of another in the nighttime with intent to commit a felony therein. Here, although the hotel probably qualifies as the "dwelling of another," there is no indication that Hannah intended to commit a felony once she got inside. Therefore, she can't be guilty of burglary.

Consequently, the worse crime she can be convicted of is trespass.

(A), (B) and (C) are not the best response,
because each of them names a crime that (as shown in the discussion of Choice (D) above) Hannah did not commit.

Answer 44

(A) is the best response,
because it correctly identifies that Damson satisfies all the elements of *both* burglary and larceny. The key here is that both burglary and larceny are "inchoate" offenses in the sense that once *one* act is complete with the *intent* to do another, the crimes are satisfied.

Damson is guilty of burglary because he satisfied all its elements: Breaking and entering the dwelling house of another, at night, with the intent to commit a felony therein. Thus, once Damson *entered* the house the *first* time – even before he actually took the silverware – he had completed the burglary, because burglary requires only the *intent* to commit a felony inside. Damson is also liable for larceny: the trespassory taking and carrying away of another's personal property, with intent to steal it. Under these facts, Damson would be liable for larceny once he took the silverware, because he did so with the intent to steal it. The wrinkle here is that Damson returned the silverware, thus renouncing his criminal purpose. However, once a criminal act is complete, it's too late to abandon it and escape liability. Thus, subsequent renunciation, or forgiveness or condonation by the victim, won't exonerate the defendant. Furthermore, note that the larceny that's involved in these facts requires some different elements than burglary does, so it's not a "lesser included offense" of burglary, and Damson can be convicted of both crimes. Since A correctly identifies that Damson will be liable for both burglary *and* larceny, it's the best response.

(B) is not the best response,

because although it correctly identifies that Damson will be guilty of burglary, it incorrectly states he'll be guilty of attempted larceny (in fact, he'll be liable for larceny as well). Damson satisfied all the elements of common law burglary, because he broke and entered the dwelling house of another at night, with an intent to commit a felony therein. Thus, once Damson *entered* the house the *first* time – even before he actually took the silverware – he had completed the burglary, because burglary only requires the *intent* to commit a felony inside. Larceny is the trespassory taking and carrying away of personal property of another, with intent to steal it. Under these facts, Damson would be liable for larceny once he took the silverware, because he did so with the intent to steal it. If you chose option B, it was probably because you focused on Damson's returning the silverware, and thought it must count somehow. In fact, it doesn't, because the crimes of burglary and larceny were already complete, and subsequent acts of repentance won't change that. Although attempt has several different tests, in general, attempted larceny would require that Damson only have come sufficiently close to committing the larceny, with the intent to commit the larceny in a specific way. Damson completed the crime, so he wouldn't be liable only for attempt. Since B only identifies one of the two crimes for which Damson will be liable, and another option identifies them both, B is not the best response.

(C) is not the best response,

because although it correctly identifies that Damson will be guilty of burglary, it incorrectly acquits Damson for larceny. As C states, Damson will be liable for burglary, because he satisfies all its elements: Breaking and entering the dwelling house of another, at night, with the intent to commit a felony therein. Thus, once Damson *entered* the house the first time – even before he actually took the silverware – he had completed the burglary, because burglary requires only the *intent* to commit a felony inside. However, Damson is *also* liable for larceny. Larceny requires the trespassory taking and carrying away of personal property of another, with intent to steal it. Under these facts, Damson would be liable for larceny once he took the silverware, because he did so with the intent to steal it. If you chose option C, it's probably because you mistook larceny for a lesser included offense of burglary, and figured Damson couldn't be liable for both. A lesser included offense is one which requires only proof of some but not all of the elements of another offense, and no other elements. As examples, attempted crimes are included in completed crimes, and voluntary manslaughter is included in murder (provocation is not considered an additional element). You may have confused burglary with robbery, which is a larceny from the person by force or fear. As a result, larceny is a lesser included offense of robbery. But the larceny that's involved in these facts requires some different elements than bur-

glary does, since burglary can involve *any* felony. Since C mistakenly acquits Damson of larceny, it's not the best response.

(D) is not the best response,

because Damson is guilty of both burglary *and* larceny. Damson will be liable for burglary because he satisfies all of its elements: Breaking and entering the dwelling house of another, at night, with the intent to commit a felony therein. Thus, once Damson *entered* the house the *first* time – even before he actually took the silverware – he had completed the burglary, because burglary requires only the *intent* to commit a felony inside. Damson is *also* liable for larceny. Larceny requires the trespassory taking and carrying away of another's personal property, with intent to steal it. Under these facts, Damson would be liable for larceny once he took the silverware, because he did so with the intent to steal it. If you chose this response, it's probably because you believed that returning the silverware would exonerate him. However, once a crime is *complete,* acts of renunciation, or condonation by the victim, will not erase the criminal liability! Since D does not recognize this, it's not the best response.

Answer 45

(B) is the best response,

because it states the felony, of these four, that's least likely to form a basis for felony murder. The key here is to identify the felony that is least "independent" from homicide. Note that the question asks for the "least likely" basis for felony murder. This means three *will* be suitable, and one *won't* be. B is the only one that *won't* be.

Felony murder requires an underlying felony that is inherently dangerous to human life, while remaining sufficiently "independent" from homicide. Such crimes traditionally include rape, robbery, arson, burglary, and kidnapping. Here, manslaughter *is* a homicide, so it *cannot* be "independent" from it. The same would go for a crime like aggravated battery. Since the question here asks the least likely basis for felony murder, and B is the *only* option that would *not* be amenable to felony murder, it's the best response.

(A) is not the best response,

because arson is one of the most likely felonies to form a basis for felony murder. Felony murder requires an underlying felony that is inherently dangerous to life, which does not require personal violence. The most common such crimes are rape, robbery, arson, burglary, and kidnapping. Arson is considered sufficiently "independent" from homicide to be covered by the felony murder rule. If you chose this response, you may have mistakenly read "least" likely for "most" likely, since most MBE questions ask for the option "most" likely to do something. However, since the question here asks for the least likely basis for felony murder, A isn't the best response.

(C) is not the best response,

because rape is a valid underlying crime for felony murder. Felony murder requires an underlying felony that is inherently dangerous to human life, while remaining sufficiently "independent" from homicide (including, traditionally, rape, robbery, arson, burglary, and kidnapping). The traditional test is to exclude those crimes requiring personal violence, but it would be a misnomer to say rape doesn't require personal violence. Nonetheless, rape is one of the traditional bases of felony murder, due to its independence from homicide. Note that the fact that only an attempt is involved here does not change the result, since the felony murder rule encompasses attempts. Since the question here asks for the least likely basis for felony murder, C is not the best response.

(D) is not the best response,

because burglary is a likely basis for felony murder. Felony murder requires an underlying felony that is inherently dangerous to human life, while remaining sufficiently "independent" from homicide, typically because the crime is said not to require personal violence. Such crimes include, traditionally, rape, robbery, arson, burglary, and kidnapping. Since the question here asks for the least likely basis for felony murder, D isn't the best response.

Answer 46

(B) is the best response,

because Sam's two friends did nothing to assist Sam's attack.

An accomplice is one who, with the intent that the crime be committed, aids, counsels, or encourages the principal before or during the commission of the crime.

Sam's friends should be acquitted as accomplices to manslaughter because the facts make clear they did not intend that Sam murder the woman, nor did they do anything during Sam's attack to aid, counsel or encourage Sam. Only after the crime was complete, when the elderly woman fell to the ground, did they urge Sam to flee.

Nor does the fact that the friends did nothing to help the woman — when assistance to her during the beating could conceivably have prevented the death — make any difference. Except in special circumstances (none of which applies here) a witness to a crime has no affirmative duty to intervene to prevent the crime or aid the victim, even if this could be easily done. Therefore, failing to render such assistance cannot give rise to criminal liability.

(A) is not the best response,

because Sam's friends could be found guilty of being accomplices even if Sam was not convicted.

An accomplice is one who, with the intent that the

crime be committed, aids, counsels, or encourages the principal before or during the commission of the crime. Under the modern view of accomplice liability, the fact that the principal has not yet been convicted of the substantive crime does not bar trial and conviction of the accomplices. If the principal were actually *acquitted*, this might bar prosecution, but that's not what happened here — a mistrial would not in most jurisdictions bar the prosecution of the alleged accomplices.

(C) is not the best response,

because urging Sam to flee was not a form of aid or counsel before or during the crime.

An accomplice is one who, with the intent that the crime be committed, aids, counsels, or encourages the principal *before or during* the commission of the crime.

Sam's friends should be acquitted because to be accomplices they would, before or during the assault on the victim, have to have aided, counseled or encouraged Sam in the attack, with the intent that the attack be committed. By definition, they could not be accomplices merely by urging Sam to flee after the crime was completed.

(D) is not the best response,

because they had no duty to intervene.

As a general matter no legal duty is imposed on any person to affirmatively act for the benefit of others. Absent one of several types of legal relationships between two parties, no legal duty is imposed on any person to affirmatively act for the benefit of others. None of those legal relationships existed here. Therefore, Sam's friends had no duty to intervene to prevent Sam's attack. Consequently, they cannot be made criminally liable for that failure to intervene.

Answer 47

(C) is the best response,

because it's theoretically correct, it applies to these facts, and it's the easiest to prove of these options. This is a somewhat difficult question because three of the responses are potential answers theoretically, but two of them are difficult to prove. The question asks for the *best* argument, which will be the one that's theoretically correct, applies to the facts, and will be the easiest to prove – and that's option C.

There are six general exceptions to the requirement of a search warrant: The search is incident to a lawful, custodial arrest; the "automobile" exception (need probable cause that vehicle contains evidence of crime, and exigent circumstances); plain view; consent; stop and frisk; and hot pursuit/evanescent evidence. The consent exception applies where one with the authority to consent offers voluntary and intelligent consent to the search. Under the third party consent exception, one is said to surrender his expectation of privacy due to the possible consent of another, and thus he assumes the risk the other will consent to a search. That's the case here. Jack authorized Paul to drive his car, and thus impliedly authorized Paul to consent to a search. Note that this is a fairly simple argument to make on these facts, because you're told that Paul consented to the search. Unlike options A and D, this argument doesn't require an analysis of reasonability or exigent circumstances, which would be difficult under these facts. Since C is the simplest and most straightforward argument, and it will result in the heroin being admissible, it's the best response.

(A) is not the best response,

because although it's theoretically correct and applies to these facts, it is not the easiest argument to make, of these four options. There are six, general exceptions to the requirement of a search warrant: The search is incident to a lawful, custodial arrest; the "automobile" exception (need probable cause that vehicle contains evidence of crime, and exigent circumstances); plain view; consent; stop and frisk; and hot pursuit/evanescent evidence. The "reasonability under the circumstances" test in option A implies either the automobile exception or the evanescent evidence exception. However, either of these would require weighing the circumstances carefully to determine if they justified a warrantless search, and even with Paul's nervous condition, such a decision may go either way. Thus, although the argument is theoretically correct and may apply to these facts, it is not as easy to prove as option C, and so A is not the best response.

(B) is not the best response,

because the facts do not mention an arrest. Even if the facts *imply* an arrest, the search here would exceed the scope of the arrest, *or* it occurred at the wrong time. If the term "arrest" in B applies to the *speeding* ticket, you'd have to ask whether the arrest is custodial or non-custodial. If it was non-custodial – as you'd expect with a simple speeding ticket – the right to search would be limited to a "stop and frisk." In that case, the trunk lid search would exceed the scope of a valid search, and the heroin would be inadmissible. If the speeding ticket arrest was custodial, the police would be entitled to conduct a "wingspan" search, and the trunk lid may or may not be included, since the scope of such searches is construed liberally. The problem with this argument is that there's nothing to suggest that the speeding ticket was a custodial arrest, and the trunk lid may not be within the scope of a custodial arrest. Looking at an arrest for heroin possession, the heroin clearly would not be admissible, because the heroin supplied the probable cause for the arrest, and thus it would have to have been found *before* the search. Otherwise, the police could make arrests at random, in the hope of finding evidence to justify the arrest afterwards. As a result, no matter which incident – the speeding ticket or the heroin possession – option B refers to, it does not give a strong argument for the

prosecution. As a result, B is not the best response.

(D) is not the best response,

because although it's theoretically correct and applies to these facts, it is not the easiest argument to make, of these four options. There are six, general exceptions to the requirement of a search warrant: The search is incident to a lawful, custodial arrest; the "automobile" exception (need probable cause that vehicle contains evidence of crime, and exigent circumstances); plain view; consent; stop and frisk; and hot pursuit/evanescent evidence. D implies the automobile exception. The problem is that there is a very questionable basis for such a search; all the police have is that Paul was speeding and looks nervous. That, in and of itself, might not justify a search of the trunk lid. Thus, although D *could* be argued, it would be a difficult argument to prove. Since there is an option – C – that forms an easier argument for the prosecutor, D is not the best response.

Answer 48

(B) is the best response,

because it correctly identifies the ground on which the evidence will be excluded. This is a tricky question because it turns on a "hidden" issue – the freshness of the information serving as a basis for the search warrant.

This is how a search warrant is issued: A policeman submits a written, signed affidavit to a neutral, detached magistrate, who decides if there is probable cause to issue the warrant. The affidavit must set forth the underlying circumstances to a degree sufficient for the magistrate to determine probable cause. If the information is *stale*, it will *defeat* probable cause by diminishing the possibility that the items in question are still at the location. That's the problem here. The information was two months old and as a result, probably too old to justify a search warrant. This is a tricky question because this is *not* an issue that would jump off the page at you. Nonetheless, it's the central issue here. Since B correctly identifies this as the reason for excluding the evidence, it's the best response.

(A) is not the best response,

because it misstates the rule of law. An informant's information *can* constitute probable cause for a search or arrest if it meets the "totality of the circumstances" test from *Illinois v. Gates* (1983). Under that test, elements determining the reliability of the informant include: the informant's prior use and reliability; the informant's status as a member of a reliable group (e.g., a minister); clarity of detail in the informant's tip, showing the informant has personal knowledge of where evidence is located; the tip includes a declaration against informant's penal interest (e.g., that he bought narcotics from the individual named). Thus, not only is the statement in option A incorrect, but it's likely that, under these facts, the Informant's tip would be sufficient grounds for a search warrant *if the information was fresh* instead of being two months old. The *age* of the information is what makes the search warrant defective, not the *source* of the information, because the two-month gap diminishes the probability that the items in question are still there. Since A misstates the law, even though it arrives at the correct result, it's not the best response.

(C) is not the best response,

because it misstates the law. In fact, "mere evidence" is what *most* searches involve. Apart from the suspect himself, it's not clear what else a search *could* involve. In order to obtain a search warrant, there must be probable cause to believe that the items in question are at the location. A search can be conducted *without* a warrant under certain circumstances (e.g. , stop and frisk, search incident to a lawful custodial arrest, evanescent evidence). Thus, the blanket statement in C is incorrect, making it not the best response.

(D) is not the best response,

because although it correctly characterizes Informant, it ignores the fact that the information was "stale," and thus cannot form the basis of a valid search warrant. As D implies, an informant's information *can* constitute probable cause for a search or arrest if it meets the "totality of the circumstances" test from Illinois v. Gates (1983). Under that test, elements determining the reliability of the informant include: the informant's prior use and reliability; the informant's status as a member of a reliable group (e.g., a minister); clarity of detail in the informant's tip, showing the informant has personal knowledge of where evidence is located; the tip includes a declaration against informant's general interest (e.g., that he bought narcotics from the individual named). Thus, the factors D names – informant's reliability in the past and the correctness of his information this time – would make his tip a valid basis for a search warrant *but for* one crucial fact: the tip was based on "stale" information – it was two months old. Stale information diminishes the probability that the items in question are still at the location. While "staleness" is a fluid concept, courts take into account whether the crime is ongoing or short-lived. Here, the age of the information would defeat the validity of the warrant. If you missed this one, take heart – it's a *very* close call. Nonetheless, since D correctly states the law, ignoring the "staleness" issue makes it not the best response.

Answer 49

(C) is the best response,

because it correctly identifies the basis on which the heroin will be admissible. This is a tricky question because it involves a "hidden" issue: Standing to object. One only has standing to claim a search or sei-

zure violated the Fourth Amendment when the evidence was obtained from a search or seizure which violated his "legitimate expectation of privacy." Rakas v. Illinois (1978). This means that even if the Defendant owns the property, or is present when the search takes place, he will have no standing to challenge the search *unless* the search violated his legitimate expectation of privacy. Under the facts here, Defendant clearly had no legitimate expectation of privacy in the back seat of Morgan's car. Thus, he cannot object to the validity of the search. Since C correctly identifies this, it's the best response.

(A) is not the best response,

because the "plain view" doctrine would not be determinative under these facts. The "plain view" doctrine provides one means by which the police can conduct a warrantless search. It states that police can make a warrantless seizure when they are on the premises for lawful purposes, and they inadvertently discover evidence in "plain view." A correctly states the facts in that, since the heroin was under the rear seat, it was not in "plain view." However, it ignores the central reason why the motion to suppress will be denied: Defendant has no standing to object to the search, since it was Morgan's car that was searched, and Defendant had no privacy interest in it. Were it *Morgan* who was being tried, the result might be different, because the *issues* would be different, since Morgan clearly would have standing to object. If the police were going to take Morgan into custody and arrest him, they could conduct a search of the entire passenger compartment (since it's considered "within the suspect's control," even if he is away from the car when the search takes place). Here, this would make the search valid. If, however, the police *didn't* intend to take Morgan into custody, they could only "frisk" him – making the search *invalid.* The "custodial arrest" issue is *unclear* on these facts.

Thus, even though option A is correct in that the heroin would *not* be covered by the plain view doctrine, it ignores the standing issue, which is central to solving this question. As a result, A is not the best response.

(B) is not the best response,

because it ignores the central issue in the case: Defendant does not have standing to object to the search. If you chose this response, it's because you overlooked the fact that *Defendant* is objecting to a search of *Morgan's* car, in which Defendant has no privacy interest.

Let's say the facts were as you took them to be – say, Morgan was on trial. The statement in B may or may not be correct – that the scope of the search was excessive. It turns on whether Morgan was going to be taken into custody. If he *was,* the police could conduct a search of the entire passenger compartment (since it's considered "within the suspect's control," even if he was away from the car when the search took place). Here, this would make the search valid. If, however, they *didn't* intend to take Morgan into custody, they could only "frisk" him – making the search *invalid.* The custodial arrest issue is unclear on these facts. Thus, even if it was Morgan on trial, option B would not be a particularly sound choice, since it wouldn't resolve the issue of whether the heroin should be admitted into evidence.

In any case, the fact that resolves the issue *conclusively* is Defendant's lack of standing to object, meaning the evidence will be admissible. Since B ignores this and in doing so arrives at an incorrect result, it's not the best response.

(D) is not the best response,

because the facts here do not indicate that Morgan was subject to a full custodial arrest – it only says Morgan was stopped for speeding. Furthermore, D ignores the central issue, which is that Defendant has no standing to object to the search. Under these circumstances, Morgan may or may not have been taken into custody – you simply don't know from these facts. If he *was* to be taken into custody, D would be correct, because the police would be entitled to search the entire passenger compartment as a search incident to a custodial arrest. However, if they *didn't* intend to take him into custody, they'd only be entitled to frisk him, and thus the search of the car would be excessive and the evidence would be inadmissible. Thus, D states an argument that cannot conclusively be made on the facts given.

What D *ignores* is that Defendant has no standing to object to the search, because he had no privacy interest in Morgan's car. *That's* what conclusively makes the evidence admissible. Thus, even though D arrives at the correct result, it's not the best response.

Answer 50

(D) is the best response,

because Henry consented to the police entering his house.

An officer of the law can make a warrantless arrest for a felony, such as robbery. The police can then make a warrantless search of an arrestee's person incident to an arrest. So the motion would have to be denied unless, prior to the moment when the police recognized that Scott matched the description of the drugstore robber, the police's presence violated some constitutional right of Scott.

The owner of a house unquestionably has the right to invite the police in — when they enter in response to such an invitation and move around the house, they are not violating the rights of a guest, as long as they stay within the scope of the owner's invitation. That's what happened here — the police were invited (by Henry) into, or to a place near, the kitchen. Since the police were authorized to be in or near the kitchen, they were entitled to be in the place from which they recognized Scott. And that recognition triggered their

right to arrest and then to search incident to arrest, all without constitutional violation.

(A) is not the best response,

because Henry's consent overrides Scott's right to contest entry.

The owner's consent to a search of (or other police entry on) a premises is binding on a non-paying guest, even if the guest refuses consent. So here, Henry's rights as a homeowner to consent to the police's warrantless entry into the house overrode Scott's right to bar the police from entering. (As a non-paying guest, as opposed to a tenant or a paying hotel guest, Scott had very limited rights, and the police's entry did not violate those rights.)

(B) is not the best response,

because the answer incorrectly mixes two aspects of the law.

Scott's mere presence at the scene of the search may in a sense have given him "standing" to protest the police's entry into the house and the kitchen. But the real question is whether Scott's constitutional rights were violated by the police presence in the kitchen. And, under the analysis in Choice (D) above, the answer to this question is no. So Choice (B) reaches the wrong result, and does so on a completely wrong (or at least irrelevant) theory.

(C) is not the best response,

because Scott's lack of ownership or possessory interest in the premises isn't what caused him to lose — Henry's consent is.

An overnight social guest has a legitimate expectation of privacy in at least parts of the home where he is staying. (In other words, the guest's lack of ownership or "other possessory interest" in the premises is not automatically fatal to his right to protest a premises search.) However, the owner's consent to a search of a premises will be binding on a non-paying guest, even if the guest refuses consent. So when Henry consented, that consent took priority over whatever privacy interest Scott may have had in the premises. Thus Choice (C) reaches the right result for the wrong reason.

Answer 51

(C) is the best response,

because the arrest was lawful, and the knife and pistol were on Jason's person.

In the case of a lawful arrest a full search of the person (and, indeed, areas within the suspect's "control") not only falls within an exception to the warrant requirement of the 4th Amendment, but is also a reasonable search under that Amendment.

Here, the arrest was legal. That's because: (1) the search warrant was valid; (2) breaking into the house to execute the warrant is allowed if there is no answer to the knock; (3) the police had the right to look in the basement for whoever was making the noises (if only to protect police safety); and (4) once the police saw Jason in physical possession of a brown suitcase with leather straps (which they had probable cause to believe contained cocaine), they had probable cause to arrest Jason for illegal drug possession.

Thus the arrest was legal because (1) it was supported by probable cause as analyzed in the prior paragraph; and (2) it fell within the search-incident-to-arrest exception to the requirement of a search warrant. (This exception is necessary here, because the original search warrant being executed didn't by itself authorize a search of anyone's body, only a search for the brown suitcase).

(A) is not the best response,
because the police acted according to requirements of warrant execution — and then the rules of arrest — as analyzed in the treatment of Choice (C).

(B) is not the best response,
because any failure to give *Miranda* warnings would not make the arrest illegal, and the validity of the seizure was guaranteed by its being incident to a valid arrest.

For the reasons given in the analysis of Choice (C), the arrest was valid, and a valid arrest permits the police to do a body search incident to that arrest. A failure to give *Miranda* warnings can only affect the admissibility of the results of questions the police ask the arrestee; the search of Jason's person, and the seizure of the weapons, did not result from any police questioning.

(D) is not the best response,
because the validity of the search and seizure comes from its being incident to a valid arrest, not because the police had reasonable grounds to believe there were weapons in the house (they didn't).

The search and seizure were valid because incident to a valid arrest, as described in the discussion of Choice (C) above. Nothing in the facts suggests that the police, at the time they entered the house, had reason to believe it contained weapons. Although the mere execution of the warrant permitted the police to check for any persons who might pose a threat to the police, it did not permit them to check for weapons. Thus, Choice (D) lists the right result but wrong explanation.

Answer 52

(C) is the best response,
because Jason's statement was not in response to any "interrogation," and only the results of interrogations can be barred by a failure to give *Miranda* warnings.

Miranda does not bar all statements made prior to the giving of Miranda rights. Statements made without any questions being asked are considered volunteered,

and admissible even if required *Miranda* warnings weren't given.

Jason's statement that "You never would have caught me with the stuff if it hadn't been for that lousy snitch Harvey" was volunteered, not made in response to any police questions. Therefore, the statement is not covered by *Miranda*.

(A) is not the best response,
because the police had the right to force the door open.

As a general rule, the officer executing the warrant must announce that he is a law enforcement officer, that he possesses a warrant, and that he is there to execute it. If the officer identifies himself and then is not answered he may use force to break into the premises described.

The facts make clear that the police followed correct procedures for executing the warrant and that their forcing open the door was reasonable. The police met the announcement requirements. They announced that they were law officers when they knocked on Jason's door and called out, "Police." They announced they possessed a warrant. And they made clear that they were there to execute the warrant when they called, "Open up." They then waited a few seconds and when they received no response they broke down the door and entered. Contrary to answer (A), this entry was permissible.

(B) is not the best response,
because Jason's statement was volunteered before the police could read him his *Miranda* rights.

Miranda does not bar all statements made prior to the giving of *Miranda* rights. The *Miranda* decision itself says that "volunteered statements of any kind" are not barred by the Fifth Amendment, and thus not affected by failure to give *Miranda* warnings. (*Miranda* covers only responses that are given in response to "interrogations" by the police.)

It's clear from the facts here that Jason's remark "You never would have caught me with the stuff if it hadn't been.... " was a spontaneous outburst, not a response to interrogation.

(D) is not the best response,
because while the motion should be denied, the reason given is not correct.

The police do indeed have the right to make a "public safety" search while making arrests, and answers to questions that the police ask during such a public-safety search don't fall within the *Miranda* rule. *N.Y. v. Quarles* (1984). But Jason's statement was not made in response to questions asked during a public-safety search, so the public-safety exception to *Miranda* doesn't apply here.

Answer 53

(A) is the best response,

because the Uzi was not found in a place a person might be found.

Incident to a lawful arrest in an arrestee's home, the officers executing the warrant may conduct a "protective sweep" of all or part of the premises, if they have a "reasonable belief" that another person who might be dangerous to the officers may be present *in the areas swept. Maryland v. Buie* (1990).

So here, the police had the right to search the house for accomplices. The Uzi, however, was found in a box on a closet shelf. Clearly the weapon was neither in plain sight nor in a place where a person could be found. Therefore, the protective-sweep exception doesn't apply. Because the Uzi was not found during a lawful search, Jason's motion to dismiss should be granted.

(B) is not the best response,

because the answer incorrectly states the applicable law — the police had the right to search the house for accomplices.

As is described in the analysis of Choice (A) above, the police had the right to check protectively for other persons. Therefore, this choice — since it says that no further search of the house was permitted once the suitcase was seized — is inconsistent with the police's right to make the protective search (which may be made at any time when the police are still on the premises and are thus vulnerable to a sudden attack from someone who might be hiding).

(C) is not the best response,

because the weapon was not in an area that could be searched.

It's true that the police were lawfully in the bedroom (under their right to make a protective sweep — see Choice (A)). But while they were in the bedroom, the police were only permitted to look in places where a person might be hiding. They therefore weren't allowed to look in small boxes, as they did here.

(D) is not the best response,

because the police did not in fact have probable cause to believe that weapons were in the house.

The search warrant itself, of course, didn't give the police the right to search the house once they found the suitcase (other than their right to do a "protective sweep" to find hidden persons). It's possible that the discovery of the weapons on Jason's person may have given the police probable cause to believe that other weapons would be found in the house. But if so, the police were required to get a new search warrant to look for those weapons (perhaps after securing the premises so that no one could destroy any weapons or contraband before the new warrant could be obtained and executed). That is, although there are a number of exceptions to the requirement of a search warrant for the search of a complete house (e.g., exigent circumstances), none of those exceptions applied here, even if the police did have probable cause to believe additional weapons would be found.

Answer 54

(A) is the best response,

because it correctly identifies that Dean's handwriting sample will be admissible. The key here is that a handwriting sample is considered *physical*, not communicative, evidence – and the Fifth Amendment only covers communicative evidence. As a result, handwriting samples are not covered by the Fifth Amendment, and will be admissible even if the suspect wasn't given the opportunity to obtain counsel, or told any other Miranda warning. Since A recognizes that the handwriting sample will be admissible, it's the best response.

(B) is not the best response,

because it does not correctly characterize the law. A handwriting sample is considered "physical" evidence. The Fifth Amendment privilege against self-incrimination refers to communicative, not physical, evidence. Thus, Dean could be required to submit to a handwriting sample without his being given his Miranda warnings. Since B suggests Dean *was* entitled to Miranda warnings before the handwriting sample was taken, it's not the best response.

(C) is not the best response,

because it misstates the law: Dean is not entitled to refuse a handwriting sample. Option C implies that Dean is entitled to avoid incriminating himself through a handwriting sample. In fact, a handwriting sample (like a fingerprint or a blood sample) is *not* a Fifth Amendment violation, because the privilege against self-incrimination refers to *communicative,* not *physical,* evidence. Handwriting samples are "physical evidence" and thus not subject to Fifth Amendment constraints. Thus, Dean would not be entitled to refuse to give a handwriting sample. Since C gives Dean a right he doesn't, in fact, have, it's not the best response.

(D) is not the best response,

because it misstates the law: Dean was not entitled to have counsel present for the handwriting sample. The two sources of the right to counsel are the Fifth Amendment and the Sixth Amendment. Under the Fifth Amendment, the suspect is entitled to counsel for the investigative stage of the prosecution, but only for custodial questioning (under Miranda), when Defendant must take part in a lineup or show up after "formal proceedings" have begun, or undercover agents elicit incriminating statements from an already-indicted suspect. The Sixth Amendment covers "critical stages" of the trial (e.g., arraignment and trial). Option D implies that a handwriting sample is the equivalent of questioning. However, the Fifth Amendment only covers *communicative,* not *physical,* evidence. Handwriting samples, like fingerprints and blood samples, are considered physical evidence, and thus are not covered by the Fifth Amendment. Since D implies otherwise, it's not the best response.

Answer 55

(C) is the best response,

because it correctly identifies that the prior convictions can be introduced at the sentencing hearing. In imposing sentences, the judge can rely on a wide variety of evidence, including hearsay, reports which are not cross-examined, and the like (somewhat different rules apply to "unusual" sentencings, e.g., the death penalty). Prior convictions are relevant to sentencing since they bear on the likelihood of defendant's rehabilitation. Since C correctly identifies that the convictions will be admissible, it's the best response.

(A) is not the best response,

because it misstates the law: Dean was *not* deprived of a fair and unbiased tribunal. At a sentencing hearing, the judge is entitled to take into account prior convictions, as a means of determining the likelihood of the defendant's rehabilitation, among other things (somewhat different rules apply to "unusual" sentencings, e.g., the death penalty). As a result, introduction of such evidence at a sentencing hearing is not a due process violation, making A not the best response.

(B) is not the best response,

because Dean was not deprived of a fair trial by the delay in introducing the prior convictions. In a usual sentencing hearing, the judge may take into account a broad spectrum of evidence, including hearsay, non-cross-examined reports, and prior convictions (somewhat different rules apply to "unusual" sentencings, e.g., the death penalty). If *anything* introducing the prior convictions at trial would have been fraught with pitfalls, since prior convictions can be a very dangerous form of character evidence (since the jury is likely to grant them undue weight). As a result, introducing the prior convictions at the sentencing hearing for the first time does not deprive Dean of a fair trial, making B not the best response.

(D) is not the best response,

because it misstates the law. Dean is not entitled to confront witnesses against him in this sentencing hearing, because a *usual* sentence will be imposed (e.g., the death penalty is not being considered). In imposing a "usual" sentence, a judge can rely on hearsay evidence as well as reports which are not cross-examined. Williams v. N.Y. (1949).

Keep in mind that when a sentence is *not* "usual," the defendant will have to be given a greater opportunity

for confrontation than otherwise – e.g., death penalty cases. However, this isn't involved in the facts here, so Dean had no right of confrontation. Since D states otherwise, it's not the best response.

Answer 56

(B) is the best response,

because it correctly identifies the reason why Simmons' testimony will not be admissible against Taylor: It was derived from Taylor's immunized testimony.

Taylor was granted immunity for his grand jury testimony. This means that he was immunized from the use of his testimony, or evidence derived from his testimony. (The other type of immunity is transactional immunity, under which, in general, the witness is immunized from prosecution for any crime related to the transaction to which the witness testifies). Here, Taylor's testimony was the *only clue* the prosecutor had to Simmons' involvement in the robbery. Thus, Simmons' testimony was derived from Taylor's immunized testimony. As a result, it cannot be used against Taylor. Since B identifies this, it's the best response.

(A) is not the best response,

because it misstates the law: The prosecutor *can* bargain away the rights of one co-defendant in a deal with another. In a way, every time a prosecutor makes a deal with one defendant, he's impacting the rights of the other, since a defendant's testimony against his co-defendant will hurt the co-defendant. Furthermore, A ignores the real reason the objection to Simmons' testimony will be sustained: because it was derived from Taylor's immunized testimony, since Taylor's testimony is the only way the prosecutor discovered Simmons. Thus, Simmons testimony against Taylor derived from Taylor's own immunized testimony, so it cannot be used against Taylor. Since A doesn't recognize this, it's not the best response.

(C) is not the best response,

because it arrives at the wrong result, and does not focus on relevant issues. The fact that the police suspected Taylor before he testified is not relevant; his *immunized testimony,* in which he identified Simmons, is the focal point here. Taylor's immunized testimony is the only source of evidence as to Simmons' identity. Since Simmons was discovered through Taylor's testimony, Simmons' testimony would be considered derived from the immunized testimony, and thus could not be used against Taylor. Thus, the police's notion that Taylor was involved *before* he testified won't be relevant.

If you chose this response, it could be because you were thinking of the other kind of immunity – *transactional* immunity – under which the witness is immunized from prosecution for any crime related to the transaction to which the witness testifies. However, the witness may nonetheless be prosecuted if the prosecution can show an independent source for the evidence – i.e., any source other than the immunized testimony. Under these facts, however, it's *use* immunity, not *transactional* immunity, that's involved – so the "independent source" concept isn't relevant. Since C states otherwise, it's not the best response.

(D) is not the best response,

because it misstates the law, and arrives at the wrong result. There are many reasons why a witness who is willing to testify may not be able to: If his testimony is cumulative evidence, if he's incompetent to testify, and many others. Thus, as a blanket statement, D is incorrect. Under these facts specifically, D ignores the fact that Simmons' testimony was derived from Taylor's immunized testimony, and thus cannot be used against Taylor. Since D fails to recognize this, it's not the best response.

Answer 57

(A) is the best response,

because it correctly identifies that the evidence is inadmissible due to an illegal stop. The stop was illegal because Officer was stopping cars *at random*. This is not permissible because such a system relies on the officer's discretion in determining whom to stop, and the intrusion is great because the driver is likely to be anxious about being stopped at random. There are two ways such a system *can* be made legal: by setting up, say, a checkpoint where *every* car is stopped and checked for license and registration. The other is to require a reasonable suspicion of illegal activity before a car is stopped. However, the random system here is illegal. Since A correctly identifies this, it's the best response.

(B) is not the best response,

because it misstates the law, and ignores the central issue here. First, use of a flashlight does not constitute a search, since it only augments the officer's vision. However, B *does* say that probable cause would be required, and that implies the correct test: In order to stop vehicles, police need a reasonable suspicion of illegal activity. Here, it's the stop *itself* that's deficient, *not* the fact that a flashlight was used to conduct a search. Since B ignores the fact that the stop itself was invalid, it's not the best response.

(C) is not the best response,

because although it correctly states the facts, it ignores the fact that the plan *itself* is invalid. The key is that the stops were made *at random*. There are two things that could make the system valid: Either require a reasonable suspicion of illegal activity for a stop, OR set up a checkpoint, and stop every car to check for license and registration. A system like this is valid because 1/ it does not rely on the officer's discretion in determining who to stop, and 2/ the intrusion is considered less

because the driver is not likely to be as anxious as he would be with a random stop. However, under these facts, the stops are purely random, and thus the plan is not valid. As a result, compliance with the plan would not make a stop valid. Since C doesn't recognize that the plan itself is deficient, it's not the best response.

(D) is not the best response,

because although the facts it states are true, it ignores the threshold issue that the stop *itself* was invalid. Had the *stop* been valid, the search would have been justified under plain view, the frisk would have been valid due to a reasonable suspicion of criminal activity and that the suspect was armed, and the discovery of drugs and the gun would have been valid. However, the stop here was *not* valid, and so everything flowing form it would be invalid as well. The stop was invalid because of the plan for random stops. Random stops are impermissible because they rely on the officer's discretion in determining who to stop, and the intrusion is great because the driver is anxious when he's randomly stopped. Instead, a stop requires either reasonable suspicion of illegal activity, or a fixed check, e.g., a checkpoint where *every* car is checked for license and registration. Since the stop itself was invalid under these facts, and D ignores this, it's not the best response.

Answer 58

(D) is the best response,

because neither provides a valid ground for dismissal.

The double jeopardy guarantee of the Fifth Amendment states that a person cannot be tried twice for the same offense. The guarantee also bars the government from trials for two different crimes if one is a "lesser included offense" of the other. However, there are two exceptions to the lesser-included-offense doctrine. One of those exceptions is that if the government could not have tried the second crime at the time it tried the first, due to circumstances beyond the government's control, the lesser-included-offense doctrine doesn't apply. That's what happened here — by the time of the original trial (or, actually, guilty plea) on reckless driving, Peggy hadn't yet died, so no manslaughter prosecution was possible. Therefore, double jeopardy doesn't apply.

Nor does the statute of limitations bar the manslaughter prosecution. The statute of limitations doesn't start to run until all facts necessary for prosecution have occurred. Here, Peggy's death was one such fact, and it occurred less than three years before the indictment, so the statute of limitations hadn't run by the date of indictment (which was the event that satisfied the statute).

(A), (B) and (C) are not the best responses,

since each of them asserts that at least one of the two grounds was valid, and neither was (as shown in the discussion of Choice (D)).

Answer 59

(C) is the best response,

because it correctly identifies the central reason why Barber's confession will be admissible. Certainly the most obvious issue where a confession is concerned is whether the Miranda warnings were required and given. Here, the Miranda warnings were *not* required because there was no custodial interrogation. An interrogation is custodial only if the individual questioned is not free to leave. Here, Barber voluntarily went to the police station, and he volunteered his confession. Under these facts, there was no time up to and including his confession when Barber was *not* free to leave. Thereafter, when the police were no longer willing to allow Barber to leave and wanted to question him further, they properly gave him his Miranda warnings. Since C correctly identifies that Barber's statement will be admissible because it was voluntarily given and he was not entitled to Miranda warnings, it's the best response.

(A) is not the best response,

because it misstates the facts, and arrives at the wrong result. Miranda warnings are only necessary when the police intend to conduct a custodial interrogation. When a person voluntarily comes to the station house, he is not considered "in custody," and as a result, is not entitled to Miranda warnings. Oregon v. Mathiason (1977). That's what's happening under these facts. Barber voluntarily came to the station, and apparently realized he was free to leave at any time (which is what distinguishes "custody" from not being in custody). His confession was completely voluntary. As a result, he would not be entitled to Miranda warnings. Note that if the police wanted to question him *after* his confession, and didn't want him to be free to leave – as they undoubtedly would have done – then they *would* have had to give him his Miranda warnings. Even then, the volunteered confession given *before* the custodial interrogation would be admissible. Since A mistakenly states that the Miranda warnings would be required at the beginning of the discussion, it's not the best response.

(B) is not the best response,

because it mischaracterizes the facts and arrives at the wrong result. The right to counsel and due process were not violated by the interrogation because it was not a custodial interrogation, and as a result the Miranda warnings were not required. An interrogation is "custodial" if the one being questioned believes he is not free to leave. Here, Barber voluntarily came to the station, and from these facts was free to leave. Since Barber was there voluntarily and *confessed* voluntarily, his right to counsel and due process were not violated. Since B doesn't recognize this, it's not the best response.

(D) is not the best response,

because although it arrives at the correct result, it misidentifies Barber's conduct as a *waiver* of his Miranda warnings, which it isn't. The issue of waiving one's Miranda rights only comes into being when the warnings are required – i.e., the police are going to conduct a custodial interrogation. At *that* point, the suspect can only waive his rights if the waiver is done knowingly, intelligently, and voluntarily – and the burden is on the *prosecution* to prove that the waiver is valid.

Here, there *was* no custodial interrogation, the Miranda warnings were not required, and so there's no issue of waiver. An interrogation is custodial only if the individual questioned is not free to leave. Here, Barber voluntarily went to the police station, and he volunteered his confession. Under these facts, there was no time when Barber was *not* free to leave. Thus, the Miranda warnings requirement was never "triggered." Since D doesn't recognize this, it's not the best response.

Answer 60

(C) is the best response,

because the inspections were allowed pursuant to a statute with reasonable requirements.

Businesses subject to extensive regulation may be subjected to warrantless, unannounced searches, at least where frequent unannounced inspections are the only effect way to enforce the regulatory requirements.

Of the various ways to achieve the aim of the statute (that is, deterring motor vehicle theft and trafficking in stolen motor vehicles), State X selected a relatively unintrusive means of inspection. All an owner would have to do is permit an inspector who showed up during normal business hours to take a physical inventory of the motor vehicles on the lot. Since the junkyard industry is a heavily regulated one, and the state has chosen a reasonably nonintrusive way of carrying out its regulation, no warrant was required.

(A) is not the best response,

because the statute has a reasonable inspection requirement.

No warrant was required, for the reason stated in the discussion of Choice (A). If the police had arbitrarily inspected Janet's business more often than others, or for improper purposes, the warrantless inspection here might nonetheless have been found to be an "unreasonable" Fourth Amendment search. But the facts say that officers periodically visit all junkyards in town, and give no hint that Janet is being singled out. Therefore, the inspection was reasonable even though warrantless.

(B) is not the best response,

because heavily regulated industries can be inspected

without a warrant.

The motion should be denied because there is no indication that the statute was in anyway a pretext. In fact, the Supreme Court has stated that businesses administered by heavy regulations that can only be enforced by unannounced or frequent inspections are subject to warrantless searches.

(D) is not the best response,

because not all commercial establishments are subject to warrantless searches.

"Ordinary" businesses — ones not subject to unusually heavy governmental regulations — are not subject to warrantless inspections, anymore than homes are. So this Choice is far too broad.

Answer 61

(C) is the best response,

because it correctly identifies that the motion should not be granted at this stage in the proceedings. Since a grand jury may hear and use *any* piece of evidence regardless of its admissibility, including hearsay and illegally obtained evidence, the filing of a motion to suppress before the proceeding is premature.

This is a tricky question, because it steers you toward analyzing the substantive merits of the motion and away from spotting the determinative procedural issue of timing. Probably, your first reaction was to analyze whether the employee's action could be considered governmental conduct which would make it subject to the Fourth Amendment. The fact pattern contains an ambiguous statement that the employee was "persuaded" by a police officer to remove a drinking glass from the defendant's office and offers no information from which to determine whether the defendant had a reasonable expectation of privacy as to the drinking glass in his office. Therefore, there aren't any concrete facts upon which to base a substantive decision.

The sketchiness of details should be an indicator to you to switch your focus and look for a different issue posed by the fact pattern. C is the best response because it recognizes that the merits of the motion are not considered at this stage.

(A) is not the best response,

because it misstates the law and does not address the relevant issue. During its deliberations, the grand jury reviews *all* evidence available to it to determine whether there is sufficient evidence to justify a trial. It does not matter whether probable cause existed, nor does it matter whether a warrant was secured or whether the circumstances supported an exception to the warrant requirement.

Furthermore, A mischaracterizes the law by implying that success on the merits of a motion to suppress would rely solely on the finding of probable cause. In fact, if there was conduct by the government and the defendant had a reasonable expectation of privacy in

regards to the glass, then, along with probable cause, it would be necessary to find that either an exception to the warrant requirement applied or that a warrant had been properly secured and executed. Therefore, probable cause would not alone be determinative.

However, this issue is irrelevant in light of the fact that the substantive merits of the motion are not considered at the grand jury stage, and that the denial of the motion should be based only on the improper timing of its filing. Since A ignores the relevant issue and otherwise misstates the law, it is not the best response.

(B) is not the best response,

because it arrives at the wrong result and ignores the central issue in the case. The relevant and determinative issue is whether the motion was filed at an appropriate time. It is easy to understand why you might have misdirected your attention and instead focused on whether there was governmental conduct involved in the search and seizure.

When confronted with a possible search and seizure violation and a question asking whether or not a motion to suppress should be granted, you are likely to focus on the facts surrounding the search and seizure to determine its legality. Here's the tip-off. The facts which are essential in determining whether the employee was acting as an agent of the police are not fully developed; there's a mere conclusory statement that the employee was "persuaded" by a police detective to remove a drinking glass from the defendant's office. Without further information, it's not possible to decide definitively whether or not the employee was acting as an agent for the government.

Since B cannot be clearly substantiated by the facts, you should be on the lookout for a hidden issue. The central issue, that a motion to suppress is premature during the grand jury proceeding, makes the determination of B's status irrelevant. As a result, B is not the best response.

(D) is not the best response,

because it arrives at the correct result, but for the wrong reason. The reason the motion should be denied is because it was filed at the wrong time. Whether or not the employee was considered a private citizen when he obtained the drinking glass will become relevant only when a motion is properly made at a later point. The facts as presented do not give you enough information to determine with sufficient certainty the status of the employee. This should indicate to you that the controlling issue does not depend on analysis of the substantive merits of the motion. Since D does not consider this and in doing so arrives at an incorrect result, it is not the best response.

Answer 62

(C) is the best response,

because it correctly identifies the constitutionally

required prerequisite for a plea hearing which is lacking in this case: that the defendant understand his right to a jury trial. In order to ensure that a defendant's guilty plea is intelligent and voluntary, a judge is constitutionally required to confirm that the defendant understands the following: the nature of the charge, the maximum possible penalty and the mandatory minimum penalty for the offense and that he is waiving his right to a jury trial as a result of pleading guilty. Although the judge did ask the defendant whether he understood that he did not have to plead guilty, he did not specifically ask the defendant whether he was aware that he was waiving his right to a jury trial. Since C identifies that the plea bargain was constitutionally deficient for this reason, it is the best response.

(A) is not the best response,

because it misstates the law. There is no constitutional requirement that a judge rule on outstanding motions before accepting a plea from a defendant. It may appear odd that Miller did not wait for an order on the motion before deciding to plead guilty, but there is no constitutional duty on the judge's part requiring him to first decide the motion. Perhaps an argument could be made that Miller's attorney did not provide him with effective counsel and should have advised him to wait for the ruling before pleading. However, that argument is irrelevant in light of the fact that there was a definite constitutional violation in that the judge did not determine whether Miller understood that he had a right to a jury trial. Since A does not correctly identify the reason for setting aside the defendant's plea, it is not the best response.

(B) is not the best response,

because it misstates the law. In order to ensure that a defendant's guilty plea is intelligent and voluntary, a judge is constitutionally required to confirm that the defendant understands the following: the nature of the charge, the maximum possible penalty and the mandatory minimum penalty for the offense and that he is waiving his right to a jury trial as a result of pleading guilty. Additionally, federal courts and some state courts require that the judge inquire as to the factual basis for the plea in order to determine its accuracy. However, this is not constitutionally required (except in the case where the defendant testifies that he is innocent, but then pleads guilty for some other reason, *e.g.,* to avoid a harsh sentence in case he is convicted). Since B erroneously states that the judge is constitutionally required to determine that the defendant actually committed the acts, it is not the best response.

(D) is not the best response,

because it incorrectly states the law. The judge is not required to determine whether the prosecutor has failed to disclose any exculpatory material. The disclosure of exculpatory evidence is a constitutional requirement the purpose of which is to guarantee a defendant

a fair trial and which is relevant at the trial stage. Since D incorrectly states that this is a constitutional requirement at the plea bargaining stage, it is not the best response.

Answer 63

(A) is the best response,

because Miller was not told he had the right to be silent.

When an individual is taken into custody by the authorities and is subjected to interrogation, he is entitled to *Miranda* warnings. When one deputy pinned Miller's arms behind his back, Miller was clearly in "custody" (he was not, and knew he was not, free to leave). When the other deputy asked demanded, "Tell us what you did with Jones ..." this was interrogation, since it was a demand for information. Therefore, the *Miranda* warnings were required. Since they weren't given, Miller's response is inadmissible. (Had he been given the warnings, he might have voluntarily waived his right to remain silent. But where the warnings aren't given, the court will not find a waiver no matter how likely the court thinks it is that the subject would have waived his rights had he been told of them.)

(B) is not the best response,

because the entry and search of the farm was not illegal.

Had the entry and search of the farm been illegal, Miller would indeed have had a good argument that his statement was the fruit of that illegality, and thus inadmissible. But the area the deputies entered was "open fields" not within the farmhouse's curtilege (see answer to next question), so Miller had no justifiable expectation of privacy in them (and no warrant was therefore required). Consequently, the deputies' entry was not a violation of the Fourth Amendment, and the fruit-of-the-poisonous-tree doctrine had no application.

In any event, Miller's failure to receive *Miranda* warnings is (as described in the treatment of Choice (A) above) the far more direct explanation of why the statement must be suppressed.

(C) is not the best response,

because there is no "hot pursuit" exception to the *Miranda* doctrine.

As the discussion of Choice (A) above shows, the *Miranda* warnings were required here. Choice (C) might be right if there were a "hot pursuit" exception to the requirement of *Miranda* warnings. But there isn't. (There's a "public safety" exception, but that's not what the choice says, and the situation here didn't fall within that exception anyway).

It's true that there's a "hot pursuit" exception somewhere in criminal procedure, but it's an exception to the requirement of a search warrant. (If the police are chasing a suspect whom they have probable cause to arrest, and he enters a dwelling, even his own, the police may follow and look for him in the premises without a warrant.) The exception has no relevance to the facts here (since you're asked about questioning, not searching).

(D) is not the best response,

because this was not the sort of emergency that triggers the "public safety" exception to the *Miranda* rule.

For the reasons described in the analysis of Choice (A) above, *Miranda* warnings were required here. It's true that there's a "public safety" exception to *Miranda*, announced in *N.Y. v. Quarles* (1984). But the doctrine applies only where unwarned questioning is dictated by "overriding considerations of public safety" (e.g., an attempt to find a weapon that may have been hidden nearby by the suspect). Here, after arresting Miller, the police had plenty of time to check for the grave based on the tip they'd received (and no danger from delay in doing so), so there was no imminent need or public danger of the sort that triggers the public-safety exception.

Answer 64

(C) is the best response,

because the scarecrow was not a part of Miller's home protected from a warrantless search.

The Fourth Amendment's protection against unreasonable searches and seizures applies not only to houses but also to the area immediately surrounding a dwelling, known as "curtilage" of the dwelling. The Supreme Court has articulated standards for determining whether a particular part of property falls within the curtilage of a person's dwelling. The inhabitant will have a justifiable expectation of privacy in those areas that do. The factors to be considered are: (1) the proximity of the home to the area claimed as curtilage; (2) whether the area is included within an enclosure that surrounds the home; (3) the nature of the uses to which the area is put; and (4) the steps taken by the resident to protect the area from observation by people passing it. *U.S. v. Dunn* (1987).

Under this 4-part test, the places entered by the deputies don't fall within the curtilege. Factor (2) might arguably point towards including the fields in the curtilege, but the other factors point the other way. In particular, a hillside 200 yards from the house is not "proximate" to the house, as factor (1) requires. (In *Dunn*, a barn just 60 yards from the farmhouse was held to be too far away to be part of the curtilege.)

Since the hillside and nearby fields weren't part of the curtilege, Miller is deemed to have no reasonable expectation of privacy as to their contents. Consequently, the police needed neither probable cause nor a warrant to search them.

(A) is not the best response,

because the deputies would need a warrant only for those areas in which Miller had an expectation of privacy.

As the analysis of Choice (C) above shows, because the hillside and fields were not part of the curtilege of the farmhouse, Miller had no expectation of privacy as to them. Consequently, no search warrant was required before the police entered.

(B) is not the best response,

because the search of Miller's fields was conducted correctly. See the analysis of Choice (C) above.

(D) is not the best response,

because the search was not illegal, but not for the reason given.

The fact that the clothing itself was not Miller's property would not cause his Fourth Amendment claim to fail. Had the police warrantlessly (and without an exception to the warrant requirement) entered a place as to which they needed a warrant, the fact that they then seized an item of property not belonging to Miller would not render the search invalid. (For instance, if they warrantlessly entered Miller's house and found Jones' clothing in Miller's bedroom, the clothing would be inadmissible).

Instead, the correct analysis is that no warrant was needed for the entry into the area where the clothing was found, for the reason given in the analysis of Choice (C) above.

STRATEGIES AND TACTICS

EVIDENCE

When it comes to Evidence questions on the MBE, there's both good news and bad news. The good news is these question virtually always require a mechanical application of the Federal Rules of Evidence (the "FRE"); however, that's the source of the bad news as well — the FRE are intricate, so you have to be *thoroughly* familiar with them in order to answer MBE Evidence questions successfully.

OUTLINE OF COVERAGE

The following outline of coverage for the Evidence portion of the MBE was adopted by the Bar Examiners for all MBEs given on or after July, 2003. It was designed to clarify what's covered on the Evidence portion of the exam. This is the most up-to-date outline of coverage released by the Bar Examiners, and your substantive study for Evidence should be centered around it.

Here's what you need to know:

I. Presentation of evidence
    A. Introduction of evidence
        1. Requirement of personal knowledge
        2. Refreshing recollection
        3. Objections and offers of proof
        4. Lay opinions
        5. Competency of witnesses
        6. Judicial notice
        7. Roles of judge and jury
        8. Limited admissibility
    B. Presumptions
    C. Mode and order
        1. Control by court
        2. Scope of examination
        3. Form of questions
        4. Exclusion of witnesses
    D. Impeachment, contradiction, and rehabilitation
        1. Inconsistent statements and conduct
        2. Bias and interest
        3. Conviction of crime
        4. Specific instances of conduct
        5. Character for truthfulness
        6. Ability to observe, remember, or relate accurately
        7. Impeachment of hearsay declarants
        8. Rehabilitation of impeached witnesses
II. Relevancy and reasons for excluding relevant evidence
    A. Probative value
        1. Relevancy
        2. Exclusion for unfair prejudice, confusion, or waste of time
    B. Authentication and verification
    C. Character and related concepts
        1. Admissibility of character
        2. Methods of proving character
        3. Habit and routine practice
        4. Other crimes, acts, transactions, and events
    D. Expert testimony and scientific evidence

1. Qualifications of witnesses
2. Bases of testimony
3. Ultimate issue rule
4. Reliability of scientific evidence
    E. Real, demonstrative, and experimental evidence
III. Privileges and other policy exclusions
    A. Spousal immunity and marital communications
    B. Attorney-client and work product
    C. Physician/psychotherapist-patient
    D. Self-incrimination
    E. Other privileges
    F. Insurance coverage
    G. Remedial measures
    H. Compromise, payment of medical expenses, and plea negotiations
    I. Past sexual conduct
IV. Writings, recordings, and photographs
    A. Requirement of original
    B. Summaries
    C. Completeness rule
V. Hearsay and circumstances of its admissibility
    A. Definition of hearsay
        1. What is hearsay
        2. Prior statements by witness
        3. Statements attributable to party-opponent
        4. Multiple hearsay
    B. Present sense impressions and excited utterances
    C. Statements of medical, emotional, or physical condition
    D. Statements for purposes of medical diagnosis and treatment
    E. Past recollection recorded
    F. Business records
    G. Public records and reports
    H. Learned treatises
    I. Former testimony; depositions
    J. Statements against interest
    K. Other exceptions to the hearsay rule

WHAT TO EXPECT

You'll face 33 Evidence questions on the MBE. Of these, approximately one-third will be based on category I (Presentation of evidence), one-third on category V (Hearsay and definition of hearsay), and one-third on categories II, III, and IV. There will be questions from each of the roman numeral topics on the exam, but not necessarily from each of the sub-topics.

Evidence questions on the MBE virtually always consist of short, focused hypotheticals. Inevitably, the hypothetical will involve a piece of evidence or an item of testimony, and you will be asked to identify the basis on which the evidence will be found admissible or inadmissible.

STUDY STRATEGIES: DETAILS, DETAILS, DETAILS

Naturally, the Bar Examiners could test you on virtually any aspect of Evidence. Since they're interested in determining whether or not you're thoroughly familiar with Evidence law, they tend to test concepts that are particularly difficult—those that are tricky either because the concept tested involves a lot of elements (e.g., some of the hearsay exceptions), or because it has a misleading, seductive name (e.g., prior inconsistent statements, Best Evidence Rule). While you should be fully prepared on every topic, pay particular attention to the following:

1. **Study only the Federal Rules of Evidence.**

    The Multistate exam follows the Federal Rules of Evidence, *not the common law*. You absolutely must keep the differences between the two straight in your mind, since this is a very easy area for the Bar Examiners to test. Look out for situations where the result under the FRE and the common law will be different. Here's an example:

    > Peters sued Davis for $100,000 for injuries received in a traffic accident. Davis charges Peters with contributory negligence and alleges that Peters failed to have his lights on at a time when it was dark enough to require them. Davis offers to have Bystander testify that he was talking to Witness when he heard the crash and heard Witness, now deceased, exclaim, "That car doesn't have any lights on." Bystander's testimony is
    >
    > A. admissible as a statement of present sense impression
    >
    > B. admissible, because Witness is not available to testify
    >
    > C. inadmissible as hearsay, not within any exception
    >
    > D. inadmissible, because of the Dead Man's Statute

    Under FRE 803(1), statements of present sense impression are admissible as an exception to the hearsay rule without requiring the speaker's availability (thus, A is the correct response). If you remembered and applied the common law rule — that present sense impressions are hearsay, not within any exception — you'd choose choice (C), and you'd be wrong.

    While we're talking about hearsay, here's a simple rule to remember. If you aren't sure whether something is hearsay or not, *try to identify the out-of-court declarant*. Remember, hearsay is an out-of-court statement offered to prove the truth of its assertion. If it's a statement, it must have a declarant. If you can't identify one (e.g., the speaker of a comment, or the writer of a document), then the item can't be hearsay.

2. **Know the requirements for the substantive use of prior inconsistent statements, identifications, and prior consistent statements, FRE 801(d)(1).**

    Questions involving these three hearsay exclusions are frequently missed, both because the exceptions are very technical and because their names may tempt you to apply them incorrectly. Here's an example:

    > Miller is tried for armed robbery of the First Bank of City.
    >
    > At the request of police, the teller who was robbed prepared a sketch bearing a strong likeness to Miller, but the teller died in an automobile accident before Miller was arrested. At trial the prosecution offers the sketch. The sketch is
    >
    > A. admissible as an identification of a person after perceiving him
    >
    > B. admissible as a past recollection recorded
    >
    > C. inadmissible as hearsay not within any exception
    >
    > D. inadmissible as an opinion of the teller

    A is a tempting response, because the item in question is, indeed, what A says it is: an identification of a person after perceiving him. Watch out, though; that's *not enough* to make the prior identification admissible: to apply this exception, the declarant must also be a currently testifying witness, subject to cross-examination. According to the facts, the teller is dead, so this exception can't possibly apply. (The correct response is C.)

    The one common factor which makes prior statements of these three types *inadmissible* is that *the facts do not satisfy the "presently testifying witness" requirement*, as illustrated by the example above;

therefore, whenever an answer choice on the MBE mentions a prior identification, prior inconsistent statement, or prior consistent statement, you can eliminate common distractors easily by checking to see if the declarant is currently testifying. If he isn't, that answer can't possibly be correct!

In addition, with prior inconsistent statements, there's something else to keep in mind. Even if a prior inconsistent statement doesn't meet all the requirements for admissibility, it will always be available, as non-hearsay, to **impeach or rehabilitate** a witness (FRE 801(c)).

3. Know the requirements of admissibility on items like authentication and expert testimony.

You need to be familiar with the **minimums required** to admit documents, photographs, expert testimony, and the like. For instance, you should know that expert testimony is **not** needed to authenticate a photograph — all that's required is a person who saw the scene in question and can testify that the photograph **fairly and accurately represents or illustrates** what it's supposed to depict. Likewise, expert testimony isn't required to authenticate a signature — anyone personally familiar with an individual's handwriting can testify as to its authenticity, as long as the familiarity was **not acquired for the purposes of the litigation**. FRE 901(b)(2). Of course, a graphologist **could** authenticate handwriting by comparing handwriting samples, without **any** personal familiarity with the individual's handwriting — but the expert testimony isn't necessary if a lay witness (who meets the above requirements) testifies. Here's an example:

> In a trial between Jones and Smith, an issue arose about Smith's ownership of a horse, which had caused damage to Jones's crops.
>
> Jones seeks to introduce in evidence a photograph of his cornfield in order to depict the nature and extent of the damage done. The judge should rule the photograph
>
> A. admissible if Jones testifies that it fairly and accurately portrays the condition of the cornfield after the damage was done
>
> B. admissible if Jones testifies that the photograph was taken within a week after the alleged occurrence
>
> C. inadmissible if Jones fails to call the photographer to testify concerning the circumstances under which the photograph was taken
>
> D. inadmissible if it is possible to describe the damage to the cornfield through direct oral testimony

The correct response is A. Under the FRE test given above, Jones is certainly qualified to authenticate the photograph. The question tries to muddy the waters here, since Jones, as the owner of the property, has reason to make the damage seem more extensive than it actually was; note, though, that the possibility of falsified evidence is an entirely unrelated matter. Here, all that counts is that Jones qualifies, under the FRE, to authenticate the photograph.

4. Be thoroughly familiar with the Best Evidence Rule.

It's important to know **exactly** what situations are covered by the Best Evidence Rule. Generally, the MBE contains relatively few questions to which the Best Evidence Rule actually applies; it is, however, a popular "distractor," because it **sounds** as though it applies to a far broader spectrum of situations than it **actually** does. Under the Best Evidence Rule, FRE 1002, **where the material terms of a writing are at issue, the "original writing" itself (which includes photocopies and carbons) must be produced. Copies and oral testimony concerning the writing's contents are permissible only on a showing that the original is unavailable and that its lack of availability is not the result of the proponent's serious misconduct.**

In simpler terms, this means there are really only **two** situations in which the Best Evidence Rule requires that the original document, if available, be introduced:

1. The terms of the writing are being proven; or
2. The witness is testifying relying on the writing.

Remember, this rule only applies to **material terms**. A common trap on the MBE is to offer a situation in which the witness is, in fact, testifying relying on a writing, but in which the **subject of the testimony is only a collateral matter** (so the Best Evidence Rule doesn't apply). Here's an example:

> Phillips purchased a suit of thermal underwear manufactured by Makorp from synthetic materials. While he was attempting to stamp out a fire, Phillips' thermal underwear caught fire and burned in a melting fashion up to his waist. He suffered a heart attack a half hour later. In a suit against Makorp, Phillips alleged that negligence and breach of warranty caused both the burn and the heart attack. Phillips testified to the foregoing.

Phillips testified that his purchase of the underwear occurred on April 17th, a fact of minor importance in the case. He stated that he could identify the date because his secretary had taken the day off to attend the first game of the baseball season and he had checked his company's payroll records to verify the date. Makorp moved to strike the testimony as to the date. The motion should be

    A. sustained, because the best evidence of the information contained in the payroll records is the records themselves

    B. sustained, because Phillips' testimony is based upon hearsay declarations contained in the payroll records

    C. overruled if the judge has personal knowledge of the date on which the baseball season opened

    D. overruled, because the payroll records relate to a collateral matter

A is a tempting choice, because Phillips *is* testifying relying on the payroll records. Note, however, that the Best Evidence Rule only applies when the **terms are material**. Here, the only purpose the payroll records served was to **bolster Phillips' memory on a "fact of minor importance"**; they have no other impact on the case. Therefore, A is not the best choice. The best response is choice D — the payroll records themselves needn't be offered, because they relate to a collateral matter.

EXAM TACTICS

1. Break the question down to its theoretical basis.

On Evidence questions, it is vitally important that you analyze questions both logically and theoretically, because Evidence law is frequently counter-intuitive. Your instinct may tell you that a piece of evidence should be inadmissible, whereas in fact, under the Federal Rules, it **is** admissible. The reverse is also true — you may believe in your heart that a piece of evidence should be admitted, but, according to the FRE, it's inadmissible hearsay. To avoid being mislead, when you read an Evidence question, you should always ask yourself: What in theory is going on here? Here's an example:

Miller is tried for armed robbery of the First Bank of City.

Miller testifies on his own behalf. On cross-examination of Miller, the prosecutor asks Miller whether he was convicted in the previous year of tax fraud. This question is

    A. proper to show that Miller is inclined to lie

    B. proper to show that Miller is inclined to steal money

    C. improper, because the conviction has insufficient similarity to the crime charged

    D. improper, because the probative value of the evidence is outweighed by the danger of unfair prejudice

If you break this question down to what's happening **theoretically and logically**, you can see that the prosecutor is attempting to impeach a witness with evidence from the witness's own mouth — in other words, "intrinsic" impeachment. He's attempting to do so by using a recent, prior conviction for a crime involving dishonesty.

Your instinct will probably tell you that this evidence should not be admissible, because, regardless of the purpose for which it is **intended**, we all know what the jury is likely to do with it — they're going to take it as evidence that Miller is inclined to steal money. Your instinct will be even stronger in this instance, since the witness is the criminal defendant himself. What the prosecutor is trying to do is, of course, an improper use of prior, unrelated acts to show character; if you analyze the facts coldly and theoretically, though, you should realize that the prosecutor's question is a proper form of intrinsic impeachment, under FRE 609(a), since the conviction isn't more than ten years old and is for a felony or a misdemeanor involving dishonesty.

If, therefore, you set aside your emotional reaction and analyze the answer choices logically, you'll find that A is the correct answer. Since the prior conviction is being used to impeach Miller, it's being used to attack his credibility — in other words, to show that he's inclined to lie. That's what A says, and it's the correct answer. (By the way, even with a "cold" analysis of the facts, you might still consider D as a potentially correct answer, because "legal relevance" is never a response you can dismiss out of hand. In this question, legal relevance is not a problem, because the evidence doesn't have the "shocking" quality of evidence normally excluded on this ground: the probative value of a tax fraud conviction is unlikely to be substantially outweighed by the probability of undue prejudice. Issues of legal relevance generally arise in instances of shocking evidence, such as severed limbs, gruesome photos, and the like.) Here's another example:

In a tort action, Fisher testified against Dawes. Dawes then called Jones, who testified that Fisher had a bad reputation for veracity. Dawes then also called Weld to testify that Fisher once perpetrated a hoax on the police.

Weld's testimony is

    A. admissible, provided that the hoax involved untruthfulness

    B. admissible, provided that the hoax resulted in conviction of Fisher

    C. inadmissible, because it is merely cumulative impeachment

    D. inadmissible, because it is extrinsic evidence of a specific instance of misconduct

Reading this question, you should, first, identify what's going on: Fisher is being impeached with extrinsic evidence (i.e., not from his own mouth) about an unconvicted bad act; such impeachment is inadmissible — evidence of unconvicted bad acts must be intrinsic in order to be valid. This example shows that, if you categorize the method being used (or the type of hearsay involved in a hearsay question) before you try to answer, you'll save time and improve your chances of answering correctly.

2. Eliminate answer choices which don't apply to the facts.

As with all MBE questions, you should attack questions by eliminating the wrong choices until you're left with only one, the correct choice. In some Evidence questions, the Bar Examiners have made this even easier for you because *some answer choices don't even apply to the facts*. Any answer choice that doesn't apply to the facts in the question *can't* be the correct response! Here's an example:

An issue in Parker's action against Daves for causing Parker's back injury was whether Parker's condition had resulted principally from a similar occurrence five years before, with which Daves had no connection.

Parker called Watts, his treating physician, who offered to testify that when she saw Parker after the latest occurrence, Parker told her that before the accident he had been working full time, without pain or limitation of motion, in a job that required lifting heavy boxes.

Watts's testimony should be

    A. admitted, because it is a statement of Parker's then existing physical condition

    B. admitted, because it is a statement made for purposes of medical diagnosis or treatment

    C. excluded, because it is hearsay not within any exception

    D. excluded, because Parker is available as a witness

A is an example of an answer choice that doesn't apply to the facts. In talking to his physician, Parker was describing his condition *before* the latest occurrence, not his condition as it existed at the time of the physical exam, which is what A suggests. Since A *misstates* the facts, it cannot be correct! (In fact, the correct response is B.)

Making such a mistake is inexcusable, since the question itself provides you with all the grounds you need to eliminate the incorrect choice. As a result, this type of mistake is graded most harshly in our scoring system. Here's another example:

Rider, a bus passenger, sued Transit Company for injuries to his back from an accident caused by Transit's negligence. Transit denies that Rider received any injury in the accident.

Rider's counsel seeks to introduce an affidavit he obtained in preparation for trial from Dr. Bond, who has since died. The affidavit avers that Dr. Bond examined Rider two days after the Transit Company accident and found him suffering from a recently incurred back injury. The judge should rule the affidavit

    A. admissible as a statement of present bodily condition made to a physician

    B. admissible as prior recorded testimony

    C. inadmissible, because it is irrelevant

    D. inadmissible, because it is hearsay, not within any exception

Here, choice A can't possibly be correct, because the facts indicate the statement was that of Dr. Bond, not that of Rider, so the statement *can't* be "a statement of present bodily condition made to a physician!" Since A doesn't correctly characterize the facts, it cannot be the correct response, and you should eliminate it immediately. (The best response is D.)

3. Know the doctrine of limited admissibility.

For some MBE questions, it's not enough to know that a piece of evidence is admissible; you must also know *for what purposes* it's admissible. A common trap in MBE questions is to make you forget that evidence may be admissible for one purpose (which is given in one of the answers) and not for another (which is given in another answer choice). You may be tricked into choosing a wrong answer if you realize that an answer choice contains a correct rule, and so choose that answer. If the rule *isn't applicable to the facts*, you'll be wrong — needlessly wrong.

Here's an example:

> Alice was held up at the point of a gun, an unusual revolver with a red-painted barrel, while she was clerking in a neighborhood grocery store. Dennis is charged with armed robbery of Alice.
>
> The prosecutor calls Winthrop to testify that, a week after the robbery of Alice, he was robbed by Dennis with a pistol that had red paint on the barrel. Winthrop's testimony is
>
> A. admissible as establishing an identifying circumstance
>
> B. admissible as showing that Dennis was willing to commit robbery
>
> C. inadmissible, because it is improper character evidence
>
> D. inadmissible, because its probative value is substantially outweighed by the danger of unfair prejudice

Here, the evidence being offered will establish an identifying circumstance — that makes what would, otherwise, be inadmissible character evidence into admissible evidence: if it were offered only to show Dennis is willing to commit robbery, it would be inadmissible, but, here, it's offered to help identify Dennis. Thus, applying the doctrine of limited admissibility, A is the correct response — not C.

Here's another example:

> In Polk's negligence action against Dell arising out of a multiple-car collision, Witt testified for Polk that Dell went through a red light. On cross-examination, Dell seeks to question Witt about her statement that the light was yellow, made in a deposition that Witt gave in a separate action between Adams and Baker. The transcript of the deposition is self-authenticating. On proper objection, the court should rule the inquiry
>
> A. admissible for impeachment only
>
> B. admissible as substantive evidence only
>
> C. admissible for impeachment and as substantive evidence
>
> D. inadmissible, because it is hearsay not within any exception

Here, the statement in Witt's deposition will be admissible under the "former testimony" hearsay exception, FRE 804(b)(1). It is available *both* for impeachment *and* as substantive evidence. It wouldn't be enough to know that the deposition will be admissible as "former testimony"; you'd need to know that the testimony is admissible for both impeachment purposes and as substantive evidence!

4. Be sensitive to clues in the facts.

It's always important to *read MBE questions carefully.* In Evidence questions, especially, careful reading of the facts can steer you toward the correct answer. Here's an example:

> Phillips purchased a suit of thermal underwear manufactured by Makorp from synthetic materials. While he was attempting to stamp out a fire, Phillips' thermal underwear caught fire and burned in a melting fashion up to his waist. He suffered a heart attack a half hour later. In a suit against Makorp, Phillips alleged that negligence and breach of warranty caused both the burn and the heart attack. Phillips testified to the foregoing.
>
> Phillips testified that his purchase of the underwear occurred on April 17th, a fact of minor importance to the case. He stated that he could identify the date because his secretary had taken the day off to attend the first game of the baseball season and he had checked his company's payroll records to verify the date. Makorp moves to strike the testimony as to the date. The motion should be
>
> A. sustained, because the best evidence of the information contained in the payroll records is the records themselves
>
> B. sustained, because Phillips' testimony is based upon hearsay declarations contained in the payroll records
>
> C. overruled if the judge has personal knowledge of the date on which the baseball season opened
>
> D. overruled, because the payroll records relate to a collateral matter

Here, a close reading of the facts alone would tell you that the testimony involves *"a fact of minor importance to the case."* As a result, the date is a *collateral issue*, so the Best Evidence Rule doesn't apply. If you read the facts carefully, you could eliminate choice A right off the bat. (In fact, the best response is D.)

5. **Dealing with common answer choices to Evidence questions.**

   a. **"The testimony is inadmissible due to its self-serving nature."**

   This is a relatively common distractor. Whenever you see an choice like this, it's *incorrect*, regardless of the facts. The self-serving nature of the testimony affects its *credibility*, not its *admissibility*.

   b. **"Admissible as *res gestae*" or "Inadmissible as testimony on ultimate issues."**

   These alternatives, especially *res gestae*, are common distractors on the MBE. ***Don't choose old rules like these.*** *Res gestae*, for instance, is a common law concept which dealt with hearsay exceptions that are now covered, under the FRE, by declarations of present bodily condition, declarations of present state of mind, excited utterances, and declarations of present sense impression. The hearsay doctrine under the FRE is far more precise than the old *res gestae* concept. The same goes for testimony on ultimate issues. This is a limitation which is not recognized under the FRE. Remember, the MBE is concerned with the present state of the law. Don't clutter up your already overtaxed memory by learning fine points of outmoded concepts, which will show up only as "distractors."

   c. **"Inadmissible because the declarant is available to testify."**

   This is a relatively common answer choice in questions dealing with hearsay. While it *can* be correct, since a few hearsay exceptions do require that the declarant be unavailable, *for the majority of hearsay exceptions, unavailability is not required.* The hallmark of the hearsay exceptions under the FRE is *trustworthiness*, not unavailability. (The hearsay exceptions which *do* require unavailability are found in FRE 804; they include prior testimony, dying declarations, declarations against interest, and statements of pedigree, as well as the "catch-all" exception.)

   d. **"Inadmissible because the probative value of the evidence is outweighed by the probability of undue prejudice."**

   If a piece of evidence is inadmissible because of this, it's not legally relevant. On the MBE, legal relevance is a *wild card* — sometimes it's the best choice, and sometimes it's not. The best thing you can do is to keep in mind the type of evidence typically excluded due to legal relevance problems: *shocking* evidence. Imagine yourself as a juror and decide whether or not the evidence would jolt your mind. Here's an example:

   > Miller is tried for armed robbery of the First Bank of City.
   >
   > The prosecution, in its case in chief, offers evidence that when Miller was arrested one day after the crime, he had a quantity of heroin and a hypodermic needle in his possession. This evidence should be
   >
   > A. admitted to prove Miller's motive to commit the crime
   >
   > B. admitted to prove Miller's propensity to commit crimes
   >
   > C. excluded, because its probative value is substantially outweighed by the danger of unfair prejudice
   >
   > D. excluded, because such evidence may be offered only to rebut evidence of good character offered by defendant

   The correct answer is C — the evidence here is not legally relevant, because it will be given prejudicial weight by the jury. Wouldn't you tend to give it more weight than it deserves, if you were a juror? An important point to remember is that, but for the legal relevance problem, the evidence would be admissible, because it would tend to prove Miller's motive to commit the crime (choice A). *Legal relevance is one of the few issues in Evidence law which requires you to do some fine line-drawing and to make judgment calls of your own. Remember — even if a piece of evidence passes every other test of admissibility, it must also be legally relevant.*

   e. **"Inadmissible because it is hearsay not within any exception."**

   As with the "legal relevance" answer choice in (d), above, the "inadmissible" choice is one that can go either way. There is a way, however, to greatly increase your chances of answering a question successfully when one of the choices is the "inadmissible" choice:

Overcome your natural instinct that every piece of evidence is admissible, somehow.

What the answer choice is **really** saying when it says *"inadmissible as hearsay not within any exception"* is "inadmissible under any other answer choice for this question." If you read it this way, it becomes obvious that **the only way to arrive at the "inadmissible" answer choice is through a process of elimination**. In fact, questions in which the "inadmissible" choice is the correct one tend to be more "cut and dried" than other Evidence questions, because, for "inadmissible" to be the correct choice, the other three alternatives must be clearly wrong. Here's an example:

> Miller is tried for armed robbery of the First Bank of City.
>
> At the request of police, the teller who was robbed prepared a sketch bearing a strong likeness to Miller, but the teller died in an automobile accident before Miller was arrested. At trial the prosecution offers the sketch. The sketch is
>
> A. admissible as an identification of a person after perceiving him
>
> B. admissible as past recollection recorded
>
> C. inadmissible as hearsay not within any exception
>
> D. inadmissible as an opinion of the teller

The correct answer here is C. This is a good example of an "inadmissible" question, because your gut reaction on reading these facts is that **the judge would find a way to admit the sketch**. Maybe the judge would, but not on any of these grounds. The sketch clearly does not fit any of the alternatives to C! It can't be alternative A, because, as stated earlier in this section, a prior identification is only admissible when the declarant is testifying; similarly, B is only applicable to witnesses. D is not applicable, because it fails to identify the sketch as hearsay (and, beyond that, lay testimony by the preparer of the sketch would be admissible). That leaves only C, which **must**, therefore, be the correct response.

f.   Avoid any answer choice stating a concept you don't recognize.

If you've prepared sufficiently for the MBE, you will not come across any correct answer choices that mention concepts you don't recognize at all. The Bar Examiners are exceptionally skillful at making nonsense concepts sound like the real thing, and these can prove a tempting trap for the unwary. Here's an example:

> Pemberton and three passengers, Able, Baker, and Charley, were injured when their car was struck by a truck owned by Mammoth Corporation and driven by Edwards. Helper, also a Mammoth employee, was riding in the truck. The issues in *Pemberton v. Mammoth* include the negligence of Edwards in driving too fast and failing to wear glasses, and of Pemberton in failing to yield the right of way.
>
> Pemberton's counsel proffers evidence showing that shortly after the accident Mammoth put a speed governor on the truck involved in the accident. The judge should rule the proffered evidence
>
> A. admissible as an admission of a party
>
> B. admissible as *res gestae*
>
> C. inadmissible for public policy reasons
>
> D. inadmissible, because it would lead to the drawing of an inference on an inference

Choice D here doesn't sound familiar to you, does it? It shouldn't — there's no such legal principle. It **sounds** like a legal principle, but it isn't one. The only way you'd choose an answer choice like this was if you weren't sufficiently prepared for the MBE. If you feel you've prepared adequately, there shouldn't be any unfamiliar concepts in correct answers choices. (By the way, the correct response here is C — subsequent remedial measures cannot be admitted to prove negligence or wrongdoing, due to public policy reasons.)

This question also illustrates two of the principles we addressed earlier: one, *res gestae* is never the correct response; two, you need to be familiar with rationales as well as the rules themselves. Here, the correct choice, C, only **implies** that the rule excluding evidence of subsequent remedial measures is involved, it doesn't state it directly. Even though it only states the rationale, it's the correct response.

g.   Avoid any answer choice which would exclude testimony because of witness incompetence.

The FRE are extremely liberal concerning competence. In fact, there are only two requirements: the witness must have personal knowledge of the matter on which he will testify (FRE 602), and he must declare that he will testify truthfully, by oath or affirmation (FRE 603). Also, whenever you see "incompetence" as a possibility on the MBE, be careful not to confuse it with **bias** — that's **normally** what's at issue when competence is raised as a possibility. Here's an example:

> Drew was tried for the July 21 murder of Victor. Drew called Wilson to testify to alibi. On cross-examination of Wilson, the prosecution asked, "Isn't it a fact that you are Drew's first cousin?" The question is
>
> A. proper, because it goes to bias
>
> B. proper, because a relative is not competent to give reputation testimony
>
> C. improper, because the question goes beyond the scope of direct examination
>
> D. improper, because the evidence being sought is irrelevant

h. How to handle any answer choice dealing with expert testimony.

You should remember the liberal bases on which expert testimony can rely. Under FRE 703 and 705, an expert may testify on three types of information: personal observation, facts presented to the expert at trial (e.g., answering a hypothetical question), or facts introduced to the expert outside the courtroom (e.g., by technicians or consultants) of the type upon which experts in his field reasonably rely. An expert may base his opinion on facts not in evidence and even on facts which could not be admitted as evidence because they're inadmissible hearsay. Thus, when you come across a question on expert testimony, look closely before you decide the testimony is inadmissible. Here's an example:

> Dever was indicted for the murder of Vickers by poison. At trial, the prosecutor calls the county coroner, Dr. Wolfe, who is a board-certified pathologist, to testify that, in accord with good practice in her specialty, she has studied microphotographic slides, made under her supervision by medical assistants, of tissue taken from Vickers' corpse and that it is Wolfe's opinion, based on that study, that Vickers died of poisoning. The slides have not been offered in evidence. Dr. Wolfe's opinion should be
>
> A. excluded, because the cause of death is a critical issue to be decided by the trier of fact
>
> B. excluded, because her opinion is based on facts not in evidence
>
> C. admitted, because Wolfe followed accepted medical practice in arriving at her opinion
>
> D. admitted, because her opinion is based on matters observed pursuant to a duty imposed by law

Here, C is the best response, because, under the test stated above, C correctly identifies that the expert testimony was based on a suitable source. Any time you face an "expert testimony" question, it pays to keep in mind how broad the realm is on which an expert may rely.

i. How to handle answer choices dealing with admissions in conjunction with offers to settle or offers to pay medical bills.

When you enter the world of admissions in relation to offers to pay medical bills and offers of compromise, you've opened a real can of worms. The FRE and the common law overlap to a small extent, and there are four different possibilities for each. Also, the rationale for excluding some of these admissions and admitting others is not at all obvious. The four possibilities under the FRE are: offers and payment of settlements themselves, admissions in conjunctions with an offer to pay a settlement, offers and payment of medical bills, and admissions in conjunction with an offer to pay medical bills.

Of these four, all are inadmissible **except** admissions in conjunction with an offer to pay medical bills.

If you remember a simple word picture, you can easily memorize this rule. First, notice that the payment of settlements or of medical bills, as well as offers to pay, are always inadmissible. Thus, it's only the admissions that you have to worry about: admissions with medical bills are admissible, whereas admissions with settlements are not. Here's a simple way to remember that: picture, in your mind, a settlement of some sort— an Indian settlement, pilgrims, whatever is easiest for you to picture. Then, picture a big, red plastic "X" laid over the settlement: it's so big the settlers are tripping over it. This should remind you that admissions in conjunction with settlements are not admissible, and, by process of elimination, that admissions with medical bills **are**. This distinction is obviously one that does not come up in every Evidence MBE question, but when it does, you'll be prepared for it!

QUESTIONS
EVIDENCE

QUESTIONS

EVIDENCE

Question 1

Plaintiff sued Defendant for illegal discrimination, claiming that Defendant fired him because of his race. At trial, Plaintiff called Witness, expecting him to testify that Defendant had admitted the racial motivation. Instead, Witness testified that Defendant said that he had fired Plaintiff because of his frequent absenteeism. While Witness is still on the stand, Plaintiff offers a properly authenticated secret tape recording he had made at a meeting with Witness in which Witness related Defendant's admissions of racial motivation.

The tape recording is

(A) admissible as evidence of Defendant's racial motivation and to impeach Witness's testimony.

(B) admissible only to impeach Witness's testimony.

(C) inadmissible, because it is hearsay not within any exception.

(D) inadmissible, because a secret recording is an invasion of Witness's right of privacy under the U.S. Constitution.

Question 2

At Devlin's trial for burglary, Jaron supported Devlin's alibi that they were fishing together at the time of the crime. On cross-examination, Jaron was asked whether his statement on a credit card application that he had worked for his present employer for the last five years was false. Jaron denied that the statement was false.

The prosecutor then calls Wilcox, the manager of the company for which Jaron works, to testify that although Jaron had been first employed five years earlier and is now employed by the company, there had been a three-year period during which he had not been so employed.

The testimony of Wilcox is

(A) admissible, in the judge's discretion, because Jaron's credibility is a fact of major consequence to the case.

(B) admissible, as a matter of right, because Jaron "opened the door" by his denial on cross-examination.

(C) inadmissible, because whether Jaron lied in his application is a matter that cannot be proved by extrinsic evidence.

(D) inadmissible, because the misstatement by Jaron could have been caused by misunderstanding of the application form.

Question 3

Defendant was charged with attempted murder of Victor in a sniping incident in which Defendant allegedly shot at Victor from ambush as Victor drove his car along an expressway. The prosecutor offers evidence that seven years earlier Defendant had fired a shotgun into a woman's home and that Defendant had once pointed a handgun at another driver while driving on the street.

This evidence should be

(A) excluded, because such evidence can be elicited only during cross-examination.

(B) excluded, because it is improper character evidence.

(C) admitted as evidence of Defendant's propensity toward violence.

(D) admitted as relevant evidence of Defendant's identity, plan, or motive.

Question 4

In a jurisdiction without a Dead Man's Statute, Parker's estate sued Davidson claiming that Davidson had borrowed from Parker $10,000, which had not been repaid as of Parker's death. Parker was run over by a truck. At the accident scene, while dying from massive injuries, Parker told Officer Smith to "make sure my estate collects the $10,000 I loaned to Davidson."

Smith's testimony about Parker's statement is

(A) inadmissible, because it is more unfairly prejudicial than probative.

(B) inadmissible, because it is hearsay not within any exception.

(C) admissible as an excited utterance.

(D) admissible as a statement under belief of impending death.

Question 5

In a federal investigation of Defendant for tax fraud, the grand jury seeks to obtain a letter written January 15 by Defendant to her attorney in which she stated: "Please prepare a deed giving my ranch to University but, in order to get around the tax law, I want it back-dated to December 15." The attorney refuses to produce the letter on the ground of privilege.

Production of the letter should be

(A) prohibited, because the statement is protected by the attorney-client privilege.

(B) prohibited, because the statement is protected by the client's privilege against self-incrimination.

(C) required, because the statement was in furtherance of crime or fraud.

(D) required, because the attorney-client privilege belongs to the client and can be claimed only by her.

Question 6

Plaintiff sued Defendant Auto Manufacturing for his wife's death, claiming that a defective steering mechanism on the family car caused it to veer off the road and hit a tree when his wife was driving. Defendant claims that the steering mechanism was damaged in the collision and offers testimony that the deceased wife was intoxicated at the time of the accident.

Testimony concerning the wife's intoxication is

(A) admissible to provide an alternate explanation of the accident's cause.

(B) admissible as proper evidence of the wife's character.

(C) inadmissible, because it is improper to prove character evidence by specific conduct.

(D) inadmissible, because it is substantially more prejudicial than probative.

Question 7

Alex and Sam were arrested for holding up a gas station. They were taken to police headquarters and placed in a room for interrogation. As a police officer addressing both started to give them the Miranda warnings prior to the questioning, Alex said, "Look, Sam planned the damned thing and I was dumb enough to go along with it. We robbed the place – what else is there to say?" Sam said nothing. Sam was escorted into another room and a full written confession was then obtained from Alex. If Sam is brought to trial on an indictment charging him with robbery, the fact that Sam failed to object to Alex's statement and remained silent after Alex had implicated him in the crime should be ruled

(A) admissible because his silence was an implied admission by Sam that he had participated in the crime

(B) admissible because a statement of a participant in a crime is admissible against another participant

(C) inadmissible because, under the circumstances, there was no duty or responsibility on Sam's part to respond

(D) inadmissible because whatever Alex may have said has no probative value in a trial against Sam

Question 8

Plaintiff's estate sued Defendant Stores claiming that Guard, one of Defendant's security personnel, wrongfully shot and killed Plaintiff when Plaintiff fled after being accused of shoplifting. Guard was convicted of manslaughter for killing Plaintiff. At his criminal trial Guard, who was no longer working for Defendant, testified that Defendant's security director had instructed him to stop shoplifters "at all costs." Because Guard's criminal conviction is on appeal, he refuses to testify at the civil trial. Plaintiff's estate then offers an authenticated transcript of Guard's criminal trial testimony concerning the instructions of Defendant's security director.

This evidence is

(A) admissible as a statement of an agent of a party-opponent.

(B) admissible, because the instruction from the security director is not hearsay.

(C) admissible, although hearsay, as former testimony.

(D) inadmissible, because it is hearsay not within any exception.

Question 9

The bus in which Pat was riding was struck from the rear by a taxi. He sued Cab Company for a claimed neck injury. Cab Company claimed the impact was too slight to have caused the claimed injury and introduced testimony that all passengers had refused medical attention at the time of the accident. Pat called a doctor from City Hospital to testify that three persons (otherwise proved to have been on the bus) were admitted to the hospital for treatment of severe neck pain within a week after the accident. The trial judge should rule the doctor's testimony

(A) admissible, because a doctor is properly qualified as an expert in medical matters

(B) admissible if other testimony established causal connection between the other passengers' pain and the accident

(C) inadmissible, because the testimony to neck pain is hearsay, not within any exception

(D) inadmissible, because the testimony is not the best evidence of the other passengers' pain and the passengers are not shown to be unavailable

Question 10

Defendant is on trial for participating in a drug sale. The prosecution calls Witness, an undercover officer, to testify that, when Seller sold the drugs to Witness, Seller introduced Defendant to Witness as "my partner in this" and Defendant shook hands with Witness but said nothing.

Witness's testimony is

(A) inadmissible, because there is no evidence that Seller was authorized to speak for Defendant.

(B) inadmissible, because the statement of Seller is hearsay not within any exception.

(C) admissible as a statement against Defendant's penal interest.

(D) admissible as Defendant's adoption of Seller's statement.

Question 11

In a federal civil trial, Plaintiff wishes to establish that, in a state court, Defendant had been convicted of fraud, a fact that Defendant denies.

Which mode of proof of the conviction is LEAST likely to be permitted?

(A) A certified copy of the judgment of conviction, offered as a self-authenticating document.

(B) Testimony of Plaintiff, who was present at the time of

the sentence.

(C) Testimony by a witness to whom Defendant made an oral admission that he had been convicted.

(D) Judicial notice of the conviction, based on the court's telephone call to the clerk of the state court, whom the judge knows personally.

Question 12

In an arson prosecution the government seeks to rebut Defendant's alibi that he was in a jail in another state at the time of the fire. The government calls Witness to testify that he diligently searched through all the records of the jail and found no record of Defendant's having been incarcerated there during the time Defendant specified.

The testimony of Witness is

(A) admissible as evidence of absence of an entry from a public record.

(B) admissible as a summary of voluminous documents.

(C) inadmissible, because it is hearsay not within any exception.

(D) inadmissible, because the records themselves must be produced.

Question 13

Passenger is suing Defendant for injuries suffered in the crash of a small airplane, alleging that Defendant had owned the plane and negligently failed to have it properly maintained. Defendant has asserted in defense that he never owned the plane or had any responsibility to maintain it. At trial, Passenger calls Witness to testify that Witness had sold to Defendant a liability insurance policy on the plane.

The testimony of Witness is

(A) inadmissible, because the policy itself is required under the original document rule.

(B) inadmissible, because of the rule against proof of insurance where insurance is not itself at issue.

(C) admissible to show that Defendant had little motivation to invest money in maintenance of the airplane.

(D) admissible as some evidence of Defendant's ownership of or responsibility for the airplane.

Questions 14-15 are based on the following fact situation.

Price sued Derrick for injuries Price received in an automobile accident. Price claims Derrick was negligent in (a) exceeding the posted speed limit of 35 m.p.h., (b) failing to keep a lookout, and (c) crossing the center line.

Question 14

Bystander, Price's eyewitness, testified on cross-examination that Derrick was wearing a green sweater at the time of the accident. Derrick's counsel calls Wilson to testify that Derrick's sweater was blue. Wilson's testimony is

(A) admissible as substantive evidence of a material fact

(B) admissible as bearing on Bystander's truthfulness and veracity

(C) inadmissible, because it has no bearing on the capacity of Bystander to observe

(D) inadmissible, because it is extrinsic evidence of a collateral matter

Question 15

Derrick testified in his own behalf that he was going 30 m.p.h. On cross-examination, Price's counsel did not question Derrick with regard to his speed. Subsequently, Price's counsel calls Officer to testify that, in his investigation following the accident, Derrick told him he was driving 40 m.p.h. Officer's testimony is

(A) admissible as a prior inconsistent statement

(B) admissible as an admission

(C) inadmissible, because it lacks a foundation

(D) inadmissible, because it is hearsay not within any exception

Question 16

Mrs. Pence sued Duarte for shooting her husband from ambush. Mrs. Pence offers to testify that, the day before her husband was killed, he described to her a chance meeting with Duarte on the street in which Duarte said, "I'm going to blow your head off one of these days."

The witness's testimony concerning her husband's statement is

(A) admissible, to show Duarte's state of mind.

(B) admissible, because Duarte's statement is that of a party-opponent.

(C) inadmissible, because it is improper evidence of a prior bad act.

(D) inadmissible, because it is hearsay not within any exception.

Question 17

Susan entered a guilty plea to a charge of embezzlement. Her attorney hired a retired probation officer as a consultant to gather information for the preparation of a sentencing plan for Susan that would avoid jail. For that purpose, the consultant interviewed Susan for three hours.

Thereafter, the prosecution undertook an investigation of Susan's possible involvement in other acts of embezzlement. The consultant was subpoenaed to testify before a grand jury. The consultant refused to answer any questions concerning her conversation with Susan. The prosecution has moved for an order requiring her to answer those questions.

The motion should be

(A) denied, on the basis of the attorney-client privilege.

(B) denied, in the absence of probable cause to believe the interview developed evidence relevant to the grand jury's inquiry.

(C) granted, because the consultant is not an attorney.

(D) granted, because exclusionary evidentiary rules do not apply in grand jury proceedings.

Question 18

Defendant is on trial for the murder of his father. Defendant's defense is that he shot his father accidentally. The prosecutor calls Witness, a police officer, to testify that on two occasions in the year prior to this incident, he had been called to Defendant's home because of complaints of loud arguments between Defendant and his father, and had found it necessary to stop Defendant from beating his father.

The evidence is

(A) inadmissible, because it is improper character evidence.

(B) inadmissible, because Witness lacks firsthand knowledge of who started the quarrels.

(C) admissible to show that Defendant killed his father intentionally.

(D) admissible to show that Defendant is a violent person.

Question 19

Plaintiff sued Defendant under an age discrimination statute, alleging that Defendant refused to hire Plaintiff because she was over age 65. Defendant's defense was that he refused to employ Plaintiff because he reasonably believed that she would be unable to perform the job. Defendant seeks to testify that Employer, Plaintiff's former employer, advised him not to hire Plaintiff because she was unable to perform productively for more than four hours a day.

The testimony of Defendant is

(A) inadmissible, because Defendant's opinion of Plaintiff's abilities is not based on personal knowledge.

(B) inadmissible, because Employer's statement is hearsay not within any exception.

(C) admissible as evidence that Plaintiff would be unable to work longer than four hours per day.

(D) admissible as evidence of Defendant's reason for refusing to hire Plaintiff.

Question 20

Plaintiff sued Defendant for personal injuries arising out of an automobile accident.

Which of the following would be ERROR?

(A) The judge allows Defendant's attorney to ask Defendant questions on cross-examination that go well beyond the scope of direct examination by Plaintiff, who has called Defendant as an adverse witness.

(B) The judge refuses to allow Defendant's attorney to cross-examine Defendant by leading questions.

(C) The judge allows cross-examination about the credibility of a witness even though no question relating to credibility has been asked on direct examination.

(D) The judge, despite Defendant's request for exclusion of witnesses, allows Plaintiff's eyewitness to remain in the courtroom after testifying, even though the eyewitness is expected to be recalled for further cross-examination.

Question 21

In a contract suit between Terrell and Ward, Ward testifies that he recalls having his first conversation with Terrell on January 3. When asked how he remembers the date, he answers, "In the conversation, Terrell referred to a story in that day's newspaper announcing my daughter's engagement." Terrell's counsel moves to strike the reference to the newspaper story. The judge should

(A) grant the motion on the ground that the best evidence rule requires production of the newspaper itself

(B) grant the motion, because the reference to the newspaper story does not fit within any established exception to the hearsay rule

(C) deny the motion on the ground that the court may take judicial notice of local newspapers and their contents

(D) deny the motion on the ground that a witness may refer to collateral documents without providing the documents themselves

Question 22

Drew is charged with the murder of Pitt. The prosecutor introduced testimony of a police officer that Pitt told a priest, administering the last rites, "I was stabbed by Drew. Since I am dying, tell him I forgive him." Thereafter, Drew's attorney offers the testimony of Wall that the day before, when Pitt believed he would live, he stated that he had been stabbed by Jack, an old enemy. The testimony of Wall is

(A) admissible under an exception to the hearsay rule

(B) admissible to impeach the dead declarant

(C) inadmissible because it goes to the ultimate issue in the case

(D) inadmissible because it is irrelevant to any substantive issue in the case

Question 23

Defendant is on trial for extorting $10,000 from Victim. An issue is the identification of the person who made a telephone call to Victim. Victim is prepared to testify that the caller had a distinctive accent like Defendant's, but that he cannot positively identify the voice as Defendant's. Victim recorded the call but has not brought the tape to court, although its existence is known to Defendant.

Victim's testimony is

(A) inadmissible, because Victim cannot sufficiently identify the caller.

(B) inadmissible, because the tape recording of the conversation is the best evidence.

(C) admissible, because Defendant waived the "best evidence" rule by failing to subpoena the tape.

(D) admissible, because Victim's lack of certainty goes to the weight to be given Victim's testimony, not to its admissibility.

Question 24

Plaintiff Construction Co. sued Defendant Development Co. for money owed on a cost-plus contract that required notice of proposed expenditures beyond original estimates. Defendant asserted that it never received the required notice. At trial Plaintiff calls its general manager, Witness, to testify that it is Plaintiff's routine practice to send cost overrun notices as required by the contract. Witness also offers a photocopy of the cost overrun notice letter to Defendant on which Plaintiff is relying, and which he has taken from Plaintiff's regular business files.

On the issue of giving notice, the letter copy is

(A) admissible, though hearsay, under the business record exception.

(B) admissible, because of the routine practices of the company.

(C) inadmissible, because it is hearsay not within any exception.

(D) inadmissible, because it is not the best evidence of the notice.

Questions 25-26 are based on the following fact situation.

Dann, who was charged with the crime of assaulting Smith, admitted striking Smith but claimed to have acted in self-defense when he was attacked by Smith, who was drunk and belligerent after a football game.

Question 25

Dann offered testimony of Employer, that he had known and employed Dann for twelve years and knew Dann's reputation among the people with whom he lived and worked to be that of a peaceful, law-abiding, nonviolent person. The trial judge should rule this testimony

(A) admissible, because it is relevant to show the improbability of Dann's having committed an unprovoked assault

(B) admissible, because it is relevant to a determination of the extent of punishment if Dann is convicted

(C) not admissible, because whether Dann is normally a person of good character is irrelevant to the specific charge

(D) not admissible, because it is irrelevant without a showing that Employer was one of the persons among whom Dann lived and worked

Question 26

On cross-examination of Employer (Dann's), the state's attorney asked Employer if he had heard that Dann often engaged in fights and brawls. The trial judge should rule the question

(A) not objectionable, because evidence of Dann's previous fights and brawls may be used to prove his guilt

(B) not objectionable, because it tests Employer's knowledge of Dann's reputation

(C) objectionable, because it seeks to put into evidence separate, unrelated offenses

(D) objectionable, because no specific time or incidents are specified and inquired about

Question 27

Dann's friend Frank was called to testify that Smith had a reputation among the people with whom he lived and worked for lawbreaking and frequently engaging in brawls. The trial judge should rule the testimony

(A) admissible to support Dann's theory of self-defense, touching on whether Dann or Smith was the aggressor

(B) admissible if Frank testifies further as to specific acts of misconduct on Smith's part of which Frank has personal knowledge

(C) inadmissible, on the question of Dann's guilt because Dann, not Smith, is on trial

(D) inadmissible, because Frank failed to lay a proper foundation

Questions 28-31 are based on the following fact situation.

Carr ran into and injured Pedersen, a pedestrian. With Carr in his car were Wanda and Walter Passenger. Passerby saw the accident and called the police department, which sent Sheriff to investigate.

All of these people were available as potential witnesses in the case of *Pedersen v. Carr*. Pedersen alleges that Carr, while drunk, struck Pedersen who was in a duly marked crosswalk.

Question 28

Pedersen's counsel wants to introduce testimony of Sheriff that at the police station Carr told Sheriff, "I think this was probably my fault." The trial judge should rule this testimony

(A) admissible as a part of the *res gestae*

(B) admissible as an admission of a party

(C) inadmissible because it includes a conclusion of law which the declarant was not qualified to make

(D) inadmissible because it constitutes an opinion rather than an admission of specific facts

Question 29

Pedersen's counsel wishes to prove that after the accident Carr went to Pedersen and offered $1,000 to settle Pedersen's claim. The trial judge should rule this evidence

(A) admissible as an admission of a party

(B) admissible as an admission to show Carr's liability, provided the court gives a cautionary instruction that the statement should not be considered as bearing on the issue of damages

(C) inadmissible since it is not relevant either to the question of liability or the question of damages

(D) inadmissible because even though it is relevant and an admission, the policy of the law is to encourage settlement negotiations

Question 30

Pedersen's counsel wants to have Sheriff testify to the following statement made to him by Walter Passenger, out of the presence of Carr: "We were returning from a party at which we had all been drinking." The trial judge should rule this testimony

(A) admissible as an admission of a party

(B) admissible as a declaration against interest

(C) inadmissible as hearsay not within any exception

(D) inadmissible because it would lead the court into non-essential side issues

Question 31

On the evening of the day of the accident, Walter Passenger wrote a letter to his sister in which he described the accident. When Walter says he cannot remember some details of the accident, Pedersen's counsel seeks to show him the letter to assist him in his testimony on direct examination. The trial judge should rule this

(A) permissible under the doctrine of present recollection refreshed

(B) permissible under the doctrine of past recollection recorded

(C) objectionable because the letter was not a spontaneous utterance

(D) objectionable because the letter is a self-serving declaration in so far as the witness, Walter, is concerned

Question 32)

Plaintiff sued Defendant for personal injuries suffered in a train-automobile collision. Plaintiff called an eyewitness, who testified that the train was going 20 miles per hour. Defendant then offers the testimony of an experienced police accident investigator that, based on his training and experience and on his examination of the physical evidence, it is his opinion that the train was going between 5 and 10 miles per hour.

Testimony by the investigator is

(A) improper, because there cannot be both lay and expert opinion on the same issue.

(B) improper, because the investigator is unable to establish the speed with a sufficient degree of scientific certainty.

(C) proper, because a police accident investigator has sufficient expertise to express an opinion on speed.

(D) proper, because Plaintiff first introduced opinion evidence as to speed.

Question 33)

Defendant is charged with murder in connection with a carjacking incident during which Defendant allegedly shot Victim while attempting to steal Victim's car. The prosecutor calls Victim's four-year-old son, whose face was horribly disfigured by the same bullet, to testify that Defendant shot his father and him.

The son's testimony should be

(A) admitted, provided the prosecutor first provides evidence that persuades the judge that the son is competent to testify despite his tender age.

(B) admitted, provided there is sufficient basis for believing that the son has personal knowledge and understands his obligation to testify truthfully.

(C) excluded, because it is insufficiently probative in view of the son's tender age.

(D) excluded, because it is more unfairly prejudicial than probative.

Question 34

Cars driven by Pugh and Davidson collided, and Davidson was charged with driving while intoxicated in connection with the accident. She pleaded guilty and was merely fined, although under the statute the court could have sentenced her to two years in prison.

Thereafter, Pugh, alleging that Davidson's intoxication had caused the collision, sued Davidson for damages. At trial, Pugh offers the properly authenticated record of Davidson's conviction. The record should be

(A) admitted as proof of Davidson's character

(B) admitted as proof of Davidson's intoxication

(C) excluded, because the conviction was not the result of a trial

(D) excluded, because it is hearsay not within any exception

Question 35

Pitt sued Dow for damages for injuries that Pitt incurred when a badly rotted limb fell from a curbside tree in front of Dow's home and hit Pitt. Dow claimed that the tree was on city property and thus was the responsibility of the city. At trial, Pitt offered testimony that a week after the accident, Dow had cut the tree down with a chainsaw. The offered evidence is

(A) inadmissible, because there is a policy to encourage safety precautions

(B) inadmissible, because it is irrelevant to the condition of the tree at the time of the accident

(C) admissible to show the tree was on Dow's property

(D) admissible to show the tree was in a rotted condition

Question 36

At Dove's trial for theft, Mr. Wong, called by the prosecutor, testified to the following: 1) that from his apartment window, he saw thieves across the street break the window of a jewelry store, take jewelry, and leave in a car; 2) that Mrs. Wong telephoned the police and relayed to them the license number of the thieves' car as Mr. Wong looked out the window with binoculars and read it to her; 3) that he has no present memory of the number, but that immediately afterward he listened to a playback of the police tape recording giving the license number (which belongs to Dove's car) and verified that she had relayed the number accurately.

Playing the tape recording for the jury would be

(A) proper, because it is recorded recollection.

(B) proper, because it is a public record or report.

(C) improper, because it is hearsay not within any exception.

(D) improper, because Mrs. Wong lacked firsthand knowledge of the license number.

Question 37

Plaintiff sued Defendant for injuries suffered in a car accident allegedly caused by brakes that had been negligently repaired by Defendant. At a settlement conference, Plaintiff exhibited the brake shoe that caused the accident and pointed out the alleged defect to an expert, whom Defendant had brought to the conference. No settlement was reached. At trial, the brake shoe having disappeared, Plaintiff seeks to testify concerning the condition of the shoe.

Plaintiff's testimony is

(A) admissible, because Defendant's expert had been able to examine the shoe carefully.

(B) admissible, because Plaintiff had personal knowledge of the shoe's condition.

(C) inadmissible, because the brake shoe was produced and examined as a part of settlement negotiations.

(D) inadmissible, unless Plaintiff establishes that the disappearance was not his fault.

Question 38

Dryden is tried on a charge of driving while intoxicated. When Dryden was booked at the police station, a videotape was made that showed him unsteady, abusive, and speaking in a slurred manner. If the prosecutor lays a foundation properly identifying the tape, should the court admit it in evidence and permit it to be shown to the jury?

(A) Yes, because it is an admission

(B) Yes, because its value is not substantially outweighed by unfair prejudice

(C) No, because the privilege against self-incrimination is applicable

(D) No, because specific instances of conduct cannot be proved by extrinsic evidence

Question 39

In Polk's negligence action against Dell arising out of a multiple-car collision, Witt testified for Polk that Dell went through a red light. On cross-examination, Dell seeks to question Witt about her statement that the light was yellow, made in a deposition that Witt gave in a separate action between Adams and Baker. The transcript of the deposition is self-authenticating. On proper objection, the court should rule the inquiry

(A) admissible for impeachment only

(B) admissible as substantive evidence only

(C) admissible for impeachment and as substantive evidence

(D) inadmissible, because it is hearsay not within any exception

Question 40

Powers sued Debbs for battery. At trial, Powers' witness Wilson testified that Debbs had made an unprovoked attack on Powers.

On cross-examination, Debbs asks Wilson about a false claim that Wilson had once filed on an insurance policy. The question is

(A) proper, because the conduct involved untruthfulness

(B) proper provided that the conduct resulted in conviction of Wilson

(C) improper, because the impeachment involved a specific instance of misconduct

(D) improper, because the claim form would be the best evidence

Question 41

While crossing Spruce Street, Pesko was hit by a car that she did not see. Pesko sued Dorry for her injuries.

At trial, Pesko calls Williams, a police officer, to testify that, ten minutes after the accident, a driver stopped him and said, "Officer, a few minutes ago I saw a hit-and-run accident on Spruce Street involving a blue convertible, which I followed to the drive-in restaurant at Oak and Third," and that a few seconds later Williams saw Dorry sitting alone in a blue convertible in the drive-in restaurant's parking lot.

Williams' testimony about the driver's statement should be

(A) admitted as a statement of recent perception

(B) admitted as a present sense impression

(C) excluded, because it is hearsay not within any exception

(D) excluded, because it is more prejudicial than probative

Question 42

Post sued Dean for personal injury alleged to have been caused by Dean's negligence. A major issue at trial was whether Post's disability was caused solely by trauma or by a preexisting condition of osteoarthritis.

Post called Dr. Cox, who testified that the disability was caused by trauma. On cross-examination, Dr. Cox testified that a medical textbook entitled *Diseases of the Joints* was authoritative and that she agreed with the substance of passages from the textbook that she was directed to look at, but that the passages were inapplicable to Post's condition because they dealt with rheumatoid arthritis rather than with the osteoarthritis that Post was alleged to have.

Dean then called his expert, Dr. Freed, who testified that, with reference to the issue being litigated, there is no difference between the two kinds of arthritis. Dean's counsel then asks permission to read to the jury the textbook passages earlier shown to Dr. Cox.

The judge should rule the textbook passages

(A) admissible only for the purpose of impeaching Cox

(B) admissible as substantive evidence if the judge determines that the passages are relevant

(C) inadmissible, because they are hearsay not within any exception

(D) inadmissible, because Cox contended that they are not relevant to Post's condition

Question 43

Plaintiff is suing Doctor for medical malpractice occasioned by allegedly prescribing an incorrect medication, causing Plaintiff to undergo substantial hospitalization. When Doctor learned of the medication problem, she immediately offered to pay Plaintiff's hospital expenses. At trial, Plaintiff offers evidence of Doctor's offer to pay the costs of his hospitalization.

The evidence of Doctor's offer is

(A) admissible as a nonhearsay statement of a party.

(B) admissible, although hearsay, as a statement against interest.

(C) inadmissible, because it is an offer to pay medical expenses.

(D) inadmissible, because it is an offer to compromise.

Question 44

Darden was prosecuted for armed robbery. At trial, Darden testified in his own behalf, denying that he had committed the robbery. On cross-examination, the prosecutor intends to ask Darden whether he had been convicted of burglary six years earlier.

The question concerning the burglary conviction is

(A) proper if the court finds that the probative value for impeachment outweighs the prejudice to Darden

(B) proper, because the prosecutor is entitled to make this inquiry as a matter of right

(C) improper, because burglary does not involve dishonesty or false statement

(D) improper, because the conviction must be proved by court record, not by question on cross-examination

Question 45

On trial for murdering her husband, Defendant testified she acted in self-defense. Defendant calls Expert, a psychologist, to testify that under hypnosis Defendant had described the killing, and that in Expert's opinion Defendant had been in fear for her life at the time of the killing.

Is Expert's testimony admissible?

(A) Yes, because Expert was able to ascertain that Defendant was speaking truthfully.

(B) Yes, because it reports a prior consistent statement by a witness (Defendant) subject to examination concerning it.

(C) No, because reliance on information tainted by hypnosis is unconstitutional.

(D) No, because it expresses an opinion concerning Defendant's mental state at the time of the killing.

Question 46

Plaintiff sued Defendant for breach of a commercial contract in which Defendant had agreed to sell Plaintiff all of Plaintiff's requirements for widgets. Plaintiff called Expert Witness to testify as to damages. Defendant seeks to show that Expert Witness had provided false testimony as a witness in his own divorce proceedings.

This evidence should be

(A) admitted only if elicited from Expert Witness on cross-examination.

(B) admitted only if the false testimony is established by clear and convincing extrinsic evidence.

(C) excluded, because it is impeachment on a collateral issue.

(D) excluded, because it is improper character evidence.

Question 47

David is being tried in federal court for criminal conspiracy with John to violate federal narcotics law. At trial, the prosecutor calls David's new wife, Wanda, and asks her to testify about a meeting between David and John that she observed before she married David.

Which of the following is the most accurate statement of the applicable rule concerning whether Wanda may testify?

(A) The choice is Wanda's

(B) The choice is David's

(C) Wanda is permitted to testify only if both Wanda and David agree

(D) Wanda is compelled to testify even if both Wanda and David object

Question 48

Phil is suing Dennis for injuries suffered in an automobile collision. At trial Phil's first witness, Wanda, testified that, although she did not see the accident, she heard her friend Frank say just before the crash, "Look at the crazy way old Dennis is driving!" Dennis offers evidence to impeach Frank by asking Wanda, "Isn't it true that Frank beat up Dennis just the day before the collision?"

The question is

(A) proper, because it tends to show the possible bias of Frank against Dennis.

(B) proper, because it tends to show Frank's character.

(C) improper, because Frank has no opportunity to explain or deny.

(D) improper, because impeachment cannot properly be by specific instances.

Question 49

Defendant is on trial for nighttime breaking and entering of a warehouse. The warehouse owner had set up a camera to take infrared pictures of any intruders. After an expert establishes the reliability of infrared photography, the prosecutor offers the authenticated infrared picture of the intruder to show the similarities to Defendant.

The photograph is

(A) admissible, provided an expert witness points out to the jury the similarities between the person in the photograph and Defendant.

(B) admissible, allowing the jury to compare the person in the photograph and Defendant.

(C) inadmissible, because there was no eyewitness to the scene available to authenticate the photograph.

(D) inadmissible, because infrared photography deprives a defendant of the right to confront witnesses.

Question 50

Paulsen sued Daly for nonpayment of a personal loan to Daly, as evidenced by Daly's promissory note to Paulsen. Paulsen called Walters to testify that he knows Daly's handwriting and that the signature on the note is Daly's. On direct examination, to identify himself, Walters gave his name and address and testified that he had been employed by a roofing company for seven years.

During presentation of Daly's case, Daly called Wilson to testify that she is the roofing company's personnel manager and that she had determined, by examining the company's employment records, that Walters had worked there only three years. The trial judge should rule that Wilson's testimony is

(A) inadmissible, because it is not the best evidence

(B) inadmissible, because it is impeachment on a collateral question

(C) admissible as evidence of a regularly conducted activity

(D) admissible as tending to impeach Walters' credibility

Question 51

Plaintiff sued Defendant for injuries sustained in an automobile collision. During Plaintiff's hospital stay, Doctor, a staff physician, examined Plaintiff's X rays and said to Plaintiff, "You have a fracture of two vertebrae, C4 and C5." Intern, who was accompanying Doctor on her rounds, immediately wrote the diagnosis on Plaintiff's hospital record. At trial, the hospital records custodian testifies that Plaintiff's hospital record was made and kept in the ordinary course of the hospital's business.

The entry reporting Doctor's diagnosis is

(A) inadmissible, because no foundation has been laid for Doctor's competence as an expert.

(B) inadmissible, because Doctor's opinion is based upon data that are not in evidence.

(C) admissible as a statement of then-existing physical condition.

(D) admissible as a record of regularly conducted business activity.

Question 52

At Defendant's trial for sale of drugs, the government called Witness to testify, but Witness refused to answer any questions about Defendant and was held in contempt of court. The government then calls Officer to testify that, when Witness was arrested for possession of drugs and offered leniency if he would identify his source, Witness had named Defendant as his source.

The testimony offered concerning Witness's identification of Defendant is

(A) admissible as a prior inconsistent statement by Witness.

(B) admissible as an identification of Defendant by Witness after having perceived him.

(C) inadmissible, because it is hearsay not within any exception.

(D) inadmissible, because Witness was not confronted with the statement while on the stand.

Question 53

PullCo sued Davidson, its former vice president, for return of $230,000 that had been embezzled during the previous two years. Called by PullCo as an adverse witness, Davidson testified that his annual salary had been $75,000, and he denied the embezzlement. PullCo calls banker Witt to show that, during the two-year period, Davidson had deposited $250,000 in his bank account.

Witt's testimony is

(A) admissible as circumstantial evidence of Davidson's guilt.

(B) admissible to impeach Davidson.

(C) inadmissible, because its prejudicial effect substantially outweighs its probative value.

(D) inadmissible, because the deposits could have come from legitimate sources.

Question 54

Pedestrian died from injuries caused when Driver's car struck him. Executor, Pedestrian's executor, sued Driver for wrongful death. At trial, Executor calls Nurse to testify that two days after the accident, Pedestrian said to Nurse, "The car that hit me ran the red light." Fifteen minutes thereafter, Pedestrian died.

As a foundation for introducing evidence of Pedestrian's statement, Executor offers to the court Doctor's affidavit that Doctor was the intern on duty the day of Pedestrian's death and that several times that day Pedestrian had said that he knew he was about to die.

Is the affidavit properly considered by the court in ruling on the admissibility of Pedestrian's statement?

(A) No, because it is hearsay not within any exception.

(B) No, because it is irrelevant since dying declarations cannot be used except in prosecutions for homicide.

(C) Yes, because, though hearsay, it is a statement of then-existing mental condition.

(D) Yes, because the judge may consider hearsay in ruling on preliminary questions.

Question 55

Defendant is on trial for robbing a bank in State A. She testified that she was in State B at the time of the robbery. Defendant calls her friend, Witness, to testify that two days before the robbery Defendant told him that she was going to spend the next three days in State B.

Witness's testimony is

(A) admissible, because the statement falls within the present sense impression exception to the hearsay rule.

(B) admissible, because a statement of plans falls within the hearsay exception for then-existing state of mind.

(C) inadmissible, because it is offered to establish an alibi by Defendant's own statement.

(D) inadmissible, because it is hearsay not within any exception.

Question 56

At Defendant's murder trial, Defendant calls Witness as his first witness to testify that Defendant has a reputation in their community as a peaceable and truthful person. The prosecutor objects on the ground that Witness's testimony would constitute improper character evidence.

The court should

(A) admit the testimony as to peaceableness, but exclude the testimony as to truthfulness.

(B) admit the testimony as to truthfulness, but exclude the testimony as to peaceableness.

(C) admit the testimony as to both character traits.

(D) exclude the testimony as to both character traits.

EVIDENCE

Answer Key

Use this Answer Key to quickly identify the correct answer to each question.

(1) B	(11) D	(21) D	(31) A	(41) C	(51) D
(2) C	(12) A	(22) B	(32) C	(42) B	(52) C
(3) B	(13) D	(23) D	(33) B	(43) C	(53) A
(4) B	(14) D	(24) B	(34) B	(44) A	(54) D
(5) C	(15) B	(25) A	(35) C	(45) D	(55) B
(6) A	(16) D	(26) B	(36) A	(46) A	(56) A
(7) C	(17) A	(27) A	(37) B	(47) A	
(8) D	(18) C	(28) B	(38) B	(48) A	
(9) B	(19) D	(29) D	(39) C	(49) B	
(10) D	(20) D	(30) C	(40) A	(50) B	

ANSWERS

EVIDENCE

Answer 1

(B) is the best response,

because the tape is admissible as a prior inconsistent statement offered to impeach the witness, but inadmissible substantively because of hearsay.

First, let's consider the recording's admissibility for impeachment. FRE 613(b) implicitly allows use of extrinsic evidence to show that a witness has made a prior inconsistent statement. ("Extrinsic evidence of a prior inconsistent statement by a witness is not admissible unless the witness is afforded an opportunity to explain or deny the same and the opposite party is afforded an opportunity to interrogate the witness thereon, or the interests of justice otherwise require.")

So here, once Witness said on the stand that Defendant had given a non-racial explanation for the firing, Witness' tape recorded statement that Defendant had given a racial explanation was extrinsic evidence tending to show a prior inconsistent statement by the witness. Consequently, the statement was admissible for impeachment under FRE 613(b), since Witness was still on the stand (and thus had a chance to explain or deny the statement).

Now, let's consider substantive admissibility. Here, the tape recording is "hearsay within hearsay." The outer level is that Witness is making a recorded, and thus out-of-court, statement. The inner level is that Witness is repeating an admission made by Defendant.

Here, the inner level is not inadmissible hearsay, because it falls within the exception for admissions introduced against the maker. See FRE 801(d)(2) (A statement is not hearsay if "The statement is offered against a party and is (A) the party's own statement...") But the outer level is hearsay that is not within any exception — Witness is making an out-of-court statement (Witness' words on the recording) offered to demonstrate the truth of the matter asserted (that Defendant made a certain admission to Witness). There is nothing in this statement ("Defendant told me he fired Plaintiff for racial reasons") that falls within any hearsay exception. Thus the statement can't come in for the substantive purpose of demonstrating that Defendant was racially motivated.

Choice (A) is not the best response,

because, as is described in the analysis of choice (B), the recording is not admissible as "evidence of Defendant's racial motivation," which is a substantive (non-impeachment-of-the-witness) purpose.

Choice (C) is not the best response,

because as is described in Choice (B), the statement is admissible for impeachment as a prior inconsistent statement of the witness.

Choice (D) is not the best response,

because no violation of the Constitution occurs when a person secretly records a conversation to which he is a party (and in any event, Witness was not a governmental actor, again preventing the recording from possibly being a constitutional violation).

Answer 2

(C) is the best response,

because Jaron cannot be impeached on a collateral issue by extrinsic evidence.

Wilcox' testimony is not relevant to any substantive issue in the case — it bears solely on Jaron's credibility. Therefore, the matter is governed by FRE 608(b), which says in part that "Specific instances of the conduct of a witness, for the purpose of attacking or supporting the witness' credibility, other than conviction of crime as provided in Rule 609, may not be proved by extrinsic evidence." In other words, once a lawyer has completed cross-examination of a witness, he must be satisfied with whatever he could bring out on cross tending to show that the witness lied on a collateral matter (i.e., a matter not pertaining to the substantive issues in the case) — the lawyer may not introduce another witness, or document, to prove that the first witness lied.

Here, the testimony of Wilcox is extrinsic evidence of specific conduct by Jason, offered for the purpose of attacking Jaron's credibility. Therefore, it is barred by the just-quoted portion of 608(b).

(A) is not the best response,

because there is no discretion to admit extrinsic evidence to impeach on a collateral issue.

If the prosecutor had presented Jaron with a document tending to show he had lied on his credit card application, *that* would be admissible in the judge's discretion, because the second sentence of Rule 608(b) says that "Specific instances of the conduct of a witness, for the purpose of attacking or supporting the witness' credibility ... may, however, in the discretion of the court, if probative of truthfulness or untruthfulness, be inquired into on cross-examination of the witness (1) concerning the witness' character for truthfulness or untruthfulness." But since the testimony here is from

Wilcox about Jaron's credibility, it's extrinsic evidence governed by the first sentence of 608(b) (quoted in the discussion of Choice (C) above), not the sentence just quoted; therefore, the judge can't use her discretion to admit it.

(B) is not the best response,

because Jaron may have "opened the door" to being asked further questions about his application on cross, but he did not (and could not) open the door to the use of extrinsic evidence to show he was lying.

As the discussion of Choice (C) indicates, once a lawyer has completed cross-examination of a witness, he must be satisfied with whatever he could bring out on cross tending to show that the witness lied on a collateral matter (i.e., a matter not pertaining to the substantive issues in the case) — the lawyer may not introduce another witness, or document, to show that the first witness lied. So nothing Jaron said could have "opened the door" to this type of extrinsic evidence.

(D) is not the best response.

because whether Jaron could have honestly misunderstood the form is irrelevant — the evidence is extrinsic evidence barred because it pertains to a collateral matter.

The first sentence of Rule 608(b), quoted in the discussion of Choice (C) above, bars extrinsic evidence to prove a collateral matter. The matter here (whether Jaron lied on his credit card application) is a collateral matter, since it pertains only to Jaron's credibility, not to any substantive issue in the case. Therefore, even if Jaron could *not* reasonably have misunderstood the meaning of the question on the application, the prosecutor was still not entitled to present a second witness (a form of extrinsic evidence) to prove either that Jaron was generally untruthful or that his testimony on cross about the application was untruthful.

Answer 3

(B) is the best response,

because evidence of prior bad acts to prove that on the present occasion the defendant acted in conformity with the character indicated by those prior bad acts is inadmissible.

FRE 404(a) states the familiar principle that "Evidence of a person's character or a trait of his character is not admissible for the purpose of proving action in conformity therewith on a particular occasion" (subject to exceptions not relevant here).

The prosecution here is trying to get the evidence in to suggest, in effect, that "Since Defendant is the sort of person who has twice before shot at victims or menaced them with a gun, he is likely to have fired the sniper shot charged here."

If the prior bad acts were extremely similar to the one charged here (e.g., they both involved the firing of sniper shots at a person, in similar circumstances and

with a similar motive), the prior acts might be admissible under FRE 404(b)'s exception for "other crimes, wrongs, or acts ... [offered] for other purposes, such as proof of motive, ... preparation, [or] plan..." But the prior acts are so different from the crime charged here — neither is a hidden sniper-style shot fired directly at a human being — that none of the exceptions in 404(b) can even plausibly apply. (It's clearly not enough that all the acts, including the one charged, involve a firearm.)

(A) is not the best response,

because evidence of prior bad acts to prove action in conformity therewith is not admissible either on direct or cross.

For the reasons described in Choice (B) above, this is "prior bad acts" evidence offered to show a propensity to act in conformity therewith. Therefore, it's forbidden by 404(a). And that's true whether the evidence is presented on direct, or elicited on cross.

If you were tempted by this answer, you may have thought that these prior bad acts could be used on cross for impeachment purposes. To understand why this is not so, first notice that there's no indication that Defendant was convicted of a crime for these prior actions. Therefore, their use for impeachment is governed by FRE 608(b) (specific instances of conduct), not 609 (impeachment by evidence of conviction of crime).

Now, 608(b) says that "specific instances of the conduct of a witness, for the purpose of attacking or supporting the witness' credibility, other than conviction of crime as provided in Rule 609 ... may, ... in the discretion of the court, *if probative of truthfulness or untruthfulness*, be inquired into on cross-examination of the witness (1) concerning the witness' character for truthfulness or untruthfulness..." As you can see by the italicized phrase, this exception applies only to prior bad acts that are probative of the witness' truthfulness. Since shootings and menacings aren't probative of truthfulness, they could not be inquired about even on the cross of Defendant.

(C) is not the best response,

because evidence of a propensity to violence is inadmissible character evidence.

The Federal Rules of Evidence embody the principle that prior crimes may not be introduced to show the defendant's character, thereby justifying the inference that he acted in conformity with that character on the present occasion. This rule is discussed in the treatment of Choice (B) above.

The present choice is literally inconsistent with the no-prior-acts-to-show-conforming-character rule, so it's clearly wrong.

(D) is not the best response,

because the prior acts offered are not sufficiently similar to bear on D's identity, plan or motive.

It's true that FRE 404(b) admits proof of "other crimes, wrongs, or acts ... [offered] for other purposes, such as proof of motive, ... plan, [or] identity..." But there's no indication that motive, plan or identity was at issue in the case, or was the purpose for which this other-bad-acts evidence was offered.

In any event, to bear on motive, plan or identity, the prior acts would have to be much more similar to the present attack than they in fact are — neither of the prior acts was a hidden sniper-style shot fired directly at a human being. (It's clearly not enough that all the acts, including the one charged, involve a firearm, or violence.)

Answer 4

(B) is the best response,

because the statement is hearsay (it was made out of court and is offered to prove the truth of the matter asserted), and is not within any exception to the hearsay rule.

First, let's look at whether the statement was hearsay. It's clearly an out-of-court declaration. And, the statement includes Parker's assertion that he's owed $10,000 by Davidson, offered to prove that Davidson does indeed owe this money. So the statement easily fits within the definition of hearsay — out-of-court statement offered to prove the truth of the matter asserted.

Now, does some exception apply? No. The two most plausible ones are the excited utterance exception (not applicable because the statement doesn't relate to the exciting event — see the discussion of Choice (C)) and the dying declaration exception (not applicable because the statement doesn't relate to the cause of impending death — see the discussion of Choice (D)).

(A) is not the best response,

because even if the statement were more prejudicial than probative, it would be inadmissible hearsay not within any exception.

Apart from the hearsay problem (see the discussion of Choice (B) above), the statement here is not all that prejudicial, so it's unlikely that the statement's probative value would be found to be "*substantially* outweighed" by the prejudicial effect, as FRE 403's balancing test requires.

(C) is not the best response,

because Parker's comment did not relate to the event causing the excitement (the accident).

FRE 803(2)'s excited-utterance exception applies to "a statement *relating to a startling event or condition* made while the declarant was under the stress of excitement caused by the event or condition." As you can see from the italicized phrase, the statement has to relate to the startling event. Parker's comment here relates solely to the debt, not to the startling event (the truck accident).

(D) is not the best response,

because Parker's comment did not concern the cause or circumstance of his death.

FRE 803(b)(2)'s dying-declaration exception applies to (in a civil case or homicide prosecution) "a statement made by a declarant while believing that death was imminent, *concerning the cause or circumstances of what the declarant believed to be impending death.*" So the statement must relate to the cause of the impending death. Since Parker's statement related only to the collection of the debt, not to the truck accident that was about to cause his death, it doesn't qualify.

Answer 5

(C) is the best response,

because Defendant was attempting to evade taxes.

The essence of the attorney-client privilege is that a client has the right not to disclose, and the right to prevent his lawyer from disclosing, any confidential communication between the two of them relating to the professional relationship. An exception to this rule — the "crime or fraud" exception — states there is no privilege if the services of the lawyer were sought or obtained to enable or aid anyone to commit or plan to commit what the client knew or reasonably should have known to be a crime or fraud.

Here, the letter constitutes Defendant's attempt to have the Lawyer conspire with Defendant to commit tax fraud. Therefore, the communication covered by the letter falls within the crime-or-fraud exception, and is therefore not privileged.

(A) is not the best response,

because acts in furtherance of a crime are not covered by attorney-client privilege.

For the reasons described in the analysis of Choice (B) above, the letter fell within the crime-or-fraud exception, and was thus not privileged. Therefore, Choice (A) is wrong.

(B) is not the best response,

because the 5th Amendment does not normally protect against the compelled disclosure of voluntarily-created testimonial documents.

The 5th Amendment protects against *compulsory* self-incrimination. The document here was voluntarily created by Defendant. Therefore, it would not be a violation of the 5th Amendment for either Defendant or the attorney to be forced to produce the document.

(D) is not the best response,

because the attorney-client privilege can be claimed by the attorney on behalf of the client.

Where the privilege exists, both the client and the attorney can claim it, but the attorney can claim the privilege only on behalf of the client. However, in the absence of evidence to the contrary, courts will presume that the attorney who claims the privilege is acting on behalf of the client. A court would certainly make this presumption here. Therefore, this choice reaches the right result (privilege does not apply), but for the wrong reason.

Answer 6

(A) is the best response,

because Defendant is not attempting to prove a character trait, but is trying to provide an alternate explanation.

An issue in the case (indeed, the core issue) is whether the accident was caused by a defective steering wheel or, instead, by some other cause not associated with Defendant. If the wife was intoxicated at the time she was driving the car, this fact would obviously make it more likely than it would otherwise be that the intoxication, not a steering-wheel defect, was the cause of the accident. Therefore, the wife's intoxication was directly relevant evidence that does not fall within any exclusion. (As to the argument that the evidence is inadmissible character evidence, see the discussion of Choice (C)).

(B) is not the best response,

because Defendant is not trying to prove a trait of Plaintiff's deceased wife's character.

If the evidence being offered by Defendant was evidence that the wife was often drunk, then the evidence would in effect be character evidence. In that event, this choice would still be wrong, because character evidence, offered to prove that the person acted in conformity therewith on a particular occasion, is generally inadmissible. FRE 404(a). But here, what's being offered is not character evidence (evidence that the wife was often or generally drunk) but rather direct evidence of behavior on the particular occasion in question (evidence that she was drunk while driving into the fatal accident). This is not character evidence at all.

(C) is not the best response,

because, although it more or less correctly states a rule, that rule does not apply on these facts.

It's true that under FRE 404(a), evidence of a person's character or a trait of character "is not admissible for the purpose of proving action in conformity therewith on a particular occasion" (with some exceptions not applicable here). It's also true that under FRE 404(b), "evidence of other ... acts is not admissible to prove the character of a person in order to show action in conformity therewith." Therefore, if Defendant were trying to show that the wife was drunk on particular occasions other than the one now in question, that evidence would indeed be excludible under 404(b)'s ban on specific-acts evidence to prove conduct in conformity with character.

But that's not what's being offered here: what's offered is direct evidence that the wife was drunk on the particular occasion in issue, and that's not "charac-

ter" evidence of any sort.

(D) is not the best response,

because proof of Plaintiff's wife's intoxication would be probative of Defendant's defense.

It's true that under FRE 403, relevant evidence may be excluded "if its probative value is substantially outweighed by the danger of unfair prejudice..." But given that the key issue in the case is "What caused the accident?", and given that the wife's intoxication, if it existed, would have tremendous probative value on the issue of the accident's cause, no court would conclude that there was a danger of "unfair" prejudice, or that that prejudice substantially outweighed the evidence's probative value.

Answer 7

(C) is the best response,

because it correctly characterizes the facts as ones that would not give rise to a duty on Sam to respond.

Under these facts, the prosecutor is attempting to admit Alex's statement against Sam. If it's admissible at all, it will be admissible as an admission by silence. However, an admission by silence is only admissible, under FRE 801(d)(2), if the person heard the accusatory statement, he was capable of denying the statement, and a reasonable person would have denied the statement were it not true, under the same circumstances. Here, the fact that Sam was in police custody makes it unlikely that a reasonable person under the same circumstances would have denied the statement, since he could reasonably feel that he didn't want to say anything in the presence of police. Since C correctly states this, it's the best response.

(A) is not the best response,

because it does not correctly apply the rule on "tacit admissions."

An admission by silence is only admissible, under FRE 801(d)(2), if the person heard the accusatory statement, he was capable of denying the statement, and a reasonable person would have denied the statement were it not true, under the same circumstances. Here, the fact that Sam was in police custody makes it unlikely that a reasonable person under the same circumstances would have denied the statement, since he could reasonably feel that he didn't want to say anything in the presence of police. Since this element is missing, the statement will not be admissible against Sam as a tacit admission, and A is not the best response.

(B) is not the best response,

because it misstates the facts: the admission here was not made during the course and in furtherance of the common plan.

An admission by a co-participant is admissible against the defendant if it was made during the course and in furtherance of the common plan. FRE 801(d)(2). Here, Alex and Sam are in police custody, and, unless they're mighty unusual robbers, they wouldn't have planned to be caught and arrested by the police. Since the common plan had ended before the time in question here, Alex's statement, as co-participant, is not admissible against Sam. Since B doesn't recognize this, it is not the best response.

(D) is not the best response,

because Alex's comment *is* of probative value in Sam's trial.

"Probative value" is another way of wording "logical relevance." That is, a piece of evidence is logically relevant if it tends to prove or disprove a material fact. The comment of Alex, a co-conspirator of Sam's, that Sam planned the hold up, would clearly make it more likely that Sam, in fact, took part in the crime. Thus, the statement may be inadmissible, but it won't be because it's irrelevant. Since D wrongly states that the comment is of no probative value, it is not the best response.

Answer 8

(D) is the best response,

because the trial testimony was a statement-within-a-statement, and the outer level was hearsay not within any exception.

Anytime the evidence in question consists of an out-of-court statement by *A* repeating another out-of-court statement by *B*, you have to analyze both *A*'s statement and *B*'s statement — if *either* statement is hearsay not falling within any exception, the combined statement cannot come in.

Here, it's true that the "inner level," i.e., the security director's statement ("Stop shoplifters at all costs") is admissible, because it's not hearsay — it doesn't assert the truth of any matter, so it can't now be being offered to prove the truth of the matter asserted therein.

But the "outer level" i.e., Guard's trial testimony about what the security director had previously said, is hearsay not within any exception. First, this testimony is hearsay, because it's being offered to show that the security director really uttered the words "Stop shoplifters at all costs" (making the shooting fall within Defendant's respondeat superior liability), and is thus offered to show the truth of the matter asserted therein.

Second, this testimony by Guard does not fall within any hearsay exception. For example, the testimony is not an admission by an agent of a party, admissible against the party, because by the time of the criminal trial, Guard was no longer working for Defendant.

Nor is Guard's trial testimony admissible under the "former testimony" exception of FRE 803(b)(1), because that exception only applies "if the party against whom the testimony is now offered, or, in a civil action or proceeding, a predecessor in interest, had an opportunity and similar motive to develop the testimony

by direct, cross or redirect examination." Defendant obviously had no opportunity or motive to cross-examine Guard at Guard's criminal trial. And of the two parties at the criminal trial (Defendant and the prosecution), neither can be said to have been in any way a "predecessor in interest" to Defendant. So the "opportunity and motive to cross-examine" requirement for admission of prior testimony is not satisfied here.

Since there are no other exceptions that might cover Guard's testimony, it's inadmissible hearsay, making the whole "package" inadmissible.

(A) is not the best response,

because the piece representing Guard's own testimony is not a party-admission, since Guard no longer worked for Defendant at the time of the statement.

This is hearsay-within-hearsay, so it's inadmissible unless both pieces (Guard's trial statement, and the security director's statement quoted by Guard) fall within a hearsay exception. As described in the analysis of choice (D), Guard's trial statement is not admissible against Defendant as an admission by a party-opponent's agent, because at the time of the statement (Guard's criminal trial), Guard was no longer employed by Defendant, and his statement was therefore no longer within the agency relationship.

(B) is not the best response,

because, although the instruction by the security director is not hearsay, it's contained within Guard's inadmissible-hearsay "outer" statement.

This choice is probably correct in concluding that the director's own statement is not hearsay — it's an instruction or command, and it's not being offered to prove the "truth" of any matter asserted therein, because there is no "matter" whose "truth" is being asserted.

On the other hand, the director's statement is contained in Guard's trial testimony, which is (inadmissible) hearsay. Therefore, although choice (B) is literally correct, it does not correctly explain the outcome.

(C) is not the best response,

because the former-testimony exception does not apply.

Former testimony, i.e. testimony given at an earlier proceeding, is an exception to the hearsay rule. Under FRE 804(b)(1), one of the requirements for the prior-testimony exception is that "the party against whom the testimony is now offered, or, in a civil action or proceeding, a predecessor in interest, [must have] had an opportunity and similar motive to develop the testimony by direct, cross, or redirect examination." Defendant had no opportunity or motive to cross-examine Guard at Guard's criminal trial, and the prosecution cannot be said to have been a "predecessor in interest" to Defendant. So the former-testimony exception does not apply.

Answer 9

(B) is the best response,

because it correctly identifies that, if a causal connection is provided, the other instances will be admissible.

Under these facts, Pat is offering evidence of other injuries from the bus accident to prove that his own injuries were caused by the accident. The problem posed by such evidence is its *relevance*. In order for such evidence to be admissible, the material circumstances must be substantially identical, and the proponent of the evidence (here, Pat) must establish the similarity.

In this question, you're told that it's already been proven that the other three passengers were involved in the same accident. Thus, the only "missing link" that Pat must prove is that their injuries came from the same accident, since this will provide the "substantial similarity" that relevance requires. Option B recognizes and resolves this issue, by focusing on the causal connection between the other passengers' injuries and the accident.

Note that option B uses the qualifier "if." That means that the reasoning need only be plausible on these facts, that it must address a central issue, and that the result must be consistent with the reasoning. Here, it's plausible that other testimony could establish that the other patients were injured in the bus accident. If that were proven, it would make the testimony relevant, which is the central issue here. As a result, B is the best response.

(A) is not the best response,

because the doctor's expert status is not relevant to the issue of admissibility here.

Under these facts, Pat is offering evidence of other injuries from the bus accident to prove that his own injuries were caused by the accident. The problem posed by such evidence is its *relevance*. In order for such evidence to be admissible, the material circumstances must be substantially identical, and the proponent of the evidence (here, Pat) must establish the similarity.

In this question, you're told that it's already been proven that the other three passengers were involved in the same accident. Thus, the only "missing link" that Pat must prove is that their injuries came from the same accident, since this will provide the "substantial similarity" that relevance requires. The doctor's qualification to speak on technical medical matters does not make such evidence relevant; it only gives him the opportunity to give *expert testimony* about medical matters. If the doctor's testimony addressed the similarity of the injuries between Pat and the other three passengers, the doctor's expert status would be relevant, but that's not what's been asked of him here. Instead, all the doctor has been asked is whether or not three other passengers from the same bus acci-

dent were admitted to the hospital that week for treatment of severe neck pain, which would not require expert testimony. As a result, A is not the best response.

(C) is not the best response,

because the testimony here does not involve hearsay.

Hearsay is an out-of-court statement offered to prove the truth of its assertion. Here, there's no out-of-court statement; the doctor is being asked whether or not three other bus passengers were admitted to the hospital for treatment of neck pain within a week of the accident. This doesn't involve recounting any out-of-court statement, and one quick way for you to identify this is that there's no out-of-court declarant.

Say the facts were different, and the doctor was being asked about the other passengers' *statements* about their neck injuries, at the time they were admitted. Even though such testimony would be hearsay – because the doctor would be repeating the patients' comments – it would be hearsay admissible under the "past physical sensation" hearsay exception, to prove the source of the injury. Statements of past physical sensation are admissible only as long as they are made to medical personnel for purposes of diagnosis or treatment (FRE 803(4)). However, under the facts here, the doctor's testimony does not involve hearsay at all; since option C doesn't recognize this, it's not the best response.

(D) is not the best response,

because it misapplies the "best evidence" rule, and ignores the central issue here.

The best evidence rule applies only when the terms of a writing are being proven, or a witness is testifying relying on a writing. It *doesn't* require that the "best evidence" for every issue be offered. Since a writing (or a related document, like an X-ray) is not involved here, there's no "best evidence" rule issue. Even if there *was* a document involved, option D doesn't identify the problem with this evidence. Under these facts, evidence of other injuries, ostensibly created by the same accident, is being offered to prove that plaintiff's injuries were caused by the accident. The problem posed by such evidence is its *relevance*. That is, there must be proof that the material circumstances between the other passengers' injuries and Pat's injuries were virtually identical. Testimony as to the other passengers' pain doesn't provide this; rather, what does so is proof that their injuries came from the same accident. Since option D doesn't recognize the central issue, and it misapplies the "best evidence" rule to these facts, it's not the best response.

Answer 10

(D) is the best response,

because Defendant's silence in these circumstances constituted his adoption of Seller's statement.

FRE 801(2)(B) codifies the common-law notion of an adoptive admission: a statement is not hearsay if it is "offered against a party and is ... (B) a statement of which the party has manifested an adoption or belief in its truth." The applicable test for adoption is whether, taking into account all circumstances, *A*'s conduct or silence justifies the conclusion that he knowingly agreed to the accuracy of *B*'s statement.

Here, it's clear that Defendant adopted Seller's statement. Seller introduced Defendant to Witness as "my partner." Defendant clearly heard and understood the statement, and it was the sort of statement that would, if untrue, have called for a denial by Defendant rather than a shaking of hands.

(A) is not the best response,

because Defendant adopted Seller's statement.

Defendant did not need to authorize Seller to speak for him. It's true that one way *A*'s statement can be used as an admission against *B* is if *B* authorized *A* to speak for him. (See FRE 801(d)(2)C).) But another way for *A*'s statement to be used as an admission against *B* is if *B* has "manifested an adoption or believe in [the statement's] truth." (FRE 801(d)(2)(B)). That's what happened here, as described more fully in the discussion of Choice (D) above.

(B) is not the best response,

because adoptive admissions are not hearsay.

The statement here was admissible as an admission against Defendant, because Defendant adopted it. (See the discussion in Choice (D)). Consequently, the statement was rendered non-hearsay by FRE 801(d)(2)(B).

(C) is not the best response,

because Defendant is not the declarant.

A statement against interest is one made by a person (the declarant), now unavailable as a witness, against that person's pecuniary, proprietary, or penal interest when made. FRE 804(b)(3) treats statements against interest as an exception to the hearsay rule.

However, there is no doctrine by which a statement made by *A* against *B*'s interest can be admitted against *B* based on *B*'s adoption of the statement. Since the declarant was *A*, the statement would have to be against *A*'s (not *B*'s) interest for it to fall within the statement-against-interest exception. And that's not what this choice specifies. (Also, even if the statement *were* somehow treated as if it were made or authorized by Defendant, the exception wouldn't apply because Defendant is present at trial and thus not unavailable.)

Answer 11

(D) is the best response,

because the clerk is not a source "whose accuracy cannot reasonably be questioned," as required for judicial notice under the FRE.

FRE 201 allows judicial notice of a fact that is "not subject to reasonable dispute" because it is either "(1) generally known within the territorial jurisdiction of the trial court" or "(2) capable of accurate and ready determination by resort to *sources whose accuracy cannot reasonably be questioned.*"

The fact here would be very unlikely to fall within category (1), since even the federal judge seems not to know it. So the only hope is category (2). The clerk of the state court might be a reasonably accurate source, but not a "source whose accuracy cannot reasonably be questioned". For instance, the clerk might be relying on a faulty memory, or might have some hidden motive to intentionally mis-state the facts. In any event, the custom in most courts (including ones following FRE 201) is not to take judicial notice of the determinations of courts other than the court which is doing the noticing.

All three of the other possibilities, by contrast, fall squarely within well-established methods of proof. (See the discussion below for each one.)

(A) is not the best response,

because a certified copy would be permitted under FRE 902(4).

FRE 902 lists a number of categories of documents that are self-authenticating. One of these is 902(4)'s category of "certified copies of public records," defined to include "a copy of an official record or report ... certified as correct by the custodian or other person authorized to make the certification." A certified copy of a record of conviction would clearly fall within this definition.

(B) is not the best response,

because testimony of someone who heard the sentence be issued would be a good means of authentication.

FRE 901(b) gives a number of illustrations of acceptable methods of authentication, i.e., of (in FRE 901(a)'s language) "evidence sufficient to support a finding that the matter in question is what its proponent claims." Since the claim is that there has been a conviction, authentication consists of evidence sufficient to find that the conviction really occurred.

The first illustration given in FRE 901(b) is (1), "Testimony of witness with knowledge" — the text of (1) recognizes authentication by means of "testimony that a matter is what it is claimed to be." So here, Plaintiff's testimony, from his own personal knowledge, that a sentence of conviction was pronounced, will qualify.

(C) is not the best response,

because Defendant's statement would be admissible as an admission.

The testimony here is a classic admission by a party-opponent. Under FRE 801(d)(2), an out-of-court statement is admissible (as an exception to the hearsay rule) if it is "offered against a party and is (1) the party's own statement..." Since the "oral admission" by Defendant that he had been convicted is a statement by Defendant being offered against him, the testimony by the witness is admissible.

Answer 12

(A) is the best response,

because this type of "absence of a public record" evidence is admissible and non-hearsay under FRE 803(10).

The fact that the records are silent here is a form of hearsay — the records are an out-of-court statement, and they're offered to say, in essence, "Because the records don't say that Defendant was incarcerated on a particular date, he was not in fact incarcerated on that date." So the silence would not, strictly speaking, be admissible unless there were a hearsay exception to cover the situation.

But there such an exception. FRE 803(10), entitled "Absence of public record or entry," says that for the purpose of proving "the absence of a record ... or the nonoccurrence or nonexistence of a matter of which a record ... was regularly made and preserved by a public office or agency," a hearsay exception is given for "testimony[] that diligent search failed to disclose the record..." Here, we know that if Defendant had been incarcerated at a particular jail on a particular date, there would be a record at the jail to that effect. So the proferred testimony that a search of the jail's collected attendance records showed no such record meets the requirements of FRE 803(10). (Notice, by the way, that Witness need not be an employee of the jail, or even of the government — *anyone* who testifies that he conducted a diligent search of the relevant records can testify to the absence of the record in question.)

(B) is not the best response,

because Witness was testifying about only the absence of a single record, not the contents of voluminous records.

FRE 1006, entitled "Summaries," says that "The content of voluminous writings ... which cannot conveniently be examined in court may be presented in the form of a chart, summary, or calculation."

Here, however, while the records Witness searched might be voluminous, the subject of his search was a single record, which he didn't find. Witness was therefore not summarizing "the content of voluminous writings."

(C) is not the best response,

because there is a hearsay exception for the absence of official records.

As described in the analysis of Choice (A) above, FRE 803(10) gives a hearsay exception for the absence of an official record. Consequently, the testimony here is not hearsay.

(D) is not the best response,

because testimony about the absence of an official record receives a hearsay exception, and the records containing the omission need not be produced under the Best Evidence Rule.

FRE 803(10), allowing testimony that a particular official record was not found after diligent search, does not include any requirement that the records that were searched be produced.

It's true that apart from hearsay issues, when the affirmative contents of a document are offered the document itself must normally be offered under the Best Evidence Rule (the FRE's general formulation of which occurs in Rule 1002). But the Best Evidence Rule is not deemed applicable to the "absence of a record" situation — testimony that a diligent search has not turned up the record is all that is required, and the mass of searched records need not be produced.

Answer 13

(D) is the best response,

because evidence of liability insurance is admissible if relevant to show ownership or control.

The Federal Rules of Evidence (like the common law) provide that evidence that a person carried or did not carry liability insurance is not admissible on the issue of whether that person acted negligently. See FRE 411, first sent. This rule bars such evidence when it is offered by a plaintiff to suggest that because the defendant was insured, the defendant was probably careless.

However, the rule does not apply where the evidence is offered for some other purpose, "such as proof of agency, ownership, or control ..." FRE 41, second sent. That's what's happening here — the evidence is being used to show that because Defendant bought a liability policy on the plane, he had ownership or control of it.

(A) is not the best response,

because the terms of the policy are not at issue, only the policy's existence.

The Best Evidence Rule (B.E.R.) states that in proving the terms of a writing or a recording, where the terms are material, the original must be produced. The rule applies to cases where there is a legally operative or dispositive document.

The B.E.R. would apply if the terms of the insurance policy were in question. But under the facts here, the terms are not in question and not material — Witness' testimony involves only the existence of the policy, not its terms. Therefore, the B.E.R. does not apply.

(B) is not the best response,

because it misstates the rule.

The rule against proof of liability insurance is not a general rule against "proof of insurance where insurance is not itself the issue" (as this choice asserts).

Instead, the rule prohibits proof of a liability policy's existence when offered to prove negligence. Where the proof is offered for another reason, the evidence is admissible. Here, the insurance is offered to show that Defendant owned or had some responsibility for the plane, so the rule against proof of insurance does not apply.

(C) is not the best response,

because such evidence is offered to suggest Defendant was probably careless.

FRE 411, first sent., says that "Evidence that a person was or was not insured against liability is not admissible upon the issue whether the person acted negligently or otherwise wrongfully." That's the very purpose that this choice posits, since it suggest that an insured plane owner would be less likely to properly maintain the plane. So this choice flies squarely in the face of FRE 411.

Answer 14

(D) is the best answer,

because it correctly identifies the testimony as extrinsic evidence on a collateral matter, which makes the evidence inadmissible.

Under these facts, Derrick's counsel is attempting to impeach Bystander with evidence not from Bystander's own mouth – that is, "extrinsic" evidence. Extrinsic evidence which only discredits a witness, without bearing on any substantive issues in the case, is called "collateral," and is not admissible. FRE 403. Here, the issues in the case involve the speed of Derrick's car, his failing to keep a lookout, and his crossing the center line. The color of his sweater is not a material issue; all Wilson's testimony will serve to do is discredit Bystander. As a result, the testimony will not be admissible, and since D recognizes this, it's the best response.

(A) is not the best response,

because it mischaracterizes the facts: the color of Derrick's sweater is not a material fact.

Under these facts, Derrick's counsel is attempting to impeach Bystander with evidence not from Bystander's own mouth – that is, "extrinsic" evidence. Extrinsic evidence which only discredits a witness, without bearing on any substantive issues in the case, is called "collateral," and is not admissible. FRE 403. Here, the issues in the case involve the speed of Derrick's car, his failing to keep a lookout, and his crossing the center line. The color of his sweater is not a material issue; all Wilson's testimony will serve to do is discredit Bystander.

Note that if the color of Derrick's sweater *was* a material fact, then Wilson's testimony would be admissible. Extrinsic evidence can be admitted to prove a number of things, including bias, contradicting facts, inconsistent statements, defects in perception or memory or capacity, certain prior convictions, or bad character for truthfulness. As a contradicting fact, Wilson's testimony

would be admissible. As it is, the color of Derrick's sweater does not bear on any of the substantive issues in the case. As a result, it is a "collateral" matter – it is relevant only to discredit a witness, Bystander. As such, it will not be admissible, under FRE 403, making A not the best response.

(B) is not the best response,

because the testimony here could *not* be admitted on the subject of Bystander's truthfulness and veracity.

Under these facts, Derrick's counsel is attempting to impeach Bystander with evidence not from Bystander's own mouth – that is, "extrinsic" evidence. Extrinsic evidence can be admitted to prove a number of things, including bias, contradicting facts, inconsistent statements, defects in perception or memory or capacity, certain prior convictions, or bad character for truthfulness. Option B addresses the last of these. However, the problem is that extrinsic evidence on a witness's bad character for truthfulness can *only* be proven via reputation or opinion testimony, under the FRE. Rule 608(a). Here, Wilson's testimony addresses a specific instance – that is, Bystander's testimony that Derrick's sweater was green. As a result, Wilson's testimony could not be admitted for the purpose option B suggests. As a result, B is not the best response.

(C) is not the best answer,

because it misstates the facts – the testimony *would* bear on Bystander's ability to observe.

Under these facts, Derrick's counsel is attempting to impeach Bystander with evidence not from Bystander's own mouth – that is, "extrinsic" evidence. Extrinsic evidence can be admitted to prove a number of things, including bias, contradicting facts, inconsistent statements, defects in perception or memory or capacity, certain prior convictions, or bad character for truthfulness. However, what option C ignores is that the issue here – Derrick's sweater being blue instead of green – is not *material,* so extrinsic impeachment will not be available to prove defects in Bystander's ability to observe.

Option C is correct, however, in concluding that the evidence is inadmissible. However, the reason it's inadmissible is that it is extrinsic evidence addressing a "collateral matter." That is, all that Wilson's testimony will do is discredit Bystander – it doesn't bear on any *material* issue in the case. It will be inadmissible on that basis. Since C doesn't recognize this, it's not the best response.

Answer 15

(B) is the best response,

because it correctly identifies the statement as an admission, and declares it admissible on that basis.

Under these facts, Price is offering Derrick's out-of-court statement to prove that Derrick was speeding. Since it's being offered to prove the truth of its assertion, the statement is hearsay. However, the statement will be admissible under the admission exclusion to the hearsay rule. The statement is an admission because it is unfavorable to the declarant, Derrick, at the time of the trial. FRE 801(d)(2). Since B identifies the correct basis on which the statement will be admissible, it's the best response.

(A) is not the best response,

because there is no basis on which to admit a prior inconsistent statement.

The basic problem with the evidence here concerns hearsay. Hearsay is an out-of-court statement offered to prove the truth of its assertion. Here, if Officer's testimony is offered to prove that Derrick was, in fact, speeding, it will have to be admissible *substantively* – that is, to prove that Derrick was, in fact, speeding. If, on the other hand, it's only being offered to impeach Derrick (in other words, calling into question his truthfulness), there *must* have been some testimony of Derrick's, on cross-examination, which contradicts the prior inconsistent statement. Here, Price is seeking to impeach Derrick with *extrinsic* evidence of a prior inconsistent statement (i.e., evidence not from Derrick's own mouth). The problem here is that Price's attorney hadn't questioned Derrick about his speed at all, on cross-examination, so there's nothing to impeach. The thing that makes this tricky is that Derrick's speed is obviously a material issue in the case. However, prior inconsistent statements are strictly limited to impeaching the witness's testimony; they can't be used substantively *unless* they were included in prior testimony.

Instead, the evidence will escape hearsay problems because it qualifies as an admission. Since A misapplies the prior inconsistent statements hearsay exclusion, it's not the best response.

The problem with extrinsic evidence of prior inconsistent statements is that it requires a *foundation.* That is, the witness must be given a chance to explain or deny (if justice so requires), before *or* after the extrinsic evidence is introduced. FRE 613(b). Without this foundation, the testimony is not admissible. Under these facts, you're told that Price's attorney had not questioned Derrick about his speed; thus, there's no foundation. Of course, Price's attorney could give Derrick a chance to explain or deny the statement *after* Officer's testimony was introduced, but without such an opportunity, Officer's testimony would be inadmissible.

Say the facts were different, and Price's attorney was seeking to impeach Derrick *intrinsically,* not *extrinsically.* Under those circumstances, a prior inconsistent statement does not require a foundation. However, here, the evidence of a prior inconsistent statement is extrinsic, and as a result it will require a foundation. Since option A doesn't recognize this, it's not the best response.

(C) is not the best response,

because it implicitly mischaracterizes the basis on which Officer's testimony will be admissible.

The central problem here addresses hearsay. Hearsay is an out-of-court statement offered to prove the truth of its assertion. Here, if Officer's testimony is offered to prove that Derrick was speeding, it is being offered as substantive evidence. Option C doesn't address this, but instead, implicitly characterizes Officer's testimony as impeachment. There are two problems with this.

First, a "foundation" refers to the admissibility of a prior inconsistent statement. Officer's testimony could not be admissible as a prior inconsistent statement, since it's being offered to impeach Derrick, and there's nothing to impeach, since Derrick didn't testify to his speed on cross-examination. (Note that the testimony couldn't be admissible *substantively* as a prior inconsistent statement, since that's only possible when the prior inconsistent statement was in prior testimony).

Second, in any case, a foundation is *not* required *before* a prior inconsistent statement is admitted, under the Federal Rules (this *was* a requirement at common law). Under the Federal Rules, the declarant can be questioned about a prior inconsistent statement *after* it has been admitted, or not at all, if justice so requires. FRE 613(b). (Incidentally, note that where the impeachment is intrinsic, not extrinsic, a prior inconsistent statement does no require a foundation).

In fact, Officer's testimony will be admissible as an admission, since it is unfavorable to the declarant, Derrick, at the time of the trial. FRE 801(d)(2). Since C doesn't recognize this, it's not the best response.

(D) is not the best response,

because it fails to realize that the testimony will be admissible as an admission.

Option D does correctly realize that there are hearsay problems with Officer's testimony. Hearsay is an out-of-court statement offered to prove the truth of its assertion. Here, if Officer's testimony is offered substantively – that is, to prove that Derrick was speeding – then it's hearsay, and it must fit a hearsay exception or exclusion to be admissible. What option D fails to realize is that the testimony will be admissible as an admission. The testimony is an admission because it's unfavorable to the declarant, Derrick, at the time of trial. Admissions are admissible as an *exclusion* from the hearsay rule. FRE 801(d)(2). Thus, the testimony is not, technically, hearsay at all.

Note that what "hearsay not within any exception" actually means is that the hearsay must not fit another option. Here, option B correctly recognizes that the testimony will be admissible as an admission. As a result, D is not the best response.

Answer 16

(D) is the best response,

because Mrs. Pence's testimony would be hearsay within hearsay, and the "outer level" is not within any exception.

The FRE defines hearsay as "a statement, other than one made by the declarant while testifying at the trial or hearing, offered in evidence to prove the truth of the matter asserted." FRE 801(c).

Anytime the evidence in question consists of an out-of-court statement by *A* repeating another out-of-court statement by *B*, you have to analyze *both A*'s statement and *B*'s statement — if *either* statement is hearsay not falling within any exception, the combined statement cannot come in.

Here, the "inner" level (Duarte's statement to Mrs. Pence's husband) is an admission being used against a party-opponent, so it falls within the admissions exception to the hearsay rule.

But the "outer" level (the husband's statement to Mrs. Pence, "Here's what Duarte told me...") is hearsay not within any exception. First, notice that the statement ("Duarte told me he'd blow my head off one day") is being offered to prove the matter asserted: it's being offered to prove that Duarte indeed made the threat. (It's also being offered for the additional not-really-hearsay inference that if Duarte made a threat to kill Husband by shooting, that's evidence tending to show that the fatal shooting of Husband by someone unknown was done by Duarte. But this "secondary" purpose doesn't detract from the fact that the primary purpose — to prove that Duarte made the threat — is a hearsay purpose.)

Now, let's look at whether the husband's statement falls within any exception. It doesn't. For instance, it doesn't fall within the state-of-mind exception, because the husband wasn't saying, "I'm scared of Duarte because he threatened to kill me..." — it's offered for the pure purpose of showing that Duarte made the threat, and that purpose doesn't qualify for state-of-mind, excited-utterance, or any other exception.

(A) is not the best response.

because the state-of-mind exception doesn't solve the problem that the husband's statement to Mrs. Pence is, separately, hearsay.

It's true that Duarte's statement alone might well be admissible as evidence of Duarte's state of mind vis a vis the husband, under FRE 803(3) (covering declarant's "then existing state of mind, emotion, sensation, or physical condition").

But the problem (as further discussed in Choice (D) above) is that what's offered is what the husband said out of court that Duarte told him out of court. So if the husband's statement (the "outer" statement) is hearsay not within an exception, the fact that Duarte's statement (the "inner" statement) falls within a hearsay

exception doesn't help.

Here, the statement by the husband is hearsay not within any exception, as shown by the analysis in Choice (D). Therefore, the combined statements of the husband and Duarte can't come in.

(B) is not the best response.

because the admissibility of statements made by, and offered against, a party-opponent doesn't solve the combined hearsay-on-hearsay problem present here.

It's true that Duarte's statement, if made directly to the testifying witness (Mrs. Pence) could be repeated by her on the stand, since then it would be a statement made by a party opponent admitted against that opponent, a non-hearsay use under FRE 801(2)(A).

But the problem (as further discussed in Choice (D) above) is that what's offered is what the husband said out of court that Duarte told him out of court. So if the husband's statement (the "outer" statement) is hearsay not within an exception, the fact that Duarte's statement (the "inner" statement) is a non-hearsay admission doesn't help.

Here, the statement by the husband is hearsay not within any exception, as shown by the analysis in Choice (D). Therefore, the combined statements of the husband and Duarte can't come in.

Answer 17

(A) is the best response,

because one who obtains a confidential communication while assisting a lawyer is covered by the attorney-client privilege.

If the interview for sentencing-preparation had been between the attorney and Susan, it's perfectly clear that the attorney-client privilege would apply. The fact that it's a non-attorney third person, not the attorney, who had the conversation with the defendant is what makes the problem interesting.

However, it's well-established that the attorney-client privilege also applies to communications between the client and a third-party non-lawyer who has been engaged by the lawyer to aid in the representation. Since the probation officer was engaged by Susan's lawyer to aid in an aspect of the defense, anything Susan told him is treated as if it had been told to the lawyer, and is therefore privileged.

(B) is not the best response,

because the attorney-client privilege's applicability makes the probable-cause issue irrelevant.

As described in the analysis of Choice (A) above, the communication is covered by the attorney-client privilege. Therefore, even if the interview did more probably than not develop evidence relevant to the grand jury's inquiry, the interview would still be privileged.

In any event, this choice misstates the criterion for grand jury questioning — as long as the matter under question has a reasonable chance of being either directly relevant or leading to relevant evidence, the proponent of the questioning need not show by "probable cause" that the questions are directly relevant to the grand jury's inquiry.

Choice (C) is not the best response,

because a non-attorney engaged by an attorney is covered by the attorney-client privilege. See the further analysis of this legal rule in the discussion of Choice (A) above.

Choice (D) is not the best response,

because the rules of privilege very much apply in grand jury proceedings. It's true that not all rules of evidence apply in grand jury proceedings (the hearsay rule, for instance), but privileges, such as the attorney-client privilege, do apply.

Answer 18

(C) is the best response,

because the beatings would tend to prove that the killing was not accidental.

Under FRE 404(b), "Evidence of other crimes, wrongs, or acts is not admissible to prove the character of a person in order to show action in conformity therewith." So if the prosecution were offering the prior beatings on the theory that "These beatings showed that Defendant had a violent character, making it more likely that he acted violently on this occasion," the evidence would be barred by the above-quoted portion of 404(b).

However, FRE 404(b) goes on to say that such other-crimes-or-wrongs evidence "may, however, be admissible for other purposes, such as proof of motive, opportunity, intent, preparation, plan, knowledge, identity, or *absence of mistake or accident*..." Here, that's exactly what's happening: Defendant has claimed that the shooting was accidental, and the prosecution is offering the prior beatings to show "absence of mistake or accident." So the evidence is admissible.

(A) is not the best response,

because the acts of violence here are not being offered as character evidence.

It's true that if the evidence were offered as pure character evidence, to show that Defendant acted in conformity with his character (character for violence, say) on the present occasion, the evidence would be barred by FRE 404(b). But as described in the analysis of Choice (C), the evidence here is being offered to show "absence of mistake or accident," not to show "character," so it's admissible.

(B) is not the best response,

because the beatings show lack of accident regardless of who started the fights.

The fact that Witness doesn't know first-hand who started the fights is irrelevant, if the mere existence of the fights would tend to show that the shooting on the present occasion was no mistake. For instance, even if the father started the two prior fights, the fact that Defendant responded by beating his father would make it at least somewhat less likely than it would otherwise be that the shooting now was an accident. So the evidence is relevant, and it's admissible (as described in Choice (C)) as tending to prove absence of accident.

(D) is not the best response,

because evidence of a character for violence is not admissible under these circumstances.

Under FRE 404(b), "Evidence of other crimes, wrongs, or acts is not admissible to prove the character of a person in order to show action in conformity therewith." So if the evidence of the prior beatings were really being offered to show that "Defendant has a character for violence, and is thus likely to have acted violently on the present occasion," the quoted sentence would apply to make the evidence inadmissible (not admissible, as this choice posits).

However, "character for violence" is not what the prior-acts evidence is being offered for. Instead (as shown in the analysis of Choice (C)), it's being offered to show absence of accident, and that purpose is admissible under 404(b).

Answer 19

(D) is the best response,

because the testimony is not hearsay, in that it is not offered for the truth of the matter asserted, but rather to show the listener's response to the assertion.

Hearsay is a statement offered to prove "the truth of the matter asserted." FRE 801(c). The matter being "asserted" in the out-of-court declaration is "Plaintiff can't work productively more than 4 hours per day." So if the statement were being offered to prove that Plaintiff couldn't in fact work more than 4 hours per day, it would be hearsay (and not within any exception).

However, Plaintiff can properly claim that this is not the purpose of introducing the former employer's statement. Plaintiff can say, "I'm offering this statement not to show that the former employer was speaking truthfully or accurately — I have no idea whether Plaintiff could or couldn't work productively — but rather to explain that at the moment I declined to hire her, my having heard this statement, not my desire to avoid hiring someone over 65, was my motivation." A court would agree — where the out-of-court statement is offered to show its effect on the listener rather than its truth, that's a non-hearsay purpose.

(A) is not the best response,

because Defendant's opinion of Plaintiff's abilities is not rendered inadmissible by the fact that it is not based on personal knowledge.

It's true that there are some types of testimony that are not admissible because not based on personal knowledge. But here, Defendant's opinion is not being offered to show that that opinion was "true." Rather, it's being offered to show that the opinion — whether "true" or not — was not based on forbidden age discrimination. Therefore, the fact that the opinion was not based on Defendant's personal experience does not make it inadmissible.

(B) is not the best response,

because Employer's statement is not offered for the truth of the matter asserted in it, and therefore cannot be hearsay.

Hearsay is an out-of-court statement offered in evidence to prove the truth of the matter asserted in the statement.

The matter asserted in the statement is that Plaintiff was incapable of working productively for more than four hours in a day. If the statement was offered to prove that Plaintiff in fact was incapable of working more than this amount, the statement would indeed be inadmissible hearsay. But that's not why it's being offered — it's being offered merely to prove that Defendant's reason for not hiring Plaintiff was this advice from Employer (whether that advice was based on real facts or not) rather than an age-discriminatory motive. And, as outlined in the discussion of Choice (D), that's not hearsay.

(C) is not the best response,

because if the statement was offered for this purpose, it would be inadmissible hearsay.

Hearsay is an out-of-court statement offered to prove the truth of the matter asserted.

The out of court statement includes the sub-statement "Plaintiff can't work more than four hours productively." (The statement also includes a recommendation, "I advise you not to hire her.") If the statement were offered to prove that Plaintiff indeed couldn't work more than four hours productively, the statement would be being offered to prove the truth of the (or a) matter asserted in it. This would make the statement hearsay. Since there is no exception that applies, the statement would be inadmissible, not admissible as this choice asserts.

Answer 20

(D) is the best response,

because the court shall exclude witnesses at the request of a party.

FRE 615 says that "At the request of a party the court shall order witnesses excluded so that they cannot hear the testimony of other witnesses..." Although the eyewitness has already testified, the fact that he is expected to be re-called for further cross means that he's still to be treated as a witness who has not yet testified. (The purpose of the sequestration rule is to pre-

vent the witness from tailoring his testimony to that of other witnesses. This purpose would be thwarted by letting the eyewitness here be in the courtroom before his re-cross.)

(A) is not the best response,

because the court has the discretion to permit inquiry into additional matters.

FRE 611(b) says that as a general rule cross "should be limited to the subject matter of the direct examination and matters affecting the credibility of the witness." But that section goes on to say, "The court may, in the exercise of discretion, permit inquiry into additional matters as if on direct examination." The court's discretion would be especially proper in this case, since Defendant is effectively the direct examiner (because Plaintiff called Defendant as an adverse, or "hostile," witness.)

(B) is not the best response,

because leading questions are not proper when the "cross" examination is really a direct examination since the party was originally called as an adverse witness.

Here, if Defendant's lawyer is conducting "cross examination" of Defendant, it must be because Plaintiff called Defendant as an adverse witness (which is, indeed, what Choice (A) specifies happened.) In that scenario, this "cross" is to be treated by the court as if it were a direct exam, since the questioner is sympathetic to the witness. In that instance, the cross should not be allowed to make use of leading questions, any more than a standard direct exam may use leading questions. (See FRE 611(c), stating the general rule that leading questions "should not be used on the direct examination of a witness except as may be necessary to develop the witness' testimony.")

(C) is not the best response,

because matters of credibility are within the scope of cross-examination.

FRE 611(b), in defining the permissible scope of cross-examination, says that the cross may include, in addition to "the subject matter of the direct examination," "matters affecting the credibility of the witness." So the fact that credibility was not placed in issue in the direct does not bar it from being covered on cross.

Answer 21

(D) is the best response,

because it correctly states that a witness may refer to collateral documents without having to produce the documents themselves.

The central issue in these facts is that Ward is testifying relying on a writing – namely, the newspaper story. Thus, there's a potential Best Evidence Rule problem. Under the Best Evidence Rule, when the terms of a writing are being proven, or the witness is testifying relying on a writing, the writing must be produced, if available. FRE 1002. However, under these facts, the only relevance the writing has is that it reinforces Ward's memory. Ward's memory is not closely related to a material issue in the case, and as such is considered "collateral." The Best Evidence Rule doesn't cover collateral matters, and, as a result, his testimony will be admissible without producing the newspaper. FRE 1004. Since D states the correct rule and applies it to these facts, it is best response.

(A) is not the best response,
because the Best Evidence Rule is not applicable to these facts.

The Best Evidence Rule, requiring that the document itself be produced if available, only applies if the terms of a writing are being proven, or the witness is testifying relying on a writing. FRE 1002. However, under these facts, the only relevance the writing has is that it reinforces Ward's memory. Ward's memory is not closely related to a material issue in the case, and as such is considered "collateral." The Best Evidence Rule doesn't cover collateral matters, and, as a result, Ward's testimony will be admissible without producing the newspaper. FRE 1004. Since A doesn't recognize this, it's not the best response.

(B) is not the best response,
because there's no hearsay problem under these facts.

Hearsay is an out-of-court statement offered to prove the truth of its assertion. Here, the out-of-court statement is that of the newspaper. However, it's not being offered to prove that Ward's daughter actually became engaged on that day; thus, it's not being offered to prove the truth of its assertion, but rather only to prove something *unrelated* to the writing: that Ward talked with Terrell that day. As a result, it's not hearsay.

Instead, what B ignores is the central issue under these facts, which involves the Best Evidence Rule. The Best Evidence Rule, requiring that the document itself be produced if available, only applies if the terms of a writing are being proven, or the witness is testifying relying on a writing. FRE 1002. However, under these facts, the only relevance the writing has is that it reinforces Ward's memory. Ward's memory is not closely related to a material issue in the case, and as such is considered "collateral." The Best Evidence Rule doesn't cover collateral matters, and, as a result, Ward's testimony will be admissible without producing the newspaper. FRE 1004. Since B ignores this issue all together, it's not the best response.

(C) is not the best response,
because it states an incorrect rule of law. Judicial notice is appropriate for both notorious facts (subject to common knowledge in the community) and manifest facts (capable of positive verification through readily accessible, undoubtedly accurate sources). FRE 201(b). The contents of local newspapers would not fit either one of these categories, since, apart from anything else, the papers could quite easily have misdated Ward's daughter's engagement announcement. (Appropriate topics for judicial notice include federal and state laws, the normal human gestation period, information available from almanacs, the validity of ballistics tests, the validity of paternity blood tests, and the like – you get the idea.)

Instead, what C fails to realize is the central issue under these facts: the applicability of the Best Evidence Rule. In fact, since the article only addresses a collateral issue – Ward's memory for the date his conversation with Terrell took place – the Best Evidence Rule does not apply, and Ward's testimony will be admissible without producing the newspaper report. Since C ignores this issue, and misstates the rule on judicial notice, it's not the best response.

Answer 22

(B) is the best response,
because it correctly identifies that the evidence will be admissible to impeach Pitt. This method of impeachment is called impeachment with prior inconsistent statements.

Note that Pitt's statement is hearsay. Hearsay is an out-of-court statement offered to prove the truth of its assertion. Here, Pitt is the out-of-court declarant, and his statement is being offered to prove that Drew was his murderer. Thus, it's hearsay. However, it'll be admissible under the "dying declaration" hearsay exception, because it was made by a person now unavailable to testify, believing he was about to die, concerning personal knowledge of the cause of death, and the statement is offered at either a criminal homicide trial or a civil wrongful death suit. Since Pitt's last statement is admissible under the "dying declaration" exception to the hearsay rule, his prior inconsistent statement can be used to impeach his credibility, since hearsay declarants *can* be impeached. (Note that the impeaching evidence would not be admissible *substantively,* since it does not fulfill the requirements of the prior inconsistent statement requirement, since a prior inconsistent statement is only admissible substantively if the statement was made under oath, at a prior proceeding, subject to perjury, and the declarant is the testifying witness.) Since B correctly states the law and applies it to these facts, it's the best response.

(A) is not the best response,
because Wall's testimony does not fit an exception to the hearsay rule; it's inadmissible hearsay. As a result, it can't be admitted to prove the truth of its assertion – that is, that Jack stabbed Wall.

Wall's statement concerning Jack is hearsay because it's an out-of-court statement offered to prove the truth of its assertion. The out-of-court statement is Pitt's: "I was stabbed by Jack..." It is being offered to prove the truth of its assertion, i.e., that Jack had stabbed him. However, the statement does not fit the most obvious exception, the "dying declaration" exception to the hearsay rule, because Pitt did not have an impending sense of death when he made the statement. FRE 804(b)(2). The rationale behind the exception is that no one wants to die with a lie on his lips; where a person thinks he's going to *live*, this is not applicable. Also, the statement will not be admissible *substantively* as a prior inconsistent statement, because Pitt is not a testifying witness, the statement was not made under oath subject to perjury, as the prior inconsistent statement exception requires. Instead, the statement will be admissible to *impeach* Pitt's dying declaration, that Drew stabbed him, because Pitt's statement about Jack contradicts his dying declaration. Since A doesn't recognize this, it's not the best response.

(C) is not the best response,

because it does not state the correct reasoning on these facts, nor the correct conclusion.

An "ultimate issue" is one which will determine liability. Under the FRE, the admissibility of a statement does not depend on whether it addresses an "ultimate issue." If you chose this response, you may have been thinking of the common law (not FRE) approach to expert testimony, which required that such testimony not address "ultimate issues." Instead, what option C fails to recognize is that the statement will be admissible to impeach Pitt's dying declaration, as a prior inconsistent statement. Since C doesn't recognize this, it's not the best response.

(D) is not the best response,

because it misstates the facts.

There are two types of relevance: Logical relevance and legal relevance. A piece of evidence is legally relevance as long as its probative value is not substantially outweighed by the probability of undue prejudice it will engender. There's no legal relevance problem under these facts. Instead, option D addresses logical relevance. A piece of evidence is logically relevant if it tends to prove or disprove a material fact. FRE 401. Evidence cannot be admissible unless it's logically relevant; however, that's no problem here, contrary to what D states. If Pitts' prior statement is true,

it will tend to prove that Pitt was lying about Drew's stabbing him, and thus make it less likely that Drew is guilty of murder. As a result, it's *extremely* relevant! Since D states otherwise, it's not the best response.

Answer 23

(D) is the best response,

because Victim will testify that the voice on the phone is similar to Defendant's, and because the Best Evidence Rule does not apply.

Authentication, the Federal Rules of Evidence say, is the condition precedent to admissibility that is satisfied

by evidence sufficient to support a finding that the matter in question is what its proponent claims. Since the prosecution is trying to establish that the voice on the phone was Defendant's, Victim's testimony that he believes the voice was victim's will have to be authenticated.

FRE 901(b)(5) gives, as an illustration of proper authentication, "Identification of a voice, whether heard firsthand or through mechanical or electronic transmission or recording, by opinion based upon hearing the voice at any time under circumstances connecting it with the alleged speaker." Since Victim has heard Defendant's voice and knows that that voice has a distinctive accent, his proposed testimony (which states that the voice had a similar distinctive accent) meets this requirement. There is no requirement that the giver of the opinion must be positive in the identification — the witness is permitted to say merely that the voice was similar, for instance having a similar distinctive accent. At that point, the jury is free to give very little weight to the evidence — the point is that the lack of certainty doesn't make the tentative identification inadmissible.

Nor does the Best Evidence Rule apply here — see the explanation of this fact in the discussion of Choice (B).

(A) is not the best response,

because Victim's testimony is admissible.

For the reasons stated in the treatment of Choice (D) above, the fact that Victim cannot conclusively identify the voice as being Defendant's does not prevent the tentative identification from being admissible.

(B) is not the best response,

because the testimony is admissible and the Best Evidence Rule (B.E.R.) does not apply.

The B.E.R. states that if the terms of a writing or a recording are to be proved, the original must be produced. The Rule does not apply to events that have by happenstance been recorded — it applies only where the terms of the recording, per se, are what are being sought to be proved.

Here, the extortion happened in a live phone call. The prosecution is proving the contents of that live phone call. The fact that Victim happened to have made a tape of the call, therefore, does not mean that the prosecution is attempting to "prove the contents" of this incidentally-created tape. So the B.E.R. doesn't apply. (It would be different if the extortion occurred when someone sent a threatening tape to Victim — then the recording *would* be subject to the B.E.R., because the prosecution's case would require it to show what the contents of the tape were.)

(C) is not the best response,

because the Best Evidence Rule (B.E.R.) wouldn't be waived by a failure to subpoena, and in any case, the

Rule is not applicable to these facts.

The B.E.R., like any evidentiary requirement, can be waived by the non-proponent party. But that waiver would have to take the form of a failure to object at trial. The opponent's mere failure to subpoena the tape would not serve as a waiver. (For example, the opponent, Defendant here, might not have known that the tape even existed.)

In any event, the B.E.R. doesn't apply to these facts, because the contents of the recording are not what's being proved. See the discussion of Choice (B) above.

Answer 24

(B) is the best response,

because the general manager's testimony was sufficient to prove that it was Plaintiff's habit to have created and mailed a cost overrun notice in circumstances like the one here.

The issue is whether the copy found in Plaintiff's files is indeed a copy of a letter that was actually sent to Defendant. Therefore, FRE 406 is relevant. That rule says that "Evidence of the habit of a person or of the routine practice of an organization, whether corroborated or not and regardless of the presence of eyewitnesses, is relevant to prove that the conduct of the person or organization on a particular occasion was in conformity with the habit or routine practice." So here, the general manager's testimony that it was the organization's habit to send such a notice as required by its contracts tends to establish that the photocopy was indeed a photocopy of a letter that was sent, as contemplated by FRE 406.

Nor is the letter here hearsay (whether within an exception or not) — see Choice (A) for an explanation.

(A) is not the best response

because the letter is not hearsay at all, since it's not offered to prove the truth of any matter asserted therein.

It's true that the letter is an "out of court declaration." But the letter is not being offered to prove the "truth of the matter asserted." The matter asserted is that there was a cost overrun. But the purpose for offering the letter in evidence is merely to show that the contractual requirement of a notice was satisfied. (The letter would be equally relevant on the issue of notice even if the letter was incorrect in its assertion that there was a cost overrun. So it's not offered to prove the truth of the matter asserted therein.)

So even though the letter would probably be admissible under the business records exception if it *were* being offered to prove the truth of the matter asserted, there's no hearsay here to require an exception. To put it another way, the phrase "though hearsay" in this choice is an incorrect conclusion of law.

(C) is not the best response,

because the letter is not hearsay at all.

See the discussion of Choice (A) for why this is so.

(D) is not the best response,

because even though the Best Evidence Rule applies, the duplicate copy is admissible.

FRE 1002's version of the Best Evidence Rule (called "Requirement of Original"), says that in proving the terms of a writing, the original writing must ordinarily be produced. So on the face of this rule, since the contents of the letter are being proved, FRE 1002 seems to require use of the original.

But FRE 1003 says that "A *duplicate is admissible* to the same extent as an original unless (1) a genuine question is raised as to the authenticity of the original or (2) in the circumstances it would be unfair to admit the duplicate in lieu of the original." Since Defendant has not raised a genuine question about the authenticity of the original, and since it would be not be unfair to admit the duplicate (Plaintiff obviously couldn't possess the original any more if its story of having sent it to Defendant is true), FRE 1003 allows use of the copy here.

Answer 25

(A) is the best response,

because it correctly applies the "Mercy Rule" to these facts.

The problem under these facts is that the evidence offered is *character* evidence, which is, as a *very* general rule, inadmissible. However, option A correctly identifies that the "Mercy Rule" will operate to make this evidence admissible. Under the "Mercy Rule," in criminal cases only, the defendant may offer pertinent character evidence to prove his innocence, in the form of reputation or opinion. The character evidence here is in the form of reputation, and, by tending to prove that Dann is a nonviolent, peace-loving person, it would tend to exonerate Dann. Since A applies to the facts and correctly states the "Mercy Rule," it's the best response.

(B) is not the best response,

because the admissibility of evidence for purposes of punishment would not be relevant to its admissibility for purposes of guilt.

The problem under these facts is that the evidence offered is *character* evidence, which is, as a very general rule, inadmissible. In fact, under these facts, the "Mercy Rule" will operate to make the evidence admissible. Under the "Mercy Rule," in criminal cases only, the defendant may offer pertinent character evidence to prove his innocence, in the form of reputation or opinion. The character evidence here is in the form of reputation, and, by tending to prove that Dann is a nonviolent, peace-loving person, it would tend to exonerate Dann.

In fact, the admissibility of evidence for purposes of sentencing does not determine its admissibility during trial at all. In imposing a sentence, once guilt is established, the judge can rely on hearsay evidence as well as reports which are not cross-examined, neither of which might be admissible at trial. *Williams v. N.Y.* (1949). Since B does not address the appropriate stage of the trial, it's not the best response.

(C) is not the best response,

because it doesn't recognize that the "Mercy Rule" will make the evidence admissible.

The problem under these facts is that the evidence is character evidence. As a general rule, character evidence is inadmissible. However, under the "Mercy Rule," in criminal cases only, the defendant may offer pertinent character evidence to prove his innocence, in the form of reputation or opinion. Here, the testimony of Employer will be relevant because Dann's reputation as a peaceful, non-violent person would suggest that he did not attack Smith without provocation.

What C suggests is that the evidence is not logically relevant: That is, Dann's general good character does not make him less likely to be guilty of the crime charged. In fact, this isn't true, because if he normally doesn't beat people up, it's less likely that he beat up Smith. In any case, the central issue here is applicability of the Mercy Rule. Since C doesn't recognize this, it's not the best response.

(D) is not the best response,

because it raises a threshold issue of competency that is not at issue under these facts.

Under FRE 602, a witness is competent to testify if he has personal knowledge of the matter on which he will testify, and he must declare that he will testify truthfully, by oath or affirmation. FRE 603. As Dann's employer, it could fairly be assumed that Employer is, in fact, competent to testify about Dann's reputation for peacefulness. Furthermore, since reputation testimony only requires that the witness be familiar with the subject's reputation, it would not be necessary to prove that he lived or worked with Dann.

Instead, what D fails to recognize is that the character evidence will be admissible under the "Mercy Rule." The "Mercy Rule" provides that, in criminal cases only, the defendant may offer pertinent character evidence to prove his innocence, in the form of reputation or opinion. Here, the testimony of Employer will be relevant because Dann's reputation as a peaceful, non-violent person would suggest that he did not attack Smith without provocation. Since D does not recognize this, it's not the best response.

Answer 26

(B) is the best response,

because it correctly states that the evidence will be admissible to impeach Employer as a reputation witness.

The problem here is that the evidence the prosecutor

is seeking is character evidence. Option A offers a way to overcome this problem. Under these facts, Employer is testifying as a reputation witness on Dann's behalf; that is, he's testifying that Dann is known as a peaceful, nonviolent person. As option A correctly identifies, he can be cross-examined about his knowledge concerning Dann's reputation. Under FRE 404(a), a reputation witness may be questioned about specific instances bearing on the reputation, since not knowing such information reflects on the witness's competence to testify as to the person's reputation in the community. Since B correctly states this rule and it applies to the facts, it's the best response.

(A) is not the best response,

because it states an incorrect rule of law: Evidence of the prior fights and brawls may *not,* in fact, be used to prove Dann's guilt. Prior specific acts of misconduct are only admissible when they have independent relevance, e.g., they prove preparation, motive, intent, knowledge, and the like, under FRE 404(b). They definitely cannot be admitted to prove defendant's guilt in this instance, since their admissibility on this basis would likely encourage a jury to convict defendant because he's a "bad person," not because he's guilty in this instance.

Instead, what option A fails to recognize is that the evidence can be used to *impeach* Employer, as a reputation witness. Under FRE 404(a), a reputation witness may be questioned about specific instances bearing on the reputation, since not knowing such information reflects on the witness's competence to testify as to the person's reputation in the community. Of course, in actuality, once the jury hears this evidence, it will immediately assume that Dann is a brawling bully who can't stay out of trouble. Nonetheless, the evidence will be admissible to impeach Employer. Since A states the incorrect rule, it's not the best response.

(C) is not the best response,

because it fails to identify that the evidence will be admissible to impeach Frank's status as a reputation witness.

Option C implicitly recognizes that the problem here is that the evidence is character evidence. Option C correctly cites the *general* rule, which is that separate, unrelated offenses are inadmissible to proof guilt or liability on a specific occasion. However, there are exceptions to this rule, and the facts here represent one of them. In this instance, the evidence will be admissible to *impeach* Frank, since, if he is not familiar with Dann's other fights, he may not be credible as a reputation witness. FRE 404(b). Since C fails to recognize this, it is not the best response.

(D) is not the best response,

because while impeachment of a reputation witness with specific instances is possible, the specific instances need not be identified as precisely as D suggests.

The problem here is that the evidence is *character* evidence, which is, as a very general rule, inadmissible. However, as option D implicitly recognizes, under FRE 404(a), a reputation witness (of which Employer is one) may be questioned about specific instances bearing on the reputation, since *not* knowing such information reflects on the witness's *competence* to testify as to the person's reputation in the community. However, the testimony here is specific enough to constitute specific acts; it clearly does not amount to opinion or reputation testimony.

If you chose this response, you may have confused the "specific acts" requirement here with the foundation requirement for prior inconsistent statements, when they're used as extrinsic impeachment. Under those facts, the witness must be given a chance to explain or deny the statement, and this would necessarily require that he know exactly which statement he's being questioned about. FRE 613. However, this isn't a problem here. Since D overstates the requirements of impeaching a reputation witness with evidence of specific acts, D is not the best response.

Answer 27

(A) is the best response,

because it correctly identifies that the reputation evidence on the victim, Smith, will be admissible to exonerate Dann. The problem here is that the evidence about Smith is *character* evidence, and character evidence is, as a *very* general rule, inadmissible. However, option A correctly recognizes the reason the testimony here will be admissible. Defendant can offer reputation and opinion evidence of victim's character where, if victim acted in conformity with his character, the conduct would tend to prove the defendant's innocence (*except* in rape cases, where such evidence is generally inadmissible). Here, the testimony will tend to prove that Smith was the aggressor, and it's in the form of reputation evidence. Since A states the correct rule and it applies to these facts, it's the best response.

(B) is not the best response,

because the admissibility of other evidence is irrelevant to the admissibility of *this* evidence.

The problem here is that the evidence about Smith is *character* evidence, and character evidence is, as a *very* general rule, inadmissible. In fact, the evidence here is admissible on its own, because defendant can offer reputation and opinion evidence of victim's character where, if victim acted in conformity with his character, the conduct would tend to prove the defendant's innocence (*except* in rape cases, where such evidence is generally inadmissible).

Option B incorrectly states that the evidence is only admissible if it is accompanied by testimony of specific acts of misconduct about which Frank knows. In fact, specific instances are *not* admissible to prove victim's

character – only reputation and opinion. If you chose this response, you may have been thinking of evidence of *habit,* which is admissible to show that a person acted in conformity with his habit on a specific occasion. Such evidence *must* be in the form of specific instances of misconduct. However, here, the evidence would not be admissible as habit evidence, because the act here – lawbreaking and frequently engaging in brawls – would be *volitional* on every occasion, and habit evidence must be "semi-automatic" (e.g., always running a certain stop sign). FRE 406. In any case, since B fails to recognize that the evidence is admissible by itself, it's not the best response.

(C) is not the best response,

because the evidence will tend to exonerate Dann even though it concerns Smith.

What option C suggests is that the evidence will be inadmissible because it's irrelevant. There are two kinds of relevance: legal relevance and logical relevance. Logical relevance, to which option C alludes, requires that a piece of evidence must prove or disprove a material fact in order to be admissible. FRE 401. Here, Dann is claiming that he only assaulted Smith in self-defense. Thus, evidence that Smith had a reputation for brawling would tend to suggest that Smith did, in fact, assault Dann on the occasion in question, making it more likely that Dann did act in self-defense. Thus, the evidence is relevant.

What option C ignores is the *character evidence* problem with this testimony. As a general rule, character evidence is inadmissible. However, the facts here fit an exception to this rule. Defendant *can* offer reputation and opinion evidence of victim's character where, if victim acted in conformity with his character, the conduct would tend to prove the defendant's innocence (*except* in rape cases, where such evidence is generally inadmissible). Since C fails to recognize this, it is not the best response.

(D) is not the best response,

because a foundation is not necessary for admission of this testimony.

The problem here is that the evidence about Smith is *character* evidence, and character evidence is, as a *very* general rule, inadmissible. However, the facts here fit an exception to the rule. Defendant *can* offer reputation and opinion evidence of victim's character where, if victim acted in conformity with his character, the conduct would tend to prove the defendant's innocence (*except* in rape cases, where such evidence is generally inadmissible). Such evidence does not require a *foundation;* instead, the testimony will be admissible if Frank is competent to testify about Smith's reputation. Under FRE 602, a witness is competent to testify if he has personal knowledge of the matter on which he will testify, and he must declare that he will testify truthfully, by oath or affirmation. FRE 603. Reputation testimony only requires that the witness be familiar with the subject's reputation, and as long as Frank is familiar with Smith's reputation, he'll be competent to testify.

If you chose this response, you were thinking of the common law rule relating to impeachment with extrinsic evidence of prior inconsistent statements. This clearly doesn't apply here. Since D states, incorrectly, that a foundation will be required for admissibility of this testimony, it is not the best response.

Answer 28

(B) is the best response,

because it correctly characterizes the statement as an admission, and concludes that it is admissible on that basis.

Option B implicitly recognizes that there's a hearsay problem under these facts. Hearsay is an out-of-court statement offered to prove the truth of its assertion. Here, the out-of-court declarant is Carr: "I think this was probably my fault." The statement is being offered to prove that Carr was at fault, so it's hearsay, and it will only be admissible if it fits a hearsay exception or exclusion. Option B correctly recognizes that the statement fits the admission of a party-opponent hearsay exclusion. An admission by a party opponent is a statement against the party's interest at the time of trial. FRE 801(d)(2). Since B correctly identifies the basis on which the statement will be admissible, it's the best response.

(A) is not the best response,

because *res gestae* is not recognized by the Federal Rules, so it cannot be the best response.

At common law, *res gestae* represented the body of spontaneous hearsay declarations which were considered admissible because of their proximity to an act or event. Under the Federal Rules, these would include declarations of present bodily or mental state, excited utterances, and present sense impressions. Even if *res gestae* were recognized by the Federal Rules, it wouldn't apply here, because Carr made the statement *at the police station,* so it probably wouldn't be sufficiently proximate to the accident to be part of *res gestae.*

Option A *does*, in fact, correctly recognize that there is a hearsay problem under these facts. Hearsay is an out-of-court statement offered to prove the truth of its assertion. Here, the out-of-court declarant is Carr: "I think this was probably my fault." The statement is being offered to prove that Carr was at fault, so it's hearsay, and it will only be admissible if it fits a hearsay exception or exclusion. Option A correctly recognizes that the statement will be admissible, but fails to recognize that this is because the statement fits the "admissions" hearsay exclusion. As a result, A is not the best response.

(C) is not the best response,

because it misstates the law, and comes to an incorrect conclusion.

What option C suggests is that Carr's statement will not be admissible because it includes an opinion as to a conclusion of law, namely, that he'll be legally liable for causing the accident ("I think this was probably my *fault"*). However, the rule is that admissions in opinion form are competent. What option C *does* implicitly cite correctly is that Carr's statement is an admission. It's an admission because it's unfavorable to Carr at the time of the trial, FRE 801(d)(2), and it's reasonable to infer from it that Carr is conscious of his guilt. In fact, the statement will be admissible as an admission, which is an exclusion from the hearsay rule. However, since C incorrectly analyzes the "opinion" aspect of the admission, and arrives at an incorrect conclusion, it's not the best response.

(D) is not the best response,

because the language here is that of an admission.

What option D suggests is that Carr's statement will not be admissible because it includes an opinion as to a conclusion of law, namely, that he'll be legally liable for causing the accident ("I think this was probably my *fault"*). However, the rule is that admissions in opinion form are competent.

Option D also ignores the fact that Carr's statement is an admission. It's an admission because it's unfavorable to Carr at the time of the trial, FRE 801(d)(2), and it's reasonable to infer from it that Carr is conscious of his guilt. In fact, the statement will be *admissible* as an admission, which is an exclusion from the hearsay rule. Since D mischaracterizes the statement here as inadmissible opinion, it's not the best response.

Answer 29

The key here is simply knowing the rule, under the Federal Rules, about admissibility of admissions in conjunction with settlement offers. It does not require any line-drawing. The thing most likely to trip you up is to confuse the Federal Rules with the common law, since your answer will differ depending on which you choose.

(D) is the best response,

because it correctly characterizes the statement as relevant and an admission, and correctly concludes that the evidence will be inadmissible due to public policy considerations.

Under these facts, what you have is a settlement offer by Carr. Since it's an out-of-court statement being offered to prove the truth of its assertion, it's hearsay. Since one could reasonably infer from the offer that Carr is conscious of his guilt, the offer would constitute an admission, since it tends to prove that Carr caused the accident. However, even though admissions are typically admissible as hearsay exclusions, there is a special rule when an admission involves a dispute settlement. Under FRE 408, admissions in conjunction with settlement offers are inadmissible to prove negligence, liability, or a claim's value. That's the case here. (Don't confuse this with admissions in conjunction with offers to pay medical bills, which *are* admissible under the FRE. Also, under common law, both types of admissions – with settlements and with medical bills — are admissible). Since D identifies the public policy which is the basis for inadmissibility, it's the best response.

(A) is not the best response,

because the public policy of encouraging settlements will make the admission inadmissible, even though, barring the fact that there's a settlement offer involved, the admission *would* be admissible. FRE 408.

Under these facts, what you have is a settlement offer by Carr. Since it's an out-of-court statement being offered to prove the truth of its assertion, it's hearsay. As A correctly recognizes, the statement is an admission, and thus potentially fits the admission by a party-opponent hearsay exclusion. The statement is an admission because one could reasonably infer from the offer that Carr is conscious of his guilt. However, what makes the statement *inadmissible* is the public policy, reflected in FRE 408, that admissions in conjunction with settlement offers are inadmissible to prove negligence, liability, or a claim's value.

If you got this wrong, it's probably because you confused the rule under the Federal Rules with the common law rule – under the common law, admissions in conjunction with settlement offers, and the settlement itself, are *admissible.* This option indicates why it's so important to take into account the differences between the Federal Rules and the common law. Since A fails to take into account the settlement aspect of the Federal Rules, it's not the best response.

(B) is not the best response,

because a limiting instruction would not make the evidence here admissible.

Limiting instructions are appropriate in relation to the "doctrine of limited admissibility," whereby evidence is admissible for one purpose, but not for another purpose (e.g., liability insurance to prove ownership, but not to prove ability to pay). Under such circumstances the evidence is generally admitted with a cautionary instruction from the judge, instructing the jury to limit the use of the evidence to its permissible purpose.

The reason this wouldn't apply here is that the evidence isn't admissible *at all.* Under these facts, what you have is a settlement offer by Carr. Since it's an out-of-court statement being offered to prove the truth of its assertion, it's hearsay. As A correctly recognizes, the statement is an admission, and thus potentially fits the admission by a party-opponent hearsay exclusion. The statement is an admission because one could reason-

ably infer from the offer that Carr is conscious of his guilt. However, what makes the statement *inadmissible* is the public policy, reflected in FRE 408, that admissions in conjunction with settlement offers are inadmissible to prove negligence, liability, or a claim's value. Since the evidence cannot be admitted at all, there's no need for a limiting instruction. (Note that if the admission *were* admissible, the limiting instruction would probably be appropriate.) Since B incorrectly implies that the statement is admissible, it's not the best response.

(C) is not the best response,

because it misstates the facts – the settlement offer *is* relevant.

In order to be admissible, a piece of evidence must be relevant. There are two aspects to relevance: Logical relevance and legal relevance. Legal relevance, which addresses "inflammatory" evidence, is not a problem here. Logical relevance requires that a piece of evidence must prove or disprove a material fact. FRE 401. Here, the relevant evidence is a settlement offer from Carr. Such a statement could be taken to mean that Carr acknowledges his own guilt. Thus, it's relevant to the issue of fault.

While option C is correct in recognizing that the evidence is inadmissible, it ignores the real reason for this: the public policy of encouraging settlement negotiations. Under these facts, what you have is a settlement offer by Carr. Since it's an out-of-court statement being offered to prove the truth of its assertion, it's hearsay. As A correctly recognizes, the statement is an admission, and thus potentially fits the admission by a party-opponent hearsay exclusion. The statement is an admission because one could reasonably infer from the offer that Carr is conscious of his guilt. However, what makes the statement *inadmissible* is the public policy, reflected in FRE 408, that admissions in conjunction with settlement offers are inadmissible to prove negligence, liability, or a claim's value. Since C doesn't recognize this, it's not the best response.

Answer 30

(C) is the best response,

because it correctly identifies that the testimony will be inadmissible because it doesn't fit within any hearsay exception. Note that what this really means is that the testimony will not be admissible under any of the other alternatives here. Option C correctly characterizes the testimony as hearsay. Hearsay is an out-of-court statement offered to prove the truth of its assertion. The out-of-court declarant is Walter Passenger: "We were returning..." It's being offered to prove that Carr was driving drunk, so it's being offered to prove the truth of its assertion. As a result, it's hearsay, and in order to be admissible, it would have to fit a hearsay exception or exclusion. Since the testimony is not admissible as an admission (option A) or a declaration against interest (option B), and D does not address the hearsay issue, then C must be the correct answer.

(A) is not the best response,

because the statement here would not qualify as an admission by a party-opponent, since the party-opponent is Carr, not Walter Passenger.

Option A correctly implies that there is a hearsay problem under these facts. Hearsay is an out-of-court statement offered to prove the truth of its assertion. The out-of-court declarant is Walter Passenger: "We were returning..." It's being offered to prove that Carr was driving drunk, so it's being offered to prove the truth of its assertion. As a result, it's hearsay, and in order to be admissible, it would have to fit a hearsay exception or exclusion. Option A suggests that the statement should be admissible under the "admission" hearsay exclusion. However, the problem is that admissions must be from a party-opponent; here, the party-opponent is Carr, not Walter Passenger. Furthermore, there's no basis on which Carr could be bound by Walter's statement. He didn't indicate his agreement, and, beyond that, there's no principal-agent relationship under which Carr could be bound by Walter's statement without specifically adopting it. Note that if the facts were different, and Carr was the declarant, not Walter, the statement *would* be admissible as an admission, because it's unfavorable to Carr, the declarant, at the time of the trial. FRE 801(d)(2). However, since it's Walter's statement, not Carr's, the statement won't be an admission, making A not the best response.

(B) is not the best response,

because the statement here would not qualify as a declaration against interest.

Option B correctly implies that there is a hearsay problem under these facts. Hearsay is an out-of-court statement offered to prove the truth of its assertion. The out-of-court declarant is Walter Passenger: "We were returning..." It's being offered to prove that Carr was driving drunk, so it's being offered to prove the truth of its assertion. As a result, it's hearsay, and in order to be admissible, it would have to fit a hearsay exception or exclusion. Option B suggests that the statement should be admissible under the "declaration against interest" hearsay exception. The statement here is not a declaration against interest, because it does not meet several of the requirements of a declaration against interest. Apart from anything else, it wasn't against Walter's financial, property, or penal interest to make the statement. The exception also requires that the declarant be unavailable to testify, that he had personal knowledge of the facts, that he knew the statement was against interest when made, and he must have had no motive to lie. FRE 804(b)(3). Here, Walter is available to testify, so he does not satisfy that element of the hearsay exception, either. Since B incorrectly characterizes the statement as a

"declaration against interest," it's not the best response.

(D) is not the best response,

because it suggests that the evidence is not relevant, or will lead to irrelevant issues.

Evidence is logically relevant if it tends to prove or disprove a material fact. FRE 401. The testimony here will be relevant, since it suggests that Carr was drunk, which is one of the issues in the case. If evidence is relevant, the possibility that it will lead to nonessential side issues is not determinative of its admissibility. Rather, the evidence here is inadmissible because it's hearsay that doesn't fit within an exception mentioned here (it's hearsay because it's an out-of-court statement offered to prove the truth of its assertion, namely, that Carr was driving drunk.)

If you chose this response, you *may* have been thinking of the "collateral matter" rule. That is, a witness cannot be extrinsically impeached with evidence that is only relevant to discredit the witness; it must also prove or disprove a substantive issue (unless it proves something considered important, like witness bias). FRE 403. However, there's no impeachment involved in these facts, so the "collateral matter" rule wouldn't come into play.

Since D does not identify the correct reason for the testimony's inadmissibility, it's not the best response.

Answer 31

(A) is the best response,

because it correctly identifies that the testimony will be admissible under the doctrine of present recollection refreshed. Under this doctrine, any item may be used to refresh the witness's memory, including leading questions, documents, or objects. If the witness, having seen the refreshing object, can testify from memory, the item will not be considered evidence (if the witness *cannot* thereafter testify from memory, then the item *may* be admissible as a past recollection recorded, if it meets the requirements of FRE 803(5)). Here, all you're told is that Pedersen's counsel is seeking to show Walter the letter to help Walter testify. This "refreshment" is valid under the present recollection refreshed rule, and since A recognizes this, it's the best response.

(B) is not the best answer,

because it misapplies the doctrine of past recollection recorded to these facts.

Under FRE 803(5), a document is only admissible as a past recollection recorded if it meets these requirements: The witness must have no present recollection of the facts, since if the document revives memory enabling the witness to testify without it, the document is inadmissible; the document must have been made at the time of the event or shortly thereafter; the document must have been based on personal knowledge, and made or adopted by the witness; the witness must verify that the document was true when made; and the document must be authenticated. If the document meets these requirements, it can then be read into evidence. The facts here indicate that, while at some point the letter here *may* qualify for this exception, at the point in time these facts indicate, the letter does not *yet* qualify for it: seeing the letter may revivify Walter's memory to the extent that he'll be able to testify from memory, without relying on the letter. In that sense, applying the doctrine of past recollection recorded here is "jumping the gun" – it should only be used as a last resort if the revivifying document does not, in fact, jog Walter's memory. As a result, B is not the best response.

(C) is not the best response,

because it ignores the fact that the letter can be used to refresh Walter's memory.

Option C implicitly recognizes that there's a hearsay problem with the letter itself. Hearsay is an out-of-court statement offered to prove the truth of its assertion. Here, the out-of-court declarant is Walter himself. However, the letter isn't being offered at all – it's merely being used to refresh Walter's memory. As a result, its use is not objectionable, under the doctrine of present recollection refreshed – the letter need not be a spontaneous utterance in order to be useful in revivifying Walter's memory.

Option C's suggestion of a spontaneous utterance refers to the present sense impression or excited utterance exceptions to the hearsay rule. Even if the letter itself *was* being offered into evidence, thus creating a hearsay problem, the "spontaneous utterance" language is not sufficiently precise for the Federal Rules of Evidence. In fact, the mere fact that the letter would not qualify as a present sense impression or excited utterance (due to its lack of proximity to the accident) would not make it inadmissible – since it quite possibly could be admissible under the past recollection recorded hearsay exception, FRE 803(5), assuming as a prerequisite that merely seeing the letter wouldn't help Walter testify from memory. In any case, since the letter can be used to revivify Walter's memory without requiring that it be a spontaneous utterance, C is not the best response.

(D) is not the best response,

because the self-serving nature of the letter would not prevent its being used to refresh Walter's memory.

Option D misses the mark in at least two respects. First, it suggests that the letter itself is being offered as evidence. In fact, it's not – all that's happening is that Pedersen's counsel is seeking to show Walter the letter to help him with his testimony. Thus, D mischaracterizes the facts.

Even if the letter *was* being offered into evidence, the self-serving nature of the letter wouldn't be a problem,

because the self-serving nature of any evidence affects its credibility, not its admissibility. Instead, if the letter itself was being offered, there'd be a hearsay problem, since it would be an out-of-court statement offered to prove the truth of what it contains – namely, Walter's recollections of the accident. Since option D mischaracterizes the facts, and cites an issue that would not determine the admissibility of evidence, it's not the best response.

Answer 32

(C) is the best response,

because the police accident investigator's testimony is admissible as that of an expert witness.

FRE 702 imposes five requirements that expert testimony must meet in order to be admissible: (1) it must be the case that *scientific, technical, or other specialized knowledge* will *assist* the trier of fact to *understand the evidence or to determine a fact in issue*; (2) the witness must be qualified as an expert by *knowledge, skill, experience, training or education*; (3) the testimony must be *based upon sufficient facts or data*; (4) the testimony must be the *product of reliable principles and methods*; and (5) the witness must have *applied these principles and methods reliably to the facts of the case.*

The proposed testimony by the investigator is proper. The investigator would be considered an expert witness and his testimony would be admissible because it satisfies the five requirements: (1) The investigator's testimony about the speed of the train will help the trier of fact to understand the evidence in the case. (2) The facts state that the police accident investigator is experienced and has received training. (3) The investigator's testimony is based on his examination of the physical evidence. (4) The techniques used by the investigator were presumably those he received in his training to become a police accident investigator, so the testimony would be the product of reliable principles and methods. (5) The investigator made his conclusion about the train's speed after applying his training and experience to the physical evidence of the case. Having satisfied all five requirements, the accident investigator's testimony is proper and admissible.

(A) is not the best response,

because it states a non-existent rule of law.

There is simply no principle that says that "there cannot be both lay and expert opinion on the same issue." (For instance, it is perfectly proper for one side to put on lay eyewitness opinion testimony about the approximate speed of the train, and for the other to put on expert scientific opinion on the same subject.)

(B) is not the best response,

because any uncertainty in the investigator's findings would go to the weight of the testimony not its admissibility.

There is no principle that scientific or other expert testimony must reach its conclusion with any particular degree of "scientific certainty." All that is required is that the conclusion be sufficiently "reliable." For the reasons discussed in Choice (C), this reliability standard is satisfied here.

To the extent that this choice is referring to the fact that the investigator is testifying merely that the speed falls within a range, instead of giving a single number, the existence of a range does not pose a problem. (Indeed, use of a range is probably more, not less, reliable, since it's less likely to give a false impression of precision.)

(D) is not the best response,

because the testimony would be admissible even if Plaintiff had not first introduced opinion evidence on the issue.

The only requirements for expert testimony are those discussed in the analysis of choice (C) above. There is no requirement that the other side have first introduced some sort of opinion evidence on the issue.

Answer 33

(B) is the best response,

because it correctly states the two competency requirements.

The Federal Rules of Evidence rules on competency of witnesses state that every person is competent to be a witness except as otherwise provided. The *only* two limitations given require that: (1) the witness have *personal knowledge* of the matter he is to testify about, and (2) the witness indicates his willingness (by oath or affirmation) to testify truthfully. See FRE 602 and 603.

Since Choice (B) correctly recites these requirements, it's the correct answer.

(A) is not the best response,

because the prosecutor does not have to persuade the judge of son's competency to testify.

The Federal Rules of Evidence rules on competency requirements of witnesses state that every person is competent to be a witness except as otherwise provided. The only two limitations given require that: (1) the witness have personal knowledge of the matter he is to testify about, and (2) the witness must declare, by oath or affirmation, that he will testify truthfully. FRE 602 and 603.

There is no requirement that the proponent of evidence first provide evidence of the witness' competence, even where the witness is underage.

(C) is not the best response,

because Victim's son's age would not affect his ability to identify Defendant.

As noted in the discussion of Choice (B), there are only two requirements regarding the witness' competence. Tender age does not constitute a failure to meet

either of those requirements.

(D) is not the best response,

because the probative value of the testimony outweighs its emotional elements.

It's true that FRE 403 says that "Although relevant, evidence may be excluded if its probative value is substantially outweighed by the danger of unfair prejudice[.]" But the son is an eyewitness who can testify on the core issue in the case, so it's wildly unlikely that a court would conclude that any "prejudice" from having him testify with his disfiguring injuries would either be "unfair" or would "substantially outweigh" the value of his eyewitness testimony about the crime.

Answer 34

(B) is the best response,

because it correctly characterizes the prior conviction as admissible to prove Davidson's intoxication.

Option B implicitly identifies that the conviction is hearsay. Hearsay is an out-of-court statement offered to prove the truth of its assertion. Here, the out-of-court declarant is the original court that convicted Davidson. The conviction is being offered to prove that Davidson was intoxicated, so it's hearsay, and it must fit a hearsay exception or exclusion to be admissible.

Option B correctly identifies that the conviction will be admissible under an exception to the hearsay rule. Under the FRE, a felony conviction is admissible to prove any fact essential to sustain the judgment. FRE 803(22). The exception expressly states that the conviction must be for a crime punishable by death, or imprisonment in excess of one year. The facts here indicate that Davidson could have been sentenced to two years in prison, so the crime is one that qualifies for this exception. Davidson's intoxication was a fact essential to the finding of guilt, since she could not have been convicted of drunk driving without such a finding. As a result, the facts here fit the "prior conviction" hearsay exception. (Note, incidentally, that Davidson's guilty plea could be admissible as an admission, since it's an acknowledgement of her guilt.) In any case, since B recognizes that the conviction will be admissible to prove Davidson's intoxication, it's the best response.

(A) is not the best response,

because it states an impermissible goal of prior convictions.

A prior conviction cannot be admitted to prove Davidson's character, since Davidson's character is not in issue here. Character evidence is only admissible when the issue involves testamentary capacity, sanity, child custody (to prove parents' character), defamation, entrapment, notice, or to impeach a reputation witness. In fact, the problem with offering evidence to prove character is that the jury is likely to find against the defendant because she's a "bad person," not because she committed the act in question.

This doesn't, however, mean that the prior conviction won't be admissible at all. In fact, it will be admissible to prove any fact essential to sustain the judgment. FRE 803(22). The exception expressly states that the conviction must be for a crime punishable by death, or imprisonment in excess of one year. The facts here indicate that Davidson could have been sentenced to two years in prison, so the crime is one that qualifies for this exception. Davidson's intoxication was a fact essential to the finding of guilt, since she could not have been convicted of drunk driving without such a finding. As a result, the facts here fit the "prior conviction" hearsay exception, and will be admissible to prove intoxication. This is an example of the doctrine of limited admissibility, in that the prior conviction will be admissible to prove Davidson's intoxication, but not her character. Since proving character is an impermissible goal under these facts, A is not the best response.

(C) is not the best response,

because the condition it raises is irrelevant; the admissibility of the conviction does not turn on whether or not it followed a trial.

Under FRE 803(22), a felony conviction is admissible to prove any fact essential to sustain the judgment. The exception expressly states that the conviction must be for a crime punishable by death, or imprisonment in excess of one year. The facts here indicate that Davidson could have been sentenced to two years in prison, so the crime is one that qualifies for this exception. Davidson's intoxication was a fact essential to the finding of guilt, since she could not have been convicted of drunk driving without such a finding. As a result, the evidence of her intoxication will be admissible into evidence, regardless of whether she underwent a trial. Since C incorrectly suggests a trial is necessary for use of the conviction, it is not the best response.

(D) is not the best response,

because while the conviction is hearsay, it *is* admissible under the prior convictions exception to the FRE, which is embodied in option A.

Option D is correct in identifying that the conviction is hearsay. Hearsay is an out-of-court statement offered to prove the truth of its assertion. Here, the out-of-court declarant is the original court that convicted Davidson. The conviction is being offered to prove that Davidson was intoxicated, so it's hearsay, and it must fit a hearsay exception or exclusion to be admissible. In fact, it fits FRE 803(22), under which a felony conviction is admissible to prove any fact essential to sustain the judgment. The exception expressly states that the conviction must be for a crime punishable by death, or imprisonment in excess of one year. The facts here indicate that Davidson could have been sentenced to two years in prison, so the crime is one that qualifies for this exception. Davidson's intoxication was a fact

essential to the finding of guilt, since she could not have been convicted of drunk driving without such a finding. As a result, the evidence of her intoxication will be admissible into evidence. Since option D doesn't recognize that this exception will make the evidence admissible, it's not the best response.

Answer 35

(C) is the best response,

because it correctly identifies the purpose for which the evidence will be admissible.

The problem here is that cutting down the tree, after a limb fell on Pitt, would be considered a subsequent remedial measure. The general rule is that subsequent remedial measures are not admissible to show negligence or wrongdoing. FRE 407. However, such evidence *is* admissible for other purposes, e.g., to show ownership, control, or to prove the opponent destroyed evidence. Option C correctly identifies why the evidence of subsequent remedial measures will be admissible here: to prove ownership. The evidence here will tend to prove that Dow *did*, in fact, own the tree, which he denies at trial. As a result, the evidence will be admissible. This question is an example of the doctrine of limited admissibility, under which a piece of evidence can be admissible for one purpose, but inadmissible for another. Since C correctly identifies this, it's the best response.

(A) is not the best response,

because it misidentifies the purpose for which the evidence is offered.

The problem here is that cutting down the tree, after a limb fell on Pitt, would be considered a subsequent remedial measure. The general rule is that subsequent remedial measures are not admissible to show negligence or wrongdoing. FRE 407. As option A points out, the rationale of this rule is a policy of encouraging safety precautions. However, what option A doesn't recognize is that there is a permissible purpose for this evidence: proving ownership of the tree. Here, Dow disputes that the tree was *his,* so ownership is an issue. His subsequently cutting down the tree would suggest that it *was* his, after all.

If you chose this response, you did so because you overlooked the fact that subsequent remedial measures *are* admissible to prove *non-wrongdoing related items,* of which ownership is one. Thus, A is not the best response.

(B) is not the best response,

because it mischaracterizes the evidence as irrelevant, and it fails to recognize a purpose for which the evidence could be admitted.

The problem here is that cutting down the tree, after a limb fell on Pitt, would be considered a subsequent remedial measure. The general rule is that subsequent remedial measures are not admissible to show negligence or wrongdoing. FRE 407. However, under these facts, Dow is denying he owns the tree; his subsequently cutting it down would prove that he does, and ownership is a permissible purpose of evidence of subsequent remedial measures.

Option B is incorrect in stating that the evidence is irrelevant to the condition of the tree when the accident occurred. A piece of evidence is logically relevant to an issue if it tends to prove or disprove the issue. Here, it's unlikely that Dow would cut down his tree if it weren't somehow damaged. His cutting it down within a week of the accident would tend to suggest that it was rotted, and *that* would tend to indicate that he was negligent in failing to care for it, or cut it down earlier. Thus, Dow's cutting down the tree would be relevant to the condition of the tree at the time of the accident. However, the evidence would not be admissible for the purpose, due to the general rule about inadmissibility of subsequent remedial measures. Since B doesn't recognize a purpose for which the evidence could be admitted, and it mischaracterizes the evidence as irrelevant, it's not the best response.

(D) is not the best response,

because it states an impermissible motive for the evidence.

Under these facts, Dow cut down the tree within a week after one of its branches fell on Pitt. If he allowed the tree to stand, once it was rotting, he'd likely be liable in negligence for Pitt's damages. However, the problem with the evidence is that cutting down the tree would be considered a subsequent remedial measure. The general rule is that subsequent remedial measures are inadmissible to prove negligence or wrongdoing. FRE 407. Thus, the evidence *could not* be admitted to prove the tree was in a rotted condition. What option D ignores is that the evidence *will* be admissible to prove ownership of the tree, since Dow denies that the tree is his, and ownership is a permissible purpose for evidence of subsequent remedial measures. Since D states an impermissible motive for the evidence, it's not the best response.

Answer 36

(A) is the best response,

because the events satisfy all the requirements of the recorded recollection exception.

FRE 803(5) recognizes a hearsay exception for a past recollection recorded. There are four elements to the exception: (1) the memorandum must relate to something of which the witness once had first-hand knowledge; (2) the record must have been made by, or adopted by, the witness when the matter was fresh in the witness' memory; (3) there must currently be some impairment of the witness' memory of the events; and (4) there is evidence that the record correctly reflects the witness' original knowledge.

Playing the tape for the jury would be proper under

the past recollection recorded hearsay exception because it satisfies all four elements of the exception. (1) The tape relates to something of which Mr. Wong once had first-hand knowledge, since Mr. Wong personally saw the events, including the license number. (2) The tape was made when the matter was fresh in Mr. Wong's memory. (3) There is an impairment of Mr. Wong's memory, since he has said that he has no present memory of the license plate number. (4) At trial, Mr. Wong is testifying that immediately after the event he listened to a playback and verified that Mrs. Wong had relayed the license number correctly.

(B) is not the best response,

because Mr. Wong is not a public official who had a duty to make the report.

There is a common-law exception to the hearsay rule for public records and reports. This exception is codified in FRE 803(8), which allows the admission of "records, reports [or] statements ... of public offices or agencies" "setting forth ... (B) matters observed pursuant to duty imposed by law as to which matters there was a duty to report, excluding, however, in criminal cases matters observed by police officers and other law enforcement personnel[.]"

The public records exception to the hearsay rule does not apply in this case because Mr. Wong (the one who made the "observation") was not a public official, nor was the report he made to the police of the break-in part of an official duty. (Even if Mr. Wong *was* a police officer, the last clause quoted above would prevent the report from coming in against Dove in Dove's criminal trial.)

(C) is not the best response,

because the tape recording of the call to the police falls within the past recollection recorded exception. (See the discussion of Choice (A) for why this is so.)

(D) is not the best response,

because Mrs. Wong did not have to have first-hand knowledge of the license number in order for the recorded recollection exception to apply.

Playing the tape for the jury would be proper under the past recollection recorded hearsay exception. The requirements of FRE 803(5)'s past recollection recorded exception do not require that witness be the one who physically made the record. All that 803(5) requires in this respect is that the record be one that is "made *or adopted* by the witness when the matter was fresh in the witness' memory." Here, when Mr. Wong immediately listened to the playback and pronounced the relayed number correct, Mr. Wong adopted the record.

Answer 37

(B) is the best response,

because the fact that Plaintiff had personal knowledge

of the shoe's condition is sufficient to allow him to testify about that condition.

Where a witness has personal knowledge about a fact, the witness is ordinarily entitled to testify about that fact. Here, Plaintiff has personal knowledge about the condition of the shoe, and is therefore entitled to testify about that condition, unless some other rule blocks the testimony. There is no such other rule that applies here.

(A) is not the best response,

because the fact that Defendant's expert was able to examine the shoe carefully is irrelevant.

Even if the Defendant's expert had not been able to examine the shoe, the Plaintiff would still have been permitted to testify about his personal knowledge of the condition.

(C) is not the best response,

because the fact that a physical object was present during settlement negotiations does not mean that testimony about the object becomes inadmissible.

It is true that FRE 408 makes inadmissible settlement offers, as well as "conduct and statements made in" settlement negotiations. But FRE 408 carefully states that the rule "does not require the exclusion of any evidence otherwise discoverable merely because it is presented in the course of compromise negotiations."

The fact that the shoe was presented to the other side during settlement negotiations falls within the last sentence of 408 quoted above, making testimony about the shoe admissible.

(D) is not the best response,

because Plaintiff does not bear the burden of establishing that the disappearance was not his fault.

If the item had been a document, and its "contents" were sought to be proved, the fact that the person seeking to testify about the contents was responsible in bad faith for the document's disappearance would cause the testimony to be excluded. (See FRE 1004: "The original is not required, and other evidence of the contents of a writing ... is admissible if (1) All originals are lost or have been destroyed, unless the proponent lost or destroyed them in bad faith.") But no such rule applies to items of physical evidence that are not writings, recordings, or photographs (i.e., items that are not subject to the Best Evidence Rule).

The court probably has discretion to exclude testimony about an item of real evidence whose disappearance has been shown to have been procured by the intentional wrongdoing of the proponent of the testimony. But even so, it certainly is not the case that the burden would be placed on the party who will be testifying to make an affirmative showing that that party was not responsible for the disappearance.

Answer 38

(B) is the best response,

because it correctly identifies the key to admissibility here – that the tape is legally relevant. A piece of evidence is legally relevant if its probative value is not substantially outweighed by the possibility of unfair prejudice.

This is an answer that you would have to choose as a result of eliminating the other answers, because it is a "threshold" issue – *every* piece of evidence must be legally relevant in order to be admissible, but it also must meet other hurdles (e.g., it cannot be inadmissible hearsay or character evidence, it must be logically relevant, it must be unprivileged, etc.). However, because the tape here will have a significant impact on the jury – it shows Dryden drunk as a skunk – B is relevant, because there *could* an issue of legal relevance. However, the evidence would not be considered sufficiently inflammatory or misleading to be excluded due legal relevance problems. When you talk about excluding evidence on this basis, you're typically talking about severed limbs, gruesome photos, and the like. Thus, since there *is* a legal relevance problem (even though the evidence would still be admissible), and none of the other answers are satisfactory, B is the best response.

(A) is not the best response,

because it does not correctly characterize the facts.

Option A suggests that Dryden's acts would be considered hearsay, but would be admissible nonetheless under the "admissions" hearsay exclusion. Hearsay is an out-of-court statement offered to prove the truth of its assertion. The problem here is that there's no assertion. While conduct *can* be considered an admission if, from it, one can reasonably infer that the actor is conscious of his guilt, this is not the case here; Dryden's conduct is non-assertive (i.e., not intended to communicate).

Even under the somewhat different common law rule, Dryden's conduct would not be considered an admission. At common law, non-assertive conduct is considered hearsay *only* if it is offered to prove the actor's *beliefs* regarding a fact in issue. Here, the evidence isn't being offered to prove Dryden knew he was blotto; it's being offered to prove that he *was* blotto.

In any case, it's the lack of a hearsay assertion that makes Dryden's conduct a non-admission. Since option A doesn't recognize this, it's not the best response.

(C) is not the best response,

because the privilege against self-incrimination would not apply to these facts.

The privilege against self-incrimination is a *testimonial* privilege; it only allows one the right not to *testify* as to incriminating matters. Here, there's no testimony involved – the evidence being offered is an out-of-court videotape of Dryden. As a result, it is not covered by the privilege.

Say the facts were different, and the prosecutor sought to question Dryden himself about his drunkenness. Of course, Dryden, as a criminal defendant, could refuse to take the stand at all. If he *did* take the stand in his own defense, he would have *waived* the privilege against self-incrimination, and he'd have to answer all relevant questions.

In any case, since option C doesn't recognize that the privilege against self-incrimination is only a testimonial privilege, which would not apply to these facts, it's not the best response.

(D) is not the best response,

because it both misstates these facts and misstates the law.

D in fact states an ostensible rule of law that's a mishmash of ideas. The "specific instances of conduct" part suggests character evidence is involved here. However, the evidence here suggests that Dryden was drunk on *this* occasion, not another one, so it's not character evidence. The "extrinsic evidence" part suggests that Dryden is being impeached, and that there may be a collateral matter involved. Dryden isn't being impeached – he isn't even testifying. And not only is a collateral matter *not* involved, but Dryden's drunkenness shortly after arrest would be very strong evidence of a central issue – his drunk driving. Since D does not apply the correct law or identify the facts correctly, it's not the best response.

Answer 39

(C) is the best response,

because it correctly states that the evidence here will be admissible both to impeach and as substantive evidence.

The essential problem here, as C recognizes, is that Witt's testimony will be hearsay. Hearsay is an out-of-court statement being offered to prove the truth of its assertion. Here, the out-of-court declarant is Witt herself: "The light was yellow." The statement is being offered, at least in part, to prove the truth of its assertion: That the light was yellow, not red. However, it's *also* being offered to impeach Witt – that is, to bring her veracity into question.

As to the issue of *substance,* you have to determine a hearsay exception or exclusion under which the evidence will fit. The out-of-court statement here is a prior inconsistent statement, made by a currently testifying witness (who can be cross-examined), and made under oath, subject to penalty of perjury. Thus, it fits the prior inconsistent statement hearsay *exclusion,* under FRE 801(d)(1)(A), and as a result it can be used substantively (that is, to prove that the light was yellow, not red). Option C correctly identifies this.

As to the issue of *impeachment,* prior inconsistent statements may be used to draw the witness's veracity into question *regardless* of the circumstances under

which the prior inconsistent statement was made. Thus, Witt's prior statement about the light being yellow will be admissible to impeach her, as well as to prove that the light was, in fact, yellow. (Note that, if a prior inconsistent statement can be used substantively, it is *always* usable for impeachment as well, since the requirements for impeachment are far less stringent.) Option C recognizes this as well.

Since C recognizes that the prior inconsistent statement will be available both substantively and for impeachment, it's the best response.

(A) is not the best response,

because it states the *common law* rule, *not* the rule under the Federal Rules of Evidence.

The essential problem here, as A recognizes, is that Witt's testimony will be hearsay. Hearsay is an out-of-court statement being offered to prove the truth of its assertion. Here, the out-of-court declarant is Witt herself: "The light was yellow." The statement is being offered, at least in part, to prove the truth of its assertion: That the light was yellow, not red. However, it's *also* being offered to impeach Witt – that is, to bring her veracity into question.

As to the issue of *substance,* you have to determine a hearsay exception or exclusion under which the evidence will fit. The out-of-court statement here is a prior inconsistent statement, made by a currently testifying witness (who can be cross-examined), and made under oath, subject to penalty of perjury. Thus, it fits the prior inconsistent statement hearsay *exclusion,* under FRE 801(d)(1)(A), and as a result it can be used substantively (that is, to prove that the light was yellow, not red). Option A doesn't recognize this.

As to the issue of *impeachment,* prior inconsistent statements may be used to draw the witness's veracity into question *regardless* of the circumstances under which the prior inconsistent statement was made. Thus, Witt's prior statement about the light being yellow will be admissible to impeach her, as well as to prove that the light was, in fact, yellow. (Note that, if a prior inconsistent statement can be used substantively, it is *always* usable for impeachment as well, since the requirements for impeachment are far less stringent.)

If you chose this response, it's probably because you confused the common law rule with the rule under the FRE. At common law, prior inconsistent statements could *only* be used to impeach. Since A does not state the rule as it appears in the FRE, it is not the best response.

(B) is not the best response,

because it does not cite the *entire* basis on which the evidence will be admissible.

The essential problem here, as D recognizes, is that Witt's testimony will be hearsay. Hearsay is an out-of-court statement being offered to prove the truth of its assertion. Here, the out-of-court declarant is Witt herself: "The light was yellow." The statement is being offered, at least in part, to prove the truth of its assertion: That the light was yellow, not red. However, it's *also* being offered to impeach Witt – that is, to bring her veracity into question.

As to the issue of *substance,* you have to determine a hearsay exception or exclusion under which the evidence will fit. The out-of-court statement here is a prior inconsistent statement, made by a currently testifying witness (who can be cross-examined), and made under oath, subject to penalty of perjury. Thus, it fits the prior inconsistent statement hearsay *exclusion,* under FRE 801(d)(1)(A), and as a result it can be used substantively (that is, to prove that the light was yellow, not red).

As to the issue of *impeachment,* prior inconsistent statements may be used to draw the witness's veracity into question *regardless* of the circumstances under which the prior inconsistent statement was made. Thus, Witt's prior statement about the light being yellow will be admissible to impeach her, as well as to prove that the light was, in fact, yellow. (Note that, if a prior inconsistent statement can be used substantively, it is *always* usable for impeachment as well, since the requirements for impeachment are far less stringent.)

The key word in B is "only," since the statement that the evidence is *only* admissible substantively is incorrect, making B not the best response.

(D) is not the best response,

because the evidence here *is* admissible both to impeach *and* substantively .

The essential problem here, as D recognizes, is that Witt's testimony will be hearsay. Hearsay is an out-of-court statement being offered to prove the truth of its assertion. Here, the out-of-court declarant is Witt herself: "The light was yellow." The statement is being offered, at least in part, to prove the truth of its assertion: That the light was yellow, not red. However, it's *also* being offered to impeach Witt – that is, to bring her veracity into question.

As to the issue of *substance,* you have to determine a hearsay exception or exclusion under which the evidence will fit. The out-of-court statement here is a prior inconsistent statement, made by a currently testifying witness (who can be cross-examined), and made under oath, subject to penalty of perjury. Thus, it fits the prior inconsistent statement hearsay *exclusion,* under FRE 801(d)(1)(A), and as a result it can be used substantively (that is, to prove that the light was yellow, not red).

As to the issue of *impeachment,* prior inconsistent statements may be used to draw the witness's veracity into question *regardless* of the circumstances under which the prior inconsistent statement was made. Thus, Witt's prior statement about the light being yellow will be admissible to impeach her, as well as to prove that the light was, in fact, yellow. (Note that, if a prior

inconsistent statement can be used substantively, it is *always* usable for impeachment as well, since the requirements for impeachment are far less stringent.)

Since D fails to recognize that the prior statement will be usable both substantively and to impeach Witt, it's not the best response.

Answer 40

(A) is the best response,

because it correctly indicates that Wilson can be impeached with this evidence.

Here, discrediting testimony is being sought from Wilson's own mouth. This is "intrinsic" impeachment. There are five general types of questions that may be used to elicit intrinsic impeachment from a witness. They are questions seeking to show bias or interest; prior inconsistent statements; certain prior convictions; bad character for honesty (including unconvicted bad acts); and sensory deficiencies (e.g., eyesight, memory, mental disability).

As this list indicates, the witness can be intrinsically impeached with evidence of his bad character for honesty. A false claim on an insurance policy would be just such an act.

Incidentally, say the facts were different, and the method of impeachment here were *extrinsic,* not *intrinsic.* The methods of extrinsic impeachment include bias; contradicting facts; inconsistent statements (require a foundation); sensory deficiencies; certain convictions; and bad character for truthfulness. While bad character for truthfulness *can* be addressed with extrinsic impeachment, *when the evidence is extrinsic, only reputation or opinion testimony may be used, under FRE 608(a).* This means that the specific instance here could *not* be used!

In any case, since A correctly states that the evidence will be usable as intrinsic impeachment, it's the best response.

(B) is not the best response,

because the conduct didn't have to result in a conviction in order to be usable for impeachment.

Here, discrediting testimony is being sought from Wilson's own mouth. This is "intrinsic" impeachment. There are five general types of questions that may be used to elicit intrinsic impeachment from a witness. They are questions seeking to show bias or interest; prior inconsistent statements; certain prior convictions; bad character for honesty (including unconvicted bad acts); and sensory deficiencies (e.g., eyesight, memory, mental disability).

Thus, while prior convictions *can* be used for intrinsic impeachment, the witness can also be intrinsically impeached with evidence of his bad character for honesty. A false claim on an insurance policy would be just such an act. Note that if the conduct *had* resulted in a conviction, it would be the type of conviction that could be used for impeachment. Under FRE 609(a), the only convictions that can be used are those no more than ten years old, for either misdemeanors involving dishonesty, or any felony. Here, the act involves dishonesty, so it wouldn't matter if it were a felony or a misdemeanor.

In any case, since B incorrectly states that the conduct must have resulted in a conviction to be usable as impeachment, it's not the best response.

(C) is not the best response,

because the impeachment *can* be in the form of a specific instance of misconduct.

Here, discrediting testimony is being sought from Wilson's own mouth. This is "intrinsic" impeachment. There are five general types of questions that may be used to elicit intrinsic impeachment from a witness. They are questions seeking to show bias or interest; prior inconsistent statements; certain prior convictions; bad character for honesty (including unconvicted bad acts); and sensory deficiencies (e.g., eyesight, memory, mental disability).

As this list indicates, the witness can be intrinsically impeached with evidence of his bad character for honesty. A false claim on an insurance policy would be just such an act.

If you chose this response, you were thinking of the rule for *extrinsic* impeachment with evidence of bad conduct. The methods of extrinsic impeachment include bias; contradicting facts; inconsistent statements (require a foundation); sensory deficiencies; certain convictions; and bad character for truthfulness. While bad character for truthfulness *can* be addressed with extrinsic impeachment, *when the evidence is extrinsic, only reputation or opinion testimony may be used, under FRE 608(a).* This means that the specific instance here could *not* be used! Thus, option C represents the rule for extrinsic impeachment, not intrinsic impeachment, making it not the best response.

(D) is not the best response,

because it erroneously applies the Best Evidence Rule to these facts.

The Best Evidence Rule only applies when the terms of a writing are being proven, or the witness is testifying relying on a writing. Under those circumstances, the document itself must be introduced, if it's available.

The Best Evidence Rule does not apply to these facts, because, although the best evidence of a writing is the writing itself, where the issue is "collateral" – here, the claim will only address Wilson's character for truthfulness – the witness's testimony will be admissible without producing the document. FRE 1004.

In fact, the claim form itself would be *inadmissible*, under the "collateral matter rule." Under that rule, "extrinsic" evidence (not from the witness's own mouth) is "collateral" and cannot be admitted if it is relevant only to discredit a witness (or it proves something

deemed material, like witness bias); if the evidence also proves or disproves a substantive issue, the evidence is admissible. FRE 403. Here, the claim form would only show that Wilson isn't honest; it wouldn't impact any issue in the case. Thus, not only is D incorrect in stating that the claim form is the only way to admit the evidence of the false claim, but it fails to recognize that the claim form wouldn't be admissible at all under the collateral matter rule. As a result, D is not the best response.

Answer 41

(C) is the best response,

because it correctly identifies the statement here as inadmissible hearsay. Note that what this *really* means is that the evidence is not admissible *under any of the other options in this question.* Of course, the evidence *could* be admissible under the catch-all exception to the hearsay rule; but it's clearly not admissible under the other options, A and B, so C must be the correct response.

Note that the statement here *is* hearsay, because it's an out-of-court statement offered to prove the truth of its assertion. The out-of-court declarant is the driver: "Officer, a few minutes ago..." The statement is being offered to prove that Dorry was the culprit, so it's hearsay. However, the statement will be admissible as neither a present sense impression nor, of course, under the fictitious hearsay exception indicated in option A, the statement of recent perception. Since C correctly identifies the evidence as hearsay, and it's not admissible under any option here, C is the best response.

(A) is not the best response,

because it states a hearsay exception that doesn't exist.

Note that option A *is* correct in characterizing the evidence as hearsay. Hearsay is an out-of-court statement offered to prove the truth of its assertion. The out-of-court declarant is the driver: "Officer, a few minutes ago..." The statement is being offered to prove that Dorry was the culprit, so it's hearsay, and in order to be admissible, it would have to fit a hearsay exception or exclusion.

The problem with option A is that it doesn't offer a viable means of admitting the hearsay statement. Statements of recent perception are not admissible under a hearsay exception. The closest real exception would be present sense impressions. The rationale of allowing present sense impressions is that the declarant has not had time to fabricate – he's responding to something that's taking place currently. If the declarant has time to reflect, he has time to fabricate, making his statement less trustworthy. Here, it's been at least a few minutes since driver saw the hit-and-run accident, so even if you read option A to refer to the "present sense impression" hearsay exception, the statement here wouldn't qualify. In any case, since A states a hearsay exception that doesn't exist, it's not the best response.

(B) is not the best response,

because the facts here would not fit the present sense impression exception to the hearsay rule.

Note that option B *is* correct in characterizing the evidence as hearsay. Hearsay is an out-of-court statement offered to prove the truth of its assertion. The out-of-court declarant is the driver: "Officer, a few minutes ago..." The statement is being offered to prove that Dorry was the culprit, so it's hearsay, and in order to be admissible, it would have to fit a hearsay exception or exclusion.

The problem here is that the statement wouldn't fit the present sense impression hearsay exception. Under FRE 803(1), a present sense impression is admissible under a hearsay exception if it was made while the declarant was perceiving an event/condition (or immediately thereafter), and it describes or explains the event/condition. Under these facts, the driver has had, according to his statement, "a few minutes" in order to think. The rationale behind the present sense impression hearsay exception is that, because the statement was made contemporaneously with the event it concerns, it will suffer no defects in memory; and, since it usually would have been made to someone else who was also present, there was an opportunity for at least one other person to correct it. Furthermore, since it was made at the time of the event, there's no time for the declarant to fabricate. Under these facts, these parameters are not satisfied, making B not the best response.

(D) is not the best response,

because the legal relevance of the evidence here is not a particular problem.

In order to be admissible, every piece of evidence must be "legally relevant"; that is, its probative value must not be substantially outweighed by the danger of unfair prejudice. This typically applies to inflammatory evidence (e.g., body parts, gruesome photos).

Here, instead, the problem is hearsay. Hearsay is an out-of-court statement offered to prove the truth of its assertion. The out-of-court declarant is the driver: "Officer, a few minutes ago..." The statement is being offered to prove that Dorry was the culprit, so it's hearsay, and in order to be admissible, it would have to fit a hearsay exception or exclusion.

Say the facts were different, and it was driver himself testifying as to what he saw (*not* what he said to Williams, because it would *still* be hearsay). The evidence still wouldn't have legal relevance problems, because there's nothing particularly prejudicial about it. Furthermore, its tremendous probative value — it's direct evidence of Dorry's guilt — would make it admissible. Since D suggests a legal relevance problem where one does not in fact exist, and it ignores the central issue

under these facts, it's not the best response.

Answer 42

(B) is the best response,

because it correctly identifies that the treatise can be read into evidence, and gives one possible source for establishing the treatise as a reliable authority: the judge.

Option B correctly recognizes that there's a hearsay problem with this evidence. Hearsay is an out-of-court statement offered to prove the truth of its assertion. Here, the out-of-court declarant is the author of the treatise. It's being offered to prove Post's injuries may not have been caused by Dean's negligence. Thus, the treatise is hearsay, and it will have to fit some hearsay exception or exclusion to be admissible.

Option B correctly recognizes that the learned treatise hearsay exception will make the passages admissible. Under the FRE, a learned treatise can be read into evidence (it *cannot* be admitted as an exhibit) if an expert witness relies on it on direct examination, or it's called to his attention on cross-examination, or it's established as reliable authority by witness's testimony or admission, other expert testimony, or judicial notice. FRE 803(18). Since B recognizes a correct basis for reading the treatise into evidence, and states that the evidence is admissible, it's the best response.

(A) is not the best response,

because it is too restrictive. While the evidence will be admissible to impeach Cox, under FRE 803(18), it will also be admissible as substantive evidence.

Option A correctly recognizes that there's a hearsay problem with this evidence. Hearsay is an out-of-court statement offered to prove the truth of its assertion. Here, the out-of-court declarant is the author of the treatise. It's being offered to prove Post's injuries may not have been caused by Dean's negligence. Thus, the treatise is hearsay, and it will have to fit some hearsay exception or exclusion to be admissible.

However, option A fails to recognize that the treatise can be read into evidence under the "learned treatise" hearsay exception. If you chose A, it's probably because you confused the common law rule with the rule under the FRE on the admissibility of learned treatises. At common law, learned treatises are only admissible as relied upon and referred to by an expert witness on direct examination, and to impeach an expert witness's testimony on cross-examination (by pointing out how his opinion differs from the source upon which he states he has relied — no *other* source can be used). However, under the FRE, a learned treatise can be read into evidence if an expert witness relies on it on direct examination, or it's called to his attention on cross-examination, or it's established as reliable authority by witness's testimony or admission, other expert testimony, or judicial notice. FRE 803(18). Thus, the textbook here will be admissible substantively. Since A is too restrictive, stating that the text-book will *only* be admissible to impeach, it's not the best response.

(C) is not the best response,

because the evidence here, although hearsay, *is* admissible under the learned treatises exception to the hearsay rule, FRE 803(18).

Option C correctly recognizes that there's a hearsay problem with this evidence. Hearsay is an out-of-court statement offered to prove the truth of its assertion. Here, the out-of-court declarant is the author of the treatise. It's being offered to prove Post's injuries may not have been caused by Dean's negligence. Thus, the treatise is hearsay, and it will have to fit some hearsay exception or exclusion to be admissible.

What option C fails to realize is that the testimony fits the "learned treatise" hearsay exception. Under the FRE, a learned treatise can be read into evidence if an expert witness relies on it on direct examination, or it's called to his attention on cross-examination, or it's established as reliable authority by witness's testimony or admission, other expert testimony, or judicial notice. FRE 803(18). Thus, the textbook here will be admissible substantively. Since C states otherwise, it's not the best response.

(D) is not the best response,

because Cox's acknowledgement of relevance is not a requirement for admissibility. Under the FRE, a learned treatise can be read into evidence if an expert witness relies on it on direct examination, or it's called to his attention on cross-examination, or it's established as reliable authority by witness's testimony or admission, other expert testimony, or judicial notice. FRE 803(18). Thus, under these facts, as long as the treatise is established as reliable authority, it can be read into evidence even if Cox things it's pure drivel. Since D erroneously states that the expert himself must acknowledge the applicability of a treatise, it's not the best response.

Answer 43

(C) is the best response,

because an offer to pay medical expenses is inadmissible to prove liability.

Although the facts don't state the purpose for which Plaintiff is offering the fact of Doctor's offer to pay expenses, let's assume that the purpose is the obvious one of trying to show liability or responsibility (on the theory that "Doctor wouldn't have offered to pay my hospital expenses unless she believed that she was or might be the cause of my problem.")

In that event, the case is clearly governed by FRE 409, which says that "Evidence of furnishing or offering or promising to pay medical, hospital, or similar expenses occasioned by an injury is not admissible to prove liability for the injury."

(A) is not the best response,

because offers to pay medical expenses fall under a separate rule.

It's true that the offer to pay expenses would not be hearsay. But there are many reasons other than hearsay for exclusion of statements, and the no-evidence-of-offers-to-pay-for-medical-expenses rule (see Choice (C) above) is one of them.

(B) is not the best response,

because the offer is not hearsay, and in any event is inadmissible for other reasons.

First, the out-of-court statement here is "I'll pay your medical expenses." That statement is being offered to supply an inference of liability ("You wouldn't have made the offer unless you thought you might be responsible or liable for my condition.") A statement is hearsay only if it's offered to prove "the truth of the matter asserted therein." Here, there is no matter whose "truth" is asserted in the out-of-court statement; the statement is merely an offer to do something. Therefore, repeating the statement in court couldn't be hearsay. (If Doctor had said, "I'm sorry my negligence caused your hospitalization," then this *would* be a statement containing an assertion of fact, which could make it hearsay.)

A second problem with this choice is that the declaration-against-interest exception to the hearsay rule applies only where the declarant is not available to testify at trial. Doctor is available to testify here, so far as we're aware. (The appropriate hearsay exception would be the one for admissions by, and offered against, a party-opponent.)

(D) is not the best response,

because Doctor's offer was unilateral and not the product of negotiation.

It's true that the fact that a party has offered to settle a claim may not be admitted on the issue of the claim's validity. See FRE 408. But the exclusion only applies to offers, or other statements, made *during the course of settlement negotiations*. The offer here was a unilateral one, not one made during settlement negotiations. (The facts tell us that the offer was made "immediately" once Doctor learned of the problem.) Therefore, it doesn't fall within the exclusion.

Answer 44

(A) is the best response,

because it most closely reflects the central issue concerning admissibility on these facts.

Under these facts, Darden, a criminal defendant, is testifying on his own behalf. The prosecutor is attempting to impeach him, intrinsically, with evidence of a six-year-old felony.

As to the technical question of whether or not this is a proper means of intrinsic impeachment, there's no real issue: It's clearly proper. Under FRE 609(a), a witness can be intrinsically impeached with conviction of any felony, as here, or any crime, felony or misdemeanor, involving dishonesty or a false statement (where the crime does not involve dishonesty, admission is within the judge's discretion, under the notes to Rule 609(a)). Thus, as to the impeachment issue standing alone, the question would be permissible.

However, option A notes that there's an overriding problem with the question: legal relevance. In order to be admissible, *every* piece of evidence must be legally relevant. Evidence is legally relevant if its probative value is not substantially outweighed by the danger of unfair prejudice. Here, there is a possibility that evidence of the prior conviction would tempt a jury to convict Darden because he's a "bad man," not because he committed the crime for which he's currently charged. Thus, there's a possibility that the evidence would be inadmissible on this basis, but it's difficult to say for sure that it *would* be. Option A avoids this problem by using the qualifier "if." That means that the reasoning need only be plausible on the facts, that it must resolve a central issue, and that the result must be consistent with the reasoning. Here, it's possible that the evidence is legally relevant; this determines whether the evidence here will be admissible; and the result is consistent with the reasoning. This, combined with the fact that the other options are clearly incorrect, makes A the best response.

(B) is not the best response,

because the prosecutor would not have a *right* to ask such a question.

Under these facts, Darden, a criminal defendant, is testifying on his own behalf. The prosecutor is attempting to impeach him, intrinsically, with evidence of a six-year-old felony.

The rule concerning intrinsic impeachment with prior convictions is found in FRE 609(a). Under FRE 609(a), a witness can be intrinsically impeached with conviction of any felony, as here, or any crime, felony or misdemeanor, involving dishonesty or a false statement (where the crime does not involve dishonesty, admission is within the judge's discretion, under the notes to Rule 609(a)). Here, burglary does not involve dishonesty, so it would be within the judge's discretion to allow the question. Thus, contrary to what B states, the prosecutor could not ask about the conviction as of right.

B also ignores the issue of legal relevance. FRE 609(a) provides that prior felony convictions can only be used to impeach *if the probative value of admitting the evidence outweighs its prejudicial effect on the defendant.* This mirrors the requirement of legal relevance, which all evidence must meet. Here, if Darden's prior conviction is admitted, there's a possibility that the jury will convict Darden because he's a "bad man," not because he committed the crime for which he's currently charged. Thus, there's a substantial danger of undue prejudice (although this wouldn't mean, necessarily, that the conviction here would be inadmissible). In any case, since B mischaracterizes the question as one of right, not discretion, and it ignores the legal relevance issue altogether, it's not the best response.

(C) is not the best response,

because it misstates the standard on which prior convictions are admissible to impeach.

Under these facts, Darden, a criminal defendant, is testifying on his own behalf. The prosecutor is attempting to impeach him, intrinsically, with evidence of a six-year-old felony.

Under the FRE, Rule 609(a), any felony (crime punishable by at least one year in prison), or any felony or misdemeanor involving dishonesty or false statement, can be used to impeach a witness (juvenile convictions or convictions more than ten years old are generally inadmissible). Where the crime does not involve dishonesty, admission of the conviction is discretionary with the judge; if it *does* involve dishonesty, admission is mandatory. Notes to FRE 609. If you chose this alternative, you may have done so because you confused the rule under the Federal Rules with the common-law trend, which is to only allow impeachment with convictions for crimes reflecting on veracity, whether they are felonies or misdemeanors. However, the FRE rule is as stated, and so C is not the best response.

(D) is not the best response,

because the conviction *can* be proven through intrinsic impeachment.

Under these facts, Darden, a criminal defendant, is testifying on his own behalf. The prosecutor is attempting to impeach him, intrinsically, with evidence of a six-year-old felony. Option D suggests that such impeachment requires that the original court record of the conviction must be introduced. In fact, that's not the case. Under FRE 609(a), a witness can be intrinsically impeached with conviction of any felony, as here, or any crime, felony or misdemeanor, involving dishonesty or a false statement (where the crime does not involve dishonesty, admission is within the judge's discretion, under the notes to Rule 609(a)). (Here, burglary does not involve dishonesty, so it would be within the judge's discretion to allow the question.)

Note that intrinsic impeachment is impeachment "from the witness's own mouth." Since it's permissible to intrinsically impeach a witness with certain prior convictions under FRE 609(a), the court record of the conviction *cannot* be a requirement – since a witness couldn't provide the court record in his own testimony.

Say the facts were different, and the impeachment was *extrinsic,* not intrinsic. Under those circumstances, prior convictions can also be used, and the court record *would* be required to prove the conviction. However, what's involved here is intrinsic impeachment, not extrinsic. Since D doesn't recognize this, it's not the best response.

Answer 45

(D) is the best response,

because the proposed testimony consists of expert opinion about whether the defendant had the requisite mental state, offered in a criminal case.

FRE 704(b) says that "No expert witness testifying with respect to the mental state or condition of a defendant in a criminal case may state an opinion or inference as to whether the defendant did or did not have the mental state or condition constituting an element of the crime charged or of a defense thereto. Such ultimate issues are matters for the trier of fact alone."

The proposed testimony here — that Defendant had the mental state required for a defense (the defense of self-defense) — falls squarely within the prohibition of FRE 704(b).

(A) is not the best response,

because the statement is not admissible, whether or not Expert believed that Defendant was speaking truthfully.

This choice is wrong because, as described in Choice (D) above, FRE 704(b) bars the proposed testimony.

Additionally, the vast majority of courts have rejected the admission of statements made under hypnosis. This is true whether the statement is offered as substantive evidence or for its bearing on the credibility of the witness' live testimony at trial.

(B) is not the best response,

because the testimony violates FRE 704(b), even though it might otherwise qualify as a prior consistent statement introduced to rebut an implied claim of fabrication.

As described in Choice (D), the statement is expressly barred by FRE 704(b).

If it weren't barred by 704(b), it might well be admissible under FRE 801(d)(1)(B), which defines as non-hearsay, and thus allows, prior statements by a witness, where "The declarant testifies at the trial or hearing and is subject to cross-examination concerning the statement, and the statement is ... (B) consistent with the declarant's testimony and is offered to rebut an express or implied charge against the declarant of recent fabrication or improper influence or motive..." It's not clear from the facts here that the prosecution is making an "express or implied charge" that Defendant has "recently fabricated" her assertion that she acted in fear for her life, but if the court were convinced that there was such a charge, and if FRE 704(b) didn't intervene, the statement here would be admissible under 801(d)(1)(B).

(C) is not the best response,

because use of the hypnosis-induced out-of-court statement by Defendant would not violate his constitutional rights.

If hypnosis-induced testimony were introduced *against* a criminal defendant, this usage might conceivably violate the defendant's criminal rights. (If the statement were induced from a third-party witness who was not available for cross-examination at trial, for instance, use of the testimony might violate the defendant's Confrontation Clause rights.) But use by a criminal defendant could never violate the constitution — whose rights would be violated? (The state itself, in the form of the prosecution, does not have "constitutional rights" vis a vis the defendant.)

Answer 46

(A) is the best response,

because it correctly states the rule on extrinsic evidence.

FRE 608(b) says that "Specific instances of the conduct of a witness, for the purpose of attacking or supporting the witness' credibility, other than conviction of crime as provided in rule 609, *may not be proved by extrinsic evidence.* They may, however, in the discretion of the court, if probative of truthfulness or untruthfulness, be *inquired into on cross-examination of the witness* (1) concerning the witness' character for truthfulness or untruthfulness..."

The present use fits the second sentence of FRE 608(b): the giving of false testimony in a prior trial is obviously "probative of untruthfulness." And Choice's (A)'s limitation to matters "elicited from Expert Witness on cross-examination" brings the situation into the second sentence (cross-examination) rather than the first sentence (extrinsic evidence).

(B) is not the best response,

because prior bad acts can be introduced only on cross-examination, but in that event need not be supported by "clear and convincing" extrinsic evidence.

As described in Choice (A) above, the prior-bad-act evidence here can only be brought out on cross. Therefore, Choice (B) is wrong since it does not include this limitation.

On the other hand, if the evidence *is* brought out on cross, it need not be supported by "clear and convincing" evidence. It's true that as a judge-made rule, the cross-examiner must have a "good faith basis" for believing that the false-testimony episode actually occurred. But such a good-faith basis, not the possession of clear-and-convincing-evidence, is all that is required for introducing the topic on cross.

(C) is not the best response,

because Defendant's testimony would be admissible if elicited on cross-examination.

If the evidence were being offered "extrinsically"

(e.g., by testimony from a different witness who witnessed the false testimony), this Choice would be correct — see the first sentence of FRE 608(b), quoted in the discussion of Choice (A) above. But the evidence would be allowed to be brought up ("elicited") on cross of Expert Witness himself, even though it relates solely to credibility rather than to a substantive issue in the case (and thus concerns a "collateral matter"). Since Choice (C) overstates the situations in which the evidence would be excluded, it's not the best answer.

(D) is not the best response,

because the evidence would be admissible if elicited on cross-examination.

Evidence of a prior bad act by the witness demonstrating the witness' poor character for truthfulness does not fall within the general ban on proof of character traits to show action-in-conformity-therewith-on-the-present-occasion. Instead, FRE 608(b) imposes specific rules governing when such evidence is admissible — as described in Choice (A), such prior-acts-of-lying evidence may be brought out only on cross of the witness whose veracity is in question, not by means of "extrinsic evidence." Therefore, Choice (D) is an incorrect statement of both the rule and the outcome.

Answer 47

(A) is the best response,

because it correctly applies the rule on spousal privilege in federal courts.

In federal courts, in criminal cases, the witness spouse holds the privilege exclusively, and can choose to testify if he/she wants, without the consent of the accused/spouse, except as to confidential communications (on which the accused/spouse can forbid testimony). Here, Wanda's potential testimony involves a conversation between David and John before Wanda even married David, so it can't involve a confidential marital communication. As a result, the choice to testify is entirely Wanda's. Since A correctly states this rule, it's the best response.

(B) is not the best response,

because it misapplies the rule on spousal privilege in federal courts.

In federal courts, in criminal cases, the witness spouse holds the privilege exclusively, and can choose to testify if he/she wants, without the consent of the accused/spouse, except as to confidential communications (on which the accused/spouse can forbid testimony). Since a confidential marital communication was not involved here, the choice is entirely Wanda's, not David's, making B not the best response.

(C) is not the best response

because it misapplies the rule on spousal privilege in federal courts.

In federal courts, in criminal cases, the witness

spouse holds the privilege exclusively, and can choose to testify if (s)he wants, without the consent of the accused/spouse, except as to confidential communications (on which the accused/spouse can forbid testimony). Since a confidential marital communication was not involved here, the choice is entirely Wanda's, and C is not the best response.

(D) is not the best response

because it misapplies the rule on spousal privilege in the federal courts.

In federal courts, in criminal cases, the witness spouse holds the privilege exclusively, and can choose to testify if he/she wants, without the consent of the accused/spouse, except as to confidential communications (on which the accused/spouse can forbid testimony). Since a confidential marital communication was not involved here, the choice is entirely Wanda's. If you chose option D, it could be because you confused the federal court rule with the common law rule in civil cases, in which the witness/spouse can be forced to testify against the party/spouse. This is not the rule in federal courts in criminal trials, so D is not the best response.

Answer 48

(A) is the best response,

because evidence of witness bias is allowed.

All courts, including the federal courts under the FRE, allow impeachment on the basis of bias. Although nothing in the FRE specifically deals with when and how a party can show a witness' bias, it's quite clear that the evidence here — which presents a strong indication that Frank dislikes Dennis and might well therefore try to injure him by false testimony — would be admitted.

(B) is not the best response,

because Frank's character isn't in question, whereas his possible bias is. As described in Choice (A) above, a party may always show that a witness (including an out-of-court declarant whose statement is serving as testimony) was biased.

(C) is not the best response,

because it isn't necessary that Frank be "given an opportunity to explain or deny."

There are very few instances under the FRE under which a person must be given an opportunity to "explain or deny" (or otherwise respond to) particular evidence. Perhaps the examiners were trying to trick you into thinking that the following FRE provision applies: "Extrinsic evidence of a *prior inconsistent statement by a witness* is not admissible unless the witness is *afforded an opportunity to explain or deny* the same and the opposite party is afforded an opportunity to interrogate the witness thereon, or the interests of justice otherwise require." (FRE 613(b).)

However, this provision clearly doesn't apply here because (1) Frank is not "a witness" for purposes of the provision (he hasn't taken the stand); and (2) showing that Frank had a bias is not the same as showing that he's made a prior statement that's inconsistent with the statement being discussed.

There is no other provision concerning an opportunity to "explain or deny" that might apply here.

(D) is not the best response,

because bias *can* be shown by specific instances.

It's clear that when *A* quotes an out-of-court statement by *B*, *A* may be cross-examined about material — including prior acts by *B* — that tends to show that *B* was biased when he made the statement. See FRE 608(b) (specific credibility-related instances of the conduct of a witness may be brought up on cross of either that witness or some other witness about whom the present witness has testified.) So in this scenario, among others, witness bias *can* be shown by specific instances.

Answer 49

(B) is the best response,

because no expert witness is required to point out the similarities between the photo and the defendant — the jury is entitled to make the comparison itself.

When an automatic device takes a picture, only a limited type of authentication is needed. A witness must testify about how the machine works, and that testimony must somehow tie the photo to the issue under question (e.g., "The photo was taken at 2:45 A.M. on Aug. 23rd, the same time a burglar alarm went off indicating that the premises had been broken into.") Since the facts tell us the expert has testified to the "reliability of infrared photography," we can presume that this type of testimony was given.

Once this has happened, no further authentication or other expert testimony is needed. The jury is deemed to be capable of comparing the image with the defendant, so as to make its own determination of whether there are interesting resemblances. (Expert testimony would be admissible — if the judge thought that it would help the jury and be "reliable" — but it's not *required*.)

(A) is not the best response,

because, for the reason explained in Choice (B) above, no expert testimony is required (though such testimony might be admissible).

(C) is not the best response,

because no eyewitness identification is needed for photos taken by automatic devices.

Where a photo is taken by an automatic device, only limited authentication (showing that the machine is reliable, and tying the photo to the episode in question) is required. What's NOT required is any testimony by a

human who says, "I saw the photo taken, and I can say it was taken at a certain time [or in a certain circumstance.]" So once the expert here testified about how the machine works (see the example in Choice (B) of testimony that would have sufficed), no "eyewitness" testimony about the taking of the photo was needed.

(D) is not the best response,

because the camera and the photos taken by it are not "witnesses" for purpose of the Confrontation Clause.

The Confrontation Clause applies only where a human being gives testimony. Where evidence is produced by an inanimate object — such as the camera here — the Clause is never triggered.

Answer 50

(B) is the best response,

because it correctly recognizes the evidence as inadmissible because it is impeachment on a collateral matter.

Under these facts, Walters is being impeached with extrinsic evidence that contradicts his direct testimony. The evidence is that he worked for his employer for only seven years instead of three, which has no bearing on any issue in the case.

The problem with this is that the impeachment violates the "collateral matters" rule. Under the "collateral matters" rule, extrinsic evidence can only be introduced to impeach a witness if it *also* bears on a *substantive* issue in the case (or if it proves something deemed important, like bias). Here, if the employment records are true, they only prove Walters is lying – they do not make any issue in the case either more or less probable.

Note that what the option doesn't mention, but implies, is that what makes the impeachment impermissible is that it's *extrinsic* impeachment – Walters *could* be impeached by asking *him* about his employment record (which would be "intrinsic" impeachment, since it's from his own mouth). Since B correctly applies this rule to the facts here, it's the best response.

(A) is not the best response,

because it incorrectly applies the Best Evidence Rule.

The Best Evidence Rule only applies when the material terms of a writing are being proven, or the witness is testifying relying on a writing. Neither of these applies to the facts here. The terms of the writing (the employment records) are not relevant to any of the issues in the trial. Instead, Walters is being impeached with extrinsic impeachment that contradicts his direct testimony. The evidence is that he worked for his employer for only seven years instead of three, which has no bearing on any issue in the case. Under the "collateral matters" rule, extrinsic evidence can only be introduced to impeach a witness if it *also* bears on a *substantive* issue in the case (or if it proves something deemed important, like bias). Here, if the records are true, they only prove Walters is lying – they do not make any issue in the case either more or less probable. As a result, the records need not be introduced, and A is not the best response.

(C) is not the best response,

because it wrongly invokes the business records exception to the hearsay rule.

While the employment records here could qualify under that exception (if the entries were made in the regular course of business, in conjunction with a business activity, entered under a duty to record, by one with personal knowledge of matters recorded or transmitted from such a person, entered at or near time of transaction, and authenticated at trial), FRE 803(6), option C is incorrect because the records haven't been offered into evidence.

Instead, what option C fails to take into account the "collateral matters" rule. Under that rule, extrinsic evidence (i.e., not from the witness's own mouth) can only be introduced to impeach a witness if it *also* bears on a *substantive* issue in the case (or if it proves something deemed important, like bias). Here, if the records are true, they only prove Walters is lying – they do not make any issue in the case either more or less probable. Since C does not recognize the "collateral matter" involved here, it's not the best response.

(D) is not the best response,

because it fails to take into account the "collateral matters" rule.

Option D correctly recognizes that the evidence here will impeach Walters, by bringing into question his credibility. However, the fact that the evidence here will impeach Walters' credibility is not enough to make it admissible, because extrinsic evidence (i.e., evidence not from the witness's own mouth) is only admissible to impeach a witness if it *also* bears on a *substantive* issue in the case (or if it proves something deemed important, like bias). Here, if the records are true, they only prove Walters is lying – they do not make any issue in the case either more or less probable. Since D does not recognize the "collateral matter" hitch here, it's not the best response.

Answer 51

(D) is the best response,

because the record here satisfies the records-of-regularly-kept-activities exception, and the statement recorded falls within the statements-for-purposes-of-medical-diagnosis exception.

We have here a statement-within-a-statement problem. That is, we have (1) a written statement by Intern (the hospital record), which is the "outer" level; and (2) an oral statement (the statement spoken by the Doctor), which is the "inner" level. For the written record to come in, both levels must either be non-hearsay or

hearsay within an exception.

Let's take the inner level first. This one falls neatly within FRE 803(4)'s hearsay exception for "Statements made for purposes of medical diagnosis or treatment and describing ... past or present symptoms ... or the inception or general character of the cause or external source thereof insofar as reasonably pertinent to diagnosis or treatment."

Now, the outer level. FRE 803(6) gives a hearsay exception for "A ... *record* ... of acts, events, conditions, opinions, or *diagnoses*, made at or near the time by, or *from information transmitted by*, a *person with knowledge*, if *kept in the course of a regularly conducted business activity*, and if it was the *regular practice* of that business activity to make the ... record ..., all as shown by the testimony of the custodian or other qualified witness[.]" The record here qualifies. Note that the fact that the record wasn't physically made by the person "with knowledge" (Doctor) doesn't matter, as long as the record was made "from information transmitted by" a person with knowledge. Since Doctor transmitted the info to Intern, the fact that Intern was the one who made the physical record is OK.

(A) is not the best response,

because establishment of Doctor's expertise is neither sufficient nor necessary for admissibility of the record.

Doctor is not giving testimony here, so he's not an "expert witness," and the foundation required for expert testimony is therefore not required. Furthermore, even if such a foundation had been laid, the record couldn't come in unless the two-levels of exceptions to the hearsay rule were established (as they were — see the discussion of Choice (D) above).

(B) is not the best response,

because at issue is the admissibility of the record, not data that is not in evidence.

When a record containing an opinion is admissible as an exception to the hearsay rule, the fact that the data on which the maker of the record relied is not in evidence is irrelevant.

In fact, this choice is a complete red herring. Even if Doctor were on the stand repeating his diagnosis, the underlying data wouldn't have to be in evidence, or even admissible — see FRE 703: "The facts or data in the particular case upon which an expert bases an opinion or inference may be those perceived by or made known to the expert at or before the hearing. If of a type reasonably relied upon by experts in the particular field in forming opinions or inferences upon the subject, the facts or data *need not be admissible in evidence* in order for the opinion or inference to be admitted."

(C) is not the best response,

because the entry records Doctor's statements, not Plaintiff's.

Statements *by a patient* regarding the patient's physical condition made to a treating physician in connection with treatment are admissible as exceptions to the hearsay rule. They fall within the much more general exception in FRE 803(3) for "A statement of the declarant's then existing state of mind, emotion, sensation, or physical condition." But the statement here wasn't made by the patient (Plaintiff) — it was made by the treating doctor. And the correct hearsay exception for Doctor's oral statement is (as discussed in Choice (D) above) is 803(4)'s exception for "statements made for purposes of medical diagnosis or treatment."

Answer 52

(C) is the best response,

because the statement was made out-of-court, is offered for the truth of the matter asserted, and does not fall within any exception.

FRE 801(c) defines hearsay as a statement, other than one made by the declarant while testifying at trial, offered in evidence to prove the truth of the matter asserted.

Witness' statement naming Defendant as his source was made by Witness after being arrested by Officer, which is to say it was not made when Witness was testifying at trial. The government seeks to offer Officer's repetition of that statement for the truth of the matter asserted in it, i.e., that Defendant was indeed the source for the drugs he is now charged with selling. So the statement is hearsay, and is inadmissible unless some exception applies.

No exception applies. For instance, the "prior inconsistent statement" exception doesn't apply for the reason stated in the analysis of Chioce (A) below, and the "identification" exception doesn't apply for the reason stated in the analysis of Choice (B) below.

(A) is not the best response,

because Witness has made only one statement.

Certain statements by a person who testifies at a trial or hearing, and is subject to cross-examination about the statements, are not hearsay. FRE 801(d)(1) says that where the declarant "testifies at the trial or hearing and is subject to cross-examination" concerning the prior statement, the prior statement is non-hearsay (and thus admissible) if it is "inconsistent with the declarant's testimony, and was given under oath subject to the penalty of perjury at a trial, hearing, or other proceeding." (801(d)(1)(A)).

This exclusion obviously doesn't apply here: the declarant is Witness, and he is not "testifying ... subject to cross-examination" at trial. (Merely appearing at the trial and refusing to answer doesn't count as "testifying," certainly not when there is a requirement of being "subject to cross-examination." And even if Witness' out-of-court statement was viewed as being both "prior" and "inconsistent," it wasn't given "under oath."

(B) is not the best response,

because Witness has refused to testify.

Certain statements by a person who testifies at a trial or hearing, and is subject to cross-examination about the statements, are not hearsay. FRE 801(d)(1)(C) says that where the declarant "testifies at the trial or hearing and is subject to cross-examination" concerning the prior statement, the prior statement is non-hearsay (and thus admissible) if it is "one of identification of a person made after perceiving the person."

This exclusion doesn't apply here. Witness has not "testified" or been "subject to cross-examination" (see the analysis of Choice (A) for more detail about why).

(D) is not the best response,

because the lack of confrontation doesn't have anything to do with the inadmissibility of the statement.

There is no general principle that an out-of-court declaration can't be introduced unless the declarant is "confronted with the statement while on the stand."

It's true that in the case of a prior inconsistent statement from a testifying witness, FRE 613(b) says that extrinsic evidence of the prior statement is inadmissible "unless the witness is afforded an opportunity to explain or deny the same and the opposite party is afforded an opportunity to interrogate the witness thereon, or the interests of justice otherwise require." But this provision doesn't come close to applying, since Witness is not a testifying witness, and the prior statement is not a "prior inconsistent statement."

It's also true that in some cases, the *defendant's* Confrontation Clause rights will constitutionally prevent an out-of-court declaration from being admitted against him. But Choice (D) refers to Witness' right to "confront" the statement while on the stand, not the defendant's right to confront the witness.

In summary, Witness had no right to be "confronted with the statement while on the stand."

Answer 53

(A) is the best response,

because it shows Davidson deposited more than he made, and is thus circumstantial evidence of guilt the admission of which does not violate any evidentiary rule.

Circumstantial evidence is evidence which, even if it is believed, does not resolve the matter at issue unless additional reasoning is used to reach the proposition to which the evidence is directed. Circumstantial evidence will be admitted only if it has probative value, that is, only if it affects the probability of the existence of a fact consequential to the action.

Evidence that Davidson deposited nearly twice his salary over a two-year period is circumstantial evidence of Davidson's embezzlement, because this evidence makes it more likely than it would otherwise be that Davidson had a major non-salary source of income. There is no evidentiary rule that would bar the admission of this very-relevant evidence.

(B) is not the best response,

because the use of Witt's testimony for impeachment purposes would violate FRE 608(b).

FRE 608(b) says that "Specific instances of the conduct of a witness, for the purpose of *attacking or supporting the witness' credibility*, other than conviction of crime as provided in rule 609, *may not be proved by extrinsic evidence*." The evidence here consists of "specific instances" of Davidson's conduct. If the evidence is being offered to "impeach" Davidson as Choice (B) specifies, it is being offered to "attack the witness' credibility," and falls within 608(b), given that there has been no criminal conviction. Therefore, the specific instances of conduct can't be proved by "extrinsic evidence" (which is what separate testimony from Witt would be). Instead, impeachment could only happen by bringing out the instances while Davidson was on the stand (e.g., "Isn't it true that according to bank records you deposited almost twice the amount of your salary?")

(C) is not the best response,

because the evidence is highly probative of embezzlement, and there is no "unfair" prejudice.

FRE 403 says that "Although relevant, evidence may be excluded if its probative value is substantially outweighed by the danger of unfair prejudice...." However, this provision wouldn't apply here because: (1) the probative value is quite large (surely a person who deposits almost twice his salary into a bank account is significantly more likely to be an embezzler than one who does not); and (2) there is minimal "unfairness" in showing that a person has made bank deposits, certainly not enough unfairness to "substantially outweigh" the major probative value of the evidence.

(D) is not the best response,

because the fact that the deposits could have been legitimate goes to weight, not admissibility.

A piece of evidence, to be admissible (assuming no special rule of exclusion applies) must merely make some issue of disputed fact more likely to be true than it would be in the absence of the evidence. The evidence doesn't have to conclusively "prove" the ultimate proposition to which it's addressed, or even render that proposition "more likely than not" true. As the idea is sometimes put, "a brick is not a wall."

Here, the fact that a person has made bank deposits of almost twice his salary in a two-year period makes it more likely that he's an embezzler than if he had only deposited the amount of his salary or less. So this evidence satisfies the standard in the prior paragraph, even though there may well be a legitimate explanation for the deposits. As the court might say, the possibility of an innocent explanation here merely "goes to weight, not admissibility."

Answer 54

(D) is the best response,

because a trial judge is allowed to use hearsay when ruling on preliminary questions.

FRE 104(a) says that "Preliminary questions concerning ... the admissibility of evidence shall be determined by the court.... In making its determination it is *not bound by the rules of evidence* except those with respect to privileges."

Pedestrian's statement to Nurse is admissible if, and only if, the statement qualified for the dying-declaration exception. That exception requires that the declarant knew or believed that he was about to die. The affidavit is relevant to that issue. It's true that the affidavit is hearsay (it's an out-of-court statement offered to prove the truth of the matter asserted, i.e., that Pedestrian really knew or believed he was dying.) And this hearsay does not fall within any exception. But under 104(a), the court may consider this inadmissible hearsay to make his preliminary ruling on the admissibility of Pedestrian's statement to Nurse.

(A) is not the best response,

because even though the affidavit is hearsay not within any exception, it may still be considered on the preliminary matter of the admissibility of the statement to Nurse.

As described in Choice (D) above, the fact that the affidavit is hearsay not within any exception does not prevent the court from using it to resolve a preliminary question about the admissibility of other evidence.

(B) is not the best response,

because (1) dying declarations are admissible in civil cases; and (2) the admissibility of the affidavit is irrelevant to whether it can be considered on the preliminary question here.

First, FRE 804(b)(2) gives a hearsay exception for "In a prosecution for homicide *or in a civil action or proceeding*, a statement made by a declarant while believing that the declarant's death was imminent, concerning the cause or circumstances of what the declarant believed to be impending death." So the proposition asserted in Choice (B) — that dying declarations can't be used except in homicide prosecutions —is simply incorrect as a matter of law.

Furthermore, even if this statement of law were true, it would be irrelevant — as described in the discussion of Choice (D) above, the judge may consider inadmissible material in ruling on an evidentiary question.

(C) is not the best response,

because (1) the affidavit is the "outer level" of a two-level hearsay statement, and that outer level doesn't qualify for the then-existing-state-of-mind exception; and (2) the affidavit's admissibility doesn't matter here anyway.

First, notice that we have hearsay-within-hearsay.

The "outer" level is Doctor's affidavit (a statement made out of court, repeating some other statement.) The "inner" level is Pedestrian's statement to Doctor. Each must satisfy a hearsay exception. It's true that the inner statement arguably qualifies for the then-existing state of mind exception (though even this is far from clear, since under FRE 803(3) "A statement of ... belief to prove the fact ... believed" does not qualify for the exception.)

But the *outer* statement is not a statement about *the declarant's* then-existing state of mind — for this purpose, the declarant is Doctor, and he's not summarizing his own then-existing state of mind (except insofar as he's making a statement of what he currently remembers Pedestrian to have said, which is inadmissible since FRE 803(3) denies the state-of-mind exception for "A statement of memory ... to prove the fact remembered.")

Since one of the two levels is inadmissible hearsay, the entire statement-within-a-statement is inadmissible. But anyway, as described in Choice (D) above, the statement need not be admissible to be considered by the judge in making a preliminary admissibility ruling.

Answer 55

(B) is the best response,

because Witness' testimony does in fact fall within the then-existing state-of-mind exception.

The out-of-court statement here is "I'm going to spend the next three days in State B," offered to show that the declarant in fact spent the next three days there. So at least in a loose sense, the declaration is being offered to prove the "truth" of the matter asserted.

FRE 803(3) gives a hearsay exception for "A statement of the declarant's then existing state of mind ... (such as intent, *plan* [or] motive...)" So to the extent that the statement here is a statement by Defendant of the fact that she currently plans to do act X, it fits within this exception as a statement of then-existing plan. (Once it comes in, it's allowable for the further inference that if Defendant planned to do act X, she probably did act X as planned.)

(A) is not the best response,

because Defendant's statement wasn't an effort to describe an event she was perceiving.

FRE 803(1)'s implementation of the present-sense-impression exception gives an exception for "A statement describing or explaining *an event or condition* made while the declarant was perceiving the event or condition, or immediately thereafter." Defendant's plan to make a trip is not an "event or condition," so the exception doesn't apply.

(C) is not the best response,

because there is no special rule against "establish[ing] an alibi by [a] defendant's own statement."

This is one of those cases where the examiners try to trick you into believing that there is a "rule" on a particular subject when there isn't. There is simply no special rule about when a prior statement by a defendant can be introduced to furnish an alibi.

Actually, a prior statement by a witness (whether she's the defendant or otherwise) gets a hearsay exception if the statement is "consistent with the declarant's testimony and is offered to rebut an express or implied charge against the declarant of recent fabrication..." FRE 801(d)(1)(B). So to the extent that the prior statement here falls within a special rule for prior statements, the rule is one of admissibility, not non-admissibility.

(D) is not the best response,

because the statement falls within the then-existing-state-of-mind hearsay exception. See the analysis of Choice (B) for an explanation of why this is so.

Answer 56

(A) is the best response,

because only the testimony about peaceableness is a "pertinent trait" of the accused.

FRE 404(a), after stating the general rule against character evidence to prove action in conformity therewith, gives an exception for "evidence of a pertinent trait of character offered by an accused[.]" Since peaceability and truthfulness are each "traits of character," the evidence will be admissible if and only if it concerns a "pertinent" trait.

What traits are "pertinent" depends on the nature of the crime charged and any defenses raised. Here, what's charged is a crime that involves violence, but not untruthfulness.

Therefore, the accused's reputation for peaceableness involves a "pertinent" trait (one who is peaceable is less likely to have committed a crime involving violence). However, the accused's reputation for truthfulness would probably be held not to be pertinent (since one who is truthful is not less likely to have committed a murder than one who is untruthful.)

(Note, however, that if Defendant took the stand and the prosecution attacked his credibility, then the "reputation for truthfulness" testimony would become admissible because the Defendant's truthfulness or untruthfulness would be in issue and thus a "pertinent" trait.)

To the extent that Choices (B), (C) and (D) each fails to admit the peaceableness testimony or admits the truthfulness testimony, it's wrong for the reasons described in the analysis of Choice (A).

STRATEGIES AND TACTICS
REAL PROPERTY

There's no getting around it — Property questions on the MBE are very tough. Unlike Evidence, where most of the questions can be solved with a mechanical application of the Federal Rules, Property questions frequently require careful analysis based on your general knowledge of the subject.

"Real Property" on the MBE consists of two distinct subjects — Real Property and Future Interests. Because Future Interests is such a complex area of law, we've separated our discussion of Property into two parts: Real Property and Future Interests. This section examines only the Real Property questions on the exam; look at the "Future Interests" portion of this book for strategies and tactics in dealing with that part of the MBE.

OUTLINE OF COVERAGE

The following outline for the Real Property/Future Interests portion of the MBE was adopted by the Bar Examiners for all MBEs given on or after July, 2003. This is the most up-to-date outline of coverage released by the Bar Examiners, and your substantive study for Real Property should be centered around it.

The Bar Examiners expect you to understand five key points about each "interest or topic" in this outline (for simplicity, we'll refer to them as the "elements" of Real Property). The Examiners have specifically noted that you need to know these key points even though they *may not be specifically listed* in the outline. These points are: (1) the *nature and characteristics* of the elements of Real Property; (2) how a particular element can be *created;* (3) how to *classify* the element; (4) the *rights of possession* and *rights of the user* of the element; and (5) the *legal and equitable remedies* stemming from that element. For instance, for Fixtures, you're expected to know the nature and characteristics of a fixture (What is a fixture? How does something become a fixture? How do you identify a fixture?), the rights of someone who installs a fixture, and the remedies for disputes arising over fixtures.

You must keep these five points in mind as you study the substantive law of Real Property — if you can master them for all the substantive elements of the outline, you'll be in great shape for this portion of the exam.

Here's what you need to know:

I. Ownership
   A. Present estates
      1. Fees simple
      2. Defeasable fees simple
      3. Life estates
   B. Cotenancy
      1. Tenancy in common
      2. Joint tenancy
   C. Future interests
      1. Reversions
      2. Remainders, vested and contingent
      3. Executory interests
      4. Possibilities of reverter, powers of termination
   D. The law of landlord and tenant
      1. Fitness and suitability of premises

   2. Types of holdings: creation and termination
      a. Terms for years
      b. Tenancies at will
      c. Holdovers and other tenancies at sufferance
      d. Periodic tenancies
   3. Assignment and subletting
   4. Rent
   5. Surrender, mitigation of damages, and anticipatory breach
   E. Special problems
      1. Rule Against Perpetuities
      2. Alienability, descendability, and devisability

   [outline is continued on next page]

II. Rights in land
   A. Covenants at law and in equity
   B. Easements, profits, and licenses
   C. Other interests in land
      1. Fixtures (including relevant application of Article 9, UCC)
      2. Scope and extent of real property
         a. Superjacent, adjacent, and subjacent space
         b. Rights in the common resources of light, air, streams, and bodies of water
         c. Nuisance
   D. Taking and aspects of zoning
III. Real property contract
   A. Relationships included
      1. Contracts to buy and sell by conveyance of realty
      2. Installment contract
   B. Creation and construction
      1. Statute of Frauds
      2. Essential terms
      3. Implied conditions or terms
         a. Time for performance
         b. Title required
         c. Burdens related to title defects
   C. Performance
      1. Fitness and suitability of premises
      2. Marketable title
      3. Risk of loss
   D. Interests before conveyance
      1. Equitable conversion
      2. Earnest-money deposits
   E. Relationships after conveyance
      1. Condition of premises
      2. Title problems
IV. Real property mortgages
   A. Types of security devices
      1. Mortgages (including deeds of trust)
      2. Land contracts as security device
      3. Absolute deeds as security
   B. Some security relationships
      1. Necessity and nature of obligation
      2. Theories: title, lien, and intermediate
      3. Rights and duties prior to foreclosure
      4. Right to redeem and clogging equity of redemption
   C. Transfers by mortgagor
      1. Distinguishing "subject to" and "assuming"
      2. Rights and obligations of transferor

3. Application of subrogation and suretyship principles
      4. Due-on-sale clauses
   D. Transfers by mortgagee (including effect of Article 3 of UCC)
   E. Discharge and defenses
   F. Foreclosure
      1. Types
      2. Rights of omitted parties
      3. Deficiency and surplus
      4. Redemption after foreclosure
      5. Deed in lieu of foreclosure
V. Titles
   A. Adverse possession
   B. Conveyancing by deed
      1. Types
      2. Necessity for a grantee
      3. Delivery (including escrows)
      4. Land description and boundaries
      5. Covenants for title
   C. Conveyancing by will
      1. Ademption
      2. Exoneration
      3. Lapse
   D. Priorities and recording
      1. Types of priority
         a. Recording acts
         b. Judgment liens
         c. Fraudulent conveyances
         d. Protection of bona fide purchasers other than under statutes
      2. Scope of coverage
         a. Recorded documents
         b. Elements required
         c. Parties protected
         d. Interests affected
      3. Special problems
         a. After acquired title (including estopped by deed)
         b. Constructive notice
         c. Forged instruments
         d. Transfers by corporations and by agents
         e. Purchase money mortgages

Of the 33 Real Property/Future Interests questions on the MBE, approximately 75% (24-25 questions) will come from categories I, II, and V, and the rest (8-9 questions) from categories III and IV. There will be questions from each of the roman numeral topics on the exam, but not necessarily from each of the sub-topics.

WHAT TO EXPECT

Property questions on the MBE tend to involve very long, complicated fact patterns. You'll also face many "series" questions, in which you're given a basic fact pattern, followed by two or three questions arising under those facts. The most difficult Property questions will probably deal with conveyances and covenants, because those concepts are so complex.

STUDY STRATEGIES

As with every Multistate subject, you should be as familiar as possible with the entire subject. There are certain topics, nonetheless, which are more likely than others to trip you up if you aren't careful. Here are some to which you should pay particular attention:

1. Remember that bona fide purchaser status does not matter between the original parties to the transaction.

Status as a bona fide purchaser — one who takes for value without notice of prior claims — is relevant primarily when examining protection under recording statutes. Bona fide purchaser status isn't relevant between the original parties; it's only relevant if **subsequent purchasers** are involved! Here's an example:

> Rogers gave Mitchell a power of attorney containing the following provision: "My attorney, Mitchell, is specifically authorized to sell and convey any part or all of my real property." Mitchell conveyed part of Rogers' land to Stone by deed in the customary form containing covenants of title. Stone sues Rogers for breach of a covenant. The outcome of Stone's suit will be governed by whether
>
> A. deeds without covenants are effective to convey realty
> B. the jurisdiction views the covenants as personal or running with the land
> C. Stone is a bona fide purchaser
> D. the power to "sell and convey" is construed to include the power to execute the usual form of deed used to convey realty

Here, Stone's status as a bona fide purchaser (BFP) — one who pays value, in good faith, without notice of any prior conveyance — would be relevant to determine if he would be protected by the recording statutes in a notice or race-notice recording statute jurisdiction. It is not relevant, however, in determining **whether or not he could sue for breach of covenants of title**! Answer choice C indicates why it's important to remember that, if a party to the lawsuit is one of the original parties to the conveyance, his status as a bona fide purchaser is not relevant. (Here, D is the best response.)

2. Be extremely familiar with the concepts of "marketable title" and the doctrine of merger.

Marketable title is a popular topic on the MBE, and there's a good reason for it: the existence and conveyance of marketable title are implied in land sale contracts, **but once the deed takes effect, the terms of the deed control.** This is important because, if a vendor contracts to sell property and later conveys the property via quitclaim deed, **there are no covenants associated with the deed! Under the doctrine of merger, the deed, not the contract, controls**.

3. Know real covenants and equitable servitudes.

These subjects make for good Multistate questions, because they involve many tricky requirements. If the requirements are met, a person can be bound by them even if they don't appear in his deed! The one issue with which you should be most familiar is **notice**, since that's the easiest one to miss. Remember that notice can be *express or implied* — for example, the mere physical appearance of a neighborhood can provide notice that a building restriction exists.

4. Know differences between recording statutes.

Know the three different kinds of recording statutes: **"pure race," "pure notice," and "race-notice."** Pure race statutes are a bit of an anomaly, because they don't require good faith, as the others do; further, pure race statutes are very rare and don't pop up on the MBE too often. They are, however, easy to spot, because, under a pure race statute, the first conveyance recorded wins (the **"first in time"** rule.)

The other two types of recording statutes — pure notice and race-notice — are easily distinguishable by **one point**: whether or not a subsequent BFP is **protected before** he records **his own** interest. Under a pure notice statute, a subsequent BFP is protected from the moment the conveyance to him takes place. Under a race-notice statute, he's not protected **until he records his own interest**. Remember, though, that, under **both** types of statutes, the purchaser must have **no actual knowledge** of a prior conveyance at the moment he takes the conveyance. If he does. he won't be a BFP and the conveyance won't be valid against the prior purchaser.

Race-notice is the most commonly tested type of recording statute on the MBE. To identify this type, watch for language such as: "No unrecorded conveyance or mortgage of real property shall be good against subsequent purchasers for value without notice, who shall first record."

EXAM TACTICS

Many of these suggestions will echo recommendations in the section "How to Attack the MBE" but will show you how the principles already covered apply especially to Property questions.

1. Read carefully!

You may be tired of hearing it, but, in Property questions, it's particularly important to **read the facts carefully**. Property questions tend to be complex, and, because they're long, they're hard to read. Nevertheless, become as involved as you can with each fact pattern so that you don't miss anything.

2. Method for eliminating wrong answers:

Because Property questions are hard, you may find it more difficult to apply a process of elimination to the answer choices. This is the order you should take:

1. Eliminate the answers that are wrong on the facts.
2. Eliminate the answers that are wrong on the law.
3. Eliminate the answers that are irrelevant. As you look through the responses, think to yourself, "Does this address — and overcome — a major obstacle to prevailing in this case?" Alternatively, ask, "Even if this were true — so what?" Here's an example:

> A brother and sister, Bruce and Sharon, acquired as joint tenants a twenty-acre parcel of land called Greenacre. They contributed equally to the purchase price. Several years later, Bruce proposed that they build an apartment development on Greenacre. Sharon rejected the proposal but orally agreed with Bruce that Bruce could go ahead on his own on the northerly half of Greenacre and Sharon could do what she wished with the southerly half of Greenacre. Bruce proceeded to build an apartment development on, and generally developed and improved, the northerly ten acres of Greenacre. Sharon orally permitted the southerly ten acres of Greenacre to be used by the Audubon Society as a nature preserve. Bruce died, leaving his entire estate to his son, Stanley. The will named Sharon as executrix of his will, but she refused so to serve.
>
> In an appropriate action to determine the respective interests of Sharon and Stanley in Greenacre, if Sharon is adjudged to be the owner of all of Greenacre, the most likely reason for the judgment will be that
>
> A. the Statute of Frauds prevents the proof of Sharon's oral agreement
>
> B. Bruce could not unilaterally sever the joint tenancy
>
> C. Sharon's nomination as executrix of Bruce's estate does not prevent her from asserting her claim against Stanley
>
> D. the recorded title of the joint tenancy in Greenacre can be changed only by a duly recorded instrument

Here, choice B misstates a rule of law. A joint tenant **can** unilaterally sever a joint tenancy by any act which disturbs one of the four unities (time, title, possession, and interest); these includes the act of one of the joint tenants in mortgaging the property (under "title" jurisdictions), as well as an act of alienation by any tenant (whether voluntary or involuntary). Since B misstates this rule, it can't be correct.

Both choices C and D focus on irrelevant facts. C cites a rule that does not support a judgment under these facts, though it may accurately state a general rule of law. As C states, the executrix of an estate can assert a claim against the estate. But the fact that Sharon can maintain such an action doesn't address the merits of the case: it's a "threshold" issue. D is also irrelevant, because recording is done for the benefit of subsequent purchasers; it does not affect the two parties currently in title; their interests could be changed without recording.

Since B misstates the law and C and D are both irrelevant, A is the only possible response. Note that the question asks for the most likely reason for the judgment. It might not be the basis **you'd** choose if you were litigating the issue, but, **of these four answer choices**, it's the one most likely to succeed. Choice A addresses and overcomes the most critical obstacle to Sharon's winning the case. Transactions involving an interest in land are covered by the Statute of Frauds, which in turn generally requires a writing to evidence the agreement. While there are numerous exceptions to the Statute of Frauds, none of the other three responses deals with them. As a result, A is the best response.

3. Beware of answers that state a result as a fact, instead of conditionally.

If an answer choice states a result as a certainty — it says, "X will prevail, **because...**," the fact that makes the answer correct must be given to you in the fact pattern of the question. On the other hand, if an answer choice says, "X will prevail, if...," that fact needn't be stated in the question. With conditional answers, you need determine only if the fact provided is central to resolving the issue; if so, the answer is correct. Here's an example:

> Lawnacre was conveyed to Celeste and Donald by a deed which, in the jurisdiction in which Lawnacre is situated, created a cotenancy in equal shares and with the right of survivorship. The jurisdiction has no statute directly applicable to any of the problems posed.

> Celeste, by deed, conveyed "my undivided one-half interest in Lawnacre" to Paul. Celeste has since died. In an appropriate action between Paul and Donald in which title to Lawnacre is at issue, Donald will

> A. prevail, because he is the sole owner of Lawnacre

> B. prevail if, but only if, the cotenancy created in Celeste and Donald was a tenancy by the entirety

> C. not prevail if he had knowledge of the conveyance prior to Celeste's death

> D. not prevail, because Paul and Donald own Lawnacre as tenants in common

Choice D is an example of what we're discussing here. If an answer choice states something as a certainty, and you can think of even **one** circumstances which makes it **inapplicable**, then it **can't** be the best response. Here, the problem doesn't state that Celeste and Donald were married when the conveyance to them took place. If they weren't married, the tenancy created was a joint tenancy. When Celeste conveyed her interest to Paul, she destroyed the joint tenancy, so Donald and Paul hold as a tenants in common. If this were the **only** possibility, D would be the best response. If, however, Celeste and Donald were married when the conveyance to them took place, the resulting tenancy would be a tenancy by the entirety, which cannot be severed by one spouse's attempt to convey his/her interest. If one spouse does so, the conveyance is meaningless: the tenancy by the entirety remains intact, and, when either spouse dies, the other spouse is left as the sole owner (due to the right to survivorship). At least one possibility exists, then, which would make D incorrect. As a result, it cannot be the best response. (B is, in fact, the best, because, if the condition it offers is satisfied, it states the correct result. Note the world of difference between D, which would require that the facts it relies on be given in the problem, and B, which **supplies** a necessary condition.)

4. Watch out for constructive notice.

Constructive notice is based on circumstances which appear in the grantee's "chain of title." Most likely to trip you up is a fact pattern containing evidence that something's amiss in a previously-recorded deed when the deed itself doesn't appear in the chain of title. If there isn't any indication of a problem in the chain of title, then **the grantee doesn't have notice of it**. (Watch out for inquiry notice, though.)

5. Questions asking for the argument that's "most likely to succeed."

On questions like this, determine **which answer choice most closely addresses the greatest obstacle to success in the case**. This will involve **some** analysis based on your own knowledge of the subject; however, you do get some help here: remember that at least one of the answer choices **must** address a central issue in order to be the best response!

You should also consider the difficulty of proof. If a point is central to the case, but will be very difficult to prove, the answer choice containing it is unlikely to be the best response. Here's an example:

> In 1970, Oscar, owner of a 100-acre tract, prepared and duly recorded a subdivision plan called Happy Acres. The plan showed 90 one-acre lots and a ten-acre tract in the center that was designated "Future Public School." Oscar published and distributed a brochure promoting Happy Acres which emphasized the proximity of the lots to the school property and indicated potential tax savings "because the school district will not have to expend tax money to acquire this property." There is no specific statute concerning the dedication of school sites.

> Oscar sold 50 of the lots to individual purchasers. Each deed referred to the recorded plan and also contained the following clause: "No mobile homes shall be erected on any lot within Happy Acres." Sarah was one of the original purchasers from Oscar.

> In 1976, Oscar sold the remaining 40 lots and the ten-acre tract to Max by a deed which referred to the plan and contained the restriction relating to mobile homes. Max sold the 40 lots to individual purchasers and the ten-acre tract to Pete. None of the deeds from Max referred to the plan or contained any reference to mobile homes.

> Assume for this question only that Pete has announced his intention of erecting a fast food restaurant on the ten-acre tract and that Sarah has filed an action to enjoin Pete. If Sarah wins, it will be because

A. Sarah has an equitable servitude concerning the use of the tract

B. Sarah, as a taxpayer, has a legal interest in the use of the tract

C. Sarah is a creditor beneficiary of Oscar's promise with respect to the tract

D. Pete is not a bona fide purchaser

Look at choice C. While Sarah could potentially prevail on this basis, it's not strong grounds for a result in her favor on these facts. In order for Sarah to be a creditor beneficiary of the Oscar/Pete contract, Oscar would have to owe Sarah a pre-existing duty, which Pete's performance will fulfill, and Sarah would have to prove that Oscar specifically intended Pete's performance to benefit her. With this fact pattern, it's unlikely that Oscar intended the Oscar/Pete contract to benefit Sarah in any significant way; in addition, it would be difficult to characterize Sarah as a creditor of Oscar's, since she only purchased a lot from him. While Sarah could, possibly, prevail on a third party beneficiary theory, these factors indicate that it would be a very difficult case to prove. As a result, it's not the best response. (A is, in fact, the best choice, partially because it's much easier to prove than C.)

6. In questions asking for the most important point — determine the fact that's *pivotal*.

The most important point in a case is the one that will determine who will prevail. Here's an example:

> In 1967 Owen held Blackacre, a tract of land, in fee simple absolute. In that year he executed and delivered to Price a quitclaim deed which purported to release and quitclaim to Price all of his rights, title and interest of Owen in Blackacre. Price accepted the quitclaim and placed the deed in his safety deposit box.

> Owen was indebted to Crider in the amount of $35,000. In September, 1971, Owen executed and delivered to Crider a warranty deed, purporting to convey the fee simple to Blackacre, in exchange for a full release of the debt he owed to Crider. Crider immediately recorded his deed.

> In December, 1971, Price caused his quitclaim deed to Blackacre to be recorded and notified Crider that he (Price) claimed title.

> Assume that there is no evidence of occupancy of Blackacre and assume, further, that the jurisdiction where Blackacre is situated has a recording statute which required good faith and value as elements of the junior claimant's priority. Which of the following is the best comment concerning the conflicting claims of Price and Crider?

> A. Price cannot succeed, because the quitclaim through which he claims prevents him from being *bona fide* (in good faith)

> B. The outcome will turn on the view taken as to whether Crider paid value within the meaning of the statute requiring this element

> C. The outcome will turn on whether Price paid value (a fact not given in the statement)

> D. Price's failure to record until December, 1971, estops him from asserting title against Crider

The key fact here is the recording statute. Since it has a good faith element, it must be either a notice or a race-notice statute (pure race statutes do not require good faith). Realizing this leads you to the correct answer — B — because, if Crider is *not* considered a *bona fide* purchaser, the common law rule of "first in time, first in right" will control, and Price will be entitled to Blackacre. If Crider *is* a BFP, he'll be entitled to protection under the recording statute. As stated earlier, the statute here must be a race-notice or pure notice statute. If it's a pure notice statute, Crider, as subsequent purchaser, will only prevail if, when the conveyance to him took place, the prior interest (Price's) had not been recorded. If it's a race-notice statute, then Crider will only prevail if, in addition to being a BFP, he records first. Under these facts, Crider would prevail regardless of which type of statute controls, because he recorded first. Thus, who wins the case turns on whether Crider would be considered a BFP, so B is the best response. Recognizing the key fact here — the type of recording statute involved — is crucial to identifying the best response!

7. Chart the facts.

The facts in property questions can be exceptionally complex. In order to effectively test your knowledge of property law (i.e., of complex concepts such as notice or adverse possession), the facts **have** to be complex. This means that it's vitally important that you chart facts on a piece of scrap paper. Otherwise, it's easy to be overwhelmed, and you can be sure that one of the incorrect responses will be a trap for those who haven't charted the question! Here's an example:

At a time when Ogawa held Lot 1 in the Fairoaks subdivision in fee simple, Vine executed a warranty deed that recited that Vine conveyed Lot 1, Fairoaks, to Purvis. The deed was promptly and duly recorded.

After the recording of the deed from Vine to Purvis, Ogawa conveyed Lot 1 to Vine by a warranty deed that was promptly and duly recorded. Later, Vine conveyed the property to Rand by warranty deed and the deed was promptly and duly recorded. Rand paid the fair market value of Lot 1 and had no knowledge of any claim of Purvis.

In an appropriate action, Rand and Purvis contest title to Lot 1. In this action, judgment should be for

    A. Purvis, because Purvis' deed is senior to Rand's

    B. Rand, because Rand paid value without notice to Purvis' claim

    C. Purvis or Rand, depending on whether a subsequent grantee is bound, at common law, by the doctrine of estoppel by deed

    D. Purvis or Rand, depending on whether Purvis' deed is deemed recorded in Rand's chain of title

This question clearly requires that you chart the facts on a piece of scrap paper so that you can keep them straight. If you chart the conveyances in this problem, it will become clear that Vine is an "interloper," so a deed from him would not be considered within the chain of title from Ogawa to Rand. Without charting the facts, it would be difficult to draw this conclusion. (D is the best answer here.)

8. Beware of answers with constitutional implications.

Keep in mind that, in order for a zoning ordinance or covenant to violate the Constitution, it must be far outside the realm of standard restrictions; therefore, if you encounter a question containing a garden variety restriction, it's unlikely to be repugnant to the Constitution, so any answer choice voiding the restriction on Constitutional grounds is likely to be wrong. Here's an example:

Ohner holds title in fee simple to a tract of 1,500 acres. He desires to develop the entire tract as a golf course, country club, and residential subdivision. He contemplates forming a corporation to own and to operate a golf course and country club; the stock in the corporation will be distributed to the owners of lots in the residential portions of the subdivision, but no obligation to issue the stock is to ripen until all the residential lots are sold. The price of the lots is intended to return enough money to compensate Ohner for the raw land, development costs (including the building of the golf course and the country club facilities), and developer's profit, if all of the lots are sold.

Ohner's market analyses indicate that he must create a scheme of development that will offer prospective purchasers (and their lawyers) a very high order of assurance that several aspects will be clearly established:

    1. Aside from the country club and golf course, there will be no land user other than for residential use and occupancy of the 1,500 acres.

    2. The residents of the subdivision will have unambiguous right of access to the club and golf course facilities.

    3. Each lot owner must have an unambiguous right to transfer his lot to a purchaser with all original benefits.

    4. Each lot owner must be obligated to pay annual dues to a pro rata share (based on the number of lots) of the club's annual operating deficit (whether or not such owner desires to make use of club and course. facilities).

Of the following, the greatest difficulty that will be encountered in establishing the scheme is that

    A. any judicial recognition will be construed as state action which, under current doctrines, raises a substantial question whether such action would be in conflict with the Fourteenth Amendment

    B. the scheme, if effective, renders title unmarketable

    C. one or more of the essential aspects outlined by Ohner will result in a restraint on alienation

    D. there is a judicial reluctance to recognize an affirmative burden to pay money in installments and over an indefinite period as a burden which can be affixed to bind future owners of land

Choice A is a good example of why it's important to be wary of "Constitutional" answers to questions that give every indication of being Property questions. Make sure you correctly eliminate every Property law possibility before you consider Constitutional implications. Here, the facts just don't give rise to a Fourteenth Amendment violation. While a judicial recognition of the scheme could be construed as state action, this does not, *per se,* amount to a Fourteenth Amendment problem, mainly because the scheme indicates no due process or equal protection problems. (In fact, the best answer is D.)

QUESTIONS
REAL PROPERTY

QUESTIONS
REAL PROPERTY

NOTE: For ease of study, we've put all **Future Interests** questions together, beginning with Question 39.

Question 1

Olivia, owner in fee simple of Richacre, a large parcel of vacant land, executed a deed purporting to convey Ripchacre to her nephew, Grant. She told Grant, who was then 19, about the deed and said that she would give it to him when he reached 21 and had received his undergraduate college degree. Shortly afterward Grant searched Olivia's desk, found and removed the deed, and recorded it.

A month later, Grant executed an instrument in the proper form of a warranty deed purporting to convey Richacre to his fiancée, Bonnie. He delivered the deed to Bonnie, pointing out that the deed recited that it was given in exchange for "$1 and other good and valuable consideration," and that to make it valid Bonnie must pay him $1. Bonnie, impressed and grateful, did so. Together, they went to the recording office and recorded the deed. Bonnie assumed Grant had owned Richacre, and knew nothing about Grant's dealing with Olivia. Neither Olivia's deed to Grant nor Grant's deed to Bonnie said anything about any conditions.

The recording act of the jurisdiction provides: "No conveyance or mortgage of real property shall be good against subsequent purchasers for value and without notice unless the same be recorded according to law."

Two years passed. Grant turned 21, then graduated from college. At the graduation party, Olivia was chatting with Bonnie and for the first time learned the foregoing facts.

The age of majority in the jurisdiction is 18 years.

Olivia brought an appropriate action against Bonnie to quiet title to Richacre.

The court will decide for

(A) Olivia, because Grant's deed to Bonnie before Grant satisfied Olivia's conditions was void, as Bonnie had paid only nominal consideration.

(B) Olivia, because her deed to Grant was not delivered.

(C) Bonnie, because Grant has satisfied Olivia's oral conditions.

(D) Bonnie, because the deed to her was recorded.

Question 2

Owner owned Greenacre, a tract of land, in fee simple. Owner executed an instrument in the proper form of a deed, purporting to convey Greenacre to Purchaser in fee simple. The instrument recited that the conveyance was in consideration of "$5 cash in hand paid and for other good and valuable consideration." Owner handed the instrument to Purchaser and Purchaser promptly and properly recorded it.

Two months later, Owner brought an appropriate action against Purchaser to cancel the instrument and to quiet title. In support, Owner proved that no money in fact had been paid by Purchaser, notwithstanding the recitation, and that no other consideration of any kind had been supplied by Purchaser.

In such action, Owner should

(A) lose, because any remedy Owner might have had was lost when the instrument was recorded.

(B) lose, because the validity of conveyance of land does not depend upon consideration being paid, whether recited or not.

(C) prevail, because the recitation of consideration paid may be contradicted by parol evidence.

(D) prevail, because recordation does not make a void instrument effective.

Question 3

Alex and Brenda owned in fee simple Greenacre as tenants in common, each owning an undivided one-half interest. Alex and Brenda joined in mortgaging Greenacre to Marge by a properly recorded mortgage that contained a general warranty clause. Alex became disenchanted with land-owning and notified Brenda that he would no longer contribute to the payment of installments due Marge. After the mortgage was in default and Marge made demand for payment of the entire amount of principal and interest due, Brenda tendered to Marge, and Marge deposited, a check for one-half of the amount due Marge. Brenda then demanded a release of Brenda's undivided one-half interest. Marge refused to release any interest in Greenacre. Brenda promptly brought an action against Marge to quiet title to an undivided one-half interest in Greenacre.

In such action, Brenda should

(A) lose, because Marge's title had been warranted by an express provision of the mortgage.

(B) lose, because there was no redemption from the mortgage.

(C) win, because Brenda is entitled to marshalling.

(D) win, because the cotenancy of the mortgagors was in common and not joint.

Question 4

Janet had a season ticket for the Scorpions' hockey games at Central Arena (Section B, Row 12, Seat 16). During the intermission between the first and second periods of a game between the Scorpions and the visiting Hornets, Janet solicited signatures for a petition urging that the coach of the Scorpions be fired.

Central Arena and the Scorpions are owned by ABC, Inc., a privately owned entity. As evidenced by many prominently displayed signs, ABC prohibits all solicitations anywhere within Central Arena at any time and in any manner. ABC notified Janet to cease her solicitation of signatures.

Janet continued to seek signatures on her petition during the Scorpions' next three home games at Central Arena. Each time, ABC notified Janet to cease such solicitation. Janet announced her intention to seek signatures on her petition again during the Scorpions' next home game at Central Arena. ABC wrote a letter informing Janet that her season ticket was canceled and tendering a refund for the unused portion. Janet refused the tender and brought an appropriate action to establish the right to attend all home games.

In this action, the court will decide for

(A) ABC, because it has a right and obligation to control activities on realty it owns and has invited the public to visit.

(B) ABC, because Janet's ticket to hockey games created only a license.

(C) Janet, because, having paid value for the ticket, her right to be present cannot be revoked.

(D) Janet, because she was not committing a nuisance by her activities.

Question 5

By a writing, Oner leased his home, Blackacre, to Tenn for a term of three years, ending December 31 of last year, at the rent of $1,000 per month. The lease provided that Tenn could sublet and assign.

Tenn lived in Blackacre for one year and paid the rent promptly. After one year, Tenn leased Blackacre to Agrit for one year at a rent of $1,000 per month.

Agrit took possession of Blackacre and lived there for six months but, because of her unemployment, paid no rent. After six months, on June 30 Agrit abandoned Blackacre, which remained vacant for the balance of that year. Tenn again took possession of Blackacre at the beginning of the third and final year of the term but paid Oner no rent.

At the end of the lease term, Oner brought an appropriate action against both Tenn and Agrit to recover $24,000, the unpaid rent.

In such action Oner is entitled to a judgment

(A) against Tenn individually for $24,000, and no judgment against Agrit.

(B) against Tenn individually for $18,000, and against Agrit individually for $6,000.

(C) against Tenn for $12,000, and against Tenn and Agrit jointly and severally for $12,000.

(D) against Tenn individually for $18,000, and against Tenn and Agrit jointly and severally for $6,000.

Question 6

Sal owned five adjoining rectangular lots, numbered 1 through 5 inclusive, all fronting on Main Street. All of the lots are in a zone limited to one- and two-family residences under the zoning ordinance. Two years ago, Sal conveyed Lots 1, 3, and 5. None of the three deeds contained any restrictions. Each of the new owners built a one-family residence.

One year ago, Sal conveyed Lot 2 to Peter. The deed provided that each of Peter and Sal, their respective heirs and assigns, would use Lots 2 and 4 respectively only for one-family residential purposes. The deed was promptly and properly recorded. Peter built a one-family residence on Lot 2.

Last month, Sal conveyed Lot 4 to Betty. The deed contained no restrictions. The deed from Sal to Peter was in the title report examined by Betty's lawyer. Betty obtained a building permit and commenced construction of a two-family residence on Lot 4.

Peter, joined by the owners of Lots 1, 3, and 5, brought an appropriate action against Betty to enjoin the proposed use of Lot 4, or, alternatively, damages caused by Betty's breach of covenant.

Which is the most appropriate comment concerning the outcome of this action?

(A) All plaintiffs should be awarded their requested judgment for injunction because there was a common development scheme, but award of damages should be denied to all.

(B) Peter should be awarded appropriate remedy, but recovery by the other plaintiffs is doubtful.

(C) Injunction should be denied, but damages should be awarded to all plaintiffs, measured by diminution of market value, if any, suffered as a result of the proximity of Betty's two-family residence.

(D) All plaintiffs should be denied any recovery or relief because the zoning preempts any private scheme of covenants.

Question 7

Ollie owned a large tract of land known as Peterhill. During Ollie's lifetime, Ollie conveyed the easterly half (East Peterhill), situated in the municipality of Hawthorn, to Abel, and the westerly half (West Peterhill), situated in the municipality of Sycamore, to Betty. Each of the conveyances, which were promptly and properly recorded, contained the following language:

The parties agree for themselves and their heirs and assigns that the premises herein conveyed shall be used only for residential purposes; that each lot created within the premises herein conveyed shall contain not less than five acres; and that each lot shall have not more than one single-family dwelling. This agreement shall bind all successor owners of all or any portion of Peterhill and any owner of any part of Peterhill may enforce this covenant.

After Ollie's death, Abel desired to build houses on one-half acre lots in the East Peterhill tract as authorized by current applicable zoning and building codes in Hawthorn. The area surrounding East Peterhill in Hawthorn was developed as a residential community with homes built on one-half acre lots. West Peterhill was in a residential area covered by the Sycamore zoning code, which allowed residential development only on five-acre tracts of land.

In an appropriate action brought by Betty to enjoin Abel's proposed construction on one-half acre lots, the court will find the quoted restriction to be

(A) invalid, because of the change of circumstance in the neighborhood.

(B) invalid, because it conflicts with the applicable zoning code.

(C) valid, but only so long as the original grantees from Ollie own their respective tracts of Peterhill.

(D) valid, because the provision imposed an equitable servitude.

Question 8

Susan owned Goldacre, a tract of land, in fee simple. By warranty deed, she conveyed Goldacre in fee simple to Ted for a recited consideration of "$10 and other valuable consideration." The deed was promptly and properly recorded. One week later, Susan and Ted executed a written document that stated that the conveyance of Goldacre was for the purpose of establishing a trust for the benefit of Benton, a child of Susan's. Ted expressly accepted the trust and signed the document with Susan. This written agreement was not authenticated to be eligible for recordation and there never was an attempt to record it.

Ted entered into possession of Goldacre and distributed the net income from Goldacre to Benton at appropriate intervals.

Five years later, Ted conveyed Goldacre in fee simple to Patricia by warranty deed. Patricia paid the fair market value of Goldacre, had no knowledge of the written agreement between Susan and Ted, and entered into possession of Goldacre.

Benton made demand upon Patricia for distribution of income at the next usual time Ted would have distributed. Patricia refused. Benton brought an appropriate action against Patricia for a decree requiring her to perform the trust Ted had theretofore recognized.

In such action, judgment should be for

(A) Benton, because a successor in title to the trustee takes title subject to the grantor's trust.

(B) Benton, because equitable interests are not subject to the recording act.

(C) Patricia, because, as a bona fide purchaser, she took free of the trust encumbering Ted's title.

(D) Patricia, because no trust was ever created since Susan had no title at the time of the purported creation.

Question 9

Olivia owned Blackacre, her home. Her daughter, Dawn, lived with her and always referred to Blackacre as "my property." Two years ago, Dawn, for a valuable consideration, executed and delivered to Bruce an instrument in the proper form of a warranty deed purporting to convey Blackacre to Bruce in fee simple, reserving to herself an estate for two years in Blackacre. Bruce promptly and properly recorded his deed.

One year ago, Olivia died and by will, duly admitted to probate, left her entire estate to Dawn.

One month ago, Dawn, for a valuable consideration, executed and delivered to Carl an instrument in the proper form of a warranty deed purporting to convey Blackacre to Carl, who promptly and properly recorded the deed. Dawn was then in possession of Blackacre and Carl had no actual knowledge of the deed to Bruce. Immediately thereafter, Dawn gave possession to Carl.

The recording act of the jurisdiction provides: "No conveyance or mortgage of real property shall be good against subsequent purchasers for value and without notice unless the same be recorded according to law."

Last week, Dawn fled the jurisdiction. Upon learning the facts, Carl brought an appropriate action against Bruce to quiet title to Blackacre.

If Carl wins, it will be because

(A) Dawn had nothing to convey to Bruce two years ago.

(B) Dawn's deed to Bruce was not to take effect until after Dawn's deed to Carl.

(C) Carl was first in possession.

(D) Dawn's deed to Bruce was not in Carl's chain of title.

Question 10

Opal owned several vacant lots in ABC Subdivision. She obtained a $50,000 loan from a lender, Bank, and executed and delivered to Bank a promissory note and mortgage describing Lots 1, 2, 3, 4, and 5. The mortgage was promptly and properly recorded.

Upon payment of $10,000, Opal obtained a release of Lot 2 duly executed by Bank. She altered the instrument of release to include Lot 5 as well as Lot 2 and recorded it. Opal thereafter sold Lot 5 to Eva, an innocent purchaser, for value.

Bank discovered that the instrument of release had been altered and brought an appropriate action against Opal and Eva to set aside the release as it applied to Lot 5. Opal did not defend against the action, but Eva did.

The recording act of the jurisdiction provides: "No unrecorded conveyance or mortgage of real property shall be good against subsequent purchasers for value without notice, who shall first record."

The court should rule for

(A) Eva, because Bank was negligent in failing to check the recordation of the release.

(B) Eva, because she was entitled to rely on the recorded release.

(C) Bank, because Eva could have discovered the alteration by reasonable inquiry.

(D) Bank, because the alteration of the release was ineffective.

Question 11

Owen owned Blackacre in fee simple, as the land records showed, when he contracted to sell Blackacre to Bryer. Two weeks later, Bryer paid the agreed price and received a warranty deed. A week thereafter, when neither the contract nor the deed had been recorded and while Owen remained in possession of Blackacre, Cred properly filed her money judgment against Owen. She knew nothing of Bryer's interest.

A statute in the jurisdiction provides: "Any judgment properly filed shall, for ten years from filing, be a lien on the real property then owned or subsequently acquired by any person against whom the judgment is rendered."

The recording act of the jurisdiction provides: "No conveyance or mortgage of real property shall be good against subsequent purchasers for value and without notice unless the same be recorded according to law."

Cred brought an appropriate action to enforce her lien against Blackacre in Bryer's hands.

If the court decides for Bryer, it will most probably be because

(A) the doctrine of equitable conversion applies.

(B) the jurisdiction's recording act does not protect creditors.

(C) Owen's possession gave Cred constructive notice of Bryer's interest.

(D) Bryer was a purchaser without notice.

Questions 12-13 are based on the following fact situation.

Seller and Buyer execute an agreement for the sale of real property on September 1, 1991. The jurisdiction in which the property is located recognized the principle of equitable conversion and has no statute pertinent to this problem.

Question 12

Assume for this question only that Seller dies before closing and his will leaves his personal property to Perry and his real property to Rose. There being no breach of the agreement by either party, which of the following is correct?

(A) Death, an eventuality for which the parties could have provided, terminates the agreement if they did not so provide.

(B) Rose is entitled to the proceeds of the sale when it closes, because the doctrine of equitable conversion does not apply to these circumstances.

(C) Perry is entitled to the proceeds of the sale when it closes.

(D) Title was rendered unmarketable by Seller's death.

Question 13

Assume for this question only that Buyer dies before closing, there being no breach of the agreement by either party. Which of the following is appropriate in most jurisdictions?

(A) Buyer's heir may specifically enforce the agreement.

(B) Seller has the right to return the down payment and cancel the contract.

(C) Death terminates the agreement.

(D) Any title acquired would be unmarketable by reason of Buyer's death.

Question 14

Six years ago, Oscar, owner of Blackacre in fee simple, executed and delivered to Albert an instrument in the proper form of a warranty deed, purporting to convey Blackacre to "Albert and his heirs." At that time, Albert was a widower who had one child, Donna.

Three years ago, Albert executed and delivered to Bea an instrument in the proper form of a warranty deed, purporting to convey Blackacre to "Bea." Donna did not join in the deed. Bea was and still is unmarried and childless.

The only possibly applicable statute in the jurisdiction states that any deed will be construed to convey the grantor's entire estate, unless expressly limited.

Last month, Albert died, never having remarried. Donna is his only heir. Blackacre is now owned by

(A) Donna, because Albert's death ended Bea's life estate *pur autre vie*.

(B) Bea in fee simple pursuant to Albert's deed.

(C) Donna and Bea as tenants in common of equal shares.

(D) Donna and Bea as joint tenants, because both survived Albert.

Question 15

Several years ago, Bart purchased Goldacre, financing a large part of the purchase price by a loan from Mort that was secured by a mortgage. Bart made the installment payments on the mortgage regularly until last year. Then Bart persuaded Pam to buy Goldacre, subject to the mortgage to Mort. They expressly agreed that Pam would not assume and agree to pay Bart's debt to Mort. Bart's mortgage to Mort contained a due-on-sale clause stating, "If Mortgagor transfers his/her interest without the written consent of Mortgagee first obtained, then at Mortgagee's option the entire principal balance of the debt secured by this Mortgage shall become immediately due and payable." However, without seeking Mort's consent, Bart conveyed Goldacre to Pam, the deed stating in pertinent part " . . . , subject to a mortgage to Mort [giving details and recording data]."

Pam took possession of Goldacre and made several mortgage payments, which Mort accepted. Now, however, neither Pam nor Bart has made the last three mortgage payments. Mort has brought an appropriate action against Pam for the amount of the delinquent payments.

In this action, judgment should be for

(A) Pam, because she did not assume and agree to pay Bart's mortgage debt.

(B) Pam, because she is not in privity of estate with Mort.

(C) Mort, because Bart's deed to Pam violated the due-on-sale clause.

(D) Mort, because Pam is in privity of estate with Mort.

Question 16

Anna owned Blackacre, which was improved with a dwelling. Beth owned Whiteacre, an adjoining unimproved lot suitable for constructing a dwelling. Beth executed and delivered a deed granting to Anna an easement over the westerly 15 feet of Whiteacre for convenient ingress and egress to a public street, although Anna's lot did abut another public street. Anna did not then record Beth's deed. After Anna constructed and started using a driveway within the described 15-foot strip in a clearly visible manner, Beth borrowed $10,000 cash from Bank and gave Bank a mortgage on Whiteacre. The mortgage was promptly and properly recorded. Anna then recorded Beth's deed granting the easement. Beth subsequently defaulted on her loan payments to Bank.

The recording act of the jurisdiction provides: "No conveyance or mortgage of real property shall be good against subsequent purchasers for value and without notice unless the same be recorded according to law."

In an appropriate foreclosure action as to Whiteacre, brought against Anna and Beth, Bank seeks, among other things, to have Anna's easement declared subordinate to Bank's mortgage, so that the easement will be terminated by completion of the foreclosure.

If Anna's easement is NOT terminated, it will be because

(A) the recording of the deed granting the easement prior to the foreclosure action protects Anna's rights.

(B) the easement provides access from Blackacre to a public street.

(C) Anna's easement is appurtenant to Blackacre and thus cannot be separated from Blackacre.

(D) visible use of the easement by Anna put Bank on notice of the easement.

Question 17

Owner owned a hotel, subject to a mortgage securing a debt Owner owed to Lender One. Owner later acquired a nearby parking garage, financing a part of the purchase price by a loan from Lender Two, secured by a mortgage on the parking garage. Two years thereafter, Owner defaulted on the loan owed to Lender One, which caused the full amount of that loan to become immediately due and payable. Lender One decided not to foreclose the mortgage on Owner's hotel at that time, but instead brought an action, appropriate under the laws of the jurisdiction and authorized by the mortgage loan documents, for the full amount of the defaulted loan. Lender One obtained and properly filed a judgment for that amount.

A statute of the jurisdiction provides: "Any judgment properly filed shall, for ten years from filing, be a lien on the real property then owned or subsequently acquired by any person against whom the judgment is rendered."

There is no other applicable statute, except the statute providing for judicial foreclosure of mortgages, which places no restriction on deficiency judgments.

Lender One later brought an appropriate action for judicial foreclosure of its first mortgage on the hotel and of its judgment lien on the parking garage. Lender Two was joined as a party defendant, and appropriately counterclaimed for foreclosure of its mortgage on the parking garage, which was also in default. All procedures were properly followed and the confirmed foreclosure sales resulted as follows:

Lender One purchased the hotel for $100,000 less than its mortgage balance.

Lender One purchased the parking garage for an amount that is $200,000 in excess of Lender Two's mortgage balance.

The $200,000 surplus arising from the bid paid by Lender One for the parking garage should be paid

(A) $100,000 to Lender One and $100,000 to Owner.

(B) $100,000 to Lender Two and $100,000 to Owner.

(C) $100,000 to Lender One and $100,000 to Lender Two.

(D) $200,000 to Owner.

Question 18

Abel owned Blackacre in fee simple. Three years ago, Abel and Betty agreed to a month-to-month tenancy with Betty paying Abel rent each month. After six months of Betty's occupancy, Abel suggested to Betty that she could buy Blackacre for a monthly payment of no more than her rent. Abel and Betty orally agreed that Betty would pay $25,000 in cash, the annual real estate taxes, the annual fire insurance premiums, and the costs of maintaining Blackacre, plus the monthly mortgage payments that Abel owed on Blackacre. They further orally agreed that within six years Betty could pay whatever mortgage balances were then due and Abel would give her a warranty deed to the property. Betty's average monthly payments did turn out to be about the same as her monthly rent.

Betty fully complied with all of the obligations she had undertaken. She made some structural modifications to Blackacre. Blackacre is now worth 50% more than it was when Abel and Betty made their oral agreement. Betty made her financing arrangements and was ready to complete the purchase of Blackacre, but Abel refused to close. Betty brought an appropriate action for specific performance against Abel to enforce the agreement.

The court should rule for

(A) Abel, because the agreements were oral and violated the statute of frauds.

(B) Abel, subject to the return of the $25,000, because the arrangement was still a tenancy.

(C) Betty, because the doctrine of part performance applies.

(D) Betty, because the statute of frauds does not apply to oral purchase and sale agreements between landlords and tenants in possession.

Question 19

Vendor owned Greenacre, a tract of land, in fee simple. Vendor entered into a valid written agreement with Purchaser under which Vendor agreed to sell and Purchaser agreed to buy Greenacre by installment purchase. The contract stipulated that Vendor would deliver to Purchaser, upon the payment of the last installment due, "a warranty deed sufficient to convey the fee simple." The contract contained no other provision that could be construed as referring to title.

Purchaser entered into possession of Greenacre. After making 10 of the 300 installment payments obligated under the contract, Purchaser discovered that there was outstanding a valid and enforceable mortgage on Greenacre, securing the payment of a debt in the amount of 25% of the purchase price Purchaser had agreed to pay. There was no evidence that Vendor had ever been late in payments due under the mortgage and there was no evidence of any danger of insolvency of Vendor. The value of Greenacre now is four times the amount due on the debt secured by the mortgage.

Purchaser quit possession of Greenacre and demanded that Vendor repay the amounts Purchaser had paid under the contract. After Vendor refused the demand, Purchaser brought an appropriate action against Vendor to recover damages for Vendor's alleged breach of the contract.

In such action, should damages be awarded to Purchaser?

(A) No, because the time for Vendor to deliver marketable title has not arrived.

(B) No, because Purchaser assumed the risk by taking possession.

(C) Yes, because in the absence of a contrary express agreement, an obligation to convey marketable title is implied.

(D) Yes, because the risk of loss assumed by Purchaser in taking possession relates only to physical loss.

Questions 20-21 are based on the following fact situation.

Owner held 500 acres in fee simple absolute. In 1960 Owner planted and obtained all required governmental approvals of two subdivisions of 200 acres each.

In 1960 and 1961 commercial buildings and parking facilities were constructed on one, Royal Center, in accordance with the plans disclosed by the plat for each subdivision. Royal Center continues to be used for commercial purposes.

The plat of the other, Royal Oaks, showed 250 lots, streets, and utility and drainage easements. All of the lots in Royal Oaks were conveyed during 1960 and 1961. The deeds contained provisions, expressly stated to be binding upon the grantee, his heirs and assigns, requiring the lots to be used only for single family, residential purposes until 1985. The deeds expressly stated that these provisions were enforceable by the owner of any lot in the Royal Oaks subdivision.

At all times since 1959, the 200 acres of Royal Center have been zoned for shopping center use, and the 200 acres in Royal Oaks have been zoned for residential use in a classification which permits both single-family and multiple-family use.

Question 20

In an appropriate attack upon the limitation to residential user by single families, if the evidence disclosed no fact in addition to those listed above, the most probable judicial resolution would be that

(A) there is no enforceable restriction because judicial recognition constitutes state action which is in conflict with the Fourteenth Amendment to the United States Constitution

(B) there is no enforceable restriction because of Owner's conflict of interest in that he did not make the restriction applicable to the 100 acres he retains

(C) the restriction in user set forth in the deeds will be enforced at the suit of any present owner of a lot in Royal Oaks residential subdivision

(D) any user consistent with zoning will be permitted but that such users so permitted as are in conflict with the restrictions in the deeds will give rise to a right to damages from owner or Owner's successor

Question 21

For this question only, assume that Owner now desires to open his remaining 100 acres as a residential subdivision of 125 lots (with appropriate streets, etc.). He has, as an essential element of his scheme, the feature that the restrictions should be identical with those he planned for the original Royal Oaks residential subdivision and, further, that lot owners in Royal Oaks should be able to enforce (by lawsuits) restrictions on the lots in the 100 acres. The zoning for the 100 acres is identical with that for the 200 acres of Royal Oaks residential subdivision. Which of the following best states the chance for success for his scheme?

(A) He can restrict use only to the extent of that imposed

by zoning (that is, to residential user by not more than four dwelling units per lot).

(B) He cannot restrict the 100 acres to residential user because of the conflicting user for retail commercial purposes in the 200 acres comprising the shopping center.

(C) He cannot impose any enforceable restriction to residential user only.

(D) Any chance of success depends upon the 100 acres being considered by the courts as a part of a common development scheme which also includes the 200 acres of Royal Oaks.

Question 22

Chase, as seller, and Scott, as buyer, enter into a written contract for the sale and purchase of land which is complete in all respects except that no reference is made to the quality of title to be conveyed. Which of the following will result?

(A) The contract will be enforceable

(B) Chase will be required to convey a marketable title

(C) Chase will be required to convey only what he owned on the date of the contract

(D) Chase will be required to convey only what he owned on the date of the contract plus whatever additional title rights he may acquire prior to the closing date

Question 23

Thirty years ago Able, the then-record owner of Greenacre, a lot contiguous to Blueacre, in fee simple, executed and delivered to Baker an instrument in writing which was denominated "Deed of Conveyance." In pertinent part it read, "Able does grant to Baker and her heirs and assigns a right-of-way for egress and ingress to Blueacre." If the quoted provision was sufficient to create an interest in land, the instrument met all other requirements for a valid grant. Baker held record title in fee simple to Blueacre, which adjoined Greenacre.

Twelve years ago Charlie succeeded to Able's title in fee simple in Greenacre and seven years ago Dorcas succeeded to Baker's title in fee simple in Blueacre by a deed which made no mention of a right-of-way or driveway. At the time Dorcas took title, there existed a driveway across Greenacre which showed evidence that it had been used regularly to travel between Main Road, a public road, and Blueacre. Blueacre did have frontage on Side Road, another public road, but this means of access was seldom used because it was not as convenient to the dwelling situated on Blueacre as was Main Road. The driveway originally was established by Baker.

Dorcas has regularly used the driveway since acquiring title. The period of time required to acquire rights by prescription in the jurisdiction is ten years.

Six months ago Charlie notified Dorcas that Charlie planned to develop a portion of Greenacre as a residential subdivision and that Dorcas should cease any use of the driveway. After some negotiations, Charlie offered to permit Dorcas to construct another driveway to connect with the streets of the proposed subdivision. Dorcas declined this offer on the ground that travel from Blueacre to Main Road would be more circuitous.

Dorcas brought an appropriate action against Charlie to obtain a definitive adjudication of the respective rights of Dorcas and Charlie. In such lawsuit Charlie relied upon the defense that the location of the easement created by the grant from Able to Baker was governed by reasonableness and that Charlie's proposed solution was reasonable.

Charlie's defense should

(A) fail, because the location had been established by the acts of Baker and Able.

(B) fail, because the location of the easement had been fixed by prescription.

(C) prevail, because the reasonableness of Charlie's proposal was established by Dorcas's refusal to suggest any alternative location.

(D) prevail, because the servient owner is entitled to select the location of a right-of-way if the grant fails to identify its location.

Question 24

Adam owns Townacres in fee simple, and Bess owns the adjoining Greenacres in fee simple. Adam has kept the lawns and trees on Townacres trimmed and neat. Bess "lets nature take its course" at Greenacres. The result on Greenacres is a tangle of underbrush, fallen trees, and standing trees that are in danger of losing limbs. Many of the trees on Greenacres are near Townacres. In the past, debris and large limbs have been blown from Greenacres onto Townacres. By local standards Greenacres is an eyesore that depresses market values of real property in the vicinity, but the condition of Greenacres violates no applicable laws or ordinances.

Adam demanded that Bess keep the trees near Townacres trimmed. Bess refused.

Adam brought an appropriate action against Bess to require Bess to abate what Adam alleges to be a nuisance. In the lawsuit, the only issue is whether the condition of Greenacres constitutes a nuisance.

The strongest argument that Adam can present is that the condition of Greenacres

(A) has an adverse impact on real estate values.

(B) poses a danger to the occupants of Townacres.

(C) violates community aesthetic standards.

(D) cannot otherwise be challenged under any law or ordinance.

Question 25

Adam owned Blackacre. Adam entered into a written three-year lease of Blackacre with Bertha. Among other provisions, the lease prohibited Bertha from "assigning this lease, in whole or in part, and from subletting Blackacre, in whole or in part." In addition to a house, a barn, and a one-car garage, Blackacre's 30 acres included several fields where first Adam, and now Bertha, grazed sheep.

During the following months, Bertha:

I. By a written agreement allowed her neighbor Charles exclusive use of the garage for storage, under lock and key, of his antique Packard automobile for two years, charging him $240.

II. Told her neighbor Doris that Doris could use the fields to practice her golf as long as she did not disturb Bertha's sheep.

Which, if any, of Bertha's actions constituted a violation of the lease?

(A) I only.

(B) II only.

(C) Both I and II.

(D) Neither I nor II.

Question 26

Art, who owned Blackacre in fee simple, conveyed Blackacre to Bea by warranty deed. Celia, an adjoining owner, asserted title to Blackacre and brought an appropriate action against Bea to quiet title to Blackacre. Bea demanded that Art defend Bea's title under the deed's covenant of warranty, but Art refused. Bea then successfully defended at her own expense.

Bea brought an appropriate action against Art to recover Bea's expenses incurred in defending against Celia's action to quiet title to Blackacre.

In this action, the court should decide for

(A) Bea, because in effect it was Art's title that was challenged.

(B) Bea, because Art's deed to her included the covenant of warranty.

(C) Art, because the title Art conveyed was not defective.

(D) Art, because Celia may elect which of Art or Bea to sue.

Question 27

At a time when Ogawa held Lot 1 in the Fairoaks subdivision in fee simple, Vine executed a warranty deed that recited that Vine conveyed Lot 1, Fairoaks, to Purvis. The deed was promptly and duly recorded.

After the recording of the deed from Vine to Purvis, Ogawa conveyed Lot 1 to Vine by a warranty deed that was promptly and duly recorded. Later, Vine conveyed the property to Rand by warranty deed and the deed was promptly and duly recorded. Rand paid the fair market value of Lot 1 and had no knowledge of any claim of Purvis.

In an appropriate action, Rand and Purvis contest title to Lot 1. In this action, judgment should be for

(A) Purvis, because Purvis' deed is senior to Rand's

(B) Rand, because Rand paid value without notice to Purvis' claim

(C) Purvis or Rand, depending on whether a subsequent grantee is bound, at common law, by the doctrine of estoppel by deed

(D) Purvis or Rand, depending on whether Purvis' deed is deemed recorded in Rand's chain of title

Question 28

Olive owned Blackacre, a single-family residence. Fifteen years ago, Olive conveyed a life estate in Blackacre to Lois.

Fourteen years ago, Lois, who had taken possession of Blackacre, leased Blackacre to Trent for a term of 15 years at the monthly rental of $500.

Eleven years ago, Lois died intestate leaving Ron as her sole heir.

Trent regularly paid rent to Lois and, after Lois's death, to Ron until last month.

The period in which to acquire title by adverse possession in the jurisdiction is 10 years.

In an appropriate action, Trent, Olive, and Ron each asserted ownership of Blackacre.

The court should hold that title in fee simple is in

(A) Olive, because Olive held a reversion and Lois has died.

(B) Ron, because Lois asserted a claim adverse to Olive when Lois executed a lease to Trent.

(C) Ron, because Trent's occupation was attributable to Ron, and Lois died 11 years ago.

(D) Trent, because of Trent's physical occupancy and because Trent's term ended with Lois's death.

Question 29)

Alpha and Beta owned Greenacre, a large farm, in fee simple as tenants in common, each owning an undivided one-half interest. For five years Alpha occupied Greenacre and conducted farming operations. Alpha never accounted to Beta for any income but Alpha did pay all real estate taxes when the taxes were due and kept the buildings located on Greenacre insured against loss from fire, storm, and flood. Beta lived in a distant city and was interested only in realizing a profit from the sale of the land when market conditions produced the price Beta wanted.

Alpha died intestate survived by Hera, Alpha's sole heir. Thereafter Hera occupied Greenacre but was inexperienced in farming operations. The result was a financial disaster. Hera failed to pay real estate taxes for two years. The appropriate governmental authority held a tax sale to recover the taxes due. At such sale Beta was the only bidder and obtained a conveyance from the appropriate governmental authority upon payment of an amount sufficient to discharge the amounts due for taxes, plus interest and penalties, and the costs of holding the tax sale. The amount paid was one-third of the reasonable market value of Greenacre.

Thereafter Beta instituted an appropriate action against Hera to quiet title in and to recover possession of

Greenacre. Hera asserted all defenses available to Hera.

Except for the statutes related to real estate taxes and tax sales, there is no applicable statute.

In this lawsuit, Beta is entitled to a decree quieting title so that Beta is the sole owner in fee simple of Greenacre

(A) because Beta survived Alpha.

(B) because Hera defaulted in the obligations undertaken by Alpha.

(C) unless Hera pays Beta one-half of the reasonable market value of Greenacre.

(D) unless Hera pays Beta one-half of the amount Beta paid for the tax deed

Question 30

Alex and Betty, who were cousins, acquired title in fee simple to Blackacre, as equal tenants in common, by inheritance from Angela, their aunt. During the last 15 years of her lifetime, Angela allowed Alex to occupy an apartment in the house on Blackacre, to rent the other apartment in the house to various tenants, and to retain the rent. Alex made no payments to Angela; and since Angela's death 7 years ago, he has made no payments to Betty. For those 22 years, Alex has paid the real estate taxes on Blackacre, kept the building on Blackacre insured, and maintained the building. At all times, Betty has lived in a distant city and has never had anything to do with Angela, Alex, or Blackacre.

Recently, Betty needed money for the operation of her business and demanded that Alex join her in selling Blackacre. Alex refused.

The period of time to acquire title by adverse possession in the jurisdiction is 10 years. There is no other applicable statute.

Betty brought an appropriate action against Alex for partition. Alex asserted all available defenses and counterclaims.

In that action, the court should

(A) deny partition and find that title has vested in Alex by adverse possession.

(B) deny partition, confirm the tenancy in common, but require an accounting to determine if either Betty or Alex is indebted to the other on account of the rental payment, taxes, insurance premiums, and maintenance costs.

(C) grant partition and require, as an adjustment, an accounting to determine if either Betty or Alex is indebted to the other on account of the rental payments, taxes, insurance premiums, and maintenance costs.

(D) grant partition to Betty and Alex as equal owners, but without an accounting.

Question 31

Santos agreed to sell and Perrine agreed to buy a described lot on which a single-family residence had been built. Under the contract, Santos agreed to convey marketable title subject only to conditions, covenants, and restrictions of record and all applicable zoning laws and ordinances. The lot was subject to a 10-foot side line setback originally set forth in the developer's duly recorded subdivision plot. The applicable zoning ordinance zones the property for single-family units and requires an 8.5-foot side line setback.

Prior to closing, a survey of the property was made. It revealed that a portion of Santos' house was 8.4 feet from the side line.

Perrine refused to consummate the transaction on the ground that Santos' title is not marketable. In an appropriate action, Santos seeks specific performance. Who will prevail in such an action?

(A) Santos, because any suit against Perrine concerning the setback would be frivolous

(B) Santos, because the setback violation falls within the doctrine *de minimis non curat lex*

(C) Perrine, because any variation, however small, amounts to a breach of contract

(D) Perrine, because the fact that Perrine may be exposed to litigation is sufficient to make the title unmarketable

Question 32

Bill owned in fee simple Lot 1 in a properly approved subdivision, designed and zoned for industrial use. Gail owned the adjoining Lot 2 in the same subdivision. The plat of the subdivision was recorded as authorized by statute.

Twelve years ago, Bill erected an industrial building wholly situated on Lot 1 but with one wall along the boundary common with Lot 2. The construction was done as authorized by a building permit, validly obtained under applicable statutes, ordinances, and regulations. Further, the construction was regularly inspected and passed as being in compliance with all building code requirements.

Lot 2 remained vacant until six months ago, when Gail began excavation pursuant to a building permit authorizing the erection of an industrial building situated on Lot 2 but with one wall along the boundary common with Lot 1. The excavation caused subsidence of a portion of Lot 1 that resulted in injury to Bill's building. The excavation was not done negligently or with any malicious intent to injure. In the jurisdiction, the time to acquire title by adverse possession or rights by prescription is 10 years.

Bill brought an appropriate action against Gail to recover damages resulting from the injuries to the building on Lot 1.

In such lawsuit, judgment should be for

(A) Bill, if, but only if, the subsidence would have occurred without the weight of the building on Lot 1.

(B) Bill, because a right for support, appurtenant to Lot 1, had been acquired by adverse possession or prescription.

(C) Gail, because Lots 1 and 2 are urban land, as distinguished from rural land and, therefore, under the circumstances Bill had the duty to protect any improvements on Lot 1.

(D) Gail, because the construction and the use to be made of the building were both authorized by the applicable law.

Question 33

Corp, a corporation, owned Blackacre in fee simple, as the real estate records showed. Corp entered into a valid written contract to convey Blackacre to Barbara, an individual. At closing, Barbara paid the price in full and received an instrument in the proper form of a deed, signed by duly authorized corporate officers on behalf of Corp, purporting to convey Blackacre to Barbara. Barbara did not then record the deed or take possession of Blackacre.

Next, George (who had no knowledge of the contract or the deed) obtained a substantial money judgment against Corp. Then, Barbara recorded the deed from Corp. Thereafter, George properly filed the judgment against Corp.

A statute of the jurisdiction provides: "Any judgment properly filed shall, for ten years from filing, be a lien on the real property then owned or subsequently acquired by any person against whom the judgment is rendered."

Afterward, Barbara entered into a valid written contract to convey Blackacre to Polly. Polly objected to Barbara's title and refused to close.

The recording act of the jurisdiction provides: "Unless the same be recorded according to law, no conveyance or mortgage of real property shall be good against subsequent purchasers for value and without notice."

Barbara brought an appropriate action to require Polly to complete the purchase contract.

The court should decide for

(A) Polly, because George's judgment was obtained before Barbara recorded the deed from Corp.

(B) Polly, because even though Corp's deed to Barbara prevented George's judgment from being a lien on Blackacre, George's filed judgment poses a threat of litigation.

(C) Barbara, because Barbara recorded her deed before George filed his judgment.

(D) Barbara, because Barbara received the deed from Corp before George filed his judgment.

Question 34

Fernwood Realty Company developed a residential development, known as the Fernwood Development, which included single-family dwellings, town houses, and high-rise apartments for a total of 25,000 dwelling units. Included in the deed to each unit was a covenant under which the grantee and the grantee's "heirs and assigns" agreed to purchase electrical power only from a plant Fernwood promised to build and maintain within the development. Fernwood constructed the plant and the necessary power lines. The plant did not supply power outside the development. An appropriate and fair formula was used to determine price.

After constructing and selling 12,500 of the units, Fernwood sold its interest in the development to Gaint Realty Investors. Gaint operated the power plant and constructed and sold the remaining 12,500 units. Each conveyance from Gaint contained the same covenant relating to electrical power that Fernwood had included in the 12,500 conveyances it had made.

Page bought a dwelling unit from Olm, who had purchased it from Fernwood. Subsequently, Page, whose lot was along the boundary of the Fernwood development, ceased buying electrical power from Gaint and began purchasing power from General Power Company, which provided such service in the area surrounding the Fernwood development. Both General Power and Gaint have governmental authorization to provide electrical services to the area. Gaint instituted an appropriate action against Page to enjoin her from obtaining electrical power from General Power. If judgment is for Page, it most likely will be because

(A) the covenant does not touch and concern the land

(B) the mixture of types of residential units is viewed as preventing one common development scheme

(C) the covenant is a restraint on alienation

(D) there is no privity of estate between Page and Gaint

Questions 35-36 are based on the following fact situation.

Orris had title to Brownacre in fee simple. Without Orris' knowledge, Hull entered Brownacre in 1950 and constructed an earthen dam across a watercourse. The earthen dam trapped water that Hull used to water a herd of cattle he owned. After twelve years of possession of Brownacre, Hull gave possession of Brownacre to Burns. At the same time, Hull also purported to transfer his cattle and all his interests in the dam and water to Burns by a document that was sufficient as a bill of sale to transfer personal property but was insufficient as a deed to transfer real property.

One year later, Burns entered into a lease with Orris to lease Brownacre for a period of five years. After the end of the five-year term of the lease, Burns remained on Brownacre for an additional three years and then left Brownacre. At that time Orris conveyed Brownacre by a quitclaim deed to Powell. The period of time to acquire title by adverse possession in the jurisdiction in ten years.

Question 35

After Orris' conveyance to Powell, title to Brownacre was in

(A) Hull

(B) Orris

(C) Burns

(D) Powell

Question 36

After Orris' conveyance to Powell, title to the earthen dam was in

(A) the person who then held title to Brownacre in fee simple

(B) Burns as purchaser of the dam under the bill of sale

(C) the person who then owned the water rights as an incident thereto

(D) Hull as the builder of the dam

Question 37

A little more than five years ago, Len completed construction of a single-family home located on Homeacre, a lot that Len owned. Five years ago, Len and Tina entered into a valid five-year written lease of Homeacre that included the following language: "This house is rented as is, without certain necessary or useful items. The parties agree that Tina may acquire and install such items as she wishes at her expense, and that she may remove them if she wishes at the termination of this lease."

Tina decided that the house needed, and she paid cash to have installed, standard-sized combination screen/ storm windows, a freestanding refrigerator to fit a kitchen alcove built for that purpose, a built-in electric stove and oven to fit a kitchen counter opening left for that purpose, and carpeting to cover the plywood living room floor.

Last month, by legal description of the land, Len conveyed Homeacre to Pete for $100,000. Pete knew of Tina's soon-expiring tenancy, but did not examine the written lease. As the lease expiration date approached, Pete learned that Tina planned to vacate on schedule, and learned for the first time that Tina claimed and planned to remove all of the above-listed items that she had installed.

Pete promptly brought an appropriate action to enjoin Tina from removing those items.

The court should decide that Tina may remove

(A) none of the items.

(B) only the refrigerator.

(C) all items except the carpet.

(D) all of the items.

Question 38

Ven owned Goldacre, a tract of land, in fee simple. Ven and Pur entered into a written agreement under which Pur agreed to buy Goldacre for $100,000, its fair market value. The agreement contained all the essential terms of a real estate contract to sell and buy, including a date for closing. The required $50,000 down payment was made. The contract provided that in the event of Pur's breach, Ven could retain the $50,000 deposit as liquidated damages.

Before the date set for the closing in the contract, Pur died. On the day that Addy was duly qualified as administratrix of the estate of Pur, which was after the closing date, Addy made demand for return of the $50,000 deposit. Ven responded by stating that he took such demand to be a declaration that Addy did not intend to complete the contract and that Ven considered the contract at an end. Ven further asserted that Ven was entitled to retain, as liquidated damages, the $50,000. The reasonable market value of Goldacre had increased to $110,000 at that time.

Addy brought an appropriate action against Ven to recover the $50,000. In answer, Ven made no affirmative claim but asserted that he was entitled to retain the $50,000 as liquidated damages as provided in the contract.

In such lawsuit, judgment should be for

(A) Addy, because the provision relied upon by Ven is unenforceable.

(B) Addy, because the death of Pur terminated the contract as a matter of law.

(C) Ven, because the court should enforce the express agreement of the contracting parties.

(D) Ven, because the doctrine of equitable conversion prevents termination of the contract upon the death of a party.

[START OF FUTURE INTERESTS QUESTIONS]

Question 39

The following facts concern a tract of land in a state which follows general United States law. Each instrument is in proper form, recorded, marital property rights were waived when necessary, and each person named was adult and competent at the time of the named transaction.

1. In 1940 Oleg, the owner, conveyed his interest in fee simple "to my brothers Bob and Bill, their heirs and assigns as joint tenants with right of survivorship."

2. In 1950 Bob died, devising his interest to his only child, "Charles, for life, and then to Charles's son, Sam, for life, and then to Sam's children, their heirs and assigns."

3. In 1970 Bill died, devising his interest "to my friend, Frank, his heirs and assigns."

4. In 1972 Frank conveyed his quitclaim deed "to Paul, his heirs and assigns whatever right, title and interest I own."

Paul has never married. Paul has contracted to convey marketable record title in the land to Patrick. Can Paul do so?

(A) Yes, without joinder of any other person in the conveyance.

(B) Yes, if Charles, Sam, and Sam's only child (Gene, age 25) will join in the conveyance.

(C) No, regardless of who joins in the conveyance, because Sam may have additional children whose interests cannot be defeated.

(D) No, regardless of who joins in the conveyance, because a title acquired by quitclaim deed is impliedly unmerchantable.

Question 40

Odum owned Brightacre (a tract of land) in fee simple. He conveyed it "to Pike, his heirs and assigns; but if Farley shall be living thirty years from the date of this deed, then to Farley, his heirs and assigns." The limitation "to Farley, his heirs and assigns" is

(A) valid, because Farley's interest is a reversion

(B) valid, because the interest will vest, if at all, within a life in being

(C) valid, because Farley's interest is vested subject to divestment

(D) invalid

Question 41

Otis owned in fee simple Lots 1 and 2 in an urban subdivision. The lots were vacant and unproductive. They were held as a speculation that their value would increase. Otis died and, by his duly probated will, devised the residue of his estate (of which Lots 1 and 2 were part) to Lena for life with remainder in fee simple to Rose. Otis's executor distributed the estate under appropriate court order, and notified Lena that future real estate taxes on Lots 1 and 2 were Lena's responsibility to pay.

Except for the statutes relating to probate and those relating to real estate taxes, there is no applicable statute.

Lena failed to pay the real estate taxes due for Lots 1 and 2. To prevent a tax sale of the fee simple, Rose paid the taxes and demanded that Lena reimburse her for same. When Lena refused, Rose brought an appropriate action against Lena to recover the amount paid.

In such action, Rose should recover

(A) the amount paid, because a life tenant has the duty to pay current charges.

(B) the present value of the interest that the amount paid would earn during Lena's lifetime.

(C) nothing, because Lena's sole possession gave the right to decide whether or not taxes should be paid.

(D) nothing, because Lena never received any income from the lots.

Questions 42-43 are based on the following fact situation.

Trease owned Hilltop in fee simple. By his will, he devised as follows: "Hilltop to such of my grandchildren who shall reach the age of 21; and by this provision I intend to include all grandchildren whenever born." At the time of his death, Trease had three children and two grandchildren.

Question 42

Courts hold such a devise valid under the common-law Rule Against Perpetuities. What is the best explanation of that determination?

(A) All of Trease's children would be measuring lives.

(B) The rule of convenience closes the class of beneficiaries when any grandchild reaches the age of 21.

(C) There is a presumption that Trease intended to include only those grandchildren born prior to his death.

(D) There is a subsidiary rule of construction that dispositive instruments are to be interpreted so as to uphold interests rather than to invalidate them under the Rule Against Perpetuities.

Question 43

Which of the following additions to or changes in the facts of the preceding question would produce a violation of the common-law Rule Against Perpetuities?

(A) A posthumous child was born to Trease.

(B) Trease's will expressed the intention to include all afterborn grandchildren in the gift.

(C) The instrument was an *inter vivos* conveyance rather than a will.

(D) Trease had no grandchildren living at the time of his death.

Question 44

Testator devised his farm "to my son, Selden, for life, then to Selden's children and their heirs and assigns." Selden, a widower, had two unmarried adult children.

In appropriate action to construe the will, the court will determine that the remainder to children is

(A) indefeasibly vested

(B) contingent

(C) vested subject to partial defeasance

(D) vested subject to complete defeasance

Questions 45-46 are based on the following fact situation.

In 1945 Owen, owner of both Blackacre and Whiteacre, executed and delivered two separate deeds by which he conveyed the two tracts of land as follows: Blackacre was conveyed "To Alpha and his heirs as long as it is used exclusively for residential purposes, but if it is ever used for other than residential purposes, to the American Red Cross." Whiteacre was conveyed "To Beta and her heirs as long as it is used exclusively for residential purposes, but if it is used for other than residential purposes prior to 1965, then to the Salvation Army." In 1950 Owen died leaving a valid will by which he devised all his real estate to his brother, Bill. The will had no residuary clause. Owen was survived by Bill and by Owen's daughter, Della who was Owen's sole heir.

For the purpose of this set of questions, it may be assumed that the common law Rule Against Perpetuities applies in the state where the land is located and that the state also has a statute providing that, "All future estates and interests are alienable, descendible, and devisable in the same manner as possessory estates and interests."

Question 45

In 1955, Alpha and Della entered into a contract with John whereby Alpha and Della contracted to sell Blackacre to John in fee simple. After examining title, John refused to perform on the ground that Alpha and Della could not give good title. Alpha and Della joined in an action against John for specific performance. Prayer for specific performance will be

(A) granted, because Alpha and Della together own a fee simple absolute in Blackacre

(B) granted, because Alpha alone owns the entire fee simple in Blackacre

(C) denied, because Bill has a valid interest in Blackacre

(D) denied, because the American Red Cross has a valid interest in Blackacre

Question 46

In 1946, the interest of the American Red Cross in Blackacre could best be described as a

(A) valid contingent remainder

(B) void executory interest

(C) valid executory interest

(D) void contingent remainder

Question 47

Morgan conveyed Greenacre, her one-family residence, to "Perez for life, remainder to Rowan, her heirs and assigns, subject, however, to First Bank's mortgage thereon." There was an unpaid balance on the mortgage of $10,000, which is payable in $1,000 annual installments plus interest at 6 percent on the unpaid balance, with the next payment due on July 1. Perez is now occupying Greenacre. The reasonable rental value of the property exceeds the sum necessary to meet all current charges. There is no applicable statute.

Under the rules governing contributions between life tenants and remaindermen, how should the burden for payment be allocated?

(A) Rowan must pay the principal payment, but Perez must pay the interest to First Bank.

(B) Rowan must pay both the principal and the interest payments to First Bank.

(C) Perez must pay both the principal and interest payments to First Bank.

(D) Perez must pay the principal payment, but Rowan must pay the interest to First Bank.

Question 48

Anders conveyed her only parcel of land to Burton by a duly executed and delivered warranty deed, which provided: To have and to hold the described tract of land in fee simple, subject to the understanding that within one year from the date of the instrument said grantee shall construct and thereafter maintain and operate on said premises a public health center.

The grantee, Burton, constructed a public health center on the tract within the time specified and operated it for five years. At the end of this period, Burton converted the structure into a senior citizens' recreational facility. It is conceded by all parties in interest that a senior citizens' recreational facility is not a public health center.

In an appropriate action, Anders seeks a declaration that the change in the use of the facility has caused the land and structure to revert to her. In this action, Anders should

(A) win, because the language of the deed created a determinable fee, which leaves a possibility of reverter in the grantor

(B) win, because the language of the deed created a fee subject to a condition subsequent, which leaves a right of entry or power of termination in the grantor

(C) lose, because the language of the deed created only a contractual obligation and did not provide for retention of property interest by the grantor

(D) lose, because an equitable charge is enforceable only in equity

Question 49

In 1965, Hubert Green executed his will which in pertinent part provided, "I hereby give, devise, and bequeath Greenvale to my surviving widow for life, remainder to such of my children as shall live to attain the age of 30 years, but if any child dies under the age of 30 years survived by a child or children, such child or children shall take and receive the share which his, her, or their parent would have received had such parent lived to attain the age of 30 years."

At the date of writing his will, Green was married to Susan, and they had two children, Allan and Beth. Susan died in 1970 and Hubert married Waverly in 1972. At his death in 1980, Green was survived by his wife, Waverly, and three children, Allan, Beth, and Carter. Carter, who was born in 1974, was his child by Waverly.

In a jurisdiction which recognizes the common-law Rule Against Perpetuities unmodified by statute, the result of the application of the rule is that the

(A) remainder to the children and to the grandchildren is void because Green could have subsequently married a person who was unborn at the time Green executed his will

(B) remainder to the children is valid, but the substitutionary gift to the grandchildren is void because Green could have subsequently married a person who was unborn at the time Green executed his will

(C) gift in remainder to Allan and Beth or their children is valid, but the gift to Carter or his children is void

(D) remainder to the children and the substitutionary gift to the grandchildren are valid

Question 50

Theresa owned Blueacre, a tract of land, in fee simple. Theresa wrote and executed, with the required formalities, a will that devised Blueacre to "my daughter, Della, for life with remainder to my descendants *per stirpes*." At the time of writing the will, Theresa had a husband and no descendants living other than her two children, Della and Seth.

Theresa died and the will was duly admitted to probate. Theresa's husband predeceased her. Theresa was survived by Della, Seth, four grandchildren, and one great-grandchild. Della and Seth were Theresa's sole heirs at law.

Della and Seth brought an appropriate action for declaratory judgment as to title of Blueacre. Guardians *ad litem* were appointed and all other steps were taken so that the judgment would bind all persons interested whether born or unborn.

In that action, if the court rules that Della has a life estate in the whole of Blueacre and that the remainder is contingent, it will be because the court chose one of several possible constructions and that the chosen construction

(A) related all vesting to the time of writing of the will.

(B) related all vesting to the death of Theresa.

(C) implied a condition that remaindermen survive Della.

(D) implied a gift of a life estate to Seth.

Question 51

For a valuable consideration, Amato, the owner of Riveracre, signed and gave to Barton a duly executed instrument that provided as follows: "The grantor may or may not sell Riveracre during her lifetime, but at her death, or if she earlier decides to sell, the property will be offered to Barton at $500 per acre. Barton shall exercise this right, if at all, within sixty days of receipt of said offer to sell." Barton recorded the instrument. The instrument was not valid as a will. Is Barton's right under the instrument valid?

(A) Yes, because the instrument is recorded.

(B) Yes, because Barton's right to purchase will vest or fail within the period prescribed by the Rule Against Perpetuities.

(C) No, because Barton's right to purchase is a restraint on the owner's power to make a testamentary disposition.

(D) No, because Barton's right to purchase is an unreasonable restraint on alienation.

Question 52

Three years ago Adam conveyed Blackacre to Betty for $50,000 by a deed that provided: "By accepting this deed, Betty covenants for herself, her heirs and assigns, that the premises herein conveyed shall be used solely for residential purposes and, if the premises are used for nonresidential purposes, Adam, his heirs and assigns, shall have the right to repurchase the premises for the sum of one thousand dollars ($1,000)." In order to pay the $50,000 purchase price for Blackacre, Betty obtained a $35,000 mortgage loan from the bank. Adam had full knowledge of the mortgage transaction. The deed and mortgage were promptly and properly recorded in proper sequence. The mortgage, however, made no reference to the quoted language in the deed.

Two years ago Betty converted her use of Blackacre from residential to commercial without the knowledge or consent of Adam or of the bank. Betty's commercial venture failed, and Betty defaulted on her mortgage payments to the bank. Blackacre now has a fair market value of $25,000.

The bank began appropriate foreclosure proceedings against Betty. Adam properly intervened, tendered $1,000, and sought judgment that Betty and the bank be ordered to convey Blackacre to Adam, free and clear of the mortgage.

The common-law Rule Against Perpetuities is unmodified by statute.

If the court rules against Adam, it will be because

(A) the provision quoted from the deed violates the Rule Against Perpetuities.

(B) the Bank had no actual knowledge of, and did not consent to, the violation of the covenant.

(C) the rights reserved by Adam were subordinated, by necessary implication, to the rights of the bank as the lender of the purchase money.

(D) the consideration of $1,000 was inadequate.

Question 53

Ortega owned Blackacre in fee simple and by his will specifically devised Blackacre as follows: "To my daughter, Eugenia, her heirs and assigns, but if Eugenia dies survived by a husband and a child or children, then to Eugenia's husband during his lifetime with remainder to Eugenia's children, their heirs and assigns. Specifically provided, however, that if Eugenia dies survived by a husband and no child, Blackacre is specifically devised to my nephew, Luis, his heirs and assigns."

While Ortega's will was in probate, Luis quitclaimed all interest in Blackacre to Eugenia's husband, Jose. Three years later, Eugenia died, survived by Jose but no children. Eugenia left a will devising her interest in Blackacre to Jose. The only applicable statute provides that any interest in land is freely alienable.

Luis instituted an appropriate action against Jose to establish title to Blackacre. Judgment should be for

(A) Luis, because his quitclaim deed did not transfer his after acquired title

(B) Luis, because Jose took nothing under Ortega's will

(C) Jose, because Luis had effectively conveyed his interest in Blackacre

(D) Jose, because the doctrine of after-acquired title applies to a devise by will

REAL PROPERTY

Answer Key

Use this Answer Key to quickly identify the correct answer to each question.

(1) B	(11) B	(21) D	(31) D	(41) D	(51) B
(2) B	(12) C	(22) B	(32) A	(42) A	(52) A
(3) B	(13) A	(23) A	(33) D	(43) C	(53) C
(4) B	(14) B	(24) B	(34) A	(44) C	
(5) A	(15) A	(25) A	(35) A	(45) C	
(6) B	(16) D	(26) C	(36) A	(46) B	
(7) D	(17) A	(27) D	(37) D	(47) A	
(8) C	(18) C	(28) C	(38) A	(48) C	
(9) D	(19) A	(29) D	(39) A	(49) D	
(10) D	(20) C	(30) C	(40) B	(50) C	

ANSWERS

REAL PROPERTY

Answer 1

(B) is the best response,

because the lack of delivery by Olivia caused the deed to Grant to be void, and there was therefore no title for Bonnie to take, regardless of whether she was a b.f.p. and regardless of whether she paid value.

For a deed to be valid, it must not only be executed but also "delivered." However, the requirement of delivery does not mean that the deed must necessarily be physically given to the grantee. Instead, the delivery requirement is satisfied by words or conduct of the grantor which evidence his intention to make his deed *presently operative*, so as to vest title in the grantee and to surrender his own control over title.

Here, there was no actual delivery of Olivia's deed for Richacre to Grant. In fact, Olivia's words and deeds made clear that she did *not* intend for the deed to be presently operative. Without delivery by Olivia, title to Richacre never vested in Grant.

Since title never vested in Grant, he had nothing to convey to Bonnie. Therefore, whether she knew or didn't know of Grant's deceit, and whether she did or didn't give value, never even become issues. And the recording act's provisions never govern the case at all.

(A) is not the best response,

because it is an incorrect legal explanation for the correct result.

As described in the analysis of Choice (B) above, title never vested in Grant because the deed to him was never delivered. Consequently, Grant had nothing to convey to Bonnie. Therefore, the fact that Bonnie paid only nominal consideration is irrelevant — even if she had paid full consideration, she still would have received nothing!

(C) is not the best response,

because Grant never received title, regardless of the fact that he eventually satisfied the conditions that Olivia had announced.

As described in the analysis of Choice (B), nothing passed to Grant, because there was no delivery. The fact that Grant later satisfied Olivia's oral conditions is irrelevant — the statement of conditions was at most a promise to make a conveyance in the future, and satisfaction of those conditions would not cause delivery to automatically occur. So even assuming that Grant met the previously-announced conditions eventually, Olivia would still be treated as never having made delivery. Since Olivia never made delivery, there never was any-

thing for Grant to convey to Bonnie. (By the way, if the eventual satisfaction of the conditions *did* cause delivery to be "retroactively valid," which it didn't, then by the doctrine of "estoppel by deed" or "after-acquired title," Bonnie might indeed end up with title, as this choice asserts.)

(D) is not the best response,

because Bonnie had no interest to record.

A deed that is defective, meaning that one of the formalities was not met or there was a failure of delivery, may be void or voidable. A deed that is found to be void will be set aside by a court, even if the property has been passed to a bona fide purchaser.

The deed Grant conveyed to Bonnie is void, because Grant had no interest to convey to Bonnie (for the delivery-related reasons described in the analysis of Choice (C)). Since Bonnie had no interest in Richacre to record, the fact that she recorded was meaningless. (Note that this would be true even if Bonnie had been a bona fide purchaser for value, which she wasn't — the $1 was obviously sham consideration, and was not enough to make her a purchaser for "value.")

Answer 2

(B) is the best response,

because consideration is not required to make a deed valid.

The valid execution of a deed requires several formalities. The presence of consideration, however, is not one of them. Therefore, even if Owner was able to prove that no money had in fact been paid by Purchaser, notwithstanding the recitation, and that no other consideration of any kind had been supplied by Purchaser, Owner would still lose.

(A) is not the best response,

because Purchaser's recording did not end Owner's right to bring suit.

The principal function of recording acts is to give a subsequent purchaser a way to check the chain of title of a piece of land.

Owner should lose, but not for the reason given. Purchaser's act of recording would not prevent Owner from recovering. One of the things that recording does is to create a rebuttable presumption that the recorded instrument is valid. Owner could still challenge the validity of the deed, i.e., rebut the presumption. However, under these facts, the deed was authentic and validly delivered, notwithstanding the lack of consideration and the false recital about it; therefore, Owner's attempt to rebut the presumption of validity from recording would fail.

(C) is not the best response,

because whether consideration was paid (and therefore how the existence of consideration can be proved) is irrelevant.

As described in the analysis of Choice (B), consideration is not required for a deed to be valid. Consequently, the fact that the parole evidence rule might allow the recitation of consideration to be proved false (a true statement), is irrelevant.

(D) is not the best response,

because the deed was valid, not an ineffective void instrument.

It's true that recordation does not validate an invalid conveyance, such as a forged or undelivered deed. However, that rule does not apply to these facts: the deed Owner gave to Purchaser is valid, since consideration is not required for the valid execution of a deed. Therefore, Owner will lose, not prevail.

Answer 3

(B) is the best response,

because the mortgage attached to the entire property, and payment of 1/2 the total amount therefore did not "free up" a 1/2 undivided interest.

The facts do not indicate whether Alex and Brenda personally guaranteed payment of the mortgage, so Brenda's case for quieting title to her undivided 1/2 interest is strongest if we assume that she did not personally guarantee payment.

But even in this most-favorable-to-Brenda scenario, Marge as mortgagee has a lien on the *entire property*. That is, she received a security interest on the full property — and the concomitant right upon default to conduct a judicial sale of the full property to get her debt repaid — regardless of whether one party paid that party's full share. In other words, Marge is entitled to say, "Who paid what is between the two of you — I've got the right to have the whole property sold at foreclosure if any part of my loan is in default and the default is not wholly cured." That's what happened here. (Brenda's remedy is a suit in contribution against Alex for 1/2 the amount she paid to Marge.)

(A) is not the best response,

because Marge did not have title in Greenacre.

A mortgage is a security interest in a property securing a loan. The fact that the mortgage instrument contained a clause in which Alex and Brenda warranted that they owned the property free of encumbrances (which is what the general warranty clause did) is irrelevant to the issue of whether Brenda is entitled to quiet title. So this choice reaches the right result, but states the wrong reason for it.

(C) is not the best response,

because the equitable doctrine of marshalling does not apply to these facts.

Marshalling is the ranking of assets in a certain order towards the payment of debts. The concept arises in equity, and means that where there are two creditors, with the senior one having two funds to satisfy his debt, that senior creditor must resort first to the fund which is not subject to demand of the junior creditor.

Marshalling would not release the property from Marge's mortgage. The concept is misapplied to this fact pattern, because the doctrine would be one a second mortgagor invoked to protect his interest from Marge's foreclosure. Under these facts there is only one mortgage on Greenacre, and as a party who joined with Alex in making the mortgage on Greenacre, Brenda would not be able to have her interest be released.

(D) is not the best response,

because Brenda would lose even if the cotenancy was joint.

Joint tenancy differs from tenancy in common only with respect to the right of survivorship, which exists as to the former but not the latter. Even had the property been in joint tenancy, the bringing of the suit to have the Brenda's half-interest released would probably have resulted in severance of the joint interest. Therefore, there is no difference in the legal analysis here between the joint-tenancy and tenancy-in-common scenarios.

Answer 4

(B) is the best response,

because tickets to a sporting event are licenses.

A ticket to a sporting event or other public function is virtually always considered a license rather than an easement. A license is a right to use the licensor's land that is revocable at the will of the licensor.

Janet's season tickets to Scorpion's hockey games at the Central Arena constituted a license granted to her by ABC, Inc. Because Janet held only a license, that interest was revocable at the will of the licensor. (If the revocation had been without proper cause, Janet would have a claim for damages, but even then a court would not award her the right to attend games. In the actual event, the fact that Janet violated the announced no-solicitation rule would probably prevent Janet from getting even damages.)

(A) is not the best response,

because ABC's right to revoke Janet's tickets arises under its rights as a licensor, not out of its "right and obligation to control activities..."

A ticket to a sporting event or other public function is nearly always considered a license rather than an easement. A license is a right to use the licensor's land that is revocable at the will of the licensor.

Although ABC may have a right and obligation to control activities on realty it owns, its right to revoke Janet's season tickets arises from the fact that it has issued Janet only a license.

(C) is not the best response,

because licenses issued for value can be revoked.

A ticket to a sporting event or other public function is nearly always considered a license rather than an easement. A license is a right to use the licensor's land that is revocable at the will of the licensor. The fact that the licensee pays value for the license does not change the license's revocability, at least in cases where (as here) the licensee does not honor the rules governing the license.

(D) is not the best response,

because the terms of Janet's license prohibited solicitation.

Janet would not need to be committing a nuisance for ABC to have the right to revoke her license. ABC granted Janet a license in the form of season tickets. That license expressly prohibited licensees from solicitations anywhere within Central Arena at any time and in any manner. When Janet violated this prohibition by soliciting signatures for her petition urging that the coach of the Scorpions be fired, ABC had the right to revoke her license, whether Janet was a "nuisance" or not.

Answer 5

(A) is the best response,

because Tenn's sublease to Agrit leaves Tenn responsible for all 24 months of unpaid rent.

An "assignment" is the transfer by the lessee of his entire interest in the leased premises. If something less, even a term one day less, is transferred, the transfer is not an assignment, but a "sublease." A sublease is a lease executed by the lessee of land or premises to a third person, conveying the same interest the lessee enjoys but for a *shorter term* than that for which the lessee holds. With a sublease, there is a relationship between the lessee and the sublessee, but there is no relationship, no privity of estate, between the lessor and sublessee. Since there is no privity of estate between the two, *the lessor cannot sue the sublessee for rent.*

Tenn's lease of Blackacre to Agrit was a sublease, because it was for a shorter time (1 year) than remained on the original lease (2 years).

Because this was a sublease, there was no privity of estate between Oner and Agrit. Therefore, Oner cannot sue Agrit for the rent not paid during the one year Agrit was in possession of Blackacre.

On the other hand, the creation of the sublease did not release Tenn from his original liability to Oner for the full rent (only a release executed by Oner could do that). Therefore, Tenn is responsible to Oner for the full

unpaid 24 months.

(B), (C) and (D) are not the best response,

because Tenn subleased Blackacre to Agrit, leaving Tenn individually liable for the full amount. See the discussion as to Choice (A).

Answer 6

(B) is the best response,

because the restriction giving grounds for equitable relief was in Peter's deed, but not in the other owners'.

The plaintiffs here are seeking to treat Sal's promise of 1-family-home-only-on-Lot-4 as both a covenant at law (insofar as the suit seeks money damages) and an equitable servitude (insofar as plaintiffs seek an injunction).

Neither a covenant at law nor an equitable servitude is enforceable unless both the burden and the benefit "touch and concern" the appropriate parcel of land. (I.e., the burden must touch and concern the defendant's land and the benefit must touch and concern the plaintiff's land.)

Here, the burden touches Betty's land: when Sal conveyed Lot 2 to Peter and simultaneously exchanged promises that Sal's remaining lot (Lot 4) and Peter's lot (Lot 2) would be restricted to single-family, Sal's promise touched and concerned Lot 4, which is the lot now owned by Betty. Furthermore, Betty was on actual notice of this burden, since the Sal-to-Peter deed was in the title report. So both the burden and the notice requirements for the running of a covenant are satisfied, as to a suit by all plaintiffs.

However, the requirement that the *benefit* have run is more problematic. That is, each plaintiff must show (for both the injunctive relief at equity and the monetary relief at law) that the benefit touched and concerned his or her particular parcel. Here, Peter satisfies this requirement — his lot (Lot 2) was expressly and intentionally benefitted by Sal's promise of the 1-family restriction. So Peter can sue on the promise — he meets all three requirements (running-of-the-burden, running-of-the-benefit and notice-to-the-defendant) for both a legal and an equitable action.

But *the other owners do not meet the running-of-the-benefit requirement.* Each took his lot without restriction, and without any return promise by Sal that Sal's then-remaining parcels would be restricted. Had there been in place a "plan of development" (say, a filed subdivision plat) showing an intent to keep the whole development 1-family residential, these other plaintiffs might succeed with an argument that Sal implicitly promised them that he'd burden his remaining lots consistently with this plan. But the facts do not indicate that any such plan existed at the time Sal sold Lots 1, 3 and 5. Therefore, no benefit of any subsequent promise by Sal was intended to benefit these owners' land, and they thus fail to meet the running-of-the-benefit requirement. Consequently, they cannot recover in either law or equity.

(A) is not the best response,

because there was no common development scheme.

As described in the prior paragraph, had there been a common development scheme in force *at the time Lots 1, 3 and 5 were conveyed*, this choice would probably be correct in saying that the plaintiff could get an injunction. But no common development scheme was in fact in force, so this choice is wrong. (But it's correct in saying that the plaintiffs don't get damages, as described in the analysis of Choice B.)

(C) is not the best response,

because damages may not be awarded to the owners other than Peter.

As noted in the analysis of Choice B, owners cannot recover at law unless they can show that there was an intent to give their parcels the benefit of the restrictive promise. Here, when Sal conveyed Lots 1, 3 and 5, there was no such intent to burden Sal's remaining lots. The fact that Sal later developed such a purpose to burden his lots doesn't help — there must have been an intent-to-burden at the time when Sal still owned the lots in question.

(D) is not the best response,

because the existence of a zoning scheme that allows the activity in question doesn't trump a stricter scheme of covenants.

If the zoning scheme was stricter, it would prevail (landowners can't by mutual agreement cause strict zoning rules to be relaxed). But the converse is not true — indeed, the whole idea of restrictive covenants is that they can be used to forbid uses that are allowed by the zoning rules.

Answer 7

(D) is the best response,

because the restriction was recorded in the deeds from Ollie to Abel and Betty.

Where a promise regarding land use is a negative one — i.e., one forbidding certain uses — the promise is called an "equitable servitude." (The name comes from the fact that an injunction is a form of equitable relief.) So whether Betty can enforce the promise depends on whether the promise is in fact a valid equitable servitude. For a person who is not a party to the original promise to enforce it as a servitude, she must show that the benefit of the promise touched and concerned her land. (If enforcement was sought against one who took from Abel, rather than against Abel himself, Betty would also have to show that the burden touched and concerned the East Peterhill parcel, and that the taker had actual or constructive notice. But since suit is against Abel, the very person whose own deed created the restriction, these requirements need not be met.)

Betty meets the touch-and-concern requirement as to her parcel, because where Lot 1 and Lot 2 are adjacent, a promise that Lot 2 won't be used in a certain way will be interpreted as benefitting the owners of Lot 1 in their use and enjoyment of their land. Since Betty meets the touch-and-concern requirement, she can get an injunction to enforce the equitable servitude even though Abel in effect made the promise to Ollie, not to her. (And this is true regardless of which transfer, to Abel or to Betty, came first, since each restriction applied to the entire Peterhill parcel, including the piece retained by Ollie.)

(A) is not the best response,

because the change does not mean that the court cannot enforce the servitude in good conscience.

There can be extreme circumstances in which a change of land use throughout an entire neighborhood might lead a court to conclude that it should no longer enforce an equitable servitude. But the mere fact that uses inconsistent with the servitude are now prevalent in adjacent parcels would not be enough. That's especially true where, as here, some of the parcels near plaintiff (i.e., any parcel on the West Peterhill side of the municipal line) are used in a way that is consistent with the restriction. See Rest., § 564, Illustr. 1 (change of neighborhood won't be cause for releasing restriction unless the restricted area *as a whole* has changed so as to no longer benefit from continued restriction.)

(B) is not the best response,

because an inconsistent zoning code is not determinative, but is only one element to be considered.

As the last sentence of the discussion of Choice (A) describes, a change of zoning or other change in land-use patterns won't cause a court to refuse enforcement of an otherwise-valid restriction unless the *entire area* in question has changed in such a way that enforcement would be of little value. So if, for instance, all of *both municipalities* surrounding Peterhill were now half-acre-zoned and on actual half-acre parcels (so that only Peterhill remained five-acre-minimum), a court might conclude that the inconsistency of the restriction with the zoning scheme and with the actual land-use patterns justified relaxing the restriction. But where, as here, use patterns on the West Peterhill side are still five-acres, the fact that the zoning code of East Peterhill is inconsistent with five-acre-minimums would not induce the court to relax the enforcement of the servitude.

(C) is not the best response,

because equitable servitudes are enforceable against subsequent purchasers who take with notice.

Courts will enforce an equitable servitude against a subsequent owner of burdened land who took with actual or constructive notice. So if, for instance, Abel sold to Cathy, Cathy would be deemed to have constructive notice of the restriction (it's in her chain of title). Consequently, Betty could get an injunction against Cathy even though Cathy was not an "original grantee." Consequently, the reasoning described in this choice is flatly incorrect.

Answer 8

(C) is the best response,

because Patricia had no notice of Ted's trust.

One who purchases from the record owner of property is eligible for the protection of the recording act, as against someone else who previously took from that same record owner. Here, Ted is the record owner (in fee simple), and Benton is a "prior transferee" from Ted. (That is, Ted created an interest in Benton by the trust document, and this interest was created prior to the conveyance to Patricia). So Patricia is in position to use the recording act to gain protection against Benton as prior transferee from the same grantor (Ted).

Only bona fide purchasers ("BFPs") are entitled to prevail against a prior transferee under recording statutes. To be a BFP, a person must: (1) be a "purchaser" (holder of a fee interest, or mortgagee or creditor), (2) take without notice (actual, constructive or inquiry) of the prior instrument; and (3) pay valuable consideration. Since Patricia (1) holds what purports to be a fee interest, (2) took without either actual or constructive notice (since she couldn't have found anything to indicate the existence of Benton's interest by looking in the public records), and (3) paid fair market value, she meets all of these requirements for getting the benefit of the recording act.

Therefore, the failure of Benton's interest to be recorded means that as against Benton, Patricia's interest takes priority, and Benton's interest is null and void.

(A) is not the best response,

because it ignores the effect of the recording act.

It may be true as a general principle that "a successor in title to the trustee takes title subject to the grantor's trust." But this is subject to the rule that a bona fide purchaser (BFP) from the trustee will take free of the unrecorded instrument by which the BFP's grantor created the trust. (If this were not true, no one could ever safely buy property — there would always be the risk that the grantor had secretly created a trust encumbering the property.)

(B) is not the best response,

because trusts creating equitable interests *are* subject to the recording act.

A beneficiary's interest in a trust is indeed, as this choice suggests, an equitable interest. (The trustee has legal title.) But this choice is false is stating that equitable interests are not subject to recording acts. Because no attempt was made to record the instrument creating the trust, the trust was not in the chain of title and Patricia took Goldacre as a BFP.

(D) is not the best response,

because a trust *was* created, and because this choice ignores the operation of the recording act.

As between Ted and Benton, the property would be deemed to be held in trust for Benton, because the transactions in which Susan conveyed to Ted and Ted later signed the trust document were certainly sufficient to create a trust. The problem is that this trust was an unrecorded instrument, and like any unrecorded instrument *will* be void against a subsequent transferee from the same grantor (Ted) who takes without notice and for value. So this choice predicts the correct result, but on incorrect reasoning.

Answer 9

(D) is the best response,

because the deed was indeed not in Carl's chain of title (since it was recorded before Dawn took title), making Carl a BFP who gets the protection of the recording act.

As between Dawn and Bruce, Bruce could rely on the doctrine of "estoppel by deed" (sometimes called "after-acquired title") to establish that he owns the property. Under this doctrine, one who makes a conveyance of property she doesn't own, and who then acquires that property, is estopped from denying the grantee's superior claim to the property. So if Dawn had never made any conveyance of Blackacre to anyone but Bruce, and Bruce sued Dawn to establish that he now owns the property rather than she, Bruce would win.

But most courts hold that the doctrine of estoppel by deed *does not apply as against a subsequent bona fide purchaser from the original grantor.* That is, most courts would say that as between Carl (the subsequent BFP from Dawn) and Bruce, Bruce cannot rely on the estoppel-by-deed doctrine, even though he recorded his title promptly. The reason is that a contrary rule would mean that Carl would have an immense burden when checking Dawn's title — he would have had to check for conveyances by Dawn dating from *before* the time when, according to the records, Dawn herself got title. For this reason, an *"early recorded document"* (one recorded as a grant by the grantor before the date when the grantor got record title) is in most courts deemed to be *outside the grantor's chain of title*. There's no guarantee that a court would follow this majority view, but (1) the court would probably do so; and (2) if the court did so, Carl would win.

(A) is not the best response,

because it ignores the possible application of the estoppel-by-deed / after-acquired-title doctrine.

This doctrine (which is summarized in the discussion of Choice (D) above) would mean that Bruce did indeed get title, even though Bruce got nothing at the time of the purported conveyance two years ago. So although Choice (A) is factually correct, it doesn't explain why Carl would win.

(B) is not the best response,

because nothing would delay Bruce's deed from taking effect.

There is nothing under these facts which would make Bruce's deed take effect after Carl's. It's possible that the doctrine of estoppel-by-deed (see the analysis in Chioce (D)) might apply. But even if it did, the doctrine would cause the conveyance from Dawn to Bruce to "relate back" to the date Dawn delivered the instrument to Bruce, not the date Dawn herself got record title. So this choice doesn't explain how things would work. (And in any event, the estoppel-by-deed doctrine probably would apply as against a subsequent purchaser for value like Carl.)

(C) is not the best response,

because Carl's possession would not give him rights greater than Bruce's fee simple.

Priority in possession generally does not affect who wins in a dispute between two people who have received conveyances of the same property. Therefore, if one ignores the possible effect of the estoppel-by-deed doctrine (see the analysis in Choice (D)), the fact that Bruce recorded before Carl would cause Bruce to win in a dispute between him and Carl even though Carl took possession first. (The fact that Carl was in possession would have put Bruce on inquiry notice of Carl's interest after the time that Carl took possession. So if Carl had received an unrecorded conveyance *before* Bruce did, Bruce might have been deprived of the ability to use the recording act. But here, Bruce, not Carl, has recorded first, so the state of Bruce's knowledge about Carl's interest is irrelevant.)

Answer 10

(D) is the best response,

because the forged release was not effective, and recording this forged document had no effect.

A person who procures record title by forging (and then recording) a deed has nothing to convey. The grantee then gets nothing, despite the apparently perfect record title. (This problem points up a major problem of recording acts — if a person procures title by a forged document that she then records, a prospective grantee from that person has no way to determine from inspection of the records that she is taking nothing. That's one of the risks that title insurance guards against.)

Therefore, Opal's forged document saying that she had unencumbered title to Lot 5 was of no effect, even when recorded. Eva loses despite the absolutely perfect appearance of Opal's record title.

(A) is not the best response,

because an owner of an interest has no obligation to check the public records to guard against fraud.

As explained in the analysis of choice (D), the forgery here was not effective. Consequently, Bank was entitled to sit back and ignore the state of the public records. A person who already holds a recorded interest has no "duty to check the records" to guard against a subsequent forgery, and thus cannot be "negligent."

(B) is not the best response,

because Eva was not entitled to rely on the records as protection against a forgery in her grantor's chain of title.

A forged instrument is void. It's void against the forger, of course, but more interestingly it's also void against one who takes from the forger (or even against anyone down the chain from the forger, until the statute of limitations has run). So Eva was not "entitled to rely on the recorded release" as a guarantee that her grantor did not obtain her an unencumbered interest by fraud.

(C) is not the best response,

because even if Eva couldn't have discovered the alteration by reasonable inquiry she would still lose.

It's true that Eva could have seen from the public records that Bank once had a mortgage on the parcel. So Eva could theoretically have asked the Bank, "Did you really release your lien on Lot 5?", and Bank might well have answered, "No." But even if a court were to rule that Eva had reason to be suspicious enough to check with Bank, or even if the court were to conclude that Bank wouldn't have answered her inquiry, Eva would still lose. That's because of the general rule (described in the discussion of Choice (D)) that a forged instrument, even when perfectly recorded, is completely ineffective when relied on by a subsequent grantee.

Answer 11

(B) is the best response,

because creditors are probably not "purchasers for value" as required for protection under the recording act.

Some recording acts have language that specifically protects judgment creditors who file their judgment after the debtor has made an unrecorded conveyance. But where the language of the recording act is ambiguous about whether judgment creditors are covered (e.g., where, as here, "purchasers for value" are what are covered), most courts have interpreted the statute so as not to cover the judgment creditor. There is no guarantee that a court would interpret the statute in this anti-creditor way, but that's at least a possibility, and of the four choices this is the most likely explanation for an anti-creditor result. (Remember, you're not asked to say how the case will come out — you're merely asked to say what the most likely rationale will be *if* the case is decided for Bryer.)

A second rationale for Cred's loss, by the way, is that

the judgment lien statute here gives a lien on "property then owned or subsequently acquired" by the debtor — a court could very plausibly conclude that this language is limited to "property then *actually* owned," not "property then owned as of record," by the debtor.

(A) is not the best response,

because the doctrine of equitable conversion does not apply to these facts.

The doctrine of equitable conversion applies to conflicts between grantor and grantee arising during the gap between the signing of the contract and the delivery of the deed. (For instance, a structure on the property may be destroyed during the gap, in which case the doctrine would mean that Bryer would be viewed as the equitable owner at the time of destruction, and would be required to close.) Equitable conversion might apply in this scenario if Cred filed her judgment during the gap (i.e., between the time when Owen contracted to sell and when he made the conveyance). But once Owen made the conveyance while Cred had not yet filed her judgment, the equitable conversion doctrine had no further application.

(C) is not the best response,

because Owen's possession would not suggest Owen had sold Blackacre to Bryer.

Under a recording statute like the one here, a subsequent bona fide purchaser (i.e., a person who gives valuable consideration and has no actual or constructive notice of the prior instrument) prevails over a prior grantee who failed to record. If Cred was trying to become covered by the recording act, and *Bryer* was in possession at the time Cred filed her lien, the fact that Bryer (not Owen, the record owner) was in possession at the date of lien filing might have been enough to cause Bryer to lose, since this possession might have put her on inquiry notice that Owen was perhaps no longer the owner. But the fact that *Owen* was still in possession didn't put Bryer on notice of anything, so it's irrelevant on these facts.

(D) is not the best response,

because being a purchaser without notice only helps the *subsequent* "purchaser" gain protection of the recording act, and the person seeking protection of the act here is Cred, not Bryer.

Recording acts protect the second, not the first, purchaser in certain circumstances. Here, it would be Cred (who can argue that she "purchased" by filing her lien), not Bryer, who is trying to get the protection of the recording act. It is the person seeking the protection of the recording act (the second purchaser), not the person resisting application of the act (the first purchaser) who needs to be "without notice." So here, the notice status of Cred might well matter (if the recording act otherwise applied to judgment lien creditors). But the notice status of Bryer, the first "purchaser," does not matter at all.

Answer 12

(C) is the best response,

because it correctly identifies the result, due to operation of the doctrine of equitable conversion. Under the doctrine of equitable conversion, during the period between the land sale contract and the conveyance, the purchaser is considered the beneficial owner of the property, and the seller has a personal property interest in the purchase price. If the seller dies before the conveyance takes place, the one entitled to his personal property is entitled to the purchase price (the one entitled to his *real* property only gets a bare legal title, which he must convey to the purchaser when the purchaser performs his duty under the contract, i.e., turns over the cash). Under these facts, Perry is entitled to Seller's personalty, so he gets all the semolians from the sale, and Rose is out of luck. Since C correctly identifies this result, it's the best response.

(A) is not the best response,

because death does not terminate a land sale contract. As long as the land sale contract is specifically enforceable, if the vendor dies before the conveyance takes place, the one to whom he willed his personal property is entitled to the purchase price, when the conveyance takes place. This is part of the doctrine of equitable conversion. If you chose this response, it could be because you thought it was covered by Restatement of Contracts §48, which terminates an *offer* on the death or insanity of either the offeror or the offeree. That's not involved here, since there's an enforceable contract already in place. Since A states the wrong rule, it's not the best response.

(B) is not the best response,

because it arrives at the wrong conclusion and states, wrongly, that the doctrine of equitable conversion does not apply to these circumstances. In fact, the doctrine of equitable conversion *does* apply to these circumstances, and its operation means that the person entitled to Seller's personal property, Perry, is entitled to the purchase price. Under the doctrine of equitable conversion, during the period between the land sale contract and the conveyance, the purchaser is considered the beneficial owner of the property, and the seller has a personal property interest in the purchase price. If the seller dies before the conveyance takes place, the one entitled to his personal property is entitled to the purchase price (the one entitled to his *real* property only gets a bare legal title, which he must convey to the purchaser when the purchaser performs his duty under the contract, i.e., turns over the cash). Since B does not state the correct rule, and arrives at the incorrect conclusion, it's not the best response.

(D) is not the best response,

because it misstates the rule of law, and, in any case, the concept of marketable title is irrelevant to these facts. Title is not rendered unmarketable by the Seller's death. A marketable title is one which, viewed objectively, is free from reasonable doubt in both law and fact, and which the reasonable buyer would accept without fear of litigation. The conveyance of marketable title is an implied covenant in land sale contracts (however, the terms of the *deed* will control once the deed is conveyed; thus, if a quit claim deed is conveyed, there will be no obligation to provide marketable title). Here, the mere fact that Seller died would not render the title unmarketable. Since the doctrine of equitable conversion is followed in the jurisdiction, there's no question that the one entitled to Seller's personal property – Perry – will be entitled to the purchase price. Thus, there is no reasonable doubt as to law and fact, and there should be no reasonable fear of litigation. In any case, the marketability of the title is not at issue here. While the conveyance of marketable title is an implied covenant in land sale contracts, it need only be marketable when the deed is conveyed; beyond that, if the deed does not contain appropriate warranties (e.g., it's a quitclaim deed), there will be no warranties of title at all. Since D misstates the law and does not apply to these facts, it's not the best response.

Answer 13

(A) is the best response,
because it correctly cites the result under the doctrine of equitable conversion, which you're told is the law in this jurisdiction (and which, in fact, most states follow). Under the doctrine of equitable conversion, if the purchaser dies during the existence of an enforceable land contract, the right to receive the land goes to his heir. Thus, as A states, the heir will be able to specifically enforce the contract. Since A states the correct rule as it applies to these facts, it's the best response.

(B) is not the best response,
because it misstates the law. Under the doctrine of equitable conversion, when the purchaser dies during the existence of an enforceable land sale contract, the right to receive the land goes to the buyer's heir (although the duty to pay is imposed on the buyer's personal representative). Thus, as long as the contract is enforceable – and the facts here indicate that there has been no breach of the agreement – the Seller does not have the right to return the down payment and cancel the contract. Since B states otherwise, it is not the best response.

(C) is not the best response,
because it misstates the law. Death does not terminate a land sale contract. As long as the land sale contract is specifically enforceable, if the vendee dies before the conveyance takes place, his heir is entitled to receive the land. This is part of the doctrine of equitable conversion, which you're told is recognized in this jurisdiction. If you chose this response, it could be because

you thought this situation was covered by Restatement of Contracts §48, which terminates an *offer* on the death or insanity of either the offeror or the offeree. That's not involved here, because the facts have progressed beyond the offer stage – there's an enforceable contract. Since C doesn't recognize this, it's not the best response.

(D) is not the best response,
because it both misstates the law, and does not apply to these facts. First, the title here is, in fact, marketable. A marketable title is one which, viewed objectively, is free from reasonable doubt in both law and fact, and which the reasonable buyer would accept without fear of litigation. The conveyance of marketable title is an implied covenant in land sale contracts (however, the terms of the *deed* will control once the deed is conveyed; thus, if a quit claim deed is conveyed, there will be no obligation to provide marketable title). Here, buyer's death would not render the title unmarketable, since, under the doctrine of equitable conversion, it's clear what happens to buyer's rights and duties: His heir receives the right to receive the land, and the duty to pay the purchase price is imposed on the buyer's personal representative. Furthermore, marketable title is not relevant to these facts, since it would refer to the quality of title contracted to be conveyed by Seller; thus, Buyer's death, and who accepts his rights and obligations, is not in issue. Since D states otherwise, it's not the best response.

Answer 14

(B) is the best response,
because it recognizes that a grant "to A and his heirs" is a grant of a fee simple interest.

A literal reading of the grant "to Albert and his heirs" would suggest that Albert's heirs take something. But a gift "to A and his heirs" has always been interpreted to mean the grant of a fee simple interest to A, with A's heirs taking nothing. Consequently, Albert had the ability to convey that same fee simple to Bea, which he did, and the fact that Donna did not join the deed is irrelevant (she had no interest to convey or not convey).

(A), (C) and (D) are not the best response,
because each choice incorrectly suggests that Donna received an interest as Albert's "heir."

Answer 15

(A) is the best response,
because Pam would have to assume Bart's mortgage to be liable under it.

When a person buys a mortgaged property without assuming the mortgage, the buyer has no liability on the mortgage. That's true even if the mortgage contains a due-on-sale clause — the clause will be enforced (and will entitle the mortgagee to accelerate the mortgage), but the clause won't cause the buyer to be deemed to have assumed the mortgage.

(B) is not the best response,

because privity of estate is not an issue in mortgage cases.

Privity of estate makes a difference in cases involving covenants at law — absence of privity of estate means that a successor to the covenantor won't be bound. But a mortgage is not a covenant running with the land, so privity of estate doesn't matter.

(C) is not the best response,

because Pam was not a party to the mortgage agreement.

A due-on-sale clause allows a lender to demand full payment of the remainder of an existing loan if the mortgagor transfers any interest in the property securing the loan without the lender's consent. The violation of the due-on-sale clause would give Mort grounds for a case against Bart, and grounds to accelerate the mortgage, but not grounds to obtain a personal judgment against Pam. Pam did not assume Bart's debt to Mort, and the violation of the due-on-sale clause did not change this fact.

(D) is not the best response,

because a mortgage is not a covenant running with the land, making privity of estate irrelevant.

Privity of estate makes a difference in cases involving covenants running with land. A covenant running with land is simply a contract between two parties, which, because it meets certain technical requirements, has the additional quality that it is binding against one who later buys the promisor's land. In determining whether a covenant runs with the land, one of the requirements is that there be privity of estate between the parties.

However, a mortgage is not a covenant running with the land. Therefore, the existence or non-existence of privity of estate as between Mort and Pam is irrelevant — Mort would only prevail against Pam if Pam expressly assumed the mortgage that existed between Bart and Mort, which she didn't.

Answer 16

(D) is the best response,

because Anna's use of the easement put Bank on notice of her interest, preventing Bank from being a purchaser "without notice" who is entitled to the protection of the recording act.

Under a recording statute like the one here, a subsequent BFP prevails over a prior grantee who failed to record by the time of the subsequent grant. But the statute gives subsequent purchaser protection only if she had no actual or constructive notice at the time of the conveyance.

The subsequent grantee will be deemed to have notice not only of matters of which he has "actual" notice, and of matters that are shown by the public records ("record notice"), but also of any matter as to which the grantee is (or should be) in possession of facts which would lead the grantee to make an investigation. This is called *"inquiry notice."* One source of inquiry notice is that if the property is in possession of one other than the record owner, the prospective grantee is under a duty to inquire about the facts that put that person into possession (since the reason may be that the possessor has an unrecorded interest).

Here, the Bank should have noticed that though the strip was shown as belonging to Beth's parcel, it was "possessed" by Anna in the form of the driveway. Had Bank made inquiry of Anna, she would (presumably) have told Bank about her easement. Consequently, Bank is deemed to have been on notice of Anna's easement, preventing Bank from being the "subsequent purchaser for value and without notice" required for protection under the recording statute. Since Anna's interest precedes Bank's, Bank could win only with the protection of the recording act, so it loses.

(A) is not the best response,

because the late recording would not have prevented Anna's rights from being subordinate to Bank's if Bank was a BFP without notice.

Recording the easement deed prior to the foreclosure action would not protect Anna's rights. If Bank was a BFP without notice of Anna's interest at the time Bank made the mortgage, Anna's interest would be subordinate to Bank's recorded mortgage, and the fact that Anna later (after the mortgage) recorded would not change this. (You can see how this would have to work this way if lenders are to be able to lend in reliance on the records — once the loan is made, the lender needs to be able to be confident that no later-filed interest can take priority over its own interest.)

(C) is not the best response,

because it ignores the operation of the recording act, and in any event misstates how the assignment of appurtenant easements works.

The easement here is, indeed, "appurtenant" rather than "in gross." (That is, it pertains to a particular benefitted parcel, Blackacre.) It's true that an easement appurtenant generally passes with the property — so if Anna sold Blackacre, the easement would pass with Blackacre, rather than being extinguished.

But here, these mechanics are irrelevant (for one thing, Anna isn't transferring her interest in Blackacre). The recording act operates completely separately from the assignment of appurtenant easements — the easement is an interest in Whiteacre, and needed to be recorded if it was not to be subordinated to a BFP of Whiteacre. (In other words, it was only Bank's inquiry notice that prevented Bank from getting protection of the recording statute vis a vis Anna's easement).

Answer 17

(A) is the best response,
because Lender One's judgment lien on the garage came ahead of Owner's equity.

When Lender One filed its judgment for the amount owed on the hotel, that lender got a lien against the garage (as well as against the hotel) for the full amount owed on the garage. So at that moment, Lender One was in the position of a second mortgagee on the garage, behind Lender Two.

Then, when Lender One purchased the hotel for $100,000 less than the mortgage balance, Lender One obtained a deficiency judgment for that $100,000 amount. This became the amount covered by the earlier-filed judgment lien, and was secured by a second position on the garage. (It's irrelevant that the hotel was bought by Lender One: the same result, a $100,000 second-position lien for Lender One on the garage, would have come into existence regardless of who bought the hotel at foreclosure, if the price paid was $100,000 less than the balance due.)

When Lender One paid $200,000 more than the outstanding Lender Two mortgage balance for the garage, this $200,000 amount was "excess," and was required to be handled the same way as if Lender Two had had no mortgage and the total purchase price was $200,000. That is, Lender One's lien now moved to first position, and was entitled to be paid in full before anything went to the equity owner (Owner). So Lender One got the first $100,000 of the excess. The balance, $100,000, went to the equity owner (Owner).

(B), (C) and (D), are not the best response,
since they involve computations that are inconsistent with this analysis. (In particular, you should have been able to immediately eliminate choices (B) and (C), since these involved payments to Lender Two. Like any mortgagee, Lender Two was not entitled to any money brought in by a foreclosure that was in excess of the money then owed to it on the mortgage.)

Answer 18

(C) is the best response,
because Betty's actions made the oral contract enforceable.

The Statute of Frauds requires that a promise to transfer or buy any interest in land be in writing. However, even if an oral contract for the transfer of an interest in land is not enforceable at the time it is made due to the lack of a writing, *subsequent acts* by the parties may render it enforceable. Under the "part performance" exception to the Statute, a party who takes action in reliance on the oral agreement will be permitted to gain enforcement of it, provided that the acts taken in part performance are "unequivocally referable" to the alleged oral agreement, i.e., are not adequately explained by some other facet of the parties' relationship.

Here, if all that had happened was that after the oral agreement, Betty had kept making approximately the same monthly payment to Abel that she had always made, Betty would have been out of luck — the court would likely have ruled that these payments could simply have been continued rents, and were therefore not "unequivocally referable" to the purchase agreement. But here, Betty paid the $25,000 in original cash, the taxes, the insurance premiums, and the maintenance costs — all things that she hadn't paid before the oral agreement. So a court would be convinced that these "extra" payments were unequivocally referable to the alleged oral agreement, since they could not be explained by the prior landlord-tenant arrangement.

(A) is not the best response,
because Betty's actions made the oral promise which violated the Statute of Frauds enforceable.

The part performance doctrine, where applicable, furnishes an exception to the Statute of Frauds. See the analysis of Choice (C) for an explanation of how and why the doctrine applies here.

(B) is not the best response,
because Betty had an enforceable contract to buy the property.

If the court had ruled that the oral agreement didn't qualify for the part performance doctrine, this might have been a correct answer (since if the court didn't enforce the oral agreement, it's unlikely that Abel would have been permitted to retain the $25,000). But as described in Choice (C) above, the oral agreement did qualify for the part performance doctrine, so the contract was enforceable.

(D) is not the best response,
because the answer incorrectly states the applicable law.

The Statute of Frauds generally applies to contracts for the purchase of land — there's no exception for "purchase and sale agreements between landlords and tenants in possession." Part performance may sometimes take a contract out of the Statute, but Choice (D) states a broad principle that's simply incorrect.

Answer 19

(A) is the best response,
because under an installment contract, marketable title need not be delivered until after the last payment.

Ordinarily, the obligation to convey a marketable title is implied. So Vendor has the obligation to convey a marketable title (among other things, a title free from encumbrances such as unsatisfied mortgages) after all installment payments have been made.

There can be circumstances in which the buyer under an installment provision has reasonable grounds for worrying about whether the vendor will be able to convey marketable title when the time comes (e.g., the vendor simply doesn't seem to have record title at all). If the buyer has such grounds for insecurity, most courts say she can demand reasonable assurances that the defect will be cured, and if the assurances are not forthcoming, can rescind or sue for breach.

But here, there are no grounds that would make a reasonable buyer insecure about whether marketable title will ultimately be forthcoming, given that the mortgage is small relative to the value of the property, that Vendor is solvent and pays the mortgage on time each month, and that 97% of the purchase price remains to be paid (so that Purchaser will have ample time to see whether the mortgage is continuing to be paid). Consequently, the fact that a very curable encumbrance happens to exist at the moment will not constitute a breach by Vendor.

(B) is not the best response,

because possession did not cause Purchaser to assume the risk that Vendor would end up not being able to convey marketable title.

A vendee who takes under an installment contract — and who (as is usually the case) takes possession before the installments are fully paid — does not "assume the risk" that the vendor won't be able to convey good title. If, for instance, the vendee has reasonable grounds for worrying about whether the vendor will have the ability to convey marketable title down the road, the vendee may be entitled to reasonable assurances that there won't be a problem (see discussion of Choice (A) above).

(C) is not the best response,

because although an obligation to convey marketable title is implied in the absence of an express agreement to the contrary, Vendor hasn't breached that obligation.

Unless the contract of sale otherwise expressly states, courts find an implied duty to convey a marketable title. The reference here to "a warranty deed sufficient to convey the fee simple" — although somewhat vague about just what type of deed has been promised — will not be found to constitute an express provision that marketable title is not required. So, since the promise is ambiguous, the usual presumption in favor of an obligation to convey marketable title will be applied. The fact that this is an installment contract does not change that presumption. However, for the reasons stated in Choice (A), Vendor has not breached that obligation, making this choice wrong.

(D) is not the best response,

because risk of loss relating to possession would not be grounds on which Purchaser could recover.

It's true that any "risk of loss" assumed by Purchaser would relate only to physical events (e.g., destruction of a structure on the land). But the fact that "risk of loss" doesn't apply does not by itself mean that Purchaser can recover damages now. Indeed, for the rea-

son given in Choice (A) (time to deliver marketable title hasn't yet arrived), Purchaser will lose, not win, so Choice (D) can't be correct.

Answer 20

(C) is the best response,

because it correctly identifies that the restriction will be enforceable by any owner in the Royal Oaks subdivision. The basis for this is an implied reciprocal servitude, which is a means by which a subsequent property owner can be bound by a covenant even if it is not present in his own deed, as long as the restriction is in deeds from the same grantor to prior purchasers, typically in the same subdivision. The prior purchasers can enforce the servitudes as long as the restriction in the earlier deeds resulted from a *general plan,* under a covenant that all properties later conveyed would be burdened by the same restriction, and the prior purchasers relied on same. There must also be notice of the restriction, either actual, constructive, or implied. This applies to the facts here. There is a general plan for Royal Oaks, and the restrictions in the deeds suggest that all lots in Royal Oaks would be so bound, and would be enforceable by any lot owner in Royal Oaks. Even if the restriction were not present in every deed, there would be, at the very least, implied notice, since a look at the subdivision would indicate that such a restriction exists (since it would be entirely populated by single-family homes). Since Royal Oaks satisfies the requirements of an implied reciprocal servitude, the current owners will be able to enforce the restriction. Since C recognizes this, it's the best response.

(A) is not the best response,

because the restriction here would be constitutional. Thus, even with judicial recognition, there would not be any conflict with the Fourteenth Amendment to the Constitution. It's when the restriction is *discriminatory* that judicial recognition would be state action in conflict with the Fourteenth Amendment. In these facts, however, there is nothing to suggest that the restriction would be unenforceable; single family restrictions are fairly common. If you chose this response, you may have been thinking of the Constitutional Law case Moore v. City of East Cleveland (1977), in which the Supreme Court found a fundamental right for related people to live together in a household, and any zoning ordinance violating this would be subject to strict scrutiny (and thus likely be a due process violation). When you think about it, that's not terribly close to these facts. Since A mistakenly states that the restriction would be unenforceable, it's not the best response.

(B) is not the best response,

because it's irrelevant. Whether or not the single-family restriction on Royal Oaks is enforceable depends on whether there is a valid restriction on the use of that land itself; in fact, there is a valid restriction in the form of an implied reciprocal servitude. Contrary to what B states, Owner's non-restricted acreage would not bear on whether or not the restriction on the 100 acres involved here is enforceable, and thus the concept of "conflict of interest" is misapplied. As a result, B is not the best response.

(D) is not the best response,

because it does not correctly apply the law. Enforcement of the restriction would be through a claim that the restriction was an implied reciprocal servitude. The correct remedy for breach of an implied reciprocal servitude is not damages, but an injunction to enforce the restriction. Option D is a muddle, because either the restriction is enforceable, in which case the other landowners would be entitled to an injunction against an errant landowner – or it's unenforceable, in which case each landowner need only comply with zoning restrictions. If the restriction *were* unenforceable, then the other landowners would certainly not be entitled to damages from a landowner violating the restriction. Since D states otherwise, it's not the best response.

Answer 21

(D) is the best response,

because it identifies the greatest obstacle to Owner's plan to have the Royal Oaks owners be able to enforce the single-family restriction against any new owners in the new 100 acres. In order to be able to enforce the restriction, the restriction would have to be characterized as an implied reciprocal servitude. The prior purchasers can enforce the servitudes as long as the restriction in the earlier deeds resulted from a *general plan,* oral or written, that all properties later conveyed would be burdened by the same restriction, and the prior purchasers relied on same. There must also be notice of the restriction to the subsequent property owner in order to bind him. The factor which will pose the greatest problem under these facts is characterizing the new 100 acres as being part of the same general plan as Royal Oaks. Note that option D does not *resolve* this issue, but merely states that Owner's *chance for success* depends on the resolution of this issue. Nonetheless, since D correctly identifies the central issue, it's the best response.

(A) is not the best response,

because the zoning will not bear on whether the restriction is enforceable. Naturally, if the restriction called for a use which was impermissible under the applicable zoning provision – e.g., the restriction called for strictly commercial use, in an area zoned strictly residential – then the zoning *would* prohibit enforcement of the restriction. However, when the zoning is less restrictive than the restriction, the enforceability of the restriction will have to be determined on its own merits. Under these facts, this will be determined by analyzing whether Royal Oaks and the new acreage could be considered a common development scheme, whereby the current owners could enforce the restriction as an implied reciprocal servitude. Since A focuses instead on zoning, it's not the best response.

(B) is not the best response,

because the restriction on the 200 acre shopping center will not be determinative of the enforceability of the restriction on the new, 100 acres. The restriction here, if enforceable by Royal Oaks lot owners as well as other owners in the new 100 acres, will be characterized as an implied reciprocal servitude. As an equitable restriction, a court would refuse to enforce it if it were inequitable to do so – if, for instance, the surrounding property had changed in use so as to make the property unsalable with the restriction. However, the mere proximity to a shopping center would not make enforcement of the single-family restriction inequitable. Thus, since B states otherwise, it's not the best response.

(C) is not the best response,

because Owner *will* be able to restrict the use to residential use. In fact, it's not the restriction as to the new 100 acres that is the difficult part of this question, but Owner's desire that the owners of Royal Oaks lots also be able to enforce the restriction! Owner can easily impose the residential restriction on, at the very least, the buyers of the new lots, by inserting a covenant in each deed, as long as this compares with applicable zoning laws. Since C states that Owner will not be able to impose *any* enforceable restriction to residential use on the new lots, it's not the best response.

Answer 22

(B) is the best response,

because it recognizes that, even though quality of title to be conveyed was not mentioned in the land sale contract, the requirement of conveying marketable title will be *implied*. The key fact here is that, since the conveyance hasn't yet taken place, the provisions of the land sale contract – including the implied warranty of marketable title – control. Marketable title is title which, viewed objectively, is free from reasonable doubt in both law and fact, and which the reasonable buyer would accept without fear of litigation. On a related matter, note that if Scott, in fact, accepts a quitclaim deed to the property, the terms of the deed will control *over* the terms of the land sale contract, under the doctrine of merger. Since a quitclaim deed conveys only Chase's interest in the property, whatever it is, without warranties of any kind, Scott would not thereafter be able to sue for breach of the implied covenant of marketable title in the land sale contract. Nonetheless, under the facts here, B states the correct rule – that Chase has a contractual obligation to convey marketable title, since that requirement is implied in land sale contracts. Thus, B is the best response.

(A) is not the best response,

because although it's correct, it doesn't address these facts as precisely as option B. The lack of mention as to the quality of title to be conveyed will not render the contract unenforceable, it's true. But this ignores the language in the question addressing the "quality of title" conveyed. A more precise answer would address not only the contract's enforceability, but the quality of title issue, also. Option B does just that. It not only recognizes that the contract will be enforceable, but goes one step further and states that the conveyance of marketable title will be an implied covenant. Since A is not as precise as another option, it's not the best response.

(C) is not the best response,

because the lack of mention of the quality of title to be conveyed does not mean that Chase need only convey what he owned on the date of the contract. Chase is bound by the terms of the land sale contract, which includes implied requirement to convey marketable title. Marketable title is title which, viewed objectively, is free from reasonable doubt in both law and fact, and which the reasonable buyer would accept without fear of litigation. If you chose this response, you confused the land sale contract with a quitclaim deed. A quitclaim deed is a deed completely without warranties (and a deed has no implied warranties). Thus, if these facts went further – and Chase conveyed the land to Scott via a quitclaim deed – Chase would, in fact, only convey what he owned at the time of the conveyance itself, *with no warranties* (that's because the land sale contract is "merged into" the deed, such that the contract's provisions don't matter once the deed is transferred). In any case, since C states an incorrect rule of law, it's not the best response.

(D) is not the best response,

because it does not state the correct rule of law. Chase is bound by the terms of the land sale contract, as well as the implied requirement to convey marketable title. Thus, his actual ownership is not relevant in terms of his obligation – if he does not convey what he contracted to convey, he'll be liable for breach. If you chose this response, it may be because you confused a land sale contract without reference to quality of title with a quitclaim deed. Under a quitclaim deed, there are no warranties, and the vendor conveys only his interest in the property, whatever it is. Once the deed is conveyed, the terms of the deed – not the land sale contract – control, under the doctrine of merger. However, under these facts, it's the land sale contract that's in force, with its implied covenant of marketable title. Alternatively, if you chose option D, you may have been thinking of the "After-Acquired Title Doctrine," also known as "Estoppel by Deed." The doctrine covers this situation: Grantor purports to convey an estate larger than the one he has; grantor subsequently acquires the title he's already purportedly conveyed;

title *automatically* passes to Grantee, by estoppel. This doctrine is not applicable here, because it involves conveyances themselves, not land sale contracts. Under these facts, it's the land sale contract that controls, since there's been no conveyance yet. Since D provides otherwise, and conditions Chase's obligation to convey only on what he actually owns by the time of the conveyance, it's not the best response.

Answer 23

(A) is the best response,

because the easement was fixed and Charlie did not have right to move it.

There are various ways of creating an easement. One of those ways is by express grant. That is what happened here. Although Charlie might argue that the grant of a "right of way" was the grant of a revocable license rather than of an easement, this argument would fail — the reference in the document to Baker "and her heirs" would convince a court that a permanent interest in land (i.e., an easement), not a revocable personal license, was intended.

The easement by express grant did not, of course, fix the location in the document. However, when Able acquiesced in Baker's building of the driveway over a particular strip of Able's property, this acquiescence acted to fix the location of the easement as being the driveway. Once that location was definitively fixed, neither Able nor his successor Charlie had the right to compel the easement holder (whether the holder was Baker or Baker's successor Dorcas) to move the location, no matter how unburdensome moving that location would have been for the easement holder.

(B) is not the best response,

because the location of the easement was fixed by grant, not prescription.

Easements can certainly be created by prescription. But that's not what happened here — rather, the easement was created by grant. Then, Able's acquiescence in having the driveway run over particular land acted to fix the location, but this, too, happened by permission, not by prescription. So this choice explains the right result by the wrong reasoning.

(C) is not the best response,

because Dorcas had the right to refuse to move the easement, regardless of the new location's reasonableness.

Once the location of the easement was fixed by the express grant in the document, together with Able's acquiescence to Baker's choice of location, that route became permanently associated with the easement, and became an interest in land. When an easement has been established over a particular route, the holder cannot be forced to accept a different route, no matter how "reasonable" the suggestion of a different route may be.

(D) is not the best response,

because the easement was defined by Able and Baker's use.

If an easement is created but not specifically located on the servient tenement, a location of sufficient size to make the intended use reasonably convenient will be implied. The owner of the servient tenement may indeed select the location of the easement so long as her selection is reasonable.

However, once the owner of the servient tenement selects the reasonable route (or acquiesces in the dominant holder's choice, as happened here), that route becomes fixed, and the dominant holder can't later be forced to allow the servient owner to change the route. So the fact that Able might have been permitted to select the original location of the right-of-way became irrelevant once the driveway was built and used.

Answer 24

(B) is the best response,

because the physical danger from debris and tree limbs may well constitute a substantial and unreasonable interference with Adam's use and enjoyment of his property.

A claim for "private nuisance" (which is the sort of nuisance claim that Adam is bringing here) occurs when the defendant unreasonably and substantially interferes with the plaintiff's use and enjoyment of his land. The fact that defendant maintains a condition on defendant's land that poses a substantial danger of causing a damaging physical invasion of plaintiff's land would suffice. So the risk from debris and large limbs that might be (and have been in the past) blown onto Adam's land may well be found to be a substantial and unreasonable interference with Adam's use and enjoyment of his property.

(A) is not the best response,

because there is no indication that the decline in property values is "substantial."

An interference with plaintiff's use and enjoyment of his property must be "substantial" in order to be actionable as a nuisance. On these facts, there is no indication that the reduction in market values is substantial.

Furthermore, any reduction in real estate values occurs throughout the "vicinity," according to our fact pattern, meaning that the harm is spread among a considerable number of landowners. A court might therefore conclude that one requirement of private nuisance — that plaintiff be one of a small number of owners to be affected by the condition — is not satisfied. (Also, the court might worry that there is no obvious limit to such suits: is a neighbor six houses down too far away?)

In any event, the "reduction in market value" factor here is simply less convincing than the very real physi-

cal danger posed by the debris and tree limbs.

(C) is not the best response,

because courts generally do not regard the creation of eyesores as a sufficiently substantial interference with neighbors' use and enjoyment of their property to support a nuisance claim. (Perhaps courts worry that allowing a cause of action for "eyesore creation" would mean that everyone in the neighborhood would be able to sue an owner with an unmowed lawn, so that the courts would have no natural stopping point.)

(D) is not the best response,

because the fact that the conduct doesn't violate a law or ordinance doesn't mean that a nuisance claim will lie.

The law of nuisance is not a "fall back" claim, such that conduct that is annoying but not violative of any law or ordinance can automatically be challenged. Adam will have to show that the conditions here cause him a substantial interference with his use and enjoyment of his property, and the fact that the condition doesn't violate a law or ordinance doesn't say anything about whether Adam can meet this standard.

Answer 25

(A) is the best response,

because Bertha's agreement with Charlie was a subletting of Blackacre, but her agreement with Doris was merely a license or easement.

A sublease is a lease executed by the lessee of land or premises to a third person, conveying the same interest the lessee enjoys (as to all or part of the property) but for a shorter term than that for which the lessee holds.

When Bertha allowed Charles to use the garage to store his car, she subleased the property. This was a sublease because Bertha gave Charles the exclusive use of a defined piece of property, the garage, for a defined term that was less than the time remaining on the master lease. The fact that the arrangement applied to only part of the premises did not prevent it from being a sublease.

Bertha's arrangement with Doris, by contrast, was merely a license or easement, as explained in the discussion of Choice (B).

(B) is not the best response,

because Bertha's agreement with Doris was a license or easement, not a sublease.

A license is a right to use the licensor's land that is revocable at the will of the licensor. An easement is a right to use the land that is not revocable. It's not clear whether the grant to Doris was a license or an easement, but regardless of which it was, it certainly wasn't a sublease, and thus didn't violate the no-subleasing/no-assignment clause. A sublease occurs when the sublessor gives the sublessee the *exclusive* right to use part of the property for a defined period of time (a period shorter than the time remaining on the master lease). Since Doris could only golf when and if this wouldn't interfere with the sheep, Doris' rights weren't exclusive, preventing the arrangement from being a sublease, and thus preventing it from violating the lease.

(C) and (D) are not the best responses,

for the reasons given in Choices (A) and (B) above.

Answer 26

(C) is the best response,

because the covenant of warranty requires defense only against suits that turn out to be meritorious.

The covenant of warranty includes a promise by the covenantor to defend on behalf of the covenantee any lawful or reasonable claims of title by a third party. So if Bea had lost the suit, she could have recovered her legal costs (and the value of the property) from Art.

But ironically, by winning against Celia, Bea lost her right to recover from Art. When Bea won versus Celia, she established that Celia's claim was without merit. At that point, Art had no obligation to reimburse her for defending this now-known-to-be-valueless claim.

(A) is not the best response,

because although in a sense Art's title was challenged, the challenge was without merit.

As discussed in the analysis of Choice (C) above, Art was obliged to defend (or cover the costs of defending) only against meritorious challenges to his vendee's title. Because Bea won against Celia, this condition was not met. So even though the quality of title that Art conveyed to Bea was being challenged, Art had no obligation to defend.

(B) is not the best response,

because the covenant of warranty required Art to defend against only meritorious claims.

As described in the discussion of Choice (C) above, Art only had an obligation to defend against a meritorious claim. Since Bea defeated Celia's claim, Celia's claim is now known not to be meritorious, so the fact that Art made a covenant of warranty was irrelevant.

(D) is not the best response,

because Celia has to sue the holder of title, Bea, not Art.

The court should decide for Art, but not for the reason given. Celia cannot elect to sue either Art or Bea. Bea presently claims to have title to Blackacre, so she, not Art, is the proper target for Celia's suit. In any event, even if Celia had had a right of election, this would make no difference — Art is only obligated to defend meritorious suits against his covenantee, and this suit is now known not to be meritorious (see the analysis of Choice (C) above).

Answer 27

(D) is the best response,

because it identifies the issue upon which either Purvis or Rand will prevail. Note that D does not *resolve* this issue, but states, instead, that the outcome of the case will *turn on how the issue is resolved*. Thus, all you needed to do to answer this question correctly was to identify the central issue. This problem is one in which it's vitally important to chart the facts, to keep track of exactly how each transaction relates to the others.

The "chain of title" refers to the string of recorded instruments reflecting prior ownership and encumbrances of a piece of property. Thus, every grantor should appear as a grantee in the land records to reflect when he received the property, and then as a grantor when he conveys it away. Furthermore, any encumbrance must at least be recited in an instrument in the chain of title in order to bind subsequent grantees. If an interest does not appear in this chain, then it will not be considered recorded and will not give constructive notice to any subsequent purchasers or encumbrancers. Under these facts, Purvis's title would not be considered within Rand's chain of title. If Rand checked the grantor-grantee index for the jurisdiction, he'd find Vine as a grantee from Ogawa, and thus the chain of title wouldn't indicate any gaps or contain any indication that something was amiss. Since Rand wouldn't have any indication that there was a problem with title, and since he's a subsequent bona fide purchaser, he'd prevail. Note that this would not be terribly unfair, since if Purvis had checked land records when Vine conveyed to *him,* he'd realize that Vine did not appear in the grantee index in any former instrument. As such, Vine would be an "interloper" and a deed from him would *not* be considered within the chain of title from Ogawa to Rand. (This problem has an added wrinkle in that title would inure automatically to the grantee, Purvis, when Ogawa conveyed to Vine, under the doctrine of "estoppel by deed.") Although it is reasonably clear how this case would be resolved, D is the best answer because it does identify the central issue.

(A) is not the best response,

because the factor it cites is not determinative of who will prevail. Purvis's deed is senior to Rand's because title passed to him before it passed to Rand, under the doctrine of estoppel by deed (also known as the "after-acquired title doctrine"). The doctrine of estoppel by deed is applicable where the grantor intends to convey an estate larger than he in fact has, and he later acquires the estate he purportedly conveyed. Under "estoppel by deed," the title inures automatically to the grantee. Here, Vine claimed to own Fairoaks in fee simple when he didn't have it; once he did, the title would inure automatically to Purvis, Vine's grantee. Here, Purvis obtained title to Fairoaks when Ogawa conveyed it to Vine, and recorded it *before* Rand recorded his interest.

However, this will not determine if Purvis is entitled to judgment in his favor, because if Rand is not bound by the conveyance to Purvis, then Rand will prevail. Rand will not be bound by Purvis if Purvis's title is deemed recorded in Rand's "chain of title." If it is *not,* then Rand will not be bound by it. Thus, the mere superiority of Purvis's title will not be determinative, making A not the best response.

(B) is not the best response,

because it cites as a conclusion a fact which is in issue. If Rand did, in fact, pay value without notice of Purvis' claim, he would prevail. However, what's at issue here is whether Rand actually had notice of Purvis's claim, since it's not clear whether Purvis' deed was recorded in Rand's "chain of title." If it *was,* then Purvis will prevail, since Rand would have had notice of Purvis' claim; if it *wasn't,* Rand will prevail, as a subsequent bona fide purchaser (for value without knowledge of prior conveyances). Since B states this as a conclusion, it's not the best response.

(C) is not the best response,

because the issue it focuses on is not determinative of the result here. Furthermore, it cites as an issue a fact that is settled at common law, viz., the doctrine of estoppel by deed. The doctrine of estoppel by deed is applicable where the grantor intends to convey an estate larger than he in fact has, and he later acquires the estate he purportedly conveyed. Under "estoppel by deed," the title inures automatically to the grantee. Here, Vine claimed to own Fairoaks in fee simple when he didn't have it; once he did, the title would inure automatically to Purvis, Vine's grantee. Here, Purvis obtained title to Fairoaks when Ogawa conveyed it to Vine, and recorded it *before* Rand recorded his interest. Thus, the issue is not whether the doctrine of estoppel by deed applies, but whether Rand is bound by Purvis's title. Since C does not address this issue, it's not the best response.

Answer 28

(C) is the best response,

because Trent's occupancy, as a tenant of Ron, satisfied all the requirements of adverse possession.

Title to real property may be acquired by adverse possession. If all the requirements are fulfilled, at the end of the statutory period title to the property passes from the owner to the possessor who claims title. The possession must typically meet the following requirements: it must be (1) open, notorious, and visible; (2) hostile; and (3) continuous for the statutory period.

Olive retained a right of reversion, effective upon Lois' demise. Lois died eleven years ago, at which point Olive's reversion became possessory. So at that point, Ron's continued constructive possession of the property (through his tenant) became adverse to Olive's ownership. This started the 10-year statutory period running against Olive.

It's true that Ron did not himself physically occupy the property. But he rented it out to Trent, by letting Trent physically occupy it and by collecting rent. So Ron would be deemed to have constructively possessed the property "openly, notoriously and visibly." That is, one in Olive's position who inspected the property would have been able to determine immediately that Trent was occupying it under a purported grant from Ron, so Olive would have been on notice that Ron was treating the property as if he owned it. Since Ron's possession (through Trent) was hostile (without Olive's consent), and continuous for more than 10 years, Ron gained title by adverse possession.

(A) is not the best response,

because although Olive had a reversion that became possessory when Lois died, Olive then lost the property through adverse possession.

Under the analysis in Choice (C), Ron gained title from Olive by adverse possession. Therefore, the fact that Olive held a reversion that became possessory when Lois died is irrelevant.

(B) is not the best response,

because Lois conveyed an interest less than her life tenancy, so the conveyance was not adverse or hostile to Olive.

A life tenant has a right to convey his interest, such as by a lease. What the life tenant cannot do is convey any estate greater than the life estate he holds.

Since Lois was entitled to convey the leasehold interest, her doing so was not "adverse" to Olive's reversion. Consequently, that lease is not what started Ron's statutory period of adverse possession running. (Instead, it was Lois' death, and Ron's collection of rents, that began the period of adverse possession, as detailed in Choice (C) above).

(D) is not the best response,

because Trent had a leasehold interest, which was not adverse to Ron, while Ron gained title to Blackacre.

It's true that once Lois died, her estate (or her heir, Ron) no longer had any interest to convey, so Ron's leasehold interest, strictly speaking, ended at Lois' death. However, the fact that Trent paid rent to Ron pursuant to what Trent apparently thought was his leasehold obligation means that Trent's possession was not "hostile" to Ron. Therefore, Trent never even began the type of possession required by the statute.

Answer 29

(D) is the best response,

because when Beta bought the tax debt, she will be deemed to have acted on Hera's behalf.

First, note that Beta and Hera were tenants in common. (Because Alpha and Beta were tenants in common, not joint tenants, Alpha's interest passed to Hera when Alpha died.)

Tenants in common (like joint tenants) owe each other a fiduciary duty of fair dealing and good faith. One aspect of that duty is that when one co-tenant buys an outstanding interest, she holds that interest on behalf of the other co-tenant(s).

So here, when Beta bought the tax deed, she was deemed to have bought on behalf of Hera as well as herself. Thus Hera received, in effect, an option to contribute (after the fact) to the tax sale, and Beta got a lien to make sure that if Hera didn't exercise that option, Beta would own the property free and clear. So now, Hera can choose either to pay her one-half share of the amount Beta paid at the tax sale (at which point Beta and Hera would each own 1/2 the tax debt and would in effect retire it), or to forfeit Hera's undivided one-half interest. (Hera is not personally liable for the one-half — the only sanction against her if she doesn't pay is to lose her one-half interest in the property.)

(A) is not the best response,

because there is no right of survivorship with a tenancy in common.

The facts tell us that Alpha and Beta held as tenants in common (not joint tenants). There is no right of survivorship under a tenancy in common. Therefore, when Alpha died intestate, his undivided one-half interest passed by the statutes of descent and Hera became a tenant in common with Beta. Consequently, Beta's surviving Alpha did not make her sole owner.

(B) is not the best response,

because neither failure to operate the property successfully nor failure to pay taxes ended Hera's rights as a tenant in common.

Generally, each co-tenant has the right to occupy the entire premises (subject to the other's right to do the same), without accounting to any absent co-tenant(s) for profits made from that occupancy. Nor does the fact that the tenant who is in possession pays more than his share of the taxes or maintenance constitute any kind of an "obligation" or "undertaking" to the other(s) that he will continue to do so, in the absence of an express contract between the two. So there were no "obligations undertaken" by Alpha, and no "default" by Hera.

(C) is not the best response,

because under the duty of fair dealing, Beta's right to purchase is shared by Hera.

When one co-tenant buys an outstanding interest in the property, the purchaser in a sense buys on behalf of all other co-tenants (see the discussion of Choice (D) above). What Beta bought here was not the whole property, but the government's tax lien on the property. At that point, Beta succeeded to the government's lien position. Hera had a right to "redeem" her interest in the property from that lien, by paying her share of the

tax debt represented by that lien. Hera was not required to pay the value of her interest in the entire property, because Beta did not own the whole property outright. (In other words, what Hera had the right to do was analogous to her right to pay off her share of an outstanding mortgage.)

Answer 30

(C) is the best response,

because either co-tenant had the right to demand partition and an accounting.

Either co-tenant has the right, at any time, to demand partition. (Courts will try to physically divide the property where this is feasible; if not, they will order the property sold and the proceeds divided. But in either event, the proceeding is referred to as "partition.")

During the course of partition, the court will order an accounting, to determine whether either party owes the other money for rents collected, taxes paid, etc. It is not clear what substantive rules will govern that analysis — for instance, jurisdictions differ on whether a co-tenant who occupies the premises himself must account for the imputed value of rent received beyond his pro rata share. But the one thing that we can be sure of is that the court will require an accounting, and that's what this choice specifies.

(A) is not the best response,

because Alex never occupied Blackacre in a "hostile" manner.

If Alex had occupied the property "hostilely" as against Angela, he might indeed have obtained title by adverse possession five years before Angela died. But it's quite clear that Angela acquiesced in Alex's keeping the rent and occupying the house, so his possession was not "hostile" and therefore never started the adverse possession clock running. (Nor did he hostilely possess vis a vis Betty, since he never denied her the right to co-occupy the premises.) So Alex did not take by adverse possession.

(B) is not the best response,

because the court would grant partition.

As explained in the answer to Choice (C) above, either co-tenant has the right, at any time, to demand partition. To the extent that this choice indicates that the court would deny partition, it's wrong (though it's correct about requiring an accounting).

(D) is not the best response,

because a court would conduct an accounting to determine if either party has an obligation to pay money to the other.

It's not clear exactly what substantive rules would apply to such questions as whether Alex has a duty to pay Betty one-half of the rents he collected from outsiders (probably he does), or whether he has the duty to pay one-half of the imputed value of his own occupancy (probably he doesn't). But the one thing that is sure is that Betty would have the right to have these matters examined in an accounting procedure.

Answer 31

(D) is the best response,

because it correctly identifies that the zoning violation will render the title unmarketable. Marketable title is title which, viewed objectively, is free from reasonable doubt in both law and fact, and which the reasonable buyer would accept without fear of litigation. Here, the zoning violation would give Perrine a reasonable fear of litigation, since he could be compelled to make the property comply with the zoning regulation. While there is a possibility he could be granted a variance and thus avoid the restrictions of the setback ordinance, there's no guarantee this would happen, and even if it did, it would still mean that the original title conveyed was not marketable. Santos's supplying marketable title is a condition to Perrine's performance; without it, Perrine is excused from performing under the contract. Since D correctly identifies that the setback violation renders the title unmarketable, it's the best response.

(A) is not the best response,

because it misstates the law. A frivolous lawsuit is one which lacks the purpose of actually determining a controversy. Under these facts, a claim against Perrine concerning the setback would certainly not be frivolous, since the setback rule has been violated. As a result, Perrine could be forced to move the house or tear down the offending portion. Since option A incorrectly states that any suit against Perrine concerning the setback would be frivolous, it's not the best response.

(B) is not the best response,

because *any* setback violation is sufficient to consider the title unmarketable. Marketable title is title which, viewed objectively, is free from reasonable doubt in both law and fact, and which the reasonable buyer would accept without fear of litigation. The doctrine *de minimis no curat lex* means that, literally, "the law is not concerned with trifles." While this doctrine generally means that substantial performance is enough for contracts, it does not apply to zoning regulations, which require *strict compliance*. A violation, no matter how small, is actionable. As a result, title to the property would not be "marketable." Since option B incorrectly states that the violation is not actionable, it's not the best response.

(C) is not the best response,

because it doesn't identify the central reason title here is not "marketable." Marketable title is title which, viewed objectively, is free from reasonable doubt in both law and fact, and which the reasonable buyer would accept without fear of litigation. While it's true

that any variation from a contract amounts to a breach of contract, this in and of itself doesn't address whether Santos will be entitled to specific performance of the contract. Perrine could only be compelled to perform if the breach was minor, and substantial performance was sufficient to require return performance, and no remedy at law would be adequate. However, the rule with zoning violations is that they require *strict*, not substantial, performance. *Any* violation could subject Perrine to litigation, which would make the title unmarketable. Since Santos's providing marketable title was a condition to Perrine's performance, Perrine will not be forced to perform, as C recognizes – however, it's not due to a breach of contract *alone,* but the fact that the breach *here* relieves Perrine of his duty to perform. Thus, C is not the best response.

Answer 32

(A) is the best response,

because Gail is strictly liable if Bill's building did not contribute to the subsidence, but not liable without negligence if Bill's building did contribute.

One of the rights incident to land is the right to "lateral support." That is, every landowner is entitled to have his land receive the necessary physical support from adjacent and underlying soil. The right to lateral support is absolute — that is, once support has been withdrawn and injury occurs, the responsible person is liable even if he used utmost care. However, the absolute right to later support exists *only with respect to land in its natural state.* If owner *A* has constructed a building, and the soil under the building subsides in part due to the acts of adjacent owner *B*, but also in part because of the weight of *A*'s building itself, *B* is not liable without negligence.

Therefore, this choice accurately states the rule.

(B) is not the best response,

because Bill's right to lateral support is not gained by adverse possession but is a right incident to his ownership of his own land.

Subject to zoning limits, a landowner is permitted to build right up to the property line. (This happens routinely in large cities.) Therefore, the fact that Bill put up his building right up against his lot line did not cause him to gain anything by adverse possession. The right to lateral support that he had was an incident of his original ownership of Lot 1.

(C) is not the best response,

because Bill has no duty to protect the improvements on Lot 1 against subsidence that would have occurred even had there been no building on that lot.

If the subsidence would not have occurred had there been no building on Lot 1, then (C) would essentially be correct — that is, Bill would lose because in the absence of negligence by Gail, the risk of damage to Bill's land would have been borne by him, and it would have been up to him to assure that his building was buttressed in such a way that an excavation on Lot 2 wouldn't damage his own building.

But this choice also implies that the risk would be born by Bill even if the excavation would have caused a cave in on Bill's lot had there been no building there. And this is not the law — as explained in the analysis of Choice (A) above, a landowner's right to lateral support means that the excavator next door, not the landowner, bears the risk of a cave-in of the landowner's unoccupied land.

(D) is not the best response,

because following the law would not be an excuse or a defense for Gail.

A's right of lateral support is violated when an adjoining owner *B* causes a cave-in that would have occurred even on an unoccupied lot — and that statement is true even if *B* has not only acted non-negligently but also followed all applicable laws.

Answer 33

(D) is the best response,

because by the time George purported to get his lien Barbara, not Corp., was the owner of Blackacre.

The statute here says that George could get a lien on property "then owned" (or after-acquired) by his judgment debtor. So if Blackacre can be viewed as still having been owned by Corp. on the day George filed, George might well win as against Barbara (because the prior unrecorded conveyance would not be good against George's lien, assuming that George was viewed as a "purchaser for value," which he might well be). But the problem for George is that a court would probably conclude that when George filed, the property was not "then owned" by Corp. That's because this type of statute is generally interpreted to exclude any property that has been properly conveyed by the judgment debtor, even if the conveyance has not been recorded.

Since George's lien isn't valid against the property because it was no longer Corp's property at the moment of filing, the lien was ineffective, and Barbara has good title.

(A) is not the best response,

because George's judgment did not affect Barbara's title.

It's only the filing of a judgment lien, not the obtaining of a judgment, that causes an encumbrance on the judgment debtor's real estate. So the fact that George got his judgment before Barbara recorded is irrelevant.

(B) is not the best response,

because any suit by George would definitely fail, so that the threat of meritless litigation would not be enough to cloud Barbara's title.

The obligation to convey marketable title does not mean an obligation to convey "perfect title," or title that could not possibly be attacked by anyone. So long as it is quite clear (not merely "barely probable") that the vendor would be found in litigation to have valid unencumbered title, the title is not unmarketable.

For the reasons described in Choice (D) above, Barbara would clearly win as against George if George sued. So the mere fact that George might file suit based on his filed judgment would not be enough to render Barbara's title unmarketable.

(C) is not the best response,

because it wasn't the fact that Barbara won the race to record that caused her to prevail.

As explained in Choice (D) above, as soon as the unrecorded conveyance to Barbara occurred, Corp. no longer owned the property, and any filing by George of his judgment that occurred after that would have had no effect. So this choice explains the correct outcome by incorrect reasoning — even if Barbara had not recorded until after George filed, Barbara would still have won because George's filing was of no effect.

Answer 34

(A) is the best response,

because it correctly identifies the basis on which Page will not be bound by the covenant: It does not "touch and concern" the land. The covenant here is ostensibly a "real" covenant, which is a promise related to land which is enforceable by (and against) subsequent holders of the land. Its requirements are that the parties must have intended that the covenant run with the land, it must "touch and concern" the land, the Statute of Frauds must be satisfied, and privity of estate must exist. Option A correctly focuses on the "touch and concern" requirement. A covenant does not "touch and concern" the land if it doesn't change the value, use, or utility of the land. Most typically, covenants that touch and concern the land are building restrictions, although even payments to homeowner's associations can qualify. However, a mere agreement to purchase electricity from the Fernwood facility would not be considered to "touch and concern" the land, it couldn't "run with" the land, and, as a result, Page would not be bound by it without his personally covenanting to do so. Since A correctly identifies the most likely basis of these four on which Page will prevail, it's the best response.

(B) is not the best response,

because it misstates the law, and, in any case, does not refer to these facts. In order for a covenant to "run with the land," the parties must have intended that the agreement would run with the land; the agreement must "touch and concern" the land; the Statute of Frauds must be satisfied; and there must be privity of estate. The requirement to which option B refers is not for a real covenant, but an implied reciprocal servitude. An implied reciprocal servitude is a means by which a subsequent property owner can be bound by a covenant not present in his own deed, but in deeds from the same grantor to prior purchasers, typically in the same subdivision. The prior purchasers can enforce the servitudes as long as the restriction in the earlier deeds resulted in a general plan that all properties later conveyed would be burdened by the same restriction, and the prior purchasers relied on same. Furthermore, there must be notice, actual, constructive, or implied, to bind the subsequent property owner in order to bind him. This isn't the case here; the covenant appeared in Page's deed, so there's no notice problem; and, in any case, a common development scheme would not require that all the dwellings are the same. Since B does not focus on the correct issue, and misstates the law on that issue, it's not the best response.

(C) is not the best response,

because it does not focus on the correct issue, and, in any case, misstates the law. Restraints on alienation are not *per se* invalid; for instance, promissory restraints are valid, as in the case of prohibitions against subletting and assignment in landlord-tenant agreements. They are viewed narrowly by courts, but they can be valid. While the covenant here would be a restraint on alienation, it would not be invalid for that reason, since if the covenant touched and concerned the land, it would be enforceable as a "real" covenant. Since C focuses on the wrong issue, it's not the best response.

(D) is not the best response,

because it is incorrect. There *is* privity between Page and Gaint, because their interests ultimately come from a common grantor: Fernwood. Thus, grantor-grantee privity exists, which suffices in most states. Instead, the problem here is the "touch and concern" requirement of a real covenant, which this covenant doesn't satisfy. Since D doesn't recognize this, and wrongly suggests that no privity exists here, it is not the best response.

Answer 35

(A) is the best response,

because Hull owns Brownacre.

This is a question where the facts are so complex that it's necessary to chart them in order to be able to arrive at the correct response. Here's basically what happens:

1950: Hull moves in, builds dam.
Adverse possession begins.
1960: Title vests in Hull by adverse possession.
1962: Hull to Burns, ineffective deed.
Result: Hull has title to land; Burns has cattle.
1963: Burns leases Brownacre from Orris for five years.
No lease. Hull still has title; Burns is not in adverse possession, because his use isn't adverse as against

Hull, the owner.
1967: Lease ends - Hull still has title.
1970: Burns leaves - Hull has title.
Orris conveys via quitclaim to Powell. Powell gets Orris's interest, which is nothing. Hull still has title.

As this chart indicates, Hull's title in Brownacre matured after his ten years of adverse possession, in 1960. Thereafter, Burns' use was permissive, and, beyond that, he didn't occupy Brownacre long enough to obtain title via adverse possession. When Orris leased Brownacre to Burns in 1963, Orris went into adverse possession of Brownacre by treating it as his, but, since the lease lasted only five years, Orris did not get title to Brownacre. Burns' five year lease would not be tacked on to Burns' possession, since he possessed Brownacre for that five year period under a lease, not a claim of ownership. The three years after the lease were adverse to Hull's ownership, but a non-permissive period cannot be tacked onto a permissive period for purposes of adverse possession. Thereafter, Orris's conveyance to Powell is irrelevant, since Orris had no interest to convey. Under these facts, once Hull gained title to Brownacre, he never surrendered it. Since A correctly identifies Hull as the owner of Brownacre, it's the best response.

(B) is not the best response,

because it states an incorrect result. Under these facts, the las time that Orris had title was before Hull's title matured, in 1960. Hull moved into adverse possession of Brownacre in 1950, because his use of Brownacre was open, notorious, continuous, hostile to Orris's interest, and exclusive. Once Hull's title matured in 1960, Orris was no longer the owner. Granting a lease to Burns in 1962 would be considered an adverse use of Brownacre, but the adverse use ended in 1967 for Orris, when the lease ended, so the use would not satisfy the statutory period of ten years. Even if Orris had been the owner after that, his quitclaiming his interest to Powell would end Orris's ownership. Since B states that Orris is still owner of Brownacre, it's not the best response.

(C) is not the best response,

because it states an incorrect result. Basically, Burns's use of Brownacre was only adverse for the three year period after his lease from Orris ran out. For the five years of Burns' ostensible lease from Orris, it was Orris whose use was adverse, not Burns – and, in any case, the use was not long enough to establish title via adverse possession. Burns' use after Hull gave possession to him was not adverse, because, at that time, Hull had title via adverse possession, and, Burns' use of it was *permissive*, not adverse, and thus title could not mature in Burns for that period. Since Burns could not be the owner of Brownacre, C is not the best response.

(D) is not the best response,

because Powell is clearly not the owner of Brownacre. In order for Powell to own Brownacre, he'd have to have received an interest from Orris. Orris didn't own Brownacre, because his title ended when Hull gained title by adverse possession in 1960. Orris's leasing the property to Burns for five years in the 1960's was the type of possession that could be adverse (since it was open, notorious, continuous, exclusive, and hostile), but it did not continue long enough for title to mature in Orris. Thus, since Orris did not own Brownacre, Powell could not, making D not the best response.

Answer 36

(A) is the best response,

because it correctly characterizes ownership of the dam as being determined by ownership of Brownacre. The ownership of the dam would pass with ownership of the land, because it's a fixture. A fixture is a chattel which has been annexed to land in such a way as to be regarded as real property. Its requirements are annexation to realty (e.g., heating system installed), appropriate to the use of the realty to which it's connected, and the intent to make a permanent accession, viewed objectively (look to, for instance, the annexor's estate in land – an owner is more likely to intend a permanent accession than a mere lessee). Here, the dam would clearly qualify as a fixture. Since A correctly identifies that the ownership of Brownacre will determine ownership of the dam, it's the best response.

(B) is not the best response,

because the facts indicate that the bill of sale was insufficient as a deed to transfer real property. The dam here would be considered a fixture, and as such would pass with ownership of the land. A fixture is a chattel which has been annexed to land in such a way as to be regarded as real property. Its requirements are annexation to realty (e.g., heating system installed), appropriate to the use of the realty to which it is connected, and the intent to make a permanent accession, viewed objectively (look to, for instance, the annexor's estate in land – an owner is more likely to intend a permanent accession than a mere lessee). Here, the dam would clearly qualify as a fixture. Since Hull's bill of sale was insufficient to transfer ownership of the dam to Burns, it remains with him. Since B states otherwise, it's not the best response.

(C) is not the best response,

because ownership of the water rights would not determine ownership of the dam. Rather, the ownership of the dam will be determined by ascertaining who owns the real property. That's because the dam here is a fixture, and as such would pass with ownership of the land. A fixture is a chattel which has been annexed to land in such a way as to be regarded as real property. Its requirements are annexation to realty (e.g., heating

system installed), appropriate to the use of the realty to which it is connected, and the intent to make a permanent accession, viewed objectively (look to, for instance, the annexor's estate in land – an owner is more likely to intend a permanent accession than a mere lessee). Here, the dam would clearly qualify as a fixture. Thus, it's the ownership of the real property that determines the ownership of the dam, not the ownership of the water rights. Since C states otherwise, it's not the best response.

(D) is not the best response,

because Hull's status as builder of the dam is irrelevant to determining its ownership, just as a general contractor doesn't automatically own every house he builds. As a fixture, the dam would belong to whoever owns the real property. A fixture is a chattel which has been annexed to land in such a way as to be regarded as real property. Its requirements are annexation to realty (e.g., heating system installed), appropriate to the use of the realty to which it's connected, and the intent to make a permanent accession, viewed objectively (look to, for instance, the annexor's estate in land – an owner is more likely to intend a permanent accession than a mere lessee). Here, the dam would clearly qualify as a fixture. Thus, it's the ownership of the real property that determines the ownership of the dam, regardless of who built the dam. Since D would condition ownership on who built the dam, it's not the best response.

Answer 37

(D) is the best response,

because none of the items was a fixture.

A tenant may not remove "fixtures" at the end of the lease term. A fixture is a chattel attached to real property so that it ceases being personal property and becomes part of the real property. So the question is which, if any, of the items here was a fixture.

The following factors, if present, argue in favor of a finding that the item is a chattel: (1) it is firmly imbedded in the real estate; (2) it is peculiarly adapted or fitted to the real estate; (3) removal would destroy the chattel, or significantly damage the real estate; and (4) the person who did the annexing (in this case, the tenant) had a substantial and permanent interest in the real estate (with a tenancy of years being the shortest, and a fee simple being the longest).

Here, all of these factors point to none of the chattels being fixtures: (1) none of the items is really "firmly embedded" in the real estate; (2) all were designed and manufactured without reference to the building's particular dimensions and characteristics, so none can be said to be "peculiarly adapted or fitted" to the real estate; (3) removal would be relatively easy and non-damaging in all cases; and (4) the affixer's (Tina's) interest at the time of affixation was very short and impermanent (a 5-year lease). Furthermore, the lease seems to contemplate that all such items can be removed (though it's not absolutely certain that these are the items the "may remove" clause was talking about).

(A), (B) and (C) are not the best responses
for the same reasons that (D) is the best choice.

Answer 38

(A) is the best response,
because the liquidated damages clause was not a measure of either Ven's anticipated or actual losses, and was therefore an unenforceable penalty.

Liquidated damages are agreed to by both parties at the time of the contract. Such liquidated damages clauses, where enforced by the court, determine the measure of damages which the court will award. In order for such a clause to be enforceable, however, it must meet this requirement: the amount fixed must be reasonable relative to either the *anticipated* loss (viewed as of the time the contract was signed) or to the *actual* loss (as determined by the passage of time).

The clause here does not meet this standard. It was not a reasonable forecast viewed as of the time the contract was made, because a loss of $50,000 in value during the contract-closing gap is highly unlikely given that the market value at the outset was $100,000 (i.e., a 50% loss of value during a relatively short 2- or 3-month period).

Nor was the amount set in the clause reasonable compared with the actual damages, since we're told that the value of the property had actually increased between the signing and the time for closing. So the clause was not reasonable relative to either the anticipated or actual loss, making it an unenforceable penalty.

(B) is not the best response,
because Pur's death does not discharge the contract.

If a contract does not call for significant personal services by a party, that party's death or incapacity generally does not terminate or discharge the contract. The reason is that the dead person's duties can be delegated to some other person and the contract continued.

So here, Pur's death did not cause the contract to terminate, since Pur's estate could continue to perform its duties under the contract.

(C) is not the best response,
because the court would not enforce an unenforceable term of a contract.

As described in Choice (A) above, the liquidated damages clause was an unenforceable penalty. Therefore, the court will not (and should not) enforce it, even though it was the express agreement of the parties. In other words, there are some types of agreements that parties are simply not permitted to make, and a penalty masquerading as a liquidated damages clause is one

of those types.

(D) is not the best response,
because although the doctrine of equitable conversion would indeed prevent the contract from terminating, that doctrine wouldn't make the liquidated damages clause enforceable.

The doctrine of equitable conversion applies to situations that arise during the gap between the signing of the contract and the delivery of the deed. If the purchaser dies while the contract is still executory, the equitable conversion doctrine applies so that (1) the person entitled to receive the decedent's estate is entitled to the land; and (2) the recipients of the personal property not only do not receive the land, but must pay any remaining portion of the purchase price out of their shares of the estate.

So here, Addy was required to pay the purchase price, so that whoever was entitled to Pur's real estate could and would receive the property.

However, this fact did not entitle Ven to keep the deposit, because (as described in Choice (A) above), the liquidated damages clause was an unenforceable penalty. Ven's remedy was to keep only that portion of the deposit that reflected any damage to him from the breach. Since the property increased in value, there was no damage (except perhaps incidental expenses like having to re-advertise the property). Therefore, Ven would have to return all or nearly all the deposit.

Answer 39

(A) is the best response,
because it correctly identifies that Paul is the owner in fee simple absolute of the land. You need only have picked up on one key fact to get this answer right: That Bob was not free to devise his interest in the land, since he owned the land in joint tenancy with Bill, and thus Bill was entitled to Bob's interest, on Bob's death, due to the right of survivorship. Bill's right would take precedence over any devise Bob ostensibly made. Once Bob dies, Bill owns the land in fee simple absolute, and the devises and conveyances thereafter transfer ownership of the land, in fee simple absolute, to Frank, then to Paul, then to Patrick. Since A correctly identifies that Paul need have no one join him in the conveyance, it's the best response.

(B) is not the best response,
because Paul can convey the land without joining anyone else in the conveyance. If you chose this response, it's because you mistakenly found that Bob could devise his interest in the land to anyone he chose. In fact, the "right of survivorship" – the hallmark of a joint tenancy as opposed to a tenancy in common – means that a co-tenant's devise of the land will be disregarded, and it will automatically go to his co-tenant. Here, this would mean that Bill becomes sole tenant. When Bill dies, his devise is valid, since there's no

co-tenant with a right of survivorship. That leaves Frank with the property in fee simple absolute. Frank is free to convey the property as he sees fit, so when he conveys it to Paul, Paul has it in fee simple absolute, and Paul is likewise free to dispose of it as he chooses. Since B incorrectly requires that Charles, Sam, and Sam's only child join in the conveyance, it's not the best response.

(C) is not the best response,

because no one else needs to join in the conveyance, since Paul owns the land in fee simple absolute. If you chose this response, it's because you didn't realize that Bob was not free to devise his interest in the land, since the land was held as a joint tenancy which had a right to survivorship – meaning that Bill would take Bob's interest in the land, regardless of any devise by Bob. Thereafter, *Bill* can dispose of the land any way he wants, since he's the sole surviving joint tenant – meaning no one has a right to survivorship as to *Bill's* interest. Since C does not recognize this, it's not the best response.

(D) is not the best response,

because it misstates the law, and, beyond that, arrives at the wrong conclusion. For one thing, the concept of merchantability is not applicable to title; it's *marketable* title that's an implied covenant of land sale contracts. Even if the correct terminology were employed here, it would still be wrong, since title by quitclaim deed means only that the vendor is conveying whatever interest in the property he, in fact, has. Since marketable title is an implied covenant of land sale contracts, if the vendor tries to pass a quitclaim deed at the closing to the vendee, the vendee can refuse to accept it. However, once the deed is passed, the vendee could not claim a breach due to failure to pass a marketable title, since the terms of the deed control under the doctrine of merger, and a quitclaim deed has no covenants associated with it whatsoever. Since D misstates the law, it cannot be the best response.

Answer 40

(B) is the best response,

because it arrives at the correct conclusion, identifies the major obstacle to the interest – the Rule Against Perpetuities – and correctly identifies that Farley's interest will overcome this obstacle. The key fact here is that, although Farley's interest is a shifting executory interest and thus subject to the Rule Against Perpetuities, it *must* vest within a life in being plus twenty-one years.

The conveyance here creates a fee simple subject to an executory interest in Pike, and a shifting executory interest in Farley (since Farley's interest does not become possessory on the natural termination of the prior estate, and it divests another grantee, not the grantor [making it a "shifting" instead of a "springing"

executory interest]). As an executory interest, the most important point about the validity of Farley's interest is whether or not it meets the Rule Against Perpetuities. In order to do so, it must vest or fail within a life in being plus twenty-one years. Here, it will vest or fail within a life in being – Farley's. Farley must be alive now, and whether or not he is to take Brightacre will be determined within a "life in being" – Farley's – since if he's alive thirty years from now, his interest vests and he takes, and if he dies, his interest will fail whenever he dies within thirty years. Since Farley's executory interest satisfies the Rule Against Perpetuities, it will be valid, making B the best response.

(A) is not the best response,

because although it arrives at the correct conclusion, it mischaracterizes the facts. Farley's interest is not a reversion, but a shifting executory interest. A reversion is a future interest arising in the grantor when he conveys an estate of shorter duration than the estate he possesses (e.g., grantor has a fee simple; he conveys a fee tail, life estate or leasehold; grantor's interest is a reversion). Here, Farley's interest cannot be a reversion because, if nothing else, he's not the grantor. Since option A does not recognize this, it cannot be the best response.

(C) is not the best response,

because although it arrives at the correct conclusion, it does not correctly characterize the facts. Farley's interest is not a vested remainder subject to divestment, but rather a shifting executory interest. The easiest way to tell if an interest is a remainder or an executory interest is to determine if it takes at the natural termination of the previous interest. Here, the previous estate is Pike's. If Farley is to take at all, his interest will divest Pike of possession thirty years from now. Since Farley's possession terminates Pike's interest at a time other than its natural termination, Farley's interest must be an executory interest, not a remainder. (By the way, Farley's interest is a "shifting" executory interest instead of a "springing" executory interest because he divests another grantee, not the grantor, of possession.) Since C does not correctly characterize the facts, it cannot be the best response.

(D) is not the best response,

because it does not arrive at the correct conclusion. Farley's interest is valid, because, although it is a shifting executory interest and thus subject to the Rule Against Perpetuities, it will vest or fail within a life in being plus twenty-one years, so it's valid. If you chose this response, it could be because mention of the "thirty years" threw you off, and made you think that the interest violates the Rule Against Perpetuities. However, the important fact here is that Farley is the life in being, and the interest will vest or fail *in his lifetime* – if he's alive in thirty years' time, it vests, and if he dies before then, the interest fails when he dies. Since D mischaracterizes Farley's interest as invalid, it's not the best response.

Answer 41

(D) is the best response,

because Lena's obligation to pay property tax is limited to the rent she received.

Since a life tenancy is by definition to be followed by another interest, a life tenant has a number of duties vis a vis the future interest. One of those duties is to pay all property taxes which come due while the life tenant holds possession of the property. However, a life tenant is liable to the holder of the future interest for property taxes only to the extent of the rents received, or the fair rental value if the life tenant occupies it.

Since the property was vacant, there were no rents, and Lena consequently had no liability to Rose for failing to pay them. And that's true even though Rose went into her pocket to pay these taxes.

(A) and (B) are not the best response,

because a life tenant's obligation to pay taxes is limited by the amount received in rent, which in this case is $0. See the discussion in Choice (D).

(C) is not the best response,

because had Lena received rental income her possession would not have given her the right to determine whether or not the taxes should be paid — in that event, she would have been liable for non-payment of taxes up to the amount of rent received. In other words, this choice states the correct result, but on wrong reasoning.

Answer 42

(A) is the best response,

because it gives the reason why the class gift will be valid under the Rule Against Perpetuities. The key fact here is that the class gift was created in a will, and thus Trease cannot have more children.

Under the Rule Against Perpetuities, an interest is only valid if it must vest, if at all, no later than twenty-one years after one or more lives in being at the creation of the interest. "Measuring lives" are the "lives in being" for purposes of the Rule. Here, Trease's children will be the measuring lives for determining the validity of the class gift. In fact, the gift here *must* vest or fail within twenty-one years of the deaths of Trease's children, since, once Trease's children die, their children can turn twenty-one after no more than twenty-one years. In fact, the key to this question is that Trease created the class gift *in his will*. Thus, the class gift would not be "created" until the will took effect, that is, Trease's death. At Trease's death, all of his children must be lives in being, since he can't have more children once he's dead (Future Interests doesn't recognize exotic things like sperm banks). Thus, he couldn't

have grandchildren who would turn twenty-one more than twenty-one years after the "measuring lives" – his children. If there's one rule that you remember for the Multistate concerning class gifts, it should be this – class gifts in grandchildren, like the one here, are valid if the gift is created in a will, *but not if the gift is created in a conveyance*. In the case of a conveyance, the grantor could have children after the conveyance takes place, and those children could have children who would turn twenty-one *after* the perpetuities period, thus violating the Rule Against Perpetuities. However, since the class gift for the grandchildren was created in a will under these facts, it will be valid. Since A implies this, it's the best response.

(B) is not the best response,

because the rule of convenience is not applicable to these facts. The rule of convenience is a rule of construction which applies to class gifts. Where there is no expression of intent that all members of a class should take, the class closes when a member of the class can call for distribution of a share of the class gift. The rule is designed to avoid delaying distribution beyond that period necessary, and at the same time avoiding rebates in the future. Its primary significance is that, under it, no after-born members can take. However, the rule would not apply here, because Trease expressly intended to include "all grandchildren whenever born." Since there is no need to construe this language, the rule of convenience will not apply, making B not the best response.

(C) is not the best response,

because there is no basis on which to employ this presumption. Trease could not have intended to include only those grandchildren born prior to his death, because he expressly included "all grandchildren whenever born." This could only be interpreted as including "after-born" children. Note that option C implies that the rule of convenience should apply to these facts. Under the rule of convenience, applicable to class gifts, where there is no expression of intent that all members of a class should take, the class closes when a member of the class can call for distribution of a share of the class gift. The rule could have applied if Trease had not specifically mentioned "all grandchildren whenever born." Had he merely said, "to all my grandchildren who shall reach the age of 21," children born after his death would not take (while those born before his death, but not 21 by the time he died, could not take a share until and unless they reached age 21). However, since Trease was explicit about his wishes and provided for *all* his grandchildren, C cannot be the best response.

(D) is not the best response,

because the Rule Against Perpetuities is interpreted strictly: an interest *must* vest or fail within a life in being plus twenty-one years in order to be valid. There isn't room for a rule of construction with the Rule Against Perpetuities, because if an interest *may, for whatever remote reason, not vest within the perpetuities period, it's not valid.* Since D states otherwise, it's not the best response.

Answer 43

(C) is the best response,

because it identifies the added condition, of these four options, which will result in a violation of the Rule Against Perpetuities. The reason is this: If Trease made the conveyance during his life, there may be members of the class whose interest does not vest or fail within the "perpetuities period" – a life in being plus twenty-one years. Say, for instance, that Trease makes the conveyance in 1989. He has three children at the time. In 1990, he has a fourth child, Farkus. Since Farkus was born after the conveyance took place, he would not be a "life in being" for purposes of the Rule Against Perpetuities. Farkus dies at age 16, in 2016, having just had a child. That child would turn 21 in 2037. Farkus's child's interest in Hilltop would make the conveyance to the grandchildren invalid, because his interest wouldn't vest until he turned 21 in 2037, which is *more* than a life in being plus twenty-one years since the conveyance took place, since his father, Farkus, wasn't a life in being in 198*9*. This is the "after-born children" problem, and it's the reason why class gifts to grandchildren, to take effect when the grand-children reach 21, *are valid only in wills, not in convey-ances.* Since C correctly identifies the circumstance which would make the class gift violate the Rule Against Perpetuities, it's the best response.

(A) is not the best response,

because the birth of a posthumous child would not change the application of the Rule Against Perpetu-ities. The Rule Against Perpetuities requires that, in order to be valid, an interest must vest or fail within a life in being plus twenty-one years at the time the inter-est was created. In fact, fetuses are considered a "life in being" for purposes of the Rule, and so you could say that there's a nine-month "grace period" for the Rule. Option A does, though, imply the correct reason-ing, which is, the grant here was valid only because it was in a will, not an inter vivos conveyance, since it's the possibility of after-born children to Trease that would invalidate the interest. The fact still remains that Trease cannot parent any more children once he dies, and so any grandchildren he has must turn twenty-one within a life in being plus twenty one years (the "life in being" being measured by Trease's children). The fact that his wife is pregnant when he dies would not change this result, so A is not the best response.

(B) is not the best response,

because it misinterprets the facts, and, in any case, the inclusion of grandchildren whenever born would not create a violation of the Rule Against Perpetuities. Trease *did* expressly include his afterborn grandchil-dren, because he stated that he intended "to include all grandchildren whenever born." Thus, the inclusion of afterborn grandchildren does not violate the Rule Against Perpetuities. The Rule Against Perpetuities requires that, in order for an interest to be valid, the interest must vest or fail within a life in being plus twenty-one years. Here, the "measuring lives" would be Trease's children. Trease's will takes effect when he dies, and, coincidentally, when he can have no more children. Thus, Trease's grandchildren cannot turn twenty-one later than twenty-one years after his chil-dren die, because once his children die, they can't have any more children of their own. Thus, when the grandchildren are born is *irrelevant.* Since B misinter-prets the facts and does not correctly apply the Rule Against Perpetuities, it's not the best response.

(D) is not the best response,

because Trease's having no grandchildren alive when he died would not make the grant violate the Rule Against Perpetuities. In order for the provision to sat-isfy the Rule Against Perpetuities, all that's required is that all the interests vest or fail within a life in being plus twenty-one years after the provision takes effect. The "measuring lives" for the purpose of this provision are Trease's children. They physically cannot have children who turn twenty-one more than twenty-one years after they die, because once Trease's children die they can't have any more children. However, it doesn't matter when the children are born vis-a-vis Trease's death, for purposes of the Rule Against Per-petuities. Since D states otherwise, it's not the best response.

Answer 44

(C) is the best response,

because it correctly characterizes the facts here as creating a vested remainder subject to partial defea-sance in Selden's children. A vested remainder sub-ject to partial defeasance is one which is created in a "class" of persons, at least one of whom is ascertained and in existence, which is certain to become posses-sory when preceding estates terminate, and is capable of being diminished by others entering the class. A remainder to children of a living person is the most common example of such a class. The remainder is vested when the first child is born, but can be dimin-ished proportionately as other children are born, until the "class" closes. Since C correctly identifies this, it's the best response.

(A) is not the best response,

because Selden's two children will have their shares reduced if Selden has any more children. The devise here created a life estate in Selden, and a class gift in the form of a remainder to Selden's children. The problem here is determining the effective date for determining the size of the class. Under the Rule of Convenience, barring intent to the contrary, the class closes on the date of the first distribution – that is, Selden's death, since that's when the interest of his children will become possessory. If Selden has children after Testator's death, they will also take a share of the farm, because membership in the class will not be determined until Selden dies. Thus, the interests of Selden's two current children cannot be completely divested, but they may be reduced (e.g., if Selden has one more child, each child will take 1/3 instead of the current 1/2). Since the interests may be reduced, the interests are not indefeasibly vested, but vested subject to partial defeasance. The key here is that the gift was created in a "class" of persons – Selden's children. Had testator instead, for instance, *named* Selden's two children – "to Selden for life, then to his children, Moe and Curly, and their heirs and assigns," the interests of Moe and Curly would be indefeasibly vested, since testator expressly intended only Moe and Curley to take. However, the facts here specifically call for distribution to a class, thus making the remainder a vested remainder subject to partial defeasance. Since A states otherwise, it's not the best response.

(B) is not the best response,

because the interests of the children are vested, not contingent. A contingent remainder is one which is either subject to a condition precedent (in other words, when the previous estate ends, the estate cannot become possessory *unless* the condition precedent has *also* occurred), or it is created in favor of an unborn person or is to be taken by an unascertained person. That's not the case here. Selden's children are certain to take; the only question is how much of a share they will receive, since their shares will decrease if Selden has more children. However, this "contingency" does not make their interest a contingent remainder. Say, instead, that the devise had been worded "to my son, Selden, for life, then to those of Selden's children who outlive him." Here, the share of each child would be contingent on his outliving Selden. This would make the interests contingent remainders. However, no such contingency exists in the facts here, so B is not the best response.

(D) is not the best response,

because, while the shares of Selden's children can be reduced, they cannot be eliminated, and thus their shares are not subject to complete defeasance. A vested remainder subject to complete defeasance is a remainder subject to a condition subsequent, but not a condition precedent – in other words, nothing stops one from taking possession, but something can take it away. Say, instead of the devise here, the devise had been worded "to Selden for life, then to Selden's son Willie and his heirs, but if Willie predeceases Selden, then to Selden's other son Amadeus and his heirs."

Here, Willie's interest is a vested remainder subject to complete divestment, because while there is no condition precedent to Willie's taking possession, it can subsequently be divested (the hallmark of a vested remainder subject to complete defeasance is the "but if" or "provided that if" language). Under the facts in this question, the interests of Selden's children are not subject to a totally divesting condition subsequent. Instead, their interests will be reduced if Selden has more children. Since D mischaracterizes the facts, it's not the best response.

Answer 45

(C) is the best response,

because it correctly identifies that Bill must join in the conveyance, since he holds a possibility of reverter in Blackacre. The key fact here is that the executory interests in the Red Cross and in the Salvation Army are invalid because they violate the Rule Against Perpetuities – and that as a result, the interest reverts to Owen and his heirs.

Owen tried to convey a fee simple determinable subject to an executory interest to Alpha, and a shifting executory interest to the Red Cross. A "fee simple determinable" is a fee simple estate that automatically terminates on the occurrence of a specified event – it's a type of defeasible fee. An executory interest is an interest, in anyone but the grantor, that *can't* become possessory on the natural termination of the prior estate (natural termination meaning, for instance, the death of a life estate holder). If an executory interest divests another grantee, it's a "shifting" executory interest; if it divests the grantor, it's a "springing" interest.

The problem here is that a future interest can't follow a defeasible fee, since the executory interest may never vest or fail, and thus violates the Rule Against Perpetuities (which requires that an interest vest or fail within a life in being plus twenty-one years). Since the executory interest must be removed, Alpha is left with a defeasible fee, and Owen and his heirs are left with a possibility of reverter. Since Owen devised all his real estate to his brother, Bill, Bill will hold the possibility of reverter.

In order to convey Blackacre, both Alpha and Bill would have to join to convey a fee simple absolute (Della needn't join in the conveyance at all). As a result, the prayer for specific performance should be denied. Since C correctly identifies the result and the reasoning behind it, it's the best response.

(A) is not the best response,

because Alpha and Della do not own a fee simple absolute in Blackacre – Bill has a possibility of reverter, and Della does not have an interest in Blackacre.

Owen tried to convey a fee simple determinable subject to an executory interest to Alpha, and a shifting executory interest to the Red Cross. A "fee simple determinable" is a fee simple estate that automatically terminates on the occurrence of a specified event – it's a type of defeasible fee. An executory interest is an interest, in anyone but the grantor, that *can't* become possessory on the natural termination of the prior estate (natural termination meaning, for instance, the death of a life estate holder). If an executory interest divests another grantee, it's a "shifting" executory interest; if it divests the grantor, it's a "springing" interest.

The problem here is that a future interest can't follow a defeasible fee, since the executory interest may never vest or fail, and thus violates the Rule Against Perpetuities (which requires that an interest vest or fail within a life in being plus twenty-one years). Since the executory interest must be removed, Alpha is left with a defeasible fee, and Owen and his heirs are left with a possibility of reverter. Since Owen devised all his real estate to his brother, Bill, Bill will hold the possibility of reverter.

Thus, in order to convey a fee simple absolute in Blackacre, Alpha and Bill would have to join in the conveyance, since Alpha owns the defeasible fee, and Bill has a possibility of reverter, which "add up" to the entire fee. Since Bill has not been joined in the conveyance, and Della has, the prayer for specific performance should be denied. Since A states otherwise, it's not the best response.

(B) is not the best response,
because Alpha does not own the whole fee simple in Blackacre. Alpha has only a defeasible fee, and so, to convey a fee simple absolute in Blackacre, Bill, the holder of a possibility of reverter, would have to join in.

Owen tried to convey a fee simple determinable subject to an executory interest to Alpha, and a shifting executory interest to the Red Cross. A "fee simple determinable" is a fee simple estate that automatically terminates on the occurrence of a specified event – it's a type of defeasible fee. An executory interest is an interest, in anyone but the grantor, that *can't* become possessory on the natural termination of the prior estate (natural termination meaning, for instance, the death of a life estate holder). If an executory interest divests another grantee, it's a "shifting" executory interest; if it divests the grantor, it's a "springing" interest.

The problem here is that a future interest can't follow a defeasible fee, since the executory interest may never vest or fail, and thus violates the Rule Against Perpetuities (which requires that an interest vest or fail within a life in being plus twenty-one years). Since the executory interest must be removed, Alpha is left with a defeasible fee, and Owen and his heirs are left with a possibility of reverter. Since Owen devised all his real estate to his brother, Bill, Bill will hold the possibility of reverter.

Thus, in order to convey a fee simple absolute in Blackacre, Alpha and Bill would have to join in the conveyance, since Alpha owns the defeasible fee, and Bill has a possibility of reverter, which "add up" to the

entire fee. Since Alpha could not convey the entire fee simple himself, B is not the best response.

(D) is not the best response,
because the American Red Cross does not have a valid interest in Blackacre.

Owen tried to convey a fee simple determinable subject to an executory interest to Alpha, and a shifting executory interest to the Red Cross. A "fee simple determinable" is a fee simple estate that automatically terminates on the occurrence of a specified event – it's a type of defeasible fee. An executory interest is an interest, in anyone but the grantor, that *can't* become possessory on the natural termination of the prior estate (natural termination meaning, for instance, the death of a life estate holder). If an executory interest divests another grantee, it's a "shifting" executory interest; if it divests the grantor, it's a "springing" interest.

The problem here is that a future interest can't follow a defeasible fee, since the executory interest may never vest or fail, and thus violates the Rule Against Perpetuities (which requires that an interest vest or fail within a life in being plus twenty-one years). Since the executory interest must be removed, Alpha is left with a defeasible fee, and Owen and his heirs are left with a possibility of reverter. Since Owen devised all his real estate to his brother, Bill, Bill will hold the possibility of reverter.

If you chose this response, it could be because you mistakenly believed the "charity-to-charity" exception to remote vesting applied to these facts. It doesn't, because for that exception to apply, *both* Alpha *and* the Red Cross would have to be charities; it's not enough if only one of them is a charity. If Alpha had been a charity, the Red Cross would have had a valid shifting executory interest in Blackacre.

As it is, Alpha and Bill would have to join in a conveyance of Blackacre. Since D states that the American Red Cross would have to join in the conveyance, and not Bill, it's not the best response.

Answer 46

(B) is the best response,
because it correctly identifies the Red Cross's interest as a void executory interest.

Owen tried to convey a fee simple determinable subject to an executory interest to Alpha, and a shifting executory interest to the Red Cross. A "fee simple determinable" is a fee simple estate that automatically terminates on the occurrence of a specified event – it's a type of defeasible fee. An executory interest is an interest, in anyone but the grantor, that *can't* become possessory on the natural termination of the prior estate (natural termination meaning, for instance, the death of a life estate holder).

The problem here is that a future interest can't follow a defeasible fee, since the executory interest may never vest or fail, and thus violates the Rule Against

Perpetuities (which requires that an interest vest or fail within a life in being plus twenty-one years). Since the executory interest must be removed, Alpha is left with a defeasible fee, and Owen and his heirs are left with a possibility of reverter.

The fact that makes this question a little bit tricky is that the Red Cross is a charity, and this could have led you to believe the "charity" exception to the Rule Against Perpetuities applies, making the Red Cross's interest valid even though it may vest remotely. However, the charity exception only applies to charity-to-charity transfers; here, Alpha is not a charity, so the exception would not apply. Since B correctly identifies that the Red Cross has an invalid executory interest in Blackacre, it's the best response.

(A) is not the best response,

because not only is the Red Cross's interest not valid, it's not a contingent remainder. In fact, the Red Cross's interest is a void executory interest, leaving Alpha with a defeasible fee and Owen with a possibility of reverter.

Owen tried to convey a fee simple determinable subject to an executory interest to Alpha, and a shifting executory interest to the Red Cross. A "fee simple determinable" is a fee simple estate that automatically terminates on the occurrence of a specified event – it's a type of defeasible fee. An executory interest is an interest, in anyone but the grantor, that *can't* become possessory on the natural termination of the prior estate (natural termination meaning, for instance, the death of a life estate holder).

The problem here is that a future interest can't follow a defeasible fee, since the executory interest may never vest or fail, and thus violates the Rule Against Perpetuities (which requires that an interest vest or fail within a life in being plus twenty-one years). Since the executory interest must be removed, Alpha is left with a defeasible fee, and Owen and his heirs are left with a possibility of reverter.

The Red Cross's interest is not a contingent remainder, because it isn't a remainder at all, since it does not become possessory on the natural termination of the preceding estate, which a remainder must do. Instead, it divests Alpha of his interest in the event that Blackacre is used for any purpose other than as a residence. Since the Red Cross's interest is not a remainder of any kind, and beyond that is not valid, A is not the best response.

(C) is not the best response,

because although the Red Cross's interest is an executory interest, it is void.

Owen tried to convey a fee simple determinable subject to an executory interest to Alpha, and a shifting executory interest to the Red Cross. A "fee simple determinable" is a fee simple estate that automatically terminates on the occurrence of a specified event – it's a type of defeasible fee. An executory interest is an

interest, in anyone but the grantor, that *can't* become possessory on the natural termination of the prior estate (natural termination meaning, for instance, the death of a life estate holder).

The problem here is that a future interest can't follow a defeasible fee, since the executory interest may never vest or fail, and thus violates the Rule Against Perpetuities (which requires that an interest vest or fail within a life in being plus twenty-one years). Since the executory interest must be removed, Alpha is left with a defeasible fee, and Owen and his heirs are left with a possibility of reverter.

If you chose this response, it could be because you mistakenly believed the "charity-to-charity" exception to remote vesting applied to these facts. It doesn't, because for that exception to apply, *both* Alpha *and* the Red Cross would have to be charities; it's not enough if only one of them is a charity. If Alpha had been a charity, the Red Cross would have had a valid shifting executory interest in Blackacre.

As it is, the Red Cross's executory interest is not valid, and since C states otherwise, it's not the best response.

(D) is not the best response,

because, although it correctly identifies the Red Cross's interest as being invalid, it wrongly characterizes the interest as a contingent remainder.

Owen tried to convey a fee simple determinable subject to an executory interest to Alpha, and a shifting executory interest to the Red Cross. A "fee simple determinable" is a fee simple estate that automatically terminates on the occurrence of a specified event – it's a type of defeasible fee. An executory interest is an interest, in anyone but the grantor, that *can't* become possessory on the natural termination of the prior estate (natural termination meaning, for instance, the death of a life estate holder).

The problem here is that a future interest can't follow a defeasible fee, since the executory interest may never vest or fail, and thus violates the Rule Against Perpetuities (which requires that an interest vest or fail within a life in being plus twenty-one years). Since the executory interest must be removed, Alpha is left with a defeasible fee, and Owen and his heirs are left with a possibility of reverter.

The Red Cross's interest in not a contingent remainder, because it isn't a remainder at all, since it does not become possessory on the natural termination of the preceding estate, which a remainder must do. Instead, it divests Alpha of his interest in the event that Blackacre is used for any purpose other than as a residence. Since the Red Cross's interest is not a remainder of any kind, D is not the best response.

Answer 47

(A) is the best response,

because it reflects the traditional rule on splitting mortgage payments between life estate holders and remainderman. That rule is that the life estate holder pays the portion of the mortgage reflecting interest, and the remainderman pays the principal. Since A reflects this rule, it's the best response.

(B) is not the best response,

because Rowan, as remainderman, will be liable only for the portion of the mortgage representing principal.

The traditional rule is that the life estate holder pays interest on any mortgage on the property, whereas the remainderman pays the principal. Under these facts, this would mean that Perez pays the interest, and Rowan pays the principal. Since B states otherwise, it's not the best response.

(C) is not the best response,

because Perez will be liable only for the portion of the mortgage representing interest.

The traditional rule is that the life estate holder pays interest on any mortgage on the property, whereas the remainderman pays the principal. Under these facts, this would mean that Perez pays the interest, and Rowan pays the principal. Since C states that Perez should be liable for the entire amount, it's not the best response.

(D) is not the best response,

because while it suggests that the payment should be split between Perez and Rowan, it has their liabilities reversed. The traditional rule is that the life estate holder pays interest on any mortgage on the property, whereas the remainderman pays the principal. Under these facts, this would mean that Perez pays the interest, and Rowan pays the principal. Since D has these the other way around, it's not the best response.

Answer 48

(C) is the best response,

because it correctly identifies that the language of the deed created only a contractual obligation for Burton, not a restriction on the use of the land. The language here is a bit misleading because it sounds as though it creates a defeasible fee. A "defeasible fee" is a fee simple estates that terminates on the occurrence of a specified event. If the estate automatically terminates when the condition occurs, the estate is known as a "fee simple determinable." If the grantor must reenter and retake the property when the condition occurs, it's a fee simple defeasible subject to a condition subsequent.

What C recognizes is that courts dislike restraints on alienation, so if there is any question as to the interpretation of a conveyance, courts will favor a fee simple absolute over a defeasible fee. As a result, Burton would be left with a fee simple absolute and a personal, contractual liability to use the property as instructed by the deed. Since C recognizes this, it's the best response.

(A) is not the best response,

because the language of the deed did not create a defeasible fee. A "defeasible fee" is one that terminates on the occurrence of a specified event. (If it terminates automatically, it's a fee simple determinable; if the grantor must actively reenter and retake the property, it's a fee simple subject to a condition subsequent.) The "subject to the understanding that" language would not impose restrictions on usage of the estate; instead, it would impose, at most, only a contractual obligation on Burton's part.

This is somewhat tricky because the language sounds as though it could create a defeasible fee estate. However, courts do not like restraints on alienation, so if there is any question as to the interpretation of a conveyance, courts will favor fee simple absolute over a defeasible fee (either a fee simple determinable or a fee simple subject to a condition subsequent). Thus, Anders would have to have worded the conveyance something like "to Burton only so long as the premises are used for a public health center, which Burton must build within one year," to create a defeasible fee. Since the conveyance did not create a fee simple determinable, A is not the best response.

(B) is not the best response,

because the language of the fee did not create a fee subject to a condition subsequent. The "subject to the understanding that" would not impose restrictions on the usage of the estate; instead, it would impose, at most, only a contractual obligation on Burton's part.

This is difficult because the language sounds as though it could create a defeasible fee estate. A "defeasible fee" is one that terminates on the occurrence of a specified event. (If it terminates automatically, it's a fee simple determinable; if the grantor must actively reenter and retake the property, it's a fee simple subject to a condition subsequent.)

However, courts do not like restraints on alienation, so if there is any question as to the interpretation of a conveyance, courts will favor fee simple absolute over a defeasible fee (either a fee simple determinable or a fee simple subject to a condition subsequent). Assuming arguendo that the language here had created restrictions on usage, it would not have created a fee simple subject to a condition subsequent anyway, but a fee simple determinable. That's because there's no language here giving Anders the power to re-enter and retake the premises; rather, the property would revert automatically to Anders. To create a fee simple subject to a condition subsequent, the conveyance would have to have been worded something like "to Burton as long as he constructs and maintains and operates on said premises a public health center, but if he ever ceases to do so, Anders or his successors can re-enter and retake the premises." Since the conveyance here does not resemble this, B is not the best response.

Real Property — Answers   339

(D) is not the best response,

because the agreement here would not have to be enforced in equity. If an obligation was created by the wording of the deed, it will be enforceable at law as a contract, since it would not be sufficient to create a restriction on the use of the estate. Since D would have the obligation enforceable only in equity, it is not the best response.

Answer 49

(D) is the best response,

because it correctly identifies that neither of the gifts created here violates the Rule Against Perpetuities. The key fact here is that Hubert created the gift *in his will,* and the day he dies is the date the interests would be considered "created."

Under the Rule Against Perpetuities, an interest must vest or fail within a life in being plus twenty-one years or the creation of the interest. Both of the classes here – the children and the substitutionary gift to the grandchildren – fulfill this requirement. The key fact here is that the *gift was created in Green's will.* Since the will does not take effect – and the interests are thus not "created," until Green dies, no more members of the class of measuring lives (the children) can be added after the interests are created. Thus, all interests created in it must vest or fail within a life in being plus twenty-one years. In fact, all the interests will be determined when the youngest of Green's children turns, or would have turned, thirty. Since D correctly identifies that the interests created here are valid, it's the best response.

(A) is not the best response,

because the interests were created in a will, not in an *inter vivos* conveyance. As a result, the remainder to the children and the grandchildren is valid.

The Rule Against Perpetuities requires that, to be valid, an interest must vest or fail within a life in being plus twenty-one years, as of the date of the creation of the interest. Here, the interests would be considered created when the will takes effect, *not* when Hubert executed the will. Thus, Green could not remarry after the instrument takes effect, unless he engages in some Frankensteinian behavior beyond the reach of the Rule Against Perpetuities.

Since Green cannot have any more once he's dead, all of his children must be lives in being when the will takes effect. Thus, his grandchildren cannot take any later than the thirtieth year after the birth of a life-in-being (namely, Hubert's children). Since these interests cannot violate the Rule Against Perpetuities, the remainder to the children and grandchildren is valid, making A not the best response.

(B) is not the best response,

for the same reasons as A: Since the interests were created in a will and not in an *inter vivos* conveyance,

the remainder to the grandchildren is valid.

The relevant date in these facts is not when the will was executed, but when Hubert dies, because that's when the interests would be deemed "created." Once Green is dead, he can neither marry again nor have any more children. Thus, his children are all lives in being when the interests come into being (Green's death), and the grandchildren's interests either vest (if their parent dies before thirty) or fails (if the parent reaches thirty) within a life in being, never mind the additional twenty-one years in the perpetuities period. Since B incorrectly states that the gift to the grandchildren will fail, it's not the best response.

(C) is not the best response,

because Green's will became operative when he died. Thus, it doesn't matter that Carter was born after Green *executed* his will.

If you chose this response, it's probably because you misapplied the rule of convenience. The rule of convenience is a rule of construction which applies to class gifts. Where there is no expression of intent that all members of a class should take, the class closes when a member of the class can call for distribution of a share of the class gift. Under the facts here, no member of the "class" – Green's children – can call for distribution until Green dies, since the gift is in his will. Thus, all his children will be included, no matter when they are born, since they have to be born before his death (or within nine months of it). To make option C be the correct answer, let's change the facts. Say Green left Greenvale to "my friend Aloysius's children." When Green dies, Aloysius has two children, Allan and Beth, and after Green's death, Aloysius has Carter. With this hypothetical devise, Carter would be excluded, since Allan and Beth could call for distribution of the gift at Green's death. However, under the facts in the problem as given, the operative date is Green's death, when his will takes effect. Since Carter was a member of the "class" by then, he'll be entitled to a share, making C not the best response.

Answer 50

(C) is the best response,

because if no condition that the remaindermen survive Della was implied, the remainder would be vested.

It's clear that the interest in Della is a life estate. The interest following Della's death is clearly a remainder, but the interesting issue is whether that remainder is vested or contingent. (All remainders are either vested or contingent.) A remainder is contingent if it is subject to a condition precedent (other than the mere expiration of the preceding estate) that must be satisfied before the remainder can become a present interest. A common type of condition precedent is the requirement that the holder of the remainder survive the holder of the previous estate (often a life estate). Thus O's bequest "to A for life, remainder to B if and only if B survives A" would create a contingent remainder in B, because the remainder can become a present interest only if B is alive at A's death.

Here, there are two most plausible interpretations of what Theresa meant by "my descendants": (1) "all of my descendants existing and identifiable at the moment of my own death" (when the remainder is being created); or (2) "all of my descendants in existence when the remainder becomes possessory" (i.e., all descendants who survive Della). If interpretation (1) is chosen by the court, the remainder would be vested, because at the moment of Theresa's death we would know everyone who was to take, and if any predeceased Della, their heirs could take. If interpretation (2) is chosen, we would not know who takes until Della dies, at which point we would look to which descendants of Theresa survived Della; in that event, the remainder would be contingent. So it is only if the court selects interpretation (2) (imputing a condition that the remaindermen must survive Della in order to take) that would cause the remainder to be contingent.

(A) is not the best response,

because if vesting occurred at the moment the will was written, the remainder would be vested, not contingent.

This choice is referring to the possibility that the court would conclude that the bequest's reference to "my descendants" meant "anyone who is my descendant viewed as of the moment when I am writing this will." If this were the interpretation, then at the moment of the will-writing, we would know everyone who could take (they're all identifiable, and their remainder interests would vest immediately even though the remainder would not become possessory until Della died). In that event, the remainders would be vested, not contingent.

(B) is not the best response,

because if all vesting were related to Theresa's death, the remainder would be vested, not contingent.

A remainder's status as vested or contingent is evaluated at the moment the interest is created. Here, the moment the interest was "created" was the moment of Theresa's death. If vesting was determined as of Theresa's death, we can say with certainty at that moment who Theresa's descendants are. So as of the moment of the interest's creation (Theresa's death), the remaindermen are identifiable and are certain to take once Della dies. So on this analysis, the remainder would be vested, not contingent (see the analysis of vested vs. contingent in the discussion of Choice (C) above).

(D) is not the best response,

because an interpretation giving a life estate to Seth is not plausible on these facts, and in any cause would not create a contingent remainder.

Theresa's will quite clearly sought to benefit Della and not Seth when it expressly granted a life estate to Della but did not mention Seth. And a parent is permit-

ted to disinherit a child by failing to make a bequest to that child. Thus there would be no reason for a court to imply a life estate to Seth.

Furthermore, even if the court somehow managed to interpret the document as creating a life interest in Seth, this would not dispose of the issue of what the status of the remainder following Seth's interest would be. (For instance, if only those of Theresa's descendants who were still alive after both Della and Seth died took, then this remainder would be contingent; but if any descendant X alive at Theresa's death received a remainder that could be passed as property on X's death if X failed to survive both Della and Seth, X's remainder would be vested, not contingent.) So on this interpretation that the document created a life estate in Seth, the court wouldn't necessarily hold that the remainder after Seth died was contingent.

Answer 51

(B) is the best response,

because it identifies Barton's right as valid. Under the contract here, Amato has given Barton a valid right of first refusal in the event that she decides to alienate Riveracre, or upon her death. This is an interesting question in that there really isn't a pressing Rule Against Perpetuities issue under these facts; however, it's clear that the other responses are incorrect, leaving B as the best response, even though it doesn't address a central issue. Since B correctly identifies Barton's interest as valid and states correct reasoning, it's the best response.

(A) is not the best response,

because recording an instrument would not make it valid; it only establishes priority. The question here asks about the validity of Barton's interest, not the priority of it *vis a vis* someone else's interest in the property, and *that's* when priority is an issue. Thus, A cannot be the best response.

(C) is not the best response,

because Amato is restricting only *her own* power to convey or devise Riveracre, by giving Barton a right of first refusal. Restraints on alienation come into question only when a grantor or testator wants to convey or dispose of property while, *at the same time,* retaining control over its alienation. While it's true that restraints on fee estates are not valid, what Amato has here is not a restraint, but merely a right of first refusal for Barton in the event that she *does* decide to unload Riveracre, since she isn't conveying or disposing of property. This will be valid, making C not the best response.

(D) is not the best response,

because there is no transfer of property involved, so there cannot be a restraint on alienation. Restraints on alienation come into question only when a grantor or testator wants to convey or dispose of property while, *at the same time,* retaining control over its alienation. What Amato has essentially done is to give Barton a right of first refusal in the event she does decide to alienate Riveracre. Since this will be valid, D is not the best response.

Answer 52

(A) is the best response,

because an option to purchase "in gross" is subject to the Rule Against Perpetuities, and this option might be exercised beyond the Perpetuities period.

The option to purchase here, although it is contingent, would be held to create an interest in land. (That is, if the holder of the fee refused to convey after using the property for non-residential purposes, the optionee could get an order of specific performance. That's enough to give the optionee a contingent interest in the land.)

The option here is "in gross" — that is, the option is not appurtenant to an interest already held by the optionee in the land. (A purchase option given to a tenant, by contrast, would not be in gross.) Options in gross are generally held to be subject to the Rule Against Perpetuities.

The Rule says that an interest is void if it might vest more than 21 years after some life in being at the time of creation of the interest. Here, the only lives that might qualify as measuring lives are Adam's and Betty's. Yet by its terms, the clause might be exercisable in the very distant future — by Adam's great-great-grandchildren, for instance, as against Betty's great-great-children. This exercise would be far after any measuring life mentioned in the document plus 21 years. Consequently, the option would be void if options in gross are subject to the Rule. (It's not absolutely certain that options in gross *would* be subject to the Rule in a particular jurisdiction. But *if* the court rules against Adam, the only plausible explanation from those given is that the court has found that the Rule applies to options in gross, and that this option violates the Rule.)

(B) is not the best response,

because Bank's rights are subordinate to the option, even though Bank may have been unaware of the option.

A mortgagee's rights are no greater than the rights held by the mortgagor at the moment the mortgage is issued. Therefore, at the moment Bank funded the purchase and took its mortgage, Bank merely obtained the right, in the event of default, to foreclose on whatever rights Betty had. Those rights were subject to the option to repurchase. The fact that Bank didn't know this is irrelevant, especially since Bank had the opportunity to inspect the deed giving Betty her rights and failed to do so.

(C) is not the best response,

because Adam's rights were not subordinated to Bank's.

This is simply not a correct statement of how the law works. If there were no Perpetuities problem, Adam's purchase option would be superior to Bank's mortgage, because the purchase option existed in the very deed creating Betty's interest, and Bank's mortgage merely gave it the right to foreclose on whatever interest Betty obtained by the deed.

(D) is not the best response,

because courts will not inquire into the adequacy of consideration.

A court will not examine the "adequacy" of the consideration, as long as the court is satisfied that there really was a bargain or exchange. Here, the court would look at the overall transaction, and would undoubtedly conclude that it represented a true bargain, in which Betty agreed to accept the land with the restriction on it, and to be faced with the chance that if she broke her covenant, the land could be taken away from her (or her heirs) for a less-than-market price. Since there was an actual bargain, the fact that the option standing alone might have been for an "inadequate" (i.e., much-less-than-market) price will be irrelevant.

Answer 53

(C) is the best response,

because it correctly identifies that the conveyance was valid. Under the will, Luis took a contingent remainder, contingent on Eugenia's dying without children surviving her, but with a husband. The facts state specifically that any interest in land is freely alienable. Thus, Luis was free to convey his contingent remainder to Jose. He did so when he quitclaimed his interest in Blackacre to Jose, since a quitclaim deed transfers whatever interest the conveyor has in the property, without any covenants. Since option C recognizes that Luis took a valid interest under the will which he later validly conveyed to Jose, it's the best response.

(A) is not the best response,

because the after-acquired title doctrine *will not* apply to these facts. The "after-acquired title doctrine," also known as "estoppel by deed," covers this situation: The grantor purports to convey an estate larger than the one he has; the grantor subsequently acquires the title he's already purportedly conveyed; title *automatically* passes to grantee, by estoppel. Here, Luis conveyed *whatever interest he had* in Blackacre. In fact, he had a contingent remainder, contingent on Eugenia's dying without children surviving her, but with a husband. Under the facts here, all interests in land are freely alienable, so Luis was free to convey his contingent remainder. Thus, once he conveys the contingent remainder to Jose, Jose takes whatever interest Luis had, and it becomes possessory whenever it would have become possessory in Luis's hands. Thus, Luis didn't transfer an estate larger than he had; he transferred *exactly* what he had – a contingent remainder. As a result, the after-acquired title doctrine would not apply, and Luis's quitclaim deed would be sufficient to convey his contingent remainder. Since A states otherwise, it's not the best response.

(B) is not the best response,

because Luis took a contingent remainder under Ortega's will. It's a contingent remainder because it's subject to a condition precedent: Eugenia's dying with a husband but no children. The facts here state that any interest in land is freely alienable; thus, Luis was free to quitclaim his interest in Blackacre to Jose. If you thought Luis had no interest in Blackacre, it could be because his interest hadn't vested when he transferred it. However, that doesn't mean it's not an interest *at all*. Since B wrongly states that Luis took no interest in Blackacre, it's not the best response.

(D) is not the best response,

because the after-acquired title doctrine would not apply to these facts. The "after-acquired title doctrine," also known as "estoppel by deed," covers this situation: The grantor purports to convey an estate larger than the one he has; the grantor subsequently acquires the title he's already purportedly conveyed; title *automatically* passes to grantee, by estoppel. Here, Luis conveyed *whatever interest he had* in Blackacre. In fact, he had a contingent remainder, contingent on Eugenia's dying without children surviving her, but with a husband. Thus, Luis didn't transfer an estate larger than he had; he transferred *exactly* what he had – a contingent remainder. Since D would wrongly apply the after-acquired title doctrine to these facts, it's not the best response.

STRATEGIES AND TACTICS
TORTS

OUTLINE OF COVERAGE

The following outline for the Torts portion of the MBE was adopted by the Bar Examiners for all MBEs given on or after July, 2003.

Important note: you should answer Torts questions according to *principles of general applicability.* On the MBE, you must assume that there is no applicable statute unless one is specified. There's one exception: where a question involves *survival actions* and *wrongful death claims*, you can assume that a statute is available. In addition, assume that joint and several liability, with *pure* comparative negligence, is the relevant rule, unless you're told otherwise.

Here's what you need to know:

I. Intentional torts
    A. Harms to the person: assault, battery, false imprisonment, infliction of emotional distress
    B. Harms to property interests; trespass to land and chattels, conversion
    C. Defenses to claims for physical harms
        1. Consent
        2. Privileges and immunities: protection of self and others; protection of property interests; parental discipline; protection of public interests; necessity; incomplete privilege
II. Negligence
    A. The duty question: including failure to act; unforeseeable plaintiffs; and obligations to control the conduct of third parties
    B. The standard of care
        1. The reasonably prudent person; including children, physically and mentally impaired individuals, professional people, and other special classes
        2. Rules of conduct derived from statutes and custom
    C. Problems relating to proof of fault, including *res ipsa loquitur*
    D. Problems relating to causation
        1. But for and substantial causes
        2. Harms traceable to substantial causes
        3. Questions of apportionment of responsibility among multiple tortfeasors, including joint and several liability
    E. Limitations on liability and special rules of liability
        1. Problems relating to "remote" or "unforeseeable" causes, "legal" or "proximate" cause, and "superseding" causes
        2. Claims against owners and occupiers of land
        3. Claims for mental distress not arising from physical harm; other intangible injuries
        4. Claims for pure economic loss
    F. Liability for acts of others
        1. Employees and other agents
        2. Independent contractors and nondelegable duties
    G. Defenses
        1. Contributory fault: including common law contributory negligence and last clear chance, and the various forms of comparative negligence
        2. Assumption of risk
III. Strict liability: claims arising from abnormally dangerous activities; the rule of *Rylands v. Fletcher* and other common law strict liability claims; defenses
IV. Products liability: claims against manufacturers and others based on defects in manufacture, design, and warning; defenses

V. Other torts
    A. Claims based on nuisance, and defenses
    B. Claims based on defamation and invasion of privacy; defenses and constitutional limitations
    C. Claims based on misrepresentations, and defenses
    D. Claims based on intentional interference with business relations, and defenses

WHAT TO EXPECT

You'll face 34 questions on Torts on the MBE. *Half* of those (17 questions) will deal solely with category II — Negligence. The remaining Torts questions will cover the other categories (I, III, IV, and V). The exam will have questions on each of the roman numeral topics, but not necessarily on each of the sub-topics.

Accordingly, Torts (and especially negligence) is a subject you can't afford to ignore when you study.

The three most common types of Torts questions on the MBE are:

1. Questions asking you Plaintiff's best claim;
2. Questions asking you Defendant's best defense; and
3. Questions asking you if Plaintiff will prevail.

The most common of these three is the third type; this also represents the most difficult type of question, because you're frequently **not told the nature of the claim**. Instead, you're told only that Plaintiff asserted a claim for damages against Defendant, and you're left to figure out what the claim is. Handling this kind of question is addressed under "Exam Tactics" below.

STUDY STRATEGIES

1. Memorize this test for negligence.

You may remember the four elements of a negligence claim from your first year of law school: duty, breach, causation and damages. This simple list is perfectly correct but not terribly helpful on the MBE. You'll find it far easier to analyze negligence questions if you memorize this test:

> Defendant must fail to exercise such care as a reasonable person in his position would have exercised; his conduct must be a breach of the duty to prevent the foreseeable risk of harm to anyone in plaintiff's position, and this breach must cause plaintiff's damages.

If you find this a bit cumbersome, keep in mind that **almost ten percent of the entire** MBE will cover **only** negligence*;* thus, your grasp of this one definition could mean the difference between passing and failing!

2. Remember the purpose of *res ipsa loquitur.*

Remember that *res ipsa loquitur* is merely one means of proving a negligence claim: it establishes a *prima facie* case of negligence **only where direct evidence of the circumstances of the injury are unclear**. If you have direct evidence of how a result came about, **res ipsa loquitur will not apply**.

In order for *res ipsa* to establish a *prima facie* case of negligence, these three elements have to exist: the event causing injury would normally not have occurred in the absence of negligence; Defendant was in exclusive control of the instrumentality causing injury; and Plaintiff must not have voluntarily contributed to the event causing his injury. Perhaps you remember the classic case of the human toe in the sealed can of food, where negligence was established by applying *res ipsa loquitur.* Keep it in mind to in deciding whether *res ipsa exists.*

3. Remember what different causes of action do.

You need to know not only the elements of various torts, but also what kinds of facts these elements **apply to**. Because Torts questions frequently don't tell you what Plaintiff is basing her claim on, it's important that you be able to determine that from the facts of the question. While you'll get clues from the answer choices as to what Plaintiff's claim must be, your knowledge of the facts to which various elements apply will help you analyze questions quickly and eliminate incorrect responses.

4. Defamation.

Defamation questions pop up on the MBE a little more often than you might guess — you're likely to face 2 or 3. While much of defamation law is straightforward, here are some elements to keep in mind:

a. Special damages:

There's only one situation where plaintiff must prove special damages as part of his defamation claim: when his claim is based on slander and is for a *slanderous* statement not within the following four *slander per se* categories:

➡ statements accusing someone of a crime;
➡ statements alleging that someone has a foul or loathsome disease;
➡ statements adversely reflecting on a person's fitness to conduct her business or trade; and
➡ statements imputing serious sexual misconduct to someone (almost always to a woman).

If a plaintiff's claim doesn't fall within one of these four categories, he must prove special damages or his claim will fail. (By the way, special damages are *pecuniary* [economic] damages, e.g., a lost job, inheritance, gift, customer). If plaintiff's claim is for libel, or slander *per se*, she doesn't have to prove special damages. This is a sneaky issue because it's easy to overlook — thus, a perfect basis for an MBE question.

b. Publication:

The Bar Examiners tend to focus a lot on the requirement of *"publication,"* i.e., that the defamatory statement be *communicated* to someone other than the plaintiff. When you're reading a question involving an allegedly defamatory statement, you should, therefore, look carefully at the facts to see if the speaker of the statement *spoke before someone else.* If he didn't make his statement to anyone other than the person claiming defamation, then there's no *actionable* defamation.

One aspect of publication that the Bar Examiners like to test is that *strict liability* is not required; the plaintiff must show that the defendant either *intended* to communicate the statement to a third person or that the defendant *negligently* publicized the statement to third persons. Watch out for situations where a third person learns of the statement *through no fault of the defendant;* in this situation, the plaintiff *cannot* recover damages for the defendant's statement. For instance, suppose that John sends Eric a letter falsely accusing him of molesting John's teenage son. Eric, who receives the letter at work, crumples it up and tosses it in the wastebasket. An hour later, David, a fellow office worker of Eric, realizing that he threw an important document into the same wastebasket by mistake, goes through the wastebasket looking for his document. In the process, he finds John's letter, reads it, and tells some of his co-workers what it says; as a result, Eric loses his job. If Eric sues John for defamation, *Eric will lose*, even though he's been harmed, because the others heard the defamatory statement *through no fault of John.*

c. Qualified privilege:

Qualified privilege addresses the level of *fault* plaintiff will have to prove in order to prevail.

If a qualified privilege exists, Plaintiff will have to prove not only that a statement was defamatory and published through fault of the Defendant, but also that it was made with *malice* — knowing falsity or a reckless disregard for the truth. Qualified privilege protects a public or private interest, and the statement will be protected if it's in furtherance of that interest. Such situations include: a former employer warning a new employer about an employee's tendency to steal, testifying to a parole board about a prisoner's shortcomings, and the like.

Remember that, when no privilege exists and there's no special defendant which causes malice to be proven (e.g., the media), *defamation is never a strict liability offense*! Instead, the plaintiff will have to prove, at the very least, negligence.

Here's the level of fault that must be proven in various circumstances:

Public figure, public issue, media defendant — malice;
Public figure, private issue, media defendant — negligence;
Private figure, media defendant — negligence;
Non-media defendant — negligence.

Thus, if defendant wasn't unreasonable in some way, he *can't* be liable for defamation under any *circumstances*. How's this most likely to come up? Well, if defendant reasonably believed the statement was true, he *can't* be liable for negligence. (Of course, if defendant is a media defendant and the issue is public, Plaintiff has more to prove; in order to prevail, he has to show that Defendant knew the statement was false or evidenced a reckless disregard for its truth or falsity; proving negligence wouldn't be enough.)

5. Don't confuse defamation and invasion of privacy.

There's an important reason for remembering this: truth is not a defense to invasion of privacy, but it's a *complete* defense to defamation.

Remember that invasion of privacy is not a tort *itself*, but is, rather an "umbrella" tort covering four separate, distinct claims: (1) appropriation of plaintiff's personality for defendant's own commercial advantage; (2) intrusion on plaintiff's affairs or seclusion; (3) publication of facts which place plaintiff in a false light; and (4) public disclosure of private facts about plaintiff. (Here's a mnemonic: **A FLIP** [**A**ppropriation, **F**alse Light, **I**ntrusion, **P**rivate].) Thus, you could say a statement's *truth* is the essence of the damage in most invasion of privacy claims, while its *falsity* is the linchpin of a defamation claim.

6. Remember the sources of strict liability.

Strict liability can be the source of a great deal of frustration on the MBE. You will frequently be tempted to choose it as a response even where it doesn't apply. Remember that strict liability is not a handy means to avoid proving fault. The easiest way to avoid the strict liability trap is to remember not just the *elements* of strict liability, but also its *sources*. If a fact pattern doesn't address those sources, then *strict liability cannot be the basis of defendant's liability*!

Like negligence, strict liability requires proof of these four elements: Duty, breach, causation, and damages. Unlike negligence, strict liability involves an *absolute* duty, *not* a duty of reasonable care. Again, like negligence, this definition won't help you very much in analyzing MBE questions. What you should keep in mind is that there are *only three ways* a defendant can be strictly liable (i.e., liable without regard to fault or intent):

1. by *keeping a wild animal;*
2. by conducting an *abnormally dangerous activity*; or
3. by *selling a defective, unreasonably dangerous product* (strict *products liability*).

Strict liability can also be imposed by case law or statute, but, if this arises in an MBE question, the question will have to supply the statute or cases, and you'd just have to recognize and apply what you're given.

The first of the three general sources — animals — is easy to spot. If someone has a skunk, chimpanzee, elephant, or other *exotic pet* (and it needn't be one you'd consider *dangerous*; it need only be nondomesticated), and the pet causes damage, the owner will be liable, no matter how careful he was about keeping the thing penned up That's because, with strict liability, it doesn't matter how careful one is — the duty is *absolute*. Also, even if a pet is domesticated, if the owner has reason to know it's dangerous (e.g., it's bitten someone before), the owner will be liable.

The second source, an abnormally dangerous activity, is one to handle carefully. It's easy to mistake any dangerous activity for an abnormally dangerous one. You may find it helpful to remember that, in general, abnormally dangerous activities *cannot be performed with complete safety no matter how much care is taken — that's why they're a source of strict liability*. Common abnormally dangerous activities include fumigation, the use of explosives, blasting, excavating, and mining.

The third source — defective, unreasonably dangerous products — is just garden-variety strict products liability (also known simply as "products liability"). The basic elements of strict products liability are laid out in Restatement of Torts 2d § 402A; however, the definition in the Restatement isn't the easiest thing in the world to remember. Here's our list of all the important things you need to know about strict product liability for the MBE:

1. DEFECT: The product must have been in a defective condition which was unreasonably dangerous to the user/consumer or his property;
2. CONTROL: the condition must have existed when it left the defendant's control;
3. CHANGES: the product must not be expected to undergo significant changes before it gets to the user (or, it must not actually undergo significant changes);
4. BUSINESS: the seller must be in the business of selling the product (that is, he can't be a casual seller or a user);
5. CAUSATION: damage must result from the defect (defendant is liable for any physical damage);
6. NO PRIVITY: defendant's duty extends to anyone foreseeably endangered by the product (this means there's no *privity requirement*).

If you take the first letter of each of these elements, and add a vowel, you get a mnemonic: **CCC BoND** (**C**ontrol; **C**hanges; **C**ausation; **B**usiness, **N**o privity; **D**efect). If you can remember the elements without a mnemonic, fine — the point is, if you can remember them, you're unlikely to be fooled by a strict product liability question.

There's an irony about strict liability that you should keep in mind: outside of products liability, strict liability is the **hardest** claim to prove. In products liability cases, however, strict liability can be the **easiest** claim to prove, because the defendant can be liable for defects created by those who came **before** him in the distribution chain, and the plaintiff doesn't have to prove any lack of care. Also remember that, aside from products liability, strict liability is difficult because it applies to a very limited number of situations.

No matter what type of strict liability question you're examining, don't forget the **proximate cause** requirement. Remember what strict liability was designed to do: compensate for damage caused by the extraordinary risks created by certain enterprises. If the consequences are outside the extraordinary risk that **created** absolute liability, the defendant won't be liable. For instance, say Barnum keeps an elephant, Jumbo, as a pet. One day, Jumbo roams over to Old MacDonald's barn next door, falls through some rotted floorboards, clambers out, and goes home. Later, Old Mac goes to the barn, and, in the darkness, falls through the hole. Old Mac's injuries would be considered sufficiently outside the risk of the strict liability imposed upon Barnum to preclude liability on strict liability grounds.

7. Products liability.

Remember two things about products liability that you might otherwise overlook:

a. It's not the only basis of liability for harm caused by products.

You must remember that there are actually **three different ways** in which someone who makes or sells a product can be held liable for injuries the product causes. They are: (1) **strict products liability;** (2) **breach of warranty;** and (3) **negligence.** Although products liability is by far the most important of the three, you can't completely forget about warranty and negligence on the MBE.

As for warranty, you should remember that it's a **separate theory** of recovery for a defective product — it's **not an element of strict products liability**. The Bar Examiners sometimes throw a warranty answer choice into a question that assumes you're suing in strict liability. Watch out! It's probably a distractor. Also, remember the two types of warranties: express and implied. Express warranties do show up on the MBE; when one does, a commonly-tested aspect is that a plaintiff who successfully sues someone for breach of warranty is entitled to the **benefit of the bargain.**

As for negligence, remember that it's **always available as an alternative theory** when a product hurts someone; therefore, in products liability questions, you should be aware that negligence might be the correct answer choice, but **only** if strict products liability isn't available (usually because one of its requirements hasn't been met). A defendant can't be liable for product-related negligence, though, unless, at a minimum, the defect was **discoverable** by reasonable means.

One situation in which you may see negligence as the correct answer choice when you may be tempted to think products liability occurs when the purchaser of a defective, unreasonably dangerous product **learns about an available safety device** but **fails to install it.** If the device is cheap, and the danger from not installing the device is great, then the purchaser may be found negligent for failing to installing the device.

b. Privity.

When a product liability claim is based on either negligence or strict liability, **privity is not an issue**, because **anyone** who could foreseeably be endangered by the product can claim. Privity is only an issue with implied warranty and representation theories. Even there, if a claim is for breach of implied warranty or a form of representation, privity is only an issue in theory, because courts in general dislike denying plaintiff recovery due to lack of privity. Also, under implied warranty, privity is unlikely to be an issue because there are differences among the states as to who's covered and the MBE is not likely to test these differences. As to representations (either misrepresentation in tort or breach of express warranty in contract), privity is not, in practice, required. Furthermore, under representation theories, the remote party **suing** need not be familiar with the representation, as long as the buyer relied on the misrepresentation (in tort), or it was part of the "basis of the bargain" (in contract). For **all** these reasons, privity is not an issue generally, and is never an issue under strict liability and negligence. Even where it is an issue, a plaintiff would almost never be denied recovery just because he didn't purchase the item himself.

c. Liability for others' fault.

An important feature of strict products liability, as discussed in #6, above, is that the defendant needn't have created the defect — it merely has to be in existence **when the product leaves his** *control*. Thus, a retailer can be liable for a manufacturer-created defect, even if the retailer didn't know about it and couldn't have discovered it. This seems counter-intuitive until you remember that the retailer won't necessarily be **ultimately** liable; he can seek indemnity from his supplier, who can seek indemnity from his supplier, and so on, until the one originally responsible for creating the defect is held liable. The retailer is, nevertheless a potential defendant.

Under negligence, as opposed to products liability, this result couldn't be further from reality. The defendant himself **must** have failed to exercise due care in order to be held liable — he can't be held liable for the negligence of those preceding him in the distribution chain. Be careful, though. A defendant's negligence can take a variety of forms. Watch out for any behavior that is characterized as **unreasonable**. Thus, if defendant didn't inspect and a reasonable person would have, or if he **did** inspect but didn't find a defect when a **reasonable** inspection would have discovered it, he'll be liable, but only because his own conduct has been unreasonable.

8. Remember how nuisance resembles strict liability.

In order to prevail on a private nuisance claim, the plaintiff need only prove an **act by defendant creating an unreasonable, substantial interference with plaintiff's use or enjoyment of property**. Focus on the interest protected, namely, the plaintiff's right to use and enjoy his land. Thus, the defendant doesn't have to intend to interfere with plaintiff's rights, and he needn't even be negligent about interfering with plaintiff's rights, in order to be liable. Nuisance resembles strict liability that way.

Why is nuisance a tricky claim? Because it's likely to come up in situations where defendant has done **everything he reasonably can in order to avoid interfering with plaintiff's use and enjoyment of property**, so it seems as though he shouldn't be liable. Here's an example:

In 1975, Utility constructed a new plant for the generation of electricity. The plant burns lignite, a low grade fuel which is available in large quantities. Although the plant was constructed in accordance with the best practicable technology, the plant emits a substantial quantity of invisible fumes. The only way Utility can reduce the fumes is by the use of scrubbing equipment that would cost $50,000,000 to install and would increase the retail price of generated electricity by 50 per cent while reducing the volume of fumes by only 20 percent. Because of the expense of such equipment and its relative ineffectiveness, no other generating plants burning lignite use such equipment.

The plant was located in a sparsely settled rural area, remote from the large city served by Utility. Farmer owned a farm adjacent to the plant. He had farmed the land for forty years and lived on the premises. The prevailing winds carried fumes from the new plant over Farmer's land. His 1975 crop was less than half the average size of this crop over the five years immediately preceding the construction of the plant. It can be established that the fumes caused the crop reduction.

Farmer's hay fever, from which he had long suffered, became worse in 1976. Physicians advised him that the lignite fumes were affecting it and that serious lung disease would soon result unless he moved away from the plant. He did so, selling his farm at its reasonable market value, which was then $10,000 less than before the construction of the plant.

If Farmer asserts a claim based on negligence against Utility for crop damages, will Farmer prevail?

A. No, because Utility was not negligent

B. No, as to 1976 crop damage, because Farmer did not mitigate damages by selling his farm in 1975

C. Yes, as to 20 per cent of his crop damage, because use of available equipment would have reduced the fumes by 20 percent

D. Yes, because operation of the plant constituted a nuisance

Remember, all Plaintiff need prove is that Defendant's act resulted in a substantial, unreasonable interference with Plaintiff's use and enjoyment of his property. That's exactly what Utility did here, so Utility will be liable because it created a nuisance: choice D.

A number of factors will determine if something is "unreasonable," including zoning, Defendant's right to reasonably use of his land, the character of the neighborhood, the value of the land, alternatives available to Defendant, who was there first, and economic benefit. None of these elements will be controlling, though; the key to a private nuisance claim is interference with one's right to use and enjoy one's property.

EXAM TACTICS

1. Questions asking for a "best argument."

When faced with this type of question, you're likely to look for *all* the arguments that will support the choices given you, so you'll fail to look to focus on the only correct answer; instead, look at these questions this way: only one of the answer choices will provide a successful claim or defense. The other three will *all* be flawed in some way, because they either don't apply to the facts or don't correctly apply the law.

2. Questions asking what plaintiff will need to prove and in which the claim is identified (e.g., nuisance, defamation).

In this kind of question, only one answer choice will supply the correct level of proof. The others will *overstate* it or *understate* it. An answer choice *overstates* the proof required if, for instance, it overstates the level of fault. An answer choice understates the proof required if, for instance, it's not specific enough, or it's not relevant. *Whenever* a claim is mentioned, think of the elements that claim requires, as well as relevant defenses, and keep those in mind as you analyze each choice.

3. Identifying claims when a question doesn't.

As you'll remember from the strategies section, Torts questions frequently don't tell you the basis for the claim (e.g., nuisance, negligence). There are, however, three important categories that are easy to define:

Intentional tort;
Negligence; and
Strict liability.

If you apply the rules on strict liability that we gave you in the "Study Strategies" section, you can easily identify where strict liability applies. Intentional torts are inherently simple to identify. That will leave you in most cases with a negligence claim.

You'll get additional help in identifying the claim if you look at the reasoning of the answer choices, because at least one will contain a material element of the correct claim. Language such as "reason to know" in answer choices is the language of negligence, since that's determined objectively. Also, in the question *itself*, the facts will suggest what Plaintiff's claim must be. If there's no intent stated or indicated, you won't base a claim on an intentional tort. If there's no basis for strict liability, you wouldn't claim it. That leaves negligence.

It's important to identify the claim specifically, since incorrect answer choices are often wrong because they are based on something that is *not relevant to plaintiff's claim* but is relevant to *another*, similar claim. If you've correctly identified the claim, you can't be fooled this way.

Here's an example of this kind of question:

> When Mary Weld visited Dugan's Alleys to participate in the weekly bowling league competition held there, she brought her 2-year-old son, Bobby, along and left him in a nursery provided by Dugan for the convenience of his customers. The children in the nursery were normally supervised by three attendants, but at this particular time, as Mary Weld knew, there was only one attendant present to care for about twenty children of assorted ages.
>
> About thirty minutes later, while the attendant was looking the other way, Bobby suddenly started to cry. The attendant found him lying on his back, picked him up, and called his mother. It was later discovered that Bobby had suffered a skull fracture.
>
> If a claim is asserted against Dugan on Bobby's behalf, will Bobby prevail?
>
> A. Yes, because Dugan owed the child the highest degree of care.
>
> B. Yes, because a 2-year-old is incapable of contributory negligence.
>
> C. No, unless Dugan or his employees failed to exercise reasonable care to assure Bobby's safety.
>
> D. No, if Mary Weld assumed the risk by leaving Bobby in the nursery.

As you can see, you're not told what the claim is for. If you apply the intentional tort - strict liability - negligence analysis to the facts here, you will see that there's no intentional tort; also, baby-sitting is not a source of strict liability; that leaves only negligence as a basis for a claim. You know that the linchpin of a negligence claim is *defendant's unreasonable conduct;* so, if defendant behaved reasonably, he can't be liable. This, coupled with the fact that choices B and D rely on defenses which don't correspond with the facts and that Choice A states incorrectly the degree of care owed, should lead you to the best response: C.

4. Where "if" is the modifier in an answer choice.

Analyze these answer choices this way:

1. The reasoning of the answer choice must be **plausible** on the facts, i.e., there can't be anything in the facts suggesting an alternative is true.
2. The answer choice must resolve a significant issue.
3. The result must be consistent with the reasoning.

5. Where "because" is the modifier in an answer choice.

If the corresponding question asks who will prevail, ask yourself: "Would these facts be necessary to make the defendant liable?" Here's an example:

> Ohner owns the Acme Hotel. When the International Order of Badgers came to town for its convention, its members rented 400 of the 500 rooms, and the hotel opened its convention facilities to them. Badgers are a rowdy group, and during their convention they littered both the inside and the outside of the hotel with debris and bottles. The hotel manager knew that objects were being thrown out of the hotel windows. At his direction, hotel employees patrolled the hallways telling the guests to refrain from such conduct. Ohner was out of town and was not aware of the problems which were occurring. During the convention, as Smith walked past the Acme Hotel on the sidewalk, he was hit and injured by an ashtray thrown out of a window in the hotel. Smith sued Ohner for damages for his injuries.

> Will Smith prevail in his claim against Ohner?

>   A. Yes, because a property owner is strictly liable for acts on his premises if such acts cause harm to persons using the adjacent public sidewalks
>   B. Yes, if the person who threw the ashtray cannot be identified
>   C. No, because Ohner had no personal knowledge of the conduct of the hotel guests
>   D. No, if the trier of fact determines that the hotel employees had taken reasonable precautions to prevent such an injury

Look at choice C. Since it uses the modifier "because," it would have to state an element required to make the defendant liable. Although you're not told the nature of the claim here, using the reasoning from Exam Tactic #3, above, you can determine that the claim must be for negligence. Furthermore, if Ohner is to be held liable, it must be due to **vicarious liability** for the actions of his employees. In order for the employees to be liable for negligence, they must have failed to exercise the care a reasonable person in their position would have exercised. Could this be true without Ohner having personal knowledge of the conduct of the hotel guests? Sure. Employers are frequently held liable for torts of their employees when they have no personal knowledge. Thus, C can't be the best response, because it offers Ohner's lack of personal knowledge as the basis for Smith's failure to prevail.

Since we're talking about modifiers, look at the other three answer choices. Choice A, another answer choice using "because," is not the best response. If you apply the rules of strict liability from the strategies section, you know that a property owner cannot be held strictly liable for the kind of conduct in this question. Choice B, using the modifier "if," also isn't correct, because, although it is plausible on the facts, it wouldn't result in Ohner's being held liable. Lastly, consider choice D. Remember, a defendant can't be held liable for negligence if his conduct was reasonable. Under these facts, it's possible that the employees were reasonable, and, if they were, Ohner couldn't be held liable. That makes D the best response.

6. Where "unless" is the modifier in an answer choice.

If an answer choice states that "Plaintiff will prevail **unless** X...," then there must be no **other** way for Plaintiff to succeed. If X doesn't exist, Defendant isn't liable.

This reasoning need only be plausible on the facts. As an example, look at the question in Tactics, above, where the correct response, C, uses "unless" as a modifier. If you apply this reasoning to it, you'd ask yourself: If Dugan or his employees exercised reasonable care, is there any way they could be liable? There isn't, since reasonable behavior precludes liability for negligence. Thus, C must be correct.

7. Negligence questions: a shortcut.

In the "Study Strategies" section, above, we gave you a definition to apply to negligence. Here's a shortcut to the correct response in some circumstances.

Look at the defendant's conduct and see if it was **reasonable**. If it was, defendant **cannot be negligent, because negligence requires unreasonable behavior**. Here's an example of why remembering this can be helpful to you:

Doctor, a licensed physician, resided in her own home. The street in front of the home had a gradual slope. Doctor's garage was on the street level, with a driveway entrance from the street.

At two in the morning Doctor received an emergency call. She dressed and went to the garage to get her car and found a car parked in front of her driveway. That car was occupied by Parker, who, while intoxicated, had driven to that place and now was in a drunken stupor in the front seat. Unable to rouse Parker, Doctor pushed him into the passenger's side of the front seat and got in on the driver's side. Doctor released the brake and coasted the car down the street, planning to pull into a parking space that was open. When Doctor attempted to stop the car, the brakes failed to work, and the car crashed into the wall of Owner's home, damaging Owner's home and Parker's car and injuring Doctor and Parker. Subsequent examination of the car disclosed that the brake linings were badly worn. A state statute prohibits the operation of a motor vehicle unless the brakes are capable of stopping the vehicle within specified distances at specified speeds. The brakes on Parker's car were incapable of stopping the vehicle within the limits required by the statute. Another state statute makes it a criminal offense to be intoxicated while driving a motor vehicle.

If Parker asserts a claim against Doctor for his injuries, Parker will probably

- A. recover, because Doctor was negligent as a matter of law
- B. recover, because Doctor had no right to move the car
- C. not recover, because his brakes were defective
- D. not recover because he was in a drunken stupor when injured

As a threshold matter, you have to determine the nature of the claim, using the reasoning from Exam Tactic #3. The tort here can't be intentional, there's no basis for strict liability, so the claim must be negligence. Remember, in order to be negligent, **Doctor must have behaved unreasonably**. Under these facts, she simply didn't: it was an emergency situation and it was reasonable to move Parker's car. Keeping this in mind, you can automatically eliminate choices A and B, both of which suggest that Parker should recover. He can't recover from Doctor because she wasn't negligent. (In fact, choice C is the best response.)

8. Handling causation issues.

Causation is one of the trickiest issues on the entire MBE. Here are some pointers to help you analyze causation issues correctly.

The most important thing to remember is not to be intimidated by multiple causes. It's easy to be overwhelmed by fact patterns where there are multiple causes of Plaintiff's damage. Remember:

THERE CAN BE MORE THAN ONE CAUSE IN FACT.

The fact that someone other than the defendant contributed to Plaintiff's damages, **doesn't, in itself, relieve the defendant of liability** if defendant's conduct was a substantial factor in causing plaintiff's damages. Here's an example:

Section 1 of the Vehicle Code of State makes it illegal to cross a street in a central business district other than at a designated crosswalk. Section 2 of the Code prohibits parking any motor vehicle so that it blocks any part of a designated crosswalk. Ped wanted to cross Main Street in the central business district of City, located in State, but a truck parked by Trucker was blocking the designated crosswalk. Ped stepped out into Main Street and carefully walked around the back of the truck. Ped was struck by a motor vehicle negligently operated by Driver.

If Ped asserts a claim against Trucker, the most likely result is that Ped will

- A. prevail, because Trucker's violation of a state statute makes him strictly liable for all injuries caused thereby.
- B. prevail, because the probable purpose of Section 2 of the Vehicle Code of State was to safeguard pedestrians using crosswalks
- C. not prevail, because Ped assumed the risk of injury when he crossed the street outside the crosswalk
- D. not prevail, because Driver's conduct was the actual cause of Ped's harm

Look at choice D: It suggests that Driver's conduct was the only cause in fact of Ped's harm, and thus Trucker's conduct **can't** be considered. This isn't correct, because defendant's conduct can be a **substantial factor** in creating Plaintiff's injuries at the same time as there are other contributing causes. D can't be correct. (B is.)

Another important point:

TRY IGNORING EVERY ACTOR EXCEPT DEFENDANT AND PLAINTIFF.

Ask yourself this: were Plaintiff's injuries within the risk created by Defendant's act? Alternatively, If Defendant was negligent, what were the risks his negligence created? This is the **heart** of proximate cause. Remember that **intervening** causes relieve the original tortfeasor of liability only if the **results of the intervening causes are unforeseeable**. Think of intervening causes as insulation and decide whether they create enough of a barrier to justify Plaintiff's not recovering. Here's an example:

Motorist arranged to borrow his friend Owner's car to drive for one day while Motorist's car was being repaired. Owner knew that the brakes on his car were faulty and might fail in an emergency. Owner forgot to tell Motorist about the brakes when Motorist picked up the car, but Owner did telephone Spouse, Motorist's wife, and told her about them. Spouse, however, forgot to tell Motorist.

Motorist was driving Owner's car at a reasonable rate of speed and within the posted speed limit, with Spouse as a passenger. Another car, driven by Cross, crossed in front of Motorist at an intersection and in violation of the traffic signal. Motorist tried to stop, but the brakes failed, and the two cars collided. If the brakes had been in proper working order, Motorist could have stopped in time to avoid the collision. Motorist and Spouse were injured.

If Motorist asserts a claim against Cross, Motorist will

A. recover the full amount of his damages, because Motorist himself was not at fault

B. recover only a portion of his damages, because Spouse was also at fault

C. not recover, because Spouse was negligent and a wife's negligence is imputed to her husband

D. not recover, because the failure of the brakes was the immediate cause of the collision

Here, it's important to strip away everyone except Motorist and Cross, because this problem is a veritable wonderland of causation issues. If you look just at what Cross did — drive through a red light — you'd come to the conclusion that Cross should be liable, because the risk created by driving through a red light is collision with another car. In fact, this alone leads you to the right answer: A.

There's one more important point to remember here:

DON'T BE THROWN BY THE FACT THAT THE INTERVENING ACTOR MAY ALSO BE LIABLE.

The negligence of intervening actors won't relieve the original tortfeasors of liability unless the results of that intervening negligence are unforeseeable. The plaintiff is free to pick his defendant, and the mere fact that he could have sued someone else **as well** doesn't exonerate the defendant. For instance, in the example directly above, Cross isn't the only one who could be held liable — certainly Owner and probably Spouse could be, as well, because they all contributed significantly to Motorist's injuries; however, that fact alone would not exonerate any one of them!

FINALLY — REMEMBER THAT THERE CAN'T BE PROXIMATE CAUSE WITHOUT CAUSE IN FACT.

If conduct is the proximate cause of damage, it must be a cause in fact as well. If there aren't any intervening acts, proximate cause must exist (as long as defendant was negligent, of course). In fact, the only time you should be concerned with proximate cause is when **remote possibilities** are involved.

QUESTIONS
TORTS

QUESTIONS

TORTS

Question 1

Traveler was a passenger on a commercial aircraft owned and operated by Airline. The aircraft crashed into a mountain, killing everyone on board. The flying weather was good.

Traveler's legal representative brought a wrongful death action against Airline. At trial, the legal representative offered no expert or other testimony as to the cause of the crash.

On Airline's motion to dismiss at the conclusion of the legal representative's case, the court should

(A) grant the motion, because the legal representative has offered no evidence as to the cause of the crash.

(B) grant the motion, because the legal representative has failed to offer evidence negating the possibility that the crash may have been caused by mechanical failure that Airline could not have prevented.

(C) deny the motion, because the jury may infer that the aircraft crashed due to Airline's negligence.

(D) deny the motion, because in the circumstances common carriers are strictly liable.

Question 2

Del's sporting goods shop was burglarized by an escaped inmate from a nearby prison. The inmate stole a rifle and bullets from a locked cabinet. The burglar alarm at Del's shop did not go off because Del had negligently forgotten to activate the alarm's motion detector.

Shortly thereafter, the inmate used the rifle and ammunition stolen from Del in a shooting spree that caused injury to several people, including Paula.

If Paula sues Del for the injury she suffered, will Paula prevail?

(A) Yes, if Paula's injury would have been prevented had the motion detector been activated.

(B) Yes, because Del was negligent in failing to activate the motion detector.

(C) No, because the storage and sale of firearms and ammunition is not an abnormally dangerous activity.

(D) No, unless there is evidence of circumstances suggesting a high risk of theft and criminal use of firearms stocked by Del.

Question 3

Because of Farmer's default on his loan, the bank foreclosed on the farm and equipment that secured the loan. Among the items sold at the resulting auction was a new tractor recently delivered to Farmer by the retailer. Shortly after purchasing the tractor at the auction, Pratt was negligently operating the tractor on a hill when it rolled over due to a defect in the tractor's design. He was injured as a result. Pratt sued the auctioneer, alleging strict liability in tort. The jurisdiction has not adopted a comparative fault rule in strict liability cases.

In this suit, the result should be for the

(A) plaintiff, because the defendant sold a defective product that injured the plaintiff.

(B) plaintiff, if the defendant failed to inspect the tractor for defects prior to sale.

(C) defendant, because he should not be considered a "seller" for purposes of strict liability in tort.

(D) defendant, because the accident was caused in part by Pratt's negligence.

Question 4

Homeowner owns a house on a lake. Neighbor owns a house across a driveway from Homeowner's property. Neighbor's house sits on a hill and Neighbor can see the lake from his living room window.

Homeowner and Neighbor got into an argument and Homeowner erected a large spotlight on his property that automatically comes on at dusk and goes off at sunrise. The only reason Homeowner installed the light was to annoy Neighbor. The glare from the light severely detracts from Neighbor's view of the lake.

In a suit by Neighbor against Homeowner, will Neighbor prevail?

(A) Yes, because Homeowner installed the light solely to annoy Neighbor.

(B) Yes, if, and only if, Neighbor's property value is adversely affected.

(C) No, because Neighbor's view of the lake is not always obstructed.

(D) No, if the spotlight provides added security to Homeowner's property.

Question 5

Driver was driving his car near Owner's house when Owner's child darted into the street in front of Driver's car. As Driver swerved and braked his car to avoid hitting the child, the car skidded up into Owner's driveway and stopped just short of Owner, who was standing in the driveway and had witnessed the entire incident. Owner suffered serious emotional distress from witnessing the danger to his child and to himself. Neither Owner nor his property was physically harmed.

If Owner asserts a claim for damages against Driver, will Owner prevail?

(A) Yes, because Driver's entry onto Owner's land was unauthorized.

(B) Yes, because Owner suffered serious emotional distress by witnessing the danger to his child and to himself.

(C) No, unless Driver was negligent.

(D) No, unless Owner's child was exercising reasonable care.

Question 6

Neighbor, who lived next door to Homeowner, went into Homeowner's garage without permission and borrowed Homeowner's chain saw. Neighbor used the saw to clear broken branches from the trees on Neighbor's own property. After he had finished, Neighbor noticed several broken branches on Homeowner's trees that were in danger of falling on Homeowner's roof. While Neighbor was cutting Homeowner's branches, the saw broke.

In a suit for conversion by Homeowner against Neighbor, will Homeowner recover?

(A) Yes, for the actual damage to the saw.

(B) Yes, for the value of the saw before Neighbor borrowed it.

(C) No, because when the saw broke Neighbor was using it to benefit Homeowner.

(D) No, because Neighbor did not intend to keep the saw.

Question 7

When Parents were told that their child, Son, should repeat second grade, they sought to have him evaluated by a psychologist. The psychologist, who charged $300, determined that Son had a learning disability. Based upon the report, the school board placed Son in special classes. At an open meeting of the school board, Parents asked that the $300 they had paid to the psychologist be reimbursed by the school district. A reporter attending the meeting wrote a newspaper article about this request, mentioning Son by name.

In a privacy action brought by Son's legal representative against the newspaper, the plaintiff will

(A) recover, because the story is not newsworthy.

(B) recover, because Son is under the age of consent.

(C) not recover, if the story is a fair and accurate report of what transpired at the meeting.

(D) not recover, if Parents knew that the reporter was present.

Questions 8-10 are based on the following fact situation.

An ordinance of City makes it unlawful to park a motor vehicle on a City street within ten feet of a fire hydrant. At 1:55 p.m. Parker, realizing he must be in Bank before it closed at 2:00 p.m., and finding no other space available, parked his automobile in front of a fire hydrant on a City

street. Parker then hurried into the bank, leaving his aged neighbor, Ned, as a passenger in the rear seat of the car. About 5 minutes later, and while Parker was still in Bank, Driver was driving down the street. Driver swerved to avoid what he mistakenly thought was a hole in the street and sideswiped Parker's car. Parker's car was turned over on top of the hydrant, breaking the hydrant and causing a small flood of water. Parker's car was severely damaged and Ned was badly injured. There is no applicable guest statute.

Question 8

If Ned asserts a claim against Parker, the most likely result is that Ned will

(A) recover because Parker's action was negligence per se.

(B) recover because Parker's action was a continuing wrong which contributed to Ned's injuries.

(C) not recover because a reasonably prudent person could not foresee injury to Ned as a result of Parker's action.

(D) not recover because a violation of a city ordinance does not give rise to a civil cause of action.

Question 9

If Parker asserts a claim against Driver for damage to Parker's automobile, the most likely result is that Parker will

(A) recover because the purpose of the ordinance is to provide access to the fire hydrant.

(B) recover because Driver's negligence was later in time than Parker's act of parking.

(C) not recover because Parker was contributorily negligent as a matter of law.

(D) not recover because Parker's action in parking unlawfully was a continuing wrong.

Question 10

If City asserts a claim against Driver for the damage to the fire hydrant and Driver was negligent in swerving his car, his negligence is

A . a cause in fact and a legal cause of City's harm.

(B) a cause in fact, but not a legal cause, of City's harm because Parker parked illegally.

(C) a legal cause, but not a cause in fact, of City's harm because Parker's car struck the hydrant.

(D) neither a legal cause nor a cause in fact of City's harm.

Questions 11-12 are based on the following fact situation.

Susie Blake, a working woman, always brought her lunch to eat in the office. One Saturday afternoon she went to Roger's Market, a local self-service grocery, and bought a can of corned beef. The can had printed on its label "A

Product of West Beef Company." The company was a reputable supplier of beef products. On Sunday evening, Susie prepared a sandwich for lunch the next day, using the can of corned beef she had bought on Saturday. When Susie bit into her sandwich at lunch time the next day, a large sliver of bone concealed in the corned beef slice pierced between her teeth, broke one off, and came to rest deep in the roof of her mouth. This accident caused her to suffer severe pain and to incur medical expenses of $700.

Susie brought two claims for damages: one against Roger's Market and the other against West Beef Company. The claims were tried together. At the trial, Susie proved all of the above facts leading up to her injury as well as the elements of her damage. West Beef Company, one of the defendants, proved that it had not processed and packed the corned beef, but that such had been done by its regular and independent supplier, Meat Packers, Inc. West Beef Company further proved that it had never obtained from Meat Packers, Inc. defective meat products, and that it had no way of knowing that the can contained any dangerous material. Roger's Market, the other defendant, proved that it had no way of knowing the content of the can was likely to cause harm, and that it had sold the products of West Beef Company for a number of years without ever having been told by a customer that the products were defective. Both defendants agreed by stipulation in open court that Meat Packers, Inc. had been guilty of negligence in packing the corned beef containing the sliver of bone.

Question 11

If Susie's claim against Roger's Market is based on a negligence theory, Susie will

(A) recover, because the negligence of Meat Packers, Inc. follows passage of title of the product to the defendant.

(B) recover, because the defendant is liable for the negligence of Meat Packers, Inc., they being joint venturers.

(C) not recover, because there was no evidence that the defendant failed to exercise due care in selling her the corned beef.

(D) not recover, because she was guilty of contributory negligence when she selected the can containing the sliver of bone.

Question 12

If Susie's claim against West Beef Company is based on the theory of strict liability in tort, Susie will

(A) recover, because the can contained a sliver of bone when the defendant sold it.

(B) recover, because any breach of warranty chargeable to Roger's Market would be imputed to the defendant.

(C) not recover, because there was no privity of contract between her and the defendant.

(D) not recover, because any breach of warranty was that of Meat Packers, Inc. and not that of the defendant.

Question 13

Vintner is the owner of a large vineyard and offers balloon rides to visitors who wish to tour the grounds from the air. During one of the rides, Vintner was forced to make a crash landing on his own property. Without Vintner's knowledge or consent, Trespasser had entered the vineyard to camp for a couple of days. Trespasser was injured when he was hit by the basket of the descending balloon.

If Trespasser sues Vintner to recover damages for his injuries, will Trespasser prevail?

(A) No, unless the crash landing was made necessary by negligence on Vintner's part.

(B) No, unless Vintner could have prevented the injury to Trespasser after becoming aware of Trespasser's presence.

(C) Yes, because even a trespasser may recover for injuries caused by an abnormally dangerous activity.

(D) Yes, if the accident occurred at a place which Vintner knew was frequented by intruders.

Questions 14-15 are based on the following fact situation.

Si was in the act of siphoning gasoline from Neighbor's car in Neighbor's garage and without his consent when the gasoline exploded and a fire followed. Rescuer, seeing the fire, grabbed a fire extinguisher from his car and put out the fire, saving Si' s life and Neighbor's car and garage. In doing so, Rescuer was badly burned.

Question 14

If Rescuer asserts a claim against Si for personal injuries, Rescuer will

(A) prevail, because he saved Si's life.

(B) prevail, because Si was at fault in causing the fire.

(C) not prevail, because Rescuer knowingly assumed the risk.

(D) not prevail, because Rescuer's action was not a foreseeable consequence of Si's conduct.

Question 15

If Rescuer asserts a claim against Neighbor for personal injuries, Rescuer will

(A) prevail, because he saved Neighbor's property.

(B) prevail, because he acted reasonably in an emergency.

(C) not prevail, because Neighbor was not at fault.

(D) not prevail, because Rescuer knowingly assumed the risk.

Questions 16-17 are based on the following diagram and fact situation.

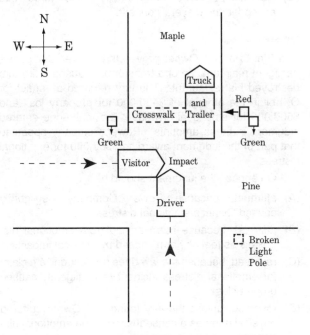

In City of State Y, Maple Street is a local public thorough-fare, designated as a one-way street for northbound traffic. Pine Street is a public thoroughfare, designated as a one-way street for eastbound traffic. Maple and Pine Streets intersect at right angles. The intersection is controlled by traffic lights. There are two sets of lights, one at the north-east corner and one at the northwest corner, for traffic on Maple Street. There are two sets of lights, one at the north-east corner and one at the southeast corner, for traffic on Pine Street.

Trucker was making a delivery to a market on the east side of Maple Street, just north of its intersection with Pine Street. There being insufficient space for his truck and enclosed trailer, he parked it with the rear of the trailer extending entirely across the crosswalk on the north side of the intersection. The height of the trailer was such that it entirely obscured the traffic light on the northeast corner from the view of traffic moving east on Pine Street. Unknown to Trucker, the traffic light at the southeast cor-ner was not functioning, because a collision seventy-two hours earlier had knocked down the pole from which the light was suspended.

Visitor, on his first trip to City, was driving east on Pine Street. Not seeing any traffic light or pole, he entered the intersection at a time when the light was red for eastbound traffic and green for northbound traffic. Driver, proceeding north on Maple Street and seeing the green light, entered the intersection without looking for any cross traffic and struck Visitor's car. Driver received personal injuries, and Visitor's car was damaged severely as a result of the impact.

Statutes of State Y make it a misdemeanor (1) to park

a motor vehicle so that any part projects into a crosswalk, and (2) to enter an intersection contrary to a traffic signal.

Question 16

If Driver asserts a claim against Trucker and establishes that Trucker was negligent, the likely result is that Trucker's negligence is

(A) a legal but not an actual cause of Driver's injuries.

(B) an actual but not a legal cause of Driver's injuries.

(C) both an actual and a legal cause of Driver's injuries.

(D) neither an actual nor a legal cause of Driver's injuries.

Question 17

If Driver asserts a claim against City, the theory on which he has the best chance of prevailing is that City

(A) is strictly liable for harm caused by a defective traffic signal.

(B) was negligent in not replacing the broken pole within seventy-two hours.

(C) had an absolute duty to maintain installed traffic sig-nals in good operating order.

(D) created a dangerous trap by not promptly replacing the broken pole.

Question 18

The warden of State Prison prohibits the photographing of the face of any prisoner without the prisoner's consent. Photographer, a news photographer, wanted to photo-graph Mobster, a notorious organized crime figure incar-cerated at State Prison. To circumvent the warden's prohibition, Photographer flew over the prison exercise yard and photographed Mobster. Prisoner, who was imprisoned for a technical violation of a regulatory statute, happened to be standing next to Mobster when the photo-graph was taken.

When the picture appeared in the press, Prisoner suf-fered severe emotional distress because he believed that his business associates and friends would think he was consorting with gangsters. Prisoner suffered no physical harm as the result of his emotional distress. Prisoner brought an action against Photographer for intentional or reckless infliction of emotional distress.

What is the best argument that Photographer can make in support of a motion for summary judgment?

(A) No reasonable person could conclude that Photogra-pher intended to photograph Prisoner.

(B) Prisoner did not suffer any physical injury arising from the emotional distress.

(C) As a news photographer, Photographer was privi-leged to take photographs that others could not.

(D) No reasonable person could conclude that Photogra-pher's conduct was extreme and outrageous as to Prisoner.

Question 19

Passenger departed on an ocean liner knowing that it would be a rough voyage due to predicted storms. The ocean liner was not equipped with the type of lifeboats required by the applicable statute.

Passenger was swept overboard and drowned in a storm so heavy that even a lifeboat that conformed to the statute could not have been launched.

In an action against the operator of the ocean liner brought by Passenger's representative, will Passenger's representative prevail?

(A) Yes, because the ocean liner was not equipped with the statutorily required lifeboats.

(B) Yes, because in these circumstances common carriers are strictly liable.

(C) No, because the storm was so severe that it would have been impossible to launch a statutorily required lifeboat.

(D) No, because Passenger assumed the risk by boarding the ocean liner knowing that it would be a rough voyage.

Question 20

Athlete, a professional football player, signed a written consent for his team's physician, Doctor, to perform a knee operation. After Athlete was under a general anesthetic, Doctor asked Surgeon, a world famous orthopedic surgeon, to perform the operation. Surgeon's skills were superior to Doctor's, and the operation was successful.

In an action for battery by Athlete against Surgeon, Athlete will

(A) prevail, because Athlete did not agree to allow Surgeon to perform the operation.

(B) prevail, because the consent form was in writing.

(C) not prevail, because Surgeon's skills were superior to Doctor's.

(D) not prevail, because the operation was successful.

Question 21

Perry suffered a serious injury while participating in an impromptu basketball game at a public park. The injury occurred when Perry and Dever, on opposing teams, each tried to obtain possession of the ball when it rebounded from the backboard after a missed shot at the basket. During that encounter, Perry was struck and injured by Dever's elbow. Perry now seeks compensation from Dever.

At the trial, evidence was introduced tending to prove that the game had been rough from the beginning, that elbows and knees had frequently been used to discourage interference by opposing players, and that Perry had been one of those making liberal use of such tactics.

In this action, will Perry prevail?

(A) Yes, if Dever intended to strike Perry with his elbow.

(B) Yes, if Dever intended to cause a harmful or offensive

contact with Perry.

(C) No, because Perry impliedly consented to rough play.

(D) No, unless Dever intentionally used force that exceeded the players' consent.

Question 22

In a trial to a jury, Owner proved that Power Company's negligent maintenance of a transformer caused a fire that destroyed his restaurant. The jury returned a verdict for Owner in the amount of $450,000 for property loss and $500,000 for emotional distress. The trial judge entered judgment in those amounts. Power Company appealed that part of the judgment awarding $500,000 for emotional distress.

On appeal, the judgment should be

(A) affirmed, because Power Company negligently caused Owner's emotional distress.

(B) affirmed, because harm arising from emotional distress is as real as harm caused by physical impact.

(C) reversed, because the law does not recognize a claim for emotional distress incident to negligently caused property loss.

(D) reversed, unless the jury found that Owner suffered physical harm as a consequence of the emotional distress caused by his property loss.

Questions 23-24 are based on the following fact situation.

Adam's car sustained moderate damage in a collision with a car driven by Basher. The accident was caused solely by Basher's negligence. Adam's car was still drivable after the accident. Examining the car the next morning, Adam could see that a rear fender had to be replaced. He also noticed that gasoline had dripped onto the garage floor. The collision had caused a small leak in the gasoline tank.

Adam then took the car to Mechanic, who owns and operates a body shop, and arranged with Mechanic to repair the damage. During their discussion Adam neglected to mention the gasoline leakage. Thereafter, while Mechanic was loosening some of the damaged material with a hammer, he caused a spark, igniting vapor and gasoline that had leaked from the fuel tank. Mechanic was severely burned.

Mechanic has brought an action to recover damages against Adam and Basher. The jurisdiction has adopted a pure comparative negligence rule in place of the traditional common-law rule of contributory negligence.

Question 23

In this action, will Mechanic obtain a judgment against Basher?

(A) No, unless there is evidence that Basher was aware of the gasoline leak.

(B) No, if Mechanic would not have been harmed had Adam warned him about the gasoline leak.

(C) Yes, unless Mechanic was negligent in not discovering the gasoline leak himself.

(D) Yes, if Mechanic's injury was a proximate consequence of Basher's negligent driving.

Question 24

In this action, will Mechanic obtain a judgment against Adam?

(A) No, because it was Mechanic's job to inspect the vehicle and repair whatever needed repair.

(B) No, unless Adam was aware of the risk that the gasoline leak represented.

(C) Yes, if a reasonable person in Adam's position would have warned Mechanic about the gasoline leak.

(D) Yes, because the car was unreasonably dangerous when Adam delivered it to Mechanic.

Question 25

Fran, who was driving at an excessive speed, applied her brakes to stop at a traffic light. Due to damp, fallen leaves, her car skidded and came to a halt perpendicular to the roadway. Sid, who was also driving at an excessive speed and was immediately behind Fran, saw Fran's car perpendicular to the roadway. Although Sid had sufficient distance to come to a slow, controlled stop, he decided not to slow down but, rather, to swerve to the left in an effort to go around Fran's car. Due to oncoming traffic, the space was insufficient and Sid's car collided with Fran's car, severely injuring Fran.

Fran filed a personal injury action against Sid in a jurisdiction in which contributory negligence is a bar to recovery.

Will Fran prevail?

(A) Yes, if the jury finds that Sid was more than 50% at fault.

(B) Yes, if the jury finds that Sid had the last clear chance.

(C) No, if the jury finds that Fran's conduct was in any way a legal cause of the accident.

(D) No, if the jury finds that, in speeding, Fran assumed the risk.

Question 26

Orderly, a male attendant who worked at Hospital, had sexual relations with Patient, a severely retarded person, in her room at Hospital.

In a tort action brought on Patient's behalf against Hospital, Patient will

(A) not prevail, if Orderly's actions were outside the scope of his employment.

(B) not prevail, if Patient initiated the relationship with Orderly and encouraged his actions.

(C) prevail, if Orderly was an employee of Hospital.

(D) prevail, if Hospital failed to use reasonable care to protect Patient from such conduct.

Question 27

The Rapido is a sports car manufactured by the Rapido Motor Co. The Rapido has an excellent reputation for mechanical reliability with one exception, that the motor may stall if the engine has not had an extended warm-up. Driver had just begun to drive her Rapido in city traffic without a warm-up when the engine suddenly stalled. A car driven by Troody rear-ended Driver's car. Driver suffered no external physical injuries as a result of the collision. However, the shock of the crash caused her to suffer a severe heart attack.

Driver brought an action against the Rapido Motor Co. based on strict liability in tort. During the trial, the plaintiff presented evidence of an alternative engine design of equal cost that would eliminate the stalling problem without impairing the functions of the engine in any way. The defendant moves for a directed verdict at the close of the evidence.

This motion should be

(A) denied, because the jury could find that an unreasonably dangerous defect in the engine was a proximate cause of the collision.

(B) denied, if the jury could find that the Rapido was not crashworthy.

(C) granted, because Troody's failure to stop within an assured clear distance was a superseding cause of the collision.

(D) granted, if a person of normal sensitivity would not have suffered a heart attack under these circumstances.

Question 28

Employer retained Doctor to evaluate medical records of prospective employees. Doctor informed Employer that Applicant, a prospective employee, suffered from AIDS. Employer informed Applicant of this and declined to hire her.

Applicant was shocked by this news and suffered a heart attack as a result. Subsequent tests revealed that Applicant in fact did not have AIDS. Doctor had negligently confused Applicant's file with that of another prospective employee.

If Applicant sued Doctor for damages, on which of the following causes of action would Applicant recover?

   I. Invasion of privacy.

   II. Negligent misrepresentation.

   III. Negligent infliction of emotional distress.

(A) III only.

(B) I and II only.

(C) II and III only.

(D) I, II, and III.

Question 29

Powell, who was an asbestos insulation installer from 1955 to 1965, contracted asbestosis, a serious lung disorder, as a result of inhaling airborne asbestos particles on the job. The asbestos was manufactured and sold to Powell's employer by the Acme Asbestos Company. Because neither Acme nor anyone else discovered the risk to asbestos installers until 1966, Acme did not provide any warnings of the risks to installers until after that date.

Powell brought an action against Acme based on strict liability in tort for failure to warn. The case is to be tried before a jury. The jurisdiction has not adopted a comparative fault rule in strict liability cases.

In this action, an issue that is relevant to the case and is a question for the court to decide as a matter of law, rather than for the jury to decide as a question of fact, is whether

(A) a satisfactory, safer, alternative insulation material exists under today's technology.

(B) the defendant should be held to the standard of a prudent manufacturer who knew of the risks, regardless of whether the risks were reasonably discoverable before 1966.

(C) the defendant should reasonably have known of the risks of asbestos insulation materials before 1966, even though no one else had discovered the risks.

(D) the asbestos insulation materials to which the plaintiff was exposed were inherently dangerous.

Question 30

While approaching an intersection with the red light against him, Motorist suffered a heart attack that rendered him unconscious. Motorist's car struck Child, who was crossing the street with the green light in her favor. Under the state motor vehicle code, it is an offense to drive through a red traffic light.

Child sued Motorist to recover for her injuries. At trial it was stipulated that (1) immediately prior to suffering the heart attack, Motorist had been driving within the speed limit, had seen the red light, and had begun to slow his car; (2) Motorist had no history of heart disease and no warning of this attack; (3) while Motorist was unconscious, his car ran the red light.

On cross motions for directed verdicts on the issue of liability at the conclusion of the proofs, the court should

(A) grant Child's motion, because Motorist ran a red light in violation of the motor vehicle code.

(B) grant Child's motion, because, in the circumstances, reasonable persons would infer that Motorist was negligent.

(C) grant Motorist's motion, because he had no history of heart disease or warning of the heart attack.

(D) deny both motions and submit the case to the jury, to determine whether, in the circumstances, Motorist's conduct was that of a reasonably prudent person.

Question 31

Hank owned a secondhand goods store. He often placed merchandise on the sidewalk, sometimes for short intervals, sometimes from 7:00 a.m. until 6:00 p.m. Pedestrians from time to time stopped and gathered to look at the merchandise. Fred had moved into an apartment which was situated immediately above Hank's store; a street-level stairway entrance was located about twenty feet to the east. On several occasions, Fred had complained to Hank about the situation because not only were his view and peace of mind affected, but his travel on the sidewalk was made more difficult. Fred owned and managed a restaurant two blocks to the west of his apartment and made frequent trips back and forth. There was a back entrance to his apartment through a parking lot; this entrance was about two hundred feet farther in walking distance from his restaurant. Once Fred complained to the police, whereupon Hank was arrested under a local ordinance which prohibited the placing of goods or merchandise on public sidewalks and imposed, as its sole sanction, a fine for its violation.

One day, the sidewalk in front of Hank's store was unusually cluttered because he was cleaning and mopping the floor of his shop. Fred and his fifteen-year-old son, Steve, saw a bus they wished to take, and they raced down the stairs and on to the cluttered sidewalk in front of Hank's store, Fred in the lead. While dodging merchandise and people, Fred fell. Steve tripped over him and suffered a broken arm. Fred also suffered broken bones and was unable to attend to his duties for six weeks.

If, prior to the day of his personal injuries, Fred had asserted a claim based on public nuisance for injunctive relief against Hank for his obstruction of the sidewalk in violation of the ordinance, the defense on which Hank would have most likely prevailed is that

(A) Fred consented to the obstruction by continuing to rent his apartment.

(B) the violation of the ordinance was not unreasonable.

(C) remedy of abatement by self-help was adequate.

(D) there was no claim for special damage.

Questions 32-36 are based on the following fact situation.

Motorco is a manufacturer of motor vehicles. A federal regulation requires that all motor vehicles manufactured for sale in the United States be equipped with seat belts for each passenger and prescribes specifications for such belts. Motorco equipped all its cars with seat belts. It purchased all the bolts used in its seat belt assemblies from Boltco and it tested samples from each shipment received.

Dunn purchased a motor vehicle manufactured by Motorco. While operating the car, with Price as a passenger in the front seat, Dunn collided with another vehicle. The collision was due solely to Dunn's negligence. Price had his seat belt fastened, but one of the bolts which anchored the belt to the frame broke. Price was thrown through the windshield, sustaining various injuries. Dunn, whose belt was fastened and held, was killed when, following the collision, the car went off the road, down an embankment, and overturned.

Subsequent to the accident, tests of the bolt that broke showed metallurgical defects. Motorco's records showed that tests of samples from the shipment in which the defective bolt was received revealed no defective bolts.

Question 32

If there is a guest law in the state where the accident happened, then in any action by Price against Motorco, that guest statute has which of the following effects?

(A) It bars recovery by Price.

(B) It bars recovery by Price unless he can prove that Dunn was guilty of more than ordinary negligence.

(C) It bars recovery by Price unless he can prove that Motorco was guilty of more than ordinary negligence.

(D) It is not relevant.

Question 33

In a negligence action by Price against Motorco, the proof needed to establish a prima facie case is

(A) only that the bolt was defective.

(B) that the bolt was defective and had not been inspected by Motorco.

(C) that the bolt was defective, was inspected by Motorco, and the defect was not discovered.

(D) that the bolt was defective and the defect would have been discovered if Motorco had exercised reasonable care in the inspection of component parts.

Question 34

In a negligence action by Price against Motorco, the negligence of Dunn will be considered to be

(A) within the risk created by the action of Motorco.

(B) the proximate cause of Price's injuries.

(C) the legal cause of Price's injuries.

(D) an independent, intervening cause of Price's injuries.

Question 35

In a negligence action by Price against Motorco, a defense that is likely to prevail is that

(A) Motorco exercised due care in testing the bolts.

(B) Dunn's negligence was the legal cause of Price's injuries.

(C) Price was a passenger in Dunn's car.

(D) Boltco, as the manufacturer of the bolts, has the sole responsibility for any defects therein.

Question 36

In an action based on strict liability in tort by Price against Boltco, Price will rely principally on

(A) *res ipsa loquitur.*

(B) warranty.

(C) privity.

(D) the fact that one of the bolts anchoring his seat was defective.

Question 37

The most generally accepted basis on which a court will hold that X has a legal duty to aid another is the recognition by X that there is immediate danger of serious harm to

(A) another human being from a stranger's wrongful conduct.

(B) his neighbor from a stranger's wrongful conduct.

(C) his cousin from a stranger's wrongful conduct.

(D) another human being from X's own non-negligent conduct.

Questions 38-42 are based on the following fact situation.

Walker, a pedestrian, started north across the street in a clearly marked north-south crosswalk with the green traffic light in her favor. Walker was in a hurry, and so before reaching the north curb on the street, she cut to her left diagonally across the street to the east-west crosswalk and started across it. Just after reaching the east-west crosswalk, the traffic light turned green in her favor. She proceeded about five steps further across the street to the west in the crosswalk when she was struck by a car approaching from her right that she thought would stop, but did not. The car was driven by Driver, 81 years of age, who failed to stop his car after seeing that the traffic light was red against him. Walker had a bone disease, resulting in very brittle bones, that is prevalent in only 0.02 percent of the population. As a result of the impact, Walker suffered a broken leg and the destruction of her family heirloom, a Picasso original painting that she was taking to her bank for safe-keeping. The painting had been purchased by Walker's grandmother for $750 but was valued at $500,000 at the time of the accident.

Walker has filed suit against Driver. Driver's attorney has alleged that Walker violated a state statute requiring that pedestrians stay in crosswalks, and that if Walker had not violated the statute she would have had to walk 25 feet more to reach the impact point and therefore would not have been at a place where she could have been hit by Driver. Walker's attorney ascertains that there is a statute as alleged by Driver, that his measurements are correct, that there is a state statute requiring observance of traffic lights, and that Driver's license expired two years prior to the collision.

Question 38

The violation of the crosswalk statute by Walker should not defeat her cause of action against Driver because

(A) Driver violated the traffic light statute at a later point in time than Walker's violation.

(B) pedestrians are entitled to assume that automobile drivers will obey the law.

(C) Walker was hit while in the crosswalk.

(D) the risks that the statute was designed to protect against probably did not include an earlier arrival at another point.

Question 39

The failure of Driver to have a valid driver's license has which of the following effects?

(A) It makes Driver liable to Walker because Driver is a trespasser on the highway.

(B) It would not furnish a basis for liability.

(C) It proves that Driver is an unfit driver in this instance.

(D) It makes Driver absolutely liable for Walker's injury.

Question 40

If Walker establishes liability on the part of Driver for her physical injuries, should Walker's recovery include damages for a broken leg?

(A) No, since only 0.02 percent of the population have bones as brittle as Walker's.

(B) No, unless a person of ordinary health would probably have suffered a broken leg from the impact.

(C) Yes, because Driver could foresee that there would be unforeseeable consequences of the impact.

(D) Yes, even though the extent of the injury was not a foreseeable consequence of the impact.

Question 41

Walker's violation of the crosswalk statute should not be considered by the jury because

(A) there is no dispute in the evidence about factual cause.

(B) as a matter of law the violation of the statute results in liability for all resulting harm.

(C) as a matter of law Driver's conduct was an independent intervening cause.

(D) as a matter of law the injury to Walker was not the result of a risk the statute was designed to protect against.

Question 42

Company designed and built a processing plant for the manufacture of an explosive chemical. Engineer was retained by Company to design a filter system for the processing plant. She prepared an application for a permit to build the plant's filter system and submitted it to the state's Department of Environmental Protection (DEP). As required by DEP regulations, Engineer submitted a blueprint to the DEP with the application for permit. The blueprint showed the entire facility and was signed and sealed by her as a licensed professional engineer.

After the project was completed, a portion of the processing plant exploded, injuring Plaintiff. During discovery in an action by Plaintiff against Engineer, it was established that the explosion was caused by a design defect in the processing plant that was unrelated to the filter system designed by Engineer.

In that action, will Plaintiff prevail?

(A) Yes, if Engineer signed, sealed, and submitted a blueprint that showed the design defect.

(B) Yes, because all of the plant's designers are jointly and severally liable for the defect.

(C) No, because Engineer owed no duty to Plaintiff to prevent the particular risk of harm.

(D) No, if Engineer was an independent contractor.

Questions 43-44 are based on the following fact situation.

Parents purchased a new mobile home from Seller. The mobile home was manufactured by Mobilco and had a ventilating system designed by Mobilco with both a heating unit and an air conditioner. Mobilco installed a furnace manufactured by Heatco and an air conditioning unit manufactured by Coolco. Each was controlled by an independent thermostat installed by Mobilco. Because of the manner in which Mobilco designed the ventilating system, the first time the ventilating system was operated by Parents, cold air was vented into Parents' bedroom to keep the temperature at 68°F (20°C). The cold air then activated the heater thermostat, and hot air was pumped into the bedroom of Child, the six-month-old child of Parents. The temperature in Child's room reached more than 170°F (77°C) before Child's mother became aware of the condition and shut the system off manually. As a result, Child suffered permanent physical injury.

Claims have been asserted by Child, through a duly appointed guardian, against Mobilco, Seller, Heatco, and Coolco.

Question 43

If Child's claim against Seller is based on negligence, then the minimum proof necessary to establish Seller's liability is that the ventilating system

(A) was defective.

(B) was defective and had not been inspected by Seller.

(C) was defective and had been inspected by Seller, and the defect was not discovered.

(D) was defective, and the defect would have been discovered if Seller had exercised reasonable care in inspecting the system.

Question 44

If Child's claims against Mobilco, Heatco, and Coolco are based on strict liability in tort, Child will probably recover against

(A) Mobilco only, because the ventilating system was defectively designed by Mobilco.

(B) Heatco only, because it was the excessive heat from the furnace that caused Child's injuries.

(C) Mobilco and Heatco only, because the combination of Mobilco's design and Heatco's furnace caused Child's injuries.

(D) Mobilco, Heatco and Coolco, because the combination of Mobilco's design, Heatco's furnace, and Coolco's air conditioning unit caused Child's injuries.

Question 45

Carver is a chemical engineer. She has no interest in or connection with Chemco. Carver noticed that Chemco's most recent publicly issued financial statement listed, as part of Chemco's assets, a large inventory of a certain special chemical compound. This asset was listed at a cost of $100,000, but Carver knew that the ingredients of the compound were in short supply and that the current market value of the inventory was in excess of $1,000,000. There was no current public quotation of the price of Chemco stock. The book value of Chemco stock, according to the statement, was $5 a share; its actual value was $30 a share.

Knowing these facts, Carver offered to purchase from Page at $6 a share the 1,000 shares of Chemco stock owned by Page. Page and Carver had not previously met. Page sold the stock to Carver for $6 a share.

If Page asserts a claim based on misrepresentation against Carver, will Page prevail?

(A) Yes, because Carver knew that the value of the stock was greater than the price she offered.

(B) Yes, if Carver did not inform Page of the true value of the inventory.

(C) No, unless Carver told Page that the stock was not worth more than $6 a share.

(D) No, if Chemco's financial statement was available to Page.

Question 46

Light Company is the sole distributor of electrical power in City. The Company owns and maintains all of the electric poles and equipment in City. Light Company has complied with the National Electrical Safety Code, which establishes minimum requirements for the installation and maintenance of power poles. The Code has been approved by the federal and state governments.

Light Company has had to replace insulators on its poles repeatedly because unknown persons repeatedly shoot at and destroy them. This causes the power lines to fall to the ground. On one of these occasions, Paul, Faber's 5-year-old son, wandered out of Faber's yard, intentionally touched a downed wire, and was seriously burned.

If a claim on Paul's behalf is asserted against Light Company, the probable result is that Paul will

(A) recover, if Light Company could have taken reasonable steps to prevent the lines from falling when the insulators were destroyed.

(B) recover, because a supplier of electricity is strictly liable in tort.

(C) not recover, unless Light Company failed to exercise reasonable care to stop the destruction of the insulators.

(D) not recover, because the destruction of the insulators was intentional.

Question 47

The city of Metropolis has an ordinance that makes it an offense, punishable by fine, for the owner of a dog to permit the dog to run unleashed on a public way.

Smythe, a police officer, observed a small dog running loose in the street. As he picked the dog up, Nelson, who was seated in her car lawfully parked at the curb, called out, "Oh, thank you, Officer for returning Fido." Smythe asked Nelson whether the dog was hers, and when she acknowledged ownership, he asked her to see her driver's license. Nelson gave her name and address, but she refused to produce a driver's license. Smythe then told her to produce her driver's license. Smythe then told her to produce her driver's license if she did not want to go to jail. Nelson responded by saying, "Isn't this ridiculous?" Smythe took her by the arm and said, "Let's go. You are under arrest."

Nelson cried out that Smythe was hurting her but he refused to release her arm, and she struck him with her free hand. Smythe then dragged Nelson from her car, forced her into his squad car, and took her to the police station.

The incident took place on the street in front of the apartment where Nelson and her aged father, Joplin, lived. Smythe did not know that Joplin had observed what took place from a window in the apartment.

If Nelson's father, Joplin, asserts a claim against Smythe for the intentional infliction of emotional distress, will Joplin prevail?

(A) Yes, if Smythe's acts caused Joplin severe emotional distress.

(B) Yes, if it is found that Smythe's behavior was extreme and outrageous with respect to Nelson.

(C) No, because Smythe did not know that Joplin was watching.

(D) No, because Joplin was not within the zone of physical danger.

Question 48

Mom rushed her eight-year-old daughter, Child, to the emergency room at Hospital after Child fell off her bicycle and hit her head on a sharp rock. The wound caused by the fall was extensive and bloody.

Mom was permitted to remain in the treatment room, and held Child's hand while the emergency room physician cleaned and sutured the wound. During the procedure, Mom said that she was feeling faint and stood up to leave the room. While leaving the room, Mom fainted and, in falling, struck her head on a metal fixture that protruded from the emergency room wall. She sustained a serious injury as a consequence.

If Mom sues Hospital to recover damages for her injury, will she prevail?

(A) Yes, because Mom was a public invitee of Hospital's.

(B) Yes, unless the fixture was an obvious, commonly used, and essential part of Hospital's equipment.

(C) No, unless Hospital's personnel failed to take reasonable steps to anticipate and prevent Mom's injury.

(D) No, because Hospital's personnel owed Mom no affirmative duty of care.

Questions 49-50 are based on the following fact situation.

Innes worked as a secretary in an office in a building occupied partly by her employer and partly by Glass, a retail store. The two areas were separated by walls and were in no way connected, except that the air conditioning unit served both areas and there was a common return-air duct.

Glass began remodeling, and its employees did the work, which included affixing a plastic surfacing material to counters. To fasten the plastic to the counters, the employees purchased glue, with the brand name Stick, that was manufactured by Steel, packaged in a sealed container by Steel, and retailed by Paint Company.

In the course of the remodeling job, one of Glass's employees turned on the air conditioning and caused fumes from the glue to travel from Glass through the air conditioning unit and into Innes' office. The employees did not know that there was common ductwork for the air conditioners. Innes was permanently blinded by the fumes from the glue.

The label on the container of glue read, "DANGER. Do not smoke near this product. Extremely flammable. Contains Butanone, Tuluol and Hexane. Use with adequate ventilation. Keep out of the reach of children."

The three chemicals listed on the label are very toxic and harmful to human eyes. Steel had received no reports of eye injuries during the ten years that the product had been manufactured and sold.

Question 49

If Innes asserts a claim against Paint Company, the most likely result is that she will

(A) recover, if she can recover against Steel.

(B) recover, because Innes was an invitee of a tenant in the building.

(C) not recover unless Paint Company was negligent.

(D) not recover, because the glue came in a sealed package.

Question 50

If Innes asserts a claim against Glass, the most likely result is that she will

(A) recover, because a user of a product is held to the same standard as the manufacturer.

(B) recover, because the employees of Glass caused the fumes to enter her area of the building.

(C) not recover, because Glass used the glue for its intended purposes.

(D) not recover, because the employees of Glass had no reason to know that the fumes could injure Innes.

Question 51

Siddon worked as a private duty nurse and on occasion worked in Doctor's Hospital. The hospital called Registry, the private duty referral agency through which Siddon usually obtained employment, and asked that in the future she not be assigned to patients in Doctors' Hospital. Registry asked the hospital why it had made the request. Doctors' Hospital sent a letter to Registry giving as the reason for its request that significant amounts of narcotics had disappeared during Siddon's shift from the nursing stations at which she had worked.

If Siddon asserts a claim based on defamation against Doctors' Hospital, Siddon will

(A) recover, because the hospital accused Siddon of improper professional conduct.

(B) recover, if Siddon did not take the narcotics.

(C) not recover, if narcotics disappeared during Siddon's shifts.

(D) not recover, if the hospital reasonably believed that Siddon took the narcotics.

Question 52

Ellis, an electrical engineer, designed an electronic game known as Zappo. Ellis entered into a licensing agreement with Toyco under which Toyco agreed to manufacture Zappo according to Ellis's specifications and to market it and pay a royalty to Ellis.

Carla, whose parents had purchased a Zappo game for her, was injured while playing the game. Carla recovered a judgment against Toyco on the basis of a finding that the Zappo game was defective because of Ellis's improper design.

In a claim for indemnity against Ellis, will Toyco prevail?

(A) Yes, because as between Ellis and Toyco, Ellis was responsible for the design of Zappo.

(B) Yes, because Toyco and Ellis were joint tortfeasors.

(C) No, because Toyco, as the manufacturer, was strictly liable to Carla.

(D) No, if Toyco, by a reasonable inspection, could have discovered the defect in the design of Zappo.

Question 53

For ten years, Vacationer and Neighbor have owned summer vacation homes on adjoining lots. A stream flows through both lots. As a result of a childhood swimming accident, Vacationer is afraid of water and has never gone close to the stream.

Neighbor built a dam on her property that has completely stopped the flow of the stream to Vacationer's property.

In a suit by Vacationer against Neighbor, will Vacationer prevail?

(A) Yes, if the damming unreasonably interferes with the use and enjoyment of Vacationer's property.

(B) Yes, if Neighbor intended to affect Vacationer's property.

(C) No, because Vacationer made no use of the stream.

(D) No, if the dam was built in conformity with all applicable laws.

Question 54

The day after Seller completed the sale of his house and moved out, one of the slates flew off the roof during a windstorm. The slate struck Pedestrian, who was on the public sidewalk. Pedestrian was seriously injured.

The roof is old and has lost several slates in ordinary windstorms on other occasions.

If Pedestrian sues Seller to recover damages for his injuries, will Pedestrian prevail?

(A) Yes, because the roof was defective when Seller sold the house.

(B) Yes, if Seller should have been aware of the condition of the roof and should have realized that it was dangerous to persons outside the premises.

(C) No, because Seller was neither the owner nor the occupier of the house when Pedestrian was injured.

(D) No, if Pedestrian knew that in the past slates had blown off the roof during windstorms.

Question 55

Pat had been under the care of a cardiologist for three years prior to submitting to an elective operation that was performed by Surgeon. Two days thereafter, Pat suffered a stroke, resulting in a coma, caused by a blood clot that lodged in her brain. When it appeared that she had entered a permanent vegetative state, with no hope of recovery, the artificial life-support system that had been provided was withdrawn, and she died a few hours later. The withdrawal of artificial life support had been requested by her family, and duly approved by a court. Surgeon was not involved in that decision, or in its execution.

The administrator of Pat's estate thereafter filed a wrongful death action against Surgeon, claiming that Surgeon was negligent in having failed to consult a cardiologist prior to the operation. At the trial the plaintiff offered evidence that accepted medical practice would require examination of the patient by a cardiologist prior to the type of operation that Surgeon performed.

In this action, the plaintiff should

(A) prevail, if Surgeon was negligent in failing to have Pat examined by a cardiologist prior to the operation.

(B) prevail, if the blood clot that caused Pat's death was caused by the operation which Surgeon performed.

(C) not prevail, absent evidence that a cardiologist, had one examined Pat before the operation, would probably have provided advice that would have changed the outcome.

(D) not prevail, because Surgeon had nothing to do with the withdrawal of artificial life support, which was the cause of Pat's death.

Question 56

Astin left her car at Garrison's Garage to have repair work done. After completing the repairs, Garrison took the car out for a test drive and was involved in an accident that caused damages to Placek.

A statute imposes liability on the owner of an automobile for injuries to a third party that are caused by the negligence of any person driving the automobile with the owner's consent. The statute applies to situations of this kind, even if the owner did not specifically authorize the mechanic to test-drive the car.

Placek sued Astin and Garrison jointly for damages arising from the accident. In that action, Astin cross-claims to recover from Garrison the amount of any payment Astin may be required to make to Placek. The trier of fact has determined that the accident was caused solely by negligent driving on Garrison's part, and that Placek's damages were $100,000.

In this action, the proper outcome will be that

(A) Placek should have judgment for $50,000 each against Astin and Garrison; Astin should recover nothing from Garrison.

(B) Placek should have judgment for $100,000 against Garrison only.

(C) Placek should have judgment for $100,000 against Astin and Garrison jointly, and Astin should have judgment against Garrison for 50 percent of any amount collected from Astin by Placek.

(D) Placek should have judgment for $100,000 against Astin and Garrison jointly, and Astin should have judgment against Garrison for any amount collected from Astin by Placek.

Question 57

Dever drove his car into an intersection and collided with a fire engine that had entered the intersection from Dever's right. The accident was caused by negligence on Dever's part. As a result of the accident, the fire engine was delayed in reaching Peters' house, which was entirely consumed by fire. Peters' house was located about ten blocks from the scene of the accident.

If Peters asserts a claim against Dever, Peters will recover

(A) the part of his loss that would have been prevented if the collision had not occurred.

(B) the value of his house before the fire.

(C) nothing if Dever had nothing to do with causing the fire.

(D) nothing, because Dever's conduct did not create an apparent danger to Peters.

Question 58

Actor, a well-known movie star, was drinking Vineyard wine at a nightclub. A bottle of the Vineyard wine, with its label plainly showing, was on the table in front of Actor. An amateur photographer asked Actor if he could take his picture and Actor said, "Yes." Subsequently, the photographer sold the photo to Vineyard. Vineyard, without Actor's consent, used the photo in a wine advertisement in a nationally circulated magazine. The caption below the photo stated, "Actor enjoys his Vineyard wine."

If Actor sues Vineyard to recover damages as a result of Vineyard's use of the photograph, will Actor prevail?

(A) No, because Actor consented to being photographed.

(B) No, because Actor is a public figure.

(C) Yes, because Vineyard made commercial use of the photograph.

(D) Yes, unless Actor did, in fact, enjoy his Vineyard wine.

Question 59

Purvis purchased a used car form Daley, a used car dealer. Knowing them to be false, Daley make the following statements to Purvis prior to the sale:

Statement 1: This car has never been involved in an accident.

Statement 2: This car gets 25 miles to the gallon on the open highway.

Statement 3: This is as smooth-riding a car as you can get.

If Purvis asserts a claim against Daley based on deceit, which of the false statements made by Daley would support Purvis' claim?

(A) Statement 1 only.

(B) Statement 2 only.

(C) Statements 1 and 2 only.

(D) Statements 2 and 3 only.

Question 60

Acorp and Beeco are companies that each manufacture pesticide X. Their plants are located along the same river. During a specific 24-hour period, each plant discharged pesticide into the river. Both plants were operated negligently and such negligence caused the discharge of the pesticide into the river.

Landesmann operated a cattle ranch downstream from the plants of Acorp and Beeco. Landesmann's cattle drank from the river and were poisoned by the pesticide. The amount of the discharge from either plant alone would not have been sufficient to cause any harm to Landesmann's cattle.

If Landesmann asserts a claim against Acorp and Beeco, what, if anything, will Landesmann recover?

(A) Nothing, because neither company discharged enough pesticide to cause harm to Landesmann's cattle.

(B) Nothing, unless Landesmann can establish how much pesticide each plant discharged.

(C) One-half of Landesmann's damages from each company.

(D) The entire amount of Landesmann's damages, jointly and severally, from two companies.

Questions 61-62 are based on the following fact situation.

Cycle Company manufactured a bicycle that it sold to Bike Shop, a retail bicycle dealer, which in turn sold it to Roth. Shortly thereafter, while Roth was riding the bicycle along a city street, he saw a traffic light facing him turn from green to amber. He sped up, hoping to cross the intersection before the light turned red. However, Roth quickly realized that he could not do so and applied the brake, which failed. To avoid the traffic that was then crossing in front of him, Roth turned sharply to his right and onto the sidewalk, where he struck Perez, a pedestrian. Both Perez and Roth sustained injuries.

Question 61

If Roth asserts a claim against Bike Shop based on strict liability in tort, will Roth prevail?

(A) Yes, if the brake failed because a defect present when the bicycle left the factory of Cycle Company.

(B) Yes, because the brake failed while Roth was riding the bicycle.

(C) No, if Roth contributed to his own injury by speeding up.

(D) No, if Bike Shop carefully inspected the bicycle before selling it.

Question 62

If Perez asserts a claim based on negligence against Cycle Company and it is found that the brake failure resulted from a manufacturing defect in the bicycle, will Perez prevail?

(A) Yes, because Cycle Company placed a defective bicycle into the stream of commerce.

(B) Yes, if the defect could have been discovered through the exercise of reasonable care by Cycle Company.

(C) No, because Perez was not a purchaser of the bicycle.

(D) No, if Roth was negligent in turning onto the sidewalk.

Questions 63-64 are based on the following fact situation.

Morris was driving north on an interstate highway at about 50 miles per hour when a tractor-trailer rig, owned and driven by Dixon, passed her. The tractor was pulling a refrigerated meat trailer fully loaded with beef carcasses hanging freely from the trailer ceiling. When Dixon cut back in front of Morris, the shifting weight of the beef caused the trailer to overturn. Morris was unable to avoid a collision with the overturned trailer and was injured.

The trailer had been manufactured by Trailco. A number of truckers had complained to Trailco that the design of the trailer, which allowed the load to swing freely, was dangerous. Dixon knew of the dangerous propensity of the trailer. A restraining device that could be installed in the trailer would prevent the load from shifting and was available at nominal cost. Dixon knew of the restraining device but had not installed it.

Question 63

If Morris asserts a claim based on strict liability in tort against Trailco, she will

(A) recover, unless Morris was negligently driving when the truck overturned.

(B) recover, because Dixon's knowledge of the dangerous propensity of the trailer does not relieve Trailco of liability.

(C) not recover, because there was no privity of contract between Morris and Trailco of liability.

(D) not recover if Dixon was negligent in failing to install the restraining device in the trailer.

Question 64

If Morris asserts a claim for her injuries against Dixon, she will

(A) prevail, if the use of a restraining device would have prevented the trailer from overturning.

(B) prevail, because Dixon is strictly liable to Morris for injuries resulting from defects in the trailer.

(C) not prevail unless Dixon was driving in a negligent manner at the time Morris was injured.

(D) not prevail, because Dixon was not the manufacturer or seller of the trailer.

Questions 65-67 are based on the following fact situation.

Poe ordered some merchandise from Store. When the merchandise was delivered, Poe decided that it was not what he had ordered, and he returned it for credit. Store refused to credit Poe's account, continued to bill him, and, after 90 days, turned the account over to Kane, a bill collector, for collection.

Kane called at Poe's house at 7 p.m. on a summer evening while many of Poe's neighbors were seated on their porches. When Poe opened the door, Kane, who was standing just outside the door, raised an electrically amplified bullhorn to his mouth. In a voice that could be heard a

block away, Kane called Poe a "deadbeat" and asked him when he intended to pay his bill to Store.

Poe, greatly angered, slammed the door shut. The door struck the bullhorn and jammed it forcibly against Kane's face. As a consequence, Kane lost some of his front teeth.

Question 65

If Poe asserts a claim based on defamation against Kane, will Poe prevail?

(A) Yes, if Kane's remarks were heard by any of Poe's neighbors.

(B) Yes, because Kane's conduct was extreme and outrageous.

(C) No, unless Kane knew that Poe owed no money to Store.

(D) No, unless Poe suffered some special damage.

Question 66

If Poe asserts a claim based on intentional infliction of emotional distress against Kane, will Poe prevail?

(A) Yes, because Kane's conduct was extreme and outrageous.

(B) Yes, because Kane was intruding on Poe's property.

(C) No, unless Poe suffered physical harm.

(D) No, if Poe still owed Store for the merchandise.

Question 67

If Kane asserts a claim of battery against Poe, will Kane prevail?

(A) Yes, because Poe had not first asked Kane to leave the property.

(B) Yes, if Poe knew that the door was substantially certain to strike the bullhorn.

(C) No, if Kane's conduct triggered Poe's response.

(D) No, because Kane was an intruder on Poe's property.

Question 68

Karen was crossing Main Street at a crosswalk. John, who was on the sidewalk nearby, saw a speeding automobile heading in Karen's direction. John ran into the street and pushed Karen out of the path of the car. Karen fell to the ground and broke her leg.

In an action for battery brought by Karen against John, will Karen prevail?

(A) Yes, because John could have shouted a warning instead of pushing Karen out of the way.

(B) Yes, if Karen was not actually in danger and John should have realized it.

(C) No, because the driver of the car was responsible for Karen's injury.

(D) No, if John's intent was to save Karen, not to harm

her.

Question 69

Patron ate a spicy dinner at Restaurant on Sunday night. He enjoyed the food and noticed nothing unusual about the dinner.

Later that evening, Patron had an upset stomach. He slept well through the night, went to work the next day, and ate three meals. His stomach discomfort persisted, and by Tuesday morning he was too ill to go to work.

Eventually, Patron consulted his doctor, who found that Patron was infected with a bacterium that can be contracted from contaminated food. Food can be contaminated when those who prepare it do not adequately wash their hands.

Patron sued Restaurant for damages. He introduced testimony from a health department official that various health code violations had been found at Restaurant both before and after Patron's dinner, but that none of Restaurant's employees had signs of bacterial infection when they were tested one month after the incident.

Restaurant's best argument in response to Patron's suit would be that

(A) no one else who ate at Restaurant on Sunday complained about stomach discomfort.

(B) Restaurant instructs its employees to wash their hands carefully and is not responsible if any employee fails to follow these instructions.

(C) Patron has failed to establish that Restaurant's food caused his illness.

(D) Patron assumed the risk of an upset stomach by choosing to eat spicy food.

Question 70

As Seller, an encyclopedia salesman, approached the grounds on which Hermit's house was situated, he saw a sign that said, "No salesmen. Trespassers will be prosecuted. Proceed at your own risk." Although Seller had not been invited to enter, he ignored the sign and drove up the driveway toward the house. As he rounded a curve, a powerful explosive charge buried in the driveway exploded, and Seller was injured.

Can Seller recover damages from Hermit for his injuries?

(A) Yes, if Hermit was responsible for the explosive charge under the driveway.

(B) Yes, unless Hermit, when he planted the charge, intended only to deter, not to harm, a possible intruder.

(C) No, because Seller ignored the sign, which warned him against proceeding further.

(D) No, if Hermit reasonably feared that intruders would come and harm him or his family.

ANSWERS
TORTS

Answer Key

Use this Answer Key to quickly identify the correct answer to each question.

(1)	C	(11)	C	(21)	D	(31)	D	(41)	D	(51)	D	(61)	A
(2)	D	(12)	A	(22)	C	(32)	D	(42)	C	(52)	A	(62)	B
(3)	C	(13)	B	(23)	D	(33)	D	(43)	D	(53)	A	(63)	B
(4)	A	(14)	B	(24)	C	(34)	A	(44)	A	(54)	B	(64)	A
(5)	C	(15)	C	(25)	B	(35)	A	(45)	C	(55)	C	(65)	D
(6)	B	(16)	C	(26)	D	(36)	D	(46)	A	(56)	D	(66)	A
(7)	C	(17)	B	(27)	A	(37)	D	(47)	C	(57)	A	(67)	B
(8)	C	(18)	D	(28)	A	(38)	D	(48)	C	(58)	C	(68)	B
(9)	A	(19)	C	(29)	B	(39)	B	(49)	A	(59)	C	(69)	C
(10)	A	(20)	A	(30)	C	(40)	D	(50)	D	(60)	D	(70)	A

ANSWERS

TORTS

Answer 1

(C) is the best response,

because Traveler's legal representative has met the requirements for *res ipsa loquitor*.

The doctrine of *res ipsa loquitor* ("the thing speaks for itself") permits the plaintiff to create an inference of the defendant's negligence without any direct evidence showing negligence. There are four requirements: (1) there must be no direct evidence of how the defendant behaved in connection with the event; (2) the event must be of a kind which ordinarily does not occur except through the negligence (or other fault) of someone; (3) the instrument which caused the injury must have been, at the relevant time, in the exclusive control of the defendant; and (4) the injury must not have been due to plaintiff's own actions.

Here, the four requirements of the doctrine are satisfied: (1) There is no direct evidence of how the defendant Airline behaved, only that the airplane carrying Traveler crashed. (2) Airplanes do not ordinarily crash except through the negligence or fault of someone. (The jury would probably be entitled to take judicial notice of this, even if Traveler's side didn't present formal proof on the subject.) (3) A jury could reasonably find that the plane was in the exclusive control of Airline and its pilots (since there is no evidence of, say, hijacking). (4) The injury suffered by Traveler was not due to his own action. Since all the requirements for res ipsa are met, the jury must be permitted to draw the inference that the plane crashed because of Airline's negligence.

(A) is not the best response,

because the *res ipsa loquitor* doctrine does not require a showing of evidence of the cause of the crash. Indeed, the purpose of the doctrine is to eliminate the need for plaintiff to provide direct evidence of why or how the accident or injury occurred.

(B) is not the best response,

because the doctrine of *res ipsa loquitor* does not require the plaintiff to negate the possibility that defendant might not have been negligent.

The second requirement for res ipsa (see the discussion in Choice (C)) is that P show that the event was of a kind which "ordinarily" does not occur except through the fault of someone. But P is *not* required to show that the event couldn't possibly have been due to a cause not involving the defendant's fault (as the phrase "negating the possibility" implies).

(D) is not the best response,

because common carriers are not strictly liable.

Common carriers (including airlines) are required to exercise a very high degree of care toward their passengers and guests, which is to say they are liable for even slight negligence. But they do not have strict liability.

Answer 2

(D) is the best response,

because Del took reasonable care by storing the rifle and bullets in a locked cabinet.

An action in tort for negligence has four elements: (1) the existence of a duty on the part of defendant to conform to a specific standard of conduct for the protection of plaintiff against an unreasonable risk of injury; (2) breach of that duty by defendant; (3) proof that the breach was the actual and proximate cause of the plaintiff's injury; and (4) damage to the plaintiff's person or property.

For Paula to make a case in negligence against Del for the harm she suffered, she would have to show that he did not exercise reasonable care to protect her against injury. The facts state that the inmate escaped from a nearby prison, and then entered Del's store by breaking and entering. Once inside, the inmate had to break into a locked cabinet to get the rifle and bullets. Unless it was foreseeable that someone would succeed in breaking and entering Del's store and the locked cabinet, steal firearms and then use them in crime, Del would not be held liable, whether or not he negligently failed to activate the store's motion dectector. Only with evidence suggesting a high risk of theft and criminal use of his firearms could Paula show that Del failed to exercise reasonable care.

(A) is not the best response,

because Del took reasonable care by storing the rifle and bullets in a locked cabinet.

Of the four elements for negligence (listed in the discussion of Choice (D) above), the second is breach of a duty on the part of defendant to conform to a specific standard of conduct for the protection of plaintiff against an unreasonable risk of injury (loosely, D's failure to behave with reasonable care). The mere fact that there was some other act which Del could have taken — activation of the motion detection — that would have prevented the injury is insufficient to make Del liable. That is, other acts taken by Del (e.g., keeping the guns in a locked cabinet inside a locked building) may have already been enough to make Del's conduct non-negligent. So choice (A) is not a good explanation of the outcome.

(B) is not the best response,

because Del had probably already met the standard of reasonable care when he locked the store and the cabinet.

For Paula to make a case in negligence against Del for the harm she suffered, she would have to show that he did not exercise reasonable care to protect her against injury. Del likely met that requirement when he locked his store and the gun cabinet, even if he was negligent in failing to activate the motion detector. Since Choice (B) asserts that Paula wins automatically because of Del's negligent failure to activate the detector — and ignores the possibility that Del's other protections met the overall standard of due care — Choice (B) is wrong.

(C) is not the best response,

because Del might be liable even under ordinary negligence principles

As the discussion of Choice (D) develops, the presence of a high risk of theft of firearms might be enough to make Del liable under ordinary negligence principles, in which case the fact that there was no abnormally dangerous activity would be irrelevant.

By the way, Choice (C) is probably correct in stating that the storage and sale of firearms and ammo is not an abnormally dangerous activity (a.d.a.) — one of the major factors in determining whether something is an a.d.a. is an "inability to eliminate the risk by the exercise of reasonable care." Locking the material up securely is a way to eliminate at least the risk of theft and subsequent use in crime, so this factor seems not to be satisfied. Thus were it not for the possibility that Del was liable under ordinary negligence principles, Choice (C) might well be correct.

Answer 3

(C) is the best response,

because the auctioneer was not a seller or distributor of the tractor Pratt purchased.

Strict liability, as usually imposed, applies only against one who is "engaged in the business of selling" the type of product involved. A court would almost certainly conclude that an auctioneer acting at the behest of a creditor to sell various mortgaged items, one of which happens to be a tractor, is not "engaged in the business of selling" tractors.

(A) is not the best response,

because it incorrectly assumes that auctioneer is a seller as defined in strict liability.

If the auctioneer was "engaged in the business of selling" tractors, choice (A) would be correct, because it essentially correctly states the principle of strict liabil-

ity (though it neglects to state that the defect must have caused the injury). But since the auctioneer is not so engaged, as covered in Choice (C), Choice (A) is wrong.

(B) is not the best response,

because auctioneer's alleged negligence would not be an element of Pratt's strict liability suit.

Since Pratt is suing in strict liability, the fact that the defendant did or did not behave in a negligent manner is irrelevant. The defendant's failure to make an inspection might be evidence of negligence, but it has no bearing on whether there is strict liability.

(D) is not the best response,

because Pratt's contributory negligence would not bar his strict liability recovery, if the requirements for such liability were otherwise met.

In states that have not adopted comparative fault principles (as the facts state is the case here), plaintiff's contributory negligence is not a defense to strict liability, because strict liability is independent of general negligence principles. (Indeed, avoiding the total bar from contributory negligence was one of the reasons many jurisdictions initially adopted strict liability.)

Answer 4

(A) is the best response,

because the interference outweighs the utility of the light.

Neighbor's suit here would be based on private nuisance. A private nuisance is a substantial, unreasonable interference with another individual's use or enjoyment of his property. Since the interference with plaintiff's use of his land must be "unreasonable," the severity of the inflicted injury must outweigh the utility of defendant's conduct. Because Choice (A) specifies that Homeowner put in the light only to annoy Neighbor, we know that there was no socially-accepted "benefit" to Homeowner from the conduct. Consequently, even a small burden to Neighbor (such as detracting from his view of the lake) would outweigh the non-existent benefits to Homeowner. Since Choice (A) is the only choice that focuses on the lack of utility of Homeowner's conduct — a necessary part of the cost-benefit analysis — it is the only correct choice.

(B) is not the best response,

because plaintiff need only show an unreasonable interference with the use of his land, not loss of market value.

Plaintiffs can win a nuisance suit by showing that the interference with their use and enjoyment of their property was substantial. There is no requirement that the value of the property have been reduced. (For instance, suppose that plaintiff made a special use of the property that the defendant interfered with, and that most buyers of the property wouldn't have made that use — plaintiff can still win, even though the special-ness of his use means that defendant's conduct didn't reduce the market value of the property.)

(C) is not the best response,

because plaintiff need only show an unreasonable interference with the use of his land.

An occasional interference with plaintiff's enjoyment of her property suffices, if the interference is substantial and unreasonable. There is no requirement that the interference be constant.

(D) is not the best response,

because the spotlight's purpose was not to add security.

If Homeowner had installed the light for the *purpose* of adding security, this Choice might well be correct, since the existence of an "unreasonable" interference with the plaintiff's enjoyment and use of her property is dependent in part on the utility of the defendant's conduct. But since the facts stipulate that the only reason Homeowner put in the light was to annoy Neighbor, the court won't consider any benefits from Homeowner's actions that didn't in fact motivate Homeowner's conduct. Consequently, this side benefit is irrelevant in weighing the costs against the benefits from the light.

Answer 5

(C) is the best response,

because Driver's unauthorized entry onto Owner's land was not an intentional act, thus preventing trespass from occurring.

If Driver was negligent, then a suit based on ordinary negligence could succeed, since Driver's negligence would have placed Owner and Owner's child in the zone of danger, and then caused emotional distress. So if Driver was negligent, Owner would prevail, making this aspect of Choice (C) correct.

If Driver was not negligent, Owner's suit could of course not successfully be based on negligence. In that event, the suit would have to be based on trespass. However, trespass requires an intentional entry onto the plaintiff's property. Here, where Driver came onto Owner's property only as the result of a skid, the required "intentional entry" would not be found. (By the way, even if Driver intentionally chose to enter on Owner's property to avoid hitting the child, the doctrine of private necessity would supply a defense to trespass.)

So this Choice is the only one that correctly turns on the culpability of Driver's conduct.

(A) is not the best response,

because the fact that Driver entered Owner's land by necessity means that Driver did not need Owner's authorization.

First, assume that Owner's suit was based on tres-pass. If so, the suit would fail for two reasons, as detailed in the treatment of Choice (C): (1) the entry was not "intentional"; and (2) the doctrine of private necessity would apply. The fact that the entry was "unauthorized" would be irrelevant.

Now, assume that Owner's suit was based on negligence. If so, the suit obviously could not succeed if Driver did not behave negligently, a factor that Choice (A) ignores. (If there were no negligence, the "unautho-rized" nature of the entry would be irrelevant.)

(B) is not the best response,

because the presence of serious emotional distress is irrelevant if Driver violated no duty.

The mere fact that the plaintiff suffered serious emo-tional distress does not make the defendant liable — the defendant must have violated some independent duty to the plaintiff. So Owner would have to establish either that: (1) Driver committed the tort of negligence (in which case severe emotional distress in the absence of physical injury would not be a barrier to recovery, given that Owner was in the "zone of dan-ger"); or (2) Driver committed trespass. Since, as detailed in the treatment of Choice (C), neither of these torts is necessarily established by the facts, Choice (B)'s focus on the distress cannot be a complete answer to why or whether Owner would win.

(D) is not the best response,

because the child's exercise of reasonable care is irrel-evant to the outcome.

First, let's assume Owner's suit is brought in negli-gence. If so, the fact that Child was or wasn't careful is irrelevant. If Child *was* careful, Driver still may or may not have behaved with reasonable care. If Child *wasn't* careful, the same is true — Driver might have been, or might have not been, careful. If Driver wasn't careful, Child's negligence would not prevent Driver's conduct from giving rise to liability — one of the common ways for a driver to be negligent is to fail to be attentive to other people's, especially children's, negligence. (Nor would Child's lack of care be imputed to Owner.)

Now, let's assume that Owner's suit is brought in trespass. Again, the fact that Child was or wasn't care-ful would be irrelevant. Either way, Driver's conduct was not an intentional and unprivileged entry onto Owner's premises (as described in Choice (C)). So Choice (D)'s focus on the carefulness of the child is completely irrelevant no matter what the legal theory of Owner's suit.

Answer 6

(B) is the best response,

because it correctly states the damages available for the tort of conversion.

The tort of conversion is the interference with a per-son's possessory rights in a chattel that is so serious as to warrant that defendant pay full value for the chattel.

Under these facts, Neighbor borrowed Homeowner's chain saw without permission, thereby interfering with Homeowner's possessory rights. The facts state that the saw broke (as opposed to becoming slightly damaged or in need of minor repair), so we can take this as a serious interference as opposed to a minor one. Under the law governing conversion, Neighbor is responsible for the full value of the saw (but can keep it). In other words, the law of conversion applies the rule, familiar from retailing, that "You break it, you own it."

The fact that Neighbor was doing something ostensibly to benefit Homeowner would be deemed irrelevant — Homeowner certainly didn't consent to this use, and indeed, Neighbor's entry onto Homeowner's land to borrow the saw without permission, and his consequent uses of it for his own purposes, would certainly be enough to outweigh any possible defense based on a desire to help Neighbor.

(A) is not the best response,

because it incorrectly states the damages for the tort of conversion.

Here "actual damages" would amount to less than the full value of Homeowner's chattel, the saw. The essence of conversion is that it is a "forced sale" of the chattel to the defendant. In other words, Homeowner is entitled to the full value of the saw before it was taken, not just the actual damage amount needed to return it to the condition it was in before Neighbor took it.

(C) is not the best response,

because it incorrectly suggests a defense to the tort of conversion.

The tort of conversion is the interference with a person's possessory rights in a chattel that is so serious as to warrant that defendant pay full value for the chattel.

Homeowner is entitled to the exclusive possession of his chattel. It is not a defense that Neighbor was acting for Homeowner's benefit. (Had Neighbor been using the saw to, say, save Homeowner's life in an emergency, the defense of necessity might apply. But here, where Neighbor was initially acting to further his own interests, and then "helping" Homeowner in a non-emergency situation, the defense would not apply.)

(D) is not the best response,

because an intent to keep the chattel is not a necessary element in conversion.

Conversion is the intentional interference with a person's possessory rights in a chattel that is so serious as to warrant that defendant pay full value for the chattel. A person who makes a temporary but serious interference with another's chattel, in a way that causes substantial damage to the chattel, has committed conversion despite his intended return (or indeed his

actual return) of the chattel soon after the taking. (For instance, if D takes P's car for a joy ride and smashes it up, the fact that D promptly returns the wrecked car to P is no defense.)

Answer 7

(C) is the best response,

because the reporter has the privilege of making a fair and accurate report of the events of a public proceeding.

The tort of invasion of privacy includes public disclosures of private facts about the plaintiff by the defendant. Plaintiff must show two elements: (a) that defendant published private information about defendant, and (b) that the matter made public is one that a reasonable person would object to having made public. A qualified privilege exists for accurate reports of public hearings, meetings, or events of sufficient public interest.

Under these facts Parents' disclosure came at a public meeting. Since the news story was a fair and accurate publication of the facts, the qualified privilege for reports of a public meeting applies, shielding the newspaper.

(A) is not the best response,

because the fact that the statements were made at a public hearing makes the issue one of whether the facts were fairly and accurately reported, not whether they were newsworthy. To put it another way, a fact disclosed at a public meeting is, ipso facto, deemed newsworthy.

(B) is not the best response,

because (1) Son's parents would probably be held to have implicitly consented to publication when they raised the issue at a public meeting; and in any event (2) the privilege to give a truthful report of matters discussed at a public meeting exists independently of whether the speaker (or the person on whose behalf the speaker spoke) consented.

(D) is not the best response,

because whether Parents knew a reporter was present or not is irrelevant to the invasion-of-privacy tort.

A privilege exists to give a truthful accounting of facts disclosed at a public meeting (as discussed in the treatment of Choice (C)). This privilege exists whether or not a speaker at that public meeting knows of the reporter's presence.

Answer 8

(C) is the best response,

because it correctly identifies that Parker did not violate a duty of reasonableness as toward Ned.

There are really two prongs to analyzing this problem: One is to determine if Parker will be negligent per se due to the statute, and, failing that, whether Parker was negligent otherwise.

The standard of care in a city ordinance *can* be the basis for a claim of negligence per se if the following four elements are met:

1. The statute provides for a criminal penalty;
2. The statute was formulated to prevent the kind of harm suffered by plaintiff;
3. Plaintiff is a member of the class the legislature intended to protect with the statute; and
4. The statute is clear as to the standard of conduct expected, and from whom and when.

This does not apply to these facts because Ned is not one of the class intended to be protected by the statute. While the question doesn't spell it out, you know from experience that you're not allowed to park near a fire hydrant to ensure that fire trucks can reach the hydrant in an emergency. Since Ned couldn't rely on the statute to establish negligence per se, he'll have to establish that Parker behaved unreasonably under a traditional negligence analysis. (By the way, negligence per se only means that the defendant cannot argue that his conduct was reasonable.)

Under regular negligence analysis, you'd have to find that Parker failed to exercise such care as a reasonable person in his position would have exercised, that this was a breach of the duty to prevent the foreseeable risk of injury to anyone in plaintiff's position, and this breach must have caused plaintiff's damages. Here, parking by a fire hydrant couldn't possibly have created the foreseeable risk that the car would flip over onto the hydrant. Thus, the lack of foreseeability means Parker was not negligent toward Ned. Since C correctly identifies this, it's the best response.

(A) is not the best response,

because negligence per se will not apply under these facts.

Violation of a statutory standard is negligence per se, as long as there is a criminal penalty, violation of the statute caused the harm, plaintiff was a member of the class intended to be protected, and the statute is clear in the standard of conduct expected. The problem here is that Ned is not the one the statute is intended to protect; instead, the purpose of such a statute is to enable fire trucks to reach the hydrant in the event of a fire. As a result, Parker will not be liable for negligence per se. (Note that this doesn't mean Parker couldn't be found negligent *at all.* Instead, what negligence per se does is to stop the defendant from arguing that his conduct was reasonable. Thus, Parker could still be found liable for ordinary negligence.) Since option A misapplies negligence per se to these facts, it's not the best response.

(B) is not the best response,

because it understates the requirements for Ned to prevail on a negligence claim.

In order for Parker to be liable in negligence, he would have to have failed to exercise such care as a reasonable person in his position would have exercised, this must have been a breach of the duty to prevent the foreseeable risk of harm to anyone in plaintiff's position, and this breach must have caused plaintiff's damages. As to causation, where there are multiple causes, defendant can be liable if his act was a "substantial factor" in causing plaintiff's damages. Thus, while a continuing wrong that contributed to Ned's injuries could be the basis of a negligence claim where there are multiple causes, option B ignores the fact that Ned's injury was not a reasonably foreseeable result of Parker's negligence, so Parker did not violate a duty toward Ned, and can't be liable as a result. Thus, B isn't the best response.

(D) is not the best response,

because it misstates the law.

In fact, the standard of care in a city ordinance *can* be the basis of a claim of negligence per se if the following four elements are met: 1. The statute provides for a criminal penalty; 2. The statute was formulated to prevent the kind of harm suffered by plaintiff; 3. Plaintiff is a member of the class the legislature intended to protect with the statute; and 4. The statute is clear as to the standard of conduct expected, and from whom and when. If these elements are satisfied, the defendant is said to be negligent per se, meaning that he cannot argue his conduct was reasonable. Thus, D's blanket statement that violation of a city ordinance does not give rise to a civil cause of action is not correct. Under these specific facts the statute won't apply because Ned was not intended to be protected by the statute – the statute was intended to keep the hydrant clear for fire trucks. However, since D offers incorrect reasoning, it's not the best response.

Answer 9

(A) is the best response,

because it correctly resolves the central issue here: The status of Parker's illegal parking.

In fact, the parking statute will be irrelevant here, because it was not designed to prevent the kind of harm involved here. Instead, it was intended to keep the hydrant clear for fire trucks. Thus, it won't be determinative of Driver's liability.

Instead, Driver will be liable if he was negligent (since plaintiff's own conduct couldn't be considered contributorily negligent – it didn't help cause his harm). While option A doesn't address Driver's negligence, you could safely infer that Driver, in swerving out of the way of an imaginary pothole, was negligent. Since A correctly identifies that the statute will not exonerate Driver, and that Driver will thus be liable, it's the best response.

(B) is not the best response,

because the timing of Driver's negligence will not be determinative of his liability. In order to prevail, Parker will have to prove that Driver failed to exercise such care as a reasonable person in his position would have exercised, and this caused (or helped cause) Parker's damages. Thus, the *timing* of the negligence won't be relevant. If you chose this response, it may be because you were thinking of Last Clear Chance, a rebuttal to a claim of contributory negligence whereby plaintiff claims that defendant should be liable for negligence even though plaintiff was contributorily negligent, because defendant had the "last clear chance" to avoid the damage. However, this line of reasoning is quite far removed from these facts, since there's been no contributory negligence raised. Since B addresses an irrelevant point, it's not the best response.

(C) is not the best response,

because Parker's negligence would not constitute negligence as a matter of law, so it can't be considered contributory negligence as a matter of law.

Negligence as a matter of law, or negligence "per se," means that a criminal statute establishes a standard of care for a civil action. This only occurs when these four elements are met:

1. The statute provides for a criminal penalty;
2. The statute was formulated to prevent the kind of harm suffered by plaintiff;
3. Plaintiff is a member of the class the legislature intended to protect with the statute; and
4. The statute is clear as to the standard of conduct expected, and from whom and when.

Fire hydrant parking ordinances are designed to keep hydrants clear in the event of a fire — they don't address accident situations like this. Since Parker wouldn't be liable for negligence per se for a car accident under these facts, he can't be contributorily negligent per se. In fact, contributory negligence probably wouldn't exonerate Driver at all, regardless of the statute, since Parker's negligence didn't cause his damages. It's no more than coincidence that Parker was parked in front of a hydrant as it relates to Driver's liability. Since C incorrectly applies contributory negligence, it's not the best response.

(D) is not the best response,

because the fact that Parker was parked illegally will not exonerate Driver. D suggests that Parker's contributory negligence should bar his claim against Driver. However, Parker's behavior would not constitute contributory negligence.

Contributory negligence is plaintiff's conduct which does not meet the standard of care for his own protection, and is the cause of his harm. Here, Driver hitting Parker's car would relieve Parker of liability, since being hit by a car is not within the risk Parker's negligence created. Instead, the fact he was parked in front

of a hydrant was coincidental as it relates to Driver's negligence. Since D doesn't recognize this, it's not the best response.

Answer 10

(A) is the best response,

because it correctly identifies that both cause in fact and proximate cause are satisfied by Driver's conduct.

Cause in fact and proximate cause are the two parts of the causation element of negligence. Cause in fact is the determination, under either the "but for" (single cause) or "substantial factor" (multiple causes) test of whether defendant brought about plaintiff's harm. Proximate cause, on the other hand, involves the policy considerations limiting the scope of liability, determined primarily on the concept of foreseeability of risks and consequences.

As A correctly identifies, Driver's negligence under these facts satisfies the cause in fact requirement. His negligence resulted in pushing Parker's car onto the hydrant. There were no other acts contributing to the harm, so the "but for" test is used — and here, the hydrant wouldn't have been damaged but for Driver's negligence. Also, since there were no intervening acts, Driver's negligence *must* satisfy the proximate cause test (since proximate cause is only really an issue where remote possibilities come into play). Apart from anything else, Parker's illegal parking occurred *before* Driver's negligence, so it didn't intervene between Driver's negligence and the damage. Since A correctly recognizes that both cause in fact and proximate cause are satisfied by Driver's negligence, it's the best response.

(B) is not the best response,

because Parker's illegal parking would not negate the proximate cause requirement.

In order to satisfy the "causation" requirement of negligence, the defendant's act must be both the cause in fact and the proximate cause of the harm. Proximate cause is the policy consideration limiting defendant's scope of liability, determined primarily on the concept of foreseeability of risks and consequences. Where there's only one cause of damage — here, Driver pushing Parker's car onto the hydrant — proximate cause is automatically satisfied, because there's no intervening cause between defendant and the harm which might relieve defendant of liability (apart from anything else, Parker's illegal parking occurred *before* Driver's negligence, so it didn't intervene). Since B doesn't recognize this, it's not the best response.

(C) is not the best response,

because it misapplies causation to these facts, and states a legal impossibility.

In order to satisfy the "causation" element of negligence, the defendant's act must be the cause in fact and the proximate cause of plaintiff's harm. Cause in fact is the determination, under either the "but for" (single cause) or "substantial factor" (multiple causes) test of whether defendant brought about plaintiff's injuries. Proximate cause, on the other hand, involves the policy considerations limiting the scope of liability, determined primarily on the concept of foreseeability of risks and consequences.

Under these facts, Driver's negligence resulted in his pushing Parker's car onto the fire hydrant. There were no intervening acts between Driver and the damage to the hydrant, and no other causes, so Driver satisfies the "but for" cause in fact determination. Also, since there were no intervening acts, he *must* satisfy the proximate cause test, as well. Not only does option C ignore this, but it states reasoning that is internally inconsistent, because while there can be cause in fact without proximate cause, there *cannot* be proximate cause without cause in fact. Since C misapplies causation and its reasoning is not logical, it's not the best response.

(D) is not the best response,

because it misapplies *both* cause in fact and proximate cause to these facts.

In order to satisfy the "causation" element of negligence, the defendant's act must be both the cause in fact and the proximate cause of the harm. Cause in fact is the determination, under either the "but for" (single cause) or "substantial factor" (multiple causes) test of whether defendant brought about plaintiff's injuries. Proximate cause, on the other hand, involves the policy considerations limiting the scope of liability, determined primarily on the concept of foreseeability of risks and consequences.

Under these facts, Driver's negligence resulted in his pushing Parker's car onto the hydrant. There were no other acts contributing to the harm, so the "but for" test is used — and here, the hydrant wouldn't have been damaged but for Driver's negligence, so it satisfies the cause in fact requirement. Also, since there were no intervening acts, Driver's negligence *must* satisfy the proximate cause test (since proximate cause is only involved with remote possibilities). By failing to recognize that the facts here satisfy both cause in fact and proximate cause hurdles, D is not the best response.

Answer 11

(C) is the best response,

because it correctly identifies why Roger's Market won't be liable: It wasn't negligent.

As in any negligence claim, a product liability suit predicated on negligence requires proof that defendant failed to exercise such care as a reasonable person in his position would have exercised, this must have been a reach of the duty to prevent the foreseeable risk of harm to anyone in plaintiff's position, and this breach must have caused plaintiff's damages. The duty varies depending on whether defendant in a manufacturer,

wholesaler, or retailer. As a retailer, Roger's Market would be liable for its own affirmative negligence in handling products. For instance, wholesalers and retailers do have a responsibility to inspect for defects if they have any reason to believe the product is likely to be defective (e.g., a broken seal).

Here, Roger's Market was not affirmatively negligent, and since the defect was *inside* the can, there was nothing to trigger Roger's duty to inspect. Thus, it cannot be liable for negligence. Since C correctly identifies this, it's the best response.

(A) is not the best response,

because it misstates the law: Negligence does not, in fact, follow passage of title.

As in any negligence claim, a product liability suit predicated on negligence requires that defendant failed to exercise such care as a reasonable person in his position would have exercised, this must have been a breach of the duty to prevent the foreseeable risk of harm to anyone in plaintiff's position, and this breach must have caused plaintiff's damages. The duty owed depends on the whether the defendant is a manufacturer, wholesaler, or retailer. As a retailer, Roger's Market would only be liable for its own affirmative negligence in handling the product. For instance, wholesalers and retailers do have a responsibility to inspect for defects if they have any reason to believe the product is likely to be defective (e.g., a broken seal).

Here, Roger's Market was not affirmatively negligent, and since the can itself was not defective, the Market did not breach a duty by failing to inspect. Furthermore, there's nothing on these facts to indicate that Roger's Market failed to exercise due care in any other respect. Since negligence requires a failure to exercise due care, Roger's Market can't be liable for negligence on these facts.

If you chose this response, you may have been thinking of strict liability, although the reasoning in option A isn't an accurate statement of that, either. However, under strict liability, the defendant is liable if the product was dangerously defective when it left his control, *even if he had nothing at all to do with its defective condition*. Thus, under strict liability, Roger's Market would get tagged with liability, and is the most likely defendant as the last one in the distribution chain (since if the product was *ever* dangerously defective, it was when it left the Market). In any case, the claim here is for negligence. Since A misstates the rule of law and fails to recognize that Roger's wasn't negligent, it's not the best response.

(B) is not the best response,

because it mischaracterizes the facts.

A joint venture is similar to a partnership, but generally it is entered into for a limited time and purpose. The two identifying elements are a common purpose and a mutual right of control. B is theoretically correct, because joint venturers are liable for the torts committed by their cohorts if the torts are committed in the scope of the venture (most joint venture cases involve automobile trips). Here, there was no mutual right of control between Meat Packers and Roger's Market, so Roger's can't be liable for Meat Packers' negligence on this basis. Instead, as a retailer, Roger's can only be liable for its own affirmative negligence in handling products. For instance, wholesalers and retailers do have a responsibility to inspect for defects if there is any reason to believe the product is likely to be defective (e.g., a broken seal). Here, Roger's was not affirmatively negligent, and there was nothing about the can to suggest it should have been checked further. Thus, Roger's cannot be liable for negligence. Since B fails to realize this, and mischaracterizes the facts, it's not the best response.

(D) is not the best response,
because the reasoning does not support a contributory negligence defense.

Contributory negligence is a defense to a negligence claim if it meets this standard: Plaintiff's conduct must not meet the standard of care for his own protection, and it must cause his harm. Here, there was nothing to trigger any alarm in Susie, since the can looked fine. To forbid her recovery for contributory negligence on this reasoning would make grocery shopping into a kind of Russian roulette. On the other hand, D does arrive at the correct conclusion – Roger's won't be liable. But it won't be because of a defense, but because Roger's wasn't negligent and Meat Packers' negligence can't be imputed to it. Under a product liability claim based on negligence, a defendant can only be liable for its *own* negligence. Since D states a defense that doesn't exist on these facts, it's not the best response.

Answer 12

(A) is the best response,
because it identifies the central reason West Beef will be liable to Susie under strict liability.

Restatement of Torts 2d §402A lays out the requirements of a strict product liability claim. Under a strict product liability claim, a seller/producer is liable if:

1. The product was in a defective condition unreasonably dangerous the user/consumer or his property;
2. When it left defendant's control (meaning defendant can be liable even if he didn't cause the defect);
3. Product must not be expected to undergo significant changes before it gets to the user/consumer (or not actually undergo such changes);
4. The seller must be in the business of selling the product (thus, defendant can't be a casual seller);
5. Damage must result from the defect (defendant is

liable for any physical damage); and
6. The duty extends to anyone foreseeably endangered by the product (meaning, there's no privity requirement).

Here, the corned beef had an unreasonably dangerous defect when it left West Beef's control. All the other elements – West Beef being in the business, and the product being unchanged after it left West – are not at issue under these facts. Thus, as A correctly identifies, the key fact here is that the sliver was in the can when West Beef sold it. While West Beef may be able to seek indemnity from Meat Packers, this doesn't change the fact that West Beef can be held liable to Susie. Since A correctly identifies that Susie will recover because the beef was defective when it left West Beef, it's the best response.

(B) is not the best response,
because the claim here is for strict liability, not breach of warranty, and even if there was an implied warranty claim, Susie would not recover. A consumer's breach of implied warranty claim cannot succeed against a manufacturer or wholesaler, only a retailer. Apart from that, B's a pretty good answer.

First, the facts here state the claim is for strict liability, not breach of warranty. Thus, even if B's reasoning was correct, it couldn't be the best response, because it misstates the facts.

Second, even if the claim here *were* for breach of warranty, Susie couldn't recover from West Beef. There are two types of breach of warranty claims: Express and implied. There are no express warranties indicated in these facts, so the claim would have to be for implied warranty. Under the implied warranty of merchantability, UCC §2-314, goods must be "fit for the ordinary purposes for which such goods are used." The corned beef here clearly would not make the grade. However, the problem with this claim is that manufacturers and wholesalers are not liable to the ultimate consumer under this theory: Only the retailer is. Thus, even if the claim here *were* for breach of warranty, it couldn't succeed, making it inconsistent with the result B states.

Since B mischaracterizes the claim here, and it misapplies the rule it states, it can't be the best response.

(C) is not the best response,
because privity is not an issue in a strict liability claim.

Under strict liability, anyone foreseeably endangered by the product is a potential plaintiff. Thus, C is incorrect in stating that privity is required.

If you chose this response, it's probably because you were thinking of an implied warranty claim. That, at least in theory, requires privity of contract; under UCC §2-318, Alternative A, only buyer, family and guest in home qualify (although most courts ignore this constraint, since they don't like denying recovery in product liability causes due to privity problems). Not only is the claim here for strict liability, not implied warranty, but a warranty claim *couldn't* succeed, because only the retailer is a potential defendant – not the manufacturer or wholesaler.

Since C misapplies the privity requirement to a strict liability claim, it's not the best response.

(D) is not the best response,

because it mischaracterizes the claim here as a *warranty* claim, when it's in fact a strict liability claim. Even if the claim here *were* for breach of warranty, the reasoning in D is off the mark. Since there's no express warranty under these facts, the claim would have to be for implied warranty, and that claim would be for breach of the implied warranty of merchantability, since the food here was not fit for the ordinary purposes for which it was intended (i.e., human consumption). Contrary to what is stated in option D, the reason the claim couldn't succeed here is that West Beef is not a retailer, and wholesalers and manufacturers are not liable to the ultimate consumer under an implied warranty theory. While D correctly identifies that Susie will not prevail, since it misidentifies the claim and offers incorrect reasoning, D is not the best response.

Answer 13

(B) is the best response,

because it recognizes the most important exception to the rule of non-liability to trespassers.

The general rule is that a landowner owes no duty to a trespasser to make his land safe, to warn of dangers on it, to avoid carrying on dangerous activities on it, or to protect the trespasser in any other way. The most important exception to the general rule of non-liability to trespassers is that once the owner has *knowledge* that a particular person is trespassing on his property, he is then under a duty to exercise reasonable care for the latter's safety.

Under these facts Vintner owed no duty to Trespasser while Trespasser remained undiscovered. However, if Vintner became aware of Trespasser before the descending balloon hit him, then Vintner would be required to exercise reasonable care to protect Trespasser's safety.

(A) is not the best response,

because Vintner does not owe Trespasser a duty to protect Trespasser from harm.

The general rule is that a landowner owes no duty to a trespasser to make his land safe, to warn of dangers on it, to avoid carrying on dangerous activities on it, or to protect the trespasser in any other way.

Here, if Trespasser brought suit under a negligence theory, he'd have to show that Vintner owed him a duty to protect Trespasser from injury. However, as just stated a landowner does not owe an undiscovered trespasser a duty to protect a trespasser in any way. Therefore, even if the balloon's crash landing was caused by Vintner's negligence, Trespasser will not be

able to make a prima facie case for negligence if (as may have been the case) Vinter was unaware of Trespasser's presence.

(C) is not the best response,

because landowners have the right to engage in dangerous activities on their own land if (as may have been the case) the owner doesn't know of the trespasser's presence.

The general rule is that a landowner owes no duty to a trespasser to avoid carrying on dangerous activities on it that might injure the trespasser. (There is an exception if the owner knows of the trespasser's presence.) So even if Trespasser could prove that balloon rides are abnormally dangerous (which is doubtful), Vintner would not be liable to him for the injury, assuming Vintner was not aware that Trespasser was present. Since Choice (C) doesn't mention Vintner's knowledge as a factor, it is not the best choice.

(D) is not the best response,

because Vintner's knowledge of frequent intruders would not make Vintner's conduct negligent.

The general rule is that a landowner owes no duty to a trespasser to make his land safe, to warn of dangers on it, to avoid carrying on dangerous activities on it, or to protect the trespasser in any other way. An exception to the general rule is that if a landowner knows a limited portion of his land is frequently used by trespassers, he must use reasonable care to make the premises safe.

However, even if an owner knows of such frequent use by trespassers, the owner will not be liable unless he behaves without due care (e.g., by failing to warn of a known danger). On the facts here, nothing suggests that the crash-landing was due to Vintner's negligence. Since Choice (D) does not factor any issue of negligence into the analysis, it is not the best choice.

Answer 14

(B) is the best response,

because it correctly identifies the central reason Si will be liable.

Si negligently set the garage on fire, placing himself in peril. (He didn't act intentionally and there's no basis for strict liability here, so Rescuer's claim will be in negligence.) Thus, ironically, he's both the negligent defendant *and* the victim of his own negligence. Negligent defendants are liable for the injuries of rescuers, since the possibility of rescue is considered foreseeable. As a result, as long as the rescuer reasonably believes help is necessary, the original negligent defendant will be liable to him. Thus, Si the tortfeasor will be liable for Rescuer's injuries for helping Si the victim. Since B correctly identifies this, it's the best response.

(A) is not the best response,

because the result of Rescuer's act will not determine

whether Si is liable to Rescuer.

Although the facts don't state it expressly, Rescuer's claim is probably a negligence claim, since Si did not act reasonably in creating the risk of fire. (It couldn't be for an intentional tort, since Si didn't intend to cause harm to Rescuer, and there's no basis for applying strict liability.)

Negligent defendants are liable for injuries to rescuers, because the possibility of rescue is considered "foreseeable." Thus, as long as the rescuer reasonably believes help is necessary, the original negligent defendant will be liable to him.

As applied to these facts, this means that as long as Rescuer had a reasonable belief help was necessary, and Rescuer was no more than negligent in aiding Si, Si will be liable to him no matter what the result of Rescuer's effort is. If he had tried to save Si and Si died, presumably Si's estate would be liable to Rescuer. Since A focuses on an element which is not relevant, it's not the best response.

(C) is not the best response,

because assumption of the risk would not exonerate Si on these facts.

Here, Si negligently set the garage on fire, placing himself in peril. Thus, he's both the negligent defendant *and* the victim of his own negligence. Negligent defendants are liable for the injuries of rescuers, since the possibility of rescue is considered "foreseeable." As a result, as long as the rescuer reasonably believes help is necessary, the original negligent defendant will be liable to him. When a rescuer *does* undertake to help, he's privileged to take steps to help without assuming any risk. Since C doesn't recognize this, it's not the best response.

(D) is not the best response,

because it misstates the facts. Here, Si negligently set the garage on fire, placing himself in peril. Thus, he's both the negligent defendant *and* the victim of his negligence. Negligent defendants are liable for the injuries of rescuers, since the possibility of rescue is considered foreseeable. Thus, D is not correct in stating that Rescuer's action was not foreseeable. As a result, it's not the best response.

Answer 15

(C) is the best response,

because it addresses the central issue here and resolves it: Neighbor won't be liable because he wasn't negligent.

Here, there's only two ways Neighbor could possibly be liable: His own acts, or vicarious liability for Si's wrongful acts. There's no pre-existing relationship justifying Neighbor's liability for Si's acts, so there's no basis for vicarious liability. As to his own behavior, Neighbor did nothing unreasonable. The only contribution he made to the whole series of events here was to

leave his car in his garage, which, without more, is not unreasonable. Without unreasonableness, there's no negligence. The thing that makes this question a little tricky is that your gut feeling is that Neighbor *should* be liable to Rescuer, because, after all, Rescuer *did* save Neighbor's property. However, this creates perhaps a *moral* duty on Neighbor's part, but not a *legal* one. Since C correctly identifies that Neighbor won't be liable because he wasn't negligent, C is the best response.

(A) is not the best response,

because the *result* of Rescuer's action is not relevant to whether or not he'll prevail.

If Neighbor is to be liable to Rescuer at all, it must be because Neighbor breached some duty toward Rescuer. Under these facts, Neighbor did simply nothing wrong. The genesis of the situation here is that Si was siphoning gas out of Neighbor's car in Neighbor's garage. Neighbor did nothing unreasonable, because leaving one's car in one's garage is, barring some unusual additional facts, not unreasonable. Thus, Rescuer's coincidentally saving Neighbor's property in his effort to save Si does not create liability for Neighbor in the absence of a breach of duty (or some basis for Neighbor to be liable for Si's act). Since A focuses incorrectly on the results of Rescuer's acts and not Neighbor's responsibility toward him, it's not the best response.

(B) is not the best response,

because it doesn't address an element which will determine Neighbor's liability.

In order for Neighbor to be liable to Rescuer, he would have to have either breached a duty toward Rescuer, or there must be some basis for holding Neighbor vicariously liable for Si's acts.

First, there's no basis for vicarious liability for Si's wrongful act, because there's no pre-existing relationship justifying it. Secondly, under these facts, Neighbor did nothing unreasonably. He merely left his car in his own garage, and this, barring some unusual additional facts, is not unreasonable. What Rescuer's acting reasonably in an emergency would do is ensure he can recover from Si, as wrongdoer, under the rescuer doctrine (since a negligent defendant is liable to anyone who attempts to help his victim, since rescue is considered "foreseeable"). Even if Rescuer had been negligent, he'd *still* be able to recover under the doctrine, from Si. Thus, Rescuer's reasonability is relevant in a claim against Si, but not against Neighbor. Since B doesn't recognize this, it's not the best response.

(D) is not the best response,

because it ignores the central issue, and misstates the facts.

D misstates the facts because assumption of the risk would not apply to Rescuer. When a rescuer reasonably believes help is necessary, he can undertake to help without assuming any risk (as long as his acts are reasonable). However, this isn't relevant in Rescuer's claim against Neighbor, but in his claim against Si, since Si, as the tortfeasor, would be the one who couldn't use assumption of the risk against Rescuer. But there's a world of difference between Si and Neighbor: Si breached a duty of reasonability by placing himself in peril, thus inviting rescue. Neighbor didn't breach a duty toward Rescuer. All he did was leave his car in his garage, which, barring other facts, is perfectly reasonable. Since D fails to recognize this, it's not the best response.

Answer 16

(C) is the best response,

because Trucker's negligence satisfies both factual and legal causation elements of Driver's injuries.

A defendant is liable for negligence if he failed to exercise such care as a reasonable person in his position would have exercised, this was a breach of the duty to prevent the foreseeable risk of harm to anyone in plaintiff's position, and this breach caused plaintiff's damages.

Causation has two elements: cause in fact, or "actual" cause, and proximate, or "legal" cause. Cause in fact is determined by either the "but for" test (one cause) or "substantial factor" (multiple cause) test. Here, Trucker's negligence and Visitor's act combined to result in Driver's injuries. Thus, if Trucker's negligence was a substantial factor in causing Driver's damages, he'll satisfy the actual cause half of causation. Under these facts, it *does,* so B is correct in identifying this.

Trucker's negligence is also a legal cause of Driver's damages. Legal cause involves the policy considerations limiting the scope of liability, determined primarily on the concept of foreseeability of risks and consequences. Basically, legal cause insulates defendants from liability for remote results. Under these facts, the question boils down to whether Trucker should be liable for Driver's injuries in light of Visitor's intervening contribution. The rule is that the tortfeasor is liable for foreseeable intervening cause. A foreseeable intervening cause is one that the defendant should reasonably anticipate under the particular circumstances. Here, Visitor's going through the red light is *exactly* the risk Trucker's negligence created, thus making Driver's damages completely foreseeable. Thus, Trucker's negligence satisfies the legal half of causation.

Since C correctly identifies that Trucker's negligence is both the legal and actual cause of Driver's injuries, it's the best response.

(A) is not the best response,

because Trucker's negligence is *both* the actual *and* the legal cause of Driver's injuries. In fact, the combination option A offers is not legally possible.

A defendant is liable for negligence if he failed to exercise such care as a reasonable person in his position would have exercised, this was a breach of the duty to prevent the foreseeable risk of harm to anyone in plaintiff's position, and this breach caused plaintiff's damages. Causation has two elements: Cause in fact, or "actual" cause, and proximate, or "legal" cause. Cause in fact is determined by either the "but for" test (one cause) or "substantial factor" (multiple cause) test. Here, Trucker's negligence and Visitor's act combined to result in Driver's injuries. Thus, if Trucker's negligence was a substantial factor in Driver's damages, he'll satisfy the actual cause half of causation. Under these facts, it *does,* so A is incorrect in stating otherwise.

If you chose this response, you may have done so by treating *Visitor's* act as the *only* cause of Driver's injuries. However, as a significant factor in creating Driver's injuries, Trucker's negligence *does* satisfy the cause in fact element of causation.

Option A is correct, however, in recognizing that Trucker's act is the legal cause of Driver's injuries. Legal cause involves the policy considerations limiting the scope of liability, determined primarily on the concept of foreseeability of risks and consequences. Basically, proximate cause insulates defendant from liability for remote results. The question here boils down to whether Trucker should be liable for Driver's injuries, in light of Visitor's intervening contribution. The rule is that the tortfeasor is liable for foreseeable intervening causes. A foreseeable intervening cause is one the defendant should reasonably anticipate under the particular circumstances. Here, Visitor's going through a red light is *exactly* the risk Trucker's negligence created, thus making Driver's damages completely foreseeable. Thus, Trucker's negligence satisfies the proximate cause half of causation.

Note that A *cannot* be correct, apart from the fact that it is incorrect on the actual cause issue, because a cause *can't* be a legal cause without also being an actual cause. Since A doesn't recognize this, it's not the best response.

(B) is not the best response,

because Trucker's negligence is *both* the actual *and* the legal cause of Driver's injuries.

A defendant is liable for negligence if he failed to exercise such care as a reasonable person in his position would have exercised, this was a breach of the duty to prevent the foreseeable risk of harm to anyone in plaintiff's position, and this breach caused plaintiff's damages.

The causation factor has two elements: cause in fact, or "actual" cause, and proximate, or "legal" cause. Cause in fact is determined by either the "but for" test (one cause) or the "substantial factor" test (multiple causes). Here, Trucker's negligence and Visitor's act combined to result in Driver's damages. Thus, if

Trucker's negligence was a substantial factor in Driver's damages, he'll satisfy the actual cause half of causation. Under these facts, it *does*, so B is correct in identifying this.

However, B misses the fact that Trucker's negligence *also* satisfies legal cause. Legal cause involves the policy considerations limiting the scope of liability, determined primarily on the concept of foreseeability of risks and consequences. Basically, legal cause insulates defendant from liability for remote results. Under these facts, the question boils down to whether Trucker should be liable for Driver's injuries in light of Visitor's intervening contribution. The rule is that the tortfeasor is liable for foreseeable intervening causes. A foreseeable intervening cause is one that defendant should reasonably anticipate under the peculiar circumstances. Here, Visitor's going through a red light is *exactly* the risk Trucker's negligence created, thus making Driver's damages completely foreseeable. Thus, Trucker's negligence satisfies the legal cause half of causation.

If you missed this, it's probably because you considered Visitor's act a *superseding* force, which cancels defendant's liability by breaking the chain of causation. However, an intervening cause is only superseding if its results are unforeseeable. Here, that's not the case, so Trucker's negligence will be considered the legal cause of Driver's damages.

While it's possible for a cause to be a factual cause and not a legal cause, Trucker's act here satisfies both. As B correctly states, an act which satisfies actual but not legal cause will mean the negligence claim will fail. However, since B ignores the fact that Trucker's negligence is the legal *and* actual cause of Driver's damages, it's not the best response.

(D) is not the best response,

because Trucker's negligence is *both* the legal *and* the actual cause of Driver's injuries.

A defendant is liable for negligence if he failed to exercise such care as a reasonable person in his position would have exercised, this was a breach of the duty to prevent the foreseeable risk of harm to anyone in plaintiff's position, and this breach caused plaintiff's damages.

Causation itself has two elements: cause in fact, or "actual" cause, and proximate, or "legal" cause. Cause in fact is determined by either the "but for" test (one cause) or "substantial factor" (multiple causes) test. Here, Trucker's negligence and Visitor's act combined to result in Driver's injuries. Thus, if Trucker's negligence was a substantial factor in Driver's damages, he'll satisfy the actual cause half of causation. Under these facts, it *does,* so B is correct in identifying this. If you chose this response, you may have done so by treating *Visitor's* act as the *only* cause of Driver's injuries. However, as a significant factor in Driver's injuries, Trucker's negligence *does* satisfy the cause in fact ele-

ment of causation.

D also misses the fact that Trucker's negligence satisfies the legal cause requirement. Legal cause involves the policy considerations limiting the scope of liability, determined primarily on the concept of foreseeability of risks and consequences. Basically, legal cause insulates defendant from liability for remote results. Under these facts, the question boils down to whether Trucker should be liable for Driver's injuries in light of Visitor's intervening contribution. The rule is that the tortfeasor is liable for foreseeable intervening causes. A foreseeable intervening cause is one the defendant should reasonably anticipate under the particular circumstances. Here, Visitor's going through a red light is *exactly* the risk Trucker's negligence created, thus making Driver's damages completely foreseeable. Thus, Trucker's negligence satisfies the legal cause half of causation. If you missed this, it's probably because you considered Visitor's act a *superseding* force, which cancels defendant's liability by breaking the chain of causation. However, an intervening cause is only superseding if its results are unforeseeable. Here, that's not the case, so Trucker's negligence will be considered the legal cause of Driver's negligence.

Since Trucker's negligence satisfies both factual and legal causation, and D states otherwise, it's not the best response.

Answer 17

(B) is the best response,

because it represents a claim which will be straightforward to prove on these facts.

In order to prevail on a claim of negligence, Driver would have to prove that City failed to exercise such care as a reasonable person in its position would have exercised, this was a breach of the duty to prevent the foreseeable risk of harm to anyone in Driver's position, and this breach caused Driver's damages. While determining if a given course of conduct is negligent requires some fine line drawing, if you apply the balancing test used to determine if conduct is negligent – the burden on defendant to avoid risk and the utility of defendant's conduct vs. the probability and probable gravity of the harm defendant's conduct is likely to cause – to these facts, it's clear that leaving a traffic signal at a busy intersection unrepaired for *three full days* would qualify.

Note that strict liability is *not* a good claim under these facts because there's no basis for imposing an absolute duty on City. The three general sources of strict liability are animals, abnormally dangerous activities, and defective, unreasonably dangerous products (statutes and case law can also be a source of strict liability). None of these apply to these facts, so while a strict liability claim would relieve Driver of proving fault, he'd be unlikely to be able to pin an absolute duty on City. Since B cites a claim which is easily provable on these facts, it's the best response.

(A) is not the best response,

because it's not likely strict liability would apply to these facts, and there's an easier option for Driver to pursue.

There are three general sources of strict liability: Animals, abnormally dangerous activities, and defective, unreasonably dangerous products (case law and statutes can also provide for strict liability). Here, traffic signals would not be a likely source of strict liability based on traditional sources, and there's no statute mandating strict liability. Maintaining traffic signals could not be an abnormally dangerous activity because the hallmark of such activities is their inability to be performed with complete safety. Here, the signals *could* be maintained in a safe manner – it's just that City dropped the ball on this occasion.

This means that Driver won't be likely to recover against City if he opts for a claim without proving fault. What's involved is a trade-off between duty and fault: Either Driver must prove an absolute duty and *no* fault (strict liability), or reasonable duty and unreasonableness (negligence). Under these facts, proving negligence will be much easier, because a three-day delay in fixing a traffic signal at a busy intersection could safely be characterized as unreasonable. Since A states a claim that is unlikely to prevail due to an unrealistic duty, it's not the best response.

(C) is not the best response,

because City would probably not have an absolute duty to maintain traffic signals, under these facts. An absolute duty of care is the basis of a strict liability claim – that is, when a duty is absolute, the tortfeasor's carefulness is irrelevant, because fault isn't an element of the action. There are three general areas where an absolute duty is imposed: Animals, abnormally dangerous activities, and defective, unreasonably dangerous products (strict liability can also be imposed by case law or statutes). Under these facts, there's no statute imposing strict liability, and the traffic signal doesn't fit any traditional source of strict liability. This means that Driver is unlikely to prevail on a strict liability claim. Maintaining traffic signals could not be an abnormally dangerous activity because the hallmark of such activities is their inability to be performed with complete safety. Here, the signals *could* be maintained in a safe manner – it's just that City dropped the ball on this occasion.

What's involved in determining which claim to press is a trade-off between duty and fault: Either Driver must prove an absolute duty and *no* fault (strict liability), or reasonable duty and unreasonable behavior (negligence). Under these facts, proving negligence will be much easier, because a three-day delay in fixing a traffic signal at a busy intersection could safely be characterized as unreasonable. As a result, pressing a claim based on absolute duty would not give Driver his best chance to prevail, making C not the best response.

(D) is not the best response,

because it does not represent a sound basis on which to hold City liable. In order for Driver to prevail, he'll have to prove a duty, be it absolute or reasonable, and breach of duty.

D suggests that City should be liable without proof of fault if its act (or omission) resulted in a dangerous trap. Creating a dangerous trap is not, in and of itself, a basis for imposing strict liability. Instead, strict liability is based on breach of an absolute duty, regardless of results. The three general sources of strict liability are animals, abnormally dangerous activities, and defective, unreasonably dangerous products (also, a statute or case law could impose strict liability). City's conduct here would not likely be a subject of strict liability, since it doesn't fit these parameters.

Instead, a better claim would be negligence, because although it requires proof of fault, the 72-hour delay in repairing the signal would easily provide this. Since D does not focus on duty and addresses an unlikely source of liability, it's not the best response.

Answer 18

(D) is the best response,

because this argument correctly states a requirement for the tort of intentional infliction of emotional distress, and shows that the requirement is not met.

To establish a prima facie case for intentional/reckless infliction of emotional distress, the following elements must be shown: (1) an act by defendant amounting to extreme and outrageous conduct, (2) intent on the part of the defendant to cause plaintiff to suffer severe emotional distress, or recklessness as to the effect of defendant's conduct, (3) causation, and (4) damages.

Here, Photographer is probably correct in arguing that no reasonable person could conclude that the conduct here satisfied requirement (1)'s "extreme and outrageous conduct" standard. As the Second Restatement puts it, the conduct must be "beyond all possible bounds of decency..." Rest. 2d, § 46, Comment d. The conduct here — which, after all, involved pursuit of a newsworthy story by use of the public airspace — does not seem to meet this standard. (In any event, none of the other arguments has any real chance of prevailing, so Choice (D) is the "best" answer even though it is not certain to prevail.)

(A) is not the best response,

because whether Photographer had the intent to photograph Prisoner or not is irrelevant, given the possibility of reckless infliction of distress.

The facts say that Prisoner is suing for "intentional or *reckless*" infliction of distress. Therefore, if Prisoner can show that Photographer recklessly disregarded both the possibility that he was including Prisoner in the photo, and the possibility that this inclusion might well cause Prisoner distress, Prisoner could win (if the "extreme and outrageous" standard were met, which it isn't). So the fact that Photographer didn't specifically intend to photograph Prisoner (even if proven) would be irrelevant. (Also, a court would probably disagree with the proposition that no reasonable person could conclude that Photographer intended to include Prisoner in the shot.)

(B) is not the best response,

because physical injury suffered by plaintiff is not an element of the prima facie case for intentional or reckless infliction of emotional distress.

To establish a prima facie case for intentional infliction of emotional distress, the following elements must be shown: (1) an act by defendant amounting to extreme and outrageous conduct, (2) intent on the part of the defendant to cause plaintiff to suffer severe emotional distress, or recklessness as to the effect of defendant's conduct, (3) causation, and (4) damages.

Because physical injury is not an element of intentional or reckless infliction of emotional distress, Choice (B) is wrong.

(C) is not the best response,

because no "extra" privilege exists for news photographers to take photographs.

News photographers do not have a special privilege exempting them from tortious conduct. In other words, if the taking and publication of a particular photo would be "extreme and outrageous" (which the photo here wouldn't, as discussed above), this would be true whether the photo was taken by a professional news photographer or by an amateur with a disposable camera.

Answer 19

(C) is the best response,

because the storm was so severe that the absence of lifeboats made no difference.

On these facts, the doctrine of "negligence per se" might have applied. This doctrine states that when a safety rule has sufficiently close application to the facts of the case at hand, an unexcused violation of that statute is "negligence per se." So here, the liner's failure to have the statutorily-required lifeboats would automatically be deemed to constitute negligence.

But the negligence per se doctrine doesn't excuse the plaintiff from showing *causation*. In particular, if compliance with the statute wouldn't have prevented the harm from occurring, then the absence of compliance couldn't have been the cause in fact of the injury, and plaintiff loses.

Here, that's what happened — the absence of the required lifeboat made no factual difference, because such a boat couldn't have been used, and thus couldn't have prevented the harm.

(A) is not the best response,

because not having the lifeboats required by the statute was not the cause of Passenger's drowning.

The "negligence per se" doctrine states that when a safety rule has sufficiently close application to the facts of the case at hand, an unexcused violation of that statute is "negligence per se." However, even where the statute is applicable to the facts of the case, the "negligence per se" does not make the defendant liable unless the plaintiff shows that there is a causal link between the act constituting the violation and the resulting injury. Here, since the presence of the boats would have made no difference, this causal relationship is lacking.

(B) is not the best response,

because common carriers such as ocean liners are not held to the strict liability standard.

It is true that common carriers are required to exercise a very high degree of care toward their passengers and guests, which is to say they are liable for even slight negligence. But this is not the same as "strict liability." So Choice (B), insofar as it asserts that strict liability applies, is simply wrong.

(D) is not the best response,

because Passenger did not knowingly assume the risk of not having lifeboats.

The assumption of risk doctrine states that a plaintiff has assumed the risk of a certain harm if she voluntarily consented to take her chances that the harm would occur. Where such an assumption of risk is shown, the plaintiff is completely barred from recovery.

Here, Passenger may well have assumed the general risk of a "rough voyage." But Passenger would not be held to have assumed the risk that the liner would fail to install statutorily-required lifeboats. Indeed, where (as here) a statutory safety requirement is intended to protect a particular class of people who can't protect themselves, courts are very hesitant to find that a member of that class assumed the risk of non-compliance. In any event, here there is no evidence at all that Passenger knowingly assumed the risk of failure to have lifeboats, so assumption of risk could not apply.

Answer 20

(A) is the best response,

because the essence of battery is lack of consent, and Athlete did not consent to Surgeon's performing the operation.

Consent is a defense to a tortious interference with a plaintiff's person or property. Even if the plaintiff gives actual consent to some type of invasion of his interests, the defendant will not be privileged if she goes substantially beyond the scope of consent and invades the plaintiff's interests in a way that is substantially different than what was consented to.

Under these facts, Athlete specifically consented in writing to having the operation performed by *Doctor*. Doctor's decision to have Surgeon to perform the operation exceeded the scope of Athlete's original consent. It doesn't matter that Surgeon was a world famous orthopedic surgeon with skills better than Doctor's, or that he successfully performed the operation — Athlete's consent applied to Doctor, not to Surgeon.

(B) is not the best response,

because the written consent form was for Doctor, not for Surgeon, to perform the operation.

A patient's consent is read relatively strictly, and for the reasons discussed above would not be found to apply to Surgeon, only to Doctor. The fact that the consent form was in writing would not change the fact that the operation here exceeded the scope of the consent.

(C) is not the best response,

because Surgeon's performing the operation is substantially different than Doctor's performing it.

Consent is a defense to a tortious interference with a plaintiff's person or property. Even if the plaintiff gives actual consent to some type of invasion of his interests, the defendant will not be privileged if she goes substantially beyond the scope of consent and invades the plaintiff's interests in a way that is substantially different than what was consented to.

Here, Athlete's consent was for Doctor to perform the operation. The consent was for Doctor personally to perform the surgery, *not* for "anyone as good as or better than Doctor." Therefore, Surgeon's performance of the operation exceeded the scope of the consent, and Surgeon's better skills didn't change this fact.

(D) is not the best response,

because the success of the surgery is not a defense.

Here Athlete specifically consented in writing to Doctor's performing the surgery. Surgeon's performance of that surgery, whatever its outcome, went substantially beyond the scope of Athlete's consent. The outcome of the surgery, successful or not, is not a defense to Surgeon's operating without consent.

Answer 21

(D) is the best response,

because intentional force that exceeded the player's consent would be an offensive contact constituting a battery.

An action for battery has three elements: (1) defendant's act bringing about a harmful or offensive contact with plaintiff's person; (2) defendant's intent to bring about such contact or to create the apprehension of immediate contact; and (3) causation.

For Perry to prevail in an action for battery he'd have to prove an offensive contact. Roughness up to the level to which Perry impliedly consented would not be deemed harmful or offensive. But consent would not be

a defense if Dever intentionally used more than the consented-to level of force.

(A) is not the best response,

because what is at issue is not the contact, but the level of contact consented to by the players in the game.

Apparent consent is that which a reasonable person would infer from plaintiff's conduct. Thus, for example, somebody who voluntarily engages in a body contact sport impliedly consents to the normal contacts inherent in playing it.

If Dever intended to strike Perry, but in a way that was consistent with the play of the game, then Perry's consent would be found to be implied by his participation in the game and his use of the same tactics.

(B) is not the best response,

because it ignores the significance of the plaintiff's consent.

What would otherwise be a harmful or offensive contact will not be actionable if it was consented to. Because Perry's participation in the rough game, and his use of the same tactics, would be found to constitute implied consent to a certain level of roughness, the mere fact that Dever intended to cause, say, an offensive contact that was consistent with the general game-play would not expose him to liability.

(C) is not the best response,

because it ignores the possibility that Dever may have exceeded the scope of the implied consent.

It's true that if Dever acted merely with the same level of roughness as previously manifested by various players in the game (including Perry), Perry would be deemed to have consented to it. But Dever may have used more than the level of force to which Perry would be found to have consented. In that event, the implied-consent doctrine wouldn't apply, and Dever could be liable.

Answer 22

(C) is the best response,

because the law does not recognize a claim for damages for emotional distress incident to negligently-caused property loss.

Where due to the defendant's negligence the plaintiff either suffers physical injury or narrowly avoids it, the plaintiff can recover for emotional distress, at least if it is accompanied by physical symptoms. But where the only injury or physical damage from the defendant's negligence is property damage, courts are unwilling to allow the plaintiff to recover for her emotional distress at the property damage. (Courts fear inflated claims and liability without a natural stopping point.) Since Owner's distress is due to the property damage (not, say, due to Owner's nearly being burned in the negligently-caused fire), this rule applies here to deprive

Owner of recovery for the distress.

(A) is not the best response,

because the law does not recognize a claim for damages for emotional distress incident to negligently-caused property loss, for the reasons discussed in Choice (C) above.

(B) is not the best response,

because the law does not recognize a claim for damages for emotional distress incident to negligently caused property loss. Emotional distress harm may be "as real" as physical harm, but courts fear that false claims of emotional harm are far easier to make, and harder to disprove, than those of physical harm. Therefore, in cases of pure property damage, they do not allow recovery of emotional distress incident to that property damage.

(D) is not the best response,

because even a showing of physical harm from the distress would not suffice.

If Owner had been threatened with imminent bodily injury from the fire, then the fact that Owner suffered physical harm from emotional distress at his near escape probably would make the difference (i.e., Owner could recover for distress because he suffered physical symptoms, and couldn't recover if he didn't have physical symptoms.) But where, as here, there was no danger to the plaintiff of bodily injury, and his emotional distress is due solely to his being upset at the property damage, courts do not allow recovery (for the reasons discussed in (C) above) even if there are physical symptoms from the distress.

Answer 23

(D) is the best response,

because a tortfeasor is liable for harm of which his negligence is a proximate cause.

Under the prevailing view of proximate cause, the defendant's negligent conduct is the (or a) proximate cause of the plaintiff's injury if (and only if) the general type of harm that occurred to the plaintiff was a reasonably foreseeable consequence of the defendant's negligent action.

Choice (D) articulates this standard. We cannot say on these facts that Mechanic's injury was in fact a proximate consequence of Basher's negligent driving — but *if it was* a proximate consequence, Mechanic would be entitled to at least partial recovery from Basher, under pure comparative-negligence principles.

By the way, the fact that the accident might have been avoided by a warning from Adam won't get Basher off the hook (see the discussion of Choice (B) for why). If Adam's failure to mention the leak constituted negligence by him, this would reduce Basher's share of the judgment under comparative negligence, but it wouldn't eliminate Basher's liability.

(A) is not the best response,

because Basher's liability arises out of his negligent driving, not his awareness of the gasoline leak.

Here, Basher's liability for the explosion began when his negligent driving caused the accident with Adam's car. If it was a foreseeable consequence of that negligent driving that some repairer of the other party's car might be hurt as a result, Basher will be liable even though he never knew precisely in what way his negligence created the special danger to the repairer. In other words, liability depends on the foreseeable consequences of the negligently-caused event (the accident), not from whether the negligent actor was or wasn't aware of how the danger arose.

(B) is not the best response,

because such a warning would not be deemed to have broken the causal link between Basher's negligent driving and the injury to Mechanic.

In general, a third party's failure to discover or warn of a danger caused by the defendant will not insulate the defendant from negligence liability, even if a warning would have eliminated the danger. Especially in a comparative-negligence jurisdiction such as the one here, even if Adam's failure to mention the leak was negligence, a court would almost certainly conclude that this failure was not a "superseding cause," and was merely co-negligence (which would serve to reduce Basher's liability to Mechanic but not eliminate it).

(C) is not the best response,

because even had Mechanic negligently failed to discover the danger, he would still be entitled to recovery.

In a pure comparative negligence jurisdiction such as the one here, the plaintiff's negligent failure to discover a danger caused by the defendant will not eliminate the defendant's liability, merely reduce it. Since Basher would be otherwise liable to Mechanic if the accident was a proximate consequence of Basher's negligent driving (see Choice (D)), this result would still be true in the face of Mechanic's negligent failure to discover the danger.

Answer 24

(C) is the best response,

because a negligent failure to warn of a danger can be the basis for negligence liability.

Normally, a defendant will not be liable in negligence for a mere failure to act (here, a failure to warn). So, for instance, if Adam was merely a bystander who observed the initial collision and gas leak, he wouldn't be liable if he stood by while Mechanic began work, and failed to warn Mechanic of the danger.

But one of the exceptions to the rule of "no liability for failure to act" exists where the danger is due to an instrument under the defendant's control. So here, because Adam owned and controlled the auto, and transferred possession of it to Mechanic, he would fall within this exception. Consequently, even though Adam didn't negligently cause the original collision or the gas leak, he inherited a duty to warn Mechanic if a reasonable person in his position would have made such a warning.

(A) is not the best response,

because Mechanic's obligation to inspect the vehicle does not erase Adam's duty to warn Mechanic.

In a contributory negligence state, this choice might conceivably be right, since Mechanic's failure to spot the danger might be found to be negligence that would bar recovery. But since we are in a comparative negligence state, this failure to discover the danger, even if negligent, would only reduce, not block, recovery. And a court would be extremely unlikely to conclude that Mechanic's failure to inspect was the sort of intervening act that should be deemed to "break the chain of causation" between Adam's negligence (if any) and the injury.

(B) is not the best response,

because it omits the possibility that even though Adam was unaware of the danger, a person of ordinary prudence would have been aware of it and would have given a warning.

For the reasons stated in Chioce (C), Adam had a duty to warn if a reasonable person in his position would have warned. The reasonable person would have warned if such a person would have been aware of the risk. So Adam's duty is measured by what the mental state of a reasonable person would have been. If Adam was unusually dumb (so that he didn't know gas leaks can lead to explosions), his dumbness would not insulate him. Since Choice (B) makes Adam's subjective awareness of the danger the sole factor, it is incorrect.

(D) is not the best response,

because it incorrectly eliminates any requirement that Adam have been negligent.

If Adam was a merchant in cars, and sold the car to Mechanic, then the fact that the car was "unreasonably dangerous" when Adam delivered it would give rise to strict liability (i.e., liability in the absence of negligence) on Adam's part. But here, Adam is not in the business of selling cars (and isn't even selling this car), so there's no strict product liability.

Nor is this a situation in which Adam has been carrying out an "abnormally dangerous activity." Consequently, the only way Adam can be liable is if his failure to warn was negligent. Since Choice (D) eliminates Adam's negligence as a factor, it is incorrect.

Answer 25

(B) is the best response,

because Sid's last clear chance wiped out the effect of

Fran's contributory negligence.

The last clear chance doctrine states that if, just before the accident, the defendant had the opportunity (the "last clear chance") to prevent the harm, and the plaintiff did not have such an opportunity, the existence of the last clear chance wipes out what would otherwise be the fatal effect of the plaintiff's contributory negligence.

The doctrine applies in (and only in) contributory-negligence jurisdictions, and allows a plaintiff to recover despite his own contributory negligence, which would otherwise be a bar to recovery if plaintiff contributed in any way to the event giving rise to the claim.

The facts tell us that (1) Sid saw Fran's peril; (2) Sid had sufficient distance to slow to a controlled stop before hitting Fran; and (3) Fran's car was halted, so she no longer had the opportunity to get out of the way. Therefore, the requirements for last clear chance seem to be satisfied. In any event, this choice says that Fran will win *if* Sid had a last clear chance, and that's definitely a correct statement of doctrine.

(A) is not the best response,

because the answer states a rule for comparative rather than contributory negligence.

Under comparative negligence a plaintiff may recover if his negligence was less serious than that of the defendant. But in a contributory negligence jurisdiction, even minor negligence by the plaintiff wipes out all recovery (assuming no doctrine like last clear chance applies).

(C) is not the best response,

because the answer does not take into consideration the last clear chance exception to contributory negligence.

As described in the discussion of choice (B), the last clear chance doctrine, if applicable, would wipe out the effects of Fran's contributory negligence. Therefore, even though Fran's conduct was a legal cause of the accident, she can recover.

(D) is not the best response,

because the assumption of risk doctrine would require Fran to know that Sid was going to try to swerve rather than coming to a stop.

The assumption of risk doctrine states that a plaintiff may be denied recovery if he knew of and voluntarily assumed the risks caused by defendant's acts. Since there is no indication that prior to the accident Fran knew of, or voluntarily assumed, the risk that Sid would behave in anything like the way he did, the doctrine has no application.

Answer 26

(D) is the best response,

because Hospital has a duty of exercise reasonable care to protect Patient, an invitee of the hospital.

Invitees are those invited onto the owner's land, expressly or impliedly, to conduct business with the landowner. The owner must exercise reasonable care for the safety of invitees.

Under these facts Hospital and Patient were engaged in a business relationship. Hospital was to provide medical services for which Patient was going to pay. Hospital invited Patient onto its premises to provide the services. As an invitee of Hospital, Patient could reasonably expect that the premises had been made safe and that Hospital would continue to use reasonable care to protect Patient from harm.

One reason this choice is the best answer is that it is the only choice that doesn't turn on whether Orderly was an employee (as opposed to, say, an independent contractor), whether he was acting within the scope of his employment, and the like. If Hospital in fact failed to use reasonable care, then the answers to these other questions don't matter. (If Hospital *didn't* fail to use due care, it might still be liable under *respondeat superior*, depending on the answer to these questions — but the one thing we know for sure is that if Hospital *did* fail to use due care, it's automatically liable.)

(A) is not the best response,

because Hospital must exercise reasonable care to protect Patient from harm, even harm from employees acting outside the scope of their employment.

The "scope of employment" analysis would matter if the basis for suit was *respondeat superior* (because then, acts taken outside the scope of employment would not trigger *respondeat superior* liability). But for the reasons discussed in Choice (D) above, Hospital would be liable without respect to *respondeat superior* if it negligently failed to protect its patients. Say, for instance, that Hospital hired X as a security guard, while negligently failing to do an easily-available check that would have shown that X had recently escaped from a prison term as a rapist. If X then raped Patient, Hospital would have primary (as opposed to derivative *respondeat superior*) liability even if X was clearly acting outside the scope of his duties when he committed the rape.

(B) is not the best response,

because Patient was not legally capable of granting consent.

Those of diminished capacity (e.g., children, people who are intoxicated or unconscious or severely mentally impaired) are deemed incapable of granting consent. Any objective manifestation of consent by the plaintiff will be ineffective, at least where the defendant knows or should know that plaintiff is not competent to give meaningful consent.

Here the facts of the case are that Patient was a severely retarded person, and was known to be such by Hospital. Therefore, whether Patient initiated the relationship or encouraged Orderly's actions is irrelevant.

(C) is not the best response,

because Hospital may be liable for Orderly's actions whether he was an employee or not.

The doctrine of respondeat superior holds that an employer is liable for any intentional tort committed by the employee where the tort is wholly or in part intended to further the employer's business. But an alternative basis of liability is landowner liability: landowners must take reasonable care to protect invitees, including harm from torts committed by non-employees committed on the premises.

Under these facts Hospital may be liable regardless of whether Orderly was an employee or not. If, as unlikely as it seems, Orderly was acting within the scope of his employment, then Hospital is liable for Orderly's intentional tort (if not criminal actions) under the doctrine of *respondeat superior*. But if, as is much more likely, Orderly was acting outside his scope of employment, then Hospital wouldn't be liable under *respondeat superior*. But Hospital would still have owed a duty of reasonable care to protect Patient. If a court found that Hospital failed to exercise that required reasonable care (e.g., by failing to check whether Orderly had a criminal record for rape), Hospital would be liable even if Orderly was an independent contractor, or was an employee acting completely outside the scope of his employment.

Answer 27

(A) is the best response,

because Driver can make a prima facie case for Rapido's strict liability.

The two central sections of the Third Restatement of Torts' statement on strict liability read as follows: "§1 One engaged in the business of selling or otherwise distributing products who sells or distributes a defective product is subject to liability for harm to persons or property caused by the defect." and "§2 A product is defective when, at the time of sale or distribution, it contains a manufacturing defect, is defective in design, or is defective because of inadequate instructions or warnings."

Driver has made a prima facie showing that satisfies the above requirements for strict liability, since a reasonable jury could find that: (1) Rapido was engaged in the business of selling or distributing cars; (2) the fact that Rapido's motor may stall if the engine has not had an extended warm-up is a design defect since an alternative design was feasible; and (3) the stalling motor and ensuing accident caused Driver's shock, which resulted in a heart attack. Driver can thus make her prima facie case, so Rapido's motion should be denied.

(B) is not the best response,

because the "crashworthiness" of the car was not at

issue on these facts.

"Crashworthiness" in a vehicle is the attribute of being able to withstand a collision without posing an unacceptably large risk of injury to the passengers. (For instance, a vehicle whose passenger compartment completely crumples even in low-speed collisions would be likely to be found to be non-crashworthy.) Non-crashworthiness can certainly be a type of defect.

However, on the facts as alleged by Driver here, the injury to her occurred from the "shock of the crash," not from any failure of the vehicle to appropriately withstand the collision. (In other words, the facts indicate that even in a perfectly crashworthy vehicle, Driver would probably have had the same shock and thus the same heart attack). Consequently, even if a reasonable jury could find that the vehicle was "defective" because it was non-crashworthy (something not at all clear on these facts), the jury would probably not be entitled to find that the defect of non-crashworthiness was the legal cause of the injury. In that event, Rapido would still win on its motion. So although the conclusion (Rapido loses on the motion) is correct, the explanation of why it loses is not correct.

(C) is not the best response,

because it was foreseeable that cars with engines that stall could be in accidents, so Troody's failure to stop was not superseding.

An intervening cause is a force that takes effect after the defendant's negligence and which contributes to that negligence in producing the plaintiff's injury. Some, but not all, intervening causes are sufficient to prevent the defendant's negligence from being considered the proximate cause of the injury. Intervening causes of this kind are usually called "superseding causes" because they supersede or cancel the defendant's liability.

An intervening cause that was "foreseeable" as something that might combine with a defect to cause an injury will generally not be deemed to be superseding cause. Here, it was perfectly foreseeable that a car that stalled due to a defect would be extra likely to be hit from the rear. Therefore, being hit from the rear was a foreseeable (and thus non-superseding) intervening cause given a "defective-because-likely-to-stall" engine.

(D) is not the best response,

because the defendant "takes the plaintiff as he finds him."

Where the defendant's negligence causes an aggravation of plaintiff's existing physical or mental illness, defendant is liable for the damages caused by the aggravation, which is to say, the tortfeasor takes the victim as he finds him.

So here, this rule means that Rapido cannot escape liability by arguing that a person of normal sensitivity would not have suffered a heart attack under these cir-

cumstances.

Answer 28

(A) (III only) is the best response,

because the lack of widespread publicity prevents invasion of privacy from applying, and Applicant cannot be the plaintiff in a suit based on negligent misrepresentation, but the facts satisfy the requirements for negligent infliction of emotional distress.

We consider the choices based on (I), (II) and (III), not A-D.

Choice (I) (Invasion of privacy): Of the four types of torts that are loosely grouped together under the rubric "invasion of privacy" (misappropriation of identity; intrusion on solitude; publicity of private life; and false light), the only two which plausibly apply are "publicity of private life" and "false light." However, both of these torts require that the fact be given "publicity." Telling the private and/or false fact to a single person or small group does not constitute "publicity." Rest. 2d § 652D, Comment a, and § 652E, Comment a. Since Doctor made the (false) disclosure to only a single person, Employer, neither of the invasion-of-privacy torts applies, making choice (I) wrong.

Choice II (Negligent Misrepresentation): One who makes a negligent misrepresentation can indeed be liable for the pecuniary consequences of that misrepresentation. However, in the words of the Second Restatement, this tort "subjects the negligent supplier of misinformation to liability *only to those persons for whose benefit and guidance it is supplied.*" Rest. 2d § 552, Comment h. Since Doctor was not intending to give benefit and guidance to Applicant, Applicant is not entitled to sue.

Choice III (Negligent Infliction of Emotional Distress): As the Restatement puts it, a person is liable for negligent infliction of emotional distress if he "should have realized that his conduct involved an unreasonable risk of causing the distress ... and ... from facts known to him should have realized that the distress, if it were caused, might result in illness or bodily harm." Rest. 2d § 313.

Doctor's conduct here satisfies this standard: (1) he should have realized that if he misread and misreported the medical facts, this would cause distress to one who was seeking a job; and (2) he should have realized that, to a job seeker, the distress from a false allegation of AIDS made to a prospective employer (who might then tell others) might well be so devastating that it might cause illness.

Answer 29

(B) is the best response,

because it is the only choice that involves setting the standard of care, rather than determining whether the defendant satisfied the appropriate standard of care.

The suit has been brought on a failure-to-warn theory. The facts stipulate that the dangers that Powell says should have been warned of were not known or knowable at the time of Powell's exposure. Therefore, the judge must at the outset answer a pure question of law: does a defendant who is selling dangerous substances have a duty to warn of their dangerousness if that dangerousness is unknown at the time? Choice (B) encapsulates this issue, since if (and only if) Acme is held to have a duty to warn of these not-yet-known dangers can a reasonable jury possibly find that Acme is liable for failing to warn.

(A) is not the best response,

because (1) the issue is irrelevant to plaintiff's failure-to-warn theory, and (2) in any event, this is a question of fact, to be left to the jury.

Plaintiff has sued on a failure-to-warn theory. Therefore, even if no satisfactory, safe alternative exists even today, there could still be a duty (even today) to warn of these unavoidable dangers. (One in plaintiff's position would be entitled to conclude that in view of the dangers, he should take a different job.) Consequently, the existence of a satisfactory alternative is simply not relevant to the claim.

In any event, even if this issue were relevant, the answer would be a pure question of fact, not law.

(C) is not the best response,

because (1) the issue posed may not even be a relevant issue; and (2) the issue is in any event a question of fact.

As to (1), the judge could quite plausibly decide (as a matter of law, and as described in Choice (B)), that Powell should be held to have had a duty to warn of not-yet-discoverable risks. If the judge so held, then the issue here (whether D in fact knew of the risks) would be legally irrelevant.

As to (2), in any event, what any defendant should reasonably have known at a particular moment is inevitably a factual issue, properly left to the jury.

(D) is not the best response,

because (1) "inherent dangerousness" is probably not an issue; and (2) even if it were, this would be a factual issue to be left to the jury.

The concept of "inherent dangerousness," to the extent that it's relevant in a product-liability suit, generally refers to the issue of "unavoidable danger." That is, if a product has some social utility, and is "unavoidably dangerous" (or as it is sometimes put, "inherently dangerous"), the defendant may be able to argue that the product is not "defective." (That's because the idea of a "defect" involves something that is "wrong," needlessly dangerous, and something that is unavoidably hazardous does not meet this standard.)

Here, the case has been brought on a failure-to-warn theory. Even if asbestos is "inherently dangerous" (and thus not defective), this fact would not spare the defen-

dant from having a duty to warn of its inherent dangers (assuming there is a duty to warn of not-yet-knowable dangers). So the inherent dangerousness of the product would be irrelevant.

In any even, even if inherent dangerousness were a relevant issue, this would be a matter of fact, not law, and thus properly left to the jury.

Answer 30

(C) is the best response,

because it was not foreseeable to Motorist that he would suffer a heart attack, and any violation of the red-light statute was not the result of an intentional act.

There is no direct evidence that Motorist failed to exercise due care. Therefore, under ordinary negligence principles, the court would clearly have to find, as a matter of law, that no reasonable jury could find Motorist liable for negligence (the only plausible basis on which Child could recover).

(Had Motorist driven in the face of knowledge that he was especially vulnerable to a heart attack, then this might be enough indication of negligence to permit the case to go to the jury. But the facts carefully make it clear that this was not the case.)

The only interesting question is whether the fact that Motorist's car drove through the red light, in violation of a statute, can give rise to an inference of negligence through operation of the doctrine of negligence per se.

Here, the court could not properly apply the negligence-per-se doctrine. Since Motorist was unconscious during the violation, Motorist did not even "commit" a violation, since an unconscious act cannot be the basis for a statutory violation. Furthermore, even treating this as a statutory violation, negligence per se would not apply because the court would conclude that any statutory violation was "excused" due to the medical emergency.

(A) is not the best response,

because violation of the motor code is not proof of Motorist's negligence per se.

As is described in the treatment of Choice (C) above, Motorist would not be deemed to have committed a voluntary violation of the statute at all, and even if he did, any violation would be excused. Therefore, the negligence per se doctrine would not be applied.

(B) is not the best response,

because the requirements of proof by inference, otherwise known as "res ipsa loquitor," are not met.

For the judge to issue a directed verdict for Child, the court would have to conclude that no reasonable jury could deny that Motorist was negligent. It is very rare fact pattern that would cause the judge to find negligence as a matter of law.

The choice's reference to an "inference" of negligence is probably intended to suggest that the doctrine of res ipsa loquitur may apply. But there are at least two impediments to applying res ipsa here: (1) it cannot be said that car accidents generally don't happen in the absence of negligence by someone (which is why res ipsa is rarely applied in car accident cases); and (2) even if res ipsa applied, it would merely entitle Child to get to the jury (i.e., supply enough evidence of negligence that a jury *could* properly find negligence), not entitle Child to a directed verdict on negligence (i.e., supply such incontrovertible evidence of negligence that the judge would conclude that no reasonable jury could find that there *wasn't* negligence.)

(D) is not the best response,

because there is no evidence of Motorist's negligence.

As discussed in Choice (C), there is no evidence at all of Motorist's negligence. Therefore, the standard for issuing a directed verdict against Child (that there is at least one element of plaintiff's prima facie case that no reasonable jury could find to have been proved) is satisfied.

Answer 31

(D) is the best response,

because it correctly identifies the basis on which Hank will prevail: Fred didn't satisfy all the elements of a public nuisance suit brought by a private individual.

A public nuisance is an act which unreasonably interferes with the health, safety or convenience of the public in general. The state normally brings such an action; if a private individual does so, he must prove he suffered special damages above and beyond the ordinary damage the public incurred. Under these facts, all Frank has done is shown that Hank created a public nuisance, by reference to the ordinance (which is probably sufficient to establish a public nuisance, since that's likely the aim of the ordinance; and, even without the ordinance, blocking sidewalks would unreasonably interfere with the public's safety). However, Fred hasn't shown any damages unique to him (e.g., blocking the entrance to his business). As a result, his failure to state special damages will defeat his claim. Since D correctly identifies this, it's the best response.

(A) is not the best response,

because such a defense would not apply to these facts. Where a nuisance suit is predicated on intent, consent could at least theoretically be a good defense, but it isn't on these facts; it would be unreasonable to force Frank to move in order to enjoy his own property.

Instead, Hank is more likely to prevail because Fred's claim doesn't satisfy the elements of a public nuisance claim brought by a private individual. A public nuisance is an act which unreasonably interferes with the health, safety, or convenience of the public in general. The state normally brings such an action, but a private individual may bring such a claim if he suffered special damages above and beyond the ordinary damage the

public incurred. Since this is one of the answer options, and the reasoning A offers will be both unlikely to succeed on these facts and will be difficult to prove, A is not the best response.

(B) is not the best response,

because it does not address why Fred's public nuisance claim will fail, and furthermore it misstates the facts.

First, the statute *may* be relevant in establishing that Hank's conduct constitutes a public nuisance. A public nuisance is an act which unreasonably interferes with the health, safety or convenience of the public in general. Thus, by passing an ordinance forbidding goods and merchandise from being placed on public sidewalks, the legislature could have been recognizing that doing so is a public nuisance. However, Hank's conduct could constitute a public nuisance *regardless* of the ordinance, since it could satisfy the elements of public nuisance without reference to the statute. Thus, the statute is not particularly significant to Fred's claim.

Furthermore, there's nothing to suggest that Hank's violation of the ordinance was reasonable. Had there been a fire in Hank's store, for instance, he'd have been privileged to violate the ordinance; however, it's possible, and more reasonable, to clean the floor by moving goods around *inside,* not unloading them onto the sidewalk. Thus, stating that Hank's violation was reasonable is not entirely accurate.

Option B's primary error, however, is its failure to recognize that Fred's claim doesn't satisfy all the elements of a public nuisance claim brought by a private individual. In order to prevail, Fred would have to prove that he suffered special damages above and beyond the ordinary damage the public incurred. Since B fails to recognize this and focuses instead on an insignificant point, it's not the best response.

(C) is not the best response,

because it does not correctly characterize the facts and would not represent a valid defense. C suggests that Hank should prevail because the claim was destroyed by Fred's removing the nuisance. Not only does this misstate the facts, but it ignores the central reason Fred's claim will fail: He doesn't satisfy the elements of a public nuisance suit brought by a private individual. In order for such a claim to succeed, Fred would have to prove that he suffered special damages above and beyond the ordinary damage the public incurred. Since there's no indication that Fred did this, his claim will fail on this basis. Since C doesn't recognize this and mischaracterizes the facts, it's not the best response.

Answer 32

(D) is the best response,

because it correctly identifies that a guest statute would be irrelevant on these facts.

An automobile guest statute makes the driver of a car liable to a gratuitous guest in the car only for something more than simple negligence (typically, gross negligence). The rationale for such statutes is twofold: Protecting hospitality (by making it more difficult for a guest to sue his host) and preventing collusion (between the driver and passenger against the driver's insurance company). Thus, it has *no* applicability when the claim is against one other than the driver. Here, in Price's claim against Motorco, he only need prove simple negligence in order to recover for negligence. Since D correctly identifies that the guest statute won't apply to these facts, it's the best response.

(A) is not the best response,

because it overlooks the fact that a guest statute wouldn't be relevant in this case. Assuming arguendo that a guest statute *did* apply, it would be unlikely to bar Price's recovery.

An automobile guest statute makes the driver of a car liable to a gratuitous guest in the car only for something more than simple negligence (typically, gross negligence). The rationale for such statutes is twofold: Protecting hospitality (by making it more difficult for a passenger to sue his host) and preventing collusion (between the driver and passenger, against the driver's insurance company).

As this definition shows, a guest statute would only be applicable to a claim by a passenger against the driver, not a claim by the passenger against the car manufacturer, as is involved here. Furthermore, even if Price had been suing Dunn, he'd unlikely be barred from recovery, as option A states. If Price had to prove gross negligence, it's not clear if he'd be able to, because all these facts tell you is that Dunn was negligent. If Dunn's conduct amounted to *simple* negligence, Price couldn't recover; if it was *gross* negligence, Price could recover. Thus, even if a guest statute were applicable here, you couldn't determine if option A was correct. In any case, since the guest statute *doesn't* apply, option A *can't* be correct.

(B) is not the best response,

because it ignores the fact that the defendant here is Motorco, not Dunn.

An automobile guest statute makes the driver of a car liable to a gratuitous guest in the car only for something more than simple negligence (typically, gross negligence). The rationale for such statutes is twofold: Protecting hospitality (by making it more difficult for a guest to sue his host) and preventing collusion (between the driver and passenger, against the driver's insurance company).

Thus, a guest statute is only relevant in a claim by a passenger against the driver of the car. Here, the claim is against the car company, and as a result a guest statute would be irrelevant. If these facts were different, and Dunn were the defendant, option B would be cor-

rect. However, since B misapplies the guest statute to the facts in the question, it can't be the best response.

(C) is not the best response,

because it ignores the fact that a guest statute would be irrelevant to these facts.

An automobile guest statute makes the driver of a car liable to a gratuitous guest in the car only for something more than simple negligence (typically, gross negligence). The rationale for such statutes is twofold: Protecting hospitality (by making it more difficult for a guest to sue his host) and preventing collusion (between the driver and passenger against the driver's insurance company). Thus, a guest statute is *only* applicable when the passenger's claim is against the *driver*. In this claim, Price would only need to prove simple negligence in order to recover for negligence. Since option C ignores the fact that a guest statute would be irrelevant here, it can't be the best response.

Answer 33

(D) is the best response,

because it correctly identifies the level of proof Price's negligence claim will require.

In order to prevail against Motorco in negligence, Price will have to prove that Motorco failed to exercise such care as a reasonable person in its position would have exercised, this must have been a breach of the duty to prevent the foreseeable risk of injury to anyone in plaintiff's position, and this breach must have caused plaintiff's damages. Here, Motorco is not the manufacturer of the defective part; thus, it will be liable only for its own, affirmative negligence (e.g., it couldn't be liable in negligence for a manufacturing flaw in the bolt, of which it had no reason to know, while Boltco could be held negligent for such a flaw).

Here, Motorco *did* inspect for flaws with the random selection process. Thus, Price would have to prove that Motorco's inspection program was not reasonable, and that a reasonable program would have resulted in the defect being discovered (thus satisfying the causation element of negligence). Since D recognizes this, it's the best response.

(A) is not the best response,

because it understates the proof Price will need for a negligence claim against Motorco.

In order to prevail against Motorco in negligence, Price will have to prove that Motorco failed to exercise such care as a reasonable person in its position would have exercised, this must have been a breach of the duty to prevent the foreseeable risk of injury to anyone in plaintiff's position, and this breach must have caused plaintiff's damages. Here, Motorco is not the manufacturer of the defective part; thus, it will be liable only for its affirmative negligence (e.g., it couldn't be liable for a negligently-created manufacturing flaw in the bolt). Of course, this could take the form of a negligent failure to inspect, or, if inspection is undertaken, it could be done negligently.

Thus, the mere fact that the bolt was defective will be insufficient to pin negligence on Motorco. Instead, it must have done *something* unreasonable in terms of either failing to inspect or incorporating the bolt into the car. If, for instance, the bolt was defective and Motorco's random testing program was reasonable, Motorco couldn't be held liable in negligence. Thus, merely proving that the bolt was defective would be insufficient for a prima facie case of negligence, making A not the best response.

(B) is not the best response,

because it understates what Price will actually need to prove for a prima facie negligence claim.

In order to prevail against Motorco in negligence, Price will have to prove that Motorco failed to exercise such care as a reasonable person in its position would have exercised, this must have been a breach of the duty to prevent the foreseeable risk of injury to anyone in plaintiff's position, and this breach must have caused plaintiff's damages. Here, Motorco is not the manufacturer of the defective part; thus, it will be liable only for its own, affirmative negligence (e.g., it couldn't be liable in negligence for a manufacturing flaw in the bolt, of which it had no reason to know, while the manufacturer, Boltco, *could* be liable for such a flaw).

Thus, merely proving that the bolt was defective and Motorco failed to inspect it would be insufficient. Instead, the failure to inspect the bolt would have to be unreasonable. A "middleman" has a duty to inspect for defects only if it has some reason to believe the product is likely to be defective. Under these facts, the bolts were inspected at random; thus, Price would have to prove that this inspection system *itself* was unreasonable. Assume that B is correct in stating that the bolt was defective and hadn't been inspected by Motorco. Without going the extra step, and proving this failure to inspect was unreasonable, Price won't have a prima facie case for negligence. Since B understates what Price will have to prove, it can't be the best response.

(C) is not the best response,

because it understates what Price will have to prove for a prima facie negligence claim.

In order to prevail against Motorco in negligence, Price will have to prove that Motorco failed to exercise such care as a reasonable person in its position would have exercised, this must have been a breach of the duty to prevent the foreseeable risk of injury to anyone in plaintiff's position, and this breach must have caused plaintiff's damages. Here, Motorco is not the manufacturer of the defective part; thus, it will be liable only for its own, affirmative negligence (e.g., it couldn't be liable in negligence for a manufacturing flaw in the bolt, of which it had no reason to know, while the manufacturer, Boltco, could be held negligent in creating such a

flaw).

Thus, proving the bolt was defective, was inspected by Motorco, and the defect was not discovered, would not be sufficient for negligence; Price would also have to prove that the failure to find the defect was *unreasonable.* Since C doesn't recognize this, it's not the best response.

Answer 34

(A) is the best response,

because it correctly analyzes the impact of Dunn's negligence on Price's claim.

The causation element of negligence has two prongs: cause in fact, or "actual" cause, and proximate, or "legal" cause. In order to be the proximate cause of an injury, the injury must be within the risk created by defendant's negligence, determined primarily on the concept of foreseeability of risks and consequences.

Under these facts, assuming Motorco was negligent, you have a cause, and then you have an intervening cause – Dunn's negligence. In order to determine if Dunn's negligence should break the chain of causation from Motorco to Price, you have to ask if its results were foreseeable. If Motorco installed the seat belt negligently, the very risk this created was that passenger would fly through the windshield in an accident. Thus, the risk of an accident is exactly what seat belts address. This question indicates how important it is to keep in mind the defendant and plaintiff in a negligence action, and focus as closely as possible on defendant's acts, minimizing any intervening acts. Since A correctly states how Dunn's negligence will impact Price's claim, it's the best response.

(B) is not the best response,

because Dunn's negligence would not be considered a proximate cause of Price's injuries, and even if it was, it would *not* break the chain of causation from Motorco to Price, and thus it couldn't be considered *the* proximate cause of Price's injuries.

The causation element of negligence has two prongs: cause in fact, or "actual" cause, and proximate, or "legal" cause. In order to be the proximate cause of an injury, the injury must be within the risk created by defendant's negligence, determined primarily on the concept of foreseeability of risks and consequences.

Under these facts, look at it this way: If Motorco was negligent in incorporating the seat belt, what was the risk this negligence created? It creates the risk that, in an accident, the seat belt would fail and the passenger would be thrown through the window. Lo and behold, that's *exactly* what happened here, vis a vis *Motorco.* Thus, even if Dunn's negligence was a proximate cause of Price's injuries, it wouldn't be *the* proximate cause.

In fact, Dunn's negligence probably isn't a proximate cause at all, if you do the same analysis for it. Considering Price was wearing a seat belt, Price's flying through the windshield would be outside the risk created by Dunn's negligence. You'd anticipate whiplash, but not going through the windshield, since the seat belt should have prevented that. As a result, Dunn's negligence would be unlikely to be a proximate cause of Price's injuries. Since B states otherwise, it's not the best response.

(C) is not the best response,

because Dunn's negligence would not be considered a legal cause of Price's injuries, and even if it was, it would *not* break the chain of causation from Motorco to Price, and thus it couldn't be considered *the* legal cause of Price's injuries.

The causation element of negligence has two prongs: cause in fact, or "actual" cause, and proximate, or "legal" cause. In order to be the legal cause of an injury, the injury must be within the risk created by defendant's negligence, determined primarily on the concept of foreseeability of risks and consequences.

Under these facts, look at it this way: If Motorco was negligent in incorporating the seat belt, what was the risk this negligence created? It creates the risk that, in an accident, the seat belt would fail and the passenger would be thrown through the window. Lo and behold, that's *exactly* what happened here, vis a vis *Motorco.* Thus, even if Dunn's negligence was a legal cause of Price's injuries, it wouldn't be *the* legal cause.

In fact, Dunn's negligence probably isn't a legal cause at all, if you do the same analysis for it. Considering Price was wearing a seat belt, Price's flying through the windshield would be outside the risk created by Dunn's negligence. You'd anticipate whiplash, but not going through the windshield, since the seat belt should have prevented that. As a result, Dunn's negligence would be unlikely to be a legal cause of Price's injuries. Since C states otherwise, it's not the best response.

(D) is not the best response,

because although it correctly characterizes Dunn's negligence, it doesn't address what effect it will have on Price's claim against Motorco.

An intervening cause is a cause coming into active operation in producing the result after defendant's negligence, and it is from a source independent from defendant's negligence. Thus, while D correctly characterizes Dunn's negligence, it doesn't state how this will affect Price's claim. If Dunn's act is merely a foreseeable intervening cause, Motorco will still be liable; if it's a superseding cause, Dunn will be solely liable for Price's injuries. A foreseeable intervening cause is one which defendant should reasonably anticipate. Here, Motorco could and should anticipate car accidents – that's the whole purpose of seat belts. Thus, even though Dunn's negligence is independent and intervening, it's *foreseeable,* and *that's* what makes Motorco liable. (An intervening cause only becomes a super-

seding cause, relieving defendant of liability, if its results were unforeseeable.) Thus, since D does not discuss how Dunn's negligence will affect Price's claim, it's not the best response.

Answer 35

(A) is the best response,

because it suggests a defense which is consistent with these facts, and would result in Motorco prevailing.

In order to prevail on a negligence claim, plaintiff must prove that defendant failed to exercise such care as a reasonable person in his position would have exercised, this must have been a breach of the duty to prevent the foreseeable risk of harm to anyone in plaintiff's position, and this breach must have caused plaintiff's damages.

The issue under these facts is whether Motorco's inspection program was reasonable. If Motorco behaved reasonably, it simply can't be negligent, because unreasonability is the lynchpin of a negligence claim. Of course, this would be useless if it didn't fit these facts. The facts tell you that Motorco tested samples from each shipment, and also that the defect in Price's bolt was metallurgical, suggesting that it was not something Motorco *should* have noticed.

Note that by suggesting Motorco was reasonable, option A doesn't offer a traditional defense to negligence (like assumption of the risk or contributory negligence), but instead negates the breach of duty element of negligence. Since this would defeat Price's negligence claim, it's a good defense, making A the best response.

(B) is not the best response,

because Dunn's negligence probably *wouldn't* be considered a legal cause of Price's injuries, and even if it were, it wouldn't exonerate Motorco.

The causation element of negligence has two prongs: cause in fact, or "actual" cause, and proximate, or "legal" cause. In order to be the proximate cause of an injury, the injury must be within the risk created by defendant's negligence, determined primarily on the concept of foreseeability of risks and consequences.

Dunn's negligence probably isn't a proximate cause at all. Considering Price was wearing a seatbelt, Price's flying through the windshield would be outside the risk created by Dunn's negligence. You might anticipate whiplash or other injuries, but not going through the windshield, since the seatbelt should have prevented that. Thus, Dunn's negligence probably wouldn't be considered a proximate cause of Price's injuries.

Even if it *were* considered a proximate cause, it wouldn't be the *only* one: Motorco's negligence would be a proximate cause as well. That's because Price's flying through the window was within the risk created by Motorco's negligently installing the seatbelt – since that's exactly what a seatbelt is designed to *prevent.*

As a result, even if Dunn's negligence were characterized as a legal cause of Price's injuries, it wouldn't break the chain of causation from Motorco to Price, and thus wouldn't be a good defense. Since B doesn't recognize this, it's not the best response.

(C) is not the best response,
because it's irrelevant.

By focusing on Price's status as passenger, option C suggests that privity is lacking between Motorco and Price, and thus Price should be denied recovery. In fact, this misstates the scope of plaintiffs in a product liability suit predicated on negligence. For such a claim, anyone foreseeably endangered by the product is a potential claimant. Since installing a seat belt for a passenger anticipates that a passenger would, indeed, sit in the seat and use the belt, Price would be within the scope of plaintiffs. In fact, it's only product liability suits based on implied warranty and representation theories that pose any *potential* privity problems, and even then, most courts ignore such constraints because they dislike denying liability on privity grounds in product liability cases.

Since C implies a defense based on lack of privity when this is, in fact, not a problem, it's not the best response.

(D) isn't the best response,
because it misstates the law and thus wouldn't provide a good defense.

As manufacturer of the bolts, if Boltco failed to exercise due care, it would certainly be liable to Price in negligence, since the failure of the bolt was a cause of Price's injuries. However, this doesn't mean that Motorco couldn't *also* be liable, if it was negligent as well. Since Motorco was a "middleman" as to the bolts, it would be negligent for its own mishandling of the product OR if it failed to inspect in light of evidence suggesting there may be a defect. Thus, merely saying that Boltco was negligent wouldn't be a good defense for Motorco. Since D doesn't recognize this, it's not the best response.

Answer 36

(D) is the best response,
because it identifies a significant element of Price's claim.

The requirements of a strict product liability claim are laid out in Restatement of Torts 2d §402A:

1. The product must have been in a defective condition unreasonably dangerous to the user/consumer or his property;
2. When it left the defendant's control (that means, defendant can be liable even if he didn't cause the defect);
3. Product must not be expected to undergo significant changes before it gets to the user/consumer (or not actually undergo such changes);

4. The seller must be in the business of selling the product (thus, he can't be a casual seller, e.g., someone selling jam to his neighbor);
5. Damage must result from the defect (defendant is liable for any physical damage);
6. Duty extends to anyone foreseeably endangered by the product (meaning, there's no privity requirement).

Under these facts, if the bolt was in fact defective such that it would break on impact, this element alone will form the lynchpin of Price's claim. Add to this the fact that no other option mentions anything that is actually part of a strict liability claim, and D must be the best response.

(A) is not the best response,
because res ipsa loquitur refers to a negligence claim, *not* a strict liability claim.

Res ipsa loquitur is a doctrine of circumstantial evidence of negligence. It establishes a prima facie case of negligence in cases where direct evidence of negligence is unclear. It requires proof that the event causing injury would not normally have occurred in the absence of negligence; defendant was in exclusive control of the instrumentality causing injury; and the plaintiff must not have voluntarily contributed to the event that caused his injury.

This is not relevant to Price's claim, because he's suing based on strict liability. All Price needs to prove is that the bolt left Boltco's control in a defective condition unreasonably dangerous to the user/consumer, the product wasn't expected to undergo significant changes before it got to the user/consumer, the seller was in the business of selling the product, and damage resulted from the defect. Since res ipsa loquitur won't be relevant to the claim, A can't be the best response.

(B) is not the best response,
because warranty would not be relevant to a strict liability claim.

The requirements of a strict product liability claim are laid out in Restatement of Torts 2d §402A:

1. The product must have been in a defective condition unreasonably dangerous to the user/consumer or his property;
2. When it left the defendant's control (that means, defendant can be liable even if he didn't cause the defect);
3. Product must not be expected to undergo significant changes before it gets to the user/consumer (or not actually undergo such changes);
4. The seller must be in the business of selling the product (thus, he can't be a casual seller, e.g., someone selling jam to his neighbor);
5. Damage must result from the defect (defendant is liable for any physical damage);
6. Duty extends to anyone foreseeably endangered by the product (meaning, there's no privity

requirement).

Thus, warranty does not bear on the claim at all. While Price may also have a claim based on implied warranty, it's not his claim under these facts, making B not the best response.

(C) is not the best response,

because privity is not relevant to a strict liability claim.

The requirements of a strict product liability claim are laid out in Restatement of Torts 2d §402A:

1. The product must have been in a defective condition unreasonably dangerous to the user/consumer or his property;
2. When it left the defendant's control (that means, defendant can be liable even if he didn't cause the defect);
3. Product must not be expected to undergo significant changes before it gets to the user/consumer (or not actually undergo such changes);
4. The seller must be in the business of selling the product (thus, he can't be a casual seller, e.g., someone selling jam to his neighbor);
5. Damage must result from the defect (defendant is liable for any physical damage);
6. Duty extends to anyone foreseeably endangered by the product (meaning, there's no privity requirement).

As #6 points out, privity of contract is not relevant to a strict liability claim. If you chose this response, you were probably thinking of a product liability claim based on implied warranty or representations, which *in theory* require privity (in most states, for breach of warranty, under UCC §2-318, Alt. A, only buyer, family, and guest in home qualify. However, most courts ignore this privity requirement.) Furthermore, under those theories, the manufacturer and retailer are not liable to the ultimate consumer – only the retailer is. Thus, even if you were thinking of one of these claims, privity could only work *against* Price – he couldn't rely on it. Since C addresses an element which is not part of a strict liability claim, it can't be the best response.

Answer 37

(D) is the best response,

because it represents the facts, of these four, under which a court is most likely to impose an affirmative duty to act.

In general, an individual has no duty to act affirmatively for the benefit of others. There are three, general exceptions to this:

1. Defendant's act created the peril;
2. A "special relationship" mandates affirmative acts (parent-child, common carrier-patron); or
3. Defendant had previously undertaken to act for plaintiff's benefit.

The wrinkle under these facts is that X's own conduct was not negligent, and all the other options specifically

involve someone's *wrongful* conduct. However, it isn't the wrongfulness that's determinative, but rather the fact that X created the peril. Since this triggers one of the exceptions to the general "no duty to aid" rule, D is the best response.

(A) is not the best response,

because one would have no duty to aid under the circumstances named.

In general, an individual has no duty to act affirmatively for the benefit of others. There are three, general exceptions to this:

1. Defendant's act created the peril;
2. A "special relationship" mandates affirmative acts (parent-child, common carrier-patron); or
3. Defendant had previously undertaken to act for plaintiff's benefit.

Thus, it's unlikely a court would impose a duty to aid a stranger imperiled by a stranger's misconduct. Since A states otherwise, it's not the best response.

(B) is not the best response,

because one would have no duty to aid under the circumstances named.

In general, an individual has no duty to act affirmatively for the benefit of others. There are three, general exceptions to this:

1. Defendant's act created the peril;
2. A "special relationship" mandates affirmative acts (parent-child, common carrier-patron); or
3. Defendant had previously undertaken to act for plaintiff's benefit.

Thus, the victim's status as a neighbor would probably not merit a legal duty to aid him, since merely being a neighbor wouldn't qualify as a "special relationship." Since B states otherwise, it wouldn't be the best response.

(C) is not the best response,

because the facts it states would be insufficient to trigger a duty to aid.

In general, an individual has no duty to act affirmatively for the benefit of others. There are three, general exceptions to this:

1. Defendant's act created the peril;
2. A "special relationship" mandates affirmative acts (parent-child, common carrier-patron); or
3. Defendant had previously undertaken to act for plaintiff's benefit.

The victim's status as cousin would not be sufficient for a "special relationship" mandating a legal duty to act. Since C states otherwise, it's not the best response.

Answer 38

(D) is the best response,

because it identifies the argument most likely to stop

the statutory standard of care from defeating Walker's claim against Driver.

Walker's violating the crosswalk statute could defeat her claim if it established contributory negligence per se. In order for the standard in a statute to govern a plaintiff's duty, it must meet these four requirements:

1   The statute must provide for a criminal penalty;
2.   The statute must have been formulated to prevent the kind of harm suffered;
3.   Plaintiff must be a member of the class the legislature intended to protect with the statute; and
4.   The statute must be clear as to the standard of conduct expected, and from whom and when.

This is the same test as is used to establish negligence per se on the part of the defendant.

The element in question under these facts is the second one – whether there is a causal relationship between the violation and the harm. Here, Walker was a few feet further along than she would have been otherwise, but the light was in her favor and she was on the crosswalk when Driver hit her. It's unlikely the statute was designed to protect against the heightened risk the violation incurred. Since D recognizes this, it's the best response.

(A) is not the best response,

because the timing of the violations will not be relevant as to whether Walker's violation of the crosswalk statute should count against her.

The only way Walker's violating the crosswalk statute could defeat her claim would be if it established contributory negligence per se. To be applicable, these four elements would have to be met:

1. The statute must provide for a criminal penalty;
2. The statute must have been formulated to prevent the kind of harm suffered;
3. Plaintiff must be a member of the class the legislature intended to protect with the statute; and
4. The statute must be clear as to the standard of conduct expected, and from whom and when.

This is the same test as is used to establish negligence per se on the part of the defendant.

Here, the most likely reason that Walker's violation should not be used against her is that the facts here don't satisfy the second element: The scope of risk the statute was intended to cover. Here, Walker was further into the street than she would have been had she not violated the statute, but she still would have been in the street, legally (since the light changed in her favor just after she stepped onto the east-west crosswalk).

Thus, it's the risks to which the statute was addressed that will result in its nonapplicability to Walker; the timing of the violations is not relevant.

If you chose this response, you may have been thinking of the doctrine of Last Clear Chance – however, that is only used by plaintiffs to rebut a claim of contributory negligence, and so wouldn't apply here. Since A

focuses on an irrelevancy, it's not the best response.

(B) is not the best response,

because the reasoning it states would not be sufficient to bar application of the statute against Walker. Even though one may assume that others will obey the law, this doesn't give one a license to act unreasonably for one's own safety. Looked at another way, Walker had no more right to rely on Driver than Drier had to rely on her.

Instead, Walker's violating the crosswalk statute could defeat her claim if it established contributory negligence per se. In order for the standard of duty in a statute to govern a plaintiff's duty, it must meet these four requirements:

1.   The statute must provide for a criminal penalty;
2.   The statute must have been formulated to prevent the kind of harm suffered;
3.   Plaintiff must be a member of the class the legislature intended to protect with the statute; and
4.   The statute must be clear as to the standard of conduct expected, and from whom and when.

This is the same test as is used to establish negligence per se on the part of the defendant.

It's the second element – the causal relationship between the violation and the harm to Walker that's in question here. In fact, her violating the statute only meant she was a few feet further into the crosswalk than she would have been had she *not* violated the statute, and this would be insufficient to bar her from recovery due to contributory negligence per se. Since B focuses on an element that would *not* stop the statute from applying to Walker's case, it's not the best response.

(C) is not the best response,

because it provides an insufficient basis on which to prevent application of the crosswalk statute. While being on the crosswalk will help Walker prevail on her claim against Driver, it will not justify by itself the nonapplication of the statute.

Instead, what will stop application of the statute is the lack of a causal connection between Walker's violation of the statute and her injuries.

Walker's violating the crosswalk statute could defeat her claim if it established contributory negligence per se. In order for the standard of duty in a statute to govern a plaintiff's duty, it must meet these four requirements:

1.   The statute must provide for a criminal penalty;
2.   The statute must have been formulated to prevent the kind of harm suffered;
3.   Plaintiff must be a member of the class the legislature intended to protect with the statute; and
4.   The statute must be clear as to the standard of conduct expected, and from whom and when.

This is the same test as is used to establish negligence per se on the part of the defendant. It's the second element – the causal relationship between the violation and the harm to Walker – that's in question here. It's unlikely that the legislature intended that the risks here were to be included under the statute, since Walker's violating the statute only meant she was a few feet further along the crosswalk than she would have been otherwise. However, the mere fact she was in the crosswalk won't make the statute inapplicable. Since C states otherwise, it's not the best response.

Answer 39

(B) is the best response,

because it correctly identifies that Driver's lapsed license will not be determinative of his liability.

Licensing statutes are typically interpreted as being designed to protect the public from incompetent drivers, and create no liability where the driver is competent but simply unlicensed. Instead, the lapsed license will be *evidence* of negligence, to be considered along with other evidence suggesting that Driver did not exercise due care. That the statute won't establish negligence doesn't mean that Driver can't be liable for negligence – it's just that it can't be relied upon for that purpose. Since B correctly identifies the impact of Driver's lapsed license, it's the best response.

(A) is not the best response,

because Driver's lack of a driver's license would not be determinative of his liability. Driver's failure to maintain his driver's license would not be considered the cause of Walker's injuries, so the statute would not be relevant in determining Driver's liability.

A statutory standard of care is applicable to a civil case of negligence, to establish negligence per se, only if these four requirements are met:

1. The statute must provide for a criminal penalty;
2. The statute must have been formulated to prevent the kind of harm suffered;
3. Plaintiff must be a member of the class the legislature intended to protect with the statute; and
4. The statute must be clear as to the standard of conduct expected, and from whom and when.

Here, licensing statutes are typically designed to protect the public from incompetent drivers, and create no liability where the driver is competent but simply unlicensed. While Driver's failure to have a license may be evidence of negligence, it won't make him liable as a trespasser on the highway. Since A states otherwise, it's not the best response.

(C) is not the best response,

because the lapsed license would *not* establish that Driver is unfit.

Licensing statutes are typically designed to protect the public from incompetent drivers, and create no liability where the driver is competent but simply unlicensed. While Driver's failure to have a license may be

evidence of negligence, it won't establish that he's unfit in this instance. Since C states otherwise, it's not the best response.

(D) is not the best response,

because there's no basis for imposing strict liability on Driver.

The most that Driver's lapsed license will do is offer evidence of negligence – it won't even establish negligence per se, because there's no causal connection between Driver's violating the statute and Walker's injuries (it's Driver's negligent driving that caused the injuries, not his driving without a license).

There are three general sources of strict liability: Animals, abnormally dangerous activities, and defective, unreasonably dangerous products (statutes and case law can also establish strict liability). Under these facts there's no indication of a basis for imposing liability without fault. Since D would hold otherwise, it's not the best response.

Answer 40

(D) is the best response,

because it correctly states the basis on which Walker will recover for her broken leg.

When a defendant acts tortiously, he's responsible for all personal injuries flowing from his conduct, even if they're unusually severe. This is known as the "eggshell skull" theory, and is usually summed up by the phrase "the defendant takes his plaintiff as he finds him." This is an easily confusible issue, because foreseeability is a central concept in the proximate cause element of negligence. However, foreseeability only determines if defendant will be liable to plaintiff *at all*. That is, if defendant's act created a risk of harm to anyone in plaintiff's position, he'll be liable for *all* plaintiff's injuries – not just the foreseeable ones. If injury to plaintiff *wasn't* foreseeable, defendant won't be liable to him *at all*, since defendant's act wouldn't be considered the "proximate cause" of plaintiff's harm. As a result, defendant's liability for plaintiff's damages comes down to all or nothing. Since D correctly states that Walker will recover even if her injuries were unforeseeably extensive, and thus impliedly applies the eggshell skull theory to these facts, it's the best response.

(A) is not the best response,

because Walker's rare bone condition would not preclude her from recovery for the broken leg.

The rule that establishes recovery for unforeseeable injuries is the "eggshell skull" theory. Under it, when one commits an intentional (or negligent) tort, he'll be responsible for all personal injuries flowing from his conduct, even if the injury is unusually severe. A common example of this is punching a hemophiliac in the nose and having him bleed to death. The explanation of results like these is that the defendant "takes his plaintiff as he finds him." Thus, as long as the tort itself is established, recovery for unusual personal injuries will be allowed. Under these facts, the liability is a given, so Walker will recover for her broken leg. Since A would deny her recovery due to the rarity of her disease, it's not the best response.

(B) is not the best response,

because the injuries an ordinary person would have suffered are irrelevant to Walker's recovery. The reasonable person standard is used to establish defendant's negligence and plaintiff's contributory negligence, but it doesn't apply to plaintiff's damages. The rule that establishes recovery for unforeseeable injuries is the "eggshell skull" theory. Under it, when one commits an intentional (or negligent) tort, he'll be responsible for all personal injuries flowing from his conduct, even if the injury is unusually severe. A common example of this is punching a hemophiliac in the nose and having him bleed to death. The explanation of results like these is that the defendant "takes his plaintiff as he finds him."

Thus, as long as the tort itself is established, recovery for unusual personal injuries will be allowed, regardless of what injuries a reasonably healthy person would have suffered. Since B would mistakenly limit Walker's recovery to what an ordinary person would have received, it's not the best response.

(C) is not the best response,

because although it arrives at the correct result, its reasoning is internally inconsistent. It isn't possible to foresee unforeseeable consequences, because if such consequences were foreseeable, they couldn't be considered unforeseeable.

Instead, the reason Walker will recover for the broken leg is application of the eggshell skull theory. That is, when defendant acts tortiously, he's responsible for all personal injuries flowing from his conduct, even if they're unusually severe. This is the "eggshell skull" theory, and is usually summed up in the phrase "the defendant takes his plaintiff as he finds him." Since C applies a logically impossible foreseeable/unforeseeable analysis to this, it can't be the best response.

Answer 41

(D) is the best response,

because it states the basis on which the statute should be kept from the jury.

If a criminal statute establishes a standard of care applicable to a civil case, it's said to establish negligence per se – that is, the violator cannot thereafter establish that his conduct was reasonable. (By the same token, as applied to plaintiff, a statute can establish contributory negligence per se.) Determining whether the statute applies is a matter of law, and thus is decided by the judge. Central to this analysis is determining whether the injury was the result of a risk the statute was designed to protect against. If it *isn't*,

then the jury will not get to consider whether the standard of care offered in the statute was met by the facts in the case. Here, Walker was a few feet further along because she violated the statute than she would have been otherwise. However, she *was* on the crosswalk and she *was* crossing with the light; thus, the judge would interpret the statute as not involving the risk of injury under these facts. Since D correctly identifies this, and the result, it's the best response.

(A) is not the best response,

because the issue isn't factual cause, but whether Walker's violation of the statute should make her contributorily negligent as a matter of law – and matters of law are decided by the judge.

If a criminal statute establishes a standard of care applicable to a civil case, it's said to establish negligence per se – that is, the violator cannot thereafter establish that his conduct was reasonable, although he may have other arguments (e.g., his violation was justified due to an emergency). The judge decides if the criminal statute establishes a standard of care, by deciding whether the statute was designed to protect the class of persons to which plaintiff belongs, against the risk of the type of harm which in fact resulted from its violation. Thus, the judge's determination will turn on an analysis of the risks the statute was aimed at, not any dispute as to cause in fact. Since A states otherwise, it's not the best response.

(B) is not the best response,

because it misstates the law, and ignores the central issue here – whether Walker's violating the statute should be considered contributory negligence as a matter of law.

If a criminal statute establishes a standard of care applicable to a civil case, it's said to establish negligence per se – that is, the violator cannot thereafter establish his conduct was reasonable (by the same token, as applied to plaintiff, a statute can establish contributory negligence per se). However, contrary to what B states, this would *not* make one liable for all harm resulting from the violation – it would *still* have to be established that there was a causal link between the violation and the harm.

In any case, the judge must, as a preliminary matter, decide if the plaintiff's injury was the result of a risk the statute was designed to protect against. If it *wasn't*, the statute will not establish a standard of care, and the jury will not have the opportunity to consider if the standard was met on the facts in the case. Since B misstates the law and ignores the central issue here, it's not the best response.

(C) is not the best response,

because it doesn't address whether Walker's violation of the statute should be considered by the jury. If Walker's conduct is considered contributorily negligent per se, she will not, as a matter of law, be able to argue that her conduct was reasonable. If the injury to plaintiff was not the result of a risk the statute was designed to guard against, the statute *cannot* apply, and should not be considered by the jury. Whether Driver's conduct was an independent intervening cause is a matter for the jury which does *not* affect the availability to the jury of the crosswalk statute. Since C states otherwise, it's not the best response.

Answer 42

(C) is the best response,

because the explosion was caused by a design defect in a part of the plant unrelated to the filter system designed by Engineer.

The only plausible basis for the suit here would have to be negligence. (Although the making of explosive chemicals may have been an "abnormally dangerous activity" — triggering strict liability — Engineer was not himself carrying out that manufacturing activity, and only the person carrying out the ultrahazardous activity has strict liability for it).

To be liable in negligence, Engineer would have to have had a duty to avoid a particular type of harm, and then to have failed to use reasonable care in carrying out that duty. If Engineer had worked on the design that contained the defect, she certainly could have been held liable in negligence. But since Engineer dealt only with the filtering system, she never undertook any duty to ascertain the safety of the other aspects of the plant design. Consequently, nothing she did (or didn't do) could possibly have constituted a failure to use reasonable care in the discharging of a duty.

(A) is not the best response,

because Engineer does not become liable for a design defect merely by including that defect in her blueprints.

The facts state that Engineer was retained to design a filter system. Her duty was to protect people from unreasonable risk of injury arising from her design. The only way to show the design for the filter system was to include the rest of the plant in which the filter system was to be installed. Showing the rest of the plant, including the design defect, does not make her liable for all injuries arising for all design defects in the plant, absent an affirmative requirement to review or inspect those other parts of the blueprints. There is no principle that would impose on an engineer such an affirmative duty to review the safety of parts of blueprints for which the engineer has had no responsibility.

(B) is not the best response,

because joint and several liability does not apply on these facts.

Where two or more tortious acts combine to proximately cause an indivisible injury to a plaintiff, each tortfeasor is jointly and severally liable for that injury.

Under these facts Engineer committed no tort. Merely including a part of the defectively designed plant in her drawings absent a requirement that she knew or should have known of the defect does not make her liable in tort for the defect. Without Engineer's having committed a tort leading to Plaintiff's injury, there can be no joint and several liability.

(D) is not the best response,

because the fact that Plaintiff brought suit against Engineer personally means that it doesn't matter whether Engineer was an independent contractor or not.

Had Plaintiff brought suit against *Company*, then perhaps Engineer's status with Company — that is, whether she was an employee or an independent contractor — might be relevant to Company's liability. However, the facts state that Plaintiff brought the action against Engineer individually. Engineer's liability will depend solely on whether Engineer behaved negligently, and that would be so (or not so) regardless of whether Company employed her or merely engaged her.

Answer 43

(D) is the best response,

because it accurately reflects the minimum proof Child's negligence claim will require.

As a retailer, Seller will only be liable in negligence due to its own affirmative negligence. Retailers only have a duty to inspect if they have reason to believe the product is likely to be defective, and even if they do have a duty to inspect, they'll only be liable if an inspection undertaken with reasonable care would have uncovered the defect. D mirrors these requirements by comparing Seller's conduct to what a retailer in the exercise of due care would have done. Since D is the only option to compare Seller's conduct to that of a reasonable retailer, it's the best response.

(A) is not the best response,

because it understates what Child will have to prove.

As a retailer, Seller will only be liable for negligence due to its own affirmative negligence. Retailers only have a duty to inspect if they have reason to believe the product is likely to be defective, and even if they *do* have a duty to inspect, they'll only be liable if an inspection undertaken with reasonable care would have uncovered the defect. Thus, merely proving that the ventilating system was defective would be insufficient.

If you chose this response, you were probably thinking of strict product liability, under which proof of the defect would be the lynchpin of Child's claim (since the system was defective when it left Seller, who was in the business of selling such products, the defect was unreasonably dangerous, and there was no significant change in the product once it left Seller). However, negligence requires some proof of lack of due care on defendant's part. Since merely proving a defect ignores this, A isn't the best response.

(B) isn't the best response,

because it understates the proof Child's negligence claim will require.

As a retailer, Seller will only be liable for negligence due to its own affirmative negligence. Retailers only have a duty to inspect if they have reason to believe the product is likely to be defective, and even if they *do* have a duty to inspect, they'll only be liable if an inspection undertaken with reasonable care would have uncovered the defect. Thus, merely proving a defect and a lack of inspection would be insufficient to pin negligence liability on Seller – Child would also have to prove that a reasonable inspection would have uncovered the defect. Since B doesn't recognize this, it's not the best response.

(C) is not the best response,

because it understates the proof Child's negligence claim will require.

As a retailer, Seller will only be liable in negligence due to its own affirmative negligence. Retailers only have a duty to inspect if they have reason to believe the product is likely to be defective, and even if they *do* have a duty to inspect, they'll only be liable if an inspection undertaken with reasonable care would have uncovered the defect. Thus, merely failing to discover the defect would not make Seller negligent unless a reasonable inspection would have uncovered the defect. Since C doesn't recognize this, it's not the best response.

Answer 44

(A) is the best response,

because it correctly identifies that Mobilco is the only one of the three potential defendants who can be liable in strict liability.

The requirements of a strict product liability claim are laid out in Restatement of Torts 2d §402A:

1. The product must have been in a defective condition unreasonably dangerous to the user/consumer or his property;
2. When it left the defendant's control (that means, defendant can be liable even if he didn't cause the defect);
3. Product must not be expected to undergo significant changes before it gets to the user/consumer (or not actually undergo such changes);
4. The seller must be in the business of selling the product (thus, he can't be a casual seller, e.g., someone selling jam to his neighbor);
5. Damage must result from the defect (defendant is liable for any physical damage);
6. Duty extends to anyone foreseeably endangered by the product (meaning, there's no privity requirement).

Here, Mobilco will be strictly liable because it satisfies every element, the most significant being that the venti-

lating system was dangerously defective when it left Mobilco's control. It's this element that exonerates Heatco and Coolco, since the heating and cooling systems weren't defective – only Mobilco's ventilating system utilizing the two, was. Since A correctly identifies this, it's the best response.

(B) is not the best response,

because Heatco will not be strictly liable for Child's injuries; only Mobilco will.

The requirements of a strict product liability claim are laid out in Restatement of Torts 2d §402A:

1. The product must have been in a defective condition unreasonably dangerous to the user/consumer or his property;
2. When it left the defendant's control (that means, defendant can be liable even if he didn't cause the defect);
3. Product must not be expected to undergo significant changes before it gets to the user/consumer   (or not actually undergo such changes);
4. The seller must be in the business of selling the product (thus, he can't be a casual seller, e.g., someone selling jam to his neighbor);
5. Damage must result from the defect (defendant is liable for any physical damage);
6. Duty extends to anyone foreseeably endangered by the product (meaning, there's no privity requirement).

The missing element under these facts is the first one. The furnace wasn't defective; it was Mobilco's improperly designed ventilating system which was dangerously defective. Thus, the fact that excessive heat came from the furnace will not furnish strict liability against Heatco. Since B states otherwise, it's not the best response.

(C) is not the best response,

because although it correctly identifies that Mobilco will be liable, it mistakenly pins liability on Heatco as well.

The requirements of a strict product liability claim are laid out in Restatement of Torts 2d §402A:

1. The product must have been in a defective condition unreasonably dangerous to the user/consumer or his property;
2. When it left the defendant's control (that means, defendant can be liable even if he didn't cause the defect);
3. Product must not be expected to undergo significant changes before it gets to the user/consumer (or not actually undergo such changes);
4. The seller must be in the business of selling the product (thus, he can't be a casual seller, e.g., someone selling jam to his neighbor);
5. Damage must result from the defect (defendant is liable for any physical damage);
6. Duty extends to anyone foreseeably endangered

by the product (meaning, there's no privity requirement).

Here, Mobilco will be strictly liable because it satisfies every element, the lynchpin being that the ventilating system was dangerously defective when it left Mobilco's control. As to Heatco, it's this element that's missing. When the furnace left Heatco, it was in proper working condition; it was only Mobilco's defective ventilating system that caused Child's injuries. Since C incorrectly states that Heatco will be strictly liable, it's not the best response.

(D) is not the best response,

because although Mobilco will be strictly liable, Heatco and Coolco will *not* be.

The requirements of a strict product liability claim are laid out in Restatement of Torts 2d §402A:

1. The product must have been in a defective condition unreasonably dangerous to the user/consumer or his property;
2. When it left the defendant's control (that means, defendant can be liable even if he didn't cause the defect);
3. Product must not be expected to undergo significant changes before it gets to the user/consumer (or not actually undergo such changes);
4. The seller must be in the business of selling the product (thus, he can't be a casual seller, e.g., someone selling jam to his neighbor);
5. Damage must result from the defect (defendant is liable for any physical damage);
6. Duty extends to anyone foreseeably endangered by the product (meaning, there's no privity requirement).

Here, Mobilco will be strictly liable because it satisfies every element, the lynchpin being that the ventilating system was dangerously defective when it left Mobilco's control. As to Heatco and Coolco, it's this element that's missing. When the furnace left Heatco, it was in working order. The same goes for the cooling system from Coolco. It was only when Mobilco incorporated the two into the ventilating system that they became dangerous and defective. Note that if the reverse were true, and Heatco and Coolco had created the defects and Mobilco *hadn't,* then Mobilco *could* be liable for the defects, even if it didn't create them – because the system would have been defective when it left Mobilco's control, and that's the relevant time frame. Thus, you can be held strictly liable for dangerous defects created by those *behind* you in the distribution chain, but not for ones created by those *in front* of you. Since D states otherwise, it's not the best response.

Answer 45

(C) is the best response,

because it adds an element which would create liability in Carver.

The central problem with these facts is that they don't indicate an active misrepresentation by Carver, and there's no duty on Carver to disclose the true value of the stock. Such a duty only arises where, for instance, there is a specific query about the matter, a special (e.g., fiduciary) relationship exists, or there are other circumstances meriting disclosure (e.g., a half-truth, subsequent information which makes prior statement misleading, or knowledge of undisclosed facts basic to a transaction). None of these apply to these facts; thus, for there to be liability, an option would have to add facts *creating* liability. That's what C does, by adding a misrepresentation – that the stock is not worth more than $6. This qualifies because it satisfies all the requirements of a misrepresentation:

1. Defendant's misrepresentation of a material past or present fact;
2. Defendant's knowledge of falsity or reckless disregard for falsity;
3. Defendant's intent to induce plaintiff's reliance;
4. Plaintiff's actual, justifiable reliance;
5. Damages.

Here, Carver, as a chemical engineer, would know the true value, where Page, who presumably doesn't share Carver's expertise, would be justified in relying on Carver's statement. Her reliance would be justifiable because Chemco's own statements show the stock's worth $5. Furthermore, Carver would clearly intend to induce Page's reliance so she could get the stock at a bargain price.

Option C is thus clever in adding facts which create liability where none existed. Since C accurately assesses Carver's liability in the light of additional facts, it's the best response.

(A) is not the best response,

because it understates what Page must prove in order to recover for misrepresentation due to nondisclosure.

Option A suggests that Carver didn't tell Page that the stock was worth more than $6 a share, but should be liable for *not* telling because Carver knew the stock was worth more. In fact, this misstates the requirements for misrepresentation based on nondisclosure.

The general rule is that misrepresentation requires some form of active concealment beyond mere silence. Exceptions to this rule include:

1. An affirmative duty to disclose (due to a half-truth, subsequent information making the prior statement misleading, or knowledge of undisclosed facts basic to a transaction);
2. A specific query about the matter;
3. Existence of a special (e.g., fiduciary) relationship between the parties.

Under these facts, there's nothing to impose a duty of disclosure on Carver. In point of fact, Carver got a bargain, with nothing illegal about it. Since A suggests

Carver had a duty to disclose the value of the stock when in fact she didn't, A can't be the best response.

(B) is not the best response,

because Carver's failure to disclose the true value of the inventory would not make her liable for misrepresentation.

The general rule is that misrepresentation requires some form of active concealment beyond mere silence. Exceptions to this rule include:

1. An affirmative duty to disclose (due to a half-truth, subsequent information making the prior statement misleading, or knowledge of undisclosed facts basic to a transaction);
2. A specific query about the matter;
3. Existence of a special (e.g., fiduciary) relationship between the parties.

Under these facts, there's nothing to trigger a duty of disclosure, so Carver cannot be liable for misrepresentation even if she didn't tell Page the true value of the inventory. Since B states otherwise, it's not the best response.

(D) is not the best response,

because the availability of the financial statement would not be relevant to Page's claim. Furthermore, as a public company, Chemco's statements *would* be available to Page, as they would be to anyone.

In any case, the statement says that the stock is worth $5, so it's not the value as stated in the statement which would furnish the basis of a misrepresentation claim, but Carver's knowledge that the statement did not reflect the true value of the stock.

Instead, Carver would only be liable if she misrepresented the value of the stock (since there's no duty to disclose under these facts). Since D does not address an element which will determine Carver's liability, it's not the best response.

Answer 46

(A) is the best response,

because it identifies the central issue in the case and resolves it satisfactorily.

First, although the question doesn't mention it, option A suggests that the claim is for negligence. It couldn't be an intentional tort since there's clearly no intent; however, what is trickier is to eliminate the possibility of strict liability, since generating electricity would be considered ultrahazardous. However, under these facts, the proximate cause element of strict liability is missing, since the result – injury due to people shooting out insulators – would be sufficiently outside the risk to deny strict liability.

Having concluded that the claim is one for negligence, you need to see what Paul would have to prove in order to succeed. He'd have to show that Light Company failed to exercise such care as a reasonable person in his position would have exercised, and this must have been a breach of the duty to prevent the foreseeable risk of injury to anyone in Paul's position, and this breach must have caused Paul's damages. The key element here is causation. That is, if Paul is to prevail, what *specifically* did Light Company fail to do? It failed to prevent the lines from falling when the insulators were destroyed. If it would have been reasonable to prevent this, Paul will prevail on a negligence claim.

Note that option A uses the modifier "if" – that means that the reasoning must be plausible on the facts, it must resolve a significant issue, and its result must be consistent with its reasoning. Option A satisfies these requirements, and so is the best response.

(B) is not the best response,

because although its reasoning is theoretically true, it is not applicable to these facts.

A cause of action based on strict liability requires proof of an absolute duty of care, breach of that duty which proximately caused plaintiff's injuries, and damages. There are three general sources of strict liability: Animals, ultrahazardous activities, and defective, unreasonably dangerous products (strict liability can also arise from statutes or case law). Certainly electricity generation would be considered an ultrahazardous activity, typically meriting application of strict liability; however, what's missing under these facts is the *proximate cause* element. The result must be within the extraordinary risk to which strict liability is addressed. Here, the result – injury due to people shooting one insulators – would be sufficiently outside the risk to deny strict liability.

This is a pretty sneaky question, because seeing electricity would automatically make you think strict liability. Of course, this doesn't mean Paul couldn't recover on some other, fault-based claim, it's just that Light Company won't be liable without fault under these facts. Since option B doesn't recognize this, it's not the best response.

(C) isn't the best response,

because it overstates the degree of care Light Company would need to exercise in order to avoid liability for negligence.

For a negligence claim to succeed, defendant must have failed to exercise such care as a reasonable person in his position would have exercised, this must have been a breach of the duty to prevent the foreseeable risk of injury to anyone in plaintiff's position, and this breach must have caused plaintiff's damages.

Under these facts, and this is, admittedly, splitting hairs, it's not Light Company's failure to stop the destruction of the insulators that caused Paul's injuries, but its failure to prevent the lines from falling *after* the insulators were destroyed, and if this latter failure was negligent, it's the source of Light Company's liability. Thus, the missing element here is causation. Since C doesn't focus accurately enough on the source of Light Company's potential liability, and another option is more accurate, C is not the best response.

(D) is not the best response,

because the fact that the insulator destruction was intentional will not, in and of itself, insulate Light Company from liability.

What D implies is that the intentional destruction of the insulators should act as a supervening cause between Light Company's negligence (assuming it exists, in the form of failing to protect the insulators) and Paul's injuries. What D ignores is that the hallmark of a supervening cause is unforeseeability. Intentional acts are generally supervening but only because they are, in most cases, unforeseeable. Here, Light Company *knew* the insulators were being destroyed. That makes the destruction only intervening, not supervening, and would bring Paul's injuries back into the scope of foreseeability. Note that this doesn't mean the people who destroyed the insulators won't be liable – of course they would be. However, Light Company will be liable as well. Since D ignores that the intentional misconduct here was foreseeable, it's not the best response.

Answer 47

(C) is the best response,

because it focuses on the missing element of Joplin's claim, and thus, as C states, would result in Smythe's prevailing.

Third parties can recover for emotional distress, where someone else is intentionally physically harmed, if:

1. They are present for the physical harm;
2. They are closely related to the injured person; and
3. The actor knows of the third party's presence, and must be able to reasonably anticipate the third party's distress that will result from the actor's conduct.

The element that's missing here is Smythe's knowledge of Joplin's presence. Had Smythe known about it, it's quite possible Joplin would prevail – even though Smythe's conduct is not extreme and outrageous vis a vis Joplin! Since C correctly identifies a central element missing on these facts, and correctly determines the outcome, C is the best response.

(A) is not the best response,

because it understates what Joplin will have to prove in order to recover, and ignores a missing element in the claim.

Third parties can recover for emotional distress, where someone else is intentionally physically harmed, if:

1. They are present for the physical harm;

2. They are closely related to the injured person; and
3. The actor knows of the third party's presence, and must be able to reasonably anticipate the third party's distress that will result from the actor's conduct.

Thus, it wouldn't be enough that Smythe's acts caused Joplin severe emotional distress; what's missing under these facts is that Smythe didn't know about Joplin's presence. Since A doesn't recognize this, it's not the best response.

(B) is not the best response,

because it states an element that Joplin need *not* prove in order to recover, and ignores a missing element to the claim Joplin will *actually* have to prove.

Third parties can recover for emotional distress, where someone else is intentionally physically harmed, if:

1. They are present for the physical harm;
2. They are closely related to the injured person; and
3. The actor knows of the third party's presence, and must be able to reasonably anticipate the third party's distress that will result from the actor's conduct.

Thus, it's not necessary that the actor's conduct be extreme and outrageous with respect to the third party, even though, under these facts, Nelson would have to prove this as part of *her* emotional distress claim against Smythe. Instead, what option B ignores is that Smythe can't be liable because he didn't realize Joplin was present. As a result, B can't be the best response.

(D) is not the best response,

because it focuses on an irrelevant point, and ignores a missing element of Joplin's claim.

Third parties can recover for emotional distress, where someone else is intentionally physically harmed, if:

1. They are present for the physical harm;
2. They are closely related to the injured person; and
3. The actor knows of the third party's presence, and must be able to reasonably anticipate the third party's distress that will result from the actor's conduct.

Thus, it's not necessary that Joplin be within the zone of physical danger. (If you chose this response, it's probably because you recognize the "zone of danger" language from an outdated emotional distress claim.) In fact, it's not the third party's fear for his own safety that determines liability, but his reaction to the harm inflicted on the victim. Thus, while his *presence* will be necessary, he needn't be in the "zone of physical danger" to recover.

Instead, what's missing under these facts is Smythe's knowledge of Joplin's presence. Since D overlooks this, it can't be the best response.

Answer 48

(C) is the best response,

because it most completely states the duty owed to Mom as an invitee.

An invitee is a person who enters onto the premises in response to an express or implied invitation of the landowner. The landowner owes the invitee a general duty to use reasonable and ordinary care in keeping the property safe for the benefit of the invitee. That duty includes the duty to inspect and correct hidden dangers and defects.

Under these facts, Mom accompanied Child, a minor patient. That makes Mom an invitee, since she entered the premises under the hospital's implied invitation. At issue then is whether Hospital used reasonable and ordinary care to keep the property safe.

The mere fact that Mom injured herself on a protruding fixture does not establish that Hospital failed to use due care to protect one in Mom's position. (For instance, the fixture may have been necessary to the functioning of the emergency room, and there may have been nothing that could reasonably have been done to make it safer for one who happened to faint near it). On the other hand, it's certainly possible that inspection of the fixture would have shown that its shape and or size posed an unreasonable risk to passersby, one which could have been easily corrected by, say, use of padding.

This choice is the only one, therefore, that turns on the relevant issue: whether Hospital's personnel took, or failed to take, reasonable steps to safeguard invitees like Mom from dangers posed by the fixture.

(A) is not the best response,

because as an invitee Hospital only owed Mom a general duty of reasonable and ordinary care.

The only way Hospital would be liable for damages suffered by Mom was if it did not exercise ordinary care. To the extent that this choice suggests that Mom automatically wins because she was an invitee, it's simply wrong as a matter of law.

(B) is not the best response,

because whether the fixture on which Mom injured herself in her fall was obvious, commonly used, and an essential part of Hospital's equipment does not go to the level of care Hospital owed Mom, or to whether Hospital failed to exercise that level of care.

For example, suppose that the fixture was *non-obvious* and rarely-used. As long as the device did not pose an unreasonable danger to those around it, Hospital would still not be liable, because Hospital would not have failed to use reasonable care in connection with the device. Conversely, even if the fixture *was* obvious, commonly-used, and essential, Hospital may have negligently failed to protect passersby from it

(e.g., by putting padding around it, if this could be done without interfering with the device's function).

(D) is not the best response,

because Hospital owed Mom the duty of care owed to an invitee, which includes affirmative aspects.

An invitee is a person who enters onto the premises in response to an express or implied invitation of the landowner. The landowner owes the invitee a general duty to use reasonable and ordinary care in keeping the property safe for the benefit of the invitee. For instance, the owner owes invitees the duty to *inspect* the property so as to identify and correct hidden dangers.

Since Mom was an invitee (see the discussion of Choice (C) above), Hospital owed her the whole package of duties that landowners owe to invitees. That included the affirmative duty to inspect and safeguard the property — for instance, if inspection would have showed that the fixture's shape or location posed an unreasonable risk of injury to passersby, Hospital owed Mom the affirmative duty of finding and correcting the condition (e.g., by installing protective padding).

Answer 49

(A) is the best response,

because it implies the only basis on which Paint Company can be liable is strict liability. How do you know this? Because under strict liability, unlike negligence, a defendant can be liable for defects created by those before it in the distribution chain, since all that's relevant is that the product had an unreasonably dangerous defect when it left defendant's control. Under *negligence,* on the other hand, a defendant can only be liable for its *own* negligence (or a negligent failure to inspect where a reasonable person *would* have inspected). Under these facts, there's no indication that Paint Company acted unreasonably, and without that, it cannot be liable for negligence. That leaves strict liability. Option A tells you that Innes can recover against Paint Company if she can recover against Steel. Under strict liability, this would be correct, because if the product was unreasonably dangerously defective when it left the manufacturer *Steel's* control, it *would have* to remain defective when it left Paint Company's control, because there's no evidence of tampering in between.

Note that option A uses the modifier "if" instead of "because." That means that the reasoning need only be plausible under these facts, not that the facts provide a sure basis for the reasoning. This is crucial under these facts because while it's possible Innes would have a strict liability claim, it's by no means a sure thing, primarily because it wouldn't be clear that the product was unreasonably, dangerously defective, and, beyond that, Paint Co. may be able to defend on the grounds of the Glass Company employees' abnormal misuse and failure to follow instructions. However, all that's required under "if" reasoning is that the reasoning plausibly applies to the facts, it resolves a significant issue, and the result is consistent with the reasoning. Since A satisfies all of these, it's the best response.

(B) is not the best response,

because it's irrelevant to Innes's claim here.

Innes's status as an entrant onto the land – either trespasser, licensee, or invitee – would only be determinative of the level of duty the *landowner* owes her as to artificial conditions on the land. Even as to an invitee – one who enters the land at the owner's express or implied invitation – the landowner only owes the invitee the duty of making the property reasonably safe for the invitee. While this may include inspecting for dangers and making them safe, it would not be reasonable for the landowner to be expected to remedy the situation here – where workmen for a tenant create the hazard – and, in any case, the claim here isn't against the *landowner,* it's against *Paint Company,* so Innes' status is irrelevant. Since B doesn't recognize this, it's not the best response.

(C) is not the best response,

because it understates Innes's possibility for recovery. She may be able to recover on strict liability grounds, not just negligence, and, beyond that, it's unlikely Paint Company was negligent. Innes *could* recover for negligence if Paint Company behaved unreasonably and she was injured as a result. A retailer can be negligent by its mishandling a product, or negligently failing to inspect in light of evidence that would lead a reasonable person to inspect the product. Under these facts, it's unlikely Paint Company behaved negligently.

On the other hand, she may be able to recover from Paint Company on strict product liability grounds. The requirements of a strict product liability claim are laid out in Restatement of Torts 2d §402A:

1. The product must have been in a defective condition unreasonably dangerous to the user/consumer or his property;
2. When it left the defendant's control (that means, defendant can be liable even if he didn't cause the defect);
3. Product must not be expected to undergo significant changes before it gets to the user/consumer (or not actually undergo such changes);
4. The seller must be in the business of selling the product (thus, he can't be a casual seller, e.g., someone selling jam to his neighbor);
5. Damage must result from the defect (defendant is liable for any physical damage);
6. Duty extends to anyone foreseeably endangered by the product (meaning, there's no privity requirement).

While it's not clear that the product here would be considered dangerously defective, if it *was,* Paint Company could be strictly liable. Since C improperly

restricts Innes to recovery for negligence, it's unlikely Paint Co. was negligent, and Innes has a potential claim for strict liability, C is not the best response.

(D) is not the best response,

because the fact that the glue came in a sealed container would not be determinative of Paint Company's liability.

What the sealed container *does* suggest is that Paint Company could not be liable for a negligent failure to inspect, since a sealed can would suggest there's nothing to "trigger" a retailer's duty to inspect. However, this really isn't an issue here, since there's nothing to suggest that an inspection would have turned up anything that the sealed can itself didn't disclose. In fact, under these facts, Paint Company would be unlikely to be liable for negligence, since it didn't do anything that seems at all unreasonable.

Thus, if Innes is to recover at all, it will be in strict liability, since under that theory Paint Company will be liable for any unreasonably dangerous defects existing when the can left Paint Company's control –even if it didn't create the defect itself. Thus, it doesn't matter that the can was sealed, or if it arrived in an armoured truck, for that matter, for purposes of strict liability. Since D attaches significance to the fact the can was sealed where in fact it's not relevant, D can't be the best response.

Answer 50

(D) is the best response,

because it correctly identifies the central reason Glass won't be liable: The employees weren't negligent.

Since the employees clearly didn't intend to injure Innes, there's only two possible ways they could be liable: Strict liability or negligence.

There are three common sources of strict liability: Animals, dangerously defective products, and ultrahazardous activities (it can also be mandated by case law or statute). Since only a seller in the business can be liable for dangerously defective products, the only possible source of strict liability would be the ultrahazardous activity option. However, it's unlikely the use of the glue here would be considered ultrahazardous, by considering the four elements that make an activity ultrahazardous: The activity involves a high risk of serious harm, there's no way to perform the activity completely safely no matter how much care is taken, the activity is not commonly engaged in in the particular community, and the danger of the activity outweighs its utility to the community. The element that's missing here is that it *is* possible to use the product safely, suggesting that the use itself is not ultrahazardous.

That leaves negligence. The lynchpin of a negligence claim is that the defendant failed to exercise the due care a reasonable person in the circumstances would have exercised. Here, the facts tell you that there was no way for the employees to know that they shared a common air duct with Innes. Thus, there was nothing unreasonable about turning on the air conditioner, since the risk of danger to Innes was not foreseeable. Since D correctly addresses the central issue under these facts and resolves it, it's the best response.

(A) is not the best response,

because it misstates the law: A user of a product is *not* held to the same standard as the manufacturer.

For instance, a manufacturer can be held liable in strict liability, whereas the user, who is not a seller in the business of selling the product, could not be held liable for strict liability. Also, negligence is determined by reasonable care in the circumstances, which will generally be considerably different for a manufacturer than for a user. Instead, Innes will only be able to recover against Glass if she proves it's employees were at least negligent in failing to realize that the fumes would get to her and injure her, since there's no basis here for strict liability. Since A misstates the law, it can't be the best response.

(B) is not the best response,

because it suggests that Glass should be held strictly liable, and there's no basis for doing so under these facts.

By stating the fact the employees caused the fumes to enter her area without mentioning any level of fault, B is applying strict liability. There are three common sources of strict liability: Animals, dangerously defective products, and ultrahazardous activities (it can also be mandated by case law or statute). Since only a seller in the business can be liable for dangerously defective products, the only possible source of strict liability would be the ultrahazardous activity option. However, it's unlikely the use of the glue here would be considered ultrahazardous, by considering the four elements that make an activity ultrahazardous: The activity involves a high risk of serious harm, there's no way to perform the activity completely safely no matter how much care is taken, the activity is not commonly engaged in in the particular community, and the danger of the activity outweighs its utility to the community. The element that's missing here is that it *is* possible to use the product safely, suggesting that the use itself is not ultrahazardous.

As a result, some degree of fault — at least negligence – would have to be proven in order for Innes to prevail. Since option B doesn't recognize this, it's not the best response.

(C) is not the best response,

because the reasoning it states would not be determinative of Glass's liability.

In order for Glass to be liable in negligence, Innes would have to prove that the Glass employees did not exercise reasonable care and she was foreseeably injured as a result. While using the glue for its intended purpose – sticking things together – may be evidence

of due care (because they weren't *misusing* the product), it wouldn't be the last word on the subject. Say the facts were different, and the employees had reason to know the air conditioner ducts were connected and that the fumes could get to Innes. In that case, Glass would be liable, since injury to someone in Innes' position would be foreseeable. Since C fails to recognize that using the glue for its intended purposes is not the deciding factor in Innes's negligence claim, it's not the best response.

Answer 51

(D) is the best response,

because it offers a defense plausible under these facts, and states a result consistent with the reasoning.

A common law claim for defamation has four requirements:

1. Defendant's defamatory statement
2. Of and concerning plaintiff
3. Negligently or intentionally communicated to at least one third person; and
4. Plaintiff's reputation damaged thereby.

In addition, some degree of fault will have to be proven, and this, under these facts, turns on whether Hospital is entitled to a qualified privilege. Without it, as a non-media defamer, Hospital would still have to be at least negligent. With a qualified privilege, Siddon would have to prove malice to recover. No matter how you decide this issue – whether malice or only negligence is required – option D would be correct, because under its reasoning Hospital wouldn't even be negligent, and so, without fault at all, it *couldn't* be liable for defamation.

A qualified privilege applies when the statement bears some relationship to a public or private interest, of either the publisher, the reader/listener, or both, or that of the general public. If the statement is in furtherance of the interest, it's protected, and it can only be destroyed by malice.

A common example of a statement covered by qualified privilege is an old employer telling a new employer of an employee's thieving tendencies. Under the facts in this question, the statement by Hospital would clearly be covered by the privilege, so Hospital could only be liable if it knew Siddon hadn't taken the narcotics, or recklessly failed to determine whether or not she had. Thus, if Hospital reasonably believed Siddon took the narcotics, it wouldn't even be negligent, let alone reckless, so it *couldn't* be liable.

Note that option D uses the modifier "if." That means that the reasoning must be plausible on the facts, it must resolve a significant issue, and the result must be consistent with the reasoning. Here, there's nothing to suggest that Hospital's belief was unreasonable. Thus, option D is plausible on the facts. This resolves a significant issue, because it means Hospital acted without fault, and thus can't be liable for defamation. Finally, the result in D mirrors this. As a result, it's the best response.

(A) is not the best response,

because although it correctly reflects the facts, it does not address the possibility that the claim was true, or the existence of a qualified privilege.

A common law claim for defamation has four requirements:

1. Defendant's defamatory statement
2. Of and concerning plaintiff
3. Negligently or intentionally communicated to at least one third person; and
4. Plaintiff's reputation damaged thereby.

In addition, some degree of fault will have to be proven. That's where qualified privilege comes into play. As a non-media defamer, *without* a qualified privilege, Hospital would have to be *negligent* for Siddon to recover. With a qualified privilege, Siddon would have to prove *malice* – knowledge of falsity or reckless disregard for the truth.

A "qualified privilege" applies when the statement bears some relationship to a public or private interest, of either the publisher, the reader/listener, or both, or the general public. If the statement is in furtherance of the interest, it's protected. A common example is an old employer warning a new employer of an employee's thieving tendencies. A qualified privilege can only be destroyed by malice, or by publishing a defamatory statement for a reason other than the protection of the interest involved.

Here, Hospital's statement would certainly be entitled to qualified privilege, so Siddon would have to prove malice – a knowing falsehood or reckless disregard for the truth. Thus, merely proving that the statement was *false* would be insufficient: Siddon would have to prove Hospital *knew* it was false or recklessly failed to determine if it was true or false. Since option B ignores the fault requirement, it's not the best response.

(B) is not the best response,

because the reasoning it states is not determinative of the outcome. Siddon *still* may not recover even if she did not take the narcotics, due to the existence of Hospital's qualified privilege to defame.

A common law claim for defamation has four requirements:

1. Defendant's defamatory statement;
2. Of and concerning plaintiff;
3. Negligently or intentionally communicated to at least one third person; and
4. Plaintiff's reputation damaged thereby.

In addition, some degree of fault will have to be proven. That's where qualified privilege comes into play. As a non-media defamer, *without* a qualified privilege, Hospital would have to be *negligent* in order for Siddon to recover. With a qualified privilege, Siddon would have to prove *malice* – knowledge of falsity or

reckless disregard for the truth.

A "qualified privilege" applies when the statement bears some relationship to a public or private interest, of either the publisher, the reader/listener, or both, or the general public. If the statement is in furtherance of the interest, it's protected. A common example is an old employer warning a new employer of an employee's thieving tendencies. A qualified privilege can only be destroyed by malice, or by publishing a defamatory statement for a reason other than the protection of the interest involved.

Here, Hospital's statement would certainly be entitled to qualified privilege, so Siddon would have to prove malice – a knowing falsehood or reckless disregard for the truth. Thus, merely proving that the statement was *false* would be insufficient: Siddon would have to prove Hospital *knew* it was false or recklessly failed to determine if it was true or false. Since option B ignores the fault requirement, it's not the best response.

(C) is not the best response,

because although its reasoning is true, it doesn't address the defamatory "sting" of the statement, and thus would not exonerate Hospital. This is an extremely sneaky issue, so don't be terribly disappointed if you missed it.

A common law claim for defamation has four requirements:

1. Defendant's defamatory statement
2. Of and concerning plaintiff
3. Negligently or intentionally communicated to at least one third person; and
4. Plaintiff's reputation damaged thereby.

In addition, some degree of fault will have to be proven. That's where qualified privilege comes into play. As a non-media defamer, *without* a qualified privilege, Hospital would have to be *negligent* for Siddon to recover. With a qualified privilege, Siddon would have to prove *malice* – knowledge of falsity or reckless disregard for the truth.

As a general matter, truth is an absolute defense to defamation. However, the truth must refer to the defamatory "sting" of the statement. Here, it's not the fact that the narcotics were missing after Siddon's shift that is *itself* defamatory, because if the hospital had been robbed during Siddon's shift, there would obviously be no adverse reflection on Siddon. Instead, it's the implication that Siddon *stole* the narcotics that is the defamatory "sting" of the statement, and *that's* what would have to be proven true in order for a defense based on truth to succeed.

What will actually determine Hospital's liability is the degree of fault required. Because the statement related to an interest of both the Hospital and the Registry, as well as any other hospitals where Siddon might work, the statement would be protected by a "qualified privilege," which can only be abrogated by malice. Thus, Hospital would have to know Siddon hadn't taken the narcotics or been reckless in determining whether she had or hadn't. Since C doesn't recognize that Hospital's liability turns on this, and instead offers an incomplete truth defense, it's not the best response.

Answer 52

(A) is the best response,

because it correctly identifies that Ellis will be responsible for indemnifying Toyco, because he created the defect.

While the facts here don't state it explicitly, Carla's claim was likely for strict liability, since she recovered from Toyco for Ellis's improper design – and under strict liability, Toyco could be liable as long as the product was dangerously defective when it left Toyco's control, Toyco was in the business of selling the product, and the product didn't substantially change between Toyco and Carla. In a negligence claim, on the other hand, Toyco could only be held liable for its *own* negligence. Since the facts here say Toyco was held liable for Ellis's defective design, that means the claim must be for strict liability.

Indemnity applies to strict liability in such a way that subsequent suppliers can seek indemnity from those before them in the supply chain, so that whoever was responsible for the defect is ultimately liable for it. This is how indemnity operates: The secondary tortfeasor (here, Toyco) pays a judgment due to the tort of the primary tortfeasor (here, Ellis). The secondary tortfeasor can seek "indemnity" from the primary tortfeasor. (A common example of this is an employer recovering from a tortfeasor employee for judgments employer paid in vicarious liability). Here, this would mean that Toyco can recover from Ellis. Since A recognizes this, it's the best response.

(B) is not the best response,

because it mischaracterizes the facts.

Joint tortfeasors are tortfeasors who act "in concert" (with an express or implied agreement) to produce a result. The damages must be indivisible between tortfeasors. Under joint liability, traditionally, each defendant is liable for all the damages (however, many states modify joint liability so that a *negligent* joint tortfeasor who pays a judgment can recover pro rata shares from other joint tortfeasors).

Under these facts, Ellis and Toyco didn't act in concert; it was Ellis's improper design which created the risk. As a result, they weren't joint tortfeasors. Even if they *were,* this *wouldn't* mean that Toyco would prevail against Ellis – at most, in some states, he could get Ellis's pro rata share of the damages. In any case, this ignores the fact that under these facts, Toyco's claim is based on *indemnity.* In indemnity claims, there is a pre-existing relationship between the two parties whereby the burden of a judgment will be shifted from a secondary to a primary tortfeasor (e.g., where employer is held vicariously liable for an employee's torts, he can

seek indemnity from the employee). Since B mischaracterizes the facts, it can't be the best response.

(C) is not the best response,

because its reasoning doesn't agree with its result. If Toyco was held strictly liable to Carla for a defect created by Ellis, then Ellis *would* have to indemnify Toyco. C states just the opposite.

While the facts don't state it explicitly, it's likely Carla's claim was for strict liability, because Carla recovered against Toyco for Ellis's improper design – and under strict liability Toyco *could* be liable as long as the product was dangerously defective when it left Toyco's control. (In a negligence claim, Toyco could only be liable for its own negligence, including a negligent failure to inspect.)

Having established that Toyco was held liable for a defect created by Ellis, it follows that Toyco could seek indemnity from Ellis. Where strict liability is involved, all subsequent suppliers can seek indemnity from those before them in the supply chain, so that the one responsible for the defect is ultimately liable. *Normally* that will be the manufacturer, but here, the defect is traceable even further back, to the designer, Ellis. Thus, C is incorrect in stating that Toyco will be unable to seek indemnity, making it not the best response.

(D) is not the best response,

because the original claim here was for strict liability, not negligence. As such, Toyco will be able to recover in indemnity from Ellis, because Toyco was held liable for a defect Ellis created.

While the facts don't state it expressly, it's likely Carla's claim was for strict liability, since she recovered from Toyco for Ellis's improper design – and under strict liability, Toyco *could* be liable as long as the product was dangerously defective when it left Toyco's control. In a negligence claim, on the other hand, Toyco could only be liable for its own negligence. This could include a negligent failure to inspect, but for *that* to exist, you'd first have to establish that Toyco was negligent in failing to inspect for defects in the design. In that case, Toyco could be liable for its own negligence, and could not recover from Ellis. However, under these facts, you're told Toyco was held liable for Ellis's improper design. Since D fails to recognize this, it's not the best response.

Answer 53

(A) is the best response,

because if Neighbor's dam unreasonably interfered with Vacationer's use and enjoyment of his property, Vacationer would have a valid claim for private nuisance.

A landowner who causes a substantial, unreasonable interference with a neighbor's use or enjoyment of his property without a valid defense is liable for private nuisance.

Most courts apply this rule in the case of water-courses, holding that an upstream owner may not completely block the flow of water if this would unreasonably interfere with a downstream owner's use and enjoyment of the latter's property. So Choice (A) best states the applicable rules of nuisance.

(B) is not the best response,

because Neighbor's desire to affect Vacationer's property is not an element of the tort of private nuisance.

As described in the treatment of Choice (A) above, private nuisance is the unreasonable interference with another's use and enjoyment of the latter's property.

Choice (B) is wrong mostly because it fails to factor in whether there has been an unreasonable interfere with Vacationer's use and enjoyment of his property. For instance, if the damming was the only way to avoid flooding of Neighbor's property, and the harm it posed to Vacationer's use and enjoyment was very small, a court would conclude that the damning was not "unreasonable," and Vacationer would lose, even though Neighbor "intended" (in the sense of knowing with substantial certainty) that Vacationer's property would be "affected" (in the sense that water would no longer flow through it).

(C) is not the best response,

because the tort nuisance covers use and *enjoyment*, not just use.

A landowner who causes a substantial, unreasonable interference with a neighbor's use or enjoyment of his property without a valid defense is liable for private nuisance.

The fact that Vacationer never goes "close" to the stream is not inconsistent with her having sustained an unreasonable interference with her "use and *enjoyment*" of her property. For instance, it's very possible that Vacationer used to like to view, from an upstairs window, the stream running through her property, and that she now has much less pleasure from the water-less view. Consequently, her "use and enjoyment" have been substantially impaired, even though in a narrow sense she never "made use" of the stream.

(D) is not the best response,

because compliance with this type of statute would not preclude liability for nuisance.

A landowner who causes a substantial, unreasonable interference with a neighbor's use or enjoyment of his property without a valid defense is liable for private nuisance. Many nuisances are not in violation of any particular law, since "positive law" (statutes, ordinances, and the like) do not purport to be the sole source of legal obligations. (For instance, a factory might get all required local permits, but might still be a private nuisance because it's unreasonably loud and noisy). Therefore, the fact that the dam satisfied the relevant affirmative laws when it was built does not foreclose

the possibility of a successful nuisance suit.

Answer 54

(B) is the best response,

because Seller should have fixed the roof and doesn't escape liability just because he sold the house.

A landowner is required to use reasonable care to ensure that the property does not pose an unreasonable danger to persons outside the property. For example, it's completely clear that if Seller still owned the house when the accident occurred, he would be liable if he should have realized that the roof posed an unreasonable danger to passersby.

The interesting question is whether the fact that Seller sold and vacated the property changes the analysis. The answer is that, at least in most jurisdictions, it does not. See Rest. 2d Torts, § 373(1) ("A vendor of land who has created or negligently permitted to remain on the land a structure or other artificial condition which involves an unreasonable risk of harm to others outside of the land ... is subject to liability to such persons for physical harm caused by the condition after his vendee has taken possession of the land." Under § 373(2), except in the case where the vendor knowingly conceals the defect, the vendor's liability under § 373(1) continues "only until the vendee has had reasonable opportunity to discover the condition and to take ... precautions.") Since one day was not enough for the buyer to discover and fix the defect, Seller remained on the hook for the defect under this rule, if (as Choice (B) hypothesizes) he was aware of the condition and the danger.

(A) is not the best response,

because Seller wouldn't be strictly liable for a defective roof.

This Choice turns only on whether the roof was "defective," not on whether Seller was negligent in any way. Therefore, the choice could be the correct answer only if some type of strict liability applied.

Strict liability does not apply to landowners. It applies only in the case of ultrahazardous activities and sales of "products." When landowners sell real estate, courts normally do not apply strict product liability, even though the structure on the real estate could be thought of as being in some sense a "product." The refusal to apply strict product liability is especially likely where, as here, the seller is an "amateur" seller (i.e., one not in the business of selling real estate).

(C) is not the best response,

because as described in the treatment of Chioce (B), the fact that Seller no longer owned or occupied the property would not be a defense, if Seller negligently failed to notice and correct the danger to persons outside the property, and the buyer hadn't yet had a chance to discover and fix the problem.

(D) is not the best response,

because the state of Pedestrian's knowledge is irrelevant on these facts.

This choice is pointing you towards the doctrine of assumption of risk — the theory is that if Pedestrian knew that slates had blown off in past storms, Pedestrian assumed the risk that this might happen here.

However, the assumption-of-risk doctrine applies only where Pedestrian's exposure to the risk is "voluntary." Where, as here, Pedestrian is using the public right of way, it's extremely unlikely that a court would conclude that Pedestrian's mere knowledge that slates had fallen in past windstorms amounted to a "voluntary" assumption of the risk that this might happen here, especially where Pedestrian might have believed that only negligently-maintained roofs were likely to have this problem. (If Pedestrian knew that speeding cars had sometimes skidded over the curb during past rainstorms, would his use of the curb constitute assumption of the risk that a speeding car would strike him? Obviously not.)

Answer 55

(C) is the best response,

because it is the only answer that correctly requires a causal link between Surgeon's asserted negligence and the injury to Pat.

A plaintiff can prevail in a negligence claim only if she proves that the defendant's negligence was the cause in fact, as well as the proximate cause, of the plaintiff's injury. Since the asserted negligence here consists of failure to consult a cardiologist, Pat's administrator must show that that failure to consult was, more probably than not, the cause in fact ("but-for cause") of the blood clot. The only way this could be true is if plaintiff shows that such a consultation would, more likely than not, have led to advice to Surgeon that if followed would have prevented the clot from occurring. Since Chioce (C) correctly asserts this requirement of a causal link between the asserted negligence and the bad outcome, it is the correct answer.

(A) is not the best response,

because Surgeon would not be liable if his negligence failed to contribute to the bad outcome.

As explained more fully in the discussion of Choice (C), even if Surgeon was negligent in not consulting a cardiologist, he cannot be liable unless that negligence was a cause-in-fact of the bad outcome. The only way the lack of a consultation could be the cause-in-fact of the bad outcome is if the consultation would probably have led to a successful outcome. Since Choice (A) does not reflect this requirement of a causal link, it is not correct.

(B) is not the best response,

because it, too, incorrectly eliminates any requirement of a causal link between the negligence and the injury.

The facts tell us enough to know that Pat has made a prima facie case of negligence (this was done by the testimony that accepted medical practice would require consultation with a cardiologist). But nothing in the facts indicates that the lack of a consultation changed the outcome, i.e., that had there been a consultation, the outcome would likely have been different. The mere fact that the *operation* caused the blot clot would not be the type of causal link required, because the doing of the operation was not itself an act of negligence; only the doing of it without a consultation constituted negligence. Since Choice (B) does not correctly reflect this requirement of a causal link between the negligent omission and the bad outcome, it is incorrect.

(D) is not the best response,

because it incorrectly assumes that there can only be one cause of the bad outcome.

If Surgeon's failure to make the consultation was *a* cause-in-fact ("but-for cause"), as well as *a* proximate cause, of Pat's death, Surgeon would be liable even though there was also another cause-in-fact / proximate cause of the death, namely the disconnecting of the life support. One bad outcome can have multiple proximate causes / causes in fact, so the fact that D was responsible for only one of the causes is no defense at all. Here, if a consultation would probably have led to use of a different procedure that would have eliminated the blot clot, the lack of a consultation would have been a cause in fact of the death (the clot would not have happened without the omission of a consultation) and a proximate cause of it (it led reasonably directly and foreseeably to the clot), which is all that is required causally.

Answer 56

(D) is the best response,

because it correctly identifies what the result will be.

Under the statute in these facts, Astin could be held liable for damage negligently caused by Garrison, since he was driving her car when the accident occurred. Thus, Placek *could* win a judgment against Astin, or Astin and Garrison jointly.

Here, you're told that Placek sued them both, and that Placek could recover $100,000 solely due to Garrison's negligence. The key is that Astin wasn't negligent *at all*. Since Astin and Garrison didn't act in concert, they couldn't be jointly liable; and Garrison caused *all* the damages, the damages aren't divisible, and several liability won't apply. Instead, indemnity will apply. Under indemnity, the secondary tortfeasor, who is without *any* fault, can seek payment for any judgment he pays due to the tort of the primary tortfeasor. The most common example of this is an employer who pays a judgment, under vicarious liability, due to the tort of an employee. Due to operation of the statute in this problem, it would also apply here (since the statute only makes available a potential defendant; it doesn't assess fault for loaning a car). Since Garrison was solely responsible for the accident, he's the only one who will ultimately be liable, and because D correctly identifies the result, it's the best response.

(A) is not the best response,

because it mistakenly pins Astin, ultimately, with half of the damages.

Contrary to what A states, Astin would recover anything she actually pays from Garrison, on grounds of indemnity. Under indemnity, the burden of a judgment is shifted from a secondary tortfeasor to a primary tortfeasor. As it applies here, Astin could recover anything she pays to Placek from Garrison, since it was solely Garrison's negligence which caused the accident. In fact, Astin is only a defendant because of the statute making her liable for any negligence by anyone driving her car. However, since Garrison was solely responsible for the accident, he's the only one who will ultimately be liable.

If you chose this response, you were probably thinking of "several" liability, where damages are divisible on a logical basis between tortfeasors, based on the damages each one caused – and each one must pay his share of the damages. However, under these facts Astin wasn't negligent *at all,* so she should be able to recover entirely from the one who was – Garrison. Since A doesn't recognize this, it's not the best response.

(B) is not the best response,

because it does not take into account operation of the statute.

Under the statute in these facts, Astin *can* be liable for damage negligently caused by Garrison, since he was driving her car when the accident occurred. Thus, Placek *could* win a judgment against Astin, which option B fails to recognize.

B *does* recognize, however, what will ultimately happen, because Garrison will indemnify Astin. Indemnity applies where a secondary tortfeasor pays a judgment due to the tort of a primary tortfeasor. That's the case here, so Astin could recover from Garrison. Since B ignores the intermediate step – that Astin could initially be held liable for some or all of the damages – it's not the best response.

(C) is not the best response,

because it understates what Astin will be able to recover from Garrison.

Under the statute in these facts, Astin could be held liable for damage negligently caused by Garrison, since he was driving her car when the accident occurred. Thus, Placek *could* win a judgment against Astin, or Astin and Garrison jointly.

However, where C goes off the track is in determining how much Astin could recover from Garrison, under the doctrine of indemnity. Indemnity applies where a

secondary tortfeasor pays a judgment due to the tort of a primary tortfeasor. That's the case here, so Astin could recover from Garrison for the *entire amount* Placek recovers from Astin, not just 50% of it, as C suggests.

If you chose this response, you were either thinking of the rule of contribution under *joint* liability, or several liability.

In joint liability, two or more tortfeasors act "in concert" (with an express or implied agreement) to produced a result. The damages must be indivisible between tortfeasors (here, the damages are completely *divisible,* since Garrison caused all the damage). While under traditional joint liability each defendant is liable for *all* the damages, many states modify this with the rule of "contribution," whereby a negligent joint tortfeasor who pays a judgment can recover pro rata shares from other joint tortfeasors.

Under *several* liability, damages are divisible on a logical basis between tortfeasors, based on the damages each caused. Here, the damages aren't divisible – Garrison caused them *all.*

As a result, *indemnity* is the correct doctrine, not joint or several liability. Since C doesn't recognize this, it's not the best response.

Answer 57

(A) is the best response,

because it correctly states exactly what damages Dever will be responsible for.

You're told under these facts that Dever was negligent. Thus, he'll be liable for any damages flowing from that negligence. Here, Peters' house was already on fire when the accident occurred; thus, that portion of the damage is not attributable to Dever. By negligently hitting a fire truck on its way to a fire, Dever created the foreseeable risk of loss to whomever's house the fire truck was heading. Here, the damages Dever caused, and for which he'll be liable, is the part of the loss that would have been prevented had the accident not occurred. Since A correctly states this, it's the best response.

(B) is not the best response,

because it overstates the damages Peters will be able to recover from Dever.

The facts here tell you that Dever was negligent. As a result, he'll be liable for those damages caused by his negligence. Here, Peters' house was already on fire *before* Dever's negligence occurred, so Dever *couldn't* be responsible for the whole house. Even if Dever hadn't been negligent at all, the firemen would only have been able to salvage part of the house, and it's only that portion for which Dever would be liable. Since B ignores this, it's not the best response.

(C) is not the best response,

because Dever will be liable for damages even if he

had no hand in starting the fire.

By negligently hitting a fire truck on its way to a fire, Dever created the foreseeable risk of loss to whomever's house the fire truck was heading. Here, the damages Dever caused, and for which he'll be liable, is the part of the loss that would have been prevented had the accident not occurred.

Of course, whoever *started* the fire will be liable *as well,* and Dever's negligence would not exonerate the arsonist (since Dever's negligence would be considered a foreseeable intervening cause of Peters' damages). However, what's at issue here is *Dever's* liability, and not having started the fire would not exonerate Dever. Since C states otherwise, it's not the best response.

(D) is not the best response,

because it doesn't correctly analyze the issue of causation on these facts.

Due to his negligence, Dever will be liable for all damages flowing from his act. Here, Dever's negligence prevented the fire truck from reaching the fire. Thus, the part of Peters' loss that would have been prevented had the accident not occurred is a direct result of Dever's negligence, since it would not have occurred "but for" Dever's negligence. Thus, it's not necessary that Dever's negligence created an "apparent danger" to Peters. Since D states otherwise, it's not the best response.

Answer 58

(C) is the best response,

because this choice correctly states the standard for the misappropriation-of-identity type of invasion of privacy.

To establish a prima facie case for invasion of privacy by appropriation of plaintiff's picture or name, only one element needs to be proved: that there was an unauthorized use by defendant of plaintiff's picture or name for commercial advantage.

Under these facts Actor consented to an amateur photographer taking his picture as he sat drinking Vineyard wine at a nightclub. He did not consent to Vineyard using his photo for commercial purposes. Vineyard's advertisement in a nationally circulated magazine was intended for Vineyard's commercial advantage. Since Choice (C) focuses on the key element of Vineyard's liability, it's the best response.

(A) is not the best response,

because Actor's consent was to the amateur photographer, not to Vineyard's commercial use.

To establish a prima facie case for invasion of privacy by appropriation of plaintiff's picture or name, only one element needs to be proved: that there was an unauthorized use by defendant of plaintiff's picture or name for commercial advantage.

Here, Actor's consent was specifically to an amateur

photographer. The scope of Actor's consent was to a single amateur photograph. He did not consent to Vineyard using that photograph for its commercial advantage. Therefore, his "consent" would not excuse Vineyard from liability.

(B) is not the best response,

because public figures retain the right not to have their image utilized for commercial advantage.

To establish a prima facie case for invasion of privacy by appropriation of plaintiff's picture or name, only one element needs to be proved: that there was an unauthorized use by defendant of plaintiff's picture or name for commercial advantage.

Here, Actor was a well-known movie star and so would be considered a public figure. While this fact might conceivably be relevant in other kinds of invasion of privacy claims, or in some defamation claims, it is irrelevant to the claim here. Therefore, Actor's status as a public figure does not exonerate Vineyard.

(D) is not the best response,

because enjoyment of a product does not convey the rights to commercial use of an image.

To establish a prima facie case for invasion of privacy by appropriation of plaintiff's picture or name, only one element needs to be proved: that there was an unauthorized use by defendant of plaintiff's picture or name for commercial advantage.

Falsity is not relevant to the appropriation form of invasion of privacy. Therefore, although Vineyard was accurate in its statement that Actor enjoyed Vineyard wine, that did not give Vineyard the right to make commercial use of Actor's image.

Answer 59

(C) is the best response.

Only statements 1 and 2 are actually warranties.

Whenever a seller makes an affirmation of fact or promise relating to goods, and the affirmation becomes part of the basis of the bargain, the seller is expressly warranting that the goods will conform with the affirmation. UCC §2-313. Contrast this with "puffery," which is an expression of mere opinion about the goods.

Here, both statements 1 and 2 would constitute express warranties. Statement 1 is an affirmation of fact – that the car has been accident-free; and statement 2 is a promise – that it'll get 25 m.p.g. Statement 3 is simply not concrete enough to constitute an express warranty. "Puffery" is determined by the specificity of the representation and the reasonability of reliance. Here, Purvis would be justified in relying on statements 1 and 2, but not statement 3. Thus, only 1 and 2 could form the basis of a suit for deceit/breach of express warranty.

Answer 60

(D) is the best response,

because it correctly analyzes how damages will be determined.

Here, both Acorp and Beeco will be liable for *some* part of Landesmann's damages, since each one's act was a "substantial factor" in causing Landesmann's damages.

Joint and several liability addresses the divisibility of damages between multiple tortfeasors. Joint liability applies where the damages are *not* divisible between tortfeasors, making each defendant liable for all the damages (some states apply the rule of contribution to negligent joint tortfeasors, such that a negligent joint tortfeasor who pays a judgment can recover pro rata shares from the other tortfeasors).

Several liability applies where the damages *are* divisible, making each defendant liable only for the damages he caused.

You can remember the difference between the two this way: Say two people are fighting over a gun and it goes off, injuring plaintiff. This is joint liability, because there's no way to apportion liability. If two people, each of whom has a gun, shoot plaintiff, causing two separate injuries, then the damages can be apportioned, and there's several liability.

Here, the percentage of Landesmann's liability each defendant caused hasn't been determined, so they'll be jointly and severally liable. (In fact, the damages are not likely to be considered divisible, so each defendant would be liable under joint liability for the entire judgment.) Since D correctly identifies this, it's the best response.

(A) is not the best response,

because it does not correctly apply principles of causation to these facts.

A negligence claim requires proof that defendant failed to exercise such care as a reasonable person in his position would have exercised, this must have been a breach of the duty to prevent the foreseeable risk of injury to anyone in plaintiff's position, and this breach must have caused plaintiff's damages. The rule used to determine causation depends on how many causes there are: A single cause involves the "but for" test, and multiple causes involve the "substantial factor" test. Here, with Acorp and Beeco each being a cause of Landesmann's damages, each one will be liable as long as his act was a "substantial factor" in creating Landesmann's damages.

Under these facts, they were. Since A would exonerate each one because it wasn't enough *alone* to cause the damages, it's not the best response.

(B) is not the best response,

because Landesmann's recovery would not depend on his ability to precisely apportion damages.

In order to prevail on a negligence claim, defendant must have failed to exercise such care as a reasonable person in his position would have exercised, this must have been a breach of the duty to prevent the foreseeable risk of injury to anyone in plaintiff's position, and this breach must have caused plaintiff's damages. Where there are multiple factual causes, as here, plaintiff need only prove that an individual defendant's act was a "substantial factor" in causing plaintiff's damages. Under these facts, this is true of *both* Acorp and Beeco. Thus, they'll each be liable, regardless of whether Landesmann can assess how much pesticide each discharged.

What the ability to apportion determines is whether Acorp and Beeco will be jointly or severally liable. If the damages are indivisible between the tortfeasors, each defendant will be liable for all the damages (although many states modify joint liability with the rule of "contribution," whereby a negligent joint tortfeasor who pays a judgment can recover pro rata shares from other joint tortfeasors). If the damages are divisible on a logical basis between tortfeasors, based on the damage each one caused, then each will only pay his share of defendant's damages. Remember the difference this way: Say two people are fighting over a gun, and it goes off, injuring plaintiff. This is joint liability, because there's no way to apportion liability. If two people with a gun each shoot plaintiff, causing two separate injuries, then the damages can be apportioned, and each will only be *severally* liable. Thus, while divisibility of damages will determine how much each defendant can be liable for, it doesn't determine if defendants will be liable. Since B states otherwise, it's not the best response.

(C) is not the best response,

because it presupposes that the damages are divisible equally. While it *may* that Acorp and Beeco will each be liable for only half of the damages, this could not be determined conclusively on these facts.

Since each of Acorp and Beeco's negligence was a "substantial factor" in causing Landesmann's damages, they'll each be liable. The central issue under these facts is: For how much? This will turn on whether or not the damages are *divisible* between them. If they are *not* divisible, joint liability will apply, and each defendant could be liable for the entire judgment. If the damages are divisible on a logical basis between them, based on the damage each one caused, they'll be severally liable, and will only have to pay a fair share of plaintiff's damages. Here, if the damages are considered severable *and* each one is responsible for exactly half of Landesmann's damages, C would be correct – each would pay half *only*. However, on these facts, it's not clear that the damages are divisible (it depends on whether the amount of pesticide each dumped was calculable), and thus what share of Landesmann's damages each must pay is not determinable. Since C presupposes settlement of an issue which is unsettled on these facts, it's not the best response.

Answer 61

(A) is the best response,

because it correctly identifies the lynchpin of Roth's strict liability claim.

The requirements of a strict product liability claim are laid out in Restatement of Torts 2d §402A:

1. The product must have been in a defective condition unreasonably dangerous to the user/consumer or his property;
2. When it left the defendant's control (that means, defendant can be liable even if he didn't cause the defect);
3. Product must not be expected to undergo significant changes before it gets to the user/consumer or not actually undergo such changes);
4. The seller must be in the business of selling the product (thus, he can't be a casual seller, e.g., someone selling jam to his neighbor);
5. Damage must result from the defect (defendant is liable for any physical damage);
6. Duty extends to anyone foreseeably endangered by the product (meaning, there's no privity requirement).

Here, option A uses the modifier "if," so the reasoning must be plausible on the facts, the reasoning must resolve a significant issue, and the result must be consistent with the reasoning.

Here, A offers as a proposition that the brake failed due to a manufacturing defect caused at Cycle Company. Since these facts don't tell *why* the brake failed, this explanation is plausible.

This resolves a significant issue because it provides the foundation of a strict product liability claim: an unreasonably dangerous defect. If brakes on a bicycle have a defect such that they fail without warning, the foreseeable result could be injury or death to the rider, and injury to bystanders, as well as property damage. As a result, such a defect could safely be characterized as unreasonably dangerous.

Having established that the reasoning is correct, the result must conform with the reasoning. Option A satisfies this as well. It *does* throw you a curve by talking about the defect being present when the bike left *Cycle Company,* not Bike Shop, the defendant in this case. However, all strict product liability requires is that the defect exist when the product leaves defendant's control (as long as no substantial changes occur thereafter). Here, if the defect existed when the bicycle left Cycle Co., then it was still there when it left Bike Shop, and Bike Shop will be strictly liable (although it can seek indemnity from the *actual* tortfeasor, Cycle Co.).

Since option A offers a plausible result on these facts, it's the best response.

(B) is not the best response,

because it states as a requirement something that Roth needn't prove in order to prevail.

The requirements of a strict product liability claim are laid out in Restatement of Torts 2d §402A:

1. The product must have been in a defective condition unreasonably dangerous to the user/consumer or his property;
2. When it left the defendant's control (that means, defendant can be liable even if he didn't cause the defect);
3. Product must not be expected to undergo significant changes before it gets to the user/consumer or not actually undergo such changes);
4. The seller must be in the business of selling the product (thus, he can't be a casual seller, e.g., someone selling jam to his neighbor);
5. Damage must result from the defect (defendant is liable for any physical damage);
6. Duty extends to anyone foreseeably endangered by the product (meaning, there's no privity requirement).

Thus, if these elements are satisfied, it isn't necessary that Roth was riding the bike when the defect caused damage. Option B may be read to suggest that it would have to be Roth, as *purchaser,* who was riding the bike, in order to recover. However, this would not be correct, because strict product liability has no privity requirement. Since B states an erroneous requirement of a strict product liability claim, it's not the best response.

(C) is not the best response,

because Roth's conduct under these circumstances could not be considered contributory negligence, and even if it could, it wouldn't be a valid defense to strict product liability under these circumstances.

Contributory negligence is only a defense to strict product liability when plaintiff knows of the danger and unreasonably exposes himself to it (note that this would also constitute assumption of the risk). Here, Roth didn't know about the defect, and in fact fully expected the brakes to work when he applied them. As a result, Bike Shop wouldn't have a valid contributory negligence defense.

In any case, Roth's speeding up would be within the scope of foreseeable risk created by the defective brakes, so Roth would prevail. Since C doesn't recognize this, it's not the best response.

(D) is not the best response,

because even a careful inspection would not relieve Bike Shop of strict product liability under these facts.

The requirements of a strict product liability claim are laid out in Restatement of Torts 2d §402A:

1. The product must have been in a defective condition unreasonably dangerous to the user/consumer or his property;
2. When it left the defendant's control (that means, defendant can be liable even if he didn't cause the defect);

3. Product must not be expected to undergo significant changes before it gets to the user/consumer (or not actually undergo such changes);
4. The seller must be in the business of selling the product (thus, he can't be a casual seller, e.g., someone selling jam to his neighbor);
5. Damage must result from the defect (defendant is liable for any physical damage);
6. Duty extends to anyone foreseeably endangered by the product (meaning, there's no privity requirement).

The hallmark of strict product liability is that it doesn't require proof of *fault,* so conversely, no matter how much care the seller exercises, he will still be liable if the above elements are met. Thus, a careful inspection would not exonerate Bike Shop.

If you chose this response you were probably thinking of a product liability claim based on negligence. There, as with any negligence claim, if the defendant acts with due care, he cannot be liable. You could assume that a careful inspection would amount to due care, so Bike Shop wouldn't be liable in *negligence* if it so acted. However, the claim here is for strict liability, so care is irrelevant. As a result, D isn't the best response.

Answer 62

(B) is the best response,
because it identifies and resolves a central issue.

As in any negligence claim, a defendant will be liable for product liability based on negligence if he failed to exercise such care as a reasonable person in his position would have exercised, this must have been a breach of the duty to prevent the foreseeable risk of injury to anyone in plaintiff's position, and this breach must have caused plaintiff's damages. There are four principle ways in which a manufacturer can be negligent: Manufacturing flaw, failure to inspect, negligent design, and failure to warn.

Here, option B uses the modifier "if," so in order to be the best response, the reasoning would have to be plausible on the facts, it would have to resolve a central issue, and the result would have to be consistent with the reasoning. First, as to plausibility, there's nothing in these facts to suggest B's reasoning *can't* be true. It's just as likely as not that the defect could have been discovered in a reasonable inspection. Second, this reasoning solves a critical issue. If reasonable care would have meant Cycle Company *would* have discovered the defect, then its *not* discovering it was unreasonable, and thus negligent. This would satisfy the "breach" element of negligence, and the other three — duty, causation, and damages — are not problematical on these facts. Finally, if Cycle Company *was* negligent, it'll be liable to Perez, since his being hit when the brakes failed is foreseeable, and option B correctly identifies this result. Thus, B's the best response.

(A) is not the best response,
because the element it states would be irrelevant in a product liability claim based on negligence, and it ignores an element negligence requires: Fault.

As in any negligence claim, a product liability suit based on negligence requires that defendant failed to exercise such care as a reasonable person in his position would have exercised, this was a breach of the duty to prevent the foreseeable risk of harm to anyone in plaintiff's position, and this must have caused plaintiff's damages. There are four principal ways a manufacturer can be negligent: Manufacturing flaw, failure to inspect, negligent design, and failure to warn. Thus, the mere fact that the bicycle was defective would not be sufficient to pin *negligence* on Cycle Company, since negligence requires proof of fault.

If you chose this response, you were thinking of a product liability claim based on strict liability. Under *that* theory, a defendant will be liable if the product had an unreasonably dangerous defect when it *left his control* (in the parlance of option A, "placed in the stream of commerce"). However, negligence is the basis of the claim here, so option A cannot be the best response.

(C) is not the best response,
because Perez needn't be a purchaser in order to prevail.

Option C suggests that Perez should lose because, as a non-purchaser, he lacks privity with Cycle Company. This is not the actual rule for a product liability suit based on negligence; in fact, the defendant's duty extends to anyone foreseeably endangered by the product. As a bystander when the bicycle brakes failed, Perez would be within the scope of potential plaintiffs. Thus, as long as he can prove Cycle Company was negligent and this resulted in his damages, he'll prevail.

If you chose this response, you were probably thinking of product liability suits based on implied warranty or representation theories, which, at least in theory, have privity constraints. However, privity *never* requires that the plaintiff be the purchaser of the product, and in practice courts dislike denying recovery due to lack of privity. In any case, the claim here is for negligence, so there are no privity requirements. Since C doesn't recognize this, it's not the best response.

(D) is not the best response,
because even if Roth was negligent, this will not prevent Perez from prevailing.

Option D suggests that if Roth's turning onto the sidewalk was negligent, it will constitute a *supervening* cause, breaking the (bicycle) chain of causation from Cycle Company to Perez. Note that option D uses the modifier "if." Thus, in order to be the best response, the reasoning must be plausible on these facts, it must resolve a central issue, and the result must be consistent with the reasoning.

Here, Roth *could* have been negligent in turning onto

the curb, but it's not likely. In order to be negligent, he'd have to have been unreasonable. He was in an emergency situation and was apparently faced with two options: Going into traffic or swerving onto the sidewalk. Given these choices, going onto the sidewalk couldn't be considered particularly unreasonable.

Even if it *were,* it wouldn't exonerate Cycle Company, because Roth's negligence would be considered foreseeable. A negligent tortfeasor will only be relieved of liability by intervening forces if their results are unforeseeable, making them *supervening* forces. To determine this, look at the foreseeable risks Cycle Company's negligence created: the risk of injury to Roth and pedestrians, and property damage, at the very least. Thus, even if Roth *was* negligent, the results here – injury to Roth and Perez – were foreseeable, so Cycle Company can't rely on any negligence by Roth as a defense. Since D doesn't recognize this, it's not the best response.

Answer 63

(B) is the best response,

because it identifies and resolves a central issue under these facts.

The requirements of a strict product liability claim are laid out in Restatement of Torts 2d §402A:

1. The product must have been in a defective condition unreasonably dangerous to the user/consumer or his property;
2. When it left the defendant's control (that means, defendant can be liable even if he didn't cause the defect);
3. Product must not be expected to undergo significant changes before it gets to the user/consumer (or not actually undergo such changes);
4. The seller must be in the business of selling the product (thus, he can't be a casual seller, e.g., someone selling jam to his neighbor);
5. Damage must result from the defect (defendant is liable for any physical damage);
6. Duty extends to anyone foreseeably endangered by the product (meaning, there's no privity requirement).

Under these facts, a sticky point is the effect of Dixon's realization that the truck was dangerous, and his failure to buy and install the restraining device. As option B states, this will *not* relieve Trailco of liability toward Morris. That's because proximate cause is analyzed the same way under strict liability as it is under negligence, making the original tortfeasor liable for the foreseeable results of intervening causes. Here, it's foreseeable that Dixon wouldn't buy and install the restraining device, so Trailco will remain liable for Morris's injuries. Since B correctly identifies this, it's the best response.

(A) is not the best response,

because it mischaracterizes the facts, and, even if it didn't, contributory negligence would not be a good defense on these facts.

The requirements of a strict product liability claim are laid out in Restatement of Torts 2d §402A:

1. The product must have been in a defective condition unreasonably dangerous to the user/consumer or his property;
2. When it left the defendant's control (that means, defendant can be liable even if he didn't cause the defect);
3. Product must not be expected to undergo significant changes before it gets to the user/consumer (or not actually undergo such changes);
4. The seller must be in the business of selling the product (thus, he can't be a casual seller, e.g., someone selling jam to his neighbor);
5. Damage must result from the defect (defendant is liable for any physical damage);
6. Duty extends to anyone foreseeably endangered by the product (meaning, there's no privity requirement).

Option A suggests that Morris will only recover if she wasn't driving negligently. Under these facts, she wasn't driving negligently, and even if she was, she could *still* recover. You're told under these facts that Morris was driving 50 m.p.h. on an interstate, and that Morris was unable to avoid colliding with the truck. This suggests she wasn't acting unreasonably, and so she couldn't be considered negligent. Even if she *was,* this type of contributory negligence would *not* be a valid defense to strict liability. In a strict liability case, it's only when plaintiff knowingly, unreasonably subjects himself to a risk of harm that a contributory negligence defense can prevail (note that this *also* constitutes assumption of the risk).

The other type of contributory negligence – plaintiff's failure to realize danger or adequately protect himself against its existence – is not a defense to strict liability. Even if Morris was negligent, it would be the latter type, and so it wouldn't relieve Trailco of liability. Since A states otherwise, it couldn't be the best response.

(C) is not the best response,

because it imposes a privity requirement where, in fact, there isn't one.

The requirements of a strict product liability claim are laid out in Restatement of Torts 2d §402A:

1. The product must have been in a defective condition unreasonably dangerous to the user/consumer or his property;
2. When it left the defendant's control (that means, defendant can be liable even if he didn't cause the defect);
3. Product must not be expected to undergo significant changes before it gets to the user/con-

sumer (or not actually undergo such changes);

4. The seller must be in the business of selling the product (thus, he can't be a casual seller, e.g., someone selling jam to his neighbor);

5. Damage must result from the defect (defendant is liable for any physical damage);

6. Duty extends to anyone foreseeably endangered by the product (meaning, there's no privity requirement).

As #6 indicates, there is no privity requirement. Product liability claims based on implied warranty and representation theories are the only ones with privity requirements, and, even under those claims, courts dislike denying liability on privity grounds in product liability cases and tend to ignore these constraints. In product liability claims grounded on negligence and strict liability, there's no privity requirement. Since C states otherwise, it's not the best response.

(D) is not the best response,

because even if Dixon *was* negligent, this will not relieve Trailco of strict product liability.

The requirements of a strict product liability claim are laid out in Restatement of Torts 2d §402A:

1. The product must have been in a defective condition unreasonably dangerous to the user/consumer or his property;

2. When it left the defendant's control (that means, defendant can be liable even if he didn't cause the defect);

3. Product must not be expected to undergo significant changes before it gets to the user/consumer (or not actually undergo such changes);

4. The seller must be in the business of selling the product (thus, he can't be a casual seller, e.g., someone selling jam to his neighbor);

5. Damage must result from the defect (defendant is liable for any physical damage);

6. Duty extends to anyone foreseeably endangered by the product (meaning, there's no privity requirement).

Option D suggests that, if Dixon was negligent in failing to install the restraining device, his negligence would constitute a supervening cause relieving Trailco of liability (the same analysis of proximate cause applies to strict liability and negligence). However, the negligence of intervening actors is only supervening if its results are unforeseeable. Here, it's completely foreseeable that truckers *wouldn't* pay extra for a restraining device, so the fact that Dixon didn't (even though Dixon may *also* be liable, for negligence), doesn't relieve Trailco of liability. Since D suggests otherwise, it can't be the best response.

Answer 64

(A) is the best response,

because it correctly identifies a basis on which Dixon

would be held liable.

First, you have to identify the nature of the claim. It can't be for an intentional tort, and strict liability wouldn't apply to Dixon, since he's not in the business of selling trucks. Outside of strict *product* liability, there's no basis for applying strict liability, since driving a truck is not an ultrahazardous activity – it *can* be undertaken with complete safety. Thus, that leaves negligence as the only likely claim.

In order to prevail on a negligence claim, Morris would have to prove that Dixon failed to exercise such care as a reasonable person under the circumstances would have exercised, this must have been a breach of the duty to prevent the foreseeable risk of injury to anyone in plaintiff's position, and this must have caused plaintiff's damages.

Under these facts, if it's unreasonable for Dixon not to have installed the restraining device, he'll be liable to Morris if it would have prevented the accident (which is plausible under these facts). Not installing the restrainer *was* unreasonable, under the balancing test used to determine negligence: The burden on the defendant to avoid risk and the utility of his conduct vs. the probability and probable gravity of harm defendant's conduct is likely to cause. Here, you're told the restraining device was cheap and readily available, Dixon knew about it and knew the truck was dangerous without it, and the harm possible without it could be death of others on the road as well as extensive property damage. Thus, Dixon was clearly negligent.

Note that A uses the modifier "if," so the reasoning must be plausible on the facts, it must resolve a central issue, and the result must be consistent with the reasoning. Here, it's clearly possible that the restraining device *could* have prevented the accident by stopping the trailer from tipping over. Dixon's failure to install it was negligent, as the balancing test above shows. Finally, A correctly states that Dixon would be liable on this basis. As a result, A is the best response.

(B) is not the best response,

because there is no basis for imposing strict liability on Dixon under these facts. There are three sources of strict liability: Animals, ultrahazardous activities, and defective, unreasonably dangerous products (statutes and case law can also impose strict liability). Trucking would not be considered ultrahazardous, since it can be undertaken with complete safety, so strict liability could not be imposed on that basis. Strict product liability similarly fails to provide a source of strict liability on these facts.

The requirements of a strict product liability claim are laid out in Restatement of Torts 2d §402A:

1. The product must have been in a defective condition unreasonably dangerous to the user/consumer or his property;

2. When it left the defendant's control (that means, defendant can be liable even if he didn't cause

the defect);

3. Product must not be expected to undergo significant changes before it gets to the user/consumer (or not actually undergo such changes);

4. The seller must be in the business of selling the product (thus, he can't be a casual seller, e.g., someone selling jam to his neighbor);

5. Damage must result from the defect (defendant is liable for any physical damage);

6. Duty extends to anyone foreseeably endangered by the product (meaning, there's no privity requirement).

The missing element under these facts is that Dixon isn't in the business of selling trucks – he's a truck-driver. Thus, he can't be held strictly liable for defects in the truck. Instead, some fault-based conduct, like negligence, will have to be proven. Since B mistakenly applies strict liability to Dixon, it's not the best response.

(C) is not the best response,

because it mistakenly limits a negligence claim against Dixon to proving that Dixon was driving negligently.

In order to be liable for negligence, defendant must have failed to exercise such care as a reasonable person in his position would have exercised, this must have been a breach of the duty to prevent the foreseeable risk of injury to anyone in plaintiff's position, and this breach must have caused plaintiff's damages.

Under these facts, while Dixon's negligent driving could form the basis of a negligence claim, it's not the *only* potential source of negligence, contrary to what C suggests. Instead, if Dixon failed to exercise due care in any way and this resulted in Morris's damages, Dixon will be liable. Specifically, if Dixon was unreasonable in failing to install the restraining device, he could be liable for negligence even if he was driving carefully when the accident occurred. Since C mistakenly limits the scope of Morris's negligence claim, it's not the best response.

(D) is not the best response,

because Dixon needn't be the manufacturer or seller of the trailer in order to be liable for negligence.

In order to be liable for negligence, defendant must have failed to exercise such care as a reasonable person in his position would have exercised, this must have been a breach of the duty to prevent the foreseeable risk of injury to anyone in plaintiff's position, and this breach must have caused plaintiff's damages.

Thus, if Dixon was negligent in some way and his negligence caused Morris's damages, he'll be liable *regardless* of the fact he didn't make or sell the trailer. For instance, if he was unreasonable in failing to buy and install the restraining device, he'll be liable to Morris if this would have prevented the accident. If you chose this response, it's probably because you thought the claim was for strict liability, not negligence, in which

case Dixon's not being in the business of selling trucks would relieve him of liability. However it's for that very reason that Morris's claim *wouldn't* be for strict liability; since Dixon isn't in the business, he *couldn't* be liable for strict liability. Since D would require that Dixon be a manufacturer or seller in order to be liable for negligence, it's not the best response.

Answer 65

(D) is the best response,

because it identifies the central issue.

Common law defamation has four elements:

1. Defendant's defamatory statement;

2. Of and concerning plaintiff;

3. Negligently or intentionally "published" to at least one third person;

4. Plaintiff's reputation damaged thereby.

In addition, plaintiff will have to prove some level of fault, depending on his and the defendant's status (e.g., media, public figure); furthermore, if the statement was slander and not within a per se category, plaintiff must prove "special" (pecuniary) damages.

As D correctly points out, the issue here is whether Poe suffered special damages. That's because the statement doesn't fit any of the slander per se categories (reflecting adversely on business/profession, or imputing a foul and loathsome disease, moral turpitude crime, or unchastity in a woman), and it's not obvious from these facts that Poe actually suffered any pecuniary loss. Such damages include things like a lost job, inheritance, gift, customers, and the like. (*General* damages, on the other hand, cover things like damage to reputation or personal relationships, and mental anguish.) Note that D says Poe won't recover *unless* he can prove special damages. That means that proving special damages must be crucial to Poe's success in order for D to be correct. In fact, if Poe fails to prove special damages, he'll lose the case entirely. Since D correctly identifies this, it's the best response.

(A) is not the best response,

because it ignores a central issue in the case.

It's true that the remark would have to have been heard by any of Poe's neighbors, in order to satisfy the "publication" requirement of defamation. (The other elements are the defamatory statement itself, of and concerning plaintiff, plaintiff's reputation damaged, and some level of fault.) However, this isn't really at issue under these facts – after all, you're told that many of the neighbors were out on their porches, and that the statement could be heard a block away.

Instead, the issue here is *damages*, because Poe will have to prove "special" (pecuniary) damages in order to prevail *at all*. That's because Kane's statement was slander, not libel, and it wasn't in one of the four slander "per se" categories (reflecting adversely on business/profession, or imputing a foul and loathsome disease, moral turpitude crime, or unchastity in a woman). Slander not within the four per se categories is the *only* type of defamation requiring proof of special damages. Under these facts, there's no indication Kane's statement resulted in any special damages for Poe, so the best response would *have* to address this issue. Since A doesn't, it's not the best response.

(B) is not the best response,

because it offers an element which is not, in fact, an element of the defamation claim.

Common law defamation has four elements:

1. Defendant's defamatory statement;
2. Of and concerning plaintiff;
3. Negligently or intentionally "published" to at least one third person;
4. Plaintiff's reputation damaged thereby.

In addition, plaintiff will have to prove some level of fault depending on his and the defendant's status (e.g., media, public figure); furthermore, if the statement was slander and not within a per se category, plaintiff must prove "special" (pecuniary) damages.

Thus, a statement can be defamatory without having to be the result of extreme and outrageous conduct, and the conduct can be extreme and outrageous without satisfying the elements of defamation. If you chose this response, you were probably thinking of an intentional infliction of emotional distress claim, which does require extreme and outrageous conduct. However, the claim here is for defamation, which does not require such conduct, so B isn't the best response.

(C) is not the best response,

because it overstates the level of fault Poe would have to prove in order to prevail.

By using the modifier "unless," B suggests that the only way Kane could be liable is if he knowingly defamed Poe. In fact, in order to recover from Kane, Poe will have to satisfy these elements: A defamatory statement, of and concerning plaintiff, negligently or intentionally published to at least one third person, and plaintiff's reputation damaged thereby. In addition, because the statement here is slander not within one of the slander per se categories (reflecting adversely on business/profession, or imputing foul and loathsome disease, moral turpitude crime, unchastity in a woman), Poe will have to prove "special" (pecuniary) damages.

On the fault issue, it's likely Poe need only prove that Kane was *negligent* in not determining the truth, not that he acted *knowingly*. Normally, non-media defamers can only be liable if they're negligent (as opposed to media defamers, where *malice* must be proven, or where a qualified privilege exists due to a special interest of the defamer, the defamed, or the general public). Even if Poe had to prove malice, reckless disregard for the truth would suffice; he still wouldn't have to prove Kane acted knowingly. Since option C overstates the level of fault Poe will have to prove, it's not the best response.

Answer 66

(A) is the best response,

because it identifies an element of Poe's claim.

An intentional infliction of emotional distress claim has four elements:

1. Extreme and outrageous conduct of defendant;
2. Defendant's intent to cause plaintiff to suffer emotional distress;
3. Causation; and
4. Damages.

Thus, the element A states – the extreme and outrageous conduct – is the lynchpin of an emotional distress claim. In fact, where creditors are concerned, a pattern of abuse, hounding and extreme conduct can form the basis for an emotional distress claim, *even if* the plaintiff really owes the money! Since none of the other elements are seriously at issue in these facts, and A identifies a central issue in the claim, it's the best response.

(B) is not the best response,

because it addresses an element that is not part of an emotional distress claim.

An intentional infliction of emotional distress claim has four elements:

1. Extreme and outrageous conduct of defendant;
2. Defendant's intent to cause plaintiff to suffer emotional distress;
3. Causation; and
4. Damages.

While Kane's invading Poe's property *might* contribute to the outrageousness of his conduct, it's not necessary. Kane could have gone up to Poe in a restaurant, undertaken the same behavior, and had it constitute emotional distress. Instead, where creditors are concerned, typically abuse, hounding and extreme conduct will form the basis for an emotional distress claim (whereas garden-variety phone calls won't). Since B states that trespass is a requirement of an emotional distress claim, where in fact it isn't, B isn't the best response.

(C) isn't the best response,

because Poe's success will not be contingent on his suffering physical harm.

An intentional infliction of emotional distress claim has four elements:

1. Extreme and outrageous conduct of defendant;
2. Defendant's intent to cause plaintiff to suffer emotional distress;
3. Causation; and
4. Damages.

While proof of damages is a requirement, this needn't be physical injury, just severe emotional distress beyond that which a reasonable person could take.

Furthermore, plaintiff can recover for embarrassment and humiliation, and punitive damages are also a possibility due to the intentional nature of the tort. Since proof of physical harm is not an element of Poe's claim, and C states that he can't recover without proof of physical harm, C can't be the best response.

(D) isn't the best response,

because it's not relevant to Poe's claim.

An intentional infliction of emotional distress claim has four elements:

1.   Extreme and outrageous conduct of defendant;
2.   Defendant's intent to cause plaintiff to suffer emotional distress;
3.   Causation; and
4.   Damages.

Thus, even if Poe actually *did* owe the store money, this would not preclude his recovery on an emotional distress claim. In fact, where creditors are concerned, a pattern of abuse, hounding and extreme conduct can form the basis for an emotional distress claim, even if the money is actually owed.

If you chose this response, you were thinking of a defamation claim, where truth is a defense. Thus, if Poe actually owed money and Kane called him a "deadbeat" in the hearing of others, even if Poe proved special damages, Kane would have a valid defense – Poe's actually being a deadbeat. However, the claim here is for emotional distress. Since D focuses on an element which is not, in fact, required by an emotional distress claim, it's not the best response.

Answer 67

(B) is the best response,

because it addresses a central issue under these facts, and resolve sit satisfactorily.

There are three elements in a prima facie claim of battery:

1.   Defendant's act bringing about harmful or offensive contact with plaintiff's person;
2.   Defendant's intent to bring about such contact OR to create the apprehension of immediate contact; and
3.   Causation.

Here, the element that's most in question is *intent,* since it's not clear from these facts that Poe intended to cause the act that knocked out a few of Kane's teeth. Thus, in order to be correct, B would have to – and does – address this issue.

B uses the modifier "if," so the reasoning must be plausible on the facts, it must address a central issue, and the result must be consistent with the reasoning. First, it's possible on these facts that Poe knew that slamming the door would make it hit the bullhorn (and consequently hit Kane), since there's nothing to suggest this *couldn't* be true. Second, this resolves a central issue – intent. Intent can take one of two forms:

either a desire that a certain result will come about, or the substantial certainty that it will, regardless of one's desire that it do so. Thus, if Poe knew the door would hit the bullhorn and force it against Kane, he could be said to *intend* that it happen. Third, the result is consistent with the reasoning, because if intent is satisfied, the other elements are straightforward, and Poe will be liable. As a result, B's the best response.

(A) is not the best response,

because it does not specifically address an element of Kane's claim.

A prima facie claim for battery has three elements:

1.   Defendant's act bringing about harmful or offensive contact with plaintiff's person;
2.   Defendant's intent to bring about such contact OR to create the apprehension of immediate contact; and
3.   Causation.

Thus, if Poe can prove these elements, and Kane has no valid defense, Poe will prevail.

The defense to which option A refers is the defense of property, which requires a request to desist, unless it would be dangerous or futile, before physical force is used. The problem with applying this to these facts is that *even if* Poe *had* asked Kane to leave first, the physical force he used would be considered excessive and thus beyond the scope of his privilege making him liable for battery.

Instead, what's at issue under these facts is the *intent* element of battery, since it's not clear under these facts that intent exists and as a result the best response would have to address this point. Since A doesn't, it's not the best response.

(C) isn't the best response,

because it does not offer a valid defense to battery.

There are three elements in a prima facie claim of battery:

1.   Defendant's act bringing about harmful or offensive contact with plaintiff's person;
2.   Defendant's intent to bring about such contact OR to create the apprehension of immediate contact; and
3.   Causation.

Option C suggests that provocation is a valid defense to battery. In fact, it's not. If the facts were different, and Kane's taunts had prompted Poe to *kill* him, the conduct may be enough to reduce murder to manslaughter (due to provocation), but that's criminal law. Instead, in tort law, provocation would have to rise to the level of justifying self defense to be a valid defense.

Instead, what's at element under these facts is the *intent* element of battery, since it's not clear under these facts that intent exists, and as a result the best response would have to address this point. Since C doesn't, and offers an invalid potential defense, it's not the best response.

(D) isn't the best response,
because the fact it offers is not determinative of Kane's recovery.

There are three elements in a prima facie claim of battery:

1. Defendant's act bringing about harmful or offensive contact with plaintiff's person;
2. Defendant's intent to bring about such contact OR to create the apprehension of immediate contact; and
3. Causation.

Option D suggests that Kane's trespasser status gave Poe the privilege to use the force he used. While there *is* a defense based on defense of property, there are two principal reasons it wouldn't apply here. First, a valid defense on this basis requires a request to desist, unless it would be dangerous or futile, before physical force is used. Under these facts there's no evidence of such a request. Second, the privilege would only entitle Poe to use *reasonable* force. Putting out a couple of teeth would exceed the scope of Poe's privilege, and constitute a battery (if the act were intentional). Since D misapplies the defense of property defense to these facts, it's not the best response.

Answer 68

(B) is the best response,
because the defense of defense-of-others would be negated if John's belief about the danger was unreasonable.

Since John has intentionally caused a harmful or offensive contact with another, he's liable for battery unless he has a defense. The only defense that plausibly applies here is "defense of others." That is, just as a person has the right to use self-defense to save himself from harm, he has that right with respect to another person who is threatened with harm (even a stranger, under the modern view).

However, the defense-of-others defense, like the right of self-defense, requires that both the actor's belief that danger exists, and his belief that the proposed conduct is a good way to deal with the danger, be reasonable. If John should have realized that Karen was not in fact in danger, this requirement for the defense-of-others defense would not exist.

(A) is not the best response,
because the fact that an alternative method of dealing with the danger might have solved the problem does not automatically mean that John's method was unreasonable.

As described in the analysis of Choice (B) above, John was entitled to the defense of defense-of-others unless either his choice of methods, or his belief in Karen's peril, was unreasonable. The mere fact that the alternative method of shouting a warning might have solved the problem doesn't mean that John's

approach was unreasonable. (For one thing, pushing Karen to the ground merely threatened minor injury, whereas if she were hit she might well be killed or seriously injured. For another, John could reasonably have believed that Karen wouldn't hear his shout, that she wouldn't know that she was the one being shouted at, or that there wasn't time for her to react if she did hear.)

(C) is not the best response,
because John might be jointly-and-severally liable with the driver.

The speeding driver would clearly be *a* cause of the injury, and would therefore likely be jointly-and-severally liable with John if John was liable. But this fact wouldn't save John from liability, if John's choice of methods (or his belief in the danger) were unreasonable. Always remember that a given injury can have multiple causes, and can thus lead to multiple tortfeasors (even if they did not act in concert) being held jointly liable.

Here, John's liability would (as discussed in the analysis of choice (B)) turn on the reasonableness of his belief in the danger, not on the existence of some other jointly-acting cause.

(D) is not the best response,
because John's intent to save Karen wouldn't immunize him if his belief in the danger was unreasonable.

As is discussed in the analysis of Choice (B), John only qualifies for the defense of defense-of-others if his belief in the existence of the danger, and his choice of methods, were reasonable. Since Choice (D) ignores this fact, and focuses only on the genuineness of John's desire to save Karen, it is incorrect.

Answer 69

(C) is the best response,
because Patron cannot prove Restaurant actually caused him to get sick.

Plaintiff bears the burden of proving by a preponderance of the evidence that defendant actually caused his injury, just as he must bear the burden of proving the other parts of his prima facie case.

Under these facts, Patron cannot produce any real evidence that Restaurant caused him to become sick. At best Patron can introduce facts that raise a mere suspicion that Restaurant was the cause. All Patron can show is that he had an upset stomach later in the evening and that various health code violations had been found at the restaurant. What he cannot show is that the meal was the but-for cause of his becoming ill; that is, but for Restaurant's actions Patron would not have become ill. In response to Patron's facts, Restaurant can show that Patron had three meals after eating in their restaurant, any of which could have caused his infection. Restaurant could also argue that the bacterium causing Patron's illness could have come from Patron's own hands. While this "no causation" defense might not work, it is Restaurant's best chance of those defenses listed.

(A) is not the best response,

because the fact that no one else became ill creates only an inference that Restaurant was not the cause.

The fact that no one else got sick certainly doesn't prove that Restaurant wasn't the cause — perhaps one employee failed to wash his hands, prepared the one dish eaten by Patron, then washed them. In any event, Restaurant is better off making the much more general argument (listed in Choice (C)) that Patron is required to make an affirmative showing that the Restaurant's negligence caused the illness, and that he has failed to carry this burden by a preponderance of the evidence.

(B) is not the best response,

because Restaurant is responsible for the acts of its employees while in the course of their duties, even if they disregard instructions.

Under the doctrine of respondeat superior, an employer is vicariously liable for the negligent acts of its employees, done within the scope of the employment. The fact that the employee has disobeyed rules formulated by the employer is not a defense. Thus as long as there was evidence that an employee failed to wash her hands and then prepared a dish eaten by Patron, the fact that this happened in violation of Restaurant's instructions would not prevent respondeat superior from applying against it.

(D) is not the best response,

because Patron brought suit for an illness caused by bacterium, not an upset stomach caused by spicy food.

The assumption of the risk doctrine bars a plaintiff from recovery if he voluntarily consented to take the chance that the harm will occur.

Here Patron may have assumed the risk of an upset stomach caused by spicy food, but he did not assume the risk of becoming ill because of a bacterium in contaminated food. Without voluntary consent, there can be no assumption of the risk.

Answer 70

(A) is the best response,

because a landowner may not use deadly force to defend property.

Defense of property is a defense to an intentional tort — one may use *reasonable* force to prevent trespass, or other interference with one's land or chattels. However, deadly force (i.e., force that is likely to cause death or serious bodily harm) cannot be used except to prevent an intrusion that is likely to cause death or serious injury to the inhabitants. When a property owner uses force indirectly, by means of an automatic mechanical device like the one here, the case is judged by the same standards as if the owner were acting directly. Consequently, if a live person in the owner's

position would not reasonably have believed that the intruder posed a serious risk of death or serious injury to the inhabitants, use of the deadly-force mechanical device would not be privileged.

By this standard, even though Seller was an outright trespasser, because he did not pose a threat of death or serious bodily harm Hermit was only be entitled to use reasonable, non-deadly force to deter him.

(B) is not the best response,

because even if the intent is only to deter, deadly force cannot be used against trespassers who do not pose a threat of death or serious injury to the inhabitants, as is more fully explained in the analysis of Choice (A).

(C) is not the best response,

because deadly force cannot be used against non-dangerous trespassers, even if a warning is given.

As is described more fully in the treatment of Choice (A), deadly force cannot be used against trespassers who do not pose a threat of death or serious injury to the inhabitants. This rule is true even if the owner gives a warning against entry. (In any event, the warning here did not even specify that serious force, posing the risk of bodily injury or death, would be used, so it's doubly unlikely to immunize Hermit from liability.)

(D) is not the best response,

because even if Hermit did reasonably fear that intruders would come to harm him or his family, Seller himself did not pose such a danger.

When an owner uses an automatic mechanical devices to protect against intruders, the situation is judged by the same standards as if the owner were personally applying the force. Therefore, the mechanical device can supply deadly force (force likely to cause death or serious bodily injury) only if the owner could do so personally on the particular occasion in question. An owner could use such deadly force only if the owner reasonably feared, in that particular situation, that the intruder posed a risk of death or serious bodily harm to the owner or other inhabitants.

Here, one in Owner's position would have realized that Seller was unlikely to pose such harm, and was instead a salesman. Since Owner would not have been entitled to use deadly force "by hand" against Seller (e.g., by shooting him), he is not protected when his automatic device applied deadly force.

QUESTIONS
PRACTICE MBE — A.M. EXAM

<u>Directions</u>: Each of the questions or incomplete statements below is followed by four suggested answers or completions. You are to choose the <u>best</u> of the stated alternatives. Answer all questions according to the generally accepted view, except where otherwise noted.

For the purposes of this test, you are to assume that Articles 1 and 2 of the Uniform Commercial Code have been adopted. You are also to assume relevant application of Article 9 of the UCC concerning fixtures. The Federal Rules of Evidence are deemed to control. The terms "Constitution," "constitutional," and "unconstitutional" refer to the federal Constitution unless indicated to the contrary. You are to assume that there is no applicable statute unless otherwise specified; however, survival actions and claims for wrongful death should be assumed to be available where applicable. You should assume that joint and several liability, with pure comparative negligence, is the relevant rule unless otherwise indicated.

QUESTIONS

PRACTICE MBE — A.M. EXAM

Question 1

Davis decided to kill Adams. He set out for Adams' house. Before he got there he saw Brooks, who resembled Adams. Thinking Brooks was Adams, Davis shot at Brooks. The shot missed Brooks but wounded Case, who was some distance away. Davis had not seen Case.

In a prosecution under a statute that proscribes attempt to commit murder, the district attorney should indicate that the intended victim(s) was (were)

(A) Adams only
(B) Brooks only
(C) Case only
(D) Adams and Brooks

Question 2

A state statute requires any person licensed to sell prescription drugs to file with the State Board of Health a report listing the types and amounts of such drugs sold if his sales of such drugs exceed $50,000 during the calendar year. The statute makes it a misdemeanor to "knowingly fail to file" such a report.

Nelson, who is licensed to sell prescription drugs, sold $63,000 worth of prescription drugs during 1976 but did not file the report. Charged with committing the misdemeanor, Nelson testified that he did a very poor job of keeping records and did not realize that his sales of prescription drugs had exceeded $50,000. If the jury believes Nelson he should be found

(A) guilty, because this is a public welfare offense
(B) guilty, because he cannot be excused on the basis of his own failure to keep proper records
(C) not guilty, because the statute punishes omissions and he was not given fair warning of his duty to act
(D) not guilty, because he was not aware of the value of the drugs he had sold

Question 3

Lender met Borrower on the street, demanded that Borrower pay a debt owed to Lender, and threatened to punch Borrower in the nose. A fight ensued between them. Mann came upon the scene just as Lender was about to kick Borrower in the head. Noting that Lender was getting the better of the fight, Mann pointed a gun at Lender and said, "Stop, or I'll shoot." If Lender asserts a claim against Mann based on assault, will Lender prevail?

(A) Yes, because Mann threatened to use deadly force
(B) Yes, unless Mann was related to Borrower
(C) No, if it was apparent that Lender was about to inflict

serious bodily harm upon Borrower
(D) No, because Lender was the original aggressor by threatening Borrower with a battery

Question 4

Peter sued Don for breach of contract. The court admitted testimony by Peter that Don and his wife quarreled frequently, a fact of no consequence to the lawsuit. Don seeks to testify in response that he and his wife never quarreled. The court

(A) must permit Don to answer if he had objected to Peter's testimony
(B) may permit Don to answer, whether or not he had objected to Peter's testimony
(C) may permit Don to answer only if he had objected to Peter's testimony
(D) cannot permit Don to answer, whether or not he had objected to Peter's testimony

Questions 5-7 are based on the following fact situation.

Ames had painted Bell's house under a contract which called for payment of $2,000. Bell, contending in good faith that the porch had not been painted properly, refused to pay anything.

On June 15, Ames mailed a letter to Bell stating, "I am in serious need of money. Please send the $2,000 to me before July 1." On June 18, Bell replied "I will settle for $1,800 provided you agree to repaint the porch." Ames did not reply to this letter.

Thereafter, Bell mailed a check for $1,800 marked "Payment in full on the Ames-Bell painting contract as per letter dated June 18." Ames received the check on June 30. Because he was badly in need of money, Ames cashed the check without objection and spent the proceeds but has refused to repaint the porch.

Question 5

Bell's refusal to pay anything to Ames when he finished painting was a

(A) partial breach of contract only if Ames had properly or substantially painted the porch
(B) partial breach of contract whether or not Ames had properly or substantially painted the porch
(C) total breach of contract only if Ames had properly or substantially painted the porch
(D) total breach of contract whether or not Ames had properly or substantially painted the porch.

Question 6

After cashing the check Ames sued Bell for $200.00. Ames probably will

(A) succeed if he can prove that he had painted the porch according to specifications

(B) succeed, because he cashed the check under economic duress

(C) not succeed, because he cashed the check without objection

(D) not succeed, because he is entitled to recover only the reasonable value of his services

Question 7

In an action by Bell against Ames for any provable damages Bell sustained because the porch was not repainted, Bell probably will

(A) succeed, because by cashing the check Ames impliedly promised to repaint the porch

(B) succeed, because Ames accepted Bell's offer by not replying to the letter of June 18

(C) not succeed, because Bell's letter of June 18 was a counter-offer which Ames never accepted

(D) not succeed, because there is no consideration to support Ames's promise, if any

Questions 8-11 are based on the following fact situation.

The State of Aurora requires licenses of persons "who are engaged in the trade of barbering." It will grant such licenses only to those who are graduates of barber schools located in Aurora, who have resided in the state for two years, and who are citizens of the United States.

Question 8

The requirement that candidates for license must be graduates of barber schools in Aurora is probably

(A) unconstitutional as an undue burden on interstate commerce

(B) unconstitutional as a violation of the privileges and immunities clause of the Fourteenth Amendment

(C) constitutional, because the state does not know the quality of out-of-state barber schools

(D) constitutional, because barbering is a privilege and not a right

Question 9

The requirement that candidates for licenses must be citizens is

(A) constitutional as an effort to ensure that barbers speak English adequately

(B) constitutional as an exercise of the state's police power

(C) unconstitutional as a bill of attainder

(D) unconstitutional as a denial of equal protection

Question 10

Assume that a resident of the state of Aurora was denied a license because she had been graduated from an out-of-state barber school. Her suit in federal court to enjoin denial of the license on this ground would be

(A) dismissed, because there is no diversity of citizenship

(B) dismissed because of the abstention doctrine

(C) decided on the merits, because federal jurisdiction extends to controversies between two states

(D) decided on the merits, because a federal question is involved

Question 11

Which of the following is the strongest ground on which to challenge the requirement that candidates for barber licenses must have been residents of the state for at least two years?

(A) The privileges and immunities clause of the Fourteenth Amendment

(B) The due process clause of the Fourteenth Amendment

(C) The equal protection clause of the Fourteenth Amendment

(D) The obligation of contracts clause

Question 12

John was fired from his job. Too proud to apply for unemployment benefits, he used his savings to feed his family. When one of his children became ill, he did not seek medical attention for the child at a state clinic because he did not want to accept what he regarded as charity. Eventually, weakened by malnutrition, the child died as a result of the illness. John has committed

(A) murder

(B) involuntary manslaughter

(C) voluntary manslaughter

(D) no form of criminal homicide

Questions 13-14 are based on the following fact situation.

Professor Merrill, in a lecture in her psychology course at a private university, described an experiment in which a group of college students in a neighboring city rushed out and washed cars stopped at traffic lights during the rush hour. She described how people reacted differently – with shock, joy, and surprise. At the conclusion of her report, she said, "You understand, of course, that you are not to undertake this or any other experiment unless you first clear with me." Four of Merrill's students decided to try the same experiment but did not clear with Merrill.

One subject of their experiment, Carr, said, "I was shocked. There were two people on each side of the car. At first I thought negatively. I thought they were going to attack me and thought of driving away. Then I quieted down and decided there were too many dirty cars in the city anyway."

Charitable immunity has been abolished in the jurisdiction.

Question 13

If Carr asserts a claim against the students who washed his car, his best theory is

(A) assault
(B) negligence
(C) invasion of privacy
(D) false imprisonment

Question 14

If Carr has a valid claim against the students, will he also prevail against the university?

(A) Yes, if the students would not have performed the experiment but for Merrill's lecture.
(B) Yes, if Carr's claim against the students is based on negligence.
(C) No, because the students were not Merrill's employees.
(D) No, because Merrill did not authorize the car as a class project.

Question 15

Oxnard owned Goldacre, a tract of land, in fee simple. At a time when Goldacre was in the adverse possession of Amos, Eric obtained the oral permission of Oxnard to use as a road or driveway a portion of Goldacre to reach adjoining land, Twin Pines, which Eric owned in fee simple. Thereafter, during all times relevant to this problem, Eric used this road between Goldacre regularly for ingress and egress between Twin Pines and a public highway.

Amos quit possession of Goldacre before acquiring title by adverse possession. Without any further communication between Oxnard and Eric, Eric continued to use the road for a total period, from the time he first began to use it, sufficient to acquire an easement by prescription. Oxnard then blocked the road and refused to permit its continued use. Eric brought suit to determine his right to continue use of the road. Eric should

(A) win, because his user was adverse to Amos and once adverse it continued adverse until some affirmative showing of a change
(B) win, because Eric made no attempt to renew permission after Amos quit possession of Goldacre
(C) lose, because his user was with permission
(D) lose, because there is no evidence that he continued adverse user for the required period after Amos quit possession

Question 16-17 are based on the following fact situation.

A brother and sister, Bruce and Sharon, acquired as joint tenants a twenty-acre parcel of land called Greenacre. They contributed equally to the purchase price. Several years later, Bruce proposed that they build an apartment development on Greenacre. Sharon rejected the proposal but orally agreed with Bruce that Bruce could go ahead on his own on the northerly half of Greenacre and Sharon could do what she wished with the southerly half of Greenacre. Bruce proceeded to build an apartment development on, and generally developed and improved, the northerly ten acres of Greenacre. Sharon orally permitted the southerly ten acres of Greenacre to be used by the Audubon Society as a nature preserve. Bruce died, leaving his entire estate to his son, Stanley. The will named Sharon as executrix of his will, but she refused so to serve.

Question 16

In an appropriate action to determine the respective interests of Sharon and Stanley in Greenacre, if Stanley is adjudged to be the owner of the northerly ten acres of Greenacre, the most likely reason for the judgment will be that

(A) the close blood relationship between Sharon and Bruce removes the necessity to comply with the Statute of Frauds
(B) Sharon's conduct during Bruce's lifetime estops her from asserting title to the northerly half of Greenacre
(C) the joint tenancy was terminated by the oral agreement of Sharon and Bruce at the time it was made
(D) Sharon has a fiduciary obligation to her nephew Stanley by reason of her being named executrix of Bruce's will

Question 17

In an appropriate action to determine the respective interests of Sharon and Stanley in Greenacre, if Sharon is adjudged to be the owner of all of Greenacre, the most likely reason for the judgement will be that

(A) the Statute of Frauds prevents the proof of Sharon's oral agreement
(B) Bruce could not unilaterally sever the joint tenancy
(C) Sharon's nomination as executrix of Bruce's estate does not prevent her from asserting her claim against Stanley
(D) the record title of the joint tenancy in Greenacre can be changed only by a duly recorded instrument

Question 18

Mary Webb, a physician, called as a witness by the defendant in the case *Parr v. Doan*, was asked to testify to statements made by Michael Zadok, her patient, for the purpose of obtaining treatment from Dr. Webb. Which of the following is the best basis for excluding evidence of

Zadok's statements in a jurisdiction with a doctor-patient privilege?

(A) An objection by Dr. Webb asserting her privilege against disclosure of confidential communications made by a patient

(B) An objection by Parr's attorney on the grounds of the doctor-patient privilege

(C) A finding by the trial judge that Zadok had left the office without actually receiving treatment

(D) The assertion of a privilege by Zadok's attorney, present at the trial as a spectator at Zadok's request, and allowed by the trial judge to speak

Question 19

A leading question is LEAST likely to be permitted over objection when

(A) asked on cross-examination of an expert witness

(B) asked on direct examination of a young child

(C) asked on direct examination of a disinterested eyewitness

(D) related to preliminary matters such as the name or occupation of the witness

Questions 20-21 are based on the following fact situation.

Passer was driving his pickup truck along a lonely road on a very cold night. Passer saw Tom, who was a stranger, lying in a field by the side of the road and apparently injured. Passer stopped his truck, alighted, and, upon examining Tom, discovered that Tom was intoxicated and in danger of suffering from exposure to the cold. However, Passer returned to his truck and drove away without making any effort to help Tom. Tom remained lying at the same place and was later injured when struck by a car driven by Traveler, who was drowsy and inattentive, had veered off the road into the field and hit Tom. Traveler did not see Tom prior to hitting him.

Question 20

If Tom asserts a claim against Passer for damages for his injuries, will Tom prevail?

(A) Yes, because by stopping and examining Tom, Passer assumed a duty to aid him.

(B) Yes, if a reasonably prudent person under the circumstances would have aided Tom.

(C) No, if Passer did not, in any way, make Tom's situation worse.

(D) No, because Tom himself created the risk of harm by becoming intoxicated.

Question 21

If Tom asserts a claim against Traveler, will Tom prevail?

(A) Yes, because Traveler was negligent in going off the road.

(B) Yes, because Tom was in a helpless condition.

(C) No, because Traveler did not see Tom before Tom was struck.

(D) No, because Tom's intoxication was the cause in fact of his harm.

Question 22

Roofer entered into a written contract with Orissa to repair the roof of Orissa's home, the repairs to be done "in a workmanlike manner." Roofer completed the repairs and took all of his equipment away, with the exception of a 20-foot extension ladder, which was left against the side of the house. He intended to come back and get the ladder the next morning. At that time, Orissa and her family were away on a trip. During the night, a thief, using the ladder to gain access to an upstairs window, entered the house and stole some valuable jewels. Orissa has asserted a claim against Roofer for damages for the loss of the jewels.

In her claim against Roofer, Orissa will

(A) prevail, because by leaving the ladder Roofer became a trespasser on Orissa's property

(B) prevail, because by leaving the ladder, Roofer created the risk that a person might unlawfully enter the house

(C) not prevail, because the act of the thief was a superseding cause

(D) not prevail, because Orissa's claim is limited to damages for breach of contract

Question 23

Homer and Purcell entered into a valid, enforceable written contract by which Homer agreed to sell and Purcell agreed to purchase Blackacre, which was Homer's residence. One of the contract provisions was that after closing Homer had the right to remain in residence at Blackacre for up to 30 days before delivering possession to Purcell. The closing took place as scheduled. Title passed to Purcell and Homer remained in possession. Within a few days after the closing, the new house next door which was being constructed for Homer was burned to the ground, and at the end of the 30-day period Homer refused to move out of Blackacre; instead, Homer tendered to Purcell a monthly rental payment in excess of the fair rental value of Blackacre. Purcell rejected the proposal and that day brought an appropriate action to gain immediate possession of Blackacre. The contract was silent as to the consequences of Homer's failure to give up possession within the 30-day period, and the jurisdiction in which Blackacre is located has no statute dealing directly with this situation, although the landlord-tenant law of the jurisdiction requires a landlord to give a tenant 30 days notice before a tenant may be evicted. Purcell did not give Homer any such 30-day statutory notice. Purcell's best legal argument in support of his action to gain immediate possession is that Homer is a

(A) trespasser *ab initio*

(B) licensee

(C) tenant at sufferance

(D) tenant from month to month

Questions 24-25 are based on the following fact situation.

Albert engaged Bertha, an inexperienced actress, to do a small role in a new Broadway play for a period of six months at a salary of $200 a week. Bertha turned down another role in order to accept this engagement. On the third day of the run, Bertha was hospitalized with influenza and Helen was hired to do the part. A week later, Bertha recovered, but Albert refused to accept her services for the remainder of the contract period. Bertha then brought an action against Albert for breach of contract.

Question 24

Which of the following is Bertha's best legal theory?

(A) Her acting contract with Albert was legally severable into weekly units.
(B) Her performance of the literal terms of the contract was physically impossible.
(C) Her reliance on the engagement with Albert by declining another acting role created an estoppel against Albert.
(D) Her failure to perform for one week was not a material failure so as to discharge Albert's duty to perform.

Question 25

Which of the following, if true, would adversely affect Bertha's rights in her action against Albert?

(A) Albert could not find any substitute except Helen, who demanded a contract for a minimum of six months if she was to perform at all.
(B) Helen, by general acclaim, was much better in the role than Bertha had been.
(C) Albert had offered Bertha a position as Helen's understudy at a salary of $100 a week, which Bertha declined.
(D) Albert had offered Bertha a secretarial position at a salary of $300 a week, which Bertha declined.

Question 26

Park sued Dent for breach of an oral contract which Dent denied making. Weston testified that he heard Dent make the contract on July 7. Dent discredited Weston, and Park offers evidence of Weston's good reputation for truthfulness. The rehabilitation is most likely to be permitted if the discrediting evidence by Dent was testimony that

(A) Weston had been promoting highly speculative stocks
(B) Weston had been Park's college roommate
(C) Weston had attended a school for mentally retarded children
(D) Weston had been out of town the whole week of July 4-10

Question 27-28 are based on the following fact situation.

Lawyers Abel and Baker are the members of the law partnership of Abel and Baker in a small town that has only one other lawyer in it. Abel and Baker do a substantial amount of personal injury work. Client was severely and permanently injured in an automobile collision when struck by an automobile driven by Motorist. Client employed the Abel and Baker firm to represent her in obtaining damages for her injuries. At the time Client employed Abel and Baker, the statute of limitations had six weeks to run on her claim. The complaint was prepared but not filed. Abel and Baker each thought that the other would file the complaint. The statute of limitations ran out on Client's claim against Motorist.

Client has filed suit against Abel and Baker for negligence. That case is on trial with a jury in a court of general jurisdiction.

Question 27

In order to establish a breach of standard of care owed to her by Abel and Baker, Client

(A) must have a legal expert from the same locality that defendants' conduct was a breach
(B) must have a legal expert from the same state testify that defendants' conduct was a breach
(C) can rely on the application of the jurors' common knowledge as to whether there was a breach
(D) can rely on the judge, as an expert in the law, to advise the jury whether there was a breach

Question 28

Client has filed suit against Abel and Baker for negligence. That case is on trial with a jury in a court of general jurisdiction.

In addition to proving that Abel and Baker were negligent, Client must establish, as a minimum, that she

(A) would have, but for her lawyers' negligence, recovered from Motorist
(B) had a good faith claim against Motorist that was lost by her lawyers' negligence
(C) was severely and permanently injured when struck by Motorist's automobile
(D) did not negligently contribute to the failure to have the complaint filed

Question 29

A state statute divides murder into degrees. First degree murder is defined as murder with premeditation and deliberation or a homicide in the commission of arson, rape, robbery, burglary or kidnapping. Second degree murder is all other murder at common law.

In which of the following situations is Defendant most likely to be guilty of first degree murder?

(A) Immediately after being insulted by Robert, Defendant takes a knife and stabs and kills Robert.

(B) Angered over having been struck by Sam, Defendant buys rat poison and puts it in Sam's coffee. Sam drinks the coffee and dies as a result.

(C) Intending to injure Fred, Defendant lies in wait and, as Fred comes by, Defendant strikes him with a broom handle. As a result of the blow, Fred dies.

(D) Defendant, highly intoxicated, discovers a revolver on a table. He picks it up, points it at Alice, and pulls the trigger. The gun discharges, and Alice is killed.

Question 30

On a camping trip in a state park, Rose discovered metal signs near a rubbish heap stating, "Natural Wildlife Area – No Hunting." She took two of the signs and used them to decorate her room at home. She is charged with violation of a state statute which provides, "Any person who appropriates to his own use property owned by the state shall be guilty of a crime and shall be punished by a fine of not more than $1,000, or by imprisonment for not more than five years, or by both such fine and imprisonment."

At trial, Rose admits taking the signs but says she believed they had been thrown away. In fact, the signs had not been abandoned.

Rose should be found

(A) guilty, because this is a public welfare offense

(B) guilty, because she should have inquired whether the signs were abandoned

(C) not guilty if the jury finds she honestly believed the signs had been abandoned

(D) not guilty unless the jury finds that the state had taken adequate steps to inform the public that the signs had not been abandoned.

Question 31

Ted frequently visited Janet, his next-door neighbor. Janet was separated from her husband, Howard. Howard resided with his mother but jointly owned the house in which Janet resided. Late one night, Ted and Janet were sitting on the bed in Janet's bedroom drinking when Howard burst through the door and told Ted, "Get out!" When Ted refused, Howard challenged him to go outside and "fight it out." Ted again refused. Howard then pulled a knife from his pocket and lunged at Ted. Ted grabbed a lamp, struck Howard on the head, and killed him. Ted is charged with murder. On a charge of murder, Ted should be found

(A) not guilty, because Ted had as much right as Howard to be in the house

(B) not guilty, because Howard attacked Ted with a deadly weapon

(C) guilty, because Ted's presence in Janet's bedroom prompted Howard's attack

(D) guilty, because Ted's failure to obey Howard's order to leave the house made him a trespasser

Question 32-34 are based on the following fact situation.

In 1990, Oscar, owner of a 100-acre tract, prepared and duly recorded a subdivision plan called Happy Acres. The plan showed 90 one-acre lots and a ten-acre tract in the center that was designated "Future Public School." Oscar published and distributed a brochure promoting Happy Acres which emphasized the proximity of the lots to the school property and indicated potential tax savings "because the school district will not have to expend tax money to acquire this property." There is no specific statute concerning the dedication of school sites.

Oscar sold 50 of the lots to individual purchasers. Each deed referred to the recorded plan and also contained the following clause: "No mobile homes shall be erected on any lot within Happy Acres." Sarah was one of the original purchasers from Oscar.

In 1996, Oscar sold the remaining 40 lots and the ten-acre tract to Max by a deed which referred to the plan and contained the restriction relating to mobile homes. Max sold the 40 lots to individual purchasers and the ten-acre tract to Pete. None of the deeds from Max referred to the plan or contained any reference to mobile homes.

Question 32

Assume for this question only that Pete has announced his intention of erecting a fast food restaurant on the ten-acre tract and that Sarah has filed an action to enjoin Pete. If Sarah wins, it will be because

(A) Sarah has an equitable servitude concerning the use of the tract

(B) Sarah, as a taxpayer, has legal interest in the use of the tract

(C) Sarah is a creditor beneficiary of Oscar's promise with respect to the tract

(D) Pete is not a bona fide purchaser

Question 33

Assume for this question only that Joe, who purchased his lot from Max, has placed a mobile home on it and that Sarah brings an action against Joe to force him to remove it. The result of this action will be in favor of

(A) Sarah, because the restrictive covenant in her deed runs with the land

(B) Sarah, because the presence of the mobile home may adversely affect the market value of her land

(C) Joe, because his deed did not contain the restrictive covenant

(D) Joe, because he is not a direct but a remote grantee of Oscar

Question 34

Assume for this question only that in 1997 the school board of the district in which Happy Acres is situated has voted to erect a new school on the ten-acre tract. In an appropriate action between the school board and Pete to determine title, the result will be in favor of

(A) Pete, because the school board has been guilty of laches

(B) Pete, because his deed did not refer to the subdivision plan

(C) the school board, because Pete had constructive notice of the proposed use of the tract

(D) the school board, because there has been a dedication and acceptance of the tract

Questions 35-38 are based on the following fact situation.

On March 1, Zeller orally agreed to sell his land, Homestead, to Byer for $46,000 to be paid on March 31. Byer orally agreed to pay $25,000 of the purchase price to Quincy in satisfaction of a debt which Zeller said he had promised to pay Quincy.

On March 10, Byer dictated the agreement to his secretary but omitted all reference to the payment of the $25,000 to Quincy. In typing the agreement, the secretary mistakenly typed in $45,000 rather than $46,000 as the purchase price. Neither Byer nor Zeller carefully read the writing before signing it on March 15. Neither noticed the error in price and neither raised any question concerning omission of the payment to Quincy.

Question 35

In an action by Quincy against Byer for $25,000, which of the following is (are) correct?

I. Byer could successfully raise the Statute of Frauds as a defense because the Byer-Zeller agreement was to answer for the debt of another.

II. Byer could successfully raise the Statute of Frauds as a defense because the Byer-Zeller agreement was for the sale of an interest in land.

(A) I only

(B) II only

(C) Both I and II

(D) Neither I or II

Question 36

Which of the following would be most important in deciding an action by Quincy against Byer for $25,000?

(A) Whether the Byer-Zeller agreement was completely integrated

(B) Whether Byer was negligent in not having carefully read the written agreement

(C) Whether Zeller was negligent in not having carefully read the written agreement

(D) Whether Quincy was a party to the contract

Question 37

In an action by Quincy against Byer for $25,000, which of the following, if proved, would best serve Byer as a defense?

(A) There was no consideration to support Zeller's antecedent promise to pay Quincy the $25,000.

(B) On March 5, before Quincy was aware of the oral agreement between Zeller and Byer, Zeller agreed with Byer not to pay any part of the purchase price to Quincy.

(C) Whatever action Quincy may have had against Zeller was barred by the statute of limitations prior to March 1.

(D) Before he instituted his action against Byer, Quincy had not notified either Byer or Zeller that he had accepted the Byer-Zeller arrangement for paying Quincy.

Question 38

If Byer refused to pay more than $45,000 for Homestead, in an action by Zeller against Byer for an additional $1,000, it would be to Zeller's advantage to try to prove that

(A) the writing was intended only as a sham

(B) the writing was only a partial integration

(C) there was a mistake in integration

(D) there was a misunderstanding between Zeller and Byer concerning the purchase price

Questions 39-41 are based on the following fact situation.

House owns his home in City. On the lawn in front of his home and within five feet of the public sidewalk there was a large tree. The roots of the tree caused the sidewalk to buckle severely and become dangerous. An ordinance of City requires adjacent landowners to keep sidewalks in safe condition. House engaged Contractor to repair the sidewalk, leaving it to Contractor to decide how the repair should be made.

Contractor dug up the sidewalk, cut back the roots of the tree, and laid a new sidewalk. Two days after House had paid Contractor the agreed price of the repair, the tree fell over onto the street and damaged a parked car belonging to Driver.

Driver has asserted claims against House and Contractor, and both defendants admit that cutting the roots caused the tree to fall.

Question 39

The theory on which Driver is most likely to prevail against House is that House is

(A) strictly liable, because the tree was on his property

(B) liable for Contractor's negligence if, to House's knowledge, Contractor was engaged in a hazardous activity

(C) liable, because he assumed responsibility when he paid Contractor for the repair

(D) liable on the basis of *respondeat superior*

Question 40

In the claim of Driver against Contractor, the best defense of Contractor is that

(A) the tree was on the property of House

(B) he repaired the sidewalk at the direction of House

(C) he could not reasonably foresee that the tree would fall

(D) he was relieved of liability when House paid for the repair

Question 41

If Driver recovers a judgment against House, does House have any recourse against Contractor?

(A) No, if payment by House was an acceptance of the work.

(B) No, because House selected Contractor to do the work.

(C) Yes, if the judgment against House was based on vicarious liability.

(D) Yes, because House's conduct was not a factual cause of the harm.

Question 42

The State of Rio Grande entered into a contract with Roads, Inc., for construction of a four-lane turnpike. Prior to commencement of construction, the legislature, in order to provide funds for parks, repealed the statute authorizing the turnpike and cancelled the agreement with Roads, Inc. Roads, Inc., sued the state to enforce its original agreement. In ruling on this case, the court should hold that the state statute cancelling the agreement is

(A) valid, because constitutionally the sovereign is not liable except with its own consent

(B) valid, because the legislature is vested with constitutional authority to repeal laws it has enacted

(C) invalid, because a state is equitably estopped to disclaim a valid bid once accepted by it

(D) invalid because of the constitutional prohibition against impairment of contracts

Question 43

The strongest constitutional basis for the enactment of a federal statute requiring colleges and universities receiving federal funds to offer student aid solely on the basis of need is the

(A) police power

(B) war and defense power

(C) power to tax and spend for the general welfare

(D) power to enforce the privileges and immunities clause of the Fourteenth Amendment

Question 44

Pace sues Def Company for injuries suffered when Pace's car collided with Def Company's truck. Def's general manager prepared a report of the accident at the request of the company's attorney in preparation for the trial, and delivered the report to the attorney. Pace demands that the report be produced. Will production of the report be required?

(A) Yes, because business reports are not generally privileged.

(B) No, because it is privileged communication from the client to the attorney.

(C) No, because such reports contain hearsay.

(D) No, because such reports are self-serving.

Question 45-46 are based on the following fact situation.

In 1930, Owens, the owner in fee simple of Barrenacres, a large, undeveloped tract of land, granted an easement to the Water District "to install, inspect, repair, maintain, and replace pipes" within a properly delineated strip of land twenty feet wide across Barrenacres. The easement permitted the Water District to enter Barrenacres for only the stated purposes. The Water District promptly and properly recorded the deed. In 1931, the Water District installed a water main which crossed Barrenacres within the described strip; the Water District has not since entered Barrenacres.

In 1935, Owens sold Barrenacres to Peterson, but the deed, which was promptly and properly recorded, failed to refer to the Water District easement. Peterson built his home on Barrenacres in 1935, and since that time he has planted and maintained, at great expense in money, time, and effort, a formal garden area which covers, among other areas, the surface of the twenty-foot easement strip.

In 1976, the Water District proposed to excavate the entire length of its main in order to inspect, repair, and replace the main, to the extent necessary. At a public meeting, at which Peterson was present, the Water District announced its plans and declared its intent to do as little damage as possible to any property involved. Peterson objected to the Water District plans.

Question 45

Peterson asked his attorney to secure an injunction against the Water District and its proposed entry upon his property. The best advice that the attorney can give is that Peterson's attempt to secure injunctive relief will be likely to

(A) succeed, because Peterson's deed from Owens did not mention the easement

(B) succeed, because more than forty years have passed since the Water District last entered Barrenacres

(C) fail, because the Water District's plan is within its rights

(D) fail, because the Water District's plan is fair and equitable

Question 46

Assume that Peterson reserved his rights and after the Water District completed its work sued for the $5,000 in damages he suffered by reason of the Water District entry. Peterson's attempt to secure damages probably will

(A) succeed, because his deed from Owens did not mention the easement

(B) succeed, because of an implied obligation imposed on the Water District to restore the surface to its condition prior to entry

(C) fail, because of the public interest in maintaining a continuous water supply

(D) fail, because the Water District acted within its rights

Question 47

In 1960 Omar, the owner in fee simple absolute, conveyed Stoneacre, a five-acre tract of land. The relevant, operative words of the deed conveyed to "Church [a duly organized religious body having power to hold property] for the life of my son, Carl, and from and after the death of my said son, Carl, to all of my grandchildren and their heirs and assigns in equal shares: provided, Church shall use the premises for church purposes only."

In an existing building on Stoneacre, Church immediately began to conduct religious services and other activities normally associated with a church.

In 1975, Church granted to Darin a right to remove sand and gravel from a one-half acre portion of Stoneacre upon the payment of royalty. Darin has regularly removed sand and gravel since 1975 and paid royalty to Church. Church has continued to conduct religious services and other church activities on Stoneacre.

All four of the living grandchildren of Omar, joined by a guardian ad litem to represent unborn grandchildren, instituted suit against Church and Darin seeking damages for the removal of sand and gravel and an injunction preventing further acts of removal. There is no applicable statute. Which of the following best describes the likely disposition of this lawsuit?

(A) The plaintiffs should succeed, because the interest of Church terminated with the first removal of sand and gravel

(B) Church and Darin should be enjoined, and damages should be recovered but impounded for future distribution

(C) The injunction should be granted, but damages should be denied, because Omar and Carl are not parties to the action

(D) Damage should be awarded, but the injunction should be denied.

Question 48

In which of the following cases is a conviction of the named defendant for robbery LEAST likely to be upheld?

(A) Johnson forced his way into a woman's home, bound her, and compelled her to tell him that her jewelry was in an adjoining room. Johnson went into the room, took the jewelry, and fled.

(B) A confederate of Brown pushed a man in order to cause him to lose his balance and drop his briefcase. Brown picked up the briefcase and ran off with it.

(C) Having induced a woman to enter his hotel room, Ritter forced her to telephone her maid to tell the maid to bring certain jewelry to the hotel. Ritter locked the woman in the bathroom while he accepted the jewelry from the maid when she arrived.

(D) Hayes unbuttoned the vest of a man too drunk to notice and removed his wallet. A minute later, the victim missed his wallet and accused Hayes of taking it. Hayes pretended to be insulted, slapped the victim, and went off with the wallet.

Questions 49-50 are based on the following fact situation.

Green is cited for contempt of the House of Representatives after she refused to answer certain questions posed by a House Committee concerning her acts while serving as a United States Ambassador. A federal statute authorizes the Attorney General to prosecute contempts of Congress. Pursuant to this law, the House directs the Attorney General to begin criminal proceedings against Green. A federal grand jury indicts Green, but the Attorney General refuses to sign the indictment.

Question 49

Which of the following best describes the constitutionality of the Attorney General's action?

(A) Illegal, because the Attorney General must prosecute if the House of Representatives directs

(B) Illegal, because the Attorney General must prosecute those who violate federal law

(C) Legal, because ambassadors are immune from prosecution for acts committed in the course of their duties

(D) Legal, because the decision to prosecute is an exclusively executive act

Question 50

If the Attorney General signs the indictment, the strongest argument Green could urge as a defense is that

(A) Green may refuse to answer the questions if she can demonstrate that they are unrelated to matters upon which Congress may legislate

(B) the House may question Green on matters pertaining to the expenditures of funds appropriated by Congress

(C) only the Senate may question Green on matters that

relate to the performance of her duties

(D) Congress may not ask questions relating to the performance of duties executed by an officer of the executive branch

Questions 51-52 are based on the following fact situation.

Congress decides that the application of the Uniform Consumer Credit Code should be the same throughout the United States. To that end, it enacts the UCCC as a federal law directly applicable to all consumer credit, small loans, and retail installment sales. The law is intended to protect borrowers and buyers against unfair practices by suppliers of consumer credit.

Question 51

Which of the following constitutional provisions may be most easily used to justify federal enactment of this statute?

(A) The obligation of contracts clause

(B) The privileges and immunities clause of the Fourteenth Amendment

(C) The commerce clause

(D) The equal protection clause of the Fourteenth Amendment

Question 52

A national religious organization makes loans throughout the country for the construction and furnishing of churches. The federal UCCC would substantially interfere with the successful accomplishment of that organization's religious objectives. The organization seeks to obtain a declaratory judgment that the federal law may not be applied to its lending activities. As a matter of constitutional law, which of the following best describes the burden that must be sustained?

(A) The federal government must demonstrate that the application of this statute to the lending activities of this organization is necessary to vindicate a compelling governmental interest.

(B) The federal government must demonstrate that a rational legislature could believe that this law helps to achieve a legitimate national interest when applied to both religious and secular lending activities.

(C) The organization must demonstrate that no reasonable legislator could think that application of the UCCC to this organization would be helpful in accomplishing a legitimate governmental objective.

(D) The organization must demonstrate a specific congressional purpose to inhibit the accomplishment of the organization's religious objectives.

Question 53-55 are based on the following fact situation.

Harry met Bill, who was known to him to be a burglar, in a bar. Harry told Bill that he needed money. He promised to pay Bill $500 if Bill would go to Harry's house the following night and take some silverware. Harry explained to Bill that, although the silverware was legally his, his wife would object to his selling it.

Harry pointed out his home, one of a group of similar tract houses. He drew a floor plan of the house that showed the location of the silverware. Harry said that his wife usually took several sleeping pills before retiring, and that he would make sure that she took them the next night. He promised to leave a window unlocked.

Everything went according to the plan except that Bill, deceived by the similarity of the tract houses, went to the wrong house. He found a window unlocked, climbed in and found silver where Harry had indicated. He took the silver to the cocktail lounge where the payoff was to take place. At that point the police arrested the two men.

If Harry were charged with burglary, his best argument for acquittal would be that

Question 53

(A) there was no breaking

(B) he consented to the entry

(C) no overt act was committed by him

(D) there was no intent to commit a felony

Question 54

Bill's best argument for acquittal of burglary is that he

(A) acted under a mistake of law

(B) had the consent of the owner

(C) reasonably thought he was in Harry's house

(D) found the window unlocked

Question 55

If Harry and Bill are charged with a conspiracy to commit burglary, their best argument for acquittal is that

(A) Bill was the alter ego of Harry

(B) they did not intend to commit burglary

(C) there was no overt act

(D) there was no agreement

Question 56-59 are based on the following fact situation.

Penn sues Duke's Bar for injuries suffered in an automobile accident caused by Chase, who had been a patron of Duke's Bar. Penn claims that Chase was permitted to drink too much liquor at Duke's Bar before the accident.

Wood, a patron of Duke's Bar, testified that on the night of the accident Chase was drunk. Wood then proposed to testify that he remarked to his companion, "Chase is so drunk he can't even stand up."

Question 56

Wood's remark to his companion is

(A) admissible as an excited utterance

(B) admissible as a prior consistent statement

(C) admissible as a statement by Wood regarding a condition he observed, made while he was observing it

(D) inadmissible if there was no evidence that Wood had expertise in determining drunkenness

Question 57

Duke's Bar called Chase to testify and expected him to say that he was sober when he left Duke's Bar; however, on direct examination Chase testified that he may have had a little too much to drink at Duke's Bar. Duke's Bar now seeks to confront Chase with his statement made on deposition that he was sober when he left Duke's Bar. Which of the following is true concerning this statement?

(A) It may be used only to refresh Chase's recollection

(B) It is admissible for impeachment and as substantive evidence that Chase was sober

(C) It is inadmissible, because Duke's Bar cannot impeach its own witness

(D) It is inadmissible, because it is hearsay not within any exception

Question 58

Penn offers evidence that, after the accident, the manager of Duke's Bar established house rules limiting all customers to two drinks per hour, with a maximum limit of four drinks per night. This evidence is

(A) admissible to show that the prior conduct of Duke's Bar was negligent

(B) admissible to show that Duke's Bar was aware of the need for taking precautionary measures

(C) inadmissible, because subsequent measures by an employee are not binding on Duke's Bar

(D) inadmissible, because its admission would discourage the taking of such remedial measures

Question 59

Penn offers evidence that, after the accident, the owner of Duke's Bar visited him at the hospital and, offering to pay all of Penn's medical expenses, said, "That's the least I can do after letting Chase leave the bar so drunk last night." The statement that Chase was drunk when he left the bar on the night of the accident is

(A) admissible as an admission by the owner of Duke's Bar that Chase was drunk when he left the bar

(B) admissible as a factual admission made in connection with an offer of compromise

(C) inadmissible as hearsay not within any exception

(D) inadmissible as a statement made in connection with an offer to pay medical expenses

Question 60

In a narcotics conspiracy prosecution against Daly, the prosecutor offers in evidence a tape recording of a telephone call allegedly made by Daly. A lay witness is called to testify that the voice on the recording is Daly's. Her testimony to which of the following would be the LEAST sufficient basis for admitting the recording?

(A) She had heard the same voice on a similar tape recording identified to her by Daly's brother

(B) She had heard Daly speak many times, but never over the telephone

(C) She had, specifically for the purpose of preparing to testify, talked with Daly over the telephone at a time after the recording was made

(D) She had been present with Daly when he engaged in the conversation in question but had heard only Daly's side of the conversation

Question 61-62 are based on the following fact situation.

Devlin was the owner of a large subdivision. Parnell became interested in purchasing a lot but could not decide between Lot 40 and Lot 41. The price and fair market value of each of those two lots was $5,000. Parnell paid Devlin $5,000, which Devlin accepted, and Devlin delivered to Parnell a deed which was properly executed, complete, and ready for recording in every detail except that the space in the deed for the lot number was left blank. Devlin told Parnell to fill in either Lot 40 or Lot 41 according to his decision and then record the deed. Parnell visited the development the next day and completely changed his mind, selecting Lot 25. He filled in Lot 25 and duly recorded the deed. The price of Lot 25 and its fair market value was $7,500.

Question 61

Immediately upon learning what Parnell had done, Devlin brought an appropriate action against Parnell to rescind the transaction. If Devlin loses, the most likely basis for the judgment is that

(A) Devlin's casual business practices created his loss

(B) the need for certainty in land title records controls

(C) the agency implied to complete the deed cannot be restricted by the oral understanding

(D) the recording of the deed precludes any questioning of its provisions in its recorded form

Question 62

Assume the following facts for this question only. Before Devlin had time to learn of Parnell's actions, Parnell sold Lot 25 to Caruso for $6,000 by a duly and properly executed, delivered, and recorded warranty deed. Caruso knew that Devlin had put a price of $7,500 on Lot 25, but he knew no other facts regarding the Devlin-Parnell transaction. Caruso's attorney accurately reported Parnell's record title to be good, marketable, and free of encumbrances. Neither Caruso nor his attorney made any further investigation outside the record. Devlin brought an appropriate action against Caruso to recover title to Lot 25. If Devlin loses, the most likely basis for the judgment is that

(A) the Statute of Frauds prevents the introduction of any evidence of Devlin's and Parnell's agreement

(B) recording of the deed from Devlin to Parnell precludes any question of its genuineness

(C) as between Devlin and a bona fide purchaser, Devlin is estopped

(D) the clean hands doctrine bars Devlin from relief

Question 63

Ohner owns the Acme Hotel. When the International Order of Badgers came to town for its convention, its members rented 400 of the 500 rooms, and the hotel opened its convention facilities to them. Badgers are a rowdy group, and during their convention they littered both the inside and the outside of the hotel with debris and bottles. The hotel manager knew that objects were being thrown out of the hotel windows. At his direction, hotel employees patrolled the hallways telling the guests to refrain from such conduct. Ohner was out of town and was not aware of the problems which were occurring. During the convention, as Smith walked past the Acme Hotel on the sidewalk, he was hit and injured by an ashtray thrown out of a window in the hotel. Smith sued Ohner for damages for his injuries.

Will Smith prevail in his claim against Ohner?

(A) Yes, because a property owner is strictly liable for acts on his premises if such acts cause harm to persons using the adjacent public sidewalks.

(B) Yes, if the person who threw the ashtray cannot be identified.

(C) No, because Ohner had no personal knowledge of the conduct of the hotel guests.

(D) No, if the trier of fact determines that the hotel employees had taken reasonable precautions to prevent such an injury.

Questions 64-65 are based on the following fact situation.

Householder resented the fact that joggers and walkers would sometimes come onto his property just beside the sidewalk in order to enjoy the feel of walking or running on grass. He put up a sign, "No Trespassing," but it did not stop the practice. He then put up a sign, "Beware of Skunk," and bought a young skunk. He took the skunk to Dr. Vet to have its scent gland removed. Unfortunately, Dr. Vet did not perform the operation properly, and the scent gland was not removed. Householder was unaware that it had not been removed.

One day Walker was out for a stroll. When she came to Householder's property, she walked on the grass alongside the sidewalk on Householder's property. The skunk came up behind Walker and sprayed her with its scent. The smell was overpowering, and she fainted. She struck her head on the sidewalk and suffered serious injuries.

Question 64

The probable result of Walker's claim against Householder is that she will

(A) recover, because the skunk was a private nuisance

(B) recover, because the skunk was not a domesticated animal

(C) not recover, because Walker was a trespasser

(D) not recover, because Dr. Vet was the cause of the injury

Question 65

If Walker asserts a claim against Dr. Vet, she will

(A) recover on the ground of negligence

(B) recover on the ground of strict liability

(C) not recover, because Walker was trespassing at the time of her injury

(D) not recover, because Dr. Vet's professional services were rendered for Householder

Question 66

In a collision case, Plaintiff offers in evidence a photograph showing the scene of the accident while the cars were still in place. A proper foundation must include, as a minimum, testimony by which of the following?

(A) The photographer

(B) A person who was present at the time the photograph was taken

(C) A person who observed the cars while they were still in place

(D) A person in whose custody the photograph has been since it was developed

Questions 67-71 are based on the following fact situation.

While negligently driving his father's uninsured automobile, 25-year-old Arthur crashed into an automobile driven by Betty. Both Arthur and Betty were injured. Charles, Arthur's father, erroneously believing that he was liable because he owned the automobile, said to Betty: "I will see to it that you are reimbursed for any losses you incur as a result of the accident." Charles also called Physician and told him to take care of Betty, and that he, Charles, would pay the bill.

Arthur, having no assets, died as a result of his injuries. Dodge, one of Arthur's creditors, wrote to Charles stating that Arthur owed him a clothing bill of $200 and that he was going to file a claim against Arthur's estate. Charles replied: "If you don't file a claim against Arthur's estate, I will pay what he owed you."

Question 67

In an action by Betty against Charles for wages lost while she was incapacitated as a result of the accident, which of the following would be Charles's best defense?

(A) Lack of consideration

(B) Mistake of fact as to basic assumption

(C) Statute of Frauds

(D) Indefiniteness of Charles's promise

Question 68

Which of the following, if true, would be significant in determining whether or not there was bargained-for consideration to support Charles's promise to Physician?

I. Physician had not begun treating Betty before Charles called him.

II. Charles had a contract with Betty.

(A) I only

(B) II only

(C) Both I and II

(D) Neither I nor II

Question 69

If Physician discontinued treating Betty before she had fully recovered and Betty brought an action against Physician for breach of contract, which of the following arguments, if any, by Physician would probably be effective in defense?

I. Betty furnished no consideration, either express or implied.

II. Physician's contract was with Charles and not with Betty.

III. Whatever contract Physician may have had with Betty was discharged by novation on account of the agreement with Charles.

(A) I only

(B) I and II only

(C) II and III only

(D) Neither I nor II nor III

Question 70

If Dodge did not file an action against Arthur's estate, would Dodge succeed in an action against Charles for $200?

(A) Yes, because Dodge had detrimentally relied on Charles's promise.

(B) Yes, because Charles's promise was supported by a bargained-for exchange.

(C) No, because Dodge's claim against Arthur's estate was worthless.

(D) No, because Charles at most had only a moral obligation to pay Arthur's debts.

Question 71

Assume that Charles, honestly believing that he owed Dodge nothing, refused to pay anything to Dodge, who honestly believed that Charles owed him $200. If Dodge then accepts $150 from Charles in settlement of the claim,

will Dodge succeed in an action against Charles for the remaining $50?

(A) Yes, because Arthur's debt of $200 was liquidated and undisputed.

(B) Yes, because Dodge honestly believed that he had a legal right against Charles for the full $200.

(C) No, because Charles honestly believed that Dodge did not have a legal right against him for the $200.

(D) No, because Charles was not contractually obligated to pay Dodge $200 in the first place.

Questions 72-73 are based on the following fact situation.

Until 1954, the state of New Atlantic required segregation in all public and private schools, but all public schools are not desegregated. Other state laws, enacted before 1954 and continuing to the present, provide for free distribution of the same textbooks on secular subjects to students in all public and private schools. In addition, the state accredits schools and certifies teachers.

Little White School House, a private school that offers elementary and secondary education in the state, denies admission to all non-Caucasians. Stone School is a private school that offers religious instruction.

Question 72

Which of the following is the strongest argument against the constitutionality of free distribution of textbooks to the students at the Little White School House?

(A) No legitimate educational function is served by the free distribution of the textbooks.

(B) The state may not in any way aid private schools.

(C) The Constitution forbids private bias of any kind.

(D) Segregation is furthered by the distribution of textbooks to these students.

Question 73

Which of the following is the strongest argument in favor of the constitutionality of free distribution of textbooks to the students at Stone School?

(A) Private religious schools, like public non-sectarian schools, fulfill an important educational function.

(B) Religious instruction in private schools is not constitutionally objectionable.

(C) The purpose and effect of the free distribution of these textbooks is secular and does not entangle church and state.

(D) The free exercise clause requires identical treatment by the state of students in public and private schools.

Question 74

On a foggy night, Vera was clubbed from behind by a man wielding a blackjack. Damon was arrested in the vicinity shortly thereafter. As they were booking Damon, the police took his photograph. They promptly showed that photograph, along with the photographs of seven people who have the same general features as Damon, to Vera. Vera identified Damon as the culprit.

At trial, Damon objects to the introduction into evidence of his out-of-court identification. His objection should be

(A) sustained, because Vera did not have a good opportunity to observe the culprit

(B) sustained, because Damon was not represented by counsel at the showing of the photographs to Vera

(C) sustained, because the action of the police in showing the photographs to Vera was unnecessarily suggestive

(D) denied

Question 75

Defendant is charged with assault and battery. The state's evidence shows that Victim was struck in the face by Defendant's fist. In which of the following situations is Defendant most likely to be **not guilty** of assault and battery?

(A) Defendant had been hypnotized at a party and ordered by the hypnotist to strike the person he disliked the most.

(B) Defendant was suffering from an epileptic seizure and had no control over his motions.

(C) Defendant was heavily intoxicated and was shadow boxing without realizing that Victim was near him.

(D) Defendant, who had just awakened from a deep sleep, was not fully aware of what was happening and mistakenly thought Victim was attacking him.

Question 76

Leader is a labor leader in Metropolis. Ten years ago he was divorced. Both he and his first wife have since married other persons. Recently, *News*, a newspaper in an other city, ran a feature article on improper influences it asserted had been used by labor officials to secure favorable rulings from government officials. The story said that in 1960 Leader's first wife, with Leader's knowledge and concurrence, gave sexual favors to the mayor of Metropolis and then persuaded him to grant concessions to Leader's union, with which Metropolis was then negotiating a labor contract. The story named Leader and identified his first wife by her former and current surnames. The reporter for *News* believed the story to be true, since it had been related to him by two very reliable sources.

Leader's first wife suffered emotional distress and became very depressed. If she asserts a claim based on defamation against *News,* she will

(A) prevail, because the story concerned her personal, private life

(B) prevail if the story was false

(C) not prevail, because *News* did not print the story with knowledge of its falsity or with reckless disregard for its truth or falsity

(D) not prevail if *News* exercised ordinary care in determining if the story was true or false

Questions 77-78 are based on the following fact situation.

In 1995, Utility constructed a new plant for the generation of electricity. The plant burns lignite, a low grade fuel which is available in large quantities. Although the plant was constructed in accordance with the best practicable technology, the plant emits a substantial quantity of invisible fumes. The only way Utility can reduce the fumes is by the use of scrubbing equipment that would cost $50,000,000 to install and would increase the retail price of generated electricity by 50 per cent while reducing the volume of fumes by only 20 per cent. Because of the expense of such equipment and its relative ineffectiveness, no other generating plants burning lignite use such equipment.

The plant was located in a sparsely settled rural area, remote from the large city served by Utility. Farmer owned a farm adjacent to the plant. He had farmed the land for forty years and lived on the premises. The prevailing winds carried fumes from the new plant over Farmer's land. His 1995 crop was less than half the average size of this crop over the five years immediately preceding the construction of the plant. It can be established that the fumes caused the crop reduction.

Farmer's hay fever, from which he had long suffered, became worse in 1996. Physicians advised him that the lignite fumes were affecting it and that serious lung disease would soon result unless he moved away from the plant. He did so, selling his farm at its reasonable market value, which was then $10,000 less than before the construction of the plant.

Question 77

If Farmer asserts a claim based on nuisance against Utility for damages for personal injuries, will Farmer prevail?

(A) No, because there is no practicable way for Utility to reduce the fumes.

(B) No, because Utility's acts constituted a public nuisance.

(C) Yes, because Farmer's personal injuries were within the scope of the liability imposed on Utility.

(D) Yes, because the generation of electricity is an ultrahazardous activity.

Question 78

If Farmer asserts a claim based on negligence against Utility for crop damages, will Farmer prevail?

(A) No, because Utility was not negligent.

(B) No, as to 1996 crop damage, because Farmer did not mitigate damages by selling his farm in 1995.

(C) Yes, as to 20 per cent of his crop damage, because use of available equipment would have reduced the fumes by 20 per cent.

(D) Yes, because operation of the plant constituted a nuisance.

Question 79-81 are based on the following fact situation.

Phillips purchased a suit of thermal underwear manufactured by Makorp from synthetic materials. While he was attempting to stamp out a fire, Phillips' thermal underwear caught fire and burned in a melting fashion up to his waist. He suffered a heart attack a half hour later. In a suit against Makorp, Phillips alleged that negligence and breach of warranty caused both the burn and the heart attack. Phillips testified to the foregoing.

Question 79

Dr. Jones, a physician, having listened to Phillips' testimony, is called by Phillips and asked whether, assuming the truth of such testimony, Phillips' subsequent heart attack could have resulted from the burns. His opinion is

(A) admissible as a response to a hypothetical question

(B) admissible because the physician's expertise enables him to judge the credibility of Phillips' testimony

(C) inadmissible, because a hypothetical question may not be based on prior testimony

(D) inadmissible, because an expert's opinion may not be based solely on information provided by lay persons

Question 80

Dr. Black, a physician, is called by Phillips to testify that, on the basis of her examination of Phillips and blood study reports by an independent laboratory, reports which were not introduced in evidence, she believes that Phillips has a permanent disability. This testimony is

(A) admissible, because such laboratory reports are business records

(B) admissible if such reports are reasonably relied upon in medical practice

(C) inadmissible unless Dr. Black has been shown to be qualified to conduct laboratory blood analyses

(D) inadmissible, because Dr. Black's testimony cannot be based on tests performed by persons not under her supervision

Question 81

Phillips testified that his purchase of the underwear occurred on April 17th, a fact of minor importance in the case. He stated that he could identify the date because his secretary had taken the day off to attend the first game of the baseball season and he had checked his company's payroll records to verify the date. Makorp moves to strike the testimony as to the date. The motion should be

(A) sustained, because the best evidence of the information contained in the payroll records is the records themselves

(B) sustained, because Phillips' testimony is based upon hearsay declarations contained in the payroll records

(C) overruled if the judge has personal knowledge of the date on which the baseball season opened

(D) overruled, because the payroll records relate to a collateral matter

Questions 82-87 are based on the following fact situation.

On March 1, Computer Programs, Inc. (CP) orally agreed with Holiday Department Store (HDS) to write a set of programs for HDS's computer and to coordinate the programs with HDS's billing methods. A subsequent memo, signed by both parties, provided in its entirety:

HDS will pay CP $20,000 in two equal installments within one month of completion if CP is successful in shortening by one-half the processing time for the financial transactions now handled on HDS's Zenon 747 computer; CP to complete by July 1. This agreement may be amended only by a signed writing.

On June 6, CP demanded $10,000, saying the job was one-half done. After HDS denied liability, the parties orally agreed that HDS should deposit $20,000 in escrow, pending completion to the satisfaction of HDS's computer systems manager. The escrow deposit was thereupon made. On July 5, CP completed the programs, having used an amount of time in which it could have earned $18,000 had it devoted that time to other jobs. Tests by CP and HDS's computer systems manager then showed that the computer programs, not being perfectly coordinated with HDS's billing methods, cut processing time by only 47%. They would, however, save HDS $12,000 a year. Further, if HDS would spend $5,000 to change its invoice preparation methods, as recommended by CP, the programs would cut processing time by a total of 58%, saving HDS another $8,000 a year.

HDS's computer systems manager refused in good faith to certify satisfactory completion. HDS requested the escrow agent to return the $20,000 and asserted that nothing was owed to CP even though HDS continued to use the programs.

Question 82

If HDS denies liability on the ground that CP had orally agreed to coordinate with HDS's methods of accounting, and CP seeks in litigation to bar introduction of that agreement because of the parol evidence rule, HDS's most effective argument is that

(A) the parol evidence rule does not bar the introduction of evidence for the purpose of interpreting a written agreement

(B) the memorandum was not a completely integrated agreement

(C) HDS detrimentally relied on the oral promise of coordination in signing the memorandum

(D) the memorandum was not a partially integrated agreement

Question 83

If CP in fact had half-completed the job on June 6, would it then have been entitled to $10,000?

(A) Yes, because June 6 was within one month of completion.

(B) Yes, because CP had done one-half of the job.

(C) No, because of a constructive condition precedent requiring at least substantial completion of the work before HDS would have a duty to pay.

(D) No, because "within one month of completion" would, in these circumstances, be interpreted to mean "within one month after completion."

Question 84

Was the escrow agreement a valid modification?

(A) Yes, because it was the compromise of an honest dispute.

(B) Yes, because the Statute of Frauds does not apply to subsequent oral modifications.

(C) No, because it was oral.

(D) No, because it was not supported by consideration.

Question 85

Assume for this question only that the programs completed on July 5 had cut processing time by one-half for all of HDS's financial transactions. Is HDS entitled to renounce the contract because of CP's delay in completion?

(A) Yes, because "CP to complete by July 1" is an express condition.

(B) Yes, because the doctrine of substantial performance does not apply to commercial contracts.

(C) No, because both parties manifested an understanding that time was not of the essence.

(D) No, because the contract did not contain a liquidated damages clause dealing with delay in completion.

Question 86

Assume for this question only that CP's delay in completion did not give HDS the right to renounce the contract and that the parties' escrow agreement was enforceable. Is CP entitled to recover damages for breach of the contract?

(A) Yes, because CP had substantially performed.

(B) Yes, because the programs would save HDS $12,000 a year.

(C) No, because shortening the processing time by one-half was an express condition subsequent.

(D) No, because HDS's computer systems manager did not certify satisfactory completion of the programs.

Question 87

Assume for this question only that CP was in breach of contract because of its four-day delay in completion and that an express condition precedent to HDS's duty to pay the contract price has failed. Can CP nevertheless recover the reasonable value of its services?

(A) Yes, because continued use of the programs by HDS would save at least $12,000 a year.

(B) Yes, because HDS was continuing to use programs created by CP for which, as HDS knew, CP expected to be paid.

(C) No, because failure of an express condition precedent excused HDS from any duty to compensate CP.

(D) No, because such a recovery by CP would be inconsistent with a claim by HDS against CP for breach of contract.

Question 88

Police Officer stopped Dexter for speeding late one night. Noting that Dexter was nervous, he ordered him from the car and placed him under arrest for speeding. By state law, Police Officer was empowered to arrest Dexter and take him to the nearest police station for booking. He searched Dexter's person and discovered a package of heroin in his jacket pocket.

Dexter is charged with possession of heroin. At trial, Dexter's motion to prevent introduction of the heroin into evidence, on the ground that the search violated his federal constitutional rights, will most probably be

(A) denied, because the search was incident to a valid custodial arrest

(B) denied, because Police Officer acted under both a reasonable suspicion and legitimate concern for his own personal safety

(C) granted, because there was no reasonable or proper basis upon which to justify conducting the search

(D) granted, if Police Officer was not in fear and had no suspicion that Dexter was transporting narcotics

Question 89

Dunn was arrested moments after a forcible rape and was prosecuted for it. The victim testified she tore the assailant's shirt. Dunn did not testify. In jury argument, Dunn's counsel urged that the state's failure to offer in evidence the shirt Dunn was wearing when arrested indicated that the evidence would be unfavorable to the state's case. In his closing argument, the prosecutor said, "If the defense had thought the clothing would show anything, they could have brought it in as evidence themselves." The prosecutor's argument is

(A) proper as rebuttal to the inference that the evidence would be unfavorable to the prosecution

(B) proper as a comment on Dunn's failure to testify

(C) improper as an argument going beyond the evidence

in the case

(D) improper as a comment on Dunn's failure to testify

Question 90

Donna was arrested and taken to police headquarters, where she was given her Miranda warnings. Donna indicated that she wished to telephone her lawyer and was told that she could do so after her fingerprints had been taken. While being fingerprinted, however, Donna blurted out, "Paying a lawyer is a waste of money because I know you have me."

At trial, Donna's motion to prevent the introduction of the statement she made while being fingerprinted will most probably be

(A) granted, because Donna's request to contact her attorney by telephone was reasonable and should have been granted immediately

(B) granted, because of the "fruit of the poisonous tree" doctrine

(C) denied, because the statements were volunteered and not the result of interrogation

(D) denied, because fingerprinting is not a critical stage of the proceeding requiring the assistance of counsel

Questions 91-92 are based on the following fact situation.

Barnes was hired as an assistant professor of mathematics at Reardon State College and is now in his third consecutive one-year contract. Under state law he cannot acquire tenure until after five consecutive annual contracts. In his third year, Barnes was notified that he was not being rehired for the following year. Applicable state law and college rules did not require either a statement of reasons or a hearing, and in fact neither was offered to Barnes.

Question 91

Which of the following, if established, sets forth the strongest constitutional argument Barnes could make to compel the college to furnish him a statement of reasons for the failure to rehire him and an opportunity for a hearing?

(A) There is no evidence that tenured teachers are any more qualified than he is.

(B) He leased a home in reliance on an oral promise of reemployment by the college president.

(C) He was the only teacher at the college whose contract was not renewed that year.

(D) In the expectation of remaining at the college, he had just moved his elderly parents to the town in which the college is located.

Question 92

Which of the following, if established, most strongly supports the college in refusing to give Barnes a statement of reasons or an opportunity for a hearing?

(A) Barnes's academic performance had been substandard.

(B) A speech he made that was critical of administration policies violated a college regulation concerning teacher behavior.

(C) Barnes worked at the college for less than five years?

(D) Barnes could be replaced with a more competent teacher.

Question 93

National regulation of predatory wild animals on federal lands is most likely

(A) constitutional, because the protection of wild animals is important to the general welfare

(B) constitutional, because Congress has authority to make regulations respecting federal property

(C) unconstitutional, because wild animals as defined by state common law are not federal property

(D) unconstitutional, because regulation and control of wild animals is retained by the states under the Tenth Amendment.

Question 94

By her validly executed will, Sallie devised a certain tract of land to her son, Ben, for his life with remainder to such of Ben's children as should be living at his death, "Provided, however, that no such child of Ben shall mortgage or sell, or attempt to mortgage or sell, his or her interest in the property prior to attaining 25 years of age: and, if any such child of Ben shall violate this provision, then upon such violation his or her interest shall pass to and become the property of the remaining children of Ben then living, share and share alike."

Sallie's will included an identical provision for each of her four other children concerning four other tracts of land. The residuary clause of the will gave the residuary estate to Sallie's five children equally. Sallie died and was survived by the five children named in her will and by eleven grandchildren. Several additional grandchildren have since been born.

In an action for a declaration of rights, it was claimed that the attempted gifts to Sallie's grandchildren were entirely void and that the interests following the life estates to Sallie's children passed to the children absolutely by the residuary clause. Assuming that the action was properly brought with all necessary parties and with a guardian ad litem appointed to represent the interests of unborn and infant grandchildren, the decision should be that

(A) the attempted gifts to grandchildren are void under the Rule Against Perpetuities

(B) the attempted gifts to grandchildren are void as unlawful restraints on alienation

(C) the provisions concerning grandchildren are valid and will be upheld according to their terms

(D) even if the provisions against sale or mortgage by the

grandchildren are void, the remainders to grandchildren are otherwise valid and will be given effect

Question 95

Seth was an elderly widower who lived alone on a small farm which he owned. Except for the farm, including the house and its furnishings, and the usual items of personal clothing and similar things, Seth owned substantially no property. Under proper management, the farm was capable of producing an adequate family income. Because of the usual deterioration accompanying old age, Seth was unable to do farm work or even to provide for his own personal needs. Seth entered into an oral contract with his nephew, Jim, by which Seth agreed to convey the farm to Jim and Jim agreed to move into the house with Seth, operate the farm, and take care of Seth for the rest of his life. The oral contract was silent as to when the land was to be conveyed. Jim, who lived about fifty miles away where he was operating a small business of his own, terminated his business and moved in with Seth. With the assistance of his wife, Jim gave Seth excellent care until Seth died intestate about five years after the date of the contract. In his final years Seth was confined to his bed and required much personal service of an intimate and arduous sort. Seth was survived by his only son, Sol, who was also Seth's sole heir and next of kin. Sol resided in a distant city and gave his father no attention in his father's final years. Sol showed up for Seth's funeral and demanded that Jim vacate the farm immediately. Upon Jim's refusal to do so, Sol brought an appropriate action for possession. Jim answered by way of a counterclaim to establish Jim's right to possession and title to the farm.

If the court's decision is in favor of Jim, it will be because

(A) the land is located in a state where the Statute of Frauds will not be applied if there has been such part performance as will result in an irreparable hardship if the contract is not performed

(B) the land is located in a state where the Statute of Frauds will not be applied if there has been such part performance that is by its very nature unequivocally referable to the contract

(C) Sol is precluded by the "clean hands" doctrine from enforcing his claim against Jim

(D) the blood relationship of uncle-nephew is sufficient to remove the necessity for any writing to satisfy the Statute of Frauds

Question 96

The following events took place in a state that does not recognize the common-law marriage. The state does recognize the common-law estate of tenancy by the entirety and has no statute on the subject.

Wade Sloan and Mary Isaacs, who were never formally married, lived together over a seven-year period. During this time Mary identified herself as "Mrs. Sloan" with the knowledge and consent of Wade. Wade and Mary maintained several charge accounts at retail stores under the names "Mr. and Mrs. Wade Sloan," and they filed joint income tax returns as Mr. and Mrs. Sloan. Within this period Wade decided to buy a home. The deed was in proper form and identified the grantees as "Wade Sloan and Mary Sloan, his wife, and their heirs and assigns forever as tenants by the entirety." Wade made a down payment of $10,000, and gave a note and mortgage for the unpaid balance. Both Wade and Mary signed the note and mortgage for the unpaid balance. Both Wade and Mary signed the note and mortgage as husband and wife. Wade made the monthly payments as they became due until he and Mary had a disagreement and he abandoned her and the house. Mary then made the payments for three months. She then brought an action against Wade for partition of the land in question. The prayer for partition should be

(A) denied, because a tenant by the entirety has no right to partition

(B) denied, because Wade has absolute title to the property

(C) granted, because the tenancy by the entirety that was created by the deed was severed when Wade abandoned Mary

(D) granted, because the estate created by the deed was not a tenancy by the entirety.

Questions 97-99 are based on the following fact situation.

Sand Company operated an installation for distributing sand and gravel. The installation was adjacent to a residential area. On Sand's grounds there was a chute with polished metal sides for loading sand and gravel into trucks. The trucks being loaded stopped on the public street below the chute.

After closing hours, a plywood screen was placed in the chute and the ladder used for inspection was removed to another section of the installation. For several months, however, a number of children, 8 to 10 years of age, had been playing on Sand's property and the adjoining street after closing hours. The children found the ladder and also discovered that they could remove the plywood screen from the chute and slide down to the street below. Sand knew of this activity.

One evening, the children were using the chute as a play device. As an automobile driven by Commuter approached the chute, Ladd, an 8-year-old boy, slid down just in front of the automobile. Commuter applied her brakes, but they suddenly failed, and she hit and injured Ladd. Commuter saw the child in time to have avoided hitting him if her brakes had worked properly. Two days previously, Commuter had taken her car to Garage to have her brakes inspected. Garage inspected the brakes and told her that the brakes were in perfect working order. Claims were asserted on behalf of Ladd by his proper legal representative against Sand, Commuter, and Garage.

Question 97

On Ladd's claim against Sand, will Ladd prevail?

(A) Yes, if Sand could have effectively secured the chute at moderate cost.

(B) Yes, because Sand is strictly liable for harm resulting from an artificial condition on its property.

(C) No, if Commuter had the last clear chance to avoid the injury.

(D) No, because Ladd was a trespasser.

Question 98

On Ladd's claim against Commuter, Commuter's best defense is that

(A) her conduct was not the cause in fact of the harm

(B) she used reasonable care in the maintenance

(C) she could not reasonably foresee Ladd's presence in the street

(D) she did not act willfully and wantonly

Question 99

On Ladd's claim against Garage, will Ladd prevail?

(A) Yes, because Garage is strictly liable in tort.

(B) Yes, if Garage was negligent in inspecting Commuter's brakes

(C) No, if Ladd was in the legal category of a bystander

(D) No, because Sand's conduct was an independent and superseding cause.

Question 100

Driving down a dark road, Defendant accidentally ran over a man. Defendant stopped and found that the victim was dead. Defendant, fearing that he might be held responsible, took the victim's wallet, which contained a substantial amount of money. He removed the identification papers and put the wallet and money back into the victim's pocket. Defendant is **not guilty** of

(A) larceny, because he took the papers only to prevent identification and not for his own use

(B) larceny, because he did not take anything from a living victim

(C) robbery, because he did not take the papers by means of force or putting in fear

(D) robbery, because he did not take anything of monetary value

QUESTIONS
PRACTICE MBE — P.M. EXAM

QUESTIONS

PRACTICE MBE — P.M. EXAM

Question 101

Al and Bill are identical twins. Al, angry at David, said, "You'd better stay out of my way. The next time I find you around here, I'll beat you up." Two days later, while in the neighborhood, David saw Bill coming toward him. As Bill came up to David, Bill raised his hand. Thinking Bill was Al and fearing bodily harm, David struck Bill.

If Bill asserts a claim against David and David relies on the privilege of self-defense, David will

(A) not prevail, because Bill was not an aggressor

(B) not prevail unless Bill intended his gesture as a threat

(C) prevail if David honestly believed that Bill would attack him

(D) prevail only if a reasonable person under the circumstances would have believed that Bill would attack him

Questions 102-103 are based on the following fact situation.

Section 1 of the Vehicle Code of State makes it illegal to cross a street in a central business district other than at a designated crosswalk. Section 2 of the Code prohibits parking any motor vehicle so that it blocks any part of a designated crosswalk. Ped wanted to cross Main Street in the central business district of City, located in State, but a truck parked by Trucker was blocking the designated crosswalk. Ped stepped out into Main Street and carefully walked around the back of the truck. Ped was struck by a motor vehicle negligently operated by Driver.

Question 102

If Ped asserts a claim against Driver, Ped's failure to be in the crosswalk will have which of the following effects?

(A) It is not relevant in determining the right of Ped.

(B) It may be considered by the trier of facts on the issue of Driver's liability.

(C) It will bar Ped's recovery unless Driver saw Ped in time to avoid the impact.

(D) It will bar Ped's recovery as a matter of law.

Question 103

If Ped asserts a claim against Trucker, the most likely result is that Ped will

(A) prevail, because Trucker's violation of a state statute makes him strictly liable for all injuries caused thereby

(B) prevail, because the probable purpose of Section 2 of the Vehicle Code of State was to safeguard pedestrians in using crosswalks

(C) not prevail, because Ped assumed the risk of injury when he crossed the street outside the crosswalk

(D) not prevail, because Driver's conduct was the actual cause of Ped's harm

Question 104

Suspecting that students in a dormitory were using narcotics, the president of a private college arranged for local police to place concealed microphones in several suites of the dormitory. Using these microphones, the college security officers recorded a conversation in which Green, a student, offered to sell marijuana to another student. The tape was turned over to the local police, who played it for a local judge. The judge issued a warrant to search Green's room. The room was searched by police, and marijuana was discovered.

Green is charged with unlawful possession of narcotics. At trial, Green's motion to prevent the introduction of the marijuana into evidence will most probably be

(A) denied, because the college president, *in loco parentis*, had the responsibility of preventing unlawful activity by students under the president's supervision

(B) denied, because there was probable cause to make the search and police obtained a warrant before commencing the search

(C) granted, because Green's privacy was unreasonably invaded

(D) granted, because the electronic surveillance was "fundamentally unfair"

Question 105

Tom had a heart ailment so serious that his doctors had concluded that only a heart transplant could save his life. They therefore arranged to have him flown to Big City to have the operation performed.

Dan, Tom's nephew, who stood to inherit from him, poisoned him. The poison produced a reaction which required postponing the journey. The plane on which Tom was to have flown crashed, and all aboard were killed. By the following day, Tom's heart was so weakened by the effects of the poison that he suffered a heart attack and died. If charged with criminal homicide, Dan should be found

(A) guilty

(B) not guilty, because his act did not hasten the deceased's death, but instead prolonged it by one day

(C) not guilty, because the deceased was already suffering from a fatal illness

(D) not guilty, because the poison was not the sole cause of death

Question 106

In which of the following situations is Defendant most likely to be **not guilty** of the charge made?

(A) Police arrested Thief and recovered goods he had stolen. At the direction of the police, Thief took the goods to Defendant. Defendant, believing the goods to be stolen, purchased them. Defendant is charged with attempting to receive stolen property.

(B) Defendant misrepresented his identity to secure a loan from a bank. The banker was not deceived and refused to grant the loan. Defendant is charged with attempting to obtain property by false pretenses.

(C) Believing that state law made it a crime to purchase codeine without a prescription, Defendant purchased, without a prescription, cough syrup containing codeine. Unknown to Defendant, the statute had been repealed and codeine could be legally purchased without a prescription. Defendant is charged with attempting to purchase codeine without a prescription.

(D) Defendant, intending to kill Selma, shot at Selma. Unknown to Defendant, Selma had died of a heart attack minutes before Defendant shot at her. Defendant is charged with attempted murder.

Question 107

Potts sued Dobbs on a product liability claim. Louis testified for Potts. On cross-examination, which of the following questions is the trial judge most likely to rule **improper**?

(A) "Isn't it a fact that you are Potts' close friend?"

(B) "Isn't it true that you are known in the community as 'Louie the Lush' because of your addiction to alcohol"?

(C) "Didn't you fail to report some income on your tax return last year?"

(D) "Weren't you convicted, seven years ago in this court, of obtaining money under false pretenses?"

Question 108

In an action to recover for personal injuries arising out of an automobile accident, Plaintiff calls Bystander to testify. Claiming the privilege against self-incrimination, Bystander refuses to answer a question as to whether she was at the scene of the accident. Plaintiff moves that Bystander be ordered to answer the question. The judge should allow Bystander to remain silent only if

(A) the judge is convinced that she will incriminate herself

(B) there is clear and convincing evidence that she will incriminate herself

(C) there is a preponderance of evidence that she will incriminate herself

(D) the judge believes that there is some reasonable possibility that she will incriminate herself

Question 109

Venner, the owner of Greenacre, a tract of land, entered into an enforceable written agreement with Brier providing that Venner would sell Greenacre to Brier for an agreed price. At the place and time designated for the closing. Venner tendered an appropriate deed, but Brier responded that he had discovered a mortgage on Greenacre and would not complete the transaction, because Venner's title was not free of encumbrances, as the contract required. Venner said that it was his intent to pay the mortgage from the proceeds of the sale, and he offered to put the proceeds in escrow for that purpose with any agreeable, responsible escrowee. The balance due on the mortgage was substantially less than the contract purchase price. Brier refused Venner's proposal. Venner began an appropriate legal action against Brier for specific performance. There is no applicable statute in the jurisdiction where Greenacre is located. Venner's best legal argument in support of his claim for relief is that

(A) as the seller of real estate, he had an implied right to use the contract proceeds to clear the title being conveyed

(B) the lien of the mortgage shifts from Greenacre to the contract proceeds

(C) under the doctrine of equitable conversion, title has already passed to Brier and the only issue is how the purchase price is to be allocated

(D) no provision of the contract has been breached by Venner

Question 110

Blackacre is a three-acre tract of land with a small residence. Olga, the owner of Blackacre, rented it to Terrence at a monthly rental of $200. After Terrence had been in possession of Blackacre for several years, Terrence and Olga orally agreed that Terrence would purchase Blackacre from Olga for the sum of $24,000, payable at the rate of $200 a month for ten years and also would pay the real estate taxes and the expenses of insuring and maintaining Blackacre. Olga agreed to give Terrence a deed to Blackacre after five years had passed and $12,000 had been paid on account and to accept from Terrence a note secured by a mortgage for the balance. Terrence continued in possession of Blackacre and performed his obligations as orally agreed. Terrence, without consulting Olga, made improvements for which he paid $1,000. When Terrence had paid $12,000, he tendered a proper note and mortgage to Olga and demanded delivery of the deed as agreed. Olga did not deny the oral agreement but told Terrence that she had changed her mind, and she refused to complete the transaction. Terrence then brought an action for specific performance. Olga pleaded the Statute of Frauds as her defense. If Olga wins, it will be because

(A) nothing Terrence could have done would have over-come the original absence of a written agreement

(B) the actions and payments of Terrence are as consis-tent with his being a tenant as with an oral contract

(C) Terrence did not secure Olga's approval for the improvements that he made

(D) Olga has not received any unconscionable benefit, and, therefore, Terrence is not entitled to equitable relief

Questions 111-115 are based on the following fact situation.

During 1996 a series of arsons, one of which damaged the Humongous Store, occurred in the City of Swelter. In early 1997 Swelter's City Council adopted this resolution:

The City will pay $10,000 for the arrest and conviction of anyone guilty of any of the 1996 arsons committed here.

The foregoing was telecast by the city's sole television station once daily for one week. Subsequently, Humongous, by a written memorandum to Gimlet, a pri-vate detective, proposed to pay Gimlet $200 "for each day's work you actually perform in investigating our fire." Thereafter, in August, 1997, the City Council by resolution repealed its reward offer and caused this resolution to be broadcast once daily for a week over two local radio sta-tions, the local television station having meanwhile ceased operations. In September, 1997, a Humongous employee voluntarily confessed to Gimlet to having committed all of the 1996 arsons. Humongous' president thereupon paid Gimlet at the proposed daily rate for his investigation and suggested that Gimlet also claim the city's reward, of which Gimlet had been previously unaware. Gimlet imme-diately made the claim. In December, 1997, as a result of Gimlet's investigation, the Humongous employee was con-victed of burning the store. The city, which has no immu-nity to suit, has since refused to pay Gimlet anything, although he swears that he never heard of the city's repealer before claiming its reward.

Question 111

In which of the following ways could the city's reward offer be effectively accepted?

(A) Only by an offeree's return promise to make a reason-able effort to bring about the arrest and conviction of an arsonist within the scope of the offer

(B) Only by an offeree's making the arrest and assisting in the successful conviction of an arsonist within the scope of the offer

(C) By an offeree's supplying information leading to arrest and conviction of an arsonist within the scope of the offer

(D) By an offeree's communication of assent through the same medium (television) used by the city in making its offer

Question 112

With respect to duration, the city's reward offer was termi-nable

(A) by lapse of time, on December 31 of the year in which it was made

(B) not by lapse of time, but only by effective revocation

(C) not by revocation, but only by lapse of a reasonable time

(D) either by lapse of a reasonable time or earlier by effective revocation

Question 113

If the city's reward offer was revocable, revocation could be effectively accomplished only

(A) by publication in the legal notices of a local newspa-per

(B) in the same manner as made, i.e., by local telecast at least once daily for one week

(C) in the same manner as made or by a comparable medium and frequency of publicity

(D) by notice mailed to all residents of the city and all other reasonably identifiable, potential offerees

Question 114

Which of the following best characterizes the relationship between Humongous and Gimlet?

(A) A unilateral offer of employment by Humongous which became irrevocable for a reasonable number of days after Gimlet commenced his investigation of the store's arson

(B) An employment for compensation subject to a condi-tion precedent that Gimlet succeed in his investigation

(C) A series of daily bilateral contracts, Humongous exchanging an express promise to pay the daily rate for Gimlet's implied promise to pursue his investiga-tion with reasonable diligence

(D) A series of daily unilateral contracts, Humongous exchanging an express promise to pay the daily rate for Gimlet's daily activity of investigating the store's arson

Question 115

In a suit by Gimlet against the city to recover the $10,000 reward, which of the following, in light of the facts given, most usefully supports Gimlet's claim?

(A) The city was benefited as a result of Gimlet's services.

(B) The city's offer was in the nature of a bounty so that the elements of contract are not essential to the city's liability.

(C) The fact that the city attempted to revoke its offer only a few months after making it demonstrated that the attempted revocation was in bad faith.

(D) Although there was no bargained-for exchange between Gimlet and the city, Gimlet's claim for the reward is supported by a moral obligation on the part of the city.

Question 116

Purvis purchased a used car from Daley, a used car dealer. Knowing them to be false, Daley made the following statements to Purvis prior to the sale:

Statement 1. This car has never been involved in an accident.

Statement 2. This car gets 25 miles to the gallon on the open highway.

Statement 3. This is as smooth-riding a car as you can get.

If Purvis asserts a claim against Daley based on deceit, which of the false statements made by Daley would support Purvis' claim?

(A) Statement 1 only

(B) Statement 2 only

(C) Statement 1 and 2 only

(D) Statements 2 and 3 only

Questions 117-119 are based on the following fact situation.

Husband and Wife, walking on a country road, were frightened by a bull running loose on the road. They climbed over a fence to get onto the adjacent property, owned by Grower. After climbing over the fence, Husband and Wife damaged some of Grower's plants which were near the fence. The fence was posted with a large sign, "No Trespassing."

Grower saw Husband and Wife and came toward them with his large watchdog on a long leash. The dog rushed at Wife. Grower had intended only to frighten Husband and Wife, but the leash broke, and before Grower could restrain the dog, the dog bit Wife.

Question 117

If Wife asserts a claim based on battery against Grower, will Wife prevail?

(A) Yes, because Grower intended that the dog frighten Wife.

(B) Yes, because the breaking of the leash establishes liability under *res ipsa loquitur.*

(C) No, because Wife made an unauthorized entry onto Grower's land.

(D) No, because Grower did not intend to cause any harmful contact with Wife.

Question 118

If Husband asserts a claim based on assault against Grower, will Husband prevail?

(A) Yes, because the landowner did not have a privilege

to use excessive force.

(B) Yes, if Husband reasonably believed that the dog might bite him.

(C) No, if the dog did not come in contact with him.

(D) No, if Grower was trying to protect his property.

Question 119

If Grower asserts a claim against Wife and Husband for damage to his plants, will Grower prevail

(A) Yes, because Wife and Husband entered on his land without permission.

(B) Yes, because Grower had posted his property with a "No Trespassing" sign.

(C) No, because Wife and Husband were confronted by an emergency situation.

(D) No, because Grower used excessive force toward Wife and Husband.

Questions 120-121 are based on the following fact situation.

Ben was the illegitimate, unacknowledged child of Fred. Fred died intestate, leaving neither spouse nor any children other than Ben. The state's law of intestate succession provides that an unacknowledged illegitimate child may not inherit his father's property. The spouse, all other blood relations, and the state are preferred as heirs over the unacknowledged illegitimate child. Ben filed suit in an appropriate court alleging that the state statute barring an illegitimate child from sharing in a parent's estate is invalid, and that he should be declared lawful heir to his father's estate.

Question 120

In challenging the validity of the state statute, Ben's strongest argument would be that

(A) there is no rational basis for preferring as heirs collateral relatives and even the state over unacknowledged children, and, therefore, the law violates the equal protection clause

(B) he has been deprived of property without due process because his fundamental right to inherit has been compromised without a compelling state need

(C) it violates the privileges and immunities clause of the Fourteenth Amendment

(D) it is a denial of procedural due process because it does not give the unacknowledged illegitimate child an opportunity to prove paternity

Question 121

The state's strongest defense of the statute would be that

(A) the authority of a state over the disposition of decedents' property located in the state is not affected by the Constitution of the United States

(B) a statute prescribing the means of disposing of the property of intestate decedents does not constitute invidious discrimination

(C) inheritance under intestate succession laws is a privilege, not a right, and therefore is not protected as property under the due process clause

(D) its interest in promoting family life and in encouraging the formal acknowledgment of paternity gives the law a rational basis

Question 122

Alice conveyed Twinoaks Farm "to Barbara, her heirs and assigns, so long as the premises are used for residential and farm purposes, then to Charles and his heirs and assigns." The jurisdiction in which Twinoaks Farm is located has adopted the common-law Rule Against Perpetuities unmodified by statute. As a consequence of the conveyance, Alice's interest in Twinoaks Farm is

(A) nothing
(B) a possibility of reverter
(C) a right of entry for condition broken
(D) a reversion in fee simple absolute

Question 123

Lawnacre was conveyed to Celeste and Donald by a deed which, in the jurisdiction in which Lawnacre is situated, created a cotenancy in equal shares and with the right of survivorship. The jurisdiction has no statute directly applicable to any of the problems posed.

Celeste, by deed, conveyed "my undivided one-half interest in Lawnacre" to Paul. Celeste has since died. In an appropriate action between Paul and Donald in which title to Lawnacre is at issue, Donald will

(A) prevail, because he is the sole owner of Lawnacre
(B) prevail if, but only if, the cotenancy created in Celeste and Donald was a tenancy by the entirety
(C) not prevail if he had knowledge of the conveyance prior to Celeste's death
(D) not prevail, because Paul and Donald own Lawnacre as tenants in common

Questions 124-128 are based on the following fact situation.

Storekeeper, the owner of a large hardware store, sells power saws for both personal and commercial use. He often takes old power saws as trade-ins on new ones. The old power saws are then completely disassembled and rebuilt with new bearings by Storekeeper's employees and sold by Storekeeper as "reconditioned saws." Purchaser, the owner and operator of a cabinetmaking shop, informed Storekeeper that he wanted to buy a reconditioned circular saw for use in his cabinetmaking business. However, the blade that was on the saw he picked out had very coarse teeth for cutting rough lumber. Purchaser told Storekeeper that he wanted a saw blade that would cut plywood. Storekeeper exchanged the coarse blade for a new one with finer teeth that would cut plywood smoothly. The new blade was manufactured by Saw-Blade Company, which

uses all available techniques to inspect its products for defects. The reconditioned saw had been manufactured by Power Saw Company.

The week after the saw was purchased, Employee, who works for Purchaser in Purchaser's cabinetmaking shop, was injured while using the saw. Employee's arm was severely cut. As a result, the cabinetmaking shop was shut down for a week until a replacement for Employee could be found.

Question 124

If Employee was injured while cutting plywood when the shaft holding the saw blade came loose when a bearing gave way and the shaft and blade flew off the saw, and if Employee asserts a claim based on strict liability in tort against Power Saw Company, Employee will probably

(A) recover if the shaft that came loose was a part of the saw when it was new
(B) recover, because Power Saw Company was in the business of manufacturing dangerous machines
(C) not recover, because Employee was not the buyer of the power saw
(D) not recover, because the saw had been rebuilt by Storekeeper

Question 125

If Employee was injured while cutting plywood when the shaft holding the saw blade came loose when a bearing gave way and the shaft and blade flew off the saw, and if Purchaser asserts a claim based on strict liability in tort against Storekeeper for loss of business because of the injury to Employee, Purchaser probably will

(A) not recover, because economic loss from injury to an employee is not within the scope of Storekeeper's duty
(B) not recover, because Storekeeper was not the manufacturer of the power saw
(C) recover, because Storekeeper knew the power saw was to be used in Purchaser's cabinetmaking business
(D) recover, because the reconditioned power saw was the direct cause of Purchaser's loss of business

Question 126

If Employee was injured while cutting plywood when the shaft holding the saw blade came loose when a bearing gave way and the shaft and blade flew off the saw, and if Employee asserts a claim based on strict liability in tort against Storekeeper, Employee probably will

(A) not recover unless Purchaser told Storekeeper that Employee would use the power saw
(B) not recover if Employee failed to notice that the shaft was coming loose
(C) recover unless Employee knew that the shaft was

coming loose

(D) recover unless Storekeeper used all possible care in reconditioning the power saw

Question 127

If Employee was cutting a sheet of plywood, and while he was doing so, the saw blade flew to pieces and severely cut Employee's arm, and if Employee asserts a claim against Storekeeper, the theory on which Employee is most likely to prevail is

(A) strict liability in tort

(B) express warranty

(C) negligence, relying on *res ipsa loquitur*

(D) negligence, relying on the sale of an inherently dangerous product

Question 128

If Employee was cutting a sheet of hard plastic, and while he was doing so, the saw blade flew to pieces and severely cut Employee's arm, and if Employee asserts a claim based on strict liability in tort against Saw-Blade Company, the defense most likely to prevail is

(A) Employee did not purchase the saw blade

(B) the blade was being put to an improper use

(C) Employee was contributorily negligent in using the blade to cut hard plastic

(D) Saw-Blade Company used every available means to inspect the blade for defects

Question 129

In which of the following situations is Defendant most likely to be guilty of common-law murder?

(A) Angered because his neighbor is having a noisy party, Defendant fires a rifle into the neighbor's house. The bullet strikes and kills a guest at the party.

(B) During an argument, Harry slaps Defendant. Angered, Defendant responds by shooting and killing Harry.

(C) Defendant drives his car through a red light and strikes and kills a pedestrian who is crossing the street.

(D) Using his fist, Defendant punches Walter in the face. As a result of the blow, Walter falls and hits his head on a concrete curb, suffers a concussion, and dies.

Question 130-134 are based on the following fact situation.

Miller is tried for armed robbery of the First Bank of City.

The prosecution, in its case in chief, offers evidence that when Miller was arrested one day after the crime, he had a quantity of heroin and a hypodermic needle in his possession.

Question 130

This evidence should be

(A) admitted to prove Miller's motive to commit the crime

(B) admitted to prove Miller's propensity to commit crimes

(C) excluded, because its probative value is substantially outweighed by the danger of unfair prejudice

(D) excluded, because such evidence may be offered only to rebut evidence of good character offered by defendant

Question 131

The prosecutor offers the testimony of a bartender that when he saw the money in Miller's wallet, he said, "You must have robbed a bank," to which Miller made no reply. This evidence is

(A) admissible to prove that Miller's conduct caused the bartender to believe that Miller robbed the bank

(B) admissible as a statement made in the presence of the defendant

(C) inadmissible, because it would violate Miller's privilege against self-incrimination

(D) inadmissible, because Miller had no reason to respond to the bartender's statement

Question 132

At the request of police, the teller who was robbed prepared a sketch bearing a strong likeness to Miller, but the teller died in an automobile accident before Miller was arrested. At trial the prosecution offers the sketch. The sketch is

(A) admissible as an identification of a person after perceiving him

(B) admissible as past recollection recorded

(C) inadmissible as hearsay not within any exception

(D) inadmissible as an opinion of the teller

Question 133

Miller testified on direct examination that he had never been in the First Bank of City. His counsel asks, "What, if anything, did you tell the police when you were arrested?" If his answer would be, "I told them I had never been in the bank," this answer would be

(A) admissible to prove Miller had never been in the bank

(B) admissible as a prior consistent statement

(C) inadmissible as hearsay not within any exception

(D) inadmissible, because it was a self-serving statement by a person with a substantial motive to fabricate

Question 134

On cross-examination of Miller, the prosecutor asks Miller whether he was convicted the previous year of tax fraud. This question is

(A) proper to show that Miller is inclined to lie

(B) proper to show that Miller is inclined to steal money

(C) improper, because the conviction has insufficient similarity to the crime charged

(D) improper, because the probative value of the evidence is outweighed by the danger of unfair prejudice

Question 135

In an effort to relieve serious and persistent unemployment in the industrialized state of Onondaga, its legislature enacted a statute requiring every business with annual sales in Onondaga of over one million dollars to purchase goods and/or services in Onondaga equal in value to at least half of the annual sales in Onondaga of the business. Which of the following constitutional provisions is the strongest basis on which to attack this statute?

(A) The due process clause of the Fourteenth Amendment

(B) The equal protection clause

(C) The commerce clause

(D) The privileges and immunities clause of the Fourteenth Amendment

Question 136

Tess occupied an apartment in a building owned by Len. She paid rent of $125 in advance each month. During the second month of occupancy, Tess organized the tenants in the building as a tenants' association and the association made demands of Len concerning certain repairs and improvements the tenants wanted. When Tess tendered rent for the third month, Len notified her that rent for the fourth and subsequent months would be $200 per month. Tess protested and pointed out that all other tenants paid rent of $125 per month. Thereupon, Len gave the required statutory notice that the tenancy was being terminated at the end of the third month. By an appropriate proceeding, Tess contests Len's right to terminate. If Tess succeeds, it will be because

(A) a periodic tenancy was created by implication

(B) the doctrine prohibiting retaliatory eviction is part of the law of the jurisdiction

(C) the $200 rent demanded violates the agreement implied by the rate charged to other tenants

(D) the law implies a term of one year in the absence of any express agreement

Question 137-138 are based on the following fact situation.

Meadowview is a large tract of undeveloped land. Black, the owner of Meadowview, prepared a development plan creating 200 house lots in Meadowview with the necessary streets and public areas. The plan was fully approved by all necessary governmental agencies and duly recorded. However, construction of the streets, utilities, and other aspects of the development of Meadowview has not yet begun, and none of the streets can be opened as public ways until they are completed in accordance with the applicable ordinances in the municipality in which Meadowview is located.

College Avenue, one of the streets laid out as part of the Meadowview development, abuts Whiteacre, an adjacent one-acre parcel owned by White. Whiteacre has no access to any public way except an old, poorly developed road which is inconvenient and cannot be used without great expense. White sold Whiteacre to Breyer. The description used in the deed from White to Breyer was the same as that used in prior deeds except that the portion of the description which formerly said, "thence by land of Black, north-easterly a distance of 200 feet, more or less," was changed to "thence by College Avenue as laid out on the Plan of Meadowview North 46 degrees East 201.6 feet," with full reference to the plan and its recording data.

Breyer now seeks a building permit which will show that Breyer intends to use College Avenue for access to Whiteacre. Black objects to the granting of a building permit on the grounds that he has never granted any right to White or Breyer to use College Avenue. There are no governing statutes or ordinances relating to the problem. Black brings an appropriate action in which the right of Breyer to use College Avenue without an express grant from Black is at issue.

Question 137

The best argument for Black in this action is that

(A) Breyer's right must await the action of appropriate public authorities to open College Avenue as a public street, since no private easements arose by implication

(B) the Statute of Frauds prevents the introduction of evidence which might prove the necessity for Breyer to use College Avenue

(C) Breyer's right to use College Avenue is restricted to the assertion of a way by necessity and the facts preclude the success of such a claim

(D) Breyer would be unjustly enriched if he were permitted to use College Avenue

Question 138

The best argument for Breyer in this action is that

(A) there is a way by necessity over Meadowview's lands to gain access to a public road

(B) the deed from White to Breyer referred to the recorded plan and therefore created rights to use the streets delineated on the plan

(C) sale of lots in Meadowview by reference to its plan creates private easements in the streets shown in the plan

(D) the recording of the plan is a dedication of the streets shown on the plan to public use

Questions 139-142 are based on the following fact situation.

Reggie offered Harriet $200 for a 30-day option to buy Harriet's land, Grandvale, for $10,000. As Harriet knew, Reggie, if granted the option, intended to resell Grandvale at a profit. Harriet declined, believing that she could find a desirable purchaser herself. Reggie thereupon said to Harriet," Make me a written 30-day offer, revocable at your pleasure, to sell me Grandvale at a sale price of $10,000, and tomorrow I will pay you $200 for so doing." Harriet agreed and gave Reggie the following document:

For 30 days I offer my land known as Grandvale to Reggie for $10,000, this offer to be revocable at my pleasure at any time before acceptance.

[Signed] Harriet

Later that day Harriet's neighbor, Norma, said to Harriet, "I know someone who would probably buy Grandvale for $15,000." Harriet asked, "Who?" and Norma replied, "My cousin Portia." Harriet thanked Norma. Several hours later, Norma telephoned Harriet and said, "Of course, if you sell to Portia I will expect the usual 5 per cent brokerage fee for finding a buyer." Harriet made no reply. The next day Harriet telephone Reggie, declared that her written offer to him was revoked, and demanded payment of $200. Reggie refused to pay. Harriet subsequently sold Grandvale to Portia for $15,000 but refused to pay Norma anything.

Question 139

In a lawsuit by Harriet against Reggie to recover $200, which of the following arguments would plausibly support Harriet's position?

I. Despite its wording, Harriet's writing was in legal effect an irrevocable offer for 30 days, given in consideration of Reggie's promise to pay $200.

II. Although Harriet's writing was an offer that Harriet could revoke at will before acceptance, such an offer was exactly what Reggie had bargained for.

III. Although Harriet's writing does not show any consideration for her act of making a revocable offer, such consideration (Reggie's promise to pay $200) can be proved by parol evidence.

(A) I and II only
(B) I and III only
(C) II and III only
(D) I, II, and III

Question 140

In a lawsuit by Harriet against Reggie to recover $200, which of the following arguments would plausibly support Reggie's position?

I. Any promise implied by Harriet in making her offer was illusory because of the revocability provision.

II. Since Harriet's offer, if any, was in writing and

involved realty, it could not be revoked by telephone.

III. Enforced payment of $200 by Reggie to Harriet would defeat Reggie's reasonable expectation if Harriet's offer was legally open for only one day.

(A) I and II only
(B) I and III only
(C) II and III only
(D) I, II, and III

Question 141

Which of the following would best describe the basis of any duty or duties created by Reggie's oral promise and Harriet's writing?

(A) Firm option
(B) Precontractual liability by promissory estoppel
(C) Unilateral contract
(D) Quasi-contractual liability

Question 142

In a lawsuit by Norma against Harriet to recover $750 as a brokerage fee, which of the following arguments would effectively support Harriet's position?

I. Harriet made no promise to pay such a fee.

II. Even if it be assumed *arguendo* that Harriet made a promise to pay such a fee, there was no bargained-for   consideration for that promise.

III. There was no effective offer and acceptance between Norma and Harriet.

(A) I and II only
(B) I and III only
(C) II and III only
(D) I, II, and III

Questions 143-147 are based on the following fact situation.

John Doe, the owner of a milk container manufacturing firm, sought to focus public attention on the milk packaging law of the State of Clinton in order to have it repealed. On a weekday at 12:00 noon, he delivered an excited, animated, and loud harangue on the steps of the State Capitol in front of the main entryway. An audience of 200 onlookers, who gathered on the steps, heckled him and laughed as he delivered his tirade. Doe repeatedly stated, gesturing expressively and making faces, that "the g-ddamned milk packaging law is stupid," and that "I will strangle every one of those g-ddamned legislators I can get hold of because this law they created proves they are all too dumb to live." After about fifteen minutes, Doe stopped speaking, and the amused crowd dispersed.

There are three relevant statutes of the State of Clinton. The first statute prohibits "all speech making, picketing, and public gatherings of every sort on the Capitol steps in front of the main entryway between 7:45 a.m.-8:15 a.m., 11:45 a.m.-12:15 p.m., 12:45 p.m.-1:15 p.m., and 4:45 p.m.-5:15 p.m., on Capitol working days."

Question 143

If Doe is prosecuted under the "Capitol steps" statute and defends on constitutional grounds, which of the following best describes the proper burden of proof?

(A) Doe would have to prove that the state did not have a rational basis for enacting this statute.

(B) Doe would have to prove that the state did not have a compelling need for this statute or that it had less restrictive means by which it could satisfy that need.

(C) The state would have to prove that it had a rational basis for enacting this statute.

(D) The state would have to prove that it had a compelling need for this statute and that there were no less restrictive means by which it could satisfy that need.

Question 144

Which of the following possible plaintiffs other than Doe would be most likely to obtain an adjudication in a federal court on the validity of the "Capitol steps" statute?

(A) A state taxpayer in the highest tax bracket

(B) A politician intending to make a campaign speech on the Capitol steps during a prohibited time

(C) A legislator who voted against the statute because he thought it unconstitutional

(D) An organization whose purpose was "to seek judicial invalidation of unconstitutional laws"

Question 145

The "Capitol steps" statute is probably

(A) constitutional both on its face and as applied to Doe

(B) constitutional on its face but unconstitutional as applied to Doe

(C) unconstitutional on its face, because it applies to all working days

(D) unconstitutional on its face, because it concerns the State Capitol

Question 146

A second state statute punishes "any person who shall intentionally threaten the life or safety of any public official for any act which he performed as part of his public office." Which of the following statements is correct concerning the possible punishment of Doe under the second statute?

(A) The statute is unconstitutional on its face.

(B) The statute is constitutional on its face, but Doe could not constitutionally be punished under it for this speech.

(C) Doe could constitutionally be punished under the statute for his speech.

(D) Doe could constitutionally be punished under the statute for his speech, but only if one or more legislators were actually present when he delivered it.

Question 147

A third state statute, enacted in 1880, makes criminal "the utterance in any public place of any blasphemy or sacrilege." Assume that there have been only a few recorded prosecutions under the 1880 statute. Doe is charged with violating its proscriptions. The charge is based wholly on the speech he delivered on the steps of the Clinton State Capitol. Which of the following constitutional defenses to this prosecution under the 1880 statute would be the LEAST likely to succeed?

(A) This statute is vague and, therefore, violates the due process clause of the Fourteenth Amendment.

(B) This statute is an establishment of religion and, therefore, violates the due process clause of the Fourteenth Amendment.

(C) Application of this statute to Doe denies him equal protection of the laws in violation of the Fourteenth Amendment.

(D) Application of this statute to Doe denies him freedom of speech in violation of the Fourteenth Amendment.

Question 148-149 are based on the following fact situation.

Peri sues Denucci for a libelous letter received by Investigator. The authenticity and contents of the letter are disputed.

Peri's attorney asks Investigator to testify that, a week before receiving the libelous letter, he had written to Denucci inquiring about Peri.

Question 148

The testimony is

(A) admissible provided this inquiry was made in the regular course of Investigator's business

(B) admissible without production of the inquiry letter or the showing of its unavailability

(C) inadmissible unless Peri's attorney has given Denucci notice of Investigator's intended testimony

(D) inadmissible unless the inquiry letter itself is shown to be unavailable

Question 149

Investigator, if permitted will testify that, "I received a letter that I cannot now find, which read:

Dear Investigator,

You inquired about Peri. We fired him last month when we discovered that he had been stealing from the stockroom.

Denucci"

The testimony should be admitted in evidence **only** if the

(A) jury finds that Investigator has quoted the letter precisely

(B) jury is satisfied that the original letter is unavailable

(C) judge is satisfied that Investigator has quoted the letter precisely

(D) judge finds that the original letter is unavailable

Questions 150-151 are based on the following fact situation.

Photo, a free-lance photographer, took a picture of Player in front of Shoe Store. Player was a nationally known amateur basketball star who had received much publicity in the press. At the time, the window display in Shoe Store featured "Jumpers," a well-known make of basketball shoes. Photo sold the picture, greatly enlarged, to Shoe Store and told Shoe Store that Photo had Player's approval to do so and that Player had consented to Shoe Store's showing the enlarged picture in the window. Shoe Store made no effort to ascertain whether Player had given his consent to Photo. In fact, Player did not even know that Photo had taken the picture. Shoe Store put the enlarged picture in the window with the display of "Jumpers" shoes. The college that Player attended believed that Player had intentionally endorsed Shoe Store and "Jumpers" shoes, and the college cancelled his athletic scholarship.

Question 150

If Player asserts a claim based on defamation against Shoe Store, will Player prevail?

(A) Yes, if Shoe Store was reckless in accepting Photo's statement that Photo had Player's approval.

(B) Yes, because the defamatory material was in printed form.

(C) No, if Shoe Store believed Photo's statement that Photo had Player's approval.

(D) No, because the picture of Player was not defamatory *per se.*

Question 151

If Player asserts a claim based on invasion of privacy against Shoe Store, will Player prevail?

(A) Yes, because Photo had no right to take Player's picture.

(B) Yes, because Shoe Store, without Player's permission, used Player's picture for profit.

(C) No, because Player was already a basketball star who had received much publicity in the press.

(D) No, because Shoe Store believed it had permission to put the picture in its window.

Question 152

Landover, the owner in fee simple of Highacre, an apartment house property, entered into an enforceable written agreement with VanMeer to sell Highacre to VanMeer. The agreement provided that a good and marketable title was to be conveyed free and clear of all encumbrances. However, the agreement was silent as to the risk of fire prior to the closing, and there is no applicable statute in the state where the land is located. The premises were not insured. The day before the scheduled closing date, Highacre was wholly destroyed by fire. When VanMeer refused to close, Landover brought an action in specific performance. If Landover prevails, the most likely reason will be that

(A) the failure of VanMeer to insure his interest as the purchaser of Highacre precludes any relief for him.

(B) the remedy at law is inadequate in actions concerning real estate contracts and either party is entitled to specific performance

(C) equity does not permit consideration of surrounding circumstances in actions concerning real estate contracts

(D) the doctrine of equitable conversion applies

Question 153

Realco Realtors acquired a large tract of land upon which Realco developed a mobile home subdivision. The tract was divided into 60 lots, appropriate utilities were installed, and a plat of the entire tract, including a Declaration of Restrictions, was properly drawn and recorded. The Declaration of Restrictions included the following: "3. Ownership and/or occupancy are restricted to persons 21 years of age or over; one family per lot." As the separate lots were sold, the deed to each lot included the following provision: "As shown on recorded plat [properly identified by page and plat book reference] and subject to the restrictions therein contained." One of the lots were purchased by Dawson, who now resides in a mobile home on the lot together with his wife and two children, aged 11 and 13. Other lot owners in the subdivision brought action against Dawson to enjoin further occupancy by the children under 21 years of age. If judgment is for Dawson, the issue that most likely will determine the case will be whether

(A) the mobile home is treated as personalty or realty

(B) the restriction constitutes an unlawful restraint on alienation

(C) enforcement of the restriction is considered a violation of the equal protection clause of the Fourteenth Amendment of the United States Constitution.

(D) the terms of the restriction are expressly repeated verbatim in Dawson's deed

Questions 154-155 are based on the following fact situation.

In the application for a life insurance policy, Mary answered in the negative the question, "Have you ever had any heart disease?" Both the application and the insurance policy which was issued provided: "Applicant warrants the truthfulness of the statements made in the application and they are made conditions to the contract of insurance." Unknown to Mary, she had had a heart disease at a very early age. The policy provided that the proceeds were not to be paid over to the named beneficiary, Mary's daughter, Joan, "until she reaches the age of 21." No contingent beneficiary was named in the policy. Mary was killed in an automobile accident two months after the policy was issued. Joan died one month later at the age of 19 from injuries incurred in the same accident.

Question 154

If the question is raised in an action against the insurance company, how is the court likely to construe the clause dealing with the truthfulness of statements in the application?

(A) The clause is a condition, and because the condition was not met, the company will not be liable.

(B) The clause is a condition, but it will be interpreted to mean, "truthfulness to the best of my knowledge."

(C) The clause is not a condition, and therefore the company may be liable even though Mary's statement was not true.

(D) The clause is not a condition but is a promise, and therefore the company will have a cause of action against Mary's estate for any losses it suffered because of Mary's misstatement.

Question 155

If no objection is made concerning Mary's misstatement in the application, how is the court most likely to construe the clause dealing with the payment of the proceeds to Joan?

(A) Joan's reaching the age of 21 is a constructive condition concurrent.

(B) Joan's reaching the age of 21 is a condition precedent to the insurance company's duty to pay anyone.

(C) Joan's reaching the age of 21 has legal significance only with respect to the time of payment.

(D) Joan's reaching the age of 21 has no legal significance.

Question 156-158 are based on the following fact situation.

Defendant became intoxicated at a bar. He got into his car and drove away. Within a few blocks, craving another drink, he stopped his car in the middle of the street, picked up a brick, and broke the display window of a liquor store. As he was reaching for a bottle, the night watchman arrived. Startled, Defendant turned, and struck the watchman on the head with the bottle, killing him. Only vaguely aware of what was happening, Defendant returned to his car, consumed more liquor, and then drove off at a high speed. He ran a red light and struck and killed a pedestrian who was crossing the street.

Relevant statutes define burglary to include "breaking and entering a building not used as a dwelling with the intent to commit a crime therein." Manslaughter is defined as the "killing of a human being in a criminally reckless manner." Criminal recklessness is "consciously disregarding a substantial and unjustifiable risk resulting from the actor's conduct." Murder is defined as "the premeditated and intentional killing of another or the killing of another in the commission of committing rape, robbery, burglary, or arson." Another statute provides that intoxication is not a defense to crime unless it negates an element of the offense.

Defendant was charged with the murder of the watch-

man and manslaughter in the death of the pedestrian. Assume that he is tried separately on each charge.

Question 156

At Defendant's trial for the murder of the watchman, the court should in substance charge the jury on the issue of the defense of intoxication that

(A) intoxication is a defense to the underlying crime of burglary if Defendant, due to drunkenness, did not form an intent to commit a crime within the building, in which case there can be no conviction for murder unless Defendant intentionally and with premeditation killed the watchman.

(B) voluntary intoxication is not a defense to the crime of murder

(C) Defendant is guilty of murder despite his intoxication only if the state proves beyond a reasonable doubt that the killing of the watchman was premeditated and intentional

(D) voluntary intoxication is a defense to the crime of murder if Defendant would not have killed the watchman but for his intoxication

Question 157

At Defendant's trial on the charge of manslaughter in the death of the pedestrian, his best argument would be that

(A) he was too intoxicated to realize he was creating a substantial and unjustifiable risk in the manner in which he was operating his car

(B) when he got in the car his acts were not voluntary because he was too intoxicated to know where he was or what he was doing

(C) the pedestrian was contributorily negligent in failing to see Defendant's car approaching

(D) he was too intoxicated to form any intent to voluntarily operate the automobile

Question 158

The state's best argument to counter Defendant's argument in the last question on the intoxication issue in the manslaughter death of the pedestrian is that

(A) intoxication is no defense to the crime charged, because manslaughter is historically a general intent crime

(B) intoxication is a defense only to a specific intent crime, and no specific intent is involved in the definition of the crime of manslaughter

(C) conscious risk-taking refers to Defendant's entire course of conduct, including drinking with the knowledge that he might become intoxicated and seriously injure or kill someone while driving

(D) whether Defendant was intoxicated or not is not the crucial issue here; the real issue is whether the manner in which Defendant was operating his car can be characterized under the facts as criminally reckless.

Questions 159-160 are based on the following fact situation.

The Federal Automobile Safety Act establishes certain safety and performance standards for all automobiles manufactured in the United States. The Act creates a five-member "Automobile Commission" to investigate automobile safety, to make recommendations to Congress for new laws, to make further rules establishing safety and performance standards, and to prosecute violations of the act. The chairman is appointed by the President, two members are selected by the President pro tempore of the Senate, and two by the Speaker of the House of Representatives.

Minicar, Inc., a minor United States car manufacturer, seeks to enjoin enforcement of the Commission's rules.

Question 159

The best argument that Minicar can make is that

(A) legislative power may not be delegated by Congress to an agency in the absence of clear guidelines

(B) the commerce power does not extend to the manufacture of automobiles not used in interstate commerce

(C) Minicar is denied due process of law because it is not represented on the Commission

(D) the Commission lacks authority to enforce its standards because not all of its members were appointed by the President

Question 160

The appropriate decision for the court is to

(A) allow the Commission to continue investigating automobile safety and making recommendations to Congress

(B) allow the Commission to prosecute violations of the act but not allow it to issue rules

(C) forbid the Commission to take any action under the act

(D) order that all members of the Commission be appointed by the President by and with the advice and consent of the Senate

Questions 161-162 are based on the following fact situation.

Johnson wanted to purchase a used motor vehicle. The used car lot of Car Company, in a remote section away from town, was enclosed by a ten-foot chain link fence. While Johnson and Sales Representative, an employee of Car Company, were in the used car lot looking at cars, a security guard locked the gate at 1:30 p.m., because it was Saturday and the lot was supposed to be closed after 1:00 p.m. Saturday until Monday morning. At 1:45 p.m. Johnson and Sales Representative discovered they were locked in.

There was no traffic in the vicinity and no way in which help could be summoned. After two hours, Johnson began to panic at the prospect of remaining undiscovered and

without food and water until Monday morning. Sales Representative decided to wait in a car until help should come. Johnson tried to climb over the fence and, in doing so, fell, and was injured. Johnson asserts a claim against Car Company for damages for his injuries.

Question 161

If Johnson's claim is based on negligence, is the defense of assumption of the risk applicable?

(A) Yes, if a reasonable person would have recognized that there was some risk of falling while climbing the fence.

(B) Yes, because Sales Representative, as Car Company's agent, waited for help.

(C) No, if it appeared that there was no other practicable way of getting out of the lot before Monday.

(D) No, because Johnson was confined as the result of a volitional act.

Question 162

If Johnson's claim is based on false imprisonment, will Johnson prevail?

(A) Yes, because he was confined against his will.

(B) Yes, because he was harmed as a result of his confinement.

(C) No, unless the security guard was negligent in locking the gate.

(D) No, unless the security guard knew that someone was in the lot at the time the guard locked the gate.

Question 163-164 are based on the following fact situation.

Albert, the owner of a house and lot, leased the same to Barnes for a term of five years. In addition to the house, there was also an unattached, two-car brick garage located on the lot. Barnes earned his living as an employee in a local grocery store, but his hobby consisted of wood carving and the making of small furniture. Barnes installed a work bench, electric lights, and a radiator in the garage. He also laid pipes connecting the radiator with the heating plant inside the house. Thereafter Albert mortgaged the premises to Good Bank to secure a loan. Barnes was not given notice of the mortgage, but the mortgage was recorded. Still later, Albert defaulted on the mortgage payments, and Good Bank began foreclosure proceedings, as it was entitled to do under the terms of the mortgage. By this time Barnes's lease was almost ended. Barnes began the removal of the equipment he had installed in the garage. Good Bank brought an action to enjoin the removal of the equipment mentioned above. Both Barnes and Albert were named as defendants.

Question 163

If the court refuses the injunction, it will be because

(A) Barnes was without notice of the mortgage

(B) the circumstances reveal that the equipment was installed for Barnes's exclusive benefit

(C) in the absence of a contrary agreement, a residential tenant is entitled to remove any personal property he voluntarily brings upon the premises

(D) the Statute of Frauds precludes the Bank from claiming any interest in the equipment

Question 164

If the equipment concerned had been installed by Albert, but the facts were otherwise unchanged, the effect on Good Bank's prayer for an injunction would be that the

(A) likelihood of Good Bank's succeeding would be improved

(B) likelihood of Good Bank's succeeding would be lessened

(C) likelihood of Good Bank's succeeding would be unaffected

(D) outcome of the litigation would depend upon whether or not the mortgage expressly mentioned personal property located on the premises

Question 165

Lester, the owner in fee simple of a small farm consisting of thirty acres of land improved with a house and several outbuildings, leased the same to Tanner for a ten-year period. After two years had expired, the government condemned twenty acres of the property and allocated the compensation award to Lester and Tanner according to their respective interest so taken. It so happened, however, that the twenty acres taken embraced all of the farm's tillable land, leaving only the house, outbuildings, and a small woodlot. There is no applicable statute in the jurisdiction where the property is located nor any provision in the lease relating to condemnation. Tanner quit possession, and Lester brought suit against him to recover rent. Lester will

(A) lose, because there has been a frustration of purpose which excuses Tanner from further performance of his contract to pay rent

(B) lose, because there has been a breach of the implied covenant of quiet enjoyment by Lester's inability to provide Tanner with possession of the whole of the property for the entire term

(C) win, because of the implied warranty on the part of the tenant to return the demised premises in the same condition at the end of the term as they were at the beginning

(D) win, because the relationship of landlord and tenant was unaffected by the condemnation, thus leaving Tanner still obligated to pay rent

Question 166-167 are based on the following fact situation.

Statutes in the jurisdiction define criminal assault as "an attempt to commit a criminal battery" and criminal battery as "causing an offensive touching."

As Edward was walking down the street, a gust of wind blew his hat off. Edward reached out, trying to grab his hat, and narrowly missed striking Margaret in the face with his hand. Margaret, fearful of being struck by Edward, pushed Edward away.

Question 166

If charged with criminal assault, Edward should be found

(A) guilty, because he caused Margaret to be in apprehension of an offensive touching

(B) guilty, because he should have realized he might strike someone by reaching out

(C) not guilty, because he did not intend to hit Margaret

(D) not guilty, because he did not hit Margaret

Question 167

If charged with criminal battery, Margaret should be found

(A) guilty, because she intentionally pushed Edward

(B) guilty, because she caused the touching of Edward whether she meant to do so or not

(C) not guilty, because a push is not an offensive touching

(D) not guilty, because she was justified in pushing Edward

Question 168

Police were concerned about an increase in marijuana traffic in Defendant's neighborhood. One night, Police Officers, accompanied by dogs trained to sniff out marijuana, went into the back yard of Defendant's house and onto his porch. Defendant and his friend were inside having dinner. The dogs acted as if they smelled marijuana. Police Officers knocked on the back door. Defendant answered the door and let them in. Defendant was immediately placed under arrest. After a brief search, Police Officers confiscated a large quantity of marijuana which they found in Defendant's linen closet.

Defendant's motion to prevent introduction of the marijuana into evidence will most probably be

(A) denied, because the search was incident to a valid arrest

(B) denied, because Defendant permitted Police Officers to enter his house

(C) granted, because under the circumstances the police activity violated Defendant's reasonable expectations of privacy

(D) granted, because this kind of detection by trained dogs has not been scientifically verified and cannot be the basis for probable cause

Question 169-172 are based on the following fact situation.

Drew was tried for the July 21 murder of Victor. In his case in chief, Drew called as his first witness, Wilma to testify to Drew's reputation in his community as "a peaceable man."

Question 169

The testimony is

(A) admissible as tending to prove Drew is believable
(B) admissible as tending to prove Drew is innocent
(C) inadmissible, because Drew has not testified
(D) inadmissible, because reputation is not a proper way to prove character

Question 170

Drew called William to testify that on July 20 Drew said that he was about to leave that day to visit relatives in a distant state. The testimony is

(A) admissible, because it is a declaration of present mental state
(B) admissible, because it is not hearsay
(C) inadmissible, because it is irrelevant
(D) inadmissible, because it is hearsay not within any exception

Question 171

Drew called Wilson to testify to alibi. On cross-examination of Wilson, the prosecution asked, "Isn't it a fact that you are Drew's first cousin?" The question is

(A) proper, because it goes to bias
(B) proper, because a relative is not competent to give reputation testimony
(C) improper, because the question goes beyond the scope of direct examination
(D) improper, because the evidence being sought is irrelevant

Question 172

Drew called Warren to testify to alibi. On cross-examination of Warren, the prosecutor asked, "Weren't you on the jury that acquitted Drew of another criminal charge?" The best reason for sustaining an objection to this question is that

(A) the question goes beyond the scope of direct examination
(B) the probative value of the answer would be outweighed by its tendency to mislead
(C) the question is leading
(D) prior jury service in a case involving a party renders the witness incompetent

Question 173

Re-direct examination of a witness must be permitted in which of the following circumstances?

(A) To reply to any matter raised in cross-examination
(B) Only to reply to significant new matter raised in cross-examination
(C) Only to reiterate the essential elements of the case
(D) Only to supply significant information inadvertently omitted on direct examination

Question 174

On March 1, Mechanic agreed to repair Ohner's machine for $5,000, to be paid on completion of the work. On March 15, before the work was completed, Mechanic sent a letter to Ohner with a copy to Jones, telling Ohner to pay the $5,000 to Jones, who was one of Mechanic's creditors. Mechanic then completed the work.

Which of the following, if true, would best serve Ohner as a defense in an action brought against him by Jones for $5,000?

(A) Jones was incapable of performing Mechanic's work.
(B) Mechanic had not performed his work in a workman-like manner.
(C) On March 1, Mechanic had promised Ohner that he would not assign the contract.
(D) Jones was not the intended beneficiary of the Ohner-Mechanic contract.

Questions 175-177 are based on the following fact situation.

BCD, a manufacturer of computers, pays its sales people a salary of $1,000 per month and a commission of 5% on billings actually rendered for machines that they sell. BCD sales people are employed at will under written agreements which provide that in order to receive a commission the sales person must be in the employment of the company when the bill is sent to the customer.

In 1976, John, a sales person for BCD, worked for eight months to get an order from Bobb Corporation for a large $750,000 computer. He consulted extensively with Bobb's top executives and worked with its operating personnel to develop detailed specifications for the new equipment. He also promised Bobb, with BCD's knowledge and approval, to assist Bobb for six months after installation in making the equipment work.

On January 1, 1977, Bobb signed an order, and on March 1 the computer was installed. On March 15, BCD fired John on the stated ground that he had failed to meet his 1975 and 1976 sales quotas. John thought that BCD was correct in this statement. Another sales person, Franklin, was thereupon assigned to service the Bobb account. On March 31, BCD billed Bobb for the computer.

Question 175

Assume for this question only that BCD's termination of John's employment was not wrongful. If John, after demand and refusal, sues BCD for the Bobb sale commission, which of the following is the most likely to result?

(A) John will win, because he had procured the sale of the computer.
(B) John will win, because he had promised Bobb to assist in making the equipment work.
(C) BCD will win, because Franklin is entitled to the commission on a *quantum meruit* basis.
(D) BCD will win, because John was not employed as a BCD sales person when Bobb was billed for the computer.

Question 176

Assume for this question only that BCD's termination of John's employment was not wrongful. If John sues BCD for the reasonable value of his services, which of the following is the most likely result?

(A) John will win, because BCD benefitted as a result of John's services.
(B) John will win, because BCD made an implied-in-fact promise to pay a reasonable commission for services that result in sales.
(C) John will lose, because there is an express contractual provision pre-empting the subject of compensation for his services.
(D) John will lose, because he cannot perform his agreement to assist the customer for six months.

Question 177

Which of the following additional facts, if shown by the evidence, would support a claim by John against BCD?

I.   BCD terminated John because Franklin is the son of the company's president, who wanted his son to have the commission instead of John.

II.   BCD and John were mistaken; John had in fact exceeded his sales quotas for 1975 and 1976.

III. John had worked for BCD as a sales person for 20 years.

(A) I only
(B) II only
(C) I and II only
(D) I, II, and III

Question 178

In 1963 Hobson was appointed to a tribunal established pursuant to a congressional act. The tribunal's duties were to review claims made by veterans and to make recommendations to the Veterans Administration on their merits. Congress later abolished the tribunal and established a different format for review of such claims. Hobson was offered a federal administrative position in the same bureau at a lesser salary. He thereupon sued the government on the ground that Congress may not remove a federal judge from office during good behavior nor diminish his compensation during continuance in office. Govern-

ment attorneys filed a motion to dismiss the action. The court should

(A) deny the motion because of the independence of the federal judiciary constitutionally guaranteed by Article III
(B) deny the motion, because Hobson has established a property right to his federal employment of the tribunal
(C) grant the motion, because Hobson lacked standing to raise the question
(D) grant the motion, because Hobson was not a judge under Article III and is not entitled to life tenure

Questions 179-180 are based on the following fact situation.

In 1960, Cattle Company paid $30,000 for a 150-acre tract of agricultural land well suited for a cattle feed lot. The tract was ten miles from the city of Metropolis, then a community of 50,000 people, and five miles from the nearest home. By 1996, the city limits extended to Cattle Company's feed lot, and the city had a population of 350,000. About 10,000 people lived within three miles of the cattle feeding operation. The Cattle Company land is outside the city limits and no zoning ordinance applies. The Cattle Company land is now worth $300,000, and $25,000 has been invested in buildings and pens.

Cattle Company, conscious of its obligations to its neighbors, uses the best and most sanitary feed lot procedures, including chemical sprays, to keep down flies and odors and frequently removes manure. Despite these measures, residents of Metropolis complain of flies and odors. An action has been filed by five individual homeowners who live within half a mile of the Cattle Company feed lot. The plaintiffs' homes are valued currently at $25,000 to $40,000 each. Flies in the area are five to ten times more numerous than in other parts of Metropolis, and extremely obnoxious odors are frequently carried by the wind to the plaintiffs' homes. The flies and odors are a substantial health hazard.

Question 179

If plaintiffs assert a claim based on public nuisance, plaintiffs will

(A) prevail if plaintiffs sustained harm different from that suffered by the public at large
(B) prevail if Cattle Company's acts interfered with any person's enjoyment of his property
(C) not prevail, because only the state may bring an action based on public nuisance
(D) not prevail, because plaintiffs came to the nuisance

Question 180

If plaintiffs assert a claim based on private nuisance, plaintiffs will

(A) prevail, because Cattle Company's activity unreasonably interfered with plaintiffs' use and enjoyment of their property

(B) prevail, because Cattle Company's activity constitutes an inverse condemnation of their property

(C) not prevail, because Cattle Company had operated the feed lot for more than 25 years

(D) not prevail, because Cattle Company uses the most reasonable procedures to keep down flies and odors

Question 181

Alan, who was already married, went through a marriage ceremony with Betty and committed bigamy. Carl, his friend, who did not know of Alan's previous marriage, had encouraged Alan to marry Betty and was best man at the ceremony. If Carl is charged with being an accessory to bigamy, he should be found

(A) not guilty, because his encouragement and assistance was not the legal cause of the crime

(B) not guilty, because he did not have the mental state required for aiding and abetting

(C) guilty, because he encouraged Alan, and his mistake as to the existence of a prior marriage is not a defense to a charge of bigamy

(D) guilty, because he was present when the crime occurred and is thus a principal in the second degree

Question 182

Defendant was charged with murder. His principal defense was that he had killed in hot blood and should be guilty only of manslaughter. The judge instructed the jury that the state must prove guilt beyond a reasonable doubt, that the killing was presumed to be murder, and that the charge could be reduced to manslaughter, and Defendant accordingly found guilty of this lesser offense, if Defendant showed by a fair preponderance of the evidence that the killing was committed in the heat of passion on sudden provocation. Defendant was convicted of murder. On appeal, he now seeks a new trial and claims error in the judge's instructions to the jury.

Defendant's conviction will most probably be

(A) affirmed, because the judge carefully advised the jury of the state's obligation to prove guilt beyond a reasonable doubt

(B) affirmed, because Defendant's burden to show hot blood was not one of ultimate persuasion but only one of producing evidence to rebut a legitimate presumption

(C) reversed, because the instruction put a burden on Defendant which denied him due process of law

(D) reversed, because presumptions have a highly prejudicial effect and thus cannot be used on behalf of the state in a criminal case.

Question 183

FBI agents, without a warrant and without permission of Mexican law enforcement or judicial officers, entered Mex-

ico, kidnapped Steven, an American citizen wanted in the United States for drug smuggling violations, and forcibly drove him back to Texas. Thereafter, the agents, again without a warrant, broke into the Texas home of Joan, wanted as a confederate of Steven, and arrested her.

Steven and Joan were both indicted for narcotics violations. Both moved to dismiss the indictment on the ground that their arrests violated the Fourth Amendment.

The court should

(A) grant the motions of both Steven and Joan.

(B) grant the motion of Steven and deny the motion of Joan.

(C) grant the motion of Joan and deny the motion of Steven.

(D) deny the motions of both Steven and Joan.

Question 184

Alice was held up at the point of a gun, an unusual revolver with a red-painted barrel, while she was clerking in a neighborhood grocery store. Dennis is charged with armed robbery of Alice.

The prosecutor calls Winthrop to testify that, a week after the robbery of Alice, he was robbed by Dennis with a pistol that had red paint on the barrel. Winthrop's testimony is

(A) admissible as establishing an identifying circumstance

(B) admissible as showing that Dennis was willing to commit robbery

(C) inadmissible, because it is improper character evidence

(D) inadmissible, because its probative value is substantially outweighed by the danger of unfair prejudice

Questions 185-186 are based on the following fact situation.

An act of Congress provides that "no federal court shall order the implementation of a public school desegregation plan that would require the transportation of any student to a school other than the school closest or next closest to this place of residence."

Question 185

Which of the following is the strongest argument for the constitutionality of the act?

(A) The Fourteenth Amendment authorizes Congress to define governmental conduct which violates the equal protection clause.

(B) Under Article III, Congress may restrict the jurisdiction of the federal courts.

(C) Transportation of students is subject to regulation by Congress because commerce is involved.

(D) Congress provides partial support for public education and is therefore entitled to establish conditions upon the expenditure of federal grants.

Question 186

Which of the following is the strongest argument **against** the constitutionality of the act?

(A) This statute unduly burdens interstate commerce.

(B) Congress cannot limit the authority of federal courts to hear and decide cases properly presented for decision.

(C) The privileges and immunities clause of the Fourteenth Amendment prohibits Congress from limiting the forms of relief afforded by federal courts.

(D) The courts, not Congress, have the primary responsibility for defining the minimum requirements of the equal protection clause of the Fourteenth Amendment.

Question 187

Maria is the owner and possessor of Goodacre, on which there is a lumber yard. Maria conveyed to Reliable Electric Company the right to construct and use an overhead electric line across Goodacre to serve other properties. The conveyance was in writing, but the writing made no provision concerning the responsibility for repair or maintenance of the line. Reliable installed the poles and erected the electric line in a proper and workmanlike manner. Neither Maria nor Reliable took any steps toward the maintenance or repair of the line after it was built. Neither party complained to the other about any failure to repair. Because of the failure to repair or properly maintain the line, it fell to the ground during a storm. In doing so, it caused a fire in the lumber yard and did considerable damage. Maria sued Reliable Electric Company to recover for damages to the lumber yard. The decision should be for

(A) Maria, because the owner of an easement has duty to so maintain the easement as to avoid unreasonable interference with the use of the servient tenement by its lawful possessor

(B) Maria, because the owner of an easement is absolutely liable for any damage caused to the servient tenement by the exercise of the easement

(C) Reliable Electric Company, because the possessor of the servient tenement has a duty to give the easement holder notice of defective conditions

(D) Reliable Electric Company, because an easement holder's right to repair is a right for his own benefit, and is therefore inconsistent with any duty to repair for the benefit of another

Questions 188-191 are based on the following fact situation.

Sartorial, Inc., a new business enterprise about to commence the manufacture of clothing, entered into a written agreement to purchase all of its monthly requirements of a certain elasticized fabric for a period of three years from the Stretch Company at a specified unit price and agreed delivery and payment terms. The agreement also provides:

1. The parties covenant not to assign this contract.

2. Payments coming due hereunder for the first two months shall be made directly by Sartorial to Virginia Wear and Son, Inc., a creditor Stretch.

Stretch promptly made an "assignment of the contract" to Finance Company as security for a $100,000 loan. Sartorial subsequently ordered, took delivery of, and paid Stretch the agreed price ($5,000) for Sartorial's requirement of the fabric for the first month of its operation.

Question 188

Which of the following accurately states the legal effect of the covenant not to assign the contract?

(A) The covenant made the assignment to Finance Company ineffective.

(B) The covenant had no legal effect.

(C) Stretch's assignment was a breach of its contract with Sartorial but was nevertheless effective to transfer to Finance Company Stretch's rights against Sartorial.

(D) By normal interpretation, a covenant against assignment in a sale-of-goods agreement applies only to the buyer, not the seller.

Question 189

Assume for this question only that the assignment from Stretch to Finance Company was effective, and that Sartorial was unaware of the assignment when it paid Stretch the $5,000. Which of the following is correct?

(A) Sartorial is liable to Finance Company for $5,000.

(B) Stretch is liable to Finance Company for $5,000.

(C) Sartorial and Stretch are each liable to Finance Company for $2,500.

(D) Neither Sartorial nor Stretch is liable to Finance Company for any amount.

Question 190

Assume for this question only that the assignment from Stretch to Finance Company was effective, and that Virginia Wear and Son, Inc., did not become aware of the original agreement between Sartorial and Stretch until after Stretch's acceptance of the $5,000 payment from Sartorial. Which of the following, if any, is (are) correct?

I. Virginia Wear and Son, Inc., was an incidental beneficiary of the Sartorial-Stretch agreement.

II. Virginia Wear and Son, Inc., has a prior right to Sartorial's $5,000 payment as against either Stretch or Finance Company.

(A) I only

(B) II only

(C) Both I and II

(D) Neither I nor II

Question 191

Assume for this question only that, two weeks after making the $5,000 payment to Stretch, Sartorial by written notice to Stretch terminated the agreement for purchase of the elasticized fabric because market conditions had in fact forced Sartorial out of the clothing manufacture business. In an immediate suit by Finance Company against Sartorial for total breach, which of the following would be useful in Sartorial's defense?

(A) Stretch's rights under its agreement with Sartorial were personal and therefore non-assignable.

(B) Stretch's "assignment of the contract" to Finance Company to secure a loan would normally be interpreted as a delegation of Stretch's duties under the contract as well as an assignment of its rights; and its duties, owed to Sartorial, were personal and therefore nondelegable.

(C) The original contract between Sartorial and Stretch was unenforceable by either party for want of a legally sufficient consideration for Stretch's promise to supply Sartorial's requirements of the elasticized fabric.

(D) Sartorial ceased in good faith to have any further requirements for elasticized fabric.

Question 192

Seth owned a vacant lot known as Richacre. Seth entered into a written contract with Bob to build a house of stated specifications on Richacre and to sell the house and lot to Bob. The contract provided for an "inside date" of April 1, 1997, and an "outside date" of May 1, 1997, for completion of the house and delivery of a deed. Neither party tendered performance on the dates stated. On May 3, 1997, Bob notified Seth in writing of Bob's election to cancel the contract because of Seth's failure to deliver title by May 1. On May 12, Seth notified Bob that some unanticipated construction difficulties had been encountered but that Seth was entitled to a reasonable time to complete in any event. The notification also included a promise that Seth would be ready to perform by May 29 and that he was setting that date as an adjourned closing date. Seth obtained a certificate of occupancy and appropriate documents of title, and he tendered performance on May 29. Bob refused. Seth brought an action to recover damages for breach of contract. The decision in the case will most likely be determined by whether

(A) Seth acted with due diligence in completing the house

(B) Bob can prove actual "undue hardship" caused by the delay

(C) the expressions "inside date" and "outside date" are construed to make time of the essence

(D) there is a showing of good faith in Bob's efforts to terminate the contract

Question 193

Metterly, the owner in fee simple of Brownacre, by quit-claim deed conveyed Brownacre to her daughter, Doris, who paid no consideration for the conveyance. The deed was never recorded. About a year after the delivery of the deed, Metterly decided that this gift had been ill-advised. She requested that Doris destroy the deed, which Doris dutifully and voluntarily did. Within the month following the destruction of the deed, Metterly and Doris were killed in a common disaster. Each of the successors in interest claimed title to Brownacre. In an appropriate action to determine the title to Brownacre, the probable outcome will be that

(A) Metterly was the owner of Brownacre, because Doris was a donee and therefore could not acquire title by quitclaim deed

(B) Metterly was the owner of Brownacre, because title to Brownacre reverted to her upon the voluntary destruction of the deed by Doris

(C) Doris was the owner of Brownacre, because her destruction of the deed to Brownacre was under the undue influence of Metterly

(D) Doris was the owner of Brownacre, because the deed was merely evidence of her title, and its destruction was insufficient to cause title to pass back to Metterly

Questions 194-196 are based on the following fact situation.

Motorist arranged to borrow his friend Owner's car to drive for one day while Motorist's car was being repaired. Owner knew that the brakes on his car were faulty and might fail in an emergency. Owner forgot to tell Motorist about the brakes when Motorist picked up the car, but Owner did telephone Spouse, Motorist's wife, and told her about them. Spouse, however, forgot to tell Motorist.

Motorist was driving Owner's car at a reasonable rate of speed and within the posted speed limit, with Spouse as a passenger. Another car, driven by Cross, crossed in front of Motorist at an intersection and in violation of the traffic signal. Motorist tried to stop, but the brakes failed, and the two cars collided. If the brakes had been in proper working order, Motorist could have stopped in time to avoid the collision. Motorist and Spouse were injured.

Question 194

If Motorist asserts a claim against Cross, Motorist will

(A) recover the full amount of his damages, because Motorist himself was not at fault

(B) recover only a proportion of his damages, because Spouse was also at fault

(C) not recover, because Spouse was negligent and a wife's negligence is imputed to her husband

(D) not recover, because the failure of the brakes was the immediate cause of the collision

Question 195

If the jurisdiction has adopted "pure" comparative negligence and Spouse asserts a claim against Cross, Spouse will

(A) recover in full for her injuries, because Motorist, who was driving the car in which she was riding, was not himself at fault

(B) recover a proportion of her damages based on the respective degrees of her negligence and that of Cross

(C) not recover, because but for the failure of the brakes the collision would not have occurred

(D) not recover, because she was negligent and her negligence continued until the moment of impact

Question 196

If Motorist asserts a claim against Owner, will Motorist prevail?

(A) Yes, in negligence, because Owner knew the brakes were faulty and failed to tell Motorist.

(B) Yes, in strict liability in tort, because the car was defective and Owner lent it to Motorist.

(C) No, because Owner was a gratuitous lender, and thus his duty of care was slight.

(D) No, because the failure of Spouse to tell Motorist about the brakes was the cause in fact of Motorist's harm.

Question 197

In which of the following situations is Defendant most likely to be guilty of larceny?

(A) Defendant took Sue's television set, with the intention of returning it the next day. However, he dropped it and damaged it beyond repair.

(B) Defendant went into Tom's house and took $100 in the belief that Tom had damaged Defendant's car to that amount.

(C) Mistakenly believing that larceny does not include the taking a dog, Defendant took his neighbor's dog and sold it.

(D) Unreasonably mistaking George's car for his own, Defendant got into George's car in a parking lot and drove it home.

Question 198

Acting on an anonymous telephone call, police went to Desmond's apartment, knocked on the door, and demanded to search it for narcotics. When Desmond refused, the police forced the door open and placed him under arrest. As they were removing him from the apartment, Desmond offered to give the officers "valuable information" in exchange for his release. Before he could say anything else, Desmond was given Miranda warnings by the police. Thereafter he told the police that he had stored some heroin in his friends' apartment and that he and his friend had been going to sell it. The heroin was recovered, and Desmond was prosecuted for conspiracy to sell narcotics and for possession of narcotics. At his trial, Desmond moved to suppress his statements. Which of the following is Desmond's best argument in support of the motion to suppress?

(A) Desmond is entitled to know the identity of his accuser, and the state cannot supply this information.

(B) The police should have given Desmond Miranda warnings prior to entry into the apartment, and the warnings were ineffectual once Desmond offered to give the police information.

(C) Desmond was intimidated by the forced entry into the apartment, and since the statements were involuntary and coerced, their use against him would violate due process of law.

(D) The statements were fruits of an unlawful arrest, and though the Miranda warnings may have been sufficient to protect his right against self-incrimination, they were not sufficient to purge the taint of the illegal arrest.

Questions 199-200 are based on the following fact situation.

Kane, a member of the legislature of State, is prosecuted in federal court for a violation of the Federal Securities Act arising out of the activities of a state-owned corporation. Kane's defense includes a claim that the alleged wrongful acts were committed in the course of legislative business and are immune from scrutiny.

Question 199

Which of the following is the strongest constitutional argument supporting Kane?

(A) Because of doctrines of federalism, federal law generally cannot be applied to state legislators acting in the course of their official duties.

(B) State legislators enjoy the protection fo the speech and debate clause of the United States Constitution.

(C) A federal court must follow state law respecting the scope of legislative immunity.

(D) To apply the Federal Securities Act to state legislators would violate the due process clause.

Question 200

Which of the following is the strongest argument against Kane's constitutional defense?

(A) Congress has plenary power under the commerce clause.

(B) Congress may impose liability on state legislators as a means of guaranteeing a republican form of Government.

(C) Congress does not significantly interfere with state government by applying this law to state legislators.

(D) Congress may impose liability on state legislators by virtue of the necessary and proper clause.

SUBJECT-MATTER BREAKDOWN
PRACTICE MBE

SUBJECT-MATTER BREAKDOWN
PRACTICE MBE

This listing tells you which questions involve which subject, for the Practice MBE.

CONSTITUTIONAL LAW

8, 9,10, 11, 42, 43, 49, 50, 51, 52, 72, 73, 91, 92, 93, 120, 121, 135, 143, 144, 145, 146, 147, 153, 159, 160, 178, 185, 186, 199, 200

CONTRACTS

Non-sales (non-UCC): 5, 6, 7, 24, 25, 35, 36, 37, 38, 67, 68, 69, 70, 71, 82, 83, 84, 85, 86, 87, 95, 110, 111, 112, 113, 114, 115, 139, 140, 141, 142, 154, 155, 174, 175, 176, 177, 192

Sales (UCC): 188, 189, 190, 191

CRIMINAL LAW

Substantive Crim. Law: 1, 2, 12, 29, 30, 31, 48, 53, 54, 55, 75, 100, 105, 106, 129, 156, 157, 158, 166, 167, 181, 197

Criminal Procedure: 74, 88, 90, 104, 168, 183, 198

EVIDENCE

4, 18, 19, 26, 27, 44, 56, 57, 58, 59, 60, 66, 79, 80, 81, 89, 107, 108, 130, 131, 132, 133, 134, 148, 149, 169, 170, 171, 172, 173, 182, 184

REAL PROPERTY

15, 16, 17, 23, 32, 33, 34, 45, 46, 61, 62, 96, 109, 123, 136, 137, 138, 152, 163, 164, 165, 187, 193

Future Interests: 47, 94, 122

TORTS

3, 13, 14, 20, 21, 22, 28, 39, 40, 41, 63, 64, 65, 76, 77, 78, 97, 98, 99, 101, 102, 103, 116, 117, 118, 119, 124, 125, 126, 127, 128, 150, 151, 161, 162, 179, 180, 194, 195, 196

PRACTICE MBE — A.M. EXAM

Answer Key

Use this Answer Key to quickly identify the correct answer to each question.

(1) B	(16) B	(31) B	(46) D	(61) C	(76) D	(91) B
(2) D	(17) A	(32) A	(47) B	(62) C	(77) C	(92) C
(3) C	(18) D	(33) A	(48) D	(63) D	(78) A	(93) B
(4) B	(19) C	(34) D	(49) D	(64) B	(79) A	(94) D
(5) C	(20) C	(35) D	(50) A	(65) A	(80) B	(95) A
(6) C	(21) A	(36) A	(51) C	(66) C	(81) D	(96) D
(7) A	(22) B	(37) B	(52) A	(67) A	(82) B	(97) A
(8) A	(23) B	(38) C	(53) D	(68) C	(83) D	(98) B
(9) D	(24) D	(39) B	(54) C	(69) D	(84) A	(99) B
(10) D	(25) A	(40) C	(55) B	(70) B	(85) C	(100) C
(11) C	(26) D	(41) C	(56) C	(71) C	(86) D	
(12) B	(27) C	(42) D	(57) B	(72) D	(87) B	
(13) A	(28) A	(43) C	(58) D	(73) C	(88) A	
(14) D	(29) B	(44) B	(59) A	(74) D	(89) A	
(15) C	(30) C	(45) C	(60) A	(75) B	(90) C	

ANSWERS

PRACTICE MBE — A.M. EXAM

Answer 1

(B) is the best response,

because it correctly identifies that Davis intended to kill Brooks and Brooks alone. The key here is distinguishing between intent and mistake.

One is said to intend a result when he desires that result or, alternatively, he knows the result is substantially certain to be caused by his conduct. Here, when Davis raised his gun to fire, he intended to kill Brooks. Admittedly, he was mistaken about Brooks's identity, but he nonetheless intended to kill Brooks. He did not intend to kill Case, but his intent to kill Brooks will be "transferred" to Case. Since B correctly identifies that Davis intended to kill Brooks, B is the best response.

(A) is not the best response,

because Davis set out to kill Adams, but the intent that actuated the actual killing was Davis' raising the gun and aiming at Brooks.

Under these facts, although Davis wanted to kill Adams, he didn't perform an act toward that end that would qualify as an attempt, since an attempt to commit a crime requires the intent to commit the crime coupled with acts which come dangerously close to accomplishing the criminal goal. There would not be enough on these facts to constitute an attempt to kill Adams. Here, Davis was *mistaken* about Brooks's identity, but he did intend to kill Brooks. Since A states that Davis intended to kill Adams, it's not the best response.

(C) is not the best response,

because Davis didn't intend to kill Case at all.

In fact, he'll be guilty of attempt to commit murder for Case's wound, because his intent to kill Brooks will be "transferred" to Case, and otherwise Davis would satisfy the requirements for attempt to commit murder (since he had the intent to commit murder, and came dangerously close to achieving his goal). Transferred intent comes about when a person intending to commit one crime accidentally commits another; the intent will be "transferred" from the person he intended to harm to the person he actually harmed. Here, when Davis raised his gun to fire, he intended to kill Brooks, not Case. Since Davis did not intend to kill Case, C is not the best response.

(D) is not the best response,

because Davis intended to kill Brooks, not Adams.

Intent here refers to what actuated Davis's raising the gun and firing. He was *mistaken* as to Brooks's identity, and although he *wanted* to kill Adams, he *intended* to kill Brooks only. Since D incorrectly states that Davis also intended to kill Adams, it's not the best response.

Answer 2

(D) is the best response,

because it correctly identifies the basis on which Nelson will avoid liability. There are two key facts here: The statute itself, which requires *knowing* behavior, and the fact that the jury believes Nelson.

This question indicates why criminal law questions involving statutes on the MBE tend to be fairly easy – because all the facts you need in order to answer the question correctly are in the question. Here, the statute itself provides that the conduct must be *knowing* in order to be culpable. The question also tells you that the jury believes Nelson did not realize he had reached the minimum of $50,000 in sales. If the jury believes this, it cannot find him guilty of knowingly failing to file. Since Nelson did not satisfy the mental element of the statutory crime, he's not guilty. Since D recognizes this, it's the best response.

(A) is not the best response,

because it focuses on an irrelevancy.

It doesn't matter how the crime would be classified, if Nelson is not guilty of it by its terms. Here, the statute requires *knowing* conduct for a violation, and the jury believes that Nelson didn't behave knowingly, so he can't be guilty. For purposes of Nelson's guilt, it just doesn't matter how the statute is classified.

What option A implicitly refers to is a *strict liability* offense, since public welfare offenses are one type of offense where one can be liable without any fault at all. Strict liability crimes help in prosecuting crimes where the mental element will be difficult to prove, *or* the harm caused is such that it's worth convicting people who lack guilty minds (e.g., gun registration statutes). Here, you don't have to analyze whether the crime should involve strict liability or not, since you're given a *statute* which *expressly* requires a given state of mind: knowledge. Since A focuses on a irrelevant point, it's not the best response.

(B) is not the best response,

because Nelson need not be excused, since his behavior is not criminal under this statute.

The concept of excuse arises when one is relieved of a duty. Here, the duty is to file when one knows that he has sold $50,000 worth of prescription drugs in a year. Not knowing one had sold $50,000 worth of drugs *would* excuse him from liability under the statute. Thus, Nelson *will* be excused from liability for his failure to keep records, *not* his failure to file. Since B would find him guilty for his failure to keep records, which is not a crime under this statute, it's not the best response.

(C) is not the best response,

because, although its conclusion is correct, it misstates the facts.

Option C implicitly suggests that the statute here is unconstitutional as a due process violation, because of its failure to give fair warning of what it proscribes. However, this doesn't accurately describe the facts. A statute would be said to give fair warning when a reasonable person would understand the behavior it proscribes. The statute here would satisfy this standard, since it's clear one has to register once he knows his sales have reached $50,000. In fact, this statute would be analogous to any taxation statute, where a failure to file is criminal.

Given that the statute is constitutional, option C's argument doesn't comport with these facts, since it's clear that Nelson *did* know about the statute and what it proscribes – his problem is simply that he didn't realize his own sales had reached the level where registration would be necessary.

Since the statute provides fair warning of what it proscribes, C is not the best response.

Answer 3

(C) is the best response,

because it correctly identifies the central issue which will determine Mann's liability. A tricky "twist" to this question is that you aren't told who threw the first punch. If Borrower did, he wouldn't be privileged to defend himself (unless the fight "escalated"), so that would call into question whether Mann could use force to protect him. The courts are split on this issue, that is, whether a third party can defend a person who wouldn't be privileged to defend himself. This question prudently avoids this issue altogether.

Note that since C uses the qualifier "if" instead of "because," you needn't determine if the facts represent the proposition in C – that Lender was about to inflict serious bodily harm on Borrower. Instead, you need only determine that it's possible this could be true under these facts, that this determines an issue central to Mann's liability, and that the result is consistent with the reasoning.

This is the rule on privilege to defend others: anyone can go to the defense of another threatened with serious bodily injury. The third party may use any force reasonably necessary for such defense (thus, unnecessary force will be subject to liability). The threat of harm to the other person must be immediate (so past attacks or future threats won't be sufficient). The courts

are split as to whether mistake, as to belief that intervention is required or that the one being attacked would be privileged to use self-defense (i.e., he was the "aggressor"), or that the force applied is called for, will be a defense.

Thus, by focusing on whether Lender appeared to be about to inflict serious bodily harm on Borrower will be the central issue determining Mann's liability. Since C correctly identifies this, and resolves it satisfactorily, it's the best response.

(A) is not the best response,

because under these facts Mann *might* be privileged to use deadly force.

The rule is that anyone can go to the defense of another threatened with serious bodily injury. The third party may use any force reasonably necessary for such defense (thus, unnecessary force will be a source of liability). The threat of harm to the other person must be immediate (so past attacks or future threats won't be sufficient). The courts are split as to whether mistake – either as to belief that intervention is required, or that the one being attacked would be privileged to use self-defense (i.e, he was the "aggressor"), or that the force applied is called for, will be a defense.

Here, option A says Mann will be liable *because* he threatened to use deadly force. However, this is not necessarily true. The facts say Lender was about to kick Mann in the head. This could well be justification for threatening deadly force. Even if Mann were *mistaken* as to the need for deadly force, in some jurisdictions he'd avoid liability anyway. Since A states as a concrete proposition that threatening deadly force will make Mann liable, and there are at least some circumstances under these facts under which it *won't*, A is not the best response.

(B) is not the best response,

because it cites a fact which is irrelevant. Mann's right to use force depends on whether he'd fit the privilege to defend another.

Note that option B uses the modifier "unless." This means that, if Mann was related to Borrower, there's no way under these facts that he could be liable. In fact, that's not true – Mann's liability does not depend on whether he's related to Borrower.

The rule is that anyone can go to the defense of another threatened with serious bodily injury. The third party may use any force reasonably necessary for such defense (thus, unnecessary force will be subject to liability). The threat of harm to the other person must be immediate (so past attacks or future threats won't be sufficient). The courts are split as to whether mistake – either as to belief that intervention is required, or that the one being attacked would be privileged to use self-defense (i.e., he was the "aggressor"), or that the force applied is called for, will be a defense.

Thus, the issue of *relationship* between the defender

and the one being defended is not relevant. If the defender fits the rule, he'll avoid liability due to the defense of privilege; if he *doesn't*, he'll be liable even if he's related to the victim.

If you chose this response, you may have been thinking of the *old* rule that provided members of the same family with the privilege to defend each other. However, this rule has given way completely to the modern rule, as stated above. Since B focuses on an irrelevant issue, it's not the best response.

(D) is not the best response,

because it implies an incorrect rule of law, and in any case focuses on an irrelevant point.

Mann's liability will turn on whether he was privileged to defend Borrower with the amount of force he used. The rule is that anyone can go to the defense of another threatened with serious bodily injury. The third party may use any force reasonably necessary for such defense (thus, unnecessary force will create liability). The threat of harm to the other person must be immediate (so past attacks or future threats won't be sufficient). The courts are split as to whether mistake, either as to belief that intervention is required or that the one being attacked would be privileged to use self-defense (i.e., he was the "aggressor"), or that the force applied is called for, will be a defense.

As a result, the fact that D cites, that Lender initially threatened Borrower, will not determine Mann's liability. In most cases, a mere threat does not *generally* justify an apprehension of immediate harm, and thus wouldn't merit the use of force. Even if Lender *were* considered the "aggressor," if deadly force were not reasonably required, Mann would be liable for using unnecessary force. Since D focuses on a point which would not determine Mann's liability, it's not the best response.

Answer 4

(B) is the best response,

because it correctly vests the judge with the discretion to admit the testimony, regardless of whether Don objected to the evidence.

When irrelevant evidence is erroneously admitted, there's no hard and fast rule as to whether or not the adversely affected party should be able to rebut it. Factors to take into account include the prejudicial nature of the evidence and whether or not the adversely affected party objected, but in the final analysis it's up to the judge as to whether or not to distract attention from the issues to allow for a rebuttal. In any case, Peter would not have any right to object to Don's rebuttal.

This is all really nitpicking Evidence law, so you certainly shouldn't lose any sleep if you missed this one. In any case, since option B recognizes the correct rule, it's the best response.

(A) is not the best response,

because it both denies the judge discretion in admitting the rebuttal testimony, and it conditions rebuttal on Don's objecting to the original evidence.

When irrelevant evidence is erroneously admitted, there's no hard and fast rule as to whether or not the adversely affected party should be able to rebut it. Factors to take into account include the prejudicial nature of the evidence and whether or not the adversely affected party objected, but in the final analysis it's up to the judge as to whether or not to distract attention from the issues to allow for a rebuttal. Since A doesn't recognize this, it's not the best response.

(C) is not the best response,

because it incorrectly conditions Don's ability to rebut the evidence on whether he objected to it.

When irrelevant evidence is erroneously admitted, there's no hard and fast rule as to whether or not the adversely affected party should be able to rebut it. Factors to take into account include the prejudicial nature of the evidence and whether or not the adversely affected party objected, but in the final analysis it's up to the judge as to whether or not to distract attention from the issues to allow for a rebuttal. Thus, while Don's objecting would weigh in his favor, it's not controlling. Since C makes Don's objecting determinative when in fact it's not, C is not the best response.

(D) is not the best response,

because it incorrectly forbids the judge discretion in deciding whether Don should be allowed to rebut Peter's evidence.

When irrelevant evidence is erroneously admitted, there's no hard and fast rule as to whether or not the adversely affected party should be able to rebut it. Factors to take into account include the prejudicial nature of the evidence and whether or not the adversely affected party objected, but in the final analysis it's up to the judge as to whether or not to distract attention from the issues to allow for a rebuttal. Option D correctly recognizes that Don's objecting to Peter's testimony isn't determinative, but it incorrectly denies the judge discretion in allowing Don's rebuttal testimony. As a result, D is not the best response.

Answer 5

(C) is the best response,

because it correctly identifies that Bell's duty to pay is only triggered by Ames's substantial performance.

Ames's performance under the contract would be considered a constructive condition precedent to Bell's performance. Constructive conditions require only *substantial* performance to trigger the other party's duty to perform (unlike *express* conditions, which require *complete* performance). Thus, if Ames didn't substantially perform, Bell's duty to pay would not exist. If Ames *did* substantially perform, Bell's failure to pay would be, as

C points out, a total breach of contract (since he failed to pay anything).

Since C correctly analyzes the effect of Ames's performance on Bell's duty to pay, it's the best response.

(A) is not the best response,

because its result and its reasoning don't agree. If in fact Ames had properly or substantially painted the porch, Bell's refusal to pay anything would be a total breach of contract, not a partial one.

As a preliminary matter, note that A uses the modifier "if"; that means that the reasoning must be plausible on the facts, the reasoning must address a central issue, and the result must be consistent with the reasoning.

First, it's plausible that Ames substantially performed his duty under the contract. The difference between a material (or total) breach and minor (or partial) breach is, naturally, one of degree. The distinction is an important one, because a *major* breach relieves the non-breaching party of his duty to perform under the contract; a *minor* breach means the non-breaching party must perform, but can sue for damages. The Restatement of Contracts §275 looks to six factors to determine if a breach is material, weighing them according to what's critical in each case:

1. To what extent has the injured party received benefits?
2. Can the injured party be adequately compensated in damages?
3. Is the breaching party "close" to full performance?
4. Will the breaching party face great hardship if termination is permitted?
5. How willful is the breach?
6. How great is the certainty of completion?

Here, if Ames substantially performed, Bell's refusal to pay would be a total breach.

Second, this reasoning addresses a central issue, because Bell's duty to pay is only triggered by Ames's substantially performing his duty under the contract, since Ames's performance will be a constructive condition precedent to Bell's performance. Under these facts it's possible that Ames substantially performed, and if he did, Bell's refusal to pay would be a total breach of contract. Since A doesn't arrive at the correct result, it's not the best response.

(B) is not the best response,

because if Ames didn't substantially perform, Bell's refusal to pay wouldn't be a breach *at all*.

Ames's performance under the contract would be considered a constructive condition precedent to Bell's performance. Constructive conditions require only *substantial* performance to trigger the other party's duty to perform (express conditions require *complete* performance). Thus, if Ames didn't substantially perform, Bell's duty to pay would not exist. If Ames *did* substantially perform, Bell's breach would be *total,* not partial, since he refused to perform his entire duty.

Note that this could be analyzed in terms of breach: A failure to substantially perform would be a major breach, relieving the other party of a duty to perform; substantial performance, which is defective in some way, involves a *minor* breach, and requires the other party to perform and sue for damages. Since B would impose Bell's duty to pay even if Ames's breach was major, it's not the best response.

(D) is not the best response,

because Bell's failure to pay is only a total breach if Ames substantially performed his duty under the contract.

Ames's performance under the contract would be considered a constructive condition precedent to Bell's performance. Constructive conditions require only *substantial* performance to trigger the other party's duty to perform (unlike *express* conditions, which require *complete* performance). Thus, if Ames didn't substantially perform, Bell's duty to pay would not exist. If Ames *did* substantially perform, Bell's failure to pay would be, as D points out, a total breach of contract (since he failed to pay anything).

Note that this could be analyzed in terms of breach: A failure to substantially perform would be a major breach, relieving the other party of a duty to perform; substantial performance, which is defective in some way, involves a *minor* breach, and requires the other party to perform and sue for damages.

Since D would impose Bell's duty to pay even if Ames's breach was major, it's not the best response.

Answer 6

(C) is the best response,

because it correctly identifies that Ames's cashing the check without objection will curtail any further recovery.

An "accord" is an agreement under which a party to a contract agrees to accept, as complete satisfaction of the contract, some performance different from that originally due under the contract. "Satisfaction" is performance of the accord, and once satisfaction takes place, both the accord *and the original contractual duty* are discharged.

Here, the good-faith dispute over whether Ames properly painted the house provides consideration for the accord (since an accord, as with any contract, requires consideration). By cashing the check without objection, Ames accepted the accord, and both the accord and the original contractual duty were discharged. Thus, Ames could not go back and sue under the original contract.

At common law, the only way generally to avoid this result would be to return the check, uncashed. Under the UCC, §1-207, Ames *could* notify Bell that the check was accepted under protest, and could thereafter sue for the rest of the money allegedly owed. While the UCC doesn't apply to these facts because housepainting is a service, not a transaction in goods, option C is nonetheless the most correct answer, and thus the best response.

(A) is not the best response,

because it ignores the existence of an accord and satisfaction, which precludes Ames from suing on the original contract.

An "accord" is an agreement under which a party to a contract agrees to accept, as complete satisfaction of the contract, some performance different from that originally due under the contract. "Satisfaction" is performance of the accord, and once satisfaction takes place, both the accord *and the original contractual duty* are discharged.

Here, the good-faith dispute over whether Ames properly painted the house provides consideration for the accord (since an accord, as with any contract, requires consideration). By cashing the check without objection, Ames accepted the accord, and both the accord and the original contractual duty were discharged. Thus, Ames could not go back and sue under the original contract.

There are two things to keep in mind in relation to option A. First, if there *hadn't* been a good-faith dispute, there would be no consideration for the accord, and Ames *could* have recovered all the rest of the money even if he cashed the check (as long as he painted the house as per the contract, of course). Second, if Bell had sent the letter, Ames had accepted the settlement, but Bell hadn't sent the check, Ames could recover the original $2,000. However, under these facts there was a valid accord and satisfaction, so Ames can't recover the additional $200. Since A doesn't recognize this, it's not the best response.

(B) is not the best response,

because the facts here would not support a finding of economic duress.

Economic duress is only a defense to enforcing a contract where one party threatens or actually commits a wrongful act which puts the other party in a position posing a serious threat to his property or finances, and there are no available means to adequately avoid or prevent the threatened loss, apart from entering the contract.

Thus, in order for economic duress to be a valid defense here, Ames would have to claim he accepted the accord under economic duress. However, the wrongfulness element is missing. Bell had a good-faith belief that Ames hadn't fulfilled his contractual duty. The fact that Ames may have been motivated to accept the accord by his money problems is no concern of Bell's. Since B doesn't recognize this, it's not the best response.

(D) is not the best response,

because it does not supply a basis for pinning Ames's recovery at $1,800.

Instead, the reason Ames will not be able to recover any more money is that there was a valid accord and satisfaction.

An "accord" is an agreement under which a party to a contract agrees to accept, as complete satisfaction of the contract, some performance different from that originally due under the contract. "Satisfaction" is performance of the accord, and once satisfaction takes place, both the accord *and the original contractual duty* are discharged.

Here, the good-faith dispute over whether Ames properly painted the house provides consideration for the accord (since an accord, as with any contract, requires consideration). By cashing the check without objection, Ames accepted the accord, and both the accord and the original contractual duty were discharged. Thus, Ames could not go back and sue under the original contract.

If you chose this response, you may have been thinking of quasi-contractual recovery, where plaintiff's damages are measured by the reasonable value of his services. However, since the accord would control here, D isn't the best response.

Answer 7

(A) is the best response,

because it correctly identifies Ames's duty and the source of that duty.

These facts involve an "accord and satisfaction" – that is, an agreement under which a party to a contract agrees to accept, as complete satisfaction of the contract, some performance different from that originally due under the contract. The "accord" is the agreement, and the "satisfaction" is its performance. The consideration for the accord is provided under these facts by the good-faith dispute over the completeness of the work. Ames agreed to the accord by cashing the check. Thus, he *impliedly* agreed to repaint the porch, since that was part of Bell's settlement offer. Since A recognizes this, it's the best response.

(B) is not the best response,

because silence is not a valid means of acceptance. All the exceptions to this general rule require *some* act by offeree – a prior agreement between the parties that silence will mean acceptance (e.g., Book of the Month Club), or offeree takes benefits or exercises dominion over what offeree offers. If, say, Bell sent the check and Ames held it for an unreasonable amount of time, that could amount to acceptance. However, there's nothing under these facts that would make Ames's silence constitute acceptance. Since B doesn't recognize this, it's not the best response.

(C) is not the best response,

because it mischaracterizes Bell's letter, and does not focus on the element that will create a duty in Ames.

First, option C says Bell's letter was a counter-offer. It

can't be, because Ames and Bell already had a contract; instead, Bell's letter was a *settlement* offer.

Second, C is incorrect in stating that Ames didn't accept the offer; Ames *did* accept it by cashing the check. This substitute agreement is called an "accord," and "satisfaction" occurred when Ames cashed the check. The consideration for the accord was provided by the good-faith dispute over the completion of the porch. Thus, the original contract was discharged, and Ames impliedly agreed to repaint the porch. Since C doesn't recognize the importance of Ames's accepting and cashing the check, it's not the best response.

(D) is not the best response,

because it mischaracterizes the facts: There *is* consideration to support Ames's promise.

What's involved under these facts is an "accord and satisfaction" – that is, an agreement under which a party to a contract agrees to accept, as complete satisfaction of the contract, some performance different from that originally due under the contract. The "accord" is the agreement, and "satisfaction" is its performance. As with any enforceable agreement, there must be consideration (or some substitute for it). Its source here is the good-faith dispute over whether the job was complete, as well as the settlement, involving detriment to both parties. By accepting and cashing the check, Ames impliedly promised to paint the porch, since that was part of Bell's settlement offer. Since D doesn't recognize this, it's not the best response.

Answer 8

(A) is the best response,

because it correctly characterizes the facts, and arrives at the correct result.

In order to be valid, a state law must pass a three-part test:

1. It must be enacted within the state's powers (e.g., police powers);
2. It must not violate any person's constitutional rights; and
3. It must not improperly burden interstate commerce.

Option A addresses the third element. In order to determine if a state statute unduly burdens interstate commerce, you need to ask two questions:

1. Does it burden interstate commerce? If it has an effect on interstate commerce, it does.
2. Is the burden outweighed by legitimate interests of the state in protecting its citizens? Consider less burdensome alternatives.

Here, as to the first element, the statute clearly affects interstate commerce – it prevents out-of-state trained hairdressers from plying their trade in Medusa. Second, the burden on interstate commerce is not outweighed by a legitimate state interest in protecting its citizens, considering available less-burdensome alter-

natives, like a state licensing exam. Since option A correctly recognizes that the statute will be unconstitutional due to its impact on interstate commerce, it's the best response.

(B) is not the best response,

because the Privileges and Immunities Clause of the Fourteenth Amendment wouldn't apply to make this statute unconstitutional.

In order to be valid, a state law must pass a three-part test:

1. It must be enacted within the state's powers (e.g., police powers);
2. It must not violate any person's constitutional rights; and
3. It must not improperly burden interstate commerce. Option B addresses the second element.

The Privileges and Immunities Clause of the Fourteenth Amendment voids those state enactments which clearly infringe privileges enjoyed by U.S. citizens. It is construed narrowly, typically being restricted to fundamental rights which are shared in common by all citizens, namely:

1. The right to travel freely from state to state;
2. To petition Congress for redress of grievances;
3. To vote for national officers
4. To assemble peaceably, and
5. To discuss matters of national legislation.

Twining v. New Jersey (1908). In fact, the Privileges and Immunities Clause of the Fourteenth Amendment has virtually no practical effect; and, in any case, the privilege of barbering would not fit under any of these categories.

If you chose this response, you may have been thinking of the *Interstate* Privileges and Immunities Clause, found in Article IV, §2 of the Constitution. That clause prevents states from discriminating against out-of-state citizens and residents (not aliens), as regards "essential activities" (e.g., pursuing one's livelihood, owning property) and "basic rights" (e.g., medical care, court access), except where the discrimination is closely related to a substantial state purpose (e.g., protecting natural resources by the state), keeping in mind less restrictive means. Since plying one's trade would be considered an "essential activity," the statute here would be a violation of the Interstate Privileges and Immunities Clause. However, that's not the clause that option B addresses. Since the statute wouldn't be unconstitutional on the basis of violating the Privileges and Immunities Clause of the Fourteenth Amendment, B is not the best response.

(C) is not the best response,

because while it provides a rationale for a licensing law, it doesn't make such a law valid.

In order to be valid, a state law must pass a three-part test:

1. It must be enacted within the state's powers (e.g.,

police powers).

2. It must not violate any person's constitutional rights.

3. It must not improperly burden interstate commerce.

Option C addresses the second element. While addressing a valid concern of the state, option C doesn't address any of the elements that would make the statute constitutional.

The central problem with this statute is its impact on interstate commerce. Where interstate commerce is an issue, there are two questions to ask:

1. Does the statute burden interstate commerce? If it has an effect on interstate commerce, it does.

2. Is the burden outweighed by a legitimate interest of the state in protecting its citizens? Consider less burdensome alternatives.

Here, the licensing statute impacts interstate commerce by preventing out-of-state barber school graduates from plying their trade in Aurora. While the state has a legitimate interest in protecting its residents from a Sweeny Todd-type barber, it could accomplish the same goal by far less burdensome means, e.g., a licensing exam of some sort. Thus, even though the state admittedly doesn't know the quality of out-of-state barber schools, this in and of itself would not make the licensing exam constitutional. Since C doesn't recognize this, it's not the best response.

(D) is not the best response,

because characterizing barbering as a privilege and not a right would not determine if the statute is constitutional.

In order to be valid, a state law must pass a three-part test:

1. It must be enacted within the state's powers (e.g., police powers).

2. It must not violate any person's constitutional rights.

3. It must not improperly burden interstate commerce.

If the statute here meets this test, it doesn't matter if barbering is classified as a privilege or a right. If barbering were considered an "essential activity," the statute would violate the Interstate Privileges and Immunities Clause. Alternatively, if barbering were a fundamental right, the statute would probably fail as a violation of Equal Protection. Thus, classifying barbering as a privilege and not a right does not, in and of itself, determine the constitutionality of the statute. Since D attaches undue significance to this classification, it's not the best response.

Answer 9

(D) is the best response,

because it correctly identifies that the facts here involve an impermissible classification.

In order for a state statute to be constitutional, it must meet these three requirements:

1. It must be enacted within the state's powers (e.g., police powers).

2. It must not violate any person's constitutional rights.

3. It must not improperly burden interstate commerce.

The citizenship requirement here involves a classification: citizens vs. non-citizens. The use of a classification system suggests that there may be an equal protection problem with the statute (thus calling into question the second element, above). In order to determine if the statute passes muster under equal protection, you have to determine the basis of the classification. Here, it's alienage – non-citizenship. Alienage is a "suspect" classification, and so, in order to be constitutional, the statute would have to pass the strict scrutiny test: it would have to be necessary to promote a compelling governmental interest.

The mere mention of the strict scrutiny test should tell you that the statute will likely fail, since it's virtually impossible for a law to pass strict scrutiny. Since option D recognizes that the statute is an equal protection violation, it's the best response.

(A) is not the best response,

because the fact that the statute helps make sure barbers speak English would not be determinative of its constitutionality.

In order for a state statute to be constitutional, it must meet these three requirements:

1. It must be enacted within the state's powers (e.g., police powers).

2. It must not violate any person's constitutional rights.

3. It must not improperly burden interstate commerce.

The citizenship requirement here involves a classification: citizens vs. non-citizens. The use of a classification system suggests that there may be an equal protection problem with the statute (thus calling into question the second element, above). In order to determine if the statute passes muster under equal protection, you have to determine the basis of the classification. Here, it's alienage – non-citizenship. Alienage is a "suspect" classification, and so, in order to be constitutional, the statute would have to pass the strict scrutiny test: it would have to be necessary to promote a compelling governmental interest. That's where the reasoning in Option A becomes relevant. It tells you that the state has an interest in ensuring that barbers speak English. While this may be necessary to ensure that barbers can understand the instructions of their English-speaking customers, this goal could not be considered a compelling interest. In fact, the mere mention of the strict scrutiny test should tell you that the statute will fail, because it's virtually impossible for a law to pass strict scrutiny.

Since option A does not address an argument that will determine the statute's constitutionality, it's not the best response.

(B) is not the best response,

because a statute's being in the exercise of the state's police power doesn't, in and of itself, make a statute constitutional; and here, this is not the central issue.

In order for a state statute to be constitutional, it must meet these three requirements:

1. It must be enacted within the state's powers (e.g., police powers).
2. It must not violate any person's constitutional rights.
3. It must not improperly burden interstate commerce.

Thus, while an exercise of the state's police power would satisfy the first element, it does not address a central problem under these facts with the second element – namely, there's a classification based on *alienage* (citizens vs. non-citizens), and thus there's an equal protection problem.

In any case, it's not clear that this statute would fall under the state's police power. Under the police power, a state enactment must involve the public health, safety, welfare, and morals. It's not clear that a classification based on citizenship addresses *any* of these, and thus B probably doesn't accurately represent the facts. However, the central issue is the equal protection problem. Since B doesn't recognize this, it's not the best response.

(C) is not the best response,

because the statute here wouldn't be considered punishment.

A bill of attainder punishes past or future conduct of specifically named individuals or ascertainable groups, without a trial. While "punishment" needn't mean a ball and chain, the statute must be intended or appear to be punishment; for instance, a statute forbidding members of the Communist Party from being labor union officials would qualify. U.S. v. Brown (1965). (While it isn't an element of a bill of attainder, and it isn't present in these facts, punishment on the basis of political beliefs or activities is the hallmark of a bill of attainder.) Here, the element of punishment is missing – non-citizens are merely prevented from barbering in Aurora. Thus, what's involved is a *classification,* which suggests an equal protection problem, not a bill of attainder. Since C doesn't recognize this, it's not the best response.

Answer 10

(D) is the best response,

because it correctly identifies that the federal court will decide the case because it has the jurisdiction to do so.

Under Article III, there are several grounds on which federal court jurisdiction can be based, including:

1. "Diversity" – that is, cases between citizens of different states, where the amount in controversy is at least $10,000;
2. "Federal question" – that is, a case arises under the Constitution, federal law, or treaties; and
3. Cases between a state and a citizen of another state.

In this case, you have a statute which classifies in-state vs. out-of-state graduates, and thus calls equal protection into question, so there's at least one issue under the federal Constitution. As a result, a federal court would have federal question jurisdiction, and be able to decide the case on the merits. Since D correctly identifies this, it's the best response.

(A) is not the best response,

because it incorrectly implies that diversity of citizenship is the *only* way to invoke federal court jurisdiction.

Diversity of citizenship – where the case is between citizens of different states, and the amount in controversy is at least $10,000 – is only one way to invoke federal jurisdiction. Federal court jurisdiction extends to, among other instances under Article III:

1. All cases which arise under the Constitution, federal laws, or treaties ("federal question" jurisdiction); and
2. Cases between a state and a citizen of another state.

Here, the case will fall under "federal question" jurisdiction. That's because the statute creates an impermissible classification, and thus involves an Equal Protection problem under the federal Constitution. Since option A would limit federal court jurisdiction to diversity jurisdiction, it's not the best response.

(B) is not the best response,

because abstention would not be appropriate under these circumstances.

Under the abstention doctrine, a federal court can abstain from deciding a constitutional issue by remanding a case to state court to resolve an unsettled or unclear issue of state law (although a federal court will typically *not* abstain if a vague statute involves freedom of speech or association, due to the potential "chill" on those rights).

Here, there's nothing vague or ambiguous about the statute. It straightforwardly categorizes barbers into in-state graduates and out-of-state graduates, and denies out-of-state graduates the ability to ply their trade in-state. Thus, the problem is an equal protection problem due to an impermissible classification. Since the abstention doctrine would not apply here, and B doesn't recognize this, it's not the best response.

(C) is not the best response,

because it mischaracterizes the facts.

It's true that federal jurisdiction extends to controversies between two states, as well as to cases between citizens of different states ('diversity" jurisdiction), "federal question" jurisdiction, and other bases, under Article III of the Constitution. The problem here is that the case in these facts involves a citizen of one state and that state – not two states. Thus, C mischaracterizes the facts. It does, in fact, arrive at the correct result – that the case will be decided on the merits. However, the correct source of jurisdiction is the existence of a federal question: there is an equal protection issue, due to the existence of a classification: in-state vs. out-of-state graduates. Since C doesn't recognize this, it's not the best response.

Answer 11

(C) is the best response,

because the existence of a classification indicates there's a likely equal protection problem under these facts.

Equal protection is triggered by a classification that determines people's rights. Here, the right to barber is determined by classifying people as two-year residents vs. none-or-less-than-two-year-residents. (The test that is applied to determine an equal protection violation is this one: Where a classification relates to who may exercise a fundamental right [First Amendment rights, procreation, marriage, conception] or it is based on a suspect classification [race or alienage], the classification must be necessary to promote a compelling governmental interest. If the legislation, on the other hand, is economic or social, the "mere rationality" test will apply: if there is a set of facts imaginable that would make the law a reasonable one to achieve a legitimate governmental purpose, the law will be upheld.) While the residency requirement here may only be subject to the "mere rationality" test, it's hard to imagine any legitimate state interest that is advanced by the two-year waiting period (and, in any case, the requirement *could* burden the fundamental right to interstate travel, thus subjecting the statute to strict scrutiny). Since the problem here is most likely challengeable on equal protection grounds, and C recognizes this, it's the best response.

(A) is not the best response,

because the Privileges and Immunities Clause of the Fourteenth Amendment would be unlikely to prohibit this statute.

The Privileges and Immunities Clause of the Fourteenth Amendment voids those state enactments which clearly infringe privileges enjoyed by U.S. citizens. It is construed narrowly, typically being restricted to fundamental rights which are shared in common by all citizens, namely:

1. The right to travel freely from state to state;
2. To petition Congress for redress of grievances;
3. To vote for national officers;
4. To assemble peaceably; and
5. To discuss matters of national legislation.

Here, the two year residency requirement would not qualify under any of these privileges. In fact, the Privileges and Immunities Clause is toothless in practice. If you chose this response, you *may* have been thinking of the Interstate Privileges and Immunities Clause, from Article IV, §2 of the Constitution. That clause prevents states from discriminating against out-of-state citizens and residents (not aliens), as regards, among other things, "essential activities" (e.g., pursuing one's livelihood). The statute here involves just such discrimination, and thus would likely be a violation of the Interstate Privileges and Immunities Clause. However, since the law wouldn't violate its Fourteenth Amendment counterpart, A isn't the best response.

(B) is not the best response,

because although there *may* be a due process violation, the facts involve a *classification,* and so an equal protection violation is more likely.

A due process violation occurs under circumstances where the effect of a state's activity amounts to a deprivation of a property interest or a right, without due process of law. Thus, as a threshold issue, you have to determine the nature of the plaintiff's interest – if it's a property interest or a right. Under due process, the only real problem with rights is if the right involved is "fundamental," because if it is, the regulation must further a "compelling interest" of the state in order to be valid (a standard which is extremely difficult to meet). The fundamental rights are the First Amendment rights, interstate travel, voting, and privacy. It's true that the two-year waiting period *may* burden the fundamental right to interstate travel. The interest in barbering *may* be a property right – after all, a student is said to have a property right in his education – but this isn't all that clear. Thus, due process is not an attractive basis on which to challenge the residency requirement, especially in light of the fact that there's a much more obvious equal protection problem, and equal protection is one of the other answer choices. (The statute classifies people into residents and non-residents to determine their rights, and it's this classification that gives rise to an equal protection problem.) Since B doesn't recognize this, it's not the best response.

(D) is not the best response,

because there's no contract in existence at the time the regulation was passed, so there *cannot* be a violation of the Obligations of Contracts Clause.

The Obligation of Contracts Clause prohibits states from passing any law which impairs the obligations of contracts. The contract must exist at the time the regulation was passed in order to be impaired by it; states *can* regulate contract formation *prospectively*. Under these facts, there's no evidence of a contract in existence which the residency requirement impairs. Since D doesn't recognize this, it can't be the best response.

Answer 12

(B) is the best response,

because it correctly identifies that John will be guilty of involuntary manslaughter.

Remember the process of elimination you should go through when you encounter a homicide problem. First, look at murder as a possibility. A murder is an unlawful killing (neither justifiable nor excusable) with malice aforethought. While malice doesn't require intent, it can be satisfied by "depraved heart;" that is, the actor disregards an unreasonably high risk of harm to human life. Here, John's omission would not rise to this level of negligence (since depraved heart is generally viewed objectively). Since he won't be guilty of murder, the next possibility is involuntary manslaughter, of which John *will* be guilty.

Specifically, John will be guilty of criminal negligence manslaughter (the other type, unlawful act manslaughter, is a manslaughter that occurs as a result of or during a malum in se misdemeanor or a felony that is not sufficient for felony murder). Predictably, criminal negligence manslaughter is manslaughter that occurs through gross or criminal negligence (either by act or omission). Criminal negligence is a somewhat stricter standard than tortious negligence, requiring a higher degree of unreasonability – however, criminal negligence, like tortious negligence, is generally judged objectively. Under the facts here, John knew the child was ill, but refused to seek help at a state clinic solely because of his pride. This kind of conduct could easily be considered a criminally negligent omission, especially in view of John's fiduciary relationship with his children. Since B best characterizes the facts here, it's the best response.

(A) is not the best response,

because John's conduct would not qualify as murder.

Common-law murder is an unlawful killing (neither justifiable nor excusable) with malice aforethought. While malice aforethought does not require ill-will, it would require either intent to kill, knowledge of death or unreasonably high risk of injury will result, or intent to commit a felony. While John will be culpable for failing to get medical attention for his child, this would not rise to the level of intent or knowledge of an unreasonably high risk of injury. As a result, A is not the best response.

(C) is not the best response,

because John's conduct would not qualify as voluntary manslaughter.

Voluntary manslaughter is essentially murder except it's committed under adequate provocation (e.g., heat of passion). Under the facts here, John didn't commit a murder; common-law murder is an unlawful killing (neither justifiable nor excusable) with malice aforethought.

While malice aforethought does not require ill-will, it would require either intent to kill, knowledge of death or unreasonably high risk of injury will result, or intent to commit a felony. While John will be culpable for failing to get medical attention for his child, this would not rise to the level of intent or knowledge of an unreasonably high risk of injury.

In any case, even if John's conduct did rise to the level of murder, he wasn't provoked, so he couldn't be guilty of voluntary manslaughter. As a result, C is not the best response.

(D) is not the best response,

because John *will* be guilty of involuntary manslaughter.

In fact, John will be guilty of involuntary manslaughter of the criminal-negligence type. criminal negligence manslaughter is manslaughter that occurs through gross or criminal negligence (either by act or omission). Under the facts here, John knew the child was ill, but refused to seek help at a state clinic solely because of his pride. This kind of conduct could easily be considered a criminally negligent omission, especially in view of John's fiduciary relationship with his children.

If you chose this response, it could be because you placed too much importance on the fact that the child died as a result of the illness. *However,* a "killing" takes place whenever a death is hastened by any time at all (e.g., killing someone who was to be executed in five minutes could still be murder, if the requisite mens rea existed). The facts here state that the child's death was hastened because he was weakened by malnutrition. Thus, John is guilty of some form of homicide, making D not the best response.

Answer 13

(A) is the best response,

because it represents the only option of these four on which Carr is likely to prevail.

Assault is any act creating an apprehension of battery, with the intent to arouse apprehension. Here, the students knew, from Professor Merrill's lecture, that their "victim" might react with shock. Furthermore, the facts indicate Carr believed at first that he was "under attack." These would be sufficient to form a basis for assault. As a result, A is the best response.

(B) is not the best response,

because a negligence claim would likely fail on these facts.

Defendant is negligent if he failed to exercise such care as a reasonable person in his position would have exercised, this must have been a breach of the duty to prevent the foreseeable risk of harm to anyone in plaintiff's position, and this breach must have caused plaintiff's damages. Keep in mind that negligence is judged objectively, against the "reasonable person" standard; what weighs *against* negligence under these facts is that whatever the students did was *intentional.* Since negligence would not likely fit these facts, B is not the best response.

(C) is not the best response,
because an invasion of privacy claim would likely fail on these facts.

"Invasion of privacy" is an umbrella tort covering four specific torts: Appropriation (defendant's appropriation of plaintiff's picture or name for defendant's own commercial advantage); Intrusion (defendant's intrusion upon plaintiff's affairs or seclusion); false light (defendant's publication of facts which place plaintiff in a false light); and private facts (defendant's public disclosure of private facts about plaintiff). None of these apply to the facts here, although the second one – intrusion on plaintiff's affairs or seclusion – is the most likely one. However, its elements indicate that it would not be a viable alternative. It requires defendant's prying or intruding upon plaintiff's affairs or seclusion, which would be objectionable to a reasonable person, and the intrusion must be into something private. Here, Carr sitting in his car would not reasonably expect seclusion or privacy, especially at a stop light. As a result, C is not the best response.

(D) is not the best response,
because a false imprisonment claim would likely fail on these facts.

False imprisonment requires proof of three elements: Defendant's act (omission) which confines or restraints plaintiff to a bounded area (plaintiff must believe there's no reasonable means of escape); defendant must *intend* to so confine or restrain plaintiff; and there must be causation. There are two elements missing under these facts: The students had no intent to confine or restrain Carr, and Carr didn't believe he had no reasonable means of escape. The facts state that he thought of driving away. Since these elements are missing, a false imprisonment claim would fail. As a result, D is not the best response.

Answer 14

(D) is the best response,
because it identifies the most likely basis on which the University could be liable – vicarious liability – and cites correct reasoning as to why the University will avoid liability.

Under vicarious liability, one is liable for another's wrongful conduct, due to a "special relationship" between them (e.g., employer-employee). To be liable, the wrongful conduct must be authorized by the master, performed under his control, or the servant must seek to advance the interests of the master. However, under these facts, it's clear Merrill did *not* intend the students to carry out the experiment, they were not under her control, and in fact she encouraged them *not* to carry out the experiment. From these facts, this was

not unreasonable, so it couldn't be negligent, so the University could not be liable for Merrill's own behavior. Since D correctly identifies the most likely result under these facts, it's the best response.

(A) is not the best response,
because it does not identify a sound basis on which the University will be liable.

If the University is to be liable for Merrill's actions, it must be due to Merrill's own negligence *or* vicarious liability. Since Merrill's behavior seems reasonable, it could not be grounds for negligence. Since the students were neither subject to Merrill's control or acting on her behalf, the University could not be liable on grounds of vicarious liability. What option A's "but/for" language addresses is not the basis of liability, but causation where there is only one cause of damage. While causation must exist for there to be tort liability, *alone* it's not enough. Since A fails to recognize this, it's not the best response.

(B) is not the best response,
because it does not provide a source of liability for the University.

Merely pressing a negligence claim against the students for negligence would be insufficient to pin liability on the University. Instead, Merrill's behavior itself must have been unreasonable, or there must be some basis to hold her vicariously liable for the acts of the students. From the facts here Merrill's behavior was not unreasonable, so the University could not be liable on that basis. As to vicarious liability, there's no liability either, since the students were neither subject to Merrill's control, nor were they acting on her behalf. Since B does not provide a basis on which the University could be held liable, it's not the best response.

(C) is not the best response,
because Merrill *could* be liable even if the students were *not* her employees (and, by the same token, even if they *were* her employees, she may not be vicariously liable).

Option C is referring to the most common form of vicarious liability: The employer-employee relationship, under which the employer is liable when the employee performs a tortious act within the scope of the employment relationship. However, the concept of vicarious liability is not *confined* to the employer-employee relationship – the University *could* be liable for the students' act if the students had acted under Merrill's direction, within her control, or to serve her interests. Under these facts, they acted *in spite* of her warning not to do so without her permission.

Even if there *had* been a pre-existing relationship justifying vicarious liability, it's unlikely it would apply here, since Merrill specifically told the students not to undertake the experiment. While a servant's doing what he is told not to do is not *determinative* on the issue of vicarious liability, it's strong evidence that he's acting outside the scope of his duties, and thus the master should not be liable.

Since C wrongly confines the vicarious liability concept to the employer-employee relationship, which is both too broad and too narrow, it's not the best response.

Answer 15

(C) is the best response,
because it correctly identifies the reason Eric will lose: his use of Goldacre was not "adverse," i.e., non-permissive. The key facts here are that Eric had oral permission from Oxnard *originally* to use the road across Goldacre, and Amos quit possession of Goldacre before acquiring title by adverse possession. What does this mean? That Eric's use of Goldacre was never adverse to the interests of the landowner, and that Amos never had any enforceable rights to Goldacre.

In order to gain an easement by prescription, one's use of another's property must be actual, open and notorious, continuous for the statutory period, exclusive, and hostile and adverse (non-permissive). Here, the facts specifically state that Eric had Oxnard's oral permission to use the road across Goldacre. The red herring here is the presence of Amos. However, Amos is merely in possession of Goldacre. The facts state that he quit possession before he acquired title to it. Thus, the elements of an easement by prescription would apply to Eric and Oxnard, *not* Eric and Amos. Since C correctly identifies this, it's the best response.

(A) is not the best response,
because it focuses on the wrong fact.

Here, it doesn't matter if Eric's use is adverse to Amos, because Amos is not the landowner – *Oxnard* is. Eric's use is not adverse to Oxnard, because the facts state that Oxnard granted Eric oral permission to use the road across Goldacre. An easement by prescription requires use of another's property that is actual, open and notorious, continuous for the statutory period, exclusive, and hostile and adverse. "Hostile and adverse" means non-permissive in this context. Here, since Eric's use was with the permission of the landowner the entire time, his use was *never* adverse. Since A does not recognize this, it's not the best response.

(B) is not the best response,
due to two principal faults.

First, B states that Eric will prevail in part because he made no attempt to renew permission when possession of Goldacre changed hands. In order to gain an easement by prescription, the use of another's property must be adverse – that is, *non*-permissive. B correctly identifies that Eric's use was permissive, but by doing so eliminates the possibility of gaining an easement by prescription based on that time. In other words, it misstates the law.

The second fault is that B suggests that Amos's quitting possession of Goldacre is relevant. It is not, because an easement by prescription is gained by adverse use against the *landowner,* not the *possessor.* Eric could only gain an easement by prescription if his use of Goldacre *as against Oxnard* was actual, open and notorious, continuous for the statutory period, exclusive, and non-permissive. Since B incorrectly states the rule of law, it's not the best response.

(D) is not the best response,
because it fails to recognize that it's not the adverse use as against *Amos* that's at issue, because Amos is not the landowner at any time under these facts.

In order for one to gain an easement by prescription, his use of another's property must be actual, open and notorious, continuous for the statutory period, exclusive, and non-permissive. Here, *another's* property means another *landowner's* property. Here, Amos is simply in possession of Goldacre; he was not the owner of Goldacre at any time (since he quit possession before his adverse use ripened into ownership). As a result, D is not the best response.

Answer 16

(B) is the best response,
principally due to estoppel.

The biggest obstacle here is getting around the fact that the agreement between Sharon and Bruce, concerning partitioning Greenacre, was not in writing. This partitioning would be considered the conveyance of an interest in land, and would therefore be covered by the Statute of Frauds. If the partitioning is not considered valid, then Sharon takes the land when Bruce dies, because a joint tenant enjoys the right to survivorship. However, you're told here that the partitioning was valid, because Stanley inherited the land from Bruce. Thus, there must be something that *overrides* the writing requirement. B identifies a factor that does just that: promissory estoppel.

Estoppel prevents one from denying something in the future due to his conduct in the past. Promissory estoppel is triggered by a gratuitous promise that is likely to, and does, induce promisee's reliance. Here, when Sharon orally agreed to the partitioning, she should have recognized that Bruce would rely on this. He in fact did so by erecting an apartment development on the northerly ten acres of Greenacre. This would relieve the writing requirement for the Statute of Frauds, and would leave Bruce and the sole owner of the northerly ten acres of Greenacre, with Sharon as the owner of the rest. Thus, when Bruce died, Stanley would be entitled to the northerly ten acres of Greenacre. Since option B recognizes the Statute of Frauds problem with these facts, and suggests a viable means of getting around it, it's the best response.

(A) is not the best response,

because it misstates the rule of law. The conveyance here would be covered by the Statute of Frauds, because it involves an interest in land. In effect, Sharon and Bruce are partitioning Greenacre. This generally requires a writing, as A recognizes; however, the familial relationship of the parties does not remove the contract from the Statute of Frauds. Since A states otherwise, it's not the best response.

(C) is not the best response,

because it misstates the rule of law.

The conveyance here (partitioning Greenacre) involves an interest in land. As such, it is covered by the Statute of Frauds, and must be in writing (or otherwise removed from it) in order to be valid. If the agreement was valid, then the joint tenancy would be terminated, and Bruce would be the sole owner of the northerly ten acres, with Sharon being the sole owner of the rest. Since the facts tell you that Stanley is adjudged to be the owner of the northerly ten acres of Greenacre, you know that the partitioning must be valid, and thus *something* must have removed it from the Statute of Frauds. However, C doesn't identify a viable means of doing so. While there are circumstances which *may* remove conveyances from the Statute of Frauds, C is wrong in saying that the oral agreement *necessarily* terminated the joint tenancy. Thus, C is not the best response.

(D) is not the best response,

for three reasons; two involve misstating the correct rule of law, and one involves misstating the facts.

For one thing, Sharon's appointment as executrix would not, in and of itself, stop her from watching out for her own interests (since executors of estates are frequently interested in the distribution of those estates). Second, even if she had *accepted* the appointment (which she didn't), she would be obligated to represent the interests of the *estate*, not the beneficiaries thereof. Finally, and most conclusively, Sharon didn't accept the appointment – the facts state that she turned it down. The fact that she is not executrix of the estate is the easiest, and most obvious, way to determine that D is not the best response.

Answer 17

(A) is the best response,

because it cites the basis, *of these four,* on which Sharon is most likely to win the case. Note that the question here asks for the *most likely reason for the judgment*. This isn't to say that it's the basis *you'd* choose if you were litigating the issue – it only means that, of these four possibilities, it's the most likely to succeed. In order to determine this, as you check through the responses, you have to think to yourself: "Does this address – and overcome – a major obstacle to winning?" In order to be correct, the response *must*

do this.

The issue here involves Bruce's and Sharon's ostensibly partitioning Greenacre. In order for Sharon to be the sole owner of all of Greenacre, the partitioning *must have been invalid,* such that when Bruce died, Sharon would be entitled to his share of Greenacre under the right to survivorship of a joint tenancy. This would be the result under a strict reading of the Statute of Frauds, since the partitioning would be considered a conveyance of an interest in land, which requires a writing to be valid; an oral agreement would not, in general, be provable. The sticky issue here is that Bruce relied on the agreement to his detriment, in constructing an apartment development on his ten acres of Greenacre. Thus, the oral agreement would probably be enforced on grounds of promissory estoppel. However, you're specifically told that Sharon prevailed here, so you have to go *against* your instinct and look for an argument on which she could prevail. Option A suggests just such an argument. As a result, A is the best response.

(B) is not the best response,

because it misstates the rule of law.

Under these facts, Bruce and Sharon were joint tenants in Greenacre. The distinguishing feature of a joint tenancy is the right to survivorship – that is, if the joint tenancy was intact when Bruce died, then Sharon would be entitled to his share in Greenacre, regardless of who he intended to inherit his share from him. The sticky issue here is, as option B implicitly recognizes, the partitioning agreement between Bruce and Sharon. If it was valid, it would leave Bruce as the sole owner of the northerly ten acres and Sharon as the owner of the rest; and that would mean that Stanley would have inherited the northerly ten acres from Bruce. Thus, in order for Sharon to prevail, the partitioning agreement must have been invalid. The problem with B is that it doesn't suggest a good argument for this. A joint tenant *can* unilaterally sever a joint tenancy, by any act disturbing one of the four unities (time, title, possession, and interest). These possibilities include one of the tenants mortgaging the property (under "title" jurisdictions), and alienation by any tenant, either voluntary or involuntary. Thus, Bruce *could* unilaterally sever the joint tenancy, and this wouldn't make a good argument for Sharon. Since B states otherwise, it cannot be the best response.

(C) is not the best response,

because although it states a correct rule of law, the rule it states does not support a judgment in Sharon's favor.

Under these facts, Bruce and Sharon were joint tenants in Greenacre. The distinguishing feature of a joint tenancy is the right to survivorship – that is, if the joint tenancy was intact when Bruce died, then Sharon would be entitled to his share in Greenacre, regardless of who he intended to inherit his share from him. The sticky issue here is, as option C implicitly recognizes, the partitioning agreement between Bruce and Sharon. If it was valid, it would leave Bruce as the sole owner of the northerly ten acres and Sharon as the owner of the rest; and that would mean that Stanley would have inherited the northerly ten acres from Bruce. Thus, in order for Sharon to prevail, the partitioning agreement must have been invalid. The problem with C is that it doesn't suggest a good argument for this.

As C states, an executrix of an estate can assert a claim against the estate. However, the fact that Sharon can maintain such an action does not address the merits of the case; Sharon's ability to sue is a "threshold" issue. Since C does not address the merits of the case, it's not the best response.

(D) is not the best response,

because it addresses an issue irrelevant to these facts.

Under these facts, Bruce and Sharon were joint tenants in Greenacre. The distinguishing feature of a joint tenancy is the right to survivorship – that is, if the joint tenancy was intact when Bruce died, then Sharon would be entitled to his share in Greenacre, regardless of who he intended to inherit his share from him. The sticky issue here is, as option D implicitly recognizes, the partitioning agreement between Bruce and Sharon. If it was valid, it would leave Bruce as the sole owner of the northerly ten acres and Sharon as the owner of the rest; and that would mean that Stanley would have inherited the northerly ten acres. Thus, in order for Sharon to prevail, the partitioning agreement must have been invalid. The problem with D is that it doesn't suggest a good argument for this.

Recording is done for the benefit of subsequent purchasers; it does *not* address the two parties to the transaction. By the same token, if the transaction *had* been recorded but Bruce and Sharon hadn't reduced their agreement to writing, it wouldn't make any difference to a disagreement between the two of them. Since D states otherwise, it's not the best response.

Answer 18

(D) is the best response,

because although it's not entirely correct, it states the best of these four options.

This is a difficult question in that *none* of the answers is truly satisfactory, and so you have to choose the best of a bad lot. The basic fact to remember here is that the privilege belongs to the *patient,* not the *doctor.*

There are seven, basic requirements for the application of a privilege:

1. Appropriate *relationship* between communicants (e.g., attorney/client, doctor/patient);
2. *Relationship existed at the time* of communication;
3. *Appropriate person is claiming* the privilege (i.e., client or patient holds privilege, not attorney or doctor);

4. There was a *communication* (i.e., verbal or communicative act);
5. The communication was made *in confidence* (presence of third parties normally destroys privilege);
6. Privilege has not been *waived* (via contract or in court);
7. There is no reason privilege should not control (e.g., legal advice sought for future wrongdoing; medical advice not in course of treatment).

Under option D, the person asserting the privilege on Zadok's behalf is one closely associated with him: His attorney. His attorney is more likely to act on his behalf than any of the people proposed by the other options. Since D most closely adheres to the requirements of asserting a privilege, it's the best response.

(A) is not the best response,

because it states an erroneous rule. Asserting a privilege has seven requirements:

1. Appropriate *relationship* between communicants (e.g., attorney/client, doctor/patient);
2. *Relationship existed at the time* of communication;
3. *Appropriate person is claiming* the privilege (i.e., client or patient holds privilege, not attorney or doctor);
4. There was a *communication* (i.e., verbal or communicative act);
5. The communication was made *in confidence* (presence of third parties normally destroys privilege);
6. Privilege has not been *waived* (via contract or in court);
7. There is no reason privilege should not control (e.g., legal advice sought for future wrongdoing; medical advice not in course of treatment).

The problem here is with the third element. A doctor simply does not have a privilege against disclosure of confidential communications made by a patient. The doctor-patient privilege rests exclusively with the patient. The problem here is that Zadok cannot object to disclosure himself. In such cases, the doctor normally asserts it on the patient's behalf. Thus, Webb could theoretically assert the privilege on Zadok's behalf. However, Webb could *not* assert the privilege on the ground suggested here – an ostensible privilege against disclosing confidential communications made by a patient. Since A states a rule that is wrong, it is not the best response.

(B) is not the best response,

because a third party is not entitled to assert the doctor-patient privilege.

Asserting a privilege has seven requirements:

1. Appropriate *relationship* between communicants (e.g., attorney/client, doctor/patient);

2. *Relationship existed at the time* of communication;

3. *Appropriate person is claiming* the privilege (i.e., client or patient holds privilege, not attorney or doctor);

4. There was a *communication* (i.e., verbal or communicative act);

5. The communication was made *in confidence* (presence of third parties normally destroys privilege);

6. Privilege has not been *waived* (via contract or in court);

7. There is no reason privilege should not control (e.g., legal advice sought for future wrongdoing; medical advice not in course of treatment).

The problem here is the third requirement. It's someone other than the privilege holder, Zadok, who's asserting the privilege. The privilege exists for the *patient's* benefit. Since Parr is not concerned with Zadok's best interests, he is clearly not the appropriate person to invoke the privilege. Thus, B is not the best response.

(C) is not the best response,

because it relies on facts irrelevant to the determination of invoking the privilege.

Asserting a privilege has seven requirements:

1. Appropriate *relationship* between communicants (e.g., attorney/client, doctor/patient);

2. *Relationship existed at the time* of communication;

3. *Appropriate person is claiming* the privilege (i.e., client or patient holds privilege, not attorney or doctor);

4. There was a *communication* (i.e., verbal or communicative act);

5. The communication was made *in confidence* (presence of third parties normally destroys privilege);

6. Privilege has not been *waived* (via contract or in court);

7. There is no reason privilege should not control (e.g., legal advice sought for future wrongdoing; medical advice not in course of treatment).

Option C addresses the second element – the existence of an appropriate relationship at the time of the communication. However, C's incorrect in that the relationship requirement was satisfied here. The applicability of the doctor-patient privilege does not depend on whether the patient *actually* received treatment, but whether the doctor-patient relationship existed at the time the confidential communication was made. This can exist in the absence of receiving actual treatment. In any case, the judge's finding that Zadok left without receiving treatment would, if anything, vie for *admitting* the evidence, not *excluding* it. This, apart from anything else, should have tipped you off to the fact that C

is not the best response.

Answer 19

(C) is the best response,

because it suggests the situation, of these four options, in which a leading question would least likely be permitted.

This is a highly unusual MBE question, since it is purely theoretical – either you know the rule, or you don't. In order to arrive at this answer, you'd need a familiarity with FRE 611(c), since the other three options are all listed under it as situations in which leading questions expressly *are* permitted. A leading question is one which would lead an average person to believe that the questioner desires one answer over another, e.g., "Didn't you see the red light?" Under FRE 611(c), leading questions are permissible on cross-examination; or on direct examination if the witness is hostile, unwilling, biased, a child, an adult with difficulty communicating; if the witness's recollection is exhausted; or the questioning concerns undisputed preliminary matters. Since C is the only remaining situation, it's the best response.

(A) is not the best response,

because it suggests, of all the options here, the one where leading questions are MOST likely to be permitted.

A leading question is one which would lead an average person to believe that the questioner desires one answer over another, e.g., "Didn't you see the red light?" Under FRE 611(c), leading questions are permissible on cross-examination; or on direct examination if the witness is hostile, unwilling, biased, a child, an adult with difficulty communicating; if the witness's recollection is exhausted; or the questioning concerns undisputed preliminary matters. Leading questions are permissible on cross-examination regardless of who the witness is, so the addition of the "expert" status does not change this result. Thus, A is not the best response.

(B) is not the best response,

because it suggests a situation in which a leading question WOULD likely be permitted.

Under FRE 611(c), leading questions are permissible on cross-examination; or on direct examination if the witness is hostile, unwilling, biased, a child, an adult with difficulty communicating; if the witness's recollection is exhausted; or the questioning concerns undisputed preliminary matters. A leading question is one which would lead an average person to believe that the questioner desires one answer over another, e.g., "Didn't you see the red light?" Such questions would clearly be useful when the testifying witness is a child. Thus, B is not the best response.

(D) is not the best response,

because it suggests a situation in which a leading question WOULD likely be permitted.

A leading question is one which would lead an average person to believe that the questioner desires one answer over another, e.g., "Didn't you see the red light?" Under FRE 611(c), leading questions are permissible on cross-examination; or on direct examination if the witness is hostile, unwilling, biased, a child, an adult with difficulty communicating; if the witness's recollection is exhausted; or the questioning concerns undisputed preliminary matters. Since D states otherwise, it's not the best response.

Answer 20

(C) is the best response,

because it most closely identifies the reason why Passer will not be liable to Tom. The key here is duty to aid, since Passer came upon Tom, who was obviously in need of help, and didn't aid him.

This is one of those questions on the MBE which is made difficult because your *instinct* is that Passer should be liable. You may feel, and rightly so, that Passer had a moral duty to stop and help Tom. This, however, doesn't equate with a legal duty, and since Passer had no legal duty to help, his merely *not* helping wouldn't render him liable.

The general rule is that there is no duty to aid unless one of these elements exist: The defendant's negligence created the peril, a "special relationship" mandates affirmative acts (e.g., parent-child), or defendant had previously undertaken to act for plaintiff's benefit. Thus, unless Passer made Tom's situation worse, he was not under a duty to help, and thus couldn't be liable. Note that C says Passer will not be liable *if* he didn't make Tom's situation worse. Where "if" is the modifier, the reasoning must be plausible on the facts, it must resolve a central issue in the question, and the result must be consistent with the reasoning. Here, it's possible that Passer didn't exacerbate Tom's condition, this resolves Passer's duty to aid, and this is the central issue here. As a result, C is the best response.

(A) is not the best response,

because the facts it cites – stopping and examining Tom – would not create liability in Passer.

The central issue here is the duty to aid. As a general rule, there is no duty to aid, unless one of these elements exist: Defendant's negligence created the peril, a "special relationship" mandates affirmative acts (e.g., common carrier-patron), or defendant has previously undertaken to act for plaintiff's benefit. Here, although Passer stopped and examined Tom, he did not make his condition worse, and it couldn't be said that he'd undertaken to act for Tom's benefit. True, Passer is a schmuck for leaving Tom in the field, but this doesn't make him legally liable. Since A states otherwise, it's not the best response.

(B) is not the best response,

because it does not state a basis on which Passer can be held liable.

What a reasonably prudent person would do under the circumstances doesn't make Passer's doing *something else* tortious; that is, it isn't what the reasonable person would do, but whether the behavior Passer undertook was *unreasonable*. This is the standard for negligence, which requires that defendant must have failed to exercise such care as a reasonable person in his position would have exercised, this must have been a breach of the duty to prevent the foreseeable risk of harm to anyone in plaintiff's position, and this breach must have caused plaintiff's damages. The problem here is duty: There isn't one. As a general rule, there is no affirmative duty to aid, unless one of these elements exist: Defendant's negligence created the peril, a "special relationship" mandates affirmative acts (e.g., parent-child), or defendant has previously undertaken to act for plaintiff's benefit. None of these exist under these facts, so Passer had no duty to aid Tom. As a result, he could not be held liable for *not* aiding Tom. Since B states otherwise, it's not the best response.

(D) is not the best response,

because it does not address Passer's liability.

If Passer was under a duty to aid Tom and didn't do so, he'd be liable, even if Tom had created the risk of harm to himself. As a general rule, one is under no affirmative duty to aid, unless one of these elements exist: Defendant's negligence created the peril, a "special relationship" mandates affirmative acts (e.g., guardian-ward), or defendant has previously undertaken to act for plaintiff's benefit. None of these exist under these facts, so Passer had no duty to aid Tom. What D *implies* is that Tom was contributorily negligent, which would be a defense to Passer's negligence. However, negligence requires breach of a duty, and here, there was no breach. Thus, even though D correctly recognizes that Passer will not be liable, it does not identify the reason why, so it cannot be the best response.

Answer 21

(A) is the best response,

because it correctly identifies the ground on which Traveler will be liable: He was negligent.

In order to be negligent, defendant must have failed to exercise such care as a reasonable person in his position would have exercised, this must have been a breach of the duty to prevent the foreseeable risk of harm to anyone in plaintiff's position, and this breach must have caused plaintiff's damages. That's the case here. The facts state that Traveler was "drowsy and inattentive." Thus, he breached his duty to drive carefully, and hitting Tom was a direct result of this breach. Although Tom was in a drunken coma in the field, this would not break the chain of causation from Traveler's negligence to Tom's injuries. Since A correctly identifies that Traveler will be liable and the principal reason why, it's the best response.

(B) is not the best response,

because the fact it cites would not determine Passer's liability. In order to be liable, Traveler's conduct would have to have been tortious, regardless of Tom's condition. Here, Traveler's conduct was negligent: He breached his duty to drive safely, and as a result injured Tom.

By mentioning Tom's "helpless condition," option B implies the Last Clear Chance doctrine. Under the doctrine, where a plaintiff is "helpless" through his own contributory negligence, and he is in a position of peril from which he cannot reasonably escape (as Tom is here), defendant will be liable if he either knew or should have known that plaintiff was in danger, in most states. Thus, regardless of whether defendant discovered plaintiff's plight and negligently failed to avoid it, or he negligently failed to discover it, he'll be liable under Last Clear Chance. This is not applicable here, because Tom would not be considered contributorily negligent: instead, it's Traveler's "inattentive" driving which directly caused Tom's injuries. Since B fails to recognize this, it's not the best response.

(C) is not the best response,

because although it correctly states the facts, it ignores the fact that the reason Traveler *didn't* see Tom is because he wasn't paying attention.

Here, Traveler will be liable for negligence, because he had a duty to drive safely, which he breached, and in doing so injured Tom. Negligence is judged *objectively* – that is, in terms of the reasonable person, *not* the tortfeasor himself. Here, Traveler *could* have and *should* have avoided hitting Tom, and he was unreasonable in not doing so. In essence, these facts are no different than if Traveler had been driving with his eyes closed – he wouldn't have seen Tom then either, but he'd clearly be liable.

Say, instead, that Traveler had been alert and driving carefully, Tom was lying in the road at a bend, and Traveler *couldn't* have seen him in time to stop. In that case Traveler wouldn't be liable, because a reasonable person couldn't avoid hitting Tom. Thus, it's not the mere fact that Traveler didn't see Tom that determines Traveler's liability. Since C states otherwise, it's not the best response.

(D) is not the best response,

because it misstates the facts: It's Traveler's conduct that *directly* caused Tom's injuries.

Option D suggests that Tom's own actions should relieve Traveler of liability to him. This would require that Tom was contributorily negligent, which would require causation. However, what option D doesn't recognize is that by passing out in a field, Tom *did not* create the possibility that he'd be run over by a car veering

off the road. Even if he *had,* this wouldn't mean that Traveler's conduct couldn't be a cause in fact of his injuries, because a result can have more than one cause in fact.

Rather, Traveler will be liable to Tom if he failed to act as a reasonable person in his circumstances would have acted, this was a breach of the duty to prevent the foreseeable risk of harm to anyone in Tom's position, and this breach caused Tom's damages. Here, Traveler was under a duty to drive carefully, and his inattentiveness was a breach of this duty. As a result, he caused a foreseeable risk of harm to anyone (or anything) on the side of the road, including Tom. As to the causation requirement, in order to satisfy the cause in fact element, Traveler's conduct need only have been a substantial factor in causing Tom's damages. It clearly was. Since D doesn't recognize this, it's not the best response.

Answer 22

(B) is the best response,

because it impliedly identifies the basis on which Roofer will be liable: Negligence.

One is negligent if he fails to exercise such care as a reasonable person in his position would have exercised, this must have been a breach of the duty to prevent the foreseeable risk of harm to anyone in plaintiff's position, and this breach must have caused plaintiff's damages. Here, by leaving the ladder in place, Roofer behaved unreasonably in creating a risk that the home could be burglarized. He left a ladder against the house, leading to a second story window which a burglar could not otherwise have reached. Coupled with the fact that no one was at home at the time, this creates a risk of unlawful entry, which Roofer's exercise of due care could have avoided. Since Roofer's negligence caused Orissa's damages and his due care would have avoided those damages, Orissa will prevail. Since B recognizes this, it's the best response.

(A) is not the best response,

because it's highly unlikely Roofer would be considered a trespasser.

Trespass requires proof of three elements: Defendant's physical invasion of plaintiff's exclusive possessory interest in real property without plaintiff's consent; defendant's intent to bring about such invasion; and causation. Under these facts, it's unlikely Roofer's presence on the property would be considered nonpermissive. Naturally, while he was *performing* his work, his presence would be considered permissive, and as a result he would be a licensee, not a trespasser. His leaving a ladder on the property overnight would not be sufficient to change his status to trespasser. Instead, what Roofer will be liable for is *negligence,* since he failed to exercise such care as a reasonable person is his position would have exercised, this was a breach of the duty to prevent the foreseeable risk of harm to anyone in Orissa's position, and this breach caused Orissa's damages. Leaving the ladder in place created the risk that a thief would take advantage of the ladder to enter the house. Since A doesn't recognize this, it's not the best response.

(C) is not the best response,

because although it correctly states the *general* rule of law, it does not apply to facts like these.

The intentional misconduct of others *only* relieves the original actor of liability *when the misconduct is unforeseeable.* Here, theft is exactly the outcome Roofer's negligence – in leaving the ladder propped up to a second story window of an unoccupied house – is likely to produce, and as such it will be considered "within the risk" Roofer's negligence created. Thus, intervening misconduct only relieves the original actor of liability when it's *not foreseeable.* Since C fails to recognize that the facts here do not fit the general rule, it's not the best response.

(D) is not the best response,

because it misstates the law: Orissa's claim is *not* limited to damages for breach of contract, and, in any case it's unlikely Orissa would be able to claim for breach of contract under these facts.

Orissa would be able to claim under the contract only if Roofer's repairs on the roof were not done "in a workmanlike manner." There is no indication of any deficiency in the repairs under these facts. Even if there *had* been, this would not have prohibited a tort claim by Orissa for Roofer's negligence in leaving the ladder against the house, since a claim under the contract and a claim in tort are not mutually exclusive. Since D states otherwise, it's not the best response.

Answer 23

(B) is the best response,

because it removes the situation from coverage by the statute mentioned in the facts.

Getting this problem correct requires a careful analysis of the facts, not merely a mechanical application of a rule of law. The key fact here is the statute, requiring 30 days' notice for eviction. What this should tell you is that Purcell's best legal argument will involve *characterizing Homer as something other than a tenant!*

Under the facts, if Homer is characterized as a tenant, it's at least possible that he would be protected by the 30 days' notice provision. Thus, Purcell's best argument would be to characterize Homer as something *other than* a tenant, if such an argument is possible on these facts. Such an argument is possible here, since Homer could be characterized as a licensee. A licensee is one with a personal privilege to enter upon the licensor's land. A license is not considered an interest in land, and it is, with exceptions that don't apply here, revocable. Here, Homer's right, created under the contract, could be construed as a license, because it could

be said that the contract creates in Homer a personal privilege to enter Purcell's land. Since Homer's possession could be characterized as a license, and doing so removes the *single greatest obstacle to Purcell's winning the case* – the statutory 30 days' notice provision – B is the best response.

(A) is not the best response,

because it does not correctly characterize the facts.

A trespasser "ab initio" is a trespasser "from the beginning." Here, Homer initially validly possessed Blackacre under a provision in the contract between him and Purcell. While his residence after the 30-day period ended might be characterized as a trespass, certainly the period *before* that could not be considered a trespass. Thus, Homer was not a trespasser "from the beginning," making A not the best response.

(C) is not the best response,

because it does not avoid the statutory 30 days' notice provision for tenants. Otherwise, C would be an attractive response, because a tenancy at sufferance is created when a tenant wrongfully maintains possession of the premises ("holds over") after the expiration of the lease. Doing so makes him liable as a trespasser, unless the lessor holds the tenant to a new tenancy (e.g., by accepting rent). However, C does not take into account the operation of the statute here, and if you chose this response, you probably overlooked the statute, too. Since characterizing Homer as a tenant would likely invoke the 30 days' notice provision which is *unfavorable* to Purcell, C is not the best response.

(D) is not the best response,

because it does not avoid the statutory 30 days' notice provision for tenants. Furthermore, D misstates the facts, since, regardless of the statute, Homer could not be characterized as a tenant from month to month.

When a tenant wrongfully maintains possession of the premises ("holds over") after the expiration of the lease, he is liable as a trespasser, unless the lessor holds the tenant to a new tenancy (e.g., by accepting rent). If the lessor does allow a new tenancy, the resulting tenancy is a tenancy from period-to-period (a/k/a "month to month"). However, the facts here indicate that Purcell *did not* accept the rent, and instead sued immediately to gain immediate possession of Blackacre. Thus, Homer could not be considered a tenant from month to month. Furthermore, D does not take into account the operation of the statute. Purcell's best legal argument would involve avoiding invocation of the 30 days' notice statute for tenants. Characterizing Homer as a tenant would *invite* invocation of the statute, not *avoid* it. Since D does not recognize this, it's not the best response.

Answer 24

(D) is the best response,

because it represents an argument on which Bertha can prevail.

First, you have to classify Bertha's duty to perform in the play. It's a constructive condition precedent to Albert's duty to pay. As a constructive condition, Bertha need only substantially perform her duties (unlike express conditions, which require strict performance). Thus, if Bertha's illness is considered a minor breach, she's substantially performed, and so Albert's duties under the contract were not relieved, and he couldn't cancel the contract (although he could recover any damages due to the breach). If, on the other hand, Bertha's absence was a *major* breach (due to a *lack* of substantial performance), then Albert *would* be able to terminate the contract. Under these facts, it's certainly arguable that Bertha's one week absence, in light of a six month contract, would not be major. If this is true, Albert's cancellation of the contract would be a major breach of contract, and Bertha would prevail. Since D recognizes this, it's the best response.

(A) is not the best response,

because such an argument could only hurt Bertha, not help her.

In order to recover from Albert, Bertha will have to prove that she did not commit a material breach of contract, and Albert did. That's because Bertha's acting in the play would be a constructive condition precedent to Albert's duty to pay her. If her illness were only a partial breach of contract, Albert could recover damages from her, but he couldn't cancel the entire contract; and in cancelling the contract as he did, he'd be liable for the entire remaining term of the six-month contract.

If, on the other hand, Bertha argues that the contract is severable into *weeks,* Albert would only be liable for the weeks or portions thereof when he refused to perform. Thus, it's advantageous for *Albert* to make this argument, not Bertha. Since A doesn't recognize this, it's not the best response.

(B) is not the best response,

because such an argument would be of no benefit to Bertha.

In order to recover from Albert, Bertha must establish that she substantially performed a constructive condition precedent of the contract – by performing in the play. This would mean that Albert wasn't entitled to cancel the contract, and he'd be liable for the rest of the six-month contract.

By claiming impossibility, Bertha would be admitting that she didn't substantially perform her duties under the contract, which would relieve Albert of *his* duty to perform, enabling him to cancel the contract.

If the tables were turned and Albert were suing Bertha for breach, impossibility would be a good defense, since her illness would excuse her from her duties under the contract. However, a plaintiff's failure to perform a constructive condition precedent to defendant's duty is virtually never excusable due to impossibility. Thus, it wouldn't be a good argument for Bertha, making B not the best response.

(C) is not the best response,

because Bertha has a *contract* to rely on; she needn't resort to promissory estoppel.

What Bertha *wants* to establish is that she substantially performed a constructive condition precedent to Albert's duty to pay (that is, that she performed in the play) and that Albert's cancellation of the contract thus constituted a major breach of contract.

If in fact her illness caused only a *partial* breach of contract, then she'll be entitled to the contract price less damages her absence caused. If, on the other hand, her absence is considered a *major* breach, then she'd only get damages due to her reliance, but these would be determined by the contract – that is, her two days' of work – not on the basis of other jobs she passed up before the contract existed.

Instead, promissory estoppel is triggered by a gratuitous promise that is likely to, and does, induce the promisee's reliance. It is a substitute for consideration to avoid injustice; it differs from consideration in that there's no bargain. The lack of an enforceable contract is a prerequisite for promissory estoppel; here, there is an enforceable contract, so promissory estoppel cannot apply. Since C doesn't recognize this, it's not the best response.

Answer 25

(A) is the best response,

because it would seriously impair Bertha's ability to prevail.

Assuming that Bertha's week off was only a partial breach of contract, Albert would still be required to perform under the contract (by hiring Bertha back when she got better), and would only be able to recover damages due to breach. However, whenever damages are available, the aggrieved party is under a duty to "mitigate," or lessen, his damages by finding substitute performance. In doing so, he need only act reasonably. If Helen was the only substitute available, and she had to have a six month contract, then Albert was reasonable in hiring her for six months, and this would preclude his hiring Bertha back. As a result, Albert wouldn't be liable to Bertha *at all,* since he was only taking reasonable action to mitigate his damages due to Bertha's breach. This would obviously significantly impact Bertha's claim, making A the best response.

(B) is not the best response,

because its reasoning would have no bearing on Bertha's rights.

By contracting to perform in the play, Bertha's performances need only be adequate. Getting better reviews than anyone else was neither an express no implied condition of Bertha's continued employment.

Instead, Bertha's rights will be governed by the contract. Under the personal services contract, Bertha would be required to perform and if she became incapable of performing, her performance would be excused. Here, Bertha's being sick for a week would be considered a partial (not total) breach of contract, meaning that Albert could only recover damages due to her absence, not cancel the contract entirely. As in any contract, an aggrieved party must mitigate damages, and here this would mean hiring a replacement. However, Helen's being a better actress is not, in and of itself, grounds for refusing to rehire Bertha. Since B doesn't recognize that the relative merit of Bertha and Helen's performances is irrelevant, it's not the best response.

(C) isn't the best response,

because Bertha's duty to mitigate would not encompass the job Albert offered her.

Assuming that Bertha's week off would be considered a partial breach of contract, Albert had no right to cancel the contract. His doing so would be a major breach, entitling Bertha to recovery. However, as with any damages, Bertha was under a duty to *mitigate* her damages. This goes for employment contracts, such that employees must look for comparable work. However, "comparable" is the operative word here. The work must involve similar duties, working conditions, and rank. Here, the understudy role is of a lower rank and pays only half of what Bertha's original role paid. Thus, her turning down the job would have no impact on her action. Since C doesn't recognize this, it's not the best response.

(D) is not the best response,

because Bertha's duty to mitigate would not encompass the job Albert offered her.

Assuming that Bertha's week off would be considered a partial breach of contract, Albert had no right to cancel the contract. His doing so would be a major breach, entitling Bertha to recovery. However, as with any damages, Bertha was under a duty to *mitigate* her damages. This goes for employment contracts, such that employees must look for comparable work. However, "comparable" is the operative word here. The work must involve similar duties, working conditions, and rank. Here, the secretarial job doesn't involve duties that are at all similar to Bertha's acting work, even though it pays more money. Thus, her turning down the job would have no impact on her action. Since D doesn't recognize this, it's not the best response.

Answer 26

(D) is the best response,

because the evidence it contains would most seriously injure Weston's credibility.

Impeachment is the means of casting adversely on the credibility of the witness. It can be accomplished via either reputation or opinion testimony, under FRE 608(a). Impeachment can show, for instance, bias or interest, contradicting facts, inconsistent statements, prior convictions, bad character for truthfulness, or sensory deficiencies (although the requirements for admitting some of these will differ, and some can only come from the witness's own mouth, not from extrinsic evidence). Rehabilitation is the effort to rehabilitate the witness's credibility on redirect examination. Typically, it can either explain facts brought out on cross-examination, or, when the witness's character for truthfulness has been attacked, evidence of the witness's good reputation for honesty may be admitted.

Here, evidence that Weston had been out of town July 4-10 would show that he could not have heard Dent make the oral contract, thus bearing adversely on his truthfulness. This is a clear case where rehabilitation would be permissible. Since D most seriously damages Park's case, it's the best response.

(A) is not the best response,

because it is not very effective discrediting evidence.

Impeachment is the means of casting adversely on the credibility of the witness. It can be accomplished via either reputation or opinion testimony, under FRE 608(a). Impeachment can show, for instance, bias or interest, contradicting facts, inconsistent statements, prior convictions, bad character for truthfulness, or sensory deficiencies (although the requirements for admitting some of these will differ, and some can only come from the witness's own mouth, not from extrinsic evidence). Rehabilitation is the effort to rehabilitate the witness's credibility on redirect examination. Typically, it can either explain facts brought out on cross-examination, or, when the witness's character for truthfulness has been attacked, evidence of the witness's good reputation for honesty may be admitted.

Here, Weston's speculation may be foolhardy, but it does not speak to his truthfulness or veracity, and thus it really doesn't impeach him. Where there's no impeachment, there's no need for rehabilitation. Since the evidence does not injure Weston's credibility as seriously as option D, A is not the best response.

(B) isn't a bad response, but it's not the best response,

because it's not as effective as option D in discrediting Weston.

Impeachment is the means of casting adversely on the credibility of the witness. It can be accomplished via either reputation or opinion testimony, under FRE 608(a). Impeachment can show, for instance, bias or interest, contradicting facts, inconsistent statements, prior convictions, bad character for truthfulness, or sensory deficiencies (although the requirements for admitting some of these will differ, and some can only come from the witness's own mouth, not from extrinsic evidence). Rehabilitation is the effort to rehabilitate the witness's credibility on redirect examination. Typically, it can either explain facts brought out on cross-examination, or, when the witness's character for truthfulness has been attacked, evidence of the witness's good reputation for honesty may be admitted.

Here, evidence that Weston had been Park's college roommate would tend to indicate that Weston *might* be willing to lie to help out Park, but standing alone it wouldn't seriously discredit him, and thus wouldn't strongly create the need for rehabilitation. Since option D is a *more* serious attack on Weston's credibility, B is not the best response.

(C) is not the best response,

because it does not address Weston's credibility.

Impeachment is the means of casting adversely on the credibility of the witness. It can be accomplished via either reputation or opinion testimony, under FRE 608(a). Impeachment can show, for instance, bias or interest, contradicting facts, inconsistent statements, prior convictions, bad character for truthfulness, or sensory deficiencies (although the requirements for admitting some of these will differ, and some can only come from the witness's own mouth, not from extrinsic evidence). Rehabilitation is the effort to rehabilitate the witness's credibility on redirect examination. Typically, it can either explain facts brought out on cross-examination, or, when the witness's character for truthfulness has been attacked, evidence of the witness's good reputation for honesty may be admitted.

Here, evidence that Weston had attended a school for the mentally retarded would reflect on his intelligence, but it would not tend to impact his truthfulness or ability to observe. Since C would not injure Weston's credibility seriously, it would not invite rehabilitation, making C not the best response.

Answer 27

(C) is the best response,

because it correctly states that expert testimony will not be necessary to determine whether Abel and Baker breached their standard of care.

This is a bit of a tricky question, because to answer it correctly, you must be able to eliminate some distractors which deal with tort law on standards of care for professionals.

Under these facts, all the jury must do is determine if Abel and Baker filed the suit within the period authorized by the statute of limitations. This is not a matter which would, on these facts, require the kind of sophistication expert testimony suggests; all an expert would do, really, is point to a deadline on a calendar. Expert testimony is necessary only where the court deter-

mines that "scientific, technical, or other specialized knowledge will assist the trier of fact to understand the evidence or to determine a fact in issue." FRE 702. Since this standard is not satisfied here, C is the best response.

(A) is not the best response,

because it erroneously suggests that expert testimony is necessary to determine breach of the standard of care, and, beyond that, it misstates the standard by which Abel and Baker would be judged.

Under FRE 702, expert testimony is only necessary where the court determines that "scientific, technical, or other specialized knowledge will assist the trier of fact to understand the evidence or to determine a fact in issue." Determining whether Abel and Baker missed their deadline would not be the kind of matter necessarily meriting expert testimony. Furthermore, the standard against which lawyers are judged is the minimum common skill of members in good standing in their profession. The "locality" requirement that option A mentions is an old concept, which is only one factor for juries to determine in modern cases in determining if the actor behaved reasonably in the circumstances, and even when this rule was applied, it was applied generally to general medical practitioners. Since A does not state the correct result or the correct standard, it's not the best response.

(B) is not the best response

because it erroneously suggests that expert testimony is necessary to determine breach of the standard of care, and, beyond that, it misstates the standard by which Abel and Baker would be judged.

Under FRE 702, expert testimony is only necessary where the court determines that "scientific, technical, or other specialized knowledge will assist the trier of fact to understand the evidence or to determine a fact in issue." Determining whether Abel and Baker missed their deadline would not be the kind of matter necessarily meriting expert testimony, because all that needs to be determined is if Abel and Baker made the deadline. Furthermore, the standard against which lawyers are judged is the minimum common skill of members in good standing in their profession. Thus, the "statewide" standard B suggests would not be appropriate for Abel and Baker. Since B misses both of these points, it's not the best response.

(D) is not the best response,

because the judge is not competent as a witness in a case, and even if he were, expert testimony is not appropriate here.

Even though the judge is (hopefully) an expert on the law, he cannot testify as to whether Abel and Baker breached their duty, since that is a matter of fact, not law, and thus it's a matter for the jury to decide. The judge cannot offer expert testimony, because judges are not competent witnesses. FRE 605.

Even if the judge could offer expert testimony, it's not merited here. Under FRE 702, expert testimony is only necessary where the court determines that "scientific, technical, or other specialized knowledge will assist the trier of fact to understand the evidence or to determine a fact in issue." Determining whether Abel and Baker missed their deadline would not be the kind of matter necessarily meriting expert testimony, because all that needs to be determined is if Abel and Baker made the deadline. Since D mistakenly states that the judge can testify as an expert witness, and it states the expert testimony is needed on a matter where it's not, in fact, merited, D not the best response.

Answer 28

(A) is the best response,

because it provides the element of causation, which is the key issue under these facts.

A defendant is negligent if he failed to exercise such care as a reasonable person in his position would have exercised, this was a breach of the duty to prevent the foreseeable risk of harm to anyone in plaintiff's position, and this breach caused plaintiff's damages.

The question itself tells you that the duty and breach are a given (because it asks you what, *in addition* to negligence, must be proven, and duty and breach are considered negligence). Client's damages are straightforward, and, in any case, no one of the four options mentions damages, so it can't be the focus of the problem. That leaves causation. Where there is one cause, the test for causation is the "but for" test: Defendant's conduct is the "cause in fact" of an event if the event would not have occurred "but for" defendant's conduct. Under these facts, this means Client would have to prove that she would have recovered damages *but for* Abel and Baker's negligence. Thus, it wouldn't be enough to claim that she *might* have recovered, or only to prove she suffered damages due to *Motorist's* negligence. Since A correctly identifies the element of causation as a requirement of negligence, and it's the element most in question on these facts, A is the best response.

(B) is not the best response,

because it suggests an *insufficient* basis for recovery.

A defendant is negligent if he failed to exercise such care as a reasonable person in his position would have exercised, this was a breach of the duty to prevent the foreseeable risk of harm to anyone in plaintiff's position, and this breach caused plaintiff's damages.

When there is one cause (as here), the "but for" test is used to determine causation: Defendant's conduct is considered the cause in fact of an event if the event would not have occurred "but for" defendant's conduct. B states that all that would be required is a possible claim against Motorist. Under the "but for" test, a negligence claim would require that Client *would* have prevailed but for the negligence. Since B states a standard

that is lower than the real standard, it's not the best response.

(C) is not the best response,

because proving that Motorist caused her injuries would not be a sufficient basis on which to recover from Abel and Baker. All *that* proves is that *Motorist* should be held liable.

In order for Abel and Baker to be held liable, Client would have to prove that their action prevented her from recovering damages from Motorist. While proving that Motorist injured her would necessarily be *part* of this claim, it wouldn't focus on Abel and Baker's liability. As a result, C is not the best response.

(D) is not the best response,

because it is not a required element of Client's case.

In order to be found negligent, Abel and Baker's conduct must have caused Client damage. What D refers to is contributory negligence, a defense which Abel and Baker would have to raise (that is, they'd have to show that Client's own negligence helped cause her damages). Here, the only possible source of contributory negligence would be Client's approaching Abel and Baker only six weeks before the Statute of Limitations ran. However, this is a weak argument, and as stated earlier, would not be Client's responsibility unless Abel and Baker claimed contributory negligence as a defense. Instead, Client will have to prove that, but for Abel and Baker's unreasonable conduct, she would have recovered damages from Motorist. Since D does not recognize this, it's not the best response.

Answer 29

(B) is the best response,

because it identifies the situation, of these four, which most likely satisfies the first degree murder statute in the problem.

As a prerequisite, you have to remember what common law murder requires: an unlawful killing (neither justifiable nor excusable) committed with malice aforethought.

The key here is to realize that Defendant's merely being angered by Sam's conduct would not be enough to reduce murder to voluntary manslaughter, since voluntary manslaughter requires that the provocation be recent enough that the actor was still in the "heat of passion" when the killing took place, and that a reasonable person would still have been in the "heat of passion," as well. The act of having to buy rat poison and put it in Sam's coffee indicates that the Defendant had time to cool off, and, by the same token, premeditate and deliberate the killing. Furthermore, the use of poison would be clear evidence of the intent to kill, thus satisfying the "malice aforethought" requirement of common law murder (which is what's missing from option C). Since option B satisfies the statute in the problem, and the use of poison would supply the "malice aforethought" requirement of common law murder, B is the best response.

(A) is not the best response,
because it would not satisfy the "premeditation and deliberation" element of the statute given in the problem.

At common law, murder requires an unlawful killing (neither justifiable nor excusable) committed with malice aforethought. Voluntary manslaughter is murder committed in the "heat of passion." In fact, under these facts, Defendant would most likely be guilty of voluntary manslaughter. The key word here is *immediately*. If Defendant was responding immediately to an insult, there's a strong possibility that he killed Robert in the *heat of passion*. That would make the killing voluntary manslaughter, not murder. Even if he were guilty of murder, he wouldn't be guilty of first degree murder, since there was no time to premeditate and deliberate, and there was no other crime being committed. As a result, A is not the best response.

(C) is not the best response,
but it's an appealing one.

The "lying in wait" in option C would certainly satisfy the premeditation and deliberation requirement of first degree murder, as given in the statute; however, the problem here is whether there was a murder at all. While murder does not require intent, it does require malice aforethought. Malice aforethought can take the form of intending to inflict great bodily injury (short of an intent to kill), or acting in spite of an unjustifiably high risk to human life. Under option C, Defendant did intend to injure Fred; however, striking Fred with a broom handle could not be considered evidence of an intent to inflict great bodily injury, since great injury would typically not result from a whack with a broom handle. As a result, C is not the best response.

(D) is not the best response,
because it would probably not satisfy the premeditation and deliberation element of the statute in the problem.

At common law, voluntary intoxication can only be used to prove a lack of capacity for specific intent crimes, and it can only be used if the defendant was intoxicated before he formulated the intent to commit the crime. Some courts restrict the use of voluntary intoxication as a defense to first degree murder. Here, Defendant's drunkenness apparently stopped him from forming the necessary mens rea for murder. As a result, he may not be guilty of murder at all, making D not the best response.

Answer 30

(C) is the best response,
because it focuses on the central issue, and, based, on the condition it provides, arrives at the correct result. The key fact here is that, while it is not expressly men-

tioned in the statute, the requirement of criminal intent will be implied. That's because the statute here would not be considered to create a strict liability offense, since those generally involve regulatory offenses or serious potential harm to the public.

As a result, Rose cannot be found guilty of any crime if she is found to lack criminal intent. An honest belief that the signs were abandoned would preclude her guilt, since she would lack the intent to appropriate public property. Note that C focuses on an element *it provides itself*. Option C states that she won't be guilty *if* the jury believes her. The use of the modifier "if" means that the reasoning must be plausible on the facts, it must address a central issue, and the result must be consistent with the reasoning. Here, it's possible that the jury could believe Rose. If the jury *does* believe her, it will believe that she did not have the requisite criminal intent, and as a result she will be found not guilty. Since C correctly identifies the central issue and resolves it satisfactorily, and its result is consistent with its reasoning, it's the best response.

(A) is not the best response,
because regardless of whether the offense is a public welfare offense, Rose would still have to have a criminal intent in order to be convicted under the statute. That's because the statute here would not be considered to create a strict liability offense, since those generally involve regulatory offenses or serious potential harm to the public. Thus, it would have to be proven that Rose intended to appropriate government property in order to be convicted. Since option A suggests Rose would be guilty even without the requisite intent, it's not the best response.

(B) is not the best response,
because it does not focus on the central issue.

The central issue under these facts is whether Rose had the requisite intent to be convicted. That's because the statute here would not be considered to create a strict liability offense, since those generally involve regulatory offenses or serious potential harm to the public.

If Rose believed the signs were abandoned, then she would not have the duty to inquire, since the two are mutually exclusive. Inquiring about whether the signs were abandoned would call into question her honesty about believing they were abandoned. Not asking about whether the signs were abandoned would thus not establish her intent to steal the signs. As a result, B is not the best response.

(D) is not the best response,
because whether the state had adequately informed the public that the signs were public property is not a central issue, and, by using the modifier "unless," option D suggests that the state's lack of notice is a prerequisite to Rose's conviction.

The central issue instead is Rose's criminal intent, since intent will have to be proven in order to find her guilty under the statute. That's because the statute here would not be considered to create a strict liability offense, since those generally involve regulatory offenses or serious potential harm to the public. If Rose lacked criminal intent, then it wouldn't matter whether the state had adequately notified the public that the signs weren't abandoned. Since D focuses on an issue that is not controlling, it's not the best response.

Answer 31

(B) is the best response,

because it correctly identifies the basis on which Ted will be exonerated: Howard's attack on Ted was unlawful.

Ted can only be guilty of murder if he committed an unlawful killing (neither justifiable nor excusable) with malice aforethought. Here, the killing was justified by self defense. Ted was entitled to use such force as reasonably seemed necessary to protect himself, because he was not the aggressor. Since he was threatened with great bodily harm or death (as evidenced by Howard's use of a knife), he was entitled to use deadly force in self-defense. Since Ted was entitled to use self-defense, and the means of self-defense he used did not exceed his privilege, he will not be guilty of murder. Since B focuses on the reason why Ted will be exonerated, it's the best response.

(A) is not the best response,

because it does not focus on a central issue.

It's not Ted's right to be in the house that will determine his guilt on a murder charge, but his conduct vis a vis Howard. He'd be guilty of murdering Howard if he unlawfully killed Howard, without justification or excuse, with malice aforethought. Even if Ted were rightfully in the house, it would not provide him with the justification to kill Howard; conversely, his trespassing on the property would not make him guilty of murder. Instead, the fact that Ted was acting in self-defense will provide him with a justification for killing Howard, and will thus exonerate him from criminal liability. Since A does not focus on a central issue, it's not the best response.

(C) is not the best response,

because it does not provide a basis for Ted's guilt.

Ted can only be guilty of murdering Howard if he unlawfully killed Howard, without justification or excuse, with malice aforethought. Ted's most likely defense is self-defense, which would provide a justification for the killing. Thus, what will determine Ted's guilt is whether or not his use of deadly force was justified because of Howard's attack. Howard's reason for attacking Ted might, if Howard had killed Ted, reduced Howard's culpability from murder to voluntary manslaughter (a "heat of passion" killing), but as long as Howard's attack was not lawful, Ted had the right to defend himself. Since C does not focus on Ted's guilt,

it's not the best response.

(D) is not the best response,

for two reasons: Ted was not a trespasser, and even if he was, Howard would not have been privileged to attack him. Ted was not a trespasser because he had the permission of one of the owners, Janet, to be on the property. Even if Ted had been a trespasser, this would not have entitled Howard to physically attack him; rather, Howard would be limited to the use of reasonable means to eject Ted from the property. Instead, Howard attacked Ted with a knife. Since he exceeded his privilege, his attack was unlawful, and Ted was entitled to defend himself. Since Howard used deadly force, Ted was entitled to defend with deadly force, thus meaning that he won't be guilty of murder. Since D mischaracterizes the facts and, beyond that, misstates the law, it's not the best response.

Answer 32

(A) is the best response,

because it applies to these facts, it would be relatively easy to prove, and it overcomes a central obstacle in the case.

This problem indicates a pattern found on many MBE Property questions – you have to be familiar with several areas of law in order to get them right. Here, you need to know contract law, to eliminate the creditor beneficiary option in C, and Constitutional Law, to eliminate the taxpayer option in B.

In order to bind a subsequent purchaser, an equitable servitude must meet the following requirements: There must be notice, whether actual, constructive, or inquiry (here, there is constructive notice); there must be an intent that it bind subsequent purchasers; and the benefit and burden both must touch and concern the land. The notice requirement is satisfied, because although Pete's deed did not refer to the restriction on use of the ten-acre tract, the restriction is present in a prior recording in the chain of title, thus satisfying "constructive notice." The intent to bind subsequent purchasers exists, because such a restriction in the deed would be meaningless otherwise. The "benefit and burden" requirement is satisfied because, according to most courts, the benefit attaches to the properties of owners of other tracts in the development, as long as the common scheme is in existence for lots sold both before and after the one in question. The restriction itself constitutes a burden. As a result, the facts here fit the requirements of an equitable servitude relatively easily, and, in doing so, would bind Pete, as a subsequent purchaser – and this is exactly what Sarah wants to do. Since A applies to the facts here, is not difficult to prove, and addresses a central issue in the case, it's the best response.

(B) is not the best response,

because, while it is factually correct, it does not provide

a strong basis for Sarah prevailing in the action.

In general, one's status as a state or municipal tax-payer would not give her a status sufficient to merit her recovery. Her status as a taxpayer gives her, at best, an indirect interest in the use of the ten-acre tract; it's her position as one of the surrounding landowners that gives her an opportunity for relief. Since B does not recognize this, it's not the best response.

(C) is not the best response,

because, while it could be factually correct, it does not provide a strong basis for Sarah prevailing in the action.

In order to be a creditor beneficiary to the Oscar/Pete contract, Oscar would have to owe Sarah a pre-existing duty, which Pete's performance will fulfill, and Sarah would have to prove that Oscar specifically intended that Pete's performance benefit *her*. Under these facts, it's unlikely that Oscar intended the Oscar/Pete contract to benefit Sarah in any significant way, and, beyond that, it would be difficult to characterize her as a creditor of Oscar's, since she only purchased a lot from him. While Sarah could, *in theory,* prevail on a third-party beneficiary theory, these factors indicate that it would be a very difficult case to prove. As a result, C is not the best answer.

(D) is not the best response,

because, although it is factually correct, it does not offer a strong basis for Sarah prevailing in the action.

A bona fide purchaser is a subsequent purchaser, who pays value, without notice of any prior convey-ance, and is of good faith. Here, Pete has *at least* con-structive notice of Oscar's intent to use the ten-acre tract for a school, since Oscar's plan was *recorded.* As a result, Pete is not a bona fide purchaser. However, Pete's non-bona fide purchaser status would only deal with his being bound by the recorded notice; it would not have a significant impact on a dispute between Pete and Sarah. Since it does not impact a major issue in the dispute, D is not the best response, even though it is factually correct.

Answer 33

(A) is the best response,

because the mobile home restriction here could easily be characterized as a covenant running with the land, and, as such, Sarah could enforce the covenant against Joe.

In order to get this question correct, you had to know the requirements of a covenant running with the land. Most importantly, you had to realize that Joe need not be *in fact* on notice of the covenant – *constructive* notice is sufficient. Since the covenant is in Joe's chain of title, he would be bound by it.

A "covenant running with the land" is a promise related to land which is enforceable by subsequent holders of the land. There are four principle require-ments: The parties must have intended that the agree-ment would run with the land; the agreement must "touch and concern" the land; the Statute of Frauds must be satisfied; and there must be privity of estate between the parties. If these requirements are met, it doesn't matter that the restriction does not appear in the remote purchaser's deed *itself.* That's the case here.

Since there is grantor-grantee privity between Oscar and Joe (since the title went from Oscar to Max to Joe), this requirement is satisfied. Since there is no indica-tion otherwise, it can be assumed that the Statute of Frauds is satisfied. An agreement concerning a build-ing restriction would "touch and concern" the land. As to the intent that the covenant run with the land, a question of fact is involved which requires an analysis of the circumstances. However, since all the fifty lots originally sold had the restriction in them, and the lots were larger, at one acre, than one would associate with a mobile home park, one could imply the intent that the restriction was intended to be a covenant running with the land. Furthermore, as a holder of a deed to which the restriction applies, Sarah would have the standing to sue. Since A recognizes all this, it's the best response.

(B) is not the best response,

because the fact it cites is irrelevant to the issues here.

The mere fact that the presence of mobile homes would adversely affect the value of Sarah's land does not mean that Sarah has a legally cognizable right to forbid their presence. As a general principle, the owner of land may put the land to any lawful use he chooses, without regard to the impact on the market value of other, neighboring properties. Thus, even if B were *true,* it would not provide a sound basis for Sarah pre-vailing. As a result, B is not the best response.

(C) is not the best response,

because it does not correctly cite the rule on covenants running with the land.

Covenants running with the land will bind subsequent purchasers of the land as long as the original parties intended that the agreement run with the land, the agreement touches and concerns the land, the Statute of Frauds is satisfied, and there is privity of estate between the covenantor and the grantee. Here, all these elements are satisfied, so the fact that Joe's deed did not contain the covenant is *irrelevant.* Thus, C is not the best response.

(D) is not the best response,

because as long as the covenant runs with the land, Joe's being a remote grantee of the original, covenant-ing party – Oscar – is irrelevant.

A covenant running with the land can only be binding if there is privity of estate between the parties. The priv-ity that exists here is "grantor-grantee" privity, which exists when a covenant is included with a conveyance of a property interest. That's the case here. Grantor-grantee privity existed with everyone from Oscar to Joe, and so Joe is bound. Since the restriction on use would be considered a covenant running with the land, and the privity requirement is satisfied, D is not the best response.

Answer 34

(D) is the best response,
because it states a sufficient basis on which the school board could prevail, and the facts here suggest that a dedication and acceptance has taken place.

Answering this question correctly turns on a strictly mechanical application of knowing *how* a school would take advantage of the provision for the school in the original subdivision plan.

In order for the school board to prevail, the land would have to have been dedicated to the public use. The facts indicate that there is no statute concerning dedication of public schools. Thus, you have to rely on the common law rule. The general rule of dedications has two requirements: The grantor must manifest his intent to "dedicate" the property to public use, and, second, the public (through the government) must manifest its intent to accept the property. Notice that option D uses the language *"since* there has been a dedication...", not "*if* there has been a dedication," so for D to be the best response, the facts would have to indicate a dedication and acceptance. These facts do. In terms of the grantor's intent to dedicate the property, Oscar both recorded the subdivision, including the tract for the "Future Public School." Oscar further manifested his intend through the brochures which emphasized the planned school. As for the public's acceptance, the school board manifested the public's acceptance through its vote to erect a new school on the ten-acre tract. Note that there *would* still have to be notice to Pete in order for the school board to prevail, and D doesn't mention this. However, *the facts are sufficiently clear as to indicating constructive notice that this would not be a major obstacle in the case,* so D's failure to mention it would not deter from its status as the best response.

(A) is not the best response,
because, although determining laches is a factual determination, these facts indicate with sufficient clarity that a court would not find the school board guilty of laches.

Laches is an equitable defense, under which a party is barred from asserting his rights if he's been "sitting on his hands" – in other words, he's waited an unreasonable length of time to assert his rights, to another's detriment. Here, the dispute is between Pete and the school board. Since Pete has only owned the ten-acre tract for one year, the question on the first requirement of laches is whether or not one year would constitute an "unreasonable length of time." As you know, "unrea-

sonability" is purely an issue of fact – however, it's unlikely that a year would constitute an unreasonable period of time. In any case, it would be difficult to say that Pete detrimentally relied on the school board's failure to assert its rights, since Pete had at least constructive notice of the proposed use for the tract, due to its appearance in the subdivision plan. Since A does not recognize this, it's not the best response.

(B) is not the best response,
because it states an insufficient basis for a decision in Pete's favor.

Because all the deeds here were recorded, and the original subdivision plan is within Pete's "chain of title," he would be on constructive notice of the intended use for the tract. Thus, the fact that his own deed does not refer to the plan would be an insufficient basis for a decision in Pete's favor. While the notice itself would not be sufficient for a decision in *the school board's* favor, since it is not enough to support a decision for Pete, B cannot be the best response.

(C) is not the best response,
because, although it is factually correct, it does not offer a sufficient basis on for a decision in the school board's favor.

Pete did have constructive notice of the intended use of for the tract, since it appears in his "chain of title," even though it does not appear on his deed itself. Thus, C is factually correct. However, it does not state a sufficient basis for a decision for the school board, since that would require that the land have been dedicated to public use. The general rule of dedications has two requirements: The grantor must manifest his intent to "dedicate" the property to public use, and, second, the public (through the government) must manifest its intent to accept the property. While Pete's notice would likely preclude a judgment in his favor, it does not provide a solid basis for judgment in the school board's favor, making C not the best response.

Answer 35

(D) is the best response.

As to alternative I:
This is not correct, because the requirement of a writing when one promises to answer for another's debts wouldn't cover the configuration of parties here.

Here, it's Byer who's promising to pay Quincy to satisfy Zeller's debt. For the statute to apply, Byer would have to be promising *Quincy* that he'd pay off Zeller's debt. Here, instead, the promise was made directly to Zeller, and as such it is not covered by the Statute of Frauds, and is enforceable without a writing. Since alternative I states otherwise, it's incorrect.

As to alternative II:
This is incorrect, because while the sale of land would

require a writing, the part applying to payment of Quincy's debt would *not* require a writing.

Alternative II correctly identifies that contracts for the sale of an interest in land must satisfy the Statute of Frauds. However, this part of Byer and Zeller's agreement *was* in writing, so II misstates the facts. Beyond that, the part of the agreement related to paying off Zeller's debt to Quincy didn't *involve* the sale of an interest in land. Instead it merely involved Byer paying off Zeller's debt to Quincy, which wouldn't require a writing. As a result, a defense based on the Statute of Frauds wouldn't hold water. Since alternative II doesn't recognize this, it's not correct.

Answer 36

(A) is the best response,

because it would seriously impair Quincy's ability to prevail.

The most significant thing to remember here is that if Byer owes Quincy as an intended beneficiary under the agreement, there is no need for this provision to be in writing, because it doesn't fall within the Statute of Frauds. Thus, in order for the written contract to be relevant, there must be *some* significance attached to the fact that the provision *wasn't* in the written contract. That's what option A provides.

The concept of "complete integration" is relevant to the Parol Evidence Rule. That rule provides that a writing that is "completely integrated" cannot be contradicted or supplemented with prior written or oral agreements, or contemporaneous oral agreements. A "completely integrated" agreement is one which the parties intended to be a final and complete statement of their agreement.

If Byer was to pay $25,000 to Quincy instead of Zeller, this would vary the written term under which Byer would pay the entire amount to Zeller. Thus, if the agreement is fully integrated, it may prevent Quincy from proving the existence of his claim *at all*. If the written contract *isn't* fully integrated, meaning that it doesn't embody the entire agreement, then Quincy *will* be able to prove his claim, since the Parol Evidence Rule doesn't bar evidence of consistent additional terms where the contract is only partially integrated. Thus, whether or not the agreement is completely integrated will have a significant impact on the case. Since A recognizes this, it's the best response.

(B) is not the best response,

because Byer's negligence in reading the agreement would have no bearing on Quincy's claim against him.

If Byer is to be liable to Quincy, he can be liable even without a writing, since the agreement to pay Quincy falls *outside* the Statute of Frauds. Thus, in order to impact Quincy's claim against Byer, there must be some relevance to the provision's not appearing in the contract (which would be present, for instance, if the contract were considered fully integrated, since the

Quincy provision would not be provable *at all* under the Parol Evidence Rule). Byer's negligence in failing to include the provision would not be relevant to Quincy's claim except that if it were written, Quincy's claim would be easier to prove. Thus, Byer's negligence alone isn't actionable because there's no causation: Byer is liable even without the writing. Since B attaches significance to Byer's negligence where none actually exists, B isn't the best response.

(C) is not the best response,

because *Zeller's* negligence couldn't be asserted by *either* party.

The existence of Byer's duty to pay Quincy depends on whether Quincy's rights as a third party beneficiary under the contract "vested." Since the provision for paying Quincy is not covered by the Statute of Frauds, it's not necessary that the agreement appear in writing. Thus, a negligence claim centering on the failure to put the agreement in writing would not succeed, because there's no *causation*. Quincy *could* recover even without a writing; a writing would only make the claim easier to prove.

Even if negligence were relevant to the claim, neither Byer nor Quincy could assert *Zeller's* negligence. Since C fails to recognize this, it's not the best response.

(D) is not the best response,

because Quincy can recover without being a party to the contract, and, beyond that, Quincy clearly *isn't* a party to the contract under these facts.

A third party *can* recover under a contract if he was an *intended beneficiary* (or, alternatively, if he was an assignee). Thus, if Quincy proves that it was the promisee's (Zeller's) intent that Quincy receive the payment from the promisor (Byer), he'd have enforceable rights under the contract. Since Quincy could recover regardless of whether he's a party or not, D, which conditions Quincy's recovery on whether he's a party to the contract, cannot be the best response.

Answer 37

(B) is the best response,

because it offers an argument that would prevent Quincy from prevailing.

An intended beneficiary to a contract only has enforceable rights under that contract when his rights "vest." Before the rights vest, the beneficiary can't stop the parties from modifying or rescinding the contract. Here, Quincy is an intended beneficiary because Zeller intended that Byer pay part of the contract price to Quincy. Determining when Quincy's rights vest traditionally required classifying him as a creditor or donee beneficiary, since the rights of the two were said to vest at different times. Since the payment was meant to extinguish a debt Zeller owed Quincy, Quincy is a creditor beneficiary (any other beneficiary is a done beneficiary). The majority traditional view is that a creditor beneficiary's rights vest only when he has detrimentally relied on the contract. However, most modern courts agree with the Restatement 2d of Contracts, §311, which ignores the creditor-donee distinction, and rather views the rights of both as vesting when one of these three events occurs:

1. The beneficiary manifests assent to the promise.
2. The beneficiary sues to enforce the promise.
3. The beneficiary justifiably relies on the promise to his detriment.

Thus, if Byer and Zeller eliminated the Quincy payment provision before Quincy even found out about the contract, Quincy couldn't *possibly* have relied on the contract, so he'd have no enforceable rights under it. Since this would stop Quincy from prevailing, it's a good defense, making B the best response.

(A) is not the best response,

because the factor it states is irrelevant, and thus would not form a good defense for Byer.

As a non-party to the Byer-Zeller contract, Quincy can only recover under the contract if he was an intended beneficiary (or an assignee). A third party is an intended beneficiary to a contract if the promisee (here, Zeller) intended that the third party (Quincy) receive benefit from the promisor's performance (here, Byer's payment). Thus, it doesn't matter *why* Zeller wants Byer to pay Quincy — all that matters is that he *wants* Byer to do so.

The only relevance of Zeller's owing Quincy money is that he's a *creditor* beneficiary (as opposed to a *donee* beneficiary), which determines, traditionally, when his rights "vest."

The only consideration that's relevant under the Byer-Zeller contract is whether there was consideration to support the contract itself. As part of the payment for the house, the Byer-Zeller contract would be supported by adequate consideration. Since A focuses on an irrelevancy, it can't supply Byer a good defense, and thus it cannot be the best response.

(C) is not the best response,

because it's not relevant to *Byer's* duty to pay Quincy.

Option C's mention of a claim barred by the Statute of Limitations addresses a consideration issue. Consideration requires bargained-for exchange and either detriment to the promisee or benefit to the promisor, and usually both. Thus, if Byer were to use this as a defense, he'd be claiming that there was no consideration underlying the promise to pay Quincy, and thus it's unenforceable.

This would not be a good defense, for two reasons. First, a promise to pay an unenforceable debt (as here — one barred by the Statute of Limitations) is enforceable *without* consideration — it's an exception to the consideration requirement. Assuming arguendo that the promise *wasn't* enforceable from Zeller to Quincy,

this *still* wouldn't be determinative of *Byer's* duty to pay Zeller.

Quincy can recover under the Byer-Zeller agreement if he was an intended beneficiary (or an assignee). This would only require that Zeller intended Quincy to get benefit from Byer's performance under the contract — that is, paying money. Thus, it wouldn't matter if Zeller owed Quincy money or not — Zeller could be giving Quincy money as a gift and Quincy would *still* have enforceable rights. The only significance of the debt is that it would make Quincy a *creditor* beneficiary instead of a *donee* beneficiary, which is only relevant, traditionally, in determining when Quincy's rights under the contract "vest," making them enforceable. As long as he's an intended beneficiary, he has enforceable rights under the contract. Thus, the State of Limitations argument would not be a good defense for Byer.

(D) is not the best response,

because Quincy's notifying the parties of his acceptance of the agreement wouldn't be relevant to his ability to prevail.

An intended beneficiary to a contract has no rights under the contract until his rights "vest." That is, until vesting occurs, he can't prevent the parties from modifying or rescinding the contract. Thus, once Quincy's rights under the Byer-Zeller contract vested, they wouldn't be able to drop the payment provision to Quincy without his consent.

When a beneficiary's rights vest depends on what type of beneficiary he is: Creditor or donee. Here, since the provision is to pay off Zeller's debt to Quincy, Quincy is a creditor beneficiary (any other type of beneficiary is a donee beneficiary). The majority traditional view is that a creditor beneficiary's rights vest only when he has detrimentally relied on the contract. However, most modern courts agree with the Restatement 2d of Contracts, §311, which ignores the creditor-donee distinction, and rather views the rights of both as vesting when one of these three events occurs:

1. The beneficiary manifests assent to the promise.
2. The beneficiary sues to enforce the promise.
3. The beneficiary justifiably relies on the promise to his detriment.

Thus, Quincy's notifying the parties of his acceptance is not a prerequisite to his rights vesting.

Since Quincy could prevail even if he didn't accept the agreement, this wouldn't be Byer's best defense. As a result, D isn't the best response.

Answer 38

(C) is the best response,

because it represents Zeller's best chance of recovering the additional $1,000.

Under these facts, it's clear that the parties *agreed* to the $46,000, and it was only a typographical error that resulted in the contract reflecting $45,000. When a mistake (or fraud) results in a written contract that doesn't accurately reflect the parties' agreement, the equitable remedy of "reformation" is appropriate – that is, the court will "reform" the contract to make it accurate. Note that what makes this a good argument for Zeller is that it not only negates the price element, but replaces it with the $46,000 figure. All the other options either don't correctly represent the facts, or don't offer an argument for using the $46,000 price instead of $45,000. Since C accomplishes this, it's the best response.

(A) is not the best response,

because it wouldn't help Zeller collect the extra $1,000. First, it doesn't comport with the facts, and second, it would not provide a legal argument for setting the contract price at $46,000 instead of $45,000.

First, in order to be a sham, it must be obvious from the objective manifestations of the parties that at least one of them didn't intend to be bound. That's not true on these facts; the agreement appears bona fide from both parties' manifestations.

Assuming arguendo that it *was* a sham, this would only make the written agreement unenforceable; it wouldn't leave an enforceable contract for $46,000. Even worse, from Zeller's perspective, is that the remaining *oral* agreement for the sale of land would be *unenforceable* due to violation of the Statute of Frauds. Thus, since Zeller won't be able to prove a sham on these facts and even if he could, it wouldn't help him, A isn't the best response.

(B) is not the best response,

because Zeller couldn't recover the extra $1,000 on this basis.

The concept of "integration" addresses whether evidence can be given of other terms under the contract. Under the parol evidence rule, a writing that is "fully integrated" cannot be contradicted or supplemented with prior written or oral agreements, or contemporaneous oral agreements. A "completely integrated" agreement is one which the parties intended to be a final and complete statement of their agreement. A partially integrated agreement, on the other hand, is one that doesn't reflect the *complete* agreement of the parties; where an agreement is partially integrated, it's final as to the terms it states, but it may be *supplemented* by consistent, additional terms.

Thus, even if the contract here was only partially integrated, Zeller still couldn't introduce evidence to contradict a written term; he couldn't prove that the price was $46,000 instead of $45,000, as provided in the contract. As a result, it doesn't help Zeller to prove that the contract was only partially integrated, and B can't be the best response.

(D) is not the best response,

both because it mischaracterizes the facts and, beyond that, it wouldn't give Zeller a basis to recover the addi-

tional $1,000.

In order to be a valid argument, a proposition must be both factually and legally plausible. Here, the facts indicate that Byer and Zeller had no disagreement as to the price; instead, the price was only mistranscribed.

Assuming arguendo that there *was* a misunderstanding as to price, this wouldn't establish what Zeller wants – that the price was $46,000. Instead, it would mean that there was *no* understanding as to price, which could, as a material missing term, perhaps torpedo the entire agreement.

Beyond *that,* Zeller would 'have to overcome the fact that he *signed* a contract for $45,000. As a general rule, a party is bound by the terms of the contracts he signs, regardless of whether he fully understands their terms.

The upshot is that it wouldn't benefit Zeller to argue that there was a misunderstanding as to price, making D not the best response.

Answer 39

(B) is the best response,

because it addresses the central issue under these facts, and resolves it in Driver's favor. The real problem here is pinning Contractor's conduct on House, since it's likely Contractor would be considered an independent contractor, which, as a general rule, would exonerate House from liability for Contractor's conduct.

An independent contractor is distinguished from an employee in that, traditionally, his physical conduct in performing services is not subject to a right of control by the employer; a servant's is. The clue under these facts is that you're told that House engaged Contractor to repair the sidewalk, "leaving it to Contractor to decide how the repair should be made." This simply suggests Contractor is an independent contractor, not an employee.

As a result, in order to prevail, Driver would have to address some basis on which *either* Contractor could be considered an employee, *or* a basis on which House could be liable for Contractor's acts as an independent contractor. There are two general grounds on which employers will be liable for the conduct of independent contractors: First, where ultra-hazardous activities are involved (e.g., demolition); or, second, the duty is non-delegable due to public policy considerations (e.g., duty of railroad to fence in tracks). Under these facts, it would be *possible* to characterize Contractor's acts as hazardous, and if they *were*, House would be liable. Note that B is stated *conditionally* – that is, *if* Contractor was engaged in hazardous activity, House will be liable. Thus, all that's required is that it be plausible on these facts that the conduct could be considered hazardous. Had B used the word "because" instead of "if," the facts would have to show conclusively that the activity *was* hazardous. As it is, B addresses the central issue and offers a plausible ground on which to resolve it in Driver's favor. As a result, it's Driver's best theory of these four options, making B the best response.

(A) is not the best response,

because it's unlikely a claim for strict liability would succeed on these facts. There are two principle problems with strict liability as it applies here: One, it's not clear that the concept of strict liability would apply to a sidewalk maintenance statute; and two, it's not clear that Homeowner would be responsible for Contractor's conduct (since Contractor created the risk).

There are three general sources of strict liability: Animals, abnormally dangerous activities, and defective, unreasonably dangerous products (strict liability can also be imposed under statute or case law). With these, there is said to be an absolute duty of care, such that where there is a breach of that duty which causes plaintiff's damages, plaintiff can recover without proving fault.

Without more, it's not clear that the facts here would merit strict liability, and even if they did, it wouldn't be due to mere ownership of the land, as option A suggests.

Furthermore, option A does not address Contractor's status as either an employee or an independent contractor. This is critical because, in general, an employer is vicariously liable for the torts of his employees, within the scope of employment, but *not* for torts of independent contractors (unless the activity is ultra-hazardous, or non-delegable due to public policy). The two are distinguishable in that, traditionally, an independent contractor's physical conduct in performing services is not subject to a right of control by the employer, and an employee's is. Under these facts, if Contractor is considered an independent contractor and the activity is non-hazardous, House will not be strictly liable even though the tree is on his property.

In fact, the best argument for Driver is to claim that the activity was hazardous and as a result House could be liable even if Contractor is considered an independent contractor. Since A ignores this, it's not the best response.

(C) is not the best response,

because merely paying for a repair would not, in and of itself, make House liable.

Instead, there would have to be some basis on which House himself should be held liable due to his own conduct, or a means by which he would be vicariously liable for Contractor's conduct. Paying for services would not be sufficient to assume liability nor to relieve Contractor of liability. Since C fails to recognize this, it's not the best response.

(D) is not the best response,

because it's unlikely that House would be liable for Contractor's conduct on grounds of respondeat supe-

rior.

Under respondeat superior, an employer is liable for the torts of his employees if the tort occurred within the scope of the employment. The problem here is that Contractor is unlikely to be considered an employee; rather, he'd be considered an independent contractor, in which case the doctrine of respondeat superior would not result in liability for House. An independent contractor is distinguished from an employee in that, traditionally, his physical conduct in performing services is not subject to a right of control by the employer; a servant's is. The tip-off under these facts is that you're told that House engaged Contractor to decide how the repair should be made. This suggests a lack of control associated with independent contractors.

Thus, in order to be correct, D would have to address some basis for House to be liable even though Contractor is likely to be an independent contractor. Since D doesn't do this, it's not the best response.

Answer 40

(C) is the best response,

because it addresses a theory that is consistent with the facts given, and will exonerate Contractor of liability.

Under these facts it's given that Contractor's act of cutting back the roots of the tree caused it to fall. Contractor didn't *intend* it to fall, and didn't apparently *know* it would fall, so Driver's most likely claim would be that Contractor was *negligent*. As a result, a good defense for Contractor would be one that defeats a negligence claim. The beauty of option C is that it avoids liability without having to claim that Contractor wasn't negligent. The rule on liability is that negligent defendants are liable only for the *foreseeable consequences* of their actions (remember Mrs. Palsgraf?). Thus, if Contractor's claim that the tree falling was not reasonably foreseeable is a sound argument on these facts, it will be a good defense. These facts indicate that such an argument *is* possible, because Contractor left five feet of roots on the side of the tree, and all the other roots completely intact. There's nothing to indicate that the tree falling certainly *was* foreseeable, so the lack of foreseeability argument is colorable. Beyond that, no other option given represents a sound defense. As a result, C is the best response.

(A) is not the best response,

because the fact it states would not relieve Contractor of liability. Even though the tree was on House's property, if Contractor's negligence resulted in Driver's damages, Contractor will be liable. As a result, A focuses on an irrelevant fact, and so cannot be the best response.

(B) is not the best response,

because it does not accurately represent the facts,

and, in any case, it would not relieve the Contractor of liability. First, under these facts it's clear that Contractor did not repair the sidewalk at the direction of House, because you're told that House hired Contractor and left it to "Contractor to decide how the repair should be made." Thus, an argument disputing this wouldn't be "rooted" in the facts, and as a result it wouldn't hold much water.

Assuming arguendo that Contractor *had* performed under House's direction, this would only provide a basis for holding House liable for Contractor's negligence on grounds of respondeat superior – it would *not* relieve Contractor of liability. A plaintiff is free to sue either the master or the negligent servant under respondeat superior (although he can, of course, collect only one judgment). In fact, even if Driver collected on a claim against House under respondeat superior, House would be able to seek indemnification (i.e., reimbursement) from Contractor. As a result, option B misstates both the facts and the law, and cannot be the best response.

(D) is not the best response,

because it does not represent a ground on which Contractor can avoid liability.

If Contractor was negligent, House's merely paying for the repairs would not absolve him of liability (and, by the same token, House would not become liable simply by paying Contractor). Instead, there would have to be some basis either for finding House *himself* engaged in tortious behavior, or a way to find him vicariously liable for Contractor's negligence. Vicarious liability would require more than mere payment – it would require that Contractor acted under House's direction, or subject to his control. Since D does not offer a theory on which Contractor can avoid liability, it's not the best response.

Answer 41

(C) is the best response,

because it cites reasoning which *would* allow House to recover from Contractor, and it is a plausible argument on these facts. Since the facts here suggest that House hired Contractor to do the repairs, and the work could be considered hazardous, it's possible House could be liable for Contractor's conduct on the basis of vicarious liability. As a result, House *could* seek indemnity (i.e., reimbursement) from Contractor, because vicarious liability is the most common circumstance to which indemnity is applied. Where one is liable for the torts of another merely because of some relationship between them (e.g., employer/employee, manufacturer/retailer), the one who is held vicariously liable can seek indemnification from the one who committed the tort.

Note that option C uses the modifier "if." That means you need only determine if the reasoning *could plausibly* fit the facts, whether it resolves a central issue, and if the result is consistent with the reasoning. Here,

House could be held liable for Contractor's tortious conduct due to vicarious liability, and if he was, he will be indemnified by Contractor. Since C correctly identifies this, it's the best response.

(A) is not the best response,

because the acceptance of the work doesn't have anything to do with whether House has any recourse against Contractor.

Instead, House's ability to seek recourse from Contractor depends on whether House is entitled to *indemnification* from Contractor. Indemnity shifts the burden of a judgment, where there are primary and secondary tortfeasors. The most common application of indemnity is vicarious liability. Where one is liable for the torts of another merely because of some relationship between them (e.g., employer-employee), the one who is held vicariously liable can seek indemnification from the one who committed the tort. Thus, the mere fact that House paid for the work would not, in and of itself, be a sufficient basis to prevent him from seeking recourse from Contractor. Since A states otherwise, it's not the best response.

(B) is not the best response,

because House's selecting Contractor, in and of itself, would be insufficient to stop House from seeking reimbursement from Contractor.

If House had been *negligent* in selecting Contractor, he wouldn't be able to seek reimbursement from Contractor (since he'd be liable for his *own* negligence under such a claim). Otherwise, House's ability to seek recourse against Contractor depends on whether he is entitled to *indemnity* for paying for Contractor's negligence. Merely selecting Contractor to do the work would not be sufficient to deny House this right. Since B states otherwise, it's not the best response.

(D) is not the best response,

because it doesn't address the central issue here: Whether House is entitled to indemnity from Contractor.

While House's lack of negligence is central to House's being reimbursed by Contractor, it does not address the issue of Contractor's liability. For instance, if Contractor weren't negligent, he wouldn't be liable either. Instead, if House is to be able to collect from Contractor, it must be because House was held liable for Contractor's conduct. Since D doesn't recognize the Contractor's part of the equation, it's not the best response.

Answer 42

(D) is the best response,

because it identifies the central reason Roads, Inc. will prevail: the repeal violates the Contracts Clause of the federal Constitution.

The Contracts Clause, Article I, §10, prohibits states

from passing any law which impairs the obligations of existing contracts. That's what the repeal here does. The state previously entered a contract with Roads, Inc. to construct a new highway. The repeal of the turnpike authorization impairs that contract. While some modification is possible, three requirements must be met:

1. The modification must serve an important and legitimate public interest.
2. It must be necessary to achieve that public interest.
3. The contract impairment must be reasonable under the circumstances (furthermore, although this doesn't apply here, a state needn't adhere to a contract where it surrenders, from the start, an essential attribute of its sovereignty (e.g., the police power).

None of these requirements are met here, and as a result, the repeal would be invalid, making the state bound by the contract. Note that the fact that the state itself is a party to the contract doesn't change this. Since D recognizes this, it's the best response.

(A) is not the best response,

because although it states a theoretically correct rule, it doesn't recognize that under *these* facts Roads, Inc. will prevail due to violation of the Contracts Clause.

A state *can* prevent itself from being liable, but once it enters into a contract, it is, as a general rule, bound by that contract. Thereafter, under the Contracts Clause, Article I, §10, it cannot pass a law which impairs the obligation of an existing contract. This said, there *are* circumstances under which *modification* is permissible. However, these requirements must be met:

1. The modification must serve an important and legitimate public interest.
2. The modification must be necessary to serve that interest.
3. The contract impairment must be *reasonable* under the circumstances (furthermore, although this doesn't apply here, a state needn't adhere to a contract where it surrenders, from the start, an essential attribute of its sovereignty (e.g., the police power).

Here, there was no important public interest served by the new law: it only moves funds from turnpike development to parks. Thus, the state wouldn't be able to repeal the statute authorizing turnpike development. Since A doesn't recognize this, it's not the best response.

(B) is not the best response,

because while it states a theoretically correct rule, it does not apply to these facts, due to operation of the Contracts Clause of the federal Constitution.

A legislature can, in general, repeal laws it's enacted. However, where doing so will violate the Contracts Clause, Article I, §10, such repeal isn't possible. The

Contracts Clause prohibits states from passing any law which impairs the obligations of existing contracts. That's what the repeal here does. The state previously entered a contract with Roads, Inc. to construct a new highway. The repeal of the turnpike authorization impairs that contract. While some modification is possible, three requirements must be met:

1. The modification must serve an important and legitimate public interest.
2. It must be necessary to achieve that public interest.
3. The contract impairment must be reasonable under the circumstances (furthermore, although this doesn't apply here, a state needn't adhere to a contract where it surrenders, from the start, an essential attribute of its sovereignty (e.g., the police power).

Thus, even though a legislature typically *can* repeal laws it's enacted, the existence of a Contracts Clause violation makes repeal invalid under these facts. Since B doesn't recognize this, it's not the best response.

(C) is not the best response,

because there's no need to resort to equitable estoppel principles; the state cannot repeal the turnpike statute due to a violation of the Contracts Clause, Article I, §10, of the federal Constitution.

What option C does is to suggest that the state will be liable on promissory estoppel grounds. Even if there weren't a Contracts Clause violation, this wouldn't apply, because estoppel only applies when there isn't an enforceable contract. Here, you're told that the state entered into a contract with Roads; there's no indication that the contract isn't enforceable.

What makes the repeal of the turnpike statute invalid is its violation of the Contracts Clause. The Contracts Clause prohibits states from passing any law which impairs the obligations of existing contracts. That's what the repeal here does. The state previously entered a contract with Roads, Inc. to construct a new highway. The repeal of the turnpike authorization impairs that contract. While some modification is possible, three requirements must be met:

1. The modification must serve an important and legitimate public interest.
2. It must be necessary to achieve that public interest.
3. The contract impairment must be reasonable under the circumstances (furthermore, although this doesn't apply here, a state needn't adhere to a contract where it surrenders, from the start, an essential attribute of its sovereignty (e.g., the police power).

Thus, the repeal is invalid, and *that's* why Roads, Inc. will prevail – not on grounds of estoppel. Since C doesn't recognize this, it's not the best response.

Answer 43

(C) is the best response,

because it offers a federal power to which a need-based student aid program is rationally related.

The welfare power addresses the federal government's power to collect taxes and spend money for all matters of national concern. In implementing this power, Congress *can* impose any reasonable conditions on the states as a prerequisite to participating in federal spending programs. Here, student aid will have a general beneficial effect on the welfare of the country. Requiring that the aid be distributed on the basis of need is a reasonable condition to place on such a program. As such, the welfare power provides a strong constitutional basis for the statute.

Incidentally, the reason that this problem requires some thought is that education is traditionally a *state* function. Congress can only pass laws rationally related to its enumerated powers (e.g., defense, interstate commerce, etc.). As this question indicates, Congress can use its spending power to indirectly achieve objectives it couldn't achieve directly pursuant to its regulatory powers (as long as it doesn't violate any independent constitutional limitations, like due process). By relying on the Welfare Clause, option C overcomes the problem that education is a state function, making it the best response.

(A) is not the best response,

because there is no federal police power, and the question here addresses a federal statute.

Under the police power, a state enactment is a valid means of achieving a legitimate state interest where the public health, safety, welfare, and morals is involved. There is no federal equivalent of the police power, although Congress can achieve many of the same ends through valid use of its powers; for instance, Congress can use its commerce power to regulate the use of interstate channels, thus prohibiting interstate transport of stolen property, misbranded goods, lottery tickets, and the like. Since option A doesn't recognize this, it's not the best response.

(B) is not the best response,

because the war and defense power would not provide a basis for a statute of this sort.

Congress gets its war and defense power from Article I, §8 of the Constitution, under which it can declare war, raise and support armed forces, and in general administer those forces. The types of regulations Congress could pass under the war power include conducting a draft, instituting economic controls in war time, excluding people from sensitive areas, and confiscating the property of enemies. In order to be upheld under an enumerated power, a statute must be rationally related to the power, or a necessary and proper means of effectuating that power. A need-based student aid program has no obvious connection with the

war power, and as such the war power wouldn't provide a strong constitutional basis for the legislation. Since B states otherwise, it's not the best response.

(D) is not the best response,

because the Privileges and Immunities Clause of the Fourteenth Amendment is not a source of constitutional power for the federal government.

The Privileges and Immunities Clause of the Fourteenth Amendment voids those state enactments which clearly infringe privileges enjoyed by U.S. citizens. It is construed narrowly, typically being restricted to fundamental rights which are shared in common by all citizens, namely:

1. The right to travel freely from state to state;
2. To petition Congress for redress of grievances;
3. to vote for national officers;
4. To assemble peaceably; and
5. To discuss matters of national legislation.

Thus, the Clause would provide a means by which to support the constitutionality of a need-based student aid program. (In fact, the Fourteenth Amendment Privileges and Immunities Clause has virtually no practical effect, since wherever it would apply, Due Process or Equal Protection would be a stronger argument against constitutionality of an action). Since D doesn't recognize this, it's not the best response.

Answer 44

(B) is the best response,

because it correctly identifies the reports as being subject to the attorney-client privilege, and as a result not subject to production in general.

A communication is subject to attorney-client privilege if it is a communication from the client to the attorney, made in confidence, concerning legal representation. A corporation is subject to the same privilege as an individual, and the general manager would be within the scope of the privilege under the modern "performance of duties" test, under which the privilege extends to any employee's communication if it was within his duties, and it was offered to advance the legal interests of the corporation. Since the communication here is within the attorney-client privilege, as B states, B is the best response.

(A) is not the best response,

because it does not correctly characterize the facts.

Option A addresses privilege. A communication of *any* kind, business report or not, is subject to attorney-client privilege if it is a communication from the client to the attorney, made in confidence, concerning legal representation. Here, the report fits this description – the general manager made the report about the accident, intended that it be read only by the attorney, and it was made in preparation for trial.

Incidentally, note that "business reports" in general

could be inadmissible as hearsay. A business record is admissible under the "business records" hearsay exception, FRE 803(6), only where it is made in the regular course of business, in conjunction with a business activity, it is entered under a duty to record, and it is entered by one with personal knowledge of the matters recorded (or it was transmitted from a person with such personal knowledge). Furthermore, it must be entered at or near the time of the transaction, and it must be authenticated at trial (normally, the custodian of the record will testify as to how the record was prepared, and attest to its identity).

Here, the communication is not just any business report, but a communication from a client to his attorney. Since A does not recognize this, it is not the best response.

(C) is not the best response,

because it ignores the central reason the report will be inadmissible: it is covered by the attorney-client privilege.

Option C suggests that business reports, in general, are inadmissible because they contain hearsay. This is not always a correct statement because business reports *can* be admissible under the "business records" exception to the hearsay rule, FRE 803(6). Under that exception, a business record is admissible if it meets these six requirements: it must be made in the regular course of business, in conjunction with a business activity; it must be entered under a duty to record; it must be entered by one with personal knowledge of matters recorded or transmitted from such a person; entered at or near the time of the transaction; and the entry must be authenticated at trial (normally, custodian of the record will testify as to how the record was prepared, and attest to its identity).

Thus, business records *can* be admissible, and option C overstates the rule by stating such reports are always inadmissible due to their hearsay content. It just so happens that the report here would not be admissible under this hearsay exception, because Def Company is not in the business of defending lawsuits; it's in some business that involves transporting goods by trucks. Thus, the report here would not be one made in the regular course of business. However, since option C states a rule that is too broad, it can't be the best response.

(D) is not the best response,

because the self-serving nature of *any* evidence does not address its admissibility.

Any piece of evidence has several obstacles it must overcome in order to be admissible. It must be logically and legally relevant, and it cannot be inadmissible hearsay, for instance. The self-serving nature of the reports will affect the weight the jury gives the reports, but it will not affect their admissibility. Since D wrongly characterizes the self-serving nature of the reports as

determining their admissibility, it is not the best response.

Answer 45

(C) is the best response,

because it correctly identifies the basis on which the Water District will prevail.

The Water District has a valid easement as to Barrenacres. While there are several bases on which an easement can be terminated, the only ones that apply to an easement in gross under these circumstances are:

1. a release, in writing
2. abandonment
3. adverse use by servient tenement holder, for statutory period
4. estoppel

The facts here indicate that none of these have been satisfied, so the easement is still in force. The general rule is that the dominant tenement holder has both the right and the duty to maintain the easement. That's what the Water District is doing.

Since the Water District's proposed acts will do no more than maintain the easement, the adverse impact on Peterson's property will not change the result. Since C correctly identifies the basis on which the Water District will prevail, it's the best response.

(A) is not the best response,

because it does not state a basis on which Peterson can prevail.

While the deed itself does not mention the easement, Peterson is on constructive notice of the easement, since it appears in his "chain of title." The facts here state that the easement was properly and timely recorded, and, as such, in most states Peterson would take subject to the easement, since an easement is considered an interest in property. Since constructive notice is sufficient to give Peterson notice of the easement, the fact that the easement did not appear on his deed *itself* is not enough for him to succeed. Note that this is yet another example of how popular a topic "constructive notice" is on the MBE. Since A does not take into account the fact that Peterson would have constructive notice of the easement, it's not the best response.

(B) is not the best response,

because it does not suggest a proper basis on which Peterson could prevail.

The Water District has a valid easement as to Barrenacres. While there are several bases on which an easement can be terminated, the only ones that apply to an easement in gross under these circumstances are:

1. a release, in writing
2. abandonment

3. adverse use by servient tenement holder, for statutory period

4. estoppel

The facts here indicate that none of these have been satisfied, so the easement is still in force. The general rule is that the dominant tenement holder has both the right and the duty to maintain the easement. That's what the Water District is doing.

In fact, it couldn't accurately be said that the Water District hadn't entered Barrenacres for forty years, because its entry has been continuous – the water pipes have been there the whole time. Nonetheless, if you chose this response you might have done so due to a notion that the equitable doctrine of laches should apply to these facts, since "forty years" indicates a length of time that that doctrine would cover. However, the doctrine of laches only applies where one has not enforced his rights for an unreasonable period of time, and another party has relied on this failure. As noted earlier, the doctrine of laches would not apply to easements, since it does not constitute a basis on which an easement could be terminated. The "abandonment" required for an easement requires more than mere non-use – there must be acts indicating a clear intent to abandon. Here, that could entail, for instance, digging up and removing the pipes, filling in the space, and not replacing them. However, the facts here indicate that the Water District still has full rights to the easement, so B is not the best response.

(D) is not the best response,

because it's irrelevant.

Assuming D were true, it wouldn't make a difference to the outcome here, since, even if the plan were fair and equitable, if it wasn't within the Water District's rights, it would be impermissible. In fact, the dominant estate holder (here, the Water District) has both the right and the duty to maintain the easement, and *this* is the basis of its right to excavate the pipe. As long as the Water District is within its rights in doing so, any damage done to the property would not be actionable. Since D would mistakenly pin the Water District's right to excavate on whether the plan is fair and equitable, it's not the best response.

Answer 46

(D) is the best response,

because it correctly identifies the basis on which the Water District will *not* be liable: it's acting within its rights as the holder of an easement.

Two rules control here: One, a subsequent property holder takes subject to outstanding interests as to which he has notice. Two, an easement holder has the right and duty to maintain the easement.

Here, Peterson has constructive notice of the easement, since the facts state that the easement was promptly and properly recorded, and as a result the easement appears in Peterson's "chain of title." Sec-

ond, the Water District's right to maintain the easement is expressly provided for in the easement, and even if it weren't, it would be implied. This would give the District the right to enter, excavate, and replace the pipes. Since there is nothing here to indicate that the District has exceeded the scope of the easement – which *would* be actionable – Peterson will not be entitled to damages, because the Water District is acting within its rights and thus cannot be liable. Since D correctly identifies the principal reason the Water District will not be liable, it's the best response.

(A) is not the best response,

because it states a factor which is irrelevant.

Option A implicitly refers to the notice requirement, since a subsequent property holder only takes subject to outstanding interests as to which he has notice. What option A fails to recognize is that the notice requirement is satisfied here. Even though Peterson's deed did not mention the easement, it appears in a recorded instrument in his "chain of title." As such, Peterson has "constructive notice" of the easement. The facts here specifically state that the Water District properly and promptly recorded the easement. As a result, Peterson bought the property subject to the easement, and cannot recover damages on the basis of lack of notice. Thus, A is not the best response.

(B) is not the best response,

because it misstates the rule of law.

An easement holder has the right and duty to maintain the easement. In these facts, the right to maintain the easement is expressly provided. Furthermore, these facts do not indicate that Water District's actions were outside the scope of the easement – it did no more than was necessary to maintain the pipes. Since the Water District acted within its rights, it should not be liable for damages, making B not the best response.

(C) is not the best response,

because the factor it contains – the public interest in a continuing water supply – would not control the resolution of this case.

Given that C is true, and that the public does have such an interest, the Water District would *still* not be entitled to *unreasonably and unjustifiably* interfere with Peterson's interest in Barrenacre. The Water District's right to enter Peterson's property is a purely private matter between Peterson and the District, and is controlled by Owens's granting the District an easement. Thus, the public interest is not relevant to the case. If you chose this response, you may have been thinking of the requirements of eminent domain, in which a governmental taking of private property must be in the public interest. Thus, if Peterson had been forced to surrender an easement in Barrenacre, the public interest would be relevant. However, there's no eminent domain issue under these facts, but only a simple, private easement. As a result, C is not the best response.

Answer 47

(B) is the best response,

because it correctly indicates that both an injunction and damages are appropriate remedies in this action.

The grant here created a life estate determinable *pur autre vie* in the Church, and a vested remainder in the grandchildren as a class. As life tenant, the Church is obliged not to unreasonably impair the value of the property. Since the Church allowed the sand and gravel to be removed, it will have to cease doing so and it will be liable for the damage already done. The added wrinkle here is that the vested remaindermen may not all exist yet, since there may yet be other grandchildren born to the "class". Thus, the appropriate remedy is to impound the damages until no more members can be added to the class of grandchildren – that is, all of Omar's children die, because only then can the class of grandchildren be established. Since B states the appropriate result, it's the best response.

(A) is not the best response,

because while it correctly recognizes that the plaintiffs should succeed, it does not give the correct reason.

The estates created in the conveyance here were a life estate determinable *pur autre vie* in the Church, and a vested remainder in the grandchildren in the form of a class gift (the class being Omar's grandchildren). As a life estate holder, the Church is obliged not to unreasonably impair the value of the property. If the life estate holder does so, his estate does not cease – however, he will be liable to the vested remainderman for the diminution in value. Since A incorrectly states that committing waste terminates the life estate, it's not the best response.

(C) is not the best response,

because it incorrectly states that damages should not be awarded because Omar and Carl are not parties to the action.

In fact, the relevant parties here are the Church and the vested remaindermen – the grandchildren and a representative for the as-yet unborn grandchildren, as a class. The church, because it is allowing waste to be committed on the premises, is liable to the vested remaindermen. It is liable for the damages done so far, and can be enjoined from continuing to remove the sand and gravel. Option C incorrectly states that damages will not be available because Omar and Carl are not parties to the action. They aren't necessary, and so C is not the best response.

(D) is not the best response,

because it incorrectly states that the injunction should be denied.

A life estate holder, as the Church is here, is obliged not to unreasonably impair the value of the property. Allowing sand and gravel to be removed would constitute waste. As a result, the Church will be liable to the vested remaindermen for the diminution in value, and will be required to stop the waste from occurring. Thus, the vested remaindermen should recover damages *and* the injunction should be granted. Since D is only half right, it is not the best response.

Answer 48

(D) is the best response,

because the element of force or fear was missing, and thus Hayes would not be liable for robbery.

The key here is simply to know the elements of robbery. Robbery is a larceny from either a person or in the presence of a person, by either force or fear. Here, Hayes's victim was not cognizant of the fact his wallet was being taken, so he wasn't in fear, and since Hayes merely removed his wallet, there wasn't force, either. The subsequent slap wouldn't be considered force for purposes of determining Hayes's guilt, because the force did not relate to the crime. While the use of force encompasses the period immediately after the taking, this only controls if the wrongdoer uses force to stop the victim from catching him or regaining the property. Under facts like the ones in option D, the force would be considered separate from the taking. Since Hayes would not satisfy the elements of robbery, he won't be guilty, making D the best response.

(A) is not the best response,

because Johnson likely would be guilty of robbery.

Robbery is a larceny from either a person or in the presence of a person, by either force or fear. The element that's most in question under the facts in option A is the larceny from the person or in the presence of a person. However, the crime would be considered in the woman's presence, since it involved the area she would control if not for the force or fear used by Johnson. Since Johnson would likely be guilty of robbery, A is not the best response.

(B) is not the best response,

because Brown would likely be guilty of robbery under these facts.

Robbery is a larceny from either a person or in the presence of a person, by either force or fear. Here, although Brown did not employ force, his confederate did, and so together they would be liable for robbery, since their conduct would fit all the elements of robbery. Since Brown would be guilty of robbery, B is not the best response.

(C) is not the best response,

because Ritter likely would be guilty of robbery.

Robbery is a larceny from either a person or in the presence of a person, by either force or fear. Here, the force was involved in compelling the woman to make the phone call. When Ritter later took the jewels, he satisfied the remaining element of robbery. Since Ritter would likely be guilty of robbery, C is not the best

response.

Answer 49

(D) is the best response,

because it recognizes that the Attorney General is not subject to direction from Congress as to whom to prosecute.

Law enforcement is an exclusively executive power. The President is the only source of executive power, under Article II, §1 of the Constitution. He can, of course, delegate those executive functions to others in the executive branch. The Attorney General is the chief law enforcement official. He can prosecute criminal activity as he sees fit, and in his discretion, he can choose not to do so, as a general rule. Since option D recognizes this, it's the best response.

(A) is not the best response,

because the Attorney General is not subject to any orders from the legislative branch.

The President is the only source of executive power, under Article II, §1 of the Constitution. Many of his duties are delegated to others within the executive branch, including the Attorney General, the chief law enforcement official. The law enforcement function is an *exclusively* executive branch power. Thus, Congress enjoys *no* law enforcement powers, and could not direct the Attorney General to prosecute anyone. Since A doesn't recognize this, it's not the best response.

(B) is not the best response,

because it misstates the law.

Law enforcement is an exclusively executive power. The President is the only source of executive power, under Article II, §1 of the Constitution. He can, of course, delegate those executive functions to others in the executive branch. The Attorney General is the chief law enforcement official. He can prosecute criminal activity as he sees fit, and in his discretion, he can choose not to do so, as a general rule. Since B states that the Attorney General *must* prosecute all federal law violators when, in fact, prosecution is generally discretionary, B is not the best response.

(C) is not the best response,

because Green's immunity from prosecution for acts committed in office would be *irrelevant* as to whether the Attorney General must prosecute her for contempt.

When someone does not comply with a Congressional investigation, contempt is the appropriate punishment. Here, Green's contempt charge is due to her failure to answer questions posed during a Congressional investigation, *not* due to any wrongdoing in the course of her duties.

Instead, the reason the Attorney General needn't prosecute is that law enforcement is exclusively an *executive* function, and thus the House of Representa-

tives, as part of the *legislative* branch, can't order the Attorney General to prosecute. Since C doesn't recognize this, it's not the best response.

Answer 50

(A) is the best response,

because it correctly identifies a basis on which Green may avoid answering the questions: they are outside Congress's power to investigate.

The Congressional power to investigate is an incident to its power to legislate, implied under the Necessary and Proper Clause. Thus, if the investigation here involved any matter on which Congress has the power to act, it could hold hearings, compel witnesses to attend, and order those witnesses to answer questions.

However, if the matters on which Green was to be questioned fell outside the scope of potential legislation, Green would not have to answer them. Since option A sets forth a solid argument for a potential defense, it's the best response.

(B) is not the best response,

because it understates the scope of permissible Congressional investigations.

The Congressional power to investigate is implied under the Necessary and Proper Clause as an incident of the power to legislate. McGrain v. Dougherty (1927). Thus, Congress can investigate all matters on which it *could* choose to act; it's not limited to matters of expenditures. It's possible the investigation under which Green was called as a witness could be permissible without addressing a Congressional expenditure. Since B understates the scope of potential Congressional investigations, it would not be a good defense for Green, making B not the best response.

(C) is not the best response,

because it misstates the grounds on which a Congressional investigation may be made.

The power of *both* houses of Congress to investigate is implied under the Necessary and Proper Clause as an incident of the power to legislate. Thus, either house could investigate any matter on which it might potentially act. This could mean either house could question Green on the performance of her duties if the investigation were within the permissible scope.

If you chose this response, you were probably thinking of the limitation on the appointment power of the President, under which some appointments can only be made with the advice and consent of the Senate. Under Article II, §2 of the Constitution, an Ambassador is just such an appointment. However, what's involved here is not an appointment, so this requirement would not apply. Since option C misstates the rule on investigations, it's not the best response.

(D) is not the best response,

because it misstates the law.

The Congressional power to investigate is an incident to its power to legislate, implied under the Necessary and Proper Clause. Thus, if the investigation here involved any matter on which Congress has the power to act, it could hold hearings, compel witnesses to attend, and order those witnesses to answer questions. Those witnesses *could* be officers of the executive branch (of which an Ambassador *is* one). Of course, matters of executive privilege need not be disclosed, but other questions can be asked and must be answered, under threat of contempt. Since option D doesn't recognize this, it's not the best response.

Answer 51

(C) is the best response,

because it's the only response that offers a source of power for the federal government.

In order to be valid, a Congressional enactment must be rationally related to one of Congress's enumerated powers, or it must be necessary and proper to effectuate such a power. Congress's power to regulate interstate commerce is found in Article I, §8, clause 3 of the Constitution. The power is exceptionally broad. Under the "affectation doctrine," Congress can regulate any activity that has any appreciable direct or indirect effect on interstate commerce. Consumer credit affects interstate commerce, so Congress will be able to enact a law governing it. Since C offers a plausible source of support for the legislation, and no other response does, it's the best response.

(A) is not the best response,

because the Contracts Clause limits *state* power; it's not a source of power for the federal government.

As a general rule, the Contracts Clause, Article I, §10 of the Constitution, prohibits states from passing laws which impair the obligations of existing contracts. Here, the law was enacted by the *federal* government, not a state; furthermore, the Contracts Clause is a *limitation* on power, not a *source* of it, and this question is looking for a source of power to justify the law. Since A doesn't recognize this, it's not the best response.

(B) is not the best response,

because the Privileges and Immunities Clause of the Fourteenth Amendment *limits* the power of the *states,* it's not a source of power for the federal government.

The Privileges and Immunities Clause of the Fourteenth Amendment voids those state enactments which clearly infringe privileges enjoyed by U.S. citizens. It is construed narrowly, typically being restricted to fundamental rights which are shared in common by all citizens, namely:

1. the right to travel freely from state to state
2. to petition Congress for redress of grievances
3. to vote for national officers
4. to assemble peaceably

5. to discuss matters of national legislation

(In fact, the Privileges and Immunities Clause of the Fourteenth Amendment has virtually no practical applications, since wherever it would apply, Due Process or Equal Protection would be a stronger argument against constitutionality.)

Even if the Privileges and Immunities Clause of the Fourteenth Amendment had any "teeth," it wouldn't apply here. Consumer credit is not a fundamental right, the law here isn't a state law but a federal one, and this clause is a limit on power, where the question here asks for the source of the power to enact the UCCC. Since B doesn't recognize this, it's not the best response.

(D) is not the best response,

because the Equal Protection Clause is triggered by a classification that determines people's rights. It *prohibits* enactments; it doesn't provide a source of power for the federal government.

Here, the law addresses fair credit practices; it doesn't create a classification. Furthermore, the question asks for the source of the federal power to enact the UCCC, not a limitation on power – which the Equal Protection Clause is. Finally, the Equal Protection Clause only addresses *state* action; it's not applicable to the federal government. Since D doesn't offer a source of power to support the law, it's not the best response.

Answer 52

(A) is the best response,

because it correctly states the burden, and places it on the correct party.

First of all, determine the kind of problem you have. There's no classification here, but rather there's a law that limits a right. Thus, the issue is one of due process, not equal protection.

Here, the law limits the exercise of religious beliefs by limiting the lending activities of a religious organization. Religion is a fundamental right; thus, a law that limits it must meet the "compelling interest" test. That is, the law must be necessary to promote a compelling governmental interest (if a right isn't fundamental, a law limiting it need only meet the "mere rationality" test – in other words, the law need only rationally relate to any possible legitimate end of government).

Once an organization or person shows that the law adversely impacts its free exercise of religion, the burden would shift to the state to prove that the statute is valid. Option A correctly recognizes this.

Incidentally, the very application of the strict scrutiny test is the kiss of death for a statute, because it's an extremely difficult standard to meet. Since A applies the right burden to the right party, it's the best response.

(B) is not the best response,

because although it correctly identifies that the federal government will have the burden of proof, it *understates* that burden.

First of all, determine the kind of problem you have. There's no classification here, but rather there's a law that limits a right. Thus, the issue is one of due process, not equal protection.

Here, the law limits the exercise of religious beliefs by limiting the lending activities of a religious organization. Religion is a fundamental right; thus, a law that limits it must meet the "compelling interest" test. That is, the law must be necessary to promote a compelling governmental interest. The test option B states is applicable to any other right: The "rational relation" test, under which a law need only rationally relate to any possible legitimate end of government.

Thus, even though B correctly identifies that the burden to prove the statute is valid falls on the government, it understates this burden, and thus it's not the best response.

(C) is not the best response,

both because it understates the burden of proof and places it on the wrong party.

First of all, determine the kind of problem you have. There's no classification here, but rather there's a law that limits a right. The law limits the exercise of religious beliefs by limiting the lending activities of a religious organization. Religion is a fundamental right; thus, a law that limits it must meet the "compelling interest" test. That is, the law must be necessary to promote a compelling governmental interest. The test option C states is applicable to any other right: The "rational relation" test, under which a law need only rationally relate to any possible legitimate end of government.

Furthermore, once a law is shown to adversely impact the free exercise of religion, it's up to the state to prove that the statute is valid; C states otherwise. Since C puts the burden on the wrong party, and understates the burden, it's not the best response.

(D) is not the best response,

because the burden is on the government to prove that the statute is valid; the organization needn't prove the government intended to inhibit the free exercise of religion in order to prevail.

First of all, determine the kind of problem you have. There's no classification here, but rather there's a law that limits a right. Here, the law limits the exercise of religious beliefs by limiting the lending activities of a religious organization. Religion is a fundamental right; thus, a law that limits it must meet the "compelling interest" test. That is, the law must be necessary to promote a compelling governmental interest (if a right isn't fundamental, a law limiting it need only meet the "mere rationality" test – in other words, the law need

only rationally relate to any possible legitimate end of government).

Furthermore, once a law is shown to adversely impact the free exercise of religion, it's up to the state to prove that the statute is valid; D states otherwise. Since D puts the burden on the wrong party, and understates the burden, it's not the best response.

Answer 53

(D) is the best response,

because it correctly identifies the element which will most likely exonerate Harry.

The common law crime of burglary requires the breaking and entering of the dwelling house of another, at night, with intent to commit a felony therein. The missing element here is intent – Harry and Bill both intended that Bill take Harry's silverware, not someone else's. Since taking Harry's silverware with Harry's consent would negate the intent to steal, there would be no criminal liability. As a result, D provides Harry's best argument, and is the best response.

(A) is not the best response,

because it misstates the facts: there *was* a breaking under these facts.

Breaking is a requirement of burglary, which can be satisfied by either actual or constructive breaking. Actual breaking is the use of force to enter; constructive breaking is the use of fraud, threat, or intimidation. Opening a window, as Bill did here, would be sufficient to constitute a "breaking." Furthermore, as a co-conspirator, Harry would be liable for Bill's actions. Since there was a breaking, Harry could not successfully argue that there wasn't one, making A not the best response.

(B) is not the best response,

because it misstates the facts. Harry consented to the entry of his own house, not the house Bill actually broke into. Harry did not have the power to consent to the entry of another's property. As a result, his ostensible "consent" would not exonerate him. B *intimates* the best response, D, since Harry's consent to take *his own* silverware *would* exonerate them both. However, since B does not correctly characterize the facts, it's not the best response.

(C) is not the best response,

because even though it is true, it wouldn't exonerate Harry.

If there was a burglary under these facts, Harry would be liable as an accessory before the fact, since that requires only that one procure, counsel or command the commission of a felony, even though he is not present, actually or constructively, at the commission of the criminal act. (Note that the modern trend is to lump together accessories before the fact, and principals in the second degree, as "accomplices." A principal in the second degree is distinguished from an accessory before the fact in that a principal in the second degree is present, actually or constructively, when the criminal act is committed.) Because C focuses on an element that isn't relevant to Harry's culpability, it's not the best response.

Answer 54

(C) is the best response,
because it would exonerate Bill.

Common law burglary requires the breaking and entering of the dwelling house of another at night, with the intent to commit a felony therein. If Bill reasonably believed he was in Harry's house, he would have entered without the intent to commit a felony, since he would believe that he was going to take the silverware with the consent of the owner, and thus wouldn't be stealing it. Thus, the existence of the fact in option C would negate the intent element of burglary, and, as a result, exonerate Bill. Since C states the best basis, of these four, for Bill being acquitted, it's the best response.

(A) is not the best response,
both because it mischaracterizes the facts, and misstates the law.

Bill's mistake here was not a mistake of law, but a mistake of fact. Beyond that, a mistake of law is not a valid defense.

Bill's mistake is a mistake of fact because, if the facts had been as he actually and reasonably believed them to be (i.e., it was Harry's house, not someone else's), he would not be liable. A mistake of fact *is* a valid defense to a criminal charge, which is the essence of the correct response – C. A mistake of law, on the other hand, occurs when one mistakenly believes his acts are not proscribed, or he's simply unaware of the law proscribing his behavior. This is *not* a valid defense to a criminal charge. Since A both misstates the facts and the law, it cannot be the best response.

(B) is not the best response,
because it misstates the facts.

Bill did *not* have the consent of the owner of the house he broke into. Harry's consent is not relevant to the issue of consent, because Harry did not have the authority to consent to entering the other house. If these facts were different, and it was Harry's house Bill broke into, then of course Harry's consent would exonerate Bill. However, since these are *not* the facts, B is not the best response.

(D) is not the best response,
because the existence of the fact D offers would not exonerate Bill.

Common law burglary requires the breaking and entering of the dwelling house of another at night, with the intent to commit a felony therein. The element upon which option D would have an impact is the "breaking" element, since it implies that there is no "breaking" if the window had been unlocked. However, this is a misstatement of the law. "Breaking" is satisfied by something as minor as turning a doorknob or lifting a latch, or, in these facts, opening the window. (On a related note, had the window been open a few inches and Bill had only had to open it the rest of the way, in most states there would be *no* breaking.) Since opening the window would satisfy the "breaking" requirement, the fact that the window was unlocked would not exonerate Bill. Since D states otherwise, it's not the best response.

Answer 55

(B) is the best response,
because it states an element that would, in fact, exonerate Bill and Harry, and it is supported by the facts here.

At common law, a conspiracy requires an agreement between at least two people, an intent to enter into such an agreement, and the intent to achieve the unlawful objective of the agreement. According to most modern courts, there must also be an act in furtherance of the conspiracy, by any conspirator. Here, if Bill and Harry did not intend to commit burglary, than the "conspiracy" did not have an illegal objective, and they would be acquitted. Thus, option B cites an element that will result in their acquittal, which is supported by the facts. As a result, it's the best response.

(A) is not the best response,
because if anything it *strengthens* the case against Bill and Harry, not weakens it.

A conspiracy requires an agreement between at least two people, an intent to enter into such agreement, and the intent to achieve the objective of the agreement. The agreement must have an unlawful objective, and, according to most modern courts, there must be an act in furtherance of the conspiracy, by any conspirator. By arguing that Bill was Harry's alter ego, Bill and Harry would strengthen the concept of an agreement, which is exactly what they don't want to do. Since A would weaken their case, it is not the best response.

(C) is not the best response,
because it misstates the facts: there *was* an overt act under these facts, since Bill performed an act in furtherance of the conspiracy.

At common law, a conspiracy requires an agreement between at least two people, an intent to enter into such an agreement, and the intent to achieve the objective of the agreement. According to most modern courts, the agreement must have an unlawful objective, and there must be an act in furtherance of the conspiracy, by any conspirator. The problem with this argument here is that there clearly was an overt act in furtherance of the conspiracy, assuming there was a conspiracy: Bill broke into the house. (Note that the only purpose of the "overt act" is to prove the existence of the conspiracy, so it need not, in fact, be illegal itself. Thus, a phone call, lock picking, attending a meeting, and the like, would suffice.)

What this ignores is that Harry and Bill didn't have an unlawful objective: they both thought Bill was going to retrieve Harry's silverware from Harry's house. Thus, the intent element is missing, not the overt act requirement. Since C doesn't recognize this, it's not the best response.

(D) is not the best response,

because although it states an argument that would, in theory, exonerate Bill and Harry, it misstates the facts. If there was, in fact, a burglary under these facts, then proving conspiracy would require that there was an agreement between Bill and Harry whereby they intended to carry out the burglary. The facts here indicate an agreement between them. However, what this ignores is that Harry and Bill didn't have an unlawful objective: they both thought Bill was going to retrieve Harry's silverware from Harry's house. Thus, the intent element is missing, not the agreement requirement. Since D misstates the facts, it is not the best response.

Answer 56

(C) is the best response,

because it correctly infers that Wood's remark will be admissible under the "present sense impression" hearsay exception.

Under FRE 803(1), a statement is admissible under this exception if it was made while the declarant was perceiving an event/condition (or immediately thereafter), and it describes or explains the event/condition. That's what Wood's statement does. Such statements are considered trustworthy – the hallmark of hearsay exceptions – because they were made contemporaneously with the event they concern, and thus the statement will suffer no defects in memory; furthermore, since such statements usually would have been made to someone else who was also present, there was an opportunity for at least one other person to correct the statements.

Note that Wood's statement is hearsay even though he's repeating it himself. A hearsay statement is an out-of-court statement offered to prove the truth of its assertion. Here, Wood's statement is offered to prove that Chase was drunk, so it's hearsay. However, since it fits the present sense impression hearsay exception, it will be admissible. Since C recognizes this, it's the best response.

(A) is not the best response,

because the facts here do not fit that Wood was excited when he made the comment.

In order to be admissible under the "excited utterance" exception to the hearsay rule, an out-of-court

statement must meet the requirements in FRE 803(2). It must have been made while declarant was under the stress of excitement, it must have been due to a startling event or condition, and it must relate to the event or condition. Such statements are considered trustworthy because the "stress of excitement" generated by the event minimizes the possibility of fabrication, since the declarant doesn't have time to consciously reflect on the event.

Under these facts, the key word is "remarked." An excited utterance would require some evidence that the declarant was under stress of excitement when the statement was made; simply "remarking" would not qualify.

Instead, Wood's statement would most likely be admissible under the present sense impression hearsay exception, FRE803(1). A statement is admissible under this exception if it was made while the declarant was perceiving an event/condition (or immediately thereafter); and it describes or explains the event/condition. That's what Wood's statement does. If you didn't realize this, it may be because you were thinking of the common law, under which present sense impressions were inadmissible. However, the MBE follows the Federal Rules, making Wood's statement admissible on that basis. Since A mistakenly categorizes this comment as an excited utterance, it's not the correct response.

(B) is not the best response,

because the statement here does not satisfy the prior consistent statement hearsay exclusion under the FRE. Under FRE 801(d)(1), a prior consistent statement of a currently-testifying declarant is admissible only if it is offered to rebut a charge (express or implied) against the witness of improper motive/influence or recent fabrication. That's clearly not the case here. If you chose option B, it's probably because you were seduced by the words themselves – "prior consistent statement" *sounds* as though it should be correct. Keep in mind that the prior statements hearsay exclusion for testifying witnesses, FRE 801(d)(1), is both extremely narrow *and* a popular MBE distractor.

Instead, Wood's statement would most likely be admissible under the present sense impression hearsay exception, FRE 803(1). A statement is admissible under this exception if it was made while the declarant was perceiving an event/condition (or immediately thereafter); and it describes or explains the event/condition. That's what Wood's statement does. If you didn't realize this, it may be because you were thinking of the common law, under which present sense impressions were inadmissible. However, the MBE follows the Federal Rules, making Wood's statement admissible on that basis. Since option B mischaracterizes Wood's testimony, it's not the best response.

(D) is not the best response,

because the appearance of drunkenness is a subject

which is appropriate for lay opinion testimony.

As a general rule – and "general" is the operative word here, since there are many exceptions – lay witnesses cannot offer opinion testimony. However, under FRE 701, where the opinion testimony is helpful to understanding witness's testimony or determining a fact in issue, and is rationally based on witness's first-hand knowledge, such lay opinion testimony will be helpful. Such testimony includes testimony concerning a person's physical appearance (e.g. weight, age, height, drunkenness, strength, etc.). Here, Wood's testimony involves Chase's appearance. Thus, it would be admissible without any evidence that Wood is a particular expert in determining drunkenness.

Beyond that, D does not address the fact that Wood's statement is hearsay. Hearsay is an out-of-court statement offered to prove the truth of its assertion. Here, Wood's statement is being offered to prove that Chase was crocked; thus, it's hearsay, and any correct response would have to address this issue. Since D doesn't do this, and it doesn't recognize that lay opinion testimony would be appropriate here, it's not the best response.

Answer 57

(B) is the best response,

because it correctly identifies that the statement here will be admissible, both substantively and to impeach Chase, under the prior inconsistent statements hearsay exclusion, FRE 801(d)(1).

Under that hearsay exclusion, prior inconsistent statements, given while testifying under oath, under penalty of perjury, at a prior proceeding, can be admitted, as long as the declarant is subject to cross-examination at the current proceeding. Such statements can be used both to impeach and to prove the substance of their assertions. That's what's going on here. The prior statement qualifies because a deposition is a prior proceeding, which resembles a "mini-trial." Chase, the declarant, is testifying and subject to cross-examination.

This question shows just how technical the prior statements hearsay exclusion *is;* however, it's a popular option with MBE questions both as the correct answer and as a distractor, so it's important to be familiar with it. It's also important to distinguish those prior inconsistent statements that can be used substantively, and those that can only be used to impeach or rehabilitate. *Any* prior inconsistent statements can be used to impeach or rehabilitate, regardless of whether they were made under oath, penalty of perjury, at a prior proceeding, and whether or not the declarant is subject to cross-examination at the current proceeding. It's only when the substance of the statement is sought to be proved that all the additional requirements kick in. Since B correctly applies the prior inconsistent statements hearsay exclusion, it's the best response.

(A) is not the best response,

because it understates the purposes for which the statement can be used, and it's not clear here that it's appropriate to use the statement for refreshment.

Virtually anything can be used to refresh the witness's memory, be it a leading question, document, or object. However, the refreshing item cannot be used unless and until the witness's present memory is exhausted. Furthermore, the refreshing object must actually be used to refresh the memory, not just to show the jury the item. It's not clear here that Chase's memory is exhausted, so refreshment probably wouldn't be merited. Even if it *were* merited, the testimony can be used to prove its substance – that is, that Chase was sober when he left Duke's Bar. That's because it fits the very narrow prior inconsistent statement hearsay exclusion to the Federal Rules, FRE 801(d)(1). Under that hearsay exclusion, prior inconsistent statements, given while testifying under oath, under penalty of perjury, at a prior proceeding, can be admitted, as long as the declarant is subject to cross-examination at the current proceeding. Such statements can be used both to impeach and to prove the substance of their assertions. That's what's going on here. The prior statement qualifies because a deposition is a prior proceeding, which resembles a "mini-trial." Chase, the declarant, is testifying and subject to cross-examination. Since A doesn't recognize that this exclusion applies, and it probably incorrectly states that the testimony can be used for refreshing Chase's memory, it's not the best response.

(C) is not the best response,

because it states an incorrect rule of law: A party *can* impeach its own witness. FRE 607. If you chose this response, it's probably because you were confusing the rule under the Federal Rules with the general, common law rule that a party cannot impeach its own witness.

Not only can Duke's Bar impeach Chase with the prior testimony, but it can use the prior testimony substantively – that is, to prove that Chase was sober when he left the Bar. That's because the prior testimony fits the very narrowly prior inconsistent statements hearsay exclusion. Under that hearsay exclusion, prior inconsistent statements, given while testifying under oath, under penalty of perjury, at a prior proceeding, can be admitted, as long as the declarant is subject to cross-examination at the current proceeding. Such statements can be used both to impeach and to prove the substance of their assertions. That's what's going on here. The prior statement qualifies because a deposition is a prior proceeding, which resembles a "mini-trial." Chase, the declarant, is testifying and subject to cross-examination. Thus, his prior testimony will be admissible both to impeach him and to prove the truth of its assertion. Since option C erroneously states that Duke's Bar can't even use the statement to impeach Chase because he's one of its own witnesses, it's not the best response.

(D) is not the best response,

because the statement here is not, in fact, hearsay at all, and it *is* admissible.

Prior inconsistent statements given while testifying under oath, under penalty of perjury, at a prior proceeding, are usable both as impeachment and substantively against a currently-testifying witness, under FRE 801(d)(1). The Rule *excludes* these statements from the hearsay rule, making them not hearsay at all.

Even if Chase's prior statement didn't fit the technical requirements of the hearsay exclusion, it would still be admissible, under FRE 801(c), to impeach him, since *any* prior inconsistent statement, no matter where or how it was made, can be used to impeach. Note that such statements are still considered non-hearsay, since they are not offered to prove the truth of their assertions, but only to prove that they were *made*.

Since D doesn't recognize that Chase's prior testimony is excluded from the hearsay rule such that it can be used both substantively and as impeachment, it is not the best response.

Answer 58

(D) is the best response,

because it correctly cites the reason for inadmissibility as the public policy against allowing evidence of subsequent remedial measures to prove negligence. FRE 407.

Here, it's quite possible that Duke's Bar instituted the new limits having realized, because of the Chase accident, that it had been negligent in failing to limit the amount customers may drink in a night. Thus, the limits could be regarded as a recognition that it had been negligent. If such remedial measures were admissible, people would be hesitant to make them, being tempted to leave a hazardous situation unchanged to avoid improvements being used against them in court.

Note, incidentally, that subsequent remedial measures *can* be used to show bias, ownership, to impeach, or show that the other party destroyed evidence. Also, in product liability cases based on defective design, a subsequently improved design can be admitted to show the design was previously defective. It's just that subsequent remedial measures can't be used to prove what's being proven here – fault. Since D recognizes this, it's the best response.

(A) is not the best response,

because it does not take into account the public policy of disallowing evidence of subsequent remedial measures to prove negligence or wrongdoing. FRE 407.

Here, it's quite possible that Duke's Bar instituted the new limits having realized, because of the Chase accident, that it had been negligent in failing to limit the amount customers may drink in a night. Thus, the limits

could be regarded as a recognition that it had been negligent. Even though the evidence would be relevant to Duke's negligence, it's expressly not admissible under FRE 407, because it if *were* admissible, people would be less inclined to correct dangerous conditions for fear the evidence of their doing so would be used in court against them. Subsequent remedial measures *can* be used to show bias, ownership, to impeach, or show that the other party destroyed evidence. Also, in product liability cases based on defective design, a subsequently improved design can be admitted to show the design was previously defective. It's just that subsequent remedial measures can't be used to prove what's being proven here – fault. Since A does not recognize this, it's not the best response.

(B) is not the best response,

because it does not take into account the public policy of disallowing evidence of subsequent remedial measures to prove negligence or wrongdoing. FRE 407.

Here, it's quite possible that Duke's Bar instituted the new limits having realized, because of the Chase accident, that it had been negligent in failing to limit the amount customers may drink in a night. Thus, the limits could be regarded as a recognition that it had been negligent. If such evidence *were* admissible, those in Duke's Bar's position would be tempted to let a dangerous condition go unchanged, so the evidence of a remedial measure could not be used against them in court. Subsequent remedial measures *can* be used to show bias, ownership, to impeach, or show that the other party destroyed evidence. Also, in product liability cases based on defective design, a subsequently improved design can be admitted to show the design was previously defective. It's just that subsequent remedial measures can't be used to prove what's being proven here – fault. Thus, B is not the best response.

(C) is not the best response,

because although it arrives at the correct result, it states the wrong reason – the employee's action probably would be binding on the bar, assuming the change was within the employee's scope of employment, under the theory of respondeat superior (and in any case, a general rule like the one stated in C – that the acts of employees are not binding on their employers – is not correct).

Note that there's no hearsay problem with the subsequent remedial measure, because it's "non-assertive conduct" – that is, it's conduct that's not intended as an assertion. Such conduct was considered hearsay at common law if it was offered to prove the actor's *beliefs* regarding a fact in issue. Thus, at common law, the four drink limit could theoretically be offered to prove that the manager believed the lack of a limit was wrong. However, under the Federal Rules, specifically Rule 801(a), non-assertive conduct is not considered hearsay at all, since it's not as likely to be fabricated as assertive conduct or words.

In any case, since C makes a general statement which doesn't comport with the principle of respondeat superior, it's not the best response.

Answer 59

(A) is the best response,

because it correctly applies the rule to these facts: admissions in conjunction with an offer to pay medical bills *are* admissible; it's admissions in conjunction with offers to settle that are *inadmissible*. Keep in mind that the offer to pay and the payment itself – of both medical bills and settlements – are inadmissible.

Option A implicitly recognizes that there's a hearsay problem here. Hearsay is an out-of-court statement offered to prove the truth of its assertion. Here, the out-of-court declarant is the owner of Duke's Bar: "That's the least I can do…" The statement is being offered to prove Chase was drunk, so it's hearsay, and must fit a hearsay exception or exclusion to be admissible. In fact, the statement constitutes an admission, since it's unfavorable to the declarant at the time of trial, and it's reasonable to infer from the statement that the owner is conscious of his guilt. FRE 801(d)(2)(note that admissions were admissible at common law as *exceptions* to the hearsay rule). Option A also recognizes another important consideration – that the statement will be admissible as an admission in conjunction with an offer to pay medical bills. Had the admission accompanied an offer to settle, the statement would have been inadmissible under the public policy of encouraging settlements.

Since A states correctly that the admission in conjunction with an offer to pay medical bills will be admissible, it's the best response.

(B) is not the best response,

because it misstates the facts, and states an incorrect rule of law. The owner isn't offering to settle the case, he's offering to pay Penn's medical expenses. For purposes of determining the admissibility of admissions, this is a crucial distinction (since admissions in conjunction with offers to settle *are not* admissible under the FRE, contrary to what B states, whereas admissions in conjunction with the payment of medical bills *are*).

Option B implicitly recognizes that there's a hearsay problem here. Hearsay is an out-of-court statement offered to prove the truth of its assertion. Here, the out-of-court declarant is the owner of Duke's Bar: "That's the least I can do…" The statement is being offered to prove Chase was drunk, so it's hearsay, and must fit a hearsay exception or exclusion to be admissible. In fact, the statement constitutes an admission, as option B states, since it's unfavorable to the declarant at the time of trial, and it's reasonable to infer from the statement that the owner is conscious of his guilt. FRE 801(d)(2)(note that admissions were admissible at common law as *exceptions* to the hearsay rule).

However, the offer here was made in conjunction with the payment of Penn's medical bills, not with a settlement offer, which is what B states. Had the admission been made in conjunction with an offer to settle, it would be *inadmissible*, due to the public policy of encouraging settlements – and B is incorrect in stating otherwise. Since B incorrectly characterizes the facts, and misstates the law, it's not the best response.

(C) is not the best response,

because it mischaracterizes the statement as hearsay, and it fails to recognize that the statement here will be admissible under one of the other alternatives – as an admission in conjunction with an offer to pay medical bills.

Hearsay is an out-of-court statement offered to prove the truth of its assertion. Here, the statement is being offered to prove that Chase was drunk. Thus, it's hearsay, and would have to fit a hearsay exception or exclusion in order to be admissible. FRE 801(d)(1) specifically *excludes* admissions by a party opponent from the hearsay rule. The owner of Duke's Bar would be considered a party opponent, and so his statement fits a hearsay exclusion. (At common law, admissions were considered *exceptions* to the hearsay rule, and admissible on that basis.) The MBE follows the Federal Rules, and C is thus incorrect in stating that an admission would be considered hearsay.

C also overlooks a public policy issue: that is, the fact that the statement will be admissible because it's an admission in conjunction with an offer to pay medical bills. The distinction that's important in this regard is between admissions in relation to medical bills, and admissions in conjunction with settlement offers. Nothing to do with settlements – be they admissions, offers, or the actual payment – are admissible in court, due to the public policy of encouraging settlements. When it comes to medical bills, admissions (like the one in these facts) are admissible, whereas the offer to pay and the payment itself are not. (Note that the rules on settlements and medical bills significantly differ between the Federal Rules and the common law. At common law, the only type of statement that's excluded in this area is the actual settlement offer and payment. All others – admissions in conjunction with a settlement offer, and admissions, offer, and payment of medical bills, are admissible.)

Since C doesn't recognize the basis here on which the statement will be admissible, it is not the best response.

(D) is not the best response,

because it misstates the rule of law.

Admissions in conjunction with an offer to pay medical bills *are* admissible. If you chose this option, it's probably because you confused the rule on admissions along with medical bills with the rule on admissions along with offers to settle. It's admissions along with offers to settle that are *inadmissible* under the FRE, Rule 408. An easy way to remember this distinction is to remember this mental picture: Picture an Indian settlement, or a pilgrim settlement, or any other kind of settlement which you can easily envision, with a giant red, plastic "X" draped over it. The "X" means that the "settlement" is not admissible. With this, you'll be remembering that admissions with settlements are not admissible (and, by exclusion, that admissions with medical bills *are* admissible). Keep in mind that the offer to pay and the payment itself of *both* medical bills *and* settlements are *inadmissible* under the FRE.

Note, incidentally, that there is a hearsay issue under these facts. Hearsay is an out-of-court statement offered to prove the truth of its assertion. Here, the statement is being offered to prove that Chase was drunk. Thus, it's hearsay, and it will have to fit a hearsay exception or exclusion in order to be admissible. FRE 801(d)(1) specifically *excludes* admissions by a party opponent from the hearsay rule. The owner of Duke's Bar would be considered a party opponent, and so his statement fits a hearsay exclusion. (At common law, admissions were considered *exceptions* to the hearsay rule, and admissible on that basis.)

In any case, since D misstates the rule of law concerning admissibility of admissions in conjunction with offers to pay medical bills, it's not the best response.

Answer 60

(A) is the best response,

because it is the only alternative under which the lay witness is not *personally familiar* with Daly's voice, and thus the recording wouldn't be admissible with this testimony alone.

The difficult thing about this question is that it's framed in the *negative*; in other words, you have to eliminate the options that give a possible basis on which the recording *could* be admitted, leaving you with the option that *couldn't* be used as a basis for admitting the recording. In this case, you'd have to reword the question in your own mind, so that instead of asking yourself "Which of the following would be the least sufficient basis for authentication?" you'd have to ask "Under which of the following circumstances will the authentication be insufficient to admit the tape?"

The rule is that a voice can be authenticated by any person who recognizes it. Under FRE 901(b)(5), *"Identification of a voice, whether heard firsthand or through mechanical or electronic transmission or recording, [can be accomplished] by opinion based upon hearing the voice at any time under any circumstances connecting it with the alleged speaker."* Here, the only thing linking the lay witness and Daly's voice is an assurance by Daly's brother that a recorded voice was Daly's; the witness herself has no personal familiarity with it. (Thus, if Daly's brother were lying or mistaken, the lay witness's testimony would be useless.) Since A states the only basis on which the lay witness *couldn't*

authenticate the tape, of these four choices, it's the best response.

(B) is not the best response,

because the lay witness could authenticate the recording on this basis since a voice can be authenticated by any person who recognizes it.

The fact that the lay witness had never heard Daly speak over the telephone would be irrelevant. Under FRE 901(b)(5), *"Identification of a voice, whether heard firsthand or through mechanical or electronic transmission or recording, [can be accomplished] by opinion based upon hearing the voice at any time under any circumstances connecting it with the alleged speaker."* Here, the lay witness satisfies this requirement because she had heard the voice many times. The rule doesn't require that the witness be familiar with the voice in the form in which it must be authenticated – here, a tape recording. Thus, the testimony here would qualify, making B not the best response.

(C) is not the best response,

because the lay witness could authenticate the recording on this basis, since any person who recognizes a voice can authenticate it.

Under FRE 901(b)(5), *"Identification of a voice, whether heard firsthand or through mechanical or electronic transmission or recording, [can be accomplished] by opinion based upon hearing the voice at any time under any circumstances connecting it with the alleged speaker."* The rule specifically provides that the circumstances under which the witness became familiar with the voice are irrelevant. As a result, it doesn't matter that the lay witness only familiarized herself with Daly's voice in order to testify – she may authenticate the tape nonetheless. Thus, C is not the best response.

(D) is not the best response,

because it represents possibly the *best* basis on which the lay witness *could* authenticate the recording. Not only would she be able to recognize the voice, but she'd be familiar with the very conversation that was recorded.

Under FRE 901(b)(5), *"Identification of a voice, whether heard firsthand or through mechanical or electronic transmission or recording, [can be accomplished] by opinion based upon hearing the voice at any time under any circumstances connecting it with the alleged speaker."* Under option D, not only would the lay witness be familiar with Daly's voice, she'd have the additional benefit of having heard the very conversation in question. The fact that she heard it in person, and not over the phone, doesn't matter, because all that's required under the rule is that she be personally familiar with the voice. As a result, this will be a perfectly adequate means of authenticating the tape, and since D states otherwise, it's not the best response.

Answer 61

(C) is the best response,

because it correctly identifies the strongest basis on which a judgment for Parnell could be based – the Parol Evidence Rule.

There are two key facts here: First, that the prior oral agreement contradicts the writing, thus invoking the Parol Evidence Rule; and second, that recording transactions is for the benefit of subsequent bona fide purchasers, not one of the parties to the transaction.

In order to prevail based on his requirement that Parnell only fill in Lots 40 or 41, Devlin would have to rely on his prior, oral understanding with Parnell. Under the Parol Evidence Rule, a writing that is "completely integrated" cannot be contradicted or supplemented with prior written or oral agreements, or contemporaneous oral agreements. A "completely integrated" agreement is one which the parties intended to be a final and complete statement of their agreement. The deed here would likely qualify, so that oral restrictions on the lot number to be included would contradict the document itself, and would not be provable.

Of course, the Parol Evidence Rule does not bar evidence of defects in contract formation, like lack of consideration, fraud, and duress, but there are no such facts evident here. For instance, there is no evidence that Parnell *fraudulently* put in the number of a more expensive lot; the facts merely indicate that he changed his mind, apparently ignorant of the difference in cost, so the Parol Evidence Rule could not be avoided on grounds of fraud.

In fact, a more appropriate remedy would be *reformation,* where the court rewords the contract to reflect the parties' true intent. However, under these facts, Devlin is attempting to say that a contract never existed, because Parnell was in breach of the "Lot 40 or 41" agreement. As such, Devlin is seeking a rescission, and, due to operation of the Parol Evidence Rule, he's unlikely to succeed. Since C recognizes this as the most likely basis for Parnell's prevailing, it's the best response.

(A) is not the best response,

because it does not form as strong a basis for the judgment as does option C.

An estoppel occurs, in facts like these, when one has done or omitted to do something, and is as a result forbidden from pleading or proving an otherwise important fact. Here, Devlin's carelessness in allowing Parnell to fill in the deed would lead to his being bound by the resultant deed – he'd be "estopped" from denying its validity.

However, what option A fails to take into account is the existence of the deed, which would constitute a written contract between Parnell and Devlin, embodying their agreement. Parnell's most likely means of prevailing is enforcing the written agreement, without resorting to estoppel. He can do so if his argument focuses on the Parol Evidence Rule. Under the Parol Evidence Rule, a writing that is "completely integrated" cannot be contradicted or supplemented with prior written or oral agreements, or contemporaneous oral agreements. A "completely integrated" agreement is one which the parties intended to be a final and complete statement of their agreement. The deed here would likely qualify, so that oral restrictions on the lot number to be included would contradict the document itself, and would not be provable.

While there are exceptions to the Parol Evidence Rule, these facts to not neatly fit into any of them. Thus, an option focusing on the Parol Evidence Rule, option C, provides a stronger basis for a judgment in Parnell's favor than the estoppel argument in A, making A not the best response.

(B) is not the best response,

because although it states a correct rule, it would not apply to these facts.

Option B suggests that the fact that the land title records show Parnell owning lot 25 means that Parnell should prevail. In fact, recording conveyances is required for the benefit of subsequent, bona fide purchasers, *not* parties to transactions themselves, so Parnell could not prevail on this basis. Instead, Parnell's prevailing depends on the oral agreement, restricting the purchase to lots 40 or 41, being *inadmissible.* Since the land title records will not be a basis on which Parnell could prevail, B is not the best response.

(D) is not the best response,

because, although it states a correct rule, Devlin – as a party to the transaction – cannot rely on it. Recording conveyances is required for the benefit of subsequent, bona fide purchasers, *not* parties to transactions themselves. Thus, had the action been between Devlin and a subsequent purchaser, option D could form the basis of a judgment in the purchaser's favor – even if the deed were, in fact, void! Here, since the dispute is between the parties to the transaction, the recording of the deed is irrelevant. Instead, Parnell's prevailing depends on the oral agreement, restricting the purchase to lots 40 or 41, being *inadmissible.* Since D doesn't recognize this, it's not the best response.

Answer 62

(C) is the best response,

because it states the most likely basis, of these four, on which Devlin will lose: Devlin is estopped from denying the validity of the deed in an action between him and a bona fide purchaser.

The key fact here is that Caruso is a bona fide purchaser, and thus *can* rely on the deed, as recorded (where Parnell, as a party to the transaction with Devlin, could *not).*

The goal of recording statutes is to protect subsequent bona fide purchasers and incumbrancers – those who pay value and take without notice of prior conveyances, in good faith. Here, Caruso is a bona fide purchaser, because he has no notice of any defects in the chain of title. The price he paid, $6,000, was a bargain compared to what Devlin asked previously, but this would not in and of itself negate his bona fide purchaser status, since it would still constitute "value" and would not, barring other facts, indicate something untoward was involved. Since the chain of title indicates that Parnell was conveying marketable title, Caruso was not obligated to look further.

D goes on to suggest that Devlin is "estopped" from denying the validity of the deed. An estoppel occurs, in facts like these, when one has done or omitted to do something, and is as a result forbidden from pleading or proving an otherwise important fact. Here, Devlin's carelessness in allowing Parnell to fill in the deed will lead to his being bound by the resultant deed – he'll be "estopped" from denying its validity. Since C recognizes this, and it forms a good basis for a decision in Caruso's favor, C is the best response.

(A) is not the best response,

because the Statute of Frauds likely would *not* prevent admission of Devlin's and Parnell's agreement; it's the Parol Evidence Rule that would have this effect.

As option A recognizes, there's an underlying Statute of Frauds issue here. Where the sale of land is concerned, the Statute of Frauds requires that an agent cannot enter into an enforceable contract for conveying an interest in land unless the agreement granting the agency authority is in writing, and subscribed by the one sought to be charged. However, under these facts, the agency is implicitly included in the deed itself, so it *is* in writing, satisfying the Statute of Frauds. Instead, it's the Parol Evidence Rule which would prohibit admission of Devlin and Parnell's prior oral agreement concerning the lot number, since it contradicts the lot number in the deed. Since A doesn't recognize this, it's not the best response.

(B) is not the best response,

because it states an incorrect rule of law: Recording a deed does not preclude any question as to its genuineness. The mere act of recording would not, for instance, make a fraudulent deed genuine. The upshot, nonetheless, might be that, *despite* the fact a deed is incorrect, *the bona fide purchaser may still prevail,* on grounds of estoppel. Since B states as a concrete rule that recording a deed means its genuineness cannot be questioned, and this is incorrect, B is not the best response.

(D) is not the best response,

because it misstates the facts: Devlin's hands are not "unclean."

Under the equitable doctrine of "unclean hands," one who has acted "unconscionably," or in a morally repre-

hensible manner, cannot recover. Here, at most Devlin has behaved negligently; there is no basis on which to attach any bad faith to his behavior. If anything, he was gullible in trusting Parnell to fill in the blank in the deed as instructed; but the creation of the agency did not involve wrongdoing. If anyone, it's Parnell who's the wrongdoer. Since D states otherwise, it's not the best response.

Answer 63

(D) is the best response,

because it identifies reasoning which is plausible on these facts, and arrives at a result consistent with the reasoning.

Under these facts, the most likely basis on which Ohner would be liable is vicarious liability for the negligence of his employees in failing to take reasonable precautions for the safety of passersby. The facts here tell you that hotel employees patrolled the hallways telling the guests to refrain from destructive conduct (of the type which injured Smith). It's clear that the employees couldn't *stop* guests from misbehaving, so it's possible that such patrols would be considered reasonable precautions to prevent injuries like Smith's. Negligence requires *unreasonable* conduct, so if the employees were *reasonable* in their behavior, there could be no basis for negligence, and Ohner would not be liable. Note that option D uses the modifier "if." As a result, you have to determine if the reasoning could plausibly fit the facts, whether it addresses a central issue, and, thereafter, if the result is consistent with the reasoning. Option D satisfies all of these, making it the best response.

(A) is not the best response,

because it misstates the law, and arrives at an incorrect result.

Without more, a property owner is *not* strictly liable for acts on his premises vis a vis *any* adjacent property, public or private. Instead, in order to be strictly liable, he'll have to engage in some activity that involves strict liability – e.g., an ultrahazardous activity, like blasting. Even if A had said that a property owner is strictly liable for *ultrahazardous* acts, it probably wouldn't fit these facts because it's unlikely that having rowdy patrons would be considered ultrahazardous. In any case, since A misstates the law and offers the wrong result, it's not the best response.

(B) is not the best response,

because it offers as reasoning an irrelevant fact.

If Ohner is to be liable, it will be because he was negligent, those he employs were negligent (making Ohner vicariously liable), or there's some basis for holding him strictly liable. If there's no basis for holding Ohner liable, it doesn't matter if the tortfeasor can't be identified – Ohner won't be any more liable than he'd be for torts *you* commit. Since B does not recognize this, it can't be the best response.

(C) is not the best response,
because it offers as reasoning an irrelevant fact.

Ohner's liability will depend on whether his conduct was tortious, whether his employees' acts were at least negligent, or whether there's some basis to hold him strictly liable. If, for instance, his employees were negligent within the scope of their employment and Smith was injured as a result, Ohner would be liable on the basis of respondeat superior *regardless* of whether he had personal knowledge of his guests' behavior. Conversely, if C were true, and personal knowledge were required for liability, Ohner could insulate himself from liability by avoiding finding out about *any* potentially tortious conduct at the hotel. While ignoring what your underlings do may insulate you from responsibility if you're President of the United States, it won't help you very much in the everyday realm of Tort Law. Since C misstates the law, it can't be the best response.

Answer 64

(B) is the best response,
because it identifies the key reason Householder will be liable.

The rule is that the owner of a wild animal is strictly liable for the animal's conduct creating damage. Thus, the point B raises – that a skunk is not domesticated – is the lynchpin of Householder's liability. The wrinkle here is that you don't typically consider a skunk "wild," in the sense of a lion or saber-toothed tiger or Tasmanian devil or animals of that ilk. Nonetheless, a skunk isn't domesticated, so it can be a source of strict liability for Householder. Since it caused Walker's damages, and Walker's damages were within the scope of the extraordinary risk created by maintaining a skunk, Householder will be strictly liable. Since B correctly identifies the basis of Householder's liability, it's the best response.

(A) is not the best response,
because the private nuisance tort would not apply to these facts.

A private nuisance is an act by defendant which creates an unreasonable, substantial interference with plaintiff's use or enjoyment of property. The interest protected is the right to use and enjoy one's land. Here, Walker *has* no right to use and enjoy the land she was on when she was injured: she's a trespasser. Thus, private nuisance *cannot* apply to these facts. Although A arrives at the right response, it ignores the real basis of liability: one is strictly liable for the torts of his pets if the pets are "wild animals," of which a skunk would be one. As a result, A is not the best response.

(C) is not the best response,
because although Walker's status will determine the duty Householder owes her as an entrant on the land,

it will not determine Householder's liability on these facts.

At common law, the landowner's duty to trespassers depended on whether they were "discovered" or "undiscovered." The landowner owes no duty to undiscovered trespassers, whereas a discovered trespasser (i.e., one whom the landowner anticipates, as here, due to Householder's knowledge the grass is used as a footpath) is owed a duty of reasonable care, generally satisfied by a warning of man-made dangers known to the landowner and unlikely to be discovered by the trespasser. The modern trend is to consolidate the duties owed to various levels of entrants into a "reasonable person" standard.

In any case, these are not relevant here because they all address levels of *fault* that will be necessary for landowner liability. Instead, here Householder will be *liable without any fault at all* because the skunk will be considered a wild animal, making Householder strictly liable for damage it creates. As a result, Walker's status as a trespasser will not relieve Householder of liability.

This is a somewhat tricky option in that your gut feeling is that Walker *shouldn't* recover because she's a trespasser. However, as many MBE questions show, you can't react instinctively to the facts. A mechanical application of the law indicates that Householder will be strictly liable to Walker, so C is not the best response.

(D) is not the best response,
because the reasoning it states would not relieve Householder of liability.

The general rule is that owners are strictly liable for the torts of wild animals they keep as pets. Thus, even if the pet is caged, has its teeth removed, a frontal lobotomy, is de-clawed, or any other type of precaution is taken, the owner will *still* be liable, because strict liability requires no proof of fault – merely keeping a wild animal as a pet will be sufficient to impose liability, if the pet causes harm, and that harm is within the extraordinary risk which merited imposing strict liability in the first place. Admittedly, Dr. Vet was negligent under these facts, and Householder could recover against him for any damages paid to Walker. Nonetheless, this does not erase the fact that Householder's skunk injured Walker, and this *alone* makes Householder liable. Since D doesn't recognize this, it's not the best response.

Answer 65

(A) is the best response,
because it correctly identifies the basis on which Dr. Vet is likely to be held liable: Negligence.

In order to be negligent, defendant must have failed to exercise such care as a reasonable person in his position would have exercised, this must have been a breach of the duty to prevent the foreseeable risk of harm to anyone in plaintiff's position, and this breach must have caused plaintiff's damages.

The wrinkle here is the duty Dr. Vet owes to Walker. The rule is that an individual owes a duty only to prevent the foreseeable risk of injury to anyone in plaintiff's position. Here, Walker, as a passerby, is exactly the class of person Dr. Vet's operation on the skunk was supposed to protect. By performing the operation negligently, he failed to prevent the foreseeable risk of harm to Walker. Note that Walker's trespassing *doesn't* change this, nor does the fact that Dr. Vet performed the operation under contract with Householder. Instead, it's a garden-variety negligence claim. Since A recognizes this, it's the best response.

(B) is not the best response,

because strict liability would not be applicable to Dr. Vet's actions under these facts.

There are three general sources of strict liability: Keeping wild animals, abnormally dangerous activities, and defective, unreasonably dangerous products (strict liability can also spring from case law or a statute). A de-scenting operation performed by a vet would not fit any of these categories, and so fault will have to be proven in order for Walker to recover from Dr. Vet. Since B doesn't recognize this, it's not the best response.

(C) is not the best response,

because Walker's being a trespasser is not relevant to determining Dr. Vet's liability to her.

An individual owes a duty only to prevent the foreseeable risk of injury to anyone in plaintiff's position. Here, the type of injury Walker suffered is exactly the type that Vet's negligence – failing to de-scent the skunk – would cause.

There are two perspectives from which you could have analyzed Walker's trespassing which would have led you to option C. First, you might have thought that because Walker was committing an intentional wrong *in general*, she doesn't deserve to recover. However, the mere fact that someone is doing something wrong doesn't entitle another to commit a tort against him (thus, during Prohibition, Carrie Nation would have been liable to the owners of speakeasies whose property she destroyed, even though they were illegally selling liquor). Second, you may have equated Walker's trespassing with contributory negligence. This doesn't hold water either because not *only* is Walker's trespassing irrelevant to Dr. Vet, but it did not involve an undue risk of harm to herself – she was merely using a footpath, which would not normally be associated with the risk of being sprayed by a skunk. Thus, Walker couldn't be forbidden from recovery due to contributory negligence. Since C fails to realize that Dr. Vet will be liable to Walker regardless of her trespassing, it's not the best response.

(D) is not the best response,

because it does not address the scope of Dr. Vet's liability in torts, and arrives at the incorrect result.

Option D addresses Dr. Vet's *contractual* responsibility. However, in tort, an individual owes a duty only to prevent the foreseeable risk of injury to anyone in plaintiff's position. Under these facts, a passerby being sprayed by the skunk was exactly what Dr. Vet's operation was supposed to prevent; by failing to adequately perform the operation, he created that risk. If you chose this response, you were probably thinking about privity concepts in Contract law, which don't apply at all in non-product liability cases in tort, and only apply in limited situations even in product liability. As a result, D is not the best response.

Answer 66

(C) is the best response,

because it correctly identifies the type of testimony required to authenticate the photograph.

Under FRE 901(a), as long as a witness, based on personal knowledge, testifies that the photograph accurately and correctly represents the facts contained therein, the photograph will be admissible. The purpose of the authentication here would be to ensure that the photograph depicts the scene of the accident. Only a person who observed the cars while they were still in place could do so. Since C correctly identifies this, it's the best response.

(A) is not the best response,

because although the photographer *could* perhaps authenticate the photograph, his testimony would not be *required*.

In order to authenticate a photograph, a witness need only testify, from personal knowledge, that the photo fairly represents what it's supposed to represent. FRE 901(a). The photo here is intended to show the configuration of the cars after the accident. If the cars were still in place when the photograph was taken, anyone who saw them in that configuration can authenticate the photograph, and the photographer won't be required. Since A overstates the authentication necessary, it's not the best response.

(B) is not the best response,

because presence when the photograph was taken isn't the relevant consideration: presence while the cars were still in place is what's required.

In order to authenticate a photo, a witness must testify, from personal knowledge, that the photo fairly represents what it's supposed to represent. FRE 901(a). Here, the photo is intended to represent the scene of the accident. It's not necessary, then, that the person authenticating the photo have actually been present when the photo was taken, as long as he saw the cars before they were moved, and can as a result verify that the photo is accurate. Since B overstates the authentication that will be necessary, it's not the best response.

(D) is not the best response,

because the custody of the photograph would not be relevant to its authentication.

Custody is typically only a problem when *real* evidence is involved, e.g., a gun used as a murder weapon, when the chain of custody is vitally important to proving the weapon *is* the murder weapon. Instead, for a photograph depicting the scene of the accident, the only important issue is whether or not the photograph accurately and correctly represents the facts contained therein, which can only be proven by the testimony of a witness so testifying from personal knowledge that that's the case. FRE 901(a). Since D focuses on an irrelevant issue, it's not the best response.

Answer 67

(A) is the best response,

because it offers a defense which is likely to prevail on these facts.

A contract has three basic elements: offer, acceptance and consideration or some substitute for consideration (e.g., promissory estoppel). Consideration requires a bargained-for exchange and either detriment to the promisee or benefit to the promisor, and typically both. Here, Charles had no legal obligation to reimburse Betty for her expenses. His promise to do so didn't create any benefit to him, and Betty didn't suffer any detriment as a result of it, either. As such, the promise would be considered *gratuitous,* and thus not enforceable.

Say instead that Betty agreed not to claim against Arthur's estate in return for Charles's promise. Then she would suffer a detriment in the form of surrendering a valid legal claim. As a result, there would be consideration. Under the facts as they exist, however, there is no consideration. Without consideration, or some substitute for it, Charles's promise is an unenforceable gratuitous promise. Since A recognizes this, it's the best response.

(B) is not the best response,

because unilateral mistake is, in general, not a good defense to breach of contract.

The rule on unilateral mistake is that where the other party (here, Betty) reasonably did not know of the mistake, the mistaken party must perform. It's only if the other party knew or should have known of the mistake, that the mistaken party's performance will be excused.

Here, Betty had no reason to know that Charles believed he was liable for the accident simply because he owned the car. Thus, mistake would not excuse Charles's performance.

If you chose this response, you were probably thinking of *mutual* mistake. As a general rule, when both parties are mistaken as to a basic assumption of fact on which the contract was created, the contract is void-

able. However, what's involved here is *unilateral* mistake. Since Charles's mistake won't relieve him of his duty to perform under the contract, mistake is not his best defense, making B not the best response.

(C) is not the best response,

because the agreement here would not fall within the Statute of Frauds.

Under the Statute of Frauds, a writing is generally required for certain contracts, including those for the sale of an interest in land, incapable of performance in less than one year, to answer for another's debt, and the like. Here, Charles's promise to Betty is a direct promise to pay her expenses. Such an agreement is not covered by the Statute of Frauds, so no writing is required to make it enforceable.

If you chose this response, you were probably thinking that Charles was covering Arthur's obligation to Betty and so the agreement was designed to answer for another's debt, and would thus be covered by the Statute of Frauds. However, Charles wasn't promising to pay Arthur's debt, but rather to cover Betty's expenses, so the Statute wouldn't apply. Charles's statement to *Physician* would be covered by this provision, because he was promising to pay Betty's debt. However, that's not the issue here, since it's Betty who's suing Charles, not Physician. Since Charles's agreement with Betty falls outside the Statute of Frauds, a writing would not be required to make the agreement enforceable, so a Statute of Frauds defense would fail. Since C states otherwise, it's not the best response.

(D) is not the best response,

because it misstates the facts.

While it's true that a promise must be sufficiently definite to be enforceable, under these facts, Charles's promise *is* definite. He offered to pay Betty for any losses the accident caused. While the exact *amount* of the damages wouldn't be predictable, this itself wouldn't make the promise unduly vague, since the damages are defined by Betty's good-faith expenses. Since D mischaracterizes Charles's promise, it can't be the best response.

Answer 68

(C) is the best response.

As to alternative I:

This would have an impact on whether or not consideration exists.

Consideration requires bargained-for exchange and either detriment to the promisee or benefit to the promisor, and typically both. Here, as to the promise to pay for Betty's treatment, Charles is the promisor and Physician is the promisee. Physician's agreement to treat Betty in response to Charles's promise would be a legal detriment, since he'd be promising to do something he's not otherwise, on these facts, obligated to do.

The reason the fact that Physician had not yet begun his treatment is important is that, if he was already treating Betty, he wouldn't have undertaken to act in response to Charles's promise, and thus there wouldn't be a bargained-for exchange. Thus, alternative I is significant in determining the existence of consideration.

As to alternative II:

This would be significant in determining the existence of consideration.

Consideration requires bargained-for exchange and either detriment to the promisee or benefit to the promisor, and typically both. Here, as to the promise to pay for Betty's treatment, Charles is the promisor and Physician is the promisee.

Here, if Charles had a contract with Betty requiring him to reimburse her for her expenses related to the accident, he'd be legally obligated to do so. Thus, his contract with Physician would represent a *discharge* of that obligation, and thus a benefit to Charles, as promisor. As a result, a contract with Betty would be significant in establishing consideration for the Charles-Physician contract. Alternative II recognizes this.

Answer 69

As to alternative I:

This would not be a good defense to Betty's breach of contract claim. It fails to take into account that Betty is an intended beneficiary of the Charles-Physician contract.

Traditionally, a contract has three elements: Offer, acceptance, and consideration or some substitute for consideration (e.g., promissory estoppel). Consideration requires a bargained-for exchange and either detriment to the promisee or benefit to the promisor. The exchange of money for treatment provides the consideration here, and so Betty isn't involved with consideration *at all.*

Instead, she is an intended beneficiary of the contract, because it was the promisee's (here, Charles's) intent that she receive the benefit of promisor's (here, Physician's) performance. As a result, she has enforceable rights under the contract, and when Physician breached his duty to complete her treatment, she could sue him directly. As a result, Betty's failure to furnish consideration would not defeat her claim, making alternative I not a good defense.

As to alternative II:

This would not be a good defense to Betty's breach of contract claim, because Betty could recover under the Charles-Physician contract even without being a party to it. That's because she's an intended beneficiary under the contract, and thus has enforceable rights under it. She's an intended beneficiary because it was promisee's (here, Charles's) intent that she receive the

benefit of promisor's (here, Physician's) performance. Thus, when Physician breached his duty to complete her treatment, she could sue him directly. Her status as a non-party would not preclude her recovery, so II can't be correct.

As to alternative III:

This would not be a good defense to Betty's breach of contract claim, because there was no novation under these facts. A novation has four requirements:

1. There must be a valid agreement in existence between the original contracting parties;
2. An agreement between the promisee (to whom the performance is owed under the contract) and a new promisor, where the new promisor undertakes the old promisor's duties and the promisee accepts the substitution;
3. An express extinction of the old promisor's duties; and
4. A new, valid agreement.

If a novation exists, the old promisor's duty is *extinguished* under the contract.

The reason there can't be a novation under these facts is that there's no evidence of an original agreement between Betty and Physician. Furthermore, it's Physician's agreement with *Charles* under which Betty would recover, as an intended beneficiary. Since III misapplies novation to these facts, it can't be correct.

Answer 70

(B) is the best response,

because it cites the central reason that Dodge will prevail: the agreement was supported by consideration.

A contract has three basic elements: Office, acceptance, and consideration or some substitute for consideration (e.g., promissory estoppel). Consideration is a bargained-for exchange and either detriment to the promisee or benefit to the promisor, and typically both. The central issue here is whether Dodge's promise not to make a claim against the estate would be sufficient to constitute consideration. In fact, it would, because consideration in the form of detriment to the promisee *can* take the form of promisee's refraining from doing something he's entitled to do – like press a valid legal claim. As long as this is bargained-for, it'll satisfy the consideration requirement. Here, it *is* bargained-for, because Charles exchanged his promise to pay Dodge for Dodge's promise not to press a claim. Note that promissory estoppel *only* applies where there's *no bargain,* and thus no contract, but only a promise (so if Charles had said, "I don't want you to sue the estate; I'll pay you what he owed you," there would be no bargained-for exchange). Since B recognizes the essence of why Dodge will succeed in his claim against Charles, it's the best response.

(A) is not the best response,

because Dodge's detriment was bargained-for, so

Dodge need not rely on promissory estoppel in order to recover.

This is what promissory estoppel does: It's a substitute for consideration to avoid injustice. It's triggered by a gratuitous promise that is likely to, and does, induce the promisee's reliance. It's not consideration because there's no bargain — but it does result in the promise being *enforceable.*

The lack of an enforceable contract is a prerequisite for promissory estoppel. Here, if there hadn't been a bargain for Dodge's agreement not to press a claim, promissory estoppel *would* apply. (Say, for instance, Charles had said, "I really don't want you to press a claim against the estate. I'll pay you what he owes you.") Thus, promissory estoppel only replaces consideration where promisee's detriment *wasn't* bargained-for. Here, Charles only agreed to pay Arthur's debt to Dodge because Dodge agreed not to claim against the estate. As a result, Dodge has a valid claim for breach of contract, and needn't rely on the equitable concept of promissory estoppel. Since A doesn't recognize this, it's not the best response.

(C) is not the best response,

because the fact that Dodge's claim turned out to be worthless would not defeat his claim.

Option C implies that because Dodge's claim turned out to be worthless, the agreement between Charles and Dodge was not supported by consideration, and thus Charles's promise wouldn't be enforceable. That's because there wouldn't be any benefit to the promisor (Charles) or detriment to the promisee (Dodge). Charles wasn't obligated to satisfy the debts of Arthur's estate, so there's no benefit to him in discharging the estate's debts; and if option C is to be believed, there's no detriment to Dodge if he gave up a worthless claim. However, this analysis of Dodge's detriment is not legally correct.

A promise not to assert a valid legal claim constitutes valid consideration. Note that the claim need only be *valid,* and sometimes not even that — it's capability of collection is irrelevant. The fact that there are no assets upon which to levy a judgment is thus not relevant. In fact, if you chose this response, it's probably because you confused worthless with invalid. A promise not to pursue an invalid claim can *only* be consideration if a reasonable person could believe the claim's well-founded, and it could be pursued in good faith. Under these facts, even if Dodge's claim were invalid, it would probably still be the basis of valid consideration. Since C focuses on an irrelevant point, it's not the best response.

(D) is not the best response,

because it disregards the fact that Charles had a *contractual* duty, not just a non-actionable moral duty.

Option D is theoretically correct in stating that, as a general rule, a moral obligation is insufficient to enforce

a promise (there are exceptions to this). However, it ignores the fact that Charles has a *contractual* duty under these facts, and *that's* the source of his liability.

A contract requires an offer, acceptance, and consideration (or some substitute for consideration, like promissory estoppel). Consideration requires a bargained-for exchange and either detriment to the promisee (Dodge) or benefit to the promisor (Charles). If you chose this response, you probably overlooked the consideration: Dodge's refraining from asserting a valid legal claim constitutes consideration, because he's refraining from something he's legally entitled to do. Thus, the contract is based on consideration and Charles has a legal, not just moral, duty to live up to his promise. Since D doesn't recognize this, it's not the best response.

Answer 71

(C) is the best response,

because it impliedly recognizes the reason Dodge won't recover: the existence of an accord and satisfaction.

Here, there is a good-faith dispute over the amount owed. The settlement constitutes an "accord" — that is, an agreement under which a party to a contract agrees to accept, as complete satisfaction of the contract, some performance different than that originally due under the contract. As with any enforceable agreement, an accord requires consideration: a bargained-for exchange and either detriment to the promisee and benefit to the promisor, and typically both. Here, there is both detriment and benefit to Charles and Dodge. Charles paid more than he believed he should but less than he might have had to pay, and Dodge got more than nothing but less than he believed he should receive. Thus, it's the very dispute itself that provides the consideration for the accord, and once the accord is "satisfied" (performed), both the accord and the original contractual duty are discharged — and Dodge is precluded from recovering any more under the original contract. Thus, while Dodge's honest belief in the validity of his claim is *part* of the consideration for the accord, it's not enough to recover the additional $50. Since C realizes that the good-faith dispute is the basis for the validity of the accord and satisfaction, it's the best response.

(A) is not the best response,

because it mischaracterizes the facts and as a result arrives at the wrong result.

If Arthur's debt *were* liquidated and undisputed, A would be correct in stating that Dodge could recover the additional $50. Under the pre-existing duty rule, there would be no consideration to support the settlement, and thus the settlement would be unenforceable and Dodge could recover the additional $50 under the original contract.

However, a "liquidated" debt is one that is *undisputa-*

bly due. Here, instead, there is a good faith dispute as to the amount of the debt, and it's this dispute that forms the basis for the settlement contract. The settlement and its performance, by the way, are an "accord and satisfaction" – an "accord" being an agreement under which a party to a contract agrees to accept, as complete satisfaction of the contract, some performance different than that originally due under the contract, and "satisfaction" being performance of the accord. Once satisfaction takes place, both the accord and the original contractual duty are discharged. As a result, Dodge couldn't go back and recover additional money under the original contract. Since A mischaracterizes the debt as liquidated and thus overlooks the consideration for the accord, it's not the best response.

(B) is not the best response,

because Dodge's belief that he was owed $200 would not, in and of itself, be sufficient for him to prevail.

Here, there is a good-faith dispute over the amount owed. The settlement constitutes an "accord" – that is, an agreement under which a party to a contract agrees to accept, as complete satisfaction of the contract, some performance different than that originally due under the contract. As with any enforceable agreement, an accord requires consideration: a bargained-for exchange and either detriment to the promisee and benefit to the promisor, and typically both. Here, there is both detriment and benefit to Charles and Dodge. Charles paid more than he believed he should but less than he might have had to pay, and Dodge got more than nothing but less than he believed he should receive. Thus, it's the very dispute itself that provides the consideration for the accord, and once the accord is "satisfied" (performed), both the accord and the original contractual duty are discharged – and Dodge is precluded from recovering any more under the original contract. Thus, while Dodge's honest belief in the validity of his claim is *part* of the consideration for the accord, it's not enough to recover the additional $50, so B isn't the best response.

(D) is not the best response,

because it misstates the facts – Charles *did* have an original $200 contractual obligation.

As with any contract, the original agreement between Charles and Dodge would require an offer, acceptance, and consideration (or some substitute for consideration) in order to be valid. The consideration was supplied by Dodge's promise not to press a valid legal claim against Arthur's estate, in exchange for Charles's promise to pay him what Arthur owed him. (You probably overlooked this if you chose this response.)

D *is* correct in stating that Dodge won't recover the additional $50, but that's because there's an accord and satisfaction under these facts. Here, there is a good-faith dispute over the amount owed. The settlement constitutes an "accord" – that is, an agreement under which a party to a contract agrees to accept, as

complete satisfaction of the contract, some performance different than that originally due under the contract. As with any enforceable agreement, an accord requires consideration: a bargained-for exchange and either detriment to the promisee and benefit to the promisor, and typically both. Here, there is both detriment and benefit to Charles and Dodge. Charles paid more than he believed he should but less than he might have had to pay, and Dodge got more than nothing but less than he believed he should receive. Thus, it's the very dispute itself that provides the consideration for the accord, and once the accord is "satisfied" (performed), both the accord and the original contractual duty are discharged – and Dodge is precluded from recovering any more under the original contract. As a result, while Dodge's honest belief in the validity of his claim is *part* of the consideration for the accord, it's not enough to recover the additional $50. Since D doesn't recognize the validity of the original contract, and ignores the accord and satisfaction, it's not the best response.

Answer 72

(D) is the best response,

because it correctly identifies the central reason the distribution is invalid: it amounts to a state authorization of discrimination.

In order to be valid, a state law must meet a three-part test:

1. It must be enacted within the state's powers (e.g., police powers);
2. It must not violate any person's constitutional rights; and
3. It must not improperly burden interstate commerce.

The distribution of free textbooks would be an exercise of the state's police power, because it aids the welfare of the public. The problem is the second element: the distribution to Little White School House is an equal protection violation. Equal protection is triggered by a classification which determines people's rights. Here, the classification is on the basis of color. While states need not outlaw discrimination, they cannot authorize or encourage it. Distributing free textbooks to a racially segregated school would encourage discrimination. Thus, the distribution will be invalid. Since D recognizes this, it's the best response.

(A) is not the best response,

because it's not factually true; education *is* aided by the free distribution of textbooks.

In order to be valid, a state law must meet a three-part test:

1. It must be enacted within the state's powers (e.g., police powers);
2. It must not violate any person's constitutional rights; and

3. It must not improperly burden interstate commerce.

Option A addresses the first element – a legitimate goal of government. The distribution of free textbooks would be an exercise of the state's police power, because it aids the welfare of the public. The problem is the second element: the distribution to Little White School House is an equal protection violation. Equal protection is triggered by a classification which determines people's rights. Here, the classification is on the basis of color. While states need not outlaw discrimination, they cannot authorize or encourage it. Distributing free textbooks to a racially segregated school would encourage discrimination. Thus, the distribution will be invalid. Since option A mischaracterizes the facts and ignores the central reason the distribution is unconstitutional, it's not the best response.

(B) is not the best response,

because it misstates the law. States *may* aid private schools; the problem here is that such a distribution would foster discrimination, and thus would constitute an equal protection violation.

In order to be valid, a state law must meet a three-part test:

1. It must be enacted within the state's powers (e.g., police powers);
2. It must not violate any person's constitutional rights; and
3. It must not improperly burden interstate commerce.

The distribution of free textbooks would be an exercise of the state's police power, because it aids the welfare of the public. The problem is the second element: the distribution to Little White School House is an equal protection violation. Equal protection is triggered by a classification which determines people's rights. Here, the classification is on the basis of color. While states need not outlaw discrimination, they cannot authorize or encourage it. Distributing free textbooks to a racially segregated school would encourage discrimination. Thus, the distribution will be invalid.

It's not the status of Little White School House as *private* that makes the distribution invalid, but the fact that it's racially segregated. Since B doesn't recognize this, it's not the best response.

(C) is not the best response,

because it misstates the law.

The Constitution does not forbid *private* bias; it only prevents states from enforcing, facilitating, encouraging, or authorizing discrimination. *Shelly v. Kraemer* (1948).

In order to be valid, a state law must meet a three-part test:

1. It must be enacted within the state's powers (e.g., police powers);
2. It must not violate any person's constitutional

rights; and
3. It must not improperly burden interstate commerce.

The distribution of free textbooks would be an exercise of the state's police power, because it aids the welfare of the public. The problem is the second element: the distribution to Little White School House is an equal protection violation. Equal protection is triggered by a classification which determines people's rights. Here, the classification is on the basis of color. While states need not outlaw discrimination, they cannot authorize or encourage it. Distributing free textbooks to a racially segregated school would encourage discrimination. Thus, the distribution will be invalid. Since C doesn't recognize this, and misstates the law, it's not the best response.

Answer 73

(C) is the best response,

because it addresses the test which must be met in order for a law to comport with religious freedoms.

In order to be valid, a state law must meet a three-prong test:

1. The law must be enacted within the state's powers (e.g., police powers);
2. It must not violate any person's constitutional rights; and
3. It must not improperly burden interstate commerce.

The issue under these facts is the second element from this test. By distributing textbooks to a private religious school, the state faces a potential problem under the Establishment Clause of the First Amendment – Congress (and the states, via the Fourteenth Amendment) cannot make a law respecting the establishment of religion. The test used to determine if a governmental action conforms with the First Amendment religion clauses is this one, from *Lemon v. Kurtzman* (1971):

1. The law must have a secular purpose;
2. It must have as its principal or primary effect neither the advancement nor the inhibition of religion;
3. It must not foster excessive government entanglement with religion.

Here, lending secular textbooks to parochial schools would improve secular education, so it would be constitutional. *Board of Education v. Allen* (1968).

Incidentally, the "entanglement" issue is a thorny one. For instance, funding field trips and lending instructional equipment to parochial schools probably isn't permissible, whereas a school lunch program is all right. You can see the hair-splitting which is sometimes done. However, since this question asks for the most likely basis on which this statute would be constitutional, and C is the only one that addresses the correct test from *Lemon v. Kurtzman*, it's the best response.

(A) is not the best response,

because it does not specifically address the constitutionality of the distribution.

In order to be valid, a state law must meet a three-prong test:

1. The law must be enacted within the state's powers (e.g., police powers);
2. It must not violate any person's constitutional rights; and
3. It must not improperly burden interstate commerce.

The fact that parochial schools fulfill an important educational function, as A states, would satisfy the first element – since education is a permissible state function under the police power. However, it's the second element that's the problem, since in distributing textbooks to a private religious school, the state faces a potential problem under the Establishment Clause of the First Amendment – Congress (and the states, via the Fourteenth Amendment) cannot make a law respecting the establishment of religion. The test used to determine if a governmental action conforms with the First Amendment religion clause is this one, from *Lemon v. Kurtzman* (1971):

1. The law must have a secular purpose;
2. It must have as its principal or primary effect neither the advancement nor the inhibition of religion;
3. It must not foster excessive government entanglement with religion.

Since option A doesn't recognize that it's the applicability of this test that's the central issue as to constitutionality of the distribution, A can't be the best response.

(B) isn't the best response,

because although it's theoretically correct, it doesn't address the constitutionality of the distribution.

In order to be valid, a state law must meet a three-prong test:

1. The law must be enacted within the state's powers (e.g., police powers);
2. It must not violate any person's constitutional rights; and
3. It must not improperly burden interstate commerce.

Thus, the mere fact that religious instruction isn't constitutionally objectionable wouldn't make distribution of textbooks to a parochial school permissible. The problem is the second element from the test – in distributing textbooks to a private religious school, the state faces a potential problem under the Establishment Clause of the First Amendment. Congress (and the states, via the Fourteenth Amendment) cannot make a law respecting the establishment of religion. The test used to determine if a governmental action conforms with the First Amendment religion clause is this one, from

Lemon v. Kurtzman (1971):

1. The law must have a secular purpose;
2. It must have as its principal or primary effect neither the advancement nor the inhibition of religion;
3. It must not foster excessive government entanglement with religion.

Since option B doesn't address the issue of constitutionality of the distribution, it's not the best response.

(D) is not the best response,

because it misstates the law.

The free exercise clause doesn't require identical treatment of students in public and private schools. Instead, in order for a statute to conform with First Amendment religious freedoms, it must meet this three-pronged test:

1. The law must have a secular purpose;
2. It must have as its principal or primary effect neither the advancement nor the inhibition of religion;
3. It must not foster excessive government entanglement with religion.

Lemon v. Kurtzman (1971).

This generally will not mean identical treatment, due to the need for the state to avoid entanglement with religion. For instance, funding school field trips and lending instructional equipment to parochial schools might not be permissible, although it would be perfectly appropriate for public schools. Since D misstates the law, it can't be the best response.

Answer 74

(D) is the best response,

because it correctly identifies that the photo identification will be admissible.

There are two separate issues here: first, whether the identification itself comports with Damon's constitutional rights, which is a criminal procedure issue; and second, whether Vera's in-court testimony is admissible, which is an evidence issue.

First, the criminal procedure problem. What's involved here is a pre-trial identification. A pre-trial identification procedure only violates due process if two elements are satisfied:

1. The identification must be unnecessarily suggestive.
2. There must be a substantial likelihood of irreparable mistaken identification.

This is a difficult standard to meet, and is clearly not met by the facts here. Furthermore, there's no right to counsel for photo identifications, so the evidence here won't be excludable on that basis.

Second, the evidence issue. More specifically, the problem is one of hearsay. Hearsay is an out-of-court statement offered to prove the truth of its assertion. Here, it's Vera's fingering of Damon, as the culprit, out-of-court, which amounts to an assertion, since she's in effect saying, "He did it!" However, as a prior identification of a person made by a presently testifying witness, the statement will be *excluded* from hearsay, under FRE 801(d)(1). There may be another evidence issue that nagged at you here, and that is that Vera didn't actually see Damon – she was clubbed from behind. However, this is an issue of credibility, and since Vera is testifying, Damon's lawyer could attack her on this issue on cross-examination. Perry Mason would certainly make mincemeat out of her. However, Vera's not having actually seen Damon doesn't make her testimony inadmissible, as D identifies. In fact, since D is the only option that correctly identifies that the photo identification will be admissible, it's the best response.

(A) is not the best response,

because it does not represent a sound basis on which to exclude Vera's pre-trial identification, and it arrives at the wrong result.

A prior identification of a person, made by a presently testifying witness, is admissible as an exclusion from the hearsay rule. FRE 801(d)(1). That's what's going on here. Vera identified Damon from the photographs. The quality of the declarant's opportunity to see the person can be attacked on cross-examination. If she didn't get a chance to see Damon, the opposing attorney will draw this out and destroy her credibility. This alone doesn't provide a sound basis on which to exclude her testimony. This is actually quite a difficult call, because an underlying issue here is the fact that Vera didn't, apparently, see Damon at all, and so you could question whether she's a competent witness as to his identity (since a witness must have personal knowledge of the matter on which he testifies, under FRE 602). However, option A gives you a hint that it's not the best response by adding the word "good" to Vera's opportunity to see Damon. *Any* opportunity, no matter how insignificant, would give her a basis for testifying; option A overstates what would be required by stating that the opportunity to observe must be "good." Since A doesn't recognize that the identification will be admissible, it is not be the best response.

(B) is not the best response,

because it misstates the law, and arrives at the wrong result.

The correct rule is that the suspect does not have a right of counsel at a photographic identification. *U.S. v. Ash* (1973). In a photo identification, the suspect is not even *present,* so the rationale of the right to counsel in line up situations – to prevent the suspect from suffering for his inability to identify and object to prejudicial conditions – does not exist.

In fact, the prior identification will be admissible as an exclusion from the hearsay rule, since it fits all the requirements of the exclusion: Vera is a presently testifying witness who can be cross-examined, and the identification was made after perceiving the one identi-

fied. FRE 801(d)(1). (If the identification weren't expressly excluded from the hearsay rule, it would be considered hearsay, because it was an out-of-court statement, in the form of assertive conduct, offered to prove the truth of its assertion – that Damon was the culprit. By identifying him, Vera was effectively saying: "That's him!") Although it's not clear from these facts *when* exactly Vera snuck a peak at Damon, Damon's lawyer will be able to attack her credibility on cross-examination. Since B ignores the fact that the identification will be admissible, and states a criminal procedure problem where in fact none exists, it's not the best response.

(C) is not the best response,

because although it states a potential theoretical basis on which to exclude the evidence, it does not apply to these facts.

A photo identification can be "unnecessarily suggestive" where, for instance, the other photos are of people who look significantly different than the suspect (e.g., of a different race). Since this focuses attention on the suspect, it's considered a due process violation. *Foster v. California* (1969). However, this doesn't apply to these facts, which state that the other seven people photographed "have the same general features as Damon." As a result, the photo identification would not be unnecessarily suggestive. Since option C states an inappropriate basis on which to exclude the pre-trial identification, and in fact the evidence is admissible as a prior identification made by a presently testifying witness, C is not the best response.

Answer 75

(B) is the best response,

because it represents the defense, of these four options, which is most likely to result in Defendant's acquittal. This is a difficult question, because none of the responses is particularly bad.

Criminal assault requires either an attempt to commit a battery, or the intentional and physical creation of fear of imminent bodily harm in the mind of the victim. Criminal battery requires unlawful application of force to the person of another, resulting in bodily injury or offensive touching. The conduct battery requires must be *voluntary,* and that's what's missing here. The facts clearly state that Defendant was in the throes of an epileptic fit when the ostensibly criminal conduct occurred. Since epilepsy is a classic situation where the actor's actions are considered involuntary, Defendant would not be liable for assault and battery by so behaving. As a result, B is the best response.

(A) is not the best response,

because the status of hypnosis as removing the voluntariness of one's actions is not a settled matter of law.

Criminal assault requires either an attempt to commit a battery, or the intentional and physical creation of fear of imminent bodily harm in the mind of the victim. Criminal battery requires unlawful application of force to the person of another, resulting in bodily injury or offensive touching. In order to be criminally liable for battery, the actor must act *voluntarily.* Defendant's state of hypnosis would suggest that he was not capable of acting voluntarily; however, not all states accept this. Since hypnosis is not a defense that would *clearly* prevail in most states, and there is another response which is more firmly grounded in law, A is not the best response.

(C) is not the best response,

because although intoxication is a potential defense, it is not at all clear under these facts whether an intoxication defense could prevail.

Criminal assault requires either an attempt to commit a battery, or the intentional and physical creation of fear of imminent bodily harm in the mind of the victim. Criminal battery requires unlawful application of force to the person of another, resulting in bodily injury or offensive touching. Option C suggests a potential defense. However, voluntary intoxication is only a defense if it negates one of the elements necessary to commit the crime. Under these facts, it isn't entirely clear whether Defendant was too drunk to appreciate the dangerousness of his behavior. Even though the facts state that Defendant didn't specifically realize Victim was nearby, his behavior could have been considered as creating an unreasonable risk nonetheless. As a result, C is not the best response.

(D) is not the best response,

because to succeed Defendant would have to prove either that his act was involuntary, or that his belief Victim was attacking him was reasonable.

Criminal assault requires either an attempt to commit a battery, or the intentional and physical creation of fear of imminent bodily harm in the mind of the victim. Criminal battery requires unlawful application of force to the person of another, resulting in bodily injury or offensive touching. In order to be criminally liable for battery, the actor must act *voluntarily.* Although the facts state that Defendant was not entirely aware of what was going on, this in and of itself would not necessarily make his actions involuntary (which is what such a defense would require). Alternatively, if Defendant argued self-defense, he would have to prove that his belief Victim was attacking him was a reasonable belief. There are not facts here to indicate Defendant could prove this. As a result, D is not the best response.

Answer 76

(D) is the best response,

because it correctly identifies the issue which will determine *News's* liability. Understanding why requires a fairly detailed knowledge of the basic hierarchy of

defamation claims against media defendants:

1. If a plaintiff is a public figure and the issue is "public" – plaintiff must prove malice (i.e., knowing falsehood or reckless disregard for the truth);
2. If plaintiff is a public figure, but the issues involves his personal, private life, plaintiff need only prove negligence, not malice;
3. If plaintiff is a private figure, plaintiff need only prove negligence, not malice;
4. Regardless of the status of the plaintiff, is the item is "newsworthy," malice must be proven.

Thus, under these facts, arriving at the correct response requires that you 1. correctly characterize Wife as a private individual (since she lacks the "notoriety" a public figure requires), and 2. apply the negligence standard to it. The "ordinary care" language in D is referring to a negligence standard, since if one uses ordinary care he *cannot* be negligent. Note that D scrupulously avoids *concluding* whether *News* was negligent or not; it uses the modifier "if" instead of "because." As with any option using "if," you have to determine if the reasoning plausibly applies to the facts, whether it resolves a central issue, and whether the result is consistent with the reasoning. These are all satisfied here. While the *News* could always have done more to check the facts, the reporter did rely on two "very reliable" sources. Thus, it's possible he used reasonable care in verifying the truth of the story, and as a result wouldn't be liable for negligence. As a rule of thumb, negligence could be shown, for instance, by a *failure* to check sources. (On a related note, malice would require more: whether the reporter entertained serious doubts about the truth of what he was printing.) Since D correctly identifies the standard that will determine if *News* is liable, and the result it offers is consistent with the reasoning, it's the best response.

(A) is not the best response,

because it only addresses *part* of what Wife would have to prove, on these facts, to prevail. Realizing why A isn't sufficient requires a quick refresher on the "hierarchy" of defamation claims against media defendants:

1. If a plaintiff is a public figure and the issue is "public" – plaintiff must prove malice (i.e., knowing falsehood or reckless disregard for the truth);
2. If plaintiff is a public figure, but the issues involves his personal, private life, plaintiff need only prove negligence, not malice;
3. If plaintiff is a private figure, plaintiff need only prove negligence, not malice.
4. Regardless of the status of the plaintiff, is the item is "newsworthy," malice must be proven.

Here, there's no real question but that Wife is a private individual, not a public figure, so the observation in A – that the issue involves her personal, private life – is not relevant (she probably couldn't be considered a public figure in relation to her husband, especially since they are long divorced and the incident alleged occurred almost thirty years ago). What *is* relevant is whether or not *News* was negligent in its fact-checking. If it was, it will be liable; if it wasn't, it won't. Since A focuses on a fact that in and of itself won't determine who'll prevail, it's not the best response.

(B) is not the best response,

because it understates the standard necessary for holding *News* liable for defamation.

A statement must be false to be defamatory – however, some level of fault will also have to be proven. With a private individual as a plaintiff, the defendant would have to have been at least *negligent* in failing to determine that what it reported was false. If you chose this response, you probably had in mind the common law rule, which made defamation a strict liability offense. Since modern courts require fault, and B doesn't recognize this, it's not the best response.

(C) is not the best response,

because even without the element it offers, *News* could *still* be liable.

The reasoning in C states the definition of malice. However, malice isn't required here. Where a media defendant and a private individual plaintiff are concerned, the rule is this: no recovery for defamation is allowed unless the defendant was at least negligent. If the defendant was negligent but without malice, the plaintiff will prevail in the action (but won't be able to claim punitives without proof of malice).

If you chose this response, it's probably because you confused the rule for public figure plaintiffs with the rule for private figures. Public figures suing for defamatory statements about public matters must prove malice in order to recover. However, since Wife will be considered a private individual – being married years ago to a local labor leader would not give her the notoriety necessary to be considered a public figure – she need only prove negligence. Note that option C *does* correctly characterize the facts, since *News* did not have malice, since malice would require, at the very least, that the reporter entertained serious doubts about the truth of what he was printing. However, since C states a standard that is stricter than the on that will apply, it's not the best response.

Answer 77

(C) is the best response,

because it identifies the central reason why Utility will be liable for Farmer's injuries.

A private nuisance – which is probably the type involved here, due to the small scope of injury – is an act by defendant which creates an unreasonable, substantial interference with plaintiff's use and enjoyment of property. Here, Utility deliberately created the fumes, and they harmed Farmer. The creator of a private nuisance is liable for all harm resulting proximately from the nuisance, both personal (including diseases like

Farmer's) and property. That's all there is to it. What's important to note here is that it doesn't matter how feasible alternatives are, like the scrubbing equipment. Once the nuisance is created, there's liability. Since C correctly identifies the central reason Utility will be liable, it's the best response.

(A) is not the best response,

because it focuses on a fact which is irrelevant.

All private nuisance requires is an act by defendant creating an unreasonable, substantial interference with plaintiff's use or enjoyment of property. Thus, the ease with which the defendant could prevent the nuisance is *irrelevant*. As a result, in nuisance, it's important to focus on the damage to plaintiff, *not* the fault of defendant. Since A ignores this, it's not the best response.

(B) is not the best response,

because it's not clear that it appropriately characterizes the facts, and even if it *does*, it would not prevent Farmer from recovering for nuisance.

The distinction between a public and a private nuisance is the scope of the injury. A public nuisance affects the community at large through an act or condition which unreasonably interferes with the health, safety, or convenience of the general public (e.g., blocking a public highway, operating a brothel). A private nuisance, on the other hand, requires an act by defendant creating an unreasonable, substantial interference with plaintiff's use or enjoyment of property. While the fumes here might affect the community in general, the facts here tell you Farmer's land is adjacent to, and downwind from, the plant, and there's no mention of others being affected. Assuming arguendo that the nuisance is public and not private, Farmer will be able to recover damages nonetheless. Normally, public nuisance suits are brought by the state. In order for a private person to recover for public nuisance, he has to prove that he suffered special damages above and beyond the ordinary damage the public incurred. Here, Farmer's proximity to the fumes, and the damages he suffered, suggest he would probably be able to recover under a public nuisance claim. Thus, since B probably does not correctly characterize the facts, and the fact it cites is irrelevant, it's not the best response.

(D) is not the best response,

because there's no causation between the ultra-hazardous activity and Farmer's damages.

Private nuisance is an act by defendant which creates an unreasonable, substantial interference with plaintiff's use or enjoyment of property. Here, it's not the electricity that creates the interference, but the fumes emitted by the plant, which is *not* an ultrahazardous activity. Had Farmer been electrocuted by downed power lines, say, there *would* be causation. In fact, Utility will be liable in nuisance for the interference created by the fumes. Thus, the ultrahazardous nature of electricity is not a central concern in this problem, making D not the best response.

Answer 78

(A) is the best response,

because it correctly identifies the main reason Utility won't be liable: it wasn't negligent.

One is only negligent if he failed to exercise such care as a reasonable person in his position would have exercised, this was a breach of the duty to prevent the foreseeable risk of harm to anyone in plaintiff's position, and this breach caused plaintiff's damages.

The lynchpin of a negligence claim is that defendant's conduct *must have been unreasonable*. If it wasn't, defendant cannot be liable for negligence. It's this unreasonability which is missing from these facts, due to a variety of factors, including the fact that Utility used the best practicable technology, the scrubbing equipment was ultra-expensive and not very effective, no other plant used the equipment, and Utility was located in a sparsely-populated area. These combine to make Utility's conduct reasonable and as a result non-negligent. Since option A recognizes this as the central issue and resolves it correctly, it's the best response.

(B) is not the best response,

because it ignores the fact that Utility was not negligent, and, in any case, imposes too strict a duty on Farmer. Under these facts Utility was not negligent because it did not behave unreasonably. The facts tell you it utilized the "best practicable technology," that no other plant has installed the ultra-expensive scrubbing equipment, and that Utility was built in a rural area, all suggesting a lack of negligence.

Assume arguendo that Utility was negligent. B *still* wouldn't be the best response, since it's unlikely Farmer's delay in selling by one year would be considered contributorily negligent; and, in any case he'd still suffer losses in the form of a lower valuation on the farm than before the Utility was built. For one thing, it may not have been obvious that the fumes would be so deleterious in 1995. And if it *were* obvious, no buyer would pay a price reflecting the pre-Utility value of the farm, so there would be no way to mitigate.

Nonetheless, the principle error B makes is ignoring Utility's non-negligence. As a result, it's not the best response.

(C) is not the best response,

because it skirts the issue of negligence.

Utility's failure to install the scrubbing equipment would only create liability if it was unreasonable *not* to do so. In fact, Utility's conduct was not negligent at all, suggested by the facts that it used the best practicable technology, the scrubbing equipment was ultra-expensive and not very effective, no other plant used the equipment, and Utility was located in a sparsely-populated area.

Say instead that not using the equipment was negligent. Then it's possible that C would adequately represent Farmer's damages. However, since C ignores the central issue, it's not the best response.

(D) is not the best response,

because it's irrelevant to Utility's liability for negligence.

Nuisance is an act creating a substantial, unreasonable interference with plaintiff's use and enjoyment of his property. Thus, a nuisance need not be unreasonable. Negligence, on the other hand, requires unreasonable behavior. As a result, D does not address an issue that will determine Utility's liability for negligence, making it not the best response.

Answer 79

(A) is the best response,

because it correctly identifies that the testimony here is admissible as a response to a hypothetical question.

Expert testimony is appropriate where the court determines that *"scientific, technical, or other specialized knowledge will assist the trier of fact to understand the evidence or to determine a fact in issue."* FRE 702. Here, physician's testimony will address the causation issue – whether or not flaming underwear could cause a heart attack. Physician's status as an expert entitles him to offer opinion evidence which would be inadmissible coming from a lay witness, and to rely on information unavailable to a lay witness.

An expert may testify on three types of information: Personal observation (under FRE 703); facts presented to the expert at trial, e.g., a hypothetical question (FRE 705); or facts introduced to the expert outside the courtroom (e.g., by technicians or consultants) of the type upon which experts in his field reasonably rely (FRE 703). Since a hypothetical question is expressly permissible under the FRE, and A recognizes this, it's the best response.

(B) is not the best response,

because it states an incorrect rule, and addresses a non-issue under these facts.

First, Phillips' credibility is not an issue here, because you're told to assume the truth of Phillips' testimony. Thus, his credibility *must* be intact.

Assuming arguendo that Phillips' credibility was an issue, Jones's status as a physician wouldn't give him expert status in determining credibility. As a threshold matter, credibility itself is not a "fact," and expert testimony is only available to assist the trier of fact to understand evidence or to determine a fact in issue. FRE 702. Beyond that, a physician's expertise gives him the ability to offer opinion testimony on medical matters. It's irrelevant to assessing the credibility of testimony, since one's status as a doctor doesn't make him into Carnak the Magnificent, a mind reader. Instead, Jones will address the causation issue: whether flaming underwear could cause a heart attack.

As a physician, he could offer expert opinion testimony on this issue, which a lay witness could not offer. Since B states otherwise, it's not the correct response.

(C) is not the best response,
because it states an incorrect rule.

An expert may testify on three types of information: personal observation (under FRE 703); facts presented to the expert at trial, e.g., a hypothetical question (FRE 705); or facts introduced to the expert outside the courtroom (e.g., by technicians or consultants) of the type upon which experts in his field reasonably rely (FRE 703). Thus, the Federal Rules specifically allow the use of hypothetical questions in expert testimony, and since there is no stated limit on the source from which hypotheticals may be drawn, there's no reason why hypotheticals couldn't be based on prior testimony. In fact, such a hypothetical is most likely to be helpful to the jury, and to be relevant. Since C doesn't recognize this, it's not the best response.

(D) is not the correct response,
because it states an incorrect rule.

An expert may testify on three types of information: personal observation (under FRE 703); facts presented to the expert at trial, e.g., a hypothetical question (FRE 705); or facts introduced to the expert outside the courtroom (e.g., by technicians or consultants) of the type upon which experts in his field reasonably rely (FRE 703). An expert could rely on other testimony, and this presumably would be from laypeople. Also, in forming a diagnosis, for instance, a physician would rely on statements made to him by laypeople, including his patient and even others, including the victim's relatives. Beyond that, when you delve a little further, Dr. Jones would not be depending solely on information provided by laypeople; to a large extent his testimony would rely on his background in medicine, the basis of his status as an expert, which would tell him whether or not flaming underwear could cause a heart attack. In any case, D is incorrect in making the blanket statement that an expert cannot rely on information provided by lay people, and as a result it's not the best response.

Answer 80

(B) is the best response,
since it correctly conditions admissibility of Dr. Black's testimony on whether such reports are reasonably relied upon in medical practice.

An expert may testify on three types of information: personal observation (under FRE 703); facts presented to the expert at trial, e.g., a hypothetical question (FRE 705); or facts introduced to the expert outside the courtroom (e.g., by technicians or consultants) of the type upon which experts in his field reasonably rely (FRE 703).

Note that option B uses the modifier "if." That means

that, in order to be correct, option B must satisfy these three requirements: 1. The reasoning must be plausible on the facts; 2. It must resolve a significant issue; and 3. The result must be consistent with the reasoning. Here, there's nothing in the facts that suggests that blood study reports aren't relied upon by physicians. If they are relied upon by physicians, this would make Dr. Black's testimony admissible, under FRE 703. Thus, option B resolves a central issue, and the result is consistent with the reasoning. As a result, B is the best response.

(A) is not the best response,
because the status of the laboratory reports as business records is *irrelevant,* since it's not the reports that are being offered into evidence, but Dr. Black's testimony based on them.

The admissibility of the testimony depends on whether expert testimony can be based on such reports. An expert may testify on three types of information: personal observation (under FRE 703); facts presented to the expert at trial, e.g., a hypothetical question (FRE 705); or facts introduced to the expert outside the courtroom (e.g., by technicians or consultants) of the type upon which experts in his field reasonably rely (FRE 703). Thus, if physicians typically rely on blood study reports conducted by independent laboratories, there will be a sound basis for Dr. Black's expert testimony. In fact, as they pertain to expert testimony, it wouldn't matter if the reports themselves were inadmissible, because expert testimony can be based on inadmissible evidence.

Incidentally, the reports themselves *could* be admissible under the business records exception to the hearsay rule, FRE 803(6). The requirements for the rule are: the entry must be made in the regular course of business, in conjunction with a business activity, entered under a duty to record, entered by one with personal knowledge of matters recorded or transmitted from such a person, entered at or near the time of the transaction, and the record must be authenticated at trial.

Since A ignores the central issue here – the admissibility of expert testimony – it's not the best response.

(C) is not the best response,
because the requirement it states would not, in fact, be a prerequisite for Dr. Black's testimony.

An expert may testify on three types of information: personal observation (under FRE 703); facts presented to the expert at trial, e.g., a hypothetical question (FRE 705); or facts introduced to the expert outside the courtroom (e.g., by technicians or consultants) of the type upon which experts in his field reasonably rely (FRE 703).

Here, option C uses the qualifier "unless." That means that there must be no other way the testimony would be admissible other than if Dr. Black were qualified to conduct such tests. In fact, that's not the case. Dr. Black would not necessarily have to be qualified to *conduct* laboratory blood analyses in order to be qualified to *analyze their results.* In any case, her ability to analyze results of blood studies would have been part of qualifying her as an expert witness in the first place. The facts here do not focus on her qualifications, and as a result C is not applicable, making it not the best response.

(D) is not the best response,

because it misstates the rule of law.

An expert may testify on three types of information: personal observation (under FRE 703); facts presented to the expert at trial, e.g., a hypothetical question (FRE 705); or facts introduced to the expert outside the courtroom (e.g., by technicians or consultants) of the type upon which experts in his field reasonably rely (FRE 703).

Thus, if physicians *normally* rely on blood studies prepared by independent labs, then this will be a proper basis for expert testimony. In any case, D states as a conclusion that expert testimony *cannot* be based on tests performed by those not under the expert's supervision, and this is a clear misstatement of the rule under the FRE. As a result, D is not the best response.

Answer 81

(D) is the best response,

because it correctly identifies that the reason for admitting the testimony is that the payroll records relate to a collateral matter, and thus the payroll records themselves are not required in order to admit the testimony.

The central issue here is applicability of the Best Evidence Rule. The Best Evidence Rule is triggered when a party wants to prove the material terms of a writing, or a witness is testifying relying on a writing. Under those circumstances, the original writing (which includes photocopies and carbons) must be produced; copies and oral testimony concerning the writing's contents are only permissible on a showing of the original's unavailability not the result of proponent's serious misconduct. FRE 1002. The rationale for this rule is that errors or gaps in memory, as well as fraud, can be avoided by allowing the trier of fact to see the writing itself, if the writing is available.

Under these facts, while the payroll records would be the best evidence of the date, the Best Evidence Rule – requiring introduction of the original document, if available – does not apply to *"writings, records, or photographs not closely related to a controlling issue."* FRE 1004(4). Here, the issue is purely collateral – reinforcing Phillips' memory. You know this because the question specifically tells you that the date is "a fact of minor importance in the case." As a result, the testimony would be admissible without offering the payroll records (or explaining their unavailability).

Note that the hearsay rule would still have to be satis-

fied, because Phillips' testimony about the payroll records would be considered hearsay: out-of-court statements (namely, those in the payroll records stating in effect that "Today is X date") being offered to prove the truth of their assertions, namely, the date of Opening Day. While D does not refer to this, it's a safe bet that the payroll records would be admissible under the business records exception to the hearsay rule, FRE 803(6). D instead confronts the main issue, which is that the testimony will be admissible without requiring that the payroll records be introduced due to the collateral nature of Phillips' memory. As a result, D is the best response.

(A) is not the best response,

because it mistakenly invokes the Best Evidence Rule.

The Best Evidence Rule is triggered when a party wants to prove the material terms of a writing, or a witness is testifying relying on a writing. Under those circumstances, the original writing (which includes photocopies and carbons) must be produced; copies and oral testimony concerning the writing's contents are only permissible on a showing of the original's unavailability not the result of proponent's serious misconduct. FRE 1002. The rationale for this rule is that errors or gaps in memory, as well as fraud, can be avoided by allowing the trier of fact to see the writing itself, if the writing is available.

Under these facts, while the payroll records would be the best evidence of the date, the Best Evidence Rule – requiring introduction of the original document, if available – does not apply to *"writings, records, or photographs not closely related to a controlling issue."* FRE 1004(4). Here, the issue is purely collateral – reinforcing Phillips' memory. You know this because the question specifically tells you that the date is "a fact of minor importance in the case." As a result, the testimony would be admissible without offering the payroll records (or explaining their unavailability). Since A states otherwise, it's not the best response.

(B) is not the best response,

because it fails to recognize that the payroll records would be admissible under the business records exception to the hearsay rule.

The Best Evidence Rule is triggered when a party wants to prove the material terms of a writing, or a witness is testifying relying on a writing. Under those circumstances, the original writing (which includes photocopies and carbons) must be produced; copies and oral testimony concerning the writing's contents are only permissible on a showing of the original's unavailability not the result of proponent's serious misconduct. FRE 1002. The rationale for this rule is that errors or gaps in memory, as well as fraud, can be avoided by allowing the trier of fact to see the writing itself, if the writing is available.

Under these facts, while the payroll records would be

the best evidence of the date, the Best Evidence Rule – requiring introduction of the original document, if available – does not apply to *"writings, records, or photographs not closely related to a controlling issue."* FRE 1004(4). Here, the issue is purely collateral – reinforcing Phillips' memory. You know this because the question specifically tells you that the date is "a fact of minor importance in the case."

While Phillips' testimony is not subject to the Best Evidence Rule, it will nonetheless be subject to the hearsay rule. The payroll records here would be considered hearsay (since they are out-of-court statements offered to prove the truth of their assertion, namely, the date of Opening Day), but they would probably be admissible under the business records hearsay exception, FRE 803(6). Under that exception, such records are admissible if the entries are made in the regular course of business, in conjunction with a business activity, entered under a duty to record, entered by one with personal knowledge of the matters recorded or transmitted from such a person, entered at or near the time of the transaction (and the records must be authenticated at trial). While there's a possibility that the records here wouldn't satisfy all these requirements, they probably would, and B states unequivocally that such records would be inadmissible hearsay. As a result, B is not the best response.

(C) is not the best response,

because it states a factor which is irrelevant to whether or not a fact is subject to judicial notice, and, in any case, the fact here would not likely be subject to judicial notice.

Option C uses the modifier "if." That means that the reasoning must be plausible on the facts, it must resolve a significant issue, and the result must be consistent with the reasoning. Here, it's plausible that the judge personally knew the date of Opening Day. However, this doesn't resolve a central issue, because the judge's personal knowledge is irrelevant to judicial notice. The only thing relevant to judicial notice is whether the fact is subject to common knowledge in the community OR capable of positive verification through readily accessible, undeniably accurate sources. FRE 201(b).

Beyond that, it's not likely that the date of Opening Day would be within the scope of judicial notice. Judicial notice can only be taken of *adjudicative* facts. FRE 201(a). Adjudicative facts are those concerning the particular event giving rise to the lawsuit. Here, what's important is the date when Phillips bought the flammable underwear; the day baseball season opens doesn't have anything to do with that, and thus it's not an adjudicative fact, and can't be subject to judicial notice.

In any case, since C conditions the admissibility of the testimony on the judge's personal knowledge of the date of Opening Day, it's not the best response.

Answer 82

(B) is the best response,

because it represents the most likely basis on which HDS could get the prior oral agreement admitted into evidence.

In order to be HDS's best argument, the reasoning must be both legally correct and applicable to these facts. Determining this requires analysis of the facts under the Parol Evidence Rule. Under that rule, a written agreement which is "completely integrated" may not be contracted or supplemented with evidence of prior written or oral agreements, or contemporaneous oral agreements. A "completely integrated" agreement is one which the parties intended to be a final and complete statement of their agreement.

A "partially integrated" agreement, on the other hand, is one which is final, but not complete. As a result, unlike a completely integrated agreement, it *may* be supplemented by consistent additional terms.

Determining whether a written agreement is partially or completely integrated is subject to a wide variety of tests, but the presumption typically is that the writing is only a partial integration barring clear evidence to the contrary. Under these facts, the very fact that there was no mention of coordination in the written agreement suggests that the writing was *not* complete even though it was final as to the terms it stated. Thus, HDS could successfully argue on these facts that the agreement was only partially integrated, and legally this would result in HDS's being able to introduce evidence of the coordination provision as a consistent additional term. Since B represents HDS's best argument both factually and legally, it's the best response.

(A) is not the best response,

because although it states a correct legal theory, it doesn't apply to the facts here.

Under the Parol Evidence Rule, a writing that is "completely integrated" cannot be contradicted or supplemented with prior written or oral agreements, or contemporaneous oral agreements. A "completely integrated" agreement is one which the parties intended to be a final and complete statement of their agreement.

While it's true that evidence may be admitted to *interpret* the agreement, the oral agreement on coordinating with HDS's methods of accounting wouldn't do that, since this isn't addressed in the written agreement *at all*. At common law, additional evidence would be admitted to interpret a term only if the contract contains an ambiguity. (Under the UCC, no ambiguity is required, but the UCC wouldn't apply here since this is likely a *service* contract, not a transaction in goods.)

In fact, the fact that this issue doesn't appear in the written contract would suggest that the written agreement didn't embody the entire agreement between the parties and thus was not completely integrated. When a writing is a *partial* integration, it may not be contradicted but it *may* be supplemented by additional, consistent terms. That's HDS's best argument for admitting evidence of the oral agreement. Since A doesn't recognize this, it's not the best response.

(C) is not the best response,

because although it implies a rule that is correct in theory, it would not apply to these facts.

Under the Parol Evidence Rule, a writing that is "completely integrated" cannot be contradicted or supplemented with prior written or oral agreements, or contemporaneous oral agreements. A "completely integrated" agreement is one which the parties intended to be a final and complete statement of their agreement. The parol evidence rule does *not* bar evidence of defects in contract formation, like lack of consideration, fraud, and duress. However, mere detrimental reliance on an oral promise would not, in and of itself, rise to the level of fraud.

Instead, HDS should argue that the written agreement was only partially integrated – that is, that it didn't represent the *complete* agreement. A partially integrated agreement *may* be supplemented by consistent additional terms. The oral "coordination" clause would likely be a consistent additional term, and this is, as a result, HDS's best chance of having it admitted. Since HDS's detrimental reliance would be insufficient by itself to allow admission of the coordination term, and C fails to recognize this, C isn't the best response.

(D) is not the best response,

because it's exactly the opposite of what HDS *would* want to argue.

A partially integrated agreement is a written agreement which does not reflect the *complete* agreement of the parties. It's final as to the terms it states, but it may be supplemented by consistent additional terms. In fact, arguing that the memo here is a partial integration is HDS's best chance of getting the coordination term admitted into evidence, since there's nothing in the contract to contradict it.

If the written contract isn't a partial integration, it's either not integrated at all, or fully integrated. HDS couldn't argue that it's not integrated because this wouldn't comport with the facts, which show that the parties intended the writing to be final as to the terms it includes. HDS wouldn't want to argue that it's completely integrated, because that would preclude admission of a prior oral agreement supplementing the written agreement, which is what the "coordination" provision would do. Since D represents an argument that would not be advantageous to HDS, it's not the best response.

Answer 83

(D) is the best response,

because it identifies the central reason CP won't be entitled to half-payment on June 6: interpretation of the payment clause.

As a general rule, contract terms are interpreted objectively, by determining what interpretation a reasonable person, knowing all that the parties know, would place on the terms. Under this question, interpretation of the payment provision centers on the meaning of "within one month of completion," since "of" *could* mean "before" *or* "after". However, if you look at the rest of the terms, "of" must mean "after," because there's no way to determine if CP satisfactorily performed under the contract until its work is complete, since that's the only time when HDS can determine if CP shortened the processing time by half. If CP didn't do so, it's not entitled to payment. (Substantial performance wouldn't suffice, because the condition here is *express,* not implied or constructive). Thus, "of" must mean "after," and CP is thus not entitled to $10,000 on June 6, one month *before* completion. Since D recognizes this, it's the best response.

(A) is not the best response,

because it doesn't reflect the interpretation that would be given to the payment provision.

As a general rule, contract terms are interpreted objectively, by determining what interpretation a reasonable person (knowing all that the parties know) would place on the terms. Under these facts, the central issue is the meaning of "within one month of completion," since "of" *could* mean "before" *or* "after." However if you look at the rest of the terms, "of" must mean "after," because there's no way to determine if CP satisfactorily performed under the contract until its work is complete, since that's the only time when HDS can determine if CP shortened the processing time by half. If CP didn't do this, it's not entitled to payment. Thus, CP's completing the work is a condition precedent to HDS's duty to pay, and nothing is due until CP is finished, and even then there's one month before payment is due. Since A doesn't recognize this, it's not the best response.

(B) is not the best response,

because it does not reflect the interpretation a court would place on the payment term.

As a general rule, contract terms are interpreted objectively, by determining what interpretation a reasonable person (knowing all that the parties know) would place on the terms. Under these facts, the issue is the meaning of "within one month of completion," and whether this means "before" or "after" completion. In fact, the rest of the contract indicates that "of" *must* mean "after" completion. Even if it *didn't,* there's *nothing* in the contract to suggest that CP is entitled to half payment when the work is half done. In fact, CP's performance under the contract would be a condition precedent to HDS's duty to pay, since this is a normal arrangement, and there's nothing in the contract to suggest that HDS and CP intended otherwise. Since C places an unreasonable interpretation on the payment provision, it's not the best response.

(C) is not the best response,

because it mischaracterizes the condition precedent here, and as a result misstates HDS's duty to pay.

In a typical contract, where one party is to perform services for another in return for payment, the services are considered a condition precedent to the duty to pay, meaning the services must be substantially performed in order to trigger the other party's duty to pay. However, that applies to conditions which are implied or constructive. Here, CP's work would be considered an *express* condition, because the duty to pay is conditioned upon CP's work resulting in a 50 percent time savings in processing. An *express* condition must be strictly met; substantial performance will not suffice.

Even if the condition wasn't express, the nature of the contract suggests that HDS's duty to pay *couldn't* be triggered by *substantial* performance, because it couldn't be determined if the 50 percent time savings was realized until the work was *fully* complete. Thus, even if the condition wasn't express, the reasoning in option C couldn't be correct, making it not the best response.

Answer 84

(A) is the best response,

because it recognizes the central reason the modification is enforceable: it's supported by consideration.

As a general rule, subsequent oral modifications are valid as long as they are supported by consideration and are not covered by the Statute of Frauds. (Note that *subsequent* modifications are *not* covered by the Parol Evidence Rule.)

Consideration requires bargained-for exchange and either detriment to the promisee or benefit to the promisor, and typically both. Detriment can take the form of one's refraining from doing something he's legally entitled to do. Here, both parties could insist on the original payment terms. Their good-faith surrendering of their rights due to an honest dispute represents, as A implies, valid consideration.

Note that the "no oral modifications" term of the contract wouldn't control, because it would be considered waived by the oral modification (ironic, isn't it?). Since A recognizes that the modification will be valid because it's supported by consideration, it's the best response.

(B) is not the best response,

because it offers a blanket statement which is not true under some circumstances.

In general, unless a contract falls within the Statute of Frauds, it is valid and enforceable without a writing. Here, since none of the traditional bases of a writing requirement apply (e.g., sale of interest in land), the only possible applicable Statute of Frauds would be under the UCC (assuming the contract would be considered a transaction in goods, not services). Where a

sale of goods is involved, the general rule is that if the goods have a price of at least $50, a writing will be required. As to modifications, if the contract as modified would fall under the Statute of Frauds, the UCC requires a writing. §2-209. Thus, the blanket statement in B is not correct, since subsequent oral modifications *may* be subject to the Statute of Frauds.

Instead, the modification won't need to be in writing because it only changes the manner of payment, and as such it wouldn't be covered by the Statute of Frauds. Thus, if the modification is enforceable otherwise, the absence of a writing won't torpedo its validity. Since B states otherwise, it's not the best response.

(C) is not the best response,

because the modification will be valid even though the contract specifically called for modifications to be in writing.

As a general rule, subsequent oral modifications to a contract are valid, as long as they aren't subject to the Statute of Frauds (which the one here wouldn't be), and as long as they are supported by consideration.

If you chose this response, you probably focused on the "no oral modification" clause of the contract. Regardless of whether the contract is governed by the UCC (as a transaction in goods), the provision will not control. At common law, such provisions are normally not enforced, because the modification *implicitly* includes an agreement by the parties to waive the writing requirement of the contract. The UCC, in theory, upholds "no oral modifications" provisions, §2-209(2), and in fact the UCC allows for waiver if retracting the waiver would be unjust due to a material change in position in reliance on the waiver. §2-209(4) and 209(5). Here, it would be unjust to retract the waiver, since HDS coughed up $10,000 in reliance on the waiver.

Thus, regardless of whether the common law or the UCC controls, the modification here can be valid even though it's oral. Since C doesn't recognize this, it's not the best response.

(D) isn't the best response,

because it misstates the facts: the modification *was* supported by consideration.

As a general rule, subsequent oral modifications are valid as long as they are supported by consideration and are not covered by the Statute of Frauds. (Note that *subsequent* modifications are *not* covered by the Parol Evidence Rule.)

Consideration requires bargained-for exchange and either detriment to the promisee or benefit to the promisor. Detriment can take the form of one's refraining from doing something he's legally entitled to do. Here, both parties could legally insist on the original payment terms. Thus, the modification represents a detriment to both of them, and as a result it's supported by consideration. Since D doesn't recognize this, it's not the best

response.

Answer 85

(C) is the best response,

because it recognizes why HDS can't renounce the contract.

Under non-UCC contracts (i.e., those not involved with transactions in goods), a reasonable delay will ordinary be considered a *minor* breach of contract, *unless* the contract itself provides that "time is of the essence," in which case *any* delay would be a *material* breach.

Here, there was only a five-day delay, and there's nothing to indicate any reason why CP should have considered the July 1 deadline essential, at the time the contract was created. Thus, the delay was only a *minor* breach, requiring that HDS pay, and recover any damages it suffered because of the delay.

Even if the UCC had applied to this contract, the "perfect tender" rule would not have applied to entitle HDS to cancel the contract. Even where the time for performance has expired, seller has the right to cure if he seasonably notifies buyer of his intent to cure *and* buyer rejected non-conforming tender which seller had reasonable grounds to believe buyer would accept. UCC §2-508. Here, CP *could* argue that the testing period after delivery would give it reason to believe HDS would accept non-conforming goods, with CP expecting to cure the defects as they came to light.

In any case, since there's no indication time was of the essence under these facts, making the delay a minor breach and thus requiring HDS to perform under the contract, C is the best response.

(A) is not the best response,

because it mischaracterizes the timing provision – it's a constructive condition, not an express condition.

Under non-UCC contracts (i.e., those not involved with transactions in goods), a reasonable delay will ordinary be considered a *minor* breach of contract, *unless* the contract itself provides that "time is of the essence," in which case *any* delay would be a *material* breach.

Here, there was only a five-day delay, and there's nothing to indicate any reason why CP should have considered the July 1 deadline essential, at the time the contract was created. Thus, the delay was only a *minor* breach, requiring that HDS pay, and recover any damages it suffered because of the delay. Thus, contrary to what option A states, HDS could *not* renounce the contract.

If you chose this response, there's a couple things in these facts that may have led you astray. First, there *is* an express condition in these facts, requiring strict compliance – it's just that the deadline provision isn't it. The express condition is the 50 percent time savings provision. Thus, even if the time savings were 49 per-

cent, CP would be in material breach, because express conditions require strict performance (although if HDS continued using the programs, CP would be entitled to quasi-contractual recovery due to HDS's unjust enrichment). Also, under the UCC, implicit in the "perfect tender" concept is the idea that time is of the essence *automatically* in all but installment contracts, such that where the sale of goods is involved *any* lateness can entitle the other party to cancel the contract (but you have to take into account the seller's right to cure). Under these facts, CP would be considered to be providing *services,* not goods, so the UCC wouldn't control (and, in fact, even if the UCC did control here, CP would be entitled to cure the defect).

In any case, since option A ignores the fact that at common law the delay wouldn't entitle HDS to cancel the contract, it's not the best response.

(B) is not the best response,

because it mischaracterizes the facts, and even if it didn't, HDS still wouldn't be allowed to renounce the contract due to the delay.

First, a "commercial" contract is one that covers a transaction in goods, which is covered by UCC Article 2. Here, the contract is primarily for *services,* not goods, so the UCC wouldn't apply. Assuming arguendo that it *did* cover goods, B would be correct in stating that the UCC rejects the substantial performance doctrine in favor of the "perfect tender" rule.

However, this probably wouldn't result in HDS's being able to renounce the contract, due to CP's right to cure. The right to cure, under UCC §2-508, is the seller's right to correct non-conforming tender. There are two aspects to the right to cure. If there is still adequate time for performance, seller can cure as long as he notifies the buyer of his intent to cure. If the time for performance has expired – as it has here – seller can *still* cure if he seasonably notifies buyer of his intent to cure *and* buyer rejected non-conforming tender which seller had reasonable grounds to believe buyer would accept. Thus, even if the UCC covered this contract, CP *could* argue that the testing period after delivery would give it reason to believe HDS would accept non-conforming goods, in this case non-conforming because they were late.

However, since the contract here is for services, not goods, the common law will apply, and the common law *does* recognize the doctrine of substantial performance as to implied and constructive conditions (only *express* conditions require *strict* performance). That is, if an implied or constructive condition is substantially performed, the other party must perform and sue for any damages he suffered. That's because substantial performance results in only a *minor,* not a *major* breach of contract. The only way a reasonable delay at common law could be considered a major breach is if the contract makes time of the essence, and the one here didn't. Thus, HDS would not be entitled to renounce the contract. Since option B doesn't recognize this, it's not the best response.

(D) is not the best response,

because the absence of a liquidated damages clause would not be determinative.

A liquidated damages clause is a contractual clause providing the amount of damages in the case of a contract breach. There are three elements to a valid liquidated damages clause: the clause must reasonably forecast the probable loss due to breach, the harm caused by the breach must be difficult to calculate, and the parties must tailor the clause to the contract's circumstances (i.e., it cannot be a penalty). While delays in completion can be covered by liquidated damages clauses, the lack of one certainly doesn't preclude recovery for delays.

Instead, HDS will be able to recover damages for the delay, although it can't cancel the contract and must perform under it. That's because the timing provision under the contract would be considered a constructive condition, requiring only substantial performance to trigger HDS's performance. Had the parties provided that "time is of the essence," the condition would be an *express* condition, and any delay would be considered a material breach, entitling HDS to cancel the contract. Since option D focuses on a concept irrelevant to resolving the issue in these facts, it's not the best response.

Answer 86

(D) is the best response,

because it implies that the reason CP won't recover is that it failed to comply with an express condition.

HDS's duty to pay was expressly conditioned on CP's shortening the processing time by one-half, this to be established by HDS's computer systems manager.

The facts here tell you that CP's program only saved 47% of the time required by each transaction. Thus, HDS's computer manager's failure to certify was in good faith, and, since CP failed to strictly satisfy an express condition precedent, HDS's performance under the contract is excused.

As to the certification, as long as the dissatisfaction is in good faith, such a condition is a valid express condition. Here, the time savings was only 47%, not 50%, so the failure to certify was in good faith. Since D implicitly recognizes that CP can't recover because HDS was entitled to cancel the contract, it's the best response.

(A) is not the best response,

because express conditions are involved, and thus substantial performance would not suffice.

HDS's duty to pay was expressly conditioned on CP's shortening the processing time by one-half, this to be established by HDS's computer systems manager.

The facts here tell you that CP's program only saved 47% of the time required by each transaction. Thus,

HDS's computer manager's failure to certify was in good faith, and, since CP failed to strictly satisfy an express condition precedent, HDS's performance under the contract is excused. Since A would require only substantial performance where *strict* performance is in fact required, it's not the best response.

(B) is not the best response,

because it doesn't focus on a relevant fact. If CP's program did any less than shorten the processing time by half, it would be a major breach of contract, thus excusing HDS's duty to perform.

HDS's duty to pay was expressly conditioned on CP's shortening the processing time by one-half, this to be established by HDS's computer systems manager.

The facts here tell you that CP's program only saved 47% of the time in each transaction. Thus, HDS's computer manager's failure to certify was in good faith, and, since CP failed to strictly satisfy an express condition precedent, HDS's performance under the contract is excused. Thus, while the fact that the programs would save HDS $12,000 a year ain't chopped liver, this alone doesn't address whether CP satisfied a condition under the contract. Thus, B isn't the best response.

(C) is not the best response,

because it mischaracterizes the condition involved here.

Under these facts, HDS's duty to pay would be triggered only by CP's shortening its processing time by 50%. Since HDS doesn't have any duty to perform until CP performs, CP's performance is a condition precedent to HDS's duty to perform.

A condition *subsequent*, on the other hand, is an event which discharges a duty to perform that had become absolute. Such conditions are rare, and are typically indicated by language like "The contract will be void if..." Insurance contracts which provide that claims must be filed within a certain period after the claim is created are the most common examples of conditions subsequent. Thus, where a condition subsequent is involved, there must already have been an absolute duty to perform, which the condition extinguishes. Here, HDS has *no* duty to perform until CP performs. Since option C doesn't correctly characterize the condition here, it can't be the best response.

Answer 87

(B) is the best response,

because it implicitly recognizes the basis of CP's recovery: quasi-contract.

A party's failure to satisfy an express condition is considered a major breach. When a party has committed a major breach, it cannot recover under the contract. Thus, where the non-party has benefitted from the party's performance, there would be unjust enrichment if the non-breaching party didn't have to pay anything.

As a result, if a party's breach is major (but not willful), the non-breaching party has benefitted from the performance, and the breaching party anticipated payment, it's entitled to the reasonable value of its services under quasi-contract.

Here, CP failed to satisfy an express condition of the contract. The contract called for a 50% time savings in processing time. However, the programs did save HDS 47%, and the lynchpin of recovery here is that HDS continued to use the programs even though they didn't comply with the contract. If HDS was allowed to continue using the programs without paying for them, it'd be unjustly enriched. Thus, CP will be entitled to quasi-contractual recovery. Since B recognizes this, it's the best response.

(A) is not the best response,

because it doesn't offer a basis on which CP can recover the reasonable value of its services.

The question tells you that CP's four-day delay is a major breach. That means that HDS's performance under the contract is *excused*. Thus, it doesn't matter if CP's program would have saved HDS six zillion dollars a year – CP didn't satisfy an express condition, and as a result HDS is not obligated to pay CP under the contract.

If CP is to recover, then, it must be on some basis other than HDS's contractual duty. In fact, CP will be able to recover in quasi-contract. The fact that supplies a source of liability for HDS is its continued use of the programs. If it continued to do so without paying for them, this would mean it was unjustly enriched. In fact, quasi-contract is appropriate in several situations, one of which – plaintiff is guilty of a material (but not willful) breach, and thus would be unable to recover contractually – applies here. Since A doesn't address a relevant point, it's not the best response.

(C) is not the best response,

because although it correctly characterizes the condition, it *ignores* a crucial fact: HDS continued to use the programs, and thus CP is entitled to quasi-contractual recovery.

The question itself tells you that CP has failed to satisfy an express condition precedent. As option C states, this excuses the other party's performance. However, this presupposes that the other party doesn't receive the benefit of the defaulting party's performance. Where the other party *does* benefit, then the defaulting party will be entitled to quasi-contractual recovery, because otherwise the non-defaulting party would be unjustly enriched. Specifically, the rule is that if a party can't recover under the contract because it committed a material (not willful) breach, it's entitled to quasi-contractual recovery.

Here, if HDS were allowed to use the programs without compensating CP, it would be unjustly enriched. As

a result, CP would be entitled to the reasonable value of its services. Since option C ignores the quasi-contractual aspect of the facts, it's not the best response.

(D) is not the best response,

because recovery by CP under quasi-contract and a claim by HDS for breach of contract *are* consistent.

CP's failure to satisfy an express condition precedent *would* entitle HDS to cancel the contract, and entitles it to any damages due to the breach. However, the factor that paves the way for CP's quasi-contractual recovery is two-fold: 1. CP's breach was material, meaning it could not recover under the contract; and 2. HDS continued to use the programs, thus meaning that if it doesn't pay for them, it would be unjustly enriched (and that's what quasi-contractual recovery is designed to avoid). Since these two claims are not inconsistent, D can't be the best response.

Answer 88

(A) is the best response,

because it addresses the central reason the motion will be denied: The search was incident to a valid custodial arrest.

The rule is that a warrantless body search may be conducted incident to any "full custody" arrest (i.e., any time the suspect is to be taken to the police station and booked). It doesn't matter whether the arrest is for a minor crime (e.g., speeding, as here), whether the arresting officer fears for his safety, or whether he believes any evidence will be found. U.S. v. Robinson (1973).

This question indicates why it's so important to determine the *purpose* of a search. Here, if a stop and frisk had been involved – e.g., Police Officer didn't plan to take Dexter into custody, or he had no probable cause to arrest Dexter – Police Officer would have required a reasonable suspicion of some criminal activity, and he could *only* conduct a protective search for weapons if he had reasonable grounds to believe Dexter was armed and dangerous. Since A correctly distinguishes a search incident to a custodial arrest from a stop and frisk, it's the best response.

(B) is not the best response,

because it states the test for a stop and frisk, not a search incident to an arrest, and in any case it's not clear that the facts indicate what B says they do.

The search that's involved here is a search incident to an arrest, because the facts state the Police Officer validly arrested Dexter. The scope of such a search is the area within the suspect's "immediate control" (a/k/a his "wingspan"). Chimel v. California (1969). The office needn't have a reasonable suspicion of criminal activity and reasonable grounds to believe the person is armed and dangerous – *that's* the test for a stop and frisk, which takes place when there's *no* probable cause to arrest. Terry v. Ohio (1968). Furthermore, option B states the motion to prevent introduction of the heroin will be denied *because* of Police Officer's suspicion and concern. The facts don't suggest that Police Officer had any legitimate grounds for concern as to his own safety, because nothing here suggests Dexter was dangerous – he was only picked up for speeding. Since B does not supply the correct test, and to some extent misstates the facts, it's not the best response.

(C) is not the best response,

because it misstates the facts: there *was* a proper basis on which to conduct a search – Dexter's arrest.

A warrantless body search may be conducted incident to any "full custody" arrest (i.e., any time the suspect is to be taken to the station to be booked). Since C ignores this fact, and as a result arrives at the wrong conclusion, it's not the best response.

(D) is not the best response,

because it applies the wrong test to the facts, and arrives at the wrong conclusion as a result.

The test to which D alludes is the test to determine the validity of a search incident to a "stop and frisk": the officer must have a reasonable suspicion of criminal activity *and* he must reasonably believe the suspect is armed and dangerous. Under these facts, Dexter was arrested for speeding, and although he was nervous, there's no strong suggestion that he would appear armed and dangerous. Thus it's probable that D correctly characterizes the facts as to "reasonable suspicion," especially since it states that "if" these facts were true, the additional facts *could be* true. However, the facts here indicate a warrantless body search was conducted as a search incident to a "full custody" arrest (i.e., suspect is to be taken to the police station and booked). As a result, Dexter's motion to prevent introduction of the heroin will be denied. Since D ignores the arrest and as a result applies the wrong test to these facts, it's not the best response.

Answer 89

(A) is the best response,

because it correctly identifies the central reason the argument will be admissible: it rebuts the defendant's argument that the shirt would have been damaging to the prosecutor's case.

As a general rule, where it would be natural for a party to introduce a certain piece of available evidence, and he doesn't do so, the other party can use this failure so as to invoke an adverse inference. Here, the prosecutor didn't offer the torn shirt as evidence, when it would seem to have been advantageous for him to do so. That's why Dunn's lawyer commented on it. However, the rest of the rule holds that once such an inference has been invoked, the other party can rebut the inference. Under normal circumstances, the other party would rebut by explaining why the evidence in question wasn't introduced. By suggesting that the shirt

wouldn't have benefitted Dunn either, the prosecutor rebutted the inference that the shirt was advantageous to Dunn. Since A recognizes that this is the basis of admitting the prosecutor's argument, it's the best response.

(B) is not the best response,

because it misstates the facts, and even if it correctly stated the facts, such an argument would violate Dunn's right against self-incrimination.

Here, the prosecutor isn't commenting on Dunn's failure to testify; he's rebutting the inference that the shirt would have hurt his case by suggesting it wouldn't have been helpful to either party. This doesn't address Dunn's failure to testify at all, and in stating that it does, B misstates the facts.

Assuming arguendo that the prosecutor did comment on Dunn's failure to testify, B is incorrect in stating that this would be proper. Any comment by the prosecutor as to the defendant's failure to testify is a violation of the Fifth Amendment privilege against self-incrimination. *Griffin v. California* (1965). Thus, the prosecutor's comment would not be proper. (Incidentally, such a comment may, however, only constitute harmless error, where the prosecutor notes defendant's failure to produce evidence rebutting testimony of the victim, where there is overwhelming evidence of defendant's guilt, and what scanty evidence defendant has is inconsistent. *U. S. v. Hasting* (1983).) Since B mischaracterizes the facts and misstates the law, it can't be the best response.

(C) is not the best response,

because it misstates the facts.

While it's true that a closing argument cannot go beyond the evidence in the case, that's not what's going on here; instead, the prosecutor is rebutting an inference invoked by Dunn's counsel.

As a general rule, where it would be natural for a party to introduce a certain piece of available evidence, and he doesn't do so, the other party can use this failure so as to invoke an adverse inference. Here, the prosecutor didn't offer the torn shirt as evidence, when it would seem to have been advantageous for him to do so. That's why Dunn's lawyer commented on it. However, the rest of the rule holds that once such an inference has been invoked, the other party can rebut the inference. Under normal circumstances, the other party would rebut by explaining why the evidence in question wasn't introduced. By suggesting that the shirt wouldn't have benefitted Dunn either, the prosecutor rebutted the inference that the shirt was advantageous to Dunn. Thus, the prosecutor didn't go beyond the evidence in the case. Since C doesn't recognize this, it's not the best response.

(D) is not the best response,

because it mischaracterizes the facts.

It's true that a comment by the prosecutor as to defendant's failure to testify is improper, as a violation of the defendant's Fifth Amendment privilege against self-incrimination. However, under these facts, the prosecutor hasn't said anything about Dunn's failure to testify. Instead, he's rebutting the inference that the shirt would have hurt his case by suggesting it wouldn't have been helpful to either party. Thus, any correct response would have to address whether the rebuttal was proper. Since D instead discusses Dunn's failure to testify, it's not the best response.

Answer 90

(C) is the best response,

because it correctly states the central reason Donna's confession will be admissible: it was volunteered.

The right to counsel under Miranda is only triggered by an *interrogation*. Here, the police showed no intention of interrogating Donna; until they did, or until there was a "critical stage" in the inquiry, they needn't have responded to her request. The mere taking of fingerprints would not in and of itself trigger the right to counsel; and volunteered confessions are admissible. Since C correctly identifies the reason why Donna's confession will be admissible, it's the best response.

(A) is not the best response,

because the police were not under a duty to grant Donna's request *immediately*.

There are only two theories on which Donna would be entitled to counsel: under the Sixth Amendment, for "critical stages" of the inquiry (e.g., trial); and under the Fifth Amendment, for "investigative" stages of the inquiry (e.g., custodial interrogations). Here, since the police did not intend to interrogate her, she wouldn't be entitled to counsel on Fifth Amendment grounds. Furthermore, since fingerprinting is not a "critical stage" of the inquiry, Donna wouldn't be entitled to counsel under the Sixth Amendment. Thus, her mere request to speak to a lawyer doesn't mean the request must be granted immediately, in and of itself. What option A fails to realize is that Donna volunteered her statement, and so it can be validly offered against her. Since A doesn't recognize this, it's not the best response.

(B) is not the best response,

because the "fruit of the poisonous tree" doctrine does not apply to these facts, and B arrives at the wrong result.

The "fruit of the poisonous tree" doctrine holds that evidence derived from unlawfully obtained evidence is inadmissible. Such "derivative" evidence is called the "tainted fruit of the poisonous tree." The reason this doesn't apply here is that there *is* no unlawfully obtained evidence, and even if Donna's confession *were* illegally obtained, it would be the direct result of the illegality – that is, the "poisonous tree" itself – not the *fruit* of it.

Say the facts were different: the police did not give Donna her Miranda warnings, they interrogated her, and she told them where they could find the gun she used to kill her husband. The gun might be considered the tainted from of the poisonous tree (unless it fits an exception to the doctrine, the three major ones being independent source, inevitable discovery, and purged taint). Here, the facts are quite different. There was no illegality in terms of Donna's confession since she *volunteered* it, and, in any case, she wasn't entitled to counsel under the Sixth Amendment because fingerprinting is not a "critical stage" of the inquiry. Since B misapplies the "fruit of the poisonous tree" doctrine to these facts, it's not the best response.

(D) is not the best response,

because although it states the correct result, it does not offer appropriate reasoning.

Although, as D states, fingerprinting is not a critical stage of the proceeding requiring the assistance of counsel, it ignores the fact that Donna's statement is a confession. Thus, while option D recognizes that there's no problem with the *Sixth* Amendment right to counsel, it doesn't address the Fifth Amendment. In fact, the reason it will be admissible is that it was *volunteered,* and thus there can't be a Fifth Amendment, "interrogation" problem. If the police had, in fact, interrogated Donna without honoring her request to see her lawyer, her confession would be *inadmissible.* Thus, the central reason that Donna's confession is admissible is because it was volunteered. Since D doesn't recognize this, it's not the best response.

Answer 91

(B) is the best response,

because it's the only option that adds a fact making Barnes's claim valid. Ironically enough, although this problem looks like a constitutional law problem, option B creates a breach of contract claim, in the form of promissory estoppel.

Under these facts, you have a state activity which is depriving Barnes of what looks like some interest or right. Thus, what's involved here is, at least on its face, a *due process* issue. Since what Barnes is contesting is the lack of some process before he was not re-hired, the issue is more specifically *procedural* due process (substantive due process involves a law limiting a right, where, depending on whether the right is fundamental, either the "compelling interest" or "rational relation" test will be used to determine the law's validity).

Under procedural due process, there need only be fair process if the right being deprived is a *property* right (or life or liberty). Thus, in order for Barnes to prevail, he'd have to claim he had a property right in his state employment. This demands more than the mere enjoyment of a benefit; an applicable federal, state, or municipal law must recognize a legitimate claim to the benefit. For instance, there's a property interest in public education, and continuing welfare benefits and utilities service. As to public employment – the issue under these facts – the existence of a property interest will similarly be determined by applicable law. Here, the state statute clearly implies that there's no property interest until a professor has tenure, which requires five years' employment; before that, a professor can be fired at will after each successive one-year contract. Thus, Barnes was *not* deprived of a property right when he was not re-hired, and there can't be a due process violation.

What option B does is to add a fact which creates a contract claim. In fact, it creates a claim based on promissory estoppel. Promissory estoppel is a substitute for consideration, used to avoid injustice. It's triggered by a gratuitous promise that is likely to, and does, induce the promisee's reliance. It's not consideration because there's no bargain – but it *does* result in the promise's being *enforceable*. If, in fact, the college president assured Barnes he'd be rehired, this is a promise on which Barnes could reasonably rely, considering that the promise came from the college president. By leasing a home, Barnes justifiably relied on the promise, making it enforceable. Since B recognizes this, it's the best response.

(A) is not the best response,

because it's irrelevant.

Under these facts, you have a state activity which is depriving Barnes of what looks like some interest or right. Thus, what's involved here is a *due process* issue. Since what Barnes is contesting is the lack of some process before he was not re-hired, the issue is more specifically *procedural* due process (substantive due process involves a law limiting a right, where, depending on whether the right is fundamental, either the "compelling interest" or "rational relation" test will be used to determine the law's validity).

Under procedural due process, there need only be fair process if the right being deprived is a *property* right (or life or liberty). Thus, in order for Barnes to prevail, he'd have to claim he had a property right in his state employment. This demands more than the mere enjoyment of a benefit; an applicable federal, state, or municipal law must recognize a legitimate claim to the benefit. For instance, there's a property interest in public education, and continuing welfare benefits and utilities service. As to public employment – the issue under these facts – the existence of a property interest will similarly be determined by applicable law. Here, the state statute clearly implies that there's no property interest until a professor has tenure, which requires five years' employment; before that, a professor can be fired at will after each successive one-year contract. Thus, Barnes was *not* deprived of a property right when he was not re-hired, and there can't be a due process violation. The fact that option A states – that tenured teachers are no more qualified than Barnes –

does not make Barnes's continued employment into a property right, and as a result it's irrelevant. Since A doesn't recognize this, it's not the best response.

(C) is not the best response,

because it doesn't address the central issue here – whether Barnes had a property right in his public employment.

Under these facts, you have a state activity which is depriving Barnes of what looks like some interest or right. Thus, what's involved here is a *due process* issue. Since what Barnes is contesting is the lack of some process before he was not re-hired, the issue is more specifically *procedural* due process (substantive due process involves a law limiting a right, where, depending on whether the right is fundamental, either the "compelling interest" or "rational relation" test will be used to determine the law's validity).

Under procedural due process, there need only be fair process if the right being deprived is a *property* right (or life or liberty). Thus, in order for Barnes to prevail, he'd have to claim he had a property right in his state employment. This demands more than the mere enjoyment of a benefit; an applicable federal, state, or municipal law must recognize a legitimate claim to the benefit. For instance, there's a property interest in public education, and continuing welfare benefits and utilities service. As to public employment – the issue under these facts – the existence of a property interest will similarly be determined by applicable law. Here, the state statute clearly implies that there's no property interest until a professor has tenure, which requires five years' employment; before that, a professor can be fired at will after each successive one-year contract. Thus, Barnes was *not* deprived of a property right when he was not re-hired, and there can't be a due process violation. The fact that option C states – that Barnes was the only teacher not re-hired – would not make Barnes's interest in his job into a property right. Since C doesn't recognize this, it's not the best response.

(D) is not the best response,

because it's irrelevant.

Under these facts, you have a state activity which is depriving Barnes of what looks like some interest or right. Thus, what's involved here is a *due process* issue. Since what Barnes is contesting is the lack of some process before he was not re-hired, the issue is more specifically *procedural* due process (substantive due process involves a law limiting a right, where, depending on whether the right is fundamental, either the "compelling interest" or "rational relation" test will be used to determine the law's validity).

Under procedural due process, there need only be fair process if the right being deprived is a *property* right (or life or liberty). Thus, in order for Barnes to prevail, he'd have to claim he had a property right in his state employment. This demands more than the mere enjoyment of a benefit; an applicable federal, state, or municipal law must recognize a legitimate claim to the benefit. For instance, there's a property interest in public education, and continuing welfare benefits and utilities service. As to public employment – the issue under these facts – the existence of a property interest will similarly be determined by applicable law. Here, the state statute clearly implies that there's no property interest until a professor has tenure, which requires five years' employment; before that, a professor can be fired at will after each successive one-year contract. Thus, Barnes was *not* deprived of a property right when he was not re-hired, and there can't be a due process violation.

What option D implies is promissory estoppel, because that's where you most frequently see expectations. However, under these facts, there was no promise from anyone related to the college, and so Barnes had no promise on which he could justifiably rely – which is the lynchpin of promissory estoppel. By moving his parents to town, Barnes was, in effect, assuming the risk that he might not be rehired. When he wasn't, the fact that he moved his folks to town doesn't make his firing, without a hearing, actionable. Since D doesn't recognize this, it's not the best response.

Answer 92

(C) is the best response,

because it impliedly recognizes the central issue here – a potential due process violation – and states why the college will prevail: Barnes was not deprived of a property right, and so there can be no due process violation.

Under these facts, you have a state activity which is depriving Barnes of what looks like some interest or right. Thus, what's involved here is a *due process* issue. Since what Barnes is contesting is the lack of some process before he was not re-hired, the issue is more specifically *procedural* due process (substantive due process involves a law limiting a right, where, depending on whether the right is fundamental, either the "compelling interest" or "rational relation" test will be used to determine the law's validity).

Under procedural due process, there need only be fair process if the right being deprived is a *property* right (or life or liberty). Thus, in order for Barnes to prevail, he'd have to claim he had a property right in his state employment. This demands more than the mere enjoyment of a benefit; an applicable federal, state, or municipal law must recognize a legitimate claim to the benefit. For instance, there's a property interest in public education, and continuing welfare benefits and utilities service. As to public employment – the issue under these facts – the existence of a property interest will similarly be determined by applicable law. Here, the state statute clearly implies that there's no property interest until a professor has tenure, which requires

five years' employment; before that, a professor can be fired at will after each successive one-year contract. Thus, Barnes was *not* deprived of a property right when he was not re-hired, and there can't be a due process violation. Thus, the lynchpin of the college's argument must be the fact that Barnes worked at the college for fewer than five years. Since C recognizes this, it's the best response.

(A) is not the best response,

because it doesn't address the central issue here: whether or not Barnes was denied due process of the law.

Under these facts, you have a state activity which is depriving Barnes of what looks like some interest or right. Thus, what's involved here is a *due process* issue. Since what Barnes is contesting is the lack of some process before he was not re-hired, the issue is more specifically *procedural* due process (substantive due process involves a law limiting a right, where, depending on whether the right is fundamental, either the "compelling interest" or "rational relation" test will be used to determine the law's validity).

Under procedural due process, there need only be fair process if the right being deprived is a *property* right (or life or liberty). Thus, in order for Barnes to prevail, he'd have to claim he had a property right in his state employment. This demands more than the mere enjoyment of a benefit; an applicable federal, state, or municipal law must recognize a legitimate claim to the benefit. For instance, there's a property interest in public education, and continuing welfare benefits and utilities service. As to public employment – the issue under these facts – the existence of a property interest will similarly be determined by applicable law. Here, the state statute clearly implies that there's no property interest until a professor has tenure, which requires five years' employment; before that, a professor can be fired at will after each successive one-year contract. Thus, Barnes was *not* deprived of a property right when he was not re-hired, and there can't be a due process violation.

The fact that option A states might be a good reason to refuse to rehire Barnes, but it doesn't address the threshold issue of whether or not he was entitled to know this was the reason he wasn't re-hired. Since his three-year employment means that he wasn't entitled to know this, and option A doesn't recognize this fact, it's not the best response.

(B) is not the best response,

because what it states would not support the college's contention, but if anything does just the opposite – it suggests a violation of Barnes's right of free speech.

Of course, the mere fact that Barnes was exercised his right to free speech would not, in and of itself, insulate him from being fired. Instead, his First Amendment rights would be balanced against the governmental interest in having public services performed efficiently. Connick v. Myers (1983). The facts that would be taken into account would include:

1. Whether there is a great need for confidentiality
2. Whether a working relationship could be undermined by criticizing a close superior
3. Whether the criticism is harmful, false, and relates to daily school operations of which only a few know, thus making rebuttal difficult
4. Whether the teacher's in-class duties and the school's daily operation would be impeded thereby
5. Whether the teacher's fitness could be questioned because the statements were without foundation

Of course, even as a public employee Barnes would have some right to speak out on matters of public importance, and speaking out on those issues alone would not justify a dismissal.

However, what option B ignores is that the college has a very clear-cut defense on due process grounds: Barnes was not denied of a property right, and thus he had no right to a hearing or reasons for his failure to be rehired. Under the state statute, Barnes would only have a right to a hearing once he was a tenured professor, because the tenure creates a property right in the job. By raising the issue of a critical speech Barnes made, the college would only enter a hornet's nest of First Amendment issues, which could potentially torpedo its defense. Since option B doesn't recognize this, it's not the best response.

(D) is not the best response,

because it would not be relevant to whether or not Barnes was entitled to a hearing and reasons for his failure to be re-hired.

Under these facts, you have a state activity which is depriving Barnes of what looks like some interest or right. Thus, what's involved here is a *due process* issue. Since what Barnes is contesting is the lack of some process before he was not re-hired, the issue is more specifically *procedural* due process (substantive due process involves a law limiting a right, where, depending on whether the right is fundamental, either the "compelling interest" or "rational relation" test will be used to determine the law's validity).

Under procedural due process, there need only be fair process if the right being deprived is a *property* right (or life or liberty). Thus, in order for Barnes to prevail, he'd have to claim he had a property right in his state employment. This demands more than the mere enjoyment of a benefit; an applicable federal, state, or municipal law must recognize a legitimate claim to the benefit. For instance, there's a property interest in public education, and continuing welfare benefits and utilities service. As to public employment – the issue under these facts – the existence of a property interest will similarly be determined by applicable law. Here, the

state statute clearly implies that there's no property interest until a professor has tenure, which requires five years' employment; before that, a professor can be fired at will after each successive one-year contract. Thus, Barnes was *not* deprived of a property right when he was not re-hired, and there can't be a due process violation.

The fact that D suggests – that Barnes could be replaced with a more competent teacher – does not address whether or not he was entitled to a hearing before he was not re-hired. As a result, D isn't the best response.

Answer 93

(B) is the best response,

because it identifies the reason why the regulation will be valid.

The regulation here involves Congressional regulation of federally-owned lands. Under Article IV, §3, clause 2 of the Constitution, Congress has the power "to dispose of and make all needful rules and regulations respecting" lands of the United States. States only have power to the extent that they reserved jurisdiction when ceding the land to the federal government (or, alternatively, to the extent that Congress has, via legislation, granted jurisdiction to the state). Under these facts, there's no indication of any basis for state jurisdiction over the federally-owned lands. Thus, Congress would have the authority to pass regulations protecting wild animals on those lands. Since option B recognizes this, it's the best response.

(A) is not the best response,

because the Welfare Clause would not empower the federal government to enact this type of legislation.

The Welfare Clause, found in Article 1, §8 of the Constitution, empowers Congress to levy and collect taxes and to provide for the general welfare, and to make all laws which are necessary and proper to implement those powers. Thus, the Welfare Clause only addresses Congress's power to collect taxes and spend money. That's not what's involved in these facts; here, protecting predatory wild animals is the aim of the legislation. As a result, the Welfare Clause could not be the source of the regulation's validity. Since A states otherwise, it's not the best response.

(C) is not the best response,

because it skirts the central issue. It's not the wild animals themselves that are the focus of the legislation, but wild animals *on federal lands,* and federal lands are the exclusive domain of the federal government.

Under Article IV, §3, clause 2 of the Constitution, Congress has the power "to dispose of and make all needful rules and regulations respecting" lands of the United States. States only have power to the extent that they reserved jurisdiction when ceding the land to the federal government (or, alternatively, to the extent that Congress has, via legislation, granted jurisdiction to the state). Under these facts, there's no indication of any basis for state jurisdiction over the federally-owned lands. Thus, the state common law definition of wild animals would not be relevant. Since option C doesn't recognize this, it's not the best response.

(D) is not the best response,

because the Tenth Amendment would not provide a source of power for the states under these facts.

Under these facts, the regulation is a federal regulation concerning federally-owned lands. While it's theoretically true that the states reserve the powers not delegated to the federal government in the Constitution, this ignores application of Article IV, §3, clause 2 of the Constitution, which expressly grants the federal government control over federally-owned lands. Since this power is expressly delegated to the Congress in the Constitution, it can't be reserved by the states under the Tenth Amendment. Since option D doesn't recognize this, it's not the best response.

Answer 94

(D) is the best response,

because it correctly recognizes that the gift to the grandchildren itself is valid, regardless of whether the restraint on alienation is invalid. (In fact, the restraint is invalid as a *disabling* restraint on alienation, and as a result it will be removed.)

The gift does not violate the Rule Against Perpetuities because the members of the class will be determined within a life in being plus twenty one years. In fact, it will be determined at Ben's death, and since he's a life in being at the time the will takes effect, the Rule Against Perpetuities is satisfied (the same goes for all Sallie's other children and grandchildren, since their gifts are identically worded). Since option D recognizes this, it's the best response.

(A) is not the best response,

because does not correctly apply the Rule Against Perpetuities to these facts.

The class gift to the grandchildren does not violate the Rule Against Perpetuities, because it will vest or fail within a life in being plus 21 years. In fact, it will be determined at Ben's death, and since he's a life in being at the time the will takes effect, the Rule Against Perpetuities is satisfied (the same goes for all Sallie's other children and grandchildren, since their gifts are identically worded).

If you chose this response, it's probably because you didn't realize that the no-sale-or-mortgage-until-age-25 provision was a disabling restraint on alienation, and figured that it wasn't until all the children were 25 that the members of the class could be determined. If this were true, the grandchildren's gift wouldn't vest or fail until a life in being (Ben's and his siblings') plus *25* years, which is outside the Perpetuities period. How-

ever, the sale or mortgage provision will be removed, because disabling restraints on alienation are always *invalid* on legal interests, like the class gift here. (A disabling restraint makes any attempted transfer invalid, which in effect makes the interest granted inalienable.) As such, the gift to the grandchildren does not violate the Rule Against Perpetuities, making A not the best response.

(B) is not the best response,

because while it correctly characterizes the restraint on alienation here as invalid, it does not correctly state the *result* of this invalidity.

The restraint on alienation here is not valid because it's a *disabling* restraint on alienation. A disabling restraint makes any attempted transfer invalid, which in effect makes the interest granted inalienable. A disabling restraint is *always* invalid on a legal interest, like the gift here. However, the result is *not* to make the gift itself invalid, but to remove the restraint. This would leave a valid gift to the grandchildren, primarily because the gift would satisfy the Rule Against Perpetuities (since the interests of the grandchildren would vest or fail at Ben's death (the same goes for all Sallie's other children and grandchildren, since their gifts are identically worded). Ben is a life in being, and the Rule Against Perpetuities only requires that interests vest or fail within a life in being *plus* 21 years). Since option B does not correctly state the result of the invalidity of the restraint on alienation, it's not the best response.

(C) is not the best response,

because the provisions are not enforceable in their entirety.

There are two principle issues under these facts: Whether the class gift is valid under the Rule Against Perpetuities, and whether the restraint on alienation is valid.

As to the Rule Against Perpetuities, it requires that, to be valid, any interest must vest or fail within a life in being plus twenty-one years. Here, the gifts to the grandchildren will be determined when Ben dies (the same goes for all Sallie's other children and grandchildren, since their gifts are identically worded). Ben was a life in being when the interest was created, as were his siblings. Thus, the gift satisfies the Rule Against Perpetuities, and C is correct in recognizing that this provision will be upheld.

However, C fails to recognize that the restraint on alienation will not be upheld. In fact, the sale-or-mortgage provision is a disabling restraint on alienation. A disabling restraint makes any attempted transfer invalid, which in effect makes the interest granted inalienable. This kind of restraint is always invalid on legal interests. As a result, it will be removed, leaving a valid class gift to the grandchildren. Since the gift to the grandchildren will be upheld but the restraint on alienation won't be upheld, C is not the best response.

Answer 95

(A) is the best response,

because it provides a sound basis for enforcing the oral contract.

The principal obstacle for Jim under these facts is finding a way to enforce the land sale contract even though it was oral. That is, Jim wants to prove that when Seth *bought* the farm, Jim *got* the farm. The problem is, land sale contracts are within the Statute of Frauds, meaning that they must be in writing to be enforceable (while Statutes of Frauds vary from state to state, land sale contracts are traditionally covered).

Since the contract here required a writing, if Jim prevailed, it means he offered some basis on which the writing requirement would be excused. Furthermore, note that Jim would want the contract *enforced,* not just quasi-contractual recovery (which would give him only the reasonable value of his services).

Option A offers just such a basis, by providing reasoning that some states view as a valid excuse from complying with the Statute of Frauds. Courts are becoming more willing to apply the reliance doctrine to Statute of Frauds problems, such that where a buyer relies on the contract and performs under it on that basis, the other party is *estopped* from pleadings the Statute of Frauds, and the performing party (here, Jim) can recover *on the contract.* Thus, while land sale contracts traditionally required payment *plus* some action explainable only by the contract's existence, modern courts *are* allowing payment to suffice based on *reliance.* While you couldn't say this was a *general* rule, option A specifically conditions the recovery on the action being in a state which *does* recognize the reliance doctrine. This, coupled with the fact that no other option would result in Jim's being able to enforce the contract, makes A the best response.

(B) is not the best response,

because although it states a theoretically correct rule of law, it would not apply to these facts; and beyond that, it wouldn't give Jim the remedy he wants (enforcing the contract) but rather recovery under quasi-contract (the reasonable value of his services).

Under the Statute of Frauds, certain types of contracts must be in writing in order to be enforceable. While the contracts covered vary somewhat from state to state, such contracts typically include, among others, those contracts incapable of performance in less than one year; contracts in consideration of marriage; contracts for the sale of an interest in land; and sale of goods and securities as covered by the UCC. As a contract for the sale of an interest in land, the contract between Seth and Jim would have to comply with the Statute of Frauds.

However, there *are* circumstances where compliance with the Statute of Frauds will be *excused.* Typically, this will occur where excuse is the only way to avoid undue hardship or fraud. Option B states the *traditional* rule: under a land sale contract, where the buyer pays in whole or in part, the seller's promise to sell is only enforceable if there is other conduct unequivocally referable to the agreement – that is, the only explanation for the payment and acts is the contract's existence. For instance, if a buyer pays and constructs buildings on the land, this would unequivocally suggest a land sale contract. However, under these facts, Jim could have performed services for Seth with the expectation of payment, not necessarily conveyance of the land. Thus, the "unequivocal referability" would be missing. Not only *that,* but using this argument would only give Jim the reasonable value of his services, *not* the farm itself (and it's the farm he wants). Since B doesn't recognize this, it's not the best response.

(C) is not the best response,

because the "clean hands" doctrine is irrelevant to these facts.

The "clean hands" doctrine is only relevant where a plaintiff seeks specific performance of a contract. Under the doctrine, a plaintiff will be denied specific performance if he's guilty of any inequitable conduct with respect to the transaction in controversy. There are two reasons why this won't apply here. First, Sol is not seeking specific performance of a contract; instead, his is a standard legal claim for possession of land. Second, while Sol may have been something of a schmuck for ignoring his father in his twilight years, this wouldn't rise to the level of inequity. Thus, the "clean hands" doctrine wouldn't be relevant to a court's decision in Jim's favor. Since C doesn't recognize this, it's not the best response.

(D) is not the best response,

because it offers an exception to the Statute of Frauds which does not, in fact, exist.

Under the Statute of Frauds, certain types of contracts must be in writing to be enforceable. While the contracts covered vary from state to state, contracts for the sale of interests in land are traditionally covered. Thus, the contract between Seth and Jim would be within the Statute of Frauds, and would generally require a writing to be enforceable.

However, there *are* circumstances where compliance with the Statute of Frauds will be *excused.* Typically, this will occur where excuse is the only way to avoid undue hardship or fraud. The mere existence of *any* familial relationship would *not* provide an excuse from satisfying the Statute of Frauds. Instead, the source of the excuse under these facts is that Jim would suffer undue hardship if the contract weren't enforced. Since option D doesn't recognize this, it's not the best response.

Answer 96

(D) is the best response,
because it correctly identifies that the tenancy here was never a tenancy by the entirety, and, beyond that, it correctly identifies the result.

A tenancy by the entirety never existed under these facts, because Wade and Mary were never married. A tenancy by the entirety is a co-tenancy which can only exist between husband and wife, it cannot be destroyed by severance, and it requires the same "four unities" as a joint tenancy (time, title, possession, and interest). Since Wade and Mary were never formally married, the tenancy here cannot be a tenancy by the entirety. Thus, all the facts about how they held themselves out as a married couple are *irrelevant,* because the opening fact tells you that the state doesn't recognize common law marriage. (This is one more example of why it's important to pay special attention to any statutes or jurisdictional policies, since they're generally key to finding the right answer.) Mary could have called herself the Masked Avenger, with the same result – she never married. Since there wasn't a tenancy by the entirety, there must have been a tenancy in common, since that's the "default" tenancy (the tenancy that results if either a joint tenancy or a tenancy by the entirety fails). A tenancy in common has these attributes: it does not involve a right to survivorship, the tenants in common can obtain their interests in the property at different times, from different instruments, and they need not have equal shares. Furthermore, a tenancy in common is partitionable. Thus, when Mary brought an action against Wade for partition, it would be granted. Since D correctly identifies this, it's the best response.

(A) is not the best response,
because although it states the correct rule of law, it does not apply to these facts.

A tenancy by the entirety is a co-tenancy that can only exist between husband and wife, it has a right of survivorship, it cannot be destroyed by severance, and it requires the same "four unities" as a joint tenancy (time, title, possession, and interest). Thus, while a tenant by the entirety has no right to partition, the tenancy here is not a tenancy by the entirety, so A is not the best response.

(B) is not the best response,
because it misstates the facts: Wade *does not* have absolute title to the property.

Both Wade and Mary are listed as grantees on the deed, and although the deed incorrectly labels them as tenants by the entirety, this does not mean that Wade takes absolute title to the property; rather, they would take title as tenants in common (since tenancy in common is the "default" co-tenancy, which applies when either a joint tenancy or a tenancy by the entirety fails). In fact, if you think about it logically, B can't be the best

response, because there's no more reason that Wade should take absolute title as there is that Mary should take it. Neither one is entitled to the whole thing. Since B incorrectly gives Wade title to the entire property, it's not the best response.

(C) is not the best response,
because it incorrectly states that there was once a tenancy by the entirety, and, beyond that, it misstates the rule of law.

A tenancy by the entirety never existed under these facts, because Wade and Mary were never married. A tenancy by the entirety is a co-tenancy which can only exist between husband and wife, it cannot be destroyed by severance, and it requires the same "four unities" as a joint tenancy (time, title, possession, and interest). Even if the tenancy here *had* been a tenancy by the entirety, Wade's mere abandonment of Mary would not sever it; they would have to divorce. Since C misstates both the rule of law and the facts, it's not the best response.

Answer 97

(A) is the best response,
because it addresses the central issue and resolves it satisfactorily.

There are two alternative sources for Sand's liability, under these facts: Attractive nuisance and landowner's duty to "discovered" trespassers. Under the attractive nuisance doctrine, landowners must use ordinary care to avoid harm to children (too young to appreciate risk), which is due to a reasonably foreseeable risk, caused by artificial conditions on the land. Also, the risk of injury must outweigh the cost of remedying the dangerous condition. Note that option A states that Sand will only be liable *if* securing the chute could be accomplished at moderate cost. That means that this must be plausibly applicable to the facts, and it must resolve a central issue in the case. That's exactly what A does, since if securing the chute could be done at moderate expense, Sand would not be exercising ordinary care by failing to do so, and would be liable due to an "attractive nuisance."

Another alternative is garden-variety landowner liability. The modern trend is to impose a duty of reasonable care on the landowner as to *all* entrants. At common law, the duty depends on the status of the entrant (e.g., licensee, invitee). A discovered trespasser (of whose presence the landowner has reason to know) is owed the duty of reasonable care for the trespasser's safety, as to artificial conditions on the property. Thus, even under standard landowner liability analysis, option A would be a good choice, since it requires reasonability. As a result, A is the best response.

(B) is not the best response,
because it misstates the standard for determining Sand's liability.

There are three general sources of strict liability: Animals, ultra-hazardous activities, and defective, unreasonably dangerous products (strict liability can also be imposed by case law or statute). There is no strict liability just because an injury occurs on one's property or an unsafe condition exists thereon; fault, at least *negligence*, must be proven. Since B would make Sand strictly liable for Ladd's injuries just because of an artificial condition on its property, it's not the best response.

(C) is not the best response,

because the doctrine of Last Clear Chance does not apply to these facts.

Last Clear Chance is used by plaintiffs to rebut a claim of contributory negligence; it states that a person with the last clear chance to avoid an act, who fails to do so, is liable. It is used to avoid the harsh results of contributory negligence.

Option C would use Last Clear Chance as a defense by Sand, not as a rebuttal by Ladd to a contributory negligence defense. Unless Commuter's conduct is considered a superceding force between Sand's negligence and Ladd's injuries, it's Sand's own negligence which will determine its liability. Since option C fails to recognize this, it's not the best response.

(D) is not the best response,

because it does not determine Sand's liability.

The duty a landowner owes to various entrants onto his land is traditionally determined by a hierarchy of duties, depending on whether the entrant is an undiscovered trespasser, a discovered trespasser, a licensee, or an invitee. A discovered trespasser is one whose presence should be known to defendant – here, you know Ladd is a discovered trespasser because the facts state that Sand knew children were using the slide. A discovered trespasser is owed the duty of reasonable care for the trespasser's safety as to artificial conditions on the land. Thus, even as a *trespasser,* Sand would owe Ladd a duty of reasonable care. This, coupled with the attractive nuisance doctrine, would require that Sand take reasonable steps for the safety of the children. Since D ignores this, it's not the best response.

Answer 98

(B) is the best response,

because it applies to these facts and would result in Commuter's prevailing.

Under these facts, the most likely claim by Ladd is negligence, since Commuter clearly did not act intentionally, and there's no basis for strict liability. In order to be negligent, one must fail to exercise such care as a reasonable person in his position would exercise, this must be a breach of the duty to prevent the foreseeable risk of harm to anyone in plaintiff's position, and this breach must cause plaintiff's damages.

Thus, one cannot be negligent if he exercises rea-sonable care. Under these facts, Commuter's having her brakes checked and OK'd would certainly be considered reasonable care. Since this argument will defeat a negligence claim (or, of course, an intentional tort claim), it's Commuter's best defense, making B the best response.

(A) is not the best response,

because it misstates the facts.

"Cause in fact" is part of the causation element, along with proximate cause, of a tort claim. Cause in fact is the determination, under either the "but for" (single cause) or "substantial factor" (multiple causes) test of whether a defendant brought about plaintiff's injuries. Here, regardless of whether Garage's actions will exonerate her, Commuter's driving into Ladd was clearly a cause in fact of Ladd's injuries. What this *ignores* is the central issue here; there must be some level of unreasonableness in order for Commuter to be liable for negligence, the most likely claim. Under these facts, Commuter's having her brakes checked and OK'd would certainly be considered reasonable care. Since A misstates the facts, it's not the best response.

(C) is not the best response,

because it misstates the facts and focuses on an irrelevant point.

The most likely claim on these facts is negligence, since Commuter did not act intentionally, and there's no basis for strict liability. In order to be liable for negligence, her conduct would have to have been unreasonable. If it *was,* she'll be liable for breaching a duty to prevent the foreseeable risk of injury to anyone in plaintiff's position. Under these facts, for a start, Ladd's presence in the street *would* be considered foreseeable, because children frequently dart out into the street. Furthermore, Commuter *did* foresee his presence because she had time to brake and avoid hitting him. In any case, option C ignores the fact that foreseeability is not relevant unless the defendant is negligent. Under these facts, it's fairly clear that Commuter was diligent in maintaining her brakes, and thus her conduct was not unreasonable and cannot be negligent. Since C misstates the facts and ignores Commuter's best argument, it's not the best response.

(D) is not the best response,

because the argument it states, although true on these facts, would not exonerate Commuter.

Since Commuter did not act intentionally here, and there's no basis for strict liability, it's clear that the claim would have to be for negligence. Negligence requires only that defendant failed to exercise such care as a reasonable person in his position would have exercised, this must have been a reach of the duty to prevent the foreseeable risk of harm to anyone in plaintiff's position, and this breach must have caused plaintiff's damages.

As a result, unreasonable behavior is the lynchpin of

a negligence claim; it does *not* require willfulness or wantonness, which are the hallmarks of recklessness. Thus, Commuter could be liable even if she makes the argument D suggests. As a result, D isn't her best defense.

Answer 99

(B) is the best response,

because it correctly characterizes the facts and arrives at a result consistent with the characterization.

Note that B uses the modifier "if," which means that the reasoning need only be plausible on these facts, it must resolve a significant issue, and the result must be consistent with the reasoning. Here, Garage's failure to spot the fault with the brakes could easily be negligent, if it was a fault that Garage, in exercising due care, should have spotted. If it *was* negligent, Garage would be liable to all foreseeable plaintiffs. A pedestrian is *exactly* the kind of person likely to be injured by faulty brakes, so Ladd would be covered. Since B identifies a plausible basis on which Garage would be liable, it's the best response.

(A) is not the best response,

because it's highly unlikely Garage would be considered strictly liable for its faulty inspection.

In order to be strictly liable, Garage would have to be involved in an abnormally dangerous activity, or be liable in strict product liability (in general, for selling any product in a defective condition unreasonably dangerous to the consumer). Strict liability can also be imposed by statute or case law, or for keeping wild animals, but none of these are present on the facts here.

Under these facts, it's unlikely checking brakes would be considered an abnormally dangerous activity, and checking brakes would most likely to be characterized as a service, not a product, thus avoiding strict product liability. In any case, strict liability is not the *only* way to find Garage liable under these facts, because it would seem possible to find fault in the form of negligence on these facts. Since A suggests Garage will be strictly liable in tort, and it's extremely unlikely this would happen, A is not the best response.

(C) is not the best response,

because it misstates the facts.

If Garage was negligent, it created the risk that Commuter's brakes would fail, causing Commuter to hit someone or something. Ladd being hit by Commuter makes him a victim of Garage's negligence, because he is precisely the plaintiff Garage's duty of reasonable care was meant to protect. Even if he had been a "bystander" – say Commuter had hit another car, and flying glass injured him – he may *still* be able to recover from Garage if he would have been considered a foreseeable plaintiff. Since C does not correctly characterize Ladd, and, in any case, does not resolve the case, it's not the best response.

(D) is not the best response,

because it mischaracterizes the facts: Sand's conduct was *not* a superseding cause.

A "superseding" cause is one coming into being after defendant's negligent act, which cancels defendant's liability by breaking the "chain of causation" from defendant's act to plaintiff's injury. The unforeseeability of the results of the subsequent force relieves defendant of liability.

Under these facts, this clearly does not apply. While Sand's act was independent, it did not come into being after Garage's act so as to cut off Garage's liability. If anything, Sand's act would be another cause of Ladd's injury, but this would not exonerate Garage as long as Garage's act was a substantial factor in producing Ladd's injuries (which is the test for causation where there are multiple causes). Since D does not recognize this, it's not the best response.

Answer 100

(C) is the best response,

because it correctly states that Defendant will not be liable for robbery, and states the correct reason why.

Robbery is a larceny either from a person or a person's presence, by either force or fear. A dead person is incapable of being put in fear, or being subject to force. As a result, robbery from a dead person is impossible. Since C correctly identifies this, it's the best response.

(A) is not the best response,

because it does not state a reason which would exonerate Defendant from liability for larceny.

Common law larceny requires only a trespassory taking and carrying away of another's personal property, with intent to steal it. Option A misstates the facts because Defendant satisfies the elements of larceny – preventing identification *is* Defendant's "own use," and would not provide a valid defense to larceny. Since A states a defense which would not exonerate Defendant, it's not the best response.

(B) is not the best response,

because it states an element which is not, in fact, a requirement of larceny.

Common law larceny requires only a trespassory taking and carrying away of another's personal property, with intent to steal it. It does not require a living victim. If you chose this response, you may have been thinking of *robbery,* which requires a living victim since it's larceny from a person with the use of force or fear, and only a living person is susceptible to force or fear. Since B adds an element which is not a requirement of larceny, it's not the best response.

(D) is not the best response,

because although it arrives at the correct conclusion – that Defendant is not guilty of robbery – it does not offer the correct reasoning.

Option D states an element which is not, in fact, a requirement of robbery. Robbery is a larceny either from a person or a person's presence, by either force or fear. The larceny element only requires that one take another's personal property – it does not require that the personal property have monetary value. While it's true that Defendant is not guilty of robbery, it's not because he took something lacking monetary value, but because the victim was dead, thus preventing the use of force or fear. Since D offers incorrect reasoning, it's not the best response.

ANSWERS

PRACTICE MBE — P.M. EXAM

Answer Key

Use this Answer Key to quickly identify the correct answer to each question.

(101)	D	(116)	C	(131)	D	(146)	B	(161)	C	(176)	C	(191)	D
(102)	B	(117)	A	(132)	C	(147)	C	(162)	D	(177)	C	(192)	C
(103)	B	(118)	B	(133)	C	(148)	B	(163)	B	(178)	D	(193)	D
(104)	C	(119)	A	(134)	A	(149)	D	(164)	A	(179)	A	(194)	A
(105)	A	(120)	A	(135)	C	(150)	A	(165)	D	(180)	A	(195)	B
(106)	C	(121)	D	(136)	B	(151)	B	(166)	C	(181)	B	(196)	A
(107)	B	(122)	B	(137)	A	(152)	D	(167)	D	(182)	B	(197)	C
(108)	D	(123)	B	(138)	D	(153)	C	(168)	C	(183)	D	(198)	D
(109)	A	(124)	D	(139)	C	(154)	B	(169)	B	(184)	A	(199)	A
(110)	B	(125)	A	(140)	B	(155)	C	(170)	A	(185)	B	(200)	C
(111)	C	(126)	C	(141)	C	(156)	A	(171)	A	(186)	D		
(112)	D	(127)	A	(142)	D	(157)	A	(172)	B	(187)	A		
(113)	C	(128)	B	(143)	D	(158)	C	(173)	B	(188)	C		
(114)	D	(129)	A	(144)	B	(159)	D	(174)	B	(189)	B		
(115)	B	(130)	C	(145)	A	(160)	A	(175)	D	(190)	D		

ANSWERS

PRACTICE MBE — P.M. EXAM

Answer 101

(D) is the best response,

because it correctly characterizes a valid self-defense claim, and plausibly fits these facts.

All a self-defense claim requires is a reasonable belief in the existence of danger, with immediate force being the only way to avoid it. Thus, D, by invoking the "reasonable person" standard, recognizes this. Note that option D uses the modifier "if" instead of "because." That means that the facts need only plausibly fit the reasoning. That's the case here. It's possible on these facts that a reasonable person would, indeed, view the gesture as threatening. Since D correctly identifies the test for self-defense, and it's consistent with these facts, it's the best response.

(A) is not the best response,

because it does not address an element which will determine the validity of David's claim of privilege

It's not whether Bill was *actually* an aggressor that counts, but whether David could *reasonably believe* in the existence of danger, with immediate force being the only way to avoid it. Thus, a valid self-defense claim focuses on the belief of the one claiming the privilege. Since A doesn't recognize this, it's not the best response.

(B) is not the best response,

because it does not address an element which will determine the validity of David's claim of privilege.

It's not how Bill intended his gesture that's relevant, but whether the gesture created in David a *reasonable belief* as to the existence of danger, with immediate force being the only way to avoid it. Thus, a valid self-defense claim focuses on the belief of the one *claiming* the privilege. Since B ignores this, it's not the best response.

(C) is not the best response,

because an honest belief is not sufficient for a self-defense claim – it must be a *reasonable* belief, as well.

Thus, if David's perception of danger was a result of his hallucinating, even if his belief was honest, he would *still* be liable because his belief wasn't reasonable. Since C ignores the objective element of the self-defense claim, it's not the best response.

Answer 102

(B) is the best response,

because it identifies the correct use of the evidence.

If Ped did not exercise due care for his own safety, his contributory negligence will bar his recovery, even if Driver was negligent. The statute will be relevant in determining Ped's negligence; so will Trucker's blocking the crosswalk, since it may indicate that Ped's violating the statute was excusable. Thus, the trier of fact should be able to examine the facts determining Ped's negligence, to see if Driver will have a valid contributory negligence defense. Since B recognizes this, it's the best response.

(A) is not the best response,

because Ped's failure to cross at the crosswalk *is* relevant to determining Ped's rights.

If failing to cross at the crosswalk were considered contributorily negligent, it would bar Ped from recovering at all (note that you're told in the instructions that contributory, not comparative, negligence is recognized). Since A mistakenly considers the evidence irrelevant, it's not the best response.

(C) is not the best response,

because it assumes that Ped was contributorily negligent. Why? Because C suggests that Driver's liability depends on the Last Clear Chance doctrine ("in time to avoid the impact" language).

Last Clear Chance is used by plaintiffs to rebut a claim of contributory negligence. It allows that a defendant with the las clear chance to avoid a negligent act, who fails to do so, is liable. However, as this definition indicates, Last Clear Chance presupposes contributory negligence. Here, Ped was only contributorily negligent if stepping off the crosswalk and around the truck amounted to a failure to exercise due care for his own safety. If anything, these facts would suggest Ped was *not* negligent; they certainly don't suggest for sure that he *was*. While Driver's seeing Ped in time to avoid the impact will be relevant to Driver's negligence, it won't be contingent on Ped's contributory negligence. Since C states otherwise, it's not the best response.

(D) is not the best response,

because negligence per se would not apply to these facts.

Negligence per se occurs when a court decides violation of a statute will amount to negligence as a matter of law. However, this only occurs in a small number of statutes, and generally only when a court finds the legislature intended for violation of the statute to amount to negligence per se. There's no evidence here that that's the case. As such, D cannot be the best

response.

Answer 103

(B) is the best response,
because it identifies that Trucker's standard of care is likely to be governed by the statute.

A criminal standard of care will govern a civil case, amounting to negligence per se, if four elements are proven: The statute provides for a criminal penalty; the statute was formulated to prevent the kind of harm plaintiff suffered; plaintiff is a member of the class the legislature intended to protect with the statute; and the statute is clear as to the standard of conduct expected, and from whom and when. The facts here likely fit this standard, because, as option B states, protecting pedestrians is the likely purpose of the statute, and the other elements are satisfied. Note that proof that the standard applies will mean that Trucker cannot claim assumption of the risk, because the statute was designed to prevent exactly the risk involved with forcing pedestrians to cross outside a crosswalk. Since B correctly identifies that Trucker will be liable for negligence because the statutory standard will determine his negligence, it's the best response.

(A) is not the best response,
because it misstates the law.

Violation of a statute could only be considered as a basis for strict liability if the statute itself so provided, or the courts had determined it should be so. Absent that, at best a statutory violation could be considered negligence per se, or, in most situations, evidence of negligence. Since A mistakenly states that Trucker will be strictly liable for violating a state statute, it's not the best response.

(C) is not the best response,
because it misstates the law: Assumption of the risk would not be a valid defense to the claim.

The assumption of the risk defense requires that one knowingly, voluntarily subject oneself to danger, thus relieving defendant of a duty toward plaintiff. Here, the statute suggests that defendant should *not* be relieved of his duty to plaintiff, because plaintiff's having to step outside the sidewalk is exactly what the statute is designed to protect *against*. As a result, Trucker could not argue that Ped assumed a risk the statute was designed to avoid. Since C states otherwise, it's not the best response.

(D) is not the best response,
because Driver's conduct will not determine Trucker's liability.

Driver's act could only relieve Trucker of liability if it were a superseding force – i.e., it arose after Trucker's liability, and its unforeseeability relieves Trucker of liability. That's not the case, because Driver's act is precisely the kind of behavior Trucker's act would likely engender. Instead, whether Trucker's act was an actual cause (a/k/a cause in fact) of Ped's injuries will be determined by the "substantial factor" causation test: If Trucker's negligence was a substantial factor in Ped's injuries, he'll be liable. Since D incorrectly exonerates Trucker on the basis of Driver's actions, it's not the best response.

Answer 104

(C) is the best response,
because it correctly identifies the central reason why the evidence will be excluded: Green's actual and reasonable expectation of privacy was violated.

While it's possible for the police to conduct electronic surveillance under a warrant, the warrant requirements are very strict, and clearly not satisfied under these facts. A wrinkle in this problem is that the college president "arranged" for the local police to bug Green's room. This implies *private* action, which is *not* circumscribed by the Fourth Amendment (only *governmental* action is covered, or those acting under police direction). Thus, the college president's acts will not make the surveillance valid. Note that *after* the surveillance, the search warrant and subsequent search are not obviously flawed; since the tape provided probable cause for a warrant, and it was apparently given by a neutral, detached magistrate. Nonetheless, the original illegal surveillance requires that the evidence be excluded at trial. Since C recognizes this, it's the best response.

(A) is not the best response,
because it does not focus on the central fact: That the police unreasonably invaded Green's privacy.

In fact, the reasoning A states would not make the evidence admissible even if the college president's acts were determinative, because his acting "in loco parentis" would not in and of itself give him the duty to make sure the students are law abiding. Rather, it's the police activity which will determine the admissibility of the evidence. A wrinkle in these facts is that the college president called in the police. If you chose option A, you may have been thinking of the rule that the Fourth Amendment does not address *private* conduct, only *official* conduct (unless the private person is closely related to the state, e.g., operating at the direction of the police). That isn't the case here. Since A does not focus on the central issue, and arrives at an incorrect result, it's not the best response.

(B) is not the best response,
because although it's correct as far as it goes, it ignores the fact that the police *initially* unreasonably invaded Green's privacy.

By placing microphones in Green's room, they violated Green's reasonable expectation of privacy, and they had no warrant to place any kind of electronic surveillance. (The requirements for doing so are strict: For a start, there must be probable cause to believe specific criminal activity has taken place or is taking place, the warrant must describe with particularity the conversations which will be heard, etc.). Here, these requirements are clearly not met, which is why the evidence will not be admissible. This aside, the latter part of the police conduct – the search warrant and the search itself – are satisfactory, as B suggests. However, since B does not recognize that the foundation for the search warrant was faulty, it's not the best response.

(D) is not the best response,

because although it arrives at the correct result, it doesn't cite the correct reasoning.

"Fundamental fairness" is not the test for determining if the electronic surveillance is unfair; rather, it's whether the person's reasonable expectation of privacy has been violated. (While electronic surveillance can be conducted under a warrant, the warrant requirements are very strict, and clearly not satisfied here). Since D does not apply the correct test to these facts, it's not the best response.

Answer 105

(A) is the best response,

because it recognizes that Dan will be guilty. The key factor here is causation – Dan did, in fact, cause Tom's death.

Criminal homicide requires causing the death of a living human being, where death occurs within a year and a day. The fortuitous plane crash would not change this result; nor would Tom's pre-existing heart condition. Dan's conduct was the cause in fact and legal cause of Tom's death. Since A correctly identifies that Dan will be guilty of criminal homicide, it's the best response.

(B) is not the best response,

because the reason it gives does not negate Dan's liability for homicide.

The plane crash was a fortuitous coincidence, but does not alter the fact that Dan's culpable. Criminal homicide is causing the death of a living human being, where death occurs within a year and a day. Here, Dan deliberately poisoned Tom, intending to kill him, and the poison did in fact kill Tom. It doesn't matter that Tom would have died without the poisoning – the key fact is that the poison did, in fact, kill him. The fortuity of saving Tom from dying in the plane crash would not exonerate Dan, so B is not the best response.

(C) is not the best response,

because its reasoning is irrelevant.

The important fact is that Dan caused Tom's death, which is what criminal homicide requires. The fact that Tom would have died anyway is not an issue. The classic example of this is the person who kills a person who is scheduled to be executed the following day. The inevitability of the result from other causes is not a

defense (since, taken to an extreme, there could be no such thing as homicide – since everyone will *eventually* die). Since C states incorrect reasoning, it's not the best response.

(D) is not the best response,

because it misstates the rule on causation.

In order to be a legal cause, the conduct or omission must be a substantial factor in bringing about the result. Under the facts here, although Tom's heart was already weakened, the poison was a substantial factor in bringing on the fatal heart attack. Beyond that, criminal homicide only requires causing a death of a living human being. Here, Dan did far more than what's necessary for homicide – he intended to kill Tom, and administered a fatal dose of poison. The fact that Tom's pre-existing heart condition contributed to his death would not exonerate Dan. Thus, D is not the best response.

Answer 106

The key here is distinguishing between legal and factual impossibility; A, B and D are all examples of factual impossibility, which is *not* a valid defense to a crime. C describes *legal* impossibility, which *is* a valid defense. What could key you in to which of these is the correct response is the fact that A, B and D all describe the *same behavior* by the defendant – mistaking the facts. Thus, *none* of them can be the best response.

(C) is the best response,

because it represents the *only* option of these four under which the defendant is likely to be acquitted.

That's because defendant has a valid *legal impossibility* defense – what he intended to do was not criminal. Here, defendant did everything he intended to do – purchasing codeine without a prescription – but his actions do not constitute a crime. This should be contrasted with factual impossibility, which arises when completion of the crime is impossible due to physical facts not known to the defendant. Factual impossibility, unlike legal impossibility, is *not* a valid defense. Even if you had forgotten which of legal and factual impossibility was a valid defense, a clue here is that the three incorrect options are all similar – the defendant makes a *factual* mistake. The nature of the defendant's misperception is fundamentally different in C, which would key you in to the likelihood that it's the best response.

(A) is not the best response,

because it depicts factual impossibility, which is not a valid defense to an attempt charge.

Factual impossibility arises when completion of the crime is impossible due to physical facts not known to the defendant. (Don't confuse this with *legal* impossibility – where what defendant intends to do is not criminal. Legal impossibility *is* a valid defense to attempt.) Under option A, defendant did not know the physical fact that the police had intercepted the stolen goods.

Had this fact not been true, defendant would be liable for receiving stolen goods. Since factual impossibility is not a valid defense to an attempt charge, defendant will likely be guilty, and, since the question asks for the option where defendant is most likely to be *not* guilty, A is not the best response.

(B) is not the best response,

because it depicts factual impossibility, which is not a valid defense to an attempt charge.

Factual impossibility arises when completion of the crime is impossible due to physical facts not known to the defendant. (Don't confuse this with *legal* impossibility – where what defendant *intends* to do is not criminal. Legal impossibility *is* a valid defense to attempt.) Under option B, defendant did not know that the banker realized his true identity. Where the victim is not deceived by the wrongdoer's lies, the defendant will be liable for attempted false pretenses. Since the question asks for the option where defendant is most likely to be acquitted, B is not the best response.

(D) is not the best response,

because it depicts factual impossibility, which is not a valid defense to an attempt charge.

Factual impossibility arises when completion of the crime is impossible due to physical facts not known to the defendant. (Don't confuse this with *legal* impossibility – where what defendant *intends* to do is not criminal. Legal impossibility *is* a valid defense to attempt.) Under option D, defendant did not know Selma was dead. Thus, his attempt to kill her was thwarted by a physical fact he didn't know – i.e., that she was already dead. As a result, defendant will be liable for attempted murder. Since the question asks for the option under which defendant is most likely to be acquitted, D isn't the best response.

Answer 107

(B) is the best response,

because it is irrelevant.

Impeachment is the means of casting adversely on the credibility of the witness. It can be accomplished via either reputation or opinion testimony, under FRE 608(a). Impeachment can show, for instance, bias or interest, contradicting facts, inconsistent statements, prior convictions, bad character for truthfulness, or sensory deficiencies (although the requirements for admitting some of these will differ, and some can only come from the witness's own mouth, not from extrinsic evidence).

As a threshold issue, any piece of evidence must be relevant in order to be admissible. Evidence is logically relevant if it tends to prove or disprove a material fact. FRE 401. If a piece of evidence is logically relevant, it may be admissible (as long as it meets other evidence requirements); if it isn't logically relevant, it's inadmissible. The problem here is that Louis's alcoholism would not reflect on his veracity, making his alcoholism irrelevant, and thus inadmissible. This would make the question improper, and as a result, since the question is looking for the improper question, B is the best response.

(A) is not the best response,

because it is a question seeking to show bias or interest, which is a proper basis for intrinsic impeachment under the FRE. This would make option A a proper matter on which to question Louis, and you're looking for an *improper* question.

Impeachment is the means of casting adversely on the credibility of the witness. It can be accomplished via either reputation or opinion testimony, under FRE 608(a). Impeachment can show, for instance, bias or interest, contradicting facts, inconsistent statements, prior convictions, bad character for truthfulness, or sensory deficiencies (although the requirements for admitting some of these will differ, and some can only come from the witness's own mouth, not from extrinsic evidence).

The impeachment here is "intrinsic" because it is sought from the witness's own mouth (impeachment from other sources is called "extrinsic" impeachment). There are five basic types of questions that can be used to elicit intrinsic impeachment from a witness. They are:

1. Bias or interest;
2. Prior inconsistent statements;
3. Prior convictions (under FRE 609(a), misdemeanors involving dishonesty and any felony, and only convictions not more than ten years old);
4. Bad character for honesty (including unconvicted bad acts); and
5. Sensory deficiencies (e.g., eyesight, memory, mental disability).

If it's true that Louis is Potts's close friend, this indicates bias, since it's possible that he would lie on Potts's behalf. Thus, the evidence will be relevant to Louis's credibility. Since A fails to recognize that the evidence here will be a proper form of intrinsic impeachment, it's not the best response.

(C) is not the best response,

because it is a question seeking to show a bad character for honesty via unconvicted bad acts, which is a proper basis for intrinsic impeachment under the FRE.

Impeachment is the means of casting adversely on the credibility of the witness. It can be accomplished via either reputation or opinion testimony, under FRE 608(a). Impeachment can show, for instance, bias or interest, contradicting facts, inconsistent statements, prior convictions, bad character for truthfulness, or sensory deficiencies (although the requirements for admitting some of these will differ, and some can only come from the witness's own mouth, not from extrinsic evidence).

The impeachment here is "intrinsic" because it is sought from the witness's own mouth (impeachment from other sources is called "extrinsic" impeachment). There are five basic types of questions that can be used to elicit intrinsic impeachment from a witness. They are:

1. Bias or interest;
2. Prior inconsistent statements;
3. Prior convictions (under FRE 609(a), misdemeanors involving dishonesty and any felony, and only convictions not more than ten years old);
4. Bad charcter for honesty (including unconvicted bad acts); and
5. Sensory deficiencies (e.g., eyesight, memory, mental disability).

The impeachment here is "intrinsic" because it is sought from the witness's own mouth (impeachment from other sources is called "extrinsic" impeachment). If it's true that Louis did not declare some income on his tax return last year, his dishonesty may encompass his testimony in court as well, and is thus relevant to his credibility. Since C fails to recognize that the evidence here will be a proper form of intrinsic impeachment, it's not the best response.

(D) is not the best response,

because it is a question seeking to show a prior conviction, which because of the crime involved is a proper basis for intrinsic impeachment under the FRE.

Impeachment is the means of casting adversely on the credibility of the witness. It can be accomplished via either reputation or opinion testimony, under FRE 608(a). Impeachment can show, for instance, bias or interest, contradicting facts, inconsistent statements, prior convictions, bad character for truthfulness, or sensory deficiencies (although the requirements for admitting some of these will differ, and some can only come from the witness's own mouth, not from extrinsic evidence).

The impeachment here is "intrinsic" because it is sought from the witness's own mouth (impeachment from other sources is called "extrinsic" impeachment). There are five basic types of questions thatcan be used to elicit intrinsic impeachment from a witness. They are:

1. Bias or interest;
2. Prior inconsistent statements;
3. Prior convictions of some types;
4. Bad charcter for honesty (including unconvicted bad acts); and
5. Sensory deficiencies (e.g., eyesight, memory, mental disability).

The impeachment here is "intrinsic" because it is sought from the witness's own mouth (impeachment from other sources is called "extrinsic" impeachment). Under FRE 609(a), a witness can be intrinsically impeached with any misdemeanor involving dishon-

esty, and *any* felony, not more than ten years old. Here, it doesn't matter if the crime involved was a felony or a misdemeanor, because it involves dishonesty. Furthermore, the option indicates that the conviction is only seven years old, so it meets the time requirement of FRE 609(a). Since D fails to recognize that the evidence here will be a proper form of intrinsic impeachment, it's not the best response.

Answer 108

(D) is the best response

because it correctly states the standard.

In both federal and state courts, a witness's proper invocation of the privilege against self-incrimination is judged under the "reasonable possibilities" test. Under it, the court must find reasonable grounds for believing the witness is subject to criminal liability (not civil liability or public disgrace), and that his answer will at least provide a link to evidence which may incriminate him, in order to allow him to remain silent. Hoffman v. U.S. (1951). Since D correctly states this rule, it's the best response.

(A) is not the best response,

because it overstates the actual standard.

In both federal and state courts, a witness's proper invocation of the privilege against self-incrimination is judged under the "reasonable possibilities" test. Under it, the court must find reasonable grounds for believing the witness is subject to criminal liability (not civil liability or public disgrace), and that his answer will at least provide a link to evidence which may incriminate him, in order to allow him to remain silent. A states a standard which is much stricter than the actual standard. As a result, it's not the best response.

(B) is not the best response,

because it overstates the standard.

In both federal and state courts, a witness's proper invocation of the privilege against self-incrimination is judged under the "reasonable possibilities" test. Under it, the court must find reasonable grounds for believing the witness is subject to criminal liability (not civil liability or public disgrace), and that his answer will at least provide a link to evidence which may incriminate him, in order to allow him to remain silent. B states a standard which is much stricter than the real standard. As a result, it's not the best response.

(C) is not the best response,

because it overstates the standard.

In both federal and state courts, a witness's proper invocation of the privilege against self-incrimination is judged under the "reasonable possibilities" test. Under it, the court must find reasonable grounds for believing the witness is subject to criminal liability (not civil liability or public disgrace), and that his answer will at least provide a link to evidence which may incriminate him, in order to allow him to remain silent. C states a standard which is slightly more strict than the real standard. As a result, it's not the best response.

Answer 109

(A) is the best response,

because it correctly identifies that Venner can use the sale proceeds to pay off the mortgage, and thus force Brier to honor the contract.

Under these facts, you're told that Venner and Brier had an "enforceable written agreement" for the sale of Greenacre. The agreement, as a land sale contract, would carry with it the implied covenant of marketable title. This means that the seller, at the closing, must convey title which, viewed objectively, is free from reasonable doubt in both law and fact, and which the reasonable buy would accept without fear of litigation. Liens, mortgages, taxes, and other encumbrances render title "unmarketable," and allow the buyer to avoid the sale. Thus, for Venner to obtain specific performance of the contract, he'd have to get around the "marketable title" problem, since on the date of the closing, there's a mortgage on Greenacre, which theoretically renders title unmarketable (and renders Venner in breach of contract).

Option A suggests a viable way to avoid the "marketable title" problem. Here, you're told that the proceeds will cover the mortgage. When that's the case, the seller has an implied right to use the proceeds of the sale to pay off the mortgage. By arguing this, Venner not only avoids being in breach of the contract, but he can enforce the contract against Brier, since this means that Brier won't have the right to cancel the contract. When you think about it, this rule comports with what you'd expect to happen, since many homeowners, in real life, couldn't buy a new home if this weren't the case. Since option A recognizes a means by which Venner can enforce the contract, it's the best response.

(B) is not the best response,

because it misstates the law.

Under these facts, you're told that Venner and Brier had an "enforceable written agreement" for the sale of Greenacre. The agreement, as a land sale contract, would carry with it the implied covenant of marketable title. This means that the seller, at the closing, must convey title which, viewed objectively, is free from reasonable doubt in both law and fact, and which the reasonable buy would accept without fear of litigation. Liens, morgages, taxes, and other encumbrances render title "unmarketable," and allow the buyer to avoid the sale. Thus, for Venner to obtain specific performance of the contract, he'd have to get around the "marketable title" problem, since on the date of the closing, there's a mortgage on Greenacre, which theoretically renders title unmarketable (and renders Venner in breach of contract).

Option B doesn't offer a viable means of avoiding the

"marketable title" problem. Although it's possible that the law of the jurisdiction may make the mortgage payable from the proceeds, and the mortgage agreement itself may insist on payoff if the property is conveyed, this doesn't remove the mortgage from Greenacre -- and that's the central problem here. A strong argument for Venner would have to address how the mortgage is removed from Greenacre, since that's what prevents Venner from enforcing the contract. Since B doesn't recognize this, it's not the best response.

(C) is not the best response,

because the doctrine of equitable conversion would not apply to these facts.

The doctrine of equitable conversion addresses the period between the signing of the land sale contract, and the closing. Under the doctrine, the vendor has a personal property interest in the property, between the signing of the contract and the closing, in the form of the balance of the purchase price owed to him; the vendee is considered the beneficial owner of the property.

What this doctrine does, as an equitable doctrine, is to allocate risks the parties didn't address. However, under these facts, marketable title *was* addressed, since the conveyance of marketable title is an implied covenant in land sale contracts. As a result, Venner impliedly assumed the risk that the title might not be marketable, and that Brier could avoid the contract on this basis. Any encumbrance on property, like the mortgage here, would render it unmarketable. Since conveying marketable title is a duty allocated to Venner under the land sale contract, Venner cannot turn to equity to avoid providing it, and the doctrine of equitable conversion won't help him. Since C doesn't recognize this, it's not the best response.

(D) is not the best response,

because it states an insufficient ground on which Venner could prevail. Of course, his underlying argument must be that he hasn't breached the contract, because if he had, he wouldn't be entitled to specific performance. However, option D, in and of itself, doesn't provide a rule allowing Venner to use the proceeds to pay off the mortgage, and enforce the contract.

Under these facts, you're told that Venner and Brier had an "enforceable written agreement" for the sale of Greenacre. The agreement, as a land sale contract, would carry with it the implied covenant of marketable title. This means that the seller, at the closing, must convey title which, viewed objectively, is free from reasonable doubt in both law and fact, and which the reasonable buy would accept without fear of litigation. Liens, morgages, taxes, and other encumbrances render title "unmarketable," and allow the buyer to avoid the sale. Thus, for Venner to obtain specific performance of the contract, he'd have to get around the "marketable title" problem, since on the date of the closing, there's a mortgage on Greenacre, which theoretically renders title unmarketable (and renders Venner in breach of contract).

Simply saying that Venner hasn't breached the contract doesn't provide an argument for enforcing the contract. In fact, the seller has an implied right to use the proceeds of the sale to pay off the mortgage, assuming the proceeds cover the mortgage (which is true, under these facts) -- and it's this implied right that makes the contract enforceable. Thus, what option D does is fail to take the extra step take by option A, in addressing the implied right and forcing Brier to honor the contract. As a result, D isn't the best response.

Answer 110

(B) is the best response,

because it identifies the central issue under these facts and resolves it in Olga's favor.

The genesis of the conflict here was the *oral* agreement for the sale of an interest in land. Such a contract falls within the Statute of Frauds, and thus must be in writing to be enforceable. However, there are circumstances under which the writing requirement will be excused, and one of them appears to be a major obstacle for Olga under these facts: Part performance. In a contract for the sale of land, if the buyer pays all or part of the purchase price AND performs some act explainable only by the contract's existence, the contract will be enforceable even without a writing. Thus, Olga would *have* to explain away Terrence's $1,000 in improvements in order to prevail, since people as a rule don't spend money improving what they believe is someone else's property. One way she could overcome this is suggested by option B: She could argue that spending $1,000 on improvements is as consistent with Terrence's being a long-term tenant as with the oral contract. That's because the buyer's act must be *unequivocally referable* to an oral contract to be excused from the writing requirement. If the action is attributable to anything else, it won't suffice.

This is an interesting problem because your gut reaction is that Terrence will *prevail,* due to part performance. Then, the question throws you for a loop by stating that *Olga* prevailed, and asking you why. In a way, the element that most made you believe Terrence should win – the $1,000 in improvements – leads you to the correct response, because it tells you the *central issue* that Olga must address in order to prevail. Since the argument in option B represents a plausible way for Olga to overcome\ the central obstacle in these facts, it's the best response.

(A) is not the best response,

because it misstates the law.

Option A has a *kernel* of truth in it, in that contracts for the sale of land are within the Statute of Frauds, and thus must be in writing to be enforceable. However, even *without* a writing, under *some* circumstances, a land sale contract will be enforced. In general, the Stat-ute of Frauds writing requirement will be excused when to do otherwise would result in fraud or undue hardship. The traditional rule is that, when the buyer pays all or part of the purchase price *and* performs some act "unequivocally referable" to the existence of the contract, the writing requirement will be *excused.* An act is "unequivocally referable" if it's explainable only by the contract's existence. Thus, it's not correct to say that there's no way to overcome a lack of a writing. Since A says this, it can't be the best response.

(C) is not the best response,

because although it addresses the central issue, it makes an argument that would benefit Terrence, not Olga.

The source of the conflict here is that contracts for the sale of land are within the Statute of Frauds and thus must be in writing to be enforceable. However, the Statute of Frauds writing requirement will be excused when to do otherwise would result in fraud or undue hardship. In a traditional rule relevant to these facts, when the buyer in a land sale contract pays all or part of the purchase price *and* performs some act "unequivocally referable" to the agreement, the writing will be *excused.* An act is "unequivocally referable" if it's explainable only by the contract's existence. Thus, the major obstacle Olga had to overcome is Terrence's $1,000 worth of improvements, which would tend to suggest that the contract existed since Terrence would be unlikely to improve someone *else's* land, for nothing. In fact, the argument C makes would support *Terrence's* position, since he wouldn't ask permission to undertake improvements on his own land. Since C addresses a factor which would not help resolve the case in Olga's favor, it's not the best response.

(D) is not the best response,

because it does not address completely the basis on which Terrence would be denied specific performance.

Specific performance is an equitable remedy, appropriate only where there's no adequate legal remedy (e.g., money damages). It's appropriate where the subject is unique (e.g., a piece of land or an antique), and/or the money value is not ascertainable. As an equitable remedy, specific performance is granted to avoid injustice. However, this would be determined primarily by the unjust *harm* to Terrence, *not* unjust enrichment to Olga. Since option D focuses on the unjust benefit to Olga and not the unjust harm to Terrence, it's not the best response.

Answer 111

(C) is the best response,

because it identifies the correct means of accepting the offer, and also the appropriate interpretation of the performance requested.

An offer for a bilateral contract seeks a return promise; an offer for a unilateral contract seeks performance. In cases where the offer is ambiguous as to whether it's seeking performance or a promise, offeree has his choice of performing or promising to perform. There are very few situations were an offer *clearly* seeks performance, instead of a return promise. However, a reward offer is just such an offer. The city clearly doesn't want someone to promise to find the arsonist – it only wants *action*. Thus, only performance would constitute acceptance.

As to the interpretation of the offer, it would be unreasonable to interpret the offer as literally requiring a private citizen to arrest and convict the arsonist. Instead, the offer would be interpreted as only requiring information *leading* to the arrest and conviction. To interpret the offer literally would confine the scope of offerees to the police (since they are generally the only ones who can conduct an arrest), and the City Council clearly didn't intend to so restrict the offer. (Apart from anything else, a policeman couldn't likely accept the reward offer due to problems of consideration underlying the contract: Catching the arsonist would be considered a policeman's pre-existing legal duty.) Since C correctly addresses the means and medium of acceptance, it's the best response.

(A) is not the best response,

because the offer here was for a *unilateral* contract, and thus it could only be accepted by performance, not a return promise.

An offer for a bilateral contract seeks a return promise; an offer for a unilateral contract seeks performance. In cases where the offer is ambiguous, as to whether it's seeking a unilateral or bilateral contract, offeree has his choice of performing or promising to perform. There are very few situations where an offer *clearly* seeks performance instead of a return promise. An offer of a reward, as in these facts, is one of them; another is where offeror specifically limits the acceptance to performance. Here, the city was looking for someone to aid in finding an arsonist, not for a promise to look for the arsonist. Thus, the only way to accept the city's offer would be by offering information leading to the arsonist's arrest. Since A ignores this, it's not the best response.

(B) is not the best response,

because it overstates what an offeree would need to do in order to accept the reward offer.

Here, because a reward is offered, the offer is seeking a *unilateral* contract. That is, the *only* way a person could accept would be through the requested performance. What B addresses is exactly what form that performance must take. This requires interpretation of the "for the arrest and conviction" language. Since the offer is being broadcast to the general public, the City Council couldn't have meant to limit the reward to any citizen who actually arrested the arsonist, since this would effectively cut out any offeree except a policeman (who would probably be precluded from accepting

since finding the arsonist would probably fulfill a pre-existing legal duty, meaning that consideration would be lacking). Instead, a reasonable interpretation would require an offeree only to offer information leading to the arrest and conviction of the arsonists: Since option B interprets the offer too literally, it's not the best response.

(D) is not the best response,

because an offeree could only accept the reward offer via performance, not a return promise; and even if a promise *were* required, it wouldn't require using the same medium as the offer.

An offer for a bilateral contract seeks a return promise; an offer for a unilateral contract seeks performance. In cases where the offer is ambiguous as to whether it's seeking performance or a promise, offeree has his choice of performing or promising to perform. There are very few situations where an offer *clearly* seeks performance instead of a return promise. However, a reward offer is just such an offer. The city obviously doesn't want a promise to perform, it wants *action* only – information about the arsonists. Thus, the communication of assent by an offeree, contrary to what D suggests, would not suffice.

Even if the offer were for a bilateral contract, offeree *could* perform instead of promising to perform, and D ignores this. In fact, even if offeree *did* have to promise to perform in return, he wouldn't have to use the same medium as the offer. Under modern rules, an acceptance may be made via any medium that is reasonable in the circumstances, as long as the offeror did not expressly limit acceptance to a particular medium. Thus, while using the same medium as the offer would generally be appropriate, it wouldn't be reasonable to expect an acceptance via television, as option D suggests. (Apart from anything else, buying the TV time alone would wipe out the reward money!) Since option D misstates the means and medium required for acceptance, it's not the best response.

Answer 112

(D) is the best response,

because it recognizes the two ways the reward offer could terminate.

As a general rule, there are six ways an offer may terminate other than via acceptance: Revocation, death or insanity, intervening illegality, rejection/counter-offer, lapse of time, or destruction of subject matter. The only two that would apply to these facts would be a revocation or a lapse of time.

Note that revocation is valid *even if* the original offerees don't see it! Since D recognizes both means of terminating the offer, it's the best response.

(A) is not the best response,

because it does not address a means of terminating the city's offer.

As a general rule, there are six ways an offer may terminate other than via acceptance: Revocation, death or insanity, intervening illegality, rejection/counter-offer, lapse of time, or destruction of subject matter. The only two that would apply to these facts would be a revocation or a lapse of time. However, while A addresses the lapse of time option, it does not offer the correct rule. There's nothing magical about December 31; instead, an offer lapses after a *reasonable* time, the reasonability being dependent on the circumstances (the offeror *can,* of course, expressly limit the duration of the offer). Option A also ignores completely the possibility of revocation, since that represents the other means by which the offer could terminate. Since A misstates the lapse of time possibility and ignores revocation all together, it's not the best response.

(B) is not the best response,

because the offer could terminate through lapse of time *as well as* by effective revocation.

As a general rule, there are six ways an offer may terminate other than via acceptance: Revocation, death or insanity, intervening illegality, rejection/counter-offer, lapse of time, or destruction of subject matter. The only two that would apply to these facts would be a revocation or a lapse of time.

Option B is correct in stating that the offer could be revoked. To do this, the city would have to offer equivalent notice to the original offerees, the radio stations probably being adequate in light of the fact that the TV station is out of business (since an ad on TV with the same frequency would be the *best* means of revocation).

However, B ignores the lapse of time possibility. An offer can be revoked by a reasonable lapse of time, the reasonability being dependent on the circumstances (of course, the offeror *can* expressly limit the duration of the offer). Since B ignores one of the two alternatives for termination of the offer, it's not the best response.

(C) is not the best response,

because the offer could terminate through revocation *as well as* by lapse of time.

As a general rule, there are six ways an offer may terminate other than via acceptance: Revocation, death or insanity, intervening illegality, rejection/counter-offer, lapse of time, or destruction of subject matter. The only two that would apply to these facts would be a revocation or a lapse of time.

Option C is correct in stating that the offer could be revoked by the lapse of a reasonable period of time. Of course, the offeror *can* expressly limit the duration of the offer, although the Council didn't do so under these facts.

However, what C ignores is that the Council could *also* revoke the offer. If you chose this response, it's

probably because you *either* felt reward offers were not, in general, revocable, *or* you focused on the TV station going out of business and figured that cut out the only means of revocation. The rule is, in fact, that general offers can be revoked by equivalent notice to the original offerees. This is normally achieved via the same medium. However, where that's not feasible, certainly a similar medium to the original offerees would suffice. Under these facts, that's the radio stations. Since C doesn't recognize this, it's not the best response.

Answer 113

(C) is the best response,

because it addresses precisely the requirements of an effective revocation of a general offer.

The original ad, containing the offer, was a "general offer" – that is, it was made to an undetermined number of offerees. As a general rule, a "general offer" must be revoked by equivalent notice to the original offerees. This typically means an ad in the same medium as the offer was made. The problem under these facts is that the medium used for the offer – the TV station – has since gone out of business, so revocation can't be accomplished that way. Under facts like these, an alternative medium reaching approximately the same audience would suffice.

Note that if the revocation meets this standard, it doesn't matter if a particular offeree heard the offer and not the revocation – the offer is nonetheless revoked as to every offeree. Note also that under these facts, the revocation run over the two radio stations would probably be adequate.e Since C states the correct means of revoking a general offer, it's the best response.

(A) is not the best response,

because the same audience would not be reached by a TV ad and a legal notice in the local newspaper.

The original ad, containing the offer, was a "general offer" – that is, it was made to an undetermined number of offerees. As a general rule, a "general offer" must be revoked by equivalent notice to the original offerees. This typically means an ad in the same medium as the offer was made. The problem under these facts is that the medium used for the offer – the TV station – has since gone out of business, so revocation can't be accomplished that way. Under facts like these, an alternative medium reaching approximately the same audience would suffice. The problem with using the legal notices column of the local newspaper is that it's unlikely to have the same audience as the local TV station. You can verify this with a simple do-it-yourself demonstration. Do you watch TV? The answer's probably yes. Do you read the legal notices? Probably not. In any case, you've got a clue under these facts as to the solution to the alternative media problem: The two local radio stations that the council used, which are more likely to reach the same audience. Since the medium suggested by option A *wouldn't* reach the same audience, it's not the best response.

(B) is not the best response,

because although it's theoretically correct, it's impossible under these facts, since the TV station is out of business.

The original ad, containing the offer, was a "general offer" – that is, it was made to an undetermined number of offerees. As a general rule, a "general offer" must be revoked by equivalent notice to the original offerees. This typically means an ad in the same medium as the offer was made. The problem under these facts is that the medium used for the offer – the TV station – has since gone out of business, which B fails to take into account.

In fact, the two local radio stations used by the council would probably do the trick. Since B doesn't address a plausible solution under these facts, it's not the best response.

(D) is not the best response,

because it overstates what the Council will have to do to revoke its offer.

The original ad, containing the offer, was a "general offer" – that is, it was made to an undetermined number of offerees. As a general rule, a "general offer" must be revoked by equivalent notice to the original offerees. This typically means an ad in the same medium as the offer was made. The problem under these facts is that the medium used for the offer – the TV station – has since gone out of business, so revocation can't be accomplished that way. Under facts like these, an alternative medium reaching approximately the same audience would suffice.

While a notice to all city residents and any other offerees would certainly suffice, it's like using a chainsaw to carve a turkey: Something much less drastic would suffice. In fact, the solution the Council chose – running the revocation on the two local radio stations – would probably be sufficient. Since D overstates the requirements of revocation, it's not the best response.

Answer 114

(D) is the best response,

because it correctly identifies the relationship as a series of contracts, not one entire contract, and that the contracts are unilateral, not bilateral.

An offer for a bilateral contract requests a promise in return; an offer for a unilateral contract requests performance. While most offers *could* be characterized as seeking a *bilateral* contract, the one here couldn't: The memo specifically requested "actual performance" for $200 per day. Thus, the individual contracts could only be created by Gimlet's commencing work on a given day. You know these are unilateral contracts because

Gimlet's under no duty to start work each day. If he does a day's investigating, he's entitled to $200; if he goes to Disneyworld instead, he hasn't breached a contract, but by the same token, he's not entitled to $200 for that day. With each new day comes the potential of a new contract, created when Gimlet commences work (since commencing work under a unilateral contract is the only means of accepting it). Since option D correctly states that a series of unilateral contracts was created here, it's the best response.

(A) is not the best response,

because it does not correctly characterize the relationship here: There are no grounds for irrevocability, and the relationship is a series of contracts, not *one* contract.

There are only two ways an offer at common law can be irrevocable: If the offeree pays for irrevocability for a period of time (that is, he buys an "option"); or, under a unilateral contract, the offer cannot be revoked once performance has begun. Here, the memo to Gimlet created a series of unilateral contracts, since Humongous was seeking performance, not a return promise, on a daily basis. Thus, when Gimlet began work *each day*, Humongous couldn't revoke its offer for the rest of *that day*, but it *could* revoke it as to the future until Gimlet commenced work again the next day. Thus, although A correctly characterized the offer as unilateral, its failure to take into account that the relationship was a series of contracts and not one large contract makes it incorrect.

If you missed this, it could be because you weren't comfortable with the "series of contracts" idea. The agreement here is for a series of contracts instead of just one big one because the performance by each party is divisible into corresponding parts: A day's investigation for $200. The significance of this would have to do with breach: If a party performs one (or more) segments of a divisible contract, he can collect under the contract for those segments even if he's breached other parts. Since A mischaracterizes the contract, it's not the best response.

(B) isn't the best response,

because it mischaracterizes the agreement as one entire contract, and mischaracterizes the condition precedent.

Here, the memo from Humongous to Gimlet created a series of unilateral contracts, since Humongous was seeking performance, not a return promise, on a daily basis. Under the contract, Gimlet was required to "actually…investigat(e)" the fire, and for each day he did so, he'd be entitled to $200. Thus, for each day Gimlet's actual investigation was an express condition precedent to Humongous's duty to pay. The *success* of the investigation was neither mentioned nor otherwise required. Since B states otherwise, it's not the best response.

(C) is not the best response,

because the daily contracts were unilateral, not bilateral.

An offer for a bilateral contract requests a promise in return; an offer for a unilateral contract requests performance. While most offers *can* be characterized as requesting a promise in return, this one couldn't: The memo specifically offered $200 "for each day's work" spent investigating the fire. Thus, Gimlet could *only* accept by working. Here's a handy way to distinguish unilateral and bilateral contracts: Under a bilateral contract, when the contract is formed, there are two rights and two duties. Under a unilateral contract, at contract formation, there's one right, and one duty. Here, if Gimlet doesn't perform, he's committed no breach because he had no duty to perform – he didn't promise he'd perform. Of course, once he undertook to act each day, he had a duty to perform diligently, but this is not the result of a promise of any kind. Here, since a series of acts was requested, a series of unilateral contracts was created. Since C mistakenly characterizes the contracts as bilateral, it's not the best response.

Answer 115

(B) is the best response,

because it's the only option that doesn't characterize the offer as a *reward.*

According to most courts, an offeree must perform in response to a reward offer in order to collect the reward. As a general rule, if the offeree acts without knowledge of the reward (as Gimlet did here), he isn't entitled to the reward and the offeror (City) isn't contractually bound to pay it.

Thus, Gimlet's best claim would have to characterize the offer as for something other than a reward. Option B would do just that. In some states, when a *public body* of some type offers a reward, the reward can be claimed\ even without knowledge of it when performance took place, making it a bounty more than a reward per se. Under these facts, assuming Gimlet partially performed before the offer was revoked, the City would be obligated to leave the offer open at least for a reasonable time in order to give Gimlet a chance to complete his investigation. (That's because, as an offer for a unilateral contract, pat performance by the offeree makes the offer irrevocable, and thus the City's revocation of the offer wouldn't defeat Gimlet's claim.) Since B offers a basis on which Gimlet can recover, and no other option does, it's the best response.

(A) is not the best response,

because it represents the minority view on rewards, and ignores the central obstacle under these facts.

As a general rule, in order to recover a reward, one must know about the reward at the time of performance. Without that knowledge, no contract is formed, and no reward is owed. The minority view is what option A reflects: If the offeror gets the benefit of the

bargain, he's required to pay.

As this rule indicates, the only way for Gimlet to prevail is to have what looks like a standard reward characterized as something *other* than a reward. Since A doesn't recognize this, it's not the best response.

(C) is not the best response,

because it mischaracterizes the facts.

The offer here was a general offer for a unilateral contract. As such, it could be revoked effectively by using the same manner as the offer was made or by a comparable medium and frequency of publicity, designed to reach approximately the same offerees. Furthermore, the offer, since it seeks a unilateral contract, could only be made irrevocable by part performance of an offeree, *acting with knowledge of the offer.* Even if Gimlet could have been considered to have partially performed before the offer was revoked, he didn't know about the offer when he did so. As a result, there was nothing to stop the City from revoking its reward offer. In fact, it could have revoked the offer the day after it was made, if it so desired – the "few months" duration by itself is not illuminating.

Of course, had there *been* evidence of bad faith, the City *could* be liable, since there is an implied duty of good faith in every contract. For instance, had a City Council member overheard that Gimlet was investigating and hurriedly had the offer revoked before Gimlet found out about it, this would suffice for bad faith. But no such facts exist here, so the city couldn't be liable, and C can't be the best response.

(D) is not the best response,

because a moral obligation, in and of itself, is not sufficient to create a contractual obligation.

Under these facts, the general offer was for a unilateral contract: Thus, it could only be accepted by performance with knowledge of the offer. With its language of "no bargained-for exchange," option D suggests that consideration was lacking. In fact, the consideration for a unilateral contract is the offeree's continued performance, and thus there's no consideration problem under these facts, but by the same token there's no liability created by a moral obligation, either. The only thing that *could* obligate the City was if Gimlet commenced performance knowing about the contract. Otherwise, the City was free to revoke the offer, as it did.

What all this implies is that Gimlet can't prevail if he treats the offer as an offer for a reward, because he didn't know about the offer when he performed, and thus can't collect on that basis. Since D doesn't recognize this and instead mistakenly creates contractual liability on the grounds of moral obligation, it's not the best response.

Answer 116

(C) is the best response.

As to Statement 1:

This is a misrepresentation of fact, and as such can form the basis for an action in deceit.

These are the requirements of deceit: Defendant's misrepresentation of a material past or present fact; Defendant's knowledge of falsity or reckless disregard for falsity; Defendant's intent to induce Plaintiffs reliance; Plaintiff's actual, justifiable reliance; and damages.

Under these facts, the key distinction is between an actual misrepresentation, and the mere expression of an opinion, which is called puffing. Puffery is not actionable - if it were, every used car salesman in the country would be out of business.

Here's how you distinguish between misrepresentation and puffing: Look at the *specificity* of the representation, and the *reasonableness* of reliance. In Statement 1, the salesman's assurance that the car had never been in an accident is both specific and a reasonable statement on which a buyer could rely – it doesn't have an opinion-like quality. Furthermore, you're told Daley knew it wasn't true; the fact that he was selling Purvis a used car suggests that he intended Purvis to rely on the statement; and since the statement was made prior to the sale, it's likely that Purvis relied on the statement, in part, in deciding to buy the car. As a result, it could form the basis of an action in deceit.

As to Statement 2:

This is a statement of fact, and as a result an action in deceit could be based on it.

These are the requirements of deceit: Defendant's misrepresentation of a material past or present fact; Defendant's knowledge of falsity or reckless disregard for falsity, Defendant's intent to induce Plaintiff's reliance; Plaintiff's actual, justifiable reliance; and damages.

The key distinction here is between an actual misrepresentation, and the mere expression of an opinion, which is called "puffing." "Puffery" is not actionable.

Here's how you distinguish between misrepresentation and puffing: Look at the *specificity* of the representation, and the *reasonableness* of reliance. Here, the assertion as to the gas mileage the car gets is both specific, and it would be reasonable for Purvis to rely on the statement. Furthermore, you're told Daley knew it wasn't true; the fact that he was selling Purvis a used car suggests that he intended Purvis to rely on the statement; and since the statement was made prior to the sale, it's likely that Purvis relied on the statement, in part, in deciding to buy the car. As a result, the gas-mileage statement could form the basis for an action in deceit.

As to Statement 3:

This statement is one of opinion, and as such it couldn't be the source of an action in deceit.

These are the requirements of deceit: Defendant's misrepresentation of a material past or present fact; Defendant's knowledge of falsity or reckless disregard for falsity; Defendant's intent to induce Plaintiff's reliance; Plaintiff's actual, justifiable reliance; and damages.

The key distinction here is between an actual misrepresentation, and the mere expression of an opinion, which is called "puffing." "Puffery" is not actionable.

Here's how you distinguish between misrepresentation and puffing: Look at the *specificity* of the representation, and the *reasonableness* of reliance. Here, Daley's statement about the quality of the ride is rather clearly his own opinion about its ride, and, beyond that, it wouldn't be reasonable for Purvis to rely on the statement. Say this was slightly different, and instead of commenting on the ride itself, Daley stated that the car was equipped with Smooth-o brand shock absorbers to give the car a smooth ride. If the car was not, in fact, equipped with Smooth-o brand shock absorbers, and Daley knew this, this statement would be an actionable misrepresentation (assuming Purvis relied on it), since although the upshot of the two statements is the same – Purvis is expecting a very smooth ride – the nature of the statement becomes one of fact and not opinion. In any case, since the statement as presented is "puffery," it's not actionable.

Answer 117

(A) is the best response,

because it identifies the central issue under these facts, resolves it, and arrives at the correct result.

The main problem with a battery claim on these facts is that Grower didn't intend that the dog bite Wife. In fact, the intent battery requires can be satisfied by the intent assault requires – that is, the intent to create the apprehension of harmful or offensive contact, followed by actual conduct. Thus, Grower's intent to frighten Wife with the threat of contact is sufficient intent for battery. Since A identifies the central element and resolves it satisfactorily, it's the best response.

(B) is not the best response,

because it's irrelevant: Res ipsa loquitur is a doctrine of circumstantial evidence of *negligence*. Here, Grower is charged with an *intentional* tort - battery.

Battery requires an intentional act resulting in harmful or offensive contact with plaintiff's person. Even if the claim had been in negligence, it's not obvious that res ipsa loquitur would apply. Res ipsa loquitur establishes a prima facie claim for negligence where the following elements are shown: The event would not normally have occurred in the absence of negligence, defendant was in exclusive control of the instrumentality causing injury, and the plaintiff did not voluntarily contribute to the event causing his injury. Here, a leash could break in the absence of negligence, so it's not likely res ipsa loquitur would attach. In any case, since the claim here is for battery, res ipsa loquitur will be irrelevant, making B not the best response.

(C) is not the best response,

because Wife's unauthorized entry was justified by *necessity*.

Under the privilege of necessity, one must be apparently facing threatened injury from a source not connected with the other party, and the invasion committed must be substantially less serious than the injury faced. Here, Wife and Husband technically were trespassers; however, they entered the property to avoid a charging bull, and since they only trampled a few plants, their entry would be privileged.

Assuming arguendo that Wife *had* been a trespasser with no necessity defense, Grower *still* would not have been entitled to attack Wife with his dog, since it would be considered unreasonable force under the circumstances, even if he was acting in defense of his property (especially since Grower had no reasonable fear for his own safety). Since Wife had a privilege of necessity in entering the property, and even without the privilege Grower's use of force was excessive, C is not the best response.

(D) is not the best response,

because it states an element which is not required for battery.

It's true that battery requires an intentional act resulting in harmful or offensive contact with plaintiff's person; however, the "intent" requirement can be satisfied by the intent to create the apprehension of harmful or offensive contact, followed by such contact, even if the contact *itself* is completely unintentional. That's the case here; Grower's intent to create the fear that he was about to "sic" his dog on Wife was enough to satisfy the intent for battery, even though Grower couldn't have intended for the leash to break (and undoubtedly didn't want it to). Since D misstates the intent requirement of battery, it's not the best response.

Answer 118

(B) is the best response,

because it identifies the central issue under these facts, and resolves it satisfactorily.

Assault requires proof of an act creating in plaintiff a reasonable apprehension of immediate harmful or offensive contact with plaintiff's person; defendant's intent to create this apprehension; and causation. Under these facts, the element most in question is Husband's apprehension, because the dog attacked Wife; thus, it's not necessarily true that *Husband* would have believed he'd be attacked. However, notice that B uses the modifier "if" instead of "because," which means that the reasoning it states need only be *plausi-*

ble on these facts, and address a central issue. Here, it's plausible that Husband had a reasonable apprehension of contact, since you could imply he was close to Wife. If that's true, then Grower will be liable for assault, since the other elements are clearly satisfied. Since B identifies the central issue in these facts and comes up with the correct result, it's the best response.

(A) is not the best response,

because although it states a correct rule of law, it does not address a cause of action for assault specifically.

Assault requires proof of an act creating in plaintiff a reasonable apprehension of immediate harmful or offensive contact with plaintiff's person; defendant's intent to create this apprehension; and causation. Thus, while Grower's use of excessive force in *this* instance will result in a valid assault claim, A is not specific enough to be the best response. In fact, applying these elements to the facts shows you that the element most in question is the first one – since the dog attacked *Wife*, you'd wonder if Husband had a reasonable apprehension of contact. Since A ignores assault entirely, it's not the best response.

(C) is not the best response,

because it states an element assault does not require.

Assault only requires proof of an act creating in plaintiff a reasonable apprehension of immediate harmful or offensive contact with plaintiff's person, defendant's intent to create this apprehension, and causation. The *contact* element is what differentiates battery from assault (also, battery can be satisfied by the intent to make contact, not just the intent to create the apprehension of immediate contact). Since C focuses on an element not required by assault, it's not the best response.

(D) is not the best response,

because Grower's intent to protect his property would not insulate him from liability under these facts.

The fact that Husband and Wife were being chased by a bull means that they entered Grower's land under the privilege of necessity. This means that Grower would not be entitled to use *any* force against them. Even if they didn't have the privilege of necessity, Grower's use of the dog would still likely be considered unreasonable force under the circumstances. Since D focuses on an element that would not be relevant under these facts, it's not the best response.

Answer 119

(A) is the best response,

because it correctly identifies the basis on which Husband and Wife will be liable: Although their entry was privileged, it was not authorized, so they'll be liable for any damage they cause.

The charging bull created the necessity that created the privilege to enter Grower's land. However, private necessity is a *qualified* privilege, requiring that the entrant pay for any damage caused. While A does not explicitly mention necessity, it does identify the essential reason Husband and Wife will be liable, so it's the best response.

(B) is not the best response,
because it's not relevant.

Without a "No Trespassing" sign, Wife and Husband would still be liable as trespassers if their entry wasn't authorized or justified; and with it, they wouldn't be liable if their entry *was* authorized or justified. In fact, under these facts Husband and Wife were privileged to enter Grower's property due to necessity: They were escaping from a bull. The reason they'll be liable for the damage to the plants is because necessity is only a *qualified* privilege, meaning any loss caused must be compensated. The existence of a "No Trespassing" sign is thus irrelevant to Husband and Wife's liability; since B states otherwise, it's not the best response.

(C) is not the best response,
because although it correctly characterizes the facts, it ignores the fact that Husband and Wife will be liable for the damage to the plants.

Husband and Wife entered Grower's land under a privilege of private necessity: They were being chased by a bull. However, the defense of private necessity is a *qualified* one, requiring that any loss caused by compensated. If you chose this response, it could be that you confused private necessity with *public* necessity, which involves a threat to the public necessitating entry (e.g., burning down a house to stop the spread of a fire). Most courts hold that public necessity is an *absolute* defense, such that the entrant will *not* be liable for damage caused. However, that's not the case here – the threat is only to Husband and Wife. As a result, they'll be liable for the damaged plants. Since C does not recognize this, it's not the best response.

(D) is not the best response,
because Grower's admittedly excessive use of force would not give them the privilege to destroy his plants.

Grower's tort liability to Husband and Wife, and Husband and Wife's liability to him, are independent. Husband and Wife entered Grower's land under a privilege of private necessity. This means that Grower could not use any force at all against them, but because the privilege is only limited, they'll be liable for any damage they cause. What Grower's use of excessive force will do is give them a claim against him for assault (Husband) and a battery (Wife). Since D does not recognize this, it's not the best response.

Answer 120

(A) is the best response,
because it correctly identifies the problem here as being one of equal protection, and it applies the correct

standard to it.

Where a classification is involved which determines people's rights, the issue is most likely one of equal protection. Here, there is a classification: Legitimate vs. illegitimate children. The test to apply in determining whether the statute is valid depends on the basis of the classification. For instance, a classification relating to who may exercise a fundamental right, or based on a suspect classification (race or alienage), requires that the classification must be necessary to promote a compelling governmental interest. If, on the other hand, economic and social legislation is concerned, the rational basis test is used: That is, if there is a set of facts imaginable that would make the law a reasonable one to achieve a legitimate governmental purpose, the law is valid. Classifications based on "sensitive" classifications, like gender and legitimacy, require application of "intermediate scrutiny". That is, the law must be substantially related to an important state interest in order to be valid. Thus, if Ben could prove that this substantially relation does not exist, he will have a valid equal protection claim.

Note that this question asks for Ben's best argument, and since option A is the only option that recognizes that these facts involve an equal protection problem, it's his best argument. Of course, that doesn't mean he'll prevail, and, in fact, he probably won't. Under Lalli v. Lalli (1978), the state's interest in the just and expeditious disposition of property makes a law denying intestate succession to intestate children valid, where the paternity of the father hasn't formally been proven sometime before his death. However, the fact that Ben won't win doesn't mean A isn't his best argument. Because it's the only option addressing the central issue, it's the best response.

(B) is not the best response,
because Ben has not been deprived of property, and there is no fundamental right to inherit, and, more importantly, the issue here is equal protection, not due process.

First, as to the property issue. It's true that due process is an issue when the effect of a state's activity amounts to a deprivation of a property interest or right (or life or liberty). Property in its most literal sense means ownership of property. However, under these facts, Ben isn't being deprived of property he owns – rather, he's seeking the right to his father's property.

Second, the fundamental right issue. When a law limits a fundamental right, it must be necessary to promote a compelling governmental interest, or else it's a due process violation. The fundamental rights are limited to these: the First Amendment rights, interstate travel, voting, and privacy. Thus, the right to inherit is not a fundamental right, but rather, any law limiting the right need only rationally relate to any possible legitimate end of government. Option B thus mischaracterizes the right to inherit as a fundamental right.

Finally, option B mischaracterizes the whole issue itself. This is how you tell the difference between a due process issue and an equal protection issue: Look to see if there's a classification involved. If there is, it's most likely an equal protection problem. If there's no classification, but the effect of the state's activity amounts to a deprivation of a property interest or right, it's a due process problem.

Here, there's quite clearly a classification involved: Legitimate vs. illegitimate children. Thus, any argument on which Ben would prevail would *have* to address equal protection, not due process. Since B doesn't recognize this, it's not the best response.

(C) is not the best response,

because the law here does not violate the privileges and immunities clause of the Fourteenth Amendment.

The privileges and immunities clause voids those state enactments which clearly infringe privileges enjoyed by U.S. citizens. It is construed narrowly, typically being restricted to fundamental rights which are shared in common by all citizens, namely:

1. The right to travel freely from state to state;
2. To petition Congress for redress of grievances;
3. To vote for national officers;
4. To assembly peaceably; and
5. To discuss matters of national legislation.

Thus, the right to inherit is not a privilege enjoyed by U.S. citizens, and as a result it does not violate the privileges and immunities clause. As a result, an argument by Ben centering on the privileges and immunities clause would not be a strong one. Since option C states otherwise, it's not the best response.

(D) is not the best response,

because it mischaracterizes the issue here as one of procedural due process instead of equal protection.

Under these facts, there's a classification involved: Legitimate vs. illegitimate children. Thus, the problem is one of equal protection. A due process problem is one where there's no classification, but the effect of a state's activity amounts to a deprivation of a property interest or right. Procedural due process (as opposed to substantive due process) involves the situation where a property right (or life or liberty) is taken by government, some fair process or procedure is required. The problem with applying this here is that due process only applies to presently enjoyed rights. Here, Ben wants the right to inherit – it's not as though he currently has it and it's being taken away from him. Thus, due process would not apply. Since D states otherwise, it's not the best response.

Answer 121

(D) is the best response.

D is the best response because it impliedly recognizes that the problem here is equal protection, and it states

the correct standard for analyzing classifications based on illegitimacy.

The hallmark of an equal protection problem is the existence of a classification that determines people's rights. Here, the inheritance rights of people is determined by their status as either legitimate or illegitimate. Illegitimacy is considered a "sensitive" classification, and thus it will be subject to intermediate scrutiny to determine its validity. Intermediate scrutiny requires that the law be substantially related to an important state interest. Under Lalli v. Lalli (1978), the state's interest in the just and expeditious disposition of property makes a law denying intestate succession to intestate children valid, where the paternity of the father hasn't formally been proven sometime before his death. This will clearly form the basis of the state's strongest argument. Since D recognizes this, it's the best response.

A is not the best response, because it misstates the law. Although a state (and not the federal government) traditionally has power over in-state property, this power – as with every state power – cannot violate the provisions of the Constitution relating to the states. One such provision is the equal protection clause. If a state statute involves an impermissible classification, it will violate the equal protection clause. Here, the classification involves legitimacy, since the statute determines the right to inherit based on whether or not a child is legitimate. Legitimacy is considered a "sensitive" classification, and as a result, in order to be valid the law would have to be substantially related to an important state interest. If it's not, the statute will be invalid, even though the state has authority to over in-state property. Since A doesn't recognize this, it's not the best response.

(B) is not the best response,

because the law could be invalid even if it doesn't constitute invidious discrimination.

"Invidious" discrimination is discrimination which is made on an undoubtedly invalid basis (e.g., alienage, religion or race). Such a law must be necessary to promote a compelling governmental interest in order to be valid, and as a result, almost any law making such a classification is invalid.

However, even if a law discriminates on a non-invidious basis – e.g., gender, legitimacy, or the legislation is economic or social – it is not automatically valid. If the law classifies people on the basis of gender or legitimacy, it will be subject to intermediate scrutiny to determine it's validity. That is, it must be substantially related to an important state interest in order to be valid. If the legislation is economic or social, it must meet the rational basis test: It is valid if there is a set of facts imaginable that would make the law a reasonable one to achieve a legitimate governmental purpose (a very easy standard to meet).

Under these facts, legitimacy is the basis of the classification. Thus, the law must be substantially related to an important state interest to be valid. If it doesn't meet this test, it will be invalid *even though* it does not constitute invidious discrimination. Since B doesn't recognize this, it's not the best response.

(C) is not the best response,

because it mischaracterizes the issue here as a due process issue; and, beyond that, it makes an invalid distinction between "privileges" and "rights."

A due process problem is triggered when the effect of a state's activity amounts to a deprivation of a property interest or right (or life or liberty). Thus, it doesn't matter whether the interest is characterized as a "privilege" or a "right," contrary to what option C states.

In any case, what's involved here is not a due process problem, but an equal protection problem, since there's a classification which determines people's rights: Legitimacy vs. illegitimacy. Thus, an argument by the state focusing on due process would not be a strong defense. Since C doesn't recognize this, it's not the best response.

Answer 122

The key fact here is that the remainder in Charles violates the Rule Against Perpetuities, since a future interest following a defeasible fee is void, except for charity to charity transfers, or when the condition involved MUST occur within a life in being plus 21 years.

(B) is the best response

because it correctly identifies Alice's interest. In order to get this correct, you had to correctly analyze two separate items: One, that Charles's interest is void because it violates the Rule Against Perpetuities; and two, the result of deleting Charles's interest.

In the conveyance, Alice sought to create a fee simple determinable subject to an executory interest in Barbara, and a shifting executory interest in Charles. As an executory interest, Charles's interest is subject to the Rule Against Perpetuities. Since it may vest many generations from now, if ever, it is void. Removing Charles's interest from the conveyance leaves Barbara with a defeasible fee, and thus leaves Alice with a possibility of reverter. When the condition is broken, if ever, Twinoaks Farm will automatically revert to Alice and her heirs. Since B correctly identifies this result, it's the best response.

(A) is not the best response,

because Alice is, in fact, left with a possibility of reverter. Alice sought to create a fee simple determinable subject to an executory interest in Barbara, and a shifting executory interest in Charles. As an executory interest, Charles's interest is subject to the Rule Against Perpetuities. Since it may vest many generations from now, if ever, it's void. Removing Charles's interest form the conveyance leaves Barbara with a defeasible fee, and thus leaves Alice with a possibility

of reverter. When, if ever, Twinoaks is used for anything but residential and farm purposes, it will revert automatically to Alice and her heirs.

If you chose this response, it's because you misinterpreted the facts here one of two ways: Either you figured the conveyance was valid as worded, or you realized that the interest in Charles violated the Rule Against Perpetuities, but believed that the result would be a fee simple absolute in Barbara. If you believed the conveyance was valid as worded, you can see that you overlooked the Rule Against Perpetuities. However, if you made the second mistake – believing Barbara takes a fee simple absolute – it's probably because you believed the conveyance created a fee simple subject to an executory interest in Barbara, *not* a defeasible fee. However, the wording of a fee simple subject to an executory interest would have to go something like this: "to Barbara and her heirs, however, if the premises are used for any purpose other than as a residence or farm, then to Charles and his heirs and assigns." You can see that this wording creates an interest, and in the next clause creates a divesting condition, which is the distinction between the two. If this problem involved a fee simple subject to an executory interest, you'd be right in believing that Barbara would be left with a fee simple absolute, because removing Charles's interest would leave Barbara with the entire fee. This is an exceptionally fine distinction to make, and if you made this mistake, it's understandable. Nonetheless, since Alice does in fact wind up with a possibility of reverter, A is not the best response.

(C) is not the best response,

because Alice's interest is a possibility of reverter, not a right of entry for condition broken.

If you chose this response, you made two mistakes: First, you characterized Barbara's interest as a fee simple subject to an executory interest instead of as a defeasible fee, and, secondly, you determined that Alice would get the "left over" interest because Charles's interest violates the Rule Against Perpetuities. You're right that Charles's interest violates the Rule Against Perpetuities; however, since a defeasible fee is involved, deleting Charles's interest means that Alice is left with a possibility of reverter. Had Barbara's interest been a fee simple subject to an executory interest, deleting Charles's interest would not leave Alice with a right of entry for condition broken; instead, removing the invalid executory interest would leave Barbara with a fee simple absolute, and Alice would be left with nothing (thus, regardless of whether Barbara's interest is a fee simple subject to an executory interest or a defeasible fee, under no circumstances could Alice, the grantor, wind up with a right of entry for condition broken; she'd either get a possibility of reverter (the "defeasible" option) or nothing (the "fee simple" option)). Barbara's interest is not a fee simple subject to an executory interest, because such an interest would require the creation of the interest in one clause, and its divestment in another, e.g., "to Barbara and her heirs, however, if the premises are used as anything other than a residence or farm, then to Charles and his heirs." Under the facts in this problem, the condition is in the same clause as the creation of the interest, so it's a defeasible fee. Since C does not correctly characterize the facts here, it's not the best response.

(D) is not the best response,
    because it mischaracterizes the facts.

    Alice could not wind up with a reversion here, because she's not certain to get Twinoaks back. Her receiving Twinoaks back depends on the use of Twinoaks; it may never be used for any other purpose, and if it isn't, Alice will never get it back. Since her future possession of Twinoaks is conditional, Alice's interest, if she gets one, must be a possibility of reverter (if Barbara's interest is a defeasible fee) or a right of entry for condition broken (if Barbara's interest is a fee simple subject to a condition subsequent). Note that this analysis disregards the effect of Charles's interest, but, since Charles's interest violates the Rule Against Perpetuities, it must be deleted. In fact, Barbara's interest here is a defeasible fee, since the divesting condition is in the same clause as the creation of the interest. (A fee simple subject to a condition subsequent would have one clause creating the interest, and one clause divesting it, e.g., "to Barbara and her heirs, but if the premises are ever used for X, then to Alice and her heirs.") Since Alice's interest is conditional on an event that may never happen, her interest cannot be a reversion, and so D is not the best response.

Answer 123

(B) is the best response,
    because it states the correct response *if* the condition it supplies is satisfied.

    The key fact here is the characterization of the tenancy. If you're familiar with co-tenancies, you know that the only two that have the right to survivorship are joint tenancies and tenancies by the entirety.

    B says that Donald will win *if* he and Celeste were tenants by the entirety in Lawnacre. Under the facts here, this is possible. A tenancy by the entirety is a tenancy that exists between husband and wife, with the right of survivorship, and it cannot be destroyed by severance. It requires the same "four unities" as a joint tenancy: in other words, the tenancy for each tenant must be created by the same instrument, the tenancy must be of the same duration, all tenants must hold an equal, undivided interest in the whole, and there must be a simultaneous vesting of interests. All of these conditions are satisfied by the facts here. However, the *"if"* makes B correct, because, if Celeste and Donald were *not* married at the time of the conveyance, a joint tenancy would result. A joint tenancy is similar to a tenancy by the entirety in most respects, but differs significantly in one respect that is crucial here: A joint

tenant *can* convey his interest away, and, in doing so, leaves a tenancy in common between the conveyee and the other tenants. Since B conditions Donald's prevailing on the existence of a tenancy by the entirety, it's the best response.

(A) is not the best response,
    because the conclusion it states *may not* be correct.

    The facts here indicate two possibilities: Celeste and Donald were *either* joint tenants, or tenants by the entirety, since those are the only two co-tenancies that feature a right to survivorship (the other co-tenancy, a tenancy in common, does not). If Celeste and Donald were married when Lawnacre was conveyed to them, the tenancy is a tenancy by the entirety, which *cannot be destroyed by severance.* In other words, Celeste's conveyance would have no effect, and, when she died, her interest would go to Donald, due to the right to survivorship. However, what makes A a wrong answer is that it states that Donald is *necessarily* the sole owner of Lawnacre, and he's not. It's equally likely that the co-tenancy created by these facts was a joint tenancy, if Celeste and Donald *weren't* married. A joint tenancy, unlike a tenancy by the entirety, *can* be destroyed by severance, i.e., one of the tenants conveying his interest in the property (in which case the joint tenancy is only destroyed as to that tenant; however, where there are only two tenants, the joint tenancy is totally destroyed). This would leave Donald and Paul as tenants in common – a co-tenancy without the right to survivorship. A states merely that Donald *is* the sole owner of Lawnacre, without taking into account that he and Paul may be tenants in common. As a result, A is not the best response.

(C) is not the best response,
    because Donald's knowledge of the conveyance before Celeste died does not control resolution of the issue here.

    If the original conveyance created a joint tenancy, Celeste's conveyance to Paul destroyed it, and Donald's knowledge of the conveyance to Paul is irrelevant; and if the original conveyance created a tenancy by the entirety, because Celeste and Donald were married, then Celeste's conveyance was meaningless, because a tenancy by the entirety cannot be destroyed by one tenant's conveying away his/her interest. Since C focuses on a fact that is not relevant to resolving this issue, it's not the best response.

(D) is not the best response,
    because it states as a *certainty* something that is only a *possibility.*

    If Celeste and Donald were not married when the conveyance to them took place, then the tenancy created was a joint tenancy. When Celeste conveyed her interest to Paul, a tenancy in common would result between Donald and Paul (since conveyance by one of the co-tenants destroys a joint tenancy, leaving a tenancy in common). If this were the *only* possibility, D would be the best response. However, if Celeste and Donald were married when the conveyance to them took place, the resulting tenancy would be a tenancy by the entirety. A tenancy by the entirety cannot be severed by one spouse attempting to convey his interest. If a spouse does so, the conveyance is meaningless; the tenancy by the entirety remains intact, and, when either spouse dies, the other is left as a sole owner (due to the right to survivorship). Thus, there exists at least one possibility, under these facts, which would make D incorrect. As a result, D cannot be the best response.

Answer 124

(D) is the best response,

because it identifies the central reason Power Saw will not be strictly liable.

Under Restatement of Torts §402A, defendant can only be liable if:

1. The product was in a defective condition unreasonably dangerous to the user/consumer or his property,
2. When it left defendant's control (meaning defendant can be liable even if he didn't cause the defect);
3. Product must not be expected to undergo significant changes before it gets to the user/consumer (or not actually undergo such changes);
4. The seller must be in the business of selling the product (thus, defendant can't be a casual seller);
5. Damage must result from the defect (defendant is liable for any physical damage);
6. and the duty extends to anyone foreseeably endangered by the product (meaning, there's no privity requirement).

Option D correctly identifies the reason Power Saw won't be strictly liable under these facts: Storekeeper disassembled and rebuilt the saw after it left Power Saw's control. This would constitute a "substantial change" under §402A, thus releasing Power Saw from strict liability. Since D correctly identifies this, it's the best response.

(A) is not the best response,

because it is not relevant to determining Power Saw's liability.

A alludes to the issue of *change* in the product between the time it left Power Saw and when it reached Employee. Under Restatement of Torts §402A, defendant can only be liable if:

1. The product was in a defective condition unreasonably dangerous to the user/consumer or his property,
2. When it left defendant's control (meaning defendant can be liable even if he didn't cause the defect);

3. Product must not be expected to undergo significant changes before it gets to the user/consumer (or not actually undergo such changes);
4. The seller must be in the business of selling the product (thus, defendant can't be a casual seller);
5. Damage must result from the defect (defendant is liable for any physical damage);

and the duty extends to anyone foreseeably endangered by the product (meaning, there's no privity requirement).

The sticky wicket under these facts is the last element: Substantial change. You're told that Storekeeper completely disassembles and rebuilds the saws. This is enough to remove Power Saw from strict liability *regardless* of whether the specific shaft was replaced, because §402A addresses the product *in its entirety*. Since A focuses on an element which will not determine Power Saw's liability, it's not relevant.

(B) is not the best response,

because the element it cites, although true, is not sufficient to hold Power Saw liable. Under Restatement of Torts §402A, defendant can only be liable if:

1. The product was in a defective condition unreasonably dangerous to the user/consumer or his property,
2. When it left defendant's control (meaning defendant can be liable even if he didn't cause the defect);
3. Product must not be expected to undergo significant changes before it gets to the user/consumer (or not actually undergo such changes);
4. The seller must be in the business of selling the product (thus, defendant can't be a casual seller);
5. Damage must result from the defect (defendant is liable for any physical damage);

and the duty extends to anyone foreseeably endangered by the product (meaning, there's no privity requirement).

As a result, it's not Power Saw's manufacturing dangerous machines that would make it liable, but selling machines that are *defective* such that they are unreasonably dangerous. Merely manufacturing power saws itself is not a basis for strict liability. In any case, option B ignores the reason Power Saw will avoid strict liability – because the saw was *overhauled* before it reached Employee. This "substantial change" releases Power Saw from liability under §402A. Since B doesn't recognize this, it's not the best response.

(C) is not the best response,

because it's irrelevant.

Strict product liability extends to anyone endangered by the defective product. According to most courts, this even includes bystanders, as well as users and consumers. Employee would fit well within this scope, since he's the intended user.

In fact, option C ignores the reason Power Saw will

escape strict liability: The saw was *overhauled* by Storekeeper after it left Power Saw. This would violate the "no substantial change" between the defendant and consumer/user, that Restatement of Torts 2d §402A requires for strict liability. As a result, C is not the best response.

Answer 125

(A) is the best response.

because it correctly identifies the central reason Storekeeper will not be liable for Purchaser's lost business: Storekeeper is only liable for personal and/or property damage caused by the defect, under Restatement of Torts 2d §402A. What makes this confusing is that under Contract law, it's possible to be liable for any losses that are considered reasonably foreseeable under the contract. These are considered "consequential" damages, and are always the result of the special situation or needs of the buyer, and not capable of mitigation by the injured party. Thus, under contract, it's *possible* the lost business could be recoverable. In strict product liability, however, it's not. Since A correctly identifies this, it's the best response.

(B) is not the best response,

because the element it cites will not determine Storekeeper's liability.

It's not the fact that Storekeeper was not the manufacturer that will keep him from being strictly liable, because one can be strictly liable without being a manufacturer. Instead, he'll avoid liability for the loss of business because it's an *economic* loss, which is not recoverable under strict liability.

First, the issue of Storekeeper's strict liability. Under Restatement of Torts 2d §402A, defendant can only be liable if:

1. The product was in a defective condition unreasonably dangerous to the user/consumer or his property,
2. When it left defendant's control (meaning defendant can be liable even if he didn't cause the defect);
3. Product must not be expected to undergo significant changes before it gets to the user/consumer (or not actually undergo such changes);
4. The seller must be in the business of selling the product (thus, defendant can't be a casual seller);
5. Damage must result from the defect (defendant is liable for any physical damage);

and the duty extends to anyone foreseeably endangered by the product (meaning, there's no privity requirement).

Thus, the focus is on the condition of the product when it leaves defendant and whether defendant is engaged in the business of selling the product – *not* whether defendant is a *manufacturer*.

Secondly, option B ignores the central reason Store-

keeper cannot be liable for the business loss – only personal and property damages are recoverable. The loss of business would be considered a non-recoverable "economic loss." Since B fails to recognize this, it's not the best response.

(C) is not the best response,

because it cites an element that is not relevant to Storekeeper's liability under strict product liability.

When a defendant is liable under strict product liability, he'll be liable for any personal or property damage caused by the defect. He will *not* be liable for purely economic losses, no matter how foreseeable they are – like business losses.

If you chose this response, you probably confused damages for product liability in tort with contractual liability. Lost business would be considered *consequential damages,* which could be recovered in a breach of contract action only if they are considered a reasonably foreseeable loss under the contract (consequential damages are always the result of the special situation or needs of the buyer, and not capable of mitigation by the injured party). Thus, if the claim in these facts were contractual, Purchaser might well be able to recover the lost business, for the reason stated in option C. However, since this problem deals with strict product liability in tort, C isn't the best response.

(D) is not the best response,

because it's irrelevant to determining damages.

Under strict product liability, Restatement of Torts 2d §402A, defendant is only liable for the personal and property damage caused by the defect. Purely economic losses – like lost business – are not recoverable, *even if* the defect is the "direct cause" of the damages, as D states, While D is relevant to causation, it's *not* relevant to damages under strict liability, making D not the best response.

Answer 126

(C) is the best response,

because it identifies reasoning which is plausible on these facts, and offers a result consistent with that reasoning.

The reasoning C offers implicitly establishes a valid contributory negligence, assumption of the risk defense. Contributory negligence is only a defense to strict product liability when the user knows the danger and unreasonably exposes himself to it; that is, contributory negligence is a defense only when it also qualifies as assumption of the risk. Here, if Employee knew the shaft was coming loose, he would certainly have been unreasonable to go on using something as dangerous as a power saw. Thus, Employee's lack of knowledge of the defect is absolutely necessary in order to defeat a contributory negligence/assumption of the risk defense. However, if he *didn't* realize the danger, he *will* recover. Since C states that Employee will recover *unless* he realized the danger, it's the best response.

(A) is not the best response,

because the factor it offers is not a requirement of a strict product liability claim.

The seller/producer's liability duty extends to anyone endangered by the defective product, under strict liability. In fact, most courts extend this duty beyond users and consumers to bystanders. If you chose this response, it *could* be because you were thinking of product liability suits based on implied warranty and representation theories, which do, in theory, involve privity problems (although courts in practice tend to ignore these limitations).

In any case, under these facts, with a strict liability claim, Purchaser would not need to tell Storekeeper that Employee would use the power saw in order for Employee to have a claim; instead, Employee would clearly be in the scope of strict liability – anyone endangered by the defective product. Since A doesn't recognize this, it's not the best response.

(B) is not the best response,

because it states reasoning which would not defeat Employee's claim, and arrives at an incorrect result.

For a start, if Employee's failure to notice the danger was not negligent, it won't be a defense at all, because Employee would have taken adequate care for his own safety. Assume arguendo that failing to notice the loose shaft was negligent. This type of contributory negligence is not, in fact a good defense to strict product liability – the type of contributory negligence that *is* a good defense is where the plaintiff knows the danger and unreasonably exposes himself to it. Thus, the only type of contributory negligence that is a defense to a strict product liability claim is the type that also qualifies as assumption of the risk. Since B doesn't state a fact that would be a valid defense to a strict product liability claim even if Employee *was* negligent in failing to notice the danger, it's not the best response.

(D) is not the best response,

because in a strict product liability claim any analysis of fault is irrelevant.

A strict product liability claim means that the duty of care is absolute. Under Restatement of Torts 2d §402A, a defendant can only be liable if:

1. The product was in a defective condition unreasonably dangerous to the user/consumer or his property,
2. When it left defendant's control (meaning defendant can be liable even if he didn't cause the defect);
3. Product must not be expected to undergo significant changes before it gets to the user/consumer (or not actually undergo such changes);
4. The seller must be in the business of selling the

product (thus, defendant can't be a casual seller);
5. Damage must result from the defect (defendant is liable for any physical damage);

and the duty extends to anyone foreseeably endangered by the product (meaning, there's no privity requirement).

Thus, no matter how careful Storekeeper is, it won't matter as long as he sells a defective product unreasonably dangerous to the user/consumer, and it causes damage. If you chose this response, you were thinking of negligence, under which the exercise of due care would be a valid defense. However, the claim here is in strict liability, where due care is not relevant. Since D states that due care would be a valid defense, it's not the best response.

Answer 127

(A) is the best response,

because it represents Employee's most attractive claim.

The key is that a strict product liability claim does not require proof of fault, and under these facts, this is crucial because Storekeeper did not do anything negligent. For a strict product liability claim, Restatement of Torts 2d §402A lays out these requirements:

1. The product was in a defective condition unreasonably dangerous to the user/consumer or his property,
2. When it left defendant's control (meaning defendant can be liable even if he didn't cause the defect);
3. Product must not be expected to undergo significant changes before it gets to the user/consumer (or not actually undergo such changes);
4. The seller must be in the business of selling the product (thus, defendant can't be a casual seller);
5. Damage must result from the defect (defendant is liable for any physical damage);

and the duty extends to anyone foreseeably endangered by the product (meaning, there's no privity requirement).

Under these facts, proving a defect making the product unreasonably dangerous will be fairly straightforward. Furthermore, Storekeeper, as the last link in the distribution chain, is Employee's best defendant, because if the blade was defective when it left *anyone's* control, it would be Storekeeper's. Also, Employee is one to whom Storekeeper owes an absolute duty, since Employee is within the scope of potential plaintiffs. Since the claim here is amenable to strict liability, and no other option represents a viable claim, A is the best response.

(B) is not the best response,

because it misstates the facts, so it cannot be Employee's best theory.

An express warranty claim, under UCC §2-313,

requires proof of a representation, the product's failure to perform as represented, causation and damages. The problem here is that there's no representation by Storekeeper. As a result, there can't be breach of express warranty, so B can't be the best response.

(C) is not the best response,

because a negligence claim requires proof of fault, and because res ipsa loquitur probably would not apply to these facts.

First, as to negligence, it would have to be proven that Defendant acted unreasonably in some respect, because this is the lynchpin of a negligence claim. Here, the facts state that the manufacturer, Saw Blade, used all available means to inspect its goods. Furthermore, the defendant, Storekeeper, as a middleman, could only be liable in negligence if it failed to inspect when there is reason to believe the product is defective. No grounds for such a belief exist in these facts.

As to res ipsa loquitur, it establishes a prima facie case of negligence only where three elements exist: The event causing injury would normally not have occurred in the absence of negligence, Defendant was in exclusive control of the instrumentality causing injury, and the plaintiff must not have voluntarily contributed to the event that caused his injury. Under these facts, apart from anything else, the instrumentality – the saw blade – was in Employee's exclusive control when the injury was caused. In any case, while a saw blade doesn't normally fly to pieces, it's not clear that this couldn't happen without negligence on someone's part. Since res ipsa loquitur would not likely apply to these facts, and negligence is not an attractive claim for Employee, C is not the best response.

(D) is not the best response,

because negligence requires proof of fault, and there's no evidence of fault on these facts.

The reasoning D states suggests that selling an inherently dangerous product is itself grounds for a negligence claim. In fact, it's not; negligence requires some unreasonability. A manufacturer/supplier can be held liable for negligence for a manufacturing flaw, failure to inspect, negligent design, or failure to war. A wholesaler/retailer is, in general, only liable for their own affirmative negligence in handling product – and, beyond that, to inspect for defects if they have any reason to believe the product is likely to be defective (e.g., a broken seal). Under these facts, whether Storekeeper is considered the manufacturer of the entire saw, or a wholesaler/supplier of Saw Blade's blade, there's no evidence Storekeeper breached any duty of care – the lynchpin of a negligence claim. Since D suggests a claim that is unlikely to succeed, it's not Employee's best claim, making D not the best response.

Answer 128

(B) is the best response,

because it offers a valid defense to strict product liability, and it fits these facts.

There are three basic defenses to a strict product liability claim: Assumption of the risk, abnormal misuse of product, and failure to follow instructions. A misuse is abnormal if it is not reasonably foreseeable. This is a good defense here, because Purchaser specifically asked for a blade that would cut plywood, and Storekeeper supplied a blade with only this use in mind. It's safe to assume that Storekeeper would have given a *different* blade for cutting hard plastic. In any case, since Storekeeper had no indication of this alternate use of the blade, it would be considered unforeseeable. Since this is in theory a good defense to a strict product liability claim, and it fits these facts, B is the best response.

(A) is not the best response,

because it does not represent a viable defense to a strict product liability claim.

The duty of a seller in strict liability extends to anyone endangered by the defective product. Employee would undoubtedly fit within this scope. If you chose this response, it's probably because you were thinking about the privity issue associated with warranty and representation theories. Even under *those,* Employee would be covered, both in theory and in practice (in fact, most courts in practice tend to ignore theoretical privity requirements in these claims). In any case, under the strict product liability claim in these facts, Employee's not being the purchaser of the blade would be irrelevant. As a result, A is not the best response.

(C) is not the best response,

because the type of contributory negligence involved under these facts – if Employee was negligent at all – would not be a valid defense to a strict product liability claim.

The only type of contributory negligence that poses a valid defense to strict product liability is the type that also qualifies as assumption of the risk: The plaintiff knows the danger and unreasonably exposes himself to it. Contributory negligence is *not* a defense where plaintiff negligently failed to discover the danger. There's no indication under these facts that Employee knowingly subjected himself to an unreasonable risk by using the blade to cut plastic instead of plywood. Thus, contributory negligence wouldn't be a good defense, making C not the best response.

(D) is not the best response,

because the reasoning it suggests is irrelevant to the success of Employee's claim.

There are three defenses to a strict product liability claim: Assumption of the risk, abnormal misuse of the product, and failure to follow instructions (contributory negligence is only a defense where it also qualifies as assumption of the risk: Where plaintiff knows the danger and unreasonably exposes himself to it). The problem with the reasoning here is that 1/ It doesn't focus on *Storekeeper,* but Saw Blade; and 2/ Due care is not a defense to strict liability, because strict liability has an *absolute* duty; due care cannot exonerate the defendant.

If the claim here were for negligence instead of strict liability, Employee would have to claim that Storekeeper was negligent in handling the product (e.g., unreasonably failing to inspect a flaw). Saw Blade's negligence could not be imputed to Storekeeper. In any case, what involved in these facts is strict liability, so any discussion of due care is irrelevant. As a result, D is not the best response.

Answer 129

(A) is the best response,

because the risk Defendant created was high enough to justify a murder conviction.

Common law murder is the unlawful killing of a human being with malice aforethought. While murder does not require *intent,* the type that does *not* require it – depraved heart murder – requires that the Defendant engage in extremely negligent conduct, which a reasonable man would realize creates a very high degree of risk to human life, and which results in death. Here, Defendant's conduct – shooting a gun into a crowded party – creates just such a risk. A wrinkle in this option is that you're told Defendant was "angered." While this might trigger thoughts of provocation – and thus voluntary manslaughter, not murder – keep in mind that the provocation must be of the type that would provoke a *reasonable person,* not just the Defendant. While a reasonable person might be provoked sufficiently to call the police under these circumstances, whipping out a gun and shooting the partying crowd would certainly be three standard deviations away from what a reasonable person would do, under the circumstances. Since A provides the facts most likely to result in a murder conviction, of these four choices, it's the best response.

(B) is not the best response,

because Defendant would likely be liable for only voluntary manslaughter, not murder.

Voluntary manslaughter is murder committed under the "heat of passion." Thus, it's an unlawful killing with malice aforethought (either intent to kill or do serious bodily injury, depraved heart, or felony murder), where the act was provoked. The provocation must be one that would provoke a reasonable person and in fact provoked the Defendant; and the Defendant must not have calmed down since the provocation, and a reasonable person would similarly not have calmed down in time for the killing. Here, you're only told that Harry slapped the Defendant during an argument, and Defendant shot him in response. Without more, it's not

crystal clear that Defendant would only be liable for voluntary manslaughter instead of murder – but what facts there are suggests it's a strong possibility. As a result, B is not the best response.

(C) is not the best response,

because it's unlikely that the risk Defendant created would be great enough to convict him of murder.

Common law murder requires an unlawful killing with malice aforethought. While malice can take several forms, the one that does not require intent – depraved heart murder – does require extremely negligent conduct, which a reasonable man would realize creates a very high degree of risk to human life. If the risk is *not* that high, but still criminally negligent, the defendant will be liable for criminal negligence-type involuntary manslaughter – which is probably the case here. While running a red light does create *some* danger to human life, without other facts, the risk would not be high enough to justify a common law conviction. As a result, C is not the best response.

(D) is not the best response,

because it's unlikely that the risk Defendant created would be great enough to justify a murder conviction.

Common law murder requires an unlawful killing with malice aforethought. While malice has several forms, the one that does not require intent — depraved heart murder, does require extremely negligent conduct, which a reasonable man would realize creates a very high degree of risk to human life. Creating a *lower* level of risk, which is still criminally negligent, would result in liability for involuntary manslaughter of the criminal negligence type. That's probably the result here. Punching Walter in the face is an act, in and of itself, which a reasonable man would not anticipate resulting in a very high degree of risk to human life. Thus, D is not the best response.

Answer 130

(C) is the best response,

because it correctly identifies the reason for inadmissibility as the fact that the evidence is not legally relevant.

A piece of evidence, apart from meeting every other hurdle of admissibility, must be legally relevant – in other words, its probative value cannot be substantially outweighed by the probability of undue prejudice. This happens most frequently with "inflammatory" evidence in criminal cases – graphic and gruesome photos, body parts, etc. However, its applicability here is reasonably straightforward, since the jury is likely to be unduly influenced by its reaction to Miller's heroin addiction. This is, of course, a judgment call, but legal relevance should always come to your mind when the evidence is particularly shocking. Since C correctly identifies the evidence here as being inadmissible due to the probability of undue prejudice it will invoke, it's the best

response.

(A) is not the best response,
because it ignores the issue of legal relevance.

Here, the prosecution is offering evidence of another instance of misconduct in order to prove Miller's guilt. The problem with such evidence is its logical *relevance*. Under the FRE, 404(b), such evidence can only be admissible when it has independent relevance, namely:

1. Knowledge;
2. Absence of mistake or accident;
3. Preparation;
4. Plan;
5. Opportunity;
6. Motive;
7. Intent;
8. Identity.

As you can see, motive is one of these. However, what this ignores is the fact that the evidence must still meet the legal relevance requirement. That is, the probative value of the evidence must not be substantially outweighed by the probability of undue prejudice. While this happens most frequently with "inflammatory" evidence in criminal cases (graphic and gruesome photos, body parts, etc.), the jury here is likely to be unduly influenced by the heroin evidence. Since A does not take this into account, it is not the best response.

(B) is not the best response,
because it states a clearly impermissible goal for the evidence.

Here, the prosecution is offering evidence of another instance of misconduct in order to prove Miller's guilt. The problem with such evidence is its logical *relevance*. Under the FRE, 404(b), such evidence can only be admissible when it has independent relevance, namely:

1. Knowledge;
2. Absence of mistake or accident;
3. Preparation;
4. Plan;
5. Opportunity;
6. Motive;
7. Intent;
8. Identity.

Evidence is never admissible to prove the defendant's propensity to commit crimes, because if a person's character is shown through such evidence, the jury is likely to be unduly influenced by its reaction to the person, not by his actions under the circumstances in question. As a result, B is not the best response.

(D) is not the best response,
because it incorrectly applies the "Mercy Rule" to these facts.

Under the mercy rule, the defendant can introduce evidence of his own good character to show he did not commit the crime in question. Once defendant has done so, prosecutor can rebut. Both defendant and prosecutor are limited to reputation and opinion evidence under the FRE. Here, the evidence is in the form of a specific act – Miller's possession of heroin and a hypodermic needle on one occasion – not reputation or opinion, so it could not be admitted under the Mercy Rule even if Miller had already offered evidence of his good character. Since D misstates the rule, it's not the best response.

Answer 131

(D) is the best response,
because it correctly states that the evidence will be inadmissible because the facts do not fit the "admission by silence" hearsay exclusion under the FRE.

An admission is a party's acknowledgement of fault. While such an affirmation is typically achieved through some positive statement, under some circumstances an admission can take the form of an omission. Under FRE 801(d)(2)(B), an admission by silence requires that the person must have heard the accusatory statement; the person must have been capable of denying the statement; and a reasonable person would have denied the statement were it not true, under the same circumstances. Here, Miller had no particular reason to respond, since the bartender's comment was not an accusatory statement. As such, it's not one Miller could be said to "adopt" by his silence. Were the situation slightly different – and the bartender had commented, "My God! You're that bank robber!" the situation would be different, since *this* statement is more of an accusation. However, these facts don't rise to the level of an accusation, and since D recognizes this, it's the best response.

(A) is not the best response,
because it's logically irrelevant.

A piece of evidence is "logically relevant" if it tends to prove or disprove a material fact. FRE 401. If it does so, it's relevant, and might be admissible if it meets other evidence requirements; if it doesn't, it's inadmissible.

The bartender's belief in Miller's guilt does not make any issue in the case either more or less likely; the bartender could believe the moon is made of green cheese, for that matter; it wouldn't have any less impact on the case.

Say the facts were different, and Miller tried to get the bartender to take a bag of money from a house, with Miller claiming, falsely, that he owned the house and the bag of money. In this case, the bartender's perception would be relevant, because he couldn't be liable for larceny without the intent to steal, and his belief that he was taking Miller's money with Miller's consent would be relevant. However, that's not the case here.

Since the bartender's belief isn't relevant in the facts in the question, A is not the best response.

(B) is not the best response,

because the admissibility of a statement does not depend solely on whether it was made in the defendant's presence.

Option B seems to refer to the "admission by silence" rule, of which it states but one of three requirements. An admission by silence, under FRE 801(d)(2)(B), requires that the person must have heard the accusatory statement, that the person must have been capable of denying the statement, and a reasonable person would have denied the statement were it not true, under the same circumstances. In fact, the statement here will not be admissible as an admission by silence, because the statement wasn't accusatory in tone, and as a result a reasonable person wouldn't have denied the statement even if it were true. In any case, since B only states part of the rule, it's not the best response.

(C) is not the best response,

because the privilege against self-incrimination does not apply to these facts.

The privilege against self-incrimination doesn't apply until police (or other government agents) undertake a custodial interrogation of Miller; it does not apply to a situation like this, where there's no interrogation, and there's no government agent doing the questioning.

In fact, Miller's silence *could* be used against him, under these facts, if it were considered an admission by silence. An admission by silence, under FRE 801(d)(2)(B), requires that the person must have heard the accusatory statement, that the person must have been capable of denying the statement, and a reasonable person would have denied the statement were it not true, under the same circumstances. In fact, the statement here will not be admissible as an admission by silence, because the statement wasn't accusatory in tone, and as a result a reasonable person wouldn't have denied the statement even if it were true. In any case, since C misapplies the privilege against self-incrimination to these facts, C is not the best response.

Answer 132

(C) is the best response,

because it correctly identifies the evidence here as inadmissible hearsay.

Remember, this doesn't mean the evidence would be inadmissible under any circumstances; what it's really saying is that the evidence would not be admissible under any of the other options. An otherwise excludable piece of hearsay evidence could always be admitted by the judge under the "catch-all" hearsay provision, FRE 803(24) and 804(b)(5).

First, the evidence *is* hearsay. Hearsay is an out-of-court statement — the teller's — offered to prove the truth of its assertion, namely that the sketched person

is Miller. The identification is the equivalent of the teller's pointing to Miller and saying, "That's him!" Thus, in order to be admissible, it would have to fit an exception or exclusion. The most likely one is the "prior identification" hearsay exclusion, under FRE 801(d). However, that *only applies to currently testifying witnesses,* and here you're told that the teller died before trial.

Since C correctly identifies the evidence as hearsay inadmissible under any of the other options, it's the best response.

(A) is not the best response,

because it misapplies the rule on admitting prior identifications.

Under FRE 801(d)(1), a prior identification by a presently-testifying witness is admissible. Note that this is *only* applicable to *presently-testifying witnesses.* Here, the teller has the ultimate excuse for not testifying — she's dead. As a result, the sketch will not fit the "prior identification" hearsay exclusion. If you chose this option, you probably did so because the facts here *sound* like they should fit the prior identification exclusion. After all, literally speaking, the sketch *is* a prior identification. However, these facts indicate why it's important to be familiar with the three hearsay exclusions for presently-testifying witnesses under FRE 801(d)(1)(prior inconsistent statements, prior consistent statements, and prior identifications). These exclusions are very narrow, and easy to misapply. An easy way to avoid mistakenly choosing one of these is to note immediately if the declarant is a presently-testifying witness; if it *isn't,* the exclusion can't possibly apply.

(B) is not the best response,

for two reasons; first, the teller isn't testifying, and second, sketches are not suitable for the past recollection recorded hearsay exception.

Under FRE 803(5), the past recollection recorded hearsay exception requires that the witness must have no present recollection of the facts; the document must have been made at the time of the event of shortly thereafter; the document must have been made based on personal knowledge, and made or adopted by the witness; and the witness must verify that the document was true when made (it must also be authenticated). If a document meets these requirements, it may be read into evidence, but it cannot be received as an exhibit unless the adverse party offers it.

With these requirements in mind, it's clear that the sketch here does not qualify. This exception is intended for documents which fail to refresh the witness's memory. Here, the teller isn't testifying, and even if she were, a simple sketch could hardly refresh her memory for Miller's face. Furthermore, a sketch is not capable of being read into evidence. Thus, B is not the best response.

(D) is not the best response,

because the evidence here is not opinion testimony, and even if it were, recognition is an acceptable form of lay opinion testimony, since it is rationally based on the perception of the witness and helpful to a determination of a fact in issue. FRE 701. (Alternatively, lay opinion testimony is admissible if it is helpful to a clear understanding of the witness's testimony.)

Thus, it's not the issue of opinion testimony that makes the sketch inadmissible, but rather it's status as hearsay. Hearsay is an out-of-court statement – the teller's – offered to prove the truth of its assertion, namely that the sketched person is Miller. The identification is the equivalent of the teller's pointing to Miller and saying, "That's him!" In order to be the best response, D would have to address a hearsay exception or exclusion making the sketch admissible. Since it ignores this point entirely, D is not the best response.

Answer 133

(C) is the best response,

because it correctly identifies the testimony as inadmissible hearsay. Remember, this only means that the evidence will not be admissible under any of the other alternatives, and that the evidence is hearsay. Both of these are satisfied here.

This is a tricky question because Miller is only reiterating his original assertion – that he had never been in the First Bank of City. However, there's a crucial difference between his saying, in court, that he'd never been in the bank, and his saying that *he told the police* he'd never been in the bank. By repeating his own, out-of-court statement, Miller's testimony becomes hearsay. The statement is hearsay because it's an out-of-court statement, offered to prove the truth of its assertion. The out-of-court declarant is Miller himself, and the statement is being offered to prove he was never in the bank. Since C correctly identifies this as hearsay, and it's not admissible under any other option, C is the best response.

(A) is not the best response,

because it incorrectly infers that the testimony will be admissible.

What option A is saying is that the evidence should be admissible substantively – that is, to prove the truth of its assertion. This presupposes that the evidence is admissible, when in fact its status as hearsay is what's at issue here.

This is a tricky question because Miller is only reiterating his original assertion – that he had never been in the First Bank of City. However, there's a crucial difference between his saying, in court, that he'd never been in the bank, and his saying that *he told the police* he'd never been in the bank. By repeating his own, out-of-court statement, Miller's testimony becomes hearsay. That's because it's an out-of-court statement, offered to prove the truth of its assertion (that Miller had never

been in the bank, and thus couldn't have robbed it). Since there is no standard hearsay exception or exclusion under which the statement would be admissible, and A doesn't address the hearsay problem at all, A is not the correct response.

(B) is not the best response,

because the statement will not be admissible as a prior consistent statement.

First, you have to identify the nature of Miller's statement. He's repeating his own, out-of-court statement to the police, and his statement is being offered to prove that he had never been in the bank (and thus couldn't have robbed it). This makes it hearsay, since hearsay is an out-of-court statement offered to prove the truth of its assertion. Option B implicitly recognizes that the statement is hearsay, and suggests that it will be admissible under the prior consistent statement hearsay exclusion.

Under FRE 801(d)(1), a prior consistent statement is only admissible (as an *exclusion* from the hearsay rule) if it is offered to rebut a charge, express or implied, against the witness of improper motive/influence or recent fabrication, and it is offered against a currently-testifying declarant. Here, Miller is currently testifying on direct examination, and there has been no allegation by the prosecution that Miller recently changed his story. As a result, his statement couldn't fit the prior consistent statement hearsay exclusion. Thus, B is not the best response.

(D) is not the best response,

because it's irrelevant. The fact that the statement is self-serving does not affect its admissibility, but its believability.

While D recognizes that the statement will be inadmissible, it ignores the reason why: The statement is inadmissible hearsay. Hearsay is an out-of-court statement offered to prove the truth of its assertion. Here, the out-of-court statement is Miller's statement to police at the time of his arrest. It's offered to prove that he was never in the bank, and thus it implies that he couldn't have robbed the bank. Thus, in the absence of an applicable exclusion or exception to the hearsay rule, the statement will be inadmissible.

The self-serving nature of the testimony won't make the statement inadmissible, because if this were true, then Miller's original, direct testimony that he had never been in the bank would be inadmissible as well. In fact, what option D addresses is Miller's motive to lie, which can – and undoubtedly will – be addressed on cross-examination. However, the self-serving nature of the statement would not exclude it from evidence. Thus, D is not the best response.

Answer 134

(A) is the best response,

because it correctly identifies the fact that the evidence

here will be admissible to impeach Miller via intrinsic impeachment.

Impeachment is the means of casting adversely on the credibility of the witness. It can be accomplished via either reputation or opinion testimony, under FRE 608(a). Impeachment can show, for instance, bias or interest, contradicting facts, inconsistent statements, prior convictions, bad character for truthfulness, or sensory deficiencies (although the requirements for admitting some of these will differ, and some can only come from the witness's own mouth, not from extrinsic evidence).

The impeachment here is "intrinsic" because it is sought from the witness's own mouth (impeachment from other sources is called "extrinsic" impeachment). There are five basic types of questions thatcan be used to elicit intrinsic impeachment from a witness. They are:

1. Bias or interest;
2. Prior inconsistent statements;
3. Prior convictions (under FRE 609(a), misdemeanors involving dishonesty and any felony, and only convictions not more than ten years old);
4. Bad character for honesty (including unconvicted bad acts); and
5. Sensory deficiencies (e.g., eyesight, memory, mental disability).

The tax fraud conviction here fits the requirements of #3, impeachment with prior convictions. Here, the conviction was for tax fraud; whether it's a felony or a misdemeanor doesn't matter, because it involves dishonesty. It fits the age requirement, because it's only a year old. If you missed this one, it could be because you were thrown since it was the criminal defendant himself testifying. However, a criminal defendant can be impeached to the same extent as any other witness, as long as he testifies, of course. Since A recognizes this, it is the best response.

(B) is not the best response,

because it indicates an impermissible goal for the evidence, even though the evidence *is* admissible.

Under the doctrine of "limited admissibility," evidence can be admitted for one purpose without being admissible for some other purpose (e.g., insurance can be admitted to show ownership but not the ability to pay). Here, it's crucial to keep in mind the purposes for which a prior criminal record can be admitted. A testifying witness can be impeached with evidence of a prior conviction, if the conviction was either a misdemeanor involving dishonesty, or any felony, and as long as the conviction is not more than ten years old. FRE 609(a). Thus, such convictions can be admitted to cast doubt on the witness's credibility, which is what impeachment does. Here, Miller's tax fraud conviction would fit the prior convictions impeachment requirements, and so it could be admitted to reflect on his credibility. B instead suggests that the evidence will be admissible to show

that Miller has a propensity to steal. Evidence of prior bad acts is *never* admissible to prove a "criminal character." Since B doesn't recognize this, B is not the best response.

(C) is not the best response,

because the similarity of the conviction to the current charge is irrelevant.

Here, it's important to keep in mind the purpose for which the evidence is being admitted. The prosecutor isn't trying to show a *modus operandi* here, and he *can't* be showing Miller's propensity to steal. Instead, he's impeaching Miller with the evidence – that is, he's trying to cast aspersions on Miller's credibility. Prior convictions can be used for this purpose, as long as the conviction is either for a misdemeanor involving dishonesty, or any felony, and it's not more than ten years old. FRE 609(a). Thus, it need not be similar to the crime charged.

If you chose this response, you were probably thinking of the rule relating to prior, specific instances of misconduct. In a criminal case, there are certain circumstances where the defendant's prior instances of misconduct can be admitted substantively. Such instances of misconduct are admissible only when they're said to have independent relevance. This relevance can be supplied when the evidence proves knowledge, absence of mistake or accident, preparation, plan, opportunity, motive, intent, or identity. Thus, if Miller had committed similar bank robberies in the past and had, say, worn a Bozo mask in all of them, and the bank robber in *this* case wore a Bozo mask, the prior instances of misconduct would be admissible to prove Miller's identity. Under those facts you can see why the similarity of crimes would be necessary to admit the other instances. However, those facts are very different from the ones here. Here, the evidence is not being offered substantively – that is, to prove its truth – but only to impeach Miller. Since the purposes are different, different rules apply.

Since C doesn't recognize that the evidence will be admissible as impeachment, it's not the best response.

(D) is not the best response,

because it incorrectly states that the evidence will be inadmissible because it isn't legally relevant.

In order to be legally relevant, the probative value of the evidence must not be substantially outweighed by the probability of undue prejudice. This is true of *any* piece of evidence, regardless of whether it satisfies every other evidence requirement. A piece of evidence is most frequently excluded due to legal relevance problems when the evidence is "inflammatory" - graphic and gruesome photos, body parts, and the like. A prior tax fraud conviction would not be sufficiently shocking to raise legal relevance problems. Instead, the conviction does just about exactly what it's supposed to do – raise questions as to the credibility of the testifying witness, who, in this case, happens to be the defendant.

Say that these facts were different, and Miller's fraud conviction had been based on defrauding a convent. In theory, the requirements of the prior conviction requirement for impeachment would be met – however, the likelihood of undue prejudice for this kind of conviction would be so much greater as to require, in all probability, that the evidence be excluded. Thus, it's the nature of the prior conviction here that clears it of any legal relevance problems. Since D doesn't recognize this, it's not the best response.

Answer 135

(C) is the best response,
because the commerce clause is the most likely means of attacking the statute.

In order to be valid, a state law must pass this three-pronged test:

1. The law must be enacted within the state's powers (e.g., police powers);
2. The law must not violate any person's constitutional rights; and
3. The law must not improperly burden interstate commerce.

Look at the statute here. It satisfies the first requirement, since the statute would serve the welfare of the Onondagans. It satisfies the second requirement, as well. It's the third requirement that, as option C recognizes, is the sticky wicket. In determining if a law "improperly" burdens interstate commerce, you have to ask two questions:

1. Does the law burden interstate commerce at all? If it has an effect on interstate commerce, it does.
2. Is the burden outweighed by legitimate interests of the state in protecting its citizens, taking into account less burdensome alternatives?

Here, requiring large businesses to spend money in-state clearly has an effect on interstate commerce, since that stops them from spending that money in other states. While the law addresses a legitimate interest of Onondaga, the burden would undoubtedly outweigh the interest. Thus, the commerce clause represents a strong basis on which to attack the statute, making C the best response.

(A) is not the best response,
because the statute here would not violate due process.

A due process problem arises when a state's activity amounts to a deprivation of a property interest or right. Here, Onondaga's new law denies businesses the right to buy goods and/or services completely within their own discretion. Thus, even though there's a due process issue, the law will be valid. That's because it's economic legislation, and as such it's only subject to the rational basis test. Thus, if the regulation is ratio-

nally related to a legitimate governmental interest and it's not arbitrary or capricious, it's not a due process violation. Here, the estate's interest is legitimate: relieving unemployment. Requiring businesses with significant sales in-state to spend half the value of their in-state revenue on Onondaga products would be rationally related to this interest. Thus, an attack based on the due process clause would not be particularly strong. Since option A doesn't recognize this, it's not the best response.

(B) is not the best response,
because the statute here would not be an equal protection violation.

An equal protection problem potentially exist when there is a classification. Here, the classification is between business with over one million dollars of Onondaga sales, and those with less than one million dollars in Onondaga sales. However, this is economic legislation, and so the "rational basis" test would be applied to determine its validity. Under the rational basis test, if there is a set of facts imaginable which would make the law a reasonable one to achieve a legitimate governmental purpose, the law does not violate equal protection. Here, the law provides a clear way to relieve the Onondaga unemployment problem, and so it would not be an equal protection violation. In fact, any time the rational basis test is used, it should raise a red flag in your mind that the legislation is valid, since the test is very difficult to fail. Since there's no equal protection violation here, the equal protection clause would not provide a strong basis on which to attack the statute. Since B doesn't recognize this, it's not the best response.

(D) is not the best response,
because the privileges and immunities clause of the Fourteenth Amendment is not violated by this statute.

The privileges and immunities clause voids those state enactments which clearly infringe the privileges enjoyed by federal citizens. It is construed narrowly, typically being restricted to fundamental rights which are shared in common by all citizens, namely:

1. The right to travel freely from state to state;
2. To petition Congress for redress of grievances;
3. To vote for national officers;
4. To assemble peaceably; and
5. To discuss matters of national legislation.

The clause is interpreted narrowly, so the facts here, which do not clearly fit under any of these categories, would not be covered by the privileges and immunities clause of the Fourteenth Amendment.

If you chose this response, you may have been thinking of the *interstate* privileges and immunities clause, found in Article IV, §2 of the Constitution. That clause serves to prohibit the states from unreasonably discriminating against out-of-state citizens, in relation to fundamental national interests. The validity of a state statute under the clause is determined by a three-part test. First, you have to determine if the statute burdens a fundamental national interest which the clause protects. Second, you have to determine if there's a substantial reason for the discrimination between in-state and out-of-state citizens. Third, you need to determine if the discrimination bears a close relation to that reason, taking into account the availability of less restrictive means. Even if you thought of this test, it doesn't apply, because the term "citizens" in the clause only addresses individuals, not aliens or corporations. In fact, neither privileges and immunities clause provides the best basis for attacking the statute: Instead, the best argument would rest on the commerce clause. Since option D doesn't recognize this, it's not the best response.

Answer 136

(B) is the best response,

because it supplies a condition which would apply to these facts, and, assuming the condition is satisfied, it reaches the correct response.

If the law of the jurisdiction prohibited evictions intended to punish the tenant for some act, the facts here would likely fit such a statute, since it would be easily provable that Len is punishing Tess for organizing the tenants. If Tess proved such facts, she would prevail. Since B recognizes this, it's the best response.

(A) is not the best response,

because although the lease here is a periodic tenancy created by implication, this does not provide a ground for Tess to succeed – since Len gave adequate notice to terminate the lease.

A periodic tenancy is a tenancy which is renewed *automatically* at the end of each "period" (e.g., week, month, quarter) unless either lessor or lessee terminates it. A periodic tenancy by implication is one where the lease is silent as to duration. The amount of notice required to terminate a periodic tenancy is the same as the length of the period. That is, if the tenancy is month-to-month, as here, a month's notice is required. Len gave just that amount of notice. Since Len complied with the requirements for terminating the lease, the fact that the lease is a periodic lease by implication does not provide a ground for Tess to prevail in a wrongful termination suit. Thus, A is not the best response.

(C) is not the best response,

because it is a misstatement of law.

The amount of rent charged to the other tenants does not create an implied agreement between Tess and Len for Tess's apartment. After all, apartment buildings frequently contain apartments of different sizes, for which different rents are charged. If the same rent is charged for every apartment, this is mere coincidence – no implied agreement would spring from it as

between Len and Tess. Since C states otherwise, it's not the best response.

(D) is not the best response,

because it is a misstatement of the law.

The amount of notice required to terminate a periodic tenancy, like the one here, depends on the length of the period. At common law, the amount of notice required is the same as the period. That is, if the tenancy is week-to-week, a week's notice is required; if it's month-to-month, a month's notice is necessary. For periods of a year or more, six months' notice is required. According to modern statutes in many states, thirty days' notice is required regardless of the period involved. Thus, it is not correct to say that the law implies a term of one year without an express agreement otherwise. Thus, D is not the best response.

Answer 137

(A) is the best response,

because it correctly identifies that Breyer does not have an easement by implication, and thus his rights should wait until College Avenue opens as a public street.

While College Avenue is still private, Breyer's right to use it depends whether he has an interest in College Avenue that would allow him use of it. Black, as owner of College Avenue, didn't expressly grant Breyer the right to use it, so, if Breyer has any easement at all, it's implied. The two most likely easements, an implied easement and an easement by necessity, both have the same stumbling block for Breyer: They both require that the two parcels of land have been under common ownership in the past. The facts here do not indicate that Whiteacre and Meadowview were ever under common ownership, so there can be no implied easement or easement by necessity. Since A correctly identifies that there is no private easement by implication, and suggests a plausible alternative, it's the best response.

(B) is not the best response,

because the Statute of Frauds would not bar evidence proving an implied easement.

This is so because implied easements are created by operation of law, *not* expression of the parties, so they *cannot* be in writing! An implied easement arises when a tract of land under one owner is divided, and one part of the land had been used for the benefit of the other part. A related easement, an "easement by necessity," arises where enjoyment of one parcel of land strictly requires use of another. These are the two most likely easements here, and, since neither one of them requires a writing, the Statute of Frauds would not apply to them. As a result, B cannot be the best response.

(C) is not the best response,

because although it is internally consistent (in that the

facts preclude the success of a claim based on a way of necessity), this is *not* the only claim that Breyer could make.

It's likely that Breyer would claim a way by necessity because the facts here make such a claim attractive, in every way but one: There is no indication here that the two parcels of land involved were *ever* under common ownership, and this is a requirement of a way by necessity. However, it's likely that Breyer would also claim that there is an implied easement, which is an easement created by operation of law. An implied easement arises when a tract of land under one owner is divided, and one part of the land had been used for the benefit of the other part. Thus, the stumbling block with Breyer's proving an implied easement is the same as for an easement by necessity: There never was common ownership of the two parcels, under these facts. Nonetheless, it's as likely that Breyer would claim an implied easement as it is that he would claim an easement by necessity, and so his *assertion* would not be limited to a way by necessity, as C claims. Thus, C is not the best response.

(D) is not the best response,

because unjust enrichment need not be addressed in order to deny Breyer the right of way.

Under the doctrine of unjust enrichment, one has received and retained property, money, or benefits which justifiably and equitably belong to another. While Breyer's use of College Avenue *could* constitute unjust enrichment, it is not necessary to go as far as proving unjust enrichment, since, if Black can prove that Breyer wouldn't be within his legal rights to use College Avenue, he needn't prove anymore. In other words, in order to recover for unjust enrichment, Black would be implying that Breyer was within his legal rights to use College Avenue, but it would be inequitable for him to do so. Here, there is no indication that Breyer is within his legal rights to use College Avenue at all, and since option A recognizes this, D is not the best response.

Answer 138

(D) is the best response,

even though it's not a particularly good response. This is a difficult question because *none* of these arguments are particularly good, and so you're forced to choose the best of a bad lot.

Since there is no statute concerning dedications mentioned here, the common law rule will control. The common law rule for dedications is that the grantor must manifest intent to make a dedication to the public use, and the public must manifest an intent to accept it. Recording the plan, indicating College Avenue, could manifest such an intent on Black's part. As to the second requirement, Breyer would have to argue that he, as a *member* of the public, accepted the dedication. This would not be typical, since normally it is a governmental body that accepts dedications (e.g., a city coun-

sel). However, D is the best of the options mentioned here, so it's the best response.

(A) is not the best response,

because it misstates the rule of law: There can be no easement by necessity *unless* the two parcels of land were once under common ownership. Here, there is no indication that the two parcels ever were commonly owned, and thus, no matter how great the necessity, there can be no easement by necessity. Since A states otherwise, it is not the best response.

(B) is not the best response,

because a mere reference to the recorded plan would not be sufficient to create rights for Breyer.

The only way for Breyer to gain rights to College Avenue from White is via an easement of some kind. If White didn't have an easement covering College Avenue, then he couldn't convey an easement to Breyer, since one cannot convey rights he doesn't have. Under the facts here, there's no express easement, and, since the two parcels of property were never under the same ownership, there can't be an implied easement or an easement by necessity. Mentioning College Avenue in the deed, as it appears in the recorded plan, would not in and of itself create an easement for White and then Breyer. Thus, B is not the best response.

(C) is not the best response,

because it misstates the facts: Breyer's property is not *in* Meadowview, so the easements appropriate to those lots would not be relevant to Breyer's rights.

Otherwise, C would be correct, since buyers of lots in Meadowview *would* be entitled to an easement over College Avenue, either expressly (which is likely), or impliedly. An easement by implication would probably be appropriate, since the lots were previously under common ownership (Black's), use of one part of the land (the Avenue) by another part must have been apparent and continuous and reasonably necessary for the enjoyment of the other lots. A subdivision like the one here likely fits these requirements. An easement by necessity requires common ownership of the dominant and servient estates at some time in the past, and the use must be strictly necessary (since the easement lasts only as long as the necessity does). This typically arises when one plot has no access to a public highway without trespassing on another plot. Here again, the facts here would likely fit an easement by necessity. However, since both of these apply to lots in *Meadowview,* this won't do Breyer any good, since his lot isn't in Meadowview. As a result, C is not the best response.

Answer 139

(C) is the best response.

As to alternative I:

This is not a good argument for Harriet, because the language couldn't be interpreted to mean that the offer was irrevocable, and the parol evidence rule would prohibit admission of any evidence disputing this. Under the parol evidence rule, a written contract that is "partially integrated" (not the *complete* agreement of the parties, but final as to terms it states) may be supplemented by consistent additional terms, but it cannot be contradicted by prior written or oral agreements, or contemporaneous oral agreements. As a result, trying to offer evidence that revocable means irrevocable would not be permitted. More importantly, arguing that the offer was, in fact, irrevocable would not be permitted.

More importantly, arguing that the offer was, in fact, irrevocable would be a strategic boo-boo for Harriet, because she immediately revoked the offer – thus, if the offer was irrevocable, she breached that provision.

As to alternative II:

This would be a good argument for Harriet, because it addresses and resolves the central issue here.

The underlying problem here is consideration: As a general rule, an offer by a non-merchant cannot be irrevocable without consideration (or some substitute for it). By the same token, if the offer is revocable at any time, it's an illusory promise, since the offeror has suffered no detriment in return for the option payment. It's this problem that a good argument for Harriet would *have* to overcome. By arguing that Reggie got what he bargained for, Harriet can overcome the problem. While in a typical option contract the offeree bargains for irrevocability, here Reggie bargained for merely a *revocable* offer. At least theoretically this is a detriment to Harriet, because she believes she can get more money from another buyer, and so *making* the offer at $10,000 might be considered a detriment. In any case, since alternative II indicates a plausible argument, it must be part of a correct response.

As to alternative III:

This would be a good argument for Harriet.

Under the parol evidence rule, a writing that is "completely integrated" cannot be contradicted or supplemented with prior written or oral agreements, or contemporaneous oral agreements. A "completely integrated" agreement is one which the parties intended to be a final and complete statement of their agreement. However, here, the agreement doesn't mention consideration at all, so it would be considered only *partially* integrated. A partial integration doesn't reflect the *complete* agreement of the parties, but it's final as to the terms it states. A partial integration *may* be supplemented with consistent additional terms. Thus, Harriet

could offer evidence of the $200 promised payment. Since alternative III recognizes this, it's a good argument for Harriet.

Answer 140

(B) is the best response.

As to alternative I:

This is Reggie's best argument, because it implicitly recognizes that consideration is the central problem here.

As a general rule, an irrevocable offer by a non-merchant requires consideration. This is an "option," and the consideration is supplied by the offeror's detriment – he cannot revoke the offer for a period of time, binding him to a set price and precluding acceptance of any other offer. *Without* the irrevocability provision, such a promise is *illusory* and thus unenforceable, because the offeror has a completely unrestricted right to renege on his promise. Thus, under these facts, if Harriet was free to renege on her promise, there's no consideration to support the option contract, and she cannot recover the $200 from Reggie. This makes alternative I an exceptionally good argument for Reggie.

As to alternative II:

This is *not* a good argument for Reggie, because it misstates the law.

Alternative II impliedly refers to the Statute of Frauds. Contracts for the sale of land fall within the Statute, and thus require a writing (as a general rule). However, *offers* for the sale of an interest in land *aren't* within the Statute, and thus needn't be in writing – nor must revocations of such offers. Instead, a revocation is accomplished by any word or act which states or implied that the offeror no longer intends to enter into the contract, as long as the offeree receives the revocation. Thus, alternative II misstates the law, since the revocation by phone would be valid.

Beyond its misstatement of the law, alternative II would not be strategically beneficial to Reggie. What he *wants* to do is argue that the payment of $200 is not required. If he bargained for and got a revocable offer, Harriet's revoking it by phone wouldn't release him from the obligation to pay the $200. Thus, even if alternative II were *legally* valid, it wouldn't be *strategically* advantageous.

If you thought this was correct, you may have been thinking of offers that limit the means of acceptance. That is, if an offeror states that the offer may only be accepted by telephone, then a letter wouldn't suffice. However, the general rule is that an acceptance may be made by any reasonable means, and, in any case, it's a revocation, not an acceptance, involved here.

As to alternative III:

This provides a reasonably good argument for Reggie, due to the objective theory of contracts. Under that theory, in determining whether there was the required mutual assent between the offeror and offeree, you have to look at what a *reasonable person* in each party's position would be led to believe by the conduct and words of the other party. This is designed to protect each of the parties' reasonable expectations. If these reasonable expectations are *not* met, the promise is illusory and thus unenforceable. Here, the question would be whether a reasonable person in Reggie's position would have paid $200 for a revocable offer, expecting it to be revoked the next day. Rather, Reggie would expect that Harriet would only revoke if she got a better offer from someone else. In any case, Reggie would reasonably expect something more than a one-day offer. Thus, Reggie would have a good argument that Harriet's revoking so soon was in derogation of his reasonable expectations, making the promise illusory and unenforceable. While this isn't a great argument, it's a good one, making alternative III an option for Reggie.

Answer 141

(C) is the best response,
because it correctly characterizes the contract here as a unilateral contract.

An offer for a unilateral contract is one which requests performance in return (unlike a bilateral contract, which requests a return promise). Here, Reggie asked Harriet to "make me a written 30-day offer..." in return for which he would pay $200. Thus, he *didn't* want a return promise, and Harriet's performing the requested act – making the written offer – constitutes consideration for the contract, making the contract enforceable. Thus, the combination of Reggie's oral promise and Harriet's writing creates a unilateral contract. Since C recognizes this, it's the best response.

(A) is not the best response,
because consideration is missing, so there cannot be a firm option.

An "option" is a means by which a non-merchant can make an irrevocable offer. The option must be supported by consideration. Typically, the offeree pays the offeror to keep the offer open for a given period of time. Without the irrevocability, an option is *illusory,* because the *offeror* has an unrestricted right to revoke the offer (and it's the restriction of this right that forms part of the consideration for the option). Here, Harriet's right to revoke at any time defeats the option. Since option A doesn't recognize this, it's not the best response.

(B) is not the best response,
because promissory estoppel only applies when consideration is lacking, and there's consideration here.

Promissory estoppel is designed to avoid injustice where consideration is lacking for a contract. It comes into being when there is a gratuitous promise that is

likely to, and does, induce promisee's reliance. As option B suggests, in theory there can be justifiable reliance on a promise before a contract is created, such as where the promisee must perform before the offer can be accepted (e.g., a businessman selling his business before he can buy a franchise). Thus, there *can* be pre-contractual promissory estoppel, which can make an offer irrevocable or enforce a promise made during preliminary negotiations. However, it doesn't apply to these facts, because Reggie bargained for, and got, a revocable offer. In promissory estoppel, the bargaining element is missing. Since promissory estoppel doesn't apply to these facts, B isn't the best response.

(D) is not the best response,
because quasi-contract only applies, to prevent unjust enrichment, where no contract exists.

Under quasi-contract, a plaintiff is entitled to recovery where he conferred a benefit on the defendant with the expectation he would be paid, defendant knew or should have known plaintiff expected to be paid, and defendant would be unjustly enriched if he got to keep the benefit without paying for it. Thus, quasi-contract only applies when a person receives benefits in the absence of an enforceable promise to pay.

This doesn't apply here because there is a contract, and thus there's no reason to turn to quasi-contractual recovery. Reggie requested that Harriet perform – i.e., make a written, revocable offer – in return for $200. Once she did so, an enforceable unilateral contract was formed, and quasi-contract isn't relevant. Since D doesn't recognize this, it's not the best response.

Answer 142

(D) is the best response.
All three are good arguments for Harriet.

As to alternative I:
This is a good argument because, to be liable under contract law, there *must* be an express or an implied promise. An implied promise arises where one has a duty to speak, and doesn't do so. Here, Harriet had no duty to respond to Norma, so there's no implied promise. While liability may be imposed on a person who receives benefits, in the *absence* of a promise to pay pursuant to quasi-contract, quasi-contract requires more than the plaintiff's expectation of being paid; it requires defendant's knowledge or reason to know of this expectation. Here, Harriet had no reason to think Norma's tip was anything but gratuitous. Thus, without a promise to pay, under these circumstances, Harriet wouldn't be liable, making alternative I a good argument.

As to alternative II:
This is a good argument because the lack of consideration would torpedo Norma's claim, even if Harriet

did promise to pay the brokerage fee.

A promise, to be enforceable, requires consideration or some substitute for consideration. Consideration is a bargained-for exchange, and either detriment to the promisee or benefit to the promisor, and typically both. Here, Norma gave everything she could have given – Portia's name – without any promise from Harriet. Thus, she didn't give the name *in response* to a promise from Harriet, and thus there was no bargain, as alternative II indicates.

There are two other points of relevance here. First, there's past consideration. If you thought there was consideration here, you were probably looking to Norma's supplying the name as consideration. However, Norma had *already* given the name when she requested the commission. Thus, giving the name would be considered pas consideration, which, as a general rule, is not sufficient to make a promise enforceable (assuming arguendo, as alternative II does, that Harriet made a promise when Norma called her about the commission). Second, since there's no consideration here, you may have thought of promissory estoppel, which is a substitute for consideration which is used to avoid injustice. Promissory estoppel arises where there is a gratuitous promise that is likely to, and does, induce promisee's reliance. Here, even if Harriet promised to pay Norma in the phone call, this didn't induce Norma's reliance, because she'd already supplied the name. Thus, not only is there no consideration, but there's no substitute for it, either.

As to alternative III:

This is a good argument for Harriet, because without an offer and acceptance, there can be no enforceable promise, because mutual assent is lacking.

An offer is, in general, a promise to do something (or refrain from doing it). Acceptance allows offeree to transform the offer into a contract by promising to do something in return (or actually doing something in return).

Here, Norma's statement on the phone didn't involve any promises, but rather an *expectation* of payment – she didn't promise to do anything in return. Furthermore, while acceptance need not be *express,* it requires *some* word or act (since silence can only be acceptance where there are *some* prior dealings to indicate silence will act as assent). Here, there's no acceptance. Since both offer and acceptance are lacking under these facts, Harriet could successfully resist payment on this basis, making alternative III a good argument for Harriet.

Answer 143

(D) is the best response.

D is the best response, because it correctly identifies both the level of the burden of proof, and the party on which it is placed.

Here, the law limits the First Amendment, fundamen-

tal right to free speech in a public place – the Capitol steps. The right to such speech is not absolute; it can be limited, for instance, by valid "time, place, and manner" regulations. In order to be valid as such a regulation:

1. The law must be neutral as to the content of the speech;
2. It must further a significant government interest which is not capable of accomplishment by less restrictive means;
3. There must be alternative media of communication available.

Thus, the law must promote a significant governmental interest; option D correctly recognizes this. Furthermore, it places the burden on the correct party. Once a law is shown to adversely impact a First Amendment right, the burden is on the state to prove that the statute is valid. Since option D correctly identifies the burden and the party on which it will be placed, it's the best response.

(A) is not the best response,

because it both places the burden on the wrong party, and it misstates the level of scrutiny the statute will undergo.

Here, the law limits the First Amendment, fundamental right to free speech in a public place – the Capitol steps. The right to such speech is not absolute; it can be limited, for instance, by valid "time, place, and manner" regulations. In order to be valid as such a regulation:

1. The law must be neutral as to the content of the speech;
2. It must further a significant government interest which is not capable of accomplishment by less restrictive means;
3. There must be alternative media of communication available.

Thus, the law must promote a significant governmental interest; option A understates the interest required by stating that the law need only meet the rational basis test. The rational basis test is used for economic and social legislation, not laws limiting First Amendment rights (among others).

Furthermore, option A misplaces the burden of proof. Once a law is shown to adversely impact a First Amendment right, the burden is on the state to prove that the statute is valid. Since A puts the burden on the wrong party, and misstates that burden, it's not the best response.

(B) is not the best response,

because although it correctly states the burden of proof, it places it on the wrong party.

Here, the law limits the First Amendment, fundamental right to free speech in a public place – the Capitol steps. The right to such speech is not absolute; it can be limited, for instance, by valid "time, place, and manner" regulations. In order to be valid as such a regulation:

1. The law must be neutral as to the content of the speech;
2. It must further a significant government interest which is not capable of accomplishment by less restrictive means;
3. There must be alternative media of communication available.

Here, option B correctly identifies this burden – it just places that burden on the wrong party. All Doe needs to prove is that his First Amendment rights were adversely impacted by the law. Then, it's up to the state to prove that the statute is valid. Since B misplaces this burden, it's not the best response.

(C) is not the best response,

because although it correctly identifies that the state bears the burden of proof, it understates that burden.

Here, the law limits the First Amendment, fundamental right to free speech in a public place – the Capitol steps. The right to such speech is not absolute; it can be limited, for instance, by valid "time, place, and manner" regulations. In order to be valid as such a regulation:

1. The law must be neutral as to the content of the speech;
2. It must further a significant government interest which is not capable of accomplishment by less restrictive means;
3. There must be alternative media of communication available.

Thus, the law must promote a significant governmental interest; option C understates the interest required by stating that the law need only meet the rational basis test. The rational basis test is used for economic and social legislation, not laws limiting First Amendment rights (among others).

Although option C understates the burden, it does place it on the correct party. Once a law is shown to adversely impact a First Amendment right, the burden is on the state to prove that the statute is valid. However, since option C understates the state's burden, it's not the best response.

Answer 144

(B) is the best response.

B is the best response, because the politician is the only individual or organization, of those mentioned in these four options, who would likely have standing to challenge the "Capitol steps" statute.

In order to press a claim, a party must have standing. Standing requires that the statute challenged must have caused or is imminently likely to cause, an injury to the party seeking review. Here, a politician intending to speak on the Capitol steps during a prohibited time would be imminently likely to suffer an injury due to

operation of the statute, since it would impact his right to free speech. As a result, the politician would likely have the standing to challenge the statute. Since B recognizes this, it's the best response.

(A) is not the best response,

because such a person would lack standing to challenge the "Capitol steps" statute.

In order to press a claim, a party must have standing. Standing requires that the statute challenged must have caused, or is imminently likely to cause, an injury to the party seeking review. Taxpayers *can* have standing by virtue of their status as taxpayers, but this wouldn't help under these facts. Taxpayers can only contest spending matters. The "Capitol steps" statute is a "time, place and manner" regulation on free speech, not a spending issue. (In fact, state taxpayers can normally challenge state or municipal *measurable* expenditures [e.g., local busing of parochial school students]). Since a taxpayer wouldn't have standing under these facts, and A states otherwise, it's not the best response.

(C) is not the best response,

because the legislator would lack standing under these facts.

In order to press a claim, a party must have standing. Standing requires that the statute challenged must have caused, or is imminently likely to cause, an injury to the party seeking review. Here, a legislator who voted against the statute due to its perceived unconstitutionality would not have suffered an injury, nor would he be imminently likely to suffer an injury, due to the statute. As a result, he'd lack standing to challenge the statute. Since C doesn't recognize this, it's not the best response.

(D) is not the best response,

because the organization would lack standing to challenge the "Capitol steps" statute.

In order to press a claim, a party must have standing. Standing requires that the statute challenged must have caused, or is imminently likely to cause, an injury to the party seeking review. Here, the organization hasn't suffered an injury due to the statute, and its mere goal of invalidating unconstitutional laws would not make it likely to suffer an injury due to operation of the statute. Since D doesn't recognize this, it's not the best response.

Answer 145

(A) is the best response.

A is the best response, because it recognizes that the statute is both valid on its face and as it applies to Doe.

Under these facts, the "Capitol steps" statute regulates speech in a public place – the state Capitol building. The government can regulate the time, place, and manner of such expression. Heffren v. International

Society for Krishna Consciousness (1981). Such regulations are valid if they meet this three-pronged test:

1. They must be neutral as to the content of the speech;
2. They must further a significant government interest which is not capable of accomplishment by less restrictive means; and
3. There must be alternative media of communication available.

Here, the purpose of the statute is clearly to promote the smooth flow of ingress and egress to and from the Capitol building, since it only bars speech in front of the entryway at "rush" or "peak" periods. This is considered a significant government interest which can validly be promoted by statutes like the one in these facts; thus, the statute is facially valid. Option A correctly identifies this.

The "as applied to Doe" language in option A refers to discriminatory application of the statute. There are three ways in which a statute can be discriminatory: 1/ It can be prima facie discriminatory; 2/ it can be racially neutral but unequally administered; or 3/ it can have an impermissible motive proven through historic background, events leading up to the statute, and statements made by government officials in the decision-making process. The statute under these facts is not discriminatory on its face, and there's no evidence of an impermissible motive. As to discriminatory application, that can only occur when the one administering the statute does so in a discriminatory fashion. There's no evidence of this under these facts. As a result, the statute would be valid as it applies to Doe. Since A recognizes this, it's the best response.

(B) is not the best response,

because the statute is both constitutional on its face *and* as it applies to Doe.

Under these facts, the "Capitol steps" statute regulates speech in a public place – the state Capitol building. The government can regulate the time, place, and manner of such expression. Heffren v. International Society for Krishna Consciousness (1981). Such regulations are valid if they meet this three-pronged test:

1. They must be neutral as to the content of the speech;
2. They must further a significant government interest which is not capable of accomplishment by less restrictive means; and
3. There must be alternative media of communication available.

Here, the purpose of the statute is clearly to promote the smooth flow of ingress and egress to and from the Capitol building, since it only bars speech in front of the entryway at "rush" or "peak" periods. This is considered a significant government interest which can validly be promoted by statutes like the one in these facts. Option B correctly identifies this, by stating that the statute is facially valid.

The "as applied to Doe" language in option B refers to discriminatory application of the statute. There are three ways in which a statute can be discriminatory: 1/ It can be prima facie discriminatory; 2/ it can be racially neutral but unequally administered; or 3/ it can have an impermissible motive proven through historic background, events leading up to the statute, and statements made by government official sin the decision-making process. The statute under these facts is not discriminatory on its face, and there's no evidence of an impermissible motive. As to discriminatory application, that can only occur when the one administering the statute does so in a discriminatory fashion. There's no evidence of this under these facts. As a result, the statute would be valid as it applies to Doe. Since B doesn't recognize this, it's not the best response.

(C) is not the best response,

because the statute here is constitutional on its face.

There are three ways in which a statute can be discriminatory, and thus unconstitutional: 1/ It can be prima facie discriminatory; 2/ It can be facially neutral but unequally administered; or 3/ It can have an impermissible motive, proven through historic background, events leading up to the statute, and statements made by government officials in the decision-making process. Option C refers to the first of these – the facial validity of the statute.

Under these facts, the "Capitol steps" statute regulates speech in a public place – the state Capitol building. The government can regulate the time, place, and manner of such expression. Heffren v. International Society for Krishna Consciousness (1981). Such regulations are valid if they meet this three-pronged test:

1. They must be neutral as to the content of the speech;
2. They must further a significant government interest which is not capable of accomplishment by less restrictive means; and
3. There must be alternative media of communication available.

Here, the purpose of the statute is clearly to promote the smooth flow of ingress and egress to and from the Capitol building, since it only bars speech in front of the entryway at "rush" or "peak" periods. This is considered a significant government interest which can validly be promoted by statutes like the one in these facts; thus, the statute is facially valid. Since C states otherwise, it's not the best response.

(D) is not the best response,

because the fact that the statute concerns the State Capitol would not make it facially unconstitutional.

There are three ways in which a statute can be discriminatory, and thus unconstitutional: 1/ It can be prima facie discriminatory; 2/ It can be facially neutral but unequally administered; or 3/ It can have an impermissible motive, proven through historic background, events leading up to the statute, and statements made by government officials in the decision-making process. Option C refers to the first of these – the facial validity of the statute.

Under these facts, the "Capitol steps" statute regulates speech in a public place – the state Capitol building. The government can regulate the time, place, and manner of such expression. Heffren v. International Society for Krishna Consciousness (1981). Such regulations are valid if they meet this three-pronged test:

1. They must be neutral as to the content of the speech;

2. They must further a significant government interest which is not capable of accomplishment by less restrictive means; and

3. There must be alternative media of communication available.

Here, the purpose of the statute is clearly to promote the smooth flow of ingress and egress to and from the Capitol building, since it only bars speech in front of the entryway at "rush" or "peak" periods. This is considered a significant government interest which can validly be promoted by statutes like the one in these facts; thus, the statute is facially valid.

If you chose this response, you probably attached too much significance to the fact that the State Capitol was involved, and its status as a public place. As the discussion here indicates, even speech in a public place can be regulated. Of course, speech in non-public fora can be regulated to a much greater degree (e.g., a private property owner, like the owner of a shopping mall, can forbid picketing or the distribution of handbills from taking place on his property; whereas private property which is the equivalent of a public place, like a company town, is subject to the reasonable exercise of first amendment rights). Under these facts, even though a public forum is involved, the statute will be valid. Since D states otherwise, it's not the best response.

Answer 146

(B) is the best response,

because it recognizes both that the statute is constitutional, and that it could not be used to punish Doe.

Here, the law is designed to forbid advocacy of unlawful conduct – specifically, threatening a public official for his performance of his public duties. The validity of such statutes is determined under the "clear and present danger" test from Brandenburg v. Ohio (1969), which provides that advocacy can only be forbidden if: 1. Its aim is to produce or incite imminent illegal action, and 2. It is likely to produce or incite such action. Here, the statute only makes illegal that conduct which intentionally threatens a public official, and would as a result qualify as criminal conduct. Thus it would clearly be *facially* valid under the Brandenburg test, just as option B states.

B is also correct in stating that Doe could not be con-victed under this statute. His speech satisfies neither prong of the Brandenburg test. His statement that he will "strangle every one of those goddamned legislators I can get hold of" is a statement of anger, not intent. Furthermore, it was unlikely to illicit illegal action, because you're told the audience was amused by his comments, not incited to attack. Since B recognizes this, and the fact that the statute is facially constitutional, it's the best response.

(A) is not the best response,

because the statute would be facially constitutional.

Here, the law is designed to forbid advocacy of unlawful conduct – specifically, threatening a public official for his performance of his public duties. The validity of such statutes is determined under the "clear and present danger" test from Brandenburg v. Ohio (1969), which provides that advocacy can only be forbidden if: 1. Its aim is to produce or incite imminent illegal action, and 2. It is likely to produce or incite such action. Here, the statute only makes illegal that conduct which intentionally threatens a public official, and would as a result qualify as criminal conduct. Thus it would clearly be *facially* valid under the Brandenburg test.

If you chose this response, you may have thought that the statute was unconstitutionally vague. A statute is only void for vagueness if a person of ordinary intelligence would not be able to tell when his conduct would be forbidden under the statute. That's not the case here, because a reasonably intelligence person would know that the statute forbids a threat on the life of a public official. The problem here is not the statute itself, but its application to Doe, since Doe's language was probably not intended as a threat, and it clearly wasn't likely to produce illegal action, because the audience laughed off Doe's comments. However, the focus of option A is the facial validity of the statute, and since it incorrectly states that the statute is facially invalid, it's not the best response.

(C) is not the best response,

because although it implicitly recognizes that the statute is constitutional, it's incorrect in stating that Doe could be validly punished under the statute.

Here, the law is designed to forbid advocacy of unlawful conduct – specifically, threatening a public official for his performance of his public duties. The validity of such statutes is determined under the "clear and present danger" test from Brandenburg v. Ohio (1969), which provides that advocacy can only be forbidden if: 1. Its aim is to produce or incite imminent illegal action, and 2. It is likely to produce or incite such action. Here, the statute only makes illegal that conduct which intentionally threatens a public official, and would as a result qualify as criminal conduct. Thus it would clearly be *facially* valid under the Brandenburg test. Option C implicitly recognizes this.

However, option C is incorrect in stating that Doe could be convicted under this statute. His speech satisfies neither prong of the Brandenburg test. His statement that he will "strangle every one of those goddamned legislators I can get hold of" is a statement of anger, not intent. Furthermore, it was unlikely to illicit illegal action, because you're told the audience was amused by his comments, not incited to attack. Since C doesn't recognize this, it's not the best response.

(D) is not the best response,

because the presence of a legislator would not make Doe punishable under this statute.

Option D implicitly recognizes that the statute here is valid. The statute is designed to forbid advocacy of unlawful conduct – specifically, threatening a public official for his performance of his public duties. The validity of such statutes is determined under the "clear and present danger" test from Brandenburg v. Ohio (1969), which provides that advocacy can only be forbidden if: 1/ Its aim is to produce or incite imminent illegal action, and 2/ It is likely to produce or incite such action. Here, the statute only makes illegal that conduct which intentionally threatens a public official, and would as a result qualify as criminal conduct. Thus it would clearly be *facially* valid under the Brandenburg test.

However, the statute couldn't be applied to Doe under these facts, even if a legislator were present. That's because the mere presence of legislators would not make Doe's statements fit the Brandenburg test. His statement that he will "strangle every one of those goddamned legislators I can get hold of" is a statement of anger, not intent. Furthermore, it was unlikely to illicit illegal action, because you're told the audience was amused by his comments, not incited to attack. In order to satisfy Brandenburg, any additional facts introduced by an option would have to change Doe's intent and the effect of the statements on the audience. Option D does neither of these, and as a result, the statute cannot be applied to Doe so as to result in his punishment. Thus, D cannot be the best response.

Answer 147

(C) is the best response.

C is the best response because equal protection would not be a good defense for Doe, and the question here is looking for the worst defense.

The equal protection clause is triggered by a classification that determines people's rights: e.g., citizens vs. aliens, men vs. women, legitimate vs. illegitimate children, in-staters vs. out-of-staters. The reason the statute here wouldn't be a good target for equal protection is that it doesn't involve a classification at all: It prohibits everyone from uttering a blasphemous or sacrilegious statement. Furthermore, there is nothing to indicate that the way the law has been administered has created disparate treatment for different groups of

people. Thus, there's no likely equal protection violation, making equal protection an invalid defense, and thus making C the best response.

(A) is not the best response,

because the due process clause would be a good defense to this action, and the question is looking for the least effective defense.

Option A suggests that the statute is void for vagueness. A statute can be unconstitutionally vague, and thus a due process violation, in one of two ways: It can simply insufficiently describe the proscribed speech (e.g., it could outlaw any speech not protected by the First and Fourteenth Amendments); or it can be drawn with insufficient clarity and definiteness to inform persons of ordinary intelligence what actions are proscribed. The theory here is that such vagueness makes the statute overbroad, such that language which is protected by the First Amendment may be proscribed by a statute.

The second situation is what's involved under these facts. Even though speech is a fundamental right, it can be regulated under one of two circumstances: Either it's not *protected* speech (i.e., it satisfies the "clear and present danger" test; if it's obscene, defamatory, or constitutes "fighting words"; it constitutes deceptive advertising (and thus impermissible commercial speech)); or if it *is* protected speech, its limitation is necessary to a compelling governmental interest. The law here doesn't address any of the "unprotected" speech possibilities. Thus, it's protected speech, and its can only be limited if the government shows this limitation is necessary for a compelling governmental interest. Under these facts, language could be blasphemous or sacrilegious without otherwise being capable of prohibition under the First Amendment. For instance, stubbing your toe on a curb and yelling "Jesus Christ!" would be prohibited under this statute, but it would be permissible under the First Amendment.

Incidentally, note the significance of the fact that very few people have been prosecuted under the statute. The interpretation given to the statute by courts could have created a meaning for the statute that would abrogate its vagueness. Since other prosecutions are lacking, this is not an avenue by which an otherwise unconstitutional statute could be made valid.

Instead, the statute is unconstitutionally vague and overbroad, and amounts to a due process violation as a result, making option A a good defense. Since the question is looking for the least successful defense, A can't be the best response.

(B) is not the best response,

because the statute could conceivably be construed as an establishment of religion, making it unconstitutional and thus making this argument a good defense.

The religion clause of the First Amendment requires

that Congress make no law respecting an establishment of religion, nor prohibiting the free exercise of religion (this provision applies to the states under the Fourteenth Amendment). The "establishment" part of the religion clause requires that laws must have a secular purpose, and not have as their principal or primary effect the advancement of religion, and the laws must not foster excessive government entanglement with religion. Here, the law prohibits only language which is offensive from a religious perspective: That is, it's blasphemous or sacrilegious. By putting this religious "gloss" on the law, the state is not being neutral as to religion. As a result, the establishment clause would be a good defense to this charge. Since the question is looking for the least successful defense, B is not the best response.

(D) is not the best response,

because a freedom of speech defense would be a good defense to this charge.

Even though speech is a fundamental right, it can be regulated under one of two circumstances: Either it's not *protected* speech (i.e., it satisfies the "clear and present danger" test; if it's obscene, defamatory, or constitutes "fighting words"; it constitutes deceptive advertising (and thus impermissible commercial speech)); or if it *is* protected speech, its limitation is necessary to a compelling governmental interest. The law here doesn't address any of the "unprotected" speech possibilities. Thus, it's protected speech, and its can only be limited if the government shows this limitation is necessary for a compelling governmental interest. No such interest is shown under these facts, nor could it likely be shown at all. Thus, Doe could use the freedom of speech argument as a defense. Since the question is looking for the least successful defense, D can't be the best response.

Answer 148

(B) is the best response

because it correctly applies the appropriate rule to these facts.

In this question, the contents of a letter are involved – Investigator's letter to Denucci, inquiring about Peri. Thus, there's at least facially a Best Evidence Rule issue. The Best Evidence Rule is triggered when a party wants to prove the material terms of a writing (or a witness is testifying relying on a writing). Then, the "original writing" (which includes photocopies and carbons) must be produced, and copies and oral testimony about the writing's contents will only be admissible when the original is shown to be unavailable for some other reason than the proponent's misconduct. FRE 1002.

The thing that makes the Best Evidence Rule inadmissible here is that no one is seeking to prove the contents of the inquiry letter. It doesn't particularly matter how the request was worded, and there's nothing

for the jury to interpret. Furthermore, it is not clear that Investigator is relying on the letter for his testimony, since he wrote the letter and could remember the contents. All that matters is that Investigator asked Denucci about Peri, and Investigator's testimony will suffice for this. Since the terms of the letter are not material to the case, Investigator's testimony will be admissible without accounting for the unavailability of the letter.

Note that once you've removed any Best Evidence problem, you've also taken care of a potential hearsay problem, as well. Had the contents of Investigator's letter been at issue, there would be a hearsay issue as well as a Best Evidence problem, because the testimony would be repeating the out-of-court statements found in the letter. Since Investigator is merely being asked if he wrote to Denucci inquiring about Peri – and this doesn't require that he repeat any out-of-court statements – there's no hearsay problem.

Since B recognizes confronts the central, Best Evidence Rule issue, and satisfactorily resolves it, it is the best response.

(A) is not the best response,

because it is irrelevant.

The admissibility of Investigator's testimony is not dependent on whether or not the inquiry was made in the regular course of business; rather, all that's necessary is that Investigator have personal knowledge of the substance of his testimony – that is, whether an inquiry was made.

What option B implies is that the testimony is hearsay, and will only be admissible if it fits the business records exception to the hearsay rule. The reason this doesn't apply is that Investigator's testimony isn't hearsay. Hearsay is an out-of-court statement offered to prove the truth of its assertion. Here, the contents of Investigator's letter aren't being offered to prove that anything in the letter was true. Rather, the only thing that's important about his out-of-court statement is that it was made – i.e., to prove that he inquired about Peri at all. As a result, it's not hearsay, and there's no need for it to fit in any exception, let alone the business records exception. Since A doesn't recognize this, it's not the best response.

(C) is not the best response

because the admissibility of Investigator's testimony would not depend on Denucci's prior notification.

The "prior notification" language addresses the issue of surprise. At common law, even though a piece of evidence is relevant, it can be excluded under some circumstances if there are factors that outweigh the probative value of the evidence. One such circumstance is unfair surprise to the opponent. The theory is that with no reasonable grounds for anticipating such proof, the opponent would be unprepared to meet it. This is addressed in the Federal Rules, in the Advisory Committee's Notes to Rule 403, where it's suggested that it's more appropriate for the affected party to seek a continuance, rather than having the evidence rejected outright, in cases of surprise. Beyond that, procedural rules involving pre-trial discovery significantly diminish the possibility of surprise. Nonetheless, there are limited circumstances under the Federal Rules where advance notice is specifically required – as in evidence of prior sexual conduct of a rape victim, in the very rare circumstances where it's admissible at all.

In any case, under these facts, there'd be no basis for excluding Investigator's testimony about the inquiry even if Peri's attorney didn't specifically know about it beforehand. The entire basis of this lawsuit was a defamatory letter. Here, Investigator's inquiry would provide the reason the defamatory letter was sent. This is close enough to a central issue that Peri's attorney should reasonably have anticipated it, thus negating the possibility of unfair surprise. Since C doesn't recognize this, it's not the best response.

(D) is not the best response,

because it incorrectly implies that the Best Evidence Rule applies to Investigator's testimony, since the Best Evidence Rule requires proof that a document is unavailable before testimony about its contents will be admissible.

The Best Evidence Rule only applies when the terms of a writing are being proven, or the witness is testifying relying on a writing. Then, the "original writing" (which includes photocopies and carbons) must be produced, and copies and oral testimony about the writing's contents will only be admissible when the original is shown to be unavailable for some other reason than the proponent's misconduct. FRE 1002.

The thing that makes the Best Evidence Rule inadmissible here is that no one is seeking to prove the contents of the inquiry letter. It doesn't particularly matter how the request was worded, and there's nothing for the jury to interpret. Furthermore, it is not clear that Investigator is relying on the letter for his testimony, since he wrote the letter and could remember the contents. All that matters is that Investigator asked Denucci about Peri, and Investigator's testimony will suffice for this. Since the terms of the letter are not material to the case, and Investigator isn't relying on the letter for his testimony, Investigator's testimony will be admissible without accounting for the unavailability of the letter. Note that Denucci's letter is an entirely different matter, since that's the letter that allegedly contains the defamatory matter. Since the terms of that letter would be material to the case, it would be covered by the Best Evidence Rule. However, what's at issue in this question is Investigator's inquiry letter, not Denucci's response. Since testimony about the inquiry letter will be admissible without proving the unavailability of the letter itself, and D doesn't recognize this, D isn't the best response.

Answer 149

(D) is the best response

because it correctly states the applicable rule: The admissibility of secondary evidence is decided on the judge's determination that the original is unavailable.

The Best Evidence Rule, which is what's involved here, is triggered when either the terms of a writing are being proven, or a witness is testifying relying on a writing. When that happens, the "original writing" (which includes photocopies and carbons) must be produced. Copies and oral testimony concerning the writing's contents are only permissible on a showing of the original's unavailability which was not the result of proponent's serious misconduct. FRE 1002. The rationale is that errors or gaps in memory, as well as fraud, can be avoided by allowing the trier of fact to see the writing itself, if it's available.

Here, the exact terms of the letter are not only material, but they form the basis of the defamation claim. As a result, the Best Evidence Rule will apply. In terms of determining unavailability, option D correctly states that the judge makes that decision. the unavailability of a document is considered a "preliminary fact" to be determined by the judge. (Preliminary facts are those that form a condition to the admission of proferred evidence. The judge decides some of these, like determining if relevant evidence is competent, if a privilege exists, the standard of trustworthiness of hearsay, if business records are in the regular course of business, and the qualifications of an expert; the jury decides others, like the relevancy of evidence, agency, authenticity, credibility, and personal knowledge.)

Incidentally, note that there's no hearsay problem here, even though the terms of a document are sought to be admitted. That's because the facts are "legally operative" – in other words, the words aren't being admitted to prove the truth of their assertion (as hearsay requires), but rather only to prove that they were made. This holds for things like the words of a will, contract, or, as here, defamation.

In any case, since option D applies the correct rule, it's the best response.

(A) is not the best response

because it does not apply the Best Evidence Rule correctly, and instead focuses on a fact which will not determine the admissibility of the testimony.

Note that the question uses the qualifier "only." That means that the correct option must address a *prerequisite* for the admission of the letter. While the precision of Investigator's testimony may affect the weight the jury gives it, it will not determine its admissibility.

The Best Evidence Rule, which is what's involved here, is triggered when either the terms of a writing are being proven, or a witness is testifying relying on a writing. When that happens, the "original writing" (which includes photocopies and carbons) must be produced.

Copies and oral testimony concerning the writing's contents are only permissible on a showing of the original's unavailability which was not the result of proponent's serious misconduct. FRE 1002. The rationale is that errors or gaps in memory, as well as fraud, can be avoided by allowing the trier of fact to see the writing itself, if it's available.

Here, the exact terms of the letter are not only material, but they form the basis of the defamation claim. As a result, the Best Evidence Rule will apply. Option A is incorrect in stating how the rule will apply. For a start, the judge must decide a "preliminary fact": the unavailability of the document. (Preliminary facts are those that form a condition to the admission of proferred evidence. The judge decides some of these, like determining if relevant evidence is competent, if a privilege exists, the standard of trustworthiness of hearsay, if business records are in the regular course of business, and the qualifications of an expert; the jury decides others, like the relevancy of evidence, agency, authenticity, credibility, and personal knowledge.) FRE 104.

As to the precision of the testimony, this does not affect the admissibility of the testimony at all. Instead, that's an issue of credibility that the jury will decide once the letter is admitted. Since A doesn't recognize this, it's not the best response.

(B) is not the best response,

because although it impliedly recognizes that the Best Evidence Rule applies to these facts, it assigns to the jury the finding of a preliminary fact – the unavailability of the letter – which is actually the judge's duty.

Note that the question uses the qualifier "only." That means that the correct option must address a *prerequisite* for the admission of the letter. While option B correctly identifies what the prerequisite is – namely, the unavailability of the letter – it simply gives that duty to the wrong entity.

The Best Evidence Rule is triggered when either the terms of a writing are being proven, or a witness is testifying relying on a writing. When that happens, the "original writing" (which includes photocopies and carbons) must be produced. Copies and oral testimony concerning the writing's contents are only permissible on a showing of the original's unavailability which was not the result of proponent's serious misconduct. FRE 1002. The rationale is that errors or gaps in memory, as well as fraud, can be avoided by allowing the trier of fact to see the writing itself, if it's available.

Here, the exact terms of the letter are not only material, but they form the basis of the defamation claim. As a result, the Best Evidence Rule will apply. Option B is incorrect in stating how the rule will apply. For a start, the judge must decide a "preliminary fact": the unavailability of the document. (Preliminary facts are those that form a condition to the admission of proferred evidence. The judge decides some of these, like determining if relevant evidence is competent, if a privilege

exists, the standard of trustworthiness of hearsay, if business records are in the regular course of business, and the qualifications of an expert; the jury decides others, like the relevancy of evidence, agency, authenticity, credibility, and personal knowledge.) FRE 104(a). Since B incorrectly places the decision on unavailability in the hands of the jury, it's not the best response.

(C) is not the best response,

because it does not apply the Best Evidence Rule correctly, and instead focuses on a fact which will not determine the admissibility of the testimony.

Note that the question uses the qualifier "only." That means that the correct option must address a *prerequisite* for the admission of the letter. While the judge will make the decision as to whether the testimony is admissible, he'll be determining whether the original is unavailable, not whether the Investigator quotes the letter precisely. The precision of Investigator's testimony will determine the weight the jury gives the testimony, not its admissibility.

The Best Evidence Rule, which is what's involved here, is triggered when either the terms of a writing are being proven, or a witness is testifying relying on a writing. When that happens, the "original writing" (which includes photocopies and carbons) must be produced. Copies and oral testimony concerning the writing's contents are only permissible on a showing of the original's unavailability which was not the result of proponent's serious misconduct. FRE 1002. The rationale is that errors or gaps in memory, as well as fraud, can be avoided by allowing the trier of fact to see the writing itself, if it's available.

Here, the exact terms of the letter are not only material, but they form the basis of the defamation claim. As a result, the Best Evidence Rule will apply. Option A is incorrect in stating how the rule will apply. For a start, the judge must decide a "preliminary fact": the unavailability of the document. (Preliminary facts are those that form a condition to the admission of proferred evidence. The judge decides some of these, like determining if relevant evidence is competent, if a privilege exists, the standard of trustworthiness of hearsay, if business records are in the regular course of business, and the qualifications of an expert; the jury decides others, like the relevancy of evidence, agency, authenticity, credibility, and personal knowledge.) FRE 104.

As to the precision of the testimony, this does not affect the admissibility of the testimony at all. Instead, that's an issue of credibility that the jury will decide once the letter is admitted. Since C doesn't recognize this, it's not the best response.

Answer 150

(A) is the best response,

because it addresses the central issue under these facts, and resolves it satisfactorily.

A defamation claim requires proof of a defamatory

statement, of and concerning plaintiff, negligently or intentionally "published" to at least one third person, and plaintiff's reputation damaged thereby. In addition, plaintiff must prove some level of *fault*, depending on his status and that of the defamer, and, if the claim is for slander not in one of the four per se categories, plaintiff will have to prove special (pecuniary) damages.

While at common law defamation was a strict liability tort, modern cases suggest that where the defamer is "private" (i.e., non-media), at least negligence must be proven. That is, under these facts, if Shoe Store *didn't* verify Photo's story and a reasonable person *would* have, the fault element of defamation would be satisfied. Here, option A would make Shoe Store liable *if* it was reckless. Note that using the modifier "if" means that the reasoning need only be *plausible* under the facts, not *given* in the facts, and the reasoning must address a central element. It's quite possible here that Shoe Store *was* objectively and subjectively unreasonable in failing to contact Player; and, if this is true, it would more than satisfy the fault requirement of a private defamer. Thus, since A addresses a central issue and resolves it, it's the best response.

(B) is not the best response,
because the form of the defamation – whether libel or slander – is irrelevant here.

The primary difference in claiming libel or slander has to do with whether plaintiff will have to prove "special" (pecuniary) damages in order to recover *at all* (if the defamation claim is for libel of any kind, or slander per se, special damages needn't be proven; for slander that is not in one of the four "per se" categories (reflecting on business/profession, imputing a foul and loathsome disease, moral turpitude crime, or unchastity in a woman), then special damages will have to be proven. Here, they would not have to be, because the photo would be considered libel; even if it were slander, since Player lost his scholarship, he'd be able to prove special damages fairly easily).

Instead, defamation requires proof of a defamatory statement, of and concerning plaintiff, negligently or intentionally "published" to at least one third person, with plaintiff's reputation damaged thereby. At common law, defamation was a strict liability offense; under modern constitutional rules, some level of fault must be proven, depending on the status of the defamer (if media) and the defamed (private individual or public figure). If the defamer is non-media, negligence must be proven. Since B addresses an irrelevant point, it's not the best response.

(C) is not the best response,
because Shoe Store's belief, *if unreasonable*, would not exonerate Shoe Store.

While defamation at common law was a strict liability offense, under modern constitutional rules a private

(i.e., non-media) defamer must be at least negligent in order to be liable: Thus, if a reasonable person would have checked into the truth of Photo's statement, and Shoe Store didn't, Shoe Store will be liable for defamation.

Option C, on the contrary, would require a *knowing* defamation, by resting Shoe Store's liability on its purely subjective belief. Since Shoe Store could be liable if its belief was merely unreasonable, C is not the best response.

(D) is not the best response,
because Player's recovery will *not* depend on whether the picture is defamatory *per se*.

Libel per se is a statement libelous "on its face;" slander per se is a defamatory, spoken statement, which does not require proof of "special" (pecuniary) damages because it falls within one of the four per se exceptions (harm business/reputation, or imputes loathsome disease, moral turpitude crime, or unchastity in a woman).

"Per se" status has an entirely different effect depending on whether the claim is based on libel or slander. Under libel, if the statement is not libelous "on its face," the plaintiff will have to prove why the statement is libelous. Here, Player will be able to do this fairly easily: The photo implied a commercial endorsement by Player, which Player didn't make. In slander, on the other hand, if the statement does not fit a per se category, in order for plaintiff's claim to succeed he *must* prove special damages. Even if the statement here were for slander instead of libel, Player would still recover, since he's got straightforward pecuniary loss: His scholarship.

Since Player's success with his claim does not turn on the issue of defamation "per se," D is not the best response.

Answer 151

(B) is the best response,
because it identifies the basis on which Shoe Store will be liable.

Invasion of privacy is an "umbrella" tort encompassing four individual torts: Defendant's appropriation of plaintiff's picture or name for defendant's own commercial advantage; defendant's intrusion on plaintiff's affairs or seclusion; defendant's publication of facts which place plaintiff in a false light; and defendant's public disclosure of private facts about plaintiff.

The first type (appropriation) is applicable to these facts, since it describes – as does option B: Shoe Store used Player's picture for profit. While "consent" would be a defense, Shoe Store did not have permission under these facts. While Shoe Store believed it had permission, if it was at least negligent in verifying its information it will be liable. Although B does not address the fault issue, negligence could safely be assumed. Since B accurately describes the tort, it's applicable to these facts, and no other option is satis-factory, B is the best response.

(A) is not the best response,
because it misstates the law, and does not focus on a central issue.

It isn't Photo's *taking* the picture which Player finds objectionable, but Shoe Store's *use* of the photo, falsely suggesting Player endorsed the shoes. In fact, merely taking one's picture, in public, is not actionable; if you're out in public, you're pretty much fair game for photographers. Just ask Madonna. Since A states oth-erwise and ignores a central issue in the case, it's not the best response.

(C) is not the best response,
because it's irrelevant.

Player's status as a celebrity would not subject him to unauthorized use of his name. In fact, it's Player's fame that *prompted* Shoe Store to misappropriate his picture for its commercial advantage; simply being famous doesn't mean Player has waived his right to sue for invasion of privacy. Instead, under these facts, Player will have a valid claim for invasion of privacy in the form of appropriating plaintiff's name or picture for commer-cial advantage. As long as he proves this, his status is irrelevant. Since C states otherwise, it's not the best response.

(D) is not the best response,
because it offers a mens rea that is stricter than the *actual* mens rea required for invasion of privacy.

D suggests that if Shoe Store *believed* it had Player's permission, it will not be liable. However, this suggests that the invasion must be *knowing* in order to be action-able. In fact, an invasion of privacy may be predicated on negligent, or objectively unreasonable, behavior. Thus, Player need only prove that Shoe Store did not verify Player's consent where a reasonable person would have done so. Since D would require a standard of care higher than the one that's really required, it's not the best response.

Answer 152

(D) is the best response,
because it correctly cites the most specific basis upon which Landover could prevail: Application of the doc-trine of equitable conversion.

Under this doctrine, the vendee is considered the beneficial owner of the property after the sales contract takes effect, leaving the vendor with a personal prop-erty interest in the property, in the form of the balance of the purchase price the vendee owes him. This com-mon law doctrine is followed by most states (a minority of states follow the Uniform Vendor and Purchaser Act, which would have the opposite result). Note that, had the contract expressly provided for risk of loss, the con-tract provision would have controlled – likewise, in the

absence of such a contractual provision, a state statute would have controlled. Since neither one of these exist under these facts, you have to look to the common law and apply the doctrine of equitable conversion. Since D correctly states that the doctrine of equitable conver-sion would apply to these facts and result in Landover's prevailing in the case, it's the best response.

(A) is not the best response,
because it relies on a fact which is irrelevant.

VanMeer's failure to insure the property is not dispos-itive of Landover's ability to recover the purchase price. In fact, VanMeer did have an insurable interest in Highacre when it was destroyed – but so did Landover, so Landover cannot prevail on this basis. Since A does not provide a good basis for a decision in Landover's favor, it cannot be the best response.

(B) is not the best response,
because although it is a correct statement of the law, it would be insufficient, under these facts, to result in a decision for Landover.

B is correct in that, in general, remedies at law (e.g., damages) are inadequate in actions where real estate is involved, since real estate is "unique." In such situa-tions, specific performance is an appropriate remedy. However, specific performance is an *equitable* remedy, meaning that equitable considerations will be taken into account to determine if it's appropriate. Option D is just such a consideration – the doctrine of equitable conversion. As a result, the fact that real estate is involved is insufficient by itself to merit specific perfor-mance, making B not the best response.

(C) is not the best response,
because it misstates the law.

Specific performance is an equitable remedy. Equita-ble remedies are granted by determining whether the remedy will be just in the circumstances. As a result, the circumstances surrounding the contract *must* be considered. Since C does not recognize this, it cannot be the best response.

Answer 153

(C) is the best response,
because the equal protection issue will determine the validity of the restriction under these facts.

Restrictions on the use of land are valid as long as they aren't repugnant to law or public policy. The restriction here creates a classification: People aged 21 and over vs. those under 21. A classification which determines people's rights – here, the right to occupy land – is the hallmark of an equal protection problem. However, this question involves one further step, because the restriction here is a private agreement between owners of land in the subdivision, and the Constitution doesn't ban purely private acts of discrimi-nation; some state action is required. What makes this an equal protection issue that the other lot owners were seeking to have the restriction enforced in court, and such enforcement constitutes state action. Thus, if the restriction is an equal protection violation, the court could not enforce it. You might argue that the classification here addresses who can exercise the fundamental right of procreation, since those living in the subdivision could not have children. In that case, the restriction would be subject to strict scrutiny, and would thus almost certainly be invalid. What this shows is that an analysis of the restriction under the equal protection clause would determine its validity, and this is the only argument of these four which will determine the lawfulness of the restriction. Thus, option C is the best response.

(A) is not the best response,
because the distinction between realty and personalty would be irrelevant here.

The restriction here addresses who may own or occupy the land. Thus, it doesn't matter how the land is occupied, whether it's realty, personalty, a gingerbread house, or a giant shoe, as long as the restriction is lawful. The distinction of realty vs. personalty would be relevant, say, to whether or not the mobile home were considered a fixture, or, alternatively, for probate purposes in determining who is entitled to the mobile home (if the decedent has willed personalty to one person and realty to someone else). The distinction isn't relevant to this restriction; the only distinction involved here is between people aged 21 and over, and those under 21. Thus, the realty vs. personalty distinction won't be the issue deciding the case, making A not the best response.

(B) is not the best response,
because the restriction here wouldn't be unlawful because it's a restraint on alienation.

A deed restriction is only an invalid restraint on alienation if landowners could not sell their lots as restricted. Otherwise, property is frequently sold with restraints, like easements and restrictions on use. Here, the property owners could clearly sell their lots to adults without children. Thus, it's not the restriction's impact on alienation that would make it unlawful. As a result, it's not the alienation issue that would decide this case. Since B states otherwise, it's not the best response.

(D) is not the best response,
because if the restriction were valid, it needn't be expressly repeated verbatim in Dawson's deed in order to bind Dawson.

As long as the property holder has, at the vest least, constructive notice of the restriction, it doesn't matter that it doesn't appear in his own deed. For instance, real covenants and equitable servitudes are binding as long as they appear somewhere in the chain of title, even if they are completely absent from the current owner's deed. Here, Dawson's deed specifically refer-

ences the plat for the subdivision; thus, he had notice of the restriction, and, if the restriction were lawful, it would be binding on Dawson even without its being repeated verbatim in his deed. Since option D discusses an issue which will not be determinative under these facts, it's not the best response.

Answer 154

(B) is the best response,
because it correctly characterizes the clause as a condition, not a promise, and addresses and resolves a central issue.

A condition is the occurrence or non-occurrence of an event that triggers, limits, or extinguishes an absolute duty to perform. While it *can* be difficult to distinguish a condition from a promise, courts consider primarily the language used (i.e., how the parties characterize the clause). Furthermore, Restatement of Contracts 2d §260 provides this guideline: If the contractual provision purports to be the words of the party of whom performance is required, the provision is a promise; if it's supposed to be the words of the other party, it's a condition. Here, taken together, these suggest that the clause is a condition. B correctly characterizes this.

More importantly, B addresses the *specific* question asked, which is how the court will construe the truthfulness warranty. What the truthfulness provision would be reasonably interpreted to do is prevent fraud by requiring truthfulness to the best of the applicant's knowledge This requires that you address the rules of contract interpretation. As a general rule, contract terms are interpreted objectively, by determining what interpretation a reasonable person (knowing all the parties know) would place on the terms. Here, it wouldn't be reasonable to require an *absolute* guarantee. The truthfulness provision would be designed to let the insurance company determine the risks its undertaking. Thus, the reasonable interpretation in option B will suffice. As a result, B is the best response.

Answer 155

(C) is the best response,
because it most precisely identifies the impact of Joan's turning 21.

Under these facts, the clause dealing with Joan turning 21 is problematic in its interpretation. That's because there's a temptation to construe Joan's turning 21 as a condition precedent to the insurance company's duty to pay, since the insurance company isn't to pay "until" Joan turns 21. However, this would not comport with the rules of contract interpretation, which requires determining what interpretation a reasonable person, knowing all the parties know, would place on the terms. Here, the parties would intend that the insurance company's duty to pay become absolute when Mary dies (since it is, after all, a life insurance policy).

Joan's turning 21 thus could *not* be a condition to the duty to pay – instead, it would only determine the *time* for performance, not *whether* the insurance company must perform. Joan's dying before age 21 only means that the proceeds will become part of her own estate, and is not relevant to Joan's being entitled to the proceeds.

Since C correctly determines that Joan turning 21 would only determine *when* the insurance company must perform, not *whether* it will have to perform, it's the best response.

(A) is not the best response,

because it mischaracterizes Joan's reaching 21 – it's not a condition at all, but only determines when proceeds are distributed.

A condition is the occurrence or non-occurrence of an event that triggers, limits, or extinguishes an absolute duty to perform. Conditions are categorized both by how they came about (express, implied, and constructive) and by the time of performance (precedent, concurrent, and subsequent). A *constructive* condition is one imposed by law, and *not* spelled out by the parties. A *concurrent* condition requires that the parties exchange performance simultaneously, each party's duty to perform being dependent on the other's. Thus, if Joan's reaching age 21 were a constructive condition concurrent here, this would mean that the insurance company's duty to pay would be triggered by Joan's turning 21. This clearly isn't the case; Joan's turning 21 isn't determinative of the insurance company's duty to pay at all. Instead, that duty becomes absolute when Mary dies – it's Mary's death that's an express condition precedent to the insurance company's duty to pay, because that's the contingency the policy addressed. All Joan's turning 21 does is determines the time for insurance company's performance. Since A doesn't recognize this, it's not the best response.

(B) is not the best response,

because Joan's turning 21 isn't a condition at all – instead, it only sets the time for insurance company's performance under the contract.

A condition is the occurrence or non-occurrence of an event that triggers, limits, or extinguishes an absolute duty to perform. A condition precedent is one that triggers the other party's duty to perform. Here, Joan's turning 21 isn't a condition because it's not the event that makes the insurance company's duty to pay absolute – *that* event is Mary's death. Instead, Joan's turning 21 only establishes the *time* for insurance company to perform. Thus, Joan's interest vested when Mary died, and when Joan died at age 19, the proceeds would become part of her own estate. Since B mischaracterizes Joan's reaching age 21 as a condition, it's not the best response.

(D) is not the best response,

because Joan's reaching age 21 *is* relevant – it deter-

mines the time for insurance company's performance.

Under the contract, the insurance company's duty to pay became absolute when Mary died. The provision concerning not paying Joan until she turned 21 would only delay a duty that was absolute. Such clauses are legal, and presumably intended to prevent the youthful beneficiary from blowing the whole wad on a Porsche. Thus, the clause *does* have legal significance, making D not the best response.

Answer 156

You have an advantage with a problem like this one, because it's fully integrated – everything you need to solve it is given to you. Thus, with this type of problem, it's particularly important to *read each statute carefully*.

(A) is the best response,

because it addresses both types of murder under the statute, and correctly applies them to the facts.

The murder statute here provides two possibilities: Either premeditated and intentional murder, OR felony murder. The intoxication statute exonerates the Defendant only if his drunkenness negates an element of the crime. A correctly identifies that Defendant cannot be guilty of felony murder *if* he was unable to form an intent to commit a felony in the murder; it further correctly states that he could only be guilty of the first type of murder in the statute if he premeditated and intentionally killed the watchman. Since A addresses both parts of the murder statutes and analyzes them correctly, it's the best response.

(B) is not the best response,

because voluntary intoxication is *potentially* a good defense to the crime of murder, since it could negate an element of the offense – namely, intent.

There are two possibilities for murder in the statute given in these facts – either premeditated and intentional killing, or killing in the commission of the named crimes, the relevant one here being burglary. However, burglary requires intent as well – the intent to commit a crime in the building broken into. Either way, if the jury found that the voluntary intoxication negated defendant's ability to form an intent, he would be acquitted. Since option B does not comport with the statutes stated in the facts it's not the best response.

(C) is not the best response,

because it incorrectly eliminates a possibility for Defendant being found guilty.

The murder statute in the question offers *two* possible bases on which Defendant could be found guilty: Either premeditated and intentional killing, OR a "felony murder"-type provision – a killing in the commission of the named crimes. Thus, the Defendant could be found guilty of murder if he's found to have committed a killing in the commission of a burglary. Note that option C *limits* Defendant's being found guilty to the *first* type of murder in the statute, by stating that Defendant's can be found guilty "only if" he premeditated and intended the killing. Here, it's possible that the court could find Defendant guilty of a killing in the commission of a burglary, without finding him guilty of premeditated, intentional killing. (Note that Defendant's intoxication couldn't exonerate him from the second type of murder without exonerating him from the first type. If Defendant was drunk enough not to form an intent, it would exonerate him from both types of murder.) Since C incorrectly limits the potential for Defendant's guilt, it's not the best response.

(D) is not the best response,
because it misapplies the intoxication defense.

The statute here clearly states that intoxication is only a defense if it negates an element of the offense. Thus, the "but for" reasoning in option D is incorrect, because it's not a question of whether Defendant's *wouldn't* have killed the watchman if he was sober, but rather whether his intoxication negated an element of the offense. It's possible for Defendant to have been intoxicated *without* having his intoxication negate an element of the offense. Thus, option D applies the intoxication defense too broadly, making it not the best response.

Answer 157

Keep in mind that *best* argument means the one that will be *easiest to prove*, and will overcome a *major obstacle in the case*.

(A) is the best response,
because proving it would exonerate the Defendant, and it is easier to prove than the potential defense in another option, B.

In the facts, we're told that intoxication is defense to a crime if it negates an element of the offense. We're also told that manslaughter, the crime in question here, is killing in a reckless manner. Recklessness requires that one act with conscious disregard of a substantial or unjustifiable risk. Thus, in order to have intoxication form a good defense, it would be sufficient if defendant proved that his intoxication prevented him from *consciously* disregarding a substantial or unjustifiable risk. That's exactly what A provides, so it's the best response.

(B) is not the best response,
because although it would theoretically form a good defense to the charge, it's too broad, and thus will be more difficult to prove than option A, which is *also* a good defense and will be easier to prove.

Under the statutes given here, intoxication is a good defense if it negates an element of the offense. The offense in question here is manslaughter, for which the statute requires criminal recklessness. Recklessness is the conscious disregard of a substantial or unjustifiable risk. Thus, all Defendant really needs to prove in order to be acquitted is that his intoxication prevented him

from *consciously* disregarding a substantial or unjustifiable risk – he need not go as far as claiming his very act of getting into the car was involuntary. Since B would require more than is actually necessary to exonerate Defendant, it's not the best response.

(C) is not the best response,
because it misapplies a tort concept to a criminal case.

Although contributory negligence could be a defense to a *civil* charge of recklessness or negligence, tort defenses do not in general apply to criminal charges. That's because tort defenses concern the *individual,* whereas criminal charges involve a wrong committed, in theory, against *the state* – thus, a defense as to the individual will not exonerate the Defendant. The fact that the pedestrian was "contributorily negligent" would, as a result, not result in Defendant's acquittal. Thus, C is not the best response.

(D) is not the best response,
because it would require *intent,* where the manslaughter statute in the question only requires *recklessness.*

Thus, even if Defendant proved he did not act intentionally, that would not acquit him – since he could act recklessly without acting intentionally. One is said to act intentionally when his conscious objective is either to engage in certain behavior or cause a certain result. Recklessness, on the other hand, requires only that one act with conscious disregard of a substantial or unjustifiable risk. As a result, Defendant could have driven the car with a conscious disregard for the requisite risk to the pedestrian, without actually intending to cause him harm (or even knowing that it was substantially certain to result). Since Defendant's proof of option D would not exonerate him, it's not Defendant's best argument, making D not the best response.

Answer 158

(C) is the best response.
The key here is to realize that the prosecutor *must work within the framework of the statutes in the problem.* Since the other three options, A, B, and D, ignore this, C is the only possible correct response.

C is the best response because it correctly identifies a basis on which the prosecutor can overcome Defendant's intoxication defense.

Defendant's intoxication defense would focus on his inability to realize that his operation of the car created a substantial and unjustifiable risk. The prosecutor could successfully circumvent that defense by going further back in time, and arguing that Defendant's conscious act of undertaking a "binge," the result of which is that he could create a substantial and unjustifiable risk to someone, would be reckless itself. Thus, it's Defendant's act of *becoming* drunk that would be the focus of the prosecutor's argument. Note that this has a benefit not shared by the other three answer options – that is, it operates within the confines of the statutes given in the problem. Since option C comports with the statutes *and* provides a sound basis for overcoming the intoxication defense, it's the best response.

(A) is not the best response,

because although it is a correct statement of the general principles involved, it ignores the intoxication statute in the problem.

The statute specifically states that intoxication is a valid defense if it negates an element of the offense. The manslaughter statute in the problem states that manslaughter requires recklessness. Recklessness is the conscious disregard of a substantial or unjustifiable risk. Thus, intoxication *could* be a defense to manslaughter. Since the statute controls, it doesn't matter what the *general* principle is.

Keep in mind that a number of states have abandoned the old general/specific intent distinction in favor of the Model Penal Code "four tier" system for categorizing mental state (purposeful, knowing, reckless, and negligent behavior). That aside, option A correctly states the general theory, because manslaughter is, indeed, historically a general intent crime, and the general rule is that voluntary intoxication is not a defense to general intent crimes. General intent crimes only require an intent to do the prohibited act without justification or excuse, but not necessarily to accomplish a wrongful result. Specific intent, on the other hand, requires an intent to accomplish a certain particular wrongful result other than just doing the act itself (thus, larceny is a specific intent crime, since one must intend to permanently deprive another of an interest in personal property; if one only intends to borrow the item, he lacks the requisite specific intent for larceny, and cannot be criminally liable for larceny). The significance of the distinction between general and specific intent crimes has two components: first, a person's specific intent cannot be presumed from the act itself, whereas general intent can be; and second, some defenses are available for specific intent crimes and not for general intent crimes – for instance, voluntary intoxication.

Nonetheless, none of this is relevant to the case in the question, since the case must be analyzed in light of the statutes given. By reading them together, it's clear that intoxication can be a defense to manslaughter, if it negates any of the elements of the offense. Since A ignores this, it cannot be the best response.

(B) is not the best response,

because, like option A, it ignores the statutes in the problem.

Under the statutes given, it's clear that intoxication *could* be a defense to manslaughter, if it negates any of the elements of the offense – regardless of whether the offense would traditionally be categorized as a general intent or a specific intent crime. Thus, regardless of the traditional principle, the statute controls. Since B states

otherwise, it's not the best response.

(D) is not the best response,

because, contrary to what it states, in order to determine whether Defendant was reckless, his intoxication must be considered.

Criminal recklessness requires that one consciously disregard a substantial or unjustifiable risk. The intoxication statute in the question itself clearly states that if intoxication negates an element of the offense, it will form a defense. Thus, it's not possible to analyze whether Defendant is guilty of manslaughter *without* analyzing whether his intoxication will exonerate him. As a result, the logic in D is faulty, making it not the best response.

Answer 159

(D) is the best response,

because it correctly identifies that the Commission lacks enforcement powers.

Under the Constitution, Congress has the power to legislate, and the President has the executive power, including the power to enforce laws. The problem under these facts is that the Commission has the power to prosecute, which is an enforcement power exclusively possessed by the President. As such, all members of the Commission would have to be appointed by the President, and approved by the Senate, under Article II, section 2 of the Constitution. Buckley v. Valeo (1976). Since the Commission wouldn't have the power of enforcement, option D represents Minicar's best argument, making D the best response.

(A) is not the best response,

because it overstates the actual standard, it probably misstates the facts, and it ignores the central issue here.

Congress may delegate its legislative power, as long as three requirements are met: 1/ Congress must actually have the power it's ostensibly delegating; 2/ The power must be of a kind capable of delegation; and 3/ Congress must set adequate standards to govern the exercise of the power delegated.

Option A addresses the third requirement – the adequacy of standards. In fact, this requirement is interpreted liberally by the courts. In one case, standards phrased in terms of "public interest, convenience or necessity" were upheld. Thus, the standards delineated in these facts – to investigate automobile safety, to make recommendations to Congress for new laws, to make further rules establishing safety and performance standards, and to prosecute violations of the Federal Automobile Safety Act – would more than suffice. Also, note that option A suggests the standards must be clear; in fact, they need only be "adequate." As a result, this would not be a good argument for Minicar.

All of this ignores the central issue here, which is that

the power involved in these facts was not Congress's to delegate. Congress has legislative power, which includes the power to investigate. However, the power enjoyed by the Automobile Commission is the power to *enforce,* which is an executive power enjoyed exclusively by the executive branch, not Congress. The first requirement of valid delegation of power by Congress is that Congress must hold the power delegated. Here, it doesn't. Since option A ignores this, it's not the best response.

(B) is not the best response,

because it misstates the law, and ignores the central issue on these facts.

Congress has broad powers over interstate commerce under Article I, §3, clause 3 of the Constitution. In fact, under the "affectation doctrine," Congress can regulate any activity that has any appreciable direct or indirect effect on interstate commerce. Clearly automobiles would qualify, since they are capable of, and do, undertake interstate travel. Thus, Congress would have the power to regulate automobiles, and a claim by Minicar that Congress overstepped its commerce power would not be a good argument.

Instead, option B ignores the fact that the power Congress delegated here was not its to delegate. Congress may delegate its legislative power, as long as three requirements are met: 1/ Congress must actually have the power it's ostensibly delegating; 2/ The power must be of a kind capable of delegation; and 3/ Congress must set adequate standards to govern the exercise of the power delegated. Congress has legislative power, which includes the power to investigate. The power enjoyed by the Automobile Commission is the power to *enforce,* which is an executive power enjoyed exclusively by the executive branch, not Congress. Thus, Congress was incapable of delegating power to the Automobile Commission, making the Commission invalid. This is Minicar's best argument. Since option B ignores this, it's not the best response.

(C) is not the best response,

because the Commission would not represent a denial of due process.

Due process is triggered by a governmental activity which amounts to a deprivation of a property interest or right. A property interest at the very least requires interests already acquired in specific benefits. Then, if that right or interest is "fundamental," the strict scrutiny test is used to determine the validity of the enactment. For economic issues, the "rational relation" test is used.

However, due process would not apply to the facts here, because due process doesn't require that a private individual or organization receive representation on a Congressional, investigative agency (as long as the workings of the agency weren't conducted in a discriminatory fashion). If the Commission itself were able to enforce laws, and it prosecuted Minicar, *then* Minicar

would be entitled to due process. Under these facts, it's not. Since C doesn't recognize this, it's not the best response.

Answer 160

(A) is the best response,

because it identifies precisely the best decision by the court., which reflects the court's duty to validate the Commission's function to the extent possible.

The problem here is that Congress delegated power to the Commission that Congress itself doesn't have: namely, the power to prosecute. That power belongs exclusively to the President, pursuant to his executive power. Congress, on the other hand, has the exclusive power to legislate, and conduct investigations pursuant to that power. Both the President and Congress can validly delegate their powers. Thus, Congress could validly delegate to the Commission all the powers mentioned in the Act *except* the power to prosecute violations of the Act (note that it Congress could validly delegate to the President the power to appoint the chairman of the Commission). By allowing the Commission to continue investigating automobile safety and making recommendations to Congress, the court would be validating the Commission's functions to the greatest extent possible in light of Congress's own legislative power. Since A recognizes this, it's the best response.

(B) is not the best response,

because prosecuting violations is the one thing the court *couldn't* allow the Commission to do.

Here, Congress delegated some of its power to the Automobile Commission. The problem is that Congress can only delegate powers it *has.* Congress has the power to legislate, and conduct investigations pursuant to its power to legislate. The President, on the other hand, exclusively holds the executive power, including the power to enforce laws. Thus, Congress doesn't have the power to enforce laws, and thus couldn't authorize the Automobile Commission to prosecute violations of the Federal Automobile Safety Act. The court could allow the Commission to issue rules, contrary to what option B states, since that is a legislative function held by Congress. Since option B does not recognize the appropriate decision by the court, it's not the best response.

(C) is not the best response,

because it is too severe. The court could allow the Commission to do everything it was authorized to do *except* prosecute violations of the Federal Automobile Safety Act.

Here, Congress delegated some of its power to the Automobile Commission. The problem is that Congress can only delegate powers it *has.* Congress has the power to legislate, and conduct investigations pursuant to its power to legislate. The President, on the other hand, exclusively holds the executive power, including the power to enforce laws. Thus, Congress doesn't have the power to enforce laws, and thus couldn't authorize the Automobile Commission to prosecute violations of the Federal Automobile Safety Act. However, the court could allow the Commission to perform all the other functions stated in the Act, because those are legislative and investigative in nature. Thus, by forbidding the Commission from taking any actions at all, the court would be too strict. Since C doesn't recognize this, it's not the best response.

(D) is not the best response,

because it's too strict: The court could uphold some of the functions delegated to the Commission by Congress, and thus stay close to Congress's original intent.

Here, Congress delegated some of its power to the Automobile Commission. The problem is that Congress can only delegate powers it *has.* Congress has the power to legislate, and conduct investigations pursuant to its power to legislate. The President, on the other hand, exclusively holds the executive power, including the power to enforce laws. Thus, Congress doesn't have the power to enforce laws, and thus couldn't authorize the Automobile Commission to prosecute violations of the Federal Automobile Safety Act. However, all the other functions of the Commission are valid delegations of Congress's duty, and Congress could authorize the President to appoint the chairman; the *only* thing repugnant about the Commission is its ostensible ability to prosecute. Thus, while requiring that all the members of the Commission be appointed by the President with Congress's approval would validate the prosecution function, such a Commission wouldn't have the power to investigate (since the legislative power is exclusively Congress's, unless Congress delegates such powers to the President, within the limitations of the separation of powers doctrine). Instead, the court should uphold the validity of the Commission to the extent possible, and that would be done by simply invalidating the prosecutorial function. Since D doesn't recognize this, it's not the best response.

Answer 161

(C) is the best response.

because it correctly addresses and resolves the central issue here.

The question asks you how assumption of the risk applies to these facts. A successful assumption of the risk defense has two elements: The individual must know and appreciate the risk, and he must freely and voluntarily assume it. Here, if there appeared no other way of getting out before Monday, then Johnson wouldn't have a choice *but* to attempt to scale the fence. Being trapped in a parking lot for what could be two days, without food or water, would be considered an "emergency situation," and in such circumstances

one can take steps to save himself without assuming any risk, unless the risk involved is out of proportion to the rights being protected. Here, faced with the prospect of drinking radiator fluid until Monday, Johnson's scaling the fence would not necessarily be unreasonable. Note that option C uses the modifier "if," meaning that it only plausibly apply to the facts, and solve a crucial issue. It does. As a result, it's the best response.

(A) is not the best response,

because it mistakenly applies a "reasonable person" standard to assumption of the risk.

There are two elements of a valid "assumption of the risk" defense: The individual must know and appreciate the risk, and he must freely and voluntarily assume it. Thus, even if a reasonable person *would* have recognized the risk, assumption of the risk requires that the plaintiff *himself* realize it (although, generally, knowledge of obvious risks will be assumed). Furthermore, option A completely ignores the *voluntariness* requirement of the defense, which is what torpedoes the defense on these facts.

If you chose this option, you may have been thinking of a contributory negligence defense, under which the plaintiff takes inadequate precautions for his own safety, regardless of knowledge or appreciation of the danger. While a reasonable person *may* have climbed the fence to escape under these circumstances, it would be a better defense on these facts than assumption of the risk. However, you're confined to assumption of the risk in this question, and since option A misstates the defense, it's not the best response.

(B) is not the best response,

because Sales Rep's behavior is not relevant to the applicability of assumption of the risk on these facts.

For an assumption of the risk defense to succeed, the individual must know and appreciate the risk, and he must freely and voluntarily assume it. While Sales Rep's waiting for help might indicate that Johnson's scaling the fence was *objectively* unreasonable, this won't mean that the assumption of the risk defense will succeed, because assumption of the risk is subjective (and, in any case, who's to say how reasonable Salesman's behavior was). Finally, Salesman's status as Car Company's agent is similarly irrelevant to applying assumption of the risk to Johnson. Since B focuses on an irrelevant point, it's not the best response.

(D) is not the best response,

because the reasoning would not be sufficient for the success or failure of the assumption of the risk defense.

In order for an assumption of the risk defense to succeed, defendant must prove two elements: One, the individual must know and appreciate the risk; and two, he must freely and voluntarily assume it. While D alludes to the central issue in this problem – that is, Johnson's confinement removed the "voluntariness" element of assumption of the risk – the "volitional act" aspect of option D is not relevant. In terms of defeating an assumption of the risk defense, it doesn't matter how the voluntariness is missing as long as it's the result of defendant's negligence (since, after all, assumption of the risk is a defense to negligence). Furthermore, option D ignores entirely the first element: the knowledge and appreciation of the risk.

If you chose this response, you were probably thinking of false imprisonment. However, false imprisonment is an *intentional* tort, requiring that Defendant *intend* to confine or restrain plaintiff, so the security guard's negligence would not suffice; and, in any case, one can assume a risk under an emergency situation without assuming risk, as long as the risk involved is in proportion to the rights being protected. None of this is of consequence here, since the assumption of the risk defense would not turn on the reasoning D states. As a result, D is not the best response.

Answer 162

(D) is the best response,

because it addresses the central issue under these facts, and resolves it satisfactorily.

A prima facie case for false imprisonment has three elements: Defendant's act/omission which confines or restraints plaintiff to a bounded area (plaintiff must believe there's no reasonable means of escape); defendant's intent to so confine or restraint plaintiff; and causation. If the guard knew someone was in the lot, you could infer that the guard intended to lock that person inside (it wouldn't be necessary to prove he intended to lock up *Johnson* specifically). Without that knowledge, it wouldn't be possible to prove the guard *intended* to falsely imprison someone. Since D focuses on the issue most in doubt on these facts – intent – and resolves it satisfactorily, it's the best response.

(A) is not the best response,

because it is insufficient to support a false imprisonment claim.

While confinement is an element of false imprisonment, there are other elements, one of which is a central issue under these facts. A prima facie claim for false imprisonment requires proof of defendant's act/omission which confines or restrains plaintiff to a bounded area (such that plaintiff believes there's no reasonable means of escape); defendant's intent to so confine or restrain plaintiff; and causation. Thus, along with the confinement, Johnson would have to prove that Car Company (through its agent) *intended* to confine him. Since A doesn't recognize that this is the missing element, it's not the best response.

(B) is not the best response,

because it relies on an element which need not be proven for false imprisonment.

A prima facie case of false imprisonment has three

elements: Defendant's act/omission which confines or restrains plaintiff to a bounded area (plaintiff must believe there's no reasonable means of escape); defendant's intent to so confine or restrain plaintiff; and causation. Thus, the fact that Johnson was harmed will impact his damages, but will not determine if his claim will prevail. Since B ignores the elements of a prima facie case for false imprisonment, it's not the best response.

(C) is not the best response,

because the mental element it states would be insufficient for a false imprisonment claim.

Option C suggests that negligence is all such a claim requires. In fact, plaintiff must prove defendant *intended* to confine or restrain plaintiff. Thus, if the guard was only negligent, Car Company wouldn't be liable. Since C suggests otherwise, it's not the best response.

Answer 163

(B) is the best response,

because it addresses the central issue of the case: Whether or not the equipment will be characterized as a fixture.

The factor B discusses – intent – is the single most important factor in determining whether a chattel has become a fixture. If the intent is that the chattel *not* be considered annexed to realty and thus not a fixture, this will be a strong indication that the chattel will be considered personalty by a court. If, as B suggests, the equipment was installed for Barnes's exclusive benefit, it would manifest an *intent* on Barnes's part that the equipment not be considered part of the realty. Under these facts, this would mean a judgment in Barnes's favor, refusing the injunction. As a result, B is the best response.

(A) is not the best response,

because it's irrelevant.

Barnes's ability to remove the equipment turns on whether it will be characterized as a fixture or not. If the equipment is not a fixture, then Barnes will be able to remove it. If it *is* considered a fixture, it becomes part of the realty, and Barnes cannot remove it (at which point notice to him *may* become important). Factors which will be taken into account in determining status as a fixture will include the annexation of the chattel to realty, the appropriateness to the use of the realty to which the chattel is connected, and the intent to make a permanent accession. Thus, the existence of the landlord's mortgage will not enter into this determination, making A not the best response.

(C) is not the best response,

because, although it states a correct rule, the rule does not address the central issue here: Whether the equipment can be characterized as "personal property" *at all.*

The major issue here is whether or not the equipment could be characterized as a "fixture." If it *is,* it will be regarded as *real* property, and Barnes cannot remove it. If it is *not,* it will retain its character as personalty, and Barnes can remove it. The status as a fixture is determined by analyzing these factors: The item's annexation to realty (e.g., heating system installed = fixture); appropriateness to the use of the realty to which it is connected (the more appropriate, the more likely it's a fixture); and, most importantly, the intent to make a permanent accession, viewed objectively (look at, e.g., any agreement, and annexor's estate in the land). Since C fails to recognize the central issue in the case, it's not the best response.

(D) is not the best response,

because, like C, it fails to address the central issue in the case: The characterization of the equipment as real or personal property.

D implies that the equipment *is* real property, since, if that's true, then the Statute of Frauds would apply (since the Statute of Frauds requires that any conveyance of real property must be in writing). However, on the facts here, it's not at all clear that the equipment would be considered part of the real property, as a "fixture." If the equipment *isn't* a fixture, the Statute of Frauds would not be relevant. A fixture is a chattel which has been annexed to land in such a way as to be regarded as real property. The status as a fixture is determined by analyzing these factors: The item's annexation to realty (e.g., heating system installed = fixture); appropriateness to the use of the realty to which it is connected (the more appropriate, the more likely it's a fixture); and, most importantly, the intent to make a permanent accession, viewed objectively (look at, e.g., any agreement, and annexor's estate in the land). Since D does not recognize that this is the central issue, it's not the best response.

Answer 164

(A) is the best response.

Here, you don't have to look far to determine what the key fact is – it *must* be the one fact that changed from the last question to this one – the status of the "annexor." In the last question, it was a tenant; in this one, it's the landowner. In order to answer this question correctly, you'd have to be familiar with the law of fixtures, and realize that the single most important factor determining whether something is a fixture is intent – and that the intent of an owner of property to annex something to realty is more likely than that of a mere tenant.

A is the best response because it correctly identifies that Albert's installing the equipment would make it more likely the equipment would be considered a "fixture," and as a result would be covered by the mortgage. If it is covered by the mortgage, the injunction

would succeed. In determining whether an item has become a "fixture," three requirements must be met: It must be "annexed" to realty (e.g., a heating system installed); it must be appropriate to the use of the realty to which it is connected; and there must be the intent to make a permanent accession, viewed objectively. It's the third requirement that's at issue here. An owner is more likely to intend a permanent accession than a mere lessee. This is at issue because the only fact that changes from the last question to this one is the status of the annexor – in the last question, it was Barnes, and in this question, it is Albert. The difference between the two is that Barnes is only a tenant, and Albert is the property owner. Thus, in terms of fixtures, Albert is more likely to intend a permanent accession. After all, a tenant will not benefit from the property's increased value, so this rule only makes sense. Since A recognizes this, it's the best response.

(B) is not the best response,

because it does not correctly apply the rules on determining "fixtures" to these facts.

A fixture is a chattel which has been attached to land in such a way as to be regarded as real property. As real property, it would be covered by Good Bank's mortgage. In determining whether an item has become a "fixture," three requirements must be met: It must be "annexed" to realty (e.g., a heating system installed); it must be appropriate to the use of the realty to which it is connected; and there must be the intent to make a permanent accession, viewed objectively. It's the third requirement that's at issue here. An owner is more likely to intend a permanent accession than a mere lessee. This is at issue because the only fact that changes from the last question to this one is the status of the annexor – in the last question, it was Barnes, and in this question, it is Albert. The difference between the two is that Barnes is only a tenant, and Albert is the property owner. Thus, in terms of fixtures, Albert is more likely to intend a permanent accession. After all, a tenant will not benefit from the property's increased value, so this rule only makes sense. Since B does not recognize this, it's not the best response.

(C) is not the best response,

for the same reason as B: It does not correctly apply the rules on determining "fixtures" to these facts.

A fixture is a chattel which has been attached to land in such a way as to be regarded as real property. As real property, it would be covered by Good Bank's mortgage. In determining whether an item has become a "fixture," three requirements must be met: It must be "annexed" to realty (e.g., a heating system installed); it must be appropriate to the use of the realty to which it is connected; and there must be the intent to make a permanent accession, viewed objectively. It's the third requirement that's at issue here. An owner is more likely to intend a permanent accession than a mere lessee. This is at issue because the only fact that changes from the last question to this one is the status of the annexor – in the last question, it was Barnes, and in this question, it is Albert. The difference between the two is that Barnes is only a tenant, and Albert is the property owner. Thus, in terms of fixtures, Albert is more likely to intend a permanent accession. After all, a tenant will not benefit from the property's increased value, so this rule only makes sense. Since C does not recognize the relevance of this, it's not the best response.

(D) is not the best response,

because it states, as a settled issue, that the equipment will be considered personal property. While an express agreement about the characterization of the equipment would control (as long as it could be severed from the realty without damaging the realty), what's involved in option D is not a characterization of the equipment, but only a mention of "personal property."

By doing so, D misses the point of these facts – the point is that it's not clear whether the equipment is realty or personalty. This depends on whether it's characterized as a "fixture" or not (since, as a fixture, it would be considered realty). A fixture is a chattel which has been attached to land in such a way as to be regarded as real property. The requirements of a fixture are annexation to realty; appropriateness to the use of the realty to which it is connected; and intent to make a permanent accession, viewed objectively. Since the equipment here *could* be characterized either way, D is not dispositive of the result of the injunction, and as a result is not the best response.

Answer 165

(D) is the best response,

because it correctly identifies that, under these facts, Tanner will still be liable to Lester for the rent on the remaining portion of the farm.

There are a couple of facts which are key to arriving at the correct result. First, Tanner has already been compensated for his portion of the condemnation. When property is condemned, the tenant is entitled to a share representing the current value of the unexpired term of the lease, less future rents payable (which will not have to be paid). Presumably, Tanner's recovery represented the unexpired term for the twenty acres' of farmland. In general, when the condemnation is only *partial,* the relationship of landlord and tenant will be unaffected. As a result, the tenant will still be liable for rent to reflect the amount of the property not condemned. Since D states this correctly, it's the best response.

(A) is not the best response,

because the facts here do not satisfy the doctrine of frustrated purpose.

In order to discharge a contractual duty due to frus-

tration of purpose, four requirements must be met. First, the frustration must be caused by a supervening act or event. Second, the supervening act or event must have been unforeseeable when the parties entered into the contract. Third, the act or event must destroy or almost destroy the purpose of the contract. Finally, both parties must have realized this purpose when the contract was formed. You should also keep in mind that courts dislike discharging contracts due to frustration of purpose. Under the facts here, there are two facts which gravitate against applying the frustration of purpose doctrine. First, there are still ten acres which were *not* taken by the government. Frustration of purpose requires that the frustration be complete or almost complete. Taking two-thirds of the land probably would not qualify. Second, Tanner has already been compensated for his interest in the property. As a result, it's unlikely that the frustration of purpose doctrine would apply, making A not the best response.

(B) is not the best response,

because it misstates the facts: there has been *no* breach of the implied covenant of quiet enjoyment.

The implied covenant of quiet enjoyment is a covenant implied in every lease which provides that, first the tenant will not be ousted by any third party with "paramount title" (superior title to the landlord), and, second, the landlord and his representatives will not interfere with the tenant's use and enjoyment of the premises. Furthermore, the tenant must leave the premises within a reasonable time after the breach in order to preserve his claim, otherwise it will be waived. What makes this argument inapplicable here is that it's not the landlord or a third party with paramount title who has interfered with Tanner's use and enjoyment, but the government. Apart from that, Tanner hasn't really been ousted from the premises – only part of the land has been taken by the government. Since there hasn't been a breach of the implied covenant of quiet enjoyment, and that's what B says, B cannot be the best response.

(C) is not the best response,

because it mistakenly characterizes condemnation of the property as the tenant's responsibility.

The tenant is only liable not to commit waste on the property. He will have no responsibility for acts outside his responsibility and control. Condemnation of the property by the government is just such an act. Since option C incorrectly blames the condemnation on Tanner, it's not the best response.

Answer 166

(C) is the best response,

because it arrives at the correct result, and focuses on the reason why Edward won't be guilty – because he didn't intend to cause an offensive touching.

The criminal assault statute in this problem requires an attempt to commit a criminal battery. Attempt has two elements: Intent, and an overt act done in further-ance of the intent, beyond mere preparation. Here, Edward had no intent to touch Margaret in any way; he was trying to retrieve his hat. Since he didn't intend to touch Margaret, he couldn't be liable for any crime that explicitly or implicitly requires intent. Since intent is an element of attempt, he can't be liable. Since C correctly identifies that this is the element that will exonerate Edward, it's the best response.

(A) is not the best response,

because it ignores the intent element of the crime, and it reaches the wrong result.

The statute under which Edward was charged, the criminal assault statute, would require that Edward attempted to cause an offensive touching. Attempt has two elements: intent, and an overt act done in further-ance of the intent, beyond mere preparation. Under these facts, this would mean that Edward would have to have intended to cause an offensive touching. How-ever, the facts indicate the only thing Edward intended to touch was his hat, not Margaret. Since he didn't intend to touch Margaret, he couldn't be found guilty of a crime involving attempt – which is what the criminal assault statute requires. Since A stops short of what would be required to convict Edward, it's not the best response.

(B) is not the best response,

because it arrives at the wrong result, and offers a standard of culpability which is *lower* than the standard in the statute given.

The statute under which Edward was charged, the criminal assault statute, would require that Edward attempted to cause an offensive touching. Attempt has two elements: intent, and an overt act done in further-ance of the intent, beyond mere preparation. Option B suggests that Edward should be culpable for merely *negligent* behavior – because he *should have realized* harm might result from his act. This is not sufficient for attempt, since attempt requires intent. Since B would hold Edward liable for assault without intent, it's not the best response.

(D) is not the best response,

because although it offers the right result, it requires *more* than the actual statute requires.

The criminal assault statute only requires *an attempt* to cause an offensive touching. D suggests that an *actual* touching is required. If you chose this response, it could be because you mistakenly believed Edward was charged with criminal battery – if he *had* been charged with criminal battery, a touching would have been required. As it is, a criminal assault only requires an attempt to commit a criminal battery, and so D is not the best response.

Answer 167

(D) is the best response,

because it recognizes that Margaret's self-defense argument will exonerate her.

One is not liable for battery when his belief in immi-nent harm is reasonable, and the amount of force used in return is reasonable. That's the case here. Margaret believed she was about to be struck by Edward, and pushed him away in response. This is an appropriate amount of force to use in response to such a threat (note that it would not have been reasonable, for instance, for Margaret to take out a revolver and shoot Edward). Since D correctly identifies the basis on which Margaret will avoid liability, it's the best response.

(A) is not the best response,

because it ignores Margaret's justification in acting as she did: She pushed Edward in self-defense.

In order for self-defense to be a valid defense, one must have a reasonable belief in imminent harm, and the amount of force used in return must be reasonable. Both of these elements exist under these facts. Were it *not* for this justification, A would be correct; however, since Margaret does have a valid defense, A is not the best response.

(B) is not the best response,

because it ignores Margaret's defense, and misstates the facts.

Factually, Margaret intended to push Edward, con-trary to what B states. (Note that criminal battery does not require intent; an act intentionally done can result in battery, in most states, even if the *touching* was only criminally negligent). Finally, B gives the incorrect result, by stating Margaret will be guilty. In fact, her defense of self-defense will exonerate her. Since B is both factually incorrect and ignores a valid self-defense claim by Margaret, it's not the best response.

(C) is not the best response,

because, although it arrives at the correct result, it mis-states the law.

A push *is* an "offensive touching," since, in most states, the least touching of another person in a rude or insolent manner or in anger is sufficient for criminal battery, as long as it's offensive (e.g., being kissed by a stranger). A good shove would certainly qualify. Since C misstates the law, it cannot be the best response.

Answer 168

(C) is the best response,

because it correctly identifies the central reason the search was illegal. There are three central reasons for this: 1/ The arrest was not valid; 2/ Even if the arrest *had* been valid, the search exceeded the scope of a search incident to an arrest; and 3/ There were no grounds for a warrantless search.

First, the arrest was not valid because the police did not meet this test for a warrantless search: there must have been facts leading a reasonable person to believe a crime had been committed, and that the suspected committed it (for a misdemeanor, some states also require that the crime have been committed in the police officer's presence). Here, probable cause for arrest didn't exist until *after* the house was searched; it certainly didn't exist before. Furthermore, arresting a person in his home, without an arrest warrant, requires exigent circumstances, since entering a house to make an arrest is extremely intrusive, and thus the Fourth Amendment requires a warrant before the intrusion can take place. Second, even if the arrest was valid, a search incident to arrest is limited to a "wingspan" search – that is, the area within the suspect's immediate control. A linen closet wouldn't qualify, unless perhaps the suspect were standing right next to it. Third, no grounds existed for a warrantless search. For a search in a person's home, there would have to be exigent circumstances to justify a search without a warrant (e.g., facts indicating the evidence would be destroyed). No such facts exist here. What the sniff test did was to establish probable cause to get a *search warrant, not* to conduct a search or make an arrest in a person's house. Since C correctly identifies that the search here was illegal due to violating Defendant's Fourth Amendment rights, it's the best response.

(A) is not the best response,

because it misstates the facts: The arrest here was not valid.

The rule for warrantless arrests is that, unless there are exigent circumstances, an arrest warrant will be necessary to arrest a person *in his home.* Dayton v. New York (1980). Beyond *that,* the police in this fact pattern didn't have grounds to arrest Defendant when they did. For a warrantless arrest for a felony, the officer must have reasonable grounds to believe that a felony has been committed, and that the one being arrested committed it (for misdemeanors, some states require in addition that the crime was committed in the officer's presence). Here, there were not reasonable grounds to arrest, since the "canine sniff" itself may be valid grounds to seek a search warrant, but not to arrest. The key attribute of an *invalid* arrest is that anything seized in the search incidental to the arrest will be *inadmissible* at trial. Say that the arrest *were* valid. The search *still* would have been invalid, because it exceeded the bounds of a search incident to an arrest. Such a search is a "wingspan" search – it encompasses the suspect and the area within his immediate control. A linen closet would not be covered by this search ()unless perhaps Defendant were standing right next to it). Since A mischaracterizes the arrest and arrives at the wrong result, it's not the best response.

(B) is not the best response,

because Defendant's act in allowing the Police into his house would not be sufficient to justify a warrantless search.

The facts say that Defendant let the police in, but this does *not* amount to his consent to a search of his house. Had he consented to a house search, naturally the search would be valid, since when one with the authority to consent offers voluntary and intelligent consent to the search, the search is valid. Here, there was no such consent, and, in fact, the search was invalid. Since B misstates the standard necessary for a consent search, and arrives at the wrong result, it's not the best response.

(D) is not the best response,

because it focuses on an irrelevant point.

Regardless of whether the use of canine "sniff" tests are scientifically verified, what they *can* form the basis of probable cause for a *search* warrant, but not for an *arrest*. Probable cause for a search warrant is supplied by facts leading a reasonable person to believe that evidence of a crime will be found at a particular location. Probable cause for a felony arrest requires facts leading a reasonable person to believe that a crime has been committed, and that the suspect committed it (for a misdemeanor, some states also require that the crime have been committed in the police officer's presence). Thus, the scientific verifiability of the sniff tests would not be required, as long as they provided a basis for probable cause. However, this ignores the central point which is that the police would have required a search warrant to search Defendant's linen closet, since there's no evidence of exigent circumstances justifying a warrantless search. (As an incidental point, say the entire police action had consisted of the dogs sniffing the house. A sniff *itself* is not considered a Fourth Amendment "search"). Since D does not focus on a relevant point, it's not the best response.

Answer 169

What's going on here? The facts, and a quick glance at the answers, suggest that the question concerns the Mercy Rule - a criminal defendant's right to introduce evidence of his good character.

(B) is the best response

because it correctly states that the testimony will be admissible to prove that Drew is innocent.

First, you have to disassemble these facts, and determine what's going on here. Drew, a criminal defendant who has not testified, is calling a witness to testify to his good character. This should trigger the "Mercy Rule" in your mind. Under the "Mercy Rule," the defendant in a criminal case may offer pertinent character evidence to prove his innocence. That's exactly what Wilma's testimony does; evidence that Drew is a "peaceable man" would contradict the prosecutor's contention that Drew murdered Victor, which makes it pertinent.

Note, incidentally, that once the defendant has offered such character evidence, the prosecutor can rebut defendant's evidence with reputation and opinion testimony as to defendant's bad character (which prosecutor couldn't otherwise do).

Since B correctly states the law and applies it to the facts here, B is the best response.

(A) is not the best response

because it's not logically relevant.

If you chose this response, you realized that the "Mercy Rule" is at issue in this question, but you didn't apply it properly. Under the "Mercy Rule," the defendant in a criminal case may offer pertinent character evidence to prove his innocence. That's exactly what Wilma's testimony does; evidence that Drew is a "peaceable man" would contradict the prosecutor's contention that Drew murdered Victor, which makes it pertinent.

The mistake A makes is to suggest that Wilma's testimony is admissible on the issue of Drew's credibility (since that's what believability addresses). Drew's honesty is not in issue *because these facts tell you that Wilma is Drew's first witness,* which means that Drew himself, as a criminal defendant, has not testified, and thus he can't be impeached. Since Drew hasn't testified, his credibility isn't relevant; his penchant for violence is. Since the evidence offered here is not logically relevant, it's not admissible, and A is not the best response.

(C) is not the best response,

because it's irrelevant.

Under the "Mercy Rule," the defendant in a criminal case may offer pertinent character evidence to prove his innocence. That's exactly what Wilma's testimony does; evidence that Drew is a "peaceable man" would contradict the prosecutor's contention that Drew murdered Victor, which makes it pertinent.

It's not necessary that the defendant testify in order to offer evidence of his good character under the Mercy Rule. Of course, if he did choose to testify, then the prosecutor could impeach him with evidence reflecting on his credibility; and, in fact, even if the defendant doesn't testify, if he invokes the Mercy Rule, the prosecutor can rebut defendant's evidence with reputation and opinion testimony as to defendant's bad character.

Since C creates a prerequisite to admitting the evidence here which does not, in fact, exist, it is not the best response.

(D) is not the best response,

because it doesn't state a correct general rule, and, in any case, it ignores application of the "Mercy Rule" under these facts.

Character evidence is, as a general rule, inadmissi-

ble to prove how a person acted in a given set of circumstances. However, "general" is the operative word here. There are many exceptions to this rule – for instance, when character is considered "in issue" (e.g., the case involves testamentary capacity, defamation, sanity, child custody, or entrapment), all three types of character evidence – reputation, opinion, and specific acts – will be admissible. FRE 404. Character evidence is also admissible to prove notice of another person's character (e.g., negligent entrustment or self-defense), or to impeach a reputation witness (with specific acts character evidence *only*). What this goes to show is that it's not correct to say, as a general rule, that reputation is not a proper way to prove character.

Instead, what D ignores is that the "Mercy Rule" will make the character evidence admissible under these facts, and when the "Mercy Rule" applies, both reputation and opinion testimony are admissible (at common law, only reputation evidence was admissible under the rule). Under the "Mercy Rule," the defendant in a criminal case may offer pertinent character evidence to prove his innocence. That's exactly what Wilma's testimony does; evidence that Drew is a "peaceable man" would contradict the prosecutor's contention that Drew murdered Victor, which makes it pertinent. Since D doesn't recognize that this applies to these facts, it's not the best response.

Answer 170

(A) is the best response

because it correctly states that the testimony here will be admissible under the present state of mind exception to the hearsay rule.

First, you have to determine what's going on here. William is being asked to testify about a statement Drew made to him, outside of court, for purposes of proving the content of the statement. Thus, it's hearsay. The statement is being offered to prove that Drew actually did what he said he was going to do - leave town - and thus he was not present at the time of the murder.

As a result, in order to be admissible, the statement will have to fit some hearsay exception or inclusion. In fact, as option A indicates, the statement fits the present state of mind hearsay exception. Under FRE 803(3), declarations of present mental state are admissible when it is offered to prove either one of two things: Direct evidence of declarant's state of mind itself, where state of mind is "in issue" and material (e.g., intent, attitude, or belief); or declarant's conduct (in following through with his stated intent). The rationale behind admitting such statements is their likely trustworthiness, since the declarant knows his own state of mind, meaning there are no perception problems, and the statement deals with present state of mind, so there can't be memory defects (necessity is also generally a factor, since when state of mind is in issue, such statements may be the only way to prove it).

Here, William's testimony will tend to prove that Drew had an alibi for the time the murder took place. Since it fits the present state of mind hearsay exception, and A recognizes this, A is the best response.

(B) is not the best response,

because it misapplies the facts – the testimony offered *is* hearsay.

Hearsay is an out-of-court statement offered to prove the truth of its assertion. The statement here is an out-of-court statement: Drew's comment, "I'm about to leave town today to visit relatives." It is being offered to prove that Drew in fact followed through with his intent to leave town. Thus, it's being offered to prove the truth of its assertion, making it hearsay, contrary to what B states.

If you missed this, then you simply mischaracterized the statement. Whenever hearsay is involved, it's easier to analyze if you take the statement, make it into a declaration – "I'm about to leave town..." – and then see if it's hearsay. Here, William, on the stand, would say, "Drew said to me, "I'm about to leave town..." Thus, he must be repeating an out-of-court statement, and that's the prerequisite of hearsay.

Even though B correctly states that the statement will be admissible, since it mischaracterizes the testimony, it is not the best response.

(C) is not the best response

because it misapplies the facts – the testimony *is* relevant.

A piece of evidence is "logically relevant" if it tends to prove or disprove a material fact. FRE 401. Here, William's testimony is relevant because it would tend to prove that Drew was not present on the day the murder took place – as a result, it helps establish an alibi.

When a question discusses "relevance," barring other facts, it's addressing logical relevance. The other type of relevance, which every piece of evidence must also meet, is *legal* relevance. Legal relevance is satisfied when the probative value of the evidence is not substantially outweighed by the probability of undue prejudice. This happens most frequently with "inflammatory" evidence in criminal cases – graphic and gruesome photos, body parts, and the like.

In any case, the evidence here is clearly logically relevant, and since C doesn't recognize this, it's not the best response.

(D) is not the best response

because it fails to recognize that the testimony fits an exception to the hearsay rule, making it admissible.

As a preliminary matter, D does correctly characterize the statement as hearsay. Hearsay is an out-of-court statement offered to prove the truth of its assertion. Here, the out-of-court statement is Drew's: "I'm about to leave town today..." It is being offered to prove the truth of its assertion – that he followed through with his intent and actually left town. This would provide Drew an alibi. Thus, the statement is hearsay.

However, what D ignores is that the statement fits an exception to the hearsay rule, for declarations of present mental state. Under FRE 803(3), declarations of present mental state are admissible when it is offered to prove either one of two things: Direct evidence of declarant's state of mind itself, where state of mind is "in issue" and material (e.g., intent, attitude, or belief); or declarant's conduct (in following through with his stated intent). The rationale behind admitting such statements is their likely trustworthiness, since the declarant knows his own state of mind, meaning there are no perception problems, and the statement deals with present state of mind, so there can't be memory defects (necessity is also generally a factor, since when state of mind is in issue, such statements may be the only way to prove it). Since Drew's statement fits this exception, and option D doesn't recognize this, it's not the best response.

Answer 171

(A) is the best response,

because it correctly states that the testimony will be admissible as evidence of bias.

First, you have to determine what's going on here. The prosecutor is attempting to impeach Wilson on cross-examination – that is, cast doubt on his credibility. He's trying to do this by means of "intrinsic" impeachment, or impeachment from Wilson's own mouth. There are five, general types of questions which are appropriate for intrinsic impeachment: Questions seeking to show 1/ Bias or interest; 2/ Prior inconsistent statements; 3/ Prior convictions (only felonies, misdemeanors involving dishonesty, and no conviction more than ten years old); 4/ Bad character for honesty; and 5/ Sensory deficiencies.

Here, if Wilson is, in fact, Drew's first cousin, it suggests bias – that is, that Wilson would be willing to lie on Drew's behalf. This obviously would have a serious impact on Wilson's credibility, and is, as a result, a strong means of impeachment. Since A applies to the facts and states the correct rule of law, it's the best response.

(B) is not the best response,

because it misstates the law, and mischaracterizes the facts.

Under the FRE, the witness is competent to testify has long as he has personal knowledge of the matter on which he will testify, and he declares that he will testify truthfully, by oath or affirmation. FRE 602-3. While Wilson's relationship to Drew will undoubtedly affect his *credibility*, it does not adversely impact his competence as a witness. B doesn't recognize this.

B also mischaracterizes the facts by stating that Wilson's testimony is reputation testimony. In fact, the prosecutor's question addresses Wilson's status as Drew's cousin, not Drew's reputation. If it did address Drew's reputation there would be an issue as to the admissibility of character evidence, but that's not the case here.

Thus, although B arrives at the correct conclusion (that the question is proper), because it misstates the law and the facts, it is not the best response.

(C) is not the best response,

because it misstates the law: A question on cross-examination can go beyond the scope of direct examination, and still be valid.

The scope of cross-examination, under FRE 611(b), is limited to matters brought up in direct examination, inferences therefrom, *and* the credibility of a witness (along with any other matters, in the judge's discretion). Here, the issue of bias - which Wilson's relationship to Drew would prove - deals with credibility, since if Wilson is Drew's cousin, he'd be more likely to lie on Drew's behalf than if he were unrelated to Drew. Thus, it doesn't matter if Wilson's relationship to Drew was not addressed on direct examination. Since the question addresses credibility, it is within the scope of cross-examination, making C not the best response.

(D) is not the best response,

because it misstates the facts.

A piece of evidence is "logically relevant" if it tends to prove or disprove a material fact. FRE 401. The material fact here is Wilson's credibility as a witness. If the evidence in question – Wilson's being Drew's cousin – is true, it would suggest that Wilson might be willing to lie on Drew's behalf. This would have a serious impact on Wilson's credibility, making it logically relevant.

Note, by the way, that the prosecutor is attempting to impeach Wilson via *intrinsic* impeachment – that is, impeachment from Wilson's own mouth. Impeachment from any other source is considered *extrinsic* impeachment. Bias is one of those types of impeachment that can be proven via *either* intrinsic or extrinsic impeachment – so, if the prosecutor wanted, he could call another witness to prove Wilson's bias.

In any case, since the evidence offered is relevant, and D doesn't recognize this, it is not the best response.

Answer 172

(B) is the best response,

because it correctly identifies that the question is objectionable because it is not legally relevant.

Here, the prosecutor is impeaching Warren by attempting to show bias. While this is a proper basis of impeachment, the testimony must still, *as with every piece of evidence,* be legally relevant. That is, if the probative value of the evidence is substantially outweighed by the probability of undue prejudice, the court will exclude the evidence. Here, the weight of the bias would be outweighed by the importance the jury would attach to the fact that Drew had been tried before on a criminal charge. In other words, the jury would be likely to use the evidence to prove that Drew is a criminal, and he should be locked up on that basis, not due to his being guilty of murdering Victor. Furthermore, the value of the evidence is not great in showing bias. Warren's being on a jury that acquitted Drew of another charge wouldn't necessarily show that Warren himself voted to acquit Drew, and even if he did, this in and of itself wouldn't make him any more or less likely to lie on Drew's behalf. Instead, the jury would likely be misled by the evidence, as option B indicates. Although such an exclusion would be within the judge's discretion, the other three alternatives are clearly wrong, so B is the best response.

(A) is not the best response,

because it misstates the law. A question on cross-examination can go beyond the scope of direct examination, and still be valid.

The scope of cross-examination, under FRE 611(b), is limited to matters brought up in direct examination, inferences therefrom, *and* the credibility of a witness (along with any other matters, in the judge's discretion). Here, the issue is credibility, which need not be addressed on direct examination in order to be cross-examinable.

The prosecutor is attempting to show that Victor lacks credibility by showing possible bias, due to Warren's being a member of a jury that previously acquitted Drew of a criminal charge. As a result, it is within the scope of cross-examination even if it wasn't addressed on direct examination, making A not the best response.

(C) is not the best response,

because although it correctly characterizes the question, it fails to recognize that leading questions are permissible on cross-examination.

A leading question is one which would lead an average person to believe that the questioner desires one answer over another (e.g., "Didn't you see the red light?"). The prosecutor's question about Warren's prior jury duty is just such a question – it's obvious that the prosecutor wants Warren to say he was on that jury. However, a question isn't necessarily improper just because it's leading. Instead, under FRE 611(c), leading questions are proper under the following circumstances:

1. On cross examination in general;
2. On direction examination only if
    a. The witness is hostile, unwilling or biased;
    b. The witness is a child, or an adult with difficulty communicating;
    c. The witness's recollection is exhausted; or
    d. The questioning concerns undisputed prelimi-

nary matters.

Anyone who ever saw Perry Mason knows that cross-examination is where leading questions are most commonly used. If you didn't remember this, it's probably because you spent your childhood in more worthwhile pursuits than sitting in front of the TV, which is admirable. Nonetheless, since C doesn't recognize that leading questions are permissible under the circumstances in these facts, it's not the best response.

(D) is not the best response,

because Warren's prior jury service would not render him incompetent.

In order to be a competent witness, under FRE 602 and 603, the witness must have personal knowledge of the matter on which he will testify, and he must declare that he will testify truthfully. While Warren's prior jury service may effect his *credibility,* in that it might make him more likely to lie on Drew's behalf, it will not affect his *competence* to testify. In any case, it wouldn't be fair to the prosecution if Drew were allowed to have Wilson declared an incompetent witness, since Wilson has already testified on Drew's behalf (although the judge could, theoretically, disqualify Wilson if he weren't competent).

Incidentally, note that this is true for jurors in other cases, but not the current case. Under FRE 606, a member of the current jury can't testify in the current case as a witness.

Since D doesn't recognize that Wilson's prior jury service won't render him an incompetent witness in the current case, it is not the best response.

Answer 173

The best response is B,

because it's the only option that addresses the correct scope of re-direct examination. This is an unusual MBE question, in that it's purely theoretical: Either you know the answer, or you don't. There's no factual analysis required.

In fact, the rule is just what B says it is: Only new, *material* matters addressed on cross-examination may be covered on re-direct, as a general rule. The judge *can,* in his discretion, allow counsel to address on re-direct a matter overlooked on direct due to an oversight, but this isn't relevant here, because the question asks you for the circumstances under which a judge *must* allow re-direct examination, not where he *may* allow it. Since B cites the correct rule, it's the best response.

(A) is not the best response

because it overstates the scope of re-direct examination.

The judge is only required to allow re-direct examination to address new, material matters addressed on cross-examination. He needn't allow it for insignificant matters addressed on cross, and thus A overstates the

scope of re-direct examination, by stating that the judge must allow re-direct to reply to *any* matter raised on cross. As a result, A is not the best response.

(C) is not the best response

because it misstates the rule.

The judge is required to allow re-direct examination to address new, material matters addressed on cross-examination. In fact, allowing a party to reiterate the essential elements of the case on re-direct would contradict FRE 403, which authorizes the judge to exclude evidence if admitting it would constitute a waste of time. Since C does not recognize the correct rule on re-direct examination, it is not the best response.

(D) is not the best response,

because it misstates the rule.

Here, the question asks you when a judge *must* allow re-direct examination of a witness. The judge is only *required* to allow re-direct examination to address new, material matters addressed on cross-examination. The material D addresses is allowable in the judge's discretion – he *may,* if he sees fit, allow re-direct on matters overlooked on direct due to an oversight. However, this is not mandatory. This answer indicates the level of precision necessary to correctly answer MBE questions correctly! Since D does not state the rule correctly, it is not the best response.

Answer 174

(B) is the best response,

because it addresses a defense which would succeed.

An assignment of contractual rights is the transfer of that right to another. It requires assignor's intent to transfer, identification of the rights to be assigned, and assignee's acceptance (which is normally presumed if the assignment is beneficial).

Under the contract here, mechanic's *right* under the contract was payment from Ohner. Thus, his letter to Jones and Ohner would serve to transfer the right to payment to Jones. This makes Jones the assignee, Mechanic the assignor, and Ohner the obligor. The result of the transfer is that Jones "stands in Mechanic's shoes" as to the right to payment. As a result, any defenses under the contract that Ohner could assert against Mechanic, he can assert against Jones. Thus, Mechanic's failure to perform under the contract would be defense Ohner could successfully assert against Jones. Since option A identifies this, it's the best response.

(A) is not the best response,

because Jones's ability to do Mechanic's work is irrelevant to Jones's recovery.

An assignment of contractual rights is the transfer of that right to another. It requires assignor's intent to transfer; identification of the rights to be assigned; and assignee's acceptance (which is normally presumed if the assignment is beneficial).

Under the contract here, Mechanic's *right* under the contract was payment from Ohner. Thus, his letter to Jones and Ohner would serve to transfer the right to payment to Jones. This makes Jones the assignee, Mechanic the assignor, and Ohner the obligor. The *result* of the transfer is that Jones "stands in Mechanic's shoes" as to the right to payment. Thus, Jones's ability to perform Mechanic's duties under the contract is irrelevant.

If you chose this response, you either confused an assignment of rights with a delegation of duties, or assumed that Mechanic assigned the *contract*, not just the right to payment, which would involve a presumption that the duties were delegated as well. Most "impersonal" duties can be delegated, and Mechanic's duty to repair the machine probably *could* be delegated, barring facts indicating that Ohner had a particular interest in receiving performance from Mechanic. However, a delegation is *not* valid where it materially increases the risk that Ohner will not receive return performance. Where Jones can't perform the work, such a delegation would be invalid. However, since only an assignment of rights is involved here, A isn't the best response.

(C) is not the best response,

because the prohibition against assignment would not be upheld.

At common law, prohibitions against assignment in a contract *can* be valid. Restatement of Contracts 2d §317. However, whether a specific prohibition can be upheld depends on how the prohibition is worded: as a *promise* or a *condition*. If the prohibition is a promise, the subsequent assignment will be valid (since the promise is said to merely destroy the right, not the power, to assign rights), and the other party could only sue for breach of covenant, for which there are generally only nominal damages. If, however, the prohibition is worded as a *condition* (e.g., "any assignment of these rights shall be void"), any subsequent assignment will be *invalid* (since it is said to destroy the right *and* the power to assign rights).

Under these facts, there's no problem of interpretation, because you're told that the non-assignment provision was a *promise* by Mechanic. Thus, the assignment would be valid. (Note that the common law, not the UCC, applies to these facts because there's no transaction in goods. Under the UCC, §9-318(4), the right to payment can *always* be assigned *regardless* of prohibitions in the agreement).

Since the prohibition against assignment would not be upheld, this would not be a good defense for Ohner, making C not the best response.

(D) is not the best response,

because Jones's not being a third party beneficiary would *not* be determinative of his recovery.

Option D suggests that the only way Jones can recover is as an intended beneficiary to the contract. While, of course, an intended beneficiary *does* have enforceable rights under a contract (once his rights vest), an assignee can recover under a contract, as well. Thus, D understates the scope of third parties who can recover under a contract.

The difference between third party beneficiaries and assignees of rights is that the rights of third party beneficiaries are created in the contract, whereas an assignment involves the subsequent transfer of rights under a contract. Under these facts, Mechanic transferred his right to payment under the contract to Jones. As such, Jones stands in Mechanic's shoes as to the right to payment. Thus, if Mechanic performs under the contract, Jones will be entitled to the payment (barring any prior defenses that accrued before Ohner found out about the assignment – e.g., Jones previously owed Ohner money). As a result, it wouldn't be in Ohner's interest to say that Jones was not the intended beneficiary of the contract, since his recovery would be as an assignee, not a beneficiary. Thus, D isn't the best response.

Answer 175

(D) is the best response,

because it addresses the central reason that John will not be entitled to the commission.

There are two key points here: The provisions of the original contract, and the fact that the termination wasn't wrongful.

Under the original contract, BCD was free to terminate John at any time. Furthermore, a salesman's being employed *when the bill was sent to the customer* was an express condition of the duty to pay the commission. As a result, in the absence of a bad faith termination, the contract terms would control in determining John's right to the commission. Here, you're told specifically that the termination wasn't wrongful. Thus, the termination was within BCD's rights, and it can't be a source of liability for BCD.

Furthermore, John *was* paid a salary for the time he put in, and thus BCD didn't receive something for nothing. A primary purpose of contracts is to allocate risks. Here, John knew what he bargained for and undertook the risk he might be rightfully terminated before the bill was sent. The thing that makes this question tough is that your gut feeling is that John deserves the commission. This answer indicates, as do so many MBE questions, why it's so important to analyze MBE questions coldly and impartially. Since D recognizes that John isn't entitled to the commission, and the central reason why, it's the best response.

(A) is not the best response,

because it ignores the existence of an express condition which was not satisfied, under these facts.

The contract between BCD and John required that

John be employed *when the bill is sent to a customer* in order to receive a commission from that sale. Thus, eligibility to receive a commission is *expressly* conditioned on John's being employed when the bill is sent. Here, John was fired on March 15, and the bill was sent on March 31. Thus, an express condition was not met, and John is not entitled to the commission. (Note that John is trying to recover under the contract, since he's seeking the sales commission, *not* the reasonable value of his services.)

If you chose this response, it's probably because your gut feeling is that John *should* be paid. Probably, if you were John, you'd stuff a raw potato up the exhaust pipe of your former boss's Mercedes – right? If you feel this way, there's an important fact you overlooked – the termination wasn't wrongful. Had BCD acted in bad faith, the result would have been entirely different. In fact, another significant point is that John was *also* receiving a salary. Thus, when John entered the employment agreement, terminable at BCD's will and with the commission-only-when-billed provision, he got what he bargained for. Since A mistakenly states that John should recover the sales commission, it's not the best response.

(B) is not the best response,

because John's promise to help Bobb will not be relevant to his claim against BCD.

John's promise to Bobb will not determine his right to the sales commission. Instead, you have to look at BCD's and John's rights and duties under the employment contract, and determine if there is some basis on which John is entitled to the sales commission. The original contract was terminable at will, so BCD could fire John on the spot, anytime. Furthermore, the contract makes employment on the date the customer is sent a bill an *express condition* of the duty to pay the salesman a commission. Of course, if BCD acted wrongfully or in bad faith, John would prevail. But this question tells you specifically that the termination wasn't wrongful. John was terminated March 15, and the bill was sent March 31; thus, he's not entitled to the sales commission.

A wrinkle here is that BCD knew John promised Bobb that he'd assist in getting the system going for six months after installation. Thus, John could argue that BCD was estopped from firing him for that period. However, the facts specifically tell you that the termination was within BCD's rights, so estoppel can't apply. Since B attaches significance to John's promise to Bobb, where little actually exists, B isn't the best response.

(C) is not the best response,

because it misstates the facts. If quantum meruit were applicable (which it isn't), it would mean *John* should get paid, not *Franklin*.

Quantum meruit ("what the thing's worth") is the measure of recovery under quasi-contract. Quasi-con-

tract is typically applied where plaintiff confers a benefit on the defendant, under circumstances where defendant would be unjustly enriched if he were allowed to retain the benefit without paying fro it. The problem with applying this here is that there *is* a contractual provision that controls, and so there is no basis for referring to quasi-contract. Under the contract here, BCD was entitled to fire John at any time. John's employment at the time a customer is billed is an express condition to his being paid a commission. Most importantly, you're told that John's termination wasn't wrongful. Thus, John's right to the commission can be determined within the four corners of the contract, without falling back on quasi-contract.

Assuming arguendo that quasi-contract were applicable, it would result in John being paid, not Franklin, since it's John's work with Bobb that resulted in the benefit to BCD. Thus, even if quasi-contract were appropriate here, option C misapplies it, so it's not the best response.

Answer 176

(C) is the best response,

because it identifies the central reason John will not be able to recover damages: The contract controls.

First, determine what claim John's making. Since he's seeking the reasonable value of his services, he must be suing under quasi-contract. However, quasi-contract only applies when there's no enforceable contract covering the situation. Here, this is where John's claim falls apart. The parties expressly addressed the compensation issue under the contract, and provided that John would only be entitled to a sales commission if he was employed *when the customer was billed*. This on its face is an enforceable provision, and there's nothing to make it unenforceable (since, most significantly, the termination wasn't wrongful). While this might not compute with your basic notions of fairness, it covers a basic risk John undertook when he entered the contract: That he might lose a commission by being rightfully fired before a customer was billed. Here, that's what happened; BCD was within its rights in firing him, and since the contract covers the situation, there's no basis for looking outside the contract to determine recovery. Since option C correctly identifies this, it's the best response.

(A) is not the best response,

because it ignores the fact that the contractual provision on commission payment will control.

Option A implies that John should recover under quasi-contract (since the reasonable value of his services would be the measure of damages, and benefit to defendant is one of the requirements of quasi-contractual recovery). However option A ignores the fact that quasi-contractual recovery is only available when there is no enforceable contractual duty.

Here, the subject of compensation for services was

fully addressed in the contract. John received a base salary and would receive commissions only if he was employed when the customer was billed. Thus, employment on that date formed an express condition to John's being paid. While this might be excused had BCD acted in bad faith in firing John, you're told that the termination was not wrongful.

What this does is eliminate any basis for quasi-contractual recovery. Quasi-contract requires not only benefit to the defendant, but also circumstances where defendant would be unjustly enriched if he were allowed to retain the benefit without paying for it. Here, BCD got nothing outside its rights under the contract, and thus, while it was enriched by John's services, it wasn't unjustly enriched. Since A would mistakenly allow quasi-contractual recovery under these facts, it's not the best response.

(B) is not the best response,

because it misstates the facts.

An implied-in-fact promise is one which is not expressly stated in words, but rather is implied by the party's words or actions. You typically see implied-in-fact promises where there's no express promise to act as consideration (e.g., when an actress hires an agent to market her services, without an express promise from the agent that he'll do so. A court will *imply* that the service promised to use reasonable efforts to sell the actress's services).

The reason this doesn't apply here is that the compensation issue was *expressly* addressed in the contract, and so it won't be necessary to determine the parties' intent by looking at their *implied* promises. John Was to be paid a base salary, and a commission on sales *only* if he was employed when the customer was billed. There's nothing to indicate the contract wasn't enforceable (a significant indication of this being that the termination wasn't wrongful). Thus, the contract will control as to compensation, and there's no justification for turning to an implied-in-fact contract. Since B doesn't recognize this, it's not the best response.

(D) is not the best response,

because if John were entitled to quasi-contractual recovery, John's inability to perform the six-months' worth of assistance wouldn't defeat his claim.

In this question, you're told that John is seeking the reasonable value of his services. This means he must be seeking quasi-contractual recovery, since that's how quasi-contractual damages are measured.

Quasi-contractual recovery is only merited when there's no contractual provision that controls. Plaintiff is entitled to quasi-contractual recovery when he confers a benefit on the defendant, under circumstances where defendant would be unjustly enriched if he were allowed to retain the benefit without paying for it. Here, there is a contract provision addressing compensation,

and the provision is enforceable (due in no small part to the fact that the termination was not wrongful).

Thus, the provision will control, and there'd be no basis for stepping outside the contract to determine the parties' rights and duties. Even if quasi-contract were applicable, John could recover the reasonable value of the benefit *already conferred* – his procuring the sale. Of course he wouldn't be able to assist Bobb, but he wouldn't be compensated for it, either. Since D mistakenly states that John's inability to assist for six months will defeat his claim, it's not the best response.

Answer 177

As to alternative I:

This would support a claim by John, because it would make his termination wrongful.

The central obstacle to John's recovery is that the contract provision on compensation would control, and thus any additional facts would have to provide a basis on which to ignore the contract. The most likely way to do this is to prove that the termination was wrongful. While the contract doesn't specifically address it, there is an implied obligation of good-faith by BCD. That's because, with a termination at will clause, if there's *no* obligation of good faith, BCD's promise could be considered illusory (since there's no underlying detriment to form consideration). BCD's firing John in order for the company president's son to get the commission would clearly constitute bad faith, and thus a reach of contract. This would make a sound basis for a claim by John, thus making alternative I a good answer.

As to alternative II:

This would support a claim by John, since it would mean that John's termination was wrongful.

The central obstacle to John's recovery is that the contract provision on compensation would control. It provided that an express condition of John's receiving a sales commission would be his employment when the bill was sent. Thus, any additional facts would have to provide a basis on which to ignore the contract. The most likely way to do this is to prove the termination was wrongful.

If there was a mistake as to John's meeting his sales quotas, this would mean that he was wrongfully fired. On this basis, he'd be entitled to the sales commission, and would support John's claim. Thus, alternative II is a good answer.

As to alternative III:

This is not a good argument for John, because it would not, by itself, justify John's recovery.

The central obstacle here is that the contract provision on compensation would control. It provided that an express condition to John's receiving a sales commission would be his employment when the bill was sent. Thus, any additional facts would have to provide a basis on which to ignore the contract. The most likely way to do this would be to prove the termination was wrongful.

John's tenure at BCD wouldn't supply a basis for avoiding the compensation provision. Were there *other* facts – for instance, BCD had previously ignored John's failure to meet his quotas, or otherwise implied that the provision wouldn't control – then the twenty year's work might be relevant. However, standing alone, it does not supply a good basis for John's claim. Thus, alternative III is not a good answer.

Answer 178

(D) is the best response.

D is the best response, because it correctly identifies the central reason why the motion to dismiss should be granted: Hobson was not a federal judge, and thus was not entitled to life tenure.

As these facts state, federal judges, serving on federal courts created pursuant to Article III of the Constitution, are entitled to lifetime tenure and undiminished pay. Had Hobson been a federal judge, he would have been entitled to both these benefits. However, Hobson wasn't a federal judge; instead, you're told he served on a tribunal created by Congress. Problematically, Congress can create tribunals under Article I of the Constitution, and lower federal courts, under Article III. The difference between a tribunal and a court depends on the functions served; a tribunal is legislative in nature, and a court, adjudicative. Here, the functions of the tribunal were legislative, and as a result Hobson wouldn't enjoy the Article III privileges of a federal judge. Instead, he'd serve at the pleasure of Congress. Thus, the motion to dismiss should be granted, because Hobson could prove no set of facts under which he'd be entitled to life tenure, an Article III privilege. Sine option D recognizes this, it's the best response.

(A) is not the best response,

because Hobson is not an Article III judge, and thus there's no issue under Article III; and even if there were an Article III issue, A misstates the law.

Congress in fact has considerable power with regard to Article III courts. Under Article III, §1 of the Constitution, the federal judicial power is "vested in one Supreme Court, and in such inferior Courts as the Congress may from time to time…establish." Congress can not only create new, inferior courts, but it can regulate the appellate jurisdiction of federal courts under Article III, §2. Thus, the federal judiciary could hardly be characterized as "independent," contrary to what option A states.

In any case, Hobson was not an Article III judge. Instead, he was a member of a legislative tribunal created by Congress. While it's true that federal judges cannot be removed from office during good behavior, nor can their pay be cut, this would not apply to Hobson. Instead, he was appointed by Congress and Congress could remove him as it saw fit. Since A doesn't recognize that Hobson wasn't a judge, it's not the best response.

(B) is not the best response,

because Hobson had no property right in his federal employment.

With the words "property right," option B suggests that Hobson's removal, without some form of fair hearing, constitutes a due process violation. When the effect of a governmental activity amounts to a deprivation of a property interest or right, there's a potential due process problem. While "property" needn't necessarily be actual, tangible land or chattels, it requires at least interests already acquired in specific benefits. As far as governmental employment is concerned, the existence of a "property" interest in continued employment is determined under applicable federal, state, or municipal law. Thus, the statute creating the job, or the employment contract, or a clear understanding must provide for termination only "for cause." Here, there's no indication that Hobson's employment was anything other than at the pleasure of Congress. He served only as a member of a tribunal, not as a federal judge, so the lifetime employment and prohibition of salary diminution applicable to federal judges wouldn't apply to him.

Even if Hobson *had* a property right in his employment, this wouldn't determine that his dismissal involved a due process violation. Instead, he'd have to establish that he wasn't granted a fair hearing pursuant to his dismissal. Here gain, there are no facts under this question to indicate this. Since B incorrectly focuses on a due process issue when none are indicated under these facts, it's not the best response.

(C) is not the best response,

because Hobson *did* have the standing to challenge his dismissal.

In order to press a claim, a party must have standing. Standing requires that the governmental action challenged must have caused or is imminently likely to cause, an injury to the party seeking review. Here, Hobson was removed from his job, so he clearly suffered an injury. While his claim isn't *valid,* since he wasn't a federal judge, this doesn't address the threshold question of whether or not he has standing. Since C doesn't recognize this, it's not the best response.

Answer 179

(A) is the best response,

because it offers the cornerstone of a public nuisance claim by private individuals.

A public nuisance is an act which unreasonably interferes with the health, safety or convenience of the public in general. Such claims are typically brought by the state. However, a private individual *can* recover for public nuisance if he suffered special damages above and beyond the ordinary damage the public incurred. Since A recognizes this, it's the best response.

(B) is not the best response,

because its reasoning is an insufficient basis for a public nuisance claim brought by private individuals.

In order for a private claim of public nuisance to succeed, the plaintiff must prove that he suffered special damages above and beyond the ordinary damage the public incurred, both in kind and degree. Thus, merely proving an interference with the use or enjoyment of property would be insufficient. If you chose this response, it's probably because you were thinking of a *private* nuisance claim, which is what the reasoning in B would support. However, a public nuisance claim is stricter, and since B fails to recognize this, it's not the best response.

(C) isn't the best response,

because it misstates the law.

While the state typically *is* the plaintiff in public nuisance actions, a private individual *may* recover for public nuisance if he suffered special damages above and beyond the ordinary damage the public incurred. Thus, the state is *not* the only potential plaintiff. Since C incorrectly restricts the claim to the state, it's not the best response.

(D) is not the best response,

because "coming to the nuisance" does not, in and of itself, defeat a nuisance claim.

Even if one moves into a neighborhood knowing about a nuisance, he is *still* entitled to the reasonable use and enjoyment of his land. Only if one moves in lacking good faith, or for the sole purpose of launching a lawsuit will "coming to the nuisance" defeat a nuisance claim. (The Restatement of Torts views "coming to the nuisance" as a factor to be considered in determining liability.) Instead, as private individuals pressing a public nuisance suit, plaintiffs will have to prove they suffered damages above and beyond the damage the public incurred. A public nuisance itself is an act which unreasonably interferes with the health, safety, or convenience of the public in general. Since the mere fact of "coming to the nuisance" alone won't determine who prevails, D is not the best response.

Answer 180

(A) is the best response,

because it correctly identifies the requirements of the private nuisance tort, in its entirety. As long as Defendant creates an unreasonable, substantial interference with Plaintiff's use or enjoyment of property, he'll be liable. It doesn't matter if he tried to minimize the interference, or if his use of the property has lasted longer than plaintiffs'. Noxious odors – as here – are a classic basis of private nuisance.

Keep in mind that these factors are not totally mean-

ingless, because there is a balancing test used to determine the unreasonability of the act: The utility of Defendant's conduct vs. the severity of Plaintiff's injury. Included in this analysis will be Defendant's right to reasonable use of his land, based on the character of the neighborhood, value of the land, and alternatives available to Defendant. Nonetheless, since A correctly identifies the elements of a private nuisance suit, and it applies to these facts, A is not the best response.

(B) is not the best response,

because it imposes a burden on plaintiff which overstates the *actual* burden.

Under private nuisance, plaintiffs need only prove an act by defendant creating an unreasonable, substantial interference with their use and enjoyment of their property. A condemnation, instead, would require the *taking* of property by an actual interference with property rights, without actually entering the property. It's easier to prove an interference than a taking, so option B imposes too heavy a burden on plaintiffs. As a result, B is not the best response.

(C) is not the best response,

because Cattle Company's years in business would not be determinative of its liability for private nuisance.

A private nuisance is an act by defendant which creates an unreasonable, substantial interference with plaintiff's use or enjoyment of property. That's it. Cattle Company's tenure on the property wouldn't give it a right to interfere with others' use and enjoyment of their property; in other words, there's nothing in nuisance analogous with adverse possession. The tenure will be a factor in determining unreasonability, but it won't be the only one. Since option C would insulate Cattle Company from liability due to the age of the business, and this is not in fact a valid defense, C is not the best response.

(D) is not the best response,

because it offers a defense which will not, in fact, relieve Cattle Company of liability for nuisance.

A private nuisance is an act by Defendant which creates an unreasonable, substantial interference with Plaintiff's use or enjoyment of property. If Defendant creates such an interference, it doesn't matter *how* he tried to lessen its impact (although the unreasonability of his act will be determined by weighing the utility of his conduct vs. the severity of injury, in which defendant's alternatives are one of the factors considered). Thus, the use of due care in minimizing the interference will not be a valid defense, since private nuisance is not predicated on negligence. Since D fails to recognize this, it's not the best response.

Answer 181

(B) is the best response.

The key here is recognizing the mental element that is

required for accessory liability: One must intend to aid in the commission of a felony.

(B) is the best response,

because it correctly identifies the central issue, Carl's mens rea, and correctly concludes that he cannot be found guilty because he didn't have the correct state of mind.

In order to liable as an accessory, one must procure, counsel or command the commission of a felony. In order to do so, one must intend that a crime be committed. Here, since Carl didn't know about the prior marriage, he had no idea he was encouraging Alan to commit bigamy. Since Carl's mistake of fact negates the intent element of the crime, he cannot be guilty. Since B correctly identifies this, it's the best response.

(A) is not the best response,

because although it arrives at the correct result, it misstates the means by which accomplice liability is determined.

One can be liable as an accessory without his conduct being the legal cause of the crime; thus, contrary to what option A states, the lack of legal causation between the accomplice's act and the criminal result will not exonerate the accomplice. In order to be liable as an accomplice, one must procure, counsel, or command the commission of a felony. If Carl had encouraged Alan to marry Betty *knowing* that Alan was already married, Carl would be liable as an accessory, regardless of whether his conduct was the legal cause of the bigamous marriage. Since A states otherwise, it's not the best response.

(C) is not the best response,

because it arrives at the incorrect result, and it misstates the law.

Contrary to what option C states, mistake of fact *is* a defense to a criminal charge if it negates the necessary mens rea. The mens rea for accomplice liability is intent — one must procure, counsel, or command the commission of a felony. This requires that the accomplice intend that the crime be committed. As a result, accomplice liability is not possible when the ostensible accomplice doesn't realize he's encouraging a felony. Since C states otherwise, and arrives at an incorrect result, it's not the best response.

(D) is not the best response,

because although it makes a correct statement as to a rule of law, it does not provide a basis on which Carl can be found guilty — and, furthermore, it arrives at an incorrect result.

It's true that presence when the crime occurs would make an accomplice to a crime a principal in the second degree, not an accessory before the fact — it's presence at the scene of the crime that distinguishes the two. However, option D does not address the central issue to any liability to Carl as an accomplice of any

kind — the fact that he didn't intend that a felony be committed. Liability as an accessory before the fact or as a principal in the second degree requires that one procure, counsel, or command the commission of a felony. Since Carl didn't know about the prior marriage, he couldn't possibly have encouraged Alan to commit bigamy. Merely being present at the scene of the crime wouldn't make Carl liable as an accomplice, so D is not the best response.

Answer 182

The best response is B,

because it correctly identifies precisely why the instructions were correct: The burden of ultimate persuasion remained with the prosecution, and the defendant only bore the burden of rebutting a presumption of murder.

First, take a close look at what's going on here. Defendant was charged with murder — that is, the killing of another, with malice aforethought,. The burden of persuasion is on the prosecution, to prove every element of the crime beyond the reasonable doubt. This burden does not shift throughout the trial. The burden of production, or "going forward," requires only that a party introduce enough evidence on an issue such that a reasonable jury could infer the fact alleged. If Defendant wants to claim an affirmative defense — like self defense or provocation — he will have the burden of going forward.

The judge's instructions create a rebuttable presumption that a killing is murder; he lays the burden of ultimate persuasion on the prosecution, to prove every element of the crime beyond a reasonable doubt; and he establishes that Defendant can rebut the presumption of murder by producing evidence that shows, by a fair preponderance, that the killing was committed under adequate provocation. Note that this doesn't shift the burden of persuasion from the prosecution to the defendant, because that would violate defendant's due process rights. Instead, it requires only that, once the state has borne its burden of proving every element beyond a reasonable doubt, the defendant has the burden of producing evidence on his affirmative defense; he must show it was more likely than not that he was adequately provoked. This reflects a fair distribution of the burden between the prosecution and the defendant, and so Defendant's conviction will be upheld.

(A) is not the best response,

because it does not address with sufficient precision, in light of another option which is more precise, exactly why Defendant's conviction will be upheld.

What option A does is to address only the state's burden of ultimate persuasion. It does not address Defendant's burden of production at all.

First, take a close look at what's going on here. Defendant was charged with murder — that is, the killing of another, with malice aforethought. The burden of persuasion is on the prosecution, to prove every element of the crime beyond the reasonable doubt. This burden does not shift throughout the trial. The burden of production, or "going forward," requires only that a party introduce enough evidence on an issue such that a reasonable jury could infer the fact alleged. If Defendant wants to claim an affirmative defense – like self defense or provocation – he will have the burden of going forward.

The judge's instructions create a rebuttable presumption that a killing is murder; he lays the burden of ultimate persuasion on the prosecution, to prove every element of the crime beyond a reasonable doubt; and he establishes that Defendant can rebut the presumption of murder by producing evidence that shows, by a fair preponderance, that the killing was committed under adequate provocation. Note that this doesn't shift the burden of persuasion from the prosecution to the defendant, because that would violate defendant's due process rights. Instead, it requires only that, once the state has borne its burden of proving every element beyond a reasonable doubt, the defendant has the burden of producing evidence on his affirmative defense; he must show it was more likely than not that he was adequately provoked.

Option A ignores entirely the Defendant's burden of going forward, which is significant, due to the potential due process violation placing a burden on a criminal defendant could create. As a result, A is not the best response.

(C) is not the best response,

because Defendant was not denied due process of law, and, because the judge correctly identified the burdens of proof for both the state and the Defendant, the conviction will be upheld.

Due process requires fairness of process in circumstances when one is being deprived of life, liberty, or property. Here, if Defendant were required to prove his *innocence,* he'd be denied due process. However, he's only required to introduce enough evidence to create a reasonable doubt in the minds of the jury that he was adequately provoked. This is only a burden of going forward, and is thus considered fair.

The burden of persuasion is on the prosecution, to prove every element of the crime beyond the reasonable doubt. This burden does not shift throughout the trial. The burden of production, or "going forward," requires only that a party introduce enough evidence on an issue such that a reasonable jury could infer the fact alleged. If Defendant wants to claim an affirmative defense – like self defense or provocation – he will have the burden of going forward.

The judge's instructions create a rebuttable presumption that a killing is murder; he lays the burden of ultimate persuasion on the prosecution, to prove every element of the crime beyond a reasonable doubt; and he establishes that Defendant can rebut the presumption of murder by producing evidence that shows, by a

fair preponderance, that the killing was committed under adequate provocation. Note that this doesn't shift the burden of persuasion from the prosecution to the defendant, because that would violate defendant's due process rights. Instead, it requires only that, once the state has borne its burden of proving every element beyond a reasonable doubt, the defendant has the burden of producing evidence on his affirmative defense; he must show it was more likely than not that he was adequately provoked. Since C mistakenly states that Defendant's due process rights were violated by the jury instructions, it's not the best response.

(D) is not the best response,

because it misstates the law: Presumptions *can,* in fact, be used by the state in a criminal case.

First, a little background. There are two types burdens of proof: The burden of persuasion, and the burden of going forward. The burden of persuasion is on the prosecution, to prove every element of the crime beyond the reasonable doubt. This burden does not shift throughout the trial. The burden of production, or "going forward," requires only that a party introduce enough evidence on an issue such that a reasonable jury could infer the fact alleged. If Defendant wants to claim an affirmative defense – like self defense or provocation – he will have the burden of going forward.

A rebuttable presumption has the effect of shifting the burden of "going forward" to the party adversely effected by the presumption. It does not shift the burden of persuasion, which cannot shift throughout the trial.

Contrary to what D states, there are many, rebuttable presumptions which operate validly on behalf of the state in a criminal case. For instance, as a general rule, people who commit crimes are sane, conscious, sober, and not operating under duress. These are, as a general rule, presumptions that operate in favor of the state, such that it need not prove in a criminal case *any* of these elements – that is, unless the defendant introduces evidence on any of these elements, or in fact any justification or excuse or affirmative defense. Thus, if the defendant introduces no evidence on any presumed fact, the jury can, but doesn't have to, find that those facts exist. However, if the defendant meets the burden of going forward – that is, he introduces enough evidence to create a reasonable doubt about a presumed fact in the minds of the trier of fact – then the state must prove the challenged fact beyond a reasonable doubt. There's nothing legally repugnant about any of this; the only presumptions that couldn't operate in the state's favor are those which address the ultimate issue of proof of a crime's elements. As a result, C's statement, that presumptions cannot operate in favor of a state in a criminal case, is incorrect, making C not the best response.

Answer 183

(D) is the best response,

because Supreme Court precedents do not furnish a defense on either grounds.

With respect to Steven, the Supreme Court held in *Ker v. Illinois* (1886) that "forcible abduction is no sufficient reason why the party should not answer when brought within the jurisdiction of the court which has the right to try him for such an offence." *Ker* was a case in which agents abducted an American citizen from a foreign country, so it's on all fours with the facts here. (And it's never been overruled).

As to Joan, the analysis is somewhat different. The warrantless entry into Joan's home to arrest her violated her Fourth Amendment rights. See *Payton v. New York* (1980) (warrant required for entry into private dwelling to arrest the inhabitant, if there are no exigent circumstances). This violation would have entitled Joan to suppress any evidence found incident to the arrest. *Payton*. But the violation does *not* entitle Joan to have the indictment dismissed, because the indictment preceded the arrest, and was not in any way the product of the later illegality. (The mere fact that the prosecution had the ability to try Joan because it had her in custody through an illegal arrest does not make a difference. "Illegal arrest does not void a subsequent prosecution." *Gerstein v. Pugh* (1975).)

In summary, neither defense works.

Neither (A), (B) nor (C) is the best response,

because each answer incorrectly asserts that at least one of the defenses will be successful.

Answer 184

What's going on here? Prosecutor is attempting to enter evidence of an unrelated instance of misconduct – the other robbery. As such, it will require independent relevance in order to be admissible.

(A) is the best response

because it correctly states that evidence of the other robbery will be admissible to establish an identifying circumstance.

Here, Prosecutor is attempting to enter evidence of an unrelated instance of misconduct – the other robbery. The danger of this is that the jury is likely to convict the defendant because he's a "bad man," not because he's guilty in this instance. Nonetheless, under FRE 404(b), evidence of other, specific instances of misconduct will be admissible when they have independent relevance. These include knowledge, absence of mistake or accident, preparation, plan, opportunity, motive, intent, and identity. Here, the evidence will do more than just identify Dennis as a habitual armed robber – it helps establish that Dennis committed the robbery by identifying an unusual circumstance, known to have occurred at Alice's robbery, which happened at another robbery Dennis committed.

The common identity will provide the "independent relevance" necessary to make the evidence admissible, and since A recognizes this, it is the best response.

(B) is not the best answer,

because it misstates the purpose for which the evidence will be admissible.

Under the doctrine of "limited admissibility," evidence may be admissible for one purpose and against one party, but not admissible for some other purpose or against some other party. For instance, insurance can be admitted to show ownership but not the ability to pay. Here, evidence of other instances of misconduct is *never* admissible to show the defendant's propensity to commit crimes, because the jury would be likely to convict the defendant because of his general criminal propensities – "since he did it before, he probably did it again" – not because he's guilty in this instance. Instead, under FRE 404(b), evidence of other, specific instances of misconduct will only be admissible when they have independent relevance. These include knowledge, absence of mistake or accident, preparation, plan, opportunity, motive, intent, and identity. Here, the evidence will establish that Dennis committed the robbery by identifying an unusual circumstance, known to have occurred at Alie's robbery, which happened at another robbery that Dennis has already been proven to have committed. Of course, it will also prove that Dennis is a habitual robber, which is going to be the most likely thing the jury will remember – wouldn't you? But since the evidence fits the requirements of FRE 404(b) on independent relevance, it'll be admissible. Since B states otherwise, it is not the best answer.

(C) is not the best answer,

because although it correct characterizes the evidence here as character evidence, and character evidence as a general rule is inadmissible, it fails to recognize that the character evidence here is admissible because it has *independent relevance*; it's not being offered for the impermissible purpose of showing Dennis's criminal propensities.

Here, the prosecutor is offering evidence of another, specific act of misconduct – Dennis's holding up Winthrop with a pistol painted red. Specific acts of misconduct *are* admissible against criminal defendants when the instances have independent relevance under FRE 404(b). These include knowledge, absence of mistake or accident, preparation, plan, opportunity, motive, intent, and identity. Here, the evidence will do more than just identify Dennis as a habitual armed robber – it helps establish that Dennis committed the robbery by identifying an unusual circumstance, known to have occurred at Alice's robbery, which happened at another robbery Dennis committed. The common identity will provide the "independent relevance" necessary to make the evidence admissible. Since C does not recognize this, it is not the best response.

(D) is not the best response,

because although it's not a bad response, it does not correctly characterize the facts. In fact, this is a reasonably tough question, because you have to do some balancing and make a judgment call.

D suggests that the evidence will not be admissible because it is not legally relevant – if the probative value of a piece of evidence is substantially outweighed by the danger of unfair prejudice it will engender, then it is not admissible, even if it satisfies every other obstacle of admissibility.

The danger here is that the jury will place too much weight on Winthrop's testimony, and convict Dennis because he's a habitual criminal, not because he committed the crime for which he's being tried – holding up Alice. However, this is a balancing test, and the fact is that Winthrop's testimony has a great deal of probative value. It was evidence of a similar robbery, only a week after Alice's alleged robbery, committed with a gun with a very unusual characteristic – a barrel painted red. While of course the jury will be prejudiced by this evidence, legal relevance addresses *unfair* prejudice, and the prejudice here would not likely be considered unfair. Instead, Winthrop's testimony is character evidence that fits the "independent relevance" requirements of FRE 404(b) – it is evidence of a common plan, and identity. Since it will not unfairly prejudice Dennis, it will be admitted. Since D doesn't recognize this, it's not the best response.

Answer 185

(B) is the best response,

because it represents a valid means by which the statute could be considered constitutional.

The main problem with the statute here has to do with equal protection. Public school desegregation plans are addressed at curing problems of equal protection; thus, by forbidding federal courts from enforcing desegregation plans, Congress seems to be acting in derogation of the Constitution.

By forbidding the federal courts from ordering the implementation of such plans, the law in these facts does an "end run" around the constitutionality issue. Under Article III, §2 of the Constitution, Congress is given the power to regulate the appellate (but not original) jurisdiction of federal courts. Thus, Congress could, for instance, stop federal courts from hearing appeals in cases involving abortion, and it could likewise stop the courts from hearing cases like the one under these facts. Since B offers a basis on which the Congressional act could be found constitutional, it's the best response.

(A) is not the best response,

because it misstates the law: Congress doesn't have the power to define equal protection violations – that's a judicial function.

The judiciary has the power to declare unconstitu-

tional the acts of other branches of government. Marbury v. Madison (1803). Congress is the exclusive holder of the legislative power, and the judiciary has the power to determine the constitutionality of Congress's actions. Thus, Congress could not determine whether its own conduct violate the equal protection clause. Since A states otherwise, it's not the best response.

(C) is not the best response,

because there's no evidence here that transportation of students would affect interstate commerce.

Congress has power to regulate interstate commerce, under Article I, §8, clause 3 of the Constitution. Under the "affectation doctrine," Congress can regulate any activity that has any appreciable direct or indirect effect on interstate commerce (states may regulate commerce when Congress intended that the states be able to regulate the activity in question). While the commerce power is admittedly broad, it would be unlikely that the power could be interpreted broadly enough to encompass the facts here. Public school desegregation would only concern local transportation, not interstate transportation, and it wouldn't have any appreciable effect on any interstate activity. As a result, the commerce power would not be a good basis for the constitutionality of the act. Since C doesn't recognize this, it's not the best response.

(D) is not the best response,

because although Congress can attach "strings" to federal grants, it couldn't do so under these facts.

Public school desegregation plans are designed to promote equal protection of the law. Presumably, failure to implement such a plan in the face of an equal protection violation would be unconstitutional. Thus, if Congress were to insist that federal courts not order desegregation, it would be promoting an equal protection violation. While Congress can attach "strings" to federal grants to encourage permissible goals, like general welfare objectives, it can't act in derogation of those goals – and that's what the argument in option D would do. As a result, D is not the best response.

Answer 186

(D) is the best response,

because it correctly identifies the most likely basis on which the statute could be found unconstitutional.

In order to understand why this is the best response, you have to look closely at exactly what this law does. When a federal court orders the implementation of a desegregation plan, it's doing so in order to remedy an equal protection violation. The only body of government that's empowered to define constitutional standards is the judiciary, not Congress, which only has legislative powers to implement Constitutional provisions, like the Fourteenth Amendment. By passing a law forbidding the federal court from remedying equal protection violations, Congress is, in effect, encroaching on the judicial function. This would be a strong argument against the constitutionality of the act, making D the best response.

(A) is not the best response,
because it misstates both the law and the facts.

First, as to the law, Congress has power over interstate commerce, so it cannot, by definition, unduly burden interstate commerce. Congress could have tandem trucks jump through flaming hoops if it wanted to, presumably.

It's *states* that cannot unduly burden interstate commerce, not federal government.

Say the statute here *was* a state statute, and thus was subject to the confines of Congress's commerce power. Option A still wouldn't be the best response, because the statute here does not unduly burden interstate commerce. Under the "affectation doctrine," Congress can regulate any activity that has any appreciable direct or indirect effect on interstate commerce. While the commerce power is admittedly broad, it would be unlikely that the power could be interpreted broadly enough to encompass the facts here. Public school desegregation would only concern local transportation, not interstate transportation, and it wouldn't have any appreciable effect on any interstate activity. Thus, even if the statute here were a state statute, it wouldn't be constitutionally repugnant. Since option A doesn't recognize that the law is federal and that it doesn't impact interstate commerce, it's not the best response.

(B) is not the best response,
because it misstates the law.

Under Article III, §1 of the Constitution, Congress has the power to establish inferior federal courts – meaning beneath the Supreme Court, not "inferior" in the sense of quality – and to change federal appellate jurisdiction. Thus, Congress could forbid federal courts from hearing cases involving desegregation cases at all. As a result, this would not be a strong argument against the constitutionality of the act. Since B states otherwise, it's not the best response.

(C) is not the best response,
because the privileges and immunities clause of the Fourteenth Amendment prohibits certain kinds of *state* actions, not *federal* actions – and the act here is Congressional.

The privileges and immunities clause voids those state enactments which clearly infringe privileges enjoyed under national citizenship. It is construed narrowly, typically being restricted to fundamental rights which are shared in common by all citizens, namely:

1/The right to travel freely from state to state;

2/To petition Congress for redress of grievances;

3/To vote for national officers;

4/To assemble peaceably; and

5/To discuss matters of national legislation.

Here, since the statute in question is a federal statute, the privileges and immunities clause could not prohibit it. Even if the statute here were a state statute, the privileges and immunities clause wouldn't be exceptionally helpful, since the due process clause and equal protection clause are more typically used to protect individual rights. However, the lynchpin of the problem with option C is that the privileges and immunities clause doesn't apply to the federal government. Since C states otherwise, it's not the best response.

Answer 187

(A) is the best response,
because it recognizes that Reliable will be liable for failing to maintain the easement.

Under these facts, there is an expressly-created easement for constructing and using overhead electric lines. Since Reliable Electric was given the right to use Maria's land, it's the "dominant" tenement holder (and Maria is the "servient" tenement holder, since it's her land that's burdened by the easement). The rule on maintaining easements is that the dominant tenement holder has both the *right* and the *duty* to maintain the easement. Thus, Reliable would have the *right* to enter Maria's land and repair the line and poles, as necessary, and Maria could not object to this interference. However, Reliable could not exceed the interference necessary for maintenance; here, its failure to maintain the line and poles resulted in an interference with Maria's land outside the scope of the easement – namely, the damage caused by the fire. As a result, Maria will be able to recover for damages to the lumber yard. Since option A recognizes this, it's the best response.

(B) is not the best response,
because although it arrives at the correct result, it misstates the responsibility of the dominant tenement holder.

Option B suggests that Reliable will be strictly liable for any damage the easement causes to the servient tenement holder. This is incorrect both in that holding an easement is not a source of strict liability, and some damage may not result in liability at all.

Strict liability has three general sources: animals, ultra-hazardous activities, and defective, unreasonably dangerous products (strict liability can also be created by statute or case law). Here, none of these are particularly applicable. Thus, strict liability cannot be applied to Reliable Electric's maintenance of the easement.

Instead, Reliable Electric's liability will have to be determined by analyzing its rights and duties as a dominant tenement holder. Under these facts, there is an expressly-created easement for constructing and using overhead electric lines. Since Reliable Electric was given the right to use Maria's land, it's the "dominant" tenement holder (and Maria is the "servient" tenement holder, since it's her land that's burdened by the easement). The rule on maintaining easements is that the dominant tenement holder has both the *right* and the *duty* to maintain the easement. Thus, Reliable has the right to enter and maintain the pole and lines, and as long as it acts within this scope, it cannot be liable for damage to Maria's land,

However, what option B fails to recognize is that the interference with Maria's land in this problem is *outside* the scope of the easement. Since Reliable failed to maintain the easement, and this resulted in damage to Maria's land *exceeding* the scope of the easement, Reliable will be liable. Since B doesn't recognize this, it's not the best response.

(C) is not the best response,

because it misstates the duty of the servient tenement holder, and arrives at the wrong result.

Under these facts, there is an expressly-created easement for constructing and using overhead electric lines, Since Reliable Electric was given the right to use Maria's land, it's the "dominant" tenement holder (and Maria is the "servient" tenement holder, since it's her land that's burdened by the easement). Option C suggests that, barring any language to the contrary, the servient tenement holder must notify the dominant tenement holder of defective conditions concerning the easement. In fact, that's not the case. Maria and Reliable *could* have included such a provision in the agreement, but they didn't, and it won't be implied.

The rule on maintaining easements is that the dominant tenement holder has both the *right* and the *duty* to maintain the easement. Thus, Reliable has the right to enter and maintain the pole and lines, and as long as it acts within this scope, it cannot be liable for damage to Maria's land. The problem is that the interference with Maria's land in this problem is *outside* the scope of the easement, Since Reliable failed to maintain the easement, and this resulted in damage to Maria's land *exceeding* the scope of the easement, Reliable will be liable.

In fact, you have a clue that option C couldn't be correct in the facts themselves. Assuming arguendo that the servient tenement holder *did* have the duty to notify the dominant tenement holder of defects, you'd have to question whether the defect here was one Maria should have recognized. All you're told is that the line was improperly maintained, and as a result it fell during a storm. It's questionable whether anyone this side of an expert on electric lines could tell, merely by looking at it, whether a line has been properly maintained. In any case, since option C places a duty on Maria which doesn't, in fact, exist, it's not the best response.

(D) is not the best response,

because it fails to recognize Reliable Electric's duty to Maria.

Under these facts, there is an expressly-created easement for constructing and using overhead electric lines. Since Reliable Electric was given the right to use Maria's land, it's the "dominant" tenement holder (and Maria is the "servient" tenement holder, since it's her land that's burdened by the easement). Option D suggests that Reliable Electric has the right to repair for its own benefit, and that this is inconsistent with the duty to repair for someone else's benefit. Not only does this misstate the rule, but it's logically incorrect.

The rule on maintaining easements is that the dominant tenement holder has both the *right* and the *duty* to maintain the easement. Thus, option D is correct in so far as it states that Reliable has a right to repair the lines; but this is only part of the correct rule, since it ignores Reliable's *duty* to Maria. Reliable has the right to enter and maintain the pole and lines, and as long as it acts within this scope, it cannot be liable for damage to Maria's land. The problem is that the interference with Maria's land in this problem is *outside* the scope of the easement. Since Reliable failed to maintain the easement, and this resulted in damage to Maria's land *exceeding* the scope of the easement, Reliable will be liable.

In any case, Reliable's right to repair for its own benefit is not inconsistent with its duty to repair for Maria's benefit. If Reliable maintains the lines, there will be no glitch in service to its customers who are serviced by the line. This has the added benefit of ensuring that there's no excessive interference with Maria's land. Thus, Reliable's rights and its duty to Maria are not inconsistent. Since D states otherwise, it's not the best response.

Answer 188

(C) is the best response,

because it correctly states that the assignment will be effective, while leaving Stretch liable for breach of contract.

Central to determining the legal effect of the prohibition is determining how it will be interpreted. Under the UCC, barring circumstances to the contrary, a prohibition against assigning the contract *only* prevents delegating duties, not assigning rights. UCC §2-210(3). Here, Stretch, by "assigning the contract" to Finance Co., likewise only assigned its *rights* under the contract – that is, its right to payment from Sartorial. §2-210(2) allows assignment unless the assignment would materially change the other party's duty, materially increase the risk the contract imposes, or materially impair the other party's chance of receiving/ return performance. None of these would occur here. Thus, option C is correct in stating that the assignment itself was effective.

The assignment aside, Stretch *would* be liable for breach of contract, since it promised not to assign the contract. While Sartorial would like only recover nominal damages, the claim itself would nonetheless be valid. Option C also recognizes this. Sine Option C correctly addresses the effectiveness of the assignment *and* the breach, it's the best response.

(A) is not the best response,

because the assignment will be valid in spite of the prohibition in the contract.

Your analysis here centers on how the prohibition provision will be interpreted. First, a covenant "not to assign the contract" would be interpreted, barring circumstances to the contrary, to prevent *only* the delegation of duties, *not* the assignment of rights. UCC §2-210(3). Here, Stretch, by "assigning the contract" to Finance Company, likewise only assigned its *rights* under the contract – that is, its right to payment from Sartorial. Since Stretch only assigned its rights under the contract to Finance, and the UCC provides that such an assignment is effective in spite of a contractual prohibition otherwise, the assignment's effective. §2-210(2) allows assignment unless the assignment would materially change the other party's duty, materially increase the risk the contract imposes, or materially impair the other party's chance of receiving\ return performance. None of these would occur here. Of course, Sartorial *will* have a claim for breach of covenant against Stretch, but this does not affect the effectiveness of the assignment.

If you chose this response, you may have been thinking of contract language that's almost the same, with dramatically different effects. Had the provision stated that "any assignment shall be void," the attempted assignment would be *voidable* at the obligor's (Sartorial's) objection. The distinction is founded on the idea that a covenant not to assign is said to destroy the right, not the power, to assign; the "void" language destroys the right *and* the power.

Since A mistakenly states that the assignment will be ineffective, it's not the best response.

(B) is not the best response,

because the covenant *will* have legal effect – Sartorial will have a claim against Stretch for breach of covenant.

The effect turns on the interpretation of the prohibition against assignment. Under the UCC, barring circumstances indicating the contrary, a prohibition against assigning the contract prevents *only* delegation of duties, *not* the assignment of rights. UCC §2-210(3). Here, Stretch, by "assigning the contract" to Finance Co., likewise only assigned its *rights* under the contract – that is, its right to payment from Sartorial. §2-210(2) allows assignment unless the assignment would materially change the other party's duty, materially increase the risk the contract imposes, or materially impair the other party's chance of receiving\ return performance. None of these would occur here. Thus, option B is correct in as far as the prohibition will have no legal effect on the validity of the assignment *itself*.

However, option B ignores that Sartorial *will* have a valid claim against Stretch for breach of covenant. While this will likely only merit nominal damages, the claim *itself* will be valid. Since the breach of covenant claim is a legal effect that option B ignores, option B isn't the best response.

(D) is not the best response,

because it misstates the law.

Under the UCC, a prohibition against assignment in the contract would apply to *both* buyer and seller. UCC §2-210. Instead, what's central to resolving this question is determining how a court would *interpret* the prohibition against assignment. Under UCC §2-210(3), a promise "not to assign this contract" refers only to a delegation of duties, *not* an assignment of rights, barring circumstances indicating otherwise. Here, Stretch is only assigning its right to payment, as security for a loan, to Finance. Thus, it's only assigning a right, and this won't be covered by the prohibition. While Stretch will be liable for breach of promise, the assignment itself will be effective. Since D misstates the application of prohibitions against assignment, and ignores the central issue, it's not the best response.

Answer 189

(B) is the best response,

because it correctly identifies that Stretch owes Finance the entire $5,000.

Under these facts, you're told that the assignment was effective. That means that Stretch's rights under the contract were extinguished, and Finance stood in Stretch's shoes as to the right to Sartorial's performance. This assignment right, like any contractual right, is enforceable. Thus, when Stretch received the payment without any right to it, Finance could recover that payment from Stretch.

Note that Finance could not seek payment from Sartorial directly because *Sartorial had not yet been notified of the assignment.* Until he *is,* performance to the assignor (Stretch) protects him from liability to the assignee (Finance). Since option B correctly identifies that only Stretch is liable to Finance, it's the best response.

(A) is not the best response,

because it's *Stretch* who'd be liable to Finance Company, not *Sartorial.*

The key to Sartorial's lack of liability to Finance is that it was *unaware of the assignment.* While you're told that the assignment was effective, this only means that Stretch's rights under the contract were transferred to Finance. It doesn't address specifically to whom Sartorial's duty of performance is owed. The rule is that, until the obligor (here, Sartorial) has knowledge of the assignment, he is free to continue rendering performance to the assignor (here, Stretch). Only once he knows of the assignment is he required to perform for the assignee (here, Finance). Even if you didn't remember this rule, there's a strong clue under these facts that option A *can't* be the best response: It makes Sartorial pay twice. Since A would mistakenly make Sartorial pay Finance, it can't be the best response.

(C) is not the best response,

because Stretch owes Finance the entire $5,000, and Sartorial owes Finance nothing.

The key to Sartorial's lack of liability to Finance is that it was *unaware of the assignment.* While you're told that the assignment was effective, this only means that Stretch's rights under the contract were transferred to Finance. It doesn't address specifically to whom Sartorial's duty of performance is owed. The rule is that, until the obligor (here, Sartorial) has knowledge of the assignment, he is free to continue rendering performance to the assignor (here, Stretch). Only once he knows of the assignment is he required to perform for the assignee (here, Finance).

Instead, Stretch would be liable to Finance for the entire $5,000, because Stretch had no right to the $5,000. A valid assignment extinguishes the contractual rights in the assignor (here, Stretch). Any rights he had were assigned to Finance, and thus Finance is entitled to the $5,000 payment. Since C doesn't recognize this, it's not the best response.

(D) is not the best response,

because although Sartorial owes Finance nothing, Stretch owes Finance $5,000.

The key to Sartorial's lack of liability to Finance is that it was *unaware of the assignment.* While you're told that the assignment was effective, this only means that Stretch's rights under the contract were transferred to Finance. It doesn't address specifically to whom Sartorial's duty of performance is owed. The rule is that, until the obligor (here, Sartorial) has knowledge of the assignment, he is free to continue rendering performance to the assignor (here, Stretch). Only once he knows of the assignment is he required to perform for the assignee (here, Finance).

However, Stretch would be liable to Finance for the entire $5,000, because Stretch had no right to the $5,000. A valid assignment extinguishes the contractual rights in the assignor (here, Stretch). Any rights he had were assigned to Finance, and thus Finance is entitled to the $5,000 payment. Sine D doesn't recognize this, it's not the best response.

Answer 190

(D) is the best response.

As to alternative I:

This is not correct, because Virginia Wear is an *intended* beneficiary, not an *incidental* beneficiary.

This distinction is important, because, as you know, intended beneficiaries have enforceable rights under a contract (once the benefits vest), and incidental benefi-

ciaries do not.

This is how you distinguish the two: Look to the intent of the promisee (the one to whom the duty in question is owed). If it is promisee's primary intent that the third party receive benefit from promisor's performance, the third party is an intended beneficiary; if he doesn't, the third party is an incidental beneficiary. Criteria to examine include a statement of intent in the contract, a close relationship between the promisee and the beneficiary, identifiability of the beneficiary before contract is discharged, and promisor's performance directly to the third party.

Here, the duty involved is the *payment,* and the promisee is Stretch (since he's the one to whom payment is owed). The contract provision indicates unequivocally that it's Stretch's intent that Virginia Wear benefit from Sartorial's performance. Thus, Virginia Wear is an intended, not an incidental, beneficiary – and alternative I is incorrect.

As to alternative II:

This is not correct, because Virginia Wear has *no* rights under the contract until it *detrimentally relies* on the contract (under the majority view).

As an intended beneficiary, Virginia Wear has enforceable rights under the contract *only* once its rights *vest.* Before the rights vest, the parties are free to modify or rescind the contract without the beneficiary's permission.

In order to determine when the rights vest, you have to determine whether Virginia Wear is a *creditor* or a *donee* beneficiary (since their rights vest at different times). A creditor beneficiary is one to whom promisee (here, Stretch) owes a pre-existing duty, which promisor's (here, Sartorial's) performance will fulfill. Here, Virginia Wear is a creditor beneficiary, because Stretch owed Virginia money. (By the way, all non-creditor beneficiaries are donee beneficiaries.)

Under the majority view, the creditor beneficiary's rights only vest when he has detrimentally relied on the contract. The minority view, and that of the Restatement, requires only that the creditor manifest assent to the promisor (here, Sartorial) paying the debt instead of the promisee (Stretch). Whichever test you use, Virginia Wear's rights hadn't vested under the contract, because it didn't even *know* about the original agreement until after the assignment. Thus, the agreement could be changed in any way without regard to Virginia Wear's interests, contrary to what alternative II provides.

Even if you were thinking that both Virginia Wear and Finance were assignees, alternative II *still* wouldn't prevail, because its assignment would have been revocable (since it didn't give valuable consideration for the assignment, it didn't foreseeably rely on the assignment to its detriment, it didn't receive payment or performance from the obligor [Sartorial], and no symbol of the assignment [e.g., bank book] was transferred). Reassigning a previous, revocable assignment gives the second assignee priority. Thus, even if you misconstrued Virginia Wear as an assignee instead of a beneficiary, alternative II would still be incorrect.

Answer 191

(D) is the best response,

because it correctly identifies the central reason Sartorial will prevail: It cancelled the contract in good faith.

The contract here was a "requirements" contract. That is, Sartorial agreed to purchase all of its requirements for elasticized fabric from Stretch, for three years. This doesn't mean that both businesses must stay in business for three years or be in breach of contract. Instead, either business can terminate operations, buy retiring or selling the business, as long as this is done in *good faith*. Thus, if the termination was done solely to avoid losses under the requirements contract, it wouldn't be valid and Sartorial would be liable for breach of contract; however, here you're told that Sartorial's discontinued need for the elastic was in good faith. Thus, this will not violate the contract. UCC §2-306(1), comment 1. Since option D provides a sound basis for a defense, it's the best response.

(A) is not the best response,

because it mischaracterizes the facts.

As a general rule, most contract rights are assignable. Option A is theoretically correct in stating that "personal" rights are not assignable. "Personal" services are those that involve personal characteristics to such an extent that it would be unfair to expect the obligor (here, Sartorial) to perform for a third party. "Personal" services typically include those of lawyers, doctors, architects, authors, artists, and the like.

Of course, personal service contracts aren't the *only* non-assignable contracts. The common law, as embodied in UCC §2-210(2), disallows assignment whenever the assignment would materially change the other party's duty, materially increase the risk the contract imposes, or materially impair the other party's chance of receiving return performance.

Under the facts here, the right owed to Stretch under the contract – to receive money – clearly was *not* personal, contrary to what option A states .Beyond that, assigning the right to receive payment wouldn't affect *Sartorial's* rights under the contract. Thus, since the right *was* assignable, arguing that it *wasn't* won't help Sartorial, making A not the best response.

(B) is not the best response,

because although it states correctly the *general* rule, it ignores the fact that the facts here would not fit the general rule.

Under UCC §2-210(4), an assignment "of the contract" constitutes *both* an assignment of rights *and* a delegation of duties, *barring language or circumstances to the contrary*. However, the facts here repre-

sent the most significant exception to this rule: Where the assignment is made as security for a loan. Under such circumstances, it's clear that a delegation of duties was *not* intended.

Note that an assignment of rights under the contract, from Stretch to Finance, would have been valid because the right to receive money is assignable. A delegation of duties wouldn't have been, since Finance is incapable, under these facts, of providing elasticized fabric, thus making it unlikely it could perform under the contract. In any case, since B doesn't recognize that the facts here don't fit the general "assignment of contract includes delegation" rule, it's not the best response.

(C) is not the best response,

because it misstates the facts: The original contract *was* supported by consideration.

The contract here was a "requirements" contract. That is, Sartorial agreed to purchase all of its requirements for elasticized fabric from Stretch, for three years. As with any contract, a requirements contract requires consideration – bargained-for exchange and either detriment to the promisee or benefit to the promisor. The consideration in a "requirements" contract is provided here by Sartorial's giving up the right to buy from anyone else, thus constituting a detriment. Thus, Sartorial could not argue that the contract was unsupported by consideration, making C not the best response.

Answer 192

(C) is the best response,

because it identifies that interpretation of the delay is the central issue in the case.

In non-UCC cases, a reasonable delay is generally *not* considered a material breach. Here, since there's no transaction in goods involved, the common law will control. Thus, absent extraordinary circumstances, known to Seth when the contract was created, that would make the May 1 deadline essential, Seth's delay would only be a minor breach, requiring that Bob perform and sue for damages.

If time *was* of the essence, *any* delay would be a material breach. Thus, this is a key issue in determining if Bob was entitled to cancel the contract.

Keep in mind that the UCC treats delays somewhat differently, due to the "perfect tender" rule under §2-601. That is, the presumption in contracts for the sale of goods is that time is of the essence. However, this isn't as strict as it sounds, due to the seller's right to cure defective performance. §2-508. Where performance is late, Seller can *still* cure, if he notifies the buyer of his intent to cure, and he had reason to believe buyer would accept the delay (the delay making the goods, in effect, non-conforming).

Since C identifies the central issue on these facts, it's the best response.

(A) is not the best response,

because it ignores the central issue where there is a delay in performance: Whether time was of the essence.

In non-UCC cases, a reasonable delay is generally *not* considered a material breach. Here, since there's no transaction in goods involved, the common law will control. Thus, absent extraordinary circumstances, known to Seth when the contract was created, that would make the May 1 deadline essential, Seth's delay would only be a minor breach, requiring that Bob perform and sue for damages.

If time *was* of the essence, *any* delay would be a material breach. Thus, this is a key issue in determining if Bob was entitled to cancel the contract.

Seth's due diligence is, at best, of minor importance in the case. If time was of the essence, Seth's diligence is entirely irrelevant; if it *wasn't*, then Seth's diligence would be relevant in determining if Seth substantially performed under the contract. However, since the significance of the delay is the central issue, and A ignores this, it's not the best response.

(B) is not the best response,

because it ignores the central issue where there is a delay in performance: Whether time was of the essence.

In non-UCC cases, a reasonable delay is generally *not* considered a material breach. Here, since there's no transaction in goods involved, the common law will control. Thus, absent extraordinary circumstances, known to Seth when the contract was created, that would make the May 1 deadline essential, Seth's delay would only be a minor breach, requiring that Bob perform and sue for damages.

If time *was* of the essence, *any* delay would be a material breach. Thus, this is a key issue in determining if Bob was entitled to cancel the contract.

If time was *not* of the essence, Bob's undue hardship could become important in determining whether Seth substantially performed under the contract (thus meriting return performance). However, since option B ignores the central issue, it's not the best response.

(D) is not the best response,

because it ignores a central issue in the case: Whether time was of the essence.

In non-UCC cases, a reasonable delay is generally *not* considered a material breach. Here, since there's no transaction in goods involved, the common law will control. Thus, absent extraordinary circumstances, known to Seth when the contract was created, that would make the May 1 deadline essential, Seth's delay would only be a minor breach, requiring that Bob perform and sue for damages.

If time *was* of the essence, *any* delay would be a material breach. Thus, this is a key issue in determining if Bob was entitled to cancel the contract.

If time was *not* of the essence, and the four-week delay was considered a minor breach, then Bob's good faith in cancelling the contract would be an issue. However, if the delay was not a material breach, Bob would probably have to perform under the contract and sue for any damages the delay cost him. Since Bob's good faith is a secondary issue at best under these facts, D is not the best response.

Answer 193

(D) is the best response,

because it focuses on the central issue and analyzes it correctly: Doris's destruction of the deed would probably be insufficient to convey title back to Metterly.

In order to make a valid gift of real property, there must be the intent to bestow a gift, coupled with delivery of the deed. Under these facts, Metterly made a valid gift to Doris. However, Doris's mere destruction of the deed, *even though it was at Metterly's request,* would probably not constitute either an intent to make a gift *or* delivery of the deed, with the most obvious shortfall being in delivery of the deed. The thing that makes these facts a bit more difficult to analyze is that Metterly is the original grantor. However, this wouldn't change the rule, and indicates why it's so important on MBE questions just to *mechanically apply rules*. In this case, doing so reveals that title to Brownacre was still in Doris, making D the best response.

(A) is not the best response,

because the factor it relies on is irrelevant, and its conclusion is incorrect.

Even though Doris did not pay for Brownacre, she can still be the owner of it. A grantor may make a gift of real property by delivering a deed, with the intent to make a gift. These requirements are satisfied here. (A "quitclaim deed" is merely a deed which conveys whatever interest the grantor had in the property; it has no warranties associated with it.) Since the conveyance was valid, Doris acquired valid title to Brownacre via quitclaim deed, making A not the best response.

(B) is not the best response,

because it misstates the law.

While the conveyance from Metterly to Doris was valid, Brownacre was never conveyed back to Metterly, because mere destruction of a deed is not sufficient for a conveyance. In order to make a gift of real property, there are two elements required: Intent to make a gift, and delivery of a deed. Here, Doris's destruction of the deed would probably not constitute delivery of the deed. Furthermore, there is no evidence that Doris intended to make a gift of the property back to Metterly, since voluntarily destroying the deed would probably not suffice. As a result, Brownacre would remain Doris's, making B not the best response.

(C) is not the best response,

because it wrongly applies undue influence to these facts, and does not focus on the central issue involved.

First, the facts do not suggest undue influence. Undue influence is a kind of constructive fraud, under which a person is deprived of his free will by another. This type of thing typically turns up in wills cases, where a schemer in the family of the testator exerts moral coercion on the testator. The kind of thing Bette Davis did to Joan Crawford in "Whatever Happened to Baby Jane?" – you know. The facts here just don't measure up. Second, option C does not focus on the central issue, which is whether, in fact, Doris's destroying the deed would constitute a valid conveyance back to Metterly. In fact, it probably would *not,* since a valid gift of real property requires an intent to bestow a gift coupled with delivery of the deed. Neither of these is apparently present here. As a result, C is not the best response.

Answer 194

(A) is the best response,

because it correctly identifies that Cross will be liable, and the central reason for this under these facts.

The thing that makes this problem tricky is that Cross was not alone in his negligence; Owner was negligent in maintaining the brakes, and Spouse was negligent in not passing along Owner's warning. However, Cross's liability to Motorist will be determined by applying the negligence elements to Cross's act, and seeing if there are any defenses. A negligence claim requires that defendant failed to exercise such care as a reasonable person in his position would have exercised, this must have been a breach of the duty to prevent the foreseeable risk of harm to anyone in plaintiff's position, and this breach must have caused plaintiff's damages.

Here, Cross breached his duty to act reasonably under the circumstances by ignoring the traffic signal, satisfying the duty and breach elements. There's no damages issue raised by these facts, so the only sticky point is causation. When there are multiple causes of an event – as is the case here – the defendant will be liable if his act was a "substantial factor" in bringing about plaintiff's damages. That's the case here – by driving into the intersection, Cross substantially contributed to Motorist's damages. Now, this doesn't mean that Owner and Spouse *wouldn't* be liable for negligence – they were negligent, too, but their negligence won't exonerate Cross!

Also, it's tempting to believe that the faulty brakes should relieve Cross of liability, since without them, Motorist could have avoided the accident. However, this won't exonerate Cross because Motorist hitting Cross is within the risk Cross's negligence created. Beyond *all* this, A correctly points out that Cross has no defense because Motorist was without fault. He neither knew, nor had reason to know, the brakes were bad. Since A correctly identifies the result and the main rea-

son for it, it's the best response.

(B) is not the best response,

because Spouse's negligence is not relevant, since her negligence cannot be imputed to Motorist.

Under these facts, Cross was negligent in failing to stop at a stop sign; owner was negligent in failing to maintain the brakes and failing to notify Motorist, and Spouse was negligent in failing to tell Motorist about the brakes. However, in Motorist's claim against Cross, all that will count is whether Cross's negligence caused Motorist's damages, and whether Spouse's negligence can be imputed to Motorist so as to bar or reduce his recovery.

Here, there are two causes of Motorist's damages: Cross and Owner. Thus, Cross will be said to have caused Motorist's damages if his conduct was a substantial factor in producing them. It clearly was. Thus, Cross will be liable for negligence unless he has a defense. Motorist was not contributorily negligent, because he had no reason to know of the brakes' condition, and Spouse's negligence can't be imputed to him merely on the basis of their marital relationship (unlike vicarious liability situations, where, for instance, an employee's negligence can be imputed to his employer). Since B would wrongly deny Motorist recovery on the basis of Spouse's negligence, it's not the best response.

(C) is not the best response,

because it misstates the law and arrives at an incorrect response.

C suggests that Spouse's negligence should be imputed to Motorist, thus denying him recovery due to contributory negligence. However, the spousal relationship hasn't been sufficient to impute negligence since women stopped wearing bustles. In the old days a woman's negligence was imputed to her husband because, in law, they were viewed as one. Today, this kind of relationship will not suffice; rather, a plaintiff is only barred from recovery by the negligence of a third party if the relationship between them is such that plaintiff would be vicariously liable for the third party's acts injuring another. Since C does not offer a basis on which Motorist will be denied liability, it's not the best response.

(D) is not the best response,

because the brake failure will not absolve Cross of liability.

In order to be liable in negligence, Defendant must have failed to exercise such care as a reasonable person in his position would have exercised, this must have been a breach of the duty to prevent the foreseeable risk of harm to anyone in plaintiff's position, and this breach must have caused plaintiff's damages.

Cross violated his duty to exercise such care as a reasonable person in his position would have exercised by driving through the red light. In order to be liable, though, causation must also be proven. The main problem with causation here is that there are *three* causes of Motorist's damages: The faulty brakes (Owner's negligence), the lack of warning (Spouse's negligence), and the car in the intersection (Cross's negligence). Where there are multiple causes, the test for causation is the substantial factor test: Defendant's conduct is said to cause an event when it was a substantial factor in producing it. That's the case here – Cross's negligence was a material element in Motorist's damages. While Owner and Spouse could be liable for *their* negligence *as well*, this alone does not relieve Cross of liability. The faulty brakes wouldn't be considered a superseding force breaking the chain of causation, because, apart from anything else, a superseding force must create results that are unforeseeable, thus removing them from the risk created by defendant's original act. Here, Motorist hitting Cross is exactly what Cross's negligence, by pulling into the intersection, would be likely to result in. Since D doesn't recognize this, it's not the best response.

Answer 195

(B) is the best response,

because it correctly applies the comparative negligence doctrine to these facts.

Under comparative negligence, Plaintiff is allowed to recover a portion of his damages from Defendant, reflecting the "percentage" of his injuries Defendant caused. Under *pure* comparative negligence, the type involved here, Plaintiff can recover damages no matter to what extent his own negligence contributed to his injuries. (Under the other type, modified comparative negligence, Plaintiff can only recover damages if his own fault caused less than a set fraction of his own injuries – typically, 50%.) Here, Spouse's act contributed to her own injuries, because her failure to warn Motorist (and her knowingly riding in a car with defective brakes) was a substantial factor in producing her injuries. Cross was also negligent because his entering the intersection was also a substantial factor in causing Spouse's damages. Thus, under comparative negligence, Spouse's recovery will be reduced proportionally with her own negligence. Since B correctly identifies that this is how comparative negligence will apply to these facts, it's the best response.

(A) is not the best response,

because Motorist's lack of fault will not be relevant to Spouse's recovery.

In a suit between Cross and Spouse, Cross's breach of duty resulting in damage to Spouse will determine the validity of the claim itself, and Spouse's negligence contributing to her own injuries will determine any defenses. Here, Cross's negligence and Spouse's negligence combined to cause Spouse's injuries, since each was a substantial factor in the accident. As a

result, Motorist's *lack* of negligence will be irrelevant – it can't be imputed to Spouse. Instead, under comparative negligence, plaintiff may recover from defendant a portion of his damages, reflecting the "percentage" of his injuries defendant caused. Thus, under these facts, Spouse's recovery would be reduced by a portion representing her negligence in failing to warm Motorist of the faulty brakes, or, alternatively, reflecting her voluntarily being a passenger in a car knowing it had faulty brakes. Since A doesn't recognize this, it's not the best response.

(C) is not the best response,

because it misapplies the rules of causation to these facts, and arrives at the wrong result.

Comparative negligence is a doctrine which lessens the harsh results of contributory negligence. Under it, Plaintiff is allowed to recover a portion of his damages from Defendant, reflecting the "percentage" of his injuries Defendant caused. Thus, comparative negligence comes into play where both defendant's and plaintiff's negligence combine to result in plaintiff's damages. Therein lies the fault in the reasoning of option C. The causation element of negligence is determined by one of two tests, depending on how many causes were involved. Where there is one cause, the "but/for" test is used; with multiple causes (as here), the "substantial factor" test is used. C makes a mistake by applying the but/for test to a multiple cause situation. Instead, Cross will be liable for negligence if his act was a "substantial factor" in producing Spouse's damages; and her recovery will be reduced proportionally, under comparative negligence, to reflect the "percentage" of her injuries resulting from her own negligence. Since C doesn't recognize this, it's not the best response.

(D) is not the best response,

because it doesn't determine Spouse's recovery under comparative negligence.

Under comparative negligence, despite his *own* negligence, Plaintiff is allowed to recover a portion of his damages from Defendant, reflecting the "percentage" of his injuries Defendant caused. Thus, comparative negligence *presupposes* plaintiff's negligence; what it requires is an assessment of the degree to which plaintiff's negligence contributed to his own injuries. Under these facts, Spouse clearly was unreasonable in failing to warn Motorist of the faulty brakes (and, as to herself, in riding in the car, considering the brake problem). This was a substantial factor in causing her injuries. Thus, she was negligent. However, option D is incorrect in stating this will bar her recovery.

If you chose D, you were thinking of contributory negligence, where *any* negligence by plaintiff bars *all* recovery. In comparative negligence, the negligence of Plaintiff and Defendant is compared. Since D fails to recognize this, it's not the best response.

Answer 196

(A) is the best response,

because it correctly identifies a basis on which Owner will be liable to Motorist.

Negligence requires that defendant failed to exercise such care as a reasonable person in his position would have exercised, this must have been a breach of the duty to prevent the foreseeable risk of harm to anyone in Plaintiff's position, and this breach must have caused Plaintiff's damages.

Here, Owner's failure to warn Motorist would be considered a breach of duty, since he didn't exercise the care a reasonable person in his position would have exercised. So much for duty and breach. Damages are not an issue under these facts, so that leaves causation. While Spouse's failure to warn Motorist was a substantial factor in causing his damages, Owner was negligent in failing to warn Motorist directly, since he had no right to rely on Spouse to pass along the message, and the warning to Spouse could not be imputed to Motorist. While it's true that you'd *expect* Spouse to pass along the message, there's no legal basis for relieving Owner of his duty. Thus, as long as Owner's failure to warn Motorist was a substantial factor in causing his damages, the causation element is satisfied. Since A summarizes the elements of negligence as they apply to these facts, and arrives at the correct conclusion, A is the best response.

(B) is not the best response,

because the reasoning does not support a finding of strict liability, and, beyond that, it's unlikely strict liability would apply to these facts.

In general, strict liability has four elements: An absolute duty of care, breach of duty, which proximately causes plaintiff's injury, and damages. There are three, general sources of strict liability: Animals, abnormally dangerous activities, and defective, unreasonably dangerous products (in addition, strict liability can be imposed by case law or statutes). Thus, it wouldn't be enough, as B suggests, merely for there to be a defect: There would also need to be an absolute duty. Owner wouldn't be liable for strict product liability, because, apart from anything else, he's not a commercial supplier of cars. Lending a defective car would not be considered an abnormally dangerous activity. Since the animal basis wouldn't apply, and there's no statutory or case law source for strict liability on these facts, Owner wouldn't be strictly liable in tort.

Remember that this doesn't mean Owner will escape liability altogether; it's just that Motorist will have to prove *some* fault, at least negligence, in order to recover (which wouldn't be difficult to prove on these facts). Since B would impose liability on Owner without proof of fault, and fault would in fact need to be proven, B isn't the best response.

(C) isn't the best response,

because no matter how slight Owner's duty was, he breached it.

In fact, where a bailment is for the exclusive benefit of the bailee, the bailor's duty will, as C states, be slight. This however doesn't mean that the bailor can run roughshod over the bailee's rights. Here, Owner's failing to tell Motorist about the faulty brakes would satisfy *any* standard of negligence, no matter how slight. Since C fails to recognize this, it's not the best response.

(D) is not the best response,

because it incorrectly states that Spouse's negligence was the sole cause of Motorist's damages.

While it's true that Spouse was negligent in failing to pass along Owner's warning, this doesn't mean that Owner is relieved of liability for failing to warn Motorist directly. Unless Owner's warning to Spouse could be imputed to Motorist (for which there is *no* basis), then Owner would be required to inform Motorist directly; that is, he had no right to rely on Spouse. Thus, while Spouse's failure to warn contributed to Motorist's damages, Owner's negligent failure to warn was also a substantial factor in causing Motorist's injuries, making him liable in negligence. Since D would improperly shift Owner's liability to Spouse, it's not the best response.

Answer 197

(C) is the best response,

because Defendant satisfies all the elements of larceny.

A larceny requires a trespassory taking and carrying away of another's personal property, with intent to steal it. Here, Defendant is laboring under a mistake of law – he mistakenly believes that larceny doesn't include taking a dog. However, mistake of law, as a general principle, is not a valid defense. However, his act fulfills all the requirements of larceny, and as a result he'd likely be convicted. Since option C presents the facts, of these four options, in which Defendant is most likely to be found guilty of larceny, it's the best response.

(A) is not the best response,

because one of the elements of larceny – the intent to steal – is missing.

A larceny requires a trespassory taking and carrying away of personal property of another, with intent to steal it. Since Defendant intended to return the TV set the following day, his intent was to borrow, not steal. As a result, he cannot be liable for larceny – *even though* the upshot of his act was the same – Sue never got her TV back intact. Since Defendant under the facts in option A would not be liable for larceny, A cannot be the best response.

(B) is not the best response,

because Defendant's belief that he had a right to the

money negated his intent to steal it.

Since larceny requires intent, Defendant could not be convicted on these facts. A larceny requires a trespassory taking and carrying away of personal property of another, with intent to steal it. Here, Defendant's "claim of right" is a valid defense to larceny, since it is not larcenous to take another's property in repayment of a debt, *as long as* it is done openly and with full explanation of why the property is being taken. The theory is that the taking is being done to repay a debt, the element of intending to deprive another of his property is missing. Although the facts here do not describe the attendant circumstances – i.e., whether the taking was done openly – and although Defendant would certainly be liable for *some* crime, it's likely that Defendant would not be liable for larceny on these facts. As a result, B is not the best response.

(D) is not the best response,

because George's mistake negated one of the elements of larceny – intent to steal.

Larceny requires the taking and carrying away of another's personal property, with the intent to steal. Even an unreasonable mistake as to ownership negates the "intent to steal" requirement, as long as the belief is honest. (Of course, the more unreasonable the belief, the less likely it is that the jury will believe the mistake was "honest.") Option D is an attractive response, because your gut reaction is that unreasonable mistake cannot be a defense to a crime. However, as noted above, it negates the intent to steal. As a result, D is not the best response.

Answer 198

(D) is the best response,

because it is theoretically correct, and it will result in suppression of Desmond's confession under these facts.

The fruit of the poisonous tree doctrine holds that any evidence derived from unlawfully obtained evidence is inadmissible. Such "derivative" evidence is called the tainted fruit of the poisonous tree. Under these facts, the "poisonous tree" is the illegal arrest. The Miranda warnings, as D notes, are not enough, in and of themselves, to "purge the taint" of the illegal arrest (although they are a factor in favour of admissibility). However, courts also consider the wrongful intent of the police, intervening acts, and the proximity in time between the illegality and the confession in determining the admissibility of the confession. Here, although there was no wrongful intent, the police were only acting on an anonymous telephone call, which is insufficient to provide probable cause for arrest. Otherwise, there are no facts in favor of admissibility – the interrogation took place soon after the illegal arrest, and there were no intervening acts. As a result, the confession is likely to be excluded on the basis of this argument. Since the argument is theoretically correct, it applies to these

facts, and it would result in suppression of the evidence, it's Desmond's best argument – and as a result D is the best response.

(A) is not the best response,

because it misstates the rule of law, and does not correctly identify the facts it implies.

First, criminal defendants, in general, are not entitled to know the identity of their accusers, because informants are generally entitled to a privilege of anonymity at common law. (There are two principle exceptions to this rule: One, when the identity has already found out by those with cause to resent the communication (e.g., the disclosure was made to other law enforcement agencies), and two, where the identity is important to establishing a defense.)). The rationale of this rule is to encourage informants to come forward with information about crimes.

Thus, the rule option A states is wrong. In any case, what option A implies is not the identity of the accuser, since that's not what's involved in these facts, but rather the use by the police of an anonymous tip. An anonymous tip *can* be the basis for an arrest or search warrant as long as it meets the "totality of the circumstances" test from Illinois v. Gates (1983). Under that test, these elements will be weighed to determine the reliability of the informant: The informants prior use and reliability, his status as a member of a reliable group (e.g., a minister), clarity of detail in the tip, showing informant has personal knowledge of where evidence is located, and the tip includes a declaration against the informant's penal interest (e.g., that he bought narcotics from the individual named). Furthermore, courts will be less strict in determining the reliability of non-criminal informants than criminal informants. Under the facts here, the tip, without more facts, wouldn't be sufficient for a warrant since it wouldn't meet this test (at least certainly not for an *arrest*). What A ignores is the central flaw in the police behavior here: the arrest was unlawful, making the confession inadmissible as the tainted fruit of the poisonous tree, the poisonous tree being the unlawful arrest. Since A misstates the law and ignores the central flaw, it's not the best response.

(B) is not the best response,

because it misstates the law, and ignores the central flaw in the behavior of the police.

The Miranda warnings requirement is triggered by the police's intent to *interrogate* in custody, not by arrest. If the arrest here were otherwise valid, the police behaved correctly by stopping Desmond and reading him his rights *before* they asked him any questions. What option B *does* is to ignore the central flaw in the police behavior: The arrest was unlawful and the confession will be considered the tainted fruit of the poisonous tree (the poisonous tree being the unlawful arrest). Since B ignores this, and misstates the law, it cannot be the best response.

(C) is not the best response,

because although it states the law correctly and it *may* be true under these facts, it does not apply to these facts as closely as option D.

If Desmond's statements were, in fact, involuntary and coerced, they would not be admissible *even though* he was given his Miranda warnings first. A confession *must* be voluntary in order to be admissible. Here, it's possible that Desmond was intimidated by the way the arrest took place, making his confession involuntary and coerced. The problem is, the facts really don't indicate that Desmond's confession was involuntary; rather, it seems more like he was ratting on his friend to secure his own release. Thus, although C correctly states the law, it does not apply to these facts with any certainty, and so is not the best response.

Answer 199

(A) is the best response,

because it recognizes that federalism is the basis of Kane's strongest argument.

Under the Tenth Amendment, the states and the people retain all rights not delegated to the Constitution. Here, the Federal Securities Act would have been passed pursuant to Congress's broad commerce power. While that power is broad, it's not absolute. The concept of state sovereignty under the Tenth Amendment would mean that *some* state functions are outside the scope of Congress's commerce power. The state's legislative functions could well be outside the ambit of federal regulation. While this isn't an airtight argument, it's the best of the four possibilities, making A the best response.

(B) is not the best response,

because the speech and debate clause does not apply to state legislators.

Under Article I, §6 of the Constitution, members of Congress enjoy immunity "for any Speech or Debate in either House." The immunity covers only "legislative acts," which include those matter which form "an integral part of the deliberative and communicating processes" of Congress. This provision does not apply to the states, and thus Kane, as a state legislator, could not use it as an argument. Even if Kane *were* a federal legislator, it's unlikely that the source of the prosecution – a Federal Securities Act violation – could be considered "legislative business." In any case, the central reason this argument is not good for Kane is that he isn't covered by speech and debate immunity as a state legislator. Since B doesn't recognize this, it's not the best response.

(C) is not the best response,

due to operation of the Supremacy Clause.

Under the Supremacy Clause, found in Article VI, §2 of the Constitution, federal law takes precedence over inconsistent state laws. That's the essence of the issue

here. Congress would have power to legislate concerning securities under its commerce power, thus making the Federal Securities Act valid. Thus, any state law contradicting the federal act would be invalid. In fact, under these facts there is no indication of any state law concerning legislative immunity. Under the Supremacy Clause, it doesn't matter – as long as Congress has to the power legislate in an area, even if a state has the power to legislate in that area as well, the federal law will control. (Note that this is only true where the power is *concurrent* – that is, held by both the federal and state governments). Since option C ignores the application of the Supremacy Clause, it's not the best response.

(D) is not the best response,

because such an application would not constitute a due process violation.

When the effect of a governmental activity amounts to the deprivation of a property interest or right, there's a potential due process problem. However, that's not what Kane's immunity argument is about. Due process has nothing to do with immunity; it has to do with fair process when a right or privilege is limited. Thus, what's at issue here is not whether Kane's rights or privileges were fairly limited, but whether he's immune from prosecution all together; as a result, there's no due process issue. Since D doesn't recognize this, it's not the best response.

Answer 200

(C) is the best response,

because it's the only response that addresses the crux of Kane's defense: Federalism.

The conflict here is between Congress's commerce power, and state autonomy. By stating that state legislative business is immune from federal scrutiny, Kane is arguing that state sovereignty under the Tenth Amendment puts some state functions outside the scope of even the broadest Congressional powers. Congress's commerce power, under which the Federal Securities Act would be passed, is a very broad power. While Congress's power would mean that it can pass laws affecting the states, the concept of federalism limits that power, such that Congress could not significantly interfere with state governmental functions.

The facts here suggest that the Federal Securities Act, as applied to Kane's case, does not constitute a significant interference with state government. Under these facts, it's not the state government itself that's under scrutiny, but rather Kane's activities regarding a state-owned corporation. This, applying the securities laws to this wouldn't address Kane's legislative functions, but rather his functions pursuant to the corporation. This would push the activity out of the ambit of traditional state functions and towards commerce, over which Congress clearly has power. This, option D addresses the central issue – federalism – and resolves it satisfactorily, making it the best response.

(A) is not the best response,

because it doesn't address the issue of federalism raised by Kane's defense.

The Federal Securities Act would have been passed by Congress pursuant to its commerce power. To say that Congress has plenary (i.e., full and complete) power under the commerce clause doesn't address the issue that, broad as the commerce power is, the concept of state sovereignty under the Tenth Amendment would mean that *some* state functions are outside the scope of that power. Since option A doesn't address the central issue, it can't be the best response.

(B) is not the best response,

because applying federal law to state legislators would not guarantee a republican form of government.

Under Article IV, §4 of the Constitution, Congress has the responsibility to "guarantee to every state...a republican form of government." This doesn't mean it has to promise that George Bush becomes president; instead, a republican government is one which derives all its powers from the people, directly or indirectly, such that the supreme power rests with the people. Congress's ability to impose liability on state legislators, while it may be valid, would do just the opposite of promoting republican government. Instead, a strong argument in favor of the validity of the law as applied to Kane would have to address his argument, which concerns the scope of Congress's ability to interfere with state government. Since B doesn't recognize this, and states an argument that if anything would be in Kane's favor, it's not the best response.

(D) is not the best response,

because the necessary and proper clause would not provide an argument to defeat Kane's defense.

Under the necessary and proper clause, Article I, §8, Congress has the power to make all laws necessary and proper to carry out its delegated powers. This means that if Congress is legislating toward a legitimate end, within the scope of the Constitution, then any means which are appropriate to reach that end, and are not prohibited, will be valid. The key word here is "prohibited." While the commerce power of Congress is broad, it is limited by the doctrine of federalism; that is, pursuant to the concept of state sovereignty under the Tenth Amendment, *some* state functions are outside the scope of that power. This is the essence of Kane's defense – that state legislative business is immune to federal regulation – and relying on the necessary and proper clause doesn't address this at all. If a Congressional enactment was not necessary and proper to effectuate a delegated power, it wouldn't be valid; but even if such an enactment comports with the necessary and proper clause, it can still be invalid due to the doctrine of federalism. Since D doesn't recognize this, it's not the best response.

ANSWER SHEETS

The following pages of answer sheets have been provided for your use. The A.M. and P.M. Practice Exam sheets are replicas of those that you will see on the Bar Exam. The individual subject answer sheet has been modified to provide you with space for your own notes, etc. Feel free to remove the individual subject answer sheet from this book and make as many copies of it as you need while working through the questions in each section. Please note that the subjects are *not* scored separately on the exam and that the individual subject answer sheet is provided for your convenience only.

For each section, fill in the corresponding oval for each answer. As you answer each question, make a note of the answers which were only good guesses, and not firmly based on your knowledge of the law, so that you can check the answers to those questions more carefully.

STRATEGIES AND TACTICS FOR THE MBE

Score Sheet

CONSTITUTIONAL LAW

SIDE 1

TEST FORM: 78526

JURISDICTION CODE

Ala.	01
Alaska	02
Ariz.	03
Ark.	04
Calif.	05
Colo.	06
Conn.	07
Del.	08
D.C.	09
Fla.	10
Ga.	11
Hawaii	12
Idaho	13
Ill.	14
Ind.	15
Iowa	16
Kans.	17
Ky.	18
La.	19
Maine	20
Md.	21
Mass.	22
Mich.	23
Minn.	24
Miss.	25
Mo.	26
Mont.	27
Nebr.	28
Nev.	29
N.H.	30
N.J.	31
N. Mex.	32
N.Y.	33
N.C.	34
N. Dak.	35
Ohio	36
Okla.	37
Oreg.	38
Pa.	39
R.I.	40
S.C.	41
S. Dak.	42
Tenn.	43
Tex.	44
Utah	45
Vt.	46
Va.	47
Wash.	48
W.Va.	49
Wisc.	50
Wyo.	51
Guam	52
Northern Marana Islands/ Saipan	53
Virgin Islands	55
All Others	56

NOTES

BE SURE EACH MARK IS DARK AND COMPLETELY FILLS THE INTENDED OVAL, AS SHOWN IN THE ILLUSTRATION AT THE RIGHT. COMPLETELY ERASE ANY MISTAKES OR STRAY MARKS.

Ⓐ ● Ⓒ Ⓓ

#					#					#					#				
1	Ⓐ Ⓑ Ⓒ Ⓓ				21	Ⓐ Ⓑ Ⓒ Ⓓ				41	Ⓐ Ⓑ Ⓒ Ⓓ				61	Ⓐ Ⓑ Ⓒ Ⓓ				81	Ⓐ Ⓑ Ⓒ Ⓓ
2	Ⓐ Ⓑ Ⓒ Ⓓ				22	Ⓐ Ⓑ Ⓒ Ⓓ				42	Ⓐ Ⓑ Ⓒ Ⓓ				62	Ⓐ Ⓑ Ⓒ Ⓓ				82	Ⓐ Ⓑ Ⓒ Ⓓ
3	Ⓐ Ⓑ Ⓒ Ⓓ				23	Ⓐ Ⓑ Ⓒ Ⓓ				43	Ⓐ Ⓑ Ⓒ Ⓓ				63	Ⓐ Ⓑ Ⓒ Ⓓ				83	Ⓐ Ⓑ Ⓒ Ⓓ
4	Ⓐ Ⓑ Ⓒ Ⓓ				24	Ⓐ Ⓑ Ⓒ Ⓓ				44	Ⓐ Ⓑ Ⓒ Ⓓ				64	Ⓐ Ⓑ Ⓒ Ⓓ				84	Ⓐ Ⓑ Ⓒ Ⓓ
5	Ⓐ Ⓑ Ⓒ Ⓓ				25	Ⓐ Ⓑ Ⓒ Ⓓ				45	Ⓐ Ⓑ Ⓒ Ⓓ				65	Ⓐ Ⓑ Ⓒ Ⓓ				85	Ⓐ Ⓑ Ⓒ Ⓓ
6	Ⓐ Ⓑ Ⓒ Ⓓ				26	Ⓐ Ⓑ Ⓒ Ⓓ				46	Ⓐ Ⓑ Ⓒ Ⓓ				66	Ⓐ Ⓑ Ⓒ Ⓓ				86	Ⓐ Ⓑ Ⓒ Ⓓ
7	Ⓐ Ⓑ Ⓒ Ⓓ				27	Ⓐ Ⓑ Ⓒ Ⓓ				47	Ⓐ Ⓑ Ⓒ Ⓓ				76	Ⓐ Ⓑ Ⓒ Ⓓ				87	Ⓐ Ⓑ Ⓒ Ⓓ
8	Ⓐ Ⓑ Ⓒ Ⓓ				28	Ⓐ Ⓑ Ⓒ Ⓓ				48	Ⓐ Ⓑ Ⓒ Ⓓ				68	Ⓐ Ⓑ Ⓒ Ⓓ				88	Ⓐ Ⓑ Ⓒ Ⓓ
9	Ⓐ Ⓑ Ⓒ Ⓓ				29	Ⓐ Ⓑ Ⓒ Ⓓ				49	Ⓐ Ⓑ Ⓒ Ⓓ				69	Ⓐ Ⓑ Ⓒ Ⓓ				89	Ⓐ Ⓑ Ⓒ Ⓓ
10	Ⓐ Ⓑ Ⓒ Ⓓ				30	Ⓐ Ⓑ Ⓒ Ⓓ				50	Ⓐ Ⓑ Ⓒ Ⓓ				70	Ⓐ Ⓑ Ⓒ Ⓓ				90	Ⓐ Ⓑ Ⓒ Ⓓ
11	Ⓐ Ⓑ Ⓒ Ⓓ				31	Ⓐ Ⓑ Ⓒ Ⓓ				51	Ⓐ Ⓑ Ⓒ Ⓓ				71	Ⓐ Ⓑ Ⓒ Ⓓ				91	Ⓐ Ⓑ Ⓒ Ⓓ
12	Ⓐ Ⓑ Ⓒ Ⓓ				32	Ⓐ Ⓑ Ⓒ Ⓓ				52	Ⓐ Ⓑ Ⓒ Ⓓ				72	Ⓐ Ⓑ Ⓒ Ⓓ				92	Ⓐ Ⓑ Ⓒ Ⓓ
13	Ⓐ Ⓑ Ⓒ Ⓓ				33	Ⓐ Ⓑ Ⓒ Ⓓ				53	Ⓐ Ⓑ Ⓒ Ⓓ				73	Ⓐ Ⓑ Ⓒ Ⓓ				93	Ⓐ Ⓑ Ⓒ Ⓓ
14	Ⓐ Ⓑ Ⓒ Ⓓ				34	Ⓐ Ⓑ Ⓒ Ⓓ				54	Ⓐ Ⓑ Ⓒ Ⓓ				74	Ⓐ Ⓑ Ⓒ Ⓓ				94	Ⓐ Ⓑ Ⓒ Ⓓ
15	Ⓐ Ⓑ Ⓒ Ⓓ				35	Ⓐ Ⓑ Ⓒ Ⓓ				55	Ⓐ Ⓑ Ⓒ Ⓓ				75	Ⓐ Ⓑ Ⓒ Ⓓ				95	Ⓐ Ⓑ Ⓒ Ⓓ
16	Ⓐ Ⓑ Ⓒ Ⓓ				36	Ⓐ Ⓑ Ⓒ Ⓓ				56	Ⓐ Ⓑ Ⓒ Ⓓ				76	Ⓐ Ⓑ Ⓒ Ⓓ				96	Ⓐ Ⓑ Ⓒ Ⓓ
17	Ⓐ Ⓑ Ⓒ Ⓓ				37	Ⓐ Ⓑ Ⓒ Ⓓ				57	Ⓐ Ⓑ Ⓒ Ⓓ				76	Ⓐ Ⓑ Ⓒ Ⓓ				97	Ⓐ Ⓑ Ⓒ Ⓓ
18	Ⓐ Ⓑ Ⓒ Ⓓ				38	Ⓐ Ⓑ Ⓒ Ⓓ				58	Ⓐ Ⓑ Ⓒ Ⓓ				78	Ⓐ Ⓑ Ⓒ Ⓓ				98	Ⓐ Ⓑ Ⓒ Ⓓ
19	Ⓐ Ⓑ Ⓒ Ⓓ				39	Ⓐ Ⓑ Ⓒ Ⓓ				59	Ⓐ Ⓑ Ⓒ Ⓓ				79	Ⓐ Ⓑ Ⓒ Ⓓ				99	Ⓐ Ⓑ Ⓒ Ⓓ
20	Ⓐ Ⓑ Ⓒ Ⓓ				40	Ⓐ Ⓑ Ⓒ Ⓓ				60	Ⓐ Ⓑ Ⓒ Ⓓ				70	Ⓐ Ⓑ Ⓒ Ⓓ				100	Ⓐ Ⓑ Ⓒ Ⓓ

NATIONAL CONFERENCE OF BAR EXAMINERS
Multistate Bar Examination

A.M. EXAM

SIDE 1

TEST FORM: 78526

BE SURE EACH MARK IS DARK AND COMPLETELY FILLS THE INTENDED OVAL, AS SHOWN IN THE ILLUSTRATION AT THE RIGHT. COMPLETELY ERASE ANY MISTAKES OR STRAY MARKS.

Ⓐ ● Ⓒ Ⓓ

1 Ⓐ Ⓑ Ⓒ Ⓓ	21 Ⓐ Ⓑ Ⓒ Ⓓ	41 Ⓐ Ⓑ Ⓒ Ⓓ	61 Ⓐ Ⓑ Ⓒ Ⓓ	81 Ⓐ Ⓑ Ⓒ Ⓓ		
2 Ⓐ Ⓑ Ⓒ Ⓓ	22 Ⓐ Ⓑ Ⓒ Ⓓ	42 Ⓐ Ⓑ Ⓒ Ⓓ	62 Ⓐ Ⓑ Ⓒ Ⓓ	82 Ⓐ Ⓑ Ⓒ Ⓓ		
3 Ⓐ Ⓑ Ⓒ Ⓓ	23 Ⓐ Ⓑ Ⓒ Ⓓ	43 Ⓐ Ⓑ Ⓒ Ⓓ	63 Ⓐ Ⓑ Ⓒ Ⓓ	83 Ⓐ Ⓑ Ⓒ Ⓓ		
4 Ⓐ Ⓑ Ⓒ Ⓓ	24 Ⓐ Ⓑ Ⓒ Ⓓ	44 Ⓐ Ⓑ Ⓒ Ⓓ	64 Ⓐ Ⓑ Ⓒ Ⓓ	84 Ⓐ Ⓑ Ⓒ Ⓓ		
5 Ⓐ Ⓑ Ⓒ Ⓓ	25 Ⓐ Ⓑ Ⓒ Ⓓ	45 Ⓐ Ⓑ Ⓒ Ⓓ	65 Ⓐ Ⓑ Ⓒ Ⓓ	85 Ⓐ Ⓑ Ⓒ Ⓓ		
6 Ⓐ Ⓑ Ⓒ Ⓓ	26 Ⓐ Ⓑ Ⓒ Ⓓ	46 Ⓐ Ⓑ Ⓒ Ⓓ	66 Ⓐ Ⓑ Ⓒ Ⓓ	86 Ⓐ Ⓑ Ⓒ Ⓓ		
7 Ⓐ Ⓑ Ⓒ Ⓓ	27 Ⓐ Ⓑ Ⓒ Ⓓ	47 Ⓐ Ⓑ Ⓒ Ⓓ	76 Ⓐ Ⓑ Ⓒ Ⓓ	87 Ⓐ Ⓑ Ⓒ Ⓓ		
8 Ⓐ Ⓑ Ⓒ Ⓓ	28 Ⓐ Ⓑ Ⓒ Ⓓ	48 Ⓐ Ⓑ Ⓒ Ⓓ	68 Ⓐ Ⓑ Ⓒ Ⓓ	88 Ⓐ Ⓑ Ⓒ Ⓓ		
9 Ⓐ Ⓑ Ⓒ Ⓓ	29 Ⓐ Ⓑ Ⓒ Ⓓ	49 Ⓐ Ⓑ Ⓒ Ⓓ	69 Ⓐ Ⓑ Ⓒ Ⓓ	89 Ⓐ Ⓑ Ⓒ Ⓓ		
10 Ⓐ Ⓑ Ⓒ Ⓓ	30 Ⓐ Ⓑ Ⓒ Ⓓ	50 Ⓐ Ⓑ Ⓒ Ⓓ	70 Ⓐ Ⓑ Ⓒ Ⓓ	90 Ⓐ Ⓑ Ⓒ Ⓓ		
11 Ⓐ Ⓑ Ⓒ Ⓓ	31 Ⓐ Ⓑ Ⓒ Ⓓ	51 Ⓐ Ⓑ Ⓒ Ⓓ	71 Ⓐ Ⓑ Ⓒ Ⓓ	91 Ⓐ Ⓑ Ⓒ Ⓓ		
12 Ⓐ Ⓑ Ⓒ Ⓓ	32 Ⓐ Ⓑ Ⓒ Ⓓ	52 Ⓐ Ⓑ Ⓒ Ⓓ	72 Ⓐ Ⓑ Ⓒ Ⓓ	92 Ⓐ Ⓑ Ⓒ Ⓓ		
13 Ⓐ Ⓑ Ⓒ Ⓓ	33 Ⓐ Ⓑ Ⓒ Ⓓ	53 Ⓐ Ⓑ Ⓒ Ⓓ	73 Ⓐ Ⓑ Ⓒ Ⓓ	93 Ⓐ Ⓑ Ⓒ Ⓓ		
14 Ⓐ Ⓑ Ⓒ Ⓓ	34 Ⓐ Ⓑ Ⓒ Ⓓ	54 Ⓐ Ⓑ Ⓒ Ⓓ	74 Ⓐ Ⓑ Ⓒ Ⓓ	94 Ⓐ Ⓑ Ⓒ Ⓓ		
15 Ⓐ Ⓑ Ⓒ Ⓓ	35 Ⓐ Ⓑ Ⓒ Ⓓ	55 Ⓐ Ⓑ Ⓒ Ⓓ	75 Ⓐ Ⓑ Ⓒ Ⓓ	95 Ⓐ Ⓑ Ⓒ Ⓓ		
16 Ⓐ Ⓑ Ⓒ Ⓓ	36 Ⓐ Ⓑ Ⓒ Ⓓ	56 Ⓐ Ⓑ Ⓒ Ⓓ	76 Ⓐ Ⓑ Ⓒ Ⓓ	96 Ⓐ Ⓑ Ⓒ Ⓓ		
17 Ⓐ Ⓑ Ⓒ Ⓓ	37 Ⓐ Ⓑ Ⓒ Ⓓ	57 Ⓐ Ⓑ Ⓒ Ⓓ	76 Ⓐ Ⓑ Ⓒ Ⓓ	97 Ⓐ Ⓑ Ⓒ Ⓓ		
18 Ⓐ Ⓑ Ⓒ Ⓓ	38 Ⓐ Ⓑ Ⓒ Ⓓ	58 Ⓐ Ⓑ Ⓒ Ⓓ	78 Ⓐ Ⓑ Ⓒ Ⓓ	98 Ⓐ Ⓑ Ⓒ Ⓓ		
19 Ⓐ Ⓑ Ⓒ Ⓓ	39 Ⓐ Ⓑ Ⓒ Ⓓ	59 Ⓐ Ⓑ Ⓒ Ⓓ	79 Ⓐ Ⓑ Ⓒ Ⓓ	99 Ⓐ Ⓑ Ⓒ Ⓓ		
20 Ⓐ Ⓑ Ⓒ Ⓓ	40 Ⓐ Ⓑ Ⓒ Ⓓ	60 Ⓐ Ⓑ Ⓒ Ⓓ	70 Ⓐ Ⓑ Ⓒ Ⓓ	100 Ⓐ Ⓑ Ⓒ Ⓓ		

A — JURISDICTION CODE

Ⓐ JURISDICTION CODE

Ⓑ APPLICANT NUMBER

Ⓒ DATE OF BIRTH

Jan. ○ Feb. ○ March ○ April ○ May ○ June ○ July ○ August ○ Sept. ○ Oct. ○ Nov. ○ Dec.

USE A
SOFT LEAD
PENCIL
ONLY

DO NOT FOLD,
STAPLE, OR
ATTACH TAPE
TO THIS SHEET

JURISDICTION CODE

Ala.	01
Alaska	02
Ariz.	03
Ark.	04
Calif.	05
Colo.	06
Conn.	07
Del.	08
D.C.	09
Fla.	10
Ga.	11
Hawaii	12
Idaho	13
Ill.	14
Ind.	15
Iowa	16
Kans.	17
Ky.	18
La.	19
Maine	20
Md.	21
Mass.	22
Mich.	23
Minn.	24
Miss.	25
Mo.	26
Mont.	27
Nebr.	28
Nev.	29
N.H.	30
N.J.	31
N. Mex.	32
N.Y.	33
N.C.	34
N. Dak.	35
Ohio	36
Okla.	37
Oreg.	38
Pa.	39
R.I.	40
S.C.	41
S. Dak.	42
Tenn.	43
Tex.	44
Utah	45
Vt.	46
Va.	47
Wash.	48
W.Va.	49
Wisc.	50
Wyo.	51
Guam	52
Northern Marana Islands/ Saipan	53
Virgin Islands	55
All Others	56

NATIONAL CONFERENCE OF BAR EXAMINERS
Multistate Bar Examination

TEST FORM: 78526

P.M. EXAM

BE SURE EACH MARK IS DARK AND COMPLETELY FILLLS THE INTENDED OVAL, AS SHOWN IN THE ILLUSTRATION AT THE RIGHT. COMPLETELY ERASE ANY MISTAKES OR STRAY MARKS.

Ⓐ ● Ⓒ Ⓓ

SIDE 1

A — JURISDICTION CODE

B — APPLICANT NUMBER

C — DATE OF BIRTH

| Month |
| Jan. |
| Feb. |
| March |
| April |
| May |
| June |
| July |
| August |
| Sept. |
| Oct. |
| Nov. |
| Dec. |

USE A
SOFT LEAD
PENCIL
ONLY

DO NOT FOLD,
STAPLE, OR
ATTACH TAPE
TO THIS SHEET

JURISDIC-
TION
CODE

Ala.	01
Alaska	02
Ariz.	03
Ark.	04
Calif.	05
Colo.	06
Conn.	07
Del.	08
D.C.	09
Fla.	10
Ga.	11
Hawaii	12
Idaho	13
Ill.	14
Ind.	15
Iowa	16
Kans.	17
Ky.	18
La.	19
Maine	20
Md.	21
Mass.	22
Mich.	23
Minn.	24
Miss.	25
Mo.	26
Mont.	27
Nebr.	28
Nev.	29
N.H.	30
N.J.	31
N. Mex.	32
N.Y.	33
N.C.	34
N. Dak.	35
Ohio	36
Okla.	37
Oreg.	38
Pa.	39
R.I.	40
S.C.	41
S. Dak.	42
Tenn.	43
Tex.	44
Utah	45
Vt.	46
Va.	47
Wash.	48
W.Va.	49
Wisc.	50
Wyo.	51
Guam	52
Northern Marana Islands/ Saipan	53
Virgin Islands	55
All Others	56